MANAGING INFORMATION TECHNOLOGY

FIFTH EDITION

E. Wainright Martin
Kelley School of Business, Indiana University

Carol V. Brown
Kelley School of Business, Indiana University

Daniel W. DeHayes
Kelley School of Business, Indiana University

Jeffrey A. Hoffer
School of Business Administration, The University of Dayton

William C. Perkins
Kelley School of Business, Indiana University

Upper Saddle River, New Jersey 07458

Library of Congress Cataloging-in-Publication Data

Managing information technology / E. Wainright Martin ... [et al.].— 5th ed.
p. cm.
Includes bibliographical references and index.
ISBN 0-13-145443-9
1. Management information systems. I. Martin, E. Wainright (Edley Wainright)

T58.6.M3568 2004
658.4'038'011—dc22

2004008087

Acquisitions Editor: Bob Horan
Editor-in-Chief: Natalie Anderson
Project Manager: Lori Cerreto
Editorial Assistant: Robyn Goldenberg
Media Project Manager: Joan Waxman
Managing Editor: John Roberts
Production Editor: Renata Butera
Permissions Supervisor: Charles Morris
Production Manager: Arnold Vila
Manufacturing Buyer: Michelle Klein
Design Director: Maria Lange
Art Director: Pat Smythe
Cover Design: Bruce Kenselaar
Full-Service Project Management: nSight, Inc.
Composition: Laserwords
Printer/Binder: Courier-Westford
Typeface: 10/12 Times New Roman

Credits and acknowledgments borrowed from other sources and reproduced, with permission, in this textbook appear on appropriate page within text.

Pearson Education LTD.
Pearson Education Singapore, Pte. Ltd
Pearson Education, Canada, Ltd
Pearson Education–Japan
Pearson Education Australia PTY, Limited
Pearson Education North Asia Ltd
Pearson Educación de Mexico, S.A. de C.V.
Pearson Education Malaysia, Pte. Ltd

10 9 8 7 6 5 4 3 2
ISBN 0-13-145443-9

BRIEF CONTENTS

CONTENTS

CASE STUDIES

PREFACE

The fifth edition of this widely used M.B.A. and advanced undergraduate textbook continues the tradition of the earlier editions by focusing on how to effectively manage information technology (IT) within organizational settings. For those of you familiar with the fourth edition, the overall structure of the book has been retained. We also continue our tradition of providing full-length, original case studies to illustrate current IT management issues.

This edition includes more than two dozen original case studies that span a wide range of topics; the authors of the textbook developed most of these, but some were written by other academic faculty colleagues. Selected cases are provided for every major section of the book, but many can also be effectively used with other book chapters as well. These case studies include camouflaged but real situations, as well as identified case studies of midsized as well as *Fortune* 500-sized firms (including BAT, Compaq, IBM, Owens Corning, and Sears).

Following an introductory chapter on the use of IT as an "enabler" of modern business strategies, in Part I we provide four chapters on technology topics (hardware, software, networking, and the data resource). In Part II we present numerous examples of three major types of IT applications: enterprise systems, managerial support systems, and e-commerce applications. Part III presents methodologies and techniques for developing, purchasing, and implementing systems, as well as for facilitating end-user computing, and Part IV discusses approaches to planning and managing IT resources and the information systems (IS) organization itself.

Textbook adopters familiar with the fourth edition will notice that the data resource chapter in Part I is a new technology chapter that brings together material found in several chapters of the fourth edition as well as new material about this key IT resource. This edition also includes a new final chapter on social, ethical, and legal issues involving IT—issues becoming more critical every year to business and IS managers. All the other chapters have been extensively revised; the chapter on e-commerce applications has been totally rewritten to reflect current e-commerce issues and applications, with a focus on both pure dot-com and "clicks-and-mortar" retailers and intermediaries (both B2C and B2B).

The new case studies in this edition deal with the implementation of an enterprise resource planning (ERP) system in one unit of a multinational company; an implementation of customer relationship management software using data warehousing; developing a sales force automation application for use in multiple divisions of a multinational company; the e-business transformation underway in a large retailer; the development of a small but successful Web retailer; the decision of what to do with a long-running project that seems destined for failure; the difficulties of outsourcing the implementation of new software; the possible use of IT to transform a company; quickly integrating the IT operations in a large merger; the decision of whether to outsource major IT organization functions; and the potential advantages of a shared services unit in a multinational firm. Several of the older cases have been updated or rewritten to make them more useful, including Mezzia, Inc., the Naval Surface Warfare Center, and Clarion School for Boys.

PURPOSE

Our objective for this edition of the textbook is to prepare advanced management students—both undergraduate and graduate—to be effective managers within organizations that are expected to grow increasingly dependent on information technologies. By learning alternative approaches to managing IT—both the opportunities and the pitfalls—students will be in a better position to participate in IS management as a business manager or as a manager of systems professionals.

The first edition of this book appeared in 1991 to fill a major gap by providing a textbook dealing with the *management* of IT; this was the subject of newly required courses in many M.B.A. programs and at the original authors' home institution (Indiana University). Today most leading M.B.A. programs include IT management as a core course, and many undergraduate programs require an upper-level course with similar content. Earlier editions of this book have been successfully used in advanced undergraduate courses, M.B.A. programs, executive M.B.A. programs, online M.B.A. programs, M.S. in IS programs, and executive education courses around the world.

This fifth edition therefore continues to build upon the authors' experiences, along with the experiences of many others, in classroom teaching at both the undergraduate and graduate levels, as well as on our extensive IT experiences in researching and consulting in the field. It also incorporates new technology advances and research findings in the rapidly changing IS field.

Our chapters and case studies also continue to reflect a documented trend in organizations today: Business managers and IT managers are increasingly relied upon to work together and play critical IT leadership roles within a business. Today's business manager needs to be aware of the current (and future) IT capabilities that can be leveraged to strategic and operational advantage, as well as the limitations and potential problems involved in the use of IT. A manager needs to understand the capabilities of a range of applications for enterprisewide functions, managerial support, and e-business, as well as best practices for acquiring and implementing new information systems. A manager also must be aware of the trade-offs in choosing to custom develop or purchase a system; the importance of prototyping, documentation, system testing, and rollout planning and execution; as well as the need for attention to security controls to preserve a system's integrity. Managers must understand how an organization's IT infrastructure affects its ability to use IT strategically and to support employees at any location around the clock. Finally, a manager needs to understand the important alternatives for managing the firm's IT resources and the IS organization itself in ways that take into account the specific organizational context.

This book, therefore, helps to prepare the student to be a more effective manager of IT as well as a more effective IT user. Throughout the text we present both the *individual* and the *organizational* perspectives. Today's graduates should be prepared to leverage IT tools to enhance their own productivity in the workplace and their career advancement, as well as for the good of an enterprise. However, managers also operate in a specific organizational context, and what they can accomplish depends upon the resources provided and the constraints imposed by their organizations. Through case studies, we provide examples of managers and IT professionals as they play different organizational roles in an attempt to effectively leverage IT.

Nevertheless, we also live in a dynamic world in which new emerging information technologies can "disrupt" old ones and yesterday's most effective IT platforms can become obsolete. Therefore, most organizations have a mix of new and "legacy" (old) hardware, software, and networks, as well as systems development approaches and managerial approaches. Managers must therefore also recognize that they will continually need to keep abreast of important IT-related developments and trends and to reassess what is possible today or not until tomorrow.

ORGANIZATION AND SCOPE

After the stage-setting opening chapter, the book consists of four parts: "Information Technology," "Applying Information Technology," "Acquiring Information Systems," and "The Information Management System." Original, real-world case studies about the management and use of IT follow the opening chapter and each of the major parts of the book. In our view, and in the views communicated to us by many other users of previous editions of this book, these original case studies offer a very effective way for demonstrating IT applications and IT management issues. The scenarios in the case studies are interesting and real, and the issues encountered are important. Discussions of these case studies tend to "drive home" some of the complexities of managing IT.

The opening chapter focuses on the role of IT in the new digital economy or e-world, which is an underlying theme for the entire book. It is followed by the Midsouth Chamber of Commerce (A) case study, which is an excellent discussion starter on the roles of both business managers and IT managers.

The chapters on technology follow; Chapters 2, 3, and 4 are completely revised, and Chapter 5 is new. These chapters are at the front of the book so that classes with a strong technology background can easily skim them, or they can be covered in traditional ways by students who are less advanced in their computer literacy. Although many of the core computer and network concepts remain unchanged, these chapters incorporate material on IT industry developments and new technologies. Enough depth is presented in these technology chapters to provide new learnings for almost all students, but the emphasis throughout the book is on understanding IT capabilities from a business perspective. The new chapter on data resources, Chapter 5, is especially important for business managers. The three case studies at the end of Part I focus on the selection of a hardware platform, learnings from an early telecommuting project, and the continued saga of implementing information systems at Midsouth Chamber of Commerce.

Part II on "Applying Information Technology," Chapters 6 through 8, focuses on the capabilities of three major types of IT applications today. Enterprise systems, covered in Chapter 6, are systems designed for the entire enterprise or major portions of it, including transaction processing systems for single functions, cross-functional ERP systems, data warehouses, intranets, and groupware. Managerial support systems, covered in Chapter 7, are applications designed to support decision makers, such as executive information systems, expert systems, data mining applications, and geographical information systems. Electronic commerce applications, covered in Chapter 8, are systems designed for interactions with suppliers, customers, and other business partners. Seven case studies are provided at the end of Part II that include topics such as the creation of a sales force automation system in a multinational company, the implementation of a customer relationship management system using data warehousing, the establishment of a Web site by a bricks-and-mortar company, the movement of a traditional retailer into the e-business world, the development of a small and successful Web-based business, and the advantages and disadvantages of going to work for a start-up IT firm.

Part III on "Acquiring Information Systems" begins with a chapter on basic IS concepts, followed by separate chapters focused on a custom application development methodology for IS professionals (systems development life cycle concepts and newer approaches such as prototyping and RAD), a modified life cycle approach for purchasing large packaged systems, IT project management, and organizational support for users developing their own systems and other end-user computing activities. These chapters are followed by an exceptional set of case studies covering the challenges associated with developing custom applications, the make-or-buy decision, purchasing applications software, business process reengineering, the "big bang" implementation of an ERP system, implementing an ERP system in one unit of a multinational company, and managing applications developed by users.

Finally, Part IV focuses on an effective "management system" required to manage IT. Chapter 14, "Setting a Direction for Information Resources," presents the entire framework for setting a direction, beginning with the information resources assessment, then the creation of an appropriate IT vision and architecture, and finally the development of both the long-run and short-run IT plans for the organization. Chapter 15, "Managing the Information Systems

Function," stresses a number of critical areas for IT management, including the role of the chief information officer, the role of the business manager, the management of outsourcing, the organization of the IS function, and special global IS management issues. The final chapter on "Social, Ethical, and Legal Issues" focuses on the legal environment and ethical issues encountered by business managers and IT professionals, as well as social issues of which these managers should be aware. With the increasingly pervasive impact of IT on all phases of modern life, we feel these topics are an appropriate conclusion to this edition of our textbook.

Eleven additional case studies follow these Part IV chapters and focus on topics such as IT planning, transforming a company through the use of IT, managing an IT organization during the first year of a merger, making an outsourcing decision, providing IT support for a new international plant, the use of shared services in a multinational firm, and dealing with an ethical dilemma.

BEHAVIORAL OBJECTIVES

At the completion of a course designed around this book, our intent is that students will:

- Be able to identify ways to use IT to leverage business opportunities in different areas of responsibility
- Be aware of current technology trends and IT-enabled business application trends
- Be able to make good IT investment decisions, including choosing the best alternative way to acquire a new system based upon the type of application and the technological and organizational context
- Be able to help oversee and guide the development or purchase of a new system that is of high quality and consistent with business goals
- Understand the need for organizations to develop an information vision, an IT architecture, and strategic and operational IT plans, and be able to participate in these processes
- Understand the key concepts of an IT infrastructure and be familiar with alternative approaches for providing and managing this infrastructure
- Be able to effectively partner with IS specialists—both internal and external to the organization—to obtain the expertise, services, and technical support required
- Participate in the development of organizational policies and government legislation related to the potential impacts of IT usage on individuals, organizations, and society.

CASE STUDIES

As described earlier, we have found that real-world case studies are especially effective teaching tools for advanced management students. Although some of the actual case studies are heavily disguised, they are all faithful depictions of actual situations in specific organizations and have been carefully selected to illustrate major concepts in the book. We are greatly indebted to the organizations and individuals who served as the sources for our own original case studies published in this book, both camouflaged and not, as well as to a few other academic colleagues who have accepted our offer to publish their own teaching cases in the textbook.

There are many lessons to be learned in each case study, often related to multiple chapters in the book. Similar to the fourth edition, we have grouped the case studies at the end of the part of the book to which they are most closely related. However, instructors may wish to use a given case study to illustrate the teaching points of chapters in a different part of the text, or an instructor may discuss a case study multiple times as the course progresses.

OTHER TEACHING AIDS

The Supplement Resource Package: www.prenhall.com/martin

A comprehensive and flexible technology support package is available to enhance the teaching and learning experience. All instructor and student supplements are available on the text's Web site: *www.prenhall.com/martin*. The Web site also includes a large number of "old favorite" case studies from earlier editions.

- *Instructor's Manual* The Instructor's Manual includes syllabi for several courses (both undergraduate and master's level) that have used this book. It also includes lecture notes on each chapter, answers to the review and discussion questions at the end of each chapter, teaching notes on the case studies, and a test bank for assistance in preparing examinations based on this book. It is available on the secure faculty section of the Martin Web site (*www.prenhall.com/martin*).
- *Test Item File and TestGen Software* The Test Item File is a comprehensive collection of multiple-choice and essay questions. The questions are rated by difficulty level and the answers are referenced by page number. The Test Item File is available in Microsoft Word and for use with the computerized Prentice Hall TestGen. TestGen is a comprehensive suite of tools for testing and assessment. It allows instructors to easily create and distribute tests for their courses, either by printing and distributing through traditional methods or by online delivery via a local area network (LAN) server. TestGen features Screen Wizards to assist you as you move through the program, and the software is backed with full technical support. Both the Test Item File and TestGen software are available on the secure faculty section of the Martin Web site.
- *PowerPoint Slides* PowerPoint slides are available that illuminate and build on key concepts in the text. Both students and faculty can download the PowerPoint slides from the Martin Web site.
- *Materials for Your Online Course* Prentice Hall supports our adopters using online courses by providing files ready for upload into both WebCT and Blackboard course management systems for testing, quizzing, and other supplements. Please contact your local PH representative or mis_service@prenhall.com for further information on your particular course.

ACKNOWLEDGMENTS

Our thanks go to our faculty colleagues at Indiana University and elsewhere who have used one or more versions of the book and have provided valuable feedback. We are also indebted to reviewers of each of the five editions of this book. The list of these colleagues and reviewers is too long to include here, but we hope that they will accept our anonymous THANKS! We also thank the many Indiana University M.B.A. and undergraduate students at the Kelley School of Business who have provided suggestions to us directly.

Special thanks go to Sue Brown, Indiana University, who was the primary author of the chapter on data resources for this edition, as well as others who assisted us in drafting important sections for the chapters in this book: Lisa D. Murphy, University of Alabama; Andrew Urbaczewski, University of Michigan-Dearborn; Madhu Rao, University of Seattle; and Ramesh Venkataraman and Dong-Gil Ko, Indiana University. We gratefully acknowledge the support of the Indiana University Institute for Research on the Management of Information Systems (IRMIS), the Kelley School of Business at Indiana University, and the EDS Corporation for the development of many of the case studies.

We are also indebted to others who have served as coauthors with us or agreed to publish their own case studies here, including: Iris Vessey, Bradley Wheeler, and Michael Williams, Indiana University; Jeanne W. Ross, Massachusetts Institute of Technology; Barbara Wixom, University of Virginia; Dale Goodhue and Hugh Watson, University of Georgia; and C. Ranganathan, University of Illinois at Chicago.

Our gratitude also goes to our families who have witnessed firsthand the time commitments required to update a textbook in the fast-moving field of IT. Finally, each author thanks the other four for their intellect, professionalism, and camaraderie, qualities that have made our coauthorship endeavors so worthwhile.

E. Wainright Martin
Carol V. Brown
Daniel W. DeHayes
Jeffrey A. Hoffer
William C. Perkins

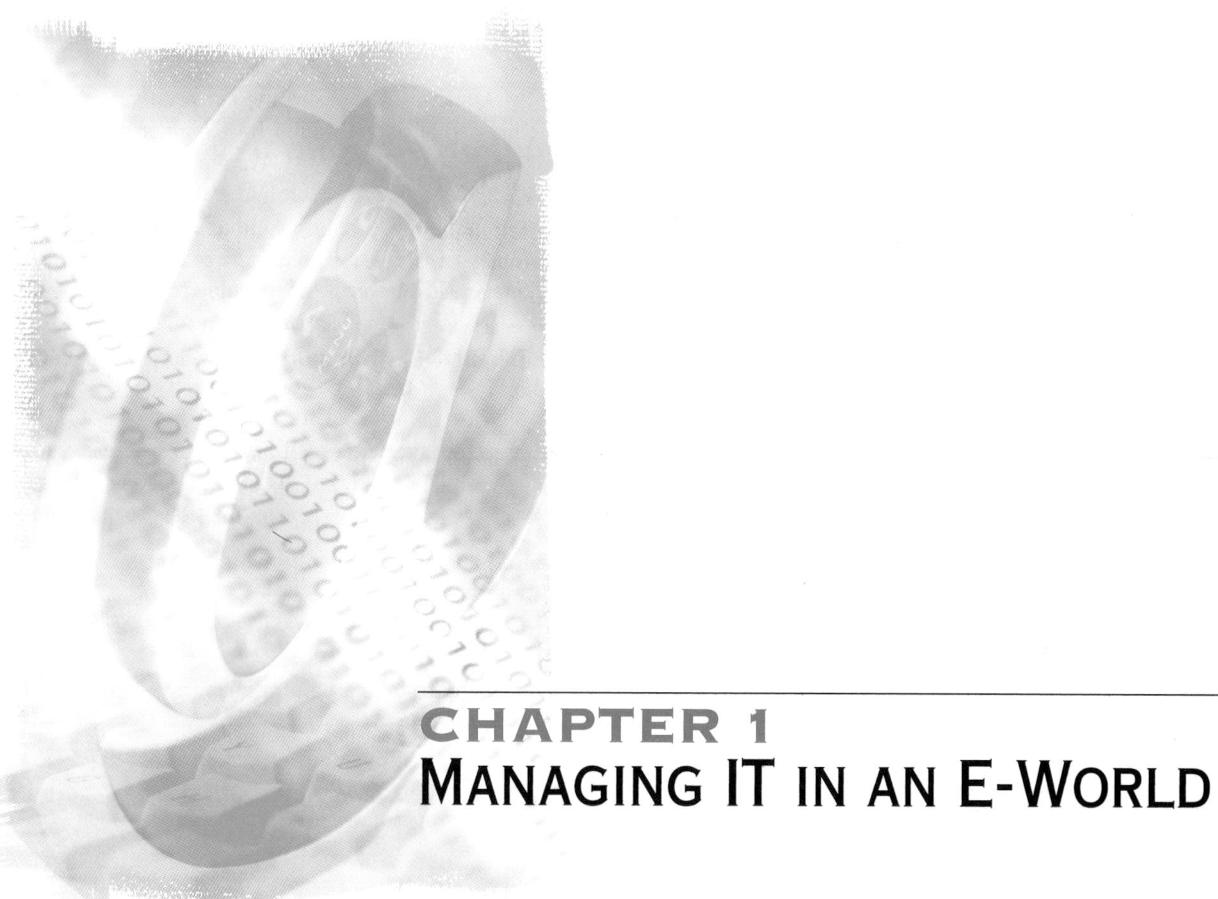

CHAPTER 1
MANAGING IT IN AN E-WORLD

THE INFORMATION REVOLUTION HAS CLEARLY ARRIVED. INVESTMENT IN information technology during the 1990s has been a major contributing factor to unprecedented gains in productivity within the United States during the early 2000s. Traditional firms have integrated the Internet into their everyday business activities. Web-based applications and Internet e-mail have become an additional channel of communication with a firm's traditional customers, its suppliers, and its shareholders.

Today we take for granted that we are part of an electronic world, or *e-world.* Many of us expect to find connections to the Internet not only in our schools and our workplace, but also in our homes. As 60 percent of U.S. homes have also invested in Internet connections for their home computers, government agencies have begun to use Web applications to provide information as well as to collect taxes and receive electronic business documents online. When we travel, we can use wireless networks at airport terminals, high-speed data connections in our hotel rooms, and Internet cafes on the streets of a city or resort town.

Businesses also recognize that they are competing in an e-world in which the technologies that they invested in yesterday could lack the business capabilities that they want today. The rules for business survival can quickly change, and an event in one part of the world can affect financial markets in countries halfway across the globe.

Being a user of **information technology** (IT) in an e-world is also clearly different from being a computer user before we had an easy-to-use browser to navigate across Web sites. Today's elementary school students learn to do research using Web-based resources, and many teens choose to use their discretionary time surfing online rather than watching television. Today's typical undergraduate student is an experienced user of e-mail and Web resources. New graduates are likely to have used the Internet to distribute a resume and to seek out or communicate online with potential employers, perhaps via a Web-based job site.

Managing IT in a business today is also very different from managing IT in a prebrowser world. Business managers expect to have access not only to data about the firm's internal

> We define **information technology (IT)** as computer technology (hardware and software) for processing and storing information, as well as communications technology for transmitting information.

operations from their desktops, but also to external market data and personal organizers with automated meeting reminders. Sales and customer support personnel expect to have access to up-to-date information about customers, as well as documents from sales force members who can be scattered across many locations. When a new business is acquired, employees expect their information systems (IS) to quickly reflect this change as well. Today's workers also typically have little patience for a computer network that is not available or an application that is not easy to use.

The primary objective of this textbook is to help prepare you to be an effective manager in an e-world. Employees with a college degree are expected to be knowledgeable about computer applications and to be ready to help plan and participate in systems implementations. Some of our readers will choose to become IT professionals working in an information systems department or to take a *business technologist* position working side-by-side with business managers and system users.

To set the stage for the remainder of the textbook, we first briefly describe some of the IT trends that are part of today's e-world. Then we present some specific examples of how IT has enabled new ways for a business to compete, for employees to work, and for people to live in a modern society. We then introduce the IS management role in today's organizations, which is a role that has evolved as IT innovations have emerged. This introductory chapter then ends with some learning objectives for each of the four parts of this textbook.

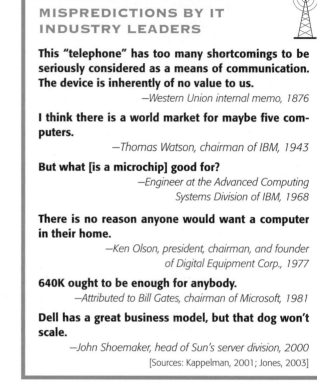

MISPREDICTIONS BY IT INDUSTRY LEADERS

This "telephone" has too many shortcomings to be seriously considered as a means of communication. The device is inherently of no value to us.

—Western Union internal memo, 1876

I think there is a world market for maybe five computers.

—Thomas Watson, chairman of IBM, 1943

But what [is a microchip] good for?

—Engineer at the Advanced Computing Systems Division of IBM, 1968

There is no reason anyone would want a computer in their home.

—Ken Olson, president, chairman, and founder of Digital Equipment Corp., 1977

640K ought to be enough for anybody.

—Attributed to Bill Gates, chairman of Microsoft, 1981

Dell has a great business model, but that dog won't scale.

—John Shoemaker, head of Sun's server division, 2000

[Sources: Kappelman, 2001; Jones, 2003]

RECENT INFORMATION TECHNOLOGY TRENDS

As a user of computers and communication devices, you are well aware that improvements in computer hardware, software, and communication networks have been dramatic and frequent over the past decade in particular. Some of you might, in fact, think that the IT industry's predictions of a "new economy" and "Internet time" led to excessive investments in IT during the late 1990s, especially in the United States. Although these criticisms could be valid, the fast rate of innovations in the IT industry has made it difficult to accurately predict the IT products and services that will be "winners" tomorrow. In fact, IT leaders in the past have publicly made some significant *mis*-predictions about technologies (see the sidebar "Mispredictions by IT Industry Leaders").

Although many of today's tools are technologically complex, they have also become easier to use—more **user-friendly**. Within a relatively short time, IT has not only become commonplace in the workplace, but also commonplace in many homes and public areas. This increased usability and availability have led to the beginnings of what has been called **ubiquitous IT**, in which computers and communications devices will touch almost every aspect of our lives.

For example, personal information devices have become so commonplace that instructions for airplane travelers include warnings about when the use of computers and cellular phones is forbidden. New airplanes are also increasingly being equipped with new technologies that include Internet access from the passenger seat of an airplane in flight. The pervasiveness of IT has also led to new battlefield tactics, in which military commanders have used their cell phones to call opposing commanders and urge them to surrender their units (Samuelson, 2003).

In Part I of this textbook, we will discuss the underlying technology concepts and their historical predecessors in much more detail. For now, let us briefly consider some of the technology developments that have led to this ubiquity of IT and to what has been called a postindustrial, digital economy.

Computer Hardware: Faster, Smaller, Cheaper

Computer-on-a-chip (microcomputer) technology was available as early as the 1970s, but the introduction of the first IBM Personal Computer (PC) in 1981 began to fuel the

Information Revolution. By the mid-1990s, desktop and portable PCs for the business and the home had become "commodity products" available from manufacturers around the world. Today's typical PC has the processing power of an organization's entire computing center of the 1960s. More important, today's PC comes with an easy-to-use operating system with graphical icons, a Web browser, point-and-click devices for screen navigation, and the capability to play music and videos—all at a cheaper price than what the same features would have cost 12 months earlier. Lightweight notebook-sized computers have also become so affordable that they have replaced many of the larger machines on the desktops of business employees and are carried into meetings and taken on business trips.

Today, even smaller, handheld computer devices have become the indispensable business tools to stay in touch with e-mail and other office documents when away from the office. As miniaturized computer devices and cellular phones have also become pervasive in all types of locations, including shopping malls and restaurants, companies have also begun to think about new applications to provide services to mobile users via these handheld devices.

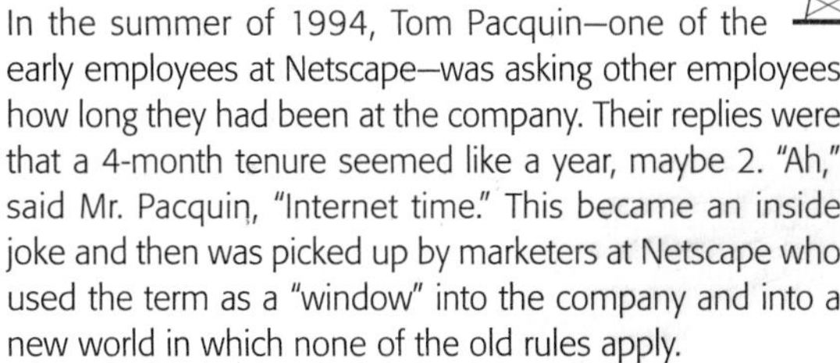

INTERNET TIME

In the summer of 1994, Tom Pacquin—one of the early employees at Netscape—was asking other employees how long they had been at the company. Their replies were that a 4-month tenure seemed like a year, maybe 2. "Ah," said Mr. Pacquin, "Internet time." This became an inside joke and then was picked up by marketers at Netscape who used the term as a "window" into the company and into a new world in which none of the old rules apply.

[Based on Gomes, 2002]

Computer Software: Standardized and Integrated

By the year 2000, some version of Microsoft Corporation's Windows software had become the standard operating system for the vast majority of microcomputers being used as desktop and portable computer "clients." Microsoft's Office Suite (word processing, spreadsheet, database, presentation, and e-mail software sold in a single bundle) and the same company's Web browser are also the *de facto* software standard throughout corporate America today, despite a U.S. government lawsuit charging Microsoft with monopolistic practices. In fact, this standard in U.S. organizations and multinational companies has been a major contributor to the ubiquity of computing and the swift emergence of today's e-world.

The 1990s also brought a tremendous growth in the availability of software packages with integrated modules that could pass common business transactions across functional groups, business divisions, and national boundaries in "real time." Today, these **enterprise system** packages have been widely adopted not only by large manufacturing and service firms based in the United States and around the globe but also by midsized and smaller firms. Some enterprise software packages have versions that have been programmed for specific industries (such as the petrochemicals industry or even higher education). With these standard enterprise system modules to build on, applications that integrate data across traditional and Web-based channels for customers and suppliers are now also available from the same early enterprise system vendors, as well as other vendors that specialize in applications for customer relationship management or supply chain management integration.

One of the early enablers of today's phenomenal progress toward software integration was the giveaway strategy of Netscape Communications, the creator of the first commercial Web browser. The Netscape browser rapidly became a standard tool for accessing the Web (see sidebar "Internet Time").

Computer Networks: High Bandwidth, Global, and Wireless

The standard browser application, along with an Internet communications standard (TCP/IP), led to an unprecedented level of IT investments in the 1990s to obtain a more global reach for employees and organizations. By the year 2000, company networks that linked employees to the Internet had become commonplace. Not only large businesses, but also small businesses and home users, could also take advantage of investments by telecommunications firms in fiber-optic lines during the late 1990s. These high-bandwidth lines sped up Web page retrieval and made possible higher-speed video access. By 2003 many home users could also buy access to high-bandwidth lines using cable modems to connect with cable lines or digital subscriber lines (DSLs) to connect via telephone lines ("land lines").

Today, companies are also investing in wireless technologies to increase the mobile access of their employees and business partners. New subscription services are available for devices that have both microcomputer and cellular capabilities, and companies have invested in developing Web pages for access by these handheld, mobile devices. Satellite and cellular technologies also can link motorists with a central support center for emergency help as well as travel services (such as GM's OnStar), accessible via a computer installed near the car driver's seat.

By the new millennium, more than half of capital expenditures by U.S.-based businesses were for IT purchases. The hardware, software, and network technologies briefly discussed above, as well as other technologies described in detail in the subsequent chapters of this textbook, have ushered in an Internet age that has already had major impacts on the way businesses compete, the way we as employees get our jobs done, and the ways we can choose to live as citizens on this planet. IT can be used today to not just enable, but also to help *shape* business strategies.

Traditional Ways to Compete

The way that businesses compete can be described in three ways (Porter, 1980):

- *Cost*—competing with other businesses by being a low-cost producer of a good or a service
- *Differentiation*—competing with other businesses by offering products or services that customers prefer due to a superiority in characteristics such as product innovativeness or image, product quality, or customer service
- *Focus*—competing on cost or differentiation within a specific market niche

Computers have been used to *lower costs* by automating transaction processing, shortening order cycle times, and providing operational data for decision making since the 1960s, when large firms invested in their first computers. In the 1980s a flood of technology innovations led to increases in IT investments that brought additional efficiency gains—such as shortening the time to develop new products with computer-aided design tools; optimizing a plant floor process with software that has captured a human expert's decision rules; and speedily changing a production line with planning systems that integrate research and development (R&D), production, and sales information.

IT has also played a significant role in enabling businesses to *differentiate* their products or services. By the 1980s firms began to gain a measurable *competitive advantage* from custom IT applications that provided

- sales personnel with information to help them better service a specific customer
- just-in-time supplies for business customers
- new information-based products such as cash management accounts or drug interaction information for healthcare providers

By the 1990s, IT applications had advanced to the extent that many firms were able to compete on *both cost and differentiation*. Some firms also used IT to transform the ways that companies in their industry had previously competed. One of the best known examples of developing IT for competitive advantage was American Airlines' SABRE reservation system, which evolved from an inventory system for American Airlines employees alone to an interorganizational system for large and small travel agencies to process airline flight reservations for American Airlines *and* its competitors.

New Ways to Compete

Although using the Internet to conduct business is still a recent innovation, we can already see some of the major ways that traditional businesses will change the way they compete in order to leverage the Internet's capabilities. For example, by the late 1990s the SABRE reservation system described above was being accessed as a Web-based reservation system for travelers and businesses via an independent intermediary (*www.travelocity.com*) as well as via the Web site for American Airlines (*www.aa.com*). However, because of the open access to the Internet, Web sites for other individual airlines, as well as other new dot-com travel sites (such as *www.expedia.com* and *www.orbitz.com*), became new online competitors, and what was once a major competitive business advantage for American Airlines' parent company was in jeopardy.

The travel industry is therefore one example of how competition in an industry has been restructured by the Internet. Consumers now have direct access to online travel businesses and electronic ticketing, which don't require an in-person visit to a local travel agency with SABRE or some other reservation system. Airline companies also need to fiercely compete on price because ticket prices are now more visible to the purchaser.

Wal-Mart, Dell, and Lands' End are three examples of preexisting companies that have been leveraging the Internet's capabilities to compete in new ways to (1) achieve additional cost efficiencies, (2) acquire the ability to mass customize their products, and (3) reach even more customers.

Wal-Mart As a large discount retailer, Wal-Mart has used Internet technology standards to increase efficiencies in its transactions with its myriad suppliers. Today it is also emerging a leader in the implementation of radio frequency identification (RFID) technologies to gain even further automation capabilities and eventually even greater cost savings.

Dell Corporation As a firm that originally sold low-cost microcomputers via phone or catalog, Dell developed software for customer service representatives to electronically capture a customer request, translate the order data into a PC system design with these components, and then electronically "summon the right resources" to fulfill the order. IT therefore enabled Dell to implement not only a low-cost business strategy, but also a "mass customization" strategy (Pine, Victor, and Boynton, 1993). In other words, Dell used IT to create a customized product using an assembly-line process. The company then leveraged the Internet's capabilities to become the first PC manufacturer to have a Web site that allowed the customer to directly place a customized order—a "self-service" application that resulted in Dell needing fewer customer service representations to take custom orders by phone.

Lands' End Another example of an original catalog company that has leveraged the Internet for mass customization is Lands' End, a clothing retailer. In this case the firm uses the Web's multimedia capabilities to facilitate custom-made purchases of clothing via its Web site. This capability was quickly implemented due to a strategic alliance with a vendor that had developed algorithms to translate customer responses into a computer-generated pattern that was shipped to an offshore manufacturer. The company also developed software to track the status of each order. Within one year of offering the first custom clothing, custom products were among its top 20 products and it had attracted new customers.

The Internet has also drastically reduced the costs for computer linkages with potential customers and suppliers in different geographic locations. For some firms the new e-world has also meant their first opportunity to sell to customers living on different continents. Small businesses can afford to conduct business electronically because of the inexpensive technologies involved. Web sites can be programmed to display screens using a different language, different currencies, and even perhaps local pricing, depending on the user's browser location or selected preference.

WORKING IN AN E-WORLD

The IT innovations in hardware, software, and networks described above have also escalated the level of IT investments to support today's **knowledge workers**, as they have become increasingly dependent on IT to do their jobs. A microcomputer on every desktop has become standard equipment in most organizations, and many workers have access to the Internet.

> Coined in the 1980s, the term **telecommuter** refers to one who works from a location outside the firm's regular offices and "commutes" via telecommunications lines in order to do his or her work.

Another major change has been the development of an IT infrastructure to support workers anytime and anywhere. Sales personnel and other traveling managers are equipped with portable computers and other mobile equipment that give them access to company data anytime (24 hours a day, 7 days a week), while working essentially anywhere (from an off-site office, home office, hotel room, airport, or on the road). Remote access to corporate records is still not always provided due to security concerns, although today the majority of Fortune 500 companies have equipped their sales forces with portable microcomputers in order to be **telecommuters**. Global access is more problematic, but anytime/anywhere access within national borders is now an expected IT service within large firms.

By 1995 measurable gains in workforce productivity due to organizational investments in IT and worker training had been reported, and the United States was able to exploit this temporary productivity advantage over other industrialized nations. When a typical graduate of a business curriculum entered the workforce for the first time, he or she could be expected to have a proficiency in personal productivity tools such as that provided by the standard productivity software suite (Microsoft Office). By 2003 the dependence of knowledge workers on IT was so pervasive that computer virus attacks could result in major productivity losses.

More Productive Teams

Today's knowledge worker also typically uses e-mail to communicate with team members when not in face-to-face settings and to share electronic work documents. Commercial software packages that support collaborative teamwork have been improved over the past decade and now typically have Web-based front ends for ease of use from internal and external networks. Videoconferencing technologies have also recently been adopted as cost-cutting measures as these technologies have improved in functionality and companies have sought to reduce travel expenditures.

Team members who telecommute are also increasingly common. For teams that have members in different time zones, some meetings might require individuals to participate in electronic conversations or videoconferencing sessions from a remote computer outside of regular office hours. In some cities environmental laws have also led to work schedules that include telecommuting for some knowledge workers, such as 4 days in the office and 1 day working outside it.

Virtual Organizations and Free Agents

Today we are also seeing the beginnings of temporary alliances between organizations and individuals in what are called **virtual organizations**. The ubiquity of IT and lowered communication costs via the Internet are making it easier for organizations to contract with other organizations or individuals in order to have access to scarce expertise, perhaps at cheaper labor costs. Some small businesses might have no real office or headquarters at all; the company might be made up of individuals scattered across different locations and might make use of talent wherever it can be found around the globe (see sidebar "Fluid Companies").

A new type of telecommuter who can do knowledge work without being at a specific work location has also emerged: the **free agent**. This means that individuals with specialized skills and IT linkages can work independently as contractors without belonging to any organization. They can post their resumes and sell their skills globally. People choose to be free agents because they have control over their schedules and what projects they work on. Organizations might want free agents because they can quickly expand and contract their human workforce without long-term obligations for salaries and benefits.

LIVING IN AN E-WORLD

Although it is too early to predict the long-term impacts of recent IT innovations on the ways we live, we do know from major technological innovations of the past, such as the automobile and the telephone, that the impacts can be far-ranging and unexpected. We also can already see impacts on our daily lives. Cell phones enable us to stay connected with family members without having to find access to a land-line service; the Internet provides access to vast amounts of "free" information that in the past required a phone call to a government agency, a reference librarian, or a company's customer service agent; and Web-based applications, such as online banking, can save us time.

The last chapter on social, ethical, and legal issues (Chapter 16) in this textbook discusses some of these issues in detail, including some "unintended" impacts such as the loss of individual privacy, vulnerability to crimes that involve "identity theft," and new social inequalities due to lack of access to computers (referred to as the digital divide, including a global digital divide). As business managers and citizens of the world, we all need to be vigilant about the implications of new IT developments and help shape their usage, as well as help our society avoid some of the potentially harmful impacts.

FLUID COMPANIES

Companies will be much more molecular and fluid. They will be autonomous business units connected not necessarily by a big building but across geographies all based on networks. The boundaries of the first will be not only fluid or blurred but in some cases hard to define.

[Don Tapscott, coauthor of Digital Capital (Byrne, 2000)]

ENVISIONING THE FUTURE

User interfaces will finally get out of their desktop metaphor... and use more natural and efficient interaction mechanisms and styles that take better advantage of our human capabilities.

—Andries van Dam

User-aware software will be capable of learning about an individual and adapting itself accordingly.

—Cherri Pancake

Ours may be the last generation that sees and readily knows the difference between real and virtual things.

—Norman I. Badler

We will create superior robots that eventually decide they have no need for us.

—Peter J. Denning

Excerpts from "The Next 1000 Years," *Communications of the ACM* [44:3 (March 2001).]

THE IS MANAGEMENT ROLE IN ORGANIZATIONS

In most organizations an **information systems (IS)** department is given the responsibility for managing the firm's IT assets: its hardware, software, networks, and IS professionals. The specific responsibilities of an IS department have continued to evolve as the range and reach of information technologies have grown.

One way to view this historical evolution of the IS management role is in the form of eras, as shown in Figure 1.1. The characteristics of the first four eras were initially envisioned by Jack Rockart of the Massachusetts Institute of Technology (Rockart, 1988), as summarized below.

Accounting Era Back-office computer automation began with accounting	IS professionals were primary decision makers but reported into an accounting function (the first corporate computer user)	Transaction processing was automated with the use of computers for single functions (transactions were aggregated and then processed in a single run or "batch" due to magnetic tape storage)
Operational Era Computer automation expanded to other functions	Business managers became more involved in systems decision making (as applications supported more business functions)	Online systems were introduced for transaction processing (made possible by direct access storage devices using magnetic disks)
Information Era IT investments to support the knowledge worker	End users became direct users of computer applications using user-friendly mainframe and microcomputer tools	Decision support systems that could "interact" with users were introduced (made possible by software tools developed for direct end-user computing)
Network Era IT investments in interenterprise systems	Business managers began to take more of an "ownership" role in IT investments	Computer networking enabled applications with business partners (custom-developed inter-organizational applications)
Internet Era IT investments to support new kinds of e-business	Top management has taken a leadership role in IT decision making to ensure that IT investments are strategically aligned with the business	The Internet and Web-based applications provide a global reach to customers and business partners (enabled by a standard communications protocol and standard Web browser)

Figure 1.1 Five IS Management Eras

> We use the term **information systems (IS) organization** to refer to the organizational department or unit that has the primary responsibility for managing IT.

In the first era (1950s to mid-1960s), the Accounting Era, IS professionals typically reported to an accounting manager, because back-office computer automation began with accounting applications, such as accounts payable. At this time computer applications were batch systems: Transactions were aggregated and then processed in a single run or "batch" due to the reliance on magnetic tape as a storage medium. Because the accounting was the first function to be automated, accountants were also the first business managers to become knowledgeable about IS. Nevertheless, the IS specialists were typically solely in charge of the development and implementation of these applications. According to Rockart, "The information systems staff swept into the department, interviewed the clerks, and designed the systems—most of which were barely understandable to anyone outside the computer hierarchy."

In the Operational Era (beginning mid-1960s), computer automation expanded to other business functions. During this era, online transaction processing also became possible due to the availability of direct access storage devices (that use magnetic disks). These technological advances made possible the development of real-time computerized systems for critical operational transactions, such as those needed for airline ticketing and manufacturing scheduling. IT specialists still dominated the development and implementation of these applications, but business (line) managers became more involved in choosing which systems to implement and participated in the development of systems requirements and system implementation.

The new application focus in the third era (late 1970s to mid-1980s), the Information Era, was the use of IT not just for transaction processing, but also for interactive decision making. End users had access to user-friendly mainframe and, later, microcomputer tools to develop decision support systems. End users were trained to develop database queries and to develop financial models for decision making. During this era the IS organization took on a new and growing role: the support of end users who could develop their own computer applications (see Chapter 13). These end-user support tasks also evolved from purchasing and installing stand-alone microcomputers, to installing local area networks (LANs), multiuse software, and shared equipment such as printers.

In Rockart's fourth era, the Network Era (beginning in the mid-1980s), firms began to actively pursue the development of custom systems that would give them a competitive advantage and business managers began to take more of an "ownership" role in IT investments. Many of these strategic applications required improved telecommunications capabilities to link across geographically distributed units of the company, as well as electronic linkages with customers, suppliers, and other business partners. With the breakup of the AT&T monopoly in 1984, the IS department also took on what became a much more complex responsibility: the operations and support of telecommunications networks.

In the first half of the 1990s, new enterprise system packages that integrated transaction data across functional "silos" became available for purchase. Large firms were among the earliest to purchase these complex systems. Multinational firms were able to implement the same enterprise system modules in non-U.S. locations by using the language and currency translation capabilities of these packages. These IT investments had very important business implications: Functions that had previously been decentralized could be consolidated (centralized) and business processes could be reengineered, for example, to provide a single point-of-contact for servicing national accounts or global customers, as well as local customers.

The fifth era in Figure 1.1, the **Internet Era**, is usually said to have begun with the widespread dissemination of the commercial Web browser. Beginning in the mid-1990s, U.S.-based businesses began to make major IT investments to develop an e-business capability. Top managers in traditional firms began to take more of a leadership role in IT decision making, because initial e-business investments required some hard decisions about how to respond to potential threats from new online (dot-com) companies and experimental applications with unknown returns. We have now begun the second decade of this Internet Era. The IS management role has evolved to include support for not only a new type of internal network (intranets) but also for remote access by customers and suppliers, including public Web sites for conducting business around-the-clock (24/7).

From these era descriptions in Figure 1.1 we can see that the IS management role has changed not only as new information technologies have expanded the firm's dependence on IT, but also as the firm's business managers have learned how to use IT in new ways.

Managing the IT Assets

Given the increased dependence on IT by businesses in all types of industries, effective management of the firm's IT assets has become a business imperative. Ross, Beath, and Goodhue (1996) argue that IT managers need to focus on managing three types of IT assets: technology, relationship, and human assets (as summarized in Figure 1.2). Some characteristics of these three assets in today's e-world are described below.

Technology Asset Managing this asset requires effective planning, building, and operating of a computer and communications infrastructure—an information "utility"—so that all employees have the right information available as needed, anytime, anywhere. Just like landline telephone users expect to receive a dial tone as they initiate a call, computer users expect a network to be up so that they can access data quickly in an easy-to-use form. Today's organizations have become so dependent on IT that when information systems are unavailable, entire departments can't get their work done, customers can't be fully supported, and suppliers can't receive orders for needed materials.

One view of an enterprise-level technology architecture, based on Weill and Broadbent (1998), is shown in Figure 1.3. The IT components layer includes the hardware, systems software, and networks that capture, process, and store transaction data. The IT services layer can be viewed from an

IT Asset	Goal
Technology	A well-defined IT architecture with sharable IT platforms and easy-to-use applications
Relationship	A working climate in which IT and business managers share the responsibility and risks, along with selected outside IT partners
Human	An appropriately skilled and supportive internal IT staff and well-managed human resources from strategic IT vendor partners.

Figure 1.2 Three IT Assets

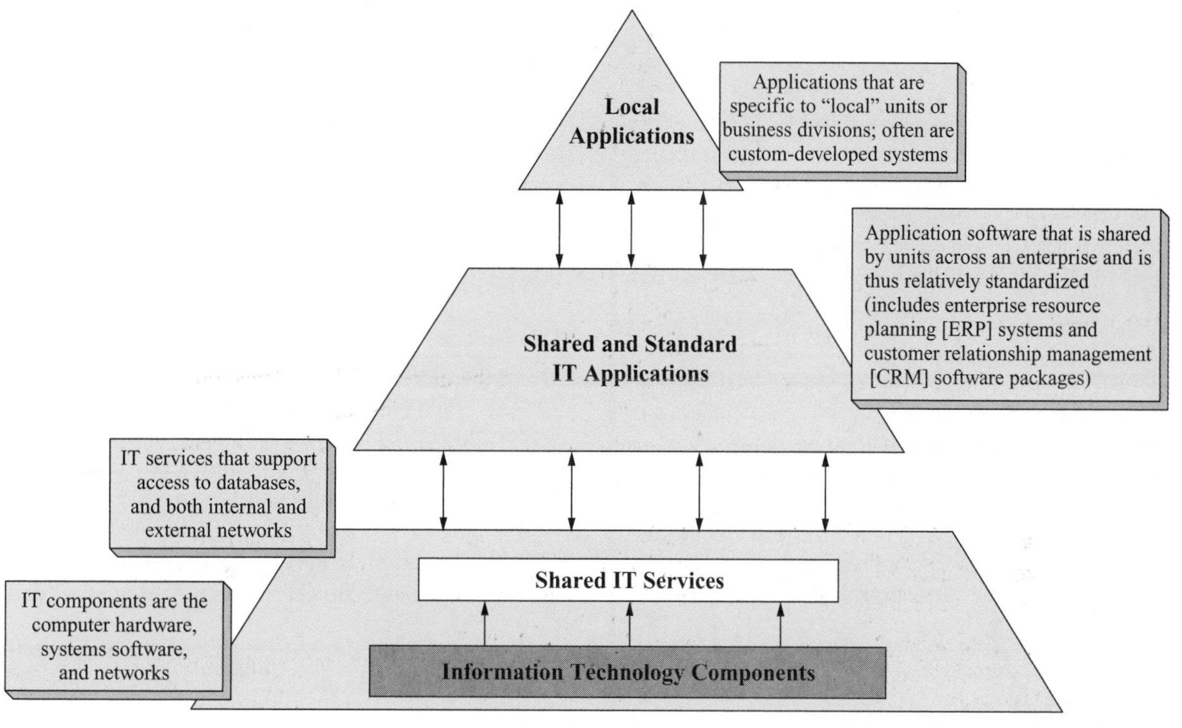

Figure 1.3 Enterprise IT Architecture (Based on Weil and Broadbent, 1998)

internal user's viewpoint: It includes support for access to e-mail services, shared databases, and both internal and external networks. (In Part I we discuss these information technologies in detail.) The IT manager is held accountable for not only ensuring reliable computer and network operations and support, but also for ensuring business continuity in the event of a virus attack or other unanticipated external event. For those organizations with Web-based retailing applications, customers cannot make a purchase if Web servers are unavailable, so the importance of IT security has escalated.

The top two layers in Figure 1.3 are application software layers. The top layer is applications that are specific to "local" units, business divisions, or specific functions; these are typically applications that have been customized to meet a specific unit's needs. The second layer from the top has grown to be much larger over the past decade. For example, enterprise system packages that support back-office transaction processing belong to this layer. (In Part II we discuss these application categories in detail.)

In a widely distributed, but poorly titled, article published in the May 2003 *Harvard Business Review* (called "IT Doesn't Matter"), Nicholas Carr argues that the primary IS management role today is to manage the costs and vulnerabilities of the computing "utility." The author also argues that because of recent investments in standard application packages, obtaining a competitive advantage from IT is an elusive goal. However, as the large number of letters to the editor published in the subsequent issue of this journal pointed out, competitive advantage doesn't come from the IT investment alone: It comes from the way that the business applies IT to meet strategic goals. Competitive advantage therefore can be achieved not only with customized applications, but also with large, complex enterprise system packages.

Relationship Asset The relationship asset has become recognized as critically important as we have evolved from the Accounting Era to the Internet Era of IS management. As seen in Figure 1.1, business managers have taken on greater decision-making roles about IT investments and are championing the development and implementation of new IT applications in order to achieve the intended business benefits.

Achieving business value from IT investments therefore requires strong working partnerships between business managers and IT managers (Brown, McLean, and Straub, 2000). According to David Pottruck (Co-CEO of Charles Schwab), IT is so integral to business today that business

BLENDING TECHNOLOGY AND THE BUSINESS

Blending technology and the more traditional business disciplines has always been a challenge, one that I recognized in my early days at another company. I volunteered to do a job in what was then "data processing," generating projects and managing them, primarily to run the internal systems of the business. I was not embraced as part of the business but rather operated in my own little domain. I had a hard time getting their attention.

This experience began to teach me some important lessons. The business managers who refused to help got the worst outcomes: Their projects were delayed, inadequate, and more expensive than we had planned. I concluded that it wasn't intentional: They couldn't appreciate the potential of their involvement. Many of them didn't see technology as integral to their business; instead, they saw IT merely as a tool. Information technology is now so integral to business that a business leader must be smart about the key elements and trade-offs.

[Adapted from Pottruck and Pearce, 2000]

leaders who do not learn how to partner with their IT leaders will not be successful (see the sidebar "Blending Technology and the Business").

In Part III of this textbook, we describe methodologies and project management techniques for acquiring and implementing new applications that require a strong relationship asset. In Part IV we describe approaches to achieving an agreed-upon level of service for different business units, which is critical for maintaining a strong relationship asset.

Human Asset Managing the human asset of an IS organization is also critical for the delivery, implementation, and ongoing operation of systems that enable an organization's strategy. Managing IT specialists is in many ways similar to managing specialists in other functional areas, but there also are some special differences due to the high rate of change in the IT industry and the nature of IT work. Today there is also an emphasis on developing alliances with domestic and offshore vendors (outsourcing) in order to lower IT operational costs and to leverage time zone and peak load differences. The pros and cons of different sourcing options and special issues associated with managing a global IT workforce are discussed in Part IV.

People Roles

Although the human IT asset focuses on IS roles (IS leaders, other IS managers, and IS professionals), the relationship asset discussed above points out the importance of IS roles for non-IS specialists (business managers and end users). The case studies in this textbook provide many examples of both the IS specialist and business manager roles that are critical for the effective management of IT in today's organizations. Some of the cases will demonstrate how to play these roles well, while others will demonstrate some of the potential pitfalls that occur when these roles are either not formally assigned or not performed well.

IS Leaders The **chief information officer** (CIO) began to emerge in the 1980s as large organizations needed high-level general managers, with both technology and business leadership experience, to manage their IT assets. If IT is to play a strategic role in the organization, IS leaders must have a close relationship with the firm's top management team—and one way to achieve that is to have in place a CIO-level position. In Part IV the IT leadership role and IT governance design choices are presented in some detail.

Other IS Managers Today's IS leadership team typically includes IS managers accountable for **data centers**, network operations, and new application solutions; many organizations also have their own IT human resource specialists to ensure that the IT human asset is well-trained and change-ready. IS managers responsible for planning, delivering, and implementing new strategic IT solutions for specific business units or functions are often physically located alongside the business managers they support. In some firms a central unit provides data center and telecommunications operations and support, while IS units responsible for application solutions report directly to a business manager.

IS Professionals Programmers, software engineers, systems analysts, database developers, Web developers, LAN administrators, and technical support providers all belong to this category. At the end of the 1990s, a shortage of IS professionals to fill such positions was estimated by the Information Technology Association of America (ITAA) to be as large as 1.2 million workers. This led many manufacturing and service firms to seek out alternative resources for technical skills, such as outsourcing firms and other service providers.

Today there is a high demand not just for skilled technical personnel, but also for individuals with a mixture of technology *and* business skills that can fill "business technologist" positions. This role requires knowledge of different business functions and softer skills, such as communication and interpersonal skills. IS professionals who have a business education as well as technical skills are expected to remain in high demand because business technology roles cannot be effectively filled by people who are not employees within the organization (such as outsourcing or other contract personnel). In some organizations IS professionals responsible for business applications work under an IS head who reports directly to a business unit manager or an IS head who reports to both IS and business leaders.

Business Managers Managers of business units are the internal customers of the IS organization. In today's e-world, the high dependence on IT for strategic business initiatives requires not just IT-literate, but IT-savvy business managers. Many strategic IT projects are therefore jointly led by business and IS managers. This is because the business managers in an organization are the most knowledgeable about what changes in business processes might be required to achieve the greatest business benefits from a new IT solution. Typical examples of key roles played by business managers that will be described in this textbook include

- serving on an advisory or oversight committee that prioritizes and approves requests for large IT investments
- being the business sponsor or "owner" of an IT project
- serving as a business process or functional expert on a project team to develop requirements for a custom application or to select a software package
- participating in the planning and execution of the rollout of a new IT application

End Users Although IS professionals are also end users of IT, in this textbook we use the term end user to refer to non-IS specialists within an organization. Not every IT project team might have end users as formal team members, but business employees frequently are relied on to give the project team information about their current work tasks and business processes, to participate in the redesign of these processes, and to evaluate designs for online application screens and reports from an end-user perspective. End users who have direct contacts with an organization's customers also play critical roles in IT projects when new systems will affect interactions with customers. In addition, many end users play critical roles in new system training, as well as ongoing "local support" for other end users who are learning new applications and computer tools. As will be discussed in Part III, some end users also develop applications using tools such as Excel, Access, and Visual Basic, and the monitoring of these applications is a business manager's responsibility.

LEARNING OBJECTIVES FOR THIS TEXTBOOK

The overall objective of this textbook is to prepare our readers to make good decisions about investing in and implementing IT solutions. Studying and discussing the technical and management topics in this textbook will prepare you to participate in the IS-business partnership needed to manage IT resources effectively. This book has been written for those who will be helping to manage IT as general managers, business managers, or as IS specialists.

Part I of this text focuses on the technology asset of the IS organization: computer systems, computer software, telecommunications/networks, and data. In order to be an effective participant in the management of IT resources, you need a base level of computer literacy. For workers in the Internet Era, this means not just gaining a fluency with IT vocabulary, but also preparing to cope with continual technology-based change. The goal is for you to increase your knowledge about fundamental technology concepts and major industry developments. From this vantage point, you can continue to grow your own knowledge base.

Part II of the text focuses on the business capabilities of three major types of software applications: enterprise systems, managerial support systems, and e-commerce applications. Understanding the IT capabilities of different categories of applications, as well as the problems that you can encounter when implementing them, is a first step toward improving your ability to identify the IT applications needed for a specific business to thrive in the Internet Era. These chapters also provide frameworks for thinking about new types of technologies and what business problems or new business opportunities they might help address.

Part III describes the methodologies and techniques for managing the development and delivery of IT projects. We begin with a chapter on IS concepts in general, then discuss in detail the methodologies for customized application development and purchasing packaged systems, all from the viewpoint of the implementing organization. A separate chapter is devoted to IT project management, including special issues related to managing IT project risks and large-scale changes in the way the business will operate after the systems implementation. The final chapter in this unit is on end-user computing management, including issues related to supporting users who are developing their own applications, as well as strategies and tactics to support and control end-user computing activities in general. Learning the key principles and guidelines in these chapters will help you avoid the application failures still being reported in the trade press.

Finally, in Part IV we devote three chapters to issues of importance for effectively managing an organization's IT assets. The first two chapters are concerned with how to develop an overall vision and strategic plan for managing the IT infrastructure and best practices for leading an IS organization. The final chapter is concerned with current legal, ethical, and social computing issues that are important for business and IT managers to address.

For this fifth edition of our textbook we have once again based our content on our own research, as well as on the research and experiences of other academic and practitioner authors. Although some of our content addresses enduring computing and management principles, other sections of this edition of the textbook required totally new or revised material due to the high rate of change in the IT profession. Our intent is to familiarize you with not only current IS management issues but also emerging ones. This edition also includes many new and revised teaching cases on IT initiatives as varied as implementing a data warehouse, automating a sales force, developing an online business, choosing an IT platform, and integrating systems after a merger.

We hope that you will use the Prentice-Hall Web site to give us feedback about what aspects of this textbook were especially helpful to you in your preparation for surviving and thriving in an e-world: *www.prenhall.com/martin*.

REVIEW QUESTIONS

1. Define what is included in the term information technology.
2. What types of productivity are associated with IT investments?
3. What are some ways that portable technologies can help employees work more effectively?
4. What are some of the IT innovations of the past two decades that have led to "ubiquitous" computing?
5. What are some ways that businesses are using the Internet to compete in new ways?
6. What is meant by the term "knowledge worker," and what IT support does this type of worker need today?
7. What are some of today's challenges for managing the technology asset (see Figure 1.2)?
8. Why has a relationship asset become so much more important in the Internet Era than in earlier computing eras described by Rockart?
9. What are some of today's challenges for managing the human asset?
10. How has the role of the business manger changed since computers were first used in business organizations?
11. What is an example of a potential "unintended" consequence of IT that needs to be monitored?
12. Briefly describe some typical ways that business managers are involved in managing IT.

DISCUSSION QUESTIONS

1. Cite some examples that show the impact that the Internet Era has had on a business function with which you are familiar (e.g., marketing, finance, operations/production, accounting, human resources).
2. Describe how your life as a student is different due to IT developments over the past decade.
3. Tomorrow's business managers need to understand how to manage IT projects, which includes learning some of the IT jargon. Identify some ways that a business manager can continue to build his or her IT knowledge.
4. Virtual organizations have been defined as temporary consortia that share costs, skills, and core competencies to develop and market products or services. Discuss how IT can enable this new type of organizational form.
5. What advantages do you see in choosing to work as a free agent? Do you see any disadvantages?
6. Using Web resources, identify some actions being taken by nonprofit organizations to help address the digital divide issue within the United States or globally.
7. Identify some Web sites that are useful resources for understanding new technology developments and tracking IS management trends.

CASE STUDY 1

MIDSOUTH CHAMBER OF COMMERCE (A): THE ROLE OF THE OPERATING MANAGER IN INFORMATION SYSTEMS

It was 7:30 P.M. on September 22, 1999, and Leon Lassiter, vice president of marketing with the Midsouth Chamber of Commerce (MSCC), was still in his office, reflecting on the week's frustrations. Lassiter had met with four territory managers, his marketing support supervisor, and a number of other members of his staff. All were upset about their lack of access to the new computer system and the problems they were having using the old PC systems. Lassiter had assured them that the problems were being addressed. He stressed that patience was needed during the ongoing conversion to the new system.

Now, during his private moment, Lassiter was beginning to recognize the problems and complexities he faced with the system conversion. The work of his marketing staff, who were unable to access the new computer system to handle their accounts, had ground to a halt. Even worse, something had happened to the data in most of the old PC systems, which meant that conference registrations and other functions had to be done manually. These inconveniences, however, were minor compared to Lassiter's uneasy feeling that there were problems with Midsouth's whole approach to the management of information technology. Lassiter knew that time was of the essence and that he might have to step in and manage the conversion, even though he had no information technology background. He wondered what he should do next.

Background

In the early 1900s, economic development in the Midsouth area was highly dependent on transportation systems. As a result of legislative decisions, many communities in the Midsouth area could not gain access to reasonable transportation services, thus retarding business and economic development. With no one to represent their concerns to Midsouth's government, a group of powerful businesspeople formed the Midsouth Chamber of Commerce to lobby the state government on the issue of transportation.

The MSCC dealt with this single issue until the 1930s, when its charter was changed to include a broader range of issues affecting the business community, including state banking laws, transportation, industrial development, and business taxes. By the mid-1980s, the MSCC, under the new leadership of President Jack Wallingford, became an aggressive advocacy organization for the business community.

The shift in the MSCC's role brought substantial change to the organization. In 1978 the MSCC had a staff of 14, a membership of 4,000, and an annual budget of $720,000. Over the years, the MSCC had been able to develop a reserve account of just over $1 million.

By 1986, the staff had grown to 24, the $1 million cash reserve had been drawn down to $250,000, and membership had dropped to 2,300, largely because of local economic problems in the early 1980s. The reserve reduction, supported by the board of directors, had fueled considerable internal growth in terms of staff and capabilities. During this time MSCC also moved into larger offices and began to computerize some manual processes.

By the late 1980s, the MSCC was considered to be the most powerful business advocacy organization in the Midsouth area and one of the most innovative in its approaches and techniques in dealing with problems facing the business community. The greatest problem facing the MSCC at the time was the growing concern that its aggressive growth might have to be curtailed because it could no longer fund its annual operating budget.

Leon Lassiter

In mid-1988, Wallingford was faced with a serious dilemma. The MSCC was projecting a $330,000 deficit for the 1989 fiscal year. Wallingford realized he was going to have to reduce both the number of staff and the number of programs or find some way to grow revenue more aggressively in the organization. Wallingford called in his vice president of public affairs and operations, Ed Wilson, and asked him to find someone new to lead the sales and marketing function.

Leon Lassiter came to the MSCC in December 1988 with 8 years of experience in sales management and marketing with American Brands, where he had recently turned down a promotion to regional sales manager. The MSCC, he reasoned, offered more of an opportunity to have an impact than at American Brands. He reported to Wallingford. Lassiter quickly began making dramatic changes. He found that the marketing support functions were better coordinated and managed than the sales functions. Additionally, although the MSCC had purchased a personal computer for sales and marketing and had installed some custom software in 1986, the system was quite limited in capability. With these facts, Lassiter began to develop an entirely new sales and marketing system based on measurable goals, documented operating procedures, and regular training programs.

Early Computerization Activity

Ed Wilson, who joined the MSCC in 1981, performed a variety of duties at the MSCC. He coordinated the legislative lobbying team, managed Midsouth's operations, and, during the time that there was no vice president of marketing, managed that function as well.

Beginning in 1986, Wilson began introducing the MSCC to the world of microcomputers and database management. Most of the staff were skeptical of the automation effort and reluctant to accept this approach. However, with the help of a systems consultant, Wilson acquired equipment and hired a programmer to write custom software in each functional area. Three primary user groups were identified: the marketing division, the operations division, and the human resources division. One IBM PC and printer were ordered for each group.

Marketing Division The marketing division's primary need was to track the activity occurring in membership. Primary uses of its computer system included:

- Developing a membership database
- Developing a prospective member database
- Making daily changes to both databases
- Generating a series of letters for personalized mail contact
- Generating prospect and member lists and labels by standard industrial classification (SIC) code, firm size (sales, employment), zip code, mailing designator, and other criteria
- Processing call-record activity by the territory managers
- Tracking member activities and concerns through a comment field
- Creating audit trails for reviewing changes
- General word processing

The marketing support area managed the database on the PC. They filled all requests for labels, lists, and changes from the sales and marketing staff. Requested changes to the member database sometimes backed up as much as 2 weeks. Lassiter felt this was unacceptable and required a 3-day turnaround on member-change activity.

Four territory managers, a marketing support supervisor, and two clerical people staffed the marketing division. The territory managers generated 75 to 80 call records per day that required database changes, letters, and invoice processing. Taking turns at the computer, both clerical people generally took a total of 12 hours to process these activities. In addition, the clerical staff processed commissions on membership sales, member cancellations, and general database maintenance. The clerical staff also prepared special-letter requests from the territory managers and performed all normal secretarial duties. Soon after the installation of the first PC system, the marketing staff began lobbying for additional capacity.

Operations Division Ed Wilson managed the operations division. Fourteen managers and support staff worked in operations. This group needed a system capable of providing financial and accounting controls, because until 1986, all payment histories and financial and accounting transactions were recorded in a ledger book and tracked by hand.

During the late 1980s, Wilson and his accounting manager set out a series of needs for the information system to meet. These included:

- The general ledger system
- Fund balances
- Accrual accounting functions
- Payment history tracking
- Commission schedules
- Membership cancellation tracking
- Report generation

In addition, Wilson wanted the operations system to be able to track legislative bills from their introduction through their demise in committee or chamber, their passage, or their veto by the governor. This information would be keyed into the system, updated as changes occurred, printed, and sent to selected staff members on a daily basis. Soon after installing one PC system to handle both functions, financial and legislative, Wilson wished he had ordered two systems for the operations division.

Human Resources Division The human resources division, with two managers and two support staff, was responsible for developing a conference and seminar tracking and reporting mechanism that would also have the capability of printing out badges for conference or seminar attendees. The division also maintained personnel records. Wilson's decision to buy a PC system for this group seemed to fit well with their needs.

From 1987 through 1992, use of the three systems grew steadily. In 1992, Wilson again hired an outside consultant to review the organization's information needs and select appropriate additional hardware and software. After a careful study, the consultant, Ted Vassici, recommended adding six more IBM PCs. In early 1993, the systems were ordered, each with HP laser printers, and allocated as follows: marketing (3), public finance (1), operations (1), and human resources (1). (See Exhibit 1 for the MSCC organization chart.)

In 1995, Vassici revised and updated the custom software used by each division. He also developed the MSCC's marketing software to sell to other membership-related organizations. Lassiter actively promoted the software, and the MSCC earned a small royalty on these sales.

Changing Times

By 1993, as a result of Lassiter's marketing and sales reorganization and Wilson's aggressive management of expenses, the MSCC was experiencing solid financial growth. While the two men were primarily responsible for the success, Wilson and Lassiter clashed on numerous occasions. Lassiter felt that much of the territory managers' work and marketing support activities could be automated to provide the MSCC with a significant reduction in labor and allied costs. Lassiter believed that a full-time systems analyst should be hired to meet the growing needs of the MSCC. Wilson, on the other hand, was worried about the cost of information systems. He felt that by maintaining the relationship with Vassici, he could control the rapidly growing demand for computer capabilities but not increase the number of employees. He knew that, as a nonprofit agency, there were limited funds for the expansion of computer capabilities. Adding a

EXHIBIT 1
MSCC Organizational Structure

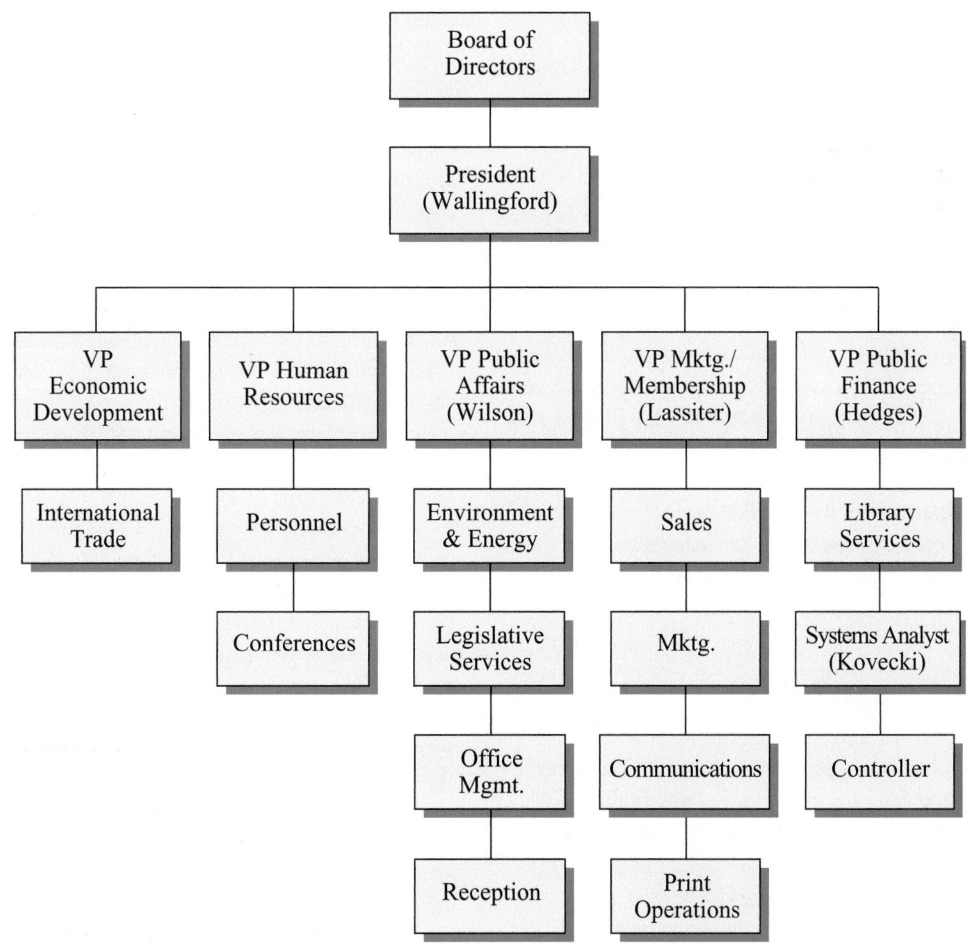

full-time systems analyst to the staff would make it significantly more difficult to contend with growing staff demands in other areas. Continuing the relationship with Vassici provided Wilson with the ability to specify exactly what Vassici worked on and what should be tabled until there was the time and budget for it.

Although Lassiter and Wilson continued to clash, Lassiter understood Wilson's desire to control costs in light of the limited resources of the MSCC. Lassiter knew that the slowly growing computer sophistication of the staff would explode once the tap was fully opened. However, Lassiter felt that the demand could be dealt with effectively once the MSCC determined the extent of the staff's needs.

In early 1996, Lassiter and Wilson joined forces on a concept by which the MSCC would offer a health insurance program to its members, now more than 4,500. Although the proposal was eventually rejected by the board of directors, Wilson and Lassiter, as a result of the study, determined that there were many revenue-producing opportunities the MSCC could pursue that would require a much higher level of information systems use. Wilson soon hired a systems analyst to increase the MSCC's capabilities.

Simon Kovecki, a young computer science graduate with no experience in a membership organization like the MSCC or with accounting software, joined the MSCC in June 1996 and spent his first 3 months on the job learning the organization and its computing systems. He worked exceptionally long hours as he struggled to understand software for which there was no documentation. Calls to Vassici for help were useless because his business had closed.

Through early 1997, Wilson continued to manage the computer systems and, with the help of Kovecki, upgraded the hardware in the PCs and printers with faster CPUs, memory upgrades, higher-capacity hard disks, and better monitors. With Kovecki's constant attention, the software continued to work relatively well. In 1997 Wilson, with Kovecki's assistance, developed an online legislative information system on a PC that was considered state of the art in the chamber of commerce industry. With this application and the growth in members and types of computer applications, the MSCC senior management began to worry about the separation of systems for membership and marketing, finance, conferences, and other applications which required constant data re-entry.

With annual dues approaching $2.8 million and approximately 4,750 member firms, the MSCC was among the largest statewide chambers of commerce in the country. By 1998, the staff had swelled to 42 and the financial reserve was nearly $2.6 million. Although Lassiter felt some satisfaction with the MSCC's growth and financial strength, he was bothered with the lack of forethought as to how the MSCC might develop a comprehensive plan to use information for competitive advantage. Wilson, too, recognized the value of information systems to an organization in the business of gathering, analyzing, and using information to affect legislative outcomes.

Catalyst for Change

By 1998, the MSCC had reached a point where change had to occur. Wallingford, at the urging of the board of directors, assigned Lassiter the additional areas of communications, graphic arts, and printing operations. Controller duties were assigned to Harry Taska, and Jeff Hedges, the new vice president of public finance, was assigned responsibility for computer operations. Wilson, nearing retirement, retained his public affairs activities and was asked to focus his efforts on developing an important public affairs project. (See Exhibit 1.)

Just after the staff changes took place, Kovecki confided to Lassiter that he was disappointed by the changes in staff responsibility. He felt he should have been elevated to manager of information systems and given additional staff. Hedges, who had little computer background, was also in charge of research on various issues of interest to the members of the MSCC as well as oversight of the controller's function. Kovecki was concerned that Hedges would not have the time to manage the growing computer operations properly.

Although the changes took place in early 1998, Lassiter had anticipated the changes in late 1997. His concern over the continued lack of attention to the information systems area led him to send out requests for information to a number of firms servicing the software needs of organizations like the MSCC. Primarily interested in sales and account tracking software, he focused on software systems from Cameo, MEI Colorado Association of Commerce and Industry, Connecticut Business and Industry Association, TelePro 2000, and Data Link. Lassiter sent the information he received from these vendors to other key managers but received little response. Wilson was involved in his new project, Taska was learning his new duties as controller, and Hedges had little time to examine the computer activities.

In August 1998, Lassiter attended a national association meeting where a session on management software led to his discovery of a small firm called UNITRAK. The company had developed a UNIX-based software system that was Y2K compliant. Lassiter was convinced that the software would meet the MSCC's needs. He based his assessment on the MSCC's current and anticipated future needs for computing capabilities that had been developed by Kovecki in 1997. (See Exhibit 2.)

Planning the New Data Processing System

Lassiter had identified areas in UNITRAK where he felt this more powerful information system would allow the MSCC to be more efficient. These improvements would enable staff members to:

- Input member information into a notes field (not then available)
- Generate telemarketing scripts that would allow "tree scripting" based on various sales objections (not then available)

EXHIBIT 2
MSCC Information Systems Needs

Information Systems Capabilities	Marketing	Operations	Public Affairs	Public Finance	Economic Development	Human Resources	Executive
Word Processing	X	X	X	X	X	X	X
Record Maintenance	X						
Legislative Services			X				
Online Publications			X			X	
List Processing	X						
Label Generation	X					X	
Database Management	X		X		X	X	
Financial Controls		X					
Conference Registration	X	X			X	X	
Seminar Registration	X	X	X			X	
Billings/Invoicing	X	X				X	
Publication Processing	X	X		X			
Data Search/Research				X			
Inventory Tracking	X	X					
Desktop Publishing	X					X	
Project Management	X	X	X		X	X	

- Utilize a statistical inquiry feature that would provide quantitative analysis of sales activity figures from all marketing activities (not attempted with the separate PC systems)

In addition, the new information system would allow territory managers to:

- Access their account information from their PCs rather than asking a staff member
- Develop letters and attachments from their PCs using information in the central database rather than manually linking information contained in several separate databases

In a memo to the management group, Lassiter commented, "The UNITRAK system not only meets our needs now, but it is also powerful enough to provide the MSCC with the room to grow over the next 5 years." The software also appeared to be user friendly, which Lassiter believed was the key to freeing up Kovecki's time. Lassiter explained the software to Hedges, who wanted the current accounting system left intact but agreed that now was the time to move forward in finding a more powerful software solution for the MSCC's problems. Hedges also agreed that other modules in the UNITRAK system could be activated at a later time.

In October 1998, Lassiter contacted Greg Ginder, president of the UNITRAK Software Corporation, and invited him to the MSCC for a demonstration of the system's capabilities. Wilson observed about 45 minutes of the three-hour demonstration and told Lassiter, "I'll support it if you want it. It will work for my project for public affairs." Hedges agreed that the new system would free up Kovecki's time and allow him to become more involved in planning and systems development. Kovecki's comments were different. He remarked, "Yeah, the software has its strengths and weaknesses and it probably would save some of my time. But, I don't like the idea of staff having uncontrolled access to so much data. It's not clear what they'll do with it."

The Proposal

Lassiter decided to move ahead quickly with a proposal to Wallingford and the board of directors. He developed simple flow charts that showed the hours it took to conduct certain activities, e.g., the staff time new member sales took with the current multiple-PC arrangement versus the time it would take with the new system. Lassiter knew that the executive committee of the board would require considerable justification to approve an "off-budget" capital expenditure that would significantly reduce reserves. He had also done some calculations to show that if the new system performed as he hoped, each territory manager would be able to generate $150,000 in increased sales through increased contacts. Although Lassiter knew this goal was aggressive and very difficult to justify, he wanted to be able to demonstrate a less-than-six-month payback if challenged by a member of the executive committee of the board.

Lassiter knew that UNITRAK would reduce the price of the software. The software was new, and UNITRAK had sold it to only one other statewide chamber of commerce organization, the Northern State Chamber of Commerce. Jeff Fritzly, vice president of marketing and development of the NSCC, told Lassiter:

> We looked at quite a few software packages as well as writing our own custom software, but our consultant chose the IBM A/S400 hardware and UNITRAK software. We purchased both the hardware and software from UNITRAK and got a good discount on the hardware. They have been very helpful and supportive of our needs.

A week before the executive committee meeting, Ginder and Lassiter agreed on a price for the software. Lassiter was pleased that the price was 30 percent less than Northern State had paid. With the help of Ginder and a member of the executive committee who headed the local branch office of IBM, Lassiter was also able to achieve an excellent discount on the A/S400. He felt this low cost was another justification for approval of the project. Lassiter also made it a point to meet with both Wilson and Hedges to keep them abreast of the negotiation and seek their advice. He felt that by increasing the level of communication with Hedges and Wilson, he would be able to gain their interest and support, which he felt was important to the success of the project.

When the executive committee of the board met in November 1998, Lassiter explained that the MSCC had reached the limit of its current system design, and that an investment in a central system connected to networked PCs was needed to allow the MSCC to meet current and future opportunities for growth. During his presentation, Lassiter said:

> While the MSCC has made significant and appropriate investments in the PC hardware necessary for the MSCC to increase its operational sophistication, we have reached the limit of these smaller machines. With the spectacular growth in revenue we've enjoyed over the last 5 years, our requirements and demands have increased dramatically. Without an immediate investment in increased capability, the MSCC's continued growth and services will be in jeopardy.

In response to challenges from the executive committee regarding what the new system would mean to the bottom line and the MSCC's reserves, Lassiter responded, "I believe we will see a 10–15 percent increase in sales and a 20 percent increase in staff productivity once the new system is operational." With these assurances and a price that would consume only 10–15 percent of reserves, the members of the executive committee complimented Lassiter on his work and approved the purchase of the software.

Implementation

Greg Ginder of UNITRAK was ecstatic over the decision and promised unlimited support at no charge to install the new system. But Kovecki continued to express concern about staff members using the new capabilities of the system. He said:

> I know that Lassiter expects this new software to be user friendly, but I'm uncomfortable with how strongly he feels about training the staff to use as many of the features as possible. He thinks that training the staff on whatever they want to learn will make the MSCC more effective, but I disagree. We would be opening Pandora's box and we would lose control over what was going on. The last thing we need is for people to be getting into things they don't need to be in.

By February 1999, Lassiter had heard nothing regarding the purchase of the new system. Kovecki told Lassiter that no one had approved the purchase order. Lassiter then questioned Hedges, who responded that he had heard nothing more and had been busy with research on issues of interest to the MSCC members. "Go ahead and purchase the software," Hedges told Lassiter. "It's your system anyway." Although Lassiter tried to explain that it was not his responsibility to implement the purchase or conversion, he felt the project would not move forward without his purchasing the software. After signing the purchase order, Lassiter handed it to Kovecki and said, "You and Hedges are the project managers. I shouldn't be involved at this point. It's up to you guys to complete the project."

On March 30, Lassiter asked Kovecki how the project was proceeding. Kovecki stated that the hardware had been delivered but that he was busy with a project of Wilson's and didn't have time to work on the new software. Lassiter went to Wilson to inquire about the anticipated length of the project Kovecki was working on and Wilson indicated it should be finished by mid-April.

Although Lassiter felt uncomfortable about pushing Hedges and Kovecki, he was beginning to feel that he would have to use his influence to get things moving. Lassiter held a meeting with his staff, informing them that a new system had been approved that would improve operations in several areas. Several staff members expressed concern that they had not been consulted or informed of the idea before its approval. Specific questions were asked regarding word processing, new member recruiting, and general processing. Lassiter, anticipating that Kovecki had studied the documentation, asked Kovecki to answer the questions. Kovecki was unable to answer the questions and indicated he needed more time to study the documentation.

Lassiter set up an appointment with UNITRAK for training for Kovecki and himself. After a positive training visit, Lassiter asked Kovecki to spend half a day with him to set up a project flow chart and anticipate potential problems, but May and June passed with little forward progress on the conversion. Lassiter had told the executive committee that the project would be completed by the end of March 1999, yet little had been accomplished.

Upon Kovecki's return from a 2-week vacation at the end of June, Lassiter asked Wallingford to intervene and to strongly urge Hedges and Kovecki to complete the project. Lassiter stated:

> It really bothered me that I had to go over Hedges' head but we were coming up on the seventh month of what should have been an easy 3-month project. It's partly my fault because I didn't establish teamwork up front, nor did I make clear early in the process the responsibilities of those participating.

The Final Phase

With Hedges' agreement, Lassiter set up 2 days of staff training for the third week in August 1999. (See Exhibit 3.) Kovecki had assured Lassiter that the system would be up by the last day of training so that the staff could immediately use the new system. Lassiter broke the training into major segments and had Kovecki set up training sites in two separate conference rooms for staff. UNITRAK sent a two-person team that would act as project managers and trainers.

The training went well with the exception of the conference and seminar segment of the software. The users brought up

EXHIBIT 3
Staff Training

TO: All Staff Members
FROM: Leon Lassiter
DATE: August 12, 1999
RE: Computer Training Schedule

The following schedule has been designed to train all staff members on the new computing system:

August 18, 1999

9:30–11:30 Marketing Support
- Susan Devine
- Ann Triplett
- Dianne Hippelheuser

11:30–12:30 Lunch

12:30–2:30 Territory Managers
- Mitch Guiet
- Jim Wagner
- Gayle Roberts
- Dave Girton

2:30–3:00 Break

3:00–3:30 General Staff
1. ____
2. ____
3. ____
4. ____
5. ____

3:30–4:00 Economic Development Staff
1. ____
2. ____
3. ____
4. ____
5. ____

4:00–4:30 Public Finance Staff
1. ____
2. ____
3. ____
4. ____
5. ____

August 19, 1999

8:30–9:00 Human Resources Staff
1. ____
2. ____
3. ____
4. ____
5. ____

9:30–10:30 Conferences Staff
- Joyce Jones
- Kathy Neeb
- Carolyn Hosford
- Dianne Hippelheuser
- Gini Raymond
- Marge Price
- Amy Kerrick

10:30–11:00 Controller Staff
1. ____
2. ____
3. ____
4. ____
5. ____

11:00–11:30 General Staff
1. ____
2. ____
3. ____
4. ____
5. ____

11:30–12:30 Lunch

12:30–1:30 Legislative Services
- Darla Barnett

1:30–2:30 Doing Word Processing
- Joyce Jones
- Dianne Hippelheuser
- Gini Raymond
- Jean Wiles
- Carolyn Hosford
- Amy Kerrick
- Kathy Neeb
- Kathleen Johnson

2:30–3:00 Break

3:00–5:00 Open

significant complaints that the new software servicing this area was not as functional and user friendly as the existing custom-written PC software. Although Lassiter suspected that a large part of the problem was that the new software was just different, he asked UNITRAK to work with the users in adapting the UNITRAK software to better meet their needs. Ginder commented:

> Because our software is relatively new to the marketplace, we are open to adjusting and changing certain aspects of the software without rewriting major portions. We feel we could learn a great deal from the MSCC that would make our software more marketable.

On the final day of training, Lassiter told Kovecki to migrate the data in the current PC systems to the new system. Kovecki told Lassiter that he was having a few problems and would conduct the migration after work, and it would be ready first thing in the morning. The next morning Kovecki, in responding to Lassiter's query as to why the system was not up, said:

> When I attempted the migration last night, less than 15 percent of the data rolled over into the proper assignments. With no documentation on the old software to refer to, it will probably take me a week to work out the bugs. In the meantime, the new system won't work and some of the data in our current PCs seems to have been corrupted. I hope we can recover the latest backup, but some of the systems haven't been backed up for more than 3 months.

Although one of the marketing division's systems had been backed up recently, the rest of the MSCC's PCs were basically inoperable. Requests for lists and labels for mailings could not be fulfilled. Word processing, payment and invoice posting, changes, list management, and so on were all inoperable or partially inoperable. UNITRAK was finding it difficult to help because Kovecki had forgotten to order a new modem that would allow UNITRAK experts remote access to the system.

Lassiter was finding it very difficult to gain information from Kovecki on the progress and status of the system conversion. It seemed that Kovecki, frustrated with the problems he was having and irritated with the staff coming to him to ask for assistance, was going out of his way to avoid the staff. Lassiter said:

> I explained to Kovecki that I wasn't trying to grill him for information, but because the staff now considered me to be the project director, I needed information with which to make decisions affecting the work flow of the staff and determine what kind of help we could request from UNITRAK.

Although Lassiter knew that the staff felt he was responsible for the new system, he felt frustrated that there was little he could do in managing the conversion. Hedges remained disengaged from the project, and Kovecki did not report to Lassiter.

The Future

It was in this situation that Lassiter found himself as he sat in his office at 7:30 P.M. in late September of 1999. Kovecki had promised that the new system would be up on each of the last several Mondays. Each Monday brought disappointment and compounded frustration to the staff. Lassiter knew that the 2 days of training had been wasted because the staff had long forgotten how to use the new system. He also guessed that Kovecki had not made the old systems Y2K compliant, so time was running out. Something had to be done—but what?

PART I
INFORMATION TECHNOLOGY

AFTER THE IMPORTANT OPENING CHAPTER, WHICH SET THE STAGE FOR THE ENTIRE book, the next four chapters constitute the information technology (IT) portion of this book. A number of technical concepts will be introduced, and a large vocabulary of technical terms will be employed. For those of you who have a background in information systems (IS), computer science, engineering, or one of the physical sciences, much of the material in this section of the book might be a review and an update of what you already know. For others, these chapters have been carefully written to introduce the non-IS specialist to IT concepts.

Chapters 2 to 5 have been written with a particular goal in mind: to convey what you as a manager need to know about IT—and the data manipulated by that technology—and to do so in a straightforward, understandable way. (For those of you considering an information systems career, these chapters provide the essential technical background upon which much of your future course work will be based.) The intent of these chapters is to give you the necessary technical background for the remainder of this book and to give you a basic understanding of IT on which you can build as you continue to learn during your career. These chapters give you the terminology and concepts to understand and communicate with IS professionals and to be an informed consumer of IT. At a minimum, these chapters should enable you to be a knowledgeable reader of IT articles in *The Wall Street Journal*, *Business Week*, *Fortune*, and similar publications.

Our overview of IT begins with a consideration of computer systems in Chapter 2. This chapter concentrates on computer hardware, the physical pieces of a computer system, but it also introduces the all-important stored-program concept. The chapter takes a look at the information systems industry and at current technology in the hardware arena. Chapter 3 discusses computer software, the set of programs that control the operations of the computer system. As a manager, your interface with the computer system is through the software. You will work directly with easy-to-use packages such as Web browsers, spreadsheets, and word processors, and you are likely to be involved in acquiring and developing other software for your particular area of an organization. This chapter surveys the key types of software in the early twenty-first century—including applications software, personal productivity packages, Web software, fourth generation languages, object-oriented and visual programming languages, and database management systems—and describes the changing nature of software.

Telecommunications and networking are the topics of Chapter 4. Virtually all computers of all sizes communicate directly (at least part of the time) with other computers by means of a variety of networks, including the world-spanning Internet. These computer networks, especially the Internet, are a major part of the current communications revolution. In fact, "network-centric computing" appears to be a key phrase of the computer industry today. Chapter 4 describes the main elements of telecommunications and networking, including transmission media and wireless communication, network topology, types of networks, and network protocols. It focuses on the business need for networking and the exploding role of telecommunications and networking.

Chapter 5 describes issues related to the data resource of an organization. These data will be processed, stored, and transmitted by a combination of hardware, software, and networking technologies. The data resource is a major organizational resource, and it must be developed and carefully managed much like other organizational assets, such as facilities, labor, and capital. This chapter focuses on data modeling and data architecture, the tools for managing data, the key principles in managing data, and data management processes and policies within organizations. A well-managed data resource is essential to the effective use of IT, and both IS and business managers play critical roles in managing the data resource.

Three teaching cases related to the technology side of managing IT have been grouped at the end of Part I. The IMT Custom Machines Company, Inc., case study investigates the choice between continued reliance on a large, mainframe-based computer system and newer IT platform alternatives: high-powered UNIX workstations or Linux-based machines. The IBM-Indiana case study describes a project in which an entire sales and sales support workforce became telecommuters, moving first to home offices and then to "mobile" computing. The Midsouth Chamber of Commerce (B) case study continues the saga—begun in Midsouth Chamber of Commerce (A) after Chapter 1 of this book—of the selection and management of hardware and software for this organization.

CHAPTER 2
COMPUTER SYSTEMS

CHAPTER 1 HAS SET THE STAGE FOR THE DETAILED STUDY OF INFORMATION technology (IT) and your role in harnessing that technology. We can now take a closer look at the building blocks of information technology and the development and maintenance of IT systems.

Our definition of IT is a broad one, encompassing all forms of technology involved in capturing, manipulating, communicating, presenting, and using data (and data transformed into information). Thus, IT includes computers (both the hardware and the software), peripheral devices attached to computers, communications devices and networks—clearly incorporating the Internet—photocopiers, facsimile machines, cellular telephones and related wireless devices, computer-controlled factory machines, robots, video recorders and players, and even the microchips embedded in products such as cars, airplanes, elevators, and home appliances. All these manifestations of IT are important, and you need to be aware of their existence and their present and potential uses in an organizational environment. However, two broad categories of IT are critical for the manager in a modern organization: computer technology and communications technology. Both of these technologies have had, and continue to have, a gigantic impact on the structure of the modern organization, the way it does its business, its scope, and the jobs and the careers of the managers in it.

Perhaps the first important point to be made in this chapter is that the division between computer and communications technology is arbitrary and somewhat misleading. Historically, computer and communications technologies were independent, but they have grown together over the years—especially in the 1980s and 1990s. Distributed systems (to be discussed in Chapter 6) exist in every industry, and these systems require the linking of computers by telecommunication lines. World Wide Web-based systems, delivered either via an intranet within the organization or via the Web itself, are becoming increasingly prevalent. Almost every manager at every level has a microcomputer on his or her desk. The computer is connected by telecommunication lines to a corporate computer and usually to the Internet. Today, the information systems organization often has responsibility for both computing and communications. The switches used in telephone networks are computers, as are the devices used to set up computer networks such as routers and gateways. It is still convenient for us to discuss computing technology as distinct from communications technology, but the distinctions are becoming even more blurred as time passes. In reality, computer/communications technology is being developed and marketed by the computer/communications industry.

This chapter concentrates on computer **hardware**, as distinct from computer **software**. Computer hardware refers to the physical pieces of a computer system—such as a CPU, a printer, and a disk drive—that can be touched. Software, by contrast, is the set of programs that controls the operations of the computer system. For the most part, our consideration of software will be deferred until Chapter 3, but the central idea behind today's computers—the stored-program concept—will be explored here to aid in our understanding of how a computer system works.

EVOLUTION OF COMPUTER SYSTEMS

At present, early in the twenty-first century, the computer/communications industry is easily the largest industry in the world in terms of dollar volume of sales. This is a remarkable statement, given that the first large-scale electronic computer was completed in 1946. The ENIAC (Electronic Numerical Integrator And Computer), which was built by Dr. John W. Mauchly and J. Presper Eckert, Jr., at the Moore School of Electrical Engineering at the University of Pennsylvania, was composed of more than 18,000 vacuum tubes, occupied 15,000 square feet of floor space, and weighed more than 30 tons (see Figure 2.1). Its performance was impressive for its day—the ENIAC could perform 5,000 additions or 500 multiplications per minute.

First Generation of Computers

The ENIAC ushered in the so-called first generation of computers, extending from 1946 through 1959. Vacuum tubes were the distinguishing technology utilized in the first generation machines. After several one-of-a-kind laboratory machines, the first production-line machines—the Sperry Rand Univac, followed shortly by the IBM 701—became available in the early 1950s. But the major success story among first generation machines was the IBM 650, introduced in 1954. The 650 was designed as a logical move upward from existing punched-card machines, and it was a hit. IBM expected to sell 50 of the 650s but, in fact, installed more than 1,000, which helped IBM gain its position of prominence in the computer industry.

Second Generation of Computers

The invention of the transistor led to the second generation of computers. Transistors were smaller, more reliable, and less expensive and gave off less heat than vacuum tubes. The second generation machines generally used magnetic cores (minute magnetizable washers strung on a lattice of wires) as their primary memory, compared to the vacuum tubes or magnetic drums, where spots were magnetized on the surface of a rotating metal cylinder, that were used in the first generation. Memory sizes were increased considerably,

Figure 2.1 The ENIAC (Courtesy of Bettmann/CORBIS)

perhaps by a factor of 20, and execution speeds increased as well, again perhaps by a factor of 20. IBM again dominated this era, largely on the strength of the popular 7000-series large machines and the record-breaking sales of the 1400-series small machines.

Third Generation of Computers

The beginning of the third generation has a specific date—April 7, 1964—when IBM announced the System/360 line of computers. The System/360, as well as third generation machines from other vendors, was based on the use of integrated circuits rather than individual transistors. Early in the third generation, magnetic cores were still used as primary memory; later, semiconductor memories replaced cores. Memory sizes and execution speeds continued to climb dramatically. With the third generation, the notion of upward compatibility was introduced. When customers outgrew (ran out of capacity with) one model in a product line, they could trade up to the next model without any reworking of implemented applications. Perhaps the most drastic change was that the third generation machines relied on revolutionary, sophisticated operating systems (complex programs), such as IBM's OS, to actually control the computer's actions. As one might expect, the System/360 and the System/370 that followed were the dominant computers of the late 1960s and 1970s (see Figure 2.2).

Fourth Generation of Computers

Unfortunately, there is no neat dividing line between the third and fourth generations of computers. Most experts and vendors would agree that we are now in the fourth generation, but they don't agree on when this generation started or how soon we should expect the fifth generation (if ever). Changes since the introduction of the System/360 have tended to be evolutionary, rather than revolutionary. New models or new lines based on new technologies were announced by all major vendors on a regular basis in the 1970s, 1980s, 1990s, and early 2000s (although many of the players have changed). Memory sizes have continued to climb, and speeds have continued to increase. An innovation later in the fourth generation was to incorporate multiple processors into a single machine. The integrated circuits of the third generation became LSI (large-scale integration) circuits and then VLSI (very-large-scale integration) circuits. Through VLSI the entire circuitry for a computer can be put onto a single silicon chip smaller than a fingernail. Communication between terminals and computers, and between computers themselves, first began during the third generation, but the use of this

Figure 2.2 A Configuration of the IBM System/360 (Courtesy of IBM Archives. Unauthorized use not permitted.)

technology came of age during the fourth. With the spread of distributed systems and various local and long-distance network arrangements, some commentators refer to communication as the distinguishing feature of the fourth generation.

The Development of Minicomputers

Parallel with the third and fourth generations, an important splintering occurred within the computer industry. As IBM and the other major vendors, such as Sperry Rand, Burroughs, NCR, Honeywell, and Control Data, competed for industry leadership with more powerful, larger machines, a number of smaller, newer firms recognized a market niche for small machines aimed at smaller businesses and scientific applications. Successful firms in this minicomputer market included Digital Equipment Corporation (DEC), Data General, and Hewlett-Packard. These minicomputers were just like the larger machines (which came to be called mainframes), except that they were less powerful and less expensive. The minicomputer vendors also worked very hard at developing easy-to-use applications software. As the minicomputer market evolved, many of the mainframe vendors, such as IBM, moved into this area.

The Development of Microcomputers

Another splintering within the industry took place in the late 1970s and 1980s with the introduction and success of the microcomputer, which is based on the computer on a chip (see Figure 2.3), or microprocessor. Apple and other companies pioneered the microcomputer business, finding a market niche below the minicomputers for home use, in very small businesses, and in the public school system. Then, in late 1981, IBM entered the market with its Personal Computer, which quickly became the microcomputer standard for the workplace. In fact, the Personal Computer, or PC, became so much of a standard that most people use the terms *microcomputer*, *Personal Computer*, and *PC* interchangeably (and we will do so in this book, as well). Subsequent developments included greatly increased speed and capabilities of microcomputers, as well as the introduction of a variety of IBM "clones" in the marketplace by other vendors. The widespread acceptance of microcomputers in the business world placed significant computing power at the fingertips of virtually every manager. The connection of all these microcomputers (as well as the connection of the larger machines) through company intranets and the worldwide Internet changed the entire face of computing in the mid- and late 1990s. The Internet and intranets will be explored in Chapter 4 as well as in Chapter 8.

BASIC COMPONENTS OF COMPUTER SYSTEMS

For historical completeness, we should note that there are really two distinct types of computers—digital and analog. Digital computers operate directly on numbers, or digits,

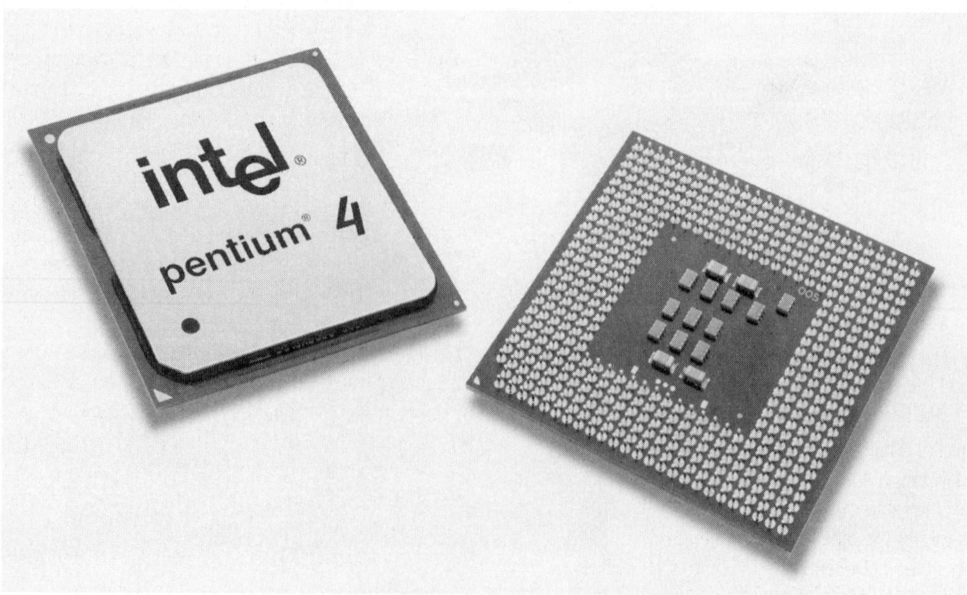

Figure 2.3 Intel® Pentium® 4 Processor Built on 90 nm (nanometer) Technology (Courtesy of Intel Corporation)

THE MICROPROCESSOR CHIP NEARS 35

In late 1971, Intel Corporation announced the first microprocessor in a trade-magazine ad that heralded "a new era in integrated electronics." But even Intel didn't anticipate the scope of the revolution it was unleashing on business and society. Today the world's chip population has swollen to nearly one trillion, including 25 billion microprocessors. Ever since Intel's first microprocessor, the 4004, these chips have grown increasingly powerful in periodic leaps and bounds (see Table 2.1). In 1996, Intel Chairman Andrew S. Grove predicted that this inexorable march would continue for at least 15 more years, perhaps 30. By 2011, he envisioned microprocessors with a billion transistors that would chew through 100,000 MIPS (millions of instructions, or operations, per second). Grove's estimates are holding true—in fact, he might well have been low in his predictions! In late 2003 the fastest Pentium 4 chips boasted 55 million transistors and speeds of 3,200 MIPS. Therefore, that 2011 chip will be crammed with the power of over 30 Pentium 4s.

Table 2.1 The Evolution of the Intel Microprocessor

Chip	Public Debut	Initial Cost	Number of Transistors	Initial MIPS
4004	11/71	$200	2,300	0.06
8008	4/72	$300	3,500	0.06
8080	4/74	$300	6,000	0.6
8086	6/78	$360	29,000	0.3
8088	6/79	$360	29,000	0,3
i286	2/82	$360	134,000	0.9
i386	10/85	$299	275,000	5
i486	4/89	$950	1.2 million	20
Pentium	3/93	$878	3.1 million	100
Pentium Pro	3/95	$974	5.5 million	300
Pentium II	5/97	$775	7.5 million	266[a]
Pentium III	2/99	$696	9.5 million	500[a]
Pentium 4	11/2000	$819	42 million[b]	1,500[a]
Pentium 4 with Hyper-Threading Technology	11/2002	$637	55 million[b]	3,060[a]
1286 (?)	2011	n/a	1 billion	100,000

[a]The numbers reported for the Pentium II, Pentium III, Pentium 4, and Pentium 4 with Hyper-Threading Technology are actually megaHertz (millions of cycles per second), not MIPS. This measure would be the same as MIPS if one instruction were executed each cycle.

[b]Intel did not make public the number of transistors on the Pentium 4 and Pentium 4 with Hyper-Threading Technology chips. The numbers in the table came from Rendleman, 2002, and might not be comparable to the other transistor figures.

Source: Business Week (December 9, 1996): 150, with updates from the Intel Web site, 1997, 1999, 2000, and 2002, and from Rendleman, 2002.

Of course, Silicon Valley-based Intel Corporation is not the only chipmaker, but it is the largest and the most important. Intel supplies over 80 percent of the all-important microprocessor chips used to power IBM and IBM-compatible microcomputers. Advanced Micro Devices (AMD), which produces Intel-compatible chips, is the only other major player in this market, with about a 15 percent market-share. Other manufacturers of processor chips (largely for more powerful machines) include IBM, Hewlett-Packard, and Sun Microsystems. IBM also produces the processor chips used in Apple microcomputers.

However, the worldwide semiconductor industry consists of much more than processor chips. Although U.S. firms dominate the processor market (all the firms mentioned above are from the United States), four of the five leading producers of the random access memory chips used in PCs are from outside the United States—Samsung Electronics (Korea), Hynix Semiconductor (Korea), Infineon Technologies (Germany), and Elpida Memory (Japan). The fifth major player is Micron Technology of the United States. Intel is at the top of the heap in terms of **flash memory** production, as used in digital cameras and music players, followed by Samsung, Toshiba (Japan), and AMD. Another rapidly growing segment of the semiconductor industry consists of **digital signal processor** (**DSP**) chips. DSP chips convert analog images or sounds in real time (meaning with essentially no delay) to a stream of digital signals. DSP chips are used at the heart of digital cellular telephones, digital audio receivers, cable modems, and handheld computers, and they are also used in traditional products such as kitchen appliances and electric motors and in new products such as hearing aids and digital-video editing systems. Texas Instruments (which, like Intel, also introduced a microprocessor chip in 1971) is the leader in sales of DSP chips, but Agere Systems (United States), Analog Devices, Inc. (United States), Infineon, Motorola, NEC Electronics (Japan), and Renesas Technology (Japan) are also major players. In another market segment, IBM is the leading producer of custom-made chips, called application-specific integrated circuits, or ASICs, followed by rivals such as Texas Instruments and NEC Electronics. Several of the chip manufacturers already mentioned, including IBM, do **foundry** work, which involves the production of chips for other companies that have been designed by those companies. The leaders in the foundry business, however, are a trio of Asian chipmakers—Taiwan Semiconductor Manufacturing Company, United Microelectronics Corporation (Taiwan), and Chartered Semiconductor Manufacturing Ltd. (Singapore). The semiconductor industry is gigantic and rapidly expanding, with worldwide revenues forecast to reach $200 billion annually by 2005.

[Adapted from Port, 1996; Rendleman, 2002; Park and Kunii, 2002; Ante, Port, Einhorn, and Park, 2003; and Edwards, Ihlwan, and Engardio, 2003]

just as humans do. Analog computers manipulate some analogous physical quantity, such as voltage or shaft rotation speed, which represents (to some degree of accuracy) the numbers involved in the computation. Analog computers have been most useful in engineering and process-control environments, but digital machines have largely replaced them even in these situations. Thus, all of our preceding discussion relates to digital computers, as does that which follows.

Underlying Structure

Today's computers vary greatly in size, speed, and details of their operation—from handheld microcomputers costing around $100 to supercomputers with price tags of more than $30 million. Fortunately for our understanding, all these machines have essentially the same basic logical structure (as represented in Figure 2.4). All computers, whether they are microcomputers from Dell or mainframes from IBM, are made up of the same set of six building blocks: input, output, memory, arithmetic/logical unit, control unit, and files. Our discussion of how computers work will focus on these six blocks and their interrelationships.

In addition to the blocks themselves, Figure 2.4 also includes two types of arrows. The broad arrows represent the flows of data through the computer system, and the thin arrows indicate that each of the other components is controlled by the control unit. A dashed line encircles the control unit and the arithmetic/logical unit. These two blocks together are often referred to as the **central processing unit**, or **CPU**, or as the **processor**. (Historically, the memory was also considered part of the CPU because it was located in the same physical cabinet, but with changes in memory technologies, memory is now regarded as a separate entity from the CPU.)

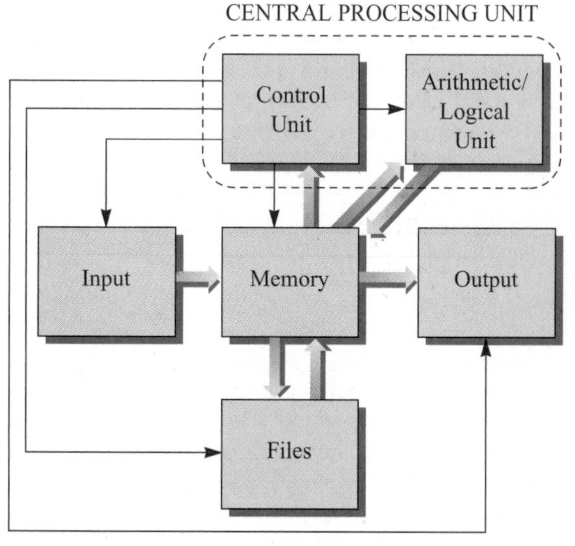

Figure 2.4 The Logical Structure of Digital Computers

Input/Output

To use a computer, we must have some means of entering data into the computer for it to use in its computations. There are a wide variety of input devices, and we will mention only the most commonly used types. The input device that you as a manager are most likely to use is a keyboard on a microcomputer or a terminal. We will talk more about microcomputers (PCs) later, but they include all the building blocks shown in Figure 2.4. A **terminal** is a simpler device than a PC; it is designed strictly for input/output and does not incorporate a processor (CPU), or at least not a general-purpose processor. Most terminals consist of a keyboard for data entry and a video display unit (a television screen) to show the user what has been entered and to display the output from the computer. The terminal is connected to a computer via some type of telecommunication line. In addition to their use by managers, terminals are widely used by clerical personnel involved in online transaction processing (to be discussed in Chapter 6). Today microcomputers are replacing many terminals.

Special types of terminals are also in widespread use as computer input devices. Point-of-sale terminals have largely replaced conventional cash registers in major department stores, and automatic teller machines (ATMs) are commonplace in the banking industry. These devices are simply terminals modified to serve a specific purpose. Like the standard terminals described above, these special-purpose devices serve as both input and output devices, often incorporating a small built-in printer to provide a hard-copy record of the transaction.

Terminals allow users to key data directly into the computer. By contrast, some input methods require that data be recorded on a special input medium before they can be entered into the computer. Until the 1980s, the most common form of computer input involved punched cards and a punched-card reader. Users keyed in data at a punched-card keypunch machine, which translated the keystrokes into holes in a punched card (employing a coding scheme known as Hollerith code). The punched cards were then carried to a punched-card reader directly attached to the computer; the reader read the cards one at a time, interpreting the holes in the cards and transmitting the data to the memory. Until the early 1980s, U.S. government checks, many credit-card charge slips, and class enrollment cards at most universities were punched cards. Computers often had a card punch attached as an output device to produce checks, enrollment cards, and other punched-card output. However, punched cards were a nuisance to handle and store, and they have disappeared because of the communications developments of the past two decades.

Other input methods employing special input media have not disappeared, although their importance has shrunk. With a key-to-tape system or a key-to-disk system, data entry personnel key in data at a microcomputer or a terminal attached to a midrange computer. The computer records the data as a series of magnetized spots (using some type of coding scheme) on the surface of a magnetic tape (similar to the tape used in a home videocassette recorder) or a magnetic disk (similar in appearance to an old-style phonograph record). After a significant quantity of data has been recorded, an output magnetic tape is created and hand-carried to the primary computer system, where it is mounted in a magnetic tape unit. This unit then reads the tape, interpreting the magnetized spots on the surface of the tape and transmitting the data to the memory.

Some input methods read an original document (such as a typed report or a check or deposit slip) directly into the computer's memory. Check processing is handled this way in the United States through the **magnetic ink character recognition** (**MICR**) input method. Most checks have the account number and bank number preprinted at the bottom using strange-looking numbers and a special magnetizable ink. After a check is cashed, the bank that cashed it records the amount of the check in magnetizable ink at the bottom of the check. A computer input device called a magnetic ink character reader magnetizes the ink, recognizes the numbers, and transmits the data to the memory of the bank's computer. **Optical character recognition** (**OCR**) is an input method that directly scans typed, printed, or hand-printed material. A device called an optical character reader scans and recognizes the characters and then transmits the data to the memory or records them on magnetic tape.

Imaging goes even further than OCR. With imaging, any type of paper document, including business forms, reports, charts, graphs, and photographs, can be read by a scanner and translated into digital form so that the document can be stored in the computer system. Then this process can be reversed so that the digitized image stored in the computer system can be displayed on a video display unit, printed on paper, or transmitted to another computer. However, the characters in the image cannot be easily processed as individual numbers or letters. Imaging is often accomplished through a specialized image-management system, which is a microcomputer-based system.

An increasingly important way of entering data into a computer is by scanning a **bar code label** on a package, a product, a routing sheet, a container, or a vehicle. Bar code systems capture data much faster and more accurately than systems in which data are keyed. Thus the use of bar codes is very popular for high-volume supermarket checkout, department store sales, inventory tracking, time and attendance records, and health care records. Bar codes are also valuable for automated applications such as automotive assembly control and warehouse restocking. There is actually a wide variety of bar code languages, called *symbologies*. Perhaps the most widely known symbology is the Universal Product Code, or UPC, used by the grocery industry.

Just as we must have a way of entering data into the computer, the computer must have a way of producing results in a usable form. We have already mentioned displaying results on a video display unit, printing a document on a small printer built into a special-purpose terminal, and punching cards. Output can also be written on a magnetic tape or a magnetic disk (such as a 3.5-inch floppy disk), which could be useful if the data will be read back later into either the same or another computer.

The dominant form of output, however, is the printed report. Computer printers come in a variety of sizes, speeds, and prices. At the lower end are serial printers, which are usually employed with microcomputers. They usually employ a nonimpact process (such as an ink-jet or laser-jet process), and they typically operate in a speed range of 3 to 15 pages per minute. Printers used with larger computers may be line printers or page printers. Line printers operate at high speeds (up to 2,200 lines per minute) and print one line at a time, usually employing an impact printing mechanism in which individual hammers force the paper and ribbon against the appropriate print characters (which are embossed on a rotating band or chain). Page printers, which produce up to 800 pages per minute, print one entire page at a time, often employing an electrophotographic printing process (like a copying machine) to print an image formed by a laser beam.

In part to counteract the flood of paper that is threatening to engulf many organizations, microfilm has become an important computer output medium. The output device is a **computer output microfilm** (**COM**) recorder that accepts the data from the memory and prepares the microfilm output at very high speeds, either as a roll of microfilm or as a sheet of film called a microfiche that contains many pages on each sheet. **Voice response units** are gaining increasing acceptance as providers of limited, tightly programmed computer output. Cable television shopping services and stock price quotation services often use voice output in conjunction with touch-tone telephone input.

A relatively new buzzword used to describe computer input and output is **multimedia**. A multimedia system uses a microcomputer to coordinate many types of communications media—text, graphics, sound, still images, animations, and video. The purpose of a multimedia system is to enhance the quality of, and interest in, a presentation, whether it is a corporate briefing, a college lecture, an elementary school lesson, or self-paced instruction. The sound and video usually come from a compact disk (CD) or digital video disk (DVD) played on a CD or DVD player built into the microcomputer. Graphics or photographs used as part of the presentation might have been scanned via an imaging system, and artwork created with a graphics program on the computer; these images are then stored in the computer's files. The key is that the microcomputer controls the entire multimedia presentation.

To summarize, the particular input and output devices attached to a given computer will vary based on the uses of the computer. Every computer system will have at least one input device and at least one output device. On the computers you will be using as a manager, keyboards, video display units, printers, CD and DVD players, and disk drives will be the most common input/output devices.

Computer Memory

At the heart of the diagram of Figure 2.4 is the **memory**, also referred to as main memory or primary memory. All data flows are to and from memory. Data from input devices always goes into memory; output devices always receive

VOICE INPUT TO COMPUTERS

Voice input to computers is becoming a reality, although we cannot converse with today's machines as easily as Starfleet officers can talk with the computer system on the *USS Enterprise*. But we are certainly moving in that direction! Economical software packages are now available to run on microcomputers operating under Windows 2000 or XP that permit users to "dictate" to the computer and have the computer produce a word-processed document. Until recently, however, the accuracy of **speech recognition software** was suspect, with the best packages achieving recognition accuracy only a little above 90 percent—nearly one error in every ten words. In late 2002 and mid-2003, *PC Magazine* tested the latest upgrades from the two leading speech recognition software packages for PCs and found that both packages achieved 95 to 98 percent accuracy after an hour of dictation, correction, and retraining. With these numbers, speech recognition software is getting close to becoming a productivity-enhancing tool—at least for users with limited typing skills, disabilities, repetitive stress injuries from overusing a computer keyboard, or no time to do anything except dictate (such as medical doctors). For most of us, speech recognition software might provide an interesting supplement to the keyboard and mouse, but it is not going to replace these traditional means of input in the short run.

PC Magazine's Greg Alwang was most impressed with the Dragon NaturallySpeaking Preferred 7 package (from ScanSoft; street price $200). After the required five minutes of training of the software, he was able to attain initial accuracy of 90 to 95 percent on dictation, depending on the document. The accuracy figure went up to 96 to 98 percent after an hour or so of use. Furthermore, NaturallySpeaking Preferred 7 contains automatic punctuation to save the user from dictating commas and periods, and it is supported on handheld Pocket PCs (more on these small computers later) so that users can dictate while on the road. IBM's ViaVoice for Windows Release 10 Pro edition (list price $190) was nearly as good on dictation accuracy, but it did not perform as well in terms of attaining hands-free operation of a PC. With NaturallySpeaking Preferred 7, Alwang was easily able to navigate around the document and correct his dictation errors by voice alone, with only minimal command errors. ViaVoice, however, required a combination of voice, keyboard, and mouse commands to navigate and make corrections.

At least in the short run, dictation to the computer is probably not the most important application of speech recognition—that honor falls to interactive voice response systems that provide up-to-date information and services through a call center, with the user providing voice input via a telephone. In this case the software runs on a server (a larger computer) at the call center. The leading suppliers of these call-center speech recognition/voice response systems are ScanSoft, Inc., and Nuance Communications. Such systems are now widely used for such activities as providing access to flight arrival and departure information, permitting phone-based Web browsing, tracking packages, and checking online brokerage accounts. At Yahoo!, subscribers pay $4.95 a month to interact with a virtual responder named Jenni, who can help them check the weather and find sports scores. Amtrak has a perky virtual attendant named Julie who provides schedule, fare, and train-status information. Users prefer these speech recognition/voice response applications to the alternative of multiple touch-tone responses, but they are expensive to develop. Amtrak has spent $4 million over 3 years on speech-related hardware, software, and integration, but the Amtrak executives think it is well worth the cost. Payback will be less than a year, based on reduced labor costs in call centers—voice systems cost about 25 cents per call, compared to about $5 for a human responder. Estimates of the size of the call-center speech recognition/voice response system market vary widely, with Giga Information Group conservatively predicting a cumulative $4 billion in sales by 2006. PC-based speech recognition software is getting close to being a mainstream application, and call-center speech recognition/voice response systems are already in the mainstream.

[Adapted from Alwang, 2002, 2003; and Keenan, 2002]

their data from memory; two-way data flows exist between files and memory and also between the arithmetic/logical unit and memory; and a special type of data flows from memory to the control unit to tell the control unit what to do next. (This latter flow is the focus of the section of this chapter entitled "The Stored-Program Concept.")

In some respects the computer memory is like human memory. Both computers and humans store data in memory in order to remember it or use it later. However, the way in which data are stored and recalled differs radically between computer memory and human memory. Computer memory is divided into cells, and a fixed amount of data can be stored in each cell. Further, each memory cell has an identifying number, called an *address*, that never changes. A very early microcomputer, for example, might have 65,536 memory cells, each capable of storing one character of data at a time. These cells have unchanging addresses varying from 0 for the first cell up to 65535 for the last cell.

A useful analogy is to compare computer memory to a wall of post office boxes (see Figure 2.5). Each box has its own sequential identifying number printed on the box's door, and these numbers correspond to the addresses associated with memory cells. In Figure 2.5 the address or identifying number of each memory register is shown in the upper-left corner of each box. The mail stored in each box changes as mail is distributed or picked up. In computer memory, each memory cell holds some amount of data until it is changed. For example, memory cell 0 holds the characters MAY, memory cell 1 holds the characters 2005, memory cell 2 holds the characters 700.00, and so on. The characters shown in Figure 2.5 represent the contents of memory at a particular point in time; a fraction of a second later the contents could be entirely different as the computer goes about its work. The contents of the memory cells will change as the computer works, while the addresses of the cells are fixed.

Computer memory is different from the post office boxes in several ways, of course. For one thing, computer memory operates on the principle of "destructive read-in, nondestructive read-out." This means that as a particular piece of data is placed into a particular memory cell, either by being read from an input device or as the result of a computation in the arithmetic/logical unit, the computer destroys (or erases) whatever data item was previously in the cell. By contrast, when a data item is retrieved from a cell, either to print out the item or to use it in a computation, the contents of the cell are unchanged.

Another major difference between post office boxes and memory cells is in their capacity. A post office box has a variable capacity depending upon the size of the pieces of mail and how much effort postal employees spend in stuffing the mail in the box. A memory cell has a fixed capacity, with the capacity varying from one computer model to another. A memory cell that can store only one character of data is called a **byte**, and a memory cell that can store two or more characters of data is called a **word**. For comparability, it has become customary to describe the size of memory (and the size of direct access files) in terms of the equivalent number of bytes, even if the cells are really words.

Leaving our post office analogy, we can note that there are several important differences between the memory of one computer model and that of another. First, the capacity

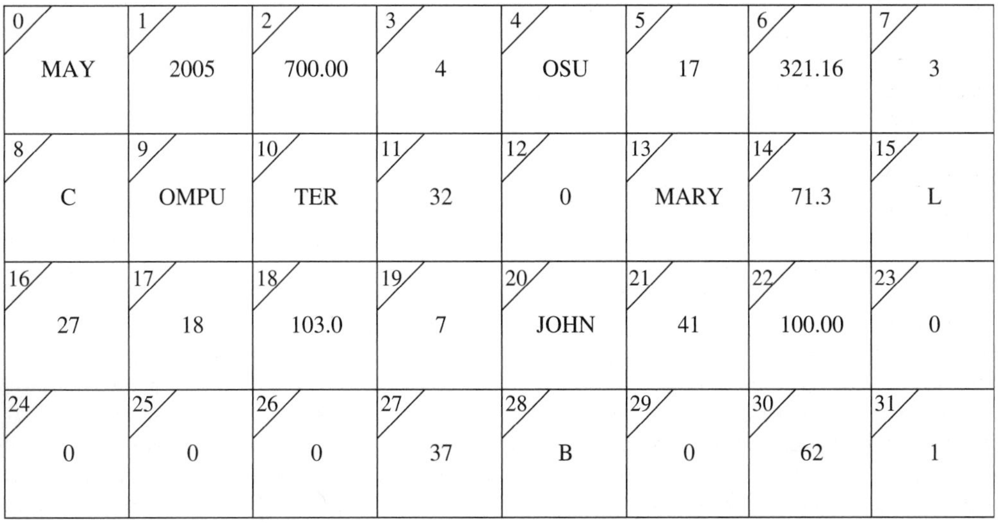

0 MAY	1 2005	2 700.00	3 4	4 OSU	5 17	6 321.16	7 3
8 C	9 OMPU	10 TER	11 32	12 0	13 MARY	14 71.3	15 L
16 27	17 18	18 103.0	19 7	20 JOHN	21 41	22 100.00	23 0
24 0	25 0	26 0	27 37	28 B	29 0	30 62	31 1

Figure 2.5 Diagram of Computer Memory

of each cell might differ. In a microcomputer each cell may hold only 1 digit of a number, whereas a single cell in a mainframe may hold 14 digits. Second, the number of cells making up memory may vary from several million to many billion. Third, the time involved to transfer data from memory to another component may differ by an order of magnitude from one machine to another. The technologies employed in constructing the memories may also differ, although all memory today is based on some variation of VLSI circuits on silicon chips.

Bits and Coding Schemes Each memory cell consists of a particular set of circuits (a small subset of the VLSI circuits on a memory chip), and each circuit can be set to either "on" or "off." Because each circuit has just two states (on and off), they have been equated to 1 and 0, the two possible values of a binary number. Thus, each circuit corresponds to a *bi*nary digi*t*, or a **bit**. In order to represent the decimal digits (and the alphabetic letters and special characters) for processing by the computer, several of these bits (or circuits) must be combined to represent a single character. In most computers eight bits (or circuits) represent a single character, and a memory cell containing a single character, we know, is called a byte. Thus, eight bits equals one byte in most machines.

Consider a particular example. Assume that we have a computer where each memory cell is a byte. (A byte can contain one character.) Then memory cell number 327, for instance, will consist of eight circuits or bits. If these circuits are set to on-on-on-on-on-off-off-on (or, alternatively, 1111 1001), this combination may be defined by the coding scheme to represent the decimal digit 9. If these bits are set to 1111 0001, this may be defined as the decimal digit 1. If these bits are set to 1100 0010, this may be defined as the letter B. We can continue on like this, with each character we wish to represent having a corresponding pattern of eight bits.

Two common coding schemes are in use today. The examples given above are taken from the Extended Binary Coded Decimal Interchange Code (commonly known as EBCDIC, pronounced eb'-si-dic). IBM originally developed EBCDIC in the 1950s, and IBM and other vendors still use it. The other common code in use is the American Standard Code for Information Interchange (ASCII), which is employed in data transmission and in microcomputers. Figure 2.6 lets you compare the ASCII and EBCDIC codes for the alphabet and decimal digits, but you do not need to know these codes—only that they exist!

The bottom line is that a coding scheme of some sort is used to represent data in memory and in the other components of the computer. In memory, circuits in a particular cell are turned on and off, following the coding scheme, to enable us to store the data until later. It turns out that circuits are also used to represent data in the control and arithmetic/logical units. In the input, output, and files, the coding scheme is often expressed through magnetized spots (on and off) on some media, such as tape or disk. In data transmission, the coding scheme is often expressed through a series of electrical pulses or light pulses. In summary, the coding scheme is vital to permit the storage, transmission, and manipulation of data.

Character	EBCDIC Binary	Character	ASCII-8 Binary
A	1100 0001	A	1010 0001
B	1100 0010	B	1010 0010
C	1100 0011	C	1010 0011
D	1100 0100	D	1010 0100
E	1100 0101	E	1010 0101
F	1100 0110	F	1010 0110
G	1100 0111	G	1010 0111
H	1100 1000	H	1010 1000
I	1100 1001	I	1010 1001
J	1101 0001	J	1010 1010
K	1101 0010	K	1010 1011
L	1101 0011	L	1010 1100
M	1101 0100	M	1010 1101
N	1101 0101	N	1010 1110
O	1101 0110	O	1010 1111
P	1101 0111	P	1011 0000
Q	1101 1000	Q	1011 0001
R	1101 1001	R	1011 0010
S	1110 0010	S	1011 0011
T	1110 0011	T	1011 0100
U	1110 0100	U	1011 0101
V	1110 0101	V	1011 0110
W	1110 0110	W	1011 0111
X	1110 0111	X	1011 1000
Y	1110 1000	Y	1011 1001
Z	1110 1001	Z	1011 1010
0	1111 0000	0	0101 0000
1	1111 0001	1	0101 0001
2	1111 0010	2	0101 0010
3	1111 0011	3	0101 0011
4	1111 0100	4	0101 0100
5	1111 0101	5	0101 0101
6	1111 0110	6	0101 0110
7	1111 0111	7	0101 0111
8	1111 1000	8	0101 1000
9	1111 1001	9	0101 1001

Figure 2.6 EBCDIC and ASCII Computer Coding Schemes

Arithmetic/Logical Unit

The **arithmetic/logical unit**, like memory, usually consists of VLSI circuits on a silicon chip. In fact, the chip pictured in Figure 2.3 is the Intel Pentium 4 processor chip used in today's top-of-the-line microcomputers. In many respects, the arithmetic/logical unit is very simple. It has been built to carry out addition, subtraction, multiplication, and division, as well as to perform certain logical operations such as comparing two numbers for equality or finding out which number is bigger.

The broad arrows in Figure 2.4 represent the way in which the arithmetic/logical unit works. As indicated by the broad arrow from memory to the arithmetic/logical unit, the numbers to be manipulated (added, subtracted, etc.) are brought from the appropriate memory cells to the arithmetic/logical unit. Next, the operation is performed, with the time required to carry out the operation varying, depending on the computer model. The speeds involved vary from several million operations per second up to billions of operations per second. Then, as indicated by the broad arrow from the arithmetic/logical unit to memory in Figure 2.4, the result of the operation is stored in the designated memory cell or cells.

Computer Files

As applications are being processed on a computer, the data required for the current computations must be stored in the computer memory. The capacity of memory is limited (although it can go over 250 billion bytes on some large machines), and there is not enough space to keep all the data for all the concurrently running programs (e.g., Microsoft Excel, Microsoft Word, Netscape Navigator, Lotus Notes) in memory at the same time. Adding additional memory might be possible, but memory is relatively expensive. In addition, memory is volatile; if the computer's power goes off, everything stored in memory is lost. To keep vast quantities of data accessible within the computer system in a nonvolatile medium but at more reasonable costs than main memory, file devices—sometimes called secondary memory or secondary storage devices—have been added to all but the tiniest computer systems. File devices include magnetic tape drives, hard (or fixed) disk drives, floppy (or removable) disk drives, and CD (or optical) drives. All but the optical drives record data by magnetizing spots on the surface of the media, using a binary coding scheme.

The broad arrows in each direction in Figure 2.4 illustrate that data can be moved from particular cells in memory to the file and that data can be retrieved from the file to particular memory cells. The disadvantage of files is that the process of storing data in the file from memory or retrieving data from the file to memory is quite slow relative to the computer's computation speed. Depending upon the type of file, the store/retrieve time could vary from a very small fraction of a second to several minutes. Nevertheless, we are willing to live with this disadvantage to be able to store enormous quantities of data at a reasonable cost per byte.

Sequential Access Files There are two basic ways to organize computer files: sequential access and direct access. With **sequential access files**, all the records that make up the files are stored in sequence according to the file's control key. For instance, a payroll file will contain one record for each employee. These individual employee records are stored in sequence according to the employee identification number. There are no addresses within the file; to find a particular record, the file device must start at the beginning of the sequential file and read each record until it finds the desired one. It is apparent that this method of finding a single record might take a long time, particularly if the sequential file is long and the desired record is near the end. Thus, we would rarely try to find a single record with a sequential access file. Instead, we would accumulate a batch of transactions and process the entire batch at the same time. (See the discussion of batch processing in Chapter 6.)

Sequential access files are usually stored on magnetic tape. A **magnetic tape unit** or magnetic tape drive is the file device that stores (writes) data on tape and that retrieves (reads) data from tape back into memory. Even with batch processing, retrieval from magnetic tape tends to be much slower than retrieval from direct access files. Thus, if speed is of the essence, sequential access files might not be suitable. On the other hand, magnetic tapes can store vast quantities of data economically. For example, a tape cartridge that can store up to 800 million bytes of data can be purchased for under $10, or a high-performance tape cartridge with a capacity of 40 billion bytes can be purchased for under $40.

Until the mid-1980s, the magnetic tape used with computers was all of the reel-to-reel variety, like old-style home tape recorders. Then 1/2-inch tape cartridges were introduced, and in 1988 the sales of magnetic tape cartridge drives overtook the sales of reel-to-reel drives for the first time. The tape cartridges are rectangular and thus easier to store than round reels, and, more importantly, the cartridges can be automatically loaded and ejected from the tape drives. With reel-to-reel, an operator must mount each individual tape; with cartridges, an operator can place an entire stack of cartridges into a hopper at one time and let the drive load and eject the individual cartridges. Thus, fewer operators are needed to handle a cartridge-based tape system.

Direct Access Files A **direct access file**, stored on a **direct access storage device (DASD)**, is a file from which it is possible for the computer to obtain a record immediately, without regard to where the record is located in the file. A typical DASD for a computer consists of a continuously rotating stack of disks (or perhaps only one disk), where each disk resembles an old-style phonograph record (see Figure 2.7). A comb-shaped access mechanism moves in and out among the disks to record on and read from hundreds of concentric tracks on each disk surface. The hard drives found on almost all microcomputers are an example of direct access files. Typical internal hard drives for PCs store from 20 to 160 billion bytes (gigabytes) and cost from $50 to $200. The speed at which data may be read from or written on a hard drive is quite fast, with transfer rates up to 100 million bytes (megabytes) per second possible.

EMC Corporation, based in Hopkinton, Massachusetts, has become the market leader in storage systems for large computers by devising a way to link together a large number of inexpensive, small hard drives (such as those used in PCs) as a substitute for the giant disk drives that were previously used. EMC has developed a specialized computer and sophisticated software to control this **redundant array of independent disks (RAID)** approach so that data can be supplied to the mainframe or other large computer rapidly, reliably, and less expensively per byte than the giant disk drive approach (Judge, 1999). As an example,

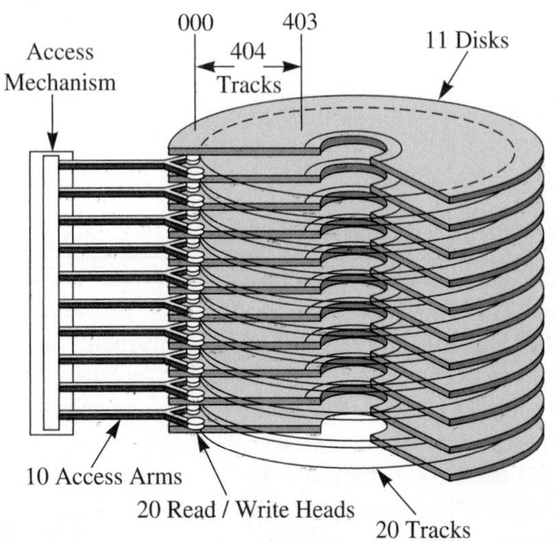

Figure 2.7 A Schematic Diagram of a Magnetic Disk Drive

EMC's Symmetrix DMX 3000 model can be configured with from 192 to 576 hard drives, each with a storage capacity of either 73 or 146 gigabytes, giving a total storage capacity from 14 terabytes (trillion bytes) up to a maximum of over 84 terabytes (EMC Web site, 2003).

In contrast to these fixed-disk, large-capacity, fairly expensive file devices, direct access devices can also be portable or employ a removable disk, be relatively small, and be quite inexpensive. For instance, a removable 3.5-inch high-density disk for a microcomputer can store up to 1.44 million bytes (1.44 megabytes) of data and costs less than 50 cents. The disk drive itself costs under $100. These 3.5-inch disks are protected by a permanent hard plastic case, but they are sometimes called floppy disks. "Floppy disk" is a misnomer for today's disks, but the name originated with their 5.25-inch predecessor disks for microcomputers, which were made of flexible plastic without sturdy cases and were in fact "floppy." The transfer rate to read to or write from a floppy disk varies, but a common transfer rate is 0.06 million bytes (megabytes) per second—a very slow rate compared to other DASDs.

A newer, higher-capacity DASD, with a removable disk, is Iomega Corporation's Zip drive. A Zip drive may be installed internally in a PC or attached externally. A Zip disk is slightly larger than a conventional floppy disk, and about twice as thick; its capacity is either 100, 250, or 750 megabytes on a single removable disk, depending upon the Zip drive. A 750-megabyte Zip drive costs about $180, and each disk for this drive is about $13; this Zip drive reads or writes at speeds up to 7.5 megabytes per second. The smaller-capacity 250-megabyte Zip drive costs about $125, and each disk for this drive is about $11; the transfer rate for reading or writing is up to 2.4 megabytes per second (Iomega Web site, 2003). These transfer rates are not particularly fast, but the low cost and durability of the Zip drive have made it quite popular for backing up and transporting large data files.

Iomega Corporation also offers an attractive line of portable hard drives to back up very large data files and move these large data files from one computer system to another. Iomega's HDD Portable Hard Drives come with capacities varying from 20 gigabytes to 60 gigabytes. The 60-gigabyte drive costs about $360 and has a maximum sustained transfer rate of 30 megabytes per second (Iomega Web site, 2003).

The newest and smallest portable DASD for PCs utilizes flash memory—as used in digital cameras and portable music players—rather than a magnetizable disk. This device goes by various names, depending upon the manufacturer or the commentator, including a Jump Drive (Lexar), DiskOnKey (M-Systems), Mini USB Drive (Iomega), flash drive, or simply keychain drive. **Keychain**

drive is perhaps the most descriptive, because the device is not much larger than the average car key (see Figure 2.8). As an example, Iomega's Mini USB Drive is available in 64, 128, and 256 megabyte sizes, with prices of about $40, $60, and $90. These keychain drives are designed to plug into a standard universal serial bus (USB) port on a PC. With a USB 2.0 port, the computer can read data from Iomega's 256-megabyte keychain drive at a rate of 5 megabytes per second and write data to the keychain drive at a rate of 3.5 megabytes per second. To use a keychain drive, take off the top of the drive, exposing the USB connector. Plug the connector into the USB port on a PC, and the computer will recognize it automatically—then just use the keychain drive as you do any other drive! The keychain drive is an economical and extremely convenient way to transport significant amounts of data. The 3.5-inch floppy disk was on its way out even before the keychain drive came on the scene, but the keychain drive should certainly hasten the floppy disk into oblivion (Armstrong, 2002, and Iomega Web site, 2003).

The key to the operation of direct access files is that the physical file is divided into cells, each of which has an address. The cells are similar to memory cells, except that they are much larger, usually large enough to store several records in one cell. Because of the existence of this address, it is possible for the computer to store a record in a particular file address and then to retrieve that record by remembering the address. Thus, the computer can go directly to the file address of the desired record, rather than reading through sequentially stored records until it encounters the desired one.

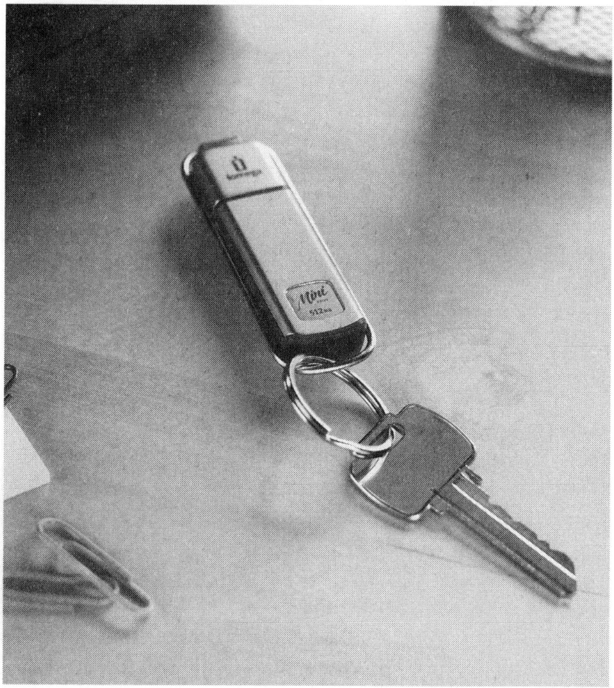

Figure 2.8 Keychain Drive: Iomega's Mini USB Drive (Photo courtesy of Iomega Corporation)

How does the computer know the correct file address for a desired record? For instance, assume that an inventory control application running on the computer needs to update the record for item number 79032. That record, which is stored somewhere in DASD, must be brought into memory for processing. But where is it? At what file address? This problem of translating from the identification number of a desired record (79032) to the corresponding file address is the biggest challenge in using direct access files. Very sophisticated software, to be discussed in Chapter 3, is required to handle this translation.

Online processing (discussed in Chapter 6) requires direct access files, and so does Web browsing. Airline reservation agents, salespeople in a department store, managers in their offices, and Web surfers from their home or office machines will not wait (and in many cases cannot afford to wait) the several minutes that might be required to mount and read the appropriate magnetic tape. On the other hand, batch processing can be done with either sequential access files or direct access files. Sequential access files are not going to go away, but all the trends are pushing organizations towards increased use of direct access files. First, online processing and Web browsing absolutely require direct access files. Second, advancements in magnetic technology and manufacturing processes keep pushing down the costs per byte of direct access files. Third, the newer optical disk technology (see the box "Optical Disk Storage") provides drastically lower costs per byte of direct access files for applications where somewhat slower data retrieval speeds are acceptable. Fourth, and most important, today's competitive environment is forcing organizations to focus on speed in information processing, and that means an increasing emphasis on direct access files.

Many major computer installations today have so many DASD units that they are collectively referred to as a disk farm. It is not unusual for a large installation to have many trillions of bytes (terabytes) of disk storage online.

Control Unit

We have considered five of the six building blocks represented in Figure 2.4. If we stopped our discussion at this point, we wouldn't have much. Thus far we have no way of controlling these various components and no way of taking advantage of the tremendous speed and capacity we have

OPTICAL DISK STORAGE

A newer type of direct access file storage for computer systems, the **optical disk**, is becoming more and more important. Some writers have argued that the optical disk might spell the end of the floppy disk: After all, rewritable versions of the optical disk are now available that have hundreds of times the capacity of a standard floppy disk, a transfer rate much faster than a floppy, and a price that is quite economical (e.g., see Wildstrom, 2000). An optical disk is made of plastic coated with a thin reflective alloy material. Data are recorded on the disk by using a laser beam to burn microscopic pits in the reflective surface (or in some cases alter the magnetic characteristics of the surface), employing a binary coding scheme.

Two primary types of optical disks are in common use with computers today: a **compact disk** (**CD**) and a **digital video disk**, or **digital versatile disk** (**DVD**). Then each of these optical disk types has three primary variations: a read-only disk (**CD-ROM** or **DVD-ROM**, where ROM stands for Read Only Memory); a recordable disk (**CD-R** or **DVD-R**, where R stands for Recordable); and a rewritable disk (**CD-RW** or **DVD-RW**, where RW stands for ReWritable). A CD has much less capacity than a DVD: Standard capacity for a CD is 700 megabytes of data or 80 minutes of audio recording, while standard capacity for a two-sided DVD is 4.7 gigabytes, more than enough for a full-length movie. Some experts believe that DVDs will eventually replace CDs and VHS videocassettes, but that won't happen overnight. A significant advantage of DVD drives is that they are backward compatible with CDs, so that a DVD drive can play all types of CDs as well as DVDs. The media are quite inexpensive, with blank CD-Rs costing under a $1, blank CD-RWs under $1.50, blank DVD-Rs under $5, and blank DVD-RWs under $7 each.

The readable CD or DVD is familiar as a way of distributing music, computer software, and even movies. It can only be read and cannot be erased; a master disk is originally created, and then duplicates can be mass produced for distribution. Thus, a readable optical disk is particularly useful for distributing large amounts of relatively stable data (such as music, computer software, a book, a movie, or multimedia material) to many locations.

A recordable optical disk was once called a **WORM** (Write Once-Read Many) disk. A recordable CD or DVD can be written on by the computer—but only once! Then it can be read many times. Recordable optical disks are quite appropriate for archiving documents, engineering drawings, and records of all types.

A rewritable CD or DVD is the most versatile form of optical disk because the data can be recorded and erased repeatedly. Writing on a rewritable optical disk is a three-step process: (1) Use laser heat to erase the recording surface; (2) use a combination of laser and magnetic technology to write on the recording surface; and (3) read, via a laser, what has been written to verify the accuracy of the recording process. This type of optical disk is a strong candidate to replace the venerable floppy disk, particularly now that software products let the user "drag" files to an optical disk (using a mouse) just like to any other drive.

One more complication arises with regard to recordable and rewritable DVDs—vendors have created multiple formats that are not always compatible. Thus, a rewritable DVD is only rewritable with the appropriate DVD writer drive. There are two different recordable formats, labeled DVD-R and DVD+R, and three different rewritable formats, labeled DVD-RW, DVD+RW, and DVD-RAM. Happily, DVD drives are beginning to appear that will read and write all major CD and DVD formats. One such drive is Iomega's Super DVD Writer/All-Format Internal Drive, priced at about $250. This drive is rated 4x2x8x when using the DVD-RW format. The numbers mean that the speed of writing on this drive is 4x (which translates to 5.5 megabytes per second), the speed of rewriting is 2x (2.75 megabytes per second), and the speed of reading is 8x (11.0 megabytes per second). When using a CD with the CD-RW format, the drive is rated 24x16x32x, which translates to writing at 3.6 megabytes per second, rewriting at 2.4 megabytes per second, and reading at 4.8 megabytes per second (Iomega Web site, 2003). (Note that the baseline 1x differs from DVD to CD: With DVD, 1x equals 1.375 megabytes per second; with CD, 1x equals 0.15 megabytes per second.)

As an example of optical storage used with large computer systems, the IBM Enhanced 3995 Optical Library C-Series uses *either* rewritable or WORM 5.25-inch removable disk cartridges, with a cartridge holding up to 5.2 gigabytes of data. The 3995 Model C38 incorporates 258 cartridges, giving a total online capacity of 1.341 terabytes (1.341 trillion bytes) for the optical library system. You can double the capacity to 2.682 terabytes by attaching a Model C18 expansion unit to the Model C38. This optical library system is capable of a sustained data transfer rate of 2.3 to 4.6 megabytes per second, with a burst data transfer rate of 6 megabytes per second.

[Portions adapted from Wildstrom, 2000; Iomega Web site, 2003; and IBM Web site, September 2003a]

described. The **control unit** is the key. It provides the control that enables the computer to take advantage of the speed and capacity of its other components. The thin arrows in Figure 2.4 point out that the control unit controls each of the other five components.

How does the control unit know what to do? Someone must tell the control unit what to do by devising a precise list of operations to be performed. This list of operations, which is called a program, is stored in the memory of the computer just like data. One item at a time from this list is moved from memory to the control unit (note the broad arrow in Figure 2.4), interpreted by the control unit, and carried out. The control unit works through the entire list of operations at electronic speed, rather than waiting for the user to tell it what to do next. What we have just described is the **stored-program concept**, which is the most important idea in all of computing.

THE STORED-PROGRAM CONCEPT

Some person must prepare a precise listing of exactly what the computer is to do. This listing must be in a form that the control unit of the computer has been built to understand. The complete listing of what is to be done for an application is called a **program**, and each individual step or operation in the program is called an **instruction**. The control unit carries out the program, one step or instruction at a time, at electronic speed.

When a particular computer model is designed, the engineers build into it (more precisely, build into its circuitry) the capability to carry out a certain set of operations. For example, a computer might be able to read an item of data keyed from a keyboard, print a line of output, add two numbers, subtract one number from another, multiply two numbers, divide one number by another, compare two numbers for equality, and perform several other operations. The computer's control unit is built to associate each of these operations with a particular instruction type. Then the control unit is told which operations are to be done by means of a program consisting of these instructions. The form of the instructions is peculiar to a particular model of computer. Thus, each instruction in a program must be expressed in the precise form that the computer has been built to understand. This form of the program that the computer understands is called the **machine language** for the particular model of computer.

Not only will the form of the instructions vary from one computer model to another, so will the number of different types of instructions. For example, a small computer might have only one add instruction, while a large one might have a different add instruction for each of several classes of numbers (such as integer, floating point or decimal, and double precision). Thus, the instruction set on some machines could contain as few as 20 types of instructions, while other machines could have more than 200 instruction types.

In general, each machine language instruction consists of two parts: an operation code and one or more addresses. The operation code is a symbol (e.g., A for add) that tells the control unit what operation is to be performed. The addresses refer to the specific cells in memory whose contents will be involved in the operation. As an example, for a hypothetical computer the instruction

Operation Code	Addresses	
A	470	500

means the computer should add the number found in memory cell 470 to the number found in memory cell 500, storing the result back in memory cell 500. Therefore, if the value 32.10 is originally stored in cell 470 and the value 63.00 is originally stored in cell 500, the sum, 95.10, will be stored in cell 500 after the instruction is executed. Continuing our example, assume that the next instruction in the sequence is

M	500	200

This instruction means move (M) the contents of memory cell 500 to memory cell 200. Thus, 95.10 will be placed in cell 200, erasing whatever was there before. (Because of nondestructive read-out, 95.10 will still be stored in cell 500.) The third instruction in our sequence is

P	200	

which means print (P) the contents of memory cell 200 on the printer, and 95.10 will be printed.

Our very short example contains only three instructions and obviously represents only a small portion of a program, but these few instructions should provide the flavor of machine language programming. A complete program would consist of hundreds or thousands of instructions, all expressed in the machine language of the particular computer being used. The person preparing the program (called a programmer) has to know each operation code and has to remember what data he or she has stored in every memory cell. Obviously, machine language programming is very difficult and time-consuming. (As we will learn in Chapter 3, programs may be written in languages that are easier for us to use and then automatically translated into machine language, so almost no one programs in machine language today.)

Once the entire machine language program has been prepared, it must be entered into the computer, using one of the input methods already described, and stored in the computer's memory. This step of entering the program in memory is called loading the program. The control unit then is told (somehow) where to find the first instruction in the program. The control unit fetches this first instruction and places it in special storage cells called registers within the control unit. Using built-in circuitry, the control unit interprets the instruction (recognizes what is to be done) and causes it to be executed (carried out) by the appropriate components of the computer. For example, the control unit would interpret the add instruction above, cause the contents of memory cells 470 and 500 to be sent to the arithmetic/logical unit, cause the arithmetic/logical unit to add these two numbers, and then cause the answer to be sent back to memory cell 500.

After the first instruction has been completed, the control unit fetches the second instruction from memory. The control unit then interprets this second instruction and executes it. The control unit then fetches and executes the third instruction. The control unit proceeds with this fetch-execute cycle until the program has been completed. Usually the instruction that is fetched is the next sequential one, but machine languages incorporate one or more branching instructions that, when executed, cause the control unit to jump to a nonsequential instruction for the next fetch. The important point is that the control unit is fetching and executing at electronic speed; it is doing exactly what the programmer told it to do, but at its own rate of speed.

One of the primary measures of the power of any computer model is the number of instructions that it can execute in a given period of time. Of course, some instructions take longer to execute than others, so any speed rating represents an average of some sort. These averages might not be representative of the speeds that the computer could sustain on the mix of jobs carried out by your organization or any other organization. Furthermore, some machines operate on four bytes at a time (microcomputers), while others operate on eight bytes at a time (many larger machines). Thus, the speed rating for a microcomputer is not comparable to the speed rating for a larger machine. In the 1980s the most commonly used speed rating was **MIPS**, or millions of instructions per second executed by the control unit. This measure has largely gone out of favor because of the "apples and oranges" nature of the comparisons of MIPS ratings across classes of computers.

Another speed rating used is **MegaFLOPS** or **MFLOPS**—millions of floating point operations per second. These ratings are derived by running a particular set of programs in a particular language on the machines being investigated. The ratings are therefore more meaningful than a simple MIPS rating, but they still reflect only a single problem area. In the LINPACK ratings, the problem area considered is the solution of dense systems of linear equations using the LINPACK software in a FORTRAN environment (Dongarra, 2003). MFLOPS ratings when solving a system of 100 linear equations include .00169 for a Palm Pilot III; 51 for an AMD K6-II (500 MHz); 62 for a Gateway G6-200 Pentium Pro; 558 for a Compaq Server D520e (667 MHz); 1,486 for an IBM eServer pSeries 655 (1.7 GHz); and 1,635 for an HP Integrity Server rx2600 (1.5 GHz). These are all single processor machines. MFLOPS ratings when solving a system of 1,000 linear equations vary from 49 for a Hewlett-Packard 9000/730 (one processor); 5,187 for a Sun UltraSPARC II (30 processors); 7,699 for an IBM RS/6000 SP Power3 (16 processors); 29,360 for a Cray T932 (32 processors); and 45,030 for a NEC SX-5/16 (16 processors) (Dongarra, 2003). Of course, these LINPACK ratings are not very meaningful for applications where input/output operations are dominant, such as most business processing.

These published speed ratings can be useful as a very rough guide, but the only way to get a handle on how various machines would handle your organization's workload is **benchmarking**. Benchmarking is quite difficult to do, but the idea is to collect a representative set of real jobs that you regularly run on your computer, and then for comparison actually run this set of jobs on various machines. The vendors involved will usually cooperate because they want to sell you a machine, but there can be severe problems in getting existing jobs to run on the target machines and in comparing the results once you get them.

Computer publications often do their own benchmarking, as illustrated in Table 2.2 in which *PC World* identifies the top seven computers in a class it calls "desktop PCs—power system." *PC World* has created a representative mix of common business applications it calls PC WorldBench 4, which it ran on all machines in this class. The performance score is a measure of how fast a PC can run this mix as compared with *PC World*'s baseline machine, a Gateway Select 1200 with a 1.2-gigaHertz (GHz) Athlon processor, 128 megabytes of memory, and a 20-gigabyte hard drive. For example, the ABS Ultimate M5 in Table 2.2 is 1.4 times as fast as the baseline system.

PC World goes on to combine this PC WorldBench 4 performance score (valued at 25 percent of the overall rating) with other factors such as price (10 percent), base configuration (10 percent), extra features (10 percent), graphics quality (15 percent), setup and ease of use (5 percent), and vendor's reliability and service (25 percent) to arrive at an overall rating for each machine, as shown in the far right column of Table 2.2.

Again, processing speeds vary across machines, but all computers use the stored-program concept. On all computers a machine language program is loaded in memory and executed by the control unit. There is a great deal more to the story of how we get the machine language program, but suffice it to say at this point that we let the computer do most of the work in creating the machine language

Table 2.2 Benchmarking: Top Seven Desktop PCs—Power System

System	Processor	Street Price	PC WorldBench 4 Performance Score[a]	Overall Rating
ABS Ultimate M5	2.2-GHz Athlon XP 3200+	$2739	140 (outstanding)	92
Dell Dimension 8300	3.2-GHz Pentium 4	$3807	127 (good)	86
Dell Dimension XPS	3.06-GHz Pentium 4	$3807	127 (good)	86
Micro Express MicroFlex 30A	2.167-GHz Athlon XP 3000+	$1999	131 (good)	86
Sys Technology Performance 3200+	2.2-GHz Athlon XP 3200+	$2690	136 (outstanding)	84
@Xi Computer MTower 3000+	2.167-GHz Athlon XP 3000+	$1993	133 (very good)	82
Acer Veriton 7600G	3-GHz Pentium 4	$1937	122 (fair)	80

[a]The descriptive labels are those assigned by *PC World.*
Source: PC World (October 2003): 144–146.

program. Neither you nor programmers working for your organization will write in machine language; any programs will be written in a language much easier and more natural for humans to understand. Chapter 3 is primarily concerned with the software, or programs, used to control computer systems.

EXTENSIONS TO THE BASIC MODEL[1]

In the previous section we considered the underlying logical structure of all digital computers, and we found that all computers are made up of the set of six building blocks shown in Figure 2.4. Now let us note that Figure 2.4 is an accurate but incomplete picture of many of today's computers. To be complete, the figure should be extended in two ways. First, today's computers (both microcomputers and larger machines) often have multiple components for each of the six blocks rather than a single component. Machines may have multiple input devices, or multiple file devices, or multiple CPUs. Second, the architecture of today's machines often includes several additional components to interconnect the basic six components. For example, magnetic disk file devices usually have a disk controller that interfaces with a data channel connected to the CPU. In this section we want to extend our basic model to incorporate these additional ideas and thus present a more complete picture of today's (and tomorrow's) computer systems.

Communications within the Computer System

Controller As a starting point for the extended model, let us note that appropriate **controllers** are needed to link input/output devices such as terminals, DASDs, and sequential access devices to the CPU and memory of large computer systems. The exact nature of the controller will vary with the vendor and the devices being linked, but the controller is usually a highly specialized microprocessor attached to the CPU (through another new component called a data channel) and to the terminals or DASDs or other devices (see Figure 2.9). The controller manages the operation of the attached devices to free up the CPU (and the data channel) from these tasks.

For example, a DASD controller receives requests for DASD read or write activity from the data channel, translates these requests into the proper sets of operations for the disk device, sees that the operations are executed, performs any necessary error recovery, and reports any problems back to the data channel (and thus to the CPU). A communications controller has the job of managing near-simultaneous input/output from an attached set of terminals, ensuring that the messages from each terminal are properly collected and forwarded to the data channel, and that responses from the data channel are properly sent to the right terminal.

Data Channel The **data channel** is just as critical as the controller. A data channel is a specialized input/output processor (yet another computer) that takes over the function

[1] The material in this section is more technical than the rest of the chapter, and it may be skipped by those readers who wish to obtain only a basic understanding of computer systems. It is included to provide a more comprehensive picture to those who are interested.

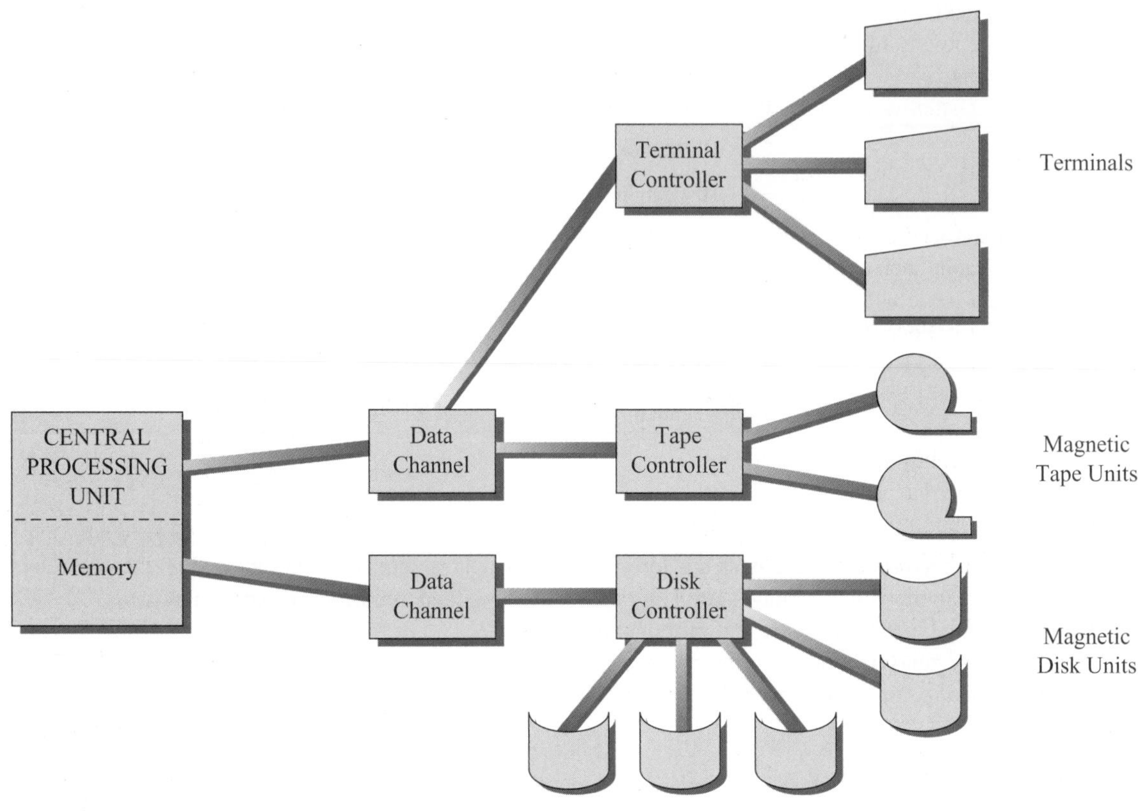

Figure 2.9 Data Channels and Controllers

of device communication from the CPU. The data channel's role is to correct for the significant mismatch in speeds between the very slow peripheral devices and the fast and critical CPU. When the CPU encounters an input/output request (including requests for disk or tape reads and writes) during the execution of a program, it relays that request to the data channel connected to the device in question (the number of data channels varies with the machine). The CPU then turns to some other job while the data channel oversees input/output.

The data channel often includes some amount of buffer storage (a special type of memory), so that it may move large blocks of data into and out of main memory at one time. In this way, the data channel has to interrupt the CPU only when it is ready to move a large data block; during most of the time the CPU can continue to process another job. The data channel, on the other hand, must wait on data transmitted from the controller as it gathers an input block, or it must wait for the controller to accept a block of output data.

Another way in which the data channel sometimes operates is by cycle stealing. In this variation, the data channel has only a small amount of buffer storage in which it receives data. For example, when this small buffer fills up during a disk read, the channel steals a cycle from the CPU and places the contents of the buffer in main memory. This operation has minimal impact on the CPU (it loses only one cycle out of thousands) and allows the data channel to employ an area of main memory as its buffer.

Cache Memory

Thus far we have considered two (or perhaps three) levels of storage devices: main or primary memory, which is very fast and quite expensive; and secondary memory, which we can subdivide into not-so-fast and not-so-expensive DASDs and slow and inexpensive sequential access storage devices (magnetic tapes). Now add **cache memory**, which was originally employed as a very high-speed, high-cost storage unit used as an intermediary between the control unit and the main memory (Grossman, 1985). The term *cache* (pronounced cash) is French for a hidden storage place. The cache is intended to compensate for one of the speed mismatches built into computer systems—in this case, that between fetching data from main memory (and moving data to the arithmetic/logical unit or other internal registers) and executing an instruction. The CPU can execute an instruction much faster than it can fetch data (which requires electronically moving the data from memory to the arithmetic/logical unit). Thus, in a conventional architecture, the critical CPU often waited for the completion of a data fetch.

With cache memory, an entire block of data is moved at one time into the cache, and then most data fetches take place from the higher-speed cache to the arithmetic/logical unit. The success of cache memory depends upon two characteristics of the data to be used by the CPU—locality of reference and data reuse. Locality of reference means that if a given piece of data is used, there is a high probability that a nearby piece of data will be used shortly thereafter. Data reuse means that a block of data will be kept in the cache until it has not been recently referenced; then it will be replaced by a block of data that has been requested. The use of cache memory should optimize the use of the critical CPU.

After its successful use as an intermediary between the CPU and main memory, cache memory was incorporated into DASD controllers. The basic idea is similar, except the speed mismatch is greater between the relatively slow DASD and the much faster data channel. Again, the keys to success of the cache are locality of reference and data reuse. A large block of data is moved from DASD to the cache, and then (hopefully) most data fetches take place from the cache rather than DASD itself. A microprocessor in the DASD controller manages the cache memory, keeping track of the frequency of reference to the data in the cache and moving blocks of data into and out of the cache in an attempt to optimize the use of the data channel (and, indirectly, the CPU). Figure 2.10 illustrates the use of cache memory both in the CPU and in a DASD controller. Cache memory (in the CPU and in the DASD controller) represents an important way in which the conventional storage hierarchy has been extended. Cache memory is becoming a part of many components of the hardware, including high-speed communication modules and special-purpose CPUs such as array processors. Even more layers may be added to the storage hierarchy as system designers seek to balance cost, capacity, and performance.

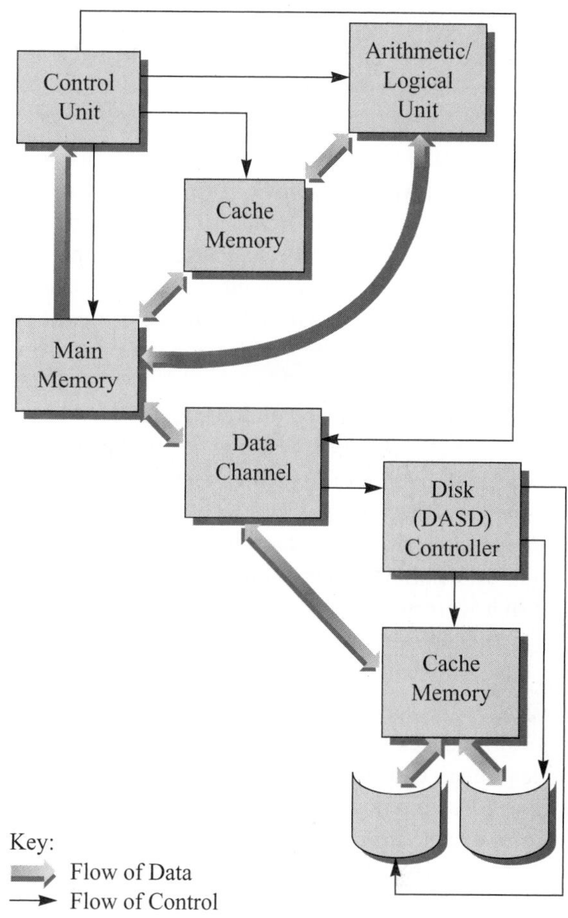

Figure 2.10 Partial Logical Structure of Computer Incorporating Cache Memory

Multiple Processor Configurations

One of the most intriguing extensions to the basic model is the use of multiple CPUs or processors as part of a single computer system. A **multiprocessor** is a computer configuration in which multiple processors (CPUs) are installed as part of the same computer system. Without using the multiprocessor terminology, we actually considered such a system when we discussed the use of data channels (which are themselves processors) with a single primary CPU. Sometimes the term *front-end processor* is used instead of data channel, but in either case the additional processor (or processors) is used to offload handling of input/output from the primary CPU.

Symmetric Multiprocessors An increasing number of larger computers now make use of multiple processors as a way of increasing their power (usually measured by throughput). In these cases, two, three, or more CPUs are installed as part of the same computer system. The term **symmetric multiprocessor** (**SMP**) refers to multiprocessor machines in which all the processors or CPUs are identical, with each processor operating independently of the others. The multiple CPUs equally share functional and timing access to and control over all other system components, including main memory and the various peripheral devices, with each CPU working in its own allotted portion of memory. One CPU might handle online transaction processing, while a second deals with engineering calculations, a third works on a batch payroll system, and a fourth operates as a Web server.

Vector Facilities An example of an asymmetric multiprocessor is a **vector facility**, a specialized multiple processor configuration designed to handle calculations involving vectors. For these calculations, the same operation is to be performed on each element of the vector. By installing a number of parallel, relatively inexpensive microprocessors (operating under control of a primary control unit and thus a single program), all these operations can be performed simultaneously. The keys to whether a vector facility is worthwhile are the percentage of the total calculations that involve vectors and the lengths of the vectors themselves. The higher the percentage and the longer the vectors, the more valuable the vector facility. For research and development activities, vector facilities are often worthwhile, but their value for most business information processing is limited.

Parallel Processors A **parallel processor (PP)** has two major differences from a vector facility. First, there is no single primary CPU in a parallel processor, and, second, the various CPUs are not always performing the same operation at the same time. For example, a parallel processing machine may have 16, 64, 256, or more processors, each of which would work on a separate piece of the same program. In order to use a parallel processing approach, the program must somehow be divided up among the processors and the activities of the various processors must be coordinated. Many supercomputers, to be discussed later in the chapter, employ a parallel processing architecture.

The term **massively parallel processor (MPP)** is used to describe machines with some large number of parallel CPUs. There is no firm guideline to distinguish between a PP and an MPP; in general, however, 32 or more parallel CPUs would be considered an MPP if the different CPUs are capable of performing different instructions at the same time, or 1,000 or more parallel CPUs would be considered an MPP if the different CPUs must all carry out the same instruction at the same time. An example of a massively parallel machine is the IBM RS/6000 SP supercomputer (code name ASCI White) purchased by the U.S. Department of Energy in 2000. This machine contains more than 8,100 microprocessors operating in parallel and is capable of 12.3 *trillion* calculations per second, which made it the world's fastest supercomputer for about 2 years.

We are just beginning to learn how to take advantage of the incredible power of parallel processing machines. At present, the user must specifically tailor his or her programs to utilize the parallel CPUs effectively. For the short term, parallel processors will be most useful in universities and research laboratories and in a few specialized applications that demand extensive computations such as extremely high-volume transaction processing.

TYPES OF COMPUTER SYSTEMS

In our earlier discussion of the various generations of computers, we introduced some terminology—microcomputers, minicomputers, and mainframes—that has been applied to different types of computer systems. Now we want to expand our taxonomy of computer types to include the full range of computer systems available today. In our discussion we will indicate the primary uses of each type of system as well as the major vendors. Our discussion must begin with a significant caveat. Although there is some agreement on the terms we will be using, there is no such agreement on the parameters defining each category or on the computer models that belong in each type. Even if there were such agreement today, there would not be tomorrow as new technologies are employed and new computer models are introduced.

Generally speaking, the boundaries between the categories are defined by a combination of cost, computing power, and purpose for which a machine is built—but the *purpose* is the dominant criterion. Listed in order of generally increasing cost and power, the categories we will use are microcomputers, workstations/midrange systems, mainframes, and supercomputers (see Table 2.3). You will note that the ranges of cost and power in Table 2.3 are often overlapping, which reflects the differences in purpose for which the machines have been designed. Remember also that MFLOPS (millions of floating point operations per second) is only a very rough comparative measure of power.

Please note that the category boundaries in Table 2.3 are extremely fuzzy. The boundary between microcomputers and workstations/midrange systems has been arbitrarily set at $3,000, but the technology employed is quite similar on both sides of this boundary (at least in terms of PCs and workstations). On the other hand, the type of work done on these classes of machines is quite different, as indicated in the table, so we have chosen to separate them. Historically, workstations and midrange systems have been considered as distinct categories, but they now overlap so much in cost, power, and applications that we have chosen to combine them in a single category that stretches all the way from microcomputers to the much larger mainframes and supercomputers. Moreover, some workstations use technology similar to supercomputers—the primary difference

Table 2.3 Types of Computer Systems

Category	Cost	MFLOPS	Primary Uses
Microcomputers	$200–$3,000	20–400	Personal computing Client in client/server[a] applications Web client Small business processing
Workstations/midrange systems	$3,000–$1,000,000	40–4,000	Departmental computing Specific applications (office automation, CAD[b], other graphics) Midsized business general processing Server in client/server applications Web server, file server, local area network server
Mainframes	$1,000,000–$20,000,000	200–8,000	Large business general processing Server in client/server applications Large Web server Widest range of applications
Supercomputers	$1,000,000–$100,000,000	4,000–100,000,000	Numerically intensive scientific calculations Very large Web server

[a]Client/server applications involve dividing the processing between a larger computer operating as a server and a smaller machine operating as a client; this idea is explored in depth in Chapter 6.

[b]CAD is an abbreviation for computer-aided design, to be discussed in Chapter 6.

might be the number of parallel processors. Low-end mainframes have significantly less power than high-end workstations/midrange systems, but have been designed for the widest possible range of applications. Some sources use the term *servers* instead of workstations/midrange systems, but we disagree with this label because a wide variety of machines including microcomputers, workstations/midrange systems, mainframes, and supercomputers can and do perform in a server capacity.

Microcomputers

Microcomputers, often called micros or **personal computers** or just PCs, cost from $300 to $3,000. They generally have less power than workstations/midrange systems, but the dividing line between these categories is faint. In general, microcomputers can be carried or moved by one person, and they usually have only a single keyboard and video display unit (which is why they are called personal computers). **Desktop PCs** are the most familiar, but PCs also come in **laptop** or **notebook** models in small briefcase-like packages weighing under 10 pounds and in newer, smaller **handheld** or **palmtop** models weighing in at a pound or (usually) less. An intriguing new variation of the notebook computer is the tablet PC, where the user writes on an electronic tablet (the video screen folded flat on top of the PC) with a digital pen (see the sidebar entitled "Is a Tablet PC Right for You?").

By the second half of the 1980s, the most popular microcomputer for business use was the IBM Personal Computer, designed around microprocessor chips built by Intel and the PC-DOS operating system (a software package) created by Microsoft. In the first decade of the twenty-first century, IBM-compatible machines still dominate the business marketplace, but the overwhelming majority of these machines are being sold by vendors other than IBM. In fact, in 2002 IBM chose to outsource the production of IBM desktop computers to Sanmina-SCI Corporation to reduce costs (Ante and Henry, 2002). (IBM continues to produce its own popular ThinkPad laptop computers.) The sales leader in the PC marketplace is Dell, which developed as a direct-sales vendor, originally by mail and telephone and now predominantly via the World Wide Web. After its 2002 acquisition of Compaq Computer, Hewlett-Packard is challenging Dell for market leadership. Other major players include a trio of Japanese firms—Fujitsu, Toshiba (both of which sell only laptop and tablet microcomputers in the United States), and NEC—as well as Gateway (which has also used the direct-sales approach, although not as successfully as Dell), and, of course, IBM. In response to competitive pressures, all the PC vendors, including Dell, Hewlett-Packard, and IBM, have lowered their prices and introduced multiple microcomputer lines.

IBM-compatible machines in the early years of the twenty-first century employ mostly Intel Pentium 4 chips, with older Pentium chips and AMD Athlon chips also in use. Most of these machines use some version of the Microsoft Windows operating system (either Windows 2000 or Windows XP).

In addition to IBM-compatible machines, the only other contender in the business environment is the Apple Macintosh. Initially, the Macintosh found tough going in the business world against the entrenched IBM microcomputers, but its easy-to-use graphical interface won it many converts in the late 1980s and early 1990s. Then Macintosh sales seemed to hit a plateau, and Apple struggled until it introduced the iMac in 1998. The colorful iMac added a spark to the Apple product line and made Apple profitable again, although Apple's market share is still very small—about 3 percent of the U.S. microcomputer market in 2003. However, Apple appears to have built a safe niche for itself through innovative products such as the very successful iPod MP3 music player; its AirPort wireless networking gear; and a new software product, iLife, which is a suite of video, music, and photography software that allows users to develop professional-looking home movies (Burrows, 2003). Between Apple and the myriad of PC-compatible vendors, the microcomputer market is extremely competitive and should remain so for the foreseeable future.

Microcomputers have been put to a myriad of uses. In the home, they have been used for record-keeping, word processing, and games; in the public schools, for computerized exercises, educational games, and limited programming; in colleges, for word processing, spreadsheet exercises (more on this in Chapter 3), presentations, and programming. In the corporate environment they are used for word processing, spreadsheets, presentations, small database applications, and programming; as terminals into larger computers; and as clients in client/server applications. Stand-alone microcomputers in a large organizational setting are a thing of the past: For managers to do their jobs, they need microcomputers linked into the corporate computer network so that they can access data and applications wherever they exist. Microcomputers have also become important for small businesses, where they do operate as stand-alone machines or on small local area networks (LANs). The growing supply of software developed for a particular type of small business (e.g., a general contractor, hardware store, or farmer), coupled with the relatively low price of microcomputers, has opened up the small business market. In the last half of the 1990s, microcomputers also became the point of entry for all types of users into the Internet and the World Wide Web—microcomputers are the universal Web client for all of us!

Workstations/Midrange Systems

Historically, workstations and midrange systems have been considered as distinct categories of computers, but they now overlap so much in cost, power, and applications that we have chosen to combine them in a single category that stretches all the way from microcomputers to the much larger mainframes and supercomputers. Somewhat arbitrarily we have defined this type of computer system as costing from $3,000 (the top of the microcomputers category) to $1,000,000 (near the bottom of the mainframes category), with power ranging from 40 to 4,000 MFLOPS.

It is enlightening to trace the roots of the two aspects of this middle-of-the-road category of computers. *Workstation* is one example of the confusing terminology that abounds in the computing field. In one use of this term, workstation means any type of computer-related device at which an individual may work. Thus, a personal computer is a workstation, and so is a terminal. However, the term workstation is also used to describe a more powerful machine that is still run by a microprocessor but might or might not be used by a single individual. This more powerful type of workstation is one of the two bases for our second category of computers. **Workstations** are, in fact, grown-up, more powerful microcomputers. Workstations at the lower end of the range

PALMTOP WARS

The smallest microcomputers—**palmtop** machines, also called handheld computers or **personal digital assistants** (**PDAs**), which weigh under a pound and cost from $200 to $800—are beginning to catch on as business tools in a big way. Early in the twenty-first century, two palmtop operating systems (and the various devices running these operating systems) dominate the marketplace: the Palm operating system and Microsoft's Windows Mobile for Pocket PC operating system. (We will talk more about operating systems in Chapter 3; for now, note that the operating system is a complex software program that controls operation of the computer.) Palm (recently renamed palmOne) has the largest market share—around 50 percent—but Microsoft is closing the gap.

Palm had first-mover advantage, with the first successful pen-based computer. With a large and growing installed base (now over 30 million Palm-powered devices sold), built on superb contact and calendar management functionality on clean-looking, user-friendly devices, Palm attracted scores of software developers who turned out thousands of varied applications to run on the Palm. Meanwhile, Microsoft had several false starts as it tried to break into the palmtop market. Microsoft's first real success occurred in 2000 with the introduction of the **Pocket PC** version of its pint-sized Windows CE operating system. Hewlett-Packard, Casio Computer, and Compaq Computer offered early Pocket PC devices, and although they offered some advantages in functionality over the Palm handhelds, they were more complex to use and more difficult to interface with the desktop PC. Numerous improvements in the Pocket PC operating system and the associated handheld devices have occurred over the past few years, as they have in the Palm operating system and Palm devices. In part because of the dominance of Microsoft in the desktop market, the Pocket PC has steadily gained market share, although it still trails Palm.

Current products using the Palm operating system include the Palm Tungsten and Zire models, the Sony Clié, and the Handspring Visor and Treo. Pocket PCs on the market include the Hewlett-Packard iPaq line (the name was inherited from Compaq Computer), the Dell Axim, and products from Toshiba, Audiovox, and ViewSonic. It is easy to synchronize both Palms and Pocket PCs with the user's desktop computer via a small "cradle" and easy-to-use software; it is also easy to synchronize the newer devices with the desktop via Bluetooth short-range wireless communication (more on this in Chapter 4). In addition, built-in Wi-Fi wireless networking (see Chapter 4) in the newer models permits both Palms and Pocket PCs to bypass the desktop PC to receive and send e-mail and to surf the World Wide Web.

Many observers believed that the palmtop market would be a replay of the desktop market, with Palm in the role of Apple, and that it was only a matter of time before the Pocket PC became the standard for the business community. Others, including Carl Zetie of Giga Information Group, believe that the market dynamics of the palmtop market are much more complex than those of the desktop, and that "there's still everything to play for—and, in fact, no guarantee that any single 'winner' must emerge" (Zetie, 2002). It is unclear whether the Microsoft advantages of built-in support for Microsoft Office documents, easy integration with Microsoft Exchange, and the Microsoft name will overcome Palm's huge advantage in installed base and available applications software. It certainly looks like the palmtop wars will continue.

[Adapted from Green, 2000; Zetie, 2002; Ewalt, 2003; and Wildstrom, July 14, 2003]

tend to have only one "station"—a keyboard and a high-quality video monitor—at which to "work," although that is not usually true for the upper-end machines. Workstations are based on the microprocessor chip, but the chips are more powerful than those used in microcomputers. Workstations were originally deployed for specific applications demanding a great deal of computing power, high-resolution graphics, or both, but they more recently have been used as Web servers, in network management, and as servers in client/server applications. (Chapter 6 will discuss client/server systems in depth.) Furthermore, because of their very strong price-performance characteristics compared to other types of computers (see Table 2.3), workstations have made inroads into the domains of traditional midrange systems (such as departmental computing and midsized business general processing) and mainframes (large business general processing). These inroads made by workstations into the midrange systems domain have been so significant that we have chosen to combine these categories for our discussion. Today it is almost impossible to decide which machines in this broader category should still be considered "workstations" and which should be considered "midrange systems."

The development of the **reduced instruction set computing** (**RISC**) chip is largely responsible for the success of this class of machines, at least at its upper end. You will recall from our earlier discussion that some computers have a large instruction set (mainframes) while others have a considerably smaller instruction set (microcomputers). The designers of the RISC chips based their work on a reduced instruction set, not on the complete instruction set used on mainframe chips. By working with a reduced

IS A TABLET PC RIGHT FOR YOU?

The newest variation of the microcomputer is the **tablet computer**, powered by the Microsoft Windows XP Tablet PC Edition operating system and manufactured by several vendors, including Acer, Fujitsu, Hewlett-Packard, Gateway, and Toshiba. All these systems provide a flat, tablet-like surface on which the user can "write" with a digital pen. Then the Windows software stores the handwriting digitally or, if you wish, converts the handwriting into type. (According to users, the conversion of handwriting into type is good, but not perfect.) For a professional person who takes lots of notes, a tablet PC seems like a great idea!

There are at least three different approaches to building a tablet computer: One of these, used by Toshiba and Acer, is a modification of the clamshell approach as used in all notebook computers. When the screen is up, the tablet PC looks like any other notebook computer (see Figure 2.11). The difference is that the screen pivots 180 degrees and folds flat over the keyboard to form a tablet (shown on the left in Figure 2.11). The second approach, used by Fujitsu, does not have a mechanical keyboard at all, so it is flat all the time—much like an electronic clipboard. The user enters data by writing with the special pen or by tapping the appropriate keys on a virtual keyboard displayed on the screen. The final approach, used by Hewlett-Packard, employs a detachable keyboard that can serve as a base somewhat like a standard notebook, or can fold behind the screen, or can be removed entirely. The H-P tablet slides into a docking station with or without the keyboard attached.

The software is the key to the successful use of a tablet PC, and the consensus seems to be that the software is getting better but is not all the way there yet (Foley, 2003, and Wildstrom, August 4, 2003). *Information Week*'s John Foley tested two tablet PC applications from Microsoft, both of which use the pen device to write on the screen in digital ink. Windows Journal was the more stable and easy-to-use of the two, having shipped as part of the Windows XP Tablet PC Edition as part of its initial release in 2002. With Windows Journal, the user takes notes and makes sketches on what appears to be endless pages of a legal pad. OneNote is an add-on to Windows released in 2003, and—although trickier to master than Journal—has a lot more capabilities: It is a note-taking application that lets the user combine handwritten or typed notes with drawings, graphics, digital photographs, audio clips, and Web pages—a true multimedia application (Foley, 2003).

The promise of the tablet PC is apparent, and—eventually—many professional workers will be using a tablet PC or one of its successors for note-taking. How soon is eventually? Is a tablet PC right for you?

[Adapted from Greene and Park, 2002; Wildstrom, 2002; Foley, 2003; and Wildstrom, August 4, 2003]

Figure 2.11 Views of the Hewlett-Packard Compaq Tablet PC TC 1000 (Courtesy of Hewlett-Packard)

instruction set, they were able to create a smaller, faster chip than had been possible previously. Variations of these RISC chips power most of the machines at the upper end of the workstations/midrange systems category today.

Turning to the second aspect of our workstations/ midrange systems category, we begin by noting that traditional **midrange systems** have always had an identity crisis—no one knew for sure what to call them or what machines belonged in this category. Until the 1990s, commentators used the label of **minicomputers** for this category (see the section entitled "Evolution of Computer Systems" earlier in this chapter). Originally, these machines were just like the larger mainframe machines, except that they were less powerful and less expensive. For a while the larger minicomputers were even called **superminicomputers**, which is a strange name, using both *super* and *mini* as prefixes. These traditional midrange systems were very important, serving as departmental computers, handling specific tasks such as office automation, and acting as the server in a client/server architecture. Many midsized businesses used one or more midrange systems to handle their corporate data processing. Some analysts suggested that the traditional midrange systems category would disappear, squeezed between increasingly powerful microcomputers and workstations from the bottom and entrenched mainframe systems from above, but that did not happen. Instead, both workstations and midrange systems have "morphed" into the complex, intertwined category that we have chosen to call **workstations/midrange systems**. These systems are primarily employed as servers for client/server applications, Web serving, file and database serving, and network management. They vary from relatively small systems that serve one user or a single department up to enterprise-wide systems that have assumed many of the roles of mainframe computers.

It can be useful to divide this category into several smaller categories. At the low end come machines that are essentially high-powered PCs, typically built around Intel microprocessors (such as the Xeon, Celeron, or Pentium 4 processor) and often using Windows NT Server, Windows 2000 Server, or Windows 2003 Server as the server operating system. It is also possible to run the UNIX or Linux operating system on these Intel-based servers, but this is not as common.[2] The major players in this market subsegment are Dell, Hewlett-Packard, IBM, and Gateway (all U.S-based firms) and NEC (Japan). Other important vendors include Sun Microsystems (United States), NCR (United States), Fujitsu (Japan), and Toshiba (Japan).

At the high end are machines that are powered either by RISC processors developed by the vendor (such as Hewlett-Packard, Sun Microsystems, or IBM) or top-of-the-line Intel microprocessors such as the Itanium 2 or Pentium 4. For the most part these high-end machines run either the Linux operating system or some variation of the UNIX operating system. In this market subsegment the leaders are IBM, Hewlett-Packard, and Sun Microsystems. Other vendors include Silicon Graphics, Inc. (United States), Fujitsu, and Dell. As an example, IBM's entry in this UNIX/Linux market subsegment is its eServer pSeries workstation (formerly RS/6000), employing IBM-developed RISC chips with copper (not aluminum) wiring. Among the many models in the eServer pSeries are the pSeries 630 with up to four processors and the pSeries 690 with up to 32 processors. The newer models in the pSeries line are powered by IBM's POWER4+ 64-bit microprocessor[3], described by IBM as a "server on a chip." The POWER4+ chip contains two processors, a high-bandwidth switch (for fast internal communications), a large memory cache, and an input/output interface—over 180 million transistors in total on a single chip! (IBM Web site, May 6, 2003) The pSeries and its predecessor RS/6000 series have been a tremendous success for IBM, with well over 1 million systems shipped to commercial and technical customers throughout the world. (See also the sidebar entitled "World's Fastest Supercomputer Revisited" later in this chapter.)

A third subcategory is made up of machines that are most identifiable with the "midrange systems" side of the mix. These machines have survived and prospered because they offer much better input/output capabilities than those from the workstations side of the mix and because an extensive array of easy-to-use commercial applications software has been developed for them. In addition, thousands of organizations have developed extensive specialized software to run on midrange systems, and these "legacy" systems cannot easily be converted to run on other types of hardware. On the other hand, these remaining midrange systems have incorporated RISC chips, have embraced UNIX and Linux, and are largely used as servers today. Thus, they are quite different from traditional midrange systems.

The primary example of such a midrange system is IBM's eServer iSeries (formerly the AS/400) family of computers. In the 1980s, IBM's System/34, System/36, and System/38 became the most popular business computers (not including microcomputers) of all time. Most of

[2] Operating systems are considered in Chapter 3. UNIX and Linux are both "open" operating systems that are used on many workstations/midrange systems, supercomputers, and now mainframes. Both open and proprietary operating systems will be discussed in Chapter 3.

[3] This means that the processor chip is capable of handling 64 bits of data at a time, whereas most microprocessor chips handle only 32 bits of data at a time.

these machines were replaced by IBM's AS/400 (which was first introduced in 1988 and has been a major success for IBM), and many additional AS/400s were sold. The name was changed in 2000 to the eServer iSeries, and the beat goes on. Today's eServer iSeries models employ 64-bit copper-based RISC technology. iSeries models vary from relatively small machines, such as the single-processor iSeries 800 with a sample configuration price tag under $25,000, to the model iSeries 890, which can incorporate as many as 32 processors and might cost hundreds of thousands of dollars. All the iSeries machines use IBM's proprietary OS/400 operating system, but even this operating system now incorporates support for the UNIX and Linux operating systems (IBM Web site, September 2003).

Mainframe Computers

The **mainframes** are the "bread-and-butter" machines of information processing and the heart of the computing systems of most major corporations and government agencies. Our earlier discussion of the evolution of computing dealt primarily with the various generations of mainframe computers. The range of mainframe power and cost is wide, with MFLOPS varying from 200 to 8,000 and cost from $1,000,000 to $20,000,000. A mainframe can handle thousands of terminals (or microcomputers acting as terminals), and the machine requires a good-sized computer room and a sizable professional staff of operators and programmer/analysts. The strength of mainframes is the versatility of the applications they can handle: online and batch processing, standard business applications, engineering and scientific applications, network control, systems development, Web serving, and more. Mainframes also operate as very large servers in a client/server environment. Because of the continuing importance of mainframes in corporate computing, a wide variety of peripheral equipment has been developed for use with these machines, as has an even wider variety of applications and systems software. This development, by the way, has been carried out by computer vendors, other equipment manufacturers, and companies that specialize in producing software, known as software houses.

Historically, competition has been fierce in the mainframe arena because of its central role in computing. The dominant vendor has been IBM since the late 1950s. The current generation of IBM mainframes is the eServer zSeries (formerly the System/390 series). The newest machines in the zSeries, code-named T-Rex but officially labeled the zSeries 990, were introduced in 2003, and they vary from a single-processor model to a 32-processor model. All these machines are built around the IBM multichip module (MCM), a grouping of 16 chips employing leading-edge copper wiring and silicon-on-insulator technology and containing over 3.2 billion transistors. The 32-processor model can have up to 256 gigabytes of main memory. Development of the zSeries 990 required 1,200 IBM developers and an investment of $1 billion over a 4-year period. A 32-processor zSeries 990 mainframe is able to process 9 billion instructions per second, a threefold improvement over IBM's previous most powerful mainframe. Furthermore, multiple systems can be combined in a Parallel Sysplex, a multisystem environment that acts like a single system. Through a combination of hardware and software, especially the z/OS operating system, a zSeries Parallel Sysplex can incorporate up to 32 individual machines, each of which can have up to 32 processors (IBM Web site, May 13, 2003).

IBM's choice of the code name for its new mainframe as it was being developed, T-Rex, is an interesting one. Some commentators have described the mainframe computer as a dinosaur nearing extinction, and IBM seems to be responding to those criticisms with the T-Rex—the most feared of the dinosaurs and, now, the most feared of the large computer systems. IBM calls the zSeries 990 "the world's most sophisticated server." IBM has maintained its preeminent position in the mainframe arena through solid technical products, excellent and extensive software, extremely reliable machines, and unmatched service.

Figure 2.12 IBM eServer zSeries 990 (Courtesy of IBM Archives. Unauthorized use not permitted.)

Competition in the mainframe arena is a little less fierce than it used to be. Two vendors, Amdahl (United States) and Hitachi (Japan), dropped out of the mainframe market in 2000. Fujitsu (Japan) purchased Amdahl, and Hitachi bowed out of the mainframe market to concentrate on other market segments. Amdahl and Hitachi are particularly interesting cases because they succeeded for many years by building machines that were virtually identical to IBM's, often with slightly newer technology, and then by selling them for a lower price. Now Fujitsu is the only remaining vendor offering IBM "plug compatible" mainframes. The only other major players in the mainframe market are Unisys (United States) and Groupe Bull (France). Unisys was formed years ago as the merger of Burroughs and Sperry (remember that Sperry built the very first production-line computer), so Unisys has been in the mainframe business a long time.

All the major mainframe vendors, including IBM, fell on hard times in the early 1990s. Because of stronger price/performance ratios from other classes of machines, especially microcomputers and workstations, the primary focus of new systems development in the first half of the 1990s was on client/server applications designed to run on these more cost-effective platforms. The last half of the 1990s saw a marked movement back to mainframes, although demand slackened before and after January 1, 2000, largely because companies were wrapped up in solving the year 2000 (Y2K) problem and then in attending to other IS problems they had let slip while working on Y2K. IBM and other vendors have introduced new technology (such as copper wiring on chips and silicon-on-insulator technology), added UNIX and Linux options to proprietary operating systems, and slashed prices drastically. The addition of Linux capability has been particularly important in the twenty-first century resurgence of the mainframe, with many companies finding out that it is more economical to run multiple Linux virtual servers on a single mainframe than to run (say) 40 Intel-based servers (Greenemeier, 2002). The role of the mainframe will continue to evolve as we move further into the twenty-first century, with more emphasis on its roles as keeper of the corporate data warehouse, server in sophisticated client/server applications, powerful Web server, and controller of worldwide corporate networks.

Supercomputers

Supercomputers are the true "number-crunchers," with MFLOPS ratings in excess of 4,000 and price tags from $1 million to $100 million (more for specialty machines). The high-end supercomputers are specifically designed to handle numerically intensive problems, most of which are generated by research scientists, such as chemists, physicists, and astronomers. Thus, most of the high-end supercomputers are located in government research laboratories or on major university campuses (even in the latter case, most of the machines are largely supported by grants from the National Science Foundation or other government agencies). Midrange supercomputers, however, have found a variety of uses in large business firms, most frequently for research and development efforts, Web serving on a massive scale, data mining, and consolidating a number of smaller servers.

Until the mid-1990s, the acknowledged leader in the high-end supercomputer arena was U.S.-based Cray Inc. However, IBM mounted a concerted effort in supercomputers in the 1990s, and IBM now clearly holds the top spot (see sidebar entitled "World's Fastest Supercomputer Revisited"). In the June 23, 2003, online listing of the world's top 500 supercomputers, the top 100 machines were distributed as follows: IBM 49, Hewlett-Packard 12, Dell and Hitachi 5 each, Cray Inc. and NEC 4 each, and 8 other vendors with 3 machines or fewer, plus 8 self-made machines (i.e., built by the using organization) (Top 500, 2003). These large computers use one or more of three high-performance computer architectures: parallel vector processing, massively parallel processing, and symmetric multiprocessing. All three of these multiprocessor arrangements were described earlier in this chapter in the section entitled "Extensions to the Basic Model." As an example, the Cray T3E can incorporate up to 2,176 MPPs and operate at speeds up to 3 teraflops (3 trillion floating point operations per second). The Cray SV1ex is based on a symmetric multiprocessing model (SMP), with up to 32 SMP nodes, each of which can consist of up to 32 processors, permitting speeds over 1 teraflop. The newest and most powerful Cray machine is the X1, which is a vector massively parallel processing machine with symmetric multiprocessing nodes. The Cray X1 is based on ultrafast individual processors capable of 12.8 gigaflops each; 64 of these processors can be installed in a single cabinet, giving up to 819 gigaflops of peak computing power. The maximum configuration for the X1 then consists of 64 cabinets containing 64 processors each, providing up to 52.4 teraflops of computing power (Cray Inc., 2002).

In addition to the vendors mentioned above, two other important vendors of midrange supercomputers are Silicon Graphics, Inc., and Sun Microsystems, both powerhouses in high-performance workstations. An interesting development in the supercomputer arena occurred in 1996 when Silicon Graphics, Inc., acquired Cray Research, thus becoming (for a time) the world's leading high-performance computing company. Cray Research continued to operate as a separate unit, focusing on large-scale supercomputers. Then in 2000, Tera Computer Company purchased Cray Research from Silicon Graphics, Inc., with the combined company renamed Cray Inc. In the supercomputer arena as in other areas, sometimes it is hard to keep up with the players!

WORLD'S FASTEST SUPERCOMPUTER REVISITED

In August 2001, the U.S. Department of Energy installed a powerful IBM RS/6000 SP supercomputer (code name ASCI White) that is dedicated to simulating nuclear explosions. The Department of Energy (DOE) computer contains more than 8,100 microprocessors and is capable of processing 12.3 *trillion* calculations per second, making it the fastest supercomputer ever built (at the time).

The DOE machine contains 512 nodes, each of which contains 16 copper-based Power3-II microprocessors, all managed by a central point-of-control running advanced management software to make the most of the hardware. (Most other microprocessors use aluminum wiring, which does not conduct electricity as well as copper and thus is slower.) The RS/6000 SP contains a switch to move data between nodes at speeds up to 800 megabytes per second. The price tag on this supercomputer was around $110 million.

A few years later, it is time for the next round of the "world's fastest supercomputer." The DOE has awarded IBM a contract valued at $216 to $267 million to build the *two* fastest supercomputers in the world, with a combined peak speed of 467 trillion calculations per second (teraflops). The first system, code named ASCI Purple, will be capable of up to 100 teraflops and will be employed to simulate the aging and operation of U.S. nuclear weapons, ensuring the safety and reliability of the stockpile without underground testing. ASCI Purple will be powered by 12,544 POWER5 microprocessors, IBM's next generation microprocessor; 64 of these microprocessors will be placed in each of 196 nodes. Then the nodes will be able to communicate with one another at the incredible rate of 12,500 billion bytes (gigabytes) per second.

The second system, code named Blue Gene/L, will take longer to develop and will be more powerful still. When completed, Blue Gene/L will employ 130,000 microprocessors and will be capable of up to 367 teraflops. Blue Gene/L will be a research machine to develop and run simulations of very complex physical phenomena of national interest, such as turbulence, prediction of material properties, and the behavior of high explosives.

The price tags for these massive supercomputers would be too steep for commercial users, but IBM uses essentially the same technology as in ASCI White, although on a much smaller scale (and thus at a more reasonable price), in the eServer pSeries 690. For example, Merck & Co., one of the world's largest pharmaceutical companies, is purchasing five pSeries 690 systems, each with 32 processors, as an addition to 2 IBM RS/6000 SP supercomputers already in use. Merck will use these supercomputers in the basic research aspects of the drug development process, including database searching and chemical property computation. IBM estimates that more than 70 percent of all IBM supercomputers sold are used for commercial applications, including tasks like Web serving on a massive scale, business intelligence and data mining (more on this in Chapter 7), handling large parallel databases, and simply consolidating large numbers of smaller servers.

[Adapted from IBM Web site, 2000; April 2002; October 2002]

SUMMARY

There is a lot more to IT than the digital computer, but there is no doubt that the computer was the key technological development of the twentieth century. The computer has had an astounding impact on organizations and on our lives, and it has captured our imaginations like no other recent development.

To summarize, all computer systems are made up of some combination of six basic building blocks: input, output, memory, arithmetic/logical unit, files, and control unit. All these components are controlled by a stored program that resides in memory and is brought into the control unit one instruction at a time, interpreted, and executed. The basic model has been extended in several directions over the years, such as by adding controllers and data channels to interface the slower peripheral devices (input, output, disks, tapes) with the much faster CPU. Many machines include a multilevel storage system including high-speed cache memory. To gain more power, multiple processors have been employed in a single computer system in a variety of configurations. Whatever the machine configuration, the computer system is still controlled by stored programs, or software. Chapter 3 explores computer software, concentrating on the programs that are most critical in running the computer system and the applications that you are most likely to encounter.

Let us end this chapter with the caveat that the numbers and specific details covered in the chapter will quickly become outdated, but the basic principles we presented should be valid for the foreseeable future.

REVIEW QUESTIONS

1. What are the distinguishing characteristics of the present, or fourth generation, computers?
2. Distinguish between microcomputers, workstations/midrange systems, mainframes, and supercomputers. Give approximate speeds (millions of floating point operations per second, or MFLOPS) and costs.

3. List the six building blocks that make up digital computers, and describe the flows of data that occur among these blocks.
4. Distinguish between the *contents* of a memory cell and the *address* of a memory cell. Distinguish between a *byte* and a *word*. Distinguish between a *bit* and a *byte*.
5. What are the advantages and disadvantages of using direct access files versus using sequential access files? Why do organizations bother to use sequential access files today?
6. Explain in your own words the importance of the stored-program concept. Include the role of the control unit in your explanation.
7. Define the expressions in italics in the following sentence copied from this chapter: "In general, each *machine language* instruction consists of two parts: an *operation code* and one or more *addresses*."
8. Provide the full names for the following acronyms or abbreviations used in this chapter.

OCR	MIPS	UPC
CPU	MPP	CD-ROM
MFLOPS	DASD	PP
CD-RW	SMP	DVD

9. Four categories of computer systems were considered in this chapter: microcomputers, workstations/midrange systems, mainframes, and supercomputers. Provide the name of at least one prominent vendor in each of these categories (and you can only use IBM once!).
10. Describe what is meant by *benchmarking*. When and how would you carry out benchmarking?
11. What is cache memory? Where would it be used, and why?
12. Distinguish between a symmetric multiprocessor computer and a parallel processor computer. Which is the most important at this time for business information processing, and why?

DISCUSSION QUESTIONS

1. From the discussion in this chapter and your own knowledge from other sources, what do you think is the most important advancement in computer hardware technology in the past 5 years? Why?
2. Carry out library or Internet research on the latest microprocessor chips available from firms such as Intel and AMD, collecting data similar to that contained in Table 2.1. Add the new information you have discovered to Table 2.1.
3. Some writers have suggested that mainframe computer systems could be squeezed out of existence in the next few years, with the incredible advances in the capabilities of workstations/midrange systems and the power of supercomputers combining to divide up the present mainframe market. What do you think? Why?
4. What are the advantages and limitations of palmtop or handheld computers? When would you use one?
5. What are the advantages and limitations of a tablet PC? Do you believe tablet PCs will be successful? Why or why not? Do you see yourself using a tablet PC in a few years?
6. As this chapter has indicated, IBM has been a dominant force in the computer industry since the late 1950s. Why do you think this is the case? More specifically, why were so many large corporations seemingly committed to "Big Blue" (as IBM is affectionately known), at least until the early 1990s?
7. Building on your answer to question 6, why did IBM suffer serious reverses in the early 1990s? Why did IBM bounce back in the latter half of the 1990s? Do you think that IBM will retain its dominant position as we move further into the twenty-first century? Why?
8. With one firm (IBM) dominating the mainframe hardware market in the United States since its inception, and with that same firm currently near the top in every segment of the hardware industry, has the computer hardware industry truly been competitive over the past five decades? Support your position.
9. List possible uses of a supercomputer in a business setting.
10. MIPS and MFLOPS were mentioned in this chapter as measures of the power of computer systems. If you were in charge of buying a new large computer system (and you might be some day), what measures of power would you want to find out? How would you go about determining these measures of power?
11. For most business information processing, what do you believe are the critical or limiting characteristics of today's computing systems—CPU speed, memory capacity, DASD capacity, data channel speed, input speed, output speed, other factors, or some combination of these factors? Justify your answer.
12. For Web serving, what do you believe are the critical or limiting characteristics of today's computing systems—CPU speed, memory capacity, DASD capacity, data channel speed, input speed, output speed, other factors, or some combination of these factors? Justify your answer.

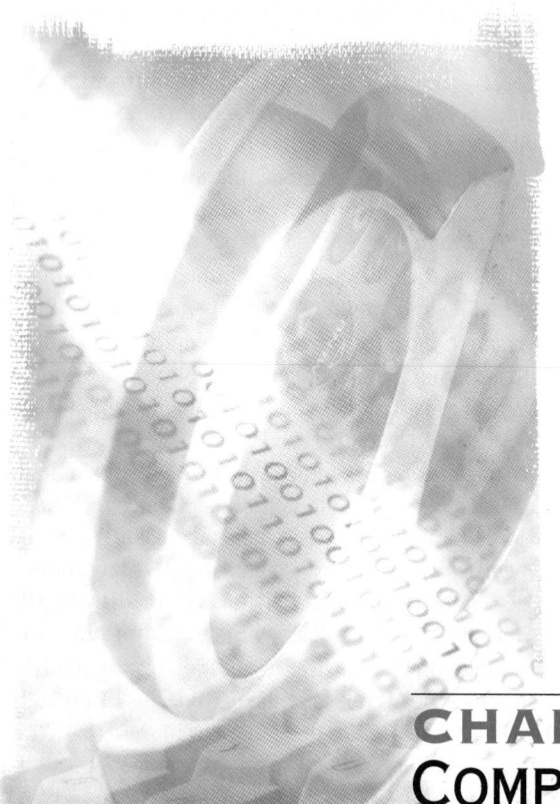

CHAPTER 3
COMPUTER SOFTWARE

IN MANY RESPECTS THIS CHAPTER IS MERELY A CONTINUATION OF CHAPTER 2, which concentrated on computer hardware, or the physical pieces of a computer system. We learned that all the hardware is controlled by a stored program, which is a complete listing (in a form that the computer has been built to understand) of what the computer is to do. Such a stored program is an example of computer software, the topic of this chapter. Software is the set of programs (made up of instructions) that control the operations of the computer system. Computer hardware without software is of little value (and vice versa). Both are required for a computer system to be a useful tool for you and your organization. Thus, this chapter will explain more fully the symbiotic relationship between computer hardware and software.

As important as understanding computer hardware is, it is even more important for you as a manager to understand software. First, appropriate software is required before hardware can do anything at all. Second, most organizations spend several times as much money on software as they do on hardware. This ratio of software to hardware costs is rapidly increasing over time. In the first decade of the twenty-first century, a software company, Microsoft Corporation, is arguably the most successful and most influential company in the entire computer arena.

Third, and most personally relevant, you will be dealing directly with a number of important software packages, such as spreadsheets, word processors, and Web browsers, whereas the only hardware you are likely to interact with is a workstation (most likely a microcomputer, not one of the higher-powered workstations discussed in the previous chapter). Whatever your job in an organization, you are also likely to be involved in software development or acquisition efforts as a member of a project team or as an end user. If your field is marketing, you might well be involved with the creation of a new sales reporting system; if your field is finance, you might develop a computer model to evaluate the impact of a possible merger; if you are an operations manager, you might participate in the development of a new inventory reporting system. (The role of the manager in software development and acquisition is discussed more fully in Chapters 10, 11, and 13.) For a variety of reasons, therefore, it is important that you understand the various types of computer software and the ways software is used within an organization.

EVOLUTION OF COMPUTER PROGRAMMING

First and Second Generation Languages

Computer software has, of course, been around as long as computer hardware. Initially, all software was written in machine language, as described in "The Stored-Program Concept" section of Chapter 2. Each instruction in a machine language program must be expressed in the precise form that the particular computer has been built to understand. If, for instance, we want to subtract the number found in memory cell 720 from the number found in memory cell 600, storing the result in cell 600, then the machine language instruction (for a hypothetical computer) would be

Operation Code	Addresses	
S	720	600

A complete program to carry out a particular application (e.g., compute the payroll or prepare a management report) would consist of hundreds or thousands of similar instructions expressed in the machine language of the particular computer. The programmer would have to look up (or memorize) each operation code and remember what data have been stored in every memory cell. Machine language programming was (and is) an exacting, tedious, time-consuming process, but it was the only option available on the earliest computers.

Computer software developers soon created **assembly languages** that used the computer itself to perform many of the most tedious aspects of programming. For example, easily remembered mnemonic operation codes are substituted for the machine language operation codes (e.g., SUB for S or SUB for something as unintelligible as 67 on some machines). Symbolic addresses are substituted for a memory cell address (e.g., GPAY for 600). Thus, if our single instruction above is part of a payroll program where we want to subtract deductions (DED) from gross pay (GPAY), we can write

SUB	DED	GPAY

Writing instructions such as this is much easier (and less error-prone) than writing machine language instructions, particularly when we consider that there are likely to be 50 different operation codes and hundreds of memory cell addresses to remember in even a moderate-sized program.

The entire assembly language program is written using instructions similar to the one above. Then the computer, under the control of a special stored program called an **assembler**,

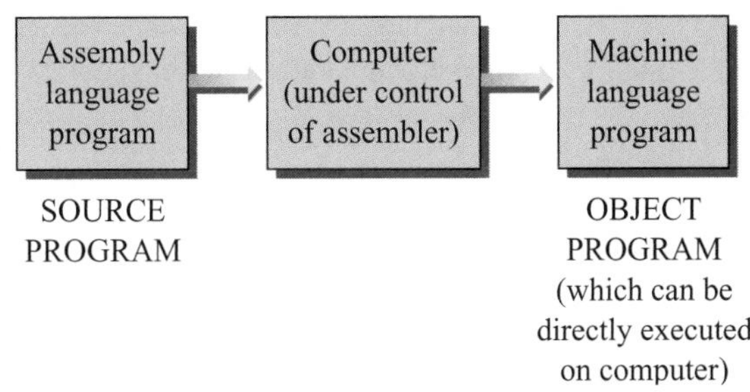

Figure 3.1 Assembler Translation Process

converts these mnemonic operation codes and symbolic addresses to the machine language operation codes and memory cell addresses. The assembler program simply keeps a table of conversions for operation codes and addresses and makes the substitutions as necessary. Figure 3.1 illustrates this translation process from the assembly language program (the program containing mnemonic codes and symbolic addresses) to the machine language program. The assembly language program is also called the **source program**, and the resulting machine language program is the **object program**. Once the translation process has been completed, the outcome machine language program is loaded into memory and carried out by the control unit (as described in Chapter 2). The machine language for a particular computer is referred to as the first generation language, or 1 GL, and the assembly language that came along later is called the second generation language, or 2 GL.

Assembly language programming was popular for business applications for many years (until about 1970), and a few major firms and some computer professionals still use assembly language.[1] Popular assembly languages have included SOAP (Symbolic Optimization Assembly Program), Autocoder, and BAL (Basic Assembly Language). Assembly language programming is much easier than machine language programming, but it still requires the programmer to employ the same small steps that the computer has been built to understand; it still requires one assembly language instruction for each machine language instruction.[2] Thus, even after

[1]The primary reason for the continued use of assembly language is computer efficiency. A well-written assembly language program will require less memory and take less time to execute than a well-written third generation or fourth generation language program.

[2]To be complete, assembly languages often provide for macroinstructions, where one macroinstruction might correspond to 5, 10, or more machine language instructions. A programmer writes a set of assembly language instructions that he or she expects to use repeatedly, and then gives this set a label (or a macroinstruction name). Then each time the macroinstruction is used in a program, the entire set of assembly language instructions is substituted for it.

the advent of assembly languages, efforts continued to make it easier to tell the computer what the user wanted done. The results are today's third and fourth generation languages (3 GLs and 4 GLs).

Third and Fourth Generation Languages

The third and fourth generation languages represent a radical departure from the first two generations. Both machine language and assembly language programming require the programmer to think like the computer in terms of the individual instructions. With 3 GLs and 4 GLs, the programmer uses a language that is relatively easy for humans to learn and use but has no direct relationship to the machine language into which it must eventually be translated. Thus, the 3 GLs and 4 GLs are designed for humans, not computers! Typically, each 3 GL or 4 GL instruction will be translated into many machine language instructions (perhaps 10 machine language instructions per 3 GL instruction, or 100 machine language instructions per 4 GL instruction). Furthermore, although each type of computer has its unique 2 GL, the 3 GLs and 4 GLs are largely machine independent. Thus, a program written in a 3 GL or 4 GL can be run on many different types of computers, which is often a significant advantage.

Third generation languages are also called **procedural languages**, because they express a step-by-step procedure devised by the programmer to accomplish the desired task. The earliest procedural language was FORTRAN (an abbreviation for FORmula TRANslator), which was developed by IBM in the mid-1950s. Other popular procedural languages include COBOL (COmmon Business Oriented Language), PL/1, BASIC, PASCAL, ADA, and C. These third generation languages (particularly FORTRAN, BASIC, C, and COBOL) are still very important today, and a later section of this chapter will expand on these introductory remarks. Estimates vary, but it is likely that at least two-thirds of the programs in use today were written in 3 GLs.

A source program in any one of these languages must be translated into the machine language object program before the computer can carry it out. For 3 GLs (and for 4 GLs), the language translator is called a **compiler** if the entire program is translated into machine language before any of the program is executed, or an **interpreter** if each source program statement is executed as soon as that single statement is translated. Historically, the BASIC language was usually interpreted, while most other 3 GLs have been compiled. However, BASIC compilers now exist, and interpreted COBOL is sometimes used during program development.

Figure 3.2 depicts the process of compiling and running a compiled procedural language program, such as C, FORTRAN, or COBOL. This process is quite similar to that used

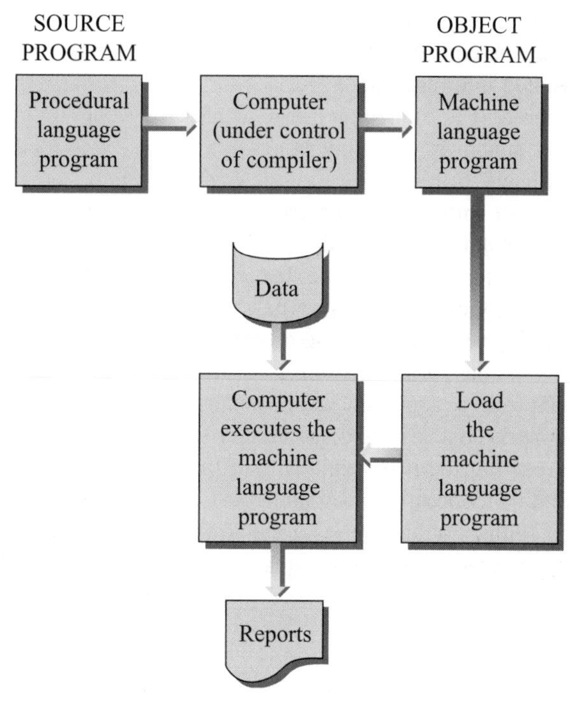

Figure 3.2 Compiling and Running a Procedural Language Program

for assembly language programming (see Figure 3.1), with the labels changed as appropriate. The key is that the entire program is translated into an object program, and then the object program is loaded and executed. Dealing with the entire program in this manner has the advantage that an efficient machine language program (one that executes rapidly) can be produced because the interrelationships among the program statements can be considered during the compilation process; dealing with the entire program has the disadvantage that the programmer does not learn about errors until the entire program has been translated.

Figure 3.3 shows the process of interpreting and running an interpretive language program, such as BASIC.

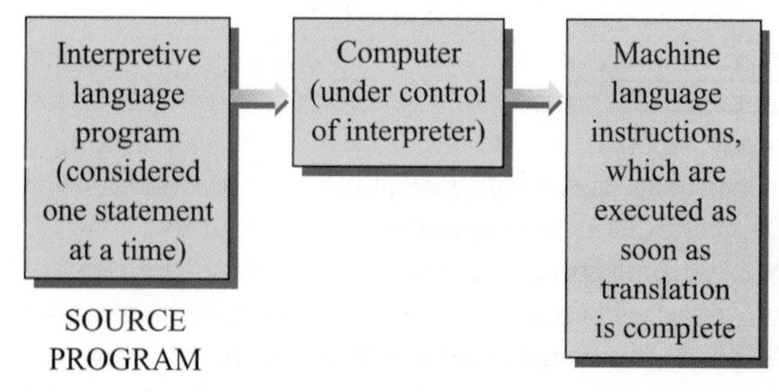

Figure 3.3 Interpreting and Running an Interpretive Language Program

With an interpreter, only one statement from the source program is considered at a time. This single statement is translated into machine language, and if no errors are encountered, it is immediately executed. The process is repeated, statement after statement. This interpretive process lends itself to interactive programming in which the programmer composes the program at a workstation, keys in one statement at a time, and is almost immediately provided feedback if an error is made. If there are no errors, output is produced immediately after the last statement is entered. The machine language program resulting from the interpretive process is usually much less efficient than one resulting from compilation because only one source program statement is being considered at a time. On the other hand, program development might be sped up because of the immediate feedback to programmers when they make an error. With an interpreter, there is often no true object program, because the machine language instructions are discarded as soon as they are executed. Furthermore, if the program is executed repeatedly, each source statement is translated again each time it is executed, which is quite inefficient compared with the compilation process.

Fourth generation languages—also called **productivity languages** and **nonprocedural languages**—are even easier to use than the third generation languages. To employ a 3 GL, the programmer must devise a step-by-step procedure to accomplish the desired result and express this procedure in the form of 3 GL statements. With a 4 GL, the computer user merely gives a precise statement of what he or she wishes to accomplish, not an explanation of how to do it. Thus, the order in which statements are given in a 4 GL is usually inconsequential. Furthermore, each 4 GL statement is usually translated into significantly more machine language instructions than a single 3 GL statement, sometimes by a factor of 100. Thus, 4 GL programs are easier to write, shorter, and less error-prone than 3 GL programs, which in turn have the same advantages over their 2 GL predecessors. Fourth generation languages, for the most part, use an interpreter to translate the source program into machine language. Please note that the 3 GLs and 4 GLs are essentially the same from one computer model to the next, but the translation programs (compilers and interpreters) must be specific to the particular computer model.

With these advantages, why aren't all programs written in 4 GLs today? First, some of the 4 GLs, like IFPS and SAS, are not general-purpose languages and cannot be used easily for many types of programs. On the other hand, FOCUS and CA-Ramis are indeed general-purpose 4 GLs. More important, many programs are not written in 4 GLs because of concern for efficient use of the computer resources of the organization. For the most part, 4 GL programs translate into longer machine language programs that take much longer to execute than the equivalent programs written in a 3 GL. (Similarly, 3 GL programs often translate into longer machine language programs that take more time to execute than the equivalent 2 GL programs.) The upshot of these arguments is that many one-time programs or infrequently used programs (such as a decision support system or a specialized management report) are written in 4 GLs, while most production programs (those that will be run every day or every week) are written in 3 GLs. In the case of infrequently used programs, human efficiency in writing the program is more important than computer efficiency in running it; for production programs, the opposite is often the case.

In the late 1990s and early 2000s, new programming languages have gained popularity that are still predominantly 3GLs but also have some 4 GL characteristics. These languages are usually described as **object-oriented programming** or **visual programming** languages. Object-oriented programming (OOP) languages such as Smalltalk and C++ came first; these languages are built on the idea of embedding procedures (called methods) in **objects,** and then putting these objects together to create an application. A newer object-oriented programming language, Java, and a visual programming language, Visual Basic, provide a graphical programming environment and a paint metaphor for developing user interfaces. These newer entries in the programming arena as well as 3 GL and 4 GL languages will be described more fully later in the chapter. Overall, the programming environment in most large organizations is now more diverse than ever, with most organizations using some combination of conventional 3 GLs, 4 GLs, object-oriented programming, and visual programming. The trend is towards more object-oriented and visual programming, but significant 4 GL programming and even more 3 GL programming is still being carried out.

KEY TYPES OF SOFTWARE

In the previous section we considered the evolution of computer programming. These programming languages—from assembly language to COBOL to FOCUS to C++ to Java—have been used over the past several decades to create an incredible array of software products, including the language translators themselves. We now want to categorize the various types of computer software that have been created and gain an understanding of how they work together.

To begin our look at the key elements of computer software, let us step back from the details and view the big picture. It is useful to divide software into two major categories:

1. Applications software
2. Support software

Applications software includes all programs written to accomplish particular tasks for computer users. In addition to our payroll computation example, applications programs would include an inventory record-keeping program, a word-processing package, a spreadsheet package, a program to allocate advertising expenditures, and a program producing a summarized report for top management. Each of these programs produces output that users need to do their jobs.

By contrast, **support software** (also called **systems software**) does not directly produce output that users need. Instead, support software provides a computing environment in which it is relatively easy and efficient for humans to work; it enables applications programs written in a variety of languages to be carried out; and it ensures that the computer hardware and software resources are used efficiently. Support software is usually obtained from computer vendors and from specialized software development companies called software houses.

The relationship between applications software and support software might be more readily understood by considering the software iceberg depicted in Figure 3.4. The iceberg's above-water portion is analogous to applications software; both are highly visible. Applications software directly produces results that you as a manager require to perform your job. However, just as the iceberg's underwater portion keeps the top of the iceberg above water, the support software is absolutely essential for the applications software to produce the desired results. (Please note that the iceberg analogy is not an accurate representation of the numbers of applications and support programs; there are usually many more applications programs than support programs.) Your concern as a manager will be primarily with the applications software—the programs that are directly relevant to your job—but you need to understand the functions of the primary types of support software to appreciate how the complete hardware/software system works.

APPLICATIONS SOFTWARE

Applications software includes all programs written to accomplish particular tasks for computer users. Portfolio management programs, general ledger accounting programs, sales forecasting programs, material requirements

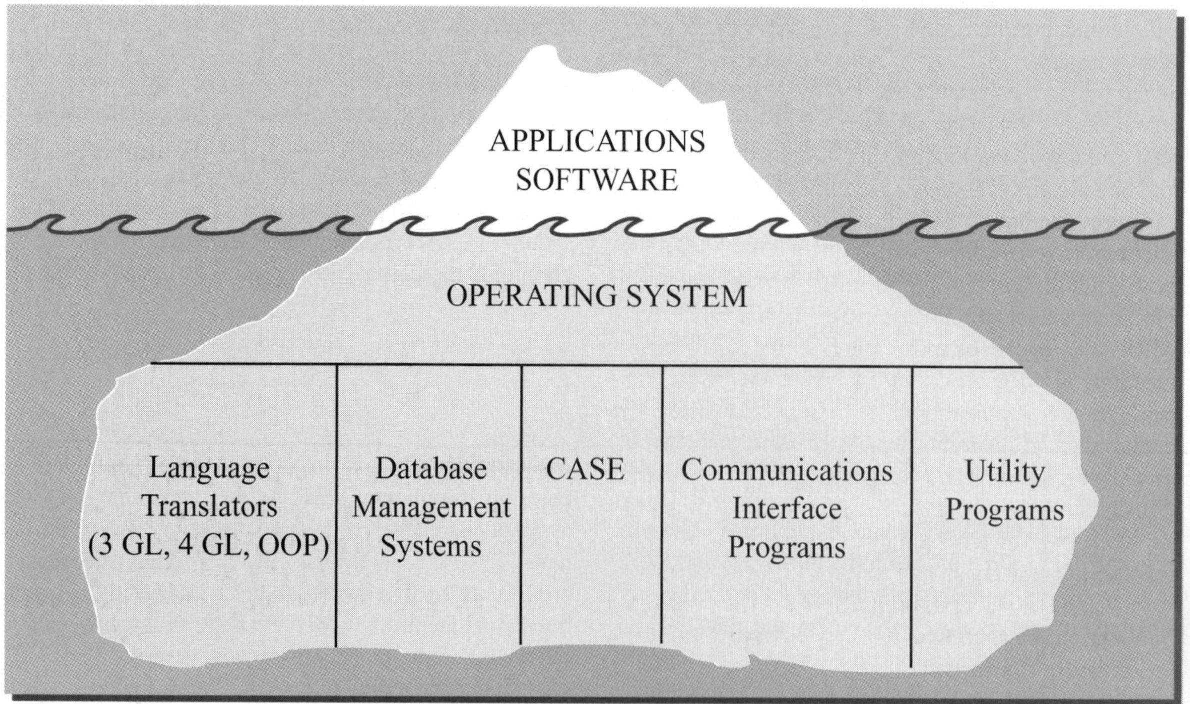

Figure 3.4 The Software Iceberg

planning (MRP) programs, electronic mail programs, and desktop publishing packages are all examples of applications software. Each of you will be using applications software as part of your job, and many of you will be involved in developing or obtaining applications software to meet your organization's needs.

Because applications software is so diverse, it is difficult to divide these programs into a few neat categories as we will do with support software later in the chapter. Instead, we will begin with a brief look at the sources of applications software, and then we will give two examples of accounting packages to illustrate the types of commercial packages that are available for purchase. Finally, we will look at personal productivity packages for handling many common applications (e.g., word processing, spreadsheets).

Where do we obtain software? Support software is almost always purchased from a hardware vendor or a software house. Only the very largest information systems organizations would even consider writing utility programs or modifying operating systems or compilers. Applications software, however, is sometimes developed within the organization and sometimes purchased from an outside source. Standard applications packages, such as word processing, database management systems, electronic mail, and spreadsheets, are almost always purchased. Applications that are unique to the organization—a one-of-a-kind production control system, a proprietary foreign exchange trading program, a decision support system for adoption or rejection of a new product—are almost always developed within the organization (or by a consulting firm or software company under contract to the organization). The vast middle ground of applications that are quite similar from one organization to the next, but which might have some features peculiar to the particular organization, might be either purchased or developed.

These middle-ground applications include accounts payable, accounts receivable, general ledger, inventory control, MRP, sales analysis, and personnel reporting. Here, the organization must decide whether its requirements are truly unique. Does the organization have the capability of developing this application in-house? What are the costs and benefits of developing in-house versus purchasing a package? This make-or-buy decision for applications software is an important one for almost every organization, and this topic will be addressed further in Chapter 11. Let us note at this point that the rising costs of software development tend to be pushing the balance towards more purchased software and less in-house development.

Until the mid-1980s virtually all software development done within an organization was done by the formally constituted information systems organization. The exceptions were engineers, scientists, and a few computer jocks[3] in other user departments. A revolution called end-user computing has occurred in the past two decades, and now end users such as you do much of the internal software development. There are at least three reasons for the end-user computing revolution. First, the information systems organization was unable to keep up with the demand for new applications software, and significant backlogs of jobs developed. Second, a more knowledgeable, more computer-oriented group of users was created through the hiring of college graduates and the use of various internal and external training programs. Third, and perhaps most significant, powerful desktop computer systems became affordable, and software vendors developed relatively easy-to-use tools that made it possible for interested, but not expert, users to carry out significant software development. These tools include the fourth generation languages and the query languages associated with database management systems. This trend toward end-user computing will continue, in our view, with many of you becoming involved in software development early in your careers. Chapter 13 explores this phenomenon of user development.

Of course, not all internal software development is now done—or should be done—by users. For the most part, information systems organizations have not shrunk because of end-user computing; they simply have not grown as rapidly as they might have otherwise. The information systems organizations (or consulting companies or software vendors) continue to develop and maintain the large, complex applications. The IS organizations also tend to develop applications that apply to multiple areas within the organization and those applications for which efficiency is paramount, such as sales transaction processing. The IS organizations employ the same tools used by end users, but they also do a substantial portion of their work using COBOL and other 3 GLs, OOP, and, in some instances, CASE (computer-aided software engineering) tools. Chapters 10 to 13 explore the various ways in which applications systems are developed or procured.

Examples of Applications Packages

Often applications software will be purchased from an outside source. To continue our look at applications software, we will consider one category of commercially available software—accounting packages—as a representative of the many categories that exist. Many commercial accounting

[3]This is not meant as a term of derision. "Computer jock" is a common term used to indicate a person who spends great quantities of time and effort working with a computer.

packages are available, but we will focus on only two such packages: one inexpensive package designed for small businesses and one somewhat more expensive package designed for midsized and larger businesses.

The package designed for smaller businesses is Peachtree Complete Accounting, with a retail price of $300 for a single-user version. This package has all the features that a small to midsized business would need, including general ledger, accounts receivable, accounts payable, inventory, payroll, time and billing, job costing, fixed asset accounting, and analysis and reporting tools. The Peachtree Today "My Business" pages, illustrated in Figure 3.5, provide a concise, graphical way for the business to review key financial information with a quick glance at a set of Web pages. The "My Business" pages display up-to-date graphical or tabular information on sales and receipts (see Figure 3.5), purchases and payables, and general ledger accounting. Other features built into Peachtree Complete Accounting include the ability to generate customer quotes, create and track sales orders and back orders, maintain an audit trail, track inventory items by detailed attributes, and customize forms, reports, and screens. *PC Magazine* gives Peachtree Compete Accounting a high rating—four out of five possible dots—and it costs $200 less than *PC Magazine*'s top-rated product. "This whale of a product is one you should consider if your inventory tracking needs are great," says *PC Magazine*'s Kathy Yakai. "Despite its large feature set, Peachtree Complete is a relatively easy program to use. Peachtree Complete's reporting capabilities have always been strong" (Yakai, 2003, p. 35).

The second package, or rather an extensive set of modules that can be purchased independently, is the ACCPAC Advantage Series Corporate Edition, produced by ACCPAC International, Inc., a subsidiary of software giant Computer Associates International, Inc. ACCPAC Advantage Series Corporate Edition (there is also an enterprise edition for medium to large businesses, a small business edition, and a discovery edition) is a Web-based, modular financial management system for midsized businesses that supports as many as 10 concurrent users. The ACCPAC software resides on a Web server, with only a Web browser needed on workstations to access the application. The central module of ACCPAC Advantage Series is the System Manager, which controls access to all ACCPAC accounting applications and information. The System Manager module manages security,

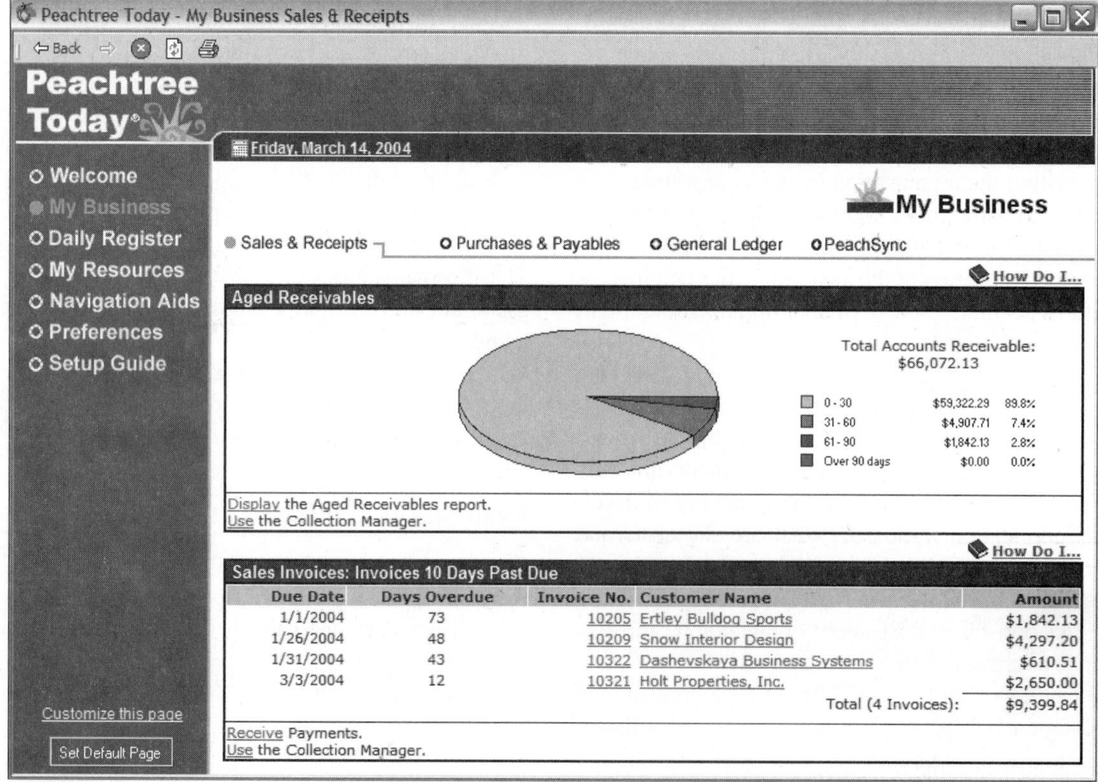

Figure 3.5 Peachtree Today "My Business" Page from Peachtree Complete Accounting (Reproduced with permission of Best Software SB, Inc. The peach device, Peachtree Complete, and Peachtree Today are registered trademarks of Best Software SB, Inc.)

ensures data integrity, handles bank reconciliation and tax processing, and permits creation of customized reports. Other available modules include General Ledger, Accounts Payable, Accounts Receivable, Inventory Control, Order Entry, Purchase Orders, U.S. Payroll, Canadian Payroll, General Ledger Consolidations, Project and Job Costing, Multicurrency, and Intercompany Transactions. The idea, of course, is for each organization to select and employ the modules needed to run its business. These modules are priced at $1,000 each. In addition, there is a fee of $900 to $1,300 per user (up to 10), depending on the database management system used with ACCPAC Advantage Series. ACCPAC options are also available, including a financial diagnostic and strategic analysis tool (CFO), an easy-to-use report generator (Query), an electronic funds transfer direct payroll option, a sales analysis tool, and a sales optimizer tool. These options cost from $500 to $1,000 each. Thus, the total cost of an ACCPAC Advantage Series installation will be much higher than that for Peachtree Complete Accounting, but ACCPAC Advantage Series will be able to handle a much larger business.

DO YOUR ACCOUNTING ON THE WEB!

Accounting for small businesses can now be done on the World Wide Web! Several companies, including Peachtree Software, make accounting software accessible via the Web so that the bookkeeper, small business owner, or other designated employee can enter accounting data, check inventory levels or financial information, and create reports from anywhere at anytime. Peachtree Software calls its online accounting service ePeachtree, and the fees are quite reasonable. The ePeachtree basic accounting service–which includes general ledger, sales and receivables, purchasing and payables, inventory, job and project tracking, and sales tax tracking–is $150 per year for a single user (plus a single outside public accountant at no additional fee), with an add-on fee of $102 per year for each additional user. ePeachtree also has available a payroll service add-on for an additional $96 per year. On its ePeachtree Web page, Peachtree stresses its security measures, including the use of Secure Sockets Layer (SSL) encryption technology and a secure "firewall" server (more on these security measures in Chapter 8). From a small business standpoint, a big plus for using ePeachtree or a similar service is that the firm never again has to spend the money or take the time to upgrade its accounting software–the vendor automatically handles all upgrades. The only software the business needs is a Web browser!

[Adapted from Peachtree Software Web site, 2003]

Personal Productivity Software

From your personal standpoint as a manager, the category of applications software that we have chosen to call **personal productivity software** is probably the most important of all. These are the packages that you and your fellow managers will use on a regular basis: word processing, spreadsheets, presentation graphics, electronic mail, desktop publishing, microcomputer-based database management systems, Web browsers, statistical packages, and other similar easy-to-use and extremely useful packages. These packages are microcomputer-based, and they have been developed with a friendly, comfortable graphical user interface (GUI).

Exciting things continue to happen in the personal productivity software area. The true beginning of this area came in 1979 with the introduction of VisiCalc, the first electronic spreadsheet. With VisiCalc, microcomputers became a valuable business tool, not just a toy or a hobby. The financial success of VisiCalc convinced many enterprising developers that there was money to be made in developing software packages that individuals and companies would buy and use. Within a few years a deluge of products appeared—a mixture of good and bad—that has not stopped flowing. The results have been truly marvelous for the businessperson with a willingness to experiment and a desire to become more productive. Most of the microcomputer products are quite reasonably priced (often a few hundred dollars), because the successful products can expect to reap large rewards on their volume of sales. Furthermore, a number of excellent publications have developed (such as *PC Magazine*, *PC World*, and *Smart Computing*), which carefully review the new products to assist us in choosing the right packages. Hardly a month goes by without the announcement of an exciting new package that might become the new VisiCalc, Lotus 1-2-3, WordPerfect, or Microsoft Excel.

Word Processing Word processing might be the most ubiquitous of the personal productivity software packages. In many organizations the first users of microcomputers were the secretaries using early word-processing packages (often WordStar). As secretaries learned the advantages of word processing, particularly the ability to make corrections in a draft without retyping the entire document, managers began to think that it might be more convenient for them, too, to have a microcomputer on their desk so that they could draft letters and reports directly at the keyboard rather than writing them out longhand. There is an art to composing at the keyboard, but once a person has the hang of it, his or her productivity (in terms of written output) can easily be doubled or tripled, as compared to writing longhand. Thus, word processing has made major inroads into the corporate world at the managerial level.

The newest versions of the popular word-processing packages make it easy to get addicted to them. For example, Microsoft Word underlines words that might be misspelled so that you can correct them as you type; lets the user change fonts, margins, and columns easily; rewrites sentences to make them grammatically correct with the click of a mouse; links any text directly to an Internet file; and converts Web files directly to Word format so they are ready to use. Another popular capability is mail merge—the ability to automatically print the same letter (with the address and salutation changed, of course) to everyone on a mailing list. Other popular word-processing packages include Corel WordPerfect, Lotus Word Pro, and Sun's StarOffice Writer. All these packages try to achieve "what you see is what you get," or WYSIWYG, and all succeed to a great extent. The idea is that the text you see on the computer screen should be as close as possible to the resulting printed text. In choosing a word processor, most of us tend to prefer whichever word processor we worked with first. Increasingly, though, organizations have settled on a standard office suite (more on this later), and thus we use the word processor included in that standard suite, usually Microsoft Word. The important thing is not which word processor you use, it is forcing yourself to choose and use any one of the better word processors in order to improve your productivity in writing.

Spreadsheets Second only to word processing in popularity are electronic spreadsheet packages, the most widely used of which is Microsoft Excel. Other popular spreadsheet packages are Lotus 1-2-3 and Corel Quattro Pro. After the early success of VisiCalc, Lotus 1-2-3 became the spreadsheet standard in the early 1980s and held that leadership position for over a decade. With the growth of software office suites and the dominance of Microsoft in the operating system arena, 1-2-3 has fallen behind Excel as the spreadsheet of choice, but Lotus is still an excellent product with a strong following.

The idea of the electronic spreadsheet is based on the accountant's spreadsheet, which is a large sheet of paper divided into many columns and rows on which the accountant can organize and present financial data. The spreadsheet approach can be used for any application that can fit into the rows and columns framework, including budget summaries for several time periods, profit and loss statements for various divisions of a company, sales forecasts for the next 12 months, an instructor's gradebook, and computation of various statistics for a basketball team.

The intersection of a row and a column is called a cell. Each row in the spreadsheet is given a label (1, 2, 3, etc., from the top down), as is each column (A, B, C, etc., from left to right), and a cell is identified by combining the designations of the intersecting row and column (see Figure 3.6). In a budget summary spreadsheet, for example, cell C4 might contain $32,150, the budgeted sales income for the second quarter. Similarly, cell C2 might contain the heading information "Second Quarter." To enter data into a cell, the cursor is positioned on that cell and the user merely keys in the appropriate data.

But the power of a spreadsheet program does not come from keying numeric data into particular cells, although that is certainly done. The power comes in part from the use of formulas to combine the contents of other cells, letting the program make the calculations rather than doing them by hand. For example, let us assume that cell C9 in our budget summary example is to contain the total income for the second quarter, which is the sum of cells C4, C5, C6, and C7. Rather than adding C4 through C7 by hand, the user enters a formula in cell C9 that tells the program to total the contents of those four cells. One way to express that formula in Microsoft Excel is = +C4+C5+C6+C7. The program then computes the sum and places it in cell C9. More importantly, if a change has to be made in one of the numerical entries, say in cell C5, the sum in cell C9 is automatically corrected to reflect the new number. This feature makes it very easy to modify assumptions and conduct "what if" analyses using a spreadsheet package.

Among the "big three" spreadsheet packages mentioned earlier, there is little difference in the basic approach, although the details do vary. The normal display when using Excel, for example, is a portion of the spreadsheet (a window) with a menu, icons, and a control area at the top of the screen. Using the arrow keys, the user navigates around the spreadsheet to the cell where the entry is to be made. Note that the window automatically changes to keep the cursor cell visible. As numerical or heading information is keyed in, it appears both in the control area at the top of the screen and in the desired cell. If a formula is keyed in, however, the formula appears in the control area while the resulting numerical value is placed in the cell. The user accesses the various commands in Excel through the menu and icons at the top of the screen. If a particular string of commands is likely to be used repeatedly, it is possible to create a "macro" (a program). The user then employs a few keystrokes to call the macro rather than entering the entire string of commands.

Projecting profit for a hypothetical company will serve as a specific spreadsheet application. The Second Company wishes to project its profit for the years 2005 through 2009, given a set of assumptions about its quantity sold, selling price, fixed expenses, and variable expenses. For example, quantity sold of the only product is assumed to be 2,000

	A	B	C	D	E	F	G
1			SECOND COMPANY PROJECTED PROFIT				
2							
3			2005	2006	2007	2008	2009
4							
5	Quantity sold		2000	2100	2205	2315	2431
6	Price		$ 50.00	$ 54.00	$ 58.32	$ 62.99	$ 68.02
7							
8	Total income		$ 100,000	$ 113,400	$ 128,596	$ 145,827	$ 165,368
9							
10							
11	Fixed costs:						
12	Rent		$ 1,000	$ 1,100	$ 1,200	$ 1,300	$ 1,400
13	Salaries		$ 20,000	$ 22,000	$ 24,200	$ 26,620	$ 29,282
14	Equipment leases		$ 4,000	$ 4,200	$ 4,410	$ 4,631	$ 4,862
15	Utilities		$ 5,000	$ 6,000	$ 7,200	$ 8,640	$ 10,368
16	Office supplies		$ 500	$ 475	$ 451	$ 429	$ 407
17							
18	Total fixed costs		$ 30,500	$ 33,775	$ 37,461	$ 41,619	$ 46,319
19							
20	Variable costs:						
21	Unit material cost		$ 8.00	$ 10.00	$ 12.00	$ 14.00	$ 16.00
22	Unit labor cost		$ 4.00	$ 4.16	$ 4.33	$ 5.11	$ 5.62
23	Unit supplies cost		$ 1.00	$ 1.00	$ 1.00	$ 1.00	$ 1.00
24							
25	Total material cost		$ 16,000	$ 21,000	$ 26,460	$ 32,414	$ 38,896
26	Total labor cost		$ 8,000	$ 8,736	$ 9,540	$ 11,820	$ 13,652
27	Total supplies cost		$ 2,000	$ 2,100	$ 2,205	$ 2,315	$ 2,431
28							
29	Total variable costs		$ 26,000	$ 31,836	$ 38,205	$ 46,548	$ 54,979
30							
31	Total costs		$ 56,500	$ 65,611	$ 75,666	$ 88,168	$ 101,298
32							
33							
34	Profit before taxes		$ 43,500	$ 47,789	$ 52,930	$ 57,660	$ 64,070

Figure 3.6 Microsoft Excel Spreadsheet

units in 2005, increasing 5 percent per year for each year thereafter. Price is assumed to be $50 per unit in 2005, increasing at 8 percent per year. Rent is $1,000 in 2005, growing at $100 per year. Similar assumptions are made for each of the other categories of fixed and variable costs. The resulting spreadsheet is shown in Figure 3.6, which indicates that the Second Company is projected to make $43,500 in profit before taxes in 2005 and $64,070 in 2009.

How were these numbers in the spreadsheet determined? Many of the numbers in the 2005 column were keyed directly in as initial assumptions. However, eight of the numbers in the 2005 column and all of the numbers in the remaining columns were determined by formulas, letting the program perform the actual calculations. For instance, 2000 was actually keyed into cell C5 and 50.00 into cell C6. Cell C8, however, contains a formula to multiply quantity sold times price, =+C5*C6. Figure 3.7 shows the formulas behind the numbers in Figure 3.6. If the cursor is positioned on cell C8 in the spreadsheet, the number 100,000 will appear in the spreadsheet but the formula =+C5*C6 will appear in the control area at the top. Similarly, cell C18 contains a formula to add the contents of cells C12, C13, C14, C15, and C16; one way of expressing this formula is =SUM(C12:C16). Cell D5, the quantity sold in 2006, also contains a formula. In this case the quantity sold in 2006 is to be 5 percent greater than the quantity sold in 2005, so the formula is =+C5*1.05. Not surprisingly, the formula in cell E5 is =+D5*1.05. Thus, any changed assumption about the quantity sold in 2005 will automatically affect both total income and profit in 2005 and quantity sold, total income, and profit in all future years. Because of this cascading effect, the impact of alternative assumptions can be easily analyzed after the original spreadsheet has been developed. This is the power of a spreadsheet package.

Database Management Systems After word processing and spreadsheets, the next most popular category of personal productivity software is microcomputer-based database management systems (DBMSs). The most widely used package is Microsoft Access; other popular packages include FileMaker Pro, Corel Paradox, Alpha Five, and Lotus Approach. dBase was the desktop DBMS leader in the 1980s but has now largely disappeared. All these packages are based on the relational data model, to be discussed in Chapter 5. The basic ideas behind these packages are the same as those to be discussed for large machine DBMSs, but the desktop DBMSs are generally easier to use. With the aid of macros and other programming tools (such as Visual Basic for Applications in the case of Access), rather sophisticated applications can be built based on these DBMS packages.

Presentation Graphics Presentation graphics is yet another important category of personal productivity software. Most spreadsheet packages incorporate significant

	A	B	C	D	E	F	G
1			SECOND COMPANY PROJE CTED PROFIT				
2							
3			2005	2006	2007	2008	2009
4							
5	Quantity sold		2000	=+C5*1.05	=+D5*1.05	=+E5*1.05	=+F5*1.05
6	Price		50	=+C6*1.08	=+D6*1.08	=+E6*1.08	=+F6*1.08
7							
8	Total income		=+C5*C6	=+D5*D6	=+E5*E6	=+F5*F6	=+G5*G6
9							
10							
11	Fixed costs:						
12	Rent		1000	=+C12+100	=+D12+100	=+E12+100	=+F12+100
13	Salaries		20000	=+C13*1.1	=+D13*1.1	=+E13*1.1	=+F13*1.1
14	Equipment leases		4000	=+C14*1.05	=+D14*1.05	=+E14*1.05	=+F14*1.05
15	Utilities		5000	=+C15*1.2	=+D15*1.2	=+E15*1.2	=+F15*1.2
16	Office supplies		500	=+C16*0.95	=+D16*0.95	=+E16*0.95	=+F16*0.95
17							
18	Total fixed costs		=SUM(C12:C16)	=SUM(D12:D16)	=SUM(E12:E16)	=SUM(F12:F16)	=SUM(G12:G16)
19							
20	Variable costs:						
21	Unit material cost		8	=+C21+2	=+D21+2	=+E21+2	=+F21+2
22	Unit labor cost		4	=+C22*1.04	=+D22*1.04	=+E22*1.18	=+F22*1.1
23	Unit supplies cost		1	1	1	1	1
24							
25	Total material cost		=+C5*C21	=+D5*D21	=+E5*E21	=+F5*F21	=+G5*G21
26	Total labor cost		=+C5*C22	=+D5*D22	=+E5*E22	=+F5*F22	=+G5*G22
27	Total supplies cost		=+C5*C23	=+D5*D23	=+E5*E23	=+F5*F23	=+G5*G23
28							
29	Total variable costs		=+C25+C26+C27	=+D25+D26+D27	=+E25+E26+E27	=+F25+F26+F27	=+G25+G26+G27
30							
31	Total costs		=+C18+C29	=+D18+D29	=+E18+E29	=+F18+F29	=+G18+G29
32							
33							
34	Profit before taxes		=+C8-C31	=+D8-D31	=+E8-E31	=+F8-F31	=+G8-G31

Figure 3.7 Cell Formulas for Microsoft Excel Spreadsheet

graphics capabilities, but the specialized presentation graphics (sometimes called business graphics) packages have even greater capabilities. Used for creating largely textual presentations, but with embedded clip art, photographs, graphs, and other media, the leaders in this field are Microsoft PowerPoint, Corel Presentations, and Lotus Freelance Graphics. For design of more complex business graphics, the leading packages are Microsoft Visio, Adobe Illustrator, CorelDraw, and Macromedia FreeHand.

World Wide Web Browsers A very important type of personal productivity software is the **Web browser** used by an individual to access information on the World Wide Web. The Web browser is the software that runs on the user's microcomputer, enabling the user to look around, or "browse," the Internet. Of course, the user's machine must be linked to the Internet via a modem connection to an Internet service provider (ISP) or a connection to a local area network (LAN), which is in turn connected to the Internet. The Web browser uses a hypertext-based approach to navigate the Internet. **Hypertext** is a creative way of linking objects (such as text, pictures, sound clips, and video clips) to each other. For example, when you are reading a document describing the Grand Canyon, you might click on the link The View from Yavapai Point to display a full-screen photograph of that view or click on the link The Grand Canyon Suite to hear a few bars from that musical composition.

Two primary Web browsers are in use in the first decade of the twenty-first century: Netscape and Microsoft's Internet Explorer. Netscape had first-mover advantage but has now been eclipsed by Internet Explorer in terms of number of users. From the user's standpoint, the great thing about this browser battle is that both products are free—the price is unbeatable! Both Microsoft and Netscape (now a subsidiary of America Online, or AOL) make money by functioning as an ISP and by developing software and applications for use on the World Wide Web.

In recent versions of Internet Explorer, Microsoft has introduced the idea of the **Active Desktop**, which Microsoft describes as a customizable "dashboard" for your Windows-based PC. The Active Desktop lets the user place both Windows icons (such as shortcuts to programs that you use frequently) and Hypertext Markup Language (HTML) elements (such as links to Web sites that you visit frequently) on the Windows home screen. The HTML elements can be dynamic, too. Users can, for example, place a Web page containing a weather report or a news feed on the desktop and have it updated at regular intervals so that the content is always fresh.

Web browsers are based on the idea of **pull technology**. The browser must request a Web page before it is sent to the desktop. **Push technology** is also important. In push technology, data are sent to the client (usually a PC) without the client requesting it. E-mail is the oldest and most widely used push technology—and certainly e-mail spam is the most obnoxious form of push technology. In the 1990s the most familiar Web example of push technology was PointCast (a free download package), which delivered customized news ticker-tape style to the user's desktop. However, this provider-to-end-user use of push technology has essentially gone out of existence (and so has PointCast) because of a flawed economic model. Other uses of push technology have been more successful. For example, it is commonplace for technology vendors (such as Microsoft) and corporations to distribute software patches and new versions of software via push technology, often on an overnight basis. Similarly, many organizations have pushed sales updates and product news to their sales representatives and field service technicians around the world. But what if the users are only occasionally online, with much of their work done offline?

BackWeb Technologies Limited—which describes itself as the "offline Web company"—has the answer with offline portal access and proactive delivery of information using its Polite technology. A **portal** is simply a standardized entry point to key information on the corporate network. When an employee is online, he or she goes through the portal to find the needed information. With the BackWeb system, a copy of the corporate portal is set up on the user's PC. When the PC is online, BackWeb's Polite technology takes advantage of otherwise unused bandwidth to update the portal's contents, such that network performance is never affected by the portal replication. Thus, the user can do most of his or her work offline using the offline portal. The newest version of BackWeb's Proactive Portal Server introduces two-way replication, which lets users work in a portal offline and then automatically replicates changes and additions once they reconnect to the network. In an important move, software giant SAP plans to package Proactive Portal Server with its mySAP software (more on SAP in Chapter 6). Offline portals, serviced by push technology, can increase the productivity of today's mobile employees when they are on the road and disconnected from the network (BackWeb Web site, 2003; and Kontzer, 2003).

Electronic Mail and Groupware We will defer a full discussion of electronic mail (e-mail) and groupware until Chapter 6, but these clearly qualify as personal productivity software. Electronic mail has become the preferred way of communicating for managers in most businesses today. It is asynchronous (no telephone tag) and unobtrusive, easy to use and precise. Groupware incorporates not only electronic mail, but also much more. Groupware has the goal of helping a group become more productive and includes innovative ways of data sharing, such as Lotus Notes' threaded discussion groups.

Other Personal Productivity Packages Desktop publishing gives the user the ability to design and print an in-house newspaper or magazine, a sales brochure, an annual report, and many other things. The more advanced word-processing packages, such as Microsoft Word and Corel WordPerfect, provide the capability to arrange the document in appropriate columns, import figures and tables, and use appropriate type fonts and styles. The popular specialized desktop publishing packages, such as Adobe PageMaker, Adobe InDesign, Adobe FrameMaker, Quark XPress, and Microsoft Publisher, are even more powerful.

There are a number of other categories of personal productivity packages. Two important security packages are Norton Internet Security[4] (from Symantec), which combines the best antivirus product with the best software firewall solution, and McAfee Internet Security (from Network Associates). We will consider computer security in more depth in Chapter 8. Personal information managers provide an easy-to-use electronic calendar plus storage of telephone numbers, addresses, and other personal information. For an individual not working as part of a group, Lotus Organizer is often the top choice; for those working in a group, groupware products such as Lotus Notes and Microsoft Outlook provide these capabilities. Goldmine Business Contact Manager (from FrontRange), ACT! (from Interact Commerce), and NOW Up to Date & Contact Manager (from Power On Software) are examples of contact management programs that let the user track past and potential customers.

A widely used and valuable package for creating, distributing, and commenting on electronic documents is Adobe Acrobat. Project scheduling software includes Microsoft Project, FastTrack Schedule (from AEC Software), and SureTrak Project Manager (from Primavera). Among the popular packages for image editing are Adobe Photoshop[4], Adobe Photoshop Elements[4] (a reduced-version package designed for hobbyists), Jasc Paint Shop Pro, and Roxio PhotoSuite. For video editing, three strong software packages are Pinnacle Studio[4], Adobe Premiere Pro, and Avid Xpress. Valuable reference packages include Rand McNally StreetFinder & TripMaker (from Global Marketing Partners), Microsoft Streets & Trips, and Microsoft Encarta (a true multimedia encyclopedia).

---

[4]*PC Magazine* named four packages as the "best desktop software products of 2002": Adobe Photoshop 7.0, Adobe Photoshop Elements 2.0, Norton Internet Security 2003, and Pinnacle Studio 8 (2003).

The list of personal productivity software presented here could certainly be extended, but today's most important categories have been mentioned. New packages and new categories will certainly be introduced in the next few years.

Office Suites New versions of the popular personal productivity software packages have been introduced every year or so in the late 1990s and early 2000s, but two other developments have been even more important in redefining the personal productivity software area. First, the key players have evolved over time, with some firms being purchased by others and some products being sold to a different vendor. IBM's purchase of Lotus Development Corporation in 1995 was perhaps the most significant shift among the players. The popular WordPerfect word-processing package has been batted around like a ping-pong ball; first Novell purchased the WordPerfect Corporation, and then Novell sold the WordPerfect package to Corel. The popular packages of 2 or 3 years ago likely still exist, but they might not have the same corporate home.

Second, an even more important development is the combining of certain of these personal productivity software packages into integrated suites of applications for use in the office. With the strong popularity of the Microsoft Windows operating system, the major software players scrambled to introduce **office suites**, also known as **application suites**, that are compatible with Windows. Of course, Microsoft, as the developer of Windows, had the inside track in terms of producing Windows software packages and a Windows office suite. In the first decade of the twenty-first century, the Microsoft Office suite is overwhelmingly the dominant entry in the marketplace. Three other office suites are worth mentioning: Corel WordPerfect Office, Lotus SmartSuite, and Sun StarOffice.

Microsoft Office (version 95, then 97, 2000, XP, and now 2003) was the first suite and has captured a dominant market share, but the other three suites have strong features, popular products, and a distinct price advantage. The Microsoft Office 2003 suite includes Word (word processing), Excel (spreadsheet), PowerPoint (presentations), and Outlook (e-mail, contacts, and scheduling) in the standard edition. The small business edition adds Publisher (desktop publishing) and a version of Outlook with Business Contact Manager, and the professional edition adds Access (database management system) to the small business package. The suggested retail price is $399 for the standard edition, $449 for the small business edition, and $499 for the professional edition. The other players in the office suite arena have had difficulty keeping up with Microsoft. Microsoft was the first mover, controls the operating system, has good individual products (although not always the best individual products), and has done a better job of integrating the individual products than Corel and Lotus.

Lotus SmartSuite Millennium Edition 9.8 includes seven primary products: Word Pro (word processing), 1-2-3 (spreadsheet), Freelance Graphics (presentations), Approach (database management system), Organizer (time management), FastSite (Web publishing), and SmartCenter (information manager). The retail price is under $300, but the street price is often under $40. Corel WordPerfect Office 11 includes three primary products in its standard edition: WordPerfect (word processing), Quattro Pro (spreadsheet), and Presentations (presentations). The professional edition adds Paradox (database management system). The retail price is about $300 for the standard edition and $400 for the professional edition, but the street price is under $40 for the standard edition and under $120 for the professional edition. The Sun StarOffice 7 office suite, which retails for $79, includes five products: Writer (word processing), Calc (spreadsheet), Impress (presentations), Draw (graphics), and Base (database management system). For all these suites, the price to upgrade from an earlier edition is considerably less than the retail price. All these suites provide excellent value for the investment. It seems clear that the future of certain personal productivity software products (word processing, spreadsheet, presentations, and database management system) lies in office suites because of the ability to move data among the various products as needed.

SUPPORT SOFTWARE

Support software has been designed to support applications software behind the scenes rather than to directly produce output of value to the user. There are several types of support software, such as the language translators we encountered earlier in this chapter. In our discussion of the evolution of computer programming, we noted that programs written in second, third, and fourth generation languages must be translated to machine language before they can be run on a computer. This translation is accomplished by support software called assemblers, compilers, and interpreters. We now want to take a systematic look at the various types of support software.

The Operating System

The most important type of support software is the operating system, which originated in the mid-1960s and is now an integral part of every computer system. The **operating system** is a very complex program that controls the operation of the computer hardware and coordinates all the other software, so as to get as much work done as possible with the available resources. Users interact with the operating system, not the hardware, and the operating system in turn controls all hardware and software resources of the computer system.

Before operating systems (and this was also before PCs), computer operators had to physically load programs and start them running by pushing buttons on the computer console. Only one program could be run at a time, and the computer was often idle while waiting for an action by the operator. Now the operator's job is much easier and the computer is used more efficiently, with the operating system controlling the starting and stopping of individual programs and permitting multiple programs to be run at the same time. The operating system on a PC also helps the user by providing an easy-to-use graphical user interface (GUI).

There are two overriding purposes for an operating system: to maximize the work done by the computer system (the throughput) and to ease the workload of computer users. In effect, the operation of the computer system has been automated through the use of this sophisticated program. Figure 3.8 illustrates some of the ways in which

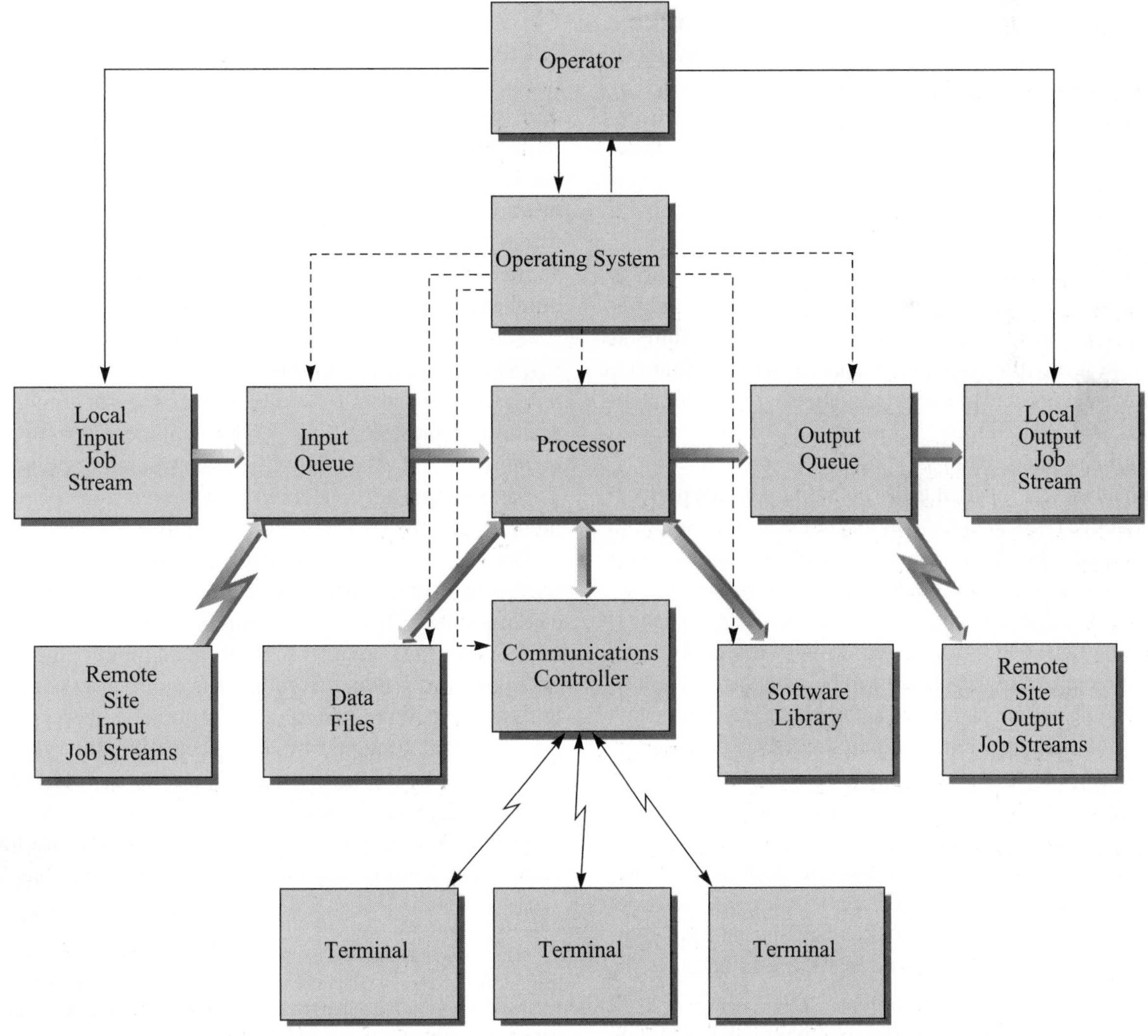

Figure 3.8 The Role of the Operating System

these purposes are advanced by the operating system. This somewhat complex diagram presents the roles of the operating system in a large computer system. To make these roles more understandable, we will concentrate on the diagram's individual elements.

First, note that the human operator at the top of the diagram interfaces only with the operating system, the local input job stream, and the local output job stream. The interface with the operating system is usually done by entering simple commands at an operator console (a specialized terminal). The interface with the local input job stream usually involves mounting tapes or changing removable disk packs, and the interface with the local output job stream means separating and distributing printed output.

The operating system, either directly or indirectly through other support software, controls everything else that takes place in Figure 3.8. It controls the inflow and outflow of communications with the various terminals and microcomputers (often through a specialized communications interface program). Using priority rules specified by the computer center manager, the operating system decides when to initiate a particular job from among those waiting in the input queue; similarly, the operating system decides when to terminate a job (either because it has been completed, an error has occurred, or it has run too long). The operating system decides which job to print next, again based on priority rules. It stores and retrieves data files, keeping track of where everything is stored (a function sometimes shared with a database management system). The operating system also manages the software library, keeping track of both support and applications programs.

The advantage of letting the operating system perform all the above tasks is that it can react at electronic speed to select the next job, handle multiple terminal sessions, select the appropriate software from the library, and retrieve the appropriate data file. Thus, the expensive and powerful central processing unit (CPU) can be kept as busy as possible, and the throughput from the system can be maximized. Further, the operating system can create a computing environment—in terms of what operators and other users see on their terminal screens and what they need to key in to instruct the operating system what to do—in which it is relatively easy to work.

A microcomputer operating system, such as Windows 2000 or Windows XP, performs many of the functions described above, although the scale is smaller and the complexity is reduced. It is still true that the user employs the operating system to start a program, to retrieve data, to copy files, and so on. The purpose of a microcomputer operating system is exactly the same as the purpose of a large machine operating system: to maximize the work done by the computer system and to ease the workload of human users.

Job Control Language As noted, it is necessary for computer users to communicate with the operating system, often by keying in instructions at a PC or terminal. These instructions must be expressed in the particular **job control language**, or **JCL**, that is understood by the operating system being used. This job control language varies significantly from one operating system to the next, both in terms of the types of instructions and the detailed syntax. For example, with the PC-DOS or MS-DOS operating system (used on IBM and IBM-compatible PCs before Windows became popular), to change directories, one types CD\ followed by the name of the new directory; to list the current directory, one types DIR; to copy a file named MEMO from the A drive to the C drive, one types COPY A:MEMO C:. These are examples of the job control language. The JCL is even simpler for a Macintosh or a PC operating under Windows 2000 or XP. In this case, the user may click or double-click on an icon to start an application or retrieve a file. The JCL is much more complex for a larger machine, but the ideas are the same. To run a payroll program, for example, JCL is used to tell the operating system the name of the program to be run, the names of the data files that are needed, instructions for output of data, and the account number to be charged, among other things.

Multiprogramming or Multitasking[5] Operating systems often incorporate two important concepts—multiprogramming (or multitasking) and virtual memory—in order to increase the efficiency of the computer's operations. These concepts are concerned with the management of the memory and the CPU time of the computer system.

On larger machines, **multiprogramming** is often employed to overlap input and output operations with processing time. This is very important because the time required for the computer to perform an input/output operation (such as reading from disk) is quite large compared to the time required to execute an arithmetic instruction. In fact, a typical computer might execute 100,000 arithmetic instructions in the time required to read a single record from a disk. Thus, it would be quite inefficient to let the CPU remain idle while input/output operations are being completed. Multiprogramming keeps the CPU busy by

[5]The material in the "Multiprogramming or Multitasking" section and the "Virtual Memory" section is more technical than the rest of the chapter, and readers who wish only to obtain a basic understanding of operating systems may skip it. It is included to provide a more comprehensive picture to those who are interested.

overlapping the input/output operations of one program with the processing time of another program.

For multiprogramming, several programs (say 5 to 10) must be located in memory at the same time. Then the operating system supervises the switching back and forth among these programs so that the CPU is almost always busy. When the currently executing program encounters an input/output instruction, an interrupt occurs and the operating system takes control. The operating system stores the status of the interrupted program in memory so that this information will be available when the interrupted program gets another shot at the CPU. The operating system then decides which of the waiting programs should be executed next, and it resets the computer with the new program's status. Then the operating system gives control to the new program, which executes until it encounters an input/output instruction. Thus, the operating system controls the switching back and forth among programs that is involved in multiprogramming.

The switching among programs in multiprogramming may be triggered by time as well as by an event (the occurrence of an input/output instruction). Time-driven multiprogramming (sometimes called **time-sharing**) is the usual mode of operation when large numbers of users are simultaneously using a computer (midrange or larger) from terminals or microcomputers serving as terminals. In this environment, each user is allocated a small slice of CPU time (e.g., a few milliseconds). When a particular user's turn arises, her program runs for those few milliseconds, carrying out thousands of instructions. Then a time interrupt occurs, and the operating system transfers control to the next user for his slice of time. Unless the number of concurrent users becomes excessively high, these bursts of available time occur so rapidly that it appears to the user that he or she is the only person using the computer.

On smaller computers, including microcomputers, the term **multitasking** is used to describe essentially the same function as multiprogramming on larger machines. In both cases the operating system controls the switching back and forth among programs stored in memory. There are two basic types of multitasking: *preemptive* and *cooperative*. In preemptive multitasking, the operating system allocates slices of CPU time to each program (the same as time-driven multiprogramming above). In cooperative multitasking, each program can control the CPU for as long as the program needs. In practice, multitasking means that a user can print a report at essentially the same time as he or she recalculates a spreadsheet, all the while monitoring for new electronic mail.

Virtual Memory[5] Whereas multiprogramming or multitasking is primarily concerned with the management of CPU time, **virtual memory** is concerned with the management of main memory. At present, virtual memory is used only on larger computer systems. Virtual memory makes it appear to the user that an unlimited amount of main memory is available, meaning that individual programs can be much larger than the actual number of memory cells. More importantly, virtual memory permits multiprogramming to operate more efficiently. How does this work?

The trick is the creative use of direct access storage devices (DASDs), with the operating system switching portions of programs (called pages) between main memory and DASDs. Unless all the programs are small, it is difficult to get enough programs stored in memory for multiprogramming to operate efficiently. For example, three large programs might occupy all of the memory, and it might be common for all three programs to be processing input/output instructions at the same time. This leaves the CPU idle, which is undesirable. The cost of adding enough real memory to store 10 programs at a time—to permit efficient multiprogramming—might be prohibitive. The virtual memory concept recognizes that only one segment of a large program is being executed at a time, while the bulk of the program is inactive. Therefore, with virtual memory, only a few pages of the program (perhaps only one) are kept in main memory, with the rest relegated to a DASD. Because only a small portion of each program is located in memory, portions of a sufficient number of programs can be stored in memory to permit efficient multiprogramming.

Of course, it is often necessary for the operating system to bring new portions of a program (new pages) into memory so they can be executed. This swapping of pages between a DASD and main memory is called, appropriately enough, paging. The size of pages varies, but each is often a few thousand bytes. When we combine the concepts of multiprogramming (switching among pages of programs already in memory) with virtual memory (requiring frequent page switches from DASDs to memory), then we begin to realize the incredible complexity of tasks carried out by the operating system.

Multiprocessing Despite the similarity between the terms, multiprocessing is quite different from multiprogramming. **Multiprocessing** refers to the processing, or work, that takes place when two or more CPUs are installed as part of the same computer system. Each CPU works on its own job or set of jobs (often using multiprogramming), with all the CPUs under control of a single operating system that keeps track of what the various CPUs are doing. This is complexity piled on complexity! It is easy to see that today's computer systems would be much less efficient and of very limited use to us without the powerful operating systems that exist and are continually being upgraded.

Sources of Operating Systems For the most part, operating systems are obtained from the manufacturer of the hardware, although some other company might have written the operating system. For example, when you buy a new microcomputer from Gateway or Dell it likely comes equipped with Windows XP, an operating system from Microsoft. Most of the popular operating systems are **proprietary systems** that were written expressly for a particular computer system. Examples are PC-DOS and MS-DOS, which are the same operating system written by Microsoft for IBM microcomputers and IBM compatibles, respectively; Windows 2000 and Windows XP, which are newer systems written for IBM-compatible microcomputers; MVS and VM, which are two alternative large machine operating systems offered by IBM; and OS/400, which is the operating system for IBM's iSeries (formerly AS/400) line of midrange systems.

In contrast to these proprietary systems, the popular UNIX operating system and the newer Linux operating system are **open systems**. UNIX and Linux are not tied to a particular computer system or hardware manufacturer. Bell Laboratories originally developed UNIX, with subsequent versions created by the University of California at Berkeley, AT&T, and a variety of hardware manufacturers. For example, Sun Microsystems and IBM have developed their own versions of UNIX—Solaris for Sun and AIX for IBM. UNIX is powerful and flexible, and it is portable in that it will run on virtually any computer with a C language compiler (UNIX was written in C; more on C later).

Linux is a cut-down version of UNIX originally written by a young Finnish programmer, Linus Torvalds, in 1991. Torvalds made his new operating system compact and flexible, and he decided to share Linux freely. The only stipulation to the free use of Linux is that if a programmer makes modifications or extensions to Linux, he or she agrees to share them with the rest of the worldwide Linux community. Torvalds then has the final say on everything that goes into Linux. Although a knowledgeable computer programmer can download Linux for free and get it operating on his or her machine, most users (including corporations) need a bit more help and buy a Linux "distribution" from a vendor such as Red Hat, Corel, and SuSE. This distribution includes the free Linux system plus additional software, documentation, and a way of installing the software. Linux received a significant boost when many of the major players in the information technology field, including IBM, Hewlett-Packard, Intel, and Dell, agreed to push its use. IBM, in fact, has made Linux the centerpiece of its information technology strategy and now offers Linux on all of its varied computer platforms, from PCs and workstations to mainframes and supercomputers. Consequently, Linux has taken market share away from UNIX and is holding down the growth of Microsoft Windows on servers.

Many of the newer computers, such as high-powered workstations and supercomputers, run only UNIX or Linux. Many computer professionals would like to see UNIX or Linux become the standard operating system for all computer systems. That appears unlikely in the foreseeable future, but the use of Linux in particular will continue to spread, at least for Web servers, network servers, and other larger machines. Some organizations have even adopted a strategy of carrying out all new applications software development in a UNIX or Linux environment and gradually moving existing applications to UNIX or Linux. In particular, many client/server applications have been designed to run on a UNIX- or Linux-based server. Linux continues to move into the large computer arena, where it is likely to coexist with vendor operating systems like VM or OS/400 in major corporate and government data processing centers.

A **server operating system**, also called a **network operating system (NOS)**, is software running on a server that manages network resources and controls the operation of a network. To state this in another way, a server OS is an operating system that has been enhanced by adding networking features. For example, a server OS allows computers on a network to share resources such as disk drives and printers; it also handles the server-side of client/server applications (more on this in Chapter 6). Major players in the server OS market include several variations of UNIX, Microsoft Windows NT Server, Microsoft Windows 2000 Server, Microsoft Windows 2003 Server, Novell NetWare, and Linux. According to the Framingham, Massachusetts-based firm IDC, Microsoft is dominant in this market, with 55 percent of the new server OSs shipped in 2002. Linux comes in second, with 23 percent of the market, followed by the various flavors of UNIX at 11 percent and Novell NetWare at 10 percent. IDC also sees continued growth for both Microsoft and Linux in the server OS arena through at least the year 2007 (Hines, 2003).

At the microcomputer level, Microsoft Windows is even more dominant, with about 94 percent of the market. The remainder is almost evenly split between Linux (for IBM-compatible machines) and Mac OS (for Apple's Macintosh machines) (Hines, 2003). Linux is growing in this market sector, but it is no real threat to Microsoft. Because most new IBM-compatible machines come preloaded with Windows XP, it is the *de facto* standard for microcomputers as of this writing.

In summary, all of the widely used operating systems in use today will continue to evolve over the next several

IS LINUX THE FUTURE?

Linux, an open source operating system with a penguin as its mascot, has become the hot software for running Web sites, with estimates indicating that well over 50 percent of the Web servers (computers that serve up Web or intranet pages) are now running the Linux operating system. Linux is also being used to run database servers, electronic mail servers, and application development servers. The result is that Linux now controls about 25 percent of the server operating system market, and that percentage appears likely to increase. Information technology managers like Linux because it is cheap and reliable and it performs well. They also feel that they need an alternative to Microsoft Windows, and they appreciate the availability of development tools through the Internet. On the negative side, the biggest concern is the limited availability of business software written for Linux. Other weaknesses cited include the existence of multiple versions of Linux and the limited availability of training and education.

Linux is also being used on computers other than midrange and low-end servers. At the high end, IBM reports that several of its customers are replacing numerous servers with new IBM zSeries mainframes running Linux. The Securities Industry Automation Corporation (SIAC), a wholly-owned subsidiary of the New York and American Stock Exchanges, replaced a number of UNIX-based servers with a single zSeries mainframe running Linux virtual servers under IBM's z/VM operating system (z/VM is the current version of IBM's VM operating system). This mainframe examines, processes, and issues e-mail activity reports on 15 to 20 million e-mail transactions a day. SIAC indicates that the use of Linux on a mainframe has resulted in reduced server and maintenance costs, greatly improved scalability, and 100 percent availability. Deutsche Telekom AG replaced 25 UNIX servers with a single IBM zSeries mainframe running two dozen virtual Linux partitions. The workload includes e-mail, internal Web sites, and network support. The benefits include higher security and reliability as well as reduced administration and operating costs. Sonera Entrum, a subsidiary of Finland's largest telecommunications company, consolidated all of its services for its digital subscriber line (DSL—more on this in Chapter 4) customers on a single zSeries mainframe running IBM's z/VM operating system with about 500 virtual Linux servers. The benefits include increased reliability, better customer service, and, most important, lower cost of operation because of reduced administration and maintenance costs.

At the low end, Linux has found its way into about 3 percent of new desktop PCs. As perhaps a sign of the times, Wal-Mart is selling $200 Linux-based PCs. In Spain, the region of Extremadura is giving away over 10,000 Linux-based PCs to residents. A new group, the Linux Desktop Consortium, has been formed to promote the use of Linux on corporate and home desktops. The movement of Linux to the desktop is slow, but Linus Torvalds, who created Linux in 1991, calls desktop Linux "inevitable." Torvalds indicated that "We already have all of the tools, in open-source software, necessary for 80 percent of the office workers in the world: an office suite including spreadsheet, word processor, and presentation program; a Web browser; graphical desktop with file manager; and tools for communication, scheduling, and personal information management" (Weiss, 2003). In addition to its use in conventional computers of all sizes, Linux is finding its way into a variety of consumer-electronics devices, including TiVo TV program recorders and Sony PlayStation video game consoles.

Linux with 25 percent of the server market? Linux on microcomputers being sold at Wal-Mart? Linux in TiVo and PlayStation? Multiple copies of Linux running on a mainframe? Perhaps Linux *is* the future.

[Adapted from Ricadela, 2002; Greene, 2003; Greenemeier, 2003; IBM Web site, 2003; Ketstetter, Hamm, Ante, and Greene, 2003; and Weiss, 2003]

years, with each becoming more complex and more powerful. Paradoxically, microcomputer operating systems will at the same time become much easier to use. It appears likely that the movement towards Linux for larger machines will continue, and that Windows will continue to dominate the microcomputer market—although Linux might make some inroads here. The server operating system market is where a major Windows-Linux battle appears to be developing.

One of the important notions in the information technology area is that of an **IT platform**, which is defined as the set of hardware, software, communications, and standards an organization uses to build its information systems. Now we are in the position to point out that the operating system is usually the single most critical component of the platform. Thus, it is common to discuss an MVS (mainframe) platform, a UNIX platform, a Windows XP platform, or a Linux platform.

Third Generation Languages

As illustrated in Figure 3.4, the underwater portion of the software iceberg includes support software in addition to the critical operating system. It is useful to divide this support software into five major categories: language translators, database management systems, CASE tools, communications interface software, and utility programs. Let us consider languages and language translators first.

The third generation languages, which are more commonly called procedural or procedure-oriented languages, are the workhorses of the information processing field. As mentioned earlier, support software in the form of compilers and interpreters is used to translate 3 GL programs (as well as 4 GL and OOP programs) into machine language programs that can be run on a computer. The procedural languages do not enjoy the near-total dominance of a decade ago, but they are still the languages of choice for many computer professionals, scientists, and engineers. During the 1990s and the early part of the 2000s, 4 GLs, DBMSs, application generators, object-oriented languages, and visual languages have gained ground on the 3 GLs (in part because of the growth of end-user computing), but they will not replace the 3 GLs in the next few years. There are several reasons why the procedural languages will remain popular. First, most computer professionals are familiar with one or more procedural languages and will be reluctant to change to something new. Second, the procedural languages tend to produce more efficient machine language programs (and thus shorter execution times) than the 4 GLs and other newer alternatives. Third, new versions of the procedural languages continue to be developed, each generally more powerful and easier to use than the previous version. For example, object-oriented versions of C, COBOL, and PASCAL are now available.

Using a procedural language requires logical thinking, because the programmer must devise a detailed step-by-step procedure to accomplish the desired task. Of course, these steps in the procedure must be expressed in the particular statement types available in the given procedural language. Writing a procedural program is generally viewed as just one stage in the entire program development process. Table 3.1 provides one possible listing of the various stages in the program development process. Note that writing the program does not occur until stage four. Stage eight is debugging, which literally means to get the bugs or errors out of the program. The most difficult stages in this program development process tend to be one and two—the proper identification of the problem and the development of an algorithm, which is a step-by-step description (in English) of the actions necessary to perform the task. In stage three, the algorithm is converted into a structure chart, which is a pictorial representation of the algorithm, or pseudocode, which is an English-language-like version of the program. Throughout the entire process, logical thinking and a logical progression of steps are required to effectively use a procedural language.

Perhaps the most significant change in the procedural languages from their beginnings is that they are more amenable to **structured programming**. A structured program is one that is divided into modules or blocks, where each block has only one entry point and only one exit point. When a program is written in this form, the program logic is easy to follow and understand, and thus the maintenance and correction of such a program should be easier than for a nonstructured program. The consequence of structured programming is that few if any transfer statements (often implemented as a GO TO statement) are required to transfer control to some other portion of the program. Therefore, structured programming is often referred to as GO TO-less programming, although the modular approach is really the central feature of a structured program. The newer versions of all the procedural languages encourage highly structured programs.

BASIC BASIC is a good place to begin a brief look at three popular procedural languages because it is the simplest of them. BASIC, which is an acronym for **B**eginner's **A**ll-purpose **S**ymbolic **I**nstruction **C**ode, was developed in

Table 3.1 Stages in the Program Development Process

Stage 1	Problem identification
Stage 2	Algorithm development
Stage 3	Conversion of algorithm to computer-understandable logic, usually in form of structure chart or pseudocode
Stage 4	Program preparation
Stage 5	Keying program into computer
Stage 6	Program compilation
Stage 7	Execution of program with test data
Stage 8	Debugging process using test data
Stage 9	Use of program with actual data

the early 1960s by John Kemeny and Thomas Kurtz at Dartmouth College. Their purpose was to create an easy-to-learn, interactive language for college students that would let the students concentrate on the thought processes involved in programming rather than the syntax.

The early versions of BASIC were interpreted rather than compiled, but BASIC compilers have popped up in the past decade or two. Unfortunately, there are many versions of BASIC developed by various computer manufacturers and software houses, and they are often incompatible. Attempts at standardization came too late, which is one reason why businesses have been loath to adopt it. Also, BASIC has historically lacked the mathematical capabilities, data management capabilities, and control structures necessary to carry out business and scientific processing efficiently. Newer versions of BASIC have addressed these shortcomings, however, as well as added the capability of developing graphical user interfaces (more on this later). These developments promise a greater role for BASIC in the future.

To illustrate BASIC, consider the following sample problem: Write a BASIC program that will find the average of a set of numbers input by the user. Use a negative number to indicate the end of the data. A BASIC program to solve this problem is shown in Figure 3.9, together with the screen dialog that occurred when the program was run on a microcomputer using a simple data set. Although the details of

BASIC PROGRAM

```
10      REM THIS PROGRAM FINDS THE AVERAGE OF A SET OF NUMBERS
20      REM     INPUT BY THE USER. A NEGATIVE NUMBER IS USED
30      REM     TO INDICATE THE END OF THE DATA.
40      PRINT "ENTER AS MANY POSITIVE NUMBERS AS YOU WISH,"
50      PRINT "WITH ONE NUMBER ENTERED PER LINE."
60      PRINT "WHEN YOU HAVE ENTERED YOUR ENTIRE SET OF NUMBERS,"
70      PRINT "ENTER A NEGATIVE NUMBER TO SIGNAL THE END OF DATA."
80      LET COUNT = 0
90      LET TOTAL = 0
100     INPUT NUMBER
110     IF NUMBER < 0 GO TO 150
120     LET TOTAL = TOTAL + NUMBER
130     LET COUNT = COUNT + 1
140     GO TO 100
150     LET AVG = TOTAL / COUNT
160     PRINT "THE AVERAGE OF YOUR NUMBERS IS"; AVG
170     PRINT "YOU ENTERED"; COUNT; "NUMBERS TOTALING"; TOTAL
180     END
```

SCREEN DIALOG WITH ABOVE BASIC PROGRAM

(Responses keyed in by user are underlined; computer responses are not underlined.)

```
OK
RUN
ENTER AS MANY POSITIVE NUMBERS AS YOU WISH,
WITH ONE NUMBER ENTERED PER LINE.
WHEN YOU HAVE ENTERED YOUR ENTIRE SET OF NUMBERS,
ENTER A NEGATIVE NUMBER TO SIGNAL THE END OF DATA.
?23
?45
?1
?78.6
?-9
THE AVERAGE OF YOUR NUMBERS IS 36.9
YOU ENTERED 4 NUMBERS TOTALING 147.6
OK
```

Figure 3.9 BASIC Program and Accompanying Screen Dialog

programming are not important, you will note that most of the instructions are quite intuitive—even the uninitiated would correctly guess the meaning of most instructions.

C For scientific and engineering programming, the most important language is C, which was written by Dennis Ritchie and Brian Kernighan in the 1970s. C is a very powerful language, but hard to use because it is less English-like and closer to assembly language than the other procedural languages. The C programming language features flexibility of use, economy of expression, versatile data structures, modern control flow, and a rich set of operators. Because of these strengths, C is widely used in the development of microcomputer packages such as word processing, spreadsheets, and database management systems, and it is gaining on FORTRAN (more on this language later) for scientific applications. Further, C has better data management capabilities than FORTRAN and other scientific languages, so it is also being used in traditional business data processing tasks such as payroll, accounting, and sales reporting.

C was originally developed for and implemented on the UNIX operating system, and its use grew as UNIX spread. In fact, the UNIX operating system was written in C. C programs have a high level of portability: A C program can usually be transported from one computer system to another—even from a mainframe to a microcomputer—with only minor changes. C has been adopted as the standard language by many college computer science departments, and it is widely used on microcomputers. On large research computers, it is not unusual for C and FORTRAN to be the only languages ever used.

C's strengths are its control structures and its mathematical features. To illustrate, suppose that the result of one trial of a simulation experiment is an estimated profit for the firm for the next year. Twenty such trials have been made, each producing an estimated profit for the next year. As an example, write a C program to compute the mean and variance of the estimated profit figures, entering in the data from the keyboard, one estimated profit figure per line.

A C program to solve this problem is given in Figure 3.10. The statements beginning and ending with /* and */ are comments. The *for* statement near the top of the program is a C statement to control repeated execution of a set of instructions. Some of the mathematical statements are obvious, and some are not, but the program gets the job done.

```
#include<stdio.h>
/* C program to compute means and variances
of simulated profit figures */

main()
{
/* Variable declaration and initialization */
  int index;
  float sum=0.0,sumsq=0.0,trial,mean,var;
/*Control repeated execution using for statement */
  for (index = 1; index <=20; ++index)
  {
     printf("Enter a profit figure:\n");
     scanf("%f",&trial);
     sum += trial;
     sumsq += trial*trial;
}/*End control for */
  mean = sum/20.0;
  var = (sumsq/19.0) - (sum*sum)/(19.0*20.0);
  printf("Mean Value is = %f\n",mean);
  printf("Variance is = %f\n",var);
}/*End of program */
```

Figure 3.10 C Program

COBOL COBOL, which is an acronym for **CO**mmon **B**usiness-**O**riented **L**anguage, is a language specifically devised for traditional business data processing tasks. It was developed by a computer industry committee (originally the short-range committee of the Conference on Data Systems Languages, or CODASYL; later the COBOL Committee of CODASYL) in order to provide an industry-wide common language, closely resembling ordinary English, in which business data processing procedures could be expressed. Since its inception in 1960, COBOL has gained widespread acceptance because it is standardized, has strong data management capabilities (relative to the other 3 GLs), and is relatively easy to learn and use. COBOL is by far the most popular language for programming mainframe computers for business applications.

COBOL programs are divided into four distinct divisions. The first two divisions are usually fairly short. The IDENTIFICATION DIVISION gives the program a name and provides other identifying information, and the ENVIRONMENT DIVISION describes the computer environment in which the program will be run. The ENVIRONMENT DIVISION is also the portion of the program that has to be changed to transport the program from one computer model to another. The DATA DIVISION, which is often quite long, defines the entire file structure employed in the program. The PROCEDURE DIVISION corresponds most closely to a BASIC or C program; it consists of a series of operations specified in a logical order to accomplish the desired task. The combination of all these divisions, especially the DATA DIVISION, makes COBOL programs quite long compared with other procedural languages. COBOL has been correctly described as a verbose language.

Our sample COBOL program is designed to compute and print monthly sales commissions for the salespersons of a large corporation. Each salesperson earns a 1 percent commission on the first $50,000 in sales during a month and a 2 percent commission on all sales in excess of $50,000. The data have already been keyed in and are stored as a data file on a magnetic disk. One record has been prepared for each salesperson, containing the person's name and sales for the month. The output is to be a line for each salesperson, showing the name, monthly sales, and sales commission. In addition, the program is to accumulate the total commissions for all salespersons and to print this amount after all the salespersons' records have been processed.

Figure 3.11 provides a COBOL program to accomplish this processing. Again, the details are not important, but

```
1      8   12
       IDENTIFICATION DIVISION.
       PROGRAM-ID. COMMISSIONS-COMPUTE.
       AUTHOR. JOE PROGRAMMER.
       ENVIRONMENT DIVISION.
       CONFIGURATION SECTION.
       SOURCE-COMPUTER. IBM-4381.
       OBJECT-COMPUTER. IBM-4381.
       INPUT-OUTPUT SECTION.
       FILE-CONTROL.
           SELECT SALES-FILE ASSIGN DA-3380-S-IPT.
           SELECT COMMISSIONS-FILE ASSIGN DA-3380-S-RPT.
       DATA DIVISION.
       FILE SECTION.
       FD SALES-FILE
           LABEL RECORD OMITTED
           RECORD CONTAINS 80 CHARACTERS
           DATA RECORD IS IN-RECORD.
       01  IN-RECORD                PICTURE X(80).
       FD  COMMISSIONS-FILE
           LABEL RECORD OMITTED
           RECORD CONTAINS 132 CHARACTERS
           DATA RECORD IS PRINT-RECORD.
       01  PRINT-RECORD             PICTURE X(132).
       WORKING-STORAGE SECTION.
       01  SALES-RECORD.
           05  NAME                 PICTURE A(30).
           05  FILLER               PICTURE X(10).
           05  SALES                PICTURE 9(8)V99.
           05  FILLER               PICTURE X(30).
       01  COMMISSION-RECORD.
           05  FILLER               PICTURE X(10).
           05  NAME-OUT             PICTURE A(30).
           05  FILLER               PICTURE X(10).
           05  SALES-OUT            PICTURE $$$,$$$,$$$.99.
           05  FILLER               PICTURE X(10).
           05  COMMISSION           PICTURE $$$$,$$$.99.
           05  FILLER               PICTURE X(47).
       77  TEMP-COMMISSION          PICTURE 9(6)V99.
       77  TOTAL-COMMISSIONS        PICTURE 9(10)V99  VALUE 0.
       77  TOTAL-COMM-EDITED        PICTURE $$,$$$,$$$,$$$.99.
       01  MORE-DATA                PICTURE X         VALUE 'Y'.
           88   THERE-IS-MORE-DATA                    VALUE 'Y'.
           88   THERE-IS-NO-MORE-DATA                 VALUE 'N'.
```

Figure 3.11 COBOL Program

```
1     8   12
      PROCEDURE DIVISION.
      MAIN-CONTROL.
          PERFORM INITIALIZATION.
          PERFORM READ-PROCESS-PRINT UNTIL THERE-IS-NO-MORE-DATA.
          PERFORM COMPLETE.
          STOP RUN.
      INITIALIZATION.
          OPEN INPUT SALES-FILE, OUTPUT COMMISSIONS-FILE.
          MOVE SPACES TO COMMISSION-RECORD.
      READ-PROCESS-PRINT.
          READ SALES-FILE INTO SALES-RECORD
              AT END MOVE 'N' TO MORE-DATA.
          IF THERE-IS-MORE-DATA
              MOVE NAME TO NAME-OUT
              MOVE SALES TO SALES-OUT
              IF SALES GREATER 50000
                 COMPUTE TEMP-COMMISSION = .01*50000+.02* (SALES-50000)
              ELSE
                 COMPUTE TEMP-COMMISSION = .01*SALES
              MOVE TEMP-COMMISSION TO COMMISSION
              WRITE PRINT-RECORD FROM COMMISSION-RECORD
                 AFTER ADVANCING 1 LINES
              ADD TEMP-COMMISSION TO TOTAL-COMMISSIONS.
      COMPLETE.
          MOVE TOTAL-COMMISSIONS TO TOTAL-COMM-EDITED.
          DISPLAY 'TOTAL-COMMISSIONS ARE' TOTAL-COMM-EDITED.
          CLOSE SALES-FILE, COMMISSIONS-FILE.
```

Figure 3.11 COBOL Program *(continued)*

note the four divisions of the program and the sheer length of this relatively simple program.

Other Procedural Languages There are many other procedural languages in addition to BASIC, C, and COBOL. The granddaddy of the procedural languages is FORTRAN. Originally introduced by IBM in the mid-1950s, it quickly became the standard for scientific and engineering programming. FORTRAN is still widely used today, in good part because of the significant investment made in the development of FORTRAN scientific software.

PL/1 (Programming Language One) was developed by IBM in the mid-1960s as a language to do both mathematical and business-oriented processing. IBM hoped that PL/1 would replace both FORTRAN and COBOL, but it obviously did not. Some companies switched from COBOL to PL/1 and have remained staunch PL/1 users, but their numbers are limited.

In the 1980s, PASCAL was often the favorite language of college computer science departments, and it was widely used on microcomputers. PASCAL has greater mathematical capabilities than BASIC, and it handles data files better than FORTRAN. However, PASCAL never caught on outside of universities except as a microcomputer language, and its popularity has now waned in favor of C.

ADA is a language developed under the direction of the U.S. Department of Defense as a potential replacement for COBOL and FORTRAN. It was first introduced in 1980 and does have strong scientific capabilities. However, it was not widely adopted outside the federal government. ADA has not disappeared, but its use has diminished even within the Department of Defense.

Special-purpose procedural languages have also been developed. For instance, SIMSCRIPT, GPSS, and SLAM are all special-purpose languages designed to help simulate the behavior of a system, such as a production line in a factory. Perl is a special-purpose language used primarily for writing Common Gateway Interface (CGI) scripts for World Wide Web applications. Our listing of procedural languages is incomplete, but it is sufficient for our purposes. The bottom line is that these workhorse languages are still important, because they are the primary languages used by the majority of computer professionals.

Fourth Generation Languages

There is no generally accepted definition of a fourth generation language, but there are certain characteristics that most 4 GLs share. They generally employ an English-like syntax, and they are predominantly nonprocedural in nature. With a 4 GL, the user merely gives a precise statement of what is to be accomplished, not how to do it (as would be done for a procedural language). For the most part, then, the order in which instructions are given in a 4 GL is unimportant. In addition, 4 GLs do not require the user to manage memory locations in the program like 3 GLs, resulting in less complex programs.

The 4 GLs employ very high-level instructions not present in 3 GLs, and thus 4 GL programs tend to require significantly fewer instructions than their 3 GL counterparts. This in turn means that 4 GL programs are shorter, easier to write, easier to modify, easier to read and understand, and less error-prone than 3 GL programs. Fourth generation languages are sometimes called very-high-level languages in contrast to the high-level third generation languages.

The roots of fourth generation languages date back to 1967, with the introduction of RAMIS (originally developed by Mathematica, Inc., and now sold by Computer Associates as CA-Ramis). Another early entry that is still is use today is FOCUS (from Information Builders, Inc.). Initially, these products were primarily available on commercial time-sharing networks (like Telenet and Tymnet), but direct sales of the products to customers took off around 1980. By the mid-1980s, FOCUS was estimated to command about 20 percent of the market, with RAMIS following with 16 percent (Jenkins and Bordoloi, 1986).

In the late 1980s and early 1990s, the 4 GL market became even more splintered as new versions of the early 4 GLs were rolled out and a wide variety of new products entered the marketplace. The emphasis of the products appearing in the 1990s was on *portability*—the ability of the 4 GL to work with different hardware platforms and operating systems, the ability to work over different types of networks (see Chapter 4), and the ability to work with different database management systems (Lindholm, 1992). In the late 1990s and early 2000s, the 4 GLs changed again. First, most 4 GLs added a Web interface so that they could be used from a PC without requiring any special software on the PC. Second, and even more important, the focus of these products shifted to **business intelligence** and the 4 GL label essentially disappeared. Today's business intelligence software tools are designed to answer queries relating to the business by analyzing data (often massive quantities of data), thereby providing "intelligence" to the business that will help it become more competitive. Of course, this focus on business intelligence is not that different from the focus of 4 GLs in the past; it really is an evolution, not a drastic change.

Some of the 4 GL products are full-function, general-purpose languages like CA-Ramis and FOCUS and have the complete functionality necessary to handle any application program. Thus, they are direct competitors with the 3 GLs. Other 4 GLs were created to handle a particular class of applications, such as statistics, decision support, or financial modeling. For example, SAS (from SAS Institute) began as a limited-purpose 4 GL focusing on decision support and modeling. SAS Business Intelligence has now expanded to an integrated suite of software for business intelligence in an enterprise, with extensive capabilities in data access, data management, data analysis, and data presentation. Among the more popular business intelligence packages today are WebFOCUS (a Web-based, business-intelligence-oriented version of FOCUS), Cognos Business Intelligence Series 7, Brio Intelligence, MicroStrategy 7i, and Microsoft Data Analyzer (MacVittie, 2002). To gain a better perspective on the nature of a 4 GL, we will take a brief look at one of the most popular and enduring 4 GLs, FOCUS.

FOCUS FOCUS is an extremely versatile general-purpose 4 GL. Versions of FOCUS are available to operate under the control of all the major operating systems mentioned earlier in this chapter. Information Builders, Inc. describes FOCUS as a "host-based reporting" system and as "the corporate standard for enterprise business information systems," while WebFOCUS is described as "the standard for enterprise business intelligence" (Information Builders Web site, 2003). FOCUS consists of a large number of integrated tools and facilities, including a FOCUS database management system, a data dictionary/directory, a query language and report generator, an interactive text editor and screen painter, and a statistical analysis package. Of particular importance, FOCUS has the ability to process data managed both by its own DBMS (FOCUS files) and by an external DBMS or external file system (non-FOCUS files). We will concentrate on perhaps the most widely used of the FOCUS capabilities, the query language and report generator.

Consider the following problem situation. A telephone company wishes to prepare a report for its internal management and its regulatory body showing the difference between customer bills under two different bill computation approaches. One of these bill computation methods is the traditional flat rate based on the size of the local calling area; the other is so-called measured service, in which the customer pays a very small flat rate for a minimum number of calls and then pays so much per call (21 cents in the example) for calls above this minimum. Massive FOCUS data files already exist containing all the necessary raw data for an extended test period, with each record including customer number, area, type of service, number of calls during the time period, and the length of the time period (in months). The telephone company wants a report for present flat rate customers in area two only, showing the difference between the two billing approaches for each customer and the total difference over all flat rate customers in area two.

Figure 3.12 shows a FOCUS program (more commonly called a FOCEXEC) that can produce the desired report.

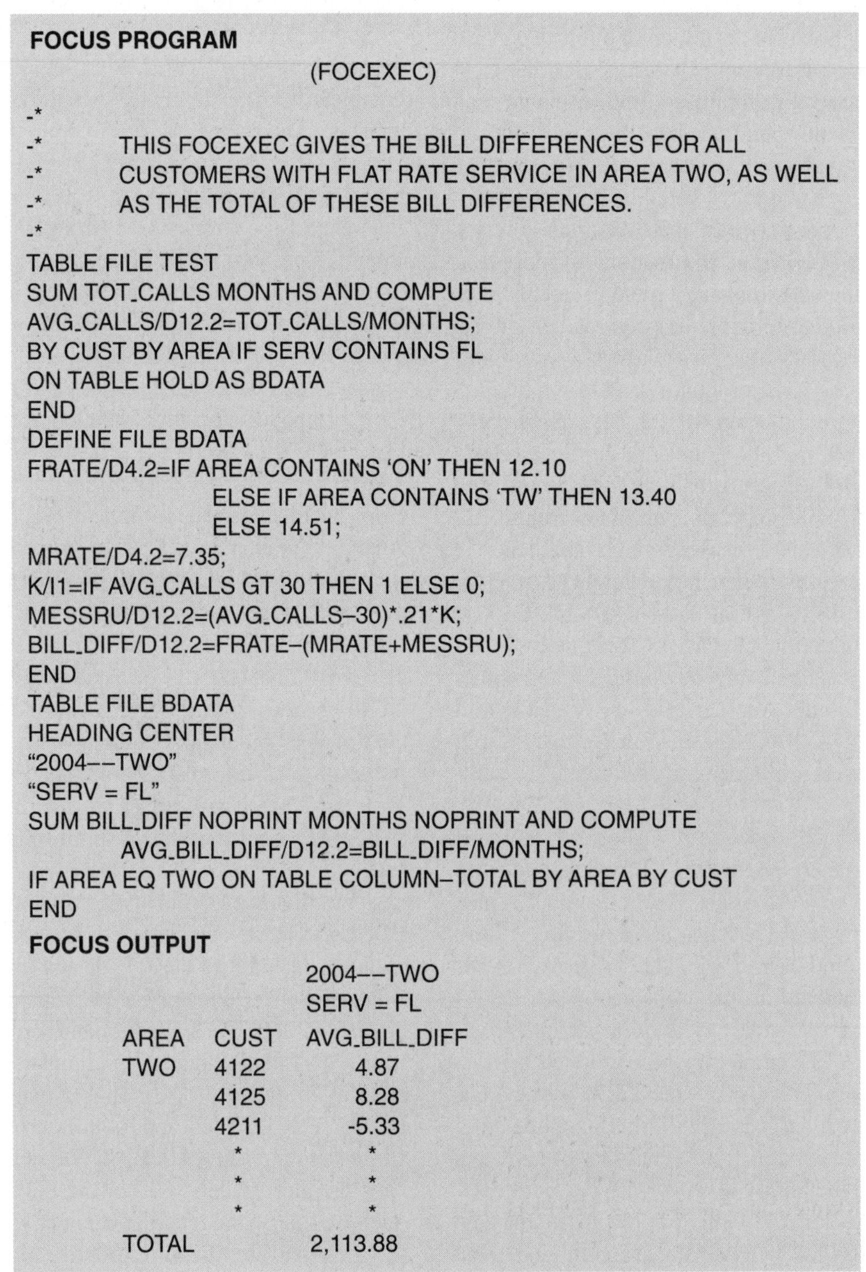

FOCUS PROGRAM

(FOCEXEC)

```
-*
-*        THIS FOCEXEC GIVES THE BILL DIFFERENCES FOR ALL
-*        CUSTOMERS WITH FLAT RATE SERVICE IN AREA TWO, AS WELL
-*        AS THE TOTAL OF THESE BILL DIFFERENCES.
-*
TABLE FILE TEST
SUM TOT_CALLS MONTHS AND COMPUTE
AVG_CALLS/D12.2=TOT_CALLS/MONTHS;
BY CUST BY AREA IF SERV CONTAINS FL
ON TABLE HOLD AS BDATA
END
DEFINE FILE BDATA
FRATE/D4.2=IF AREA CONTAINS 'ON' THEN 12.10
                 ELSE IF AREA CONTAINS 'TW' THEN 13.40
                 ELSE 14.51;
MRATE/D4.2=7.35;
K/I1=IF AVG_CALLS GT 30 THEN 1 ELSE 0;
MESSRU/D12.2=(AVG_CALLS–30)*.21*K;
BILL_DIFF/D12.2=FRATE–(MRATE+MESSRU);
END
TABLE FILE BDATA
HEADING CENTER
"2004--TWO"
"SERV = FL"
SUM BILL_DIFF NOPRINT MONTHS NOPRINT AND COMPUTE
         AVG_BILL_DIFF/D12.2=BILL_DIFF/MONTHS;
IF AREA EQ TWO ON TABLE COLUMN–TOTAL BY AREA BY CUST
END
```

FOCUS OUTPUT

```
                    2004--TWO
                    SERV = FL
        AREA   CUST   AVG_BILL_DIFF
        TWO    4122       4.87
               4125       8.28
               4211      -5.33
                 *          *
                 *          *
                 *          *
        TOTAL           2,113.88
```

Figure 3.12 FOCUS Program and Output

As with our 3 GL examples, the individual instructions are not important, but let us consider the major pieces of the program. After some initial comments, the program begins with the TABLE command, which calls the query/report generator function of FOCUS. The data file is called TEST. Up to the first END, the instructions sum the variables TOT_CALLS and MONTHS for each customer in each area if the type of service is FL, and then divide one sum by the other to get an average number of calls per month (AVG_CALLS). The DEFINE FILE BDATA computes the rates by the two approaches as well as the difference between the two rates, storing these computed values in the temporary file BDATA. Finally, the TABLE FILE BDATA computes the average bill difference, AV_BILL_DIFF, and prints the report shown at the bottom of Figure 3.12.

Note that the FOCUS program is not particularly intuitive, but it is quite short for a reasonably complex problem. It is also largely nonprocedural in that the order of most statements does not make any difference. Of course, the conditional IFs and BYs must be appropriately placed.

Future Developments The fourth generation languages are evolving even more rapidly than those in the third generation, particularly with the addition of easy-to-use business intelligence options and easy-to-interpret graphical output and colorful displays. Furthermore, with the increasing capabilities of today's computers, the lack of efficiency of execution of 4 GL programs vis-à-vis 3 GL programs is of little concern. For these reasons and others mentioned earlier (increasing computer sophistication of managers, continuing backlogs in the information systems department), the use of 4 GLs will continue to grow. The strongest element of growth will come from end-user computing, but information systems departments will also shift towards 4 GLs, especially for infrequently used applications.

Fifth generation languages will also emerge in the twenty-first century, although it is too soon to be specific about their form and functionality. One possibility is that the fifth generation languages will be **natural languages**, in which users write their programs in ordinary English (or something very close to it). Users will need little or no training to program using a natural language; they simply write (or perhaps verbalize) what they want done without regard for syntax or form (other than that incorporated in ordinary English). At present there are no true natural languages, but some restricted natural language products have been developed that can be used with a variety of database management systems and 4 GLs. Commercial developments in the natural language area have, however, been slower than expected.

Markup Languages

Before turning to object-oriented programming languages, we should mention the markup languages, which are neither 3 GLs, 4 GLs, nor OOP languages. Currently the best known of the markup languages is **HTML**, or **Hypertext Markup Language**. HTML is used to create World Wide Web pages, and it consists of special codes inserted in the text to indicate headings, bold-faced text, italics, where images or photographs are to be placed, and links to other Web pages, among other things. VRML, or virtual reality modeling language, provides the specifications for displaying three-dimensional objects on the Web; it is the 3-D equivalent of HTML. HTML and the other markup languages are not really programming languages in the sense that we have been using this term; they are simply codes to describe the way the completed product (the Web page, the 3-D object, and so on) is to appear.

XML, or **eXtensible Markup Language**, is destined to become even more important than HTML. XML is used to facilitate data interchange among applications on the Web; it is really a metalanguage standard for specifying a document markup language based on plain-text tags. Let's see what this means. XML was developed by the W3C, the World Wide Web Consortium, whose goal is to develop open standards for the Web. Other W3C standards are **HTTP** (**Hypertext Transfer Protocol**) and HTML.

XML is a pared-down version of SGML (standard generalized markup language), which was itself developed by the International Standards Organization (ISO) in 1986. HTML is another subset of SGML with which we are more familiar. Both HTML and XML employ plain-text tags (i.e., made up of ordinary letters, numbers, and special characters) as a way to "mark up" a document. However, the similarities between HTML and XML end there. HTML tags tell a Web browser how to display various elements on a Web page, while XML tags identify the nature of the associated data. For example, one XML tag might identify a customer name as a customer name, another might identify a customer's address as an address, another might identify a number as a product number, and yet another might identify the quantity sold as the quantity sold. Entire sets of XML tags are being defined for particular industries and situations.

The key is that XML is a metalanguage: For each industry or unique situation, a set of XML tags can be created to identify the data elements employed in that situation. XML makes it relatively easy to identify and share data in order to achieve data integration across organizational boundaries. XML is "extensible" in that new tags can be defined as needed, and XML allows the separation of the presentation of the data from the data themselves. Through the use of text tags, for example, a company can identify specific pieces of data on a Web page (such as a customer order) and can extract the desired data for use in another application. It seems likely that the use of XML tags in Internet documents might eventually replace electronic data interchange, or EDI (see Chapter 8 for more on EDI). EDI depends upon carefully designed, rather cumbersome formatting of the data to be exchanged; XML replaces that formatting with customized tags. Thus, XML provides an easy and effective way to identify and share data.

An XML specification (like HTML) consists of tags (enclosed in angle brackets: < >). However, XML tags are intended to convey the meaning of data, not the presentation format. For example, an HTML tag such as <H1>This data to be displayed in Heading 1 format</H1> tells the browser to display data using the Heading 1 format. By contrast, the XML tags given below are an attempt to represent the meaning of the data related to games.

```
<Game type="College Football" date="10/11/2003">
   Indiana vs. Northwestern. This was an overtime game.
   <Score team="Indiana">31</Score>
   <Score team="Northwestern">37</Score>
</Game>
```

The top-level tag <Game> specifies that what follows are details about a game. The attributes for Game (type and date) provide specific details about the information that follows. The end of details about the game is indicated by the</Game> tag. One of the key features of XML is its ability to have nested tags, i.e., tags within tags. The "Score" tags provide an example of how one can use this feature to add meaning to the information contained within the <Game></Game> tags.

XML tags (unlike HTML tags) are not fixed. Programmers can use any tags that suit an application's needs. However, all applications that are going to process a given set of data need to understand and agree upon the tag names they intend to use. It is important to realize that data specified using XML do not provide any indication as to how to display the data. The data display for a set of XML documents is controlled by the use of XSL (extensible style language) specifications. These specifications indicate how to display XML data in different formats, such as HTML.

Object-Oriented Programming

In the early years of the twenty-first century, the hottest programming languages (at least in terms of interest and experimentation) are not 4 GLs or natural languages, but **object-oriented programming (OOP)** languages. OOP is

THE SEMANTIC WEB

Just as it seems that people and businesses are getting the knack of using the World Wide Web somewhat effectively, a bigger and better network—the Semantic Web—is coming along. Led by Timothy Berners-Lee, the father of the present Web, a collaborative effort is underway under the auspices of the World Wide Web Consortium (W3C) to have key aspects of the new Semantic Web in place by 2005. The Semantic Web will be a smart network that will appear to understand human language and will make computers almost as easy to work with as other humans. The basic idea is to annotate any type of data, any content on the Web, with specialized tags that will identify the data's meaning and the context in which the data exist. Then computers will be able to process semantic relationships between items to respond to human language queries as if they truly understand the words being used.

Building the Semantic Web will require three key items of software. The first item is XML, or eXtensible Markup Language, as described in the "Markup Languages" section of this chapter. The XML tag is a label to identify an item as a part number, or a price, or a photograph of a product—but these tags do not explain the specific meaning of the part number, price, or photograph. Instead, the tags will point to a combination dictionary and thesaurus for XML tags, called the RDF, or Resource Description Framework, which is the second required item of software. The RDF, for instance, will permit the computer to understand that two different tags—say <purchase> and <buy>—actually mean the same thing. The third required piece of software is the ontology, an online encyclopedia that lays out the detailed relationships among XML terms and RDF concepts.

To illustrate the use of the future Semantic Web, consider the hypothetical case of an automobile manufacturer that needs to find the perfect part for a new car that is under development. The manufacturer could instruct a semantic search tool to find a bolt that is lightweight, resistant to heat, and a specific size, that costs less than one cent, and that can be delivered to the plant at a particular time each week. By accessing the semantic tags in online product catalogs from a variety of suppliers, the search tool could compare and evaluate the options and present the manufacturer with a list of bolts that best meet the stated criteria. It is the semantic tags, and the ability of the computer to process those tags and understand the semantic relationships among them, that permit the computer to accomplish this task.

Just as the World Wide Web was the most important software innovation in the 1990s, the Semantic Web is quite likely to be the most important software innovation in the first decade of the twenty-first century. "We expect the Semantic Web to be as big a revolution as the original Web itself," says Richard Hayes-Roth, Hewlett-Packard Co.'s chief technology officer for software (Port, 2002, p. 97).

[Adapted from Port, 2002; and Ewalt, 2002]

not new (it dates back to the 1970s), but it has received renewed attention because of the increased power of workstations and the excellent GUIs that have been developed for these workstations. OOP requires more computing power than traditional languages, and a graphical interface provides a natural way to work with the OOP objects. OOP is neither a 3 GL nor a 4 GL, but an entirely new paradigm for programming with roots in both the procedural 3 GLs and the nonprocedural 4 GLs. Creating the objects in OOP is somewhat akin to 3 GL programming in that the procedures (called methods) are embedded in the objects, while putting the objects together to create an application is much closer to the use of a 4 GL.

The fundamental ideas of OOP are to create and program various objects only once and then store them for reuse later in the current application or in other applications. These objects might be items used to create the user interface, like a text box or a check box, or they might represent an entity in the organization, such as Employee or Factory.

One of the first OOP languages was Smalltalk, a language developed by researchers at Xerox to create a way that children could learn how to program. Smalltalk never really took off as a children's programming tool, but it was used marginally in the business world. Managers thought programming would become more efficient if programmers only had to create objects once, and then were able to reuse them in later programs. This would create a "toolbox" from which programmers could just grab the tool they needed, insert it into the program, fine-tune it to meet the specific needs of the program, and be done.

The most prominent OOP languages today are C++, an object-oriented version of the original C language, and Java, a platform-independent language developed by Sun Microsystems. C++ is a superset of the C language, in that any C program can also be a C++ program, but C++ introduces the power of reusable objects, or classes. Java is a general-purpose programming language well-suited for use on the World Wide Web, and it has quickly gained widespread acceptance by most vendors and by programmers everywhere.

Java programs come in three flavors: stand-alone applications, applets, and servlets (see the section of this chapter entitled "Languages for Developing Web Applications"). Stand-alone applications are run on your desktop, whereas **applets** are programs that are downloaded from a Web server and run on your Web browser. Servlets are programs that reside in and are run on a Web server. Java programs are designed to run on a **Java virtual machine**, a self-contained operating environment (including a Java interpreter) that behaves as if it is a separate computer. Such an operating environment exists for most operating systems, including UNIX, Linux, Macintosh OS, and Windows, and this virtual machine concept implements the "write once, run anywhere" portability that is Java's goal. The Java virtual

J2EE VS. .NET

Java 2 Enterprise Edition (**J2EE**) and **.NET** are two competing frameworks proposed by an alliance of companies led by Sun Microsystems and Microsoft, respectively, as platforms for application development on the Web using the object-oriented programming paradigm.

J2EE, as the name suggests, is based on the Java language. In fact, J2EE is not the name of a product. Instead, it is a collection of 13 different Java-based technologies put together in a particular fashion. Thus, theoretically it is possible to buy each of these technologies from different vendors and mix-and-match them as needed. In practice, however, it is typical for a company to buy a product that implements the J2EE specification from a single vendor. Popular choices in this regard include Websphere from IBM, Weblogic from BEA, and SunOne from Sun. One of the key advantages of J2EE is that because everything is Java-based, the products can be run on a variety of platforms, e.g., Windows, UNIX, and Linux.

By contrast, applications written for Microsoft's .NET framework are designed to run only on the Windows platform. However, unlike J2EE, where one is limited to using Java as the programming language, in .NET a programmer can choose among a variety of languages such as VB.NET, C#, J# (a variant of Java), and even C++. In fact, within a single application a programmer can, for example, choose to write portions of the program in VB.NET and others in C#.

There has been a lot of debate as to which framework is better. The answer depends on several tangible and intangible factors. In the end, we think that the decision regarding which technology to adopt will be based largely on the following factors:

- *Available programmer expertise*
- *Complexity of the Web application* For large applications that have significant scalability and security requirements, the J2EE framework provides the flexibility needed to achieve the desired architectural and performance goals.
- *Degree of Web services support needed* Both J2EE and .NET are quite comparable in terms of their support for Web services standards including XML. The difference lies in the fact that support for XML is an integral part of the .NET framework, whereas at this time XML support has to be "bolted on" in J2EE.

machine has no access to the host operating system (whatever it is), which has two advantages:

- *System independence* A Java application will run exactly the same regardless of the hardware and software involved.
- *Security* Because the Java virtual machine has no contact with the host operating system, there is almost no possibility of a Java application damaging other files or applications.

Other object-oriented languages that are gaining prominence are those that are part of the .NET framework from Microsoft. Introduced in early 2002, the .NET framework allows programmers to write programs in a variety of OOP languages, including Visual Basic .NET (abbreviated as VB.NET), C# (pronounced "C sharp"), and J# (pronounced "J sharp") (see the sidebar entitled "J2EE vs. .NET").

As an example of an OOP program, consider Figure 3.13(A), written in Visual Basic 6.0. It is important to note that Visual Basic 6.0 is actually considered to be a

```
Private Sub btnCalculate_Click()
' Declare variables
Dim sClasses(3) As Single
Dim sMean, sHigh, sLow As Single, x As Integer
' Initialize variables
sClasses(0) = CSng (txtCalculus.Text)
sClasses(1) = CSng (txtChemistry.Text)
sClasses(2) = CSng (txtHistory.Text)
sClasses(3) = CSng (txtEnglish.Text)
sMean = 0
sHigh = 0
sLow = 100
' Do calculations
For x = 0 To 3
        sMean = sMean + sClasses (x) / 4
        If sClasses (x) > sHigh Then
                sHigh = sClasses (x)
        End If

        If sClasses (x) < sLow Then
                sLow = sClasses (x)
        End If
Next x
' Write out results
txtStatistics.Text = "Your average grade is" & sMean & vbCrLf
txtStatistics.Text = txtStatistics.Text & "Your highest grade is" & sHigh & vbCrLf
txtStatistics.Text = txtStatistics.Text & "Your lowest grade is" & sLow
End Sub
---------------------------
Private Sub btnClear_Click()
' Clears the contents of the text boxes
txtChemistry.Text = " "
txtCalculus.Text = " "
txtEnglish.Text = " "
txtHistory.Text = " "
txtStatistics.Text = " "
End Sub
---------------------------
Private Sub Exit_Click()
' Quits the program
End
End Sub
```

Figure 3.13(A) Visual Basic Program

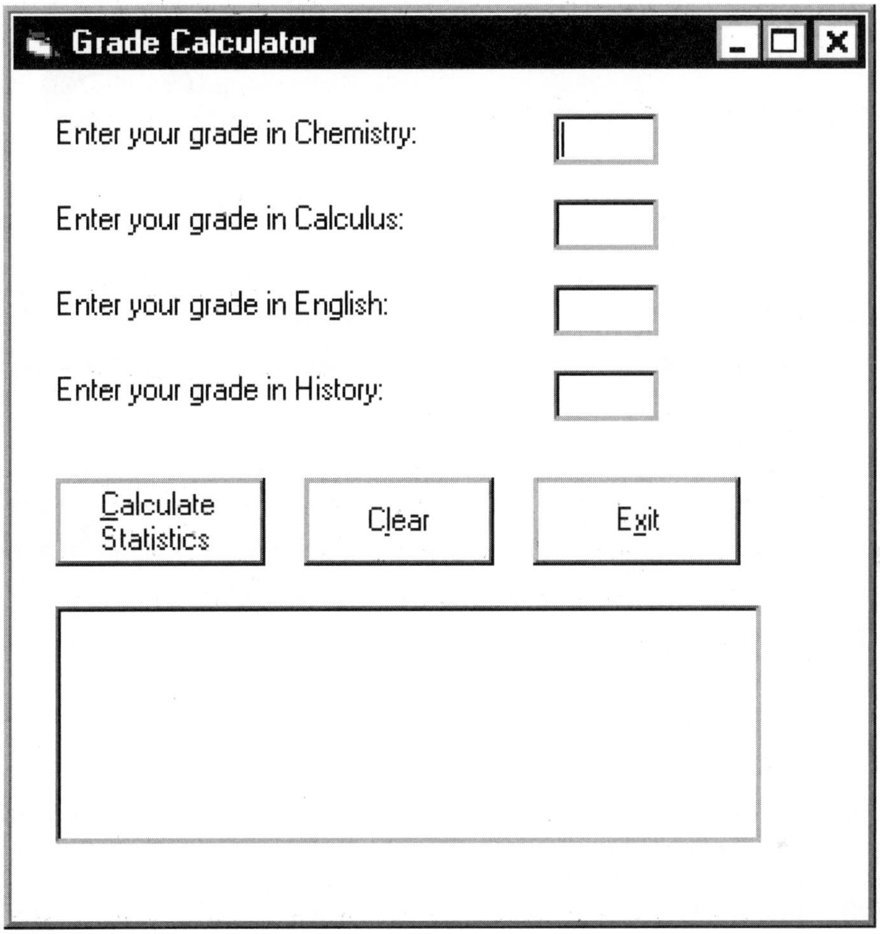

Figure 3.13(B) Visual Basic Screen Layout

pseudo-OOP language, because it supports most, but not all, features of an OOP language (see below for these features). Visual Basic 6.0 is a very popular language for developing applications. Figure 3.13(A) is a simple Visual Basic program designed to compute the average, highest, and lowest grades of a college student. Figure 3.13(B) shows the screen layout (GUI interface) designed for this application, using Visual Basic's click, drag, and drop tools. The user enters his or her grades in Chemistry, Calculus, English, and History, and the program computes the average, highest, and lowest grades. Note that the program itself looks very much like a 3 GL program, while the screen design becomes a much simpler task in Visual Basic (or any OOP language) than in a 3 GL.

To work with an OOP language, one must think in terms of objects. The programmer must start by defining those entities that are referred to as classes. A class is the blueprint or specifications for creating an object. To work with the class, we must create an instance of the class, which is then referred to as the object. An object has attributes, or properties, that can be set by the programmer, or even by the user when the program is running, if the programmer desires. An object also has methods—predefined actions taken by the object. Objects can also respond to events, or actions taken upon the object. Objects, properties, methods, and events can all be a bit difficult to comprehend at first, so let's use an example that might be more familiar to you—the family dog.

We can think of a dog and identify various attributes, which programmers call properties, to differentiate one dog from another dog. Each dog has height, weight, color, coat thickness, eye color, snout shape, and many other features that might differ from other dogs (see Figure 3.14 left). Each of these properties thus has a value. Each dog, independent of its property values, also does several actions; programmers call these methods. Eat, sleep, run, and fetch are examples of these methods. Dogs also respond to several actions done to them; these are called events. Hearing their name called, being petted, or even being kicked are examples of events to which the dog responds

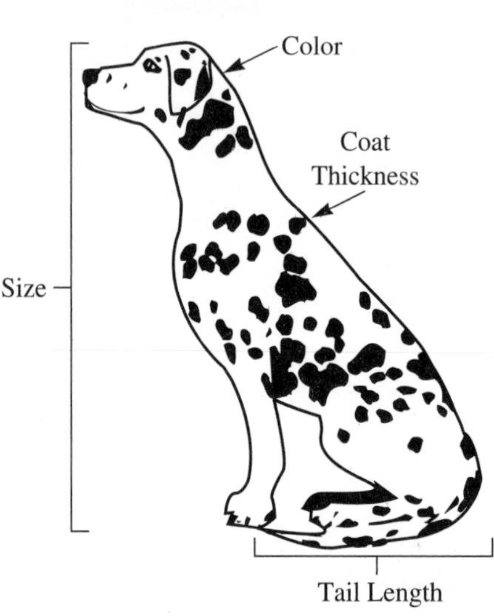

All are examples of properties

The dog wags its tail in response to an *event*, being petted

Figure 3.14 A Dog as an Object

(see Figure 3.14 right). The code in Figure 3.15 shows an example of a class called Dog, written in Java.

We said that to work with a class, we must create an instance of the class called an object—this process is called instantiation. From our class definition of a dog (Figure 3.15), we know that it has various properties, methods, and events. For a family without a pet, however, all that family has is a class definition. When the family goes to the animal shelter to rescue a furry friend, they now have an instance of the class, or an actual dog.

The code in Figure 3.16 shows how a Dog can be instantiated from the class definition in Figure 3.15. We instantiate a new Dog and then call the display method in the newly created dog object.

Objects also have two important features that make them even more useful. One of them is encapsulation. Encapsulation allows the object's creator to hide some (or even all) of the object's inner workings from other programmers or users. This keeps the object's integrity very high, exposing only parts of the object that will not cause the object to crash. Let's apply this to our dog example. For a dog to survive, it needs vitamins, nutrients, proteins, and carbohydrates. These items must get into the dog's bloodstream and be carried to the muscles and organs that need them. However, we as dog owners do not try to inject the items directly into the bloodstream or the organs; we merely buy dog food at the store and set it out for our pet. The dog eats the food and digests it, and the nutrients are carried to their proper places. You could thus say that the digestive system of the dog has been encapsulated. We do not need to know how it works, nor in most cases do we even care. It has been created to work the way it is, although if it were to start behaving incorrectly, we might take the dog to see a programmer—the veterinarian!

The second feature is called inheritance. Inheritance means that we can create subclasses and superclasses from classes, and they then automatically have properties, methods, and events of their related class. For example, if I have a class called animal, I know that dog should be a subclass of animal. A dog is a type of animal (not the other way around) and should take on the properties, methods, and events of the class animal. Visual Basic does not support inheritance, which is the primary reason that it is not a true OOP language.

Object-oriented programming is one of the most sought-after skills in the job market of the early twenty-first century. Despite OOP's supposed natural way of thinking about the world, it is difficult to find good object-oriented programmers. Older programmers who learned programming in structured languages like C and COBOL often do not want to be retrained, and some younger programmers do not like OOP languages because they can be very difficult to learn.

```
public class Dog{
    double height;
    double weight;
    String color;

        public Dog (double someheight, double someweight, String somecolor)
    {
        height = sometype;
        weight = someweight;
        color = somecolor;
    }

        //methods
        public void sleep() {
        //code to make a dog sleep will go here
        }
        public void run() {
        //code to make a dog run will go here
        }

        public Object fetch() {
        //code to make a dog fetch will go here
        //this method will return the item fetched
        }
    public void display()
    {
    System.out.println("The Height of Animal is: " + height);
    System.out.println("The Weight of Animal is: " + weight);
    System.out.println("The Color of the Animal is: " + color);
    }
}
```

Figure 3.15 Java Class Called Dog

It can also take longer to develop an object-oriented program than a structured program, and objects must be reused several times before any overall cost and time savings are realized.

```
public class AnimalTest
{
    public static void main(String args[])
    {
        Animal myanimal;

        myanimal = new Dog("10.5", 30,"Black");
        myanimal.display();
    }
}
```

Figure 3.16 Java Instantiation of a New Dog

Languages for Developing Web Applications

The emergence of the Internet has led to the increasing need for developing Web-based applications. Although these applications range in complexity from very simple applications that allow user registration to applications that enable business-to-business transactions, they all have the following things in common:

- All Web applications are based on an n-tier architecture (where n >= 2). The typical system consists of three tiers: a user interface (client), a Web or application server, and a database server.
- The user interacts with the system (on his or her machine) through Web-based forms. Data entered into the forms are sent to the server, where a server application program processes them. This program

WHY IS OBJECT TECHNOLOGY VALUABLE?

One reason that the term "object oriented," or "OO," is often confusing is that it is applied so widely. We hear about object-oriented user interfaces, object-oriented programming languages, object-oriented design methodologies, object-oriented databases, even object-oriented business modeling. A reasonable question might be: Is this term used because OO has become a synonym for "modern and good," or is there really some substantial common thread across all these object-oriented things?

I believe that there is such a common thread, and that it makes the object paradigm useful in all these diverse areas. Essentially it is a focus on the "thing" first and the action second. It has been described as a noun-verb way of looking at things, rather than verb-noun. At the user interface, first the object is selected, then the action to be performed on the object. At the programming language level, an object is asked to perform some action, rather than a procedure called to "do its thing" on a set of parameters. At the design level, the "things" in the application are defined, then the behavior (actions) of these things is described.

Object technology provides significant potential value in three areas, all closely related: productivity, maintainability, and paradigm consistency. We must change application development from a people-intensive discipline to an asset-intensive discipline. That is, we must encourage and make feasible the widespread reuse of software components. It is exactly in this "reusable component" arena that object technology can contribute significantly. The aspects of object technology that help in reuse are encapsulation (which allows the developer to see a component as a "black box" with specified behavior) and inheritance (which encourages the reuse of code to implement identical behavior among different kinds of objects).

[Radin, 1996]

might write parts of this information to a database (residing on a different machine).

The most common user interface encountered by users is an HTML form. This form might either be static or dynamic (i.e., produced by a program). An example of a dynamic HTML form that can be used to order grocery items is shown at the top of Figure 3.17. The ASP.NET code needed to generate this page is shown below the HTML form. Please note that the user simply enters the heading, the labels, the items in the list, and the possible values of these items, and the code is automatically generated by Active

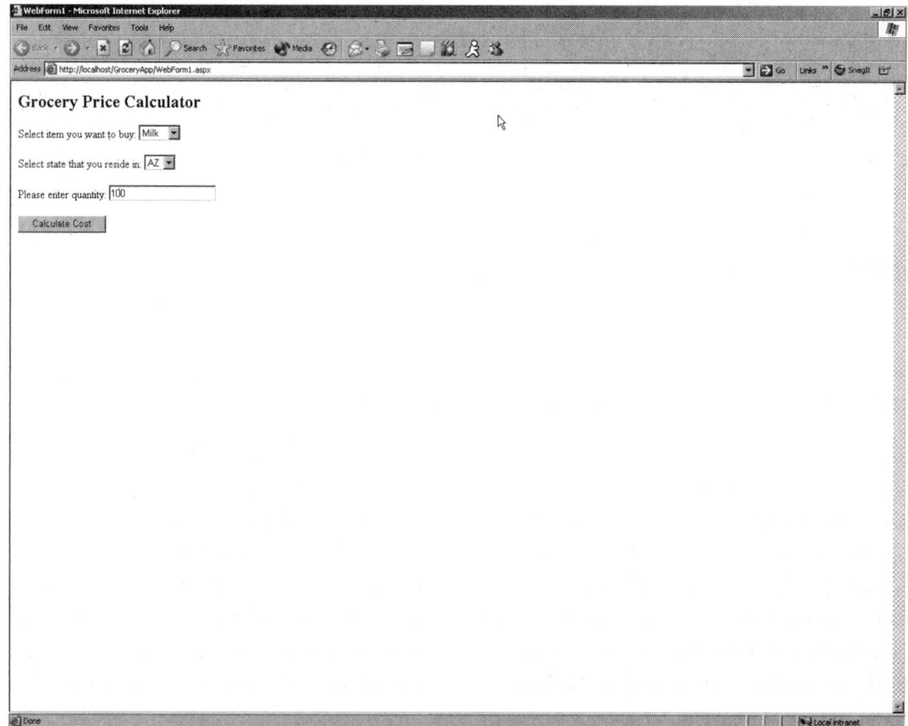

Figure 3.17 Grocery Store HTML Form and Accompanying Code

```
<%@ Page Language="vb" AutoEventWireup="false" Codebehind="WebForm1.aspx.vb"
Inherits="GroceryApp.WebForm1"%>
<!DOCTYPE HTML PUBLIC "-//W3C//DTD HTML 4.0 Transitional//EN">
<HTML>
	<HEAD>
		<title>WebForm1</title>
		<meta name="GENERATOR" content="Microsoft Visual Studio.NET 7.0">
		<meta name="CODE_LANGUAGE" content="Visual Basic 7.0">
		<meta name="vs_defaultClientScript" content="JavaScript">
		<meta name="vs_targetSchema" content="http://schemas.microsoft.com/intellisense/ie5">
	</HEAD>
	<body>
		<form id="Form1" method="post" runat="server">
			<P>
				<asp:Label id="Label1" runat="server" Width="340px" Height="40px" Font-
				Bold="True" Font-Size="Large">Grocery Price Calculator</asp:Label></P>
			<P> </P>
			<P>
				<asp:Label id="label3" runat="server" Width="242px">Select item you want
				to buy:</asp:Label>
				<asp:DropDownList id="item" runat="server">
					<asp:ListItem Value="Eggs">Eggs</asp:ListItem>
					<asp:ListItem Value="Milk">Milk</asp:ListItem>
					<asp:ListItem Value="OJ">OJ</asp:ListItem>
				</asp:DropDownList></P>
			<P> </P>
			<P>
				<asp:Label id="label2" runat="server" Width="242px">Select state that you reside
				in:</asp:Label>
				<asp:DropDownList id="state" runat="server">
					<asp:ListItem Value="IN">IN</asp:ListItem>
					<asp:ListItem Value="AZ">AZ</asp:ListItem>
					<asp:ListItem Value="IL">IL</asp:ListItem>
				</asp:DropDownList></P>
			<P> </P>
			<P>
				<asp:Label id="Label4" runat="server" Width="164px">Please enter
				quantity:</asp:Label>
				<asp:TextBox id="Qty" runat="server"></asp:TextBox></P>
			<P> </P>
			<P>
				<asp:Button id="Submit" runat="server" Width="183px" Text="Calculate
				Cost"></asp:Button></P>
		</form>
	</body>
</HTML>
```

Figure 3.17 Grocery Store HTML Form and Accompanying Code (continued)

Server Pages (ASP). The code is a mixture of general HTML tags and some tags that are specific to ASP.NET, e.g., asp:DropDownList. The *runat* portion of the form specifies that a program on the server that generated this page should be called when the user clicks on the button of type Submit (labeled Calculate Cost) on the form. The data from each of the user interface elements are passed on to the program on the server.

The program that processes the data is shown in Figure 3.18. This program retrieves the data from the form and stores the data items in session variables named item, state, and qty, respectively. After this, the program redirects control to the next page that needs to be displayed—that is, confirm.aspx. However, before this page is loaded, the load function shown in Figure 3.19 is called. Here, we retrieve the values stored in the session and assign them to various elements of our page to be displayed. The result is the new page shown in Figure 3.19.

The example shown in Figures 3.17 through 3.19 is written using ASP.NET. All Web application development

```
Public Sub submit_Click(s As Object, e As EventArgs)

Session.add("item", item.SelectedItem.Text)
Session.add("state", state.SelectedItem.Text)
Session.add("qty", Qty.Text)
Response.sendRedirect("confirm.aspx")

End Sub
```

Figure 3.18 Program to Process Data from Grocery Store HTML Form

technologies or server-side programming environments operate using a similar model in that they all provide mechanisms for generating dynamic Web pages, encoding complex business logic on the server-side as well as reading and writing to a variety of database management systems. Common examples of server-side programming environments are CGI using Perl, Java Servlets and Java Server Pages (JSP), Microsoft's Active Server Pages (ASP, ASP.NET), and Allaire's ColdFusion. Currently, Java Servlets/JSP (for all platforms, especially UNIX and Linux) and ASP/ASP.NET (primarily for Windows) are the preferred technologies for developing e-business solutions.

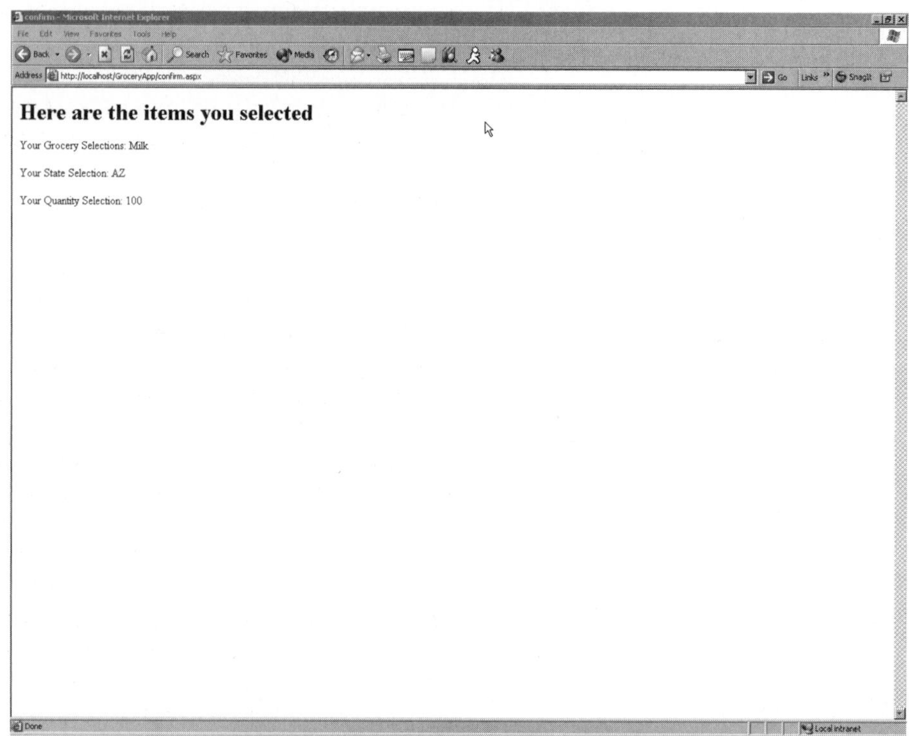

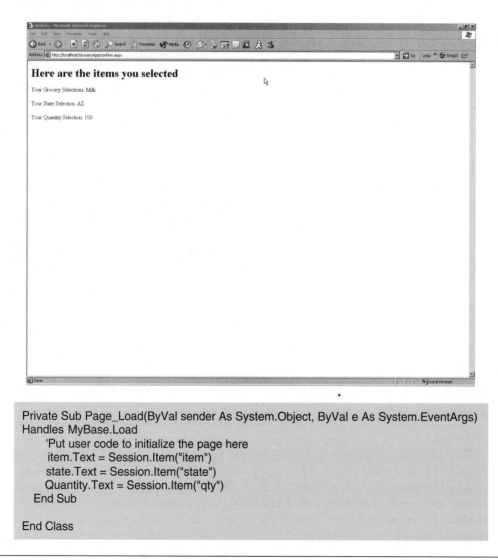

```
Private Sub Page_Load(ByVal sender As System.Object, ByVal e As System.EventArgs)
Handles MyBase.Load
      'Put user code to initialize the page here
      item.Text = Session.Item("item")
      state.Text = Session.Item("state")
      Quantity.Text = Session.Item("qty")
   End Sub

End Class
```

Figure 3.19 Grocery Store Confirmation Web Page and Code That Generates It

Database Management Systems

A **database management system (DBMS)** is support software that is used to create, manage, and protect organizational data. A database management system works with the operating system to store and modify data and to make data accessible in a variety of meaningful and authorized ways.

A DBMS adds significant data management capabilities to those provided by the operating system. The goal is to allow a computer programmer to select data from disk files by referring to the content of records, not their physical location. This makes programming easier, more productive, and less error-prone. Also, this allows systems professionals responsible for database design to reorganize the physical organization of data without affecting the logic of programs, which significantly reduces maintenance requirements. These objectives are given the umbrella term *data independence*. For example, a DBMS would allow a programmer to specify retrieval of a customer record based only on knowledge of the customer's name or number. Furthermore, once the customer record is retrieved, a DBMS would allow direct reference to any of the customer's related order or shipment records (even if these records are relocated or changed). Thus, a DBMS allows access to data based on content (e.g., customer number) as well as by association (e.g., orders for a given customer).

A **database** is a shared collection of logically related data that is organized to meet the needs of an organization. A related term is a *data warehouse*, a very large database or collection of databases, to be considered in Chapter 6. A DBMS is the software that manages a database. A DBMS is a very complex and often costly software package, ranging in price from under $500 for a personal computer product to $200,000 or more for a DBMS on a large mainframe computer.

The various types of DBMSs in use today will be explored more fully in Chapter 5. For now, let us note that the **relational DBMS** is the most common type of DBMS. With the relational model, the data are arranged into simple tables, and records are related by storing common data in each of the associated tables. Many DBMS products use the relational model, including Microsoft Access and SQL Server from Microsoft Corporation, Paradox by Corel, DB2 by IBM, and Ingres by Computer Associates.

File Organization The computer files are stored on the disk using the file organization provided by the operating system and special structures added by the DBMS. Although their exact details can be treated as a "black box" in most cases, it is useful to know some of the terminology and choices. Three general kinds of file organizations exist: sequential, direct, and indexed (see Figure 3.20).

A **sequential file organization** arranges the records so that they are physically adjacent and in order by some sort key (usually the unique key that distinguishes each record from another). Thus, a sequential customer file would have the records arranged in order by customer name or identifier. Sequential files use very little space and are fast to use when the records are to be retrieved in order, but they are inefficient when searching for a particular record because they must be scanned front to back. Also, when records are added or deleted, the whole file must be rearranged to accommodate the modifications, which can be time-consuming.

A **direct file organization** also uses a key for each record, but records are placed and retrieved so that an individual record can be rapidly accessed. The records are located wherever they can most quickly be retrieved, and the space from deleted records can be reused without having to rearrange the file. The most typical method employed is a hashing function. In this case, the record key, such as the customer number, is mathematically manipulated (by some algorithm) to determine the location of the record with that key. It is possible that several keys can "collide" to the same location, but such synonyms are easily resolved. Direct files are extremely fast for accessing a single record, but because the keys that exist at any point in time are usually arbitrary, sequential processing of direct files requires a long and tedious scan and usually sorting of the records.

Indexed file organizations provide a compromise between the sequential and direct access capabilities. The record keys only are arranged in sequence in a separate table, along with the location of the rest of the data associated with that key (this location field in the table is called a pointer). This "lookup" table or index is similar to a card catalog in a library, in which the author name, book title, and topics are different types of keys and the book catalog number is a pointer to its location in the library. To access the records sequentially, the table is completely scanned one entry at a time, and as each entry is encountered, its associated data record is retrieved. To access the records individually, the table is scanned until a match with the desired key is found and only the desired record is retrieved; if no match is found, an error is indicated. Because the table is quite small (just enough space for the key and location of every record, compared to possible hundreds or thousands of characters needed for the whole record—remember the analogy of the card catalog in a library), this scan can be very fast (certainly considerably faster than scanning the actual data). For a very large table, another table can be created to access the first table (which is, of course, nothing more than a specialized file itself). Popular names for such methods of indexes on top of indexes are indexed sequential access method (ISAM) and virtual storage access method (VSAM).

Sequential File Organization

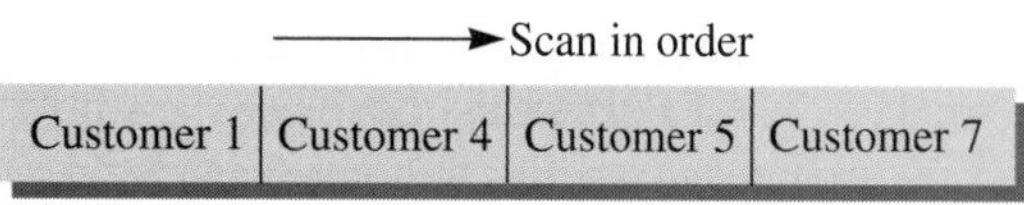

Direct File Organization

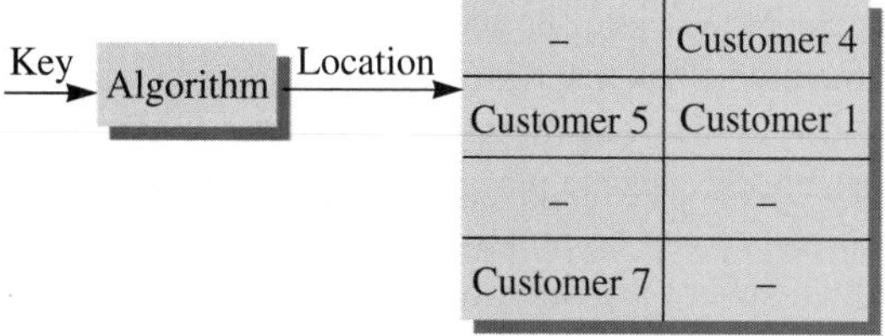

Indexed File Organization

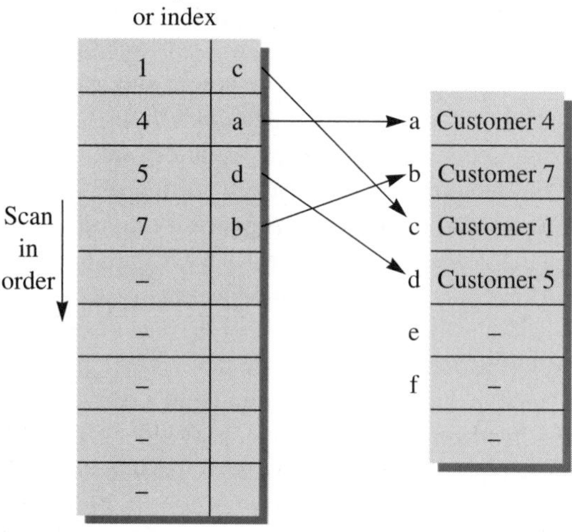

Figure 3.20 File Organizations

Finally, because in a database we want to be able to access records based upon content (e.g., by customer number) as well as by relationship (e.g., orders for a given customer), a DBMS along with the operating system must also provide a means for access via these relationships. Record keys and location pointers are these means. For example, we could store pointers in a customer record and its associated order records to link all these related records together (see Figure 3.21). Such a scheme is called *chaining* or a *list structure*. Alternately, we could store the customer number in each of its associated order records and use tables or hashing functions to locate the related record or records in other files. Relational DBMSs use this scheme.

Database management systems are a very important type of support software, and this section has introduced some basic ideas about a DBMS, a database, and file organization. Chapter 5 will return to these topics as part of a broader treatment of the data resource.

CASE Tools

It was originally predicted that CASE tools would have a major impact on computer professionals, and that has been true for some professionals in some firms. However, the growth of the use of CASE tools has been much slower than anticipated. **CASE**, an acronym for **computer-aided software engineering**, is actually a collection of software tools to help automate all phases of the software development life cycle. (The life cycle for software development is discussed in Chapters 9 and 10.) In those firms that have adopted CASE tools—and there are many of them—CASE has radically changed the jobs of systems analysts and programmers. In particular, the job of the analyst or programmer involves more up-front work in clearly defining the problem and expressing it in the particular specifications required by the CASE tool. Then the tool assists in the back-end work of translating the specifications to the required output, such as a data flow diagram (see Chapter 9) or a COBOL program.

There has been a recent surge in the use of CASE tools for object-oriented development based on the **Unified Modeling Language**, or **UML**. UML is a general-purpose notational language for specifying and visualizing complex software, especially large, object-oriented projects. Examples of such UML-based CASE tools are IBM's Rational Rose and Borland's Together. We will defer a more complete treatment of CASE software until Chapter 10, where we will explore the variety of CASE tools and their role in the systems development process. For now, note that CASE is only beginning to make an impact. CASE has the potential of providing a productivity boost to an area of the company (the information systems organization) that needs such a boost.

Communications Interface Software

Communications interface software has become increasingly important with the explosion in the number of local area networks (LANs) and wide area networks (WANs) and with the growing importance of the Internet and the World Wide Web. We have already discussed perhaps the most important type of communications interface software, the Web browser, which is software that runs on the user's computer enabling the user to look around, or "browse," the Internet. We will defer discussion of LAN and WAN software until Chapter 4, but we will consider several other types of communications interface software now.

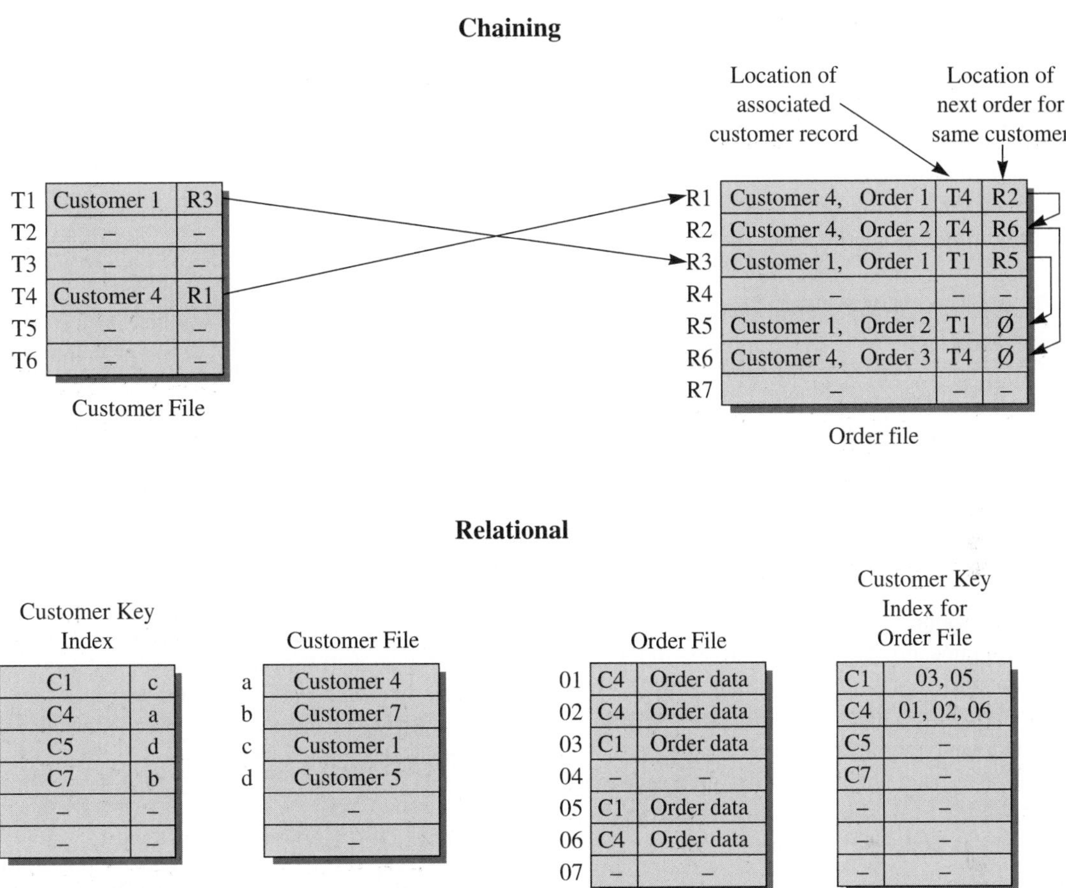

Figure 3.21 Schemes for Relationships Between Files

Communications packages on large computers with many attached workstations have the awesome task of controlling the communications of these workstations, or terminals, with the central computer. This software collects the messages from the terminals, processes them as necessary, and returns the responses to the proper terminals. These packages are often designed to work closely with a particular operating system. For example, IBM's CICS (Customer Information Control System) and TSO (Time Sharing Option) are communications packages designed to work with IBM's MVS operating system (now called the z/OS operating system). Similarly, IBM's CMS (Conversational Monitor System) is designed to work with the VM operating system (now z/VM). IBM has also created versions of CICS that work with AIX, IBM's UNIX operating system; Solaris, Sun's UNIX operating system; and HP-UX, Hewlett-Packard's UNIX operating system. These UNIX/CICS combinations made it much easier for IBM's customers to move their applications to UNIX and provide evidence of the importance of UNIX. More recently, IBM has also created a version of CICS to work with Windows NT Server. Microcomputer communications packages (in workstations attached to large computers) have the much simpler task of making the microcomputer act as if it were a particular type of terminal that can be handled by the large computer communications package.

In addition to the Web browser, two additional items of communication interface software became important in the last decade. **Telnet** is a communications interface package designed to permit a user to log into a remote computer from whatever computer he or she is currently using. The key is that the computer currently being used must be attached to the same network as the remote computer. In some cases this "same network" might be a LAN on a corporate or educational campus, while in other cases this network might be the worldwide Internet. The user invokes the Telnet program and identifies the remote computer he or she wishes to log into. The connection is made, and then the user simply logs into the remote computer as if he or she were on-site. One of this textbook's authors taught in

Europe for several summers, and he has a computer account at the European university. He regularly logs into that European computer via Telnet to carry out business there. Another valuable communications interface package is **FTP**, which is short for **File Transfer Protocol**. This package is designed to transfer files from one computer system to another. In effect, the user logs into the two computer systems at the same time, and then copies files from one system to the other. The files being transferred might be programs, textual data, images, and so on.

Utility Programs

This is obviously a catch-all category, but an important one nevertheless. On large computers, utility software includes programs that load applications programs into an area of memory, link related programs and subprograms, merge two files of data, sort a file of data into a desired sequence (e.g., alphabetical order on a particular data item), and copy files from one place to another (e.g., from a DASD to magnetic tape). Utility programs also give the user access to the software library. In most cases the user communicates with these utility programs by means of commands in the job control language. On a microcomputer, utility programs are used to zip (compact) and unzip large files for easier transport, to reorganize the hard drive to gain disk space, to check for computer viruses, and for many other tasks.

THE CHANGING NATURE OF SOFTWARE

In the process of investigating the various categories of computer software, we have noted many of the important trends in the software arena. Building upon our earlier discussions, we can explicitly identify the significant developing patterns in the software field, emphasizing those that have the most direct relevance to you as a manager. The following are seven key trends that we have identified:

1. More complexity of hardware/software arrangements.
2. Less concern with machine efficiency.
3. More purchased applications, and more portability of these applications from one computer platform to another. Conversely, more use of open source (free or inexpensive) support software, such as Linux.
4. More programming using object-oriented and visual languages, especially Java and Visual Basic .NET.
5. More emphasis on applications that run on intranets and the Internet, especially using the World Wide Web.
6. More user development.
7. More use of personal productivity software on microcomputers.

More Complexity of Hardware/Software Arrangements

To a much greater extent, varying configurations of hardware will be tied together by sophisticated software packages. We discussed multiprocessing and parallel processing, which involve multiple CPUs in one machine controlled by the operating system. Another way of configuring machines is to cluster several computers together, sharing common disk devices, all under control of their separate operating systems. Applications software is being split among machines as organizations move to multi-tier client/server or Web-based arrangements. With Web-based systems, the only software stored on the workstation is the browser, but there often are both an applications server and a database server involved in running the application. These more complex hardware/software arrangements have little direct impact on you as a manager; they are ways in which computer systems will be made more powerful to assist in the efficient and effective running of a business.

Less Concern with Machine Efficiency

The cost per instruction on computers will continue to drop dramatically, as it has for the past four decades. That is, machine cycles will continue to get cheaper. On the other hand, personnel costs, both for computer professionals and managers, will continue to climb. Thus, as time passes, we will be more concerned with human efficiency and less concerned with machine efficiency. This reduced concern for machine efficiency has both direct and indirect impacts on you as a manager. It means that software tools that improve human efficiency, such as visual and object-oriented languages, query languages, and CASE tools, will become more popular for computer professionals and, where appropriate, for managers. It also will lead to the development of executive workstations with voice and natural language interfaces, which are terribly inefficient from the machine standpoint.

More Purchased Applications

The higher personnel costs for computer professionals mean higher costs for in-house development of new applications software. In addition, the present backlogs for internal development of new applications are not going to disappear in the short run. The demand for new applications is also not going to slacken, particularly with the infusion of an increasing number of computer-literate managers into organizations. Add to this mix a vigorous software industry marketing an incredible variety of software packages, and it is easy to predict a continuing growth in purchased applications software. Furthermore, more of the purchased applications will be portable from one computing platform to another or will work with a variety of support software (especially database management systems). This gives companies more flexibility in their choice of computing platforms.

Another major reason for purchasing software is to correct internal business processes that are not working as well as they should. Most software packages designed to handle standard business tasks such as payroll, accounts payable, general ledger, and material requirements planning incorporate excellent procedures in the package, and by implementing the package the organization is required to adopt these improved procedures. Thus, the organization is forcing the "reengineering" of its processes by implementing the software package. This is particularly true for so-called enterprise resource planning packages, which we will discuss in Chapter 6. The advantage to you of the trend towards more purchased applications is that you will be able to get new applications you need implemented more quickly; the disadvantage is that the purchased software might not be able to do precisely what you want done in the way in which you want it done.

Although organizations are likely to purchase *more* of their applications in the future, it might be that they purchase *less* of their support software. The rising popularity of open source support software, such as the Linux operating system, means that more applications software is being developed to run on these open source platforms. As time goes on, organizations might be able to spend more of their information technology budget on applications and less on support software.

More Programming Using Object-Oriented and Visual Languages

In part because of the emphasis on GUIs, Visual Basic .NET, Java, and similar object-oriented and visual programming languages will gain even more widespread acceptance. These languages lend themselves to developing GUI interfaces such as those used on the World Wide Web, and many believe that they are easier to learn and use than the traditional 3 GLs. The increased use of these languages is also consistent with the lessened concern over machine efficiency noted above, because they tend to produce quite inefficient code. From the manager's perspective, the use of these languages will tend to give you the applications you need more quickly, and the GUI will make the screens more attractive and easier for you and your employees to use.

More Emphasis on Applications That Run on Intranets and the Internet

This is a very important and powerful trend, but we are somewhat premature in introducing it at this point in the book. We will explore the idea of intranets and the Internet in the next chapter. After that discussion this trend will be more meaningful. For now, note that intranets are networks operating within an organization that use the same technology as the worldwide Internet, and that the Internet is a network of networks spanning the globe. More and more organizations are creating or buying applications that run on their internal intranet or the Internet because it is both easy and economical to make these applications available to everyone who needs them.

More User Development

This trend hits close to home because you and your fellow managers will carry out more software development efforts yourselves. For the most part, you will work with personal productivity software, 4 GLs, and query languages that are easy to learn and use. Why will this increase in user development occur? Because it is easier and quicker for you to develop the software than to go to the information systems organization and work with them on the development (often after an extensive wait). This will be the case for many situations where you need a one-time or infrequently used report, or a decision support system to help you with a particular decision. Managers will continue to rely on the information systems organization (or on purchased software) for major ongoing systems, such as production control, general ledger accounting, and human resource information systems. Because of its importance to you as managers, we have devoted the entirety of Chapter 13 to user application development.

More Use of Personal Productivity Software

This final trend is the most important one for most of you. The use of personal productivity software, especially Web browsers, spreadsheet packages, and database management systems, will grow for managers and other professionals. Packages with a well-designed GUI will increasingly be the software of choice, because a GUI makes the software easier to learn and use. Your workstation, linked to a LAN and the worldwide Internet (see Chapter 4), will become as indispensable as your telephone (and eventually will *become* your telephone). You will use it almost every hour of every working day for electronic mail, Web browsing, word processing, spreadsheets, database management, presentation graphics, and other applications. In fact, most of you will find the microcomputer so essential that you will carry a notebook version or an even smaller palmtop computer with you when you are out of your office.

THE SOFTWARE COMPONENT OF THE INFORMATION SYSTEMS INDUSTRY

Many software products have been mentioned in this chapter, as well as many software vendors, but we lack a frame of reference from which to view the software subindustry. There are two primary groups of players in the software arena: hardware manufacturers and software houses. Many of the major hardware vendors—companies such as IBM, Sun Microsystems, Hewlett-Packard, Fujitsu, and Unisys—have a major presence in the mainframe/midrange/server computing market. In this big/midrange machine market, customers usually buy their operating systems and much of their support software from their hardware vendors—and sometimes a large proportion of their applications software as well. Thus, many of the major players in the hardware market are also major players in the software market. For example, IBM, the largest hardware vendor, is the second largest software vendor in the world in terms of revenue, trailing only Microsoft.

The software houses form an interesting and competitive group, although they are increasingly dominated by a single firm. Microsoft is the largest and most influential software house, and its dominance is growing. Microsoft is based in Redmond, Washington, and until 2000 was headed by Bill Gates, reportedly the richest person in the world. Gates is still the Chairman of the Board and Chief Software Architect of Microsoft. Other major software vendors include Computer Associates, based in Islandia, New York, which produces a variety of mainframe and PC-based software packages, with particular strength in mainframe database, job scheduling, security, and systems management software; Oracle (Redwood Shores, California), which began by specializing in mainframe DBMSs but has now branched out into other areas, notably enterprise resource planning systems (integrated software to run a business); SAP (Germany), which is the market leader in the enterprise resource planning area with its R/3 package; PeopleSoft (Pleasanton, California), which moved into the number two position in enterprise resource planning systems with its 2003 purchase of J. D. Edwards for $1.7 billion in stock; and Novell Inc. (Provo, Utah), a major provider of network management and network security software, as well as Web services packages. Until 1995, Lotus Development Corporation would have been listed as a major player in this group, but IBM bought it that year. The hottest Lotus product, and certainly one of the big reasons for IBM's interest, is Lotus Notes, a groupware product designed to aid in information transfer and efficient communication among large groups of people. IBM continues to buy promising software houses, including its 2003 purchase of Rational Software for $2.1 billion in cash. Rational, which now operates as a division of IBM Software, produces software to assist in the development of major applications, especially when using an object-oriented approach. In addition to these big software houses, there is a multitude of medium-sized to small-sized software firms. Many of the smaller firms tend to rise and fall rapidly based on the success or failure of a single product, and many small firms have gone bankrupt when they tried and failed to develop additional products.

A third group of players in the software subindustry, not as important as the first two, is the consulting firms. The key players are changing so rapidly that it is difficult to keep up, as the major public accounting firms spin off or sell off their consulting practices, sometimes to hardware vendors (IBM purchased PricewaterhouseCoopers Consulting). For the most part, the software developed and sold by these firms has been an outgrowth of their consulting practices and thus tends to be applications software geared to particular industries in which they have consulted extensively. There are also many smaller firms in the information systems arena that are difficult to categorize either as a software house or a consulting firm because they truly operate as both. Their consulting jobs often involve writing or modifying software for a particular firm and then moving to another firm within the same industry to do a similar job.

To complete the software story, we should mention that some excellent software can be obtained from noninformation systems companies that have developed software for their own use and then later decided to market the product. The software business is dominated, however, by the software houses and the hardware manufacturers. In Chapter 11, we will discuss the option of purchasing applications software.

SUMMARY

Both computer hardware and software are required for a computer system to perform useful work. The hardware actually does the work—adding two numbers, reading a record from disk, printing a line—but the software controls all of the hardware's actions. Thus, understanding software is critical to comprehending how computer systems work. From a financial perspective, most organizations spend several times as much money on software as they spend on hardware. Also, managers deal directly with a variety of software packages but rarely deal with hardware other than their own workstation. For all these reasons, software is a vital topic for aspiring managers to understand.

Figuratively speaking, software comes in a variety of shapes and sizes. Applications software consists of all programs written to accomplish particular tasks for computer users; support software establishes a relatively easy-to-use computing environment, translates programs into machine language, and ensures that the hardware and software resources are used efficiently. The most important piece of support software is the operating system that controls the operation of the hardware and coordinates all of the other software. Other support software includes language translators, communications interface software, database management systems, and utility programs.

Applications software is often developed within the organization using third generation procedural languages like COBOL or C, fourth generation nonprocedural languages like FOCUS or SAS, or newer languages such as C++ or Java. Historically, nearly all the internal software development has been carried out by computer professionals in the information systems organization. In the last decade or so, however, more of the development has been done by end users (including managers), using 4 GLs and DBMS query languages. The trend that affects managers even more is the growing availability and use of personal productivity software such as spreadsheets and database management systems. We anticipate that these trends toward more user development of software and more use of personal productivity packages will continue and will strengthen.

Almost all of an organization's support software and an increasing proportion of its applications software is purchased from outside the firm. The hardware manufacturers appear to supply the bulk of the support software and some of the applications programs for larger computers. Independent software houses (not associated with hardware manufacturers) are particularly important sources of mainframe applications software and microcomputer software of all types. Consulting firms are also a valuable source of applications software. When purchasing software, the organization must consider the quality and fit of the software package and the services and stability provided by the vendor.

Hopefully, this chapter has provided you with sufficient knowledge of computer software to begin to appreciate the present and potential impact of computers on your organization and your job.

REVIEW QUESTIONS

1. Briefly describe the four generations of computer programming languages, concentrating on the major differences among the generations. How does object-oriented programming fit into these generations? How does HTML fit into these generations? How does XML fit into these generations?
2. List at least five categories of personal productivity software packages. Then concentrate on one of these categories and describe a representative product in that category with which you are somewhat familiar. Provide both strong points and weak points of the particular product.
3. What are the purposes of an operating system? What are the primary tasks carried out by a mainframe operating system?
4. Differentiate between multiprogramming and multiprocessing.
5. Explain the concept of virtual memory. Why is it important?
6. List the six major categories of support software.
7. Explain the concept of structured programming. Why is it important?
8. What are the primary advantages of a fourth generation language over a third generation language? What are the primary disadvantages?
9. What are the primary characteristics of an object-oriented language? How does an object-oriented language differ from a third generation language or a fourth generation language?
10. Explain the difference between push and pull technology, and give an example of each.
11. Three general types of file organizations were described in the text: sequential, direct, and indexed file organizations. In general terms, describe how each type of file organization works. It might be helpful to draw a diagram to depict each type of file organization.
12. For what does the CASE acronym stand? In general, what is the purpose of CASE tools? What types of individuals are most likely to use CASE tools?
13. List at least three independent software houses (not associated with a computer vendor) that are major players in the software component of the information systems industry. List any software products that you

regularly use and indicate the firm that developed each product.

14. Some of the acronyms used in this chapter are listed below. Provide the full names for each of these acronyms.

JCL	HTML
4 GL	OOP
DBMS	DASD
COBOL	CASE
XML	BASIC

DISCUSSION QUESTIONS

1. From the discussion in this chapter and your own knowledge from other sources, what do you think is the most important advancement in computer software in the past 5 years? Why?
2. Which one category of personal productivity software is of most value to you now as a student? Why? Within this category, what is your favorite software package? Why?
3. Which one category of personal productivity software do you expect to be of most value to you in your career? Why? Is this different from the category you selected in the previous question? Why or why not?
4. Based on your own computing experience and your discussions with other computer users, which one category of personal productivity software needs the most developmental work to make it useful to managers? What type of development is needed?
5. List the pros and cons of the involvement of managers in the end-user computing revolution. What strengths and weaknesses do managers bring to the software development process? Is it appropriate for managers to be directly involved in applications software development?
6. In the mid-1980s, a movement developed within the information systems industry to "stamp out COBOL" and replace it with 4 GLs and other productivity tools. Manifestations of this movement included the slogan to "Kill the COBOL programmer" (not literally, of course) and T-shirts bearing the word COBOL within the international symbol for "not permitted" (a red circle with a red line diagonally across the word COBOL). Do you think the movement will ever be successful? Why?
7. You have probably had experience with at least one procedural (3 GL) language, either in high school or college. What are the strengths and weaknesses of the particular language that you know best? Based on what you have gleaned from the text, what primary advantages would a nonprocedural 4 GL offer over the 3 GL that you know best? What disadvantages? What primary advantages would a natural language offer over the 3 GL that you know best? What disadvantages?
8. Based on your reading in this chapter and other sources, what do you believe are the primary advantages of an object-oriented language over a third generation language or a fourth generation language? What are the primary disadvantages?
9. The sidebar entitled "J2EE vs. .NET" introduced the differences between these two competing frameworks for developing Web applications. Explore J2EE and .NET in more detail by discussing the two frameworks with programmers you know and by conducting research using the Web. Are there other differences between the two frameworks? How would you modify the conclusions provided in the "J2EE vs. .NET" sidebar?
10. Why is the concept of a Java virtual machine important? How does running a Java applet on a Java virtual machine differ from running a Microsoft VB.NET application on your Web browser?
11. As you have read in newspapers and magazines, one firm seems to dominate the worldwide software market—Microsoft. With this degree of dominance by one firm, has the software subindustry truly been competitive, particularly over the past decade? Support your position.
12. In the late 1990s the U.S. government, joined by several state governments, brought suit against Microsoft, arguing that Microsoft unfairly exercised monopoly power in the software industry. What is the current status of the federal government suit in the court system? What is the current status of the suit filed by the various state governments?

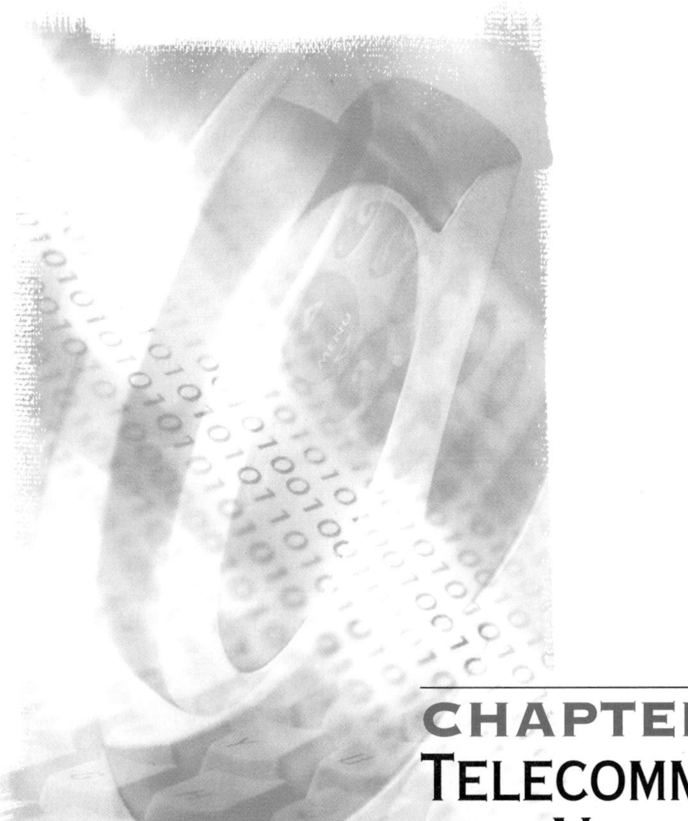

CHAPTER 4
TELECOMMUNICATIONS AND NETWORKING

THIS CHAPTER IS THE THIRD OF A QUARTET OF CHAPTERS DEVOTED TO the building blocks of information technology. So far we have considered hardware and software, but there are two more critical building blocks to go. The hardware and software must have *data* to be processed to produce useful results, and the data resource is the focus of Chapter 5. If every computer were a stand-alone unit with no connection to other computers or computer-related equipment, then hardware and software and data would be the end of the story as far as computers are concerned. In fact, until about 30 years ago, that *was* the end of the story. Today, however, virtually all computers of all sizes communicate directly with other computers by means of an incredible variety of networks. For computers in organizations, these networks include intraorganizational local area networks (LANs), backbone networks, and wide area networks (WANs) as well as the worldwide Internet. For home computers, the most important network is the Internet. In addition to computer (or data) communications, today's organizations also depend heavily on voice (telephone) and image (video and facsimile) communication. This chapter explores the increasingly important topic of telecommunications and networking.

This chapter's goal is to cover only the telecommunications and networking technology that you as a business manager need to know. You need to understand the roles and general capabilities of various types of transmission media and networks, but you do not need to know all the technical details. You certainly need to know the important terminology and concepts relating to telecommunications and networking. Most important, you need to understand the interrelationships among hardware, software, and telecommunications and networking so that you can use the full gamut of information technology to increase your productivity and your organization's effectiveness.

Change is everywhere in the information technology domain, but nowhere is change more evident and more dramatic than in the realm of telecommunications and networking. A communications revolution is taking place that directly or indirectly affects the job of every manager, and the primary catalyst is the Internet and the World Wide Web (an application that runs on the Internet).

The breakup of American Telephone & Telegraph (AT&T) in 1984 created an environment in which a large number of firms competed to develop and market telecommunications equipment and services. Partially because of this increased competition, innovation in the telecommunications and networking arena has been at an all-time high. Digital networks, fiber-optic cabling, cellular telephones, the ability to send both voice and data over the same wires at the same time, and wireless networks have contributed to the revolution.

At the same time, most large U.S. businesses have restructured internally to reduce layers of middle management and create a leaner organization (as introduced in Chapter 1). They have also decentralized operations in order to respond more quickly to market opportunities and competitors' actions and have created cross-functional teams to improve business processes and carry out projects. The net result of these internal changes is that communication has become more important than ever for the remaining, often geographically dispersed, managers. They need rapid, reliable voice and data communication with other parts of the company and with suppliers and customers. Small businesses are also more dependent upon communication than ever before, and developments such as local area networks (LANs), cellular telephones, and increased functionality of the public wired telephone network have helped fill this need. Internal needs and external competition and innovation combined to create a latter-twentieth-century communications revolution that is continuing into the new millennium. The aim of this chapter is to help you become a knowledgeable participant in the communications revolution.

THE NEED FOR NETWORKING

Let us be more precise in justifying the need for networking among computers and computer-related devices such as printers. Why do managers or other professionals working at microcomputers need to be connected to a network? Why are small computers often connected to larger machines? Why are laser printers often attached to a LAN? Why is it critical for many businesses to be connected to the Internet? In our judgment, there are five primary reasons for networking.

NETWORKS WILL CHANGE EVERYTHING

In the early 1990s, Paul Saffo, a fellow at the Institute for the Future, developed a fascinating set of forecasts about the effect of information technologies on the way we would work, play, and conduct business in the years to come. So far, his projections have been right on. "The short answer is that networks will change everything," said Saffo. "In the next 5 years, networks will be supporting a shift to business teams from individuals as the basic unit of corporate productivity. In the 10-year time frame, we'll see changing organizational structures. In 20 to 30 years, we'll see a shift so fundamental, it will mean the end of the corporation as we know it." According to Saffo, organizations have started down the path to a pervasive interconnectivity of workstations that will result in an entirely new "virtual" corporate structure.

[Adapted from Wylie, 1993]

Sharing of Technology Resources

Networking permits the sharing of critical (and often expensive) technology resources among the various users (machines) on the network. For example, by putting all the microcomputers in an office on a LAN, the users can share a variety of resources, such as a high-speed color printer that is a part of the network. The users can also share software that is electronically stored on a file server (another microcomputer designated for that particular purpose). All these devices are connected by wiring and are able to communicate with one another under control of a LAN software package called a server (or network) operating system. When a particular user wants to print a color brochure or a color transparency, it is sent electronically from the user's machine to the network printer.

Sharing resources is also important for larger computers. It is quite common for mainframes or midrange computers to share magnetic disk devices and very high-speed printers. Further, wide area networks (WANs) permit the sharing of very expensive resources such as supercomputers. The National Science Foundation has funded five national supercomputer centers across the United States, and researchers from other universities and research laboratories are able to share these giant machines by going through their local computer network into a national high-speed backbone network such as Abilene (more on this network later in the chapter).

Sharing of Data

Even more important than the sharing of technology resources is the sharing of data. Either a LAN or a WAN permits users on the network to get data (if they are authorized to do so) from other points, called nodes, on the network. It is very important, for example, for managers to be able to retrieve overall corporate sales forecasts from corporate databases to use in developing spreadsheets to project future activity in their departments. In order to satisfy customers, automobile dealers need to be able to locate particular vehicle models and colors with specific equipment installed. Managers at various points in a supply chain need to have accurate, up-to-date data on inventory levels and locations. Accountants at corporate headquarters need to be able to retrieve summary data on sales and expenses from each of the company's divisional computer centers. The chief executive officer, using an executive information system (see Chapter 7), needs to be able to access up-to-the-minute data on business trends from the corporate network.

In some instances data might be retrieved from a commercial, public database external to the firm, such as LexisNexis or Dow Jones Newswires.

Of course, the ultimate sharing of data is now occurring via the **World Wide Web** on the Internet. By conservative estimates, there are now at least 600 million users of the Web at sites around the world, and this number continues to grow rapidly. Each of these users has easy (and often free) access to an incredible array of information on any topic. The user begins by using a search engine such as Google or a favorite reference site, and then follows hypertext-based links to seek out the desired data. In short, the Web has created a new and exciting way of sharing data.

Distributed Data Processing and Client/Server Systems

With **distributed data processing**, the processing power is distributed to multiple computers at multiple sites, which are then tied together via telecommunications lines. **Client/server systems** are a variant of distributed systems in which the processing power is distributed between a central server system, such as a mainframe, midrange computer, or powerful workstation, and a number of client computers, which are usually desktop microcomputers. Distributed and client/server systems tend to reduce computing costs because of their reliance on more cost-effective microcomputers and workstations.

There are many examples of distributed systems. One is the use of laptop computers by a company's sales force, where orders and sales data are transmitted over the telephone network to the corporate computer center. A second example is the use of a client/server application for general ledger accounting, with desktop microcomputers as the clients and a high-powered workstation as the server. In most cases such a package is implemented over a LAN in a single building or a cluster of buildings (a campus). A third example, also a client/server system, involves the creation of a commercial real estate database on a server located at the real estate firm's main office. The client machines are microcomputers located in the firm's branch offices or customer offices, with the clients and server linked via the public telephone network. In any case, it is the existence of a telecommunications network that makes distributed data processing a feasible and often attractive arrangement.

Enhanced Communications

Networks enhance the communications process within an organization (and between organizations) in many important ways. The telephone network has long been a primary means of communication within and between organizations. Electronic mail over the corporate computer network has become a mainstay of communication in many major organizations in the past decade or so, and the development of the Internet has extended the reach of these electronic mail systems around the world. Electronic bulletin boards (including internal, regional, and national bulletin boards) and mass electronic mailing lists for people with common interests permit multiparty asynchronous communication on an incredible array of topics. Instant messaging permits synchronous text communication over the Internet. And video communication, especially videoconferencing, provides a richer medium to permit more effective communication.

Direct data communication links between a company and its suppliers or customers, or both, have been successfully used to give the company a strategic advantage (this topic is more fully explored in Chapter 8). The SABRE airline reservation system is a classic example of a strategic information system that depends upon communication provided through a network. Recent developments to be discussed later in this chapter—such as Integrated Services Digital Network (ISDN) and digital subscriber line (DSL)—permit both voice and data communications to occur over the same telecommunications line at the same time. Starting with "plain old telephone service" (POTS) networks and continuing with today's LANs, WANs, and the Internet, networks have enhanced the communication process for individuals and organizations.

Marketing Outreach

In the last decade the Internet has become an important new marketing channel for a wide variety of businesses. Marketing is communication, of course, but it is a very specialized type of communication. Most midsized and larger business firms have a major presence on the World Wide Web, with extensive Web sites providing information on the firms' products and services and, in many cases, an online ordering capability. Many smaller firms are also using the Web for marketing outreach, perhaps by creating a Yahoo! store. Chapter 8 will consider the wide variety of marketing activities undertaken on the World Wide Web.

AN OVERVIEW OF TELECOMMUNICATIONS AND NETWORKING

Networking—the electronic linking of geographically dispersed devices—is critical for modern organizations. To participate effectively in the ongoing communications revolution, managers need to have a rudimentary understanding of the various telecommunications and networking options available to their organizations.

The prefix *tele-* simply means operating at a distance. Therefore **telecommunications** is communications at a distance. There are a number of other terms or abbreviations that are used almost interchangeably with telecommunications: data communications, datacom, teleprocessing, telecom, and networking. We prefer telecommunications because it is the broadest of these similar terms. It includes both voice (telephone) and data communications (including text and image). Teleprocessing means that the computer processing is taking place at a distance from where the data originates, which obviously requires telecommunications. Networking is the electronic linking required to accomplish telecommunications.

One might think that only a wire, or some other conduit, is needed for telecommunications, but it is much more complex than that! To begin a detailed consideration of telecommunications, first consider the primary functions performed by a telecommunications network, as listed in Table 4.1. The most obvious of these functions is the *transmission* of voice or data, or both, using the network and the underlying media. The *processing* involves making sure that an error-free message or data packet gets to the right destination. Subfunctions of processing include editorial, conversion, and routing. *Editorial* involves checking for errors and putting the communication into a standardized format, and *conversion* includes any necessary changes in the coding system or the transmission speed when moving from one device on the network to another. In networks where alternative paths are possible between the source and the destination of a communication (particularly WANs and the Internet), *routing*—choosing the most efficient path—is an important task. Closely related to the processing function is *network control*, which includes keeping track of the status of various elements of the system (e.g., which elements are busy or out of service) and, for some types of networks, checking each user periodically to see if the user has a communication to send. A not-so-obvious but critical function is the provision of an *interface* between the network and the user; hopefully this interface will make it easy and efficient for a manager or any other network user to send a communication. The next major section explores the variety of ways in which the functions listed in Table 4.1 can be delivered.

Table 4.1 Functions of a Telecommunications Network

Function	Brief Description
Transmission	Movement of voice and/or data using network and underlying media
Processing	Ensuring that error-free communication gets to right destination
Editorial	Checking for errors and putting communication into standardized format
Conversion	Changing coding system or speed when moving from one device to another
Routing	Choosing most efficient path when multiple paths are available
Network control	Keeping track of status of network elements and checking to see if communications are ready to be sent
Interface	Handling interactions between users and the network

KEY ELEMENTS OF TELECOMMUNICATIONS AND NETWORKING

We believe that you as a business manager need to understand certain key elements about telecommunications and networking to participate effectively in the communications revolution—to know what the options are for the business systems you need. These key elements include certain underlying basic ideas, such as analog versus digital signals and switched versus private lines; the variety of transmission media available; the topology (or possible arrangements) of networks; the various types of networks, including LANs and WANs; and the network protocols employed on these networks. This section will be rather technical and will involve a number of difficult concepts, so it might require some effort on your part to keep sight of the big picture of telecommunications.

Analog and Digital Signals

Perhaps the most basic idea about telecommunications is that the electronic signals sent on a network may be either analog or digital, depending on the type of network. Historically, the telephone network has been an **analog network**, with voice messages sent over the network by having some physical quantity (e.g., voltage) continuously vary as a function of time. This analog signal worked fine for voice transmission because it required the significant variations provided by an analog signal (corresponding to variations in human speech characteristics) and was insensitive to minor degradations in signal quality. On the other hand, computer data consist of a string of binary digits, or bits—a string of zeros and ones—to represent the desired characters. The form of this computer data does not mesh well with analog transmission. First, only two distinct signals—representing zeros and one—need to be sent, and second, the data are extremely sensitive to degradations in signal quality. Noise in a telephone line could easily cause a zero to be interpreted as a one or vice versa, and the entire message might become garbled. Because of this problem with noise, data cannot be sent directly over the analog telephone network.

Two solutions are possible to the problem of transmitting computer data. The original solution, and one that is still widely used, is to convert the data from digital form to analog form before sending it over the analog telephone network. This conversion is accomplished by a device called a **modem**, an abbreviation for a *mo*dulator/*dem*odulator (see Figure 4.1). Of course, the data must be reconverted from analog form back to digital form at the other end of the transmission line, which requires a second modem. The conversion (or modulation) carried out by the modem may be of different types. Figure 4.2 illustrates the use of amplitude modulation (two different voltage levels to represent 0 and 1), frequency modulation (two different frequencies of oscillations to represent 0 and 1), and phase modulation (the use of a phase shift to represent the change from a 0 to a 1 or vice versa). The use of modems and the analog telephone network is an acceptable way to transmit data for many applications, but it is severely limited in terms of transmission speeds and error rates.

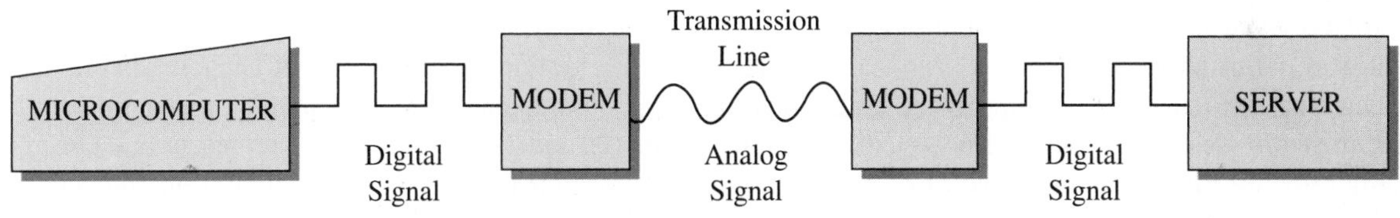

Figure 4.1 The Use of Modems in an Analog Network

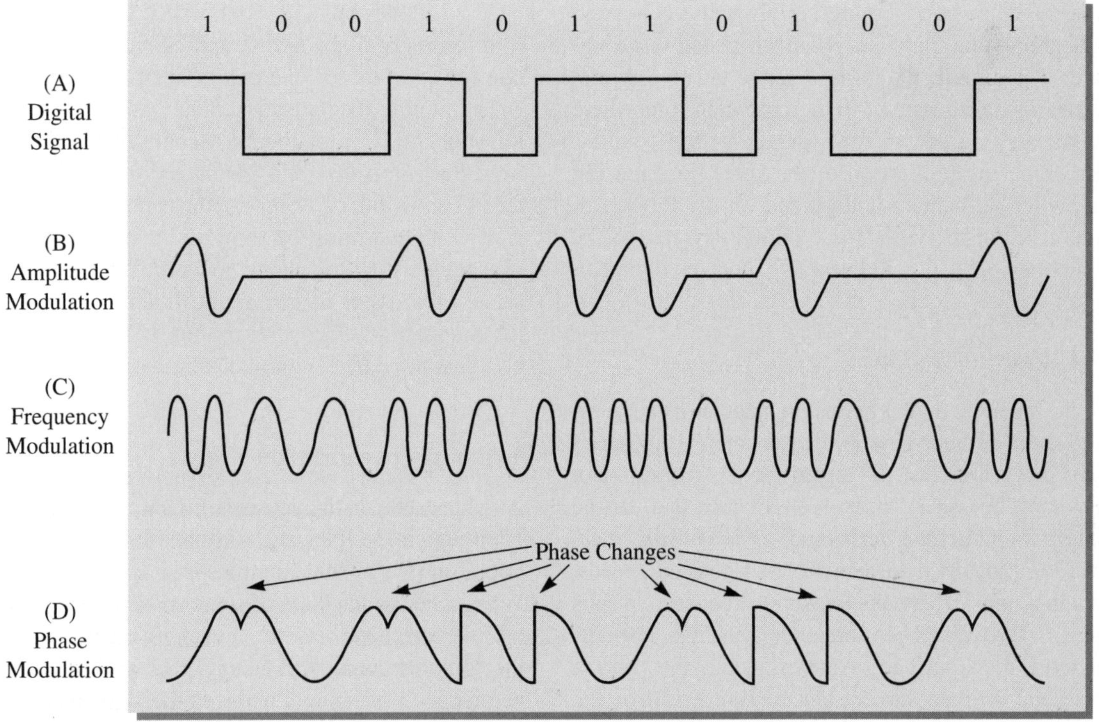

Figure 4.2 Digital and Analog Signals. (Adapted from Andrew S. Tanenbaum, *Computer Networks.* 4th ed. © 2003. Reprinted by permission of Prentice Hall, Inc., Upper Saddle River, New Jersey.)

The second and longer-term solution to the problem of transmitting computer data is to develop **digital networks** specifically designed to directly transmit zeros and ones, as in Figure 4.2 (A). Digital networks have the advantages of potentially lower error rates and higher transmission speeds, and modems are no longer necessary. Because of these advantages, the networks that have been specifically created for the purpose of linking computers and computer-related devices are digital. Furthermore, the telephone network is gradually being shifted from an analog to a digital network. Digital services such as ISDN and DSL (to be explored later in this chapter) are now available in many parts of the United States for users seeking higher-speed access to the Internet over the public telephone network.

This shift of the telephone network from analog to digital is due in part to the increasing volume of data being transmitted over the network, but there is also a significant advantage to transmitting voice signals over a digital network. Digital voice transmission can provide higher quality transmission—less noise on the line—just as digital recording provides higher fidelity CDs. Most of our telephone instruments are still analog devices, so the signal sent from the instrument to the nearest switching center (which may be operated either by the telephone company or your own organization) is still an analog signal. These telephone switches, however, are rapidly being converted from analog to digital switches. When the analog voice signal arrives at a digital switch, it is converted to a digital voice signal for transmission to a digital switch somewhere else, which may be across town or across the country. Thus, an increasing proportion of the voice transmission between switching centers is digitized. In the future our telephone instruments will also be digital devices, so the entire telephone network will eventually become digital.

Speed of Transmission

Whether the signal is digital or analog, another basic question is the speed of transmission. Please note that by speed we *do not* mean how fast the signal travels in terms like miles per hour, but rather the volume of data that can be transmitted per unit of time. Terms such as *bandwidth*, *baud*, and *Hertz* (*Hz*) are used to describe transmission speeds, whereas a measure such as bits transmitted per second (bits per second, or bps) would be more understandable. Happily, the three terms mentioned above are essentially the same as bits per second in many circumstances. **Bandwidth** is the difference between the highest and the lowest frequencies (cycles per second) that can be transmitted on a single medium, and it is a measure of the medium's capacity. (Sometimes it is necessary to divide the bandwidth into multiple channels, all carried on a single medium, to utilize the entire capacity. Thus, the transmission speeds we discuss are really data rates for the one or more channels carried on the single medium.) **Hertz** is simply cycles per second, and **baud** is the number of signals sent per second. If each cycle sends one signal that transmits exactly one bit of data, which is often the case, then all these terms are identical. To minimize any possible confusion, we will talk about bits per second, or bps, in this chapter. In information technology publications, *baud* was formerly used for relatively slow speeds such as 2,400 baud (2,400 bits per second) or 14,400 baud (14,400 bps), while *Hertz* (with an appropriate prefix) was used for higher speeds such as 500 megaHertz (500 million bps) or 2 gigaHertz (2 billion bps). More recently, the term *baud* has fallen into disfavor, but *Hertz* is still widely used in PC advertisements. For clarity, we will stick with *bps* in this chapter.

The notion of bandwidth, or capacity, is important for telecommunications. For example, approximately 50,000 bits (0s and 1s) are required to represent one page of data. To transmit this page using a 14,400 bps modem over an ordinary analog telephone line would take 3.5 seconds. If one were transmitting a large data file (such as customer accounts), that bandwidth or capacity would be unacceptably slow. On the other hand, to transmit this same page over a 128,000 bps (128 kbps) DSL line would take only four-tenths of a second. Graphics require approximately one million bits for one page. This would require a little over a minute for transmission at 14,400 bps over an analog telephone line, or about 8 seconds over a 128 kbps DSL line. Full-motion video transmission requires the enormous bandwidth of 12 million bps, and thus data compression techniques must be employed to be able to send video over the existing telephone network. The bandwidth determines what types of communication—voice, data, graphics, stop-frame video, full-motion video—can reasonably be transmitted over a particular medium.

Types of Transmission Lines

Another basic distinction is between private (or dedicated) communication lines and switched lines. The public telephone network, for example, is a switched-line system. When a communication of some sort (voice or data) is sent over the telephone network, the sender has no idea what route the communication will take. The telephone company's (or companies') computers make connections between switching centers to send the communication over the lines they deem appropriate, based on such factors as the length of the path, the amount of traffic on the various routes, and the capacity of the various routes. This switched-line system usually works fine for voice communications. Data communications, however, are more sensitive to the differences in line quality over different routes and to other local phenomena, such as electrical storms. Thus, a data communication sent from Minneapolis to Atlanta over the telephone network might be transmitted perfectly at 11 A.M., but another communication sent from Minneapolis to Atlanta 15 minutes later (a different connection) might be badly garbled because the communications were sent via different routes.

One way to reduce the error rate is through private lines. Most private lines are dedicated physical lines leased from a common-carrier company such as MCI, Sprint, or AT&T. A company might choose to lease a line between Minneapolis and Atlanta to ensure the quality of its data transmissions. Private lines also exist within a building or a campus. These are lines owned by the organization for the purpose of transmitting its own voice and data communications. Within-building or within-campus lines for computer telecommunications, for example, are usually private lines.

The last basic idea we wish to introduce is the difference among simplex, half-duplex, and full-duplex transmission. With **simplex transmission**, data can travel only in one direction. This one-way communication is rarely useful, but it might be employed from a monitoring device at a remote site (monitoring power consumption, for example) back to a computer. With **half-duplex transmission**, data can travel in both directions but not simultaneously. **Full-duplex transmission** permits data to travel in both directions at once, and, therefore, provides greater capacity, but it costs more than half-duplex lines. Ordinary telephone service is full-duplex transmission, allowing both parties to talk at once, while a Citizen's Band (CB) radio provides half-duplex transmission, allowing only one party to transmit at a time. Modems sometimes have a switch that lets the user choose between full-duplex and half-duplex operation, depending upon the type of transmission desired.

Transmission Media

A telecommunications network is made up of some physical medium (or media) over which communications are sent. Five primary media are in use today: twisted pair of wires, coaxial cable, wireless, satellite (which is a special form of wireless), and fiber-optic cable.

Twisted Pair When all uses are considered, the most common transmission medium is a **twisted pair** of wires. Most telephones are connected to the local telephone company office or the local private branch exchange (PBX) via a twisted pair. Similarly, many LANs have been implemented by using twisted pair wiring to connect the various microcomputers and related devices. A twisted pair consists of two insulated copper wires, typically about 1 millimeter thick, twisted together in a long helix. The purpose for the twisting is to reduce electrical interference from similar twisted pairs nearby. If many twisted pairs will run parallel for a significant distance—such as from a neighborhood to a telephone company office—it is common to bundle them together and enclose them in a protective sheath.

The transmission speeds attainable with twisted pairs vary considerably, depending upon such factors as the thickness of the wire and the distance traveled. On the analog voice telephone network, speeds from 14,400 to 56,000 bps are commonplace. When a digital service such as ISDN or DSL is used on the telephone network, speeds of 128,000 bps are typical, while inbound DSL speeds might be even higher, up to 1.544 million bps. Much higher speeds—16 million bps and more—can be obtained when twisted pairs are used in LANs. Multiple twisted pairs in a single cable can support speeds up to 100 million bps when used in a Fiber Distributed Data Interface (FDDI) or Fast Ethernet LAN, or even up to 1 billion bps (1 gbps) with Gigabit Ethernet (more on these LAN types later). The speeds of twisted pair and other media are summarized in Table 4.2.

Coaxial Cable **Coaxial cable**, or **coax** for short, is another common transmission medium. A coaxial cable consists of a heavy copper wire at the center, surrounded by insulating material. Around the insulating material is a cylindrical conductor, which is often a woven braided mesh. Then the cylindrical conductor is covered by an outer protective plastic covering. Figure 4.3 illustrates the construction of a coaxial cable.

Table 4.2 Telecommunications Transmission Speeds

Transmission Medium	Typical Speeds
Twisted pair—voice telephone	14.4 kbps–56 kbps
Twisted pair—digital telephone	128 kbps–1.544 mbps
Twisted pair—LAN	10 mbps–100 mbps
Coaxial cable	10 mbps–1 gbps
Wireless LAN	6 mbps–54 mbps
Microwave	50 kbps–100 mbps
Satellite (per transponder)	50 kbps–100 mbps
Fiber-optic cable	100 mbps–100 gbps

KEY: bps = bits per second
kbps = thousand bits per second, or kilo bps
mbps = million bits per second, or mega bps
gbps = billion bits per second, or giga bps

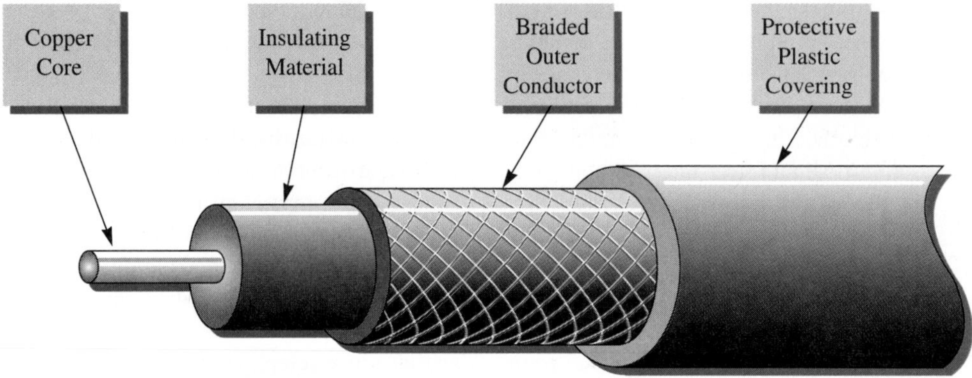

Figure 4.3 Construction of a Coaxial Cable

Because of its construction, coaxial cable provides a good combination of relatively high transmission speeds and low noise or interference. Two kinds of coaxial cable are in widespread use—**baseband coax**, which is used for digital transmission, and **broadband coax**, which was originally used for analog transmission but which is now used for digital transmission as well.

Baseband coax is simple to use and inexpensive to install, and the required interfaces to microcomputers or other devices are relatively inexpensive. Baseband offers a single digital transmission channel with data transmission rates ranging from 10 million bits per second (10 mbps) up to perhaps 1 billion bps (1 gbps), depending primarily on the distances involved (longer cables mean lower data rates). Baseband coax was widely used for LANs and for long-distance transmission within the telephone network, although much of this coax has now been replaced by fiber-optic cabling.

Broadband coax, which uses standard cable television cabling, was originally installed for analog transmission of television signals, but it increasingly employs digital transmission. A single broadband coax can be divided into multiple channels, so that a single cable can support simultaneous transmission of data, voice, and television. Broadband data transmission rates are similar to those for baseband coax, and high transmission speeds are possible over much longer distances than are feasible for baseband coax. Because of its multiple channels and additional capacity, broadband coax has been more enduring than baseband. Broadband coax is still widely used for cable television and LANs that span a significant area, often called metropolitan area networks.

Wireless Strictly speaking, wireless is not a transmission medium. **Wireless** is broadcast technology in which radio signals are sent out into the air. Wireless communication is used in a variety of circumstances, including cordless telephones, cellular telephones, wireless LANs, and microwave transmission of voice and data.

A **cordless telephone** is a portable device that may be used up to about 1,000 feet from its wired telephone base unit. This permits the user to carry the telephone to various rooms in a house or take it outdoors on the patio. By contrast, a **cellular telephone** (carried in a pocket, purse, or briefcase) may be used anywhere as long as it is within range—about 8 to 10 miles—of a cellular switching station. At present, these cellular switching stations are available in all metropolitan areas of the United States and most rural areas. The switching stations are low-powered transmitter/receivers that are connected to a cellular telephone switching office by means of conventional telephone lines or microwave technology. The switching office, which is computer-controlled, coordinates the calls for its service area and links the cellular system into the local and long-distance telephone network.

Wireless LANs are growing in popularity. They have the obvious advantage of being reasonably easy to plan and install. A wireless system provides networking where cable or wire installation would be extremely expensive or impractical, such as in an old building. A wireless LAN also permits users of mobile devices such as handheld or laptop computers to connect to the LAN (and thus the Internet) whenever they are within range of a wireless access point, such as in a coffee shop or an airport terminal. A wireless LAN is less secure than a wired LAN and more susceptible to interference, which might increase the error rate and force the wireless LAN to operate at a slower data rate. Most wireless LANs operate in the range of 6 to 11 million bps, with a few newer wireless LANs operating at speeds up to 54 mbps.

Microwave has been in widespread use for long-distance wireless communication for several decades. Microwave is line-of-sight transmission—there must be an unobstructed

WAL-MART PUSHES RFID

Wal-Mart has decided that it is time to get serious about the introduction of **radio frequency identification**, or **RFID**, as a successor to the now-familiar bar codes. Wal-Mart's Chief Information Officer Linda Dillman recently announced that the company will require its 100 top suppliers to begin using RFID for selected applications by January 2005. Wal-Mart's action will likely force other retailers to adopt RFID to remain competitive, and its wider use will bring down the costs, which is critical for RFID to be successful.

RFID tags, which are about the size of a postage stamp, combine tiny chips with an antenna. When a tag is placed on an item, it automatically radios its location to RFID readers on store shelves, checkout counters, loading bay doors, and possibly shopping carts. With RFID tags, inventory is taken automatically and continuously. RFID tags can cut costs by requiring fewer workers for scanning items; they also can provide more current and more accurate information to the entire supply chain. According to analyst Emme P. Kozloff, Wal-Mart could save $8.4 *billion* a year by 2007 by installing RFID in many of its operations.

For widespread RFID use to become a reality, however, costs must come down and other potential problems must be resolved. At present, tags run about 10 cents apiece, and RFID won't be feasible until this cost is under a penny. Wal-Mart and other retailers also have to worry about possible radio interference, and they have the difficult job of convincing consumers that the tags are not a threat to personal privacy. However, with Wal-Mart pushing it, RFID seems destined to play a significant role on the retail scene.

[Adapted from Khermouch and Green, 2003]

straight line between the microwave transmitter and the receiver. Because of the curvature of the Earth, microwave towers have to be built, typically about 25 to 50 miles apart, to relay signals over long distances from the originating transmitter to the final receiver. These requirements for towers, transmitters, and receivers suggest that microwave transmission is expensive, and it is, but long-distance microwave is less expensive than burying fiber-optic cable in a very long trench, particularly if the right of way for that trench has to be obtained. Microwave is widely used for long-distance telephone communication and, to a lesser extent, for corporate voice and data networks; transmission speeds up to 100 mbps are possible.

Other line-of-sight transmission methods exist in addition to microwave. For short distances (such as from one building to another), laser or infrared transmitters and receivers, mounted on the rooftops, are often an economical and easy way to transmit data.

Satellite A special variation of wireless transmission employs **satellite communication** to relay signals over very long distances. A communications satellite is simply a big microwave repeater in the sky; it contains one or more transponders that listen to a particular portion of the electromagnetic spectrum, amplify the incoming signals, and retransmit back to Earth. A modern satellite may have around 40 transponders, each of which can handle an 80 mbps data transmission, 1,250 digital voice channels of 64 kbps each, or other combinations of data channels and voice channels. Transmission via satellite is still line-of-sight transmission, so a communication would have to be relayed through several satellites to go halfway around the world (see Figure 4.4).

One interesting, but annoying, aspect of satellite transmission is the substantial delay in receiving the signal because of the large distances involved in transmitting up to the satellite

DR. PEPPER GOES WIRELESS

Dr. Pepper/Seven Up Inc., of Plano, Texas, is trying something new: monitoring the operation of its vending machines via wireless technology. Isochron Data Corp. is conducting the pilot test for Dr. Pepper. For the pilot, Isochron has installed a specialized microcomputer (hardware and software from VendCast) and a two-way paging device (from Motorola) in a dozen vending machines. The VendCast software collects inventory, sales, and "machine-health" data at each vending machine, and then, on a daily basis, the VendCast server at Isochron's network operations center polls each machine. A dome antenna atop the vending machine allows broadcast and reception via a narrowband personal communications services wireless network run by SkyTel Communications. The data are aggregated and stored at Isochron, and then—with the VendCast client software installed on their PCs—managers and sales personnel at Dr. Pepper can access the data via a secured Web site. Rick Harris, manager of channel research at Dr. Pepper, is excited about the business value of the data being collected, both for daily operations and in the potential for data mining (see Chapter 7). "Information like this is a great asset to have to consider new placements of vending machines, or locations where multivendor machines might be warranted, such as in front of a Wal-Mart or high-traffic supermarket." Harris indicates that a Dr. Pepper salesperson can use the data "to plan loading of trucks and truck routes. Ideally, he'd like to spend his time filling an 80 percent empty machine rather than one that's maybe only 30 percent depleted."

[Adapted from Lais, 2000]

BLUETOOTH IS HERE!

Harald Bluetooth was a tenth-century Viking king in Denmark. Now a new wireless technology named in his honor allows communication among a wide variety of devices, such as mobile telephones, desktop and notebook computers, palmtop computers, DVD players, and printers, eliminating cables and permitting communication where it used to be impossible. **Bluetooth** is short-range radio technology that has been built into a microchip, enabling data to be transmitted wirelessly at speeds of 1 million bits per second. The price for Bluetooth cards (including the microchip) is a bit steep—$100 for a 3Com Bluetooth PC Card and $129 for a Palm Bluetooth Card in late 2003—but the price is expected to drop as demand grows. The Bluetooth Special Interest Group's founding members were two leading mobile phone manufacturers, Ericsson and Nokia; two leading notebook computer vendors, IBM and Toshiba; and Intel, the leading producer of microprocessor chips. They have been joined by many other companies, including Agere, Microsoft, and Motorola as promoter members. The Bluetooth Special Interest Group has developed Bluetooth technology standards that are available free of royalties to any company that wishes to use them. Products using Bluetooth technology have to pass interoperability testing prior to release. Thus far, more than 1,000 Bluetooth products of all kinds are available for purchase, and Bluetooth support is embedded in leading operating systems such as Microsoft Windows XP, Apple Computer's Mac OS X, and Palm OS.

The possibilities are endless for the use of Bluetooth. By adding Bluetooth cards (containing the microchip) to a notebook computer and a palmtop, a business traveler is able to synchronize the data in a notebook computer and palmtop simply by placing both devices in the same room. Bluetooth can eliminate the need to use cables to connect the mouse, keyboard, and printer to a desktop computer. An array of Bluetooth-equipped appliances, such as a television set, a stove, a thermostat, and a home computer, can be controlled from a cellular phone—all from a remote location, if desired. The Bluetooth Special Interest Group has designed the microchips to include software controls and identity coding to ensure that only those units preset by their owners can communicate. As a specific example, Federal Express (FedEx) is using Bluetooth technology in the handheld computers—called the PowerPad—that all FedEx couriers will carry with them during pickup and delivery cycles each day to collect package tracking information, provide dispatch messages to couriers, communicate with dispatch centers, and exchange information with other devices such as printers and signature capture devices. Interest in Bluetooth is strong, and a new Frost & Sullivan research report indicates that shipments of Bluetooth devices will double in 2003, to 70 million units shipped. Watch out for the Viking king! Bluetooth is here!

[Adapted from Bluetooth Web site, 2003, and Clark, 2003]

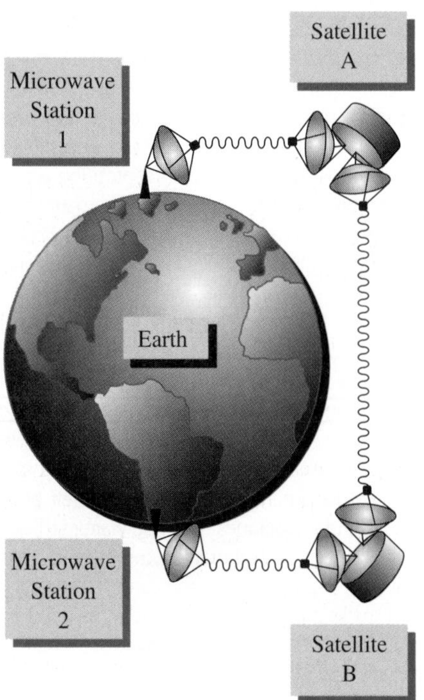

Figure 4.4 Satellite Communications

and then back down to Earth. This is particularly true for the geostationary earth orbit (GEO) satellites, which are positioned 22,000 miles above the equator such that they appear stationary relative to the Earth's surface. The minimum delay for GEO satellites is just under one-third of a second, which is an order of magnitude larger than on fiber-optic connections or Earth-bound microwave covering the same ground distance.

Interest in the use of satellites by corporations was heightened in the 1990s by the development of Ku-band satellite technology and the new very small aperture terminals (VSATs). VSATs are small satellite dishes with a 3-foot or smaller antenna, which are much less costly than their bigger cousins. Ku-band broadcasts at a higher frequency than the older C-band, and thus a smaller antenna can receive the signals. A typical VSAT data transmission rate up to a satellite is 19.2 kbps, with rates from the satellite to the VSAT of 512 kbps or more.

Another recent development is the interest in low earth orbit (LEO) satellites, which orbit at a distance of only 400 to 1,000 miles above the Earth—compared to 22,000 miles above the earth for GEO satellites. Because of their rapid motion, it takes a large number of LEO satellites for a complete system; on the other hand, because the satellites are close to the Earth, the ground stations need less power for communication and the round-trip delay is greatly reduced. Several years ago (1997) it appeared as though nearly 1,700 LEO satellites would be launched by 2006—more than 10 times the 150 commercial satellites in orbit at that time (Schine, et al., 1997)—but that is not happening. Let's see why.

The first major LEO project was Iridium, which launched 66 satellites to offer mobile telephony, paging, and data communication services. Investors in the $5 billion Iridium project included Motorola, Lockheed Martin, and Sprint; Motorola managed the project. The satellites were all flying and the Iridium system went live in 1998, with two-page advertisements splashed in major magazines such as *Business Week*. The Iridium customer would have an individual telephone number that would go with him or her anywhere on Earth, enabling the customer to make and receive calls from even the most remote places on the globe. Unfortunately, the prices to use the Iridium service were too high and it never caught on. Iridium filed for bankruptcy in 1999, and for a time it appeared likely that the satellites would be allowed to fall out of orbit. But Iridium got a second chance! A group of investors paid $25 million for the satellites and other assets of the original Iridium (quite a bargain!), and started satellite telephone service again in March 2001 (Ewalt, 2001). The old Iridium needed 1 million customers to break even; the new Iridium needed only tens of thousands. Many of these customers came from the U.S. military, which signed a deal for unlimited use for up to 20,000 soldiers. The British military is another customer, as are many news media representatives (Maney, 2003). The cost is still substantial for the reborn Iridium, but not nearly as high as before: The telephone, which weighs a little under a pound, costs about $1,500, and calls cost $1.50 per minute. In addition, there is a $60 activation fee and a $20 monthly subscription fee.

A competing LEO satellite system, Globalstar, has also had a troubled history. With its 48 LEO satellites, Globalstar does not provide complete coverage of the planet, but it does offer service in over 100 countries. The cost of Globalstar's Skyline 120 plan (in the United States and the Caribbean) is $50 per month for 120 included minutes (42 cents per minute), plus 75 cents per minute for additional minutes.

The plug was pulled on a third proposed LEO satellite system, named Teledesic, in October 2002. The original plan for Teledesic, which was sponsored by Craig McCaw (who built McCaw Cellular before selling it to AT&T), Bill Gates (Microsoft), and Boeing, was to create a 288-satellite network to provide low-cost, high-speed Internet access, corporate networking, and desktop videoconferencing. The number of satellites was later reduced to 30, each with a larger "footprint" on the Earth, but even that plan was cancelled in 2002 before any Teledesic satellites were launched. All these LEO satellite systems seemed like good ideas at the time they were planned, but the expenses involved were massive. Furthermore, the LEO systems took so long from concept to deployment that competing, less expensive technologies—such as cell phones, DSL, and cable—had made massive inroads into the potential market before the satellites were launched.

Fiber Optics The last and newest transmission medium—**fiber-optic** cabling—is a true medium, not a broadcast technology. Advances in optical technology have made it possible to transmit data by pulses of light through a thin fiber of glass or fused silica. A light pulse can signal a 1 bit, while the absence of a pulse signals a 0 bit. An optical transmission system requires three components: the light source, either an LED—a light-emitting diode—or a laser diode; the fiber-optic cable itself; and a detector (a photodiode). The light source emits light pulses when an electrical current is applied, and the detector generates an electrical current when it is hit by light.

Fiber optics are much faster than other media and require much less space because the fiber-optic cable is very small in diameter. Fiber-optic cables are more secure because the cables do not emit radiation and, thus, are very difficult to tap. They are also highly reliable because they are not affected by power-line surges, electromagnetic interference, or corrosive chemicals in the air. These benefits are leading telephone companies to use fiber optics in all their new long-distance telephone lines, lines connecting central office sites, and most of their new local lines from central office sites to terminuses located in subdivisions. (The advantages of speed and security are obvious; the size is important because many of the cable ducts already installed lack room for more coax, but can hold the thinner fiber-optic cabling.) The high cost of the required equipment and the difficulty of dealing with the tiny fibers make this an unattractive medium for most LANs, except when it is used as a backbone to connect multiple LANs and where very high speeds or high security needs exist.

Transmission speeds for fiber range up to 1 billion bits per second (1 giga bps or 1 gbps) for large diameter fiber (50 to 100 micron[1] core, which does not include any protective covering) to as high as 100 gbps for small diameter fiber (10 microns or less). The fact that the smaller diameter fiber has much larger capacity might be surprising, but light reflections are greatly reduced with a smaller fiber—the light ray bounces around less—permitting higher transmission speeds. The large diameter fiber is multimode, meaning that

[1]A micron is one-millionth of a meter or one-thousandth of a millimeter.

several light rays are traversing the fiber simultaneously, bouncing off the fiber walls, while the small diameter fiber is single mode, with a single light ray at a time propagated essentially in a straight line without bouncing. Single-mode fiber, unfortunately, requires higher-cost laser light sources and detectors than multimode fiber. In a recent development, the light ray sent through a single-mode fiber can be split into 80 or more different colors, each carrying its own stream of data. In this process, called dense wave division multiplexing, prisms are used to send these multiple colors down a single fiber. Today, much of the fiber being installed by telephone companies is 8-micron single-mode fiber with a transmission speed, using wave division multiplexing, of 10 gbps. The outside diameter (including protective covering) of this single-mode fiber is only 125 microns, which is about one-fiftieth the outside diameter of a typical coaxial cable. Thus, both the speed and size advantages of fiber optics are significant.

Topology of Networks

The starting point for understanding networks is to recognize that all telecommunications networks employ one or more of the transmission media discussed previously. But what do the networks look like in terms of their configuration or arrangement of devices and media? The technical term for this configuration is the topology of the network. There are five basic network topologies—bus, ring, star, hierarchical or tree, and mesh (see Figure 4.5)—plus an unlimited number of variations and combinations of these five basic forms.

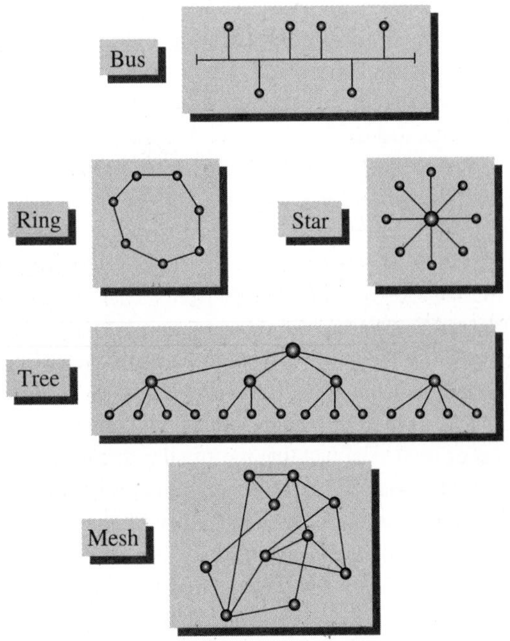

Figure 4.5 Network Topologies

Bus The simplest topology is the linear or **bus topology**. With the bus, all network devices share a single length of cable (coax, fiber, or twisted pair). One of the network devices is usually a file server with a large data storage capacity. An obvious advantage of the bus is the wiring simplicity. A disadvantage is its single-point failure characteristic. If the bus fails, nodes on either side of the failure point cannot communicate with one another.

Ring The **ring topology** is similar to the bus except that the two ends of the cable are connected. In this case, a single cable runs through every network device, including (usually) a file server. The wiring for the ring is slightly more complicated than for the bus, but the ring is not as susceptible to failure. In particular, a single failure in the ring still permits each network device to communicate with every other device.

Star The **star topology** has a mainframe or midrange computer, a file server (usually a microcomputer), or a networking device at its center, with cables (or media of some type) radiating from the central device to all the other network devices. This design is representative of many small-to-medium computer configurations, with all workstations and peripherals attached to the single midrange computer. It is also encountered in LANs. Advantages of the star include ease of identifying cable failure, because each device has its own cable; ease of installation for each device, which must only be connected to the central device; and low cost for small networks where all the devices are close together. The star's primary disadvantage is that if the central device fails, the whole network fails. A cost disadvantage might also be encountered if the network grows, for a separate cable must be run to each individual device, even if several devices are close together but far from the central device.

Tree The fourth basic topology is the **tree**, or hierarchical. This topology is sometimes called a hierarchical star, because with some rearrangement (spreading the branches out around the central device), it looks like an extension of the star. The configuration of most large and very large computer networks is a tree, with the mainframe at the top of the tree connected (through data channels) to terminal controllers such as a multiplexer[2] and perhaps to other

[2]A multiplexer is a device, usually located at a site remote from the mainframe or central device, whose function is to merge ("multiplex") the data streams from multiple low-speed input devices, such as terminals and microcomputers, so that the full capacity of the transmission line to the central device is utilized.

smaller computers. Then these terminal controllers, or smaller computers, are, in turn, connected to other devices such as terminals, microcomputers, and printers. Thus, the tree gets "bushy" as one traverses it from top to bottom.

The tree has the same primary disadvantage as the star. If the central device fails, the entire network goes down. On the other hand, the tree arrangement possesses a great deal of flexibility. The cost disadvantage of the star might not appear when devices are added to the network, for the use of intermediate devices (multiplexers, small computers) removes the necessity of connecting every device directly to the center.

Mesh In a **mesh topology** most devices are connected to two, three, or more other devices in a seemingly irregular pattern that resembles a woven net, or a mesh. A complete mesh would have every device connected to every other device, but this is seldom done because of the cost. The public telephone network is an example of a mesh topology; another example is the system of networks that makes up the Internet.

The ramifications of a failure in the mesh depend upon the alternative paths or routes available in the vicinity of the failure. In a complex mesh, like the telephone network, a failure is likely to have little impact, except on the devices directly involved.

More Complex Networks Now the fun begins, because the previous five network topologies can be combined and modified in a bewildering assortment of networks. For example, it is quite common to attach multiple bus or ring LANs to the tree mainframe computer network. Two ring LANs may be attached via a fiber-optic cable, which is in effect a very simple bus network.

National and international networks are much more complex than those we have considered thus far, because the designers have intentionally built in a significant amount of redundancy. In this way, if one transmission line goes out, there are alternative routes to almost every node or device on the network. As an example, the **vBNS+** network (originally the very high-performance Backbone Network Service, or vBNS) operated by MCI is shown in Figure 4.6. vBNS+, which was developed through a cooperative agreement between MCI and the National Science Foundation (NSF), links NSF-supported supercomputer centers (labeled on Figure 4.6) and provides points of presence (PoPs) where other users (including both researchers and commercial users) may link into vBNS+ from the Internet. vBNS+ employs a dual backbone topology based upon rings connecting the east and west coasts, with the addition of a link from Chicago to Memphis, a loop up to Seattle, extra links in the northeastern United States, and spurs going off the ring to other sites. As another example, the long-distance telephone network is a mesh topology, with numerous paths possible to connect most metropolitan areas.

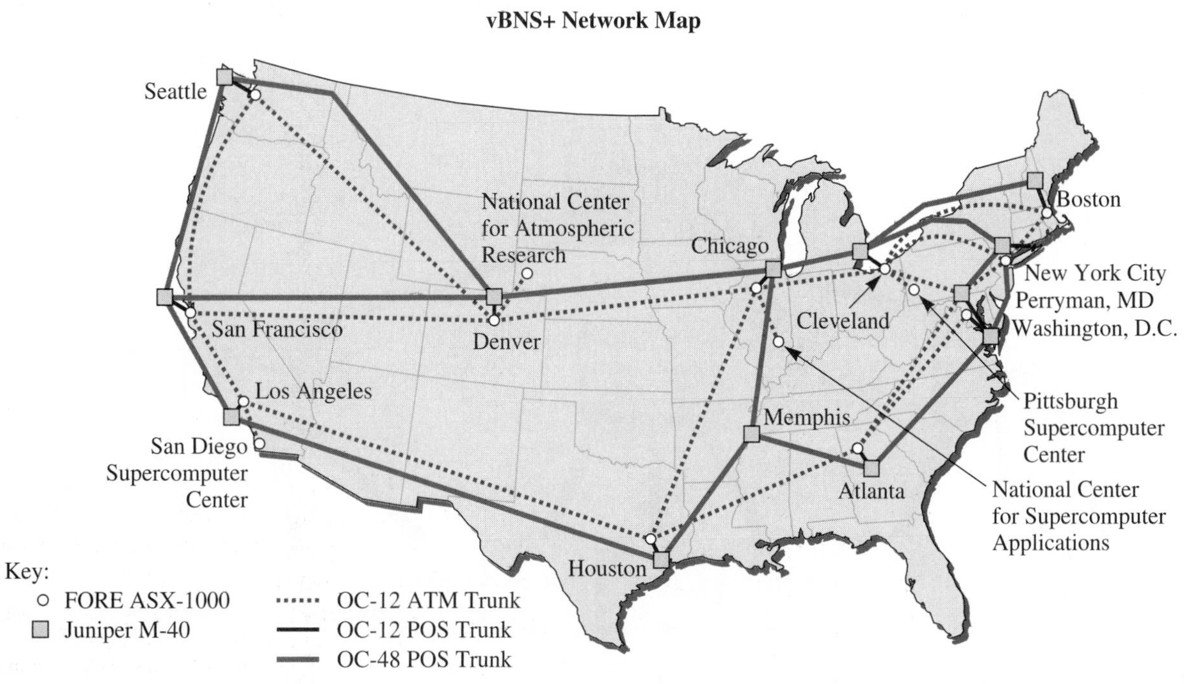

Figure 4.6 vBNS+ Network Map

Types of Networks

Thus far we have considered two key elements of telecommunications networks: the transmission media used to send the communications and the arrangement or topology of the networks. Now we turn to the categorization of networks into basic types. Please note that the categories employed here are somewhat arbitrary—but we believe extremely useful—and might differ from those used in other references. The types of networks to be described include computer telecommunications networks, private branch exchange (PBX) networks, local area networks (LANs), backbone networks, wide area networks (WANs), the Internet, and Internet2.

Computer Telecommunications Networks It is almost easier to describe this initial type of network by what it is not. It is not a PBX network, a LAN, or a WAN. What we are calling a **computer telecommunications network** is the network emanating from a single medium, large, or very large computer, or a group of closely linked computers. This type of network usually is arranged as a tree (see Figure 4.5) with coaxial cable and twisted pair as the media. Until the early 1980s, this was usually the only type of network (except for the telephone network) operated by an organization that did business in one building or a group of adjacent buildings (a campus). In many organizations even today the predominant communication with the central computer is through the computer telecommunications network. This type of network is controlled by the central computer, with all other devices (e.g., terminals, microcomputers, and printers) operating as subordinates or "slaves" on the network. IBM's mainframe architecture was originally based on this type of network, although LANs and other network types may now be linked to a mainframe or large computer.

This is not a bad arrangement, but it puts a tremendous communications control burden on the central computer. For this reason it is quite common to add a front-end processor or communications controller to the network—between the central computer and the rest of the network—to offload the communications work from the central computer (see Figure 4.7). A front-end processor or communications controller is another computer with specially designed hardware and software to handle all aspects of telecommunications, including error control, editing, controlling, routing, and speed and signal conversion.

PBX Networks **Private branch exchanges**, or **PBXs**, have been around for many years, but today's digital PBXs have extensive capabilities not possessed by their

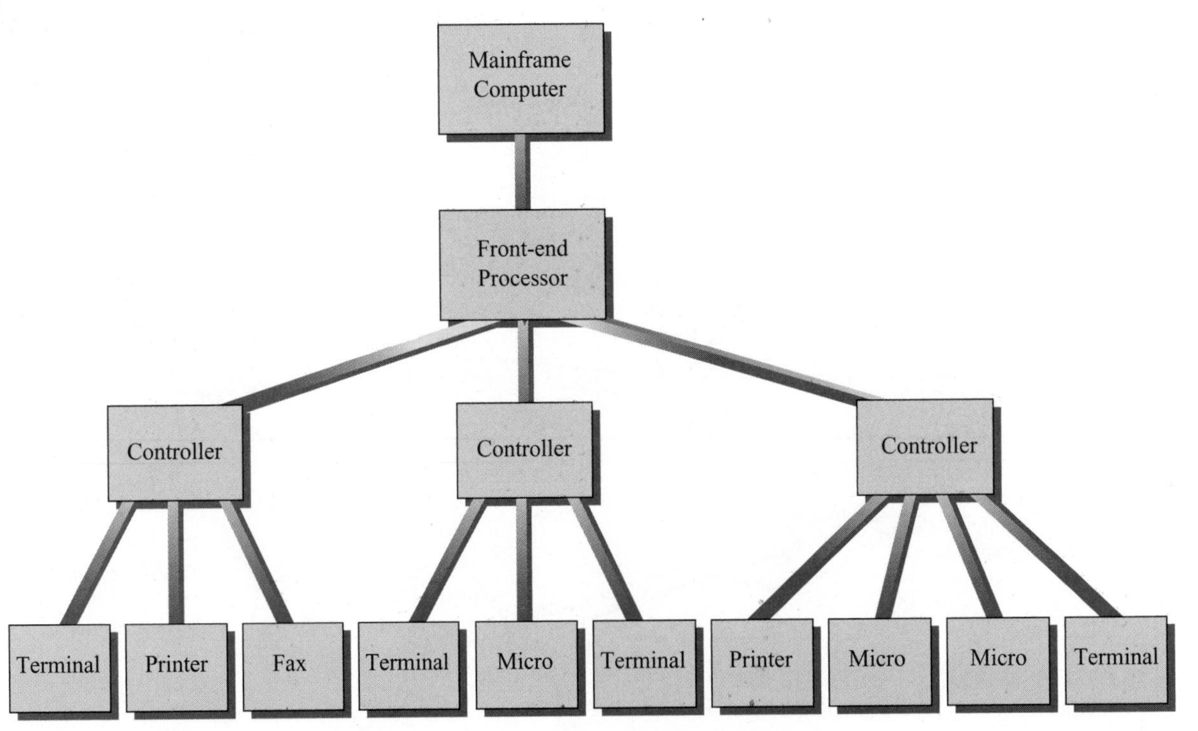

Figure 4.7 Computer Telecommunications Network

predecessors. The initial PBXs were switchboards run by human operators to operate an internal telephone system within an organization. Later PBXs worked in the same way except that electromechanical relays performed the switching rather than human operators. Today's digital PBX consists of a digital switch operated by a built-in computer, and the PBX has the capability of simultaneously handling communications with internal analog telephones, digital microcomputers and terminals, mainframe computers, and the external telephone network. The newest PBXs are IP-enabled (Internet Protocol-enabled), meaning that they can handle the new IP digital telephones running over wiring that was formerly reserved for data communications. IP telephony is sometimes referred to as voice-over-IP telephony. Figure 4.8 provides a schematic representation of a PBX.

It is obvious from Figure 4.8 that a PBX can serve as the central device in a star or a tree network. The media used are typically some combination of coax, twisted pair, and fiber (if high speeds are essential). If a mainframe computer is attached to the PBX, the PBX can function as the front-end processor for the mainframe. In terms of the telephone network, the PBX translates analog telephone signals to digital form before sending them over the digital network. Except for telephone instruments, all the devices shown in Figure 4.8 are digital, including the ISDN devices to be discussed later.

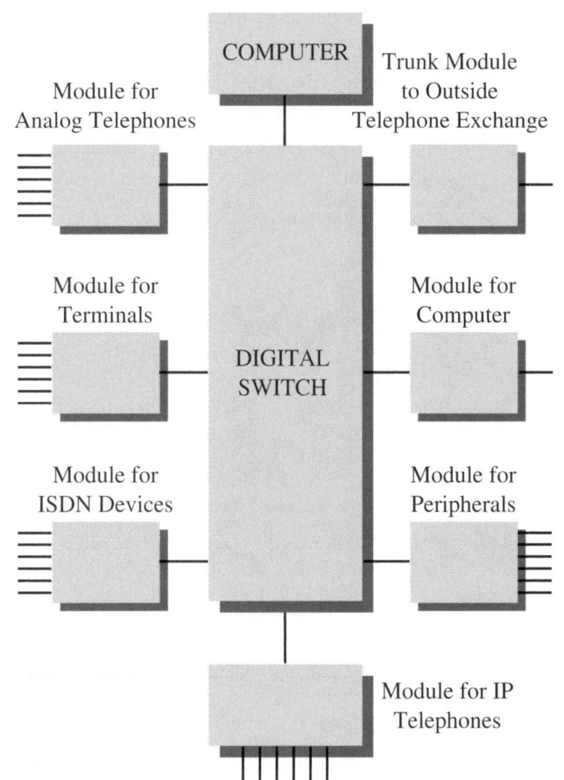

Figure 4.8 Schematic Representation of a PBX

A PBX has several advantages. It can connect all, not just some, of the telecommunications devices in a building or campus; it can use existing telephone wiring, which is a major advantage; it can carry voice and data over the same network; it can connect in a transparent way to the external telephone network; and it has a very high potential throughput rate. On the negative side, the maximum speed for a single channel (as distinct from overall throughput) is fast enough for telephone and most terminal traffic but painfully slow for shipping a large computer file from the mainframe to a remote server. PBXs are also complex and expensive pieces of equipment.

Local Area Networks A **local area network (LAN)** is first and foremost a *local* network—it is completely owned by a single organization and generally operates within an area no more than 2 or 3 miles in diameter. LANs are data networks that generally have a high data rate of several million bps or more.

A LAN differs from a computer telecommunications network in that a LAN contains a number of intelligent devices (usually microcomputers) capable of data processing rather than being built around a central computer that controls all processing. In other words, a LAN is based on a peer-to-peer relationship, rather than a master-subordinate relationship. A LAN differs from a PBX network in that a LAN handles only data[3], is not part of the telephone system, and requires new wiring. But a LAN does have a great deal in common with a PBX network in that both are aimed at establishing communication between a variety of devices in order to share data and resources and to facilitate office or factory automation. Thus, PBXs and LANs are often seen as competing technologies.

LANs exist in a variety of topologies, but four of these—for which standards have been developed by the Institute for Electrical and Electronic Engineers (IEEE) and subsequently adopted by both national and international standards organizations—are clearly dominant today. These four LAN standards are officially designated as IEEE 802.3 (contention bus design), IEEE 802.4 (token bus design), IEEE 802.5 (token ring design), and IEEE 802.11, including 802.11a, 802.11b, and 802.11g (wireless design).

Wired Local Area Networks. The **contention bus** design was originally developed by Xerox and subsequently adopted by Digital Equipment Corporation (now part of

[3]With the growth of IP telephony, this statement is not strictly true in all instances. IP telephony, based on the Internet Protocol (to be discussed later in this chapter), sends voice over the same networks used for data, and that network may include a LAN.

Hewlett-Packard) and Novell, among others. This design is usually referred to as **Ethernet**, named after the original Xerox version of the design. The contention bus is obviously a bus topology (see Figure 4.5), usually implemented using coaxial cable or twisted pair wiring. Communication on an Ethernet LAN is usually half-duplex—that is, communication in both directions is possible, but not simultaneously. The interesting feature of this design is its contention aspect—all devices must contend for the use of the cable.

With Ethernet, devices listen to the cable to pick off communications intended for the particular device and determine if the cable is busy. If the cable is idle, any device may transmit a message. Most of the time this works fine, but what happens if two devices start to transmit at the same time? A collision occurs and the messages become garbled. The devices must recognize that this collision has occurred, stop transmitting, wait a random period of time, and try again. This method of operation is called a **CSMA/CD protocol**, an abbreviation for carrier sense multiple access with collision detection. In theory, collisions might continue to occur and thus there is no upper bound on the time a device might wait to send a message. In practice, a contention bus design is simple to implement and works very well as long as traffic on the network is light or moderate (and thus there are few collisions).

The original Ethernet design, now called **shared Ethernet**, employs a contention *bus* as its logical topology, but it is usually implemented as a physical *star* arrangement (see Figure 4.9). The usual way of creating a shared Ethernet LAN is to plug the cables from all the devices on the LAN into a **hub**, which is a junction box containing up to 24 ports into which cables can be plugged. Embedded inside the hub is a linear bus connecting all the ports. Thus, shared Ethernet operates as a logical bus but a physical star.

Switched Ethernet is a newer variation of Ethernet providing better performance at a higher price. The design is similar to shared Ethernet, but a switch is substituted for the hub and the LAN operates as a logical star as well as a physical star. The switch is smarter than a hub—rather than passing all communications through to all devices on the LAN, which is what a hub does, the switch establishes separate point-to-point circuits to each device and then forwards communications only to the appropriate device. This switched approach dramatically improves LAN performance because each device has its own dedicated circuit, rather than sharing a single circuit with all devices on the network. Of course, a switch is considerably more expensive than a simple hub.

The **token bus** design employs a bus topology with coaxial cable or twisted pair wiring, but it does not rely on contention. Instead, a single token (a special communication or message) is passed around the bus to all devices in a specified order, and a device can only transmit when it has the token. Therefore, a microcomputer must wait until it receives the token before transmitting a message; when the message is sent, the device sends the token on to the next device. After some deterministic period of time based on messages sent by other devices, the device will receive the token again.

The token bus design is central to the **Manufacturing Automation Protocol (MAP)**, which was developed by General Motors and adopted by many manufacturers. MAP is a factory automation protocol (or set of standards)

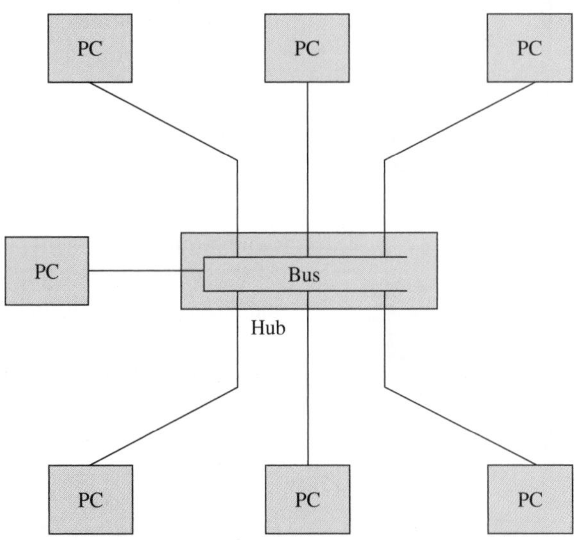

Figure 4.9 Shared Ethernet Topology: Logical Bus, Physical Star

designed to connect robots and other machines on the assembly line by a LAN. In designing MAP, General Motors did not believe it could rely on a contention-based LAN with a probabilistic delay time before a message could be sent. An automobile assembly line moves at a fixed rate, and it cannot be held up because a robot has not received the appropriate message from the LAN. Therefore, General Motors and many other manufacturers have opted for the deterministic token bus LAN design.

The third LAN standard is the **token ring**, originally developed by IBM, which combines a ring topology (see Figure 4.5) with the use of a token as described for the token bus. A device attached to the ring must seize the token and remove it from the ring before transmitting a message; when the device has completed transmitting, it releases the token back into the ring. Thus, collisions can never occur, and the maximum delay time before any station can transmit is deterministic. The usual implementation of a token ring involves the use of a wire center into which cables from individual devices are plugged, creating a physical star but a logical ring.

All three types of wired LAN designs are widely used today. Token bus dominates the manufacturing scene, and Ethernet leads token ring by a wide and growing margin in office applications. But the hottest type of LAN in the early twenty-first century is the wireless LAN, to which we will now turn.

Wireless Local Area Networks. **Wireless LANs**, commonly known as **Wi-Fi** (short for wireless fidelity), represent only a small proportion of LANs in operation today, but a rapidly growing proportion. Wi-Fi technology has obvious advantages for people on the move who need access to the Internet in airports, restaurants, and hotels. Wi-Fi is also gaining acceptance as a home or neighborhood network (see the sidebar entitled "Making Wi-Fi Work"), permitting an assortment of laptop and desktop computers to share a single broadband access point to the Internet. Wireless LANs are also moving into the corporate and commercial world, especially in older buildings and confined spaces where it would be difficult or impossible to establish a wired LAN or where mobility is paramount. Even in newer buildings, wireless LANs are often being employed as *overlay networks.* In such cases Wi-Fi is installed in addition to wired LANs so that employees can easily move their laptops from office to office and can connect to the network in places such as lunchrooms, hallways, and patios (Dennis, 2002, p. 266).

Today's wireless LANs use one of four standards incorporated in the IEEE 802.11 family of specifications. All four standards use the shared Ethernet design (logical bus, physical star; see Figure 4.10) and the **CSMA/CA protocol**, which is an abbreviation for carrier sense multiple access with collision avoidance. CSMA/CA is quite similar to CSMA/CD used in traditional Ethernet, but it makes greater efforts to avoid collisions. In one approach to collision avoidance, any computer wishing to transmit a message

MAKING WI-FI WORK

Millions of people are setting up wireless networks. Here's how it's done, using a network with a PC and one or more laptops.

1. Get a high-speed net connection. You can subscribe to a cable-modem or DSL phone service for about $40 a month. The modem is usually free, and you can do the installation yourself in a few minutes.
2. Buy a Wi-Fi access point. The size of a clock radio, this box includes an Internet router and a two-way Wi-Fi radio. It costs $100 to $250.
3. Connect access point to modem and desktop. Plug cables into the back of the modem and PC. Install the software on the PC and follow the directions.
4. Buy a wireless antenna for each laptop. These credit-card devices run $30 to $50.
5. Install antenna and antenna software on laptop. Install the antenna before you install the software, or it won't work properly.
6. Congratulations! Your network is up and running. Test the signal strength by wandering around with the laptop.
7. Whoops! The signal is weak. Most people find reception in their homes is hampered by walls and other obstructions. Signal strength will remain stronger if you move upstairs or downstairs just above or below the access point.
8. Don't panic! You have options. You can buy a signal booster, which attaches to the router and costs about $100. You can sometimes boost the strength of the router's signal online, with help from the manufacturer's service department.
9. Telecommuting? O.K., panic! If you work at home with a laptop that has been configured for the office, you may need to reconfigure it with help of your employer.
10. Expand! Now that you have connected the desktop and laptop to your network, you can buy another antenna to include your TiVo, digital home theater, or gaming console in the network.

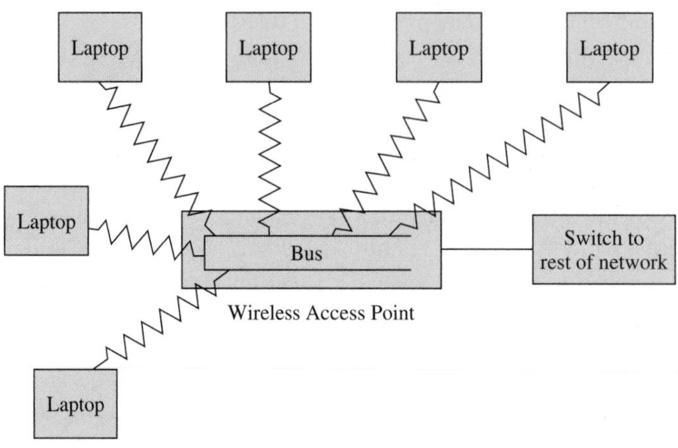

Figure 4.10 Wireless Local Area Network Topology

first sends a "request to transmit" to the wireless access point. If no other computer is transmitting, the wireless access point responds by sending a "clear to transmit" signal to all computers on the wireless LAN, specifying the amount of time for which the network is reserved for the requesting computer.

In order to establish a wireless LAN, a wireless **network interface card (NIC)** must be installed in each computer. The wireless NIC was referred to as an antenna in the "Making Wi-Fi Work" sidebar, but it is really more than that—the NIC is a short-range radio transceiver that can send and receive radio signals. At the heart of a wireless LAN is the **wireless access point**, or **WAP**, which is a radio transceiver that plays the same role as a hub in a wired Ethernet LAN. The WAP receives the signals of all computers within its range and repeats them to ensure that all other computers within the range can hear them; it also forwards all messages for recipients not on this wireless LAN via the wired network.

The most popular wireless LAN standard in the early twenty-first century is 802.11b, which operates in the 2.4 GHz (gigaHertz) band at data rates of 5.5 to 11 mbps. The range of 802.11b LANs is typically 300 to 500 feet, which is greater than that of 802.11a, the next most widely used wireless LAN standard. The 802.11a standard operates in the 5.8 GHz band at data rates up to 54 mbps. The problem with 802.11a is that the range is only about 150 feet; in fact, the 54 mbps data rate can be sustained reliably only within about 50 feet of the WAP. The newest standard is 802.11g, which uses a different form of multiplexing in the 2.4 GHz band to achieve the same range as 802.11b (300 to 500 feet) with data rates up to the 54 mbps of 802.11a. Currently 802.11g products are more expensive than those

WIRELESS MOOCHERS

Wireless Internet access—known by the term Wi-Fi, for wireless fidelity—is quickly gaining popularity among people seeking high-speed Internet connections when they are away from their home or office. The signal from a typical wireless access point (WAP) only extends for about 300 feet in any direction, so the user must find a "hot spot" to be able to access the Internet while on the road. Sometimes hot spots are available for free or for a small fee. For instance, some Schlotzsky's delicatessens, Omni Hotels, and Hampton Inns offer hot spots for free; some McDonald's restaurants, Starbucks coffee shops, and Borders bookstores offer hot spots for a fee. By the end of 2003, Gartner Group estimates that there will be 29,000 Wi-Fi hot spots in North America, ranging from retail establishments to entire city neighborhoods.

The hot spots work; they do attract customers—and moochers! The manager of a Hampton Inn in Michigan reports seeing local salespeople, who were not staying in the hotel, lurking in the lobby or sitting in cars as they checked their e-mail or surfed the Web using the hotel's wireless network. A homeowner in Oregon confirms that a digital moocher was parked at the end of his driveway using a hot spot that the homeowner had set up to share with his neighbors. One executive could not get a room at a Wyndham Hotel offering wireless access, so he checked into another hotel without Wi-Fi and ended up driving back to the Wyndham several times to check his e-mail in the lobby. Another executive sat outside a closed Starbucks after midnight, in frigid temperatures, to check his e-mail. Wi-Fi is growing in popularity, and enthusiasts will go to great lengths to find hot spots!

[Adapted from Wingfield, 2003]

for 802.11b, but 802.11g's higher data rate should make it an attractive alternative for new wireless LANs.

Higher-Speed Wired Local Area Networks. LAN technology continues to advance in the first decade of the twenty-first century. The top speed of a traditional Ethernet LAN is 10 mbps, but **Fast Ethernet,** operating at 100 mbps, is being used in many newer LANs (and backbone networks, to be discussed in the next section) where greater capacity is needed. Fast Ethernet uses the same CSMA/CD architecture and the same wiring as traditional Ethernet. The most popular implementations of Fast Ethernet are *100 Base-T*, which runs at 100 mbps over category 5 twisted-pair cabling (four pairs of wires in each cable), and *100 Base-F*, which runs at 100 mbps over multimode fiber-optic cable (usually two strands of fiber joined in one cable). Although the wiring for Fast Ethernet could handle full-duplex communication, in most cases only half-duplex is used.

Even newer and faster than Fast Ethernet is **Gigabit Ethernet**, with speeds of 1 billion bits per second and higher. The fastest Ethernet in general use is 1-gbps Ethernet, commonly called *1 GbE*. 1 GbE running over twisted-pair cables is called *1000 Base-T*; amazingly, 1000 Base-T still runs over one category 5 cable (four pairs of wires) by using an ingenious procedure to send streams of bits in parallel. There are two versions of 1 GbE when running over fiber-optic cabling: *1000 Base-SX* uses multimode fiber, and *1000 Base-LX* uses either multimode fiber or single-mode fiber depending on the distances involved (up to 1,800 feet with multimode fiber or over 16,000 feet with single-mode fiber). 1 GbE is often used in backbone networks, to be discussed in the next section. 10-gbps Ethernet is currently under development, and several researchers have proposed 40-gbps Ethernet. 10-gbps Ethernet, called *10 GbE*, will run over multimode fiber for short distances and single-mode fiber for longer distances, using full-duplex communication between only two computers at a time. Ethernet speeds keep going up, suggesting that Ethernet will continue to be the preferred networking approach for high-speed LANs and backbone networks for the foreseeable future.

Just as Fast Ethernet is sort of a traditional Ethernet grown up, so is **Fiber Distributed Data Interface (FDDI)** related to a traditional token ring LAN. A traditional token ring LAN operates at a maximum speed of 16 mbps. By contrast, FDDI employs a token ring architecture to deliver 100 mbps. FDDI was originally developed to operate with fiber-optic cable (hence the name) but now operates on either copper media (usually category 5 twisted-pair cable) or fiber-optic cabling. FDDI is actually a dual-ring technology, with each ring running in the opposite direction to improve fault recovery. With FDDI, the primary ring is active until a fault is detected, at which time the secondary ring is activated. Although still in use today, the future of FDDI seems limited because of advances in Ethernet technology.

Backbone Networks

Backbone networks are the in-between networks—the middle distance networks that interconnect LANs in a single organization with each other and with the organization's WAN and the Internet. For example, the corporate headquarters of a large firm might have multiple buildings spread out over several city blocks. Each floor of a large building might have its own LAN, or a LAN might cover an entire smaller building. All these LANs must be interconnected to gain the benefits of networking—enhanced communications, the sharing of resources and data, and distributed data processing. In addition, the LANs must also be connected to the company's WAN and, in most cases, to the Internet. A backbone network is the key to internetworking (see Figure 4.11).

The technology involved in backbone networks is essentially the same as that described for LANs, but at the high end. The medium employed is usually either fiber-optic cabling or twisted-pair cabling, providing a high data transmission rate, often 100 mbps or more. The topology may be a ring (FDDI) or a bus (Fast Ethernet or Gigabit Ethernet) or some combination. The only new terminology we need to introduce relates to the hardware devices that connect network pieces together or connect other networks to the backbone network.

We have already introduced the hub, the switch, and the wireless access point. A hub, we know, is a simple device into which cables from computers are plugged; it may also be used to connect one section of a LAN to another. Hubs forward every message they receive to all devices or sections of the LAN attached to it, whether or not they need to go there. A **wireless access point** is the central device in a wireless LAN that connects the LAN to other networks. A **bridge** connects two LANs, or LAN segments, when the LANs use the same protocols, or set of rules (more on this later); a bridge is smart enough to forward only messages that need to go to the other LAN. A **router**, or a **gateway** (a sophisticated router), connects two or more LANs and forwards only messages that need to be forwarded but may connect LANs that use different protocols. For example, a gateway is used to connect an organization's backbone network to the Internet. A **switch** connects more than two LANs, or LAN segments, that use the same protocols. Switches are very useful to connect several low speed LANs (e.g., a dozen Ethernet LANs running at 10 mbps) into a

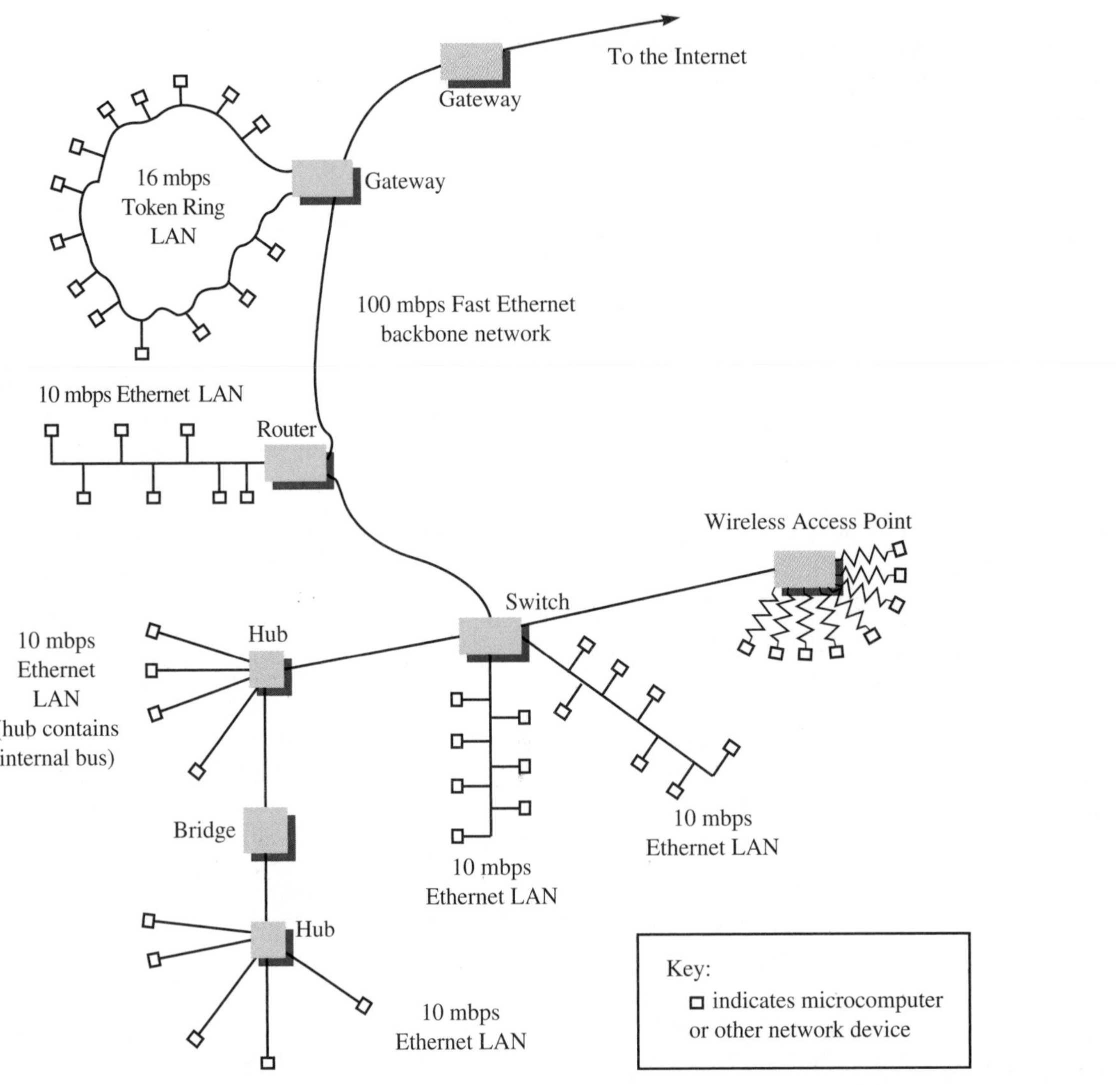

Figure 4.11 Sample Backbone Network

single 100 mbps backbone network (running Fast Ethernet). In this case the switch operates very much like a multiplexer. The top vendors of these hardware devices include Cisco, 3Com, and Lucent Technologies.

Wide Area Networks Today's more complex, more widely dispersed organizations need **wide area networks (WANs)**, also called long-haul networks, to communicate both voice and data across their far-flung operations. A WAN differs from a LAN in that a WAN spans much greater distances (often entire countries or even the globe), has slower data rates (usually below 622 mbps), and is usually owned by several organizations (including both common carriers and the user organization). In addition, a WAN employs point-to-point transmission (except for satellites), whereas a LAN uses a multiaccess channel (such as the bus and ring). We will note some exceptions, but for the most part WANs rely on the public telephone network.

DDD and WATS. The easiest way to set up a WAN is to rely on ordinary public telephone service. **Direct Distance Dialing (DDD)** is available through the local telephone company and a long-distance carrier—AT&T, MCI, Sprint, or others—and can be used for voice and data communications between any two spots served by the telephone network. Of course, the speed for data transmission is quite limited (up to 56 kbps, depending upon the modem), data error rates are relatively high, and the cost per hour is very expensive. **Wide Area Telephone Service (WATS)** is also available, in which the organization pays a monthly fee for (typically) unlimited long-distance telephone service using the ordinary voice circuits. WATS has the same advantages and disadvantages as DDD. However, the cost per hour of WATS is somewhat less than DDD, but the customer pays for it whether it is used or not, while DDD is only paid for when it is used. DDD is appropriate for intermittent, limited-volume data transmission at relatively slow speeds, while WATS is used for more nearly continuous, somewhat larger volumes of data to be transmitted at relatively slow speeds.

Leased Lines. Another, sometimes attractive, alternative is to lease dedicated communications lines from AT&T or another carrier. If a manufacturing company has three plants geographically separated from corporate headquarters (where the mainframe computer or large servers are located), it might make sense to lease lines to connect each of the three plants to headquarters. These leased lines are generally coaxial cables, microwave, or fiber-optic cables of very high capacity, and they are less prone to data errors than ordinary voice lines. The leased lines are expensive, ranging from hundreds of dollars per month for distances of a few miles up to tens of thousands of dollars per month for cross-country lines.

The most common leased lines operate at a data transmission rate of 1.544 mbps and are referred to as **T-1 lines**. In order to effectively use this high data transmission rate, organizations must employ multiplexers at each end of a T-1 line to combine (or separate) a number of data streams that are, individually, much less than 1.544 mbps.

Leased lines with capacities higher than T-1 are also available. Four T-1 lines are combined to create a T-2 trunk, with a capacity of 6.312 mbps, but T-2 trunks have largely been bypassed in favor of T-3 trunks (consisting of seven T-2s), with a data transmission capacity of nearly 45 mbps. T-3 links are available between major cities, although the costs are much higher than for T-1 lines. T-4 trunks also exist (made up of six T-3s), with a huge capacity of 274 mbps.

The newest and highest capacity leased lines (and also the most expensive) are fiber-optic transmission lines, or SONET lines. **SONET**, which is an abbreviation for **Synchronous Optical Network**, is an American National Standards Institute (ANSI) approved standard for connecting fiber-optic transmission systems. Data transmission rates for SONET lines are shown in Table 4.3. Note that the slowest SONET transmission rate (OC-1) of nearly 52 mbps is faster than the T-3 rate of 45 mbps. All the links in the vBNS+ network shown in Figure 4.6 are SONET lines, with the faster of the two dual backbones operating at OC-48 (2.488 gbps) and the slower dual backbone and all other links operating at OC-12 (622 mbps). vBNS+ is truly a high-performance, high-bandwidth network.

Table 4.3 SONET Circuits

SONET Level	Data Transmission Rate
OC-1	51.84 mbps
OC-3	155.52 mbps
OC-9	466.56 mbps
OC-12	622.08 mbps
OC-18	933.12 mbps
OC-24	1.244 gbps
OC-36	1.866 gbps
OC-48	2.488 gbps
OC-192	9.953 gbps
OC-768	39.812 gbps

Key: mbps = million bits per second
gbps = billion bits per second

Satellite. Satellite microwave communication is being used by an increasing number of organizations that are setting up a WAN. The satellite or satellites involved are owned by companies such as Loral Space and Communications, Hughes Electronics Corporation, and Intelsat, and the user organization leases a portion of the satellite's capacity. The user organization either provides its own ground stations or leases time on a carrier's ground stations, as well as communication lines to and from those ground stations. The use of Ku-band transmission with relatively inexpensive VSAT ground stations is making satellite transmission very popular for organizations with many remote locations. Both Kmart and Wal-Mart, for example, use VSAT networks to link their thousands of stores with their corporate headquarters. V-Crest Systems, a member of the Volkswagen Group, runs a VSAT network for all the Porsche, Audi, and Volkswagen dealerships throughout the United States. Through the VSAT network, V-Crest provides information services for order placement, warranty processing, parts and vehicle location, customer tracking, financing, insurance, accounting, inventory control, and service management.

ISDN. Another way of implementing a WAN is an **Integrated Services Digital Network (ISDN)**. ISDN is a set of international standards by which the public telephone network is offering extensive new telecommunications capabilities (including simultaneous transmission of voice and data over the same line) to telephone users worldwide.

So-called narrowband ISDN is now available in many areas of the world. ISDN is digital communication, using the same twisted pairs already used in the present telephone network.

ISDN capabilities are made possible by hardware and software at the local telephone company office and on the organization's premises (such as a digital PBX) that divide a single telephone line (twisted pair) into two types of communication channels. The B, or bearer, channel transmits voice or data at rates of 64 kbps, faster than is possible using a modem. The D, or data, channel is used to send signal information to control the B channels and to carry packet-switched digital data.

So far, two narrowband ISDN services have been offered. The basic rate offers two B channels and one 16 kbps D channel (a total data rate of 144 kbps) over a single twisted pair. Each basic rate line is capable of supporting two voice devices and six data devices, any two of which can be operating simultaneously. The primary rate provides 23 B channels and one 64 kbps D channel (for a total data rate of 1.544 mbps) over two twisted pairs. Although not yet widely available, broadband ISDN—using fiber-optic cabling—offers data transmission rates of over 150 mbps. Therefore, ISDN provides a significant increase in capacity while still using the public telephone network.

Further, the D channel brings new capabilities to the network. For instance, the D channel can be used for telemetry, enabling remote control of machinery, heating, or air conditioning at the same time the B channels are being used for voice or data transmission. The D channel can also be used for single-button access to a variety of telephony features, such as call-waiting and display of the calling party's number.

A number of innovative uses of ISDN have been implemented. In a customer service application, an incoming call from a customer comes in over one of the B channels. The D channel is used to automatically signal the file server to send the customer's record to the service representative's workstation over the second B channel. In a marketing application, a salesperson sends alternative specifications or designs to a potential buyer's video screen over one B channel while simultaneously talking to the buyer over the second B channel.

The developments in ISDN are a part of the digitization of the public telephone network. However, ISDN has never caught on in a big way, and it now seems destined to be bypassed by other digital developments such as DSL (to be covered in a later section) and IP (Internet Protocol) telephony. At present, ISDN service is available on most telephone lines in the United States. But ISDN service is still relatively expensive. As an example, to obtain a basic rate ISDN line from SBC (a regional Bell operating company), the installation fee is $113 and the monthly line charge is about $40 for voice and data services. In addition, an ISDN modem is required. What advantages does this ISDN line provide? ISDN permits the user to be a more effective telecommuter (working from home), to share a computer screen display with another user at a distant location, to conduct desktop videoconferencing, to transfer large data files with ease, and to access the Internet at 128 kbps (combining the two B channels), over twice as fast as an ordinary modem.

Packet-Switched Networks. **Packet-switched networks** are quite different from the switched-circuit (DDD and WATS, ISDN) and dedicated-circuit (leased lines, satellite) networks previously described. In switched- and dedicated-circuit networks, a circuit is established between the two computers that are communicating, and no other devices can use that circuit for the duration of the connection. In contrast, a packet-switched network permits multiple connections to exist simultaneously over the same physical circuit. **Packet switching** is a store-and-forward data transmission technique. Communications are sent over the common carrier network, divided into packets of some fixed length, perhaps 300 characters (see Figure 4.12). Control information is attached to the front and rear of this packet, and it is sent over a communications line in a single bundle. Packet switching is quite different from usual voice and data communications, where the entire end-to-end circuit is tied up for the duration of the session. With packet switching, the network is used more efficiently because packets from various users can be interspersed with one another. The computers controlling the network will route each individual packet along the appropriate path.

A **packet assembly/disassembly device** (**PAD**) is used to connect the user organization's internal networks (at each of its locations) to the common carrier network. The organization must, of course, pay a fee to make use of the common carrier network. In some cases the user organization provides the PADs and pays a fixed fee for a connection into the common carrier network plus a charge for the number of packets transmitted. In other cases the user organization might contract with a firm that manages and operates the entire WAN for the user organization, including the PADs needed at each location. This contracting-out practice used to be called a **value added network**, or **VAN**, but that terminology has largely disappeared. Today such a packet-switched WAN is usually called a managed network. In the United States, managed network services are available from AT&T, Sprint, MCI, and Infonet Services Corporation. Packet-switched networks are quite common,

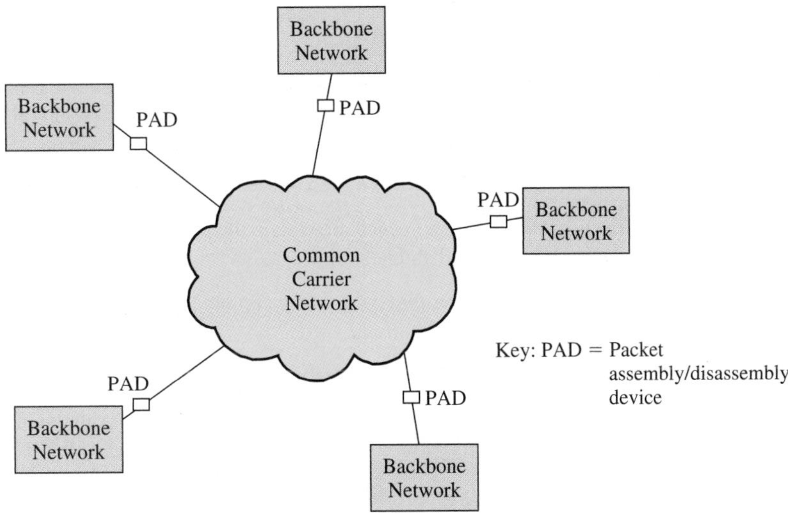

Figure 4.12 Packet-Switched Network Connecting Five Organizational Locations

including some networks like vBNS+ that serve a limited audience and others like the Internet that are available to anyone or any organization that wishes to buy the networking service.

ATM. One of the newer entries on the WAN as well as the backbone network scene is **ATM**, or **Asynchronous Transfer Mode**. ATM is based on the idea of packet switching as described earlier. For ATM, each packet is rather small—a total of 53 bytes, including 48 bytes of data and 5 bytes of control information attached to the front of the packet. ATM was originally created for use in WANs to carry both data and voice traffic, which helps explain the small packet size—the small packet is an appropriate size for voice traffic, but it is very small for data traffic. ATM is a telecommunications standard for broadband ISDN.

ATM does not really describe a line transmission technology, such as contention bus or token ring; it is a switching technology with usual speeds from 155 mbps in each direction up to 622 mbps. ATM operates as a full-duplex circuit, so the total throughput varies from 310 mbps (155 mbps times 2) up to 1.24 gbps (622 mbps times 2). An ATM network uses switches arranged in a mesh topology (see Figure 4.5), usually running on fiber-optic cables or category 5 twisted-pair cables. In brief, ATM is fast packet switching with short, fixed-length packets.

Because of the fast data transmission rates, ATM networks gained a foothold in the WAN arena and in backbone networks; they were also used in some LANs. However, ATM uses protocols that differ from the Internet's Transmission Control Protocol/Internet Protocol (TCP/IP), so it is necessary to convert ATM addresses into TCP/IP addresses (and back) to access the Internet from an ATM network. Thus, with the ascendancy of the Internet, ATM fell into disfavor. ATM has had some successes, and it is now widely used deep within the public telephone network (Tanenbaum, 2003, p. 62). It is not, however, a common choice for WANs or backbone networks.

Virtual Private Networks. A **virtual private network (VPN)** provides the equivalent of a private packet-switched network (as discussed earlier) using the public Internet. A VPN provides a moderate data rate (up to 2 mbps) at a very reasonable cost, but the network's reliability is low. To establish a VPN, the user organization places a VPN device (a special router or switch) on each Internet access circuit to provide access from the organization's networks to the VPN. Of course, the user organization must pay for the access circuits and the Internet service provider (ISP). The VPN devices enable the creation of VPN *tunnels* through the Internet. Through the use of encapsulation and encryption, these tunnels ensure that only authorized users can access the VPN. The primary advantages of VPNs are low cost and flexibility, while the disadvantages include low reliability, unpredictable transmission speeds, and security concerns. An organization can create a VPN itself, or it can contract with a vendor such as AT&T or MCI to manage and operate the VPN.

Internet Almost last, but certainly not least, of the network types we will consider is the ubiquitous Internet. The Internet could be considered a gigantic WAN, but it is really

Table 4.4 Internet Applications

Name of Application	Purpose of Application
Electronic mail, or e-mail	Easy-to-use, inexpensive, asynchronous means of communication with other Internet users
Instant messaging	Synchronous communication system that enables the user to establish a private "chat room" with another individual to carry out text-based communication in real time over the Internet
Usenet newsgroups	Internet discussion groups, which are essentially huge electronic bulletin boards on which group members can read and post messages
Listserv	Mailing list such that members of a group can send a single e-mail message and have it delivered to everyone in the group
File Transfer Protocol, or FTP	Permits users to send and receive files, including programs, over the Internet
Gopher	Menu-based tool that allows the user to search for publicly available data posted on the Internet by digging through a series of menus until the sought-after data are located
Archie	Allows the user to search the publicly available anonymous FTP sites to find the desired files
Veronica	Allows the user to search the publicly available Gopher sites using key words until the sought-after data are located
World Wide Web, or the Web	Hypertext-based tool that allows the user to traverse, or surf, the Internet by clicking on a link contained in one document to move to another document, and so on; these documents might also include video clips, recordings, photographs, and other images

much more than that. The **Internet** is a network of networks that use the TCP/IP protocol (to be discussed later in the chapter), with gateways (connections) to even more networks that do not use the TCP/IP protocol. By January 2003 there were approximately 172 million hosts (number of IP addresses that have been assigned a name) on the Internet (Internet Software Consortium, 2003). An "educated guess" of the number of Internet users in September 2002 was 605 million, with over 182 million users in Canada and the United States (Nua.com, 2003). An incredible array of resources—both data and services—is available on the Internet, and these resources are drawing more users, which are drawing more resources, in a seemingly never-ending cycle.

The Internet has an interesting history, dating back to 1969 when the U.S. Department of Defense created ARPANET[4] to link a number of leading research universities. Ethernet LANs incorporating TCP/IP networking arrived in the early 1980s, and NSFNET was created in 1986 to link five supercomputer centers in the United States. NSFNET served as the backbone (the underlying foundation of the network, to which other elements are attached) of the emerging Internet as scores of other networks connected to it. Originally, commercial traffic was not permitted on the Internet, but this barrier was broken in the late 1980s and the floodgates opened in the early 1990s. In 1995 the National Science Foundation withdrew all financial support for the Internet, and began funding vBNS+ (see Figure 4.6)—which is sometimes considered as part of Internet2 (to be discussed next).

The Internet has no direct connection to the U.S. government or any other government. Authority rests with the Internet Society, a voluntary membership organization. The governing body of the society is the Internet Architecture Board, which is entirely made up of volunteers. Similarly, the Internet receives no government support now that NSF funding has ended. Users pay for their own piece of the Internet. For an individual, this usually means paying an Internet service provider (ISP) a monthly fee to be able to dial a local number and log into the Internet. The smaller ISPs, in turn, pay a fee to hook into the Internet backbone, which is a network of high-bandwidth networks owned by major ISPs such as AT&T, UUNet/MCI, Sprint, and Aleron.

The Internet provides the four basic functions summarized in Table 4.4: electronic mail, remote login, discussion groups, and the sharing of data resources. Electronic mail was really the first "killer app" of the Internet—the first application that grabbed the attention of potential users and turned them into Internet converts. Electronic mail provides an easy-to-use, inexpensive, asynchronous means

[4]ARPANET is a creation of the Advanced Research Projects Agency of the U. S. Department of Defense. Much of the pioneering work on networking is the result of ARPANET, and TCP/IP was originally developed as part of the ARPANET project.

of communication with other Internet users anywhere in the world. A newer variant of electronic mail, **instant messaging (IM)** is a synchronous communication system that enables the user to establish a private "chat room" with another individual to carry out text-based communication in real time over the Internet. Typically, the IM system signals the user when someone on his or her private list is online, and then the user can initiate a chat session with that individual. Major players in the IM market are America Online, Yahoo!, Microsoft, and IBM Lotus.

Remote login permits a user in, say, Phoenix, to log into another machine on which she has an account in, say, Vienna, using a software program such as Telnet. Then she can work on the Vienna machine exactly as if she were there. Discussion groups are just that—Internet users who have gathered together to discuss some topic. **Usenet newsgroups** are the most organized of the discussion groups; they are essentially a set of huge electronic bulletin boards on which group members can read and post messages. A **listserv** is a mailing list such that members of the group can send a single e-mail message and have it delivered

IM ABUSE IS RAMPANT IN WORKPLACE

Whatever it is that workers are doing with instant messaging, work is far down the list, a security company said in a study.... Abusive language, gossip, sexual advances, and complaints are among the chief uses of instant messaging in the workplace, the company [Blue Coat Systems] found during a survey of U.S. and U.K. workers with access to IM applications. Among the potential problems caused by IM abuse: lost productivity, potential exposure to litigation, compliance violations, risk of leaking confidential information, attachment of viruses, and transmission of links to illegal or malicious Web sites, among others.

"There are currently 40 million business users of IM, and there are genuine business benefits to the immediacy of IM," said Steve Mullaney, Blue Coat's marketing VP. "The technology is not going to go away. But left unchecked, instant messaging could ultimately cause more business problems than it solves."

The solution, from [Blue Coat's] point of view, is to make IM a full member of the enterprise IT club, subject to the same level of restriction, monitoring, and enforcement as e-mail, Internet use, and other better-established applications. Blue Coat also recommended development of company policies regarding appropriate use of instant messaging, basing those policies on a "log it, manage it, control it" triad.

[Ferrell, 2003]

to everyone in the group. This usually works fine as long as users remember whether they are sending a message to an individual in the group or to the entire group. Do not use the reply function in response to a listserv message unless you intend your reply to go to the entire group!

The sharing of data resources is a gigantic use of the Internet. **File Transfer Protocol**, or **FTP**, is a program that permits users to send and receive files, including other programs, over the Internet. For ordinary FTP use, the user needs to know the account name and password of the remote computer in order to log into it. Anonymous FTP sites have also been set up, however, which permit any Internet user to log in using "anonymous" as the account name. As a matter of courtesy (and to track accesses), most anonymous FTP sites ask that the user enter his e-mail address as the password. Once logged in, the user may transfer any files located at that anonymous FTP site. **Gopher** is a menu-based tool that allows you to search for publicly available information posted on the Internet by digging (like a gopher) through a series of menus until you find what you want. **Archie** is a tool that allows you to search the publicly available anonymous FTP sites worldwide to find files. And **Veronica** performs a similar function with Gopher sites, searching the publicly available Gopher sites using key words to identify the data you are after.

Early in the twenty-first century, FTP is still popular, but Gopher, Archie, and Veronica have largely disappeared, subsumed by the tremendous capabilities of the **World Wide Web**, or **WWW**, or just the **Web**. The Web is a hypertext-based way of traversing, or "surfing," the Internet. With hypertext, any document can contain links to other documents. By clicking on the link with the computer mouse, the referenced document will be retrieved—whether it is stored on your own computer, one down the hall, or one on the other side of the world. More than this, the Web provides a graphical user interface (GUI) so that images, photographs, sound bites, and full motion video can be displayed on your screen as part of the document (provided your computer is appropriately equipped). All this material is delivered to your computer via the Internet. The World Wide Web is the second "killer app" of the Internet, and it has accelerated the already rapid telecommunications revolution.

To use the World Wide Web, the user's machine must have a Web browser program installed. This software package permits the machine to access a Web server, using either a dial-up telephone connection (with a modem) or a direct connection through a LAN. As noted in Chapter 3, the most popular browser is Microsoft's Internet Explorer. When a user first logs into the Web, she is connected to a "home" server at her ISP or her own organization. She can then surf the Web by clicking on hypertext links, or she can search for a particular topic using a Web crawler, or "search engine" program. Or, if she knows the address of the site she wishes to visit—this address is called the **Uniform Resource Locator (URL)**—she can enter the address directly into her browser. For Web site addresses, or URLs, she expects to visit frequently, she can save the address as a "bookmark" in her browser so that all she must do is click on the appropriate bookmark to return to the Web site.

In the early days of the Web (say, 1992 to 1995), a great deal of factual information was on the Web, but very little of commercial interest. Today, however, all major organizations, and many lesser ones, have a significant presence on the Web. The Web gives businesses a new way to provide information about their products and services, a new way to advertise, and a new way to communicate with customers and suppliers and potential customers and suppliers. With increasing frequency, the Web is being used to complete sales, particularly of products, such as software, that can be delivered via the Internet and of products such as books, CDs, and clothes, that can be delivered via regular mail. (We will talk more about electronic commerce via the Web in Chapter 8.) Designing appealing Web pages has become an art—firms want to make sure that their pages convey the right image. Figures 4.13 and 4.14 show the home pages of two leaders in the information technology field, Microsoft and Hewlett-Packard.

DSL, Cable Modem, and Satellite. How does an individual user access the Internet? In the workplace, most users are connected to a LAN, which in turn is connected to the organizational backbone network, and then to the Internet. From home or a small office, connections are most often made from a dial-in modem, operating at speeds up to 56 kbps. ISDN service is also available in most parts of the United States with data transfer rates up to 128 kbps. Early in the twenty-first century, three newer, higher-speed alternatives burst on the scene: **digital subscriber line (DSL)**, **cable modem** connection, and **satellite** connection. Taken together, these are referred to as **broadband** connections.

DSL is a service offered by telephone companies using the copper wires already installed in homes and offices; it uses a sophisticated modulation scheme to move data over the wires without interfering with voice traffic—that is, both a voice conversation and an Internet hookup can be active at the same time over a single DSL line. DSL is sometimes called a "last mile" technology in that it is used only for connections from a telephone switching station to a home or office, not for connections between switching stations. Data transfer rates on DSL are very fast, varying from 384 kpbs to 1.544 mbps downstream from the Internet to the home or office machine and usually 128 kbps upstream from the home or office machine to the Internet. This differential in upstream and downstream speed is not usually a problem, because users typically do not send as much data *to* the Web as they receive *from* the Web. Furthermore, the DSL line is dedicated to the single user, so these speeds are guaranteed. As an example of the costs, self-installation of the SBC Yahoo! DSL basic package in Indianapolis is almost free—as part of a special offer, the $99 modem is offset by a $99 instant credit if the user signs a 1-year agreement. A network interface card is included if needed. Activation is free, and the user needs to pay only taxes and a $14.95 shipping and handling fee. The monthly fee for the first year is $26.95, which does not include regular voice telephone service but does include basic Yahoo! ISP service. There is a $200 charge for a technician to install DSL.

A cable modem connection is very competitive to DSL in both price and speed. In this case the service is obtained from the cable television company and the data are transmitted over the coaxial cables already used by television. These cables have much greater bandwidth than twisted pair copper wires, but traditionally they transmitted data only in one direction—from the cable television company to the home. Reengineering of the cable television system was necessary to permit the two-way data flow required for Internet connections. Current download speeds with a cable modem range up to 3 mbps, with upload speeds considerably slower (256 kbps is common). However, cable modem speeds might be degraded because users are sharing the bandwidth of the coaxial cable; as more users in a neighborhood log into the Internet, the slower the speed of the connections. As an example of the costs, the installation charge for Cox Communications cable modem service in Phoenix is $100, or the customer can use a free self-installation kit. A cable modem costs $90, and the customer might be able to get it free as part of a special offer. Then the monthly service charges are $39.95 for cable television customers. No additional ISP is needed; Cox Communications provides the connection to the Internet.

The third alternative, a satellite connection, tends to be the most expensive option, but for customers in rural areas it might be the only choice. The uplink operates from 50 to 128 kbps, with the downlink from 400 to 700 kbps with bursts up to 1.5 mbps. Satellite broadband connections can be one-way service or two-way service. For one-way service, the customer must contract with a wired ISP (dial-up, DSL, or cable modem) for the uplink, while the satellite supports the downlink. The downlink is just like the usual terrestrial link, except that the satellite transmits data to the computer via a satellite dish at the customer's home or office. The two-way satellite service transmits and receives

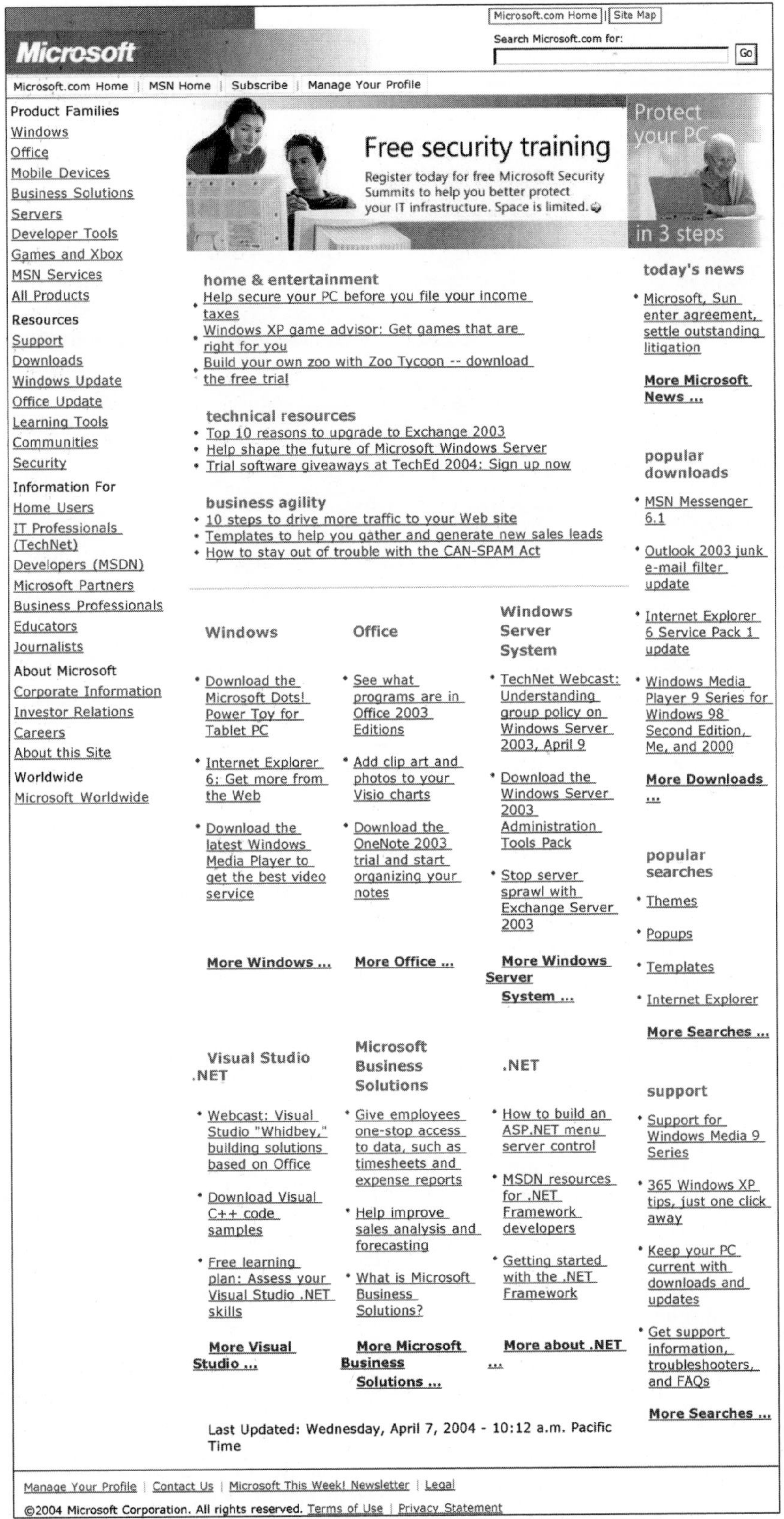
Microsoft.com Home | Site Map
Search Microsoft.com for:
Go
Microsoft
Microsoft.com Home | MSN Home | Subscribe | Manage Your Profile
Product Families
Windows
Office
Mobile Devices
Business Solutions
Servers
Developer Tools
Games and Xbox
MSN Services
All Products
Resources
Support
Downloads
Windows Update
Office Update
Learning Tools
Communities
Security
Information For
Home Users
IT Professionals (TechNet)
Developers (MSDN)
Microsoft Partners
Business Professionals
Educators
Journalists
About Microsoft
Corporate Information
Investor Relations
Careers
About this Site
Worldwide
Microsoft Worldwide
Free security training
Register today for free Microsoft Security Summits to help you better protect your IT infrastructure. Space is limited.
Protect your PC in 3 steps
home & entertainment
Help secure your PC before you file your income taxes
Windows XP game advisor: Get games that are right for you
Build your own zoo with Zoo Tycoon -- download the free trial
technical resources
Top 10 reasons to upgrade to Exchange 2003
Help shape the future of Microsoft Windows Server
Trial software giveaways at TechEd 2004: Sign up now
business agility
10 steps to drive more traffic to your Web site
Templates to help you gather and generate new sales leads
How to stay out of trouble with the CAN-SPAM Act
today's news
Microsoft, Sun enter agreement, settle outstanding litigation
More Microsoft News ...
popular downloads
MSN Messenger 6.1
Outlook 2003 junk e-mail filter update
Internet Explorer 6 Service Pack 1 update
Windows Media Player 9 Series for Windows 98 Second Edition, Me, and 2000
More Downloads ...
Windows
Download the Microsoft Dots! Power Toy for Tablet PC
Internet Explorer 6: Get more from the Web
Download the latest Windows Media Player to get the best video service
More Windows ...
Office
See what programs are in Office 2003 Editions
Add clip art and photos to your Visio charts
Download the OneNote 2003 trial and start organizing your notes
More Office ...
Windows Server System
TechNet Webcast: Understanding group policy on Windows Server 2003, April 9
Download the Windows Server 2003 Administration Tools Pack
Stop server sprawl with Exchange Server 2003
More Windows Server System ...
popular searches
Themes
Popups
Templates
Internet Explorer
More Searches ...
Visual Studio .NET
Webcast: Visual Studio "Whidbey," building solutions based on Office
Download Visual C++ code samples
Free learning plan: Assess your Visual Studio .NET skills
More Visual Studio ...
Microsoft Business Solutions
Give employees one-stop access to data, such as timesheets and expense reports
Help improve sales analysis and forecasting
What is Microsoft Business Solutions?
More Microsoft Business Solutions ...
.NET
How to build an ASP.NET menu server control
MSDN resources for .NET Framework developers
Getting started with the .NET Framework
More about .NET ...
support
Support for Windows Media 9 Series
365 Windows XP tips, just one click away
Keep your PC current with downloads and updates
Get support information, troubleshooters, and FAQs
More Searches ...
Last Updated: Wednesday, April 7, 2004 - 10:12 a.m. Pacific Time
Manage Your Profile | Contact Us | Microsoft This Week! Newsletter | Legal
©2004 Microsoft Corporation. All rights reserved. Terms of Use | Privacy Statement

Figure 4.13 Microsoft Home Page (Reproduced with permission from Microsoft Corporation)

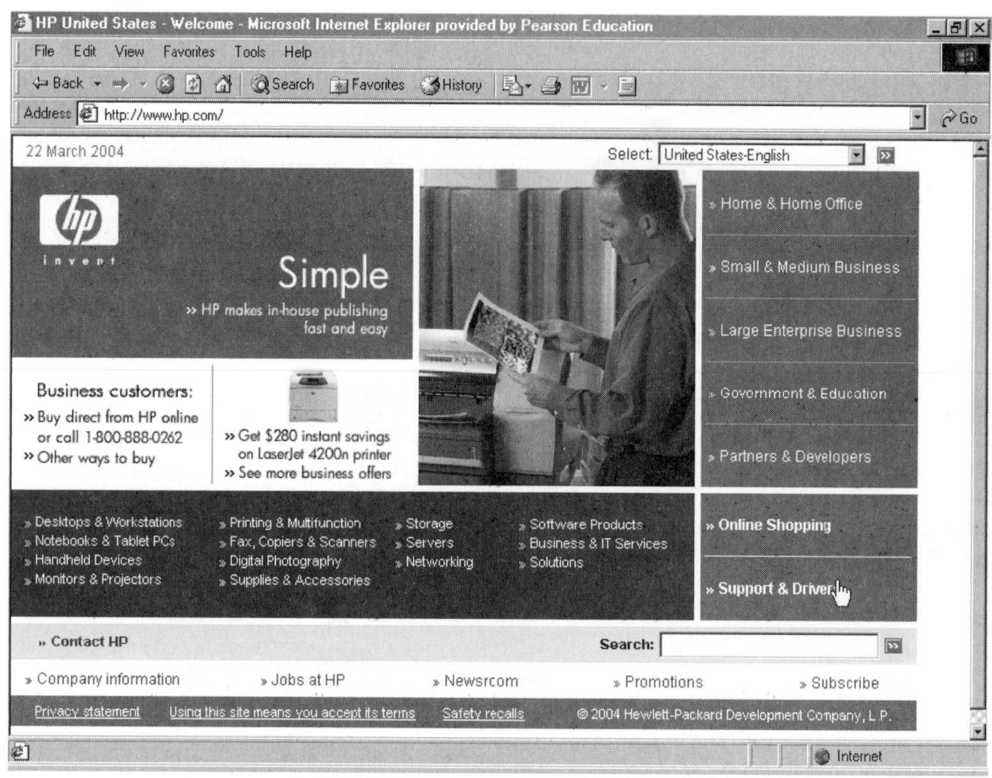

Figure 4.14 Hewlett-Packard Home Page (Reproduced with permission of Hewlett-Packard Company)

signals directly via the satellite without needing a ground line to support the connection for the upstream portion of the broadband service. As an example of a two-way satellite service, DirecWay (from Hughes Network Systems) is available from any location in the United States with a clear view of the southern sky. With a 1-year service agreement, the installation fee is $600 (including a satellite dish, a modem, and installation) and the monthly charge is $59.99.

In the battle to provide high-speed Internet access, cable modem connections have a strong early lead over DSL. In mid-2003 there were about 22 million broadband users in the United States, with roughly two-thirds of them connected by cable modem and 30 percent connected via DSL (Crockett, Ihlwan, and Yang, 2003; Jesdanun, 2003). Both cable modem and DSL users have been growing rapidly, and that growth should continue. However, the United States is far behind several other nations, including South Korea, Japan, and Canada, in the proportion of households with broadband service. In South Korea, three-fourths of all households have broadband service, and the data rates are roughly triple U.S. rates at a monthly cost that is just over half the average U.S. cost. In Japan, 27 percent of households have broadband service, compared to 18 percent in the U.S. Broadband in Japan averages 10 mbps for only $23 a month. Broadband adoption in Canada is up to 36 percent of all households. If the U.S. is to catch up, it will require efforts on the part of the government to remove regulatory roadblocks and perhaps provide tax incentives for broadband investments, efforts on the part of service providers to reduce prices and increase speeds, efforts on the part of venture capitalists to promote broadband content startup companies, and efforts on the part of content developers to promote legal file-sharing (Crockett, Ihlwan, and Yang, 2003).

Intranets. An important spin-off from the success of the Internet has been the creation of **intranets** within many large organizations. An intranet is simply a network operating within an organization that employs the TCP/IP protocol. In most cases, an intranet consists of a backbone network with a number of connected LANs. Because the protocol is the same, the organization may use the same Web browser, Web crawler, and Web server software as it would use on the Internet; however, the intranet is not accessible from outside the organization. It might or might not be possible for people within the organization to access the Internet.

DENIAL-OF-SERVICE ATTACKS, WORMS, VIRUSES PLAGUE THE INTERNET

It seems as though every month we read about—or experience first-hand—reliability and security problems on the Internet, such as denial-of-service attacks, worms, and viruses. In July 2003, Microsoft's Web site was inaccessible for almost 2 hours when a denial-of-service attack overwhelmed the site with traffic. Another denial-of-service attack hit the Web site of Knight Ridder's 31 daily newspapers (including the Miami Herald, the Philadelphia Inquirer, and the San Jose Mercury News) for several hours in September 2003. These denial-of-service attacks most likely came from one or more small programs, readily available for downloading from the Web, that were planted in the computers of unsuspecting users all over the world. Then, at some signal from the mastermind, the programs in these multiple computers started requesting access to the Microsoft or Knight Ridder site, over and over and over again. With these repeated requests from multiple computers, all in a matter of seconds, the sites simply could not handle the traffic and were essentially shut down. This congestion is like repeatedly dialing a telephone number so that everyone else dialing the same number will always get a busy signal. Thus, the perpetrators "denied service" to the legitimate users of the Web sites.

Viruses and worms are quite similar; both can play havoc with the operation of an infected computer. A virus is a program or piece of code that is loaded onto your computer without your knowledge and against your wishes; it can attach itself to other programs and can replicate itself. A worm is a special type of virus that can replicate itself and use memory but that cannot attach itself to other programs. Among the many virus and worm attacks in 2003 were the Slammer attack in January, which infected vulnerable computers by exploiting a known flaw in Microsoft's SQL Server 2000 database program; the Blaster attack in early August, which affected newer versions of Microsoft Windows through a vulnerability in its Remote Procedure Call interface; and the Sobig attack in late August, which worked to identify hiding spots for the worm and more e-mail addresses to propagate itself. Among the many repercussions of these attacks, the Slammer attack disrupted operations for police and fire dispatchers outside Seattle, who had to resort to pencil and paper for hours, and the Blaster attack brought portions of CSX Transportation's 23,000-mile rail network to a halt and delayed Amtrak's Washington, D.C. commuter trains by 2 hours. On a more personal note, the Blaster worm infected the home computer of one of this book's authors, forcing him to restart his computer multiple times until he was able to remove the worm. The Internet is important to all of us, and it is becoming even more important, but it has a long way to go to achieve reliability and security.

[Adapted from Bridis, 2003; Foley, 2003; Kreiser and Hulme, 2003; Babcock, 2003; and Associated Press, 2003]

Some commentators have referred to the Internet as the "information superhighway." That is wrong, as Bill Gates, the chairman of Microsoft, has pointed out in his book, *The Road Ahead* (1995). The Internet is merely the predecessor of the information superhighway; we are not there yet. Before we have a true information superhighway, we need gigantic increases in bandwidth, more reliability and security (see the sidebar entitled "Denial-of-Service Attacks, Worms, Viruses Plague the Internet"), more accessibility by the entire population, and more applications. We are only beginning to scratch the surface of possibilities for the Internet and the information superhighway beyond.

Internet2 In reality, **Internet2** is not a network type, although it does run a leading-edge, very high-bandwidth network; it is a not-for-profit consortium of over 200 universities, working in partnership with over 60 leading technology companies and the U.S. government, to develop and deploy advanced network applications and technologies. Internet2 hopes to accelerate the creation of tomorrow's Internet, a true "information superhighway." The three primary goals of Internet2 are to

- create a leading-edge network capability for the national research community
- enable revolutionary Internet applications based on a much higher-performance Internet than we have today
- ensure the rapid transfer of new network services and applications to the broader Internet community

Internet2's "leading-edge network for the national research community" is named Abilene, and its operation center is in Indianapolis (see Figure 4.15). This is a very high-performance network, with all but one of the links in Figure 4.15 operating at 9.953 gbps (OC-192). You can go online at *loadrunner.uits.iu.edu/weathermaps/Abilene* and see how busy the network currently is. Abilene is a backbone network used by the Internet2 universities; it provides an effective interconnection among regional networking aggregation points, called gigaPoPs[5], that have been formed by the Internet2 universities. Created by the Internet2 community, Abilene is a partnership of Internet2, Qwest Communications, Cisco Systems, Nortel Networks, and Indiana University. Please note that Abilene is engaged in a

[5]PoP is an abbreviation for point of presence—a place where an interconnection to Abilene can be made—and giga suggests that the speed of the interconnection can be in the billions of bits per second.

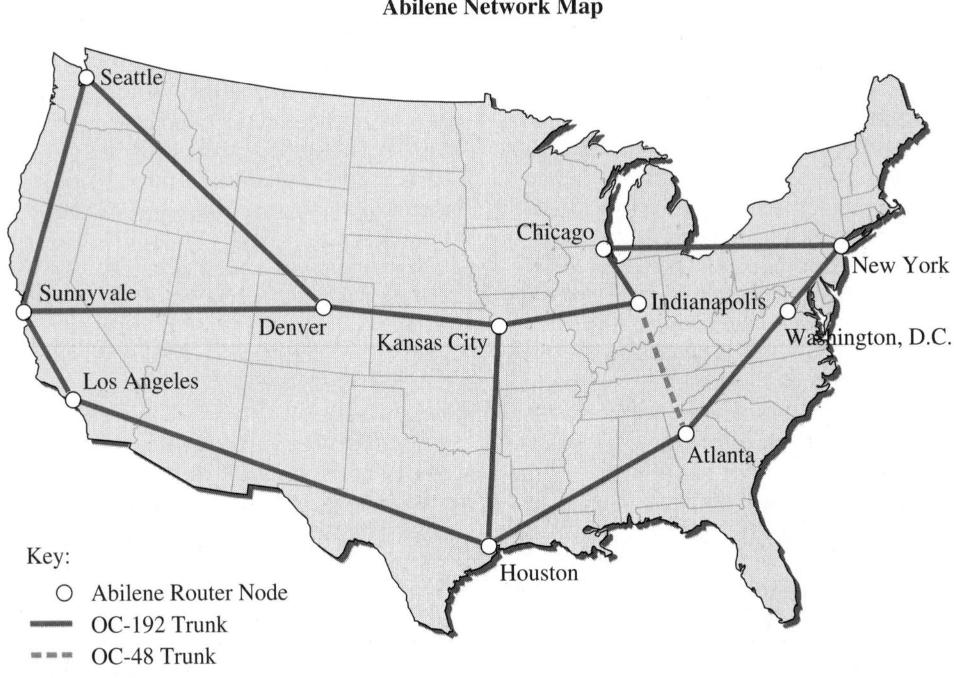

Figure 4.15 Abilene Network Map

healthy, even cooperative sort of competition with vBNS+, another very high-performance network operated by MCI (see Figure 4.6). There is a significant overlap of vBNS+ customers and Internet2 members, and MCI engineers have participated in several Internet2 projects. In fact, the vBNS+ and Abilene networks have a connection through the network access point in Chicago. vBNS+, Abilene, and the other Internet2 projects are the precursors of tomorrow's Internet.

Network Protocols

There is only one more major piece to our network puzzle. How do the various elements of these networks actually communicate with one another? The answer is by means of a **network protocol**, an agreed-upon set of rules or conventions governing communication among elements of a network, or, to be more precise, among layers or levels of a network. In order for two network elements to communicate with each other, they must both use the same protocol. Therefore, the protocol truly enables elements of the network to communicate with one another.

Without actually using the protocol label, we have already encountered several protocols. LANs, for example, have four widely accepted protocols: contention bus, token bus, token ring, and wireless. Historically, the biggest problem with protocols is that there have been too many of them (or, to look at the problem in another way, not enough acceptance of a few of them). For example, IBM and each of the other major hardware vendors created their own sets of protocols. IBM's set of protocols is collectively termed Systems Network Architecture or SNA. IBM equipment and equipment from another vendor, say, Hewlett-Packard, cannot communicate with each other unless *both* employ the same protocols—IBM's, or H-P's, or perhaps another set of "open systems" protocols. The big challenge involved in integrating computers and other related equipment from many vendors into a network is *standardization* so that all use the same protocols!

In the past two decades considerable progress has been made in standardization and acceptance of a set of protocols—although we are not ending up where most commentators would have predicted in the late 1980s. At that time, it appeared that the **OSI** or **Open Systems Interconnection Reference Model**, developed by the International Organization for Standardization (ISO), would become the standard set of protocols. The OSI model defines seven layers (see Figure 4.16), each of which will have its own protocol (or protocols). The OSI model is only a skeleton, with standard protocols in existence for some layers (the four LAN protocols are part of the data link layer), but with only rough ideas in other layers. All major computer and telecommunications vendors—including IBM—announced their support for the OSI model, and it appeared that OSI was on its way.

For better or worse, the movement toward the OSI model was essentially stopped in the 1990s by the explosion

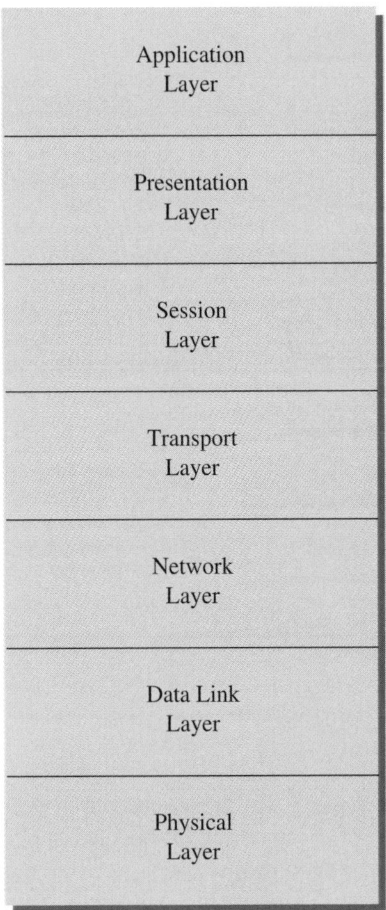

Figure 4.16 Seven Layers of the OSI Reference Model

of the role of the Internet and the creation of numerous intranets within major organizations. Both the Internet and intranets employ TCP/IP, or Transmission Control Protocol/Internet Protocol, as their protocol. TCP/IP is not part of the OSI reference model, and it is a less comprehensive set of protocols than OSI, correspondingly roughly to two of the seven OSI layers. Both the OSI model and TCP/IP are important, for different reasons, so we will explore both sets of protocols. The OSI model provides an extremely useful framework for considering computer networks, so it is a good place to begin. The TCP/IP model, augmented with some other ideas, is the *de facto* standard set of protocols for networking in the early twenty-first century, so we will turn to TCP/IP after considering the OSI model.

OSI Reference Model Because of the importance of the OSI model, and because it will give us a conceptual framework to understand how communication takes place in networks, we will briefly discuss each of the layers in the OSI model and an example of how data can be transmitted using the model (see Figure 4.17). This is a very complex model because it must support many types of networks (e.g., LANs and WANs) and many types of communication (e.g., electronic mail, electronic data interchange, and executive information systems[6]).

Physical Layer. The physical layer is concerned with transmitting bits (a string of zeros and ones) over a physical communication channel. Electrical engineers work at this level, with typical design issues involving such questions as how many volts should be used to represent a 1 and how many for a 0.

Data Link Layer. For the data link layer to work, data must be submitted to it (by the network layer) in the form of data frames of a few hundred bytes. Then the data link adds special header and trailer data at the beginning and end of each frame, respectively, so that it can recognize the frame boundaries. The data link transmits the frames in sequence to the physical layer for actual transmittal and also processes acknowledgment frames sent back by the data link layer of the receiver and makes sure that there are no transmission errors.

Network Layer. The network layer receives a packet of data from the transport layer and adds special header data to it to identify the route that the packet is to take to its destination. This augmented packet becomes the frame passed on to the data link layer. The primary concern of the network layer is the routing of the packets. The network layer often contains an accounting function as well in order to produce billing information.

Transport Layer. Although not illustrated by Figure 4.17, the transport layer is the first end-to-end layer encountered. In the lower layers of the OSI model, the protocols are between a sending device and its immediate neighbor, then between the neighbor and its immediate neighbor, and so on, until the receiving device is reached. Starting with the transport layer and continuing through the three upper layers, the conversation is directly between the layer for the sending device and the corresponding layer for the receiving device. Thus, the upper four layers are end-to-end protocols.

The transport layer receives the communication (of whatever length) from the session layer, splits it into smaller blocks if necessary, adds special header data defining the network connection(s) to be used, passes the packet(s) to the network layer, and checks to make sure that all the packets

[6]These applications and others will be explained in Chapters 6–8.

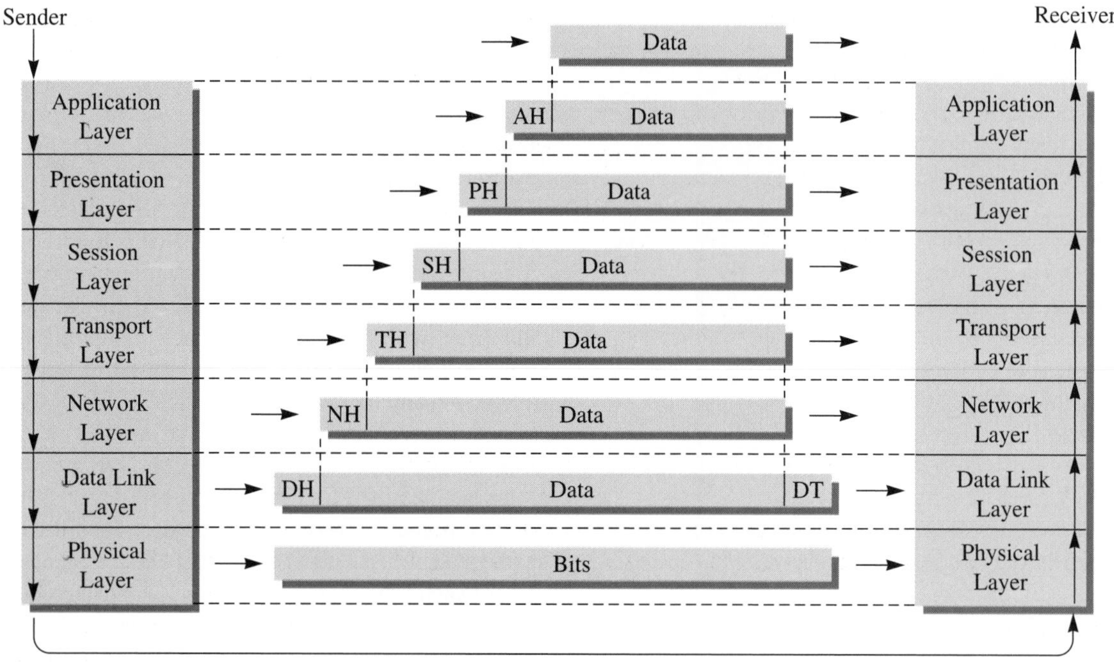

Figure 4.17 Data Transmission Based on OSI Model

arrive correctly at the receiving end. If the network connection requires multiplexing for its efficient use, the transport layer also handles this (and in a manner transparent to the higher layers).

Session Layer. Through the session layer, users on different machines may establish sessions between them. For most applications the session layer is not used, but it would allow a user to log into a remote computer or to transfer a file between two computers. The session layer may provide several services to the users, including dialog control (if traffic can only move in one direction at a time) and synchronization (so that a portion of a communication received need not be retransmitted even if the network fails).

Presentation Layer. The presentation layer, unlike the lower layers, is concerned with the information to be transmitted, rather than viewing it as a string of bits. The presentation layer accepts as input the communication as internally coded by the sending device and translates it into the standard representation used by the network. (The presentation layer on the receiving device reverses this process.) In addition, the data may be cryptographically encoded if it is especially sensitive. Like the layers below and above, the presentation layer adds a header to the data before sending it to the layer below.

Application Layer. The uppermost layer deals with the wide variety of communications-oriented applications that are directly visible to the user, such as electronic data interchange, file transfer, electronic mail, and factory floor control. There will always be differences across different terminals or systems, and a protocol is required for each application (usually implemented in software) to make each of these devices appear the same to the network. For a group of users to communicate using electronic mail, for example, the devices they employ must all use the same application layer/electronic mail protocol. The OSI electronic mail protocol, known as MOTIS, gained acceptance in some parts of the world but has largely been replaced by SMTP, which is at least unofficially part of the TCP/IP model.

Data Transmission Using the OSI Model. Figure 4.17 provides an illustration of data transmission based on the OSI model. The sender has some data to be transmitted to the receiver. The sender, for example, might be a manager at a workstation who wishes to transmit a query to the corporate executive information system located on a large server in another state. The manager types in a query, which is temporarily stored in the workstation in electronic form. When the manager hits the Enter key, the query (data) is given to the application layer, which adds the application header

(AH) and gives the resulting augmented data item to the presentation layer. The presentation layer converts the item into the appropriate network code, adds a presentation header (PH), and passes it on to the session layer. The session layer might not do anything, but if it does, it will end by attaching a session header (SH) and passing the augmented item to the transport layer. The transport layer does its work, adds a transport header (TH), and sends the resulting packet to the network layer. The network layer, in turn, does its work, adds a network header (NH), and sends the resulting frame to the data link layer. The data link layer accepts the frame, adds both a header (DH) and a trailer (DT), and sends the final bit stream to the physical layer for actual transmission to the receiver.

When the bit stream reaches the receiver, the various headers (and trailer) are stripped off one at a time as the communication moves up through the seven layers until only the original query arrives at the receiver, which, in our example, is a large server. Perhaps the easiest way to understand this entire process is that the original data go through a multilevel translation process (which is really much more than translation), with each layer acting as if it were directly communicating with the corresponding receiving layer. Most important, the entire process should take place in a device/system independent way that is totally transparent to the user.

TCP/IP **TCP/IP**, or **Transmission Control Protocol/ Internet Protocol**, is not part of the OSI reference model, although it roughly corresponds to the network and transport layers. TCP/IP is used in many non-Internet networks, including vBNS+ and Abilene, as well as in the UNIX and Linux operating systems and in Microsoft Windows. Most important, TCP/IP is the protocol used on the worldwide Internet and on numerous intranets operating within organizations. Thus TCP/IP, not OSI, has become the *de facto* standard protocol for networking around the world. Nevertheless, TCP/IP is only a partial set of protocols, not a fully developed model. Thus computer scientists and commentators have, in effect, developed an augmented TCP/IP model. First we will consider the TCP/IP protocols themselves, and then we will turn to the extended TCP/IP model.

The IP portion of the TCP/IP protocol corresponds roughly to the network layer of the seven-layer model, while the TCP portion corresponds approximately to the transport layer. TCP/IP accepts messages of any length, breaks them into pieces smaller than 64,000 bytes, sends the pieces to the designated receiver, and makes sure that the pieces are correctly delivered and placed in the right order (because they might arrive out of sequence). TCP/IP does not know the path the pieces will take and assumes that communication will be unreliable. Thus, substantial error-checking capabilities are built into TCP/IP itself to ensure reliability.

The original Internet developers envisioned the complete networking protocol as having four layers—the networking and transport layers as the middle layers, with a hardware layer below these two layers and an application layer above them (Dennis, 2002, p. 14). From a practical standpoint, this four-layer view of the world is not too different from the OSI model, because the presentation and session layers are often not used. The four-layer model's hardware layer then corresponds to both the data link and physical layers of the OSI model. In this extended TCP/IP model, the application layer includes protocols such as SMTP (for e-mail), HTTP (for Web pages), and FTP (for file transfer). The transport layer is TCP, of course, and the network layer is IP. Then the hardware layer would include the various LAN standards, ATM, FDDI, ISDN, SONET, and DSL, among others. This extended TCP/IP model represents reality in terms of the standard set of networking protocols in the early twenty-first century.

SNA The extended TCP/IP model, perhaps with some ideas borrowed from the OSI model, clearly represents the future in terms of network protocols. Nevertheless, IBM's **Systems Network Architecture (SNA)** remains an important standard. SNA, like OSI, is really a suite or grouping of protocols. IBM created SNA to allow its customers to construct their own private networks. In the original 1974 version of SNA, only a simple tree topology emanating from a single mainframe was permitted. By 1985, however, arbitrary topologies of mainframes, minicomputers, and LANs were supported.

SNA is a very complicated suite of protocols because it was designed to support the incredible variety of IBM communication products, teleprocessing access methods, and data link protocols that existed before SNA. We do not need to explore the details of the SNA suite, but it might be useful to note that the newer OSI model was patterned after SNA in several ways: Both employ the concept of layering, use seven layers, and incorporate essentially the same functions. The contents of the two sets of layers, however, are quite different, especially in the middle three layers (called the network, transport, and session layers in OSI). Although IBM still supports SNA, it also supports both TCP/IP and elements of the OSI model under the umbrella of its late-1980s **Systems Application**

Architecture (SAA), which is really a philosophy rather than a set of protocols.

We now have all the pieces of the network puzzle. Network protocols provide the means by which various elements of telecommunications networks can communicate with one another. Thus, networks consist of physical media, arranged according to some topology, in a particular type of network, with communication throughout the network permitted through the use of particular protocols.

THE EXPLODING ROLE OF TELECOMMUNICATIONS AND NETWORKING

We have already stressed the critical role of telecommunications and networking several times, but to make the point even stronger, we will discuss how the role of telecommunications and networking is exploding in organizations today. In fact, many authorities suggest that the network (not the computer) is the most critical and most important information technology of the future. To illustrate this explosion, we will consider four areas of operation in which telecommunications networks are of critical and growing importance.

Online Operations

The dominant activities of many organizations have now been placed online to the computer via a network. For banks and other financial institutions, teller stations (as well as automated teller machines) are all online. Tellers directly update your account when you cash a check or make a deposit. The bank does not care what branch in what city you use, because your account is always up-to-date. Not quite as obviously, insurance companies have most of their home office and branch office activities online. When an insurance claim is made or paid, when a premium is paid, or when a change is made to a policy, those activities are entered online to the insurance company network. These and other financial institutions (such as brokerage firms and international banks) simply could not operate as they do without telecommunications networks.

The computerized reservations systems of the major airlines are another example of an indispensable use of online systems. Virtually all travel agencies in the United States are now online. Computerized reservation systems constitute the core marketing strategy of the major airlines. The major airlines introduce new versions of their reservation systems every few years, with significant new features built into each revision. For example, Delta, United, and American Airlines provide LANs to link travel agency microcomputers, permitting the agencies to integrate a wide variety of travel agency management applications with reservations processing. All this activity makes sense when one considers that the airlines make more money on their reservation systems, per dollar spent, than they make flying passengers. Historically, the airlines make 8 to 10 percent profit overall in a good quarter, while the reservation systems, through user fees and increased sales, make as much as 20 percent profit.

In the late 1990s the airlines and private vendors moved one step further by giving users the ability to make their own reservations online, effectively bypassing travel agents entirely. Each of the major airlines has its own Web site where users can buy tickets and select seats on future flights. Even more capability is available on the Web sites of three major online travel companies: Travelocity (part of Sabre Holdings, a spin-off from American Airlines), Expedia (developed by Microsoft, and now part of USA Interactive, formerly USA Networks), and Orbitz (created by five airlines—American, Continental, Delta, Northwest, and United). These sites provide information, process ticket sales for flights from all airlines, and offer other travel services such as hotel and rental car reservations. To access Travelocity, go to *www.travelocity.com* ; for Expedia, the Web site is *www.expedia.com*; and for Orbitz, go to *www.orbitz.com*.

Connectivity

Connectivity is a very popular buzzword among major U.S. and international corporations. Most large (and many smaller) organizations now provide every managerial and professional employee a personal workstation, and these workstations are connected to a network structure (often an intranet) so that each employee has access to every person, and every system, with which he or she might conceivably need to interact.

Connectivity to persons and organizations outside the firm is also important. American Hospital Supply Corporation created a strategic advantage by providing connectivity with the hospitals it served. DaimlerChrysler Corporation has installed a system to tie its dealers to the corporation so that deviations from expected sales are spotted quickly. All the automobile manufacturers are stressing connectivity with their suppliers so that they can adjust orders efficiently. Thus, connectivity throughout the customer-manufacturer-supplier chain is a critical element.

Electronic Data Interchange and Electronic Commerce

Electronic data interchange, or **EDI**, will be covered more completely in Chapter 8, but it is certainly part of the exploding role of networking. EDI is a set of standards and hardware and software technology that permits business documents (such as purchase orders, invoices, and price lists) to be transferred electronically between computers in separate organizations. For the most part, the transmission of EDI documents takes place over public networks, including the Internet. The automobile industry is perhaps the most advanced in the use of EDI, but many other firms and industries have also adopted this technology.

Electronic commerce (also called e-business) is a broad term that incorporates any use of telecommunications and networking to conduct commercial activities. EDI is part of electronic commerce, but the most explosive electronic commerce area involves commerce over the World Wide Web. Electronic commerce includes online catalogs, online ordering, online payment for goods and services, and sometimes online delivery of products. A number of virtual stores and shopping malls have been set up on the Web, and an incredible array of products is offered. One interesting and colorful electronic commerce venture is described in the sidebar "Virtual Florist." Electronic commerce over the Web is burgeoning, and there is no end in sight. The authors of this book, for example, have purchased software and electronic books on the Web and immediately downloaded them; registered online for conferences; made hotel and airline reservations; and purchased books, CDs, and a variety of gifts on the Web for offline delivery. Shopping on the Web is becoming important for most consumers. As you will learn in Chapter 8, electronic commerce is even more important for businesses than for consumers.

VIRTUAL FLORIST

The Virtual Florist is an Internet Web site operated by the Internet Florist, St. Paul, Minnesota, with a URL of *www.virtualflorist.com.* The home page includes the Virtual Florist logo of a bouquet of yellow tulips appearing to come out of a computer screen, as well as a seasonal animated message, e.g., "Send a boo-tiful arrangement" (at Halloween) or "Bring the colors of the season inside" (in November). The home page has two primary segments, Have FRESH FLOWERS Delivered Today and Send a FREE Virtual Flower Card, as well as a tab to enable a recipient to pick up a virtual flower card. You may send anyone a virtual bouquet or virtual card (as long as he or she has an e-mail address), and it really is free! The user picks out the appropriate virtual bouquet or card from among a large number of screen displays of beautiful flowers and interesting cards. After the user personalizes the bouquet or card with a message, an e-mail message is sent to the lucky person who is to receive the bouquet. Then the recipient "picks up" the bouquet from the Virtual Florist Web site and it is displayed on his or her screen. After several days, the virtual bouquet and all records are destroyed. Of course, what the Virtual Florist wants the user to do is return to this site to order a real bouquet. Clicking on "Have FRESH FLOWERS Delivered Today" links the user to the Internet Florist home page, and to the wide selection of roses, blooming plants, fresh arrangements, stuffed animals, balloons, and flower arrangements for special occasions such as a birthday, anniversary, or birth of a baby. The user may order online via the Web or call a toll-free telephone number. In most cases same day delivery is available anywhere in the United States or Canada if the order is submitted by 2 P.M. in the time zone of the delivery.

[Adapted from Virtual Florist Web site, 2003]

Marketing

In addition to electronic commerce, telecommunications is being used for many exciting projects in the marketing area. Two examples are the use of laptop microcomputers by salespersons and the use of telecommunications for telemarketing and customer support. All business organizations sell products and services, although the distribution channels vary widely. The sales function is often performed either by sales representatives employed by the firm or by independent agents aligned with the firm (e.g., an insurance agent). In either case, telecommunications is being widely used to provide support for the sales personnel. In the last few years, instant messaging (IM) has become an important tool for customer support, especially for firms such as online retailer Lands' End and most of the major Wall Street stock and bond traders.

This sales support is not always as direct as the two examples above. Such support often takes the form of online information describing product or service characteristics and availability. This up-to-the-minute information makes the sales representative or agent more competitive and increases the organization's profitability (as well as increasing the chances of retaining productive sales personnel). The importance of this instantaneous information is apparent for a St. Louis-based Merrill Lynch stockbroker talking to a client who is considering the purchase of a stock on the New York Stock Exchange, but it is almost as critical for a parts clerk at a Honda dealership in Oregon dealing with a disgruntled customer. The parts clerk can use his networked computer to check the availability of a needed part in Honda regional warehouses in the United States and can immediately place the order from the nearest warehouse that has the part.

THE TELECOMMUNICATIONS INDUSTRY

There are three major segments of the telecommunications industry: (a) carriers, who own or lease the physical plant (cabling, satellites, cellular towers, and so forth) and sell the service of transmitting communications from one location to another; (b) equipment vendors, who manufacture and sell a wide range of telecommunications-related equipment, including LAN software and hardware, routers, hubs, wireless access points, digital switches, multiplexers, cellular telephones, and modems; and (c) service providers, who operate networks and deliver services through the network, or provide access to or services via the Internet. This third segment includes America Online, Microsoft Network, Yahoo!, and a wide variety of ISPs.

As an important historical footnote, the entire complexion of the telecommunications industry changed in 1984 with the breakup of AT&T into the long-distance telephone and equipment-centered AT&T and the regional Bell operating companies (RBOCs). Although the various pieces that resulted from the divestiture were still large, there was no longer a single monolithic entity in control of most telecommunications in the United States. Just before the AT&T breakup, technological developments in long-haul communications (microwave, satellites, and fiber optics) made the development of long-distance networks to compete with those of AT&T economically feasible. Thus came the rise of MCI, Sprint, and other long-distance carriers. Furthermore, court decisions and management policies served to effectively split AT&T (and each of the regional operating companies) into two businesses—regulated and nonregulated. The original carrier portion of the business was still regulated, but the nonregulated portion could now compete actively in the computer/communications equipment market. AT&T, and to a lesser extent the operating companies, became major players as equipment vendors.

The 1984 AT&T divestiture also had significant managerial implications for the telecommunications function in a user organization. Prior to 1984 the telecommunications manager had a relatively easy job, dealing with AT&T for almost all of his or her telecommunications needs and receiving high-quality, reliable service for a regulated price. After divestiture, the job got much tougher. Now the manager has to deal with a variety of carriers and equipment vendors (often including AT&T), and also has to make sure that all the various pieces fit together.

The twenty-first century will bring even further change, not all of it predictable, to the telecommunications industry. In much of the world the government-owned telephone carriers have shifted to private ownership. In the United States, the Telecommunications Reform Act of 1996 resulted in increased competition for telephone service (both voice and data). To a great extent, everything is now up for grabs: Within limits specified by the act, the local telephone companies may enter the long-distance market and perhaps the cable television market; the cable television operators may enter the local and long-distance telephone markets; and the long-distance telephone companies may enter the local service market and perhaps the cable television market.

The growth of mobile telephony has changed the landscape, and it appears likely that telephony over the Internet will result in further change. In late 2003 there were 147 million cell phones in the United States, compared to 187 million traditional phone lines. At the present rate of growth, mobile phones will overtake the regular telephone business in 2005 (Rosenbush, et al., 2003, p. 110). The players in the telephone industry are changing as well, with the RBOCs recombining to form megacompanies such as SBC, Verizon, and BellSouth. Perhaps the more things change, the more they stay the same: The Bell companies are numbers one (Verizon), two (Cingular, formed by BellSouth and SBC), and three (AT&T Wireless, spun off from parent AT&T) in the wireless telephone market. The telecommunications equipment manufacturers, including such firms as Lucent Technologies, Nortel Networks, and Alcatel, had disastrous financial results in the years surrounding the turn of the twenty-first century but seem to be recovering as we near the midpoint of the new century's first decade. These are exciting—and nerve-racking—times for companies in the broadly defined telecommunications industry.

THE TELECOM REVOLUTION CONTINUES . . .

. . . IN FIBER OPTICS TO THE HOME

Telecom revolutions have a way of sneaking up on you. The latest upheaval may be upon us—and it's the result of rare industry cooperation. In late May, Verizon Communications, SBC Communications, and BellSouth announced that they would jointly develop standards that will allow them to roll out ultrafast fiber-optic lines right to customers' doorsteps. All three have begun to lay fiber in select neighborhoods, including a Verizon project in suburban Virginia. Fiber to the home would boost connectivity speeds by a factor of 20, making current DSL and cable broadband services run like mules next to a Kentucky Derby champion. Faster lines could unleash an explosion of new services, ranging from video-on-demand to more realistic games. "A few years from now," says Danny Briere, CEO of researcher TeleChoice Inc., "we'll look back at this [pact] as a milestone."

[Crockett, Haddad, and Rosenbush, 2003, p. 68]

. . . IN SENSOR NETWORKS

Already, companies from British supermarket Tesco PLC to Shell Oil Co. have deployed first generation [sensor] systems to monitor inventories and check the status of pumps at gas stations. That's just the beginning. Within 5 years, these sensor computers could be shrunk to the size of a grain of sand and deployed over much of the globe, resulting in thousands of new networks. Look for them to be scattered across farms and battlefields to monitor minute chemical and temperature changes and slapped onto trucks and shipping boxes to trace inventory automatically.

Sensor networks promise a mammoth extension of the Internet. To date, the Web has been a showcase for the human brain. It specializes in the words, numbers, music, and images that mankind produces. With sensors, the network stretches to the far vaster field of global activity. This means such networks can cover every single thing that moves, grows, makes noise, or heats up. Potentially, much of the world will be bugged. Moreover, these bugs will be doing most of the work. "Most of the data traffic won't be between human beings this time around but between these silicon cockroaches," says Bob Metcalfe, the networking pioneer who has invested in Ember Corp., a sensor-network startup in Boston.

[Green, 2003, p. 100]

. . . IN NETWORK-ENABLED UTILITY COMPUTING

The concept is one of the most compelling in the history of computing: make information technology as easy to use as plugging into an electrical outlet. This idea is commonly called utility computing, and many experts believe it's going to sweep the infotech world like a digital tidal wave. IBM, for one, is spending $800 million this year on marketing its vision of utility computing, which it calls e-business on demand.

"We think this is the third major computing revolution—after mainframes and the Internet," says analyst Frank Gillett of Forrester Research. The idea is that the power plant-like computing systems of the future will operate both at remote data centers and within a company's offices—under a variety of novel payment schemes. Whatever setup, the systems can be managed by the company's own tech staff or by outsiders. And rather than requiring customers to buy computer servers outright for use inside their own walls, hardware makers, including IBM, Sun Microsystems, and Hewlett-Packard, each offer computing-as-used payment options.

[Hamm and Burrows, 2003, p. 96]

SUMMARY

The telecommunications and networking area has existed for considerably longer than computer hardware and software, but the developments in all three areas have merged in the past two decades to put more emphasis on telecommunications than ever before. The late 1990s and the early 2000s are the era of networking. Networks provide enhanced communication to organizations and individuals and permit the sharing of resources and data. They are also essential to implement distributed data processing and client/server systems. The exploding role of telecommunications and networking is evident in many organizational activities, including online operations, EDI, and electronic commerce. There is an intense desire to improve organizational communications through universal connectivity. A communications revolution is underway, with networking—and particularly the Internet—at the heart of it.

The technology of telecommunications and networking is extremely complex, perhaps even more so than computer hardware and software. By concentrating on a number of key elements, we have developed a managerial-level understanding of networks. Communication signals may be either analog or digital. It is easier to transmit data digitally, and there is a concerted movement toward digital transmission today. Networks employ a variety of transmission media (such as coaxial and fiber-optic cable) and are configured in various topologies (such as rings and trees). Major network types include computer telecommunications networks, emanating from a mainframe or midrange computer; digital PBX networks for both voice and data; LANs for high-speed communication within a restricted area; backbone networks to connect LANs together, and possibly to connect to WANs and the Internet; WANs for communication over a long haul; and the Internet. The Internet, and especially the World Wide Web, has been front-page news over the past several years as the world becomes wired. WANs and the Internet are highly dependent upon facilities owned and operated by the telephone companies and other carriers. To enable the devices attached to any type of network to communicate with one another, protocols (or rules of operation) have to be agreed upon. The success of the Internet has led to the acceptance of TCP/IP as today's *de facto* networking protocol.

We have now covered three of the four building blocks of information technology: hardware, software, and telecommunications and networking. In the next chapter we focus on the data to be processed by the hardware and software and moved around on the networks. Whatever your personal managerial career involves, you are likely to be working both directly and indirectly with hardware, software, networking, and data. Knowledge of information technology is essential for understanding its present and potential impact on your organization and your job.

REVIEW QUESTIONS

1. What are the primary reasons for networking among computers and computer-related devices?
2. Explain the difference between analog and digital signals. Is the trend is towards more use of (a) analog or (b) digital signals in the future?
3. What is a modem? When and why are modems necessary? What is a cable modem, and how does it differ from a traditional modem?
4. List the primary types of physical media in use in telecommunications networks today. Which of these media has the fastest transmission speed? The slowest transmission speed?
5. Describe the similarity between the bus and the ring topology; then describe the similarity between the star and the tree topology.
6. Identify the following acronyms or initials:

LAN	LEO	PBX
WAN	FTP	ISDN
RFID	FDDI	SONET
DSL	vBNS+	EDI

7. Explain how packet switching works. Why is packet switching important?
8. What is the Internet? What is an intranet? How are they related?
9. What is the World Wide Web, and how does it relate to the Internet?
10. Three important protocols discussed in this chapter are OSI, TCP/IP, and SNA. In one or two sentences per protocol, tell what these names stand for and describe the basic purposes of these three protocols.
11. What is Bluetooth? Give examples of its use.
12. What is a denial-of-service attack?

DISCUSSION QUESTIONS

1. Review Question 2 refers to the trend toward more digital (rather than analog) communication. In your judgment, what are the primary causes of this trend?
2. Discuss the advantages and disadvantages of the four primary types of local area networks—contention bus, token bus, token ring, and wireless.
3. A PBX network is often viewed as an alternative to a local area network. What are the advantages and disadvantages of a PBX network vis-à-vis a local area network?
4. What are the key differences between a LAN and a WAN? Are the differences between a LAN and a WAN becoming larger or smaller? Explain.
5. As noted in the chapter, the most common transmission medium is the twisted pair. Is this likely to continue to be true? Why or why not?
6. Explain the differences between accessing the Internet via a modem, ISDN, DSL, a cable modem, and satellite. Which of these access mechanisms are likely to become more important in the future?
7. List the seven layers of the OSI reference model, and give a description of the role of each layer in one or two sentences.
8. Why is the idea of a standard network protocol, such as the OSI reference model, important? What are the advantages and disadvantages of developing a single standard protocol?
9. Has the popularity of the Internet and the related adoption of TCP/IP by many organizations and networks helped or hindered the movement towards a single standard protocol such as OSI? Why?
10. Find out what types of computer networks are used at your organization (either the university at which you are taking this course or the company for which you work). Does your organization have an intranet? Does

your organization have one or more LANs? What types of LANs does your organization use? Does your organization operate a WAN? Is your organization linked to the Internet? Speculate on why your organization has developed this particular network structure.

11. Consider a large company with which you are somewhat familiar (because of your own work experience, a parent's work experience, a friend's work experience, or your study of the company). Use your imagination to suggest new ways in which the Internet could be used in this company.
12. Consider a particular small business with which you are familiar (as a customer, as a current or former employee, as a relative of the owner). Describe the current telecommunications employed by the business. In what ways might telecommunications and networking be used to improve the profitability of this business? Consider, as appropriate, such ideas as the use of facsimile communication, telemarketing, enhanced communication through a local area network, a Web home page, and cellular phones for employees.
13. What is Internet2, and how does Internet2 relate to the present Internet? What is the importance of Internet2 developments?
14. Discuss the advantages and disadvantages of wireless communication, such as Bluetooth and wireless LANs, compared to wired communication. Using your knowledge and your personal crystal ball, will wireless communication become more or less important in the future? Why?
15. Cellular telephone service has certainly become more important vis-à-vis wired telephone service over the past decade. Will this trend continue? How will the trend toward cellular service be affected by other developments in telephony such as massive increases in bandwidth through fiber-optic technology and the wider use of telephony over the Internet?

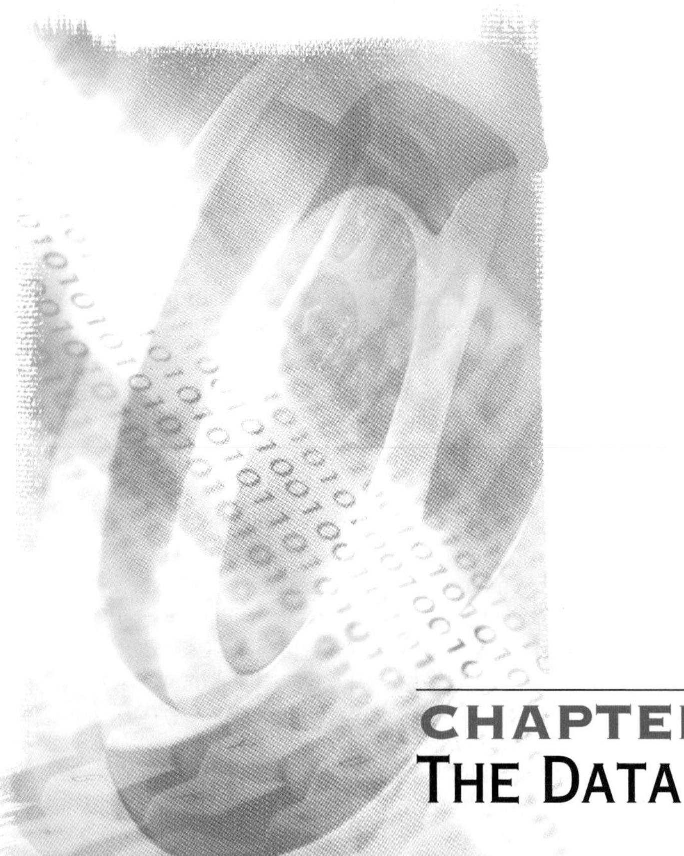

CHAPTER 5
THE DATA RESOURCE

THIS IS THE CONCLUDING CHAPTER OF PART I OF THIS BOOK, WHICH HAS been devoted to information technology. The previous three chapters have discussed computer systems, computer software, and telecommunications and networking—all clearly information technology topics. It is our contention that there is a fourth information technology component that is just as critical as those three—the data that are processed by the hardware and software and sent through the network both before and after processing. All four IT components are essential for an information technology system to produce results that are meaningful and valuable for you and your organization. This chapter focuses on the all-important data resource.

The data resource consists of the facts and information an organization gathers while conducting business and in order to conduct business. The data resource's components include numeric, text, audio, video, and graphical data collected both within the organization and from sources external to it. The variety and volume of data that are available to organizations has led to data being recognized as a major organizational resource, to be managed and developed like other assets, such as facilities, labor, and capital. In fact, many observers of trends in business believe that the organizations that will excel in the twenty-first century will be those that manage data and organizational knowledge as a strategic resource, understand the usefulness of data for business decisions, and structure data as efficiently as they do other assets.

Organizations are now able to collect more data than ever before through normal business activity, through the recording of data transactions from POS (point-of-sale) terminals, and via Web and electronic commerce sites. All this data can be an asset only if they are available when needed, and this cannot occur unless an organization actively organizes and manages its data. Financial resources are available to build a new plant or to buy raw materials only if a financial manager and other business managers have planned for enough funds to cover the associated cash requirements. A new product can be designed only if engineering and personnel managers have anticipated the needs for certain skills in the work force. A business certainly would not ever think about *not* planning and managing facilities, labor, and capital. Similarly, data must be planned and managed.

The effort to manage organizational data is the responsibility of every business manager. In addition, a special management unit, usually called data or database administration, often provides overall organizational leadership in the data management function. Furthermore, some organizations have built knowledge management functions and appointed a chief knowledge officer. Every manager in an organization has some financial, personnel, equipment, and facilities/space responsibilities. Today, data must be added to this list of managed assets.

WHY MANAGE DATA?

One way to view the importance of managing the data resource is to consider the following questions:

- What would your company do if its critical business data, such as customer orders, product prices, account balances, or patient histories, were destroyed? Could the organization function? For how long?
- What costs would your company incur if its database were damaged? Are the data irreplaceable? How would business operations change without the computerized data?
- How much time does your organization spend reconciling inconsistent data? Do account balances in your department always agree with those in central accounting? What happens when these figures do not agree? Do marketing and engineering always use the same product identifiers? Are there problems with providing custom products because of different specifications by sales and engineering? Can you track a customer order all the way from receipt through production to shipping and billing in a consistent, logical way?
- How difficult is it to determine what data are stored about the part of the business you manage? What data exist about customer sales in a particular market? In what databases do these data reside? What is the meaning of these data (e.g., do the data include lost sales, blanket orders, special orders, private label sales)? How can you gain access to these data?

Although managing data as a resource has many general business dimensions, it is also important for the cost-effective development and operation of information systems. Poor systems development productivity is frequently due to a lack of data management, and some methods, such as prototyping, cannot work unless the source of data is clear and the data are available. Systems development time is greatly enhanced by the reuse of data and programs as new applications are designed and built. Unless data are cataloged, named in standard ways, protected but accessible to those with a need to know, and maintained with high quality, the data and the programs that capture and maintain them cannot be reused.

There are both technical and managerial issues regarding the data resource. The next section examines the technical aspects of managing the data resource. It provides an overview of the most common tools used by database administrators (DBAs) and systems analysts for describing and managing data. As responsibilities for managing the data resource are distributed to the business units, these topics also become important to all managers.

TECHNICAL ASPECTS OF MANAGING THE DATA RESOURCE

The Data Model

A key element in the effective management of data is an overall map for business data—a **data model**. A manufacturing company would never think about building a new product without developing a detailed design and using common components and parts from existing products where appropriate. The same is true for data. Data entities, such as customer, order, product, vendor, market, and employee, are analogous to the components of a detailed design for a product. Just as the detailed blueprint for a product shows the relationships among components, the data model shows the relationships among the data entities.

Data modeling involves both a methodology and a notation. The methodology includes the steps that are followed to identify and describe organizational data entities, and the notation is a way to show these findings, usually graphically. Several possible methodologies are introduced in the following paragraphs, but the reader is referred to texts on database management for a discussion of data modeling notations. Figure 5.1 shows a sample data model. Specifically, it is an **entity-relationship diagram (ERD)** that captures entities (i.e., customer, order, product) and their relationships (i.e., submits, includes).

The entity-relationship diagram is the most commonly accepted method for representing the data needs in an organization. It consists of **entities**, or the things about which data are collected, and **attributes**, the actual elements of data that are to be collected. The model in Figure 5.1 could have the attributes of customer last name, customer first name, customer street, customer city, and so

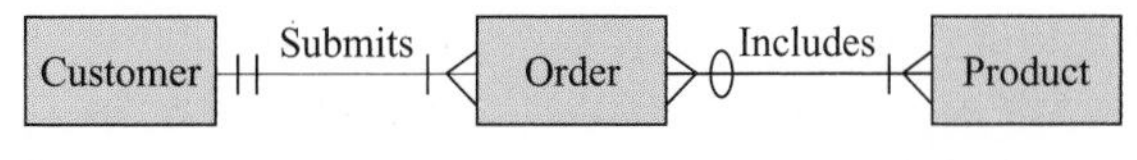

Figure 5.1 Entity-Relationship Diagram

on to represent the data that would be captured about each customer. Relationships among the entities are delineated, and the result is a picture representing the organization's data needs. Because of its nontechnical nature, the ERD is a very useful tool for facilitating communication between end users who need the data and database designers and developers who will create and maintain the database.

Data Modeling

The role of data modeling as part of IS planning is essential. In practice, two rather different approaches are followed—one top-down, called enterprise modeling, and one bottom-up, called view integration. Many organizations choose to do both approaches because they are complementary methods that emphasize different aspects of data and, hence, check and balance each other.

The **enterprise modeling** approach involves describing the organization and its data requirements at a very high level, independent of particular reports, screens, or detailed descriptions of data processing requirements. First, the work of the organization is divided into its major functions (such as selling, billing, manufacturing, and servicing). Each of these functions is then further divided into processes and each process into activities. An activity is usually described at a rather high level (e.g., "forecast sales for next quarter"). This three-level decomposition of the business is depicted in Figure 5.2.

Given a rough understanding of each activity, a list of data entities is then assigned to each. For example, quarterly forecasting activity might have the entities product, customer order history, and work center associated with it.

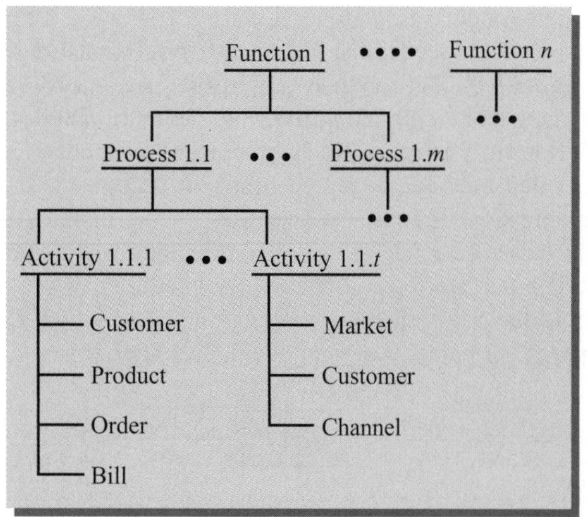

Figure 5.2 Enterprise Decomposition for Data Modeling

The lists of entities are then checked to make sure that consistent names are used and the meaning of each entity is clear. Finally, based on general business policies and rules of operation, relationships between the entities are identified and a **corporate data model** is drawn. Priorities are set for what parts of the corporate data model are in need of greatest improvement, and more detailed work assignments are defined to describe these more clearly and to revise databases accordingly.

Enterprise modeling has the advantage of not being biased by a lot of details, current databases and files, or how the business actually operates today. It is future-oriented and should identify a comprehensive set of generic data requirements. On the other hand, it can be incomplete or inaccurate because it might ignore some important details. This is where the view integration approach can help.

In **view integration**, each report, computer screen, form, document, and so on to be produced from organizational databases is identified (usually starting from what is done today). Each of these is called a user view. The data elements in each user view are identified and put into a basic structure called a normal form. **Normalization**, the process of creating simple data structures from more complex ones, consists of a set of rules that yields a data structure that is very stable and useful across many different requirements. In fact, normalization is used as a tool to rid data of troublesome anomalies associated with inserting, deleting, and updating data. When the data structure is normalized, the database can evolve with very few changes to the parts that have already been developed and populated.

After each user view has been normalized, they are all combined (or integrated) into one comprehensive description. Ideally, this integrated set of entities from normalization will match those from enterprise modeling. In practice, however, this is often not the case because of the different focuses (top-down and bottom-up) of the two approaches. Therefore, the enterprise and view-integrated data models are reconciled and a final data model is developed.

Data modeling methods are neither simple nor inexpensive to conduct. They require considerable time, organizational commitment, and the assignment of very knowledgeable managers and data specialists. In order to deal with these concerns, certain guidelines have been developed:

- *Objective* The modeling effort must be justified by some clear overriding need, such as coordination of operational data processing, flexibility to access data, or effectiveness of data systems. The less clear the goal, the higher the chance for failure.

- *Scope* The coverage for a data model must be carefully considered. Generally, the broader the scope, the higher the chances for failure. Scope choices include corporate-wide, division, areas with particular high-impact needs, and a particularly important or willing business function (e.g., sales).
- *Outcome* Choices here include a subject area database definition (e.g., all data about customers), identification of common data capture systems to be shared by several departments (replacing current separate databases), managerial and strategic databases (see Figure 5.3, which will be referred to several times in this chapter) and access services to support the information needs of these levels of management, and a more nebulous architecture for future databases. The more uncertain the outcome, the lower the chances for success.
- *Timing* Few organizations can put all systems development on hold while a complete data model is developed. It is possible, for example, to do only a high-level data model (with just major data categories), and then fill in details as major systems projects are undertaken. This evolutionary approach might be more practical, but it must be done within the context of an initial overall, general enterprise data model.

Regardless of the approach, data modeling represents a radical change to the more traditional approach of making short-term fixes to systems. A business manager often simply wants access to needed data and is not interested in waiting for an entire data model to be built. Unless an overall data management approach is taken, however, the inconsistencies and excessive costs of poorly managed data will consume the integrity and viability of the data resource.

It should be clear that data modeling is not an issue of centralized versus decentralized control. In fact, the data administration approach (with database administrators) emphasizes placing decision-making power in the hands of those most knowledgeable about the data. Some managers (both business and IS), however, will resist data planning and modeling because they sense a loss of influence.

Database Architecture

Although a **database** is a shared collection of logically related data, organized to meet the needs of an organization, the **database architecture** refers to the way in which the data are structured and stored in the database. A related term is a **data warehouse**, a very large database or collection of databases, to be discussed in more detail in Chapter 6. When selecting among database architectures, it is important to consider the types of data to be stored

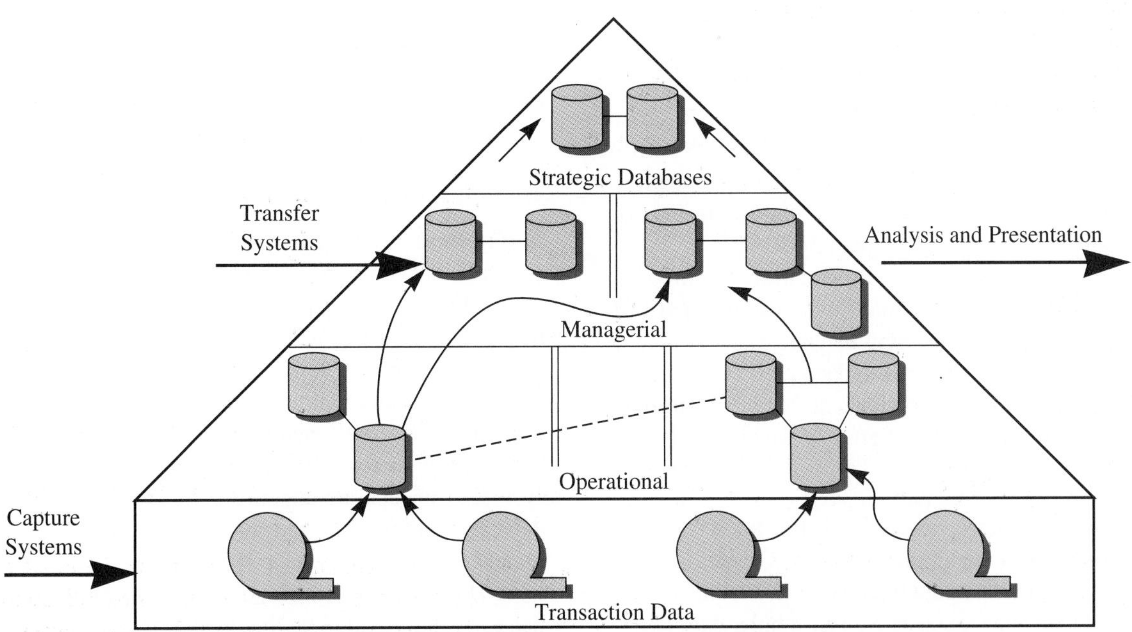

Figure 5.3 The Data Pyramid

and how they will be processed and used. The six basic architectures are:

1. Hierarchical Characterized by the IBM product Information Management System (IMS)—data are arranged in a top-down organization chart fashion.

This method of storing data is similar to an organization chart, with the senior managers, or the most general level of data, at the top. In order to access the data at the lower levels, you must follow a path through the hierarchy from top to bottom, and left to right. This method of storing data is quite useful when there are large volumes of data to be processed and the processing mechanisms are reasonably consistent over time. The primary drawbacks of this architecture stem from the fact that in order to access data, the data's *structure* must be carefully mapped out in the programs. Thus, if the structure changes, all programs accessing the data must be changed as well. This connection between the database structure and the programs that access it is known as **structural dependence**.

2. Network A good example is Integrated Database Management System (IDMS) from Computer Associates—data are arranged like the cities on a highway system, often with several paths from one piece of data to another.

The network model is also useful for high-volume transaction processing environments, and it provides increased flexibility over the hierarchical model. Similar to the hierarchical model, the network model's structure must be mapped to the programs that access the data. Thus, program modifications are quite complex and require specialized expertise.

3. Relational Many such products exist, including Microsoft Access and SQL Server from Microsoft Corporation, Paradox by Corel, DB2 and SQL/DS by IBM, and Ingres by Computer Associates—data are arranged into simple tables, and records are related by storing common data in each of the associated tables.

This is the most common organizational approach to organizing data. In a relational model, **structural independence** is achieved, meaning that programs that access the data do not need to know the database's structure. This results in a much more adaptable and flexible environment in which programs can be altered relatively easily when business processes change.

4. Object-oriented Among the better known products are GemFire from GemStone Systems, ObjectStore from Progress Software, and Objectivity/DB—data can be graphics, video, and sound as well as simpler data types.

With this approach, attributes (data) and methods are encapsulated in object classes, and relationships between classes are shown by nesting one class within another. This is the newest approach to organizing and storing data, and has as its primary advantage the ability to capture complex data types (e.g., video).

5. Object-relational This hybrid approach to organizing data capitalizes on the capability of object-oriented databases to handle complex data types, and on the inherent simplicity of the relational data model.

Although object-oriented data modeling tends to be well-suited to engineering and scientific applications, the object-relational approach is more appropriate for business applications. Companies such as IBM, Oracle, and FirstSQL provide object-relational database products.

6. Multidimensional Data warehouses are built in a multidimensional format in such a way that the logical format of the data can be viewed as a cube, consisting of facts and dimensions about those facts.

Each cell in the cube holds facts relevant to the intersection of the dimensions. Thus, a cell might contain information about date, time, location, and salesperson associated with a particular sale. Another way of viewing this model is as a star schema. This view is consistent with the cube, where the facts would be contained in a central table and the dimensions would be contained in surrounding tables that are all related to the fact table. The multidimensional approach enables faster processing of large amounts of data—something difficult to accomplish in a relational environment. The primary challenges of this model are defining the specificity level of the data and identifying all the appropriate dimensions necessary for the wide variety of individuals using the data.

Tools for Managing Data

A **database management system (DBMS)** is support software that is used to create, manage, and protect organizational data. A database management system works with the operating system to store and modify data and to make data accessible in a variety of meaningful and authorized ways. For most computer systems, the DBMS is separate from the operating system, although the trend appears to be placing some DBMS functions either in the operating system or in separate attached computer processors called database servers. The purpose of this trend is to achieve greater efficiency and security.

A DBMS adds significant data management capabilities to those provided by the operating system. The goal is to allow a computer programmer to select data from disk files by referring to the content of records, not their physical location (i.e., structural independence). This makes programming easier, more productive, and less error-prone. Also, this allows systems professionals responsible for database design to reorganize the physical organization of data without affecting the logic of programs, significantly reducing maintenance requirements. These objectives are given the umbrella term **data independence**. For example, a DBMS would allow a programmer to specify retrieval of a customer record based only on knowledge of the customer's name or number. Furthermore, once the customer record is retrieved, a DBMS would allow direct reference to any of the customer's related order or shipment records (even if these records are relocated or changed). Thus, a DBMS allows access to data based on content (e.g., customer number) as well as by association (e.g., orders for a given customer).

A DBMS is a very complex and costly software package, ranging in price from under $500 for a personal computer product to over $200,000 for a DBMS on a large mainframe computer. By purchasing a DBMS, an organization is able to draw upon a larger pool of programmers and systems designers who are familiar with the package. This reduces training costs and gives them more choices for hiring database professionals.

From a managerial point of view, a DBMS helps manage data by providing the following functions:

- *Data Storage, Retrieval, Update* Providing a variety of commands that allow easy retrieval and presentation as well as modification of data
- *Backup* Automatically making copies of the database and the updates made to it to protect against accidental damage or deliberate sabotage
- *Recovery* The ability to restore the database after damage or after inaccurate data have gotten into the database
- *Integrity Control* Ensuring that only valid data are entered into the database (so that, for example, data values only in a permissible range are entered)
- *Security Control* Ensuring that only authorized use (reading and updating) is permitted on the database
- *Concurrency Control* Protecting the database against anomalies that can occur when two or more programs attempt to update the same data at the same time
- *Transaction Control* Being able to undo changes to a database when a program malfunctions, a user cancels a business transaction, or the DBMS rejects a business transaction that updates several database records

Today, the most popular type of DBMS used to develop new systems is relational. A relational DBMS allows each entity of the data model to be viewed as a simple table, with the columns as the data elements and the rows as different instances of the entity. Also, simple and high-level relational query languages make programming much simpler than with other types of DBMSs (which often use third generation programming languages). The real power of these systems comes from being able to retrieve related data from multiple tables easily.

Not all relational systems are identical, so there has been considerable effort to standardize on one style, allowing each DBMS vendor to concentrate on extra features beyond the standard and on performance issues. **SQL** (structured query language), developed by the independent (of any particular vendor) **American National Standards Institute (ANSI)**, is a standard query language prevalent in both large machine and personal computer DBMSs. Some relational DBMSs have been designed from this standard; others permit users to work either with SQL commands or the native set of commands designed for that system. This standard allows an organization to transfer training, experience, and programs more easily between DBMSs, to more easily convert from one DBMS to another, and to make it easier to have a mix of DBMSs without duplicating support groups.

A relatively recent trend is to make the DBMS (using SQL as the standard) a kind of engine on which other support software is built. This can be done by putting the DBMS into a separate computer processor, called a **database machine** or **database server**, or by having system and application software refer to a software DBMS using SQL. Some operating systems now include an SQL-based **DBMS engine** that handles the manipulation of data, so DBMS and other software vendors (e.g., vendors of enterprise resource planning [ERP] systems) can concentrate on issues of user interface, not data management. This standardization of data management functions should make it easier to share data across different applications and decision support system generators because they will all use the same database structures and processing logic from the engine.

Data Dictionary/Directory

The **data dictionary/directory**, or **DD/D**, is a central encyclopedia of data definitions and important usage descriptions. The DD/D is a database about data and is a common source for data definitions for database software, system developers, and business managers.

The DD/D contains a definition of each entity, relationship, and data element of a database. It also retains descriptions of the display format, integrity rules, security restrictions, volume and sizes, and physical location, as well as a list of the application systems that use these data.

The DD/D is invaluable to database analysts and business managers. For example, a marketing manager could query the DD/D to find out what kinds of data are kept in a database about customer market segmentation. By using key words that were assigned to each data definition and by scanning data descriptions, the DD/D would develop a list of data elements that deal with this topic. Business managers can then determine which of these are most relevant to their needs and develop queries or report requests to the proper databases to retrieve these data. In a sense, the DD/D acts as a card catalog to the data library. The DD/D is also valuable to assess the impact of planned changes to a database. For example, if an organization is considering changing the meaning of a data element, it would be useful to know which databases need to be modified to reflect the change. Physical database designers can also use the DD/D to find statistics about data volume, size, and usage needs in order to design efficient data organizations.

Ideally, an organization would develop the DD/D before, or at the same time as, its first DBMS, but this is not usually the case. As mentioned earlier, a DD/D can facilitate many of the responsibilities of database administrators. In fact, not having a DD/D makes it so difficult to coordinate the evolution of databases that it is more likely that independent and inconsistent databases will arise when no DD/D is used. The DD/D is one of the soundest investments than can be made toward achieving the goals of data management.

Database Programming

Data processing activity with a database can be specified in either procedural programs written in a 3 GL or via special-purpose languages developed for database processing. In a relatively new development, languages such as eXtensible Markup Language (XML) and Java allow access to a database from a Web site. In the case of a 3 GL program, additional and more powerful instructions are added to the vocabulary of the programming language. For example, in a customer and order database the storage of a new order record not only necessitates storing the order data themselves but also updating various linkages that tie together a customer record with its associated order records. In a regular 3 GL program, instructions to write new data to the customer record, its index, the order record, and its indexes would have to be provided individually. With the commands available through the special enhancements to the language provided by the DBMS, only one instruction is needed in the program and all the associated indexes and records are updated automatically, which makes the programming task more productive and less error-prone.

A DBMS also frequently provides a 4 GL, nonprocedural special-purpose language, called a **query language**, for posing queries to the database. For example, the following is a query in the SQL/DS command language:

```
SELECT ORDER#, CUSTOMER#, CUSTNAME,
   ORDER-DATE FROM CUSTOMER, ORDER
   WHERE ORDER-DATE > '04/12/05'
   AND CUSTOMER.CUSTOMER# =
   ORDER.CUSTOMER#
```

This is all that is required to request the display of the order number and date from each order record, plus the customer number and name from the associated customer record, for orders placed after April 12, 2005. The equivalent COBOL program might require 10 or more procedure division instructions. The popularity of such products as Access, Paradox, Ingres, and several SQL-based language products is due in great measure to the existence of such easy-to-use query languages.

MANAGERIAL ISSUES IN MANAGING DATA

Having considered key technical issues involved in managing data, let us now turn to *managerial* issues. How to plan for data, to control data integrity, to secure access to and use data, and to make data accessible are important to the business manager. As with any business resource, quality sources for data must be identified and the data acquired; enough space must be available for data storage; obsolete data must be identified, disposed of, or archived; and usage of data must be accounted for, and, if appropriate, usage fees should be charged to those utilizing the data. These are not just issues for the IS organization—the business manager should be equipped to deal with these issues as well.

Principles in Managing Data

Successful management of the data resource depends on understanding certain key guidelines:

The Need to Manage Data Is Permanent. Any organization has customers or clients, whether these are other organizations, individual consumers, or patients. Whether a company makes to stock or to order, there are vendors or suppliers, orders or reservations, products or services, and employees. Further, irrespective of how accounting, selling, billing, or any other management activity is performed, there still will be data about customers, vendors, orders, products, and employees. Data values might change, new customers might be added, products discontinued, and employees hired and retired, but a company will always have customers, products, employees, and other entities about which it needs to keep current data. Occurrences of data are volatile, but the existence of data is persistent and the need for excellent data management is constant.

Business processes change, and so must information systems. If the company decides to change a sales forecasting method, programs will have to be rewritten, but customer, order, and general economic condition data are still needed. In fact, if data are well-managed, many of the databases will remain relatively unchanged when an organization decides to change the way it does business. At the same time, the programs that analyze, process, and report information might change drastically. Thus, data are fundamental to the business. Data remain over time and need to be managed over time.

Data Can Exist at Several Levels. Although the business retains vast amounts of data, there might be relatively few basic classes of data on which to base most information. One way to organize data is called the data pyramid (as depicted in Figure 5.3). Although new data can enter this pyramid at any level, most new data are captured at the base of the pyramid in operational databases. These databases contain the business transaction history of customer orders, purchases from suppliers, internal work orders, changes to the general ledger, personnel transfers, and other day-to-day business activities. Managerial control and strategic databases are typically subsets, summaries, or aggregations of operational databases, with key external data as supplements. For example, a database for sales forecasting (a managerial function) might contain past monthly summaries of sales by product family or geographical area derived from customer orders and product data. These data might be supplemented with external economic indicators and sales force judgments to produce sales estimates needed for production planning and scheduling.

When managerial databases are constructed from sources other than internal, shared operational databases, there can be significant inconsistencies. For example, the sales organization might track customer orders in a local database before passing these on to order entry. If they use these figures for forecasting final sales, they might not consider canceled orders, orders rejected due to insufficient credit, returned goods, or sales not met because of inadequate production capacity. These information items might not be considered because they enter the business at other points of contact with the customer. A well-run organization must consider all the transactions that define sales level to be able to build an accurate sales forecasting system.

Developing an understanding of the relationships between data in various databases is a critical element of managing the data resource. Ideally, aggregate data will be derived from operational data, not collected separately (and, hence, inconsistently), and different databases will receive data transferred from a common source. The systems that populate these databases, move data, and produce reports are described later in this chapter.

Application Software Should Be Separate From the Database. One goal of data management is **application independence**, the separation, or decoupling, of data from applications systems. This concept, embodied in Figure 5.3, is further illustrated in Figure 5.4.

In this figure the processing of data into **information** is viewed like the processing of the raw and component material resources into final products in a manufacturing company. Raw data are captured or received, inspected for quality, and stored in the warehouse. Data in storage are used in the production of any authorized information product (e.g., report). Data are retrieved from the warehouse when needed but, unlike raw materials, are not consumed when used. As data become obsolete, they are replaced with new data. Data are transferred to other parts of the organization or other organizations when authorized. As data are processed into information, this information is added to the warehouse, similar to the entry of products into finished goods storage. All operations and work centers use the raw material warehouse to produce information products (e.g., reports), but individual work centers (applications) have their own work-in-process inventory of data and receive a few kinds of data that are not shared among other applications. Thus, data are cataloged, managed, and, at least conceptually, stored centrally, where they can be kept safe and uncontaminated for use throughout the business.

The central point of Figure 5.4 is that data and applications software must be managed as separate entities. When treated separately, data are not locked inside applications, where their meaning and structure are hidden from other applications that also require these data.

Applications Software Can Be Classified by How They Treat Data. The concept of application independence suggests that different data processing applications can be classified into three groups, based upon their role in

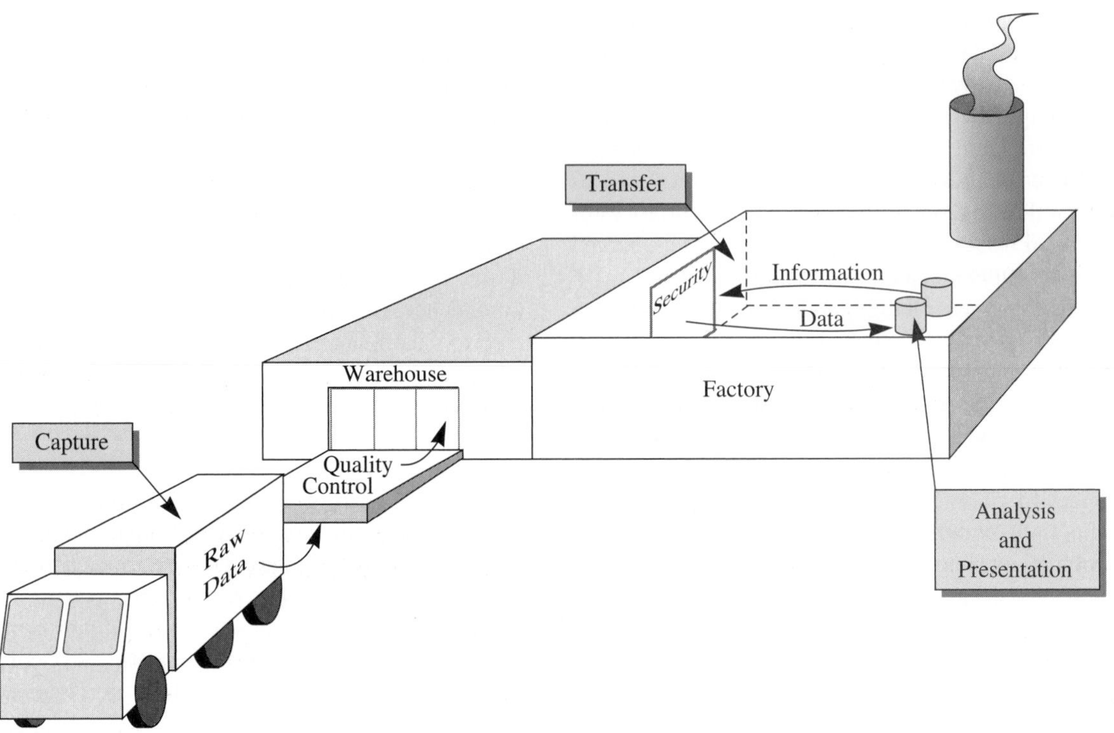

Figure 5.4 Categories of Information Processing with Application Independence

managing data: data capture, data transfer, and data analysis and presentation, as shown in Figure 5.3.

The process of transforming data into information useful for transaction management or higher-level decision making includes these steps:

1. *Data capture* **Data capture applications** gather data and populate the database. They store and maintain data in the data pyramid of Figure 5.3. Ideally, each datum is captured once and fully tested for accuracy and completeness. Responsibility for ensuring the quality of data capture systems might be distributed across the organization. Localized data capture applications are developed for data with an isolated use or data for which coordination across units is not required. Still, because localized data might eventually be useful somewhere else in the organization (and they must then be consistent across sites), an inventory of data elements (kept in the data dictionary) must be maintained of all database contents.
2. *Data transfer* **Data transfer applications** move data from one database to another. These applications are often called bridges or interfaces because they connect related databases. Once raw data are captured, they might be copied to various databases where they are stored for specific purposes. For example, customer order data might be stored in multiple subject or target area databases supporting production scheduling, billing, and customer service. Also, this kind of application extracts and summarizes data, as well as distributes copies of original data. Ideally, this transfer would be event-triggered; that is, if new basic data are captured or changed in value, messages are sent as needed to all other databases that build on these data to alert these databases that changes have occurred.
3. *Data analysis and presentation* **Data analysis and presentation applications** provide data and information to authorized persons. Data might be summarized, compared to history, reformulated into graphs, or inserted into documents being developed using a word processor. Data might be input to a decision support system or executive information system (to be discussed in Chapter 7). Data analysis and presentation applications can draw upon any and all data from databases the business manager receiving the presentation is authorized to see. Data and the way they are presented should be independent, and those who

determine the format for presentation should not necessarily control the location and format for capture and storage of data.

Applications Software Should Be Considered Disposable. A significant result of application independence is the creation of **disposable applications**. In many organizations, older systems cannot be eliminated or easily rewritten because applications and data are so intertwined. When the presentation capabilities of an application system become obsolete, but the application also maintains data that are essential to the business, an inefficient system might have to be kept alive only for its data access capabilities. With application independence, a company can replace the capture, transfer, and presentation software modules separately when necessary. Presentation systems are often the most volatile types of application, and these types of systems provide management with business value. In addition, with modern programming languages and system generators, business managers can customize their own presentation and analysis software to meet personal needs.

Data Should Be Captured Once. Another implication of the separation of data from applications is that data should be captured at one source and, even when not shared from one common database, synchronized across different databases. It is simply too costly for an organization to capture the same data multiple times and reconcile differences across applications. For example, not long ago, a university discovered during a review of its application systems that 17 different systems captured a student's home address. The redundant data management cost was estimated at several hundred thousand dollars per year. Thus, an IT architecture based on application independence permits a more responsive, flexible, and beneficial approach for managing the data resource.

Figure 5.3 illustrates one way to view the data architecture (more on the information architecture, which includes the data architecture, in Chapter 14). The **data architecture** of an organization should contain an inventory of the uses of data across the business units. The architecture should also include a plan to distribute data to various databases to support the analysis and presentation needs of different user groups. The same data might be stored in multiple databases because that is the most efficient architecture to deliver data to users. To ensure that data are current, accurate, and synchronized across the organization, however, key business data should be captured once and transferred between databases as needed.

There Should Be Strict Data Standards. Because the same and similar data are used in various application software, data must be clearly identified and defined so that all users know exactly what data they are manipulating. Further, shared databases and data transfer systems require that database contents be unambiguously defined and described. The central responsibility in managing the data resource is to develop a clear and useful way to uniquely identify every instance of data and to give unambiguous business meaning to all data. For example, an organization must be able to distinguish data about one customer from data about another. Furthermore, the meaning of such data as product description and product specification must be clear and distinct.

Figure 5.5 lists the five types of **data standards** that must be established for a business: identifiers, naming, definition, integrity rules, and usage rights. Business managers, not IS managers, have the knowledge necessary to set these standards and therefore should actively participate in the standards-setting process.

1. *Identifier* The identifier is a characteristic of a business object or event (a data entity) that uniquely distinguishes one instance of this entity from every

Identifier:	Unique value for each business entity
Naming:	Unique name or label for each type of data
Definition:	Unambiguous description for each type of data
Integrity Rule:	Specification of legitimate values for a type of data
Usage Rights:	Security clearances for a type of data

Figure 5.5 Types of Data Standards

other instance. For example, an employee number is a distinctive feature of each employee, and a unique bill-of-lading number clearly identifies each shipment. It is not uncommon to find applications in different units of a business using different identifiers for the same entity. As long as there is a one-for-one match of identifier values across the various systems, there is not a problem, but usually there is no such compatibility. The ideal identifier is one that is guaranteed to be unique and is stable for a long time. For example, a hospital might wish to use a social security number to identify a patient. Also, identifiers related to meaningful data tend not to be desirable because they are not stable. For example, a customer identification number based on geographical region and standard industrial classification (SIC) code will no longer be valid if a customer moves or changes primary businesses. Thus, it is wise to design a meaningless, sequentially assigned code as the identifier, and use such data as geographical location and SIC code as other descriptive data.

2. *Naming* Distinct and meaningful names must be given to each kind of data retained in organizational databases. If two data elements have the same name, their meaning will be confusing to users. If the same data element is referred to by different names that are never associated, business managers will think that these are different pieces of data. Many organizations develop a naming scheme or template for constructing all data names, with common terms to be used for different elements of the scheme. For example, a data name of employee-monthly-pay indicates which entity, which time period, and which type of data. Each of the three components of this data name would be limited to a restricted vocabulary; for example, the time period would have values such as daily and weekly, and abbreviations for each could be assigned. Standard names make naming new data elements easier and give a user a quick start on knowing what data are on a report or in a certain database.
3. *Definition* Each data entity and element is given a description that clarifies its meaning. The definition should apply to all business circumstances and users. Terms such as customer, employee, and product might, surprisingly, not have universal meaning. For example, does customer refer to someone who has bought from you or any potential consumer of your products or services? Over the years different parts of the business might have developed their own interpretation of such terms, so definitions must be constructed through review by a broad range of organizational units.
4. *Integrity rules* The permissible range or set of values must be clear for each data element. These integrity rules add to the meaning of data conveyed by data definitions and names. For example, a data element of region is probably limited to some set of valid values based upon sales territories or some other artificial construct. In addition, a central and single standard for valid values can be used by those developing all data capture applications to detect mistakes. Also, because exceptions might be permitted, the integrity rules might specify who can authorize deviations or under what circumstances values outside of the valid set can be authorized.
5. *Usage rights* These standards prescribe who can do what and when to each type of data. Such security standards state the permissible uses for every type of data (e.g., whole databases, individual files in a database, particular records, or data elements in a file). For example, a business manager might be restricted to retrieving only the employee-monthly-pay data element, only during regular business hours, from an authorized terminal, and only about herself and those people she supervises.

These data standards should be retained in a standards database called a data dictionary/directory (DD/D), as discussed earlier. This central repository of data about data helps users learn more about organizational databases. Database management systems should also use the DD/D to access and authorize use of data.

The Data Management Process

A manager of real estate, personnel, or finances is familiar with the basic but essential functions necessary to manage effectively those resources. Figure 5.6 lists the generic functions for managing any business resource. This section examines each of these functions within the context of data management. An important point to note is that, as with other resources, every business manager should be involved, in some way, in every one of these functions for data.

1. Plan Data resource planning develops a blueprint for data and the relationships among data across business units and functions. As with most plans, there will be a macro-level data plan, typically called an enterprise data model, to identify data entities and relationships among the entities and more detailed plans to define schedules for the implementation of databases for different parts of this blueprint. The plan identifies which data are required, where they are used in the business, how they will be used (i.e., what they

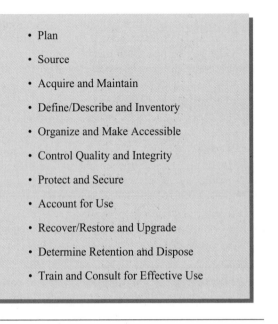

- Plan
- Source
- Acquire and Maintain
- Define/Describe and Inventory
- Organize and Make Accessible
- Control Quality and Integrity
- Protect and Secure
- Account for Use
- Recover/Restore and Upgrade
- Determine Retention and Dispose
- Train and Consult for Effective Use

Figure 5.6 Asset Management Functions

will be used to produce), and how much data are expected. This plan must then be communicated to all business functions that are involved in aspects of data resource management. For example, system capacity planning must be informed of this schedule, along with data and processing volumes, so that adequate computer and network technology can be in place to operate and access these databases.

2. Source Decisions must be made about the timeliest and highest-quality source for each data element required. For example, should customer sales data be collected at point-of-sale or entered later? Concerns over error rates, frequency of changes, chance of lost paper documents, technology costs, training requirements, and many other factors will influence this decision. For data to be acquired from sources external to the organization, the quality, cost, and timeliness of these sources need to be considered. For example, different market research organizations might collect competitive sales data from retail outlets or telephone surveys. When selecting an external data source, the original source, the reliability of the data, the timing of when the data are needed and when they were collected, the precision and detail collected, and other factors should be checked.

3. Acquire and Maintain Once the best sources for data are identified and selected, data capture systems must be built to acquire and maintain these data. Changes in data need to be broadcast to all databases that store these data. Users of the data need to know when the data are refreshed and perhaps automatically be informed of exceptional conditions (such as inventory stockout, stock price below a critical level, or receipt of an especially large customer order). Appropriate applications systems need to be built to track data acquisition and transfer. For example, suppose electronic files of customer list data are sent to telemarketing vendors for a promotional campaign and results are returned via the Internet. A system is needed to confirm that all files were sent and received, that all customers on the list were called, and that a status is received on each.

4. Define/Describe and Inventory A basic step in managing any resource is defining what is being managed. For a real estate manager, each property must be described, standards and scales must be set to define the size and shape of each building or land parcel, and terminology must be defined to refer to different pieces of each building. Similarly, in managing data, each data entity, data element, and relationship must be defined, a format for storage and reporting established, and the organization of the data described so users know how to access the data. As mentioned earlier, a data inventory catalog must be maintained, usually using a DD/D, where all data definitions and descriptions are kept, volume statistics on data are maintained, and other data about data (such as access rights and integrity rules) are stored. All users can go to the data dictionary to find out what data exist and what the data mean.

5. Organize and Make Accessible Databases need to be designed so that data can be retrieved and reported efficiently and in the format that business managers require. Data should be arranged and stored so that information can be produced easily. Although most of the work here is rather technical, this physical arrangement of data cannot be done unless potential uses of the data are well-defined, and this task is best done by business managers. The two aspects of data usage necessary for proper organization are what data are required and how the data are to be selected. For example, database designers need to know if customer data will be selected by markets, geographical regions, what products they have bought, through what sales staff they buy, or other criteria. Orders of magnitude improvements in processing speed can be achieved when the data organization is well-tuned to the processing requirements. Of course, wise choices of database designs can similarly achieve significant reductions in the cost of maintaining and processing data.

One highly popular method for making data accessible to many people in an organization is the data warehouse

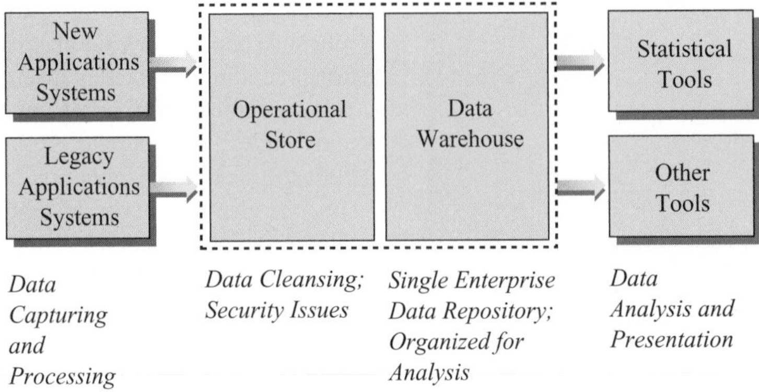

Figure 5.7 The Data Warehouse

(see Chapter 6 for more on data warehousing). Figure 5.7 depicts how a large division of a furniture manufacturer recently implemented a data warehouse. Prior to the creation of the data warehouse, the company operated several legacy applications systems, each containing data difficult to extract but needed by other units in the company. Likewise, because of the way data were organized, it was difficult to analyze the data residing in these application systems. A data warehouse was created whereby certain data from each existing system and data from new systems that were built were extracted on a regular basis and put in the operational store. In this facility the data were cleansed and organized for analysis (e.g., by product versus by order) and transferred to the data warehouse. Analysts thus have data available from each plant and for all product lines. With the data warehouse in place, the furniture manufacturer is beginning to employ data mining techniques (to be discussed in Chapter 7) to aid in areas such as analysis and forecasting. Eventually, improvements in forecasting ability and reductions in lost analyst time from the creation of this data warehouse are estimated to generate a 31 percent return on investment.

BIRTH OF A LEGEND

If your job has anything to do with data warehouses, you have heard of the tale about the correlation between purchases of diapers and purchases of beer. The statistical oddity, duly reported in at least 200 articles, is variously attributed to Wal-Mart, Thrifty PayLess stores, or an unidentified grocery chain. Whichever, the retailer supposedly rearranged its shelves and sold more diapers and more beer.

Where did this tale start? It appears to have come from one Thomas Blischok, now chief executive of Decisioneering Group in Scottsdale, Arizona. As vice president of industry consulting for NCR, he was doing a study for American Stores' Osco Drugs in 1992 when he discovered dozens of correlations, including one connecting beer and diapers in transactions between 5 P.M. and 7 P.M.

Blischok recounted the tale in a speech, and it became the stuff of consultants' pitches, trade magazine articles, and ads. But did Osco rearrange its beer or diaper shelves as a result? Nope.

[Rao, 1998]

6. Control Quality and Integrity As with employee certification, audits of financial records, and tests for hazardous materials or structural defects in buildings, quality and integrity controls must be placed on the data resource. The concept of application independence implies that such controls must be stored as part of the data definitions and enforced during data capture and maintenance. In addition, periodic checks of databases should be made as part of the audit of financial records. As with other quality assurance functions, the check of data quality should be assigned to an organization that is not directly responsible for storing and managing the data.

Data quality is an especially critical issue when data are considered a corporate asset (see the sidebar entitled "Good, Clean Data"). The more data are used to support organizational operations, the cleaner the data should be. For example, when the data are combined with a CRM (customer relationship management) application, data quality problems can lead to mismanaged relationships and result in lost sales. Data are essential in ERP (enterprise resource planning) systems, CRM, and data warehousing. The quality of the data has a direct relationship to the quality of the processes performed by these systems.

7. Protect and Secure The rights each manager has to each type of data must be defined. Privileges for use of data might include definition, retrieval, insertion, deletion,

TOO MUCH OF A GOOD THING?

Does a growing data warehouse eat up too much storage and cash?

Not according to Dave Beulke, principal consultant with Pragmatic Solutions, an Alexandria, Virginia-based consulting firm. "Adding more storage is not a critical cost factor in scaling up a data warehouse," he says. "After all, disk storage costs have been falling dramatically in the past three years."

Beulke offers these tips for managing the warehouse project:

- Split workloads among many servers, clusters, or mainframe systems logical partitions.
- Provide virtually instantaneous fall-over and backup capabilities to ensure that you keep serving your customers.
- Since the amount of input/output increases with the size of the database, I/O-intensive functions should be split across several parallel processes and CPUs.
- Organize information for effective use by your customers, such as year-to-year comparisons of marketing campaigns or any time period examinations of milestone events.
- Secure high-level sponsorship.
- Ensure that management is focused on the data warehouse's prime purpose. Many projects suffer from "scope creep" as more activities are sought from more departments.

[Singer, 2000]

GOOD, CLEAN DATA

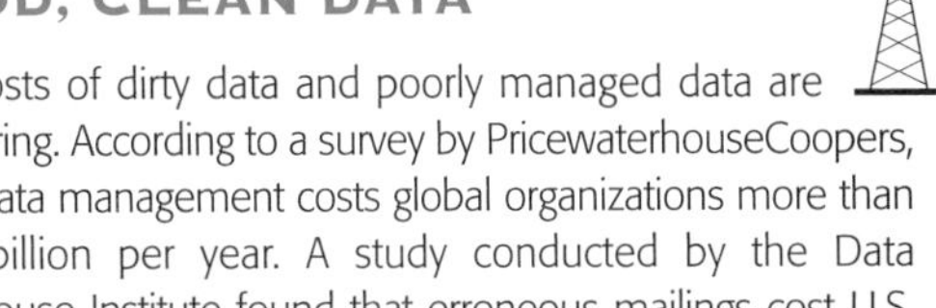

The costs of dirty data and poorly managed data are staggering. According to a survey by PricewaterhouseCoopers, poor data management costs global organizations more than $1.4 billion per year. A study conducted by the Data Warehouse Institute found that erroneous mailings cost U.S. business about $611 billion in 2002.

Data quality is a critical issue that is slowly coming to the forefront in businesses today. Two key reasons for poor data quality are the rush to install new systems and the failure to take an integrated view of the organization's data. In the rush to install a new system, many organizations fail to look critically at their existing data. Often, these new systems support a single function, and while the data might get cleaned up for that function, the source of the errors is often overlooked.

There are several critical steps in a data quality initiative:

1. Establish processes to *prevent* errors.
   a. Assign a person in each area to verify the data's quality.
   b. Structure databases so that fields are consistent across areas.
2. Clean up existing errors.
3. Verify that third-party data suppliers provide clean data.
4. Focus on the critical data.
5. Don't rely too heavily on cleanup tools; focus on prevention instead.

[Adapted from Turek, 2003, and Betts, 2001]

update, and retrieval of the datum by itself or in combination with other values. For example, a business manager might be permitted to see the salaries of everyone in his department but might not be able to match names with salaries. Privileges can be assigned to programs, databases, files, individual records or data elements, terminals, and workstations. Use of other equipment, data, and programs might be limited by time of day or days of the week. The decision on who has the right to do what with data is a delicate balance between the need to protect the quality and integrity of data by protecting a valuable asset from damage or theft and the right of individuals to have easy access to the data they need in their jobs. Because security is so important and can be dysfunctional if managed improperly, security should be considered when databases and application systems are originally built and not developed as an afterthought.

8. Account for Use Because there is considerable cost to capture, maintain, and report data, these costs must be identified and an accounting system developed to report them. Further, an organization might choose to distribute the costs to appropriate responsibility centers. Two conditions make accounting for the use of data especially difficult as compared to other information resources. First, frequently the organizational unit responsible for acquiring data is not the primary user of the data. Second, usage is shared because data are not consumed from usage. The operating system and database management systems can capture the actual costs of computer disk storage and computer processing time. The real issue is to develop a fair charging scheme that promotes good management of data but does not deter beneficial use. Because the value of data is so elusive, the linkage of readily identifiable costs to value is difficult. At a minimum, the costs for data storage and processing and who uses which data can be determined. Of course, how to charge to recover these costs is a separate and more difficult issue.

9. Recover/Restore and Upgrade When an asset becomes old or damaged, it is often renovated and put back into operation. When an employee's skills become obsolete

EXHIBIT 2

The U.S. Custom Machine Industry Production Capacity Additions from 1965 to 1995

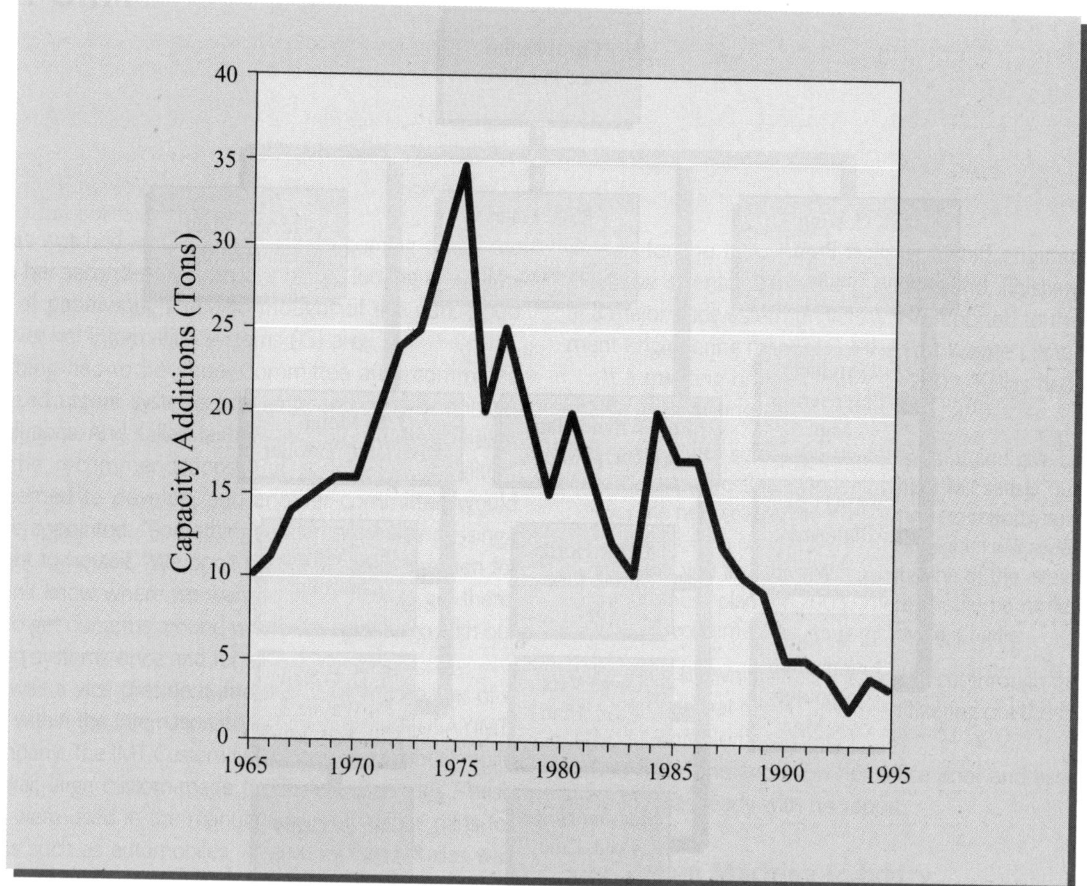

that the custom machine industry might return to a robust building program by 2005.

International Machine and Tool

International Machine and Tool used a matrix-style organization throughout its operations, modeled after the structure of other large, Europe-based global companies. Dr. Wilhelm Schlein, chairman of IMT, summarized the organization as "a federation of national companies with a global coordination center—a distributed organization which has many homes." Schlein's strategy for building a decentralized, multidomestic enterprise was critical to achieving IMT's goal of "think global, act local."

One side of IMT's matrix organization was country-based. Each country manager (president of the national holding company) was responsible for financial targets for all of IMT's products and services in that country. Country presidents coordinated synergistic relationships across IMT operations within the country (e.g., the same distribution and service networks). They were also responsible for maintaining relationships with national government officials.

The second side of IMT's matrix was technology-based (product classes) and reported through a separate transnational technology management group, called a business group (BG). The mission of each BG was to support shared knowledge and operations among many international factories in the same industry. BG leaders served as business strategists who set global "rules of the game" and then let local managers (like Kallas) pilot the execution.

In 2002, IMT had eight international custom machine factories, two of which were located in the United States. The U.S. plants represented nearly one-half of IMT's global capacity. The combined capacity of the Chicago and Fort Wayne plants was far larger than any in the other countries.

Kallas reported to two managers in the matrix, the U.S. country manager and a Custom Machine BG manager, who often had conflicting goals. While she had to increase return on assets to support the U.S. country manager, she simultaneously was encouraged to maintain a leading technology position by the BG head. As was true for all custom machine factories, Kallas' division paid about one percent of sales to the BG for global research and development projects.

Carol L. Kallas

With more than 18 years of custom machine engineering experience, Kallas was widely known and highly respected throughout the custom machine industry. Earlier in her career, Kallas had worked her way through several engineering and manufacturing management positions at WILMEC. She had always been active in the industry by chairing and working on technical committees of various professional associations.

However, Kallas was not actively involved in the use of the information systems at IMT. Her personal use of a computer was limited to preparing short documents, maintaining a calendar, constructing and reviewing reports, sending e-mail at work, and browsing the Internet from home. She felt that her hectic schedule made it impossible to use the personal computer in her office for more than 50 minutes a day.

In 1999, Kallas was appointed a vice president of IMT Custom Machines Company, Inc. (CMCI), the IMT subsidiary in the United States. On the "country side" of the matrix, CMCI reported through the IMT-USA holding company in New York, which in turn reported to IMT's world headquarters in Bonn. On the BG side of the matrix, Kallas reported to the managing director of the Custom Machine BG. The headquarters for the business group was in Milan, Italy.

Shortly after taking the job, Kallas and other division managers worked with the IMT-USA president to develop universally applicable (to all IMT-USA companies) statements of the corporate mission, principles, and vision. After considerable discussion and many revisions, the IMT-USA president disseminated the final product on March 26, 1999. (See Exhibit 3.)

EXHIBIT 3
IMT-USA Mission, Guiding Principles, and Vision Statements

The following was taken from a presentation given by the IMT-USA President on March 26, 1999.

Mission
- Serve U.S. customers to their individual needs and total satisfaction.
- Create an organizational environment that allows all IMT-USA's employees to add value.
- Promote an atmosphere of thirst and eagerness to perform that allows delegation of responsibility to the lowest possible organizational level and attracts good people.
- Generate a sense of urgency and results orientation in the development of capital and human resources to ensure proper return for both our employees and our shareholders.
- Expand the horizon of the organization to share in and contribute to our worldwide core competencies.

Guiding Principles
- Create a sense of urgency—concentrate on priority actions rather than procedural issues.
- Promote a unifying culture: "can do—do it."
- Remove barriers to performance.
- Shift organizational focus to servicing the customers and beating the competition.

Vision
- Demonstrate leadership in serving the U.S. marketplace in its transition to cleaner industry, where products are more efficiently produced, distributed, and applied.

The Fort Wayne Plant

The work environment at the Fort Wayne plant over the prior 25 years was dynamic, to say the least. Over that period, the plant first transitioned from a busy single-product factory into a stagnant operation that nearly closed due to a lack of orders. A few short years later, it evolved into a facility that supported three technically different products (large horizontal, large vertical, and medium horizontal custom machines), each originating from a different company with different engineering design systems. In 2002, IMT's Fort Wayne facility was producing near its capacity and was staffed with about 1,200 employees.

Until the mid-1990s, all the engineering and marketing operations for the Fort Wayne and Chicago plants were located in Cleveland, Ohio (200 miles from Fort Wayne and 350 miles from Chicago). In 1995, IMT closed the Cleveland site and transferred the engineering and marketing staffs to either Fort Wayne or Chicago.

As the Fort Wayne plant evolved to support multiple product lines, a number of informal procedures emerged to handle day-to-day situations. These undocumented processes worked well enough, despite the incompatibilities among the three machine technologies, which used three separate drafting systems as well as unique manufacturing processes. Very little capital had been invested in upgrading operations during the last several years of WILMEC's ownership. In fact, it was not until IMT had completed its purchase of WILMEC that a major capital upgrade was even considered. Low margins and strict capital budget limits always prevented significant upgrades. As a result, the informal processes continued under IMT ownership, as company executives focused on making the acquisition show a profit.

In early 1996, the plant was reorganized into three "machine-type" product lines, each operating as a separate product line and profit center. In June 1997, CMCI's quality assurance manager, Edward Fortesque, completed the mission statement for CMCI. (See Exhibit 4.) Finally, the company's reorganization was coming together.

CMCI's Information Systems

Charles Browning began his investigation shortly after receiving his charge from Carol Kallas. By mid-September 2002, he had uncovered considerable data about the information systems at Fort Wayne and Chicago.

Support for Fort Wayne's information systems was split into two groups: an engineering systems (ES) group and a management information systems (MIS) group (again see Exhibit 1). The ES group consisted of eight of the 25 people who reported to Dr. Michael C. King, Fort Wayne's development engineering manager. Dr. King had been trained as an engineer and was known as an industry-wide expert on the design of automated fabrication technologies.

Twenty MIS support staff members reported to Bill Gears, who in turn reported to Joe O'Neil, the division MIS manager. Chicago had its own one-person MIS "group" who reported directly to O'Neil. O'Neil reported through the division controller's organization. O'Neil was a former IBM employee with extensive experience on large mainframes and on the IBM AS/400

EXHIBIT 4
Mission/Vision Statement
IMT Custom Machine Company, Inc.

The following was issued throughout the Fort Wayne plant on June 25, 1997 by Edward Fortesque, Manager of Quality Assurance.

Mission
- To be recognized as the outstanding custom machine manufacturer in the world.

Goals
- *Provide market leadership*
  - Customer satisfaction
    - Quality
    - Reliability
    - Delivery
    - Service
  - Serve the market with optional products and services
  - Be the technology leader
- *Achieve business (operational) excellence*
  - Zero failures
  - On-time performance
  - Low throughput time for orders through the factory
  - High productivity of labor
  - Return on capital employed >30% (pre-tax)
  - Revenue to total compensation growth of at least 5% per year

Vision
- To be perceived by each of our customers as superior to the best of our competitors in the overall quality of our products and services.

EXHIBIT 5
Fort Wayne MIS Direction and Objectives
IMT Custom Machine Company, Inc.

The following was issued to top division and plant management on July 30, 2002, by Joe O Neil, division MIS manager.

Direction
- Pursue a more structured MIS strategy with a reasonable and manageable level of risk that will be consistent with our being a leader in the custom machine industry.
- Develop and execute a plan that will continually upgrade our hardware, software, applications, database, and network environments to accomplish the above.

Objectives
- Recognize our business is designing and producing custom machines, not chasing ever-changing computer technology and theories.
- Coordinate MIS strategy with our business objectives of:
  - Zero defects
  - Low throughput time
  - ROCE (return on capital employed) of 30%
- Control our own destiny.
- Minimize risk and hidden costs.
- Work from a total systems architecture plan to:
  - Develop an applications architecture
  - Select the hardware plan required to best accomplish our goals
- Maintain an integrated environment that supports the various functions of our division.

platform. He had been the MIS manager at another IMT site before coming to Fort Wayne in 1998.

On July 30, 2002, O'Neil circulated a memo to the top division and plant managers that summarized his objectives for Fort Wayne's MIS group. (See Exhibit 5.) O'Neil later told Browning, "I do not have a formal mission for the MIS group, but essentially I am looking to provide an adequate, responsive, and economical network structure of data processing support for all sites within the division."

Browning found that a variety of computing hardware was used to support the division. (See Exhibit 6.)

The division operated an IBM mainframe located at Fort Wayne that could be used by anyone in the division at no direct charge. All lease and operating costs for the mainframe were covered in the division's overhead. When they joined the company, new engineers and other professionals were supplied with a mainframe user account, a personal computer (PC) equipped with a board to enable it to communicate with the mainframe, and several PC software packages for local work. The mainframe arrived in March 1999 on a 5-year lease. A mainframe upgrade in 2001 was driven by the need for improvements in computer-aided drafting (CAD) response time and an increasing number of users. From 1999 to 2001, 65 new users throughout the factory and front offices were connected to the mainframe.

CMCI also had an IBM AS/400 that it had inherited from General Engineering. Immediately after the acquisition, MIS personnel attempted to create a facility to move data between the two mainframes, but that proved to be difficult. Most exchanges were done by "pulling" data from one system to the other. Although a routine (called AMSERV) was available to "push" data to the other system, its use was not fully understood. Another reason AMSERV was not used was that the receiver's data file could be updated without the user's knowledge. As a result, data security issues slowed the practice of sharing data between the two systems. In sequential applications, where data were created in one system and used by another, identical data files were needed on each system.

EXHIBIT 6

Computing Systems and Applications: IMT Custom Machine Company, Inc.*

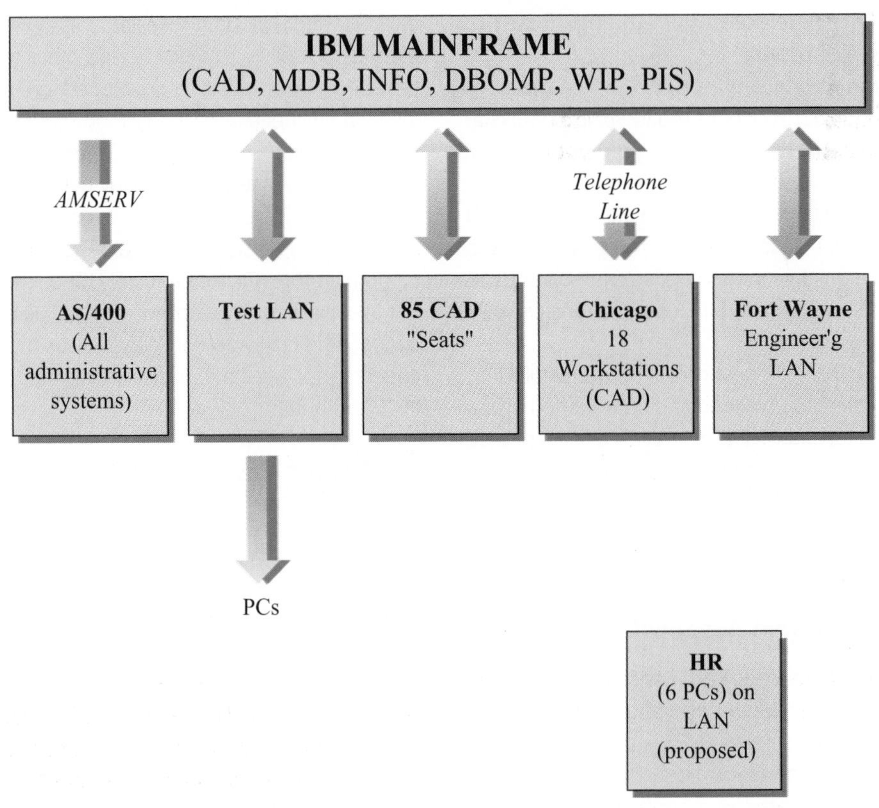

* Applications are in parentheses

From 2001 on, the heaviest use of the mainframe was by drafting and engineering staff. IMT Fort Wayne used IBM's CAD product on the mainframe. The CAD application, along with additional drafting and engineering programs, represented about 65 percent of mainframe use. Total usage in August 2002 was estimated at approximately 54 percent of the mainframe's CPU capacity.

The division also used personal computers extensively. The policy at Fort Wayne was that anyone who needed a PC could get one. Financial justification was not necessary, as PCs were considered a tool. Fort Wayne's standard PC configuration included the latest Intel processor running the latest version of Microsoft Windows as well as the Microsoft Office suite and several other popular packages—all connected to an ink jet printer. PCs were obtained under a three-year lease from a local supplier.

Many users felt that the lack of sufficient mainframe software support and lengthy systems development time on the part of the MIS group had been partially compensated by the use of PCs. For example, production scheduling in major work centers in the factory was done with a spreadsheet on PCs. However, the principal use for many PCs was as a "dumb" terminal to the mainframe for database inquiry or sending e-mail. In addition, secretaries and engineers routinely used PC word processing to write memos. Of the 300 users on Fort Wayne's mainframe, about 210 were accessing it through PCs. The remaining users were CAD users.

The division also had powerful personal workstations for technical work. As of 2002, Fort Wayne had six IBM workstations used by the development engineering group for special projects. They were connected through a local area network (LAN). Several Sun workstations were also linked into the LAN during the previous year. Personnel at the Chicago facility used 18 IBM CAD workstations for normal production work. At Fort Wayne, there were also 25 Sun and IBM workstations used for the production of drawings.

Drawings made in Chicago on workstations were stored on Fort Wayne's mainframe and uploaded and downloaded over a high-speed dedicated telephone line. Chicago's designers liked their CAD stations, but were having trouble with the connection between the mainframe and the Chicago LAN. Tom Goodman, the MIS support person in Chicago, told Browning, "I feel like we are the beta site for linking sites together."

Data Flow and Functional Responsibilities

Exhibit 7 illustrates the generalized data flow among the main functional areas of the Fort Wayne operation. Of the seven functions, only the human resources (HR) department was not connected to the main information flow. The remaining six organizational areas participated in a continuous sequential flow of information.

The flow of business information started with the interaction between marketing and the customer. Information originated from the customer when a technical description or specification (a "spec") was sent to IMT for a new machine. The length of the spec could be from ten to several hundred pages. A marketing engineer would then read the spec and enter his or her interpretation of it into a mainframe negotiation program. The negotiation program (MDB), inherited from WILMEC, required the input of about fifty computer screens of data, and was written in COBOL. For presentations, marketing used Excel and PowerPoint on their PCs.

If a marketing engineer had a question about a spec, he or she called a design engineer or another local expert. Most estimates had to be turned around in 10 working days. Because of the volume of requests and a staff of only two engineers covering all of the United States, negotiations were sometimes very hectic. Mike Truelove, a marketing engineer, told Browning, "We do the best we can, but we miss some things from time to time. Almost always after winning the order, we go back and negotiate with the customer over what we missed."

Another frequently used mainframe application was a query system (called INFO) automatically linked to data from the negotiation program. It was used to analyze data from ongoing negotiations as well as contracts after they were won or lost.

The administration and finance group was the home for most business support systems. The purchase order, accounts payable, and accounts receivable systems were applications used by purchasing, receiving, and other groups. All three systems had been custom developed on the AS/400 by the General Engineering MIS staff (some of whom now worked at CMCI). Although wages and salaries were maintained locally, an external data service company handled the payroll.

As of 2002, human resources used only stand-alone computers. HR had plans to install a LAN that operated customized corporate programs for handling HR functions, including benefits and pension/investment plans. There were no plans to connect the LAN with Fort Wayne's mainframe due to security concerns for the confidential personnel records residing on HR's computers.

Production Requirements

Each machine the company made was electrically and mechanically custom designed to a customer's exact specifications. Customization requirements, when mixed with the complexities of the economic and engineering limits, required sophisticated computer programs for modeling and design work. In 2002, Fort Wayne had three separate design systems, one for each of the three types of custom machines. Design engineers for each product line were experts on their own programs.

The first step in design engineering was to receive electronically the data previously entered into the negotiation program. The process entailed pulling the data records from the negotiation database. The design engineer reread the customer's spec and decided which additional data needed to be added to the

EXHIBIT 7
Data Flow Among Functional Areas*
IMT Custom Machine Company, Inc.

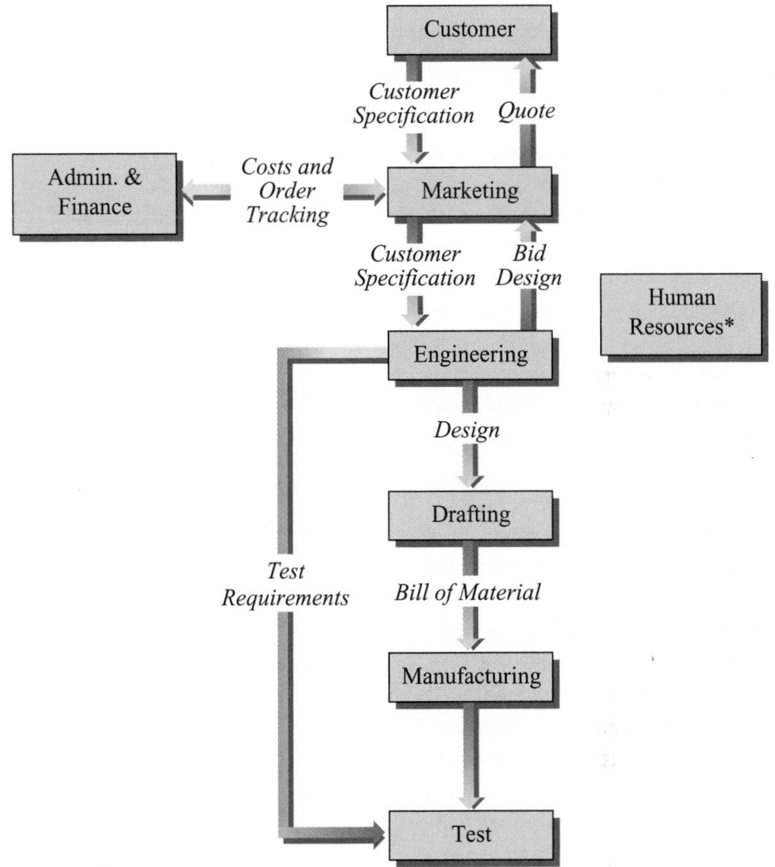

* Uses only applications supported by IMT-USA.

input files for the design program. The program then generated a design that the engineer reviewed in detail and often revised. After the design was accepted by the engineer, the electronic computer file and a paper folder with completed job forms were sent to a drafting supervisor for completion.

The ES group had created all of Fort Wayne's design systems. The number of routines used by each of the three systems was a relative measure of system size and complexity. Large vertical had about 500 routines, medium horizontal had about 400 routines, and large horizontal had about 2,400 routines.

All drafting at Fort Wayne and Chicago was performed on a CAD applications system. At Fort Wayne, the CAD application ran on the IBM mainframe, and in Chicago it ran on the local IBM workstations. There were 85 CAD "seats" at Fort Wayne and 18 at Chicago. (A "seat" is equivalent to one hardware CAD setup with a high-resolution screen, keyboard, function-button box, and a pointing device that worked like a mouse.) During the prior 5 years, additional programs had been written to take output automatically from the design programs and create CAD drawings or references to drawings of standard parts. About 60 percent of the drawings for the average 4,000 parts per machine were created in this way. The remaining 40 percent of drawings had to be created by a draftsman from the design specifications. All jobs were reduced to drawings prior to being released to the factory.

A standard part drawing included the material specification on the drawing. Assembly work orders contained the bill of material (BOM). Having CAD and the design programs on the same platform made the development of the automatic drawing programs very convenient. Jennifer Velan, an engineer in the development group, told Browning, "There are things we have been able to do with this setup that would be impossible if the jobs were split between two separate systems."

When all the drawings for a machine were completed, the BOM was manually transferred from the drawings into the BOM database system, called DBOMP. DBOMP was originally written by IBM and extensively modified for Fort Wayne in the 1990s to handle bills of material for the vertical type machines. When production of the medium and large horizontal machines was transferred to Fort Wayne, DBOMP's limitations forced many "work-arounds." For example, when the General Engineering large horizontal technology was moved to Fort Wayne, it was discovered that DBOMP could not handle the longer General Engineering drawing numbers. Moreover, there was no one at Fort Wayne who knew the DBOMP code well enough to make a change in the software.

The work-in-process (WIP) inventory tracking system for the shop floor at Fort Wayne was very limited and worked only for items required for the main aisle assembly area. It could only handle made-to-order parts, not stock items. The system worked by having a main aisle supervisor request a "pull" from the storeroom to get parts delivered. The tracking systems for items within feeder aisles were done either manually or on a spreadsheet. Each item's information was maintained by its respective aisle. The WIP main aisle tracking system resided on the mainframe, and the data were loaded by hand from the DBOMP.

The parts inventory system (PIS) was very limited and similar to the tracking system except that it worked off all stocked inventory items for the main and all feeder aisles. It used a process identical to the WIP system.

The MIS group was backlogged in supporting the rapid changes occurring at the Fort Wayne plant. The lead time on most system upgrades was 3 weeks for emergencies and 6 to 9 months for non-emergencies. When a computerized system failed to provide needed functionality, paper systems were created to support information needs.

Because each custom machine was a significant investment—between $2 million and $8 million—all machines were fully tested at Fort Wayne or Chicago and the testing was personally witnessed by an employee or agent of the customer company. The test department, along with the witness, certified that every machine met the customer's test requirements set forth in the specification.

Scheduling information and other test details were forwarded to the test department by hand. Test information was written on a form that was interpreted or copied from the customer specification in marketing and engineering. The biggest complaint from the test department was that sometimes the marketing department did not properly interpret the customer's test requirement specifications. A failed or unnecessary test that resulted from misinterpreting a customer's specification could cost IMT well over $100,000.

The test department had several personal computers connected to a LAN. Although all PCs in the test department were also connected to the mainframe, this connectivity was used only occasionally. The test department was a part of the quality assurance organization at Fort Wayne, which was responsible for the data and production of the test reports sent to customers. Electronic test result data, however, remained only on the test department's LAN. The test department maintained its own LAN applications.

Personnel Issues

Browning uncovered some additional information about the information systems personnel at the company. The programmers in MIS had extensive backgrounds in COBOL and in RPG for the AS/400. None of them, however, knew the UNIX operating system or its related programming languages. Of the 14 programmers, four had over 25 years experience at Fort Wayne, two had about 12 years, and the remaining eight had 3 years or less.

Engineers who supported the engineering system in the development group had significant backgrounds in scientific computing and four had some experience with UNIX. Each engineer had more than 10 years of experience with the company. One of the recently added programmers in the engineering systems group knew UNIX very well.

Browning heard many comments during his investigation that suggested that the MIS and engineering systems staff at Fort Wayne always made the systems work—despite the constant change.

Browning concluded that as a result of employing informal systems, work-arounds, and an extraordinary amount of human effort, Fort Wayne was profitable in 2001—its first profitable year in several years. Slowly, things were stabilizing at Fort Wayne—the informal systems were being corrected and formalized. Restructuring into three product lines had helped to clarify the focus and purpose of operations systems and procedures. Overall, the primary reason many staff members saw progress was that each product line was allowed independent control and responsibility.

Computer systems support, however, remained an issue. The engineering systems group supported engineering and drafting, and the MIS group supported everything else. The HR organization was not considered a local issue because its applications were supported by the corporate MIS group in New York (IMT-USA). A small group within MIS maintained all PCs and miscellaneous computer hardware for all the functional groups across the plant.

Support for Engineering and Drafting Systems

Browning also discovered an ongoing debate over where the IT support for the engineering and drafting systems should be located. Browning summarized the three alternatives that arose from the debate on a legal pad at his desk:

1. *In the engineering support systems group:* Arguments for leaving support for engineering and drafting in the development engineering line of authority were strong. The design and drafting programs produced models for the three product line technologies. The three principal people supporting these design systems were engineers with strong computer backgrounds. Two of the three had master's degrees in engineering. Support for these programs required a balance of custom machine design knowledge, creativity, and programming. By working close to the user engineers in the product line, the support engineers could update the systems rapidly. The engineers feared that MIS programmers had little understanding of the underlying design technology. Some of the engineers speculated that the MIS people might make coding changes that "would cost millions to correct once a design was committed and the parts were made."
2. *In the product lines:* Arguments for product line support of engineering systems included the fact that product line engineers had extensive firsthand knowledge of how the system was used. As a result, feedback on problems would be more obvious to those who supported the system. Furthermore, it could be argued that ultimate control of the software should be in the hands of each of the profit centers. They should have the option to regulate the level of computer support based on their own strategy. However, if the engineering systems support responsibilities were located within the product lines, a programmer would need to be transferred from the engineering support systems group to each of the product lines.
3. *In the MIS group:* Arguments for MIS-based support of engineering and drafting systems included an alignment of all computer-related functions in one functional group—thus providing a common responsibility point for all computer support and integrated applications. Product line and development engineering would have to submit change requests that were more completely documented. Support through MIS would guarantee that coding changes would be better documented. If support were the responsibility of the product line engineers, MIS people argued that the end result might be "spaghetti code," which no one but the original programmer could understand.

The Move to a Common Machine Design System

Browning discovered that in early 2002, Kallas had received instructions that her subsidiary would have to use a redeveloped set of custom machine design programs from Germany. The BG management team believed it was appropriate to institute a common custom machine design system across all factories. The BG strategy was based on porting the German programs onto a UNIX workstation platform and then distributing and supporting it worldwide. When the announcement was made that the German programs would be used, however, none of the programs would work with UNIX. Nor did the German developers possess more than a few years of total experience in the UNIX environment.

A New Marketing and Negotiation System

Browning learned that marketing and engineering saw the existing negotiation program as inefficient and ineffective. Two years of studying how the IMT division should do business with its customers led the marketing group to propose a reengineered "front-end information" system. The proposed system would include capabilities to optically scan in all customer proposals, including text. Customer specs could then be analyzed and processed more quickly.

The proposed system had an initial price tag of over $2.5 million. The original idea for the system was conceived in the marketing department, which employed two staff engineers and an independent outside consultant as its own IS expert. Only recently had MIS been involved with planning the system. The project was being led by the division strategic planning manager, which isolated the project from division MIS and engineering input. Hardware purchases were to begin in November 2002, and the system was to be completed and operational by the end of 2003.

CMCI's Interface to Field Sales

Browning discovered that IMT's field sales group had itself been planning a new system for transferring order information to the factories. The new system, called SPEC, was planned to come on line in late 2003. By mid-2003, each factory was to have installed a LAN to accommodate the data downloaded from field sales personnel. As of September 2002, SPEC was plagued with delays because staff could not arrive at a consensus on the exact information that should be transmitted to each of the factories.

New Software Design Tools

After asking some questions in the controller's office, Browning found that payments from Fort Wayne and Chicago accounted for 25 percent of the funds used for the BG's R&D development budget. IMT's MIS group felt that about 30 percent of its investment was received back in the form of useful information technologies while the remaining 70 percent benefited production hardware improvements. The BG was definitely committed to additional investments in UNIX application tools.

Various software engineering and applications development tools had been mentioned, but the specific software and the number of seats that would be leased or purchased had not been finalized as of the end of September 2002.

Bill of Material (BOM) System Replacement

The production scheduling people told Browning that the DBOMP system was nearly 15 years old and could not handle the new German-developed design system that was to replace the three older systems. To support the new design system and its subsequent BOM structure, a new BOM system would be required. Fort Wayne systems staff had identified a system that would run on the IBM mainframe and could be acquired at no cost. The program, called PUFR, was free because it was in the process of being discarded by IMT-USA's corporate MIS group. The only requirement was that Fort Wayne MIS staff had to support PUFR.

By September 2002, over 4,000 staff hours had been consumed by Fort Wayne MIS personnel trying to make PUFR operational. Projections suggested that approximately 10 percent more work had to be done in order to get PUFR into a test mode. To get this far, Fort Wayne systems had already purchased additional modules that were not originally included in the free IMT corporate version of PUFR. The effort had also included converting some of the approximately 400 auxiliary programs that used the old DBOMP format. Occasional discussions of replacing PUFR "in a few years" were heard in the halls.

Browning's Meeting with Kallas

Browning summarized the findings of his six-week investigation at an October 2002 meeting with Kallas that went as follows:

"The best way to characterize the current information systems situation at Fort Wayne is as a lot of manual points where data are transferred between a patchwork of old, semiautomatic, outdated processes. The result is that since each place where information is transferred has a probability of introducing a new error, checking and rechecking is necessary to ensure integrity. And since the outdated processes require constant fixes and work-arounds, the newer processes never move ahead. What we really need is a clear vision to guide our decisions today, so we can be ready for tomorrow."

"I was afraid of that, Charlie. So do we have any options?" asked Kallas.

"We do." replied Browning. "But first we really need to develop a vision, architecture, and strategy statement for all information systems consistent with our business objectives. I see three options for the basic information technology architecture."

"Let me hear the first one," replied Kallas.

"OK," said Browning. "The first option is to move towards a centralized, likely IBM, computing environment. Under this option, we would commit to staying with the mainframe for all important applications, discourage the use of the Sun and IBM workstations, maybe allow the use of Linux on the mainframe, and eliminate the AS/400. This approach would maximize use of the lower cost, energy-efficient mainframe.

"Our commitment to the mainframe would have to be long term. To continue to maintain a large central mainframe and acquire new applications and full access for all users would require a systematic plan. The plan would include porting all the major AS/400 applications to the mainframe to assure central use, support, and control. Major mainframe packages would be reviewed for upgrades that could handle Fort Wayne's current capacity and requirements. Older packages used in Fort Wayne would be phased out over the next 5 years. PCs connected through LANs to the mainframe would do spreadsheet and word processing work, but almost all computational work would be done on the mainframe."

"OK," remarked Kallas. "I can see that as feasible even though a lot of people would be upset. Our engineers have become accustomed to using the Sun and IBM workstations whenever they want to. What is option two?"

"I call option two workstation computing," said Browning. "Here we would follow a strategy whereby the mainframe is phased out completely over time. At the same time, we would make significant investments in Sun and IBM workstations running UNIX, as well as PCs, big servers, and LANs. We could allow the use of Linux on the workstations. Such an architecture would allow migration to a full client/server environment.

"Our plans for a long-term shift to a distributed UNIX environment would include the migration of all applications to the new environment. A high-speed network would be installed to link all computers. Data and application servers would be distributed by functional areas and profit centers (e.g., marketing, development engineering, human resources, and testing). CAD seats would be slowly transferred from the mainframe to dedicated workstations. During the transition period, the mainframe would be connected to the network and available for access from all workstations.

"One database would serve the entire UNIX network system, but local databases could also exist as necessary. PCs would be linked via LANs, and gateways would be installed to bridge between networks.

"As CAD and other major applications were shifted off the mainframe, it would be downsized to a smaller, compatible midrange mainframe. The process could be expected to take approximately 10 years and two mainframe downgrades before all of Fort Wayne's applications would be migrated to UNIX workstations."

"All right," said Kallas, "but wouldn't this one be a lot more expensive and create a kind of 'disintegrated' computing environment? I have heard of other companies going this route only to have to reassert central control in a few years."

"It sure has that potential," said Browning. "And you are right ... it will likely be more expensive than the mainframe option, given what has happened to the cost of mainframes over the last several years.

"Before you decide, let me explain option three. This one is even more risky. We could go to a Linux environment. In this option, we would pursue a course of abandoning the mainframe, but converting the complete computing platform to a Linux environment. Though it is similar to UNIX as an operating system, Linux-based solutions offered by companies like Red Hat, IBM, and Nortel Information Network could cluster standard PCs or servers together to accomplish the same power as multiple UNIX workstations, a mainframe, or a supercomputer. While Linux started as a plaything for some younger computer junkies, it is now getting to be a mainstream offering by many of the major vendors. In the past few years, several large companies have adopted this environment for their architecture.

"Given the diversity of our needs across the company, the Linux solution could also provide more than adequate flexibility. Utilizing services provided by a recognized supplier like IBM, specialty Linux companies, or the in-house programming staff, Linux solutions could be used for anything from tracking quality control to managing machines and monitoring production. Furthermore, to accompany the resulting processing power, some providers of Linux solutions have guaranteed 99.7 percent or higher uptime to their Linux clients. I read that Linux has been useful for automobile simulations at DaimlerChrysler and Ford. In addition, the platform's durability has been proven at Amerada Hess and other oil companies through their exploration activities. Nevertheless, this is a major leap from IMT's current conservative environment."

"I guess," replied Kallas. "But at least we ought to consider it. Any more options?"

"Just one, to be complete," replied Browning. "We could consider just waiting and watching carefully. This option says do nothing fundamental at the present time. We wait and see what develops. We would decide on specific system changes only as circumstances force us to make decisions. Following the 'watch carefully' option would mean that each decision would be made in response to immediate demands. As part of this approach, we could bring in Linux and let some people experiment with it. If Linux is the wave of the future as some people claim, maybe the best idea is to not make a commitment now. It is not clear that Linux is ready for prime time now. But some experimenting could determine in a few years if it really is a long-term solution for the company."

A Decision and Direction for IMT IS

"OK," said Kallas. "Having the options is very helpful. I appreciate all the time you put into the project. Let me think about the options and make a decision."

After Browning left the office, Kallas began to reflect on the options he had presented. Change was going to be painful. Although Browning had captured the basic strategy alternatives, there were many considerations to take into account before a decision could be made on which option to follow. Years of neglect, restructuring, and a growing organization had finally caught up with CMCI's information systems. Kallas also recognized that changes in the division's IS architecture might require organizational changes as well. A decision had to be made soon. Or did it? Now the only question was, what to do?

CASE STUDY I-2

TELECOMMUTING AT IBM-INDIANA

International Business Machines Corp. (IBM), a leader of the computer revolution, became one of the outstanding success stories of the second half of the twentieth century. By the 1970s IBM had about 70 percent of the computer market and was highly respected for its progressive management and its integrity. A pioneering multinational, IBM operates worldwide and typically derives over half its revenues from outside the United States.

Up through the early 1980s, IBM continued spectacular growth, but it also became more bureaucratic and slow-moving. Soon after career IBMer John Akers took over the helm in 1985, IBM's profit margins began to slip, and it became obvious that IBM faced a troubled future. Over the years Akers downsized IBM from over 405,000 to around 300,000 employees worldwide, attempted to focus IBM more on the needs of its customers, reorganized the company twice, cut IBM's product development cycle time in half, and replaced most of the IBM product line with very competitive hardware. However, IBM continued to lose market share and profit margin and had unprecedented losses in 1991 and 1992. (See Exhibit 1.) Furthermore, IBM stock dropped from $176 in 1987 to $49 in 1992. In early 1993, Akers resigned and the IBM board decided that an outsider was required to turn IBM around.

After much speculation about possible candidates and a widely publicized search, Louis V. Gerstner was named IBM's CEO. Gerstner had started his career with McKinsey & Company, joined American Express and rose to its presidency, and in 1989 he was hired as CEO by RJR Nabisco Holdings Inc. to lead a recovery after a takeover battle that saddled that company with $25 billion in debt.

Concentrating on downsizing and customer service, Gerstner targeted IBM's worldwide employment at 225,000, to be achieved by the end of 1994, and told IBM employees: "I start with the premise that our customers are looking for us to deliver solutions to their problems. So we've got to get back to delivering superior solutions to our customers."

The Telecommuting Project

In June, 1992, Michael W. Wiley became general manager of IBM's operations in the state of Indiana. Wiley was a second-generation IBMer who started as a salesman in 1980 and moved rapidly up through increasingly responsible staff and line marketing jobs to become administrative assistant to Senior Vice President George Conrades before taking over in Indiana.

During 1992, IBM continued to downsize and Indiana reduced its head count by about 30 percent. In 1992, IBM had its worst overall financial results ever, and word was out that Indiana faced the prospect of similar head-count reductions in 1993. In February, 1993, John F. Frank, new operations manager for the state, made his first visit to the new IBM building in Evansville that was part of his responsibility. Frank recalls:

> It was a gorgeous new building looking out over the Ohio River, and we had just moved into it in May, 1991. Although IBM did not own it, it had been built for IBM and was one of the most expensive buildings in Evansville.
>
> That Tuesday, this beautiful building was virtually empty. I looked across a big room full of desks of marketing people, who were all out talking to customers, and I could have shot a shotgun in any direction without hurting anyone. I was shown through beautiful conference rooms and classrooms, most of which were empty. I couldn't figure out why we had all this space that must have been costing us a fortune. It wasn't just the real estate cost, but also the occupancy costs—the information technology, support staff, utilities, taxes—that were killing us. So I spent my time on the plane on the way back making a rough estimate of what it was costing us to run all the IBM buildings in the state of Indiana.
>
> When I got home at 9:30 P.M., I called Mike Wiley and told him that I thought we could save a minimum of two of three million dollars in Indiana in the first year, and three to four million a year from then on, by reducing our real-estate costs. After I went over my rough figures with him, Mike said, "Let's make it happen!"

When Frank called, Wiley was preparing for a meeting in Chicago with the Midwestern Area vice president and his

 Its development was supported by the Institute for Research on the Management of Information Systems (IRMIS), Kelley School of Business, Indiana University.

EXHIBIT 1

IBM Ten-Year Revenues and Income (in millions) and Stock Prices (to nearest dollar)

	1992	1991	1990	1989	1988	1987	1986	1985	1984	1983
Revenue	64,523	64,792	69,018	62,710	59,681	54,217	51,250	50,056	45,937	40,180
Operating Income	8,199	9,489	15,249	13,553	12,617	11,269	11,175	14,281	14,446	13,216
Net Income	(6,865)	(564)	6,020	3,758	5,491	5,258	4,789	6,555	6,582	5,485
Stock Price (high)	101	140	123	131	130	176	162	159	129	134
Stock Price (low)	49	84	95	94	104	102	119	118	99	92

counterpart general managers to talk about how many head-count reductions would be required to meet the area's profitability targets. Wiley recalls:

> With our strategy of providing value to the customer by solving problems, the last thing I wanted to do was to eliminate more people. We solve problems with highly skilled, highly specialized people, and I was convinced that we should cut everything else before reducing our competitive advantage by cutting productive people. So when John called me with his idea of saving big money by reducing facilities costs, I told him we had 3 days to put together a proposal to take with me to the meeting in Chicago so that I could present it as an alternative to cutting people.

They put together a team consisting of Wiley, Frank, and the chief financial and chief information people for Indiana. Frank recalls:

> We spent 36 hours straight putting the plan together. When I made the proposal I knew a little about telecommuting, but I didn't know much about the details. It was late-night trips to the library researching what other companies were doing that prepared us to put together a rough plan. This plan called for reducing our real estate in Indiana by 65 percent by moving all of our client-related personnel out of the traditional office environment into offices in their homes.

IBM-Indiana's proposal to substitute telecommuting for head-count reductions was accepted by Midwestern Area management. This proposal would not affect people whose main workplace was an office. Rather, only IBM people who spent most of their time with customers and worked in their offices only 30 percent to 40 percent of the time were to telecommute. Those people whose main workplace was an office would continue to work at an IBM location.

The Telecommuting Environment

There were four important components of IBM-Indiana's telecommuting environment: home office equipment, communications facilities, shared workspace at the IBM location, and reengineered work support processes. Since the major initial motivation for telecommuting was to reduce costs, the project team did not plan to provide an *ideal* office environment, but rather to provide a *satisfactory* environment with a minimal investment.

The home office equipment provided included an IBM PC with a standard set of software, an IBM Proprinter dot-matrix printer, a desk, a chair, and a two- or four-drawer filing cabinet. The PC provided was usually the machine that had been in the telecommuter's IBM building office. Standard software installed on each PC before it left the IBM location included word processing, presentation software, spreadsheet software, FaxWorks for sending and receiving faxes, and standard telecommunications software for getting into IBM's LAN and mainframe IS facilities. The desks, chairs, and filing cabinets had been used in the IBM offices that were being phased out. An employee could opt to take a cash allowance for any piece of equipment and furnish it himself or herself, but everyone had to use the IBM–provided standard software. IBM configured the PC, installed the software, and moved all the equipment to the employee's home.

Good communications support would be critical to the success of telecommuting. In addition to the employee's existing telephone facilities, IBM provided two more telephone lines into the home office, one for voice and another for data. IBM also furnished a 14.4 kilobaud fax and data modem and an AT&T 722 telephone with the following features: two lines (one personal and one IBM), speaker phone, conference between lines one and two, memories to store numbers and access codes, and hold and flash buttons. IBM paid the installation charges and monthly bills for these lines.

IBM intended that an inbound caller should never get a "no answer" or a busy signal, and the caller should be able to talk to a knowledgeable person if he or she wished. This concept was implemented as follows: Any call to the employee's IBM extension was automatically forwarded to the home office phone. If that line was busy or was not answered after three rings, the call was sent to the employee's phonemail box, where it was answered by the employee's personal message that indicated when the call would be returned. The phonemail message also instructed the caller to touch certain keys to reach a live person, and those calls were forwarded to the customer service center to be handled by the people there.

There were two types of shared workspace at the IBM office locations. First, there were small cubicles equipped with a telephone and a PC with the standard software networked to laser printers and the IBM internal computer systems. One of these work areas was provided for every four telecommuters, and they were available on a first-come, first-served basis. A few enclosed offices were also provided that could be scheduled by managers or teams for private conferences. Although these offices also contained telephones and PCs, there were too few of them to allow their use as work space so managers were expected to use the small cubicles for everything except private conferences or team meetings.

The IBM location also included a conference room or rooms for group meetings, a mail room, a secretarial support center, and an administrative support center. Each telecommuter was also provided with a file drawer near the cubicles.

IBM-Indiana also downsized its office support group and decided to use people provided by an outside contractor instead of IBM employees to perform this function. In Indianapolis they established several support groups: an administrative services group that handled time cards, expense accounts, keeping publications tables up to date, and other administrative functions; a secretarial pool that scheduled the use of shared offices, set up meetings and teleconferences, and performed other secretarial duties; a word processing pool that typed letters and contracts, prepared graphics for presentations, and prepared proposal documents and meeting handouts; and a mailroom crew that distributed mail and faxes, handled copying, and distributed the output sent from home offices to central office printers.

Virtually all work support processes had to be redesigned to function in this new environment. For example, how do you schedule meetings and teleconferences when no one is around the office? Does the secretary call each participant to find feasible times, and then call back to notify each person of the time chosen? Do you use e-mail for these communications? They decided to rely on the PROFS[1] calendar function to schedule meetings and teleconferences. PROFS makes it possible for a secretary to enter a list of people and the length of the meeting, and the computer searches for a time when all the participants are available to meet. But to make this work, everyone had to maintain his or her schedule of activities on the computer, and these schedules had to be accurate and up to date. At first, some people did not keep their online calendar up to date, but the secretaries went on and scheduled meetings based on the calendars, and those who missed important meetings soon learned their lesson.

The processes that had to be redesigned ranged from how to submit an expense account to how to get a proposal prepared. Not only did someone have to decide how to perform each of these activities, but they also had to provide training and written descriptions to all 300 telecommuters. The office support staff prepared a thick reference manual describing the new processes and then converted it to an online help system.

The Implementation Process

Wiley recalls setting up the team to implement telecommuting:

> We couldn't have done this without a small group of creative thinkers—visionaries like John Frank—who also have the talent to organize and manage this kind of complex change.
>
> I asked them how quickly we could implement telecommuting, and they said they thought we could do it in 9 months. We couldn't wait that long, so I told them they had to get it done in 90 days. Now I wish I had told them to do it in 30 days. The faster you can get it done, the less chaos and resistance you have from your people. When they get in the new environment and see it work, they realize it makes sense, they see where they fit in, they learn what to do, and they do it.

There was a lot to do in 3 months. The team had to identify the needs of the telecommuters and define the specific technology to be used to meet those needs. They had to determine who would telecommute and who would not. They had to plan and schedule the activities necessary to move more than 300 telecommuters' offices to their homes. This planning and scheduling took about a month, so they had only 60 days to do the following:

- Purchase modems, software, and phone equipment
- Secure the necessary furniture
- Upgrade the local office telephone switches
- Set up each of the PCs with proper features and software
- Provide 3 days of training on the new tools for each telecommuter
- Reengineer all support processes
- Prepare homes, including new telephone lines
- Deliver the equipment to each telecommuter's home
- Vacate the freed-up office space
- Remodel remaining office space to adapt it to new uses

There were a number of issues that had to be resolved on the fly, such as the tax and liability status of the equipment being moved out into employees' homes and how to deal with security issues relating to access to IBM confidential systems. There was a lot going on at once—for example, they had construction projects going on in six locations in the state at one time. But

[1] IBM's Professional Office System (PROFS) is an integrated office software system that runs on a mainframe. Among its many functions, PROFS provides electronic mail, a calendar function that keeps a person's schedule and can make it available to others, and document preparation, distribution, and retrieval capabilities.

they got it all done and had some 300 people telecommuting, and the freed-up real estate ready for release, in 90 days!

Motivating the Change to Telecommuting

Wiley knew that the move to telecommuting was going to be a tremendous change for the people involved, and he took responsibility for leading the charge. He put a lot of effort into selling the idea and motivating those who were reluctant to telecommute, and he was one of the first people in the state to move out of his office.

Wiley sold the move to telecommuting primarily as a way to save 50 IBM jobs in the state. He also expounded other benefits of telecommuting, such as providing more effective service to customers, eliminating the time and stress of commuting into the office, eliminating parking problems, and providing more time at home with family by allowing more flexible time management. But with the history of downsizing that IBM had been through, saving jobs was the justification that most everyone accepted. According to Frank:

> When we announced the move to telecommuting, about half of the people involved were eager to go. Many who were initially reluctant were quickly convinced by Mike Wiley's explanation of why telecommuting was necessary. But the remaining group included most of our managers, who were used to private offices with secretaries answering their phones and providing plenty of one-on-one support. Wiley took the reluctant managers into a room and told them: "I know you are uncomfortable with this. I know this is bruising your egos, because IBM has conditioned you to expect these perks. But if we don't have the guts as a management team to make radical changes in these dire circumstances, we are headed for disaster. We need to show the rest of the company what can be done. If we aren't willing to give up some perks everyone will know that management doesn't understand what is going on. So I'm asking you to fully endorse this." Out of about 20 managers, only one transferred out.

Wiley agrees that the managers had the greatest problems coping with this change. He says:

> Those managers who had always been focused on the customer and had been out with their people helping them solve problems were eager to adopt telecommuting as a productivity enhancement. But the ones who had problems were those who were hung up on the prestige of an office and a secretary, who would come in and sign onto their e-mail and their voice mail and sit in their office all day instead of being out with their customers. Not only did they have a problem with prestige, but they had a problem with what to do all day if they didn't have an office to come to. They had to ask the question: "What marketable skills do I really have?" And if they had none, then they had to go get a skill that brings some value to our customers or there would be no reason for them to be here.

According to Frank, about 25 percent of the telecommuters went along reluctantly with the change. However, after experiencing the new environment, and after some improvements in the support technology provided, about half of this 25 percent converted to supporters of the concept. Frank notes:

> It is kind of ironic. Many of those people who did not want to go are now the ones who are writing testimonials and volunteering to go around and talk to other employees and say: I did not want to do this; I had five kids at home; My house was too small; etc. But it works—it has advantages that compensate for the problems.
>
> Still, about 10 percent of our people will probably not be happy with telecommuting for any of a number of reasons. It could be personal in nature, or it could be that they just can't be happy changing from what they have been used to for many years.

Reactions of the Telecommuters

During the process and afterward, the team solicited feedback via e-mail from all the participants and used this feedback to identify and reduce the problems that were revealed.

Positive Reactions

The vast majority of the telecommuters agreed that telecommuting was good for IBM, and many felt that it was an improvement for them personally. Many respondents reported that they were pleased with the impact of telecommuting on their productivity and job satisfaction:

> Telecommuting is the best idea that we have come up with in all the time I have worked with IBM. My productivity is much higher than before and, hopefully, we have saved a lot of real-estate expense.

> I can honestly say that you would have to threaten to FIRE ME to get me to go back to the traditional environment. I am almost ashamed of how much time and money I wasted in the office in my career. It has gotten to the point that I refuse to go to the office unless it is absolutely necessary because it is so unproductive.

> This has been the greatest single boon to my productivity since I've been in IBM. I have become much more organized because I have everything I need in one place instead of in my car, on my desk, at the customer site, or at home. I also find that I do many small things at odd hours; for example, I do most of my PROFS while my kids are in the shower.

> I am finding that I spend a lot less time at home than I imagined. Where before there was always 'the office' to go to for mail, notes, etc., I know that I can do that stuff for a short time after the kids go to bed and clear it up and get it off my mind, but still be home. I think this has let me spend more and better time with customers.

Some telecommuters were pleased that they no longer had to drive back and forth to the office:

> My workload has increased dramatically this year, and this program has allowed me to work the extra hours I need without taking a trip downtown or walking down a dark alley to my car. The net is that I can work whenever I want, I can work safe, and I don't need to spend time traveling. That is worth a lot to me.

I live approximately 75 miles from the office, so telecommuting has been a real time and car saver for me.

Many people were pleased with the improvements in their lifestyles resulting from telecommuting, especially the ability to spend more time with their children.

I have found that I spend less time at home than I thought I would, but I very much like the flexibility. I can eat an early dinner with the family because of special plans for the evening, then come back to my desk at 10:00 P.M. to cover just a few more things. Also, I now have the option of sitting at home in my jeans, free from traffic, suits and tall buildings, and asking myself: How can I absolutely best spend my time to get the needed results? This freedom allows more creativity in my thinking about what is needed to get the job done.

My typical workday has me hitting my office at 6:30, getting things done when previously I would have been starting the drive into the office. A great benefit is the ability to eat breakfast with my children, whom I previously seldom saw before 6:00 P.M.

Not all the feedback was strictly serious. Someone sent in his top ten reasons why telecommuting should be fun:

10. Lunch is cheaper and usually resembles dinner the night before.
9. The printer is closer and isn't backed up or jammed.
8. The coffee is fresher, and the brand doesn't upset your stomach.
7. You can impress your friends because YOU have an IBM PC at home.
6. The coffee mugs don't have green fuzz in the bottom.
5. You have to keep your desk clean or your spouse will.
4. Now the neighbors *really* wonder what you do for a living.
3. It gives new meaning to the term "business casual."
2. The chances are better for being the ninth caller for the cash song.

AND THE NUMBER ONE REASON . . .

1. When you want something thrown out you don't have to write "Trash" on it and trip over it for 3 days before it disappears.

Concerns of the Telecommuters

Although most of the telecommuters ended up supporting the change to telecommuting, some of the supporters reported concerns. Several telecommuters were troubled by the lack of interaction with peers that they very much missed, and some noted that the lack of casual contact made it much more difficult to exchange information and work as a team:

I miss the camaraderie of the branch. It's hard to get informal communication going between teams, and tracking projects is a little rougher.

The loss of the group-work setting has been a major psychological adjustment which most people are not yet over. The interaction with peers shortened the time required to accomplish many tasks because we were able to 'group together' for many short, impromptu meetings to decide strategy, plans, etc. This is very much missing and missed.

The grapevine thing is missing. Face it, we all like to know what's going on. We don't know what's happening out there anymore. We eat lunch alone. We don't exchange news items that concern our customers. There is no networking, no socialization, no moral support.

Wiley recognized that lack of social contact and casual communication would be problems, and he has encouraged IBM-Indiana offices to set up special occasions, such as weekly office luncheons, to provide opportunities for interaction. IBM-Indiana has also found it necessary to be intentional about communication by scheduling meetings to substitute for the informal communication that took place when everyone was in the office. They also make heavy use of teleconferencing to substitute for face-to-face meetings.

Some telecommuters noted that it was more difficult to communicate than before.

It is almost impossible to contact someone in the branch in under eight hours. If you are in a situation where you need a resource quickly, you are in trouble.

The one drawback seems to be playing telephone tag more often. It is a lot harder to speak with a real person unless you set up meetings or conference calls.

Some people expressed concern about never being away from the work environment:

The only disadvantage I see is that we are working a lot more hours this way. It's just too tempting to jump on the system on weekends and during the evenings. Vacations will be forced to be 'away from home' vacations in order to really get away from it all.

It is very hard to separate personal life from work when you can never really get away from the office. It is always just down the hall!

Those few who did not support telecommuting seemed to be quite frustrated by this new environment.

I am very dissatisfied with the working environment of telecommuting and do not feel that shared workspace at the office is a workable alternative.

Contrary to the PROFS note relating how telecommuting is a good deal, it's not. I ended up dedicating one room of my house to it. My house is not air-conditioned, and it is pretty uncomfortable sitting on a two-hour conference call in that environment. The correlation between mileage, lunch, etc., is ridiculous.

Problems with the Initial Technological Support

There were a number of significant problems with the technological support provided initially. One telecommuter reported his frustration with these problems:

> System configurations are inadequate, printing is a major-league problem, the phone system does not yet support this concept, and shared work space isn't adequate. These problems seem minor, but they add up to so much chaos and disruption that I find it difficult to get my job done.

The phone system was one of the most difficult problems, because it was very difficult to forward calls to the telephone where a person was working when in the IBM office. That meant incoming calls would end up in voice mail. Also, in some areas the phone company could not transfer a call to the IBMers' voice mail when their home phone was busy or unanswered, so all incoming calls had to go directly into voice mail to make sure that all calls were picked up. Two typical comments:

> The area that causes the most difficulty is getting my calls when I am in the downtown office. Not being able to have a customer call you back at the desk where you are sitting, but instead call your voice mail is frustrating.

> We must get our office phones to ring at our homes and then roll over to voice mail. Our current environment of our customers not being able to reach us directly is NOT working out well, and our not being able to reach each other efficiently is greatly affecting our productivity.

One of the most common problems with the initial technology was the difficulty of getting letter-quality printing done:

> Yesterday I directed several printouts to the 3820 printer at the office. I stopped in for a few minutes this morning to pick up the printouts only to find that the printers were broken (again). So far I've spent three hours redirecting stuff to other printers. Not very productive!

The IBM internal information systems and the difficulty of accessing them from home offices provided many frustrations:

> Our equipment and programs are exactly what we tell our customers to move away from as quickly as possible. I am still working on an obsolete PC and applications that do not work properly. Our online systems are very old and out of date. Much productivity gain could be realized by new equipment, better software, and a more up-to-date network.

> We MUST provide remote access to some of our most basic IS tools. It boggles my mind that from my home I can pull up a sales report that would be very attractive to a competitor, yet I cannot look at an on-order record to check an install date or a feature code.

One of the lessons learned from the previous feedback was that success of telecommuting is heavily influenced by the supporting technology that is available. IBM-Indiana soon replaced the dot-matrix printers that had been provided for the home offices with Lexmark laser printers, which greatly alleviated the printing problems. The telecommuting team also worked to upgrade the communications facilities, and Wiley has devoted a lot of effort to improving the IBM information systems setup.

The Change to "Mobility"

In the fall of 1993, the IBM ThinkPad laptop was made available as an exchange for desktop PCs on very favorable terms. This enabled IBM-Indiana to switch to ThinkPads that fall and to upgrade from telecommuting to "mobility." The term *mobility* refers to an environment in which workers can access information and perform their work anywhere and at any time. Wiley and Frank would have preferred mobility to telecommuting from the beginning, but because their first objective was major cost savings, they were initially unable to afford the technology investment required for mobility.

The technology involved in implementing mobility requires laptop computers and may also include cellular data communications, alphanumeric pagers, and dial-in LANs. In Indiana, going from telecommuting to mobility involved replacing the desktop PCs with IBM ThinkPad laptop computers loaded with essentially the same operating system and applications software as the PCs they replaced, so it was easy for the telecommuters to convert to the use of the new machines.

IBM-Indiana also replaced the data lines to homes with dial-in access to LANs in the IBM offices. Not only was the dial-in access less expensive, but the employees could dial in from anywhere, not just their homes. In addition, alphanumeric pagers were furnished to many employees. IBM-Indiana considered cellular communications, but decided the additional cost of that technology could not be justified except in special cases. IBM-Indiana also experimented with the use of a pen-based version of the ThinkPad for some people.

Evaluation of the Results

After the telecommuting project was implemented, Wiley invited IBM to send in a financial team from outside the state to evaluate the results. This team reported that IBM had saved $3.2 million in 1993 and that they would save $5 million a year in 1994 and each year afterward, which was far better than Frank's original estimates. In addition, Wiley was convinced that the productivity of the telecommuters had been significantly enhanced. "I know that my own productivity has improved by at least 20 percent since I moved my office home," Wiley asserts.

Impressed with the results of telecommuting in Indiana, the Midwestern area in late 1993 adopted the mobility concept. John Frank became the leader of the effort to extend what had been done for 300 people in Indiana to some 2,500 people throughout the Midwest.

As of March 1994, the concept of mobility was being embraced throughout IBM, although only a few locations were as far along with it as was Indiana.

CASE STUDY I-3

MIDSOUTH CHAMBER OF COMMERCE (B): CLEANING UP AN INFORMATION SYSTEMS DEBACLE

As Sage Niele, the newly appointed vice president of operations and chief financial officer for the Midsouth Chamber of Commerce (MSCC), walked over to the microwave in her office, she recalled her excitement when she first started in this position. Only a few weeks earlier, Sage was the owner/operator of a successful information systems and financial consulting business that kept her in the office or on the road an average of 80 hours per week. With a family and dreams of a simpler life, Sage decided to start working for someone else, where she thought her schedule would be much less hectic. Today, it did not seem as though her life had changed that much. She was still working 80 hours a week, and her life was just as hectic as before. Sage thought that she could see hope on the horizon, however.

A few days after Sage began her position, Leon Lassiter, MSCC president, gave her the daunting task of managing the MSCC's information systems. In most organizations, this role would be challenging, but it was especially so at MSCC due to its history. Over the last several months, the MSCC had been receiving what it considered erroneous charges from its software vendor and consultant, Data Management Associates (DMA). DMA had been charging the MSCC for work related to errors in and/or the implementation of the relational database system and customized report-writing software the MSCC had purchased nearly 2 years earlier. Now it was clear that this was another incident in a long history of poor operational decisions for the MSCC's information systems. And it was Sage's job to correct the situation and build a direction for the future.

As Sage looked down at the calendar, she realized that she had just 2 more days until her 100-day action plan was due to Lassiter, on September 24, 2003. Among her list of things "to do" was to determine the deficiencies of the current information system, to ascertain the MSCC's future information system needs, and to investigate the alternatives that existed should the MSCC need to scrap the DMA system. Beyond that, however, some items needed to be fixed immediately—including the deteriorating relationship with DMA and the implementation of the new software. While she knew that she did not have all the answers now, her 100-day plan had to lay out a process for getting the answers.

Given Sage's consulting experience, she decided the best way to start was to investigate the troubled history of the MSCC's information systems to help find the clues necessary to avoid disaster in the future. "How ironic," she thought. "The situation at the MSCC has the same potential to explode as the popcorn does when I hit the start button."

The Midsouth Chamber of Commerce

A more extensive description of the MSCC and its history and computing systems can be found in Case Study 1, Midsouth Chamber of Commerce (A).

The Midsouth Chamber of Commerce (MSCC) was created in the early part of the twentieth century, but its information systems history began in 1986 when personal computers and database management were first introduced into the organization by Ed Wilson, the vice president of public affairs. Many staff members were skeptical of the automation effort and reluctant to accept this approach. However, with the help of Jon Philips, a small business consultant, Wilson acquired the equipment and hired a programmer to write custom software for each functional area—the marketing division, the operations division, and the human resources division. One IBM PC and printer were ordered for each group.

From 1987 through 1992, the use of these three systems grew steadily. In 1992, Wilson selected another outside consultant, Ted Vassici, to review the organization's information systems needs and to select the hardware and software solutions the MSCC required. After a careful study, Vassici recommended six more IBM workstations. And in 1995, Vassici revised and updated the custom software used by each division and developed marketing software at the request of Leon Lassiter, the vice president of marketing.

In June 1996, Wilson hired a systems analyst, Simon Kovecki—a recent computer science graduate—to increase the MSCC's computing capabilities. Through early 1997, Wilson managed the computer systems and with the help of Kovecki, upgraded the hardware with more powerful CPUs, memory upgrades, higher capacity hard drives, and better monitors. Under Kovecki's watchful eye, the systems operated very reliably.

The Necessity for Change

By 1998, Lassiter was bothered by the lack of a comprehensive information systems plan that would provide the MSCC with a competitive advantage. Even though the system was stable, Lassiter felt the information systems area needed more attention, and eventually he sent out requests for information to a number of firms servicing the software needs of organizations like the MSCC. In August 1998, Lassiter attended a national association meeting where a session on management software led to Lassiter's discovery of a small firm called UNITRAK, which had developed a Y2K-compliant UNIX-based software system that Lassiter felt the MSCC should consider—based on his (and Kovecki's) 1997 assessment of the MSCC's current and anticipated divisional needs.

Planning the New Data Processing System

Lassiter had identified features provided by the UNITRAK software that he felt would allow the MSCC to be more efficient—including quicker access to account information, the ability to use a centralized database of information, and increased quantitative analysis of activities. In a memo to the management group, Lassiter commented, "The UNITRAK system not only meets our needs today, but this user-friendly package is also powerful enough to provide the MSCC with the room to grow over the next 5 years." Eventually, management agreed to move forward with this project.

In October 1998, Lassiter invited Greg Ginder, president of the UNITRAK Software Corporation, to give a short demonstration of the system's capabilities. Wilson observed about 45 minutes of the three-hour demonstration and told Lassiter, "I'll support it if you want it. It will work for my project in public affairs." Kovecki's comments were different. He remarked, "The software has its strengths and weaknesses and it probably would save some of my time. But, I don't like the idea of the staff having uncontrolled access to so much data. It's not clear what they'll do with it." Lassiter was able to convince the MSCC board of directors to approve the purchase of the UNITRAK system, including an IBM AS/400 computer system and the UNITRAK software.

Implementation of the System

Despite Lassiter's interest and urging, implementing the new system took much longer than was planned. Delays in issuing the purchase order and testing the software only added to the time to make the system operational. Training finally took place in August 1999. The training went well but data migration became a serious problem. On the final day of training, Lassiter told Kovecki to migrate the data in the current PC systems to the new system. Kovecki had considerable problems doing so as less than 15 percent of the data rolled over into the proper assignments. Because there was no documentation on the old software to refer to, it took him until the end of 1999 to get the system up and running. In the meantime, most of the MSCC PCs were essentially inoperable. Requests for lists and labels for mailings could not be fulfilled. And word processing, payment and invoice posting, data changes, and list management were very difficult during this time.

Lassiter was also finding it very difficult to gain information from Kovecki as to the progress and status of the system conversion. It seemed that Kovecki, frustrated with the problems he was having and irritated with the staff coming to him to ask for assistance, was going out of his way to avoid staff members.

UNITRAK came through, however, and by the end of the year the system was not only up and running but was also Y2K compliant—all at no additional cost (beyond the initial hardware and software cost) to the MSCC. Problems still remained, however, as it soon became clear that the system had severe limitations—most importantly the lack of a relational database management system. And by mid-2000, a more severe problem cropped up—UNITRAK was experiencing serious financial problems and its president decided to move its software towards a Windows-based (and away from its current UNIX-based) environment. Soon thereafter, UNITRAK's existing support staff was dismissed and the MSCC was left with no technical support. To alleviate this problem, Lassiter hired an outside consultant, Zen Consulting, to write programs, generate new reports, and assist in the maintenance/support of the software.

Moving Past the UNITRAK Implementation

In September 2000, Kovecki became concerned about his future with the MSCC. As a result, he resigned to take a position with a local law firm operating a similar hardware platform. In late October, Dick Gramen, a former staff computer trainer for a locally based insurance broker, was hired to replace Kovecki. Gramen came from an IBM RS/6000 computing environment where he established and maintained a mainframe and a local area network. Gramen, however, had no experience working with the AS/400 computer and did not think much of it.

Additionally, Gramen had no previous exposure to the UNI-TRAK software or trade associations generally. Soon after he arrived, Gramen realized that this new environment would be very difficult to learn as he struggled with even the most basic system management tasks. These struggles made him wonder why the MSCC's needs could not be satisfied on an RS/6000 and a personal computing network.

Determined to confirm his views, Gramen consulted one of his college roommates, John Harter, about the proper system for the MSCC to have in place. Harter was now an RS/6000 consultant. Harter said,

> Obviously, Dick, I'm going to tell you to buy the IBM RS/6000 system. The RS/6000 is the perfect system for your type of organization. It runs UNIX so UNITRAK should operate on it. IBM has changed the nameplate on the unit—to an eServer pSeries designation—but the system is still essentially the same. And it should be simpler for you to maintain. I have to be honest with you, though. It's going to be a tough sell to your board. There are cheaper systems out there that would also meet your needs. If you do get the RS/6000 system, however, our company could provide some support if you had difficulties.

Gramen was certain that with the help of Harter and by avoiding the learning curve on the old system, he would be able to handle the maintenance and support and succeed at the MSCC. Now, all he had to do was to convince the MSCC's managers to move to the RS/6000 system. So, one month into his tenure, Gramen began by telling Leon Lassiter, the vice president of marketing,

> The MSCC can no longer afford to stay with its current computer hardware platform. The AS/400 just cannot meet your needs today, let alone tomorrow. The current online legislative information services system is maxed out, and without new hardware I just can't support the emerging political action program. If we don't get this situation addressed soon . . .

Eventually, this combination of reasons led Lassiter to support Gramen's general hardware proposal. Lassiter was very pleased that finally the IS person was taking some initiative. He was convinced that the MSCC's information systems were the key to maintaining Midsouth's preeminence among business trade associations, and thus the key to its financial success. Lassiter was also fearful that the MSCC would not be able to be of real value to its members in the legislative tracking arena without a change. As a result, Lassiter told Gramen to quietly pursue acquisition cost estimates.

Gramen realized, however, that if he were to be successful in moving the MSCC to the new hardware, he would have to have support from the president of the association, Jack Wallingford. When Gramen approached Wallingford, however, he was not prepared for the response:

> Dick, I agree that we may need entirely new hardware, but we cannot repeat the problems that occurred with our previous information system purchase. We made some pretty serious errors when we purchased the UNITRAK system and those simply cannot occur again. And we don't have anyone from IBM on our board any longer. Plus, I don't see how you can make this decision yet. You have not had enough time to learn about our current hardware (the AS/400 system), software (UNITRAK), our data structure, or even what the MSCC is engaged in and how the organization operates.

To alleviate some of Wallingford's concerns, Gramen agreed to arrange several meetings throughout the first quarter of 2001 with members of senior management for the purpose of outlining the organization's IS needs and the general operations of the MSCC.

Moving to the IBM RS/6000

After listening to Gramen outline the gravity of the situation, Ed Wilson decided to help Gramen by going to Lassiter and Wallingford individually to persuade each to support the RS/6000 system. Lassiter's support was of the greatest importance, though, due to his influence within the executive committee and the fact that his division was the largest user of information systems. Nevertheless, when Wilson went to Lassiter, Lassiter was incensed:

> I told Gramen to *quietly* pursue acquisition cost estimates so that we would be prepared when we knew exactly what we needed. Apparently he did not honor my request. I am not willing to rush into this blindly and I will not support taking this to the executive committee until we know what we need. We can't just rush into a purchase.

Even though Lassiter's logic was sound, Wilson remained convinced that something needed to be done immediately—with or without Lassiter's support. Subsequently, even though they knew doing so would alienate Lassiter, Wilson and Gramen took their proposal to the executive committee. Wilson began,

> Ladies and gentlemen, this decision is one that must be made expeditiously. The high cost of paying a consultant to support and maintain the UNITRAK software on hardware that is undersized is becoming a drain on our increasingly scarce resources. And with needs in the legislative services arena on the horizon, we must act quickly before we can no longer serve our members well. Our proposal is the perfect solution to this crisis situation. From a technology standpoint, the IBM RS/6000 technology is state-of-the-art with impeccable stability and reliability. As important, however, is that we have received assurances from IBM that they will recommend a software vendor to meet our needs once a purchase is made. This proposal gives us the best of all worlds.

Uncharacteristically, Lassiter sat in the back of the room listening in complete silence. He felt confident that even without his input the executive committee—comprised of CEOs from twenty of the top companies in the state—would never accept this proposal. Because of the economic downturn in 2000 and, in Lassiter's opinion, the limitations of the UNITRAK software

EXHIBIT 1

Midsouth Chamber of Commerce, Revenues vs. Expenditures (1995–2003)

Year Ended October 31	Revenues	Expenditures	Difference
1995	1,853,402	1,565,522	287,880
1996	1,968,185	1,799,287	168,898
1997	2,115,646	1,903,688	211,958
1998	2,278,019	2,110,010	168,009
1999	2,561,345	2,381,965	179,380
2000	2,515,601	2,720,121	(204,520)
2001	2,698,045	3,189,617	(491,572)
2002	2,783,365	3,197,345	(413,980)
2003	3,468,698	3,642,836	(174,138)

system, the MSCC's revenue growth had slowed considerably while its expenditures continued to increase. (See Exhibit 1.) This had quickly sliced the MSCC's financial reserves in half to just over $1 million which would make an off-budget purchase difficult to justify.

Lassiter, however, had miscalculated the power of the crisis argument, as the executive committee instructed Wilson and Gramen to inquire into the acquisition cost of the RS/6000 with only one limitation—that they use "due diligence" in developing the entire information systems solution.

Realizing that the MSCC was starting down a dangerous path, Lassiter drafted a memo to Wallingford and Wilson in which he wrote,

> The MSCC must hire an outside consultant to conduct a thorough needs analysis and establish a long-range vision and IS goals before any decisions are made. Furthermore, we must recognize and learn from the mistakes we made with our first system. Hardware and software decisions cannot be made in isolation.

Neither Wallingford nor Wilson responded to his memo.

Enter Data Management Associates (DMA)

Immediately after the meeting of the executive committee, Gramen contacted IBM for its recommendation on an appropriate vendor. Without hesitation the IBM representative suggested a local value-added reseller (VAR) that not only sold and installed IBM hardware, but that also, for a fee, would search for software solutions that matched the MSCC's needs with the proposed RS/6000 hardware platform. With Gramen's shaky understanding of these matters, this seemed like the ideal solution. Because his friend, John Harter, worked for the local VAR, Gramen thought that this approach was the right way to go.

This arrangement, however, turned out to be far from ideal. Without ever visiting the MSCC—and based only on Gramen's view of the MSCC's operations and information systems needs—the VAR (for a $5,000 fee) contacted Data Management Associates (DMA) on behalf of the MSCC. DMA was a 54-employee operation located 61 miles from the MSCC offices and was headed by Dittier Rankin, a Stanford University alumnus and computer science Ph.D. DMA had recently undergone a shift in its focus and had begun developing custom software for small trade associations and local chambers of commerce throughout the country. Nonetheless, even with their lack of significant experience, the VAR was confident in DMA's abilities. After several phone conversations between Gramen and DMA, arrangements were made for DMA to demonstrate its capabilities at the DMA office in May of 2001.

While the meeting only lasted 45 minutes, Wilson and Gramen left it very impressed. With screen shots, report samples, and specification sheets in hand, Gramen was prepared to present this proposal to the executive committee. In the interim, however, a new situation had developed. John Hilborn, one of Lassiter's most trusted friends—and a member of the MSCC's executive committee—approached Lassiter inquiring about his silence at the prior meeting. Hilborn was not pleased with what he had heard. As a result, at the next executive committee meeting, Hilborn asked Lassiter—during Gramen's presentation—for his input on the proposal. With that cue, Lassiter only made one comment: "Guys, if the proposed solution turns out to be ideal for the MSCC it would be pure luck, as the software selection process has not been comprehensive." And then Lassiter sat down.

Those few words unnerved Gramen and made several members of the executive committee very uncomfortable. Immediately, a motion passed to table the proposal for a month while more information was gathered from and about DMA.

With his proposal—and potentially his job—on the line, Gramen arranged for DMA's president and two other members of DMA's management to visit the Chamber's offices and conduct an IS needs analysis. Those individuals visited for 2 days. They spent the morning of the first day providing a complete overview of DMA and demonstrating, on a laptop, the capabilities of the software system they offered. The remaining day and a half was spent interviewing the MSCC's staff on their job duties, on how they used the current system, and on any unmet needs they could identify.

Additionally, Lassiter provided DMA with a very complete look at his division's IS needs and his personal vision of the information system that the MSCC needed. Additionally, in an effort to explain the MSCC's capabilities and to impress upon DMA the diversity and complexity of its operations, Lassiter gave DMA lots of materials. These included examples of every report and every type of document that the existing system could produce as well as explanations of the purpose and meaning (to the MSCC) of the information in each of these reports. Furthermore, he gave DMA an operations manual, detailing each task of each employee in the marketing division, and a lengthy report on the information that was currently in the database that could not be retrieved and printed in a useable report format. In all, this was a two-foot-deep stack of reports and data. Lassiter was also unwilling to allow DMA to leave until he was given a detailed thesis on DMA's capabilities and its software systems.

After two weeks, and in time for the June 2001 executive committee meeting, Rankin reported that DMA had reviewed the information gathered on its fact-finding visit and had successfully analyzed the IS needs of the MSCC. In doing so, DMA determined that its Association Plus software was the ideal match for the MSCC's needs and the RS/6000 platform. Lassiter remained undeterred, however, as he urged the approval of travel funds to allow someone to visit at least one DMA customer to see the software in action. The executive committee, in deference to Lassiter—and to the fact that his division was by far the most extensive user of the current information system—agreed to delay the final decision and to approve funds to send him and Gramen to visit the Lake Erie Chamber of Commerce—one of DMA's most recent clients.

More Visits/Interviews

While DMA had willingly given out the Lake Erie Chamber of Commerce's (LECC) name, this proved to be a bad choice for DMA. One hour into their visit, Gramen and Lassiter met with LECC's president, George Franks. Mr. Franks explained,

> We were thoroughly impressed with DMA when we went through our due diligence process. They showed us reports and screen shots that gave all of us hope that this was our panacea. But guys, we have had serious and persistent data conversion problems from the moment of implementation. And, I still don't know whether we will ever see any value from this system.

With this information in hand, Lassiter (and a reluctant Gramen) reported these findings back to the executive committee. Even though Gramen continued to argue that time was of the essence, the executive committee needed additional assurances. As such, they sent Lassiter and Gramen to DMA headquarters with two goals: (1) to determine what DMA's capabilities were, and (2) to see an operational version of DMA's software.

Immediately upon arriving at DMA headquarters, Lassiter and Gramen were given a tour and were introduced to some of DMA's senior staff. Soon thereafter they were led into a conference hall where they were treated to a lengthy demonstration of what appeared to be a fully operational version of DMA's software. However, DMA had actually used the MSCC's data and reports to prepare sample reports and screenshots to create the appearance of a fully operational software system. As one former DMA employee would later tell Sage Niele,

> They used the sample reports and other information they received from Lassiter to create representative screens and reports. DMA so badly wanted to get into the trade association market with a big customer like the MSCC that they believed if they could just land this contract they could develop the software and stay one step ahead of the MSCC. The long and short of it is that they sold "vaporware."

During the demonstrations, Lassiter and Gramen repeatedly asked for and received assurances that DMA could, with "relatively minor and easily achievable modifications," develop the software and convert the UNITRAK database to produce the demonstrated reports and lists for the MSCC. To every question and contingency raised, DMA responded that the development would be no problem, and that, additionally, the MSCC would receive the source code if it purchased the software.

Satisfied with what they had seen, Lassiter and Gramen flew home. At the August 2001 executive committee meeting, they reported that this system (the RS/6000 and the DMA software) was acceptable for purchase. Hearing this, the executive committee instructed Gramen to request design specifications and specific cost estimates on this software system. Under the new configuration, a relational database management system called Progress, created by DMA, would be loaded on the RS/6000. (See Exhibit 2.) Existing data were to be converted by DMA into the new system. In addition, DMA was to use its Association Plus software to enable the MSCC's staff to produce the desired

EXHIBIT 2
Midsouth Chamber of Commerce, DMA's System Configuration

Association Plus DMA Developed Custom Software	**Results** User-Friendly Reporting Tool
Progress Relational Database Management Software	
IBM RS/ 6000 Computer	

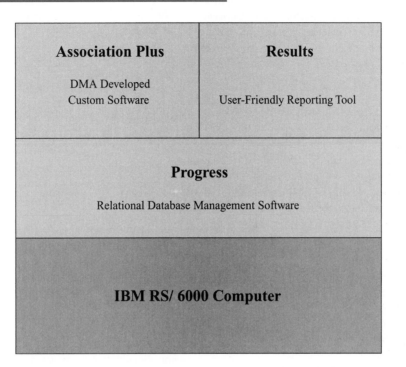

reports, lists, and other documents through a user-friendly report-writer software package known as Results. These detailed estimates were presented at the September 2001 executive committee meeting where they were approved. The total price was $277,000. Gramen immediately contacted DMA and asked the company to prepare a proposed contract.

The DMA Contract

In late September, DMA sent its standard contract to Gramen for the acquisition of the Progress relational database management system, the Association Plus custom software module, and several packaged software components. When the proposed contract arrived, Gramen, recognizing that he had neither the expertise nor the inclination to review the contract, sent the contract to Wallingford with a note saying, "It looks fine." Wallingford signed the contract and within the day it was headed back to DMA without any other staff member nor the corporate counsel or any outside specialist having reviewed the document.

Had someone with greater legal acumen reviewed the contract, however, they would have immediately recognized that it was extremely one-sided and contained none of the assurances that Lassiter and Gramen were given during their visit. In laymen's terms, it gave no specific or quantifiable performance standards for the services to be provided and gave DMA the right to increase the price of services and products provided at its discretion, while limiting DMA's financial and performance liabilities.

Troubles in Implementing the DMA Software

Nevertheless, for the first time in several years, excitement filled the air at the MSCC as it appeared as if a new computing era had begun. On November 11, 2001, the MSCC held a kick-off celebration and invited DMA management to help commemorate the event. Just as important, however, were the meetings associated with this celebration. In these meetings DMA was attempting to set the project's implementation schedule by determining (1) the complexity of the various customization components, (2) the length of time necessary to implement the customized software, and (3) the tasks that the MSCC needed to complete in order to facilitate the conversion. By the end of that day, the broad outline of an implementation schedule had been laid out with the first week of July 2002 set as the target completion date.

Two weeks after the initial meetings, Stacey Porter, a DMA consultant, arrived at the MSCC offices to install the first version of the telemarketing module and to provide training on the constituents, territory management, and committees modules. This training served as the staff's first look at the software. The territory managers, however, were not impressed with the layout or content of the software, as it often forced them to work through more than twenty screens to perform relatively simple tasks. As a result, Lassiter demanded a significant rewrite of the territory management module, and by March 2002, similar delays were a part of the PAC, accounting, meetings, and legislative modules as well.

With the scheduled conversion to the DMA software quickly approaching and delays becoming the norm, Gramen and Wallingford decided to continue running the old system until the staff was completely comfortable with the new system. Within 3 months, however, even though the DMA software was still not fully operational, the MSCC abandoned this directive as it had simply become too expensive to pay the consulting fees to keep UNITRAK operational.

As implementation pushed into late July, DMA began encountering substantial problems converting the membership database from UNITRAK into the DMA custom software package. As progress ground to a halt on the software installation, Lassiter summoned Gramen and Porter into his office. During this meeting, the working relationship between the MSCC and DMA began to deteriorate further as Gramen warned Porter, "I think we've been pretty patient with you so far, but that is about to change. I've heard of far less serious situations ending up in court before. And I know you understand that this all falls on you."

The Start of Additional Problems

Further complicating this relationship had been a series of billing issues. In the process of installing the system, DMA ran into a myriad of problems with solutions in one area often leading to problems in other areas. By the middle of July 2002, no less than five MSCC staff members were in regular contact with DMA identifying problems and requesting assistance. As a result, DMA had quickly used up the development hours specified in the contract, and had subsequently started billing the MSCC for the work beyond the free hours guaranteed.

As the problems worsened, Lassiter became increasingly involved in the daily implementation problems. Feeling as if he was the only one who could right the ship, Lassiter went to Wallingford and argued that he should be given the responsibility of overseeing the entire project. Wallingford gladly consented to Lassiter's request.

Immediately, Lassiter arranged a conference call between himself, Gramen, and Porter to address the many outstanding items past completion date. In the call Lassiter emphasized,

> We are in our eleventh month, and we still cannot use your software to close our books each month. This is completely unacceptable. You could at least provide the system documentation you promised so that we can reduce our own learning curve. It's no wonder that you cannot get the more complicated modules complete, though. All I've been making is simple requests and for some reason you can't meet them. And one more thing, we were promised the source code when our negotiations began, and now I've been told by one of your team members that this will cost us $20,000. What type of dishonest organization are you running? This is completely unacceptable and my patience is thinning. If this situation doesn't improve. . . .

The exchanges between DMA and the MSCC continued to become increasingly strained, and disagreements on what items were and were not promised as part of the system installation became a key point of contention. Given the nature of the relationship, Lassiter ordered that all DMA billings were to be carefully reviewed by Gramen for inappropriate charges. Furthermore, Lassiter asked to review the DMA contract.

There first appeared to be a glimmer of hope, as the contract specified that roughly half the cost of the software system had been due as a down payment with the balance due upon Gramen signing acceptance certificates after the satisfactory installation of each individual module. After meeting with Gramen, however, Lassiter learned that although none of the acceptance certificates had been signed, the full system had nonetheless been paid for in full. Lassiter could not believe that they had given up one of the most important pieces of leverage that the MSCC had. Lassiter quickly decided it was time to go back to Wallingford for his input.

"Jack, we have two problems," Lassiter said. "First, it goes without saying that there are serious problems with the software and with DMA's capacity to support and deliver it. Just as important, however, is that Dick does not seem to have the requisite ability to maintain and support the hardware platform and is really of little value in terms of overseeing or solving problems with the software implementation. As a result, we are completely dependent on DMA for this project's success or failure. I think it's time we go in a different direction."

Wallingford replied, "I agree with you. I trust your judgments in these matters. But before we go any farther, there is something I want to tell you. I am planning on retiring at the end of the year. This week the executive committee will appoint a search committee and begin accepting resumes from interested parties. I really would like you to consider applying for this position."

Lassiter was speechless, but by this point he no longer had any desire to stay with the MSCC. In his mind, he had taken the marketing effort at the MSCC about as far as he could—especially given the information system's limitations. Lassiter had already received a lucrative offer to be the chief operating officer of a local investment management company and was ready to accept it. Lassiter was not alone, however, as Ed Wilson had just had a final interview with a new government policy think tank. But, while Lassiter did not throw his name into consideration, Wilson did because his final outside interview had not gone well. Nevertheless, the search committee was acutely aware that Wilson would just be a temporary fix as he was nearing retirement; Lassiter was their preference.

As a result, after reviewing the other available candidates again, two search committee members contacted Lassiter and urged him to apply. After two lengthy meetings—in which the two members intimated that they would not take no for an answer—Lassiter relented and agreed to have his name offered for the presidency. At the November 2002 meeting two weeks later, the board of directors ratified that selection.

A Lack of Progress

The search for a president had not slowed down the MSCC's problems, however. In late November 2002, Lassiter gave Porter an updated list of problems with the software—as compiled by MSCC staff—and asked her to estimate the time to address these tasks in hours. Three weeks later DMA sent back the time estimates and a series of work orders with cost estimates. DMA indicated in that correspondence that it would initiate the work when the orders were signed and returned by the MSCC. Lassiter refused to sign the work orders and informed DMA that he considered the work to be part of the initial installation and that DMA was in breach of contract.

On January 1, 2003, Lassiter officially took over as president, and shortly thereafter, Ed Wilson announced he would retire on June 30. Instead of replacing him, Lassiter decided to disperse his duties among existing staff members. Knowing that he had to shed some of his IS development responsibilities and realizing that he could no longer afford to leave Gramen as the sole person responsible for the MSCC's information systems, Lassiter began looking for a candidate with a strong management, information systems, and financial background to oversee the MSCC's information systems and to serve as chief financial officer. In the interim he had Gramen report directly to him while temporarily retaining the role of overseer of the ever-tenuous relationship with DMA.

Meanwhile, DMA seemed to be creating as many problems as it fixed. Confidence in the new software was dwindling, and paper systems began to proliferate as some modules were not installed and others were completely non-operational. Due to the slow response time, the staff often had to work evenings and weekends to complete simple tasks, which further diminished morale. In addition, the integrity and dependability of the membership database had become increasingly suspect as a result of the data conversion problems and the general unreliability of the system.

At the end of January, Rankin and Porter spent a full day in meetings with the MSCC staff and senior management. Each division outlined its problems and frustrations with the software system. By the final meeting that day, Lassiter was livid, "We have to bring the initial installation to an end! It is time for your company to deliver the system that we contracted for. I am tired of missed deadlines, unreturned phone calls, and partial solutions."

"I understand your frustration, Mr. Lassiter," Rankin said. "But I want to reiterate our desire to keep you as a customer. We will redouble our efforts to finish the installation, and I will personally send a letter to you outlining the dates for completion of the outstanding problems."

Two months later, Gramen and Porter held a conference call to once again discuss the discrepancies between the promised and actual delivery dates. Per Lassiter's instructions, they also requested and received a listing of DMA's client list. Lassiter instructed Gramen to conduct a phone survey of these businesses to determine their level of satisfaction with DMA. To Lassiter's dismay, this phone survey revealed that there was overwhelming dissatisfaction with DMA's products and services. The Lake Erie and Great Lakes Chambers were already in litigation with DMA due to contract non-performance and many of their other clients were calling for a multi-party lawsuit.

On May 7, Lassiter sent Rankin another letter outlining the items still unfinished and demanding a speedy resolution to these problems. In response, Rankin instructed Porter to phone Lassiter with a pointed message. "Mr. Lassiter," Porter said, "I just wanted to let you know that DMA has already incurred $250,000 of expenses it has not charged you in an attempt to meet your concerns. Nevertheless, DMA has decided to discontinue programming support for the MSCC until the Chamber pays its outstanding invoices."

"In that case," Lassiter responded, "I guess we'll see you in court." At which point the phone conversation ended abruptly.

Enter Sage Niele

On June 30, 2003, Ed Wilson retired—although he was retained as a part-time consultant and given the title of the political action committee's executive director—and Sage Niele arrived as vice president of operations and chief financial officer. Niele held an MBA from the Wharton School of Business and had previously performed systems manager responsibilities for a large pharmaceutical company in the Midsouth area. More recently, she had operated her own information systems and financial consulting business. With two small children at home she had decided to pursue something less rigorous and time-consuming than running her own business, but it soon became clear to her that this position might not fit that billing.

A few days into her new position, Lassiter met with Niele in his office:

> Sage, it's good to have you on board. I need you to begin a planning and assessment process to determine the deficiencies of the current information system, along with the MSCC's needs, and the alternatives that exist in the event the MSCC needs to scrap the DMA system and start over. From this day forward, you are to be the exclusive contact person between the MSCC and DMA. I have begun the process of finding a suitable, top-notch replacement for Dick, which will help you in

your cause. I'll give him 2 months to find a new job, but we have to let him go.

That next week, Lassiter, Niele, and Gramen met with an attorney specializing in computer software contracts who had also been a past chairman and current executive committee member of the MSCC. Lassiter outlined the situation for her, but her assessment was far worse than Lassiter had imagined.

"The way I see this contract," she began, "The MSCC has few, if any remedies. I wish you had contacted me earlier—before the contract was signed. The absence of performance standards leaves you with only one real remedy, the avoidance of payment. Because you have already made full payment, you have given a tacit acceptance of the software system. From speaking with Leon earlier, I understand that your goal is to either receive reimbursement and the source code from DMA—so you can hire a consultant to make the software usable—*or* to get your money back and buy another system. These outcomes are unlikely. In my opinion, you need to tone down your demeanor with DMA and try to get as much additional progress out of them as possible until you decide what to do. If DMA does get serious about cutting off their support, pay what you think you owe and we'll go after them for specific performance."

Taking that advice to heart, several additional pieces of correspondence were internally generated and sent to DMA with a more temperate tenor. Meanwhile, Niele continued to send DMA payments for only those items the MSCC deemed to be billable. Each time she crossed her fingers that DMA would not pull the plug.

With the help of the MSCC librarian, Niele identified a list of eight software packages that would run on an RS/6000 hardware platform, that were designed for use in a trade association environment, and that appeared to be worthy of further investigation. At the same time, she began interviewing MSCC staff members to prepare an inventory of the current system deficiencies as well as the needs for the future. An outgrowth of this effort was the creation of an *ad hoc* information systems committee that she used to help flatten her learning curve about the MSCC and its current information systems.

Furthermore, Niele also spoke with Lassiter and key board members to determine their vision for the operational future of the MSCC. And Niele arranged for six CEOs from the executive committee to have their IS managers or other key IS staff members serve on a steering committee to assist her in evaluating systems alternatives. Not only did that give her additional points of view, but she hoped this would make it easier to sell her final recommendation to the executive committee.

Unfortunately, Niele also knew that her assessment of the current situation and the alternatives she had identified to date would not be attractive to the executive committee. On a legal pad in her office, she wrote down the problems as she saw them: (1) The modules will likely never become operational, (2) DMA is unwilling to commit the resources necessary to finish the job, (3) the DMA relationship is still deteriorating quickly, (4) any costs already itemized are likely sunk due to poor contracting, (5) it will be expensive to start over from scratch, and (6) it is equally expensive to do nothing. Now the big question was, where to go from here?

As the microwave sounded to signal that her popcorn was ready, Sage wondered which problems she would be putting to an end through her recommendations and which problems she would create by making additional changes.

PART II
APPLYING INFORMATION TECHNOLOGY

CHAPTERS 6 THROUGH 8 OFFER A COMPREHENSIVE VIEW OF THE APPLICATIONS OF information technology (IT) in organizations. Rapid changes in underlying technologies, business conditions, management methods, and types of applications make it important for managers to develop a clear understanding of the ways to take advantage of IT applications for accomplishing their own work, as well as for business growth and survival.

The purpose of these three chapters is to increase awareness and understanding of how IT can be used in an organizational setting. Chapters 6 and 7 focus on IT applications *within* a particular organization: enterprise systems—systems that support the entire enterprise or large portions of it (Chapter 6)—and managerial support systems—systems designed to provide support to a specific manager or group of managers (Chapter 7). The enterprise systems chapter covers transaction processing systems in general, enterprise resource planning, data warehousing, customer relationship management, office automation, groupware, intranets, and factory automation applications. Among the managerial support systems discussed are decision support and group support systems, geographic information systems, knowledge management applications, expert systems, neural networks, and virtual reality applications. At the beginning of Chapter 6 we also introduce several concepts critical to the understanding of IT applications, including batch versus online processing and client/server systems.

The focus of Chapter 8 is e-business, or electronic commerce applications, which are designed to interact with customers, suppliers, and other business partners. The chapter begins by considering the Internet technologies that enable e-commerce applications and the roles that legal and regulatory environments play. Frameworks are provided for evaluating business opportunities and threats at the industry level and e-business models at the firm level. After discussing the potential benefits of business-to-consumer (B2C) and business-to-business (B2B) applications in general, specific examples of successful direct retailing sites (e.g., Amazon.com and Dell, Inc.) and e-business intermediaries (e.g., eBay and Yahoo!) are described in detail.

The chapter ends with some considerations for developing a good Web site from a customer perspective.

After studying these three chapters, you should have a more complete understanding of the range of IT applications available to today's organizations. You should also begin to have a fuller understanding of how the role of information systems (IS) managers has evolved now that today's organizations have become highly dependent on computer applications and services to conduct business in traditional and new online ways.

Part II concludes with a set of seven original teaching cases. The Midstate University Business Placement Office case study looks at the information system that supports the day-to-day operations of a university placement office and provides management information to the office's managers. The MaxFli Sales Force Automation System case study describes a multiphase project to provide information via handheld computers to sales teams located in different South American countries. The First American Corporation case study is an excellent example of implementing a customer relationship management system that utilizes data warehousing tools at a major financial institution.

Four teaching cases address issues related to e-commerce applications. Batesville Casket's World Wide Web Site provides an early example of a traditional manufacturing firm attempting to exploit the new communications and marketing channel provided by the Internet. The Sears, Roebuck and Co. case study describes a traditional retail firm's challenges to becoming a clicks-and-mortar firm, up until its acquisition of a successful clicks-and-mortar catalog firm (Lands' End). The final two case studies involve startup firms. The Cliptomania Web Store case study tells the story of a small startup becoming a successful B2C business. And finally, the Mezzia, Inc., case study describes a software startup that is positioning the business as a B2B intermediary; it also addresses the advantages and disadvantages of going to work for a startup versus a more traditional firm in the IT industry.

CHAPTER 6
ENTERPRISE SYSTEMS

INFORMATION TECHNOLOGY (IT) IS A KEY ENABLER FOR ORGANIZATIONS of all sizes, both public and private. Businesses and other organizations are not the same as they were a decade ago. They are more complex but have fewer layers of management; they tend to offer more customized products and services; they are increasingly international in scope; and they are heavily dependent on the accurate and timely flow of information. And this change in organizations is accelerating, not decelerating.

As a current or future manager, you must be aware of IT and its potential impact on your job, your career, and your organization. You cannot afford to leave consideration of IT solely to the information systems (IS) specialists. As a business manager, you must perform many critical roles if you and your organization are to be successful: conceptualize ways in which IT can be used to improve performance; serve as a consultant to the IS specialists who are developing or implementing applications for your organization; manage the organizational change that accompanies new IT applications; use the technology applications and help enhance them; and facilitate the successful implementation of new IT applications.

Where do we start getting you ready for your new roles? We start with an *awareness* of how IT is being used in a variety of organizations. The first five chapters of this book have already begun the process of building awareness of IT applications. This chapter and the following two chapters will provide a systematic introduction to a wide variety of IT applications. We think you will be impressed with the breadth of areas in which IT is being employed to make organizations more efficient and effective. We hope these three chapters will stimulate your thinking about potential applications in your present or future organization. Most of the obvious applications are already in place. Nearly every organization uses a computer to handle its payroll, keep inventory records, and process accounts receivable and payable; almost every organization uses a telephone system and facsimile machines. But many applications remain to be discovered, most likely by managers like you.

APPLICATION AREAS

To consider a topic as broad as IT applications, some type of framework is needed. We have divided applications into those that are *interorganizational* systems and those that are *intraorganizational* systems. Electronic commerce or e-business applications, including electronic data interchange (EDI) systems, represent obvious examples of interorganizational systems, or systems that span organizational

CRITICAL ISSUES OF IS MANAGEMENT

For 14 years—from 1988 through 2001—Computer Sciences Corporation conducted an annual survey of senior IS executives at leading manufacturing and service companies worldwide to identify the top issues they were facing. In the most recent survey, the top two issues were "optimizing enterprise-wide IS services" and "optimizing organizational effectiveness." Enterprise resource planning (ERP) systems, together with applications such as groupware and data warehousing (all covered in this chapter), are aimed at providing high-quality, consistent IS services throughout the organization. IT applications such as customer relationship management, groupware, data mining, decision support systems, expert systems, and executive information systems provide managers with the information and the tools they need for effective decision making. These applications are considered in this chapter and the next.

The third-place concern in the survey was "organizing and utilizing data." A variety of IT applications, including data warehousing, data mining, groupware, decision support systems, executive information systems, knowledge management systems, and ERP systems (topics covered in this chapter and the next chapter), help organize and utilize data to improve the organization's performance. Number four on the list of critical issues was "connecting to customers, suppliers, and/or partners electronically." Numerous IT applications, including electronic mail, groupware, ERP systems, electronic data interchange, and especially e-business applications (topics covered in this chapter and Chapter 8), help build the electronic connection between an organization and its trading partners.

In the aftermath of 9/11, it is no surprise that the fifth-place concern in the survey was "protecting and securing information systems." None of the application areas discussed in Chapters 6 through 8 focuses primarily on this issue, although security considerations are paramount in the implementation or upgrading of any application. We will return to the topic of protecting and securing information systems in the final two chapters of this book. Number six on the list of critical issues was "updating obsolete systems," which is exactly what organizations try to do when they implement ERP systems and other enterprise-wide applications, as discussed in this chapter. Thus, the topics covered in this chapter and the next two chapters directly relate to five of the top six critical issues for IS executives.

[Survey results from Computer Sciences Corporation, 2001]

boundaries. The importance of applications that link businesses with their end consumers (B2C) or link businesses with other business customers or business suppliers (B2B) has been fueled by the growth of the Internet. Knowledge about e-business applications is so important today that we devote all of Chapter 8 to this topic.

To provide some structure to the broad range of intraorganizational systems, we have divided these applications into two major categories: enterprise systems, designed to support the entire enterprise (organization) or large portions of it, and managerial support systems, designed to provide support to a specific manager or a small group of managers. This chapter covers enterprise systems, such as transaction processing systems and groupware, as well as the critical concept of client/server architecture. Chapter 7 deals with systems specifically designed to support managers, such as decision support systems and expert systems.

Figure 6.1 lists these two major categories of applications, along with representative application areas that fall within each category. This figure provides the primary framework for our discussion of intraorganizational IT applications in this chapter and the following chapter. Please note that the application areas are neither unique nor exhaustive. For example, some specific applications fall in two or more application areas (such as enterprise resource planning systems also being transaction processing systems). Further, it is easy to argue that an application area such as groupware is both an enterprise system and a management support system. Somewhat arbitrarily, we have chosen to discuss group support systems, which is an important subset of groupware concerned with supporting the activities of a small group in

Enterprise Systems
- Transaction Processing Systems
- Enterprise Resource Planning Systems
- Data Warehousing
- Customer Relationship Management
- Office Automation
- Groupware
- Intranets
- Factory Automation

Managerial Support Systems
- Decision Support Systems
- Data Mining
- Group Support Systems
- Geographic Information Systems
- Executive Information Systems
- Business Intelligence Systems
- Knowledge Management Systems
- Expert Systems
- Neural Networks
- Virtual Reality

Figure 6.1 Types of Application Systems

a specific task or a specific meeting, as a management support system while discussing the broader category of groupware as an enterprise system. Despite these caveats, however, the application areas given in Figure 6.1 encompass the overwhelming majority of specific applications, and the terminology reflects standard usage.

CRITICAL CONCEPTS

Before we turn to specific examples of the various application areas, we must consider a number of important concepts that are intertwined throughout all the applications. An understanding of these concepts is a prerequisite to an understanding of the applications.

Batch Processing versus Online Processing

One of the fundamental distinctions for computer applications is **batch processing** versus **online processing**. In the early days of computers, all processing was batched. The organization accumulated a batch of transactions and then processed the entire batch at one time. For example, all inventory transactions (in and out) were recorded on paper during the day. After the close of business for the day, the transactions were keyed into a type of computer-readable medium, such as magnetic tape. The medium was then physically carried to the computer center, and the entire inventory was updated by processing that day's batch against the master inventory file on the computer. By the beginning of the next business day, the master inventory file was completely up-to-date and appropriate inventory reports were printed. Figure 6.2 represents this batch processing approach in a simplified form.

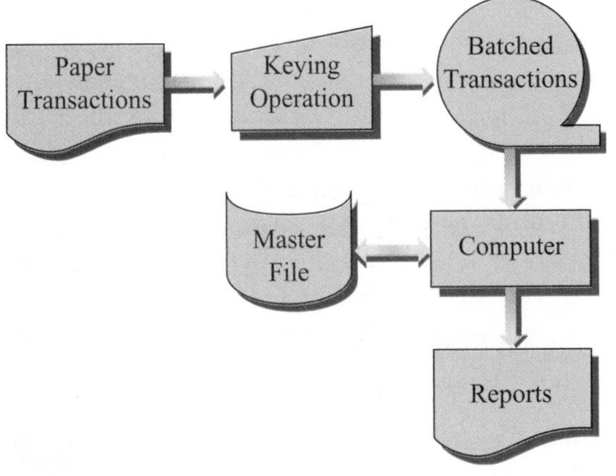

Figure 6.2 Batch Processing (simplified)

The major problem with batch processing is the time delay involved before the master file is updated. Only at the beginning of the business day, for example, will the master inventory file be up-to-date. At all other times the company does not really know how many units of each product it has in stock.

As the technology improved, online processing was developed to avoid the time delay in batch processing. With a fully implemented online system, each transaction is entered directly into the computer when it occurs. For example, in an online inventory system a shipping clerk or sales clerk enters the receipt or sale of a product into a workstation (a sophisticated cash register) connected by a telecommunications line to the server computer, which holds the inventory master file. As soon as the entry is completed, the computer updates the master file within a fraction of a second. Thus, the company always knows how many units of each product it has in stock. Figure 6.3 depicts such an **online system**.

A fully implemented online system is also called an **interactive system**, because the user is directly interacting with the computer. The computer will provide a response to the user very quickly, usually within a second. Not all online systems, however, are interactive. Some systems, often called **in-line systems**, provide for online data entry, but the actual processing of the transaction is deferred until a batch of transactions has been accumulated.

A fully online system has the distinct advantage of timeliness. Why then aren't all present-day systems online? There are two reasons—cost and the existence of so-called natural batch applications. In most cases batch systems are much less expensive to operate than their online counterparts. There are usually significant economies associated with batching, both in the data-entry function and the transaction processing. But if the data-entry function can be accomplished when the original data are captured (such as with a sophisticated cash register), an online data entry/batch processing system might be less expensive than a straight batch system. The decision of batch versus online becomes a trade-off between cost and timeliness. In general, online

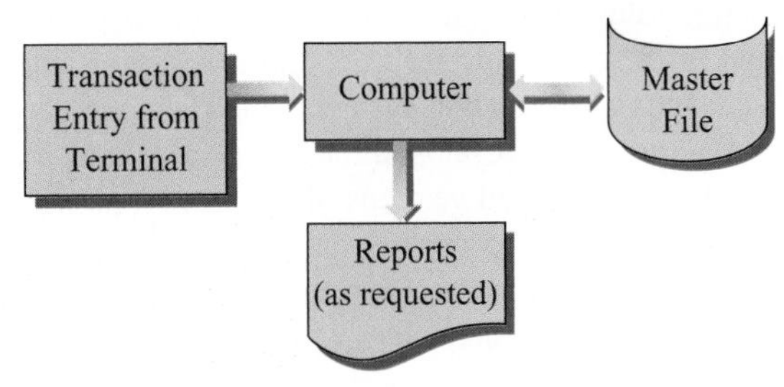

Figure 6.3 Online Processing

costs per transaction have been decreasing and the importance of timeliness has been increasing. The result is that most applications today use online data entry and an increasing proportion also use online processing.

The exception to this movement to online processing has been the natural batch applications. An organization's payroll, for example, might be run once a week or once every two weeks. There is no particular advantage to the timeliness of online processing; the organization knows when the payroll must be run. Even in this instance, there might be advantages to online data entry, to permit convenient changes in employees, exemptions, deductions, and wage rates. Thus, hybrid online data entry/batch processing systems will continue to exist.

Functional Information Systems

Instead of considering the two major categories and associated application areas of Figure 6.1, it is possible to create a framework based strictly on the organization's primary business functions—a **functional information systems** framework. For example, consider an organization in which the primary business functions are production, marketing, accounting, personnel, and engineering. Applications may then be categorized as part of the production information system, part of the marketing information system, or part of the accounting information system, and so on. This functional approach is simply an alternative way of classifying applications.

In this alternative view, the overall IS is composed of multiple subsystems, each providing information for various tasks within the function. In turn, each functional subsystem consists of a possibly interrelated series of subsubsystems. For example, the production information system is likely to include interrelated subsystems for sales forecasting, production planning, production scheduling, material requirements planning, capacity requirements planning, personnel requirements planning, materials purchasing, and inventory. The marketing information system may include subsystems for promotion and advertising, new product development, sales forecasting (hopefully tied into the production sales forecasting subsystem), product planning, product pricing, market research, and sales information. The accounting information system, which is generally the oldest and most fully developed functional system, is likely to include computerized versions of the entire journal and ledger system, plus a cost or responsibility accounting system and a financial reporting system for preparing reports for stockholders and other external groups.

One of the most important trends in the latter 1990s and the early 2000s is the movement toward integration of these functional information systems. Often these integration efforts have begun by focusing on a **business process**—the chain of activities required to achieve an outcome such as order fulfillment or materials acquisition—rather than on functions. Such a focus on process makes it easier to recognize where formerly distinct information systems are related and thus where they should be integrated (e.g., use common data and perform an activity only once). Sometimes the internal information systems department has developed these integrated systems, but more often software packages called enterprise resource planning (ERP) systems have been purchased from outside vendors. We will return to these ERP systems later in the chapter.

Vertical Integration of Systems

Another important characteristic of some systems is that they operate across levels of the organization or, in some instances, across independent firms occupying different levels in an industry hierarchy, such as an automobile manufacturer and the associated independent dealers. (More on these interorganizational systems will be covered in Chapter 8.) A system that serves more than one vertical level in an organization or an industry is called a **vertically integrated information system**. For example, in a single firm, a vertically integrated sales information system may capture the initial sales data and produce invoices (acting as a transaction processing system), summarize these data on a weekly basis for use by middle managers in tracking slow- and fast-selling items as well as productive and unproductive salespeople (acting as a decision support system), and further analyze these data for long-term trends for use by top managers in determining strategic directions (acting as an executive information system).

In a somewhat similar way, a national fast-food chain might develop a sales information system with modules both for operating units (company stores and franchises) and for the national organization. Thus, data collected at the store level using the operating unit module are already in the appropriate form to be processed by the national organization module. These basic data are transmitted via telecommunication lines to the national organization on a periodic basis, perhaps each night. The extent of vertical integration is an important characteristic of applications.

Distributed Systems and Client/Server Systems

Distributed systems, sometimes called **distributed data processing**, refers to a mode of delivery rather than a traditional class of applications like transaction processing or decision support systems. With distributed systems, the processing power is distributed to multiple sites, which are then tied together via telecommunications lines. Local area networks (LANs) and wide area networks (WANs) are both used to support distributed systems. We should note that there are a variety of operational functions that can be distributed, including data collection and entry, data editing and error correction, file location, and processing. In our view, only the last function—processing—represents distributed systems. Whether or not the processing power is distributed, it is often appropriate to distribute data collection and entry as well as data editing and error correction to the sites at which the transactions occur (e.g., the sales floor in a department store and the dock in a warehouse). File location, however, would never be distributed unless at least some processing power is also distributed.

Thus, we are defining distributed systems as systems in which computers of some size (microcomputers, midrange computers, mainframes, and so forth) are located at various physical sites at which the organization does business (headquarters, factories, stores, warehouses, office buildings) and in which the computers are linked by telecommunication lines of some sort in order to support some business process. The economics of distributed systems are not perfectly clear, but have tended to favor distribution. For the most part, communication and support costs go up with distributed systems while computer costs go down. Placing smaller microcomputers and workstations at noncentral sites is generally less expensive than expanding the capacity of a large system at the central site. Distributed systems do have disadvantages, such as greater security risk because of easy accessibility, dependence on high-quality telecommunications lines, and greater required coordination across sites. In most instances, however, the disadvantages are outweighed by the economic advantages. The distributed mode of computing has become the norm for business firms around the world.

In the 1990s a particular type of distributed system known as a **client/server system** moved to center stage, and this type of system continues to enjoy the spotlight in the twenty-first century. With this type of system, the processing power is distributed between a central server computer, such as a midrange computer or a powerful workstation, and a number of client computers, which are usually desktop microcomputers. The split in responsibilities between the server and the client varies considerably from application to application, but the client usually provides the graphical user interface (GUI), accepts the data entry, and displays the immediate output, while the server maintains the database against which the new data are processed. The actual processing of the transaction may occur on either the client or a server. For example, in a retail client/server application, the client might be the sophisticated cash register on the sales floor while the server is a workstation in the back office. When a credit sale is made, the data are entered at the register and transmitted to the server, the server retrieves the customer's record and updates it based on the sale, the server returns a credit authorization signal to the register, and the sales document is printed at the register. At the close of the billing cycle, the server prepares the bills for all the customers, prints them, and produces summary reports for store management.

Now that we have a general idea about the nature of a client/server system, let us explore the three building blocks of such a system. First, the client building block, usually running on a PC, handles the user interface and has the ability to access distributed services through a network. Sometimes the client also does the processing. Second, the server building block, usually running on a bigger machine (a high-end PC, workstation, midrange computer, or even a mainframe), handles the storage of data associated with the application. This associated data might be databases, groupware files (to be discussed later), Web pages, or even objects for object-oriented programs. Sometimes the server (or even another server) does the processing. The third building block is **middleware**, a rather vague term that covers all the software needed to support interactions between clients and servers. The *Client/Server Survival Guide* refers to middleware as "... the slash (/) component of client/server. In this first approximation, middleware is the glue that lets a client obtain a service from a server."[1]

Middleware can be divided into three categories of software: server operating systems, transport stack software, and service-specific software. The server operating system, also called a network operating system, has the task of creating a *single-system image* for all services on the network, so that the system is transparent to users and even application programmers. The user does not know what functions are performed where on the network—it looks like a single system. The primary server operating systems are Microsoft Windows NT Server, Microsoft Windows 2000 Server, Microsoft Windows 2003 Server, Novell NetWare, several variations of UNIX, and Linux. Transport stack software allows communications employing certain protocols, such as Transmission Control Protocol/Internet Protocol (TCP/IP) (see Chapter 4), to be sent across the network. The server operating system often encompasses some elements of the needed transport stack

---

[1]Orfali, Robert, Dan Harkey, and Jeri Edwards. *Client/Server Survival Guide*, 3rd ed. (New York: John Wiley & Sons, Inc., 1999), 44.

software, but other middleware products might also be required. The service-specific software is used to carry out a particular service, such as electronic mail or the World Wide Web's Hypertext Transfer Protocol (HTTP).

Consider the split in responsibilities between the client and the server. The question is where the actual processing of the application is done. Originally, all client/server systems had only **two tiers**—a client tier and a server tier. If most of the processing is done on the client, this is called a *fat client* or *thin server* model. If most of the processing is done on the server, then it is a *thin client* or *fat server* model. For example, Web servers and groupware servers are usually fat servers (i.e., the processing is largely done on the server for Web and groupware applications), while database servers are usually thin servers (i.e., the processing is largely done on the client). In the mid-1990s **three-tier client/server systems** became popular. In the most popular three-tier configuration, an application server that is separate from the database server is employed. The user interface is housed on the client, usually a PC (tier 1), the processing is performed on a midrange system or workstation operating as the application server (tier 2), and the data are stored on a large machine (often a mainframe or midrange computer) that operates as the database server (tier 3).

Let us consider some examples of client/server systems. A regional Bell operating company created a three-tier expense reporting system for use by its thousands of employees, and a natural gas company developed a three-tier facilities management application to improve decision making on the maintenance of its natural gas wells. An east-coast electric utility company used a three-tier approach to revamp its customer service system. The new system enables the utility's 450 service representatives to gain access to the multiple databases the company maintains on its 1.5 million customers. The service representatives use PCs as clients (tier 1) working through four servers that process the customer inquiries (tier 2) by accessing data from the company mainframe (tier 3). For a more complete description of a three-tier client/server application, see the sidebar entitled "Processing Prescription Drug Claims at Liberty Health."

In the early twenty-first century, there is a renewed emphasis on the thin client model to service remote areas, small locations, and traveling employees, where it is difficult to update the client software regularly. As an example, Maritz Travel Company, a $1.8 billion travel management company, used a thin client approach based on Microsoft Corp.'s Windows NT Terminal Server Edition and MetaFrame software, from Citrix Systems, Inc. With the Citrix approach, applications execute on a server and are merely displayed on the client, with the client acting as a "dumb" terminal. Maritz initially licensed 15,000 Citrix users and plans to extend the applications to nearly 50 of its remote offices. Richard Spradling, the chief information officer of Maritz, identifies many advantages to the thin client approach. According to Spradling, it is much easier to update only the servers; users automatically access the most current version of an application; performance of the applications has improved; and, over time, Maritz will spend less money on hardware by purchasing thin client devices rather than standard PCs or other fat clients (Wilde, 1999).

PROCESSING PRESCRIPTION DRUG CLAIMS AT LIBERTY HEALTH

Liberty Health is a supplemental health insurer based in Markham, Ontario. After a slow start in its efforts to migrate to client/server technology, Liberty Health concentrated on getting its most mission-critical system—processing claims for prescription drugs sold at more than 3,500 pharmacies across Canada—into a three-tier environment. The clients were PCs, running Windows, located in the pharmacies (tier 1); the application servers were Sun workstations and Hewlett-Packard midrange systems (tier 2); and the database server was a Unisys mainframe computer (tier 3). Programmers initially used the C and C++ programming languages to develop the tier 1 and tier 3 components of the system. They used a specialized development tool, BEA Systems' Tuxedo, to develop the transaction processing component (tier 2). Later development work was done using Information Advantage's DecisionSuite. Transaction volumes have grown substantially over the period since the point-of-sale prescription claims system became operational, and the system has handled the increased volume without difficulty, according to Bob Jackson, Liberty Health's IT development support officer.

[Adapted from Ruber, 1997]

TRANSACTION PROCESSING SYSTEMS

Let us begin our survey of applications with the "granddaddy" applications, the ones that started it all—**transaction processing systems**. These systems process the thousands of transactions that occur every day in most organizations, including sales; payments made and received; inventory shipped and received; hiring, firing, and paying employees; and paying dividends. In addition to producing the documents and updated records that result from the transaction processing (such as invoices, checks, and orders), these systems produce a variety of summarized reports that are useful to upper-level management.

Transaction processing systems are life-or-death systems for "paperwork" organizations, such as banks and insurance companies, and critical systems for the overwhelming majority of medium and large organizations. These systems were the first computerized systems, and they still use the majority of large-machine computing time in most organizations. For the most part, these transaction processing systems can be justified by traditional cost-benefit analysis. These systems are able to process transactions more rapidly and more economically (and certainly more accurately) than a manual (human) system. Transaction processing systems might be mainframe-based or midrange-based, or they might be two-tier or three-tier client/server systems. Most of the latest systems being implemented are client/server systems, but there are many, many mainframe- or midrange-based transaction processing systems still in use.

As a manager, you do not need to know the details of these systems. You only need to have an understanding of a transaction processing system's general nature, importance, and complexity. Therefore, we will limit our discussion to two representative transaction processing systems for single business functions—payroll and a sales order entry system.

Payroll System

At first glance, a payroll system seems fairly simple. Operators input the number of hours worked for each employee (usually employing online data entry), and the system batch processes these transactions to produce payroll checks. While this one-sentence description is correct, it represents only the tip of the iceberg, because it involves only about 10 percent of the system. The payroll processing subsystem also must keep year-to-date totals of gross income, social security income, individual deductions, various categories of taxes, and net income. It also must incorporate the ability to compute federal, state, and local taxes, as well as social security contributions, and it must handle both mandatory and voluntary deductions.

What other subsystems are necessary? Figure 6.4 lists the primary subsystems in most payroll systems and the tasks the subsystems must accomplish. Thus, the payroll system is both commonplace and complex. The payroll system is usually easy to justify on a cost-benefit basis because it would take an incredible number of payroll clerks to complete a modern payroll and maintain all the associated records.

Subsystems to accomplish:

- Payroll processing, including updating year-to-date master file
- Capture hours-worked data
- Add/delete employees
- Change deduction information for employees
- Change wage rates and salaries
- Creation of initial year-to-date master file
- Calculate and print payroll totals for pay period, quarter, and year
- Calculate and print tax reports for pay period, quarter, and year
- Calculate and print deduction reports for pay period, quarter, and year
- Calculate and print W-2 forms at end of year
- Interface with human resources information system
- Interface with budget information system

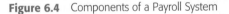

Figure 6.4 Components of a Payroll System

Order Entry System

We will illustrate a mainframe- or midrange-based order entry system, but an order entry system could certainly employ client/server technology. The basic idea behind an online order entry system is simple. As orders are received (whether in person, by mail, or by telephone), the sales representative enters the information into the system. The data entry might be via a microcomputer on the sales representative's desk or possibly through a point-of-sale transaction recording system (a sophisticated cash register that doubles as a terminal). The computer then updates the appropriate files and prints an invoice, either at the point-of-sale terminal, the sales representative's desk, or in the computer center.

Once again, this basic explanation tells only a small part of the story. Figure 6.5 provides a more complete description and shows how each transaction (sale) interacts with as many as six files on the computer system. In addition to the invoice, more than a dozen types of computer output might be generated. For example, the computer can check the credit status of the customer and reject the sale if the customer's credit limit will be exceeded. If the item ordered is in stock, a multipart shipping document is printed; if the item is not in stock, a message is sent (via the PC) to the customer to ask if he or she wants to backorder the item. Periodically or on demand, the order entry system will print out sales reports organized by item or by customer, customer statements, inventory reports, backorder status reports, and

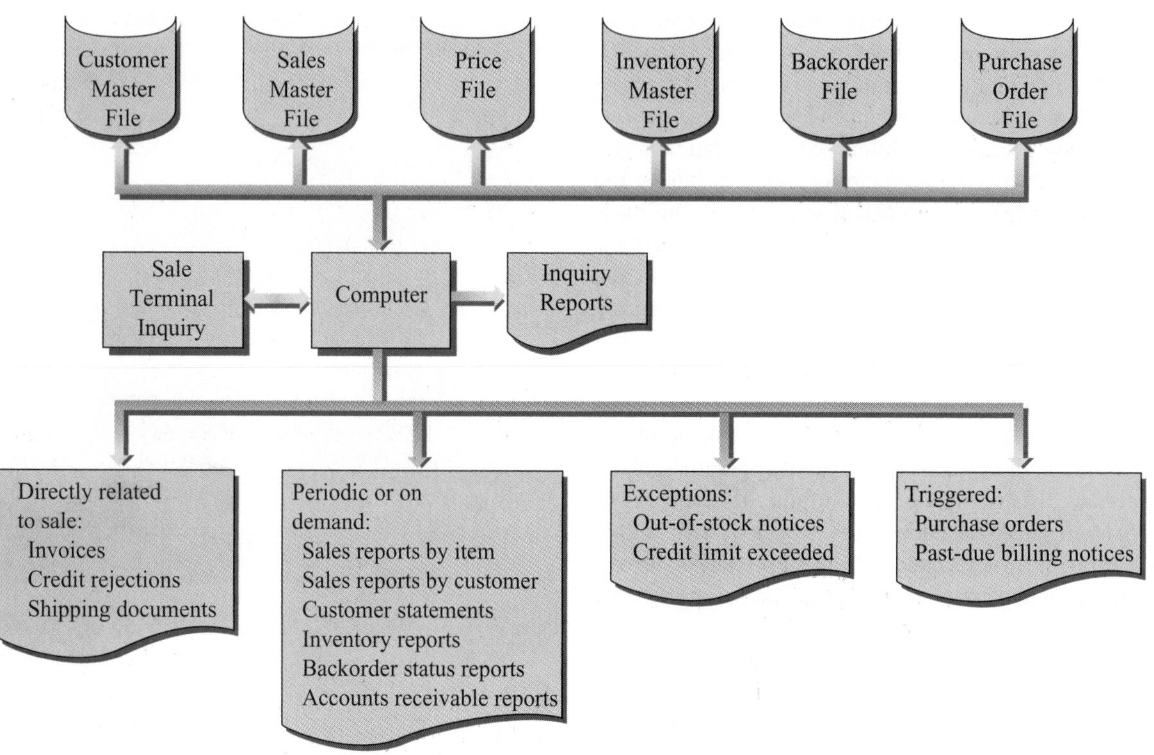

Figure 6.5 Online Order Entry System

accounts receivable reports. The system will also generate reports when exception conditions occur, such as when an item is out of stock or when a customer attempts to exceed the established credit limit. In these cases management action might be necessary. The order entry system can automatically print out purchase orders when an item is out of stock; it can also print out past-due billing notices for customers. A primary advantage of such an online system is that inquiries can be answered in a few seconds.

An important order entry system variant is an interorganizational system in which the orders are placed directly by the customer or the customer's computer (more on e-business applications in Chapter 8). An early, pre-Internet example was the American Hospital Supply Corporation's ASAP system in which order entry terminals, linked to AHSC's computer, were placed on the customers' (hospitals') premises, and hospital personnel placed orders themselves by keying them in. This made placing orders much more convenient for the customers and at the same time greatly reduced the delays and costs associated with printing and mailing order forms. More recently, orders have been placed by the customer's computer to the seller's computer using electronic data interchange (EDI)—which will be discussed in Chapter 8. By the late 1990s, the World Wide Web had taken the order entry process one step further by making it easy for both consumers and businesses to do their own order entry via a Web browser and an Internet connection. For example, many businesses use the Web to order networking equipment from Cisco Systems, and both businesses and consumers use the Web to order PCs from Dell Inc. In fact, several of the authors of this book have used the Web to order PCs from Dell.

ENTERPRISE RESOURCE PLANNING SYSTEMS

Enterprise resource planning (ERP) systems are also transaction processing systems, but they go well beyond traditional transaction processing system functionality—and thus deserve treatment as a separate application area. An ERP system is a set of integrated business applications, or modules, that carry out common business functions such as general ledger accounting, accounts payable, accounts receivable, material requirements planning, order management, inventory control, and human resources management. Usually these modules are purchased from a software vendor. In many cases a company might buy only a subset of these modules from a particular vendor, mixing them with modules from other vendors and with the company's existing applications.

An ERP system differs from earlier approaches to developing or purchasing business applications in at least two ways. First, the ERP modules are integrated, primarily through a common set of definitions and a common database. As a transaction is processed in one area, such as the receipt of an order, the impact of this transaction is immediately reflected in all other related areas, such as accounting, production scheduling, and purchasing. Second, the ERP modules have been designed to reflect a particular way of doing business—a particular set of business processes. Unlike a functional IS approach, ERP systems are based on a value-chain view of the business in which functional departments coordinate their work. To implement an ERP system, then, a company is committing to changing its business processes. If a company is purchasing an ERP system, the company might need to change its processes to conform to those embedded in the software package. The company adapts to the ERP software package, not vice versa.

Why has ERP become such a hot topic in the late 1990s and early 2000s, with most large and medium-sized firms either installing ERP systems or seriously thinking about it? The benefits from ERP will be specific to a given firm, but some common benefits have emerged. In many cases the companies are not happy with the old way of doing business—by separate functional departments—and they do not have the *integration* of applications (and therefore the data) to support their decision-making and planning needs. The current applications often do not "talk" to each other, making it a time-consuming and difficult job to gather data, present a coherent picture of what is happening in the firm, and make informed decisions and plans. This situation is not new, but, until recently, packaged solutions were not available to companies. The cost to develop a set of integrated applications internally is prohibitive; even if the company had the IS resources to perform the task, it would take years. From previous reengineering efforts, many companies know that their internal business processes need to be changed, and they believe that the best and easiest way to fix them is by adopting the processes built into an ERP system that can be purchased. Thus, implementing an ERP system is a way to force business process reengineering.

Then, to add to the demand for an ERP system, along came the year 2000 problem. In the mid- to late 1990s, it became clear to many companies that their key application programs would cease to function correctly when dates past December 31, 1999, were used. When these programs were coded—often using COBOL—the programmers allowed only two digits to represent the year. They did not imagine that their programs, written in the 1970s and 1980s, would still be used when the millennium arrived. For companies with this problem, the effort and cost to change every reference from a two-digit year to a four-digit year in their programs would be substantial. Adopting an ERP system, which was developed in the 1990s and correctly provided for dates beyond the year 2000, seemed to be an easy, albeit expensive, solution to the **Year 2000 problem**. Rarely was the year 2000 problem the sole reason to implement an ERP system, but if the company was not happy with its existing, nonintegrated set of applications, then the year 2000 problem might well have tipped the balance.

WHY PURCHASE AN ERP PACKAGE?

In a recent research study, three researchers–including one of the authors of this book–identified seven benefits gained by purchasing an ERP package. Three of these factors were overall business benefits, two were IT-related benefits, one benefit included both business and IT benefits, and the final factor was the avoidance of year 2000 maintenance costs. The three overall business benefits were data integration (improving access to data across business units, functions, processes, and the enterprise), new ways of doing business (implementing redesigned business processes, moving to a process orientation, and reducing costs of doing business), and global capabilities (supporting globalization with common processes and country-specific capabilities). The flexibility/agility benefit provided both business benefits (supporting competitive agility and business growth) and client/server architecture benefits. The two IT-related benefits were IT purchasing benefits (achieving time, cost, and reliability advantages from purchasing as opposed to building the system) and IT architecture cost reduction (reducing costs associated with systems operations and maintenance).

In considering the relative importance of these seven benefits, the authors distinguished between the purchase of an ERP by a company for its *value-chain* activities of materials management, production and operations, and sales and distribution, and the purchase of an ERP for *support* activities such as financial accounting and human resources. Data integration was the most highly sought-after benefit for both value-chain and support purchasers, and it was significantly more influential for value-chain purchasers than for support purchasers. Global capabilities were rated significantly higher by value-chain purchasers than support purchasers. Both IT purchasing benefits and year 2000 compliance were rated higher by support purchasers.

[Adapted from Brown, Vessey, and Powell, 2001]

It should be emphasized that implementation of an ERP system is extremely difficult because the company must change the way it does business. Further, ERP systems are very expensive. A typical large-scale ERP implementation costs tens of millions of dollars and takes a year or more. These implementation costs include not only the software licenses but also hardware and network investments and often consulting costs.

Further, choosing the right ERP software is a difficult task. The leading vendors are SAP, PeopleSoft, Inc. (which purchased ERP vendor J. D. Edwards in 2003), Oracle, and Baan; several smaller companies also offer ERP software. For ERP purchases, there are strong arguments for picking a single vendor, such as the tight integration of applications that is possible and the standardization of common processes. On the other hand, choosing a single vendor could also reduce flexibility for the adopting company. A "best of breed" or mix-and-match approach with multiple vendors might enable the company to meet more of its unique needs and reduce reliance on a single vendor; conversely, such an approach typically makes implementation more time-consuming and complicates system maintenance. With either approach, it is usually essential to employ the vendor or another consulting firm, or both, to assist in the implementation process. For large, multidivisional firms, implementing an ERP system is a very complex, challenging task that needs the best minds and careful attention of internal IS specialists, internal business managers, and external consultants. Most ERP implementations show positive results, but not always right away (see the sidebar entitled "Enterprise Systems Show Results, But Not Always Right Away"). The potential payoff of an ERP system, in terms of better information for strategic and operational decision making and planning, and greater efficiency, profitability, and growth, makes the efforts and the costs worthwhile.

ENTERPRISE SYSTEMS SHOW RESULTS, BUT NOT ALWAYS RIGHT AWAY

The infamous reputation of enterprise systems (ERP, CRM) is lots of money for little value. Yet more than three-quarters of companies implementing enterprise systems say they've achieved at least half of the value they initially expected from the technology, according to a study by Accenture. The companies that extracted value had two things going for them: time and follow-through. Within a year of implementation, most companies failed to realize many hoped-for benefits, such as reduced headcount and more accurate business planning. But after two years, the majority saw payback of every type of benefit except increased revenue.

[Ware, November 1, 2003]

The complexity of installing enterprise-wide systems has led to some spectacular failures in recent years. High-flying shoemaker Nike, Inc., stumbled last quarter [i.e., the first quarter of 2001], when problems related to a complex installation of supply chain software from i2 Technologies, Inc., forced it to write off $100 million in inventory and miss its sales goals. In the last two years, both Phoenix, Arizona-based PETsMART, Inc., and Hershey, Pennsylvania-based candy maker Hershey Foods Corp. saw revenues suffer as a result of problems implementing ERP systems from SAP. "The lesson learned from failures like Nike is that having to customize complex environments can kill you," says Joshua Greenbaum, principle of Enterprise Applications Group, in Daly City, California.

[Orzech, 2001]

An Example ERP System: SAP R/3

The most popular of the ERP systems is SAP R/3, developed by a German firm, SAP AG, headquartered in Walldorf, Germany. On the strength of the R/3 system and its newer Web-based variant mySAP, SAP is one of the top software firms in the world. According to an SAP brochure, 19,000 organizations worldwide run SAP software solutions. These organizations use SAP software at more than 60,000 locations in 120 countries.

SAP R/2 was a mainframe-based ERP; R/3 is a client/server system employing a common, integrated database with shared application modules. SAP R/3 handles both TCP/IP and Systems Network Architecture (SNA) communication protocols. SAP developed R/3 using its own fourth generation language (4 GL), named ABAP/4, which is the key piece of SAP's ABAP/4 Development Workbench. Customers may use ABAP/4, if they wish, to modify or enhance the standard R/3 modules. However, ABAP/4 will be of primary interest to companies that wish to employ an integrated 4 GL toolkit to develop applications, including managerial support systems, in addition to SAP standard modules. In 1999, SAP launched mySAP, which is both an umbrella concept for SAP's strategy of allowing its users to work through the World Wide Web *and* a brand name for the new Web-enabled versions of its R/3 software. Included under the mySAP label are a wide variety of enterprise software modules, including a robust ERP module (see Figure 6.6 and Figure 6.7).

The family of SAP R/3 software products fits the general description of an ERP system given above. It is a tightly integrated system consisting of numerous modules. A company may choose to implement some or all of these

Analytics
- Strategic enterprise management
- Business analytics

Financials
- Financial accounting
- Managerial accounting
- Financial supply chain management
- Manager self-service

Human Resources
- Employee transaction management
- Employee lifecycle management
- E-recruiting
- Employee relationship management
- Employee self-service
- HR analytics

Operations
- Purchase order management
- Inventory management
- Production management
- Maintenance and quality
- Delivery management
- Sales order management

Corporate services
- Real estate management
- Incentive and commission management
- Travel management

Figure 6.6 Key Functional Areas of mySAP ERP

modules. Most important, implementation of R/3 requires that the company change its business processes to conform to the processes built into the software.

Let us take a closer look at SAP R/3 and mySAP. At the very heart of an SAP implementation is the SAP R/3 Enterprise Core. Extensions can be added to the R/3 Enterprise Core, as desired, in various application areas—financials, supply chain management, product lifecycle management, human resources, and travel management. SAP R/3 Enterprise consists of the Core, the Extensions, and the SAP Web Application Server.

At the next level up in terms of comprehensiveness, mySAP ERP is a bundled ERP solution that incorporates SAP R/3 Enterprise as its core and adds mySAP Human Resources, mySAP Financials, and SAP NetWeaver. NetWeaver is SAP's integration and application platform to ensure seamless interaction with virtually any other SAP or non-SAP software. Figure 6.6 lists the key functional areas of mySAP ERP. Note that mySAP ERP is a relatively comprehensive package, with strength in the operations area as has historically been the case for SAP.

In addition to the modules bundled in mySAP ERP, other available modules in the mySAP Business Suite include business intelligence, customer relationship management, enterprise portal, marketplace, mobile business, product lifecycle management, supplier relationship management, and supply chain management (see Figure 6.7 for a sample of the key capabilities for each module). In the human resources module, the employee self-service area is an interesting one—it gives employees more active participation in the organization's human resources programs by permitting them to review and update their own address

Business Intelligence
- Data warehousing
- Business intelligence platform and tools

Customer Relationship Management
- Marketing, sales, and service
- Analytics
- E-commerce

Enterprise Portal
- Knowledge management
- Collaboration

ERP
- *See Figure 6.6*

Financials
- Strategic enterprise management
- Financial supply chain management
- Corporate services such as real estate management

Human Resources
- Employee lifecycle management
- Employee relationship management
- Employee transaction management

Marketplace
- Business partner management
- Self-service procurement
- Supplier enablement

Mobile Business
- Mobile business applications, including
  - Mobile asset management
  - Mobile time and travel
  - Mobile supply chain management

Product Lifecycle Management
- Lifecycle data management
- Program and project management
- Quality management

Supplier Relationship Management
- Contract management
- Plan-driven or self-service procurement
- Supplier connectivity

Supply Chain Management
- Supply chain planning
- Collaborative planning, forecasting, and replenishment
- Vendor-managed inventory

Figure 6.7 mySAP Business Suite Modules (in bold), with a Sample of Key Capabilities for Each Module

data, submit travel expenses or leave applications, view and print summary pay information, and check their own benefits selections and vacation balances. The names and sample capabilities of the modules should provide a reasonable understanding of what most of the modules do, but let us expand on three relatively new modules. Business intelligence provides a data warehousing capability within R/3 (more on data warehousing shortly), as well as tools to extract key information from the warehouse. Enterprise portal provides a secure, unified entry point into the organization's knowledge base as well as a comprehensive collaboration environment. Marketplace provides support for e-business on a robust, secure platform; marketplace provides self-service procurement, forward and reverse auction capabilities (more on this in Chapter 8), and, for suppliers, automated order management, up-to-date content delivery, and efficient customer billing.

All the above mySAP modules are generic software packages that would work in most businesses. In addition, the early years of the twenty-first century have seen the development of *industry solutions* by SAP and other ERP vendors that are tailored to the special needs of particular industries. SAP, for example, currently offers 23 specific industry solutions, including automotive, banking, chemicals, health care, insurance, pharmaceuticals, and retail. The trend is for more specialization of ERP packages, with variations for smaller businesses being introduced and more industry solutions under development.

Companies may choose to implement some or all of the SAP modules. Motorola's Semiconductor Products Sector, for example, chose to use the human resources modules, including payroll. Motorola, Inc., purchased the payroll module as a solution to the year 2000 problem. Motorola has implemented SAP payroll and employee record-keeping for all 25,000 U.S.-based employees, which, at the time it was installed, made it the largest North American R/3 payroll implementation. ERP implementation is such a challenging task that most companies employ a consulting firm to assist them; in Motorola's case, Price Waterhouse served as the consultant (SAP, 1997). DIRECTV, a unit of Hughes Electronics Corp. headquartered in El Segundo, California, chose to implement SAP R/3 modules for financials, materials procurement, and project tracking and costing to support its extremely rapid growth, which was largely through acquisition. DIRECTV, using Deloitte & Touche as its consulting partner, installed the R/3 modules as well as an Oracle database on a Hewlett-Packard HP 9000 server. According to DIRECTV Chief Information Officer Bob Pacek, the implementation went smoothly: "We went from a handshake to going live in only 11 months." He attributes that accomplishment to DIRECTV's decision to avoid customization insofar as possible (Wreden, 1999). MassMutual Financial Group is implementing several modules of mySAP, including employee self-service, payroll, and benefits administration from the human resources area; general ledger, budget, treasury, fixed assets, and travel and expenses from the financials area; and business-to-business procurement (buying) (SAP, 2000).

In contrast to these partial applications, Hyundai Motor Company is deploying mySAP modules, including the SAP automotive industry solution, to consolidate and automate its supply chain, financial, human resources, and procurement processes in its first North American assembly plant, now under construction in Montgomery, Alabama (Bacheldor, February 3, 2003). As part of an outsourcing agreement with EDS, Dial Corporation is scrapping enterprise software packages from Oracle, Siebel Systems, and Manugistics and moving to a single suite from SAP. The SAP implementation will include manufacturing, supply chain, finance, accounting, performance management, and customer relationship management software and is expected to cost $35 million, including licenses, implementation services, and maintenance. According to Dial Chief Information Officer Evon Jones, Dial went with SAP because "SAP and the processes with SAP's software are regarded as best in class and will drive operational efficiencies, particularly when you start to get greater visibility within your supply chain" (Bacheldor, July 25, 2003).

For more detailed descriptions of SAP implementations at several firms, see the section entitled "What is the Experience with ERP?" in Vollmann, Berry, Whybark, and Jacobs (2004, pp. 123–130). Also see the sidebar entitled "Toyota Motorsport Accelerates Formula One Operations with SAP." Today, Web-enabled ERP software systems are still a hot commodity.

DATA WAREHOUSING

In order to create a data warehouse, a firm pulls data from its operational systems—the transaction processing systems we have just discussed—and puts the data in a separate "data warehouse" so that users may access and analyze the data without endangering the operational systems. Thus, **data warehousing** is the establishment and maintenance of a large data storage facility containing data on all (or at least many) aspects of the enterprise. If the data warehouse is to be useful, the data must be accurate, current, and stored in a useable form; in addition, easy-to-use data access and analysis tools for managers and other users must be provided to encourage full use of the data.

TOYOTA MOTORSPORT ACCELERATES FORMULA ONE OPERATIONS WITH SAP

SAP announced that Toyota Motorsport GmbH, Toyota's German-based motorsport subsidiary, is implementing software from SAP's automotive industry solution to streamline ERP processes across its Formula One racing operations. Toyota Motorsport is replacing its existing, nonintegrated systems with SAP for Automotive, including mySAP Product Lifecycle Management, mySAP Supply Chain Management, mySAP Human Resources, and mySAP Financials.

Having won seven world championship titles with its World Rally Championship program, Toyota decided to enter Formula One racing in 1999. The entire car, including the engine and chassis, is completely designed and constructed at Toyota Motorsport's headquarters in Cologne, Germany. In order to operate a Formula One racing program, 20,000 to 30,000 made-to-order parts are required, and these parts must be quickly available. Further, the parts must be analyzed on an ongoing basis. Toyota Motorsport felt that SAP software was the best choice to efficiently manage the enormous amount of data required for the racing program's success, as well as to control its supply chain, production, and financial processes cost effectively.

"Applying knowledge effectively translates into competitive edge," said Thomas Schiller, IT general manager for Toyota Motorsport. "After comprehensive evaluation of several vendors, we found that SAP could best enable the solid data foundation that is critical to our business. SAP gives us a strategic advantage, ensuring high availability of reliable information across our operations to make faster and more informed decisions. With its integrated solutions and powerful scope of functionality, SAP enables us to effectively execute these decisions and accelerate our production and supply chain processes."

[Adapted from SAP, 2003]

Establishing a data warehouse is time-consuming and expensive. Three types of software tools are needed: warehouse construction software, warehouse operation software, and warehouse access and analysis software. Warehouse construction software is required to extract relevant data from the operational databases, make sure the data are clean (free from error), transform the data into a useable form, and load the data into the data warehouse (see Figure 6.8). Software tools to construct the warehouse include products such as Advantage Data Transformer (from Computer Associates), IBM DB2 Warehouse Manager, Informatica Powercenter, Oracle Warehouse Builder, and SAS/Warehouse Administrator.

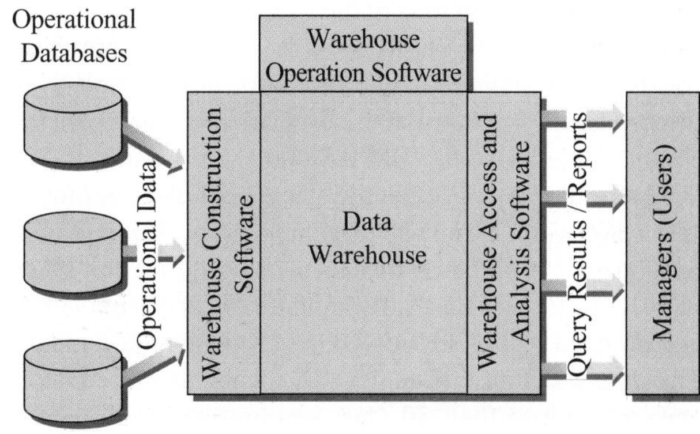

Figure 6.8 Key Elements of Data Warehousing

Operation software is required to store the data and manage the data warehouse. Data warehouse storage is typically accomplished by database management systems such as Advantage Ingres (from Computer Associates), IBM DB2, Microsoft SQL Server, NCR Teradata, Oracle, and Sybase; specialized warehouse management software is offered by Computer Associates, IBM, Information Builders, SAS Institute, and others.

The widest variety of software tools is available in the warehouse access and analysis area. Information catalog tools, such as Computer Associates' PLATINUM Repository, tell the user what is in the warehouse. Analysis and reporting tools enable a user to produce customized reports from the data warehouse, perhaps on a regular basis. Among these tools are Information Builders' WebFOCUS, MicroStrategy's 7i, Oracle's Darwin, and SAS Institute's Enterprise Miner. Visualizing the data might be important, using tools such as Computer Associates' CleverPath Forest & Trees and SAS Institute's SAS/INSIGHT. Some software packages, such as IBM's DB2 Universal Database Data Warehouse Edition, include tools to accomplish warehouse construction, operation, and access and analysis. This IBM product incorporates Intelligent Miner Modeling, Visualization, and Scoring modules to accomplish warehouse access and analysis. We will defer further consideration of these analysis tools until the next chapter, when we consider decision support systems, data mining, and executive information systems in more detail. In our judgment, creation and maintenance of the data warehouse is an enterprise system, while these end-user reporting and analysis tools are designed for management support—the topic of Chapter 7.

Companies of all shapes and sizes are successfully using data warehousing. Let us consider some examples. Gart Sports, a retailer with annual revenues of $681 million, acquired Sportmart in 1997 to become the largest sporting goods chain west of the Mississippi River. Among Gart's most essential tasks after the Sportmart purchase was the consolidation of the inventory information from the two firms' separate databases. Gart chose to create the combined database on IBM AS/400 servers using IBM's DB2 database management system. Gart also employed JDA Software Group's Merchandising Management System as its warehouse management software, combined with JDA's Retail Ideas software used to carry out queries and produce reports to satisfy Gart's unique requirements. The data warehouse occupies 400 gigabytes of disk storage, with more than 50 Gart employees accessing the warehouse. In addition to using the warehouse to manage inventory, Gart also produces performance-related reports for budget management and analysis of store operations as well as to assess the effectiveness of its advertising strategies by product and geography (Singer, 2000).

Harrah's Entertainment, with 18 casinos in 8 states, has annual revenues of $2 billion. Harrah's has created a data warehouse to track and analyze customer spending in all its casinos through its Total Gold system. All major guest transactions are captured, including those at slot machines and gaming tables, through the use of a magnetic membership card. To encourage use of the card, members receive vouchers or coupons each time it is used. John Boushy, senior vice president of information technology and marketing services, believes that "The information and analytical capabilities resulting from our new warehouse enable us to understand our customers better, to determine what adds value to each individual, and to market to them in a highly customized fashion." Boushy adds, "The system can predict a customer's profitability, even with very little transaction information. This enables us to react quickly to changes in behavior that may indicate possible attrition." Harrah's has implemented its data warehouse on an NCR massively parallel processor server, using NCR's Teradata database and warehousing software. The setup cost of the new data warehouse, which is capable of handling more than 100 terabytes of data, was about $2 million for hardware, software, and conversion expenses. Boushy expects payback of this cost within two years. According to Boushy, "Our warehouse has enabled us to develop world-class relationship marketing capabilities, which are leading to greater profits" (Singer, 1999).

Continental Airlines, Inc., won the 2003 Data Warehouse Institute Award for the best enterprise data warehouse. The original objective of the warehouse was to accurately forecast passenger bookings, but it is now used for a much wider variety of applications, including revenue management, customer relationship management, fraud detection, and management of crew payrolls. Continental's data warehouse, which is based on hardware and software from NCR's Teradata division, incorporates data from 41 sources, including flight schedules, seat inventory, revenue and ticketing data, profiles of OnePass frequent flyers, employee records, and crew payrolls. Thirteen hundred employees in 35 departments have access to the data, with most using Brio Software's query and reporting software. According to Continental, the data warehouse has been a big success, with millions of dollars in savings as well as revenue increases of several million dollars.

As user demands on the warehouse increased over time, Continental's data warehousing team reworked the data warehouse to operate on a near-real-time basis. The mainframe and COBOL tools that originally handled the transformation and loading of the data have been replaced by custom-built C++ software running on a network of Windows-based servers. Now users analyze flight operations and reservations data that is only seconds old. The data warehouse's near-real-time architecture and automated data transformation capabilities are two of the best practices that earned Continental the best enterprise data warehouse award (Whiting, July 28, 2003). Data warehousing has the potential to let companies understand and utilize the data that they are already collecting as they run their businesses.

CUSTOMER RELATIONSHIP MANAGEMENT

A type of application that often pulls much of its data from the organization's data warehouse is **customer relationship management**, or **CRM**. A CRM system attempts to provide an integrated approach to all aspects of interaction a company has with its customers, including marketing, sales, and support. The goal of a CRM system is to use technology to forge a strong relationship between a business and its customers. To look at CRM in another way, the business is seeking to better manage its own enterprise around customer behaviors.

A variety of software packages have been created to manage customer relationships, but most depend upon capturing, updating, and utilizing extensive profiles of individual customers. These profiles are often stored in a data warehouse, and data mining (discussed in Chapter 7) is used to extract relevant information about the firm's customers. Furthermore, customer profiles are made available online to all those in the company who might interact with a customer. In addition, Web-based front-ends have been

BANKING ON A WAREHOUSE AT FIRST UNION

After more than 80 acquisitions, First Union Corporation, of Charlotte, North Carolina, is now the nation's sixth largest bank and eighth largest brokerage, with assets of $230 billion and operating earnings of $3.7 billion. First Union needed a large, integrated data warehouse to incorporate the data from the legacy systems and customer databases of its acquisitions as well as its own legacy systems and databases. First Union made the decision to build the new warehouse, with a capacity of 27 terabytes, on an IBM RS/6000S platform running an Informix relational database management system. Analysts at First Union employ SAS Institute software products to carry out high-end data modeling and data mining on the data warehouse, and the analyses are proving valuable to the bank.

The story does not end with the data warehouse. First Union took the data warehousing approach one step further by creating a targeted, easily used **data mart**, which is simply a smaller, more focused version of a data warehouse created for "drop-in shopping," much like a neighborhood convenience mart. First Union designed its data mart, known as Sigma, to analyze customer profitability and to deliver customized marketing more efficiently. Sigma, which runs on the same RS/6000S with the same Informix relational database as the data warehouse, extracts all its information from the warehouse. Sigma is considerably smaller than the data warehouse—only five terabytes. Executives and sales managers access the data mart using MicroStrategy's DSS Web software (a browser-based, easy-to-use data analysis tool) on the First Union intranet. In total, about 250 analysts, managers, and executives access the warehouse and the data mart.

By evaluating the performance of products, branches, and regions, and using cross-selling analyses, First Union has increased revenues, customer satisfaction, and employee productivity. First Union also hopes to expand its commercial business with small-business customers by determining which delivery channels are the most popular and then enhancing service in those areas. Bob DeAngelis, manager of First Union's Enterprise Knowledge Group, believes that studying the interactions with customers is critical. "This enables us to better match our offerings and service levels with the customers' needs, including the assignment of relationship managers to those customers with complex relationships."

[Adapted from Singer, 1999]

created so that a customer can interact with the company online to obtain information about products and services offered by the company, to place an order, to check on the status of an existing order, to seek answers from a knowledge base, or to request service. CRM software packages enable organizations to market to, sell to, and service customers across multiple channels, including the Web, call centers, field representatives, business partners, and retail and dealer networks.

The CRM market is quite fragmented, with many of the newer options focused on a specific industry or market—so-called vertical CRM applications. One useful way of viewing the CRM market divides it into the following five segments (Schwartz, 2003):

- *Traditional out-of-the-box CRM* This segment includes all the enterprise vendors, including CRM industry leader Siebel Systems, Inc., Oracle, PeopleSoft, and SAP. These applications have a great deal of horizontal functionality, such as call center support, sales-force automation, and marketing support. It is often necessary for the company's IT department, perhaps with the assistance of a consulting firm, to customize the software by adding some elements and removing others to fit the specific business or industry needs.
- *Traditional CRM with templates for specific vertical industries* All the major enterprise vendors except Oracle offer this option, each with CRM solutions available in 20 or more vertical categories. The company's IT department selects the functionality needed for the specific business; it is often necessary for the IT department or a consultant to customize the template to meet the firm's specific needs.
- *Traditional out-of-the-box CRM with application development hooks* This segment sounds similar to the previous "templates" approach, but in reality is quite different. In this category, vendors provide a series of reusable software objects that can be combined as needed to build an application best suited to the company's needs. Vendors in this segment include E.piphany, Chordiant Software, Kana Software, Inc., and Oracle. The reusable objects incorporate the basic CRM functionality needs for every business as well as the most common needs within a variety of industries.
- *Industry-specific vertical CRM packages* This category has seen the most growth in the early twenty-first century, with packages available in most major vertical industries. For example, in the retail industry, key vendors are Blue Martini Software, JDA

Software Group, Inc., and Retek, Inc. In the consumer goods industry, vendors include CAS and MEI Group; in financial services, leading vendors are Chordiant Software, Metavante Corporation, Pegasystems Inc., and Pivotal Corporation. Firepond, Inc., Kana Software, Inc., and Pegasystems are three key vendors in the health care industry. Other leading vendors include Reynolds and Reynolds Company in the automotive industry, Interface Software, Inc., in the legal arena, and Dendrite International in the pharmaceutical industry.

- *Custom solutions from vertical systems integrators* Vendors in this category include Accenture, Computer Associates, IBM Global Services, and Unisys. A custom solution tends to be very expensive but might be necessary for companies with unique or very specific business or industry needs. In most cases the **systems integrator** will start with a vertical template and add functionality as necessary.

Without calling them CRM applications, we have already described two examples of CRM projects using a data warehouse: Harrah's Entertainment and First Union Corporation. Other examples abound: Online brokerage Quick & Reilly Inc. is using Siebel's sales-force automation tools to offer its customers investment options based on what it already knows about them. Quick & Reilly began investing $10 million in call-center and sales-force automation software in 1998. Within 6 months of initial implementation, the CRM system boosted the rate at which brokers convert sales prospects into customers by up to 20 percent. "That's a real return on investment," said Edward M. Garry, Quick & Reilly's vice president for customer relationship management (Kerstetter, Hamm, and Greene, 2002).

Pharmaceutical manufacturer Eli Lilly & Company has implemented sales-force automation, call-center, and other CRM applications from Siebel to support its efforts in branding its drugs (Lilly manufactures antidepressant Prozac as well as many other drugs). "Branding is more important to drug companies nowadays," said Roy Dunbar, chief information officer at Lilly. "Patients used to call their doctors; now, a patient on one of our drugs can pick up the phone and call us." Based on its CRM systems, Lilly has initiated the Lilly Answer Center, which uses the Web and call-center technology to stay in close contact with customers (Greenemeier, September 22, 2003).

A CRM implementation in a pharmaceutical company also helps drive sales and improve the bottom line. With CRM, a drugmaker can identify which physicians are most receptive to their salespeople, calculate potential revenue from physician relationships, and customize interactions with high-priority physicians. Kos Pharmaceuticals Inc., a manufacturer of drugs to treat chronic cardiovascular and respiratory diseases, implemented CRM in 2003 for its 500 sales representatives. "Our sales staff is growing, and we needed to make sure they communicate with each other, especially if they're calling on the same doctors," said Lisa Barry, senior manager of sales systems at Kos. "The sales force seems happier [with the CRM in place], and the physicians like that different sales reps can tell a continuous story" (Greenemeier, October 29, 2003).

In perhaps the largest implementation of CRM software ever, Hewlett-Packard is scrapping a number of different CRM applications across its business channels and installing the eBusiness Applications package from Siebel Systems, Inc., as a unified platform. The CRM project will consolidate Hewlett-Packard's direct and indirect sales channels, including thousands of direct-sales representatives, marketing professionals, contact-center representatives, and partner resellers. Eventually, the project could involve over 50,000 users. "From a customer-experience perspective, it was absolutely imperative to move rapidly," said Mike Overly, vice president of customer operations for HP Global Operations. Hewlett-Packard expects to gain a unified view of customers across all channels and drive operating efficiencies, saving the company tens of millions of dollars (Dunn, 2003). In the early 2000s many companies have publicly stated that they were becoming more customer-focused—and some companies are carrying through on such statements in a very significant way by installing a CRM system.

OFFICE AUTOMATION

Office automation refers to a set of office-related applications that might or might not be integrated into a single system. The most common applications are electronic mail, word processing, voice mail, copying, desktop publishing, electronic calendaring, and document imaging, along with document preparation, storage, and sharing.

Office technology has taken major strides since World War II. Document preparation has evolved from manual typewriters, to electric typewriters with a moving carriage, to the IBM Selectric typewriters with the "golf ball" typing element, to memory typewriters, to expensive terminals connected to a minicomputer, to stand-alone microcomputers, and now to microcomputers linked via a LAN. Copying has moved from mimeograph machines to fast photocopiers and facsimile machines. The telephone has moved from a simple instrument with no dial or keys to a

CRM: DESPERATELY SEEKING SUCCESS

Not all CRM projects are successes, but that does not seem to be deterring corporate investment in CRM applications. An AMR Research study shows that only 16 percent of CRM initiatives have returned value to the company. The remaining projects include some that have failed but more that are unclear whether they have succeeded or failed because the companies have not defined successes or goals for their CRM projects. "Companies must define their CRM strategy up front, and that strategy will define what success looks like and which metrics are important," according to Kevin Scott, a senior research analyst with AMR Research.

Despite these mixed results, 35 percent of executives surveyed in a recent *CIO Magazine* Tech Poll indicated that their organizations will launch CRM projects in the next year. Similarly, a recent IDC forecast calls for a 6.7 percent annual growth rate for CRM expenditures from 2002 to 2007, resulting in $12.1 billion in CRM software annual revenue by 2007.

Given this continued growth in CRM projects with only limited success thus far, what must companies do to give their CRM initiatives the best chance of succeeding? *CIO Magazine* suggests three best practices:

- Be prepared for organizational change–collaboration across the enterprise will be required.
- Keep it simple–make sure your application has an easy-to-use interface and that your vendor will work with you to provide user training.
- Align your vendor's definition of success with your own–make sure your vendor understands your company's definition of success.

[Adapted from Ware, August 1, 2003]

dial telephone, and then from a simple touch-tone telephone to a versatile touch-tone instrument with features such as automatic redial, call forwarding, call waiting, multiparty calling, and caller identification. To a great extent, however, these devices still do not talk to each other today—but IT will change that! In the office of the future, these devices and others will be connected via an integrated voice/data/image network, as shown in Figure 6.9. In our discussion of the components of this figure, we will mention those connections that exist today.

Word Processing and Application Suites

A number of excellent word-processing packages have been developed for microcomputers, the most common workstations in today's offices. Microsoft Word is clearly the market leader, but there is also support for Corel WordPerfect and Lotus Word Pro. As noted in Chapter 3, these software packages are typically sold as part of an application suite that includes spreadsheet, presentation, database, and possibly other applications. The advantage of a suite is that it is possible to copy and paste from one application to another in the same suite; for instance, a Microsoft Office user can copy a portion of an Excel spreadsheet to the clipboard and paste the portion directly into a Word document she is preparing. In a small office or high-print-volume situation, a high-quality printer can be connected directly to a PC. It is more common, however, for office PCs to be on a LAN so documents can be sent electronically from the preparing workstation to a high-quality printer, as depicted in Figure 6.9.

Electronic Mail

Electronic mail (e-mail) systems permit rapid, asynchronous communication between workstations on a network, eliminating telephone tag. Most systems incorporate such features as sending a note to a distribution list, forwarding a note to someone else with an appended message, replying to a note without reentering the address, and filing notes in electronic file folders for later recall. All the authors of this book use electronic mail on a regular basis, and we feel we could not do without it.

Of course, there are potential drawbacks to e-mail communication. Because it is so easy to use, the volume of e-mail can become overwhelming, particularly standard messages sent to a distribution list. Spam—unsolicited e-mail that most of us regard as junk—is the bane of e-mail users in the decade of the 2000s. E-mail is also less personal because it is dependent on text signals alone (but see the sidebar "E-mail Smileys for All Occasions"). Some people use offensive words and phrases that they would never use in face-to-face conversation, called "flaming." Privacy issues arise because of the opportunity for electronic monitoring by supervisors. For most organizations and most users, however, these drawbacks are totally overshadowed by the advantages of rapid, asynchronous communication.

Variants of e-mail include electronic bulletin boards, listservs, computer conferencing, chat rooms, and, most recently, instant messaging (IM). An electronic bulletin board is a repository (a disk on a computer) on which anyone with access to the bulletin board and the computer account number can post messages and read other messages. Bulletin boards can be operated within an organization (employing

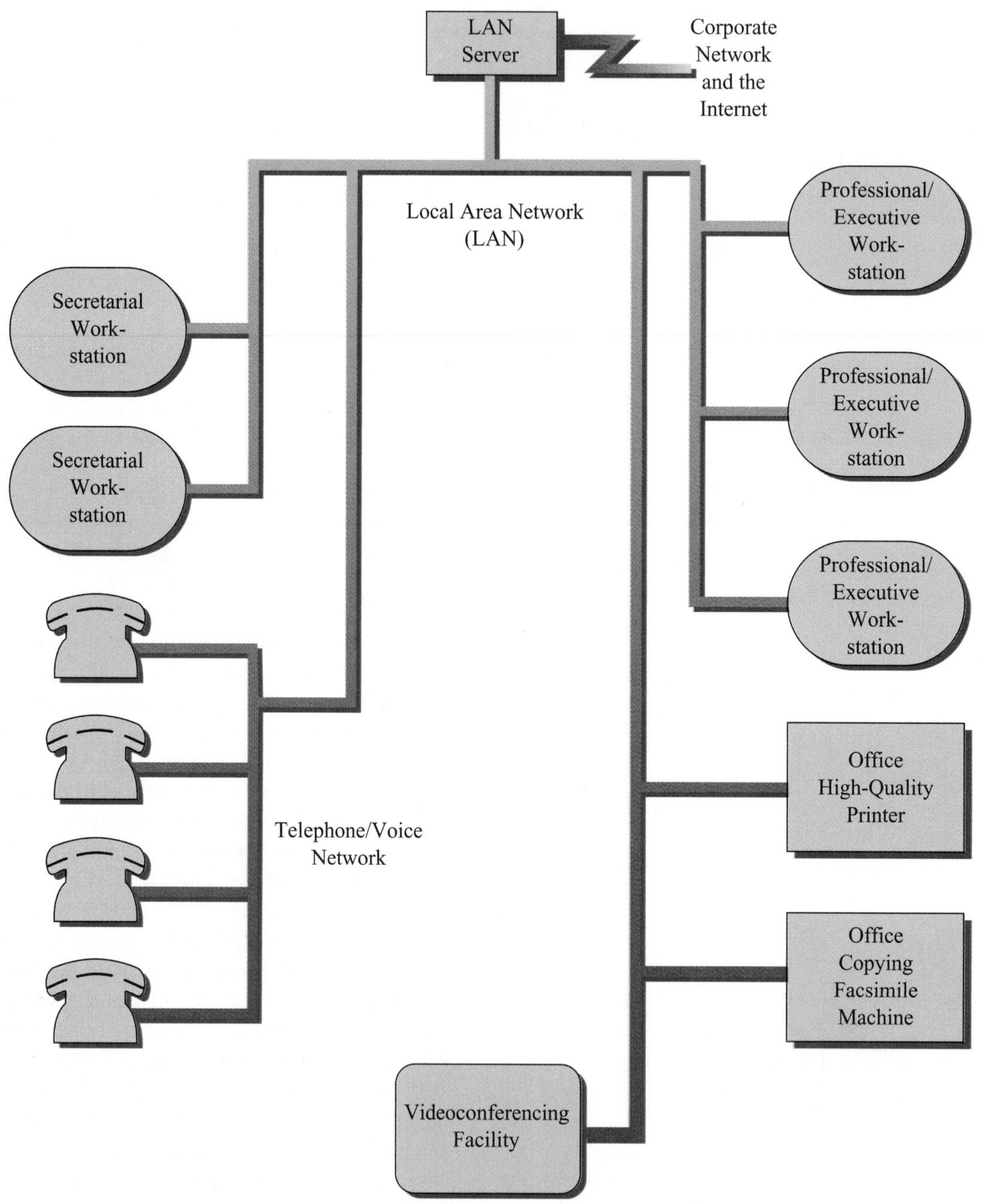

Figure 6.9 Office of the Future Network

the usual communication links), or over the Internet. A listserv is a computerized mailing list that accepts a message sent to the listserv address and forwards it to everyone on the particular mailing list.

Computer conferencing is similar to a bulletin board, but it is set up around a particular topic. For example, a professional society can set up a computer conference to consider changes in its annual meeting program. The announcement of the topic and the Web address (or account number) at which the conference will be held are published in the society's newsletter, which can be distributed electronically via a listserv. Users participate in the conference by logging into the conference, entering an opinion, and reading other participants' opinions. Chat rooms are real-time versions

E-MAIL SMILEYS FOR ALL OCCASIONS

As e-mail has spread through corporate America and around the world, new conventions for communication have been created. Perhaps the most humorous of these conventions is the digital smiley face and the numerous variations which have evolved from the original smiley. When you tilt your head to the left and use your imagination, the original digital smiley :-) looks like a little face with a colon for eyes and a hyphen for a nose. The use of this digital smiley at the end of an e-mail message means something like "just kidding," as in the following message copied from an electronic bulletin board. The subject is uncontrollable scalp flaking, and one writer is proposing a new remedy: "I find that rinsing my scalp with vinegar will cut down on it for a while, if you don't mind smelling like a salad :-)"

But the variants of the digital smiley are even more fun. Here are some variants along with their interpretations:

:-(	I'm unhappy
:-D	I'm laughing
B-)	I'm cool
:*)	I'm drunk
{(:-)	I have a toupee
}(:-(	I have a toupee and it's windy
:-8	I'm talking out of both sides of my mouth
[:-)	I'm wearing a Walkman
d:-)	I'm a baseball player
:-?	I'm smoking a pipe
<<<<(:-)	I'm a hat salesman
':-)	I accidentally shaved off one eyebrow

Try creating your own smileys and spice up your own e-mail messages!

[Adapted from Miller, 1992]

of computer conferencing (synchronous communication) conducted on the Internet, with an incredibly wide array of topics. IM is a synchronous communication system that enables the user to establish a private chat room with another individual to carry out text-based communication in real time over the Internet.

The first popular e-mail systems were mainframe or minicomputer-based, which makes sense because e-mail predated client/server systems. They were also designed to run under proprietary operating systems (e.g., not UNIX). Examples are Digital Equipment's VaxMail and ALL-IN-ONE and IBM's OfficeVision and PROFS (Professional Office System). The more advanced mainframe-based systems, such as PROFS, packaged e-mail together with electronic calendaring and other related features. In this mainframe environment, the e-mail system runs on the mainframe, with the workstation being used as a terminal. With PROFS, the main menu included a calendar with the current date highlighted, a clock, a message area where other users could directly communicate with this workstation, and a menu of other choices, such as process schedules (electronic calendaring), open the mail, search for documents, and prepare documents. Some of these mainframe e-mail systems are still in use, although they are not as popular as they once were because they do not have a GUI interface or the functionality of the newer groupware systems.

The second wave of e-mail systems was designed to run on UNIX servers (high-powered workstations running the UNIX operating system). Popular systems include Pine and Elm. This type of e-mail system runs on the server, with the PC being used as a terminal; again, there is no GUI interface. These systems do not have the functionality of mainframe systems like PROFS, but they are much more economical to operate on a per-user or per-message basis. It should come as no surprise that many colleges and universities still use these UNIX systems.

The development of POP-servers and POP-mail demonstrates how PC-based front-ends can be used to provide a friendlier interface for users. POP stands for post office protocol, and POP-mail is based on an analogy with post office boxes. To use POP-mail, a POP-client such as Eudora or Pegasus must be loaded on the PC. Various e-mail systems, including Pine, can be used as a POP-server. All incoming mail is kept on the POP-server until the user logs on and asks for mail to be downloaded to his or her own machine; this is analogous to traditional mail being kept in a post office box until the patron opens the box and empties it. The user processes the mail on his or her own machine, using the GUI provided by Eudora or Pegasus. The user can read mail, throw some of it away, store some in electronic file folders, and prepare responses to some of it. After processing the mail on the PC, the user reopens a connection to the POP-server on the host computer and uploads any outgoing messages.

The third wave of e-mail systems were LAN-based client/server software systems that incorporated well-designed GUI interfaces, complete with small inboxes, outboxes, wastebaskets, attractive fonts, color, and other GUI features. Some examples are cc:Mail by Lotus and

Microsoft Mail. If an organization wants e-mail only, these packages are sufficient. LAN-based e-mail systems were very popular in the 1990s, but have largely been replaced in the 2000s by the more robust groupware systems such as Lotus Notes/Domino and Microsoft Outlook/Exchange. A variation of this third wave of client/server e-mail systems is Internet mail, which has become very popular for small business and home use. For Internet mail, the client software is the user's Web browser, and the server software is located on a high-powered Web server operated by an Internet service or software provider. The user must, of course, have access to the Internet via an Internet service provider (ISP) or an organizational link to the Internet. Examples of these Internet mail systems, which are usually free, are Microsoft Hotmail, Netscape Mail, and Juno E-mail on the Web.

Progressive organizations, however, are ready to move beyond simple e-mail. They want the greater functionality of the older mainframe systems plus the GUI interface of the POP-mail and LAN-based systems. They want electronic calendaring and document sharing. The answer is groupware. We will discuss groupware as a separate category of applications below, after we have completed our discussion of the office of the future. Groupware is, in fact, a significant step toward the hypothetical office of the future.

Future Developments

Today, the telephone/voice network in most companies is totally independent of the computer/data network. In the office of the not-so-distant future, these networks will be combined into one integrated office network. Newer workstations include a voice receiver and a voice speaker and can function as a telephone. Some users are already using their workstations to make telephone calls over the Internet. When the technology has matured and the appropriate connections to the office and external networks have been made, the functions of today's telephones are likely to be totally subsumed by the workstation itself.

Today, almost all offices have facsimile machines to receive electronically transmitted documents and produce a hard copy version. Faxes can also be sent and received via a PC. However, conventional copying machines are still stand-alone devices. In the future, the copying machine will be integrated into the office network and will absorb the function of the stand-alone facsimile device. Single or multiple copies of a document may be printed either at the copying machine, from a workstation in the same office, or from a remote site. The all-in-one machines (printer, copier, scanner, and facsimile), such as the Hewlett-Packard OfficeJet d155xi, are early examples of these integrated devices.

Document storage is another evolving area of office automation. It is not unusual for today's organizations to store their business documents online, often using magnetic or optical disk technology (discussed in Chapter 2). More and more of these documents will be stored digitally in the future, particularly with the growing use of imaging technology. With imaging, any type of paper document—including reports, graphs, and photographs—can be read by a digital scanner and translated into digital form so that it can be stored in the computer system. Later this process can be reversed, so that the digitized image stored in the computer system can be printed on paper, displayed on a video display unit, or transmitted to another workstation.

A facility possessed by a limited but growing number of organizations—a videoconferencing facility—is shown at the bottom of Figure 6.9. Such facilities permit face-to-face, or, more properly, image-to-image meetings and conferences without the need for costly and time-consuming travel. By tying the videoconferencing facility into the integrated office network, computer-generated reports and graphics can also be shared during the conferences.

Whereas separate videoconferencing facilities work well for larger group meetings, desktop videoconferencing is now a reality, and as quality improves it will become quite popular for one-on-one and small group conferences. The screen on a desktop PC is so small, however, that we do not think desktop videoconferencing will prove satisfactory for large group conferences. Splitting an already small screen into multiple smaller images will reduce the sense of being there, reducing the effectiveness of the conference. Thus, we believe that the office of the future will include a separate videoconferencing facility (usually a conference room) where a large group of people can participate in a conference with a large group at another location.

As an example of both group and desktop videoconferencing, let us consider the newest offerings from Polycom, Inc., headquartered in Pleasanton, California. With its 2001 acquisition of PictureTel Corporation, Polycom solidified its position as the worldwide market leader in voice- and videoconferencing. Polycom iPower 9000 Series group videoconferencing units have list prices from \$15,500 to \$26,500 per unit for the iPower 9400 and from \$18,000 to \$29,000 per unit for the top-of-the-line iPower 9800. In each case the lower figure is the price of the base system with no monitors and support for only IP network connection; the higher figure includes a dual monitor package and the ability to connect to an additional type of network. Polycom iPower 9000 Series units operate at 30 frames per second (comparable to television quality) when operating at 256 kbps and above. This network speed can be obtained via a LAN connection, digital subscriber line (DSL), cable modem, or combined Integrated Services Digital Network (ISDN) lines. Included in the iPower 9800 is a feature, called Limelight, that causes the camera to focus on the current speaker. Limelight works by triangulating from the sounds received at four tiny, built-in microphones in order to focus on the speaker or, if several people are speaking almost at once, to zoom out and show all the people who are speaking. Another capability included in the iPower 9800 is ImageShare, a unique tabletop interface that lets users access a laptop computer and share its screen display with other videoconferencing participants. At the desktop level, Polycom's ViaVideo II, with a list price of $599 and a street price of $529 or less, is a compact, portable system that plugs into the universal serial bus (USB) port on a standard PC. The ViaVideo II is designed to operate at 15 frames per second (fps) at network speeds from 32 kbps up to 320 kbps (motions will appear jerky at 15 fps), or at 30 fps at network speeds above 320 kbps. This desktop system does not provide large-system picture quality, but it does provide full-screen, full-motion video with full duplex audio when used with an appropriate network connection.

In summary, the ideal office network shown in Figure 6.9 does not exist. Offices have secretarial and professional/executive workstations in ever-increasing numbers, and these devices are usually linked via a LAN. Today telephony is not typically accomplished on the same network, and the facsimile machine is not on the LAN. The use of videoconferencing is increasing, but still not commonplace.

As organizations move toward office automation, they have learned some important lessons. First, the process of office automation must be coordinated—each office unit cannot go its own way. The various islands of automation must be made compatible. In most organizations the IS organization has been given the responsibility for corporate-wide office automation. Second, the emphasis must be on the information requirements—the problems being solved—in office automation as in other IT applications. Third, training and education of all parties involved is a necessary prerequisite for a successful system. Fourth, office automation should be an evolutionary process, moving toward the mythical office of the future, but not expecting to get there overnight. Fifth, the redefinition of the functions of the office and the restructuring of individual roles are required to achieve the maximum benefits of office automation.

GROUPWARE

Earlier in this chapter, we argued that ERP systems deserved treatment as a separate application area because of their currency and importance, despite the fact that ERP systems are, indeed, transaction processing systems. Now we wish to make the same argument for including groupware as an application area vis-à-vis office automation. Clearly, groupware is part of office automation, but it is a very critical part that deserves special attention.

Groupware is an industry term that refers to soft*ware* designed to support *groups* by facilitating collaboration, communication, and coordination. Nowadays, the term **collaboration** or the phrase **collaborative environment** is often used as a synonym for groupware. In choosing a groupware product, the decision maker must decide what functions are required and seek a product (or a combination of products) that provides these features. Some groupware features are electronic mail, electronic bulletin boards, computer conferencing, electronic calendaring, group scheduling, sharing documents, electronic whiteboards, meeting support systems, workflow routing, electronic forms, desktop videoconferencing, learning management systems, and IM. None of the leading groupware packages provide all the functions that a company might want, but in many cases add-on packages can be purchased to fill the gaps.

One might guess that the heart of a successful general-purpose groupware product is electronic mail, and that might be right—but the key feature that put industry leader Lotus Notes[2] in the top position is its outstanding ability to share documents of all types. Electronic calendaring and group scheduling are also important, and these have been strengths of Novell GroupWise. The third major player, Microsoft Exchange[3], is a relative newcomer in this market, but Exchange has easily passed GroupWise to move into the number two position (Emigh, 2003). Other players in the groupware marketplace include Oracle with its Collaboration Suite, Thruport Technologies with its HotOffice product, Groove Networks with its Groove Workspace product, and Web Crossing. All the groupware

[2]Actually, Lotus Notes is the name of the client program that runs on a PC. Lotus Domino is the name of the server program. However, it is common for users to refer to the Lotus Notes/Lotus Domino combination as a Lotus Notes groupware system.

[3]In this case, Microsoft Exchange is the name of the server program, while Microsoft Outlook is the name of the client program that runs on a PC. However, it is common for users to refer to the Microsoft Outlook/Microsoft Exchange combination as a Microsoft Exchange groupware system.

players are moving to support real-time collaboration based on presence awareness, or the ability to detect others' online availability (which is the key technology underlying IM). An interesting specialized groupware area deals with electronic meeting support systems, and we will talk more about this area in the next chapter.

Groupware, like ERP systems, is a growth area in the software industry as well as an evolving area (see the sidebar entitled "Real-Time Collaboration"). To gain a greater understanding of this area, let us take a closer look at a leading groupware product, Lotus Notes.

An Example Groupware System: Lotus Notes

Lotus Development Corporation's first important product was 1-2-3, and it became the dominant spreadsheet package in the 1980s and early 1990s. The second important product was Notes, a groupware system originally featuring strong document-sharing features and a reasonable e-mail package that has grown into a more full-featured product. Notes—and Lotus's expertise in developing PC and client/server software—were important to IBM, which paid $3.5 billion to purchase Lotus in 1995. IBM was already a software powerhouse, as we have noted earlier in this book, but its strength was in large machine software. IBM believed it needed to bolster its PC software prowess to compete with Microsoft in that market, and it also wanted the Notes groupware product. IBM has allowed Lotus to operate as a separate business unit, and so far the buyout seems to have benefited both IBM and Lotus. Notes continues to be the leader in the groupware marketplace (in terms of number of "seats"), followed by second-place contender Microsoft Exchange.

Users can configure the welcome page of Lotus Notes to their liking; Figure 6.10 shows the slightly customized welcome page used by one of the authors of this book. At the top left of the screen is the menu bar containing the menus of commands used to perform tasks within Notes. Just below the menu bar is a row of icons that permit the user to perform tasks quickly by clicking the mouse on an icon. Below the row of icons is an address box. To go to a Web address you have not visited before, enter the Uniform Resource Locator (URL) in the address box; to go to a page you have previously visited, click the down arrow at the right end of the address field and select the appropriate URL from the drop-down list. To the right of the menu bar is the navigation bar that allows you to navigate in Notes just as you would in a Web browser (Notes is, in fact, a Web browser). Down the left side of the screen are the bookmark buttons, which represent a powerful way to navigate to Web pages as well as to Notes databases, views, and documents. In the big area of the screen, the upper left quadrant shows the most recent entries in the user's Notes inbox, the upper right quadrant shows the "to do" list and calendar entries for the current day, and the lower half contains "hot spot" links to the user's mail, calendar, contacts (address book), "to do" list, and personal journal.

REAL-TIME COLLABORATION

Many business-technology managers see a lot of value in using the Internet to keep people in constant and instantaneous communication with one another, yet they're not certain when that vision will become reality. It's happening, but only in bits and pieces, as with telecommuters who communicate with co-workers using IM and employees who attend project-team meetings via Web conferencing. This concept, known as real-time collaboration, focuses on the person-to-person aspect of a company's broader collaboration strategy. On occasion, technologies such as IM and Web conferencing are being used to collaborate in real time with customers, partners, and suppliers.

But are the technologies and concept advanced enough to build a strategic organizational plan around real-time collaboration? That's a question business-technology managers are asking, and there are numerous challenges to achieving that goal in the near future. Many of the technologies available don't follow standards and don't link to each other easily, and the performance of multimedia delivery over the Internet hasn't reached a high degree of consistency. Then there are the cultural issues involved in getting people to embrace a completely different way of working. "Real-time collaboration apps aren't ready for prime time," says Forrester Research analyst Erica Rugullies.

On a positive note, analysts think it will be only a few years before big visions for real-time collaboration are realized. Big-name vendors such as IBM Lotus Software, Microsoft, Oracle, Siemens, and Sun Microsystems are promising—and in some cases already offering—collaboration tools that embrace standards-based technologies such as XML, Web services, Java 2 Enterprise Edition, and voice over IP. The resulting flexibility will let collaborative components be sewn together to create an always-on architecture. The plan from the IT community is to let collaborative features be embedded in various enterprise applications, launched from numerous communication tools, and consumed by just about any device. "There's a larger vision here than a group of disconnected services," says Rob Koplowitz, senior director of product marketing for Oracle. "Customers are beginning to see this as an infrastructure play."

[Kontzer, November 17, 2003]

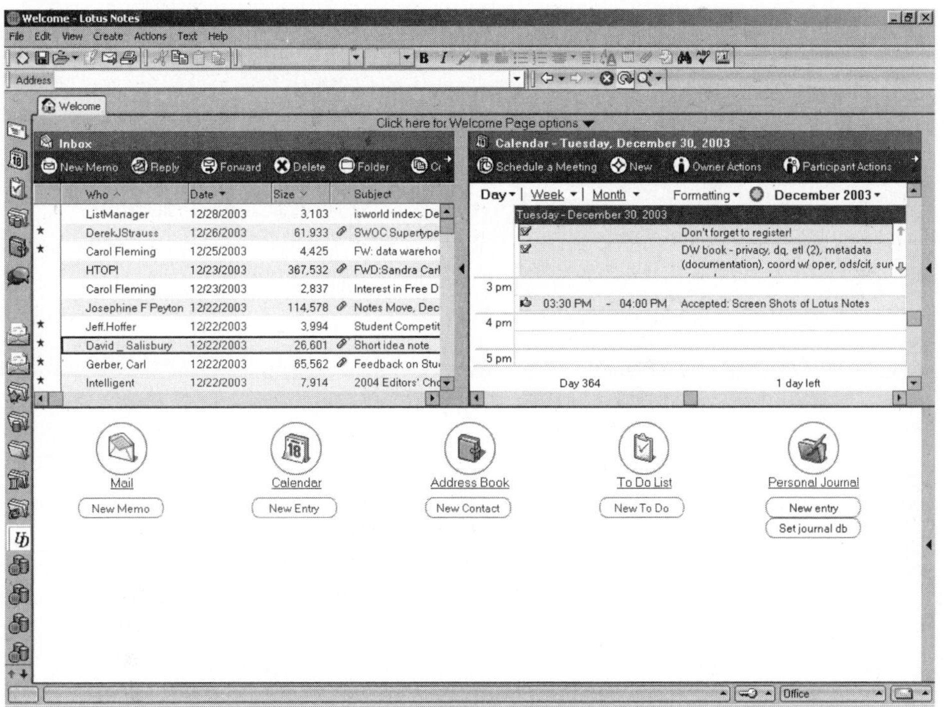

Figure 6.10 Lotus Notes® Welcome Page (Copyright © 2004 IBM Lotus Software. Lotus Notes is a registered trademark of IBM Lotus Software. Used with permission of IBM Lotus Software.)

Some established Notes users prefer to work from the workspace page, shown in Figure 6.11, which served the function of the welcome page in earlier versions of Notes. The workspace page also contains the menu bar, the row of icons, the navigation bar, and the bookmark bar. Now, however, most of the screen is occupied by the workspace, which in turn contains icons representing databases. These databases are the heart of Notes; each contains a collection of documents relating to the same topic. The database on the left is the mailbox, which is an entry point into the e-mail features of Notes. The other databases refer to a university address book, a personal address book, personal bookmarks, a personal Web navigator, and two databases related to applications. The user opens a database by double-clicking on the relevant icon.

When the user opens the mailbox—either by clicking the mail bookmark button on the left side of any page (the top icon, which looks like a piece or mail) or the mail hot spot in the bottom area of the welcome page—the inbox view of the mailbox is displayed, as shown in Figure 6.12. In addition to the bars and icons appearing on the welcome or workspace page, a view action bar appears above the listing of e-mail messages in the larger window to the right. The actions listed relate to the current view. For the inbox view, the entries are new memo, reply, forward, delete, folder (i.e., move to folder), copy into, and tools; all these, except tools, are common actions used in processing e-mail. Most of the screen is divided into a navigation pane on the left and an active view pane on the right. In the inbox view, the active view pane lists the user's mail messages, tells who sent the message, the date it was sent, the size of the message, and the subject assigned by the sender. To open a message a user double-clicks on it. A star immediately to the left of the sender's name indicates unread messages. The navigation pane on the left lists a number of views and folders that can be used to manage the mail. For instance, the folder "drafts" contains messages you are working on but have not yet sent; the "to do" folders contain task lists that have been created by the user; and the set of file folders with names such as Academic Dishonesty, Accounting, ACM, and Administrative Committee constitute the electronic filing system for this user. Notes also has a valuable electronic calendaring feature that you access by clicking on the calendar bookmark button on the left side of the page (the second icon, which looks like a page of a desk calendar) or by clicking on the calendar hot spot on the welcome page. Several different calendar views are available, including a one-day view, a one-week view, and a one-month view.

As mentioned above, the real strength of Notes is its document-sharing abilities. This is done through various shared databases. Some of the databases might be set up so that the user can only read documents, not modify them or

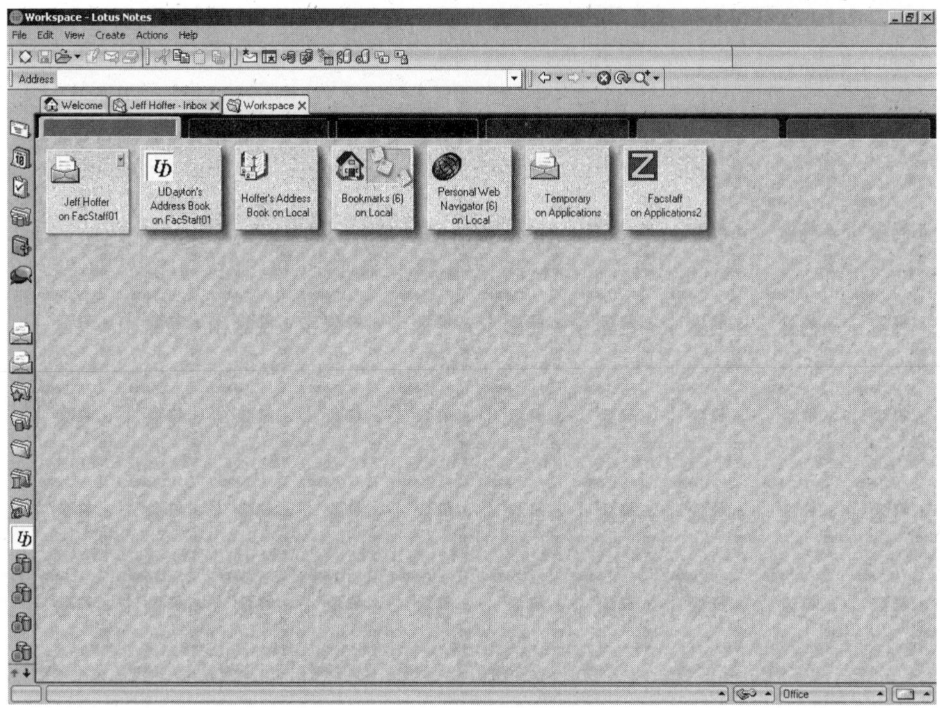

Figure 6.11 Lotus Notes® Workspace Page (Copyright © 2004 IBM Lotus Software. Lotus Notes is a registered trademark of IBM Lotus Software. Used with permission of IBM Lotus Software.)

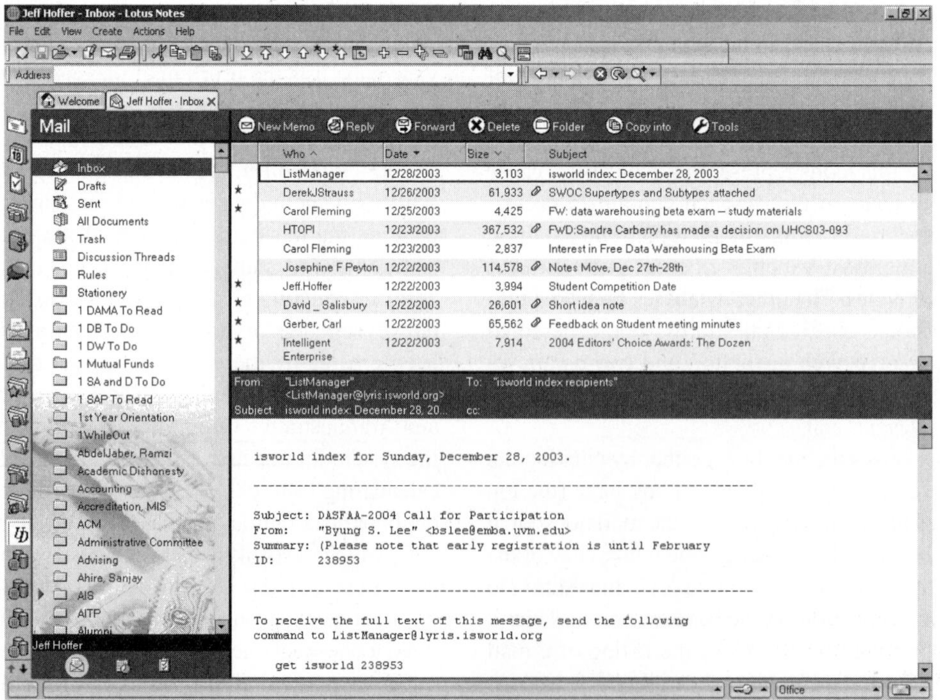

Figure 6.12 Lotus Notes® Inbox (Copyright © 2004 IBM Lotus Software. Lotus Notes is a registered trademark of IBM Lotus Software. Used with permission of IBM Lotus Software.)

add new ones; in other databases, such as discussion groups, all participants are encouraged to enter into the discussion. We already said that to open a database from the workspace page, the user double-clicks on its icon. To open a database from any other page, first click on the database bookmark button on the left side of the page (this button appears to be a cylinder, or a hard drive, in front of a file folder). This opens the database bookmark page, showing all the databases that the user has bookmarked. (These bookmarked databases are likely to be the same as those represented by database icons on the workspace page.) The user opens a database by double-clicking on the relevant database listing. What if the user has not bookmarked the desired database? The database bookmark page also contains "Find a Database" and "Browse for a Database" selections. The opening screen of any database looks similar to Figure 6.12, with appropriate tool buttons, a navigation pane to the left, and a list of topics or documents in the view pane to the right. The user double-clicks on a document to display it.

How does all this work? Lotus Notes is a client/server system, with the large files (databases) stored on the server, which Lotus calls a "Domino server powered by Notes." The user can opt to store databases on the PC hard drive, but master copies of the large corporate or departmental databases of documents are stored on the server. Corporate files are replicated from one Notes server to another on a regular basis, so that everyone in the organization has access to the same version of a document. The Lotus Notes client, operating on a PC, is used to access the server with appropriate password protection. This access might either be directly across a LAN or via a dial-up modem. Any Web browser on the Internet can also access Notes. Of course, the Notes client is itself a Web browser. A major advantage of using Notes as the browser is that Notes gives you the ability to store copies of Web pages as documents in a Notes database.

Finally, another strength of Lotus Notes is its ability to serve as a development platform, allowing companies to create their own Notes applications customized for their needs. In fact, a growing number of these specialized applications are available commercially through third-party vendors, including project management, human resources, help desk, document management, health care, sales and marketing, and imaging applications.

AT HERTZ, LOTUS NOTES/DOMINO IS #1

Hertz rents cars from approximately 7,000 locations in more than 150 countries. Given this global span, Hertz employees must communicate and collaborate on an ongoing basis with people all over the world. Forms must be completed and routed to people in other offices or countries. Changes in policies and regulations must be quickly distributed to a widely dispersed workforce. To streamline these and other global tasks, Hertz depends increasingly on IBM Lotus Notes and Domino and on related Lotus technologies such as IBM Lotus Instant Messaging, Web Conferencing, Team Workplace, and Domino.Doc.

"For us, Lotus Domino is key to efficiency," says Claude Burgess, senior vice president of technology and e-business at Hertz. "It takes so many of the mundane procedures we have as a global organization and lets us automate them to cut costs, eliminate travel, speed processes, and add security. The processes won't go away, and so making them more efficient is extremely important."

One Domino application that touches the lives of most of Hertz's 15,000 Lotus Notes users is its home-grown eForms system. With eForms, Hertz employees can electronically complete and process any of about 500 types of forms that used to exist only on paper. "With eForms I can submit the forms in seconds," says Burgess. "Our Domino-based workflow application routes it to the appropriate people automatically, and any questions or annotations stay with the form, creating a history for the next person who gets it and eliminating questions that slow things down." Burgess indicates that eForms has reduced the amount of paper Hertz prints by 70 percent and has greatly speeded up forms processing. "Form contents are more secure, and we don't lose data. Everything is routed and processed correctly not just by luck, but because the software makes it happen."

Other Lotus communication and collaboration applications at Hertz include:

- The use of IBM Lotus Team Workplace to create Web-based workrooms where project teams formed to digitize processes within the company can manage the associated documents and track progress.
- The use of Domino.Doc to publish the company's employee policy and procedure manual, as well as other internal documents. Domino.Doc is a Domino-based solution that enables collaborative document management throughout the entire document life cycle.
- The use of Lotus Web Conferencing to hold regular meetings between multidisciplinary teams in dispersed locations. "For instance," Burgess indicates, "we can all be looking at a graphical display of information while making changes to it on the shared screen as the team interaction dictates."
- The use of Lotus Domino Everyplace to send critical information to profit center managers' phones, personal digital assistants (PDAs), or other mobile devices. "These people are always on the move, and aren't often in their office or at their desks to receive messages," says Burgess. "But the faster we can get them crucial information, such as a last-minute change in fleet availability, the better they're able to do their jobs."

[Adapted from IBM, 2003]

INTRANETS

The notion of an intranet was introduced in Chapter 4: An **intranet** is a network operating within an organization that employs the TCP/IP protocol, the same protocol used on the Internet. In most cases an intranet consists of a backbone network with a number of connected LANs. Because the protocol is the same, the organization may use the same Web browser, Web crawler, and Web server software that it would use on the Internet. The intranet, however, is not accessible from outside the organization. The organization decides whether or not people within the organization have access to the Internet.

An intranet presents some incredible advantages to the organization. If an organization already has an internal network of interconnected LANs plus an operating Web server and Web browsers on most workstations, as most organizations do, then implementing an intranet is a relatively easy task involving some programming on the Web server. With minimal effort the full functionality of a localized World Wide Web, including e-mail and document sharing, is available within the organization. The Web browser is a "universal client" that works with heterogeneous platforms. Furthermore, virtually no training is needed to implement an intranet because users already know how to use a browser. Deploying a new intranet application is simple—just send an e-mail message containing the URL (address) of the new application to users.

Even if the organization does not have a Web server and Web browsers, the costs are not overwhelming. Web browsers are inexpensive or free, and a minimal Web server complete with software can be obtained for well under $10,000. Intranets are easy enough to set up that in some organizations the first intranet was set up by end users (such as engineers), not by the IS organization, to enable sharing of particular documents.

Intranets serve a variety of important uses within organizations. None is more important than those of the CareWeb intranet at the Boston-based CareGroup HealthCare System. The CareGroup includes six hospitals, 2,500 health care professionals, and 800,000 patients in the northeastern United States. The CareWeb intranet, introduced in 1998, consolidates medical records from geographically dispersed patients, clinics, and laboratories into a single clinical database and makes these records accessible to health care professionals via a Web browser.

In April 2000 the Secure Patient/Physician Communication application, a clinical database, was implemented on the CareWeb intranet. "With our clinical systems on the Web, if I am an E. R. doctor and a 53-year-old patient rolls in with chest pain, I am able to compare that day's events with what happened [to him] a year ago," say Dr. John Halamka, chief information officer of CareGroup. Furthermore, CareGroup officials firmly believe that CareWeb has enabled them to increase the quality of patient care while reducing expenses by about $1 million per year.

With patients' medical histories available on the intranet, health care professionals can easily determine information such as past surgeries, medications used, and allergies. Patients can also access their own medical records over the intranet—as long as they have a browser and the requisite password—to check prescriptions and request referrals to specialists. Another intranet application gives insurance providers access to CareWeb so that insurance transactions can be conducted over the Web. Insurance providers can transmit information on benefits and eligibility of patients to CareGroup, and CareGroup has made referral and authorization applications available on the intranet. Soon it will be possible to submit claims over CareWeb. Nearly 300 applications are currently available on CareWeb. They run the gamut from those discussed above to a signature authorization program to financial analysis to medical analysis, such as an application used for calculating kidney functions (Henry, 2000).

At Seagate Technology, Inc., the world's largest manufacturer of disk drives, an intranet and an associated secure extranet permit Seagate's sales force, distributor representatives, and representatives of original equipment manufacturers (OEMs) that use Seagate components to access timely and accurate information on Seagate product availability and pricing. The notion of an **extranet** will be explored more fully in Chapter 8, but it refers to an Internet-based application that permits key trading partners (in this case distributors and OEMs) to access another organization's intranet. Seagate has implemented 15 client/server applications on its intranet to support its forecasting, quoting, and order management activities; there are up to 1,000 users of these critical applications.

The fact that the Seagate intranet is available to key trading partners has made development of applications more challenging. Seagate has chosen to use a Java-based approach to building applications and employs Marimba's Castanet software to deliver and manage the client/server applications. When a new or updated application is completed, an IS professional loads it on a centralized server that also hosts a Castanet Transmitter. When users log on, the Castanet Tuner on their desktop or laptop automatically downloads the latest version of the Java-based application. The use of Java and Castanet permits the client software to be kept up-to-date easily on the wide variety of PCs used by distributors, OEMs, and Seagate's sales force. With its intranet applications,

Seagate has significantly improved its sales processes by providing current, easily accessible information on product availability, pricing, and sales volumes to its sales staff and its key trading partners (Earthweb.com, 2000).

When originally introduced, intranets were seen as competing with full-service groupware products such as Lotus Notes and Microsoft Exchange (Varney, 1996). Both fostered communication within the organization. Intranets did not provide the full range of groupware services, but they were much less expensive. Over time, intranets and groupware have grown closer together. Groupware has fully embraced the Internet, and groupware clients such as Lotus Notes are now Web browsers. Today many intranets employ the groupware client as the Web browser. At the same time, intranets became so complex and cumbersome to use that it was necessary to provide some structure, some organization so that users could find what they needed on the intranet. The answer was a **portal**—software that provided a structure and thus easier access to internal information via a Web browser. (If the organization desires, those external to the organization can also use portals, but that is a topic for Chapter 8.) This added software meant that intranets became more expensive. Portal software is available from a large variety of software firms, both large and small, including groupware vendors IBM, Microsoft, and Oracle. Among other portal vendors are BEA Systems, Corechange, Plumtree, Sun Microsystems, Sybase, and Vignette Corp.

IBM, for example, has built a gigantic intranet using its own groupware tools. According to IBM officials, the company's intranet is now a staple provider of information to employees. A recent internal survey found that 54 percent of IBM employees rank the intranet as among their three preferred sources of company information. Almost two-thirds of IBM employees rate the intranet as a tool that is critical to their performance, with the same proportion indicating that it is a time-saver.

IBM has been using the intranet for employee-to-employee collaboration, including a gigantic World Jam, when all employees worldwide were invited to log into a marathon chat session over a 72-hour period. More than 50,000 employees logged into World Jam to participate in 10 moderated discussion forums considering themes relevant to day-to-day life at the world's largest IT company. IBM also uses the intranet to provide information on all facets of work life, including health care benefits, unit performance updates, expense accounting, procurement, and stock purchasing. The intranet is working—more than 80 percent of IBM's U.S. employees who enrolled for health benefits last year did so via the intranet, and more than 140,000 received their health benefits information entirely online. The bottom line for IBM was about $1 million in savings (Mcdougall, 2001).

FACTORY AUTOMATION

The roots of **factory automation** lie in (1) numerically controlled machines, which use a computer program, or a tape with holes punched in it, to control the movement of tools on sophisticated machines, and in (2) **material**

POWERFUL PORTALS

The clunky intranet has given way to sophisticated corporate portals, and analysts predict these portals may soon become the new metaphor for desktop computing in business. Portals were once viewed merely as a way to provide easy access to internal information via a Web browser. But a new wave of software has helped the concept of in-house portals evolve into much more. This new generation of portals is so easy to use and effective in providing access to crucial data, reports, applications, and processes that many companies are using portals as their new desktop, replacing the Windows start button and a variety of commonly used applications.

A wide range of large companies and organizations are rolling out portals that are expected to cut costs, free up time for busy executives and managers, and add to the bottom line. That has prompted some to describe company portals as the next "killer application."

In simple terms, a company portal is an internal World Wide Web. The portal's home page, or start page, is displayed in a Web browser and generally includes search engines, as well as essential tools such as an appointment calendar and e-mail interface. Portal products are software suites that contain scores of applications that perform a variety of functions. Portal software vendors also offer special utilities—Plumtree Software calls them "gadgets"—that let users add other features such as stock tickers, clocks, and hotel, restaurant, and weather information. More sophisticated portals provide strategic, company-specific data.

Corporate information and technology managers say the portals they're rolling out this year are already contributing millions of dollars to the bottom line. Others say their return on investment will be measured in minutes and hours of employee time that is better and more profitably used.

[Konicki, 2000]

requirements planning (**MRP**) systems, which rely on extensive data input to produce a production schedule for the factory and a schedule of needed raw materials. The newer **computer-integrated manufacturing** (**CIM**) combines these basic ideas not only to let the computer set up the schedules (as with MRP) but also to carry them out through control of the various machines involved (as with numerically controlled machines).

Computer-integrated manufacturing is one of the primary ways by which manufacturers are facing the challenges of global competition. Through the various components of CIM, manufacturers are increasing productivity and quality while simultaneously reducing the lead time from the idea stage to the marketplace for most products. A list of strong proponents of CIM reads like a who's who of manufacturing—General Motors, John Deere, Ford Motor Co., Weyerhaeuser, FMC, and Kodak, among others.

CIM systems fall into three major categories: engineering systems, manufacturing administration, and factory operations. Table 6.1 lists the acronyms used in this section on factory automation. The engineering systems are aimed at increasing the productivity of engineers and include such systems as computer-aided design and group technology. Manufacturing administration includes systems that develop production schedules and monitor production against these schedules; these systems are usually termed manufacturing resources planning systems. Factory operations include those systems that actually control the operation of machines on the factory floor. Computer-aided manufacturing and shop floor control are examples of such systems.

Table 6.1 Abbreviations Used in Factory Automation

Acronym	Full Name
CIM	computer-integrated manufacturing
CAD	computer-aided design
CAE	computer-aided engineering
GT	group technology
CAPP	computer-aided process planning
MRP	material requirements planning
MRP II	manufacturing resources planning
SCM	supply chain management
CAM	computer-aided manufacturing
AGV	automated guided vehicle
MAP	Manufacturing Automation Protocol
SFC	shop floor control

Engineering Systems

Computer-aided design (**CAD**) is perhaps the most familiar of the engineering systems. CAD involves the use of computer graphics—both two-dimensional and three-dimensional—to create and modify engineering designs. **Computer-aided engineering** (**CAE**) is a system designed to analyze the functional characteristics of a design and simulate the product performance under various conditions in order to reduce the need to build prototypes. CAD and CAE permit engineers to conduct a more thorough engineering analysis and to investigate a wider range of design alternatives. Advanced CAD/CAE systems store the information they generate in a database that is shared with the other components of CIM, such as CAM.

Group technology (**GT**) systems logically group parts according to physical characteristics, machine routings through the factory, and similar machine operations. On the basis of these logical groupings, GT is able to identify existing parts that engineers can use or modify rather than design new parts, simplifying the design and manufacturing processes. **Computer-aided process planning** (**CAPP**) systems plan the sequence of processes that produce or assemble a part. During the design process, the engineer retrieves the closest standard plan from a database (using the GT classification of the new part) and modifies that plan rather than starting from scratch. The resulting plans are more accurate and more consistent, thereby reducing process planning and manufacturing costs.

Manufacturing Administration

Manufacturing resources planning (**MRP II**) systems usually have three major components: the master production schedule, material requirements planning, and shop floor control. The master production schedule component sets the overall production goals based on forecasts of demand. The MRP component then develops a detailed production schedule to accomplish the master schedule, using parts explosion, production capacity, inventory, and lead-time data. The shop floor control component releases orders to the shop floor based on the detailed production schedule and the actual production accomplished thus far. To use a recent buzzword, MRP II systems attempt to implement just-in-time (JIT) production. Note that MRP II does not directly control machines on the shop floor; it is an information system that tries to minimize inventory and employ the machines effectively and efficiently.

In our discussion of ERP systems earlier in this chapter, we noted that MRP is often one of the key modules of an ERP system. Thus, such an ERP system ties together the manufacturing production schedule with the other important aspects of running an enterprise, including sales and distribution, human resources, and financial reporting. The latest type of manufacturing administration system, however, goes beyond ERP and outside the boundaries of the firm itself: **Supply chain management (SCM)** systems are designed to deal with distribution and transportation of raw materials and finished products throughout the supply chain and to incorporate constraints caused by the supply chain into the production scheduling process. These supply chain management systems are often interorganizational in nature (a customer and its suppliers) and are commonly implemented by an SCM module from an ERP vendor or an SCM package from a vendor such as i2 or Manugistics.

Factory Operations

Factory operations systems go a significant step further than MRP II—they control the machines. By definition, **computer-aided manufacturing (CAM)** is the use of computers to control manufacturing processes. CAM is built around a series of computer programs that control automated equipment on the shop floor. In addition to computer-controlled machines such as automated drill presses and milling machines, CAM systems employ automated guided vehicles (AGVs) to move raw materials, in-process materials, and finished products from one workstation to another. AGVs are loaded using robot-like arms and then follow a computer-generated electronic signal (often a track under the floor that has been activated) to their next destination. Workers are used only to maintain the equipment and handle problems. Because job setups (preparing a machine to work on a new part) are automated and accomplished in minimum time, CAM permits extremely high machine utilization. With the low setup time, very small batches (even as small as one) can be produced efficiently, shortening production lead times and reducing inventory levels.

As this brief description has implied, a CAM system is very sophisticated and requires a great deal of input data from other systems. Product design data would come from CAD, process design data from CAPP, and the master production schedule and material requirements from MRP II. The CAM system must also be able to communicate electronically with the machines on the shop floor.

The manufacturing communications network is likely to employ the **Manufacturing Automation Protocol (MAP)**, pioneered by General Motors and now accepted by nearly all major manufacturers and vendors. MAP is a communications protocol (a set of rules) to ensure an open manufacturing system. With conformance to MAP by all vendors, seamless communication between all equipment on the factory floor—regardless of the vendor—is possible. MAP is a user-driven effort, and the details of the concept are evolving. Nevertheless, MAP is a reality in factory automation upon which future systems will be based.

Within factory operations applications, **shop floor control (SFC)** systems are less ambitious than CAM but are still important. These systems provide online, real-time control and monitoring of machines on the shop floor. For example, the SFC system might recognize that a tool on a particular milling machine is getting dull (by measuring the metal that the machine is cutting per second) and signal this fact to the human operator on duty. The operator can then take corrective measures, such as instructing the SFC to change the tool or changing it himself or herself, depending on the system.

SCM HELPS DELIVER THANKSGIVING TURKEYS

Perdue Farms produces more than 48 million pounds of chicken products and almost 4 million pounds of turkey products each week. For Thanksgiving, Perdue will ship roughly 1 million whole turkeys–and all these turkeys will arrive at the supermarkets within 24 hours of processing. This logistics task is much easier for Perdue because the company invested $20 million in Manugistics supply chain management software, including forecasting and supply chain planning tools. With the aid of the SCM system, Perdue has gotten much better at delivering the right number of turkeys to the right customers at the right time, according to Chief Information Officer Don Taylor. "As we get to November, we have live information at our fingertips," he says.

Perdue also uses technology to make sure its products arrive fresh. Each of its delivery trucks is equipped with a global positioning system, so dispatchers always know where the trucks are and can send out replacement trucks if necessary. Some supermarkets have vendor-management inventory control systems, which allow Perdue to track sales of its products in real time. "We're always looking at new technologies as they come along to see what makes sense for us," Taylor says. And SCM certainly makes sense for Thanksgiving turkeys.

[Adapted from Luttrell, 2003]

Robotics

Outside the broad area of CIM, robotics is one other aspect of factory automation that deserves mention. Robotics is, in fact, one branch of the artificial intelligence tree. (Artificial intelligence, especially expert systems and neural networks, is discussed in the next chapter.) With robotics, scientists and engineers are building machines to accomplish coordinated physical tasks in the manner of humans. For over two decades, robots have been important in manufacturing to accomplish simple but important tasks, such as painting and welding. Robots perform repetitive tasks tirelessly, produce more consistent high-quality output than humans, and are not subject to such dangers as paint inhalation or retinal damage. Newer robots incorporate a certain amount of visual perception and thus are able to perform assembly tasks of increasing complexity. Industrial robots are expensive, but they are becoming economically viable for a wider range of tasks as their capabilities are extended. Robots and CIM are producing a vastly different "factory of the future" based on IT.

SUMMARY

Early in the twenty-first century, virtually all large and mid-sized businesses and an increasing number of small businesses depend on enterprise IT systems. These systems support almost every function of the business, from procuring raw materials to planning the production schedule to distributing the product, from recording and summarizing sales figures to keeping track of inventory, from paying employees and suppliers to handling receivables, from maintaining the organization's financial records to enabling employees to communicate more effectively. Modern organizations simply cannot do business without enterprise IT systems.

Transaction processing systems are central to the operations of almost every business. These workhorse systems, which were the very first IT applications installed in most businesses, process the thousands of transactions that occur every day, including sales, payments, inventory, and payroll. In recent years many larger businesses have turned to enterprise resource planning (ERP) systems as a way to achieve an integrated set of transaction processing applications. ERP systems typically consist of a number of modules to handle the sales and distribution, manufacturing, financial reporting, and human resources areas, and the organization can buy a subset of these modules to satisfy its needs.

Transaction processing systems handle the volume of transactions generated as a firm does business, and they also produce summary reports on these transactions. They do not, however, provide this transactional data in a form that enables managers to use the data in decision-making activities—data warehousing does this. With data warehousing, organizational data are made accessible from a storage area that is distinct from that used for operational transaction processing. When combined with easy-to-use analysis tools—which are discussed in the next chapter—the data warehouse becomes a critical information resource for managers to enable strategic and operational decision making.

Office automation systems affect every knowledge worker in a firm. Word processing, electronic calendaring, electronic mail, and many other applications are most commonly delivered via an employee's PC attached to the organization's network. Groupware is an increasingly popular way of providing office automation functionality in an integrated package. Lotus Notes, the most popular groupware package today, provides an excellent document-sharing capability as well as calendaring, e-mail, and other features. Intranets—networks within an organization that employ Internet standards—offer employees easy access to an organization's internal information via a Web browser. Factory automation, especially computer-integrated manufacturing, applies IT to the task of increasing efficiency and effectiveness in the manufacturing process.

As important as these various enterprise systems are, they are certainly not the whole story in terms of IT applications. Chapter 7 focuses on managerial support systems designed to provide support to a manager or managers, and Chapter 8 explores the topic of e-business applications.

REVIEW QUESTIONS

1. Consider the enterprise systems application areas listed in Figure 6.1. Which application area developed first? Which one is most common today? What is a "hot" application area today?
2. Describe the fundamental differences between batch processing and online processing. What is in-line processing?
3. What is a vertically integrated information system? Give an example.
4. What is a client/server system? What is a client? What is a server? Why would an organization choose to implement a client/server system?
5. Define middleware. What are the three categories of middleware?
6. List the primary categories of modules that are likely to be offered by a major ERP vendor.
7. What are the primary reasons for implementing an ERP system?
8. What aspects of the automated office are you most likely to encounter in the workplace today? In the future, what additional features are likely to be added to the automated office?
9. What is groupware? What are the features likely to be included in a groupware product?

10. What is an intranet? Why would an intranet be implemented?
11. Some of the most important acronyms used in the factory automation area are listed below. Provide the full names for each of these acronyms and give a one-sentence explanation of each term.

CIM	MAP
CAD	GT
MRP	MRP II

DISCUSSION QUESTIONS

1. Differentiate between a two-tier client/server system and a three-tier client/server system. Differentiate between a fat client and a thin client. Why would a firm choose one of these approaches over the others when implementing a client/server system?
2. In review question 5 above, you listed the three categories of middleware. In one sentence for each, define the three categories. Explain the role of each category and how they interact.
3. In this chapter, payroll and order entry were used as examples of transaction processing systems. Another example with which all of us are somewhat familiar is the check-processing system employed by your bank. Consider how the check-processing system is similar to (and different from) the two examples in this chapter. Is the check-processing system likely to be batch, online, or some hybrid? What subsystems would be required to operate the check-processing system?
4. Several reasons why firms are finding it difficult to implement an ERP system were given in this chapter. Identify these reasons. Which reasons do you think are most important and why?
5. Every large organization has large files or databases containing data used in operating the business. How does a data warehouse differ from these operational files or databases? Why are these differences important?
6. Consider an office environment with which you are somewhat familiar. What changes have occurred in the preparation of documents (such as reports and letters) over the past decade? Why do you think these changes have occurred? Have they been technology-driven or people-driven, or both?
7. Based on your reading and knowledge from other sources, in what ways has the phenomenon of the Internet influenced office automation?
8. Many large firms have adopted groupware, and others are still using older mainframe-based, UNIX server-based, or LAN-based e-mail systems. What explains this difference? Why have some firms quickly moved to groupware, whereas others are moving more slowly?
9. The terminology employed in factory automation is often confusing, in part because the names are so similar and in part because the subareas do indeed overlap. Carefully distinguish among CIM, CAD, CAE, CAM, and CAPP, indicating any overlaps.
10. All of us come into contact with distributed systems almost every day, even if it is only while shopping at Wal-Mart or Sears. Describe a distributed system with which you have come in contact. In your view, what are the advantages and disadvantages of this system? Is the system you described a client/server system?

CHAPTER 7 MANAGERIAL SUPPORT SYSTEMS

MANAGERIAL SUPPORT SYSTEMS ARE THE TOPIC OF THIS SECOND OF three chapters devoted to our survey of information technology (IT) application areas. Managerial support systems are designed to provide support to a specific manager or a small group of managers, and they include applications to support managerial decision making such as group support systems, executive information systems, and expert systems. In contrast, the previous chapter dealt with enterprise systems designed to support the entire organization or large portions of it, such as transaction processing systems, data warehousing, groupware, and intranets. Together these two chapters provide a relatively comprehensive picture of the applications of IT within a single organization (*intraorganizational* systems). To complete the survey of IT applications, Chapter 8 will focus on *e-business applications* that span organizational boundaries, including B2C and B2B applications using the Internet. Taken as a set, these three chapters encompass the great majority of IT applications in use today.

The enterprise systems discussed in the previous chapter are critical for running a business or any other type of organization, and you will be dealing with many such enterprise systems, especially transaction processing systems and groupware. Nevertheless, these enterprise systems have been designed to support the organization as a whole, not you in particular or even a group of managers. Managerial support systems, in contrast, are intended to directly support you and other managers as you make strategic and tactical decisions for your organizations. For example, interactive decision support systems (DSSs) are designed to help managers and other professionals analyze internal and external data. By capturing the expertise of human experts, expert systems advise nonexperts in a particular decision area. Group support systems are designed to make group work, especially meetings, more productive. Executive information systems (EISs) provide easy-to-navigate summary data for the managers of an organization. This chapter will explore these and other managerial support systems that are increasingly important in running modern organizations.

DECISION SUPPORT SYSTEMS

A **decision support system (DSS)** is a computer-based system, almost always interactive, designed to assist a manager (or another decision maker) in making decisions. A DSS incorporates both data and models to help a decision maker solve a problem, especially a problem that is not well structured. The data are often extracted from a transaction processing system or a data warehouse, but that is not always the case. The model might be simple, such as a profit-and-loss model to calculate profit given certain assumptions, or complex, such as an optimization model to suggest loadings for each machine in a job shop. DSSs and many of the systems discussed in the following sections are not always justified by a traditional cost-benefit approach; for these systems many of the benefits are intangible, such as faster decision making and better understanding of the data.

Figure 7.1 shows that a DSS requires three primary components: model management to apply the appropriate model, data management to select and handle the appropriate data, and dialog management to facilitate the user interface to the DSS. The user interacts with the DSS through the dialog management component, identifying the particular model and data set to be used, and then the DSS presents the results to the user through this same dialog management component. The model management and data management components largely act behind the scenes, and they vary from relatively simple for a typical spreadsheet model to quite complex for a mathematical programming-based scheduling model.

An extremely popular type of DSS is a pro forma financial statement generator. Using a spreadsheet package such as Lotus 1-2-3 or Microsoft Excel, a manager builds a model to project the various elements of the organization or division financial statement into the future. The data employed are historical financial figures for the organization. The initial (base) model incorporates various assumptions about future trends in income and expense categories. After viewing the results of the base model, the manager performs a series of "what-if" analyses by modifying one or more assumptions to determine their impact on the bottom line. For example, the manager might explore the impact on profitability if the sales of a new product grew by 10 percent per year, rather than the 5 percent incorporated in the base model. Or the manager might investigate the impact of a higher-than-expected increase in the price of raw materials, such as 7 percent per year instead of 4 percent per year. This type of financial statement generator is a simple but powerful DSS for guiding financial decision making.

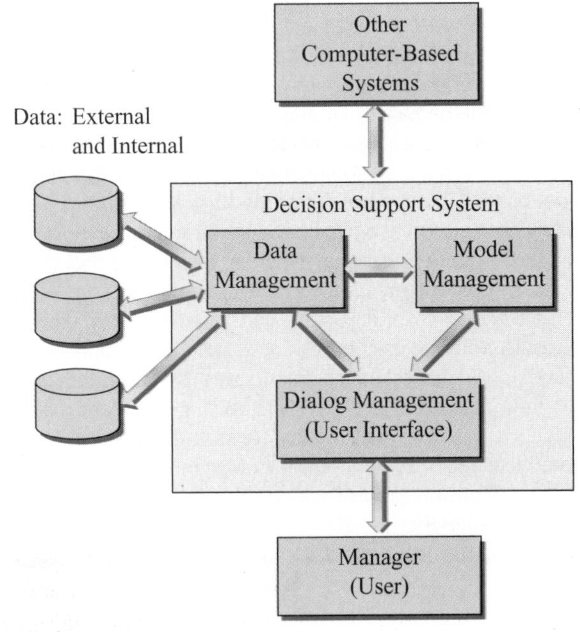

Figure 7.1 Decision Support Systems Components

An example of a DSS driven by transactions data is a police-beat allocation system used by a California city. This system enables a police officer to display a map outline and call up data by geographic zone, which shows police calls for service, types of service, and service times. The system's interactive graphics capability lets the officer manipulate the maps, zones, and data to consider a variety of police-beat alternatives quickly and easily and takes maximum advantage of the officer's judgment.

Other DSS examples include an interactive system for capacity planning and production scheduling in a large paper company. This system employs detailed historical data and forecasting and scheduling models to simulate overall performance of the company under differing planning assumptions. A major oil company developed a DSS to support capital investment decision making. This system incorporates various financial routines and models for generating future plans; these plans can be displayed in either tabular or graphic form to aid in decision making. A major airline uses a DSS to help aircraft controllers deal with aircraft shortage problems that might arise at an airport because of delayed or canceled incoming flights or mechanical problems for aircraft on the ground. The DSS, which uses a network optimization modeling technique, helps controllers use spare aircraft more effectively as well as evaluate possible delay-and-swap options. Over an 18-month period, this DSS saved the airline more than $500,000 in delay costs.

All the DSS examples cited are more properly called **specific DSSs**. These are the actual applications that assist in the decision-making process. In contrast, a

A POTPOURRI OF DSS EXAMPLES

Virtually every issue of *Interfaces* contains a discussion of one or more new DSSs. To illustrate, we briefly describe three quite different decision support systems presented in the July–August 2002 and January–February 2003 issues of *Interfaces*.

"STEP-UP: A decision support system for transforming the dislocated U.S. defense workforce" (Vitolo and Vance, 2002) describes a DSS developed to assist in the retraining and placement of workers who lose their jobs when a defense facility (in this case, the Philadelphia Naval Shipyard and Base) is closed. STEP-UP was developed by a Penn State research team based at the Center for Applied Behavioral Studies and was funded by a grant from the U.S. Department of Labor. STEP-UP requires three data components: an extensive profile for each dislocated worker, a listing of available job positions in growth industries in the general area of the closed base, and a compendium of training programs available in the area. STEP-UP provides flexible matching capabilities to help dislocated workers identify potential job matches or evaluate training programs that will prepare the worker for available jobs. Working with a counselor, the dislocated worker can use STEP-UP to probe the job market based on his or her competencies, "knowledge, skills, and abilities," or achievements such as a certification or a license. Where skills gaps with available positions exist, STEP-UP suggests appropriate training. Employers can also use STEP-UP to identify suitable candidates for job openings. STEP-UP is currently installed at two locations of the Private Industry Council of Philadelphia and is regularly used by 15 to 20 managers, counselors, and job-placement specialists. Since its inception, STEP-UP has supported processing of over 15,000 clients and has recorded job openings for almost 2,000 employers. STEP-UP is fundamentally a counseling support system, and it seems to be a very useful tool.

In the same issue of *Interfaces*, Gupta, Peters, Miller, and Blyden (2002) describe a DSS to help the distribution network of Pfizer/Warner-Lambert (with annual sales of over $30 billion) plan its operations. The DSS actually consists of five models—three are simulation models that work together to support long-run planning of warehouse capacities in the network, a fourth is a mathematical programming model that produces plans for distribution of Pfizer/Warner-Lambert products over the planning horizon, and the fifth is an inventory investment model employing multiple approaches suggested in the inventory management literature (such as the traditional item-level statistical safety-stock model and high-level square-root-of-N models). Based on these principal components, variations of the DSS have been used for a variety of strategic and tactical decision making, including determining whether the company should expand the number of regional distribution centers, deciding on the best long-term U.S. distribution network for the consolidation of the premerger Warner-Lambert and Pfizer networks, and setting up a new pharmaceutical delivery network. At the operational level, a DSS has been developed that contains a toolkit of diagnostic models, analyses, and standardized reports designed to monitor distribution and transportation operations, identify opportunities for improving short-run operations, and provide information to support immediate decisions. The quantified benefits of Pfizer/Warner-Lambert's DSS include annual savings of over a half million dollars in freight costs, the elimination of customer deductions of several hundred thousand dollars annually, and the creation of a strategic manufacturing technology plan that could save $5.9 million annually.

A quite different type of DSS has been developed for Continental Airlines to minimize the costs of schedule disruptions caused by unexpected events such as inclement weather, aircraft mechanical problems, and crew unavailability (Yu, Argüello, Song, McCowan, and White, 2003). Because of such disruptions, crews might not be properly positioned to service their remaining scheduled flights. CALEB Technologies has developed the CrewSolver DSS to generate optimal or near optimal crew-recovery solutions to cover open flights and return crews to their original schedules in a cost-effective manner while honoring government regulations, contractual rules, and quality-of-life requirements. CrewSolver is a real-time, always available DSS operated by a crew coordinator from a graphical user interface. CrewSolver employs live operational data from the system operation control database as well as a complete crew file. When a disruptive event occurs, the crew coordinator requests a recovery solution, and CrewSolver employs a mathematical programming model (solved by a heuristic-based search algorithm) to generate up to three solutions, from which the crew coordinator chooses one. Solutions consist of reassigning crews from one flight to another, deadheading crews to cover a flight or return back to base, holding crews at their current location, assigning crews additional duty periods, moving a crew's layover to a different city, and using reserve crews to cover flights left uncovered by active crews. The results from the use of CrewSolver have been impressive: Continental Airlines estimates that it saved $40 million during 2001 from the use of CrewSolver to recover from four major disruptions: snowstorms that hit Newark, New Jersey just before New Year's Eve and again in March, heavy rains that closed the Houston airport for a day in June, and the terrorist attacks on September 11, 2001.

decision support system generator is a software package that provides a set of capabilities to build a specific DSS quickly and easily (Sprague and Carlson, 1982). In the previous pro forma financial statement example, Microsoft Excel or Lotus 1-2-3 can be viewed as a DSS generator, whereas a specific Excel or 1-2-3 model to project financial statements for a particular division of a company is a specific DSS.

DATA MINING

In Chapter 6 we introduced data warehousing—the idea of a company pulling data from its operational systems and putting the data in a separate data warehouse so that users may access and analyze the data without interfering with the operational systems. In that discussion we touched on the variety of software tools available for analysis of data in the warehouse, but deferred a more complete discussion until this chapter. Our argument was that the creation and maintenance of the data warehouse is an enterprise system, in that the data warehouse supports the entire organization by making the data available to everyone, whereas the analysis of the data is performed by and/or for a single manager or a small group of managers and is, therefore, a managerial support system. Without explicitly mentioning it, we have already begun the more detailed discussion of these tools for analyzing data in the warehouse, for the DSSs described in the previous section often pull the data they need directly from the organizations' data warehouses.

Data mining employs a variety of technologies (such as decision trees and neural networks) to search for, or "mine," "nuggets" of information from the vast quantities of data stored in an organization's data warehouse. Data mining, which is sometimes considered a subset of decision support systems, is especially useful when the organization has large volumes of transaction data in its warehouse. The concept of data mining is not new, although the term became popular only in the late 1990s. For at least two decades, many large organizations have used internal or external analysts, often called management scientists, to try to identify trends, or patterns, in massive amounts of data by using statistical, mathematical, and artificial intelligence techniques. With the development of large-scale data warehouses and the availability of inexpensive processing power, a renewed interest in what came to be called data mining arose in recent years.

Along with this renewed interest came a variety of high-powered and relatively easy-to-use commercial data mining software packages. Among these packages are Oracle 9i Data Mining and Oracle Data Mining Suite (formerly Darwin), SAS Enterprise Miner, IBM Intelligent Miner for Data (as well as related products IBM Intelligent Miner Modeling, Visualization, and Scoring), and KnowledgeSEEKER, KnowledgeSTUDIO, and KnowledgeExcelerator from Angoss Software Corp. *Datamation*'s Data Mining and Business Intelligence Product of the Year for 2003 is SAS Text Miner, which has the ability to handle textual information, pulling data out of letters, memos, medical records, and documents of all kinds and finding themes and patterns in these documents (Gaudin, 2003). These packages vary widely in cost, ranging [illegible]
some desktop packages to o[illegible]
packages that run on large s[illegible]
required to fully utilize the capa[illegible]
hensive packages.

What are the decision technique[illegible]
data mining? One key technique, dec[illegible]
ded in many of the packages. A decision [illegible]
structure that is derived from the data to [illegible]
decisions that result in various outcomes—th[illegible]
end points. When a new set of decisions is prese[illegible]
information on a particular shopper, the decisio[illegible]
predicts the outcome. Neural networks, a branch of [illegible]
intelligence to be discussed later in this chapter, are in[illegible]
rated in most of the high-end products. Other popular t[illegible]
niques include linear and logistic regression; associatio[illegible]
rules for finding patterns of co-occurring events; clustering for market segmentation; rule induction, the extraction of if-then rules based on statistical significance; nearest neighbor, the classification of a record based on those most similar to it in the database; and genetic algorithms, optimization techniques based on the concepts of genetic combination, mutation, and natural selection.

For completeness, let us introduce a term related to data mining, but with a difference—**online analytical processing**, or **OLAP**. OLAP has been described as human-driven analysis, whereas data mining might be viewed as technique-driven. OLAP is essentially querying against a database, employing OLAP software that makes it easy to pose complex queries along multiple dimensions, such as time, organizational unit, and geography. The chief component of OLAP is the OLAP server, which sits between a client machine and a database server. The OLAP server understands how data are organized in the database and has special functions for analyzing the data. In contrast, data mining incorporates such techniques as decision trees, neural networks, and genetic algorithms. An OLAP program extracts data from the database and structures it by individual dimensions, such as region or dealer. Data mining software searches the database for patterns and relationships, employing techniques such as neural networks.

Of course, what you can do with data mining is more important to you as a manager than the decision techniques employed. Typical applications of data mining are outlined in Table 7.1. Whatever the nature of your business, the chances are good that several of these applications could mean increased profits. Most of these applications focus on unearthing valuable information about your customers.

Many examples of successful data mining operations have been reported in IT magazines. Farmers Insurance Group, a Los Angeles-based provider of automobile and homeowners insurance, uses data mining to develop

Uses of Data Mining

ion	Description
selling	Identify products and services that will most appeal to existing customer segments and develop cross-sell and up-sell offers tailored to each segment
istomer nurn	Predict which customers are likely to leave your company and go to a competitor and target those customers at highest risk
Customer retention	Identify customer characteristics associated with highest lifetime value and develop strategies to retain these customers over the long term
Direct marketing	Identify which prospects should be included in a mailing list to obtain the highest response rate
Fraud detection	Identify which transactions are most likely to be fraudulent based on purchase patterns and trends
Interactive marketing	Predict what each individual accessing a Web site is most likely interested in seeing
Market basket analysis	Understand what products or services are commonly purchased together (e.g., beer and diapers) and develop appropriate marketing strategies
Market segmentation	Segment existing customers and prospects into appropriate groups for promotional and evaluation purposes and determine how to approach each segment for maximum results
Payment or default analysis	Identify specific patterns to predict when and why customers default on payments
Trend analysis	Investigate the difference between an average purchase this month versus last month and prior months

competitive rates on its insurance products. For example, Farmers used IBM's DecisionEdge software to mine data on owners of sports cars. Typically, these drivers are categorized as high-risk and thus pay high insurance premiums. However, Farmers discovered that a sizeable group of sports-car owners are married, 30 to 50 years old, own two cars, and do *not* have a high risk of accidents. Farmers adjusted the premiums for this group downward and believes that the company gained a competitive advantage in this market segment (Davis, 1999).

Vermont Country Store (VCS), a Weston, Vermont-based catalog retailer of traditional clothing, personal items, and housewares, uses SAS Institute's Enterprise Mining data mining software to segment its customers to create appropriate direct marketing mailing lists. "We concentrate on profitability, which we have learned can be increased by identifying the top echelon of customers and mailing them the larger catalog," according to Erin McCarthy, manager of statistical services and research at VCS. VCS also uses data mining to determine the mailing lists to be used for special campaigns. For example, VCS uses Enterprise Miner to research Christmas buying patterns and create a special Christmas campaign list, selecting just customers who order during the holidays. These customers can be even further segmented by their level of purchases and the types of products they buy, with focused catalogs sent to each separate group. "Our ultimate goal," says McCarthy, "is to be able to limit, or stabilize, the number of contacts we have with customers and still grow our market. For instance, if we're going to mail a catalog to a certain group of people five times a year, we want to know the best five offers to make them. Data mining is helping us do that" (Dickey, 1999).

Florida Hospital, an 11-campus, Orlando-based healthcare organization, has implemented IBM's Intelligent Miner in an effort to identify relationships in its patient data. Florida Hospital's initial data mining project was to predict which patients suffering from congestive heart failure were most likely, after being treated and released, to be readmitted or, even worse, to die. Data mining identified unsuspected clusters of data involving patient care that the hospital used as a starting point for making changes in its clinical procedures. In another study, the hospital used Intelligent Miner to investigate patterns associated with the care being given by individual physicians and the total charges they generate. That study is helping the hospital's chief medical officers establish standard care guidelines and clinical best practices. Early in 2000, Florida Hospital created a new standard care plan for patients with pneumonia and acute pneumonia. "We're using Intelligent Miner to validate whether patients on the standard care plan at one campus do better than those who are not on the plan at other campuses," reports Alexander Veletsos, information systems director at the hospital (Gwynne, 2000).

Data mining *requires* a well-designed and well-constructed data warehouse with well-maintained data in it. Before any organization thinks about data mining, it must ensure that it is capturing essential data and that the data are complete and accurate. For example, Merck-Medco, the prescription mail-order unit of pharmaceutical giant Merck & Co., Inc., based in Montvale, New Jersey, had to spend four years working on its unwieldy database of patient and treatment records before it had a warehouse ready for data mining. At Merck-Medco, this became a major data reengineering effort to clean up the data (ensure that they are

DATA MINING WORKS AT MERCK-MEDCO

Evan Marks, vice president for marketing at Merck-Medco, believes that the company's data mining system, named ExpeR$_x$t, "helps you ask the right questions and deliver your information even if you're not sure what patterns you're looking for." One pattern the system has uncovered is already saving Merck-Medco customers millions of dollars.

Using ExpeR$_x$t, Merck-Medco analyzed the effectiveness of certain treatments for gastric-intestinal ailments. Cost data led Merck-Medco to seek alternative treatments to the most frequently prescribed drug. The result was identification of an alternative and less costly drug that could prove effective for many patients and could even work more quickly. "Data mining didn't tell us about the new treatment," says Marks, "but it did indicate that many of our customers had high costs in this area, and that led us to look for alternatives in the medical literature."

The new drug saved one Merck-Medco client with two million employees about $10 million in prescription drug costs. Merck-Medco has since applied the program to many other customers, helping to cut their costs by an average of 10 to 15 percent with just this one change.

Overall, ExpeR$_x$t is now used by 400 analysts throughout Merck-Medco, and Marks expects to find similar cost-saving alternative treatments through the use of data mining.

[Adapted from McCarthy, 1997]

internally consistent) and align the data into a meaningful framework within which data mining could be conducted. However, the effort appears to be worth it at Merck-Medco, as reported in the sidebar "Data Mining Works at Merck-Medco" (McCarthy, 1997). Data mining offers exciting possibilities for learning about customers, particularly for companies that have well-established data warehouses.

GROUP SUPPORT SYSTEMS

Group support systems (GSSs) are an important variant of DSSs in which the system is designed to support a group rather than an individual. GSSs, sometimes called group DSSs or electronic meeting systems, strive to take advantage of the power of a group to make better decisions than individuals acting alone. GSSs are a specialized type of groupware (see Chapter 6) that is specifically aimed at supporting meetings. Managers spend a lot of their time in group activity (meetings, committees, conferences); in fact, some researchers have estimated that middle managers spend 35 percent of their work week in meetings and that top managers spend 50 to 80 percent of their time in meetings. GSSs represent an attempt to make these group sessions more productive.

GroupSystems, developed at the University of Arizona (and now marketed by GroupSystems.com, formerly Ventana Corporation), is an excellent example of GSS software (Nunamaker, et al., 1991, GroupSystems.com Web site, 2003). GroupSystems customers include major corporations such as Agilent Technologies, Boeing, Ernst & Young, Lucent, and PricewaterhouseCoopers, and government organizations such as the Federal Aviation Administration, Federal Reserve Bank, U.S. Department of Education, and the U.S. Army, Navy, and Air Force. In a typical implementation (see Figure 7.2), a computer-supported meeting room is set up containing a PC for each participant, all linked by a local area network (LAN). A large public screen facilitates common viewing of information when this is desired. GroupSystems, which is installed on each machine in the network, provides computerized support for idea generation, organizing ideas, prioritizing (such as voting), and policy development (such as stakeholder identification).

Each participant in a group session (for example, a brainstorming session) has the opportunity to provide input anonymously and simultaneously via the PC keyboard. This can encourage creative thinking because no one can be ridiculed for a "stupid idea." Each idea or comment is evaluated on its merits rather than by who offered it. Similarly, in a voting session the participants will not be swayed by how someone else votes. Thus, a GSS such as GroupSystems should generate more high-quality ideas as well as decisions that truly represent the group.

Recent work in the GSS area has moved beyond support of the traditional group session. The new focus is to

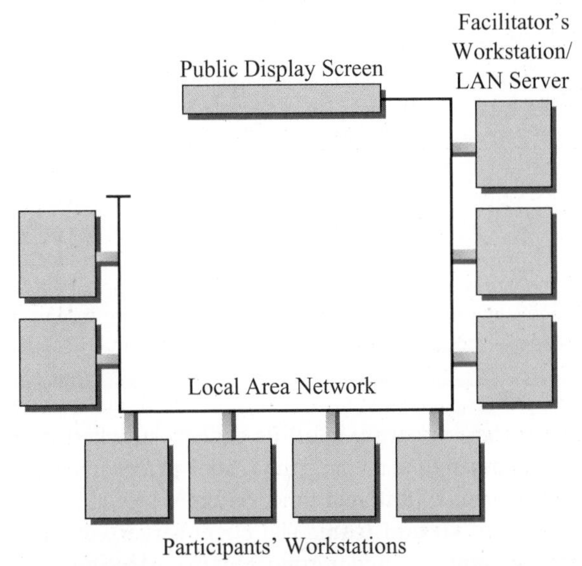

Figure 7.2 Group Support System Layout

GSS WORKS FOR EASTMAN CHEMICAL, NOKIA TELECOMMUNICATIONS

Eastman Chemical wanted to have creative problem-solving sessions to generate ideas in order to better meet customer needs, but the company found that traditional meetings were unproductive and time-consuming. Eastman installed GroupSystems, and it has paid off in a major way. In a recent GroupSystems session, 400 ideas were generated during a 2-hour session with nine people. During the same GSS session, similar ideas were combined and weighted voting was employed to pick out the top ideas for implementation. Dr. Henry Gonzales, manager of polymer technology at Eastman, stated, "We found that with GroupSystems, we had more unusual ideas, a richer pool to choose from, and we got to the point a lot faster. I did a study and calculated that the software saved 50 percent of people's time, and projected a cost savings of over $500,000 for the 12 people [who used the GSS] during a year's time. So we bought another license, and are upgrading to another facility so more people can use the technology."

Finland-based Nokia, the world's second largest cellular telephone manufacturer, had developed an environmental policy with the objective of sustainable development in accordance with the International Chamber of Commerce charter. To implement this policy, the switching platforms research and development department decided that it was necessary to integrate environmental issues into the design process. To make this happen, idea-generating workshops using GroupSystems were held for the product design experts. As an example, the initial GroupSystems workshop generated 90 pages of ideas, voting results, and survey results, providing valuable feedback on both environmental and other aspects of product design.

The environmental ideas produced by the GSS sessions were carefully examined and rewritten as check lists, which in turn became the heart of Nokia's new "Design for Environment" system. The result was the integration of "Design for Environment" into the product design at key "influencing points" in the product life cycle process, such as writing requirements and specifications.

[Adapted from GroupSystems.com Web site, 2003]

NEGOTIATION SUPPORT SYSTEMS

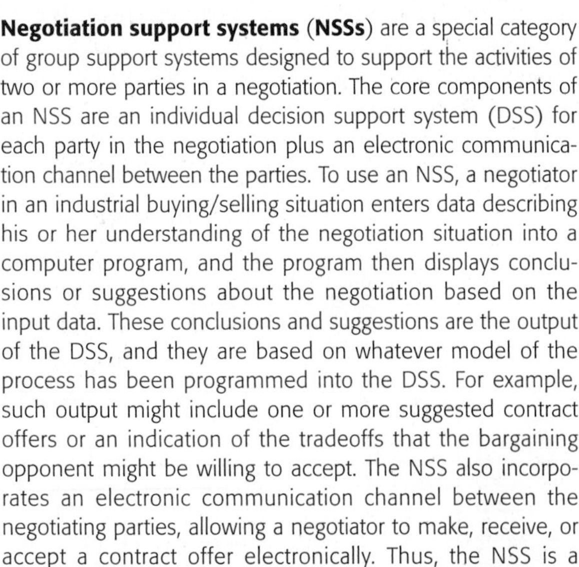

Negotiation support systems (NSSs) are a special category of group support systems designed to support the activities of two or more parties in a negotiation. The core components of an NSS are an individual decision support system (DSS) for each party in the negotiation plus an electronic communication channel between the parties. To use an NSS, a negotiator in an industrial buying/selling situation enters data describing his or her understanding of the negotiation situation into a computer program, and the program then displays conclusions or suggestions about the negotiation based on the input data. These conclusions and suggestions are the output of the DSS, and they are based on whatever model of the process has been programmed into the DSS. For example, such output might include one or more suggested contract offers or an indication of the tradeoffs that the bargaining opponent might be willing to accept. The NSS also incorporates an electronic communication channel between the negotiating parties, allowing a negotiator to make, receive, or accept a contract offer electronically. Thus, the NSS is a bargaining aid available to the negotiator if and when he or she chooses to use it.

One of the authors of this book has been involved in an ongoing series of laboratory experiments to assess the impact of NSS use. In these studies, which have used both students and purchasing managers as subjects, an early version of an NSS does appear to have added value to the negotiation process. Both the students and the managers, on average, arrived at better contracts (higher joint outcomes and more balanced contracts) when they used the NSS than when they did not use the NSS. The students took longer for the negotiation when they used the NSS, but the managers took *less* time with the NSS. In a more recent not-yet-published study, all negotiations were conducted over the World Wide Web, with negotiators arriving at better contracts when they have the use of a DSS than when they do not. As encouraging as these results are, there is a long way to go before NSSs can be of practical value in real-world negotiations.

[Adapted from Perkins, Hershauer, Foroughi, and Delaney, 1996]

support the work team in all its endeavors, whether the team is operating in a "same time, same place" traditional meeting or in a "different time, different place" mode—that is, as a **virtual team**. The client/server version of GroupSystems, called GroupSystems MeetingRoom, provides rich support for a "same time, same place" traditional meeting, while GroupSystems OnLine allows group members to use GroupSystems over the World Wide Web or an intranet, or both, via a standard Web browser, permitting group members to participate in the group session no matter where they are or when they are able to contribute.

GEOGRAPHIC INFORMATION SYSTEMS

Geographic information systems (GISs), spatial decision support systems (SDSSs), location-based services, geodemographics, computer mapping, and automated routing are names for a family of applications based on manipulation of relationships in space. Geographic technologies such as GISs capture, store, manipulate, display, and analyze data spatially referenced to the earth. As Figure 7.3 shows, GISs—a generic term for systems that specialize in geographic data—feature a rich user display and an interactive environment that is highly engaging to human decision makers.

Fields as diverse as natural resource management, public administration, NASA, the military, and urban planning have been using GISs for four decades. Scientists, planners, oil and gas explorers, foresters, soldiers, and mapmakers have matured this technology, developing sophisticated capabilities for creating, displaying, and manipulating geographic information. In the 1990s geographic technologies came to the attention of business users as the power of desktop computing merged with widespread access to geographic data. In the new century geographic technologies are moving into key business functions enabled by technologies such as radio frequency identification (RFID) tags, global positioning system (GPS) satellite transmitters and receivers, and spatial capabilities now included in production quality database management systems (DBMSs). More important, many firms are learning that most business data have inherent spatial meaning.

Business Adopts Geographic Technologies

Geographic technologies in business were a well-kept secret for many years; the earliest business adopters of GISs seldom talked about it because of its competitive value. Firms such as Arby's and McDonald's—whose ability to succeed depends on being in a better location than competitors—used GISs for site location to become among the first

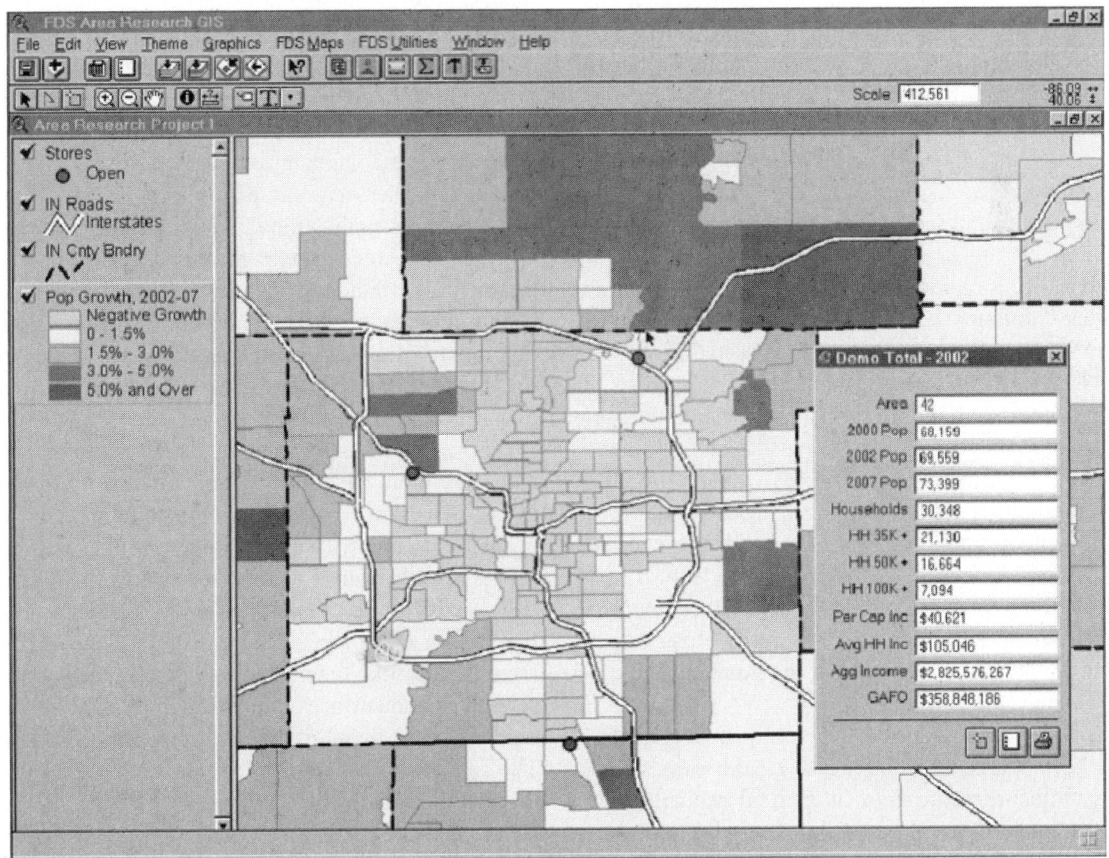

Figure 7.3 Department Store Analysis (Reprinted courtesy of Environmental Systems Research Institute, Inc. Copyright © 2003 Environmental Systems Research Institute, Inc. All rights reserved.)

to recognize the business benefits of geographic technologies. Other applications include market analysis and planning, logistics and routing, environmental engineering, and the geographic pattern analysis bankers use to show that they do not "redline" areas—that is, unfairly deny loans by location. Today, many sources provide high quality geographically encoded data; few companies need to digitize maps or photographs.

As these examples illustrate, many functional areas in business are using geographic technologies such as GISs to recognize and manage their geographic dependencies. The research arm of Federated Department Stores, Inc. (which operates over 450 Macy's, Bloomingdale's, The Bon Marché, Burdines, Goldsmith's, Lazarus, and Rich's-Macy's stores in 34 states, Guam, and Puerto Rico) is an example: Beginning in the late 1990s, Federated used a GIS for simple map production and analysis. Dozens of proprietary, industry, and public data sources including internal sales information were underutilized because of the difficulty of linking them. Because many of their most experienced retail analysts had little interest in computing, the capabilities languished until a team of five analysts identified a GIS as a key integration capability (*ArcNews Online*, 2003). The resulting system came together just in time to support a major business initiative to find sites for a new type of small store in existing markets. The GIS allowed comparison between potential and actual performance in hundreds of existing markets; mapping the data clearly showed untapped potential and supported market development (see Figure 7.3).

Furthermore, location-dominated businesses such as retailing are learning how to use spatial analysis to support more than site location (see the sidebar later in this chapter entitled "Beyond Location, Location, Location"). Sears is a notable example of building from a site-location competence to bring spatial capabilities to logistics and, along the way, improve customer service for Sears, Homelife, and Brand Central stores. Home delivery "hit rate" (delivery within the window) improved from 78 percent to over 90 percent while reducing the delivery window from 4 to 2 hours, something customers truly valued. Other benefits included lower mileage per stop, increased deliveries per truck, and eventually a reduction in the number of warehouses operated (*ArcNews*, 1996).

It is hard to find an industry or government agency that does not have spatial analysis needs. Health care, transportation, telecommunication, homeland security, law enforcement, natural resources, utilities, real estate, banking, and media all need to locate people or assets, or both, in space and to predict their behavior. For example, the National Center for Health Statistics at the Centers for Disease Control and Prevention uses a GIS to improve policy making by mapping health concerns ranging from diseases to homicides (NCHS, 2004).

What's Behind Geographic Technologies

Two approaches to representing spatial data are widely used: the raster approach and the vector approach. Both types of data have been commonly managed in a data model that stores related data in layers known as coverages or themes. Recently, a new model, the geodatabase model, has emerged based on object-oriented data concepts.

Raster-based GISs rely on dividing space into small, equal-sized cells arranged in a grid. In a GIS these cells (rasters) can take on a range of values and are aware of their location relative to other cells. Like pixels on a computer screen, the size of the cells relative to the features in the landscape determines the resolution of the data. Satellite imagery and other remote sensing applications exploit the ability of the raster approach to identify patterns across large areas. Although this approach offers continuous data, objects of interest must be inferred or extracted from the rasters, making the precision of the original data collection crucial.

Raster approaches have dominated business applications in natural resources. Analysis of raster data using statistical techniques and mathematical models allows meteorologists to distinguish rain from snow and foresters to identify diseased areas within a forest. Precision farming is a recent application that uses raster-based GISs with GPS satellite receivers to plan and deliver the specific treatment (herbicide, pesticide, fertilizer) only to the part of the field that needs it. In addition to achieving cost savings by avoiding unneeded chemical use, precision farming can reduce environmental problems and improve overall soil quality and retention (*GPS World*, 1995).

Vector-based GISs have seen widespread use in public administration and utilities and are the most common approach used in business. Vector systems associate features in the landscape with either a point, a line, or a polygon. Points are often used to represent small features such as ATMs, customer addresses, power poles, or items in motion, like trucks. Lines are for linear features such as roads and rivers and can be connected in networks. Polygons represent areas and surfaces, including lakes, land parcels, and regions—such as sales territories, counties, and zip codes. The relationships between the vector elements are called their topology; topology determines whether features overlap or intersect. Vector systems can distinguish, for example, an island in a lake, two roads crossing, and customers within a 2-mile radius of a retail site. However, vector data are not continuous; the resulting overlaps and gaps between features affect presentation and analysis, and thus must be explicitly dealt with by specialized personnel.

The most common data model for both vector and raster data is the **coverage model** in which different layers or themes represent similar types of geographic features in the same area and are stacked on top of one another (see Figure 7.4). Like working with transparent map overlays, layers allow different geographic data to be seen together, and they facilitate geographic manipulation and analysis.

Questions that geographic analysis can answer include the following:

- What is adjacent to this feature?
- Which site is the nearest one?
- What is contained within this area?
- Which features does this element cross?
- How many features are within a certain distance of a site?

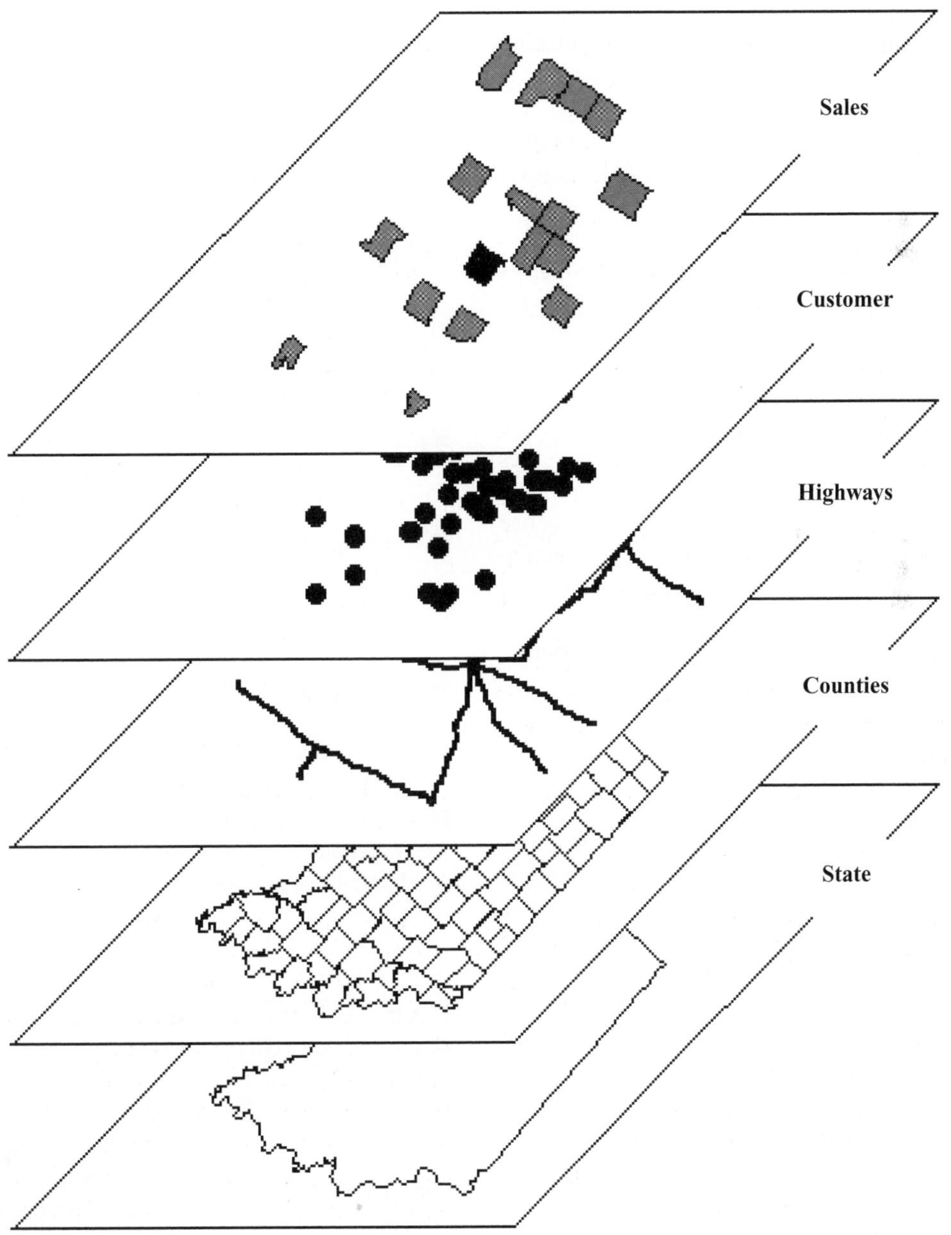

Figure 7.4 Map Layers in a GIS

Infinite zoom, panning and centering, finding the distance between two points, querying and labeling features, and changing symbols and colors on demand are basic capabilities for any GIS. Desktop GISs also provide for spatial manipulation such as intersection and union, the assignment of geographic references to addresses through geocoding, and standard query language support for interacting with attribute data. Once limited to high-end workstations, advanced GIS applications are now moving to the desktop and even the palmtop to automate sophisticated decision support tasks such as finding the shortest/fastest/safest route from A to B or grouping sales or service territories to minimize internal travel distance, equalize potential, or omit the fewest prospects.

Although the coverage data model facilitates incorporation of data from different sources into a single map for analysis and presentation, it is limited in its ability to relate objects to each other or to link objects in the system by their behavior in the world. A new model, called the **geodatabase model**, draws on object-oriented database concepts, which do not require the spatial data to be stored in separate indexes from their attributes (as vector data require) or that all items in the database be the same size (as raster data require) (Zeiler, 1999). In the geodatabase model, a feature such as a land parcel is defined not just by spatial references but by business rules which might specify its relationship to other objects such as adjacent parcels (e.g., "has at least one contiguous boundary"), owners ("has only one"), or administrative units ("is in only one fire district"). Further, this approach results in fewer problems with data accuracy while accommodating raster, vector, surface, address, coordinate, and other spatial data in one database.

Issues for Information Systems

Business applications of GISs are often initially introduced into a company to support a single user such as a market researcher. However, the power of GISs cannot be contained, and soon it spreads within and across groups, as we see with the Sears story above. Few IS organizations are in a position to develop a geographic application from scratch, but thanks to the maturity of GIS tools, this is seldom necessary. Desktop geographic systems contain scripting languages and support application program interfaces with popular desktop software packages as well as map object libraries (such as MapObjects from ESRI and MapX from MapInfo Corp.) and Internet-based interactive mapping application packages (such as Microsoft Corp.'s MapPoint Web Service).

Data sources for GISs include internal sources such as customer databases and warehouse locations and external ones such as street networks and advertising media market maps purchased from data vendors. Both new users and IS personnel are often unfamiliar with cost and quality issues for geographic data. For example, although geographic files for zip codes are often included at no additional cost in packaged desktop GIS software, the U.S. Postal Service updates zip codes on an ongoing basis, resulting in a decay in the accuracy of existing data sources. Additional issues emerge when geographic data are needed for an area outside the United States; if the data are available, they might be less accurate, more difficult to obtain, and more expensive.

Vendors for geographic technologies are seldom household words in IS; major players include Environmental Systems Research Institute (ESRI), MapInfo, AutoCAD, Microsoft, Tactician, and Intergraph Corp. GISs are increasingly integrated and integratable—map-enabled Web sites, which were an advanced technology a few years ago, are now available as an add-in using eXtensible Markup Language (XML) and .NET. Ongoing developments in geographic technologies include

- more advanced graphics, particularly three-dimensional and dynamic modeling to simulate movement through time and space, such as the path of a hurricane
- geography in your hand—the continued proliferation of spatial technologies into handheld devices for consumer use in location-based services
- linking spatial capability with wireless capability—not just access to data whenever you need it, but deployment and redeployment of the right assets—both human and nonhuman—to the right place
- radio frequency identification (RFID) technologies, which are dropping in cost and spurring new applications of spatial location to inexpensive objects, even individual garments and consumer products
- use of spatial technologies to tame out-of-control data warehouses and point-of-sale (POS) data (see the sidebar entitled "Beyond Location, Location, Location")

EXECUTIVE INFORMATION SYSTEMS/BUSINESS INTELLIGENCE SYSTEMS

The key concept behind an **executive information system (EIS)** is that such a system delivers online current information about business conditions in an aggregate form easily accessible to senior executives and other managers. An EIS is designed to be used directly by these managers without the assistance of intermediaries.

BEYOND LOCATION, LOCATION, LOCATION—GISs AND RETAILER LOYALTY CARD PROGRAMS

Not surprisingly, retailing has been one of the first business sectors to embrace GISs (e.g., Baker and Baker, 1993). Recently, retailers have come to see how geographically-enabled tools can help build traffic at existing stores (not just locate new ones) while taming the large volumes of data collected via point-of-sale (POS) systems. Researchers at the University of Alabama found distinct spatial patterns in the adoption of a customer loyalty card program for a major national retailer (disguised at the request of the firm). GIS made quick work out of address matching to analyze the first year's shopping behavior for nearly 18,000 loyalty program customers in a large Midwestern U.S. city, seamlessly incorporated census data on 300,000 people in the market area, and even determined the influence of billboard locations. Key insights that could come only from GIS-enabled spatial analysis include:

- Close proximity (living within 0.6 mile) to an innovator—someone adopting in the first 2 days—increased by 13.2 percent the chances you would join the program during the first year.
- Of course, distance from home to the store matters, but GIS shows that the distance effect was much stronger than expected. For each mile away from the store you live, you are 13.4 percent less likely to join the loyalty card program.
- Billboard locations were crucial. Nonadopters were, on average, 5.1 miles away from a billboard (compared to 2.5 miles for first-week adopters); even within a 3-mile ring of the store, nonadopters live farther from the nearest billboard than adopters.

People are always someplace in space, whether at home, working, shopping, or traveling. Retailers who understand the importance of location are exploiting the power of spatial analysis to make more effective decisions not just about store location, but about the spatial effect of different marketing innovations and strategies.

[Adapted from Allaway, Murphy, and Berkowitz, 2004]

An EIS uses state-of-the-art graphics, communications, and data storage methods to provide the executive easy online access to current information about the status of the organization.

Dating only to the late 1980s in most cases, EISs represent the first real attempt to deliver relevant summary information to management in online form. Originally, EISs were developed for just the two or three top executive levels in the firm, but that caused many problems of data disparity between the layers of management. The most important internal data—dealing with suppliers, production, and customers—are generated under the control of lower-level managers, and they need to know what is being reported higher up in the organization. As a result, today the user base in most companies has been broadened to encompass all levels of management in the firm—and sometimes even managers in customer and supplier organizations.

EISs employ transaction data that have been filtered and summarized into a form useful for the executives in the organization. In addition, many successful EISs incorporate qualitative data such as competitive information, assessments, and insights. This emphasis on competitive information has become so important in the last few years that many organizations now call their EISs **business intelligence systems** or **competitive intelligence systems** (see the sidebar entitled "Global Competitive Intelligence at Dow AgroSciences"). In summary, an EIS is a hands-on tool that focuses, filters, and organizes an executive's information so he or she can make more effective use of it.

Let us take Geac Performance Management (formerly Comshare MPC) as an example of a software platform for developing an EIS/business intelligence system. Geac Performance Management has its roots in an earlier product named Commander EIS, but it has now moved beyond a relatively simple EIS that summarizes data for top managers to a full-blown management planning and control system. Geac Performance Management is a client/server and intranet-based software tool consisting of a number of modules to monitor, measure, and manage business performance. Available modules include strategy management, planning, budgeting, financial consolidation, forecasting, and management reporting and analysis. If additional EIS/business intelligence features are desired, a companion product from Geac named Comshare Decision can be used to develop customized business intelligence, decision support, and OLAP applications as part of a comprehensive EIS. The client for Geac Performance Management is simply a Web browser.

Geac Performance Management permits customization of a large number of easy-to-use and easy-to-interpret displays to present key information to managers; the software package allows business users to view information in whatever way makes sense to them, including charts, graphs, maps, spreadsheets, ad hoc queries and calculations, and even proactive personal alerts when a specified condition occurs. In addition, it provides exception monitoring, an intelligent "drill-down" capability to identify relevant detailed information, multiple business perspectives (such

GLOBAL COMPETITIVE INTELLIGENCE AT DOW AGROSCIENCES

"Have you heard the latest about Monsanto? Can you believe the recent program Bayer launched? Rumors, news, and updates on competitors are everywhere. Yet how do we make sense of it all and stay focused on the information that really matters? Thanks to the newly launched Global Competitive Intelligence (GCI) Web site, all Dow AgroSciences employees can now efficiently learn competitive information while sharing what they hear in the marketplace." These lines begin an internal newsletter article that announced GCI to Dow AgroSciences employees in 1999.

In 1997, Dow AgroSciences management set an objective of establishing competitive intelligence as part of its company's culture. Eighteen months prior to this decision, two independent "skunk works" projects had yielded positive business results. The skunk works approaches were simple. One involved establishing Hypertext Markup Language (HTML) pages posted to a Web site on the company's intranet, where competitive information was posted and accessible by password. The other approach involved assigning an individual within each business unit as a competitive intelligence "focal point." Competitive information was fed to these focal points, who then distributed the information to all other focal points by e-mail, who in turn distributed information to sales and marketing personnel where appropriate.

Based on the business benefits realized from these early approaches, competitive intelligence was established as a global center of expertise within Dow AgroSciences. The result was the Global Competitive Intelligence (GCI) system. GCI is an intranet-based system that utilizes an Oracle database and is supported by a network of human resources (focal points) covering global operations. The intranet interface is simple to use yet is driven by a powerful database. The system is accessible to any Dow AgroSciences employee throughout the globe via the company's intranet. Currently, four levels of access have been built into the database. Level 1, which includes public information about the industry and competitors, is accessible to all employees who have access to the intranet. Competitive intelligence focal points and selected managers have access to additional information at Level 2, including public articles provided by a news service as well as reported competitive activities (rumors). Level 2 also includes detailed competitive profiles, updated annually. Level 3 is reserved for top management use, and Level 4 is for database administration.

The GCI system provides competitive observations and published news to permit employees to gain a clearer understanding of a competitor's strategy. Key competitive companies are profiled annually with the results of the analyses posted to dynamic pages within GCI. Information used in profiling companies includes corporate and divisional strategy assumptions, a history of business agreements, plant locations and research and development sites, product sales, financial assumptions, key personnel, and a SWOT analysis (see Chapter 14 for a discussion of SWOT analysis). Dow AgroSciences has integrated information from the GCI system into its business planning cycle and utilizes the analyses for licensing and acquisition activities. Through the use of the GCI system, the company has a designated network of people responsible for collecting, analyzing, and sharing competitive information with the entire organization on a global basis.

[Adapted from Fowler, 2000]

as region or product), multiple scenarios for planning (best, worst, most likely), and charting of cause/effect linkages among plan elements. Examples of Geac Performance Management displays are shown in Figure 7.5. Other leading commercial EIS products include SAS/EIS from SAS Institute, PilotWorks from Pilot Software, and Executive Dashboard from Qualitech Solutions. Commercial business intelligence platforms, which perform many of the same functions but are more narrowly focused than the EIS products, include Business Objects Enterprise 6.1, Cognos Enterprise Business Intelligence, Hyperion Performance Suite, and MicroStrategy 7i Business Intelligence Platform.

Perhaps the earliest EIS described in print is the management information and decision support (MIDS) system at the Lockheed-Georgia Company (Houdeshel and Watson, 1987). The sponsor for MIDS was the Lockheed-Georgia president, and a special staff reporting to the vice president of finance developed the system. An evolutionary approach was used in developing MIDS, with only a limited number of displays developed initially for a limited number of executives. For example, a display might show prospective customers for a particular type of aircraft or might graphically depict both forecast and actual sales over the past year.

Over time, more displays were developed and more executives were added to the system. The initial version of MIDS in 1979 had only 31 displays developed for fewer than a dozen senior executives. By 1985, 710 displays had been developed, 30 senior executives and 40 operating managers were using the system, and the mean number of displays viewed per user per day was up to 5.5. Many factors had to come together for MIDS to be successful, but perhaps the most important was that the system delivered the information (based on quantitative and qualitative data) that senior executives needed for them and their company to be successful.

More recently, EISs have been created and used successfully in many other large companies such as Phillips Petroleum, Dun & Bradstreet Software, Coca-Cola Company,

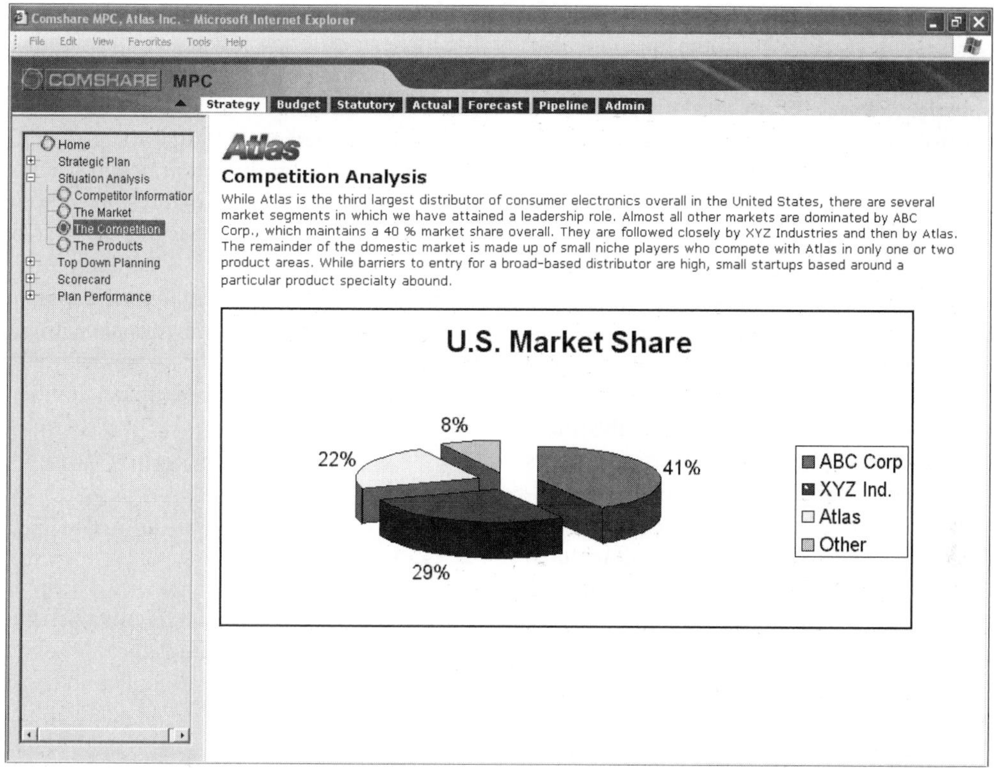

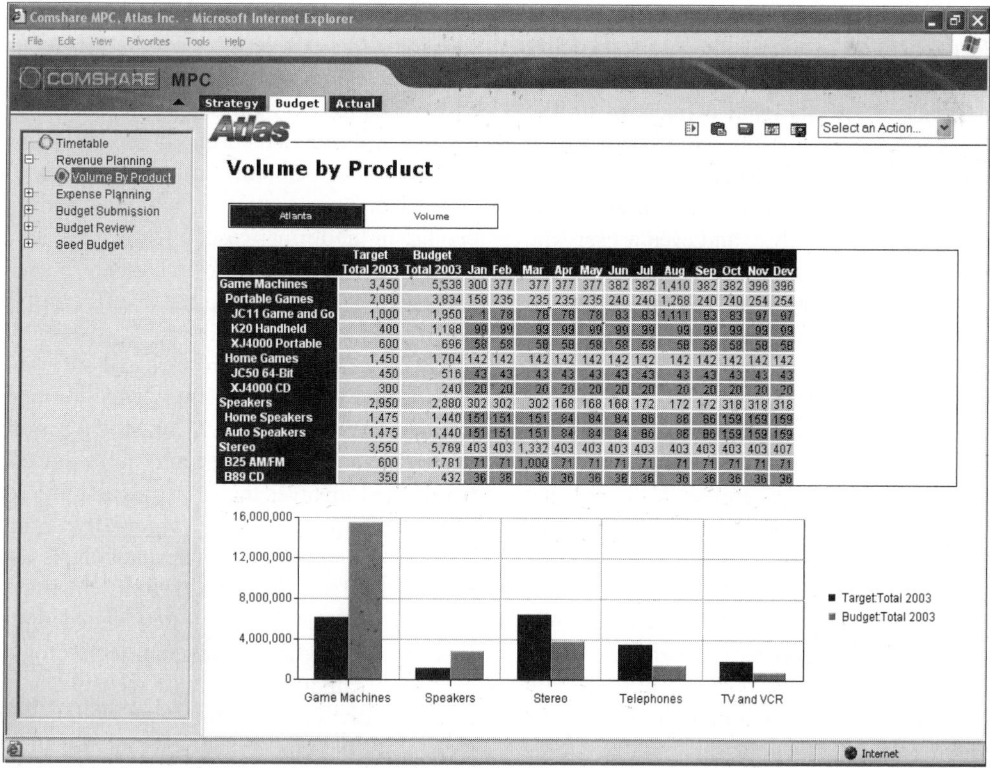

	Target Total 2003	Budget Total 2003	Jan	Feb	Mar	Apr	May	Jun	Jul	Aug	Sep	Oct	Nov	Dev
Game Machines	3,450	5,538	300	377	377	377	377	382	382	1,410	382	382	396	396
Portable Games	2,000	3,834	158	235	235	235	235	240	240	1,268	240	240	254	254
JC11 Game and Go	1,000	1,950	1	78	78	78	78	83	83	1,111	83	83	97	97
K20 Handheld	400	1,188	99	99	99	99	99	99	99	99	99	99	99	99
XJ4000 Portable	600	696	58	58	58	58	58	58	58	58	58	58	58	58
Home Games	1,450	1,704	142	142	142	142	142	142	142	142	142	142	142	142
JC50 64-Bit	450	516	43	43	43	43	43	43	43	43	43	43	43	43
XJ4000 CD	300	240	20	20	20	20	20	20	20	20	20	20	20	20
Speakers	2,950	2,880	302	302	302	168	168	168	172	172	172	318	318	318
Home Speakers	1,475	1,440	151	151	151	84	84	84	86	86	86	159	159	159
Auto Speakers	1,475	1,440	151	151	151	84	84	84	86	86	86	159	159	159
Stereo	3,550	5,769	403	403	1,332	403	403	403	403	403	403	403	403	407
B25 AM/FM	600	1,781	71	71	1,000	71	71	71	71	71	71	71	71	71
B89 CD	350	432	36	36	36	36	36	36	36	36	36	36	36	36

Figure 7.5 Example Geac Performance Management Displays (Courtesy of Geac Computer Corporation Limited. Copyright © 2003 Geac Computer Corporation Limited.)

Fisher-Price, Conoco, Inc., and CIGNA Corporation. The following paragraphs focus on four other companies that have recently installed EISs.

Based in Calgary, Alberta, Petro-Canada is a leader in the Canadian petroleum industry. Petro-Canada's oil and gas division has recently used Comshare Decision to create an integrated information system with easier, more consistent, and timely access to information for business decision-making processes—an EIS. Petro-Canada calls the new system "The Dashboard Project," which means having the key performance measures and analytical data available for view on a dashboard so that managers can look forward through the "windshield of opportunity." By using Comshare Decision's integrated solution for analysis and performance measurement, all levels of decision makers have access to the same numbers and views and have confidence that the data are current, correct, and verifiable. The new system provides a single user interface for all required information in an intuitive, flexible manner, including executive views, graphs, charts, drill-down capabilities, alarms, and alerts. Furthermore, the data visualization capabilities let decision makers have the data presented in the way that makes most sense for them (*DM Review*, 2000).

Domino's Pizza, Inc., with retail sales exceeding $3 billion per year, has also gone with the Comshare Decision approach to developing an EIS. "The rich functionality of the Web interface will allow us to provide consistent delivery whether the user is at our headquarters, in one of our regional offices, in our international offices, or on the road," states George Azrak, vice president of information systems development at Domino's Pizza. "Comshare gives us a lot of flexibility to tailor the system for an executive, middle manager, heavy-duty analyst, and even a user who is just looking for some packaged information—we can serve all our users. And the data visualization techniques for detecting hidden problems in operational data are a big hit with our users" (Geac Web site, 2003).

Dean Health System, a Madison, Wisconsin-based health care organization, originally used Comshare Decision to develop an EIS to provide its geographically diverse, multispecialty clinics with the ability to carry out detailed analysis and reporting at the local level. In 2003, Dean Health System took a further step by using the Geac Performance Management budgeting module to integrate and improve its budgeting process enterprise-wide. According to Ron Thomas, decision support administrator at Dean Health System, the enhanced EIS "will empower our departmental directors with immediate access to information they need to be accountable for the success of their operations." Krispy Kreme Doughnut Corporation, which produces more than 2.7 billion doughnuts a year, implemented all modules of Geac Performance Management to create its comprehensive EIS. "Formerly, we used a combination of financial reporting and consolidation software and spreadsheets," said Frank Hood, CIO of Krispy Kreme. "Those systems and processes left little time for analysis of the information, were not tightly integrated to many of our data stores, and were just too cumbersome and fragmented for us to ever realize the benefits of a true performance management system. We believe the increase in integration combined with gains in analytical reporting efficiency [through the use of Geac Performance Management] will translate into improvements in operational and management effectiveness" (Geac Web site, 2003).

KNOWLEDGE MANAGEMENT SYSTEMS

Knowledge management systems (KMSs) are systems that enable individuals and organizations to enhance learning, improve performance, and, hopefully, produce long-term sustainable competitive advantage. Simply stated, a KMS is a system for managing organizational knowledge. A KMS may be designed to support "communities of practice" focusing on different key knowledge areas; in this case the KMS enables connections from people to people (e.g., expert directories), people to knowledge (e.g., knowledge repositories), and people to tools (e.g., community calendars, discussion forums). On the other hand, a KMS may consist of elaborate structuring of knowledge content (e.g., taxonomies), carefully packaged and disseminated to people. In the former case, a KMS is all about technology, while in the latter case the technology is necessary but not central. We will return to these different types of KMSs later in this section.

KMSs use various hardware and software applications to facilitate and support **knowledge management (KM)** activities. What then is KM? KM is a set of management practices that is practical and action-oriented. In other words, KM involves the strategies and processes of identifying, creating, capturing, organizing, transferring, and leveraging knowledge to help individuals and firms compete (O'Dell and Grayson, 1998). KM is concerned with behavior changes to reflect new knowledge and insights. KM is not about relying on technology to improve processes; rather, KM relies on recognizing the knowledge held by individuals and the firm. Therefore, a KMS is the technology or vehicle that facilitates the sharing and transferring of knowledge for the purpose of disseminating and reusing valuable knowledge that, once applied, enhances learning and improves performance.

Why has KMS received so much attention recently, and why are so many projects labeled KMS projects? There are two explanations. First, one trigger leading to the development of KM and KMS is related to firm valuation. For example, Microsoft's net value was estimated by examining its market value based on stock prices minus net assets. The enormous difference was attributed to the knowledge held by individuals and the organization (e.g., routines, best practices). In a similar time frame, "knowledge assets" began to appear on a few firms' balance sheets in their annual reports. Hence, there is a growing awareness and consensus that "knowledge" will enable firms to differentiate themselves from others and to compete effectively in the marketplace.

Second, tangible benefits accrue from implementing KM and KMS initiatives. Although the benefits are specific to a given firm, there are both *operational improvements* and *market improvements*. Operational improvements focus on internal activities and include cost savings (e.g., faster and better dissemination of knowledge), efficient processes (e.g., best practices), change management processes (e.g., behavior changes), and knowledge reuse (e.g., high quality standards). In contrast, market improvements focus on external activities such as performance (e.g., increased sales), cost savings (e.g., lower costs of products and services), and customer satisfaction.

The goal of a KMS is to tap into the knowledge of the individual and the organization and disseminate it throughout the firm to derive operational and market improvements. Furthermore, a KMS is different from other systems because it considers the content contained within the system—that is, the system is only as good as what is in it! Based on a study of more than two dozen successful KMSs recently implemented in various firms, there are three KMS characteristics that need to be considered in describing a KMS: First, the extent to which there is formal management and control of the KMS; second, the focus of the KM processes, such as knowledge creation, capture, organization and packaging, access, search and dissemination, and application; and third, the extent to which reusability of knowledge is considered (e.g., the 80-20 rule, or 20 percent of the knowledge content that potentially could be contained in a KMS is likely to be of most value to 80 percent of the users) (Dennis and Vessey, 2003).

A KMS might have very little formal management and control, as in the case of "communities of practice" (COPs). Designed for individuals with similar interests, a COP KMS provides a vehicle to allow members of such a community to exchange ideas, tips, and other knowledge that might be valuable to the members of the community. There is no formal management or control of such a KMS; rather, the members are responsible for validating and structuring their knowledge for use within the KMS. Each member of the COP is responsible for the knowledge content, with a great likelihood that such knowledge will be applicable to only a few members. In other words, there is very little, if any, organizing and packaging of knowledge, making the search and applicability even more difficult. Hopefully, there will be occasions where a single item of knowledge content will be important to many members of the COP, although these occasions might be few in number.

In contrast, a KMS might have extensive formal management and control. There might be a KM team to oversee the process of validating the knowledge prior to dissemination. Such a team provides structure, organization, and packaging for how knowledge is to be presented to the users. These dedicated resources ensure that knowledge content entered into the KMS has been thoroughly examined and that it will meet the 80-20 rule.

This discussion does not imply that a KMS must be characterized as binary—that is, having either little or extensive formal management and control, knowledge processing, or knowledge reusability. Rather, there is a spectrum of KMSs that are designed to meet the specific needs of a given firm. In the case of a COP KMS, it is not clear whether the focus is either operational or market improvements. On the other hand, the KM team approach attempts to accomplish both operational and market improvements. Although KMSs are still growing with much room for advancement, many firms observe their KMS evolving from one form to another as they learn from their experience and as their strategic needs and resources change. Such evolution suggests that firms are enjoying the benefits accrued from tapping into their employees' and organizational knowledge. Moreover, they find a strategic need to continue their efforts to unveil the hidden treasures within and outside their organizational boundaries.

Two Recent KMS Initiatives within a Pharmaceutical Firm

Corporate KMS A KM team was formed to develop an organization-wide KMS serving multiple communities of practice. The operation of a community of practice involves a combination of software and processes. Each community has a designated coordinator whose job is to ensure that the community thrives (some communities have two or three coordinators). The coordinators are volunteers and receive no extra compensation; however, they do tend to become highly visible members of their communities. The coordinator performs many specific functions such as welcoming new members, developing and maintaining standards of conduct and standards for knowledge within the community, maintaining the community calendar, monitoring the discussion forums, ensuring the knowledge in the community is appropriate, serving as the primary point of contact and external ambassador for the community, and many other items.

The portal software used to support the communities of practice provides approximately 150 tools of which only a handful are regularly used. The three most commonly used tools are the discussion forum, tips, and calendar. As the name suggests, the discussion forum is a tool that enables question-and-answer discussions among members of the community. Any member of the community can pose a question or a request in the discussion forum, which is available to all members. Likewise, all members can respond to the items posted in the discussion. Each discussion item in the forum is typically started as its own thread and there are often two or three active discussion threads, depending on the community's size. The community's coordinator typically reviews the items in the discussion forum and archives older discussions. Sometimes the coordinator will decide that a particular item is useful and relevant over the long term and should be moved to the tips area. In that case the coordinator or the contributors to the discussion will prepare a more formal version to be stored in the tips area.

The tips tool enables any member of the community to write a short entry that documents some sort of best practice advice that the contributor believes might be of interest to the community as a whole. The full text of all tips is searchable, so the members of the community can find tips of interest.

The coordinator maintains the community calendar. Members of the community typically e-mail the coordinator with suggested calendar items, which the coordinator posts. Typical calendar items include face-to-face meetings held by part or all of the community, seminars and workshops offered by members of the community, and more formal presentations likely to be of interest to the community.

Field Sales KMS A different KM team was formed to lead the development of the field sales KMS. Unlike the corporate KMS, this KM team's mission was to design and build *both* the content and the structure of the KMS. Therefore, a knowledge taxonomy was developed so that knowledge about each of the drugs sold by the firm was organized separately. Sales representatives would have access to knowledge only about the drugs they sold.

Sales operations and brand management would develop initial drafts of the knowledge content, which they would provide to the KM team. The KM team would format the documents and put them in the proper locations in the KMS according to the taxonomy. Although the system was intended to be the primary knowledge repository used by the field sales representatives and the sales managers, all knowledge communication with the field sales representatives was expected to be conducted through the field sales KMS. Instead of mailing paper marketing materials and advisories, for example, managers would now create them in Word and PowerPoint and post them into the field sales KMS.

The KM team also realized that it was important to enable the field sales representatives themselves to contribute sales tips and practical advice for use by other sales representatives. However, because of strict government regulatory control over communication with the physicians, all such tips needed first to be approved by the firm's legal department. A formal four-step process was therefore developed for validating all content sent in from the field sales representatives. Tips were first vetted by the KM team itself to make sure the content was coherent and complete. Next, the tip was submitted to the legal group to ensure that the content was consistent with all rules, regulations, and good promotional practice guidelines. Then the tip was sent to the brand management team to ensure that it was consistent with the marketing strategy for the drug. Next, the tip was sent to the sales operations group for peer review by a panel of five sales representatives to ensure the contribution had real value. Finally, once the tip had been approved, it was entered into the field sales KMS. Although this sounds like a lengthy process, most tips were processed within 2 weeks of receipt. Field sales representatives were rewarded by receiving sales points for each tip that was ultimately accepted (these points were part of the usual commission structure received by all sales representatives; the points received for each tip were equivalent to approximately \$60).

Although there were several iterations of user interfaces to best align with changing taxonomies, the knowledge structure for the current system was designed in what the team called a "T-structure," which had two distinct parts. Across the top of the "T" (and presented horizontally near the top of the Lotus Notes screen) was the general sales knowledge designed to be pertinent to all sales divisions. This contained knowledge on topics such as rules and guidelines for sales promotions, templates for sales processes, forms for sales functions, and directories with phone numbers of key experts within the U.S. business unit. Down the middle of the "T" (and presented vertically near the left edge of the Lotus Notes screen) was the division-specific knowledge, which typically pertained to drugs sold by that division. This contained information such as fundamental sales information on the drugs sold by the sales representatives, competitive analyses, results in recent drug trials, and letters from expert physicians. Tips and best practices submitted by the field sales representatives would either fit across the top or down the side of the screen depending on whether they focused on general sales knowledge or on product-specific knowledge.

ARTIFICIAL INTELLIGENCE

The idea of **artificial intelligence (AI)**, the study of how to make computers do things that are currently done better by people, is about 50 years old, but only in the last two decades have computers become powerful enough to make AI applications commercially attractive. AI research has evolved into six separate but related areas; these are natural languages, robotics, perceptive systems (vision and hearing), genetic programming (also called evolutionary design), expert systems, and neural networks.

The work in **natural languages**, primarily in computer science departments in universities and in vendor laboratories, is aimed at producing systems that translate ordinary human instructions into a language that computers can understand and execute. Robotics was considered in the previous chapter. **Perceptive systems** research involves creating machines possessing a visual and/or aural perceptual ability that affects their physical behavior. In other words, this research is aimed at creating robots that can "see" or "hear" and react to what they see or hear. With **genetic programming** or **evolutionary design**, the problem is divided into multiple segments, and solutions to these segments are linked together in different ways to breed new "child" solutions. After many generations of breeding, genetic programming might produce results superior to anything devised by a human. Genetic programming has been most useful in the design of innovative products such as a satellite support arm with a novel shape that prevents vibrations from being transmitted along the truss, and General Electric Co.'s energy-efficient halogen light bulb, which is 48 percent brighter than a standard halogen bulb (Port, 2000).

The final two branches of AI are the ones most relevant for managerial support. The **expert systems** branch is concerned with building systems that incorporate the decision-making logic of a human expert. A newer branch of AI is **neural networks**, which is named after the study of how the human nervous system works, but which in fact uses statistical analysis to recognize patterns from vast amounts of information by a process of adaptive learning. Both these branches of AI are described in more detail in the following sections.

EXPERT SYSTEMS

How does one capture the logic of an expert in a computer system? To design an expert system, a specialist known as a knowledge engineer (a specially trained systems analyst) works very closely with one or more experts in the area under study. Knowledge engineers try to learn everything they can about the way in which the expert makes decisions. If one is trying to build an expert system for estate planning, for example, the knowledge engineer works with experienced estate planners to see how they do their job. What the knowledge engineer has learned is then loaded into the computer system, in a specialized format, in a module called the knowledge base (see Figure 7.6). This knowledge base contains both the inference rules that are followed in decision making and the parameters, or facts, relevant to the decision.

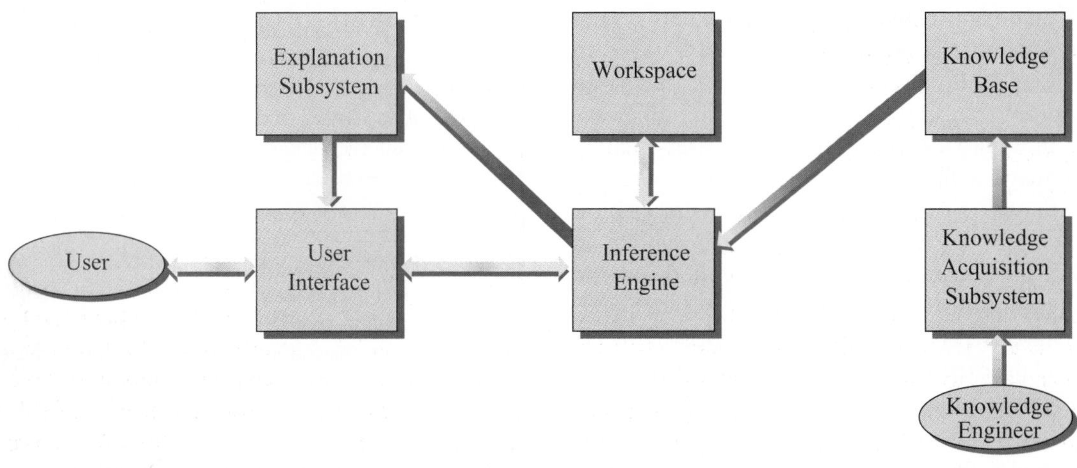

Figure 7.6 Architecture of an Expert System

The other major pieces of an expert system are the inference engine and the user interface. The inference engine is a logical framework that automatically executes a line of reasoning when supplied with the inference rules and parameters involved in the decision; thus, the same inference engine can be used for many different expert systems, each with a different knowledge base. The user interface is the module used by the end user—for example, an inexperienced estate planner. Ideally, the interface is very user-friendly. The other modules include an explanation subsystem to explain the reasoning that the system followed in arriving at a decision, a knowledge acquisition subsystem to assist the knowledge engineer in recording inference rules and parameters in the knowledge base, and a workspace for the computer to use as the decision is being made.

Obtaining an Expert System

Is it necessary to build all these pieces each time your organization wants to develop and use an expert system? Absolutely not. There are three general approaches to obtaining an expert system, and only one of them requires construction of all these pieces. First, an organization can buy a fully developed system that has been created for a specific application. For example, in the late 1980s, Syntelligence, Inc., developed an expert system called Lending Advisor to assist in making commercial lending decisions for banks and other financial institutions. Lending Advisor incorporated the many factors involved in approving or rejecting a commercial loan, and it was installed in several banks. In general, however, the circumstances leading to the desire for an expert system are unique to the organization, and in most cases this "off-the-shelf" expert system option is not viable.

Second, an organization can develop an expert system itself using an **artificial intelligence shell** (also called an **expert systems shell**). The shell, which can be purchased from a software company, provides the basic framework illustrated in Figure 7.6 and a limited but user-friendly special language with which to develop the expert system. With the basic expert system functions already in place in the shell, the system builder can concentrate on the details of the business decision being modeled and the development of the knowledge base. Third, an organization can have internal or external knowledge engineers custom-build the expert system. In this case the system is usually programmed in a special-purpose language such as Prolog or Lisp. This final approach is clearly the most expensive, and it can be justified only if the potential payoff from the expert system is quite high and no other way is possible.

Examples of Expert Systems

Perhaps the classic example of an expert system is MYCIN, which was developed at Stanford University in the mid-1970s to diagnose and prescribe treatment for meningitis and blood diseases. General Electric Co. created an expert system called CATS-1 to diagnose mechanical problems in diesel locomotives, and AT&T developed ACE to locate faults in telephone cables. Schlumberger, Ltd., an international oil company, developed an expert system named Dipmeter to give advice when a drill bit gets stuck while drilling a well. These examples and others are concerned with diagnosing problem situations and prescribing appropriate actions, because experts are not always present when a problem occurs.

Diagnosis of a different sort is made by an expert system at the American Stock Exchange that has been built to help detect insider trading on the exchange. This expert system, named Market Surveillance, is designed to support analysts in making recommendations on whether to open

EXPERT SYSTEM HELPS CAMPBELL KEEP THE SOUP STIRRING

Campbell Soup Company makes its soup in hydrostatic canned food product sterilizers, or cookers, that are over 70 feet tall and incorporate a variety of equipment. Cooker malfunctions can mean significant lost production time, which Campbell obviously tries to minimize. When Aldo Cimino, an expert at diagnosing cooker problems, announced his pending retirement, Campbell decided to "clone" the expertise of this 44-year veteran diagnostician by building an expert system. "Decades of expertise that had benefited Campbell were on the verge of walking out the door forever," said Alan Carr, Campbell's director of business systems. "Several goals were quickly determined [for the new expert system]. The expert system would have to be able to replace Aldo Cimino, and it should be useful as a training tool for production and maintenance engineers."

Campbell hired a team from Texas Instruments (TI) to create the expert system, named COOKER, using TI's Personal Consultant as the expert systems shell. The team watched Cimino perform his job and conducted extensive interviews with him over a period of several weeks; then the information provided by Cimino was captured in a series of rules placed in the knowledge base. The expert system was implemented on a PC deployed on the factory floor so that it could be quickly used by workers when problems arose. Early returns suggest that COOKER is working quite well, and that Aldo Cimino is enjoying his retirement.

[Adapted from *I/S Analyzer*, 1995]

an investigation of suspected insider trading. The relevant database of stock price activity is entered into the expert system, and the analyst responds to a series of questions from the system. The output consists of two scores—the first is the probability that an investigation should be opened and the second is the probability that an investigation should not be opened (Exsys Inc., 2003).

Earlier we mentioned that expert systems were used to assist in making commercial lending decisions as early as the 1980s. Today, over one-third of the top 100 commercial banks in the United States and Canada use FAST (Financial Analysis Support Techniques) software for credit analysis. This expert-systems-based software gives a credit analyst access to the expertise of more experienced analysts, speeding up the training process and increasing productivity. FAST also provides a complete range of traditional analytical reports on both a historical and a pro forma basis (Exsys Inc., 2003).

Expert systems often serve in an advisory role to decision makers of all kinds. For example, the IDP (individual development plan) Goal Advisor is an expert system that assists a supervisor and an employee in setting short-range and long-range employee career goals and the developmental objectives to reach these goals. Nestle Foods has developed an expert system to provide information to employees on their pension fund status. Using the expert system, an employee can conduct a private "interview" with a pension fund expert and ask what-if questions about benefits. The expert system enables the employee to make more knowledgeable personal financial planning decisions without requiring extensive personnel department consultation. EXNUT is an expert system developed by the National Peanut Research Laboratory and the U.S. Department of Agriculture to help peanut farmers manage irrigated peanut production. Based on extensive data collected from individual peanut fields throughout the growing season, EXNUT makes recommendations for irrigation, fungicide treatment, and pest management. The results are quite positive: The fields managed by EXNUT have consistently produced higher yields and high-quality peanuts using less water and less fungicide than those managed without the expert system (Exsys Inc., 2003).

Scheduling is another important area for expert systems. Expert systems currently in use include a truck routing and scheduling system that determines the sequence of stops on a route to provide the best service and a factory design system that organizes machines and operators to provide an efficient flow of materials through the factory and use the resources efficiently. As another example, General Motors created the Expert Scheduling System, or ESS, to generate viable manufacturing schedules. GM used both IntelliCorp's Knowledge Engineering Environment expert system shell and the Lisp programming language to build the system. ESS incorporates heuristics that had been developed by an experienced factory scheduler into the system, and it also links directly into GM's computer-integrated manufacturing (CIM) environment so that real-time plant information is used to generate the plant floor schedules (*I/S Analyzer*, 1995).

Some expert systems specialize in sifting through massive sets of rules or other data, sometimes called case-based reasoning. The United Nations employs an expert system called the Entitlements System to interpret the

EXPERT SYSTEMS PAYING OFF FOR SOME FIRMS

Once touted as potentially revolutionizing business operations, you don't hear much about expert systems these days, although proponents claim more enterprises than you might expect have adopted them. But can expert systems help your enterprise run leaner and smarter?

In the early days of expert systems, "there was too much technobabble that wasn't backed up by actual business cases," admitted Mike Will, director of research and development for Picodoc Corp., which develops tools for creating relatively small expert systems. Systems created with Picodoc's product, PicoXpert, have no more than 500 rules and run on the Palm handheld platform.

At a higher level are automated network-based expert systems. Sometimes these systems are built into other products, such as the network protocol analysis and monitoring developed by Network Instruments. According to Douglas Smith, president of Network Instruments, the expert component starts working after the software identifies a specific event such as a delay in data transmission. "The system examines all the streams of data," Smith explained. "It can determine, say, whether the delay is network-based or just that somebody left to go to the bathroom. It saves IT shops a lot of time."

At the high end are mainframe-based expert systems deployed by organizations such as airlines and huge shippers used for efficiently deploying equipment and crews. Will claimed that it would be exorbitantly expensive for those organizations to hire enough people to perform such ongoing analyses. Yet, deploying aircraft and crews inefficiently would result in untold losses for those companies, he claimed.

The bottom line, Will acknowledged, is that, while expert systems can make many companies operate more efficiently, they had better be ready to invest a lot of time and, in many cases, money, developing and tweaking them.

[Haskin, 2003]

complex salary regulations for all employees of the U.N. Secretariat worldwide. The pay for U.N. employees is determined by a base salary plus entitlements, and the entitlements include benefits based on location of work plus other contractual agreements. The rules and regulations for the entitlements fill three volumes of several hundred pages each. Using PowerModel software from IntelliCorp, the U.N. has built an expert system that determines and applies entitlements automatically, employing an online knowledge base containing the entitlements rules. The expert system also reassesses the entitlements whenever an employee's status changes (Baum, 1996).

NEURAL NETWORKS

Whereas expert systems try to capture the expertise of humans in a computer program, neural networks attempt to tease out meaningful patterns from vast amounts of data. Neural networks can recognize patterns too obscure for humans to detect, and they adapt as new information is received.

The key characteristic of neural networks is that they *learn*. The neural network program is originally given a set of data consisting of many variables associated with a large number of cases, or events, in which the outcomes are known. The program analyzes the data, works out all the correlations, and then selects a set of variables that are strongly correlated with particular known outcomes as the initial pattern. This initial pattern is used to try to predict the outcomes of the various cases, and these predicted results are compared to the known results. Based on this comparison, the program changes the pattern by adjusting the weights given to the variables or by changing the variables. The neural network program then repeats this process over and over, continuously adjusting the pattern in an attempt to improve its predictive ability. When no further improvement is possible from this iterative approach, the program is ready to make predictions for future cases.

This is not the end of the story. As more cases become available, these data are also fed into the neural network and the pattern is once again adjusted. The neural network learns more about cause-and-effect patterns from this additional data, and its predictive ability usually improves accordingly.

Commercial neural network programs (actually, these are shells) are available for a reasonable price, but the difficult part of building a neural network application is data collection and data maintenance. Still, a growing number of applications are being deployed. Neural networks are typically used either to predict or categorize, but to do so in an inductive manner rather than deductively. Table 7.2 lists examples of current uses of neural networks.

Here are some examples of neural networks. BankAmerica uses a neural network to evaluate commercial loan applications. American Express uses a neural system to read handwriting on credit card slips. The state of Wyoming uses a neural system to read hand-printed numbers on tax forms. Oil giants Arco and ChevronTexaco are using neural networks to help pinpoint oil and gas deposits below the Earth's surface. Mellon Bank installed a neural network credit card fraud detection system. When a credit card is swiped through the card reader in a store, the transaction is sent to Mellon's neural system. By analyzing the type of transaction, the amount spent, the time of day, and other data, the neural network makes a fraud prediction in 45 seconds or less and either denies the transaction or feeds the predictive score to a human analyst who makes the final decision. Spiegel Catalog, Inc., which depends on catalogs to generate sales for its mail-order business, uses a neural network as a way of pruning its mailing list to eliminate those who are unlikely to order from Spiegel again.

Neural networks are also being used to manage portfolios. Deere & Company's pension fund has been using neural networks to manage its portfolio of over $100 million since 1993. The fund monitors a pool of 1,000 U.S. stocks on a weekly basis. For each stock a neural network models the future performance of the stock as a function of the stock's exposure to 40 fundamental and technical factors and provides an estimate of its weekly price change. The company then selects a portfolio of the top 100 stocks and allocates the fund proportionately based on predicted

Table 7.2 Uses of Neural Networks

Categorization	Prediction/Forecasting
Credit rating and risk assessment	Share price forecast
Insurance risk evaluation	Commodity price forecast
Fraud detection	Economic indicator predictions
Insider trading detection	Process control
Direct mail profiling	Weather prediction
Machinery defect diagnosis	Future drug performance
Character recognition	Production requirements
Medical diagnosis	
Bacteria identification	

LOAN STAR

Household Financial Corporation is a $10 billion consumer finance business with headquarters in Prospect Heights, Illinois, and 1,400 branch offices in 46 states. In the late 1990s, Household developed an object-oriented software system named Vision to integrate all phases of the consumer lending process; Vision also connects to an intelligent underwriting system that returns lending decisions in minutes rather than hours or days. Built into the Vision system are neural network components that help Household make smarter decisions about its customers.

For instance, say a credit card holder calls, irate about a late fee. He's not a profitable customer for the company; he carries a single card with little or no balance and has spurned Household offers for credit insurance products and equity loans. Why should the Household service rep cancel the late fee? Vision knows why. The system "takes into consideration the potential lifetime value of the customer," says Ken Harvey, now Household's chief information officer.

Turns out this customer took out a school loan six years ago and a small auto finance deal for a used car three years ago from another company. His modest income has gone up significantly two years running. Considering these variables, Vision can recognize this late fee as a first offense by a recent college graduate who handles his finances well and may be in the market for significant new loans in the next year. Vision authorizes the service rep to waive the fee. Then the system can prompt the rep with suggestive selling for this now-happy customer—does he know that Household can pay off that old car loan and offer attractive terms on a loan for a newer vehicle?

Taken in sum, the system ties the company more closely to existing and prospective customers. Loan approvals are faster, sales proposals more targeted, and customer service more responsive. Cutting out the waiting game and creating more desirable products helps Household forge a customer intimacy that ultimately translates to profits, which in today's stock-market-driven environment is the ultimate in enterprise value.

[Slater, 2000]

returns. The annual pension fund return has been well in excess of industry benchmarks (NeuroDimension, 2000).

Another use of neural networks is in targeted marketing, where marketing campaigns are targeted to potential customers who have the same attributes that resulted in sales for previous campaigns. A security system has been developed that uses neural technology to recognize a person's face to grant that person access to a secured area. Washington, D.C.-based start-up Psynapse has based its network intrusion protection system named Checkmate on a neural network; Checkmate conducts a real-time assessment of each visitor to a network, and if it notes behavior that indicates an attempted security breach, it automatically terminates the intruder's access (Orzech, 2002).

Neural networks have also been used to forecast the number of admissions to a hospital on a given day and to discover relationships among the admissions data that are not otherwise visible. In this study neural networks produced forecasts of the same overall quality as traditional methods, but in less than half the time. Furthermore, neural networks were able to prove the value of a specific medical treatment through analysis of the admissions data; this treatment had long been claimed to be beneficial but proving the benefit had been difficult until neural networks came along (Z Solutions, 2003).

In the late 1980s and 1990s, expert system and neural network applications received a great deal of hype in the popular press. The AI applications were supposedly going to solve many of the decision problems faced by managers. Today, industry has adopted a more realistic view of AI applications: AI is not a panacea, but there are a significant number of potentially valuable applications for AI techniques. Each potential application must be carefully evaluated. The result of these careful evaluations has been a steady growth, but not an explosion, in the development and use of expert systems and neural networks to help businesses cope with problem situations and make better and more consistent decisions.

VIRTUAL REALITY

Virtual reality is a fascinating application area with rapidly growing importance. **Virtual reality**, or **VR**, refers to the use of computer-based systems to create an environment that seems real to one or more senses (usually including sight) of the human user or users. The ultimate example of VR is the holodeck aboard the U.S.S. Enterprise on *Star Trek: The Next Generation*, where Data can be Sherlock Holmes in a realistic setting with realistic characters and where Jean-Luc Picard can play the role of a hard-boiled private eye in the early twentieth century.

VR exists today, but with nowhere near the reality of the Enterprise's holodeck. You might have played a video game where you don a head-mounted computer display and a glove to get directly into the action. The use of VR in a non-entertainment setting falls primarily into three categories—training, design, and marketing. Training examples will be presented first, followed by examples of the use of VR in design and in marketing.

The U.S. Army uses VR to train tank crews. Through multiple large video screens and sound, the soldiers are seemingly placed inside a tank rolling across the Iraqi desert, and they have to react as if they were in a real tank battle. In the field of medicine, medical students are learning through collaboration and trial-and-error on virtual cadavers, which is much less expensive than using actual bodies. As an example, researchers have created 3-D animations of hematomas—bleeding between the skull and brain—of virtual patients who have suffered head damage in an automobile accident. Using a virtual-reality head-mounted display and virtual-reality gloves, students work together to diagnose and treat the patient (Hulme, 2002).

Amoco has developed a PC-based VR system, called "truck driVR," for use in training its drivers. Amoco believed that the VR system was a cost-effective way of testing how well its 12,000 drivers performed under a variety of hazardous driving conditions. This immersive VR system, which cost approximately $50,000 to develop, employs a helmet that holds the visual and auditory displays and completely immerses the user in the virtual world. To make truck driVR realistic, multiple views are provided to the user, including views of both left and right rear-view mirrors that are displayed only when the user moves his or her head to the left or right (*I/S Analyzer*, 1997).

Duracell also employs VR for training. Duracell was installing new equipment to manufacture a new line of rechargeable batteries, and the company needed to train its factory personnel on the new equipment in a safe and cost-effective manner. The Duracell system, which is nonimmersive (no helmet or special glasses), also runs on a PC and incorporates a parts familiarization module, an operations module, and a troubleshooting module. With this system the user is able to completely explore the new piece of equipment within the desktop virtual world. "With the use of that special mouse [a Magellan space mouse], the user can walk around it [the equipment], they can get underneath it, they can get on top of it," says Neil Silverstein, a training manager at Duracell. "They can fly into the smallest crevices of the machine, something that you can never do in the real world because you might lose a finger." Duracell is quite pleased with the results. The training is standardized and completely safe, and there is no need for on-the-job training (*I/S Analyzer*, 1997).

VR use in training might become even more prominent as the result of a project called Virtual Environments for Training, which is a collaboration among the Center for Advanced Research in Technology for Education, the Lockheed Martin Space Systems Advanced Technology Center, and the University of Southern California Behavioral Technology Laboratories. The purpose of this project is to develop training systems that integrate VR with a tutoring system that uses natural dialogue and "learns." For example, an intelligent martial arts tutor would learn the student's fighting style and thus become increasingly difficult for the student to beat. The intelligent tutor would also know what the student has already learned and adjust the training accordingly. The training would take place within an immersive virtual environment, using head-mounted displays and input devices such as 3-D mice and data gloves (Wohl, 2000).

Superscape Inc. specializes in the creation of innovative, high-quality, interactive 3-D applications. Superscape created interactive training materials that visualize a Ford Motor Company factory floor, including forklift trucks, to make plant workers more aware of the potential hazards on the factory floor. The company teamed with Discovery.com to build an application named "Inside the space station," which permits online PC users to control the 3-D space station environment, including docking the space shuttle, rotating solar panels, and manipulating mechanical arms. Superscape has also been heavily involved in the development of 3-D games, including the Harry Potter game for LEGO. The company's Swerve technology has been developed to create games for wireless devices, including the newer mobile phones. Among the games developed using Superscape Swerve technology are MotoGP, Jet Fighter, Astrosmash 3D, Chesscapade, and Speedboat Race (Superscape, 2003).

On the design side, several automobile manufacturers have used VR to assist in the design of automobiles. With this system, an automotive engineer—usually wearing special glasses and a special glove to be able to interact with the system—is able to sit in the driver's seat of a future automobile. The engineer turns the steering wheel and uses buttons and knobs as though he or she were in a real car. By letting the engineer get the feel of this future car, the manufacturer hopes that problems in the dashboard and controls design can be corrected before actual—and expensive—prototypes are even built.

An air conditioning/furnace manufacturer is using VR to permit engineers to walk through an existing or proposed product. By walking through a furnace, for example, the engineer gets a perspective of the design from a completely different vantage point. The engineer starts thinking of all the ways in which the design could be improved that were not obvious before. VR also allows the mock-up of products long before physical prototypes are created. This enables designers to get the real look and feel of the product and even get feedback from focus groups. Imagine sitting in the cab of a large farm combine before it is ever built and getting an understanding of the line of sight that the operator will have. Is the steering wheel blocking important gauges? Where should the mirrors be placed?

VR is increasingly being used for marketing on the Web. Interactive 3-D images of a company's products and services are beginning to appear on company Web sites; these images provide a more comprehensive view of the product as well as differentiate the Web site from those of competitors. Internet Pictures Corp., or iPIX, headquartered in Oak Ridge, Tennessee, is the leader in a field that the company calls "immersive imaging"—the capture, processing, hosting, and distribution of rich media to Internet sites and Internet-enabled devices. Of particular interest are the "virtual tours" created by iPIX for the real estate industry, the travel and hospitality industry, and educational institutions. On these virtual tours, the user logs on the appropriate Web site and can experience a 360-degree view from a particular camera location. If you are house-hunting, you can get a 360-degree view of the living room and the kitchen in a home for sale; if planning a vacation, you can get a 360-degree view of the grounds and the lobby of a resort hotel; if selecting a college, you can get a 360-degree look at key buildings on campus. Figure 7.7 shows a virtual-tour view of the living room of a home for sale in Las Vegas. By using the buttons at the bottom of the picture, the user can turn a full 360 degrees in either direction, stop the movement, or zoom in and out. An even newer use of immersive imaging is to capture up-to-date information about assets in order to be prepared for an emergency. Immersive imaging can provide visual documentation of the layout of facilities and the location of critical elements, such as exits and fire extinguishers, for use by emergency workers; it can also verify compliance with regulatory guidelines (Internet Pictures Corporation, 2003; Ortiz, 2003).

The development of VR is in its infancy, and it will be a long time before anything remotely approaching the Enterprise's holodeck is possible. Nevertheless, many vendors are developing VR hardware and software, and numerous valuable VR applications are beginning to appear.

Figure 7.7 Hometour 360° Virtual Tour of Living Room (Courtesy of Homestore, Inc. Copyright © 2004 Homestore, Inc.)

HOW TO DESIGN CARS AND SCARE CHILDREN

Robert DeBrabant decided to use GM's cutting-edge 3-D virtual-reality technology to entertain 370 children visiting the automaker on its most recent "Take Your Child to Work" day. He had designers create a pterodactyl cartoon character that pokes its beak directly into the faces of the kids sitting in the room and wearing specially designed headsets. The image proved to be a bit too true-to-life: One little girl screamed and started crying.

DeBrabant runs GM's Envisioning Center, a three-screened, theaterlike room where engineers view three-dimensional images of model-car designs. They can view the images from any angle, and at such exact scale that they can walk up to the screen and use rulers to measure the width and height of any detail. Designers can change a car's color at the click of a mouse. They can even reconfigure the way lighting and background affects a model.

The center allows for meticulous inspection of design detail. For example, a designer can manipulate the image of the car until it almost seems that he or she can reach into the interior and manipulate the steering wheel. "Designers can study how much headroom a driver has, how ergonomic the dashboard controls are, and make absolutely sure that every aspect of the vehicle is perfect," DeBrabant says. Engineering teams on different continents frequently interact in virtual reality using the center's collaboration capability and can manipulate the 3-D models as easily as their U.S. counterparts.

[Konicki, 2002]

SUMMARY

We have now completed our two-chapter survey of *intraorganizational* IT application areas. Chapter 6 focused on application areas that support the entire organization or large portions of it, including transaction processing systems, data warehousing, and office automation. At the conclusion of Chapter 6, we argued that modern organizations cannot do business without these enterprise IT systems. In this chapter we have concentrated on managerial support systems such as DSSs, EISs, and neural networks. These managerial support systems are just as critical to the individual managers in a business as the enterprise systems are to the firm as a whole. Modern managers simply cannot manage effectively and efficiently without managerial support IT systems.

Several types of managerial support systems are designed to support *individual* managers in their decision-making endeavors *without* the aid of artificial intelligence. Decision support systems (DSSs), data mining, geographic information systems (GISs), and executive information systems (EISs) all fall into this broad grouping.[1] A DSS is an interactive system, employing a model of some sort, that assists a manager in making decisions in a situation that is not well structured. The prototypical example of a DSS is carrying out what-if analyses on a financial model. Data mining is concerned with digging out nuggets of information from a data warehouse, again using a model; thus data mining can be considered as a subset of the broader DSS construct. A geographic information system is based on spatial relationships; many, but not all, GISs incorporate a model and are used as a DSS. In contrast, an EIS does not usually involve a model. An EIS provides easy online access to current aggregate information about key business conditions. A business intelligence system is a newer variant of an EIS incorporating special tools to capture and display competitive information. In general, a DSS, data mining, or a GIS provides specific information of value to a manager working on a particular problem, while an EIS provides aggregated information of value to a wide range of managers within the firm.

Group support systems (GSSs) and knowledge management systems (KMSs) provide support to a *group* of managers, although in quite different ways. A GSS provides support to a group of managers engaged in some sort of group activity, most commonly an in-person meeting, whereas a KMS is a system for managing organizational knowledge and sharing it with the appropriate group. A GSS, which is a specialized type of groupware, consists of software running on a LAN that permits all meeting participants to simultaneously and anonymously make contributions to the group discussion by keying in their ideas and having them displayed on a large public screen, if desired. The software facilitates various group tasks, such as idea generation, organizing ideas, prioritizing, and policy development. With a KMS, knowledge may be shared within a community of practice (a group of managers with similar interests) via knowledge repositories, discussion forums, and community calendars, or within a broader grouping of employees via a carefully structured package of knowledge content.

[1]This generalization is not entirely correct. Data mining, in particular, may incorporate neural networks—a branch of artificial intelligence—as a technique employed to mine data. Nevertheless, the authors believe that the groupings of managerial support systems given here provide a useful way of summarizing the chapter.

Artificial intelligence (AI) is used to support the *individual* manager in our third grouping of managerial support systems. By capturing the decision-making logic of a human expert, an expert system provides nonexperts with expert advice. A neural network teases out obscure patterns from vast amounts of data by a process of adaptive learning. In both cases the user is led to better decisions via AI. Closely related to AI is virtual reality, where computer-based systems create an environment that seems real to one or more human senses. Virtual reality has proved particularly useful for training and design activities, and it is increasingly being used for marketing on the Web.

We hope that these two chapters have convinced you of the value of these intraorganizational systems. But how does an organization, or an individual manager, acquire one of these potentially valuable systems? The complete answer to this question will have to wait until Part III of this book, entitled "Acquiring Information Systems," but we already have some clues.

The enterprise systems, for example, are primarily large-scale systems that would be purchased from an outside vendor or custom developed by the internal IS organization or an external consulting firm. In particular, enterprise resource planning, office automation, groupware, and factory automation are almost always purchased from an outside vendor. These are all massive systems that require similar functionality across a wide variety of firms. Of course, the internal IS department or a consultant may customize them to the organization. Data warehousing and intranets are often implemented with purchased package software, but there might also be internal or consultant development. Historically, the internal IS organization developed most transaction processing systems, but even these systems are likely to be purchased today, as shown by the growth of ERP systems, unless the firm's requirements are unique.

By contrast, the business manager or a consultant (internal or external to the firm) is likely to develop many managerial support systems expressly for the manager. In most cases the business manager or consultant would start with an underlying software tool (such as a DSS generator, expert systems shell, neural network program, or data mining tool) and develop a specific implementation of the tool that satisfies the need. The manager is unlikely, however, to develop a group support system, EIS, or KM system; these multi-user systems are more akin to enterprise systems in terms of their acquisition.

All these methods of IT system acquisition—purchase of a fully-developed system, development by the internal IS organization or an external consultant, and end-user development—will be explored in detail in Part III.

REVIEW QUESTIONS

1. Describe the three primary components that make up any decision support system and how they interact.
2. Explain the difference between a specific decision support system (DSS) and a DSS generator. Give an example of each.
3. Describe two examples of specific DSSs that are being used to assist in decision making. You may use examples from the textbook or other examples you have read about or heard about.
4. Negotiation support systems (NSSs) and group support systems (GSSs) are both variants of DSSs. Explain how an NSS and a GSS differ from other DSSs.
5. Explain both data warehousing and data mining. How are they related?
6. List at least two techniques (decision technologies) that are used in data mining.
7. List at least three uses of data mining.
8. What is the purpose of a group support system (GSS)? What are the potential advantages and disadvantages of using a GSS?
9. Compare the raster-based and vector-based approaches to geographic information systems (GISs). What are the primary uses of each approach?
10. What are the distinguishing characteristics of an executive information system (EIS)? Why have these systems become a part of business intelligence in many companies?
11. What is knowledge management, and what is a knowledge management system? How does the concept of a community of practice relate to knowledge management?
12. Briefly describe the several areas of artificial intelligence (AI) research. Indicate why we in business are most interested in the expert systems and neural networks areas.
13. What are the three general approaches to obtaining an expert system? What are the pluses and minuses of each approach?
14. Describe two examples of expert systems that are being used to assist in decision making. You may use examples from the textbook or other examples you have read about or heard about.
15. Describe two examples of neural networks that are being used to assist in decision making. You may use examples from the textbook or other examples you have read about or heard about.

16. Describe two examples of the use of virtual reality in an organizational setting. You may use examples from the textbook or other examples you have read about or heard about.

DISCUSSION QUESTIONS

1. Review question 5 asked about the relationship between data warehousing and data mining. In addition to data mining, which of the other application areas discussed in this chapter may be used in conjunction with data warehousing? Explain.
2. Two of the important topics in this chapter are decision support systems (DSSs) and expert systems. Based on your reading of this chapter, you have undoubtedly noticed that these two application areas have a great deal in common. What are the primary distinctions between DSSs and expert systems?
3. Compare group support systems, as described in this chapter, with groupware, as described in Chapter 6. How do these two application areas relate to one another? Which one is most important today? Do you think this will be true in the future?
4. Several examples of geographic information systems were mentioned in the chapter. Consider an industry or a company with which you have some familiarity and identify at least one possible application of GISs in the industry or company. Explain why you think this is a good prospect for a GIS application.
5. Explain the concept of "drilling-down" as used in executive information systems (EIS). Is drilling-down used in other IT applications? How do these applications relate to EIS?
6. Explain the original role that was to be played by an EIS and then describe how this role has been modified over time. Why has this role change occurred?
7. According to the trade press, the success record of knowledge management systems has been spotty. Why do you think this is? What steps must organizations take to give their knowledge management efforts the best chances of succeeding?
8. Several examples of expert systems were mentioned in the chapter. Consider an industry or a company with which you have some familiarity and identify at least one possible application of expert systems in the industry or company. Explain why you think this is a good prospect for an expert system application.
9. Several examples of neural networks were mentioned in the chapter. Consider an industry or a company with which you have some familiarity and identify at least one possible application of neural networks in the industry or company. Explain why you think this is a good prospect for a neural network application.
10. Which of the application areas considered in this chapter is most useful to a small to mid-sized business? Defend your answer.

CHAPTER 8
E-COMMERCE APPLICATIONS

As discussed in Chapter 1, today we are in the early years of an e-world: a new digital economy in which a global network of computers links individuals, organizations, and nations in real time. Chapter 6 and Chapter 7 focused on enterprise-wide applications and managerial support systems. This chapter focuses on **electronic commerce** (e-commerce) applications that are designed to extend an organization's reach beyond its own organizational boundaries and to interact with customers, suppliers, and other business partners.

Although e-commerce applications to conduct business transactions beyond organizational boundaries did not originate with the Web, the development of the first commercial Web browser (Netscape Navigator) in the mid-1990s led to an explosive demand for the development of commercial Web sites: hypertext applications stored on Web servers connected to the Internet. By the end of the 1990s, online ways of gathering information and conducting business had become a new way of doing business for many U.S.-based businesses, and new terminology had entered the vernacular to describe them.

> **Electronic commerce** is the electronic transmission of buyer/seller transactions and related information between individuals and businesses or between two or more businesses that are trading partners.

For example, one of the most visible phenomena has been the emergence of new businesses that communicate with their customers online and gain revenues entirely based on traffic to their Web sites, referred to as "pure-plays" or **dot-coms** (an artifact of the suffix ".com" in the Internet domain address for commercial organizations). Between 2000 and 2002, many of these dot-com firms closed, and many investors lost money due to stock holdings or venture capital invested in dot-com and related information technology (IT) companies.

However, at the same time that this dot-com meltdown was occurring, traditional (bricks-and-mortar) businesses that existed before the Web were continuing to learn how to design and implement e-commerce applications to complement, extend, or even transform their ways of doing business—and to regain some of the market share won by the dot-com start-ups in the preceding years. Traditional companies that integrate *offline and online* business strategies are referred to today as "bricks-and-clicks" or **clicks-and-mortar** firms.

In the following section we give a brief history of the Internet and the major IT innovations that led to its rapid growth. (For detailed discussions, see the technology chapters in Part I.) Since legal and regulatory environments also have affected the

Internet's growth, we also provide a brief discussion of some important legislative impacts. (For a fuller discussion of these issues, see Chapter 16 in Part IV.)

We then turn to a discussion of the Internet's potential influence on strategic opportunities and threats at both the industry level and the individual business level. Examples of successful business-to-consumer (**B2C**) and business-to-business (**B2B**) applications for different types of e-business models (including direct-to-customer retailing and online intermediaries) will then be described in detail. The chapter ends with a discussion of what makes a good Web site from a customer perspective.

Continued growth in e-commerce application investments has been forecast for the near future due to the proven advantages of conducting business via the Internet: This open communications network of networks has a relatively cheap entry cost, a transmission speed measured in microseconds or seconds, a multimedia communications capability via the Web, and a global reach to other businesses as well as a growing number of potential customers. A more theoretical explanation for why the Internet is likely to become an even more attractive vehicle for e-commerce in the coming years is provided by **Metcalfe's Law**, which states that

> *the value of a network to each of its members is proportional to the number of other users, expressed as* $(n^2 - n) / 2$.

Stated differently, there are increasing returns to be gained as more and more organizations create Web sites and more individuals gain access to the Internet.

E-COMMERCE TECHNOLOGIES

The *commercial* history of the Internet is actually quite short. The Internet has its roots in **ARPANET,** a network of federal government and research and development firms in the private sector that grew to include educational institutions and other nonprofit organizations outside of the United States. In 1991 the nonprofit organization in the United States responsible for managing the Internet backbone at that time (the National Science Foundation) lifted the original ban on commercial usage of the Internet. In 1994 the first commercial **Web browser** was released as a free product by its developers in an attempt to quickly build demand for its software and services. The rapid diffusion of first the Netscape browser and then Microsoft's browser (Internet Explorer), quickly ushered in the opportunity for businesses connected to the Internet anywhere in the world to reach individual consumers and other businesses.

Today, the Internet is a network of computer networks that use the Transmission Control Protocol/Internet Protocol (TCP/IP) protocol with gateways to even more networks that do not use the TCP/IP protocol. The Web (World Wide Web) is a subset of the Internet, with multimedia capabilities. Web documents are composed in standard markup languages (Hypertext Markup Language [HTML]) and stored on servers around the globe with standard addresses (Uniform Resource Locators [URLs]) that are accessible via a hypermedia protocol (Hypertext Transfer Protocol [HTTP]). Initially, these Web technologies were created for a scientific community to exchange documents.

No single organization owns the Internet; each organization or end user pays for its software and hardware (for clients and servers) and network access. Beginning in 1993, the rights for registering Web site addresses (domain names) were held solely by a U.S. federal contractor, Network Solutions Inc., but site registration is now overseen by ICANN, the Internet Corporation for Assigned Names and Numbers.

Figure 8.1 summarizes some of the major IT developments since the commercial introduction of the browser. Commercial organizations initially created a "Web presence" with hyperlinked text documents for their stakeholders (customers, shareholders) and the public. Web technologies to support interactivity with the user were then developed, along with flashier designs to capture the "eyeballs" of Web site visitors. By 1998 the term Web "portal" emerged to refer to sites that were designed to be a user's initial gateway to other Web sites.

Technologies for B2C Applications

The implementation of secure ways to transmit sensitive transactions and a standard for credit card processing by 1998 were catalysts for the development of Web sites with online sales and service capabilities. By this time the Internet had become a proven channel for supply chain and customer-facing business interactions that held the potential for a competitive advantage. Web developers began to focus on technologies not only to improve the online sales or auction bidding experiences, but also to provide new channels for around-the-clock customer service. The collection of clickstream metrics and personal data from Web site users, as well as the acceptance of Web "**cookies**" stored on the user's hard drive, enabled the customization of Web sites for the individual or organizational user. Web browsers also continually improved in functionality and ease-of-use, and by the new millennium they provided a standard interface to access interactive multimedia (audio, video, animation), with essentially no special end-user training.

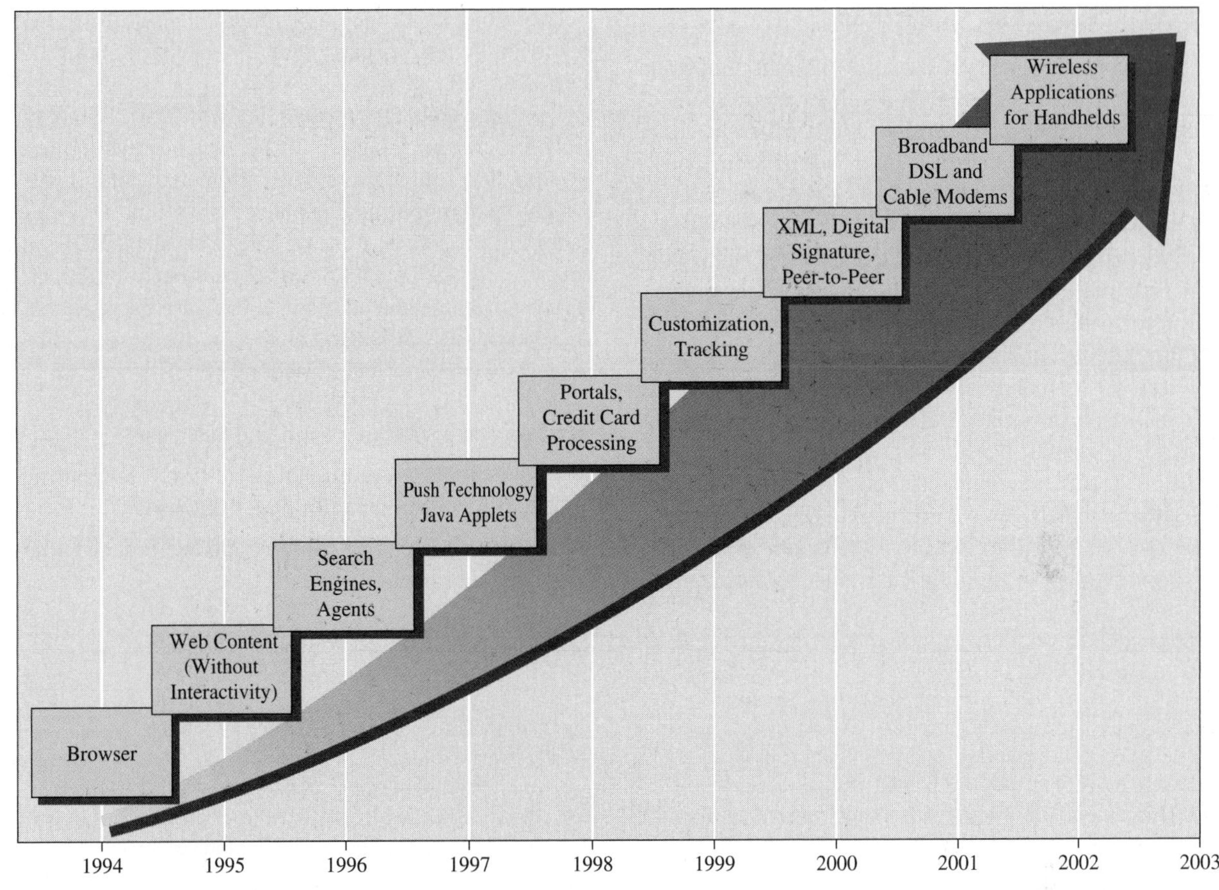

Figure 8.1 Internet Technology Innovations for E-Commerce

Compared to e-mail or the telephone, the Web is therefore a richer communications medium, even with the narrowband connections using "plain old" telephone lines or wireless networks. However, in the United States during the early 2000s, broadband access via cable modems or digital subscriber line (DSL) telephone lines became increasingly available in, or near, U.S. cities or towns with a sizable population: between May and November 2003 alone, at-home broadband connections in the United States increased by 27 percent (Nielsen/Net Ratings, 2003). Increased broadband access to the home users also enabled virtual reality applications in which a consumer can "walk through" a mall, be "measured" for clothing, "try out" a toy, or "view" real estate that is for sale.

By 2004 handheld cellular devices with Internet access that had been more heavily used in other countries (e.g., Finland and Japan), were also fueling IT innovations for mobile e-commerce applications (**m-commerce**). The rate of growth of m-commerce applications in the United States is expected to be dependent on the emergence of standard and secure wireless networks, as well as applications designed to address the constraints of small, handheld devices that might only be used for short periods of time and in physical environments with very different characteristics (e.g., noise, lighting) than the typical portable laptop computer.

The past decade has also seen technology innovations that enable peer-to-peer (**P2P**) applications. The promise of P2P was rapidly recognized due the fast rise of a music-sharing service (using an MP3 standard) via the Napster.com Web site. However, the initial version of the Web site was short-lived: it was found to be in violation of U.S. copyright laws and shut down by the federal government. Today, other Web sites facilitate P2P file-sharing between client computers using a different business model, and a similar concept, called **grid computing**, that takes advantage of unused computer processing power on desktops to accomplish massive parallel processing computations.

Technologies for B2B Applications

From an economic standpoint, one of the most important technology advances has been the development of standards for a markup language (eXtensible Markup Language, or **XML**) to facilitate the transmission of business documents via B2B applications. XML standards have been endorsed by the cross-industry World Wide Web Consortium (**W3C**), and XML has become a standard language for enabling e-business activities due to its precise "tagging" capabilities. XML also enables a flexible, low-entry form of **electronic data interchange,** or **EDI** applications).

Before the commercialization of the Internet, many companies had developed IT solutions for e-commerce with trading partners based on agreed-upon standards for business document transmission, using proprietary applications that became known as EDI. By the early 1990s over half of the Fortune 1000 had implemented EDI applications using a private telecommunications network of leased lines or a value-added network (VAN) provided by a third party (see the sidebar entitled "How EDI Works").

For large discount retailers like Wal-Mart, EDI applications became an integral part of their business strategies. For large manufacturers, the automated data flows between business partners enabled just-in-time (JIT) manufacturing processes. For example, Chrysler's EDI system in the early 1990s supported 17 million transactions per year with a portion of its 1,600 external suppliers. For these large firms, the costs of developing these customized systems were more than offset by benefits such as

- reduced cycle times for doing business
- cost savings for automated transaction handling and the elimination of paper documents
- improved interfirm coordination and reduced interfirm coordination costs

HOW EDI WORKS

EDI is usually implemented by computer-to-computer communication between organizations. A customer sends a supplier a purchase order or release to a blanket order via a standard electronic document. There is no manual shuffling of paperwork and little, if any, reentering of data. The supplier's computer system checks that the message is in an acceptable format and sends an electronic acknowledgment to the customer. The electronic order then feeds the supplier's production planning and shipping systems to schedule the shipment.

When the order is ready to ship, the supplier sends the customer an electronic notice of the pending shipment. The customer's computer checks that the shipment information corresponds to the order and returns a message authorizing the shipment. The supplier then sends a message that includes the truck number, carrier, approximate arrival time, and bill of lading. The customer's computer alerts the receiving dock of the expected arrival; receiving personnel visually verify the shipment upon arrival for quality, and the shipment is accepted.

A contract signed by EDI business partners determines when an electronic order is legally binding, which could be when it is delivered, after the message is read, or after it has been checked. A contract also determines whether all messages must be acknowledged. Usually, the customer must guarantee that if it issues a correctly formatted and acknowledged order, then it is obliged to accept and pay for the requested goods.

The technical success of EDI depends on standards. Standards for EDI are necessary because computer file formats, forms, data and transaction definitions, and the overall methods of processing data can vary considerably across companies and especially across countries. Standards provide a way to decouple the different EDI participants as much as possible, yet still facilitate data exchange.

An electronic business document is called a transaction set. Header and trailer records contain batch control information, such as the unique identifiers of the sender and receiver, a date, the number of line segments, and so on. Each transaction set also has a unique identification number and a time stamp. An EDI translation program converts an incoming EDI format so that it can be read by an application program, and vice versa.

The specific standard for a transaction set is established between the business partners of an EDI relationship. EDI standards are of three types: proprietary formats designed for one or more organizations and their trading partners, industry-specific formats that are designed to match specific industry needs (e.g., automotive), and generic formats for use by any trading partners. In some industries a major industry player or a consortium of companies have established a standard, whereas in other industries a formal body with large representation may have established a standard.

The American National Standards Institute (ANSI) has coordinated standard-setting activities in the United States. ANSI X.12 formats exist for standard documents in many U.S. industries—including chemicals, automotive, retail merchants, textiles, and electrical equipment. Some of these U.S. standards were developed by an industry group. For example, the Automotive Industry Action Group (AIAG) was created by Ford, General Motors, and Chrysler along with 300 large suppliers. For some industries, the usage of uniform standards for product identification (product codes) is also key to EDI cost savings.

Nevertheless, according to Senn (2000), fewer than 100,000 out of the several million potential business users of EDI applications within the United States had implemented EDI due to constraints such as

- start-up coordination challenges (including EDI standard agreements and legal issues)
- start-up and ongoing IT costs for one or more of the trading partners (including the maintenance of the proprietary systems and the high costs of third-party VANs)

Because of these EDI shortcomings and the development of a secure digital signature capability (see the sidebar entitled "Digital Signatures"), industry watchers projected that B2B applications would grow very rapidly in the first half-decade of the new millennium. Although this projected rate of growth was overly optimistic, and Web-based XML is still considered less efficient than proprietary EDI applications for well-defined, repetitive, and high-volume transactions with business partners, the usage of Web forms with XML "tags" in combination with extranet applications is expected to continue to grow.

DIGITAL SIGNATURES

Digital signatures use cryptography to convert data into a secret code for transmission over a public network. These technologies are often considered the most secure and reliable form of electronic signature because they use public-key infrastructure technologies to ensure that the electronic message has not been altered during transmission.

Say you wanted to draft and complete a contract with a customer using a digital signature. To do so, you'd first have to acquire a digital certificate—the electronic equivalent of an ID card. Several companies, including VeriSign and Entrust Technologies, are licensed to issue such certificates. Once you sign up, the provider transmits the certificate to your computer. You also receive two digital keys—one private and one public.

To sign a document, you enter a password or PIN and affix your electronic signature—the private key—to the document. The person or company receiving your document would then use the public key to unlock your certificate and verify that the signature is valid. Once confirmed, they could sign the document using their own digital tools and return it to you. Throughout the process, the software documents the date and time of each signing, while built-in security measures ensure that the documents haven't been altered anywhere along the process.

[J. Brown, 2000]

Web technologies have also been used to develop e-marketplaces (or exchanges) hosted by buyers, suppliers, third-party service providers, or a consortia of buyers or suppliers. The recent trend has been for companies to create their own B2B applications to support bids from their preferred suppliers or customer orders, using off-the-shelf software from software vendors such as Ariba, Inc., and Commerce One, Inc., that supports alternative EDI transmission methods. However, the economic recession in the United States that began in March 2000 severely "dampened" the rate of investments in Internet-related B2B innovations. After the huge IT expenditures for Y2K and euro compliance had been paid for, an e-business "reality check" set in and the venture capitalists began to demand profits, not just promises, from the Internet-related start-ups. Despite this slow-down in IT innovations, the growth of the commercial usage of the Internet has continued to evolve as traditional companies have learned to leverage earlier IT innovations *as well as business innovations*. The economic slowdown has also led to a better balance between the demand and supply of IT personnel who are skilled in Web technologies.

Technologies for IT Security

One of the biggest potential constraints to the diffusion of Internet-based e-commerce applications for consumers, as well as for businesses, was the initial lack of security for Internet transactions. Two major security issues are how to control access to a computer that is physically networked to the Internet and how to ensure that the security of a given communication, such as a business transaction, is not violated.

The primary way to control access to corporate or individual computers is by means of a **firewall**. Firewalls are devices that sit between the Internet and an organization's internal network (or an individual's computer) in order to block intrusions from unauthorized users and hackers from remote sites. A firewall can be a router, a personal computer, a host, or a collection of hosts. A company's public Web site typically sits outside the firewall, and many firms use outside vendors to host their external Web sites for not only security reasons but also for peak load balancing. Unknown to the Web site user, a company's Web site may therefore be on a vendor's server, and e-mail or other communications may initially be received by a third party, not a computer (or person) internal to the company that owns the domain name.

Encryption is the primary way to ensure the security of a business transaction or other communication. Today's encryption systems are based on two decoding keys and

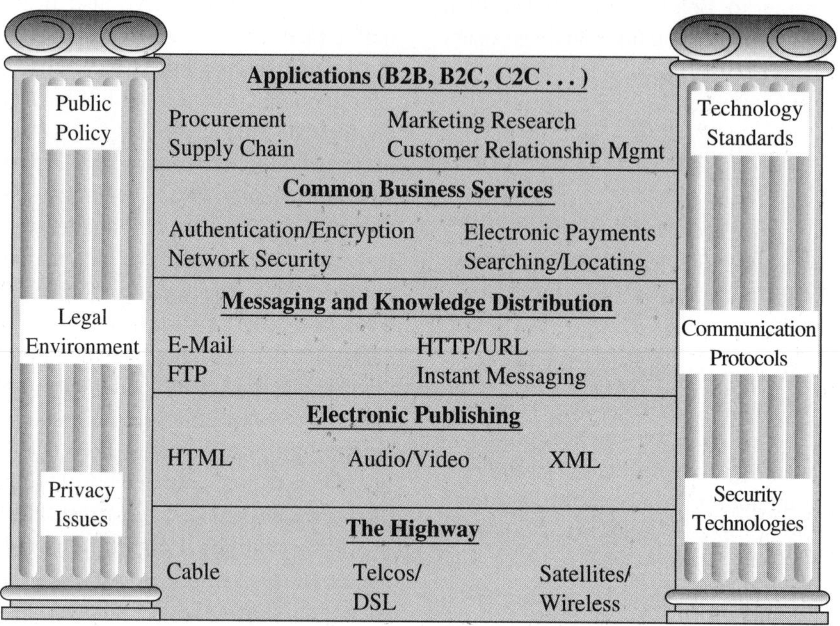

Figure 8.2 E-Commerce Framework (Adapted from Applegate, Holsapple, et al. 1996; Kalakota and Whinston, 1996)

mathematical principles for factoring a product into its two prime numbers. One decoding key is used to encipher (code) a message; a second decoding key is used to decipher it. The enciphering key makes it easy to encode a message, but deciphering requires a key available only to the message's intended recipient. If the enciphering key is the product of two very large prime numbers, the key is expected to have a relatively long life before being vulnerable to a hacker. For example, it took a group of 600 academics and hobbyists using computers of 1993 vintage just under 1 year to identify the two prime numbers for a 129-digit product. A somewhat larger product is estimated to be indecipherable within a person's lifetime (Gates, 1995).

An Internet standard for secure transactions for payment via credit card systems was initiated in 1996 by a consortium that included banks, two major credit card players (MasterCard and Visa), and other major industry players (GTE, IBM Corp., Microsoft Corporation, Netscape). The first version of this new standard, Secure Electronic Transaction (SET), was released in June 1997. Similarly, the implementation of a digital signature capability was viewed as a catalyst for B2B applications.

Companies have also made IT security investments in order to protect the corporation from intentional attacks and viruses that originate with Internet communications. In particular, programs that exploit security flaws in Microsoft's operating systems or application programs have been major targets. In most cases software vendors had already identified the flaws, but companies had not kept up-to-date with security patches made available on the vendor's Web site. As discussed in some detail in Chapter 16, denial-of-service and intentional virus attacks are criminal acts, and the legal systems of national governments need to play strong legislative and oversight roles to help businesses and individuals avoid the high costs of recovering from intentional security breaches.

As shown in Figure 8.2, the IT applications, services, and communications technologies that enable e-commerce depend on two types of pillars: a technology pillar and a legal and regulatory environment pillar. The standards for the Web have evolved under the guidance of consortia such as the W3C, industry consortia, as well as various watchdog groups. These activities are part of the right-hand support pillar in Figure 8.2. The left-hand support pillar includes actions by governments and legal systems, which we will discuss in the following section.

LEGAL AND REGULATORY ENVIRONMENT

Given the Internet's origins and short commercial life, the legal and regulatory environment in the United States has played a major role in shaping the Internet's capabilities for e-commerce as it exists today. However, we expect the role of the U.S. government to be less dominant in the coming years, as the Internet user population grows and the global **digital divide** becomes less severe.

Below we briefly discuss four issues that have been at the forefront of public concern within the United States: tax policies, copyright laws, antitrust (monopoly) laws, and privacy issues.

Tax Policies

Within the United States, taxes on sales of products and services are collected at the state level. Given the lack of physical geography associated with online purchase transactions over the Internet, the development of a uniform sales tax policy requires federal action. During the years of early Internet growh under President Bill Clinton, the executive branch of the federal government supported a "hands-off" policy for taxing Web-based sales as a deliberate attempt to foster the growth of a global superhighway. The government's vision was for a national information superhighway that would link homes, businesses, and government, and IT innovations for e-commerce were expected to fuel the development of the infrastructure to make this a reality.

In October 2001 this federal policy was scheduled to be reconsidered by Congress, and opposition to a hands-off policy had been growing under lobbying efforts by groups such as the National Retail Federation and the International Council of Shopping Centers. However, the September 11, 2001 terrorist attacks on the United States diverted attention from sales tax revenues to security concerns, and the hands-off policy was not replaced. By 2004, however, many state governments had begun taxing Internet purchases, and there was a multi-state government initiative underway to develop an interstate tax program with common collection and audit procedures (referred to as the Streamlined Sales Tax Project).

Copyright Laws

In the United States most major software vendors have been involved in a copyright suit at some time in the recent past. In 2001 the most closely watched copyright suit involved the P2P file-sharing service operated by Napster.com, which was found to be in violation of copyright laws and was closed down. In 2004 the court challenge by The SCO Group against the GPL licensing of the Linux operating system is expected to continue to receive considerable media attention.

Given the galloping rate of IT innovations, software copyrights have been difficult to enforce at a national level. Intellectual copyright laws in general also continue to be difficult to enforce at an international level, as the laws that exist in the United States are not upheld by many countries outside Western Europe and North America.

Antitrust Laws

The two biggest antitrust lawsuits by the Department of Justice against IT industry companies have involved monopoly violations by AT&T and Microsoft.

The 1982 ruling against AT&T ("Ma Bell") led to the 1984 creation of regional carriers ("Baby Bells") as local carriers. The 1996 Telecommunications Act opened up retail markets still further and led to mergers among Baby Bells and other carriers. By 2004 the telecommunications industry was still a hypercompetitive industry that included cable, wireless, regional carriers, long-distance providers, and Internet service providers (ISPs) competing against one another, acquiring spin-offs, and merging with one another.

In early 2000 a federal court judge ruled that Microsoft was in violation of antitust laws due to its tight coupling of its Windows operating systems and its Internet Explorer browser. However, the potential penalty of splitting up Microsoft into two companies—one company for systems software (e.g., Windows) and one company for application software (e.g., Microsoft Office suite)—was not invoked. By the end of 2003, Microsoft products still dominated the desktop operating system, browser, and office productivity suite markets.

Whether the U.S. and European antitrust laws will become an obstacle to global competition for IT industry companies in the near future is an unanswered question. However, one irony is already apparent: a key enabler for the rapid diffusion of the Internet has been the existence of Microsoft products as industry "standards" not only in the United States but also in most multinational firms.

Privacy Issues

The first privacy legislation within the United States dates from the 1970s. However, privacy issues associated with individual consumer data have gained significant attention within the United States with the growth of e-commerce applications and the continued introduction of new technologies to capture consumer data and behaviors, including the usage of cookies. To date, privacy-rights advocacy groups have played a major role in ensuring that companies have, and uphold, privacy standards. For example, when a top Internet advertising firm, DoubleClick, revealed its plans for user profiling (by combining anonymous data about Web surfers with personal information stored in other consumer databases), advocacy groups sent out an alert, the Federal Trade Commission (FTC) began to investigate, and DoubleClick aborted its plan (see also the discussion in Chapter 16).

Watchdog groups and nonprofit organizations have also been a deterrent to individual data misuse by Web site owners. By end of 2002, more than 90 percent of U.S.-based retailing Web sites provided explicit statements of their own privacy policies—what the firm will or will not do with any individual data collected from usage of their Web site (E-Tailing Group, 2002). Independent organizations also administer programs that validate a firm's responsible behavior toward Web site visitors, and the approved commercial Web site typically displays a visible logo signalling their validated trustworthiness (see the sidebar entitled "TRUSTe Trustmark").

TRUSTe TRUSTMARK

TRUSTe believes that an environment of mutual trust and openness will help make and keep the Internet a free, comfortable, and richly diverse community for everyone. As an Internet user, you have a right to expect online privacy and the responsibility to exercise choice over how your personal information is collected, used, and shared by Web sites. The TRUSTe program was designed expressly to ensure that your privacy is protected through open disclosure and to empower you to make informed choices.

A cornerstone of our program is the TRUSTe "trustmark," an online branded seal displayed by member Web sites. The trustmark is awarded only to sites that adhere to established privacy principles and agree to comply with ongoing TRUSTe oversight and consumer resolution procedures. Privacy principles embody fair information practices approved by the U.S. Department of Commerce, Federal Trade Commission, and prominent industry-represented organizations and associations. The principles include:

- **Adoption and implementation of a privacy policy** that takes into account consumer anxiety over sharing personal information online.
- **Notice and disclosure** of information collection and use practices.
- **Choice and consent**, giving users the opportunity to exercise control over their information.
- **Data security and quality and access** measures to help protect the security and accuracy of personally identifiable information.

[TRUSTe Web site, accessed January 2004. Logo used with permission of TRUSTe.]

However, it should be kept in mind that until now the U.S. brand of capitalism and the U.S. laws protecting freedom of expression have been the primary shapers of e-commerce because of the historical roots of the Internet and the Silicon Valley innovations of the past decade. As more non-U.S. businesses conduct e-commerce via the Internet, the influence of U.S. approaches will be less dominant, and international agreements are expected to become more important.

STRATEGIC OPPORTUNITIES AND THREATS

Frameworks for thinking about a firm's strategic opportunities and threats have been developed by management strategy guru Michael E. Porter since the early 1980s. In particular, management strategists have used Porter's **competitive forces model** to help businesses anticipate and plan strategic responses to the competitive forces within a firm's industry (Porter, 1985; Porter and Millar, 1985). The five competitive forces are: supplier power, customer power, the threat of new entrants (same products/services), the threat of substitute products/services, and the responses of competitors within the same industry to any of these same forces.

Porter's competitive forces model can also be a useful starting place for thinking about the commercial opportunities and threats introduced by the Internet at the industry level. Figure 8.3 summarizes Porter's general predictions due to the influence of the Internet from the perspective of a traditional company: potential opportunities are shown with a plus (+) sign, potential threats with a minus (–) sign (Porter, 2001).

Looking first at the opportunities due to the Internet that Porter identifies, Porter concludes that (1) the procurement of supplies via the Internet can increase the traditional company's power over its suppliers, (2) the size of a potential market is expanded due to the Internet, and (3) powerful distribution channels between the traditional company and its customers can be eliminated. The first and third opportunities here refer to the potential to bypass companies between the producer or service provider and the customer for that product or service.

However, as can be seen in Figure 8.3, Porter also identifies a large number of threats to the traditional company due to the Internet. Among these threats are:

1. There is a migration to price competition because it's difficult to keep product or service offerings proprietary.
2. The widening of the geographic markets increases the number of potential competitors.

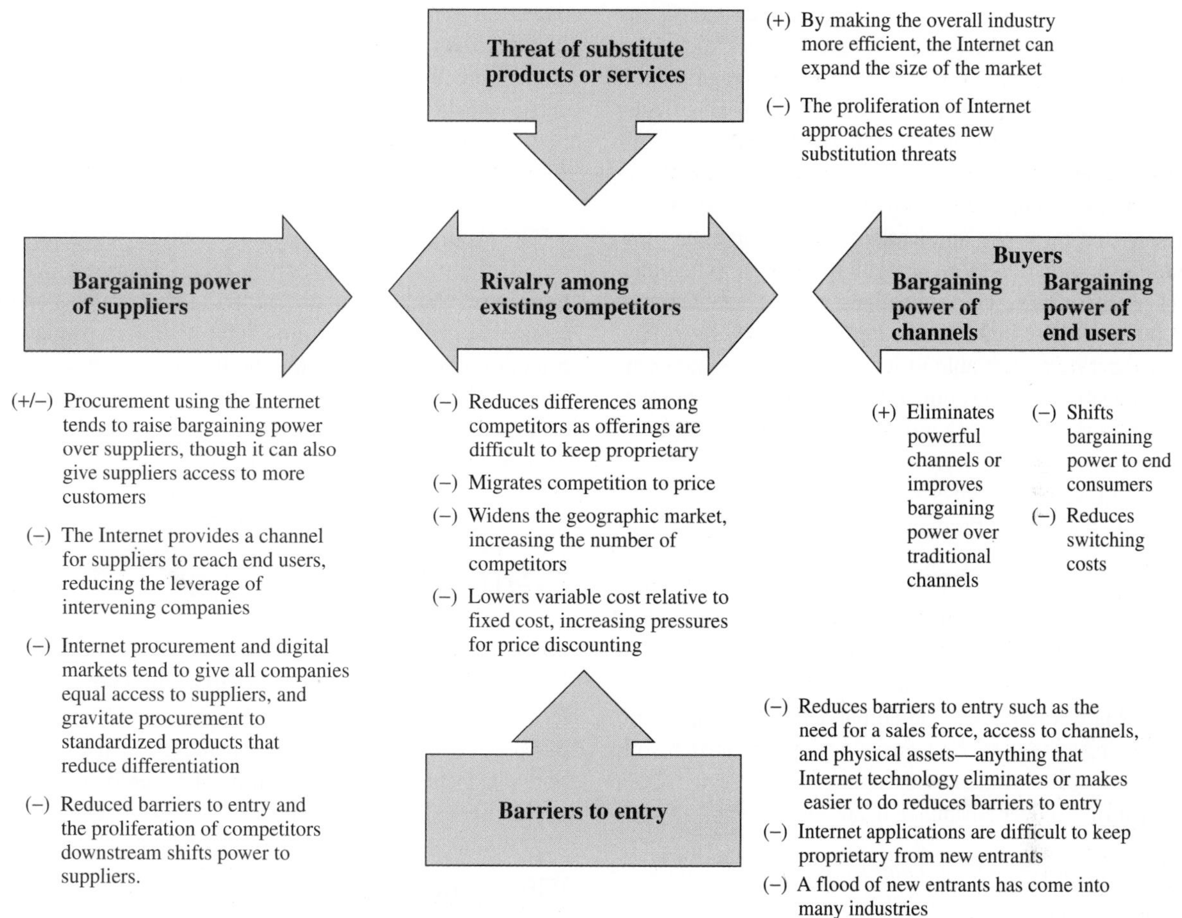
How the Internet Influences Industry Structure
Threat of substitute products or services
(+) By making the overall industry more efficient, the Internet can expand the size of the market
(–) The proliferation of Internet approaches creates new substitution threats
Bargaining power of suppliers
Rivalry among existing competitors
Buyers
Bargaining power of channels
Bargaining power of end users
(+/–) Procurement using the Internet tends to raise bargaining power over suppliers, though it can also give suppliers access to more customers
(–) The Internet provides a channel for suppliers to reach end users, reducing the leverage of intervening companies
(–) Internet procurement and digital markets tend to give all companies equal access to suppliers, and gravitate procurement to standardized products that reduce differentiation
(–) Reduced barriers to entry and the proliferation of competitors downstream shifts power to suppliers.
(–) Reduces differences among competitors as offerings are difficult to keep proprietary
(–) Migrates competition to price
(–) Widens the geographic market, increasing the number of competitors
(–) Lowers variable cost relative to fixed cost, increasing pressures for price discounting
(+) Eliminates powerful channels or improves bargaining power over traditional channels
(–) Shifts bargaining power to end consumers
(–) Reduces switching costs
Barriers to entry
(–) Reduces barriers to entry such as the need for a sales force, access to channels, and physical assets—anything that Internet technology eliminates or makes easier to do reduces barriers to entry
(–) Internet applications are difficult to keep proprietary from new entrants
(–) A flood of new entrants has come into many industries

Figure 8.3 How the Internet Influences Industry Structure (Reprinted by permission of *Harvard Business Review*. "How the Internet Influences Industry Structure," by Michael Porter. *Harvard Business Review* March 2001. Copyright © 2004 by the Harvard Business School Publishing Corporation. All rights reserved.)

3. The Internet reduces or eliminates some traditional barriers, such as the need for an in-person sales force and distribution channels.
4. Customers increase their bargaining power as the Internet reduces switching costs for the customer.

The third threat captures the concern that new dot-com competitors might be able to quickly chip away at a traditional firm's profit margins (Ghosh, 1998) due to the ease and speed with which a Web site can be introduced. The first and fourth threats suggest that it will be much more difficult for a company to compete based on differentiation—i.e., the differentiation of the company's products or services based on quality, customer service, or some other unique value perceived by the customer.

Of course, there is a potential danger in using competitive models that were initially based on ways of doing business in earlier decades. For example, Porter's model fosters single-industry thinking, but the Internet provides the potential for cross-industry alliances and marketplaces not possible in the offline world. Porter's 5-force model was conceptually developed two decades ago, when we did not have a global computer network to link commercial businesses with one another and to people across the world. Another potential shortcoming is the masking of the potential for new kinds of dot-com intermediaries to exist between a firm and its customers, as well as between a firm and its suppliers. As will be seen from our examples in subsequent sections of this chapter, the digital nature and global reach of the Internet also makes possible new online aggregators of information and business transactions between multiple buyers and sellers.

When considering the strategic opportunities and threats associated with the Internet, two pre-Internet "lessons" about using IT to provide a competitive advantage should also be considered. The first pre-Internet lesson is that a competitive advantage is likely to be sustainable for an appreciable time if the IT application was designed to leverage a unique competitive capability or strength of the company that owns the application, as this makes the impact of the application more difficult to replicate (Clemons, 1991). For example, IT applications using new handheld computer technologies that were implemented by Frito-Lay, Inc., in the 1980s were able to leverage a preexisting competitive capability of the company: a superior sales and distribution workforce. The handheld computers enabled the direct sales force to be even more effective in pricing promotions for different types of retail outlets that sold its highly perishable food products. IT also eliminated a lot of evening paperwork for the salesperson.

A second pre-Internet lesson was that although sometimes an early-mover advantage is possible, "first movers"—that is, firms that implement an innovative IT application first—do not necessarily gain a sustainable competitive advantage. Marc Andreessen, the cofounder of Netscape, who saw the company lose its first-mover advantage to Microsoft, has warned of the pitfalls of assuming that there will be a long-term first-mover advantage in an Internet era:

> *Most first movers end up lying facedown in the sand, with other people coming along and learning from their mistakes. . . . Being the first mover with the right approach is very important. Being the first mover with the wrong approach means you're dead.*
>
> —MARK ANDREESSEN (as quoted in Anders, 2001)

For example, American Airlines was *not* the first airline to develop an online reservation system for travel agents to connect to but instead was a fast follower with its SABRE rservation system. Initially, the SABRE system saved the travel agent the time and cost of calling an AA salesperson. When the airline industry was deregulated in 1978, the system was expanded to service reservations for all major airline carriers, who paid a transaction fee for each ticket sold. Its parent firm (the AMR Corporation) continued to invest in its online reservation system and expanded its offerings to include other travel industry businesses that relied on travel agents for some of their sales (such as hotels and rental cars). It became the market leader in airline ticket sales and gained control over a primary sales channel for the travel industry; by the end of the 1990s it was one of the largest privately owned computer systems in the world. The SABRE group was also one of the first in the travel industry to form strategic alliances with businesses in other industries, such as an alliance in which Citibank credit card purchases earned frequent flyer credits with American Airlines. These investments were able to provide a sustainable competitive advantage for AMR for almost three decades.

In the e-world of the second half of the 1990s, the SABRE group initially leveraged its earlier online reservation system and alliances with travel businesses to launch a B2C Web site (Travelocity.com) that bypassed its traditional intermediary: the travel agent. However, within a few years it had lost its differentiation advantages and was competing with other online intermediaries primarily on price: as predicted by Porter, the Internet lowered the entry barriers, and the new competition led to lower switching costs for the customer and price visibility that before had only been visible to the travel agent.

E-BUSINESS MODELS

Porter's 5-forces model establishes a starting point for thinking about competitive moves within an industry. Before looking at new business models for e-commerce from the perspective of an individual company, let us first discuss the potential benefits for two dominant types of e-commerce applications: B2C and B2B.

B2C Applications

The growth of business-to-consumer (B2C) e-commerce worldwide depends on the number of consumers that have Internet access. Between 2000 and 2002 the number of U.S. consumers who bought a product online increased 78 percent, the number who made a travel reservation online increased 90 percent, and the number who did banking online increased by 164 percent (Pew, 2002). The demographics of Web users within the United States have also become more mainstream (Greenspan, 2004): The number of men and women is approximately equal and the largest age group of Americans (ages 30 to 49) is also the largest user group (47 percent of total users).

The 1999 Christmas holiday season is usually pointed to as a major event in the e-commerce evolution: Online shopping approached 1 percent of holiday retail sales within the United States for the first time. By 2003 the percentage of online sales had approached 5 percent. In addition, Web sites are beneficial to users not only for online purchasing, but also for other types of prepurchase and postpurchase support. For example, based on one survey of Web users during the 2000 holiday period, 24 percent actually bought gifts online, but another 32 percent used the sites for price comparisons and the remaining 45 percent used the Web to look for gift ideas online (Schwartz, 2001).

The potential seller benefits from B2C applications will, of course, depend on the market in which the seller competes and whether companies in the industry traditionally have sold directly to consumers. However, as summarized in Figure 8.4, the potential benefits include lower sales channel costs, an extended customer reach, an around-the-clock sales and service capability, as well as new ways to do market research. If a product or service can be digitized, it might also be possible to complete not only an online sale, but also an immediate online distribution of the product or service to the customer.

B2B Applications

Although the early B2B applications were proprietary EDI systems using private networks that were not economically feasible for many smaller businesses, by the early 1990s there was a large installed base of these systems. Because these proprietary systems were also highly reliable and efficient, it has taken several years for businesses to be willing to invest in Internet technologies to either complement or replace these early proprietary systems. Similar to the benefits achievable with EDI applications, B2B applications via the Internet can increase the speed and decrease the transaction costs for transactions with business suppliers and business customer.

In addition, however, B2B applications via the Internet can be used to achieve other benefits: (1) linkages with new suppliers and new business customers, including the creation of new marketplace exchanges for buyers and sellers that have no geographic boundaries, and (2) improved relationships with suppliers and customers. Stated differently, B2B e-commerce enables firms to optimize a "web" of transactions and relationships between buyers and sellers (Applegate et al., 1996). Many of these applications use extranets and are a type of supply-chain system (as described in Chapter 6). Although the predictions for the growth of this type of B2B e-commerce were too optimistic at the end of the 1990s, the expectation is that both the United States and Europe will make major B2B technology investments during the first decade of the new millennium (CyberAtlas, 2002).

Just as new dot-com companies emerged for B2C or C2C e-commerce, dot-com companies for B2B e-commerce began to emerge in the mid-1990s. Many of these dot-com companies were a new kind of online intermediary: exchanges that created a marketplace in cyberspace for buyers and sellers. However, just as there was a dot-com meltdown for B2C sites beginning in March 2000, a large number of early dot-com B2B sites also closed down by the end of 2002.

Figure 8.5 provides one explanation for the lack of survival of the B2B dot-coms that were a new type of online intermediary: independent intermediaries will not survive if there are highly consolidated buyer markets or highly consolidated seller markets.

Stated differently, the survival of an independent intermediary depends on the fragmentation of both its buyers and sellers: It needs to compete in a marketplace in which there is a highly fragmented base of sellers as well as a highly fragmented base of buyers. As shown in Figure 8.5, if the number of buyers is small, the buyers will have a lot of "buyer power" and will not likely want to pay an independent intermediary for an online service that they could provide themselves. Similarly, if the number of sellers is small, the sellers will theoretically use their own supplier power rather than pay an intermediary for an online service that they could provide themselves.

Another alternative is for a group of buyers or sellers to band together, as a consortium or other type of alliance, to create their own intermediary. One example of this consortium approach is Covisint (pronounced coh-viz-int), which

Seller Benefits	Buyer Benefits
24/7 access to customer for sales and support	Sales and service anytime, anywhere
Lower costs from online channel	Easy access to product/service information
Multimedia opportunities for marketing	Easy access to product/service pricing
New ways to research potential markets	Agents to help find things, compare costs, and complete a sale
New ways to distribute (if product/service can be digitized)	Immediate delivery of digitized product/service
Global reach to buyers	Global access to sellers

Figure 8.4 Potential Benefits to Sellers and Buyers

- If Buyers and Sellers are Fragmented, **Independent Intermediaries** are likely to be successful.

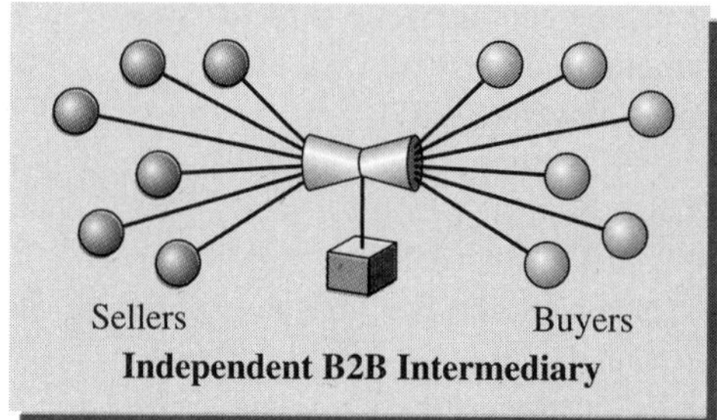

- If **Sellers** are Concentrated, Sellers are likely to dominate.

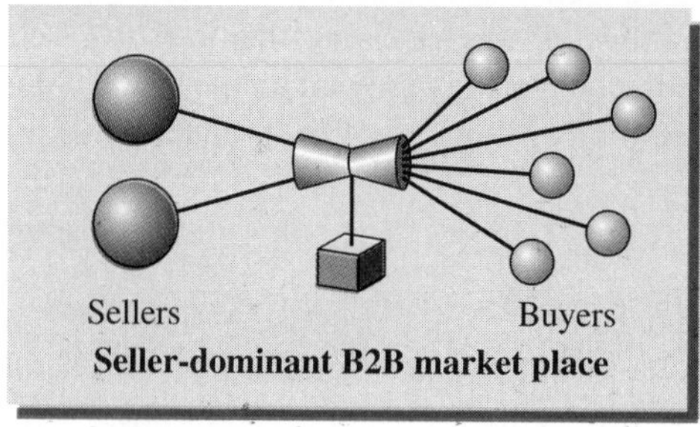

- If **Buyers** are Concentrated, Buyers are likely to dominate.

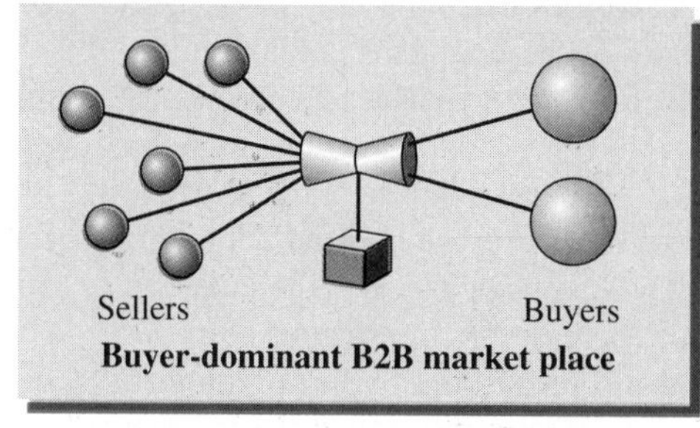

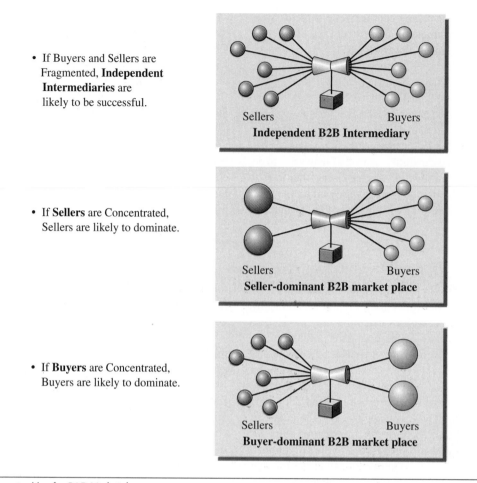

Figure 8.5 Opportunities for B2B Marketplaces

was an intermediary established by the Big 3 automobile manufacturers. However, like Covisint, such a consortium might also face operational and information-sharing constraints due to government regulations about competitor collaboration or resistance among the competing companies for other reasons.

Another explanation for the meltdown of independent online B2B intermediaries is that companies prefer to make their own procurement deals with other businesses rather than purchase through an intermediary. This appears to be true when the products being purchased are production materials that need to meet company-specific and product-specific requirements: The companies would rather have software to run their own exchange or just electronically communicate with their suppliers.

For the procurement of commodity MRO supplies (materials, repair, and operations), however, the usage of some sort of public or private B2B exchange might be more likely as companies seek to achieve cost savings. However, to capture the benefits of an exchange requires investing in new software as well as standardizing procedures (CyberAtlas, 2002). Ariba is an example of a software vendor that assists large business customers in creating their own private exchanges with potential suppliers; these B2B software vendors may also still host an online purchasing exchange for smaller businesses that cannot afford to set up their own private exchange.

Atomic Business Models

Both consultants and academic authors have focused on identifying sustainable models that individual firms can use to leverage the capabilities of the internet for B2C or B2B applications. For example, in their book *Place to Space*, Weill and Vitale (2001) identify eight "atomic" business models that can be used alone or in combinations. Summary descriptions of these eight models (based on Straub, 2004) are provided in Figure 8.6.

Business Model	Description	Customer *Relationship* Owner	Customer *Data* Owner	Customer *Transaction* Owner
1. Content provider	Provides content (e.g., information, digital products, services via intermediaries)	No	No	No
2. Direct-to-customer	Provides goods or services directly to customer, often surpassing traditional channel players	Yes	Yes	Yes
3. Full-service provider	Offers a full range of services in one domain (e.g., financial, health care) directly as well as via complementors attempting to own the primary customer relationship	Yes	Yes	Yes
4. Intermediary	Brings together buyers and sellers by concentrating information (e.g., search engines, auctions)	Yes	Yes	No
5. Shared infrastructure	Brings together multiple competitors to cooperate by sharing common IT infrastructure	No	Yes	Yes
6. Value net integrator	Coordinates value net (or value chain) activities by gathering, synthesizing, and distributing information	No	Yes	No
7. Virtual community	Facilitates and creates loyalty to an online community of people with a common interest, enabling interaction and service provision (Note: virtual communities facilitate cross-selling and up-selling)	Yes	Yes	No
8. Single point of contact	Provides a firm-wide, single point of contact, consolidating all services provided by a large, multibusiness organization (by customer events)	Yes	Yes	Yes

Figure 8.6 Eight Business Models and Their E-Business Assets (Based on Weill and Vitale 2001, Straub 2004)

Weill and Vitale argue that the value propositions for these eight business models differ according to the degree to which three e-business assets are captured *online*:

- *The Customer Transaction* The ability to capture revenues from the online transaction (revenues from selling a product or providing a service or facilitating such a sale or service; for example, fees might be collected from a business seller for selectively highlighting a seller's products or from a buyer who uses the site to help select a seller).
- *The Customer Data* The ability to capture online data that yield insights about the customer's purchasing needs (and to use that data to increase revenues via cross-selling to the customer or providing the information to other businesses).
- *The Customer Relationship* The ability to influence a customer's behaviors (such as being able to provide to a customer an online purchase recommendation that the customer "trusts" because of an established relationship with the Web site).

As shown in Figure 8.6, for example, in a direct-to-customer e-business model, the owner of the Web site captures all three assets online: the transaction, the customer data, and the customer relationship. In an intermediary e-business model, however, the customer transaction takes place between the buyers and sellers that the intermediary brings together. The intermediary can, however, capture data about the customer's purchasing or information needs and also can establish a relationship with the customer as a trusted business intermediary.

Below we provide examples of dot-com and clicks-and-mortar companies that have been successful in developing several of these e-business models.

DIRECT-TO-CUSTOMER EXAMPLES

In a direct-to-customer model, the seller and buyer communicate directly. When a traditional manufacturing firm sets up an e-business site for direct communications with its customers, this often means that it is bypassing a distribution channel traditionally used in the past: Its customer can bypass this traditional sales and customer service channel and can communicate directly with the product's manufacturer. When a traditional direct retailer sets up an e-business site, this means that a customer now has an additional channel that can be used to gather information or communicate directly with the retailer. The customer can still go to a store or telephone a catalog retailer, but now the customer also has the option of using the retailing Web site.

In contrast, for a new dot-com business, customer communications are primarily (if not completely) via the Internet. In addition, the new dot-com business is faced with a significant logistics challenge: the development of efficient offline processes and information systems to complete the order fulfillment process. The inadequate order fulfillment capabilities of dot-coms in general became widely recognized after the publicized delivery failures for online holiday purchases in 1999. This major execution weakness by online retailers also contributed to the wake-up call among venture capitalists and the rapid closing of dot-com Web sites by the end of 2000.

Weill and Vitale also distinguish direct-to-customer models based on whether the products being sold are produced by the company that has the Web site or are products produced by a third party. Firms that sell third-party products online, rather than their own products, face the greatest hurdles at developing a successful online strategy. As can be seen from Porter's 5-forces model (Figure 8.3 above), third-party retailers face the threat of lower barriers to entry for new competitors, as well as the threat of increased competition based on price.

Below we describe three examples of successful implementations of a direct-to-customer e-business model:

- Amazon (*www.amazon.com*), a dot-com pioneer in online retailing of third-party products that had its first profitable fiscal year in 2003
- Dell Corporation (*www.dell.com*), a traditional direct seller of made-to-order microcomputers, which has leveraged a sales channel via the Web to become a market leader
- Lands' End (*www.landsend.com*), a traditional catalog company that developed the capability to give online tools to customers that enable them to make orders for new custom clothing via its Web site

Amazon.com

One of the dot-coms most widely associated with the rise of the Internet is Amazon.com. Its founder, Jeff Bezos, has been recognized as a visionary in e-tailing and as committed to delivering its promises to customers. Amazon was able to use its early-mover position to quickly "brand" itself as a trusted dot-com retailer. This strong dot-com brand also helped Amazon to have the financial backing it needed before it could reach profitability, which did not occur until almost a decade after it was founded (fiscal year 2003).

Amazon.com was named after the Earth's biggest river. Launched as a totally online retailer in 1994, the site initially displayed the slogan "Earth's Biggest Bookstore." However, the company quickly expanded its online offerings to include other products found in physical bookstores, such as music CDs and videos. The Web site had more than 1 million customers after 2 years in operation, and by May 2000 it had 17 million customers.

Initially, Amazon.com was a new entrant that was a major threat only to traditional booksellers, including two bricks-and-mortar chains (Borders Books and Barnes & Noble) that in the mid-1990s were pursuing an aggressive offline growth strategy: the building of superstores. However, by mid-1999 (when venture capital in the United States was still plentiful), Amazon began to expand into other consumer products and created a multistore online mall, and thus became a competitor of Wal-Mart and Sears, Roebuck and Co.

Amazon.com's home page (see Figure 8.7) therefore includes tabs to its Web-based stores that sell a wide range of consumer goods, from electronics to kitchenware to outdoor furniture. Amazon has also expanded its business model to sell used books and has an auction capability (see Intermediary Models discussion below). The Amazon site also prominently displays logos of other retailers, including those essentially "hosted" by Amazon.com. For example, Amazon's year 2000 holiday revenues were significantly helped by its alliance with the traditional retailer Toys R Us. In contrast, in the year 2000 its major online bookseller competitor, Barnesandnoble.com (or bn.com), was pursuing an expansion into digital books for downloading and online course materials for students who registered with Barnes & Noble University. By 2004, Amazon.com listed on its Web site the names of two traditional department stores among its featured retailer partners: the discount retailer Target and the more upscale Marshall Field's.

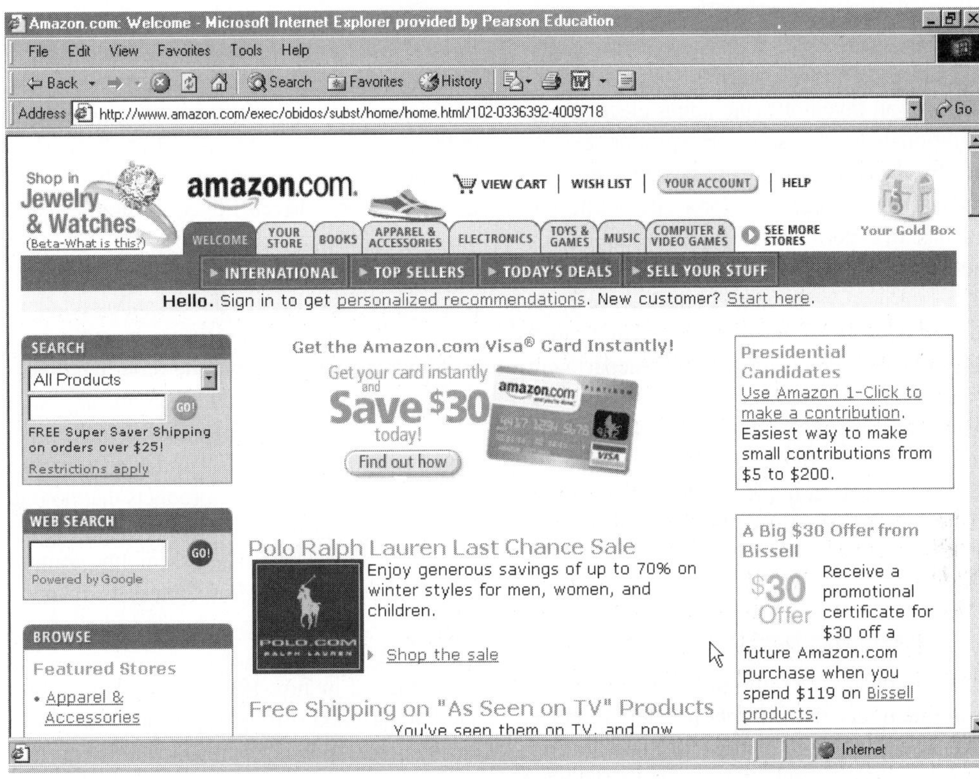

Figure 8.7 Amazon.com Home Page (© 2004 Amazon.com, Inc. All rights reserved.)

Amazon was able to develop these profitable clicks-and-mortar retailing alliances because of its widely recognized capability of providing a superior online shopping experience for its customers. It patented its "one-click" sales capability and also was the first to develop a tailoring capability that provides purchase recommendations based on a return customer's purchases and those by other online customers.

The excerpts from a 2000 review published in the *Wall Street Journal* by the personal computing critic Walter Mossberg in the sidebar "Online Shopping at Amazon.com" describes the customer experience on this site. Mossberg also refers to the virtual "community" that Amazon established by having customers share their candid opinions about purchases they had made (book reviews); in later years the Web site offered opportunities to chat with others with the same interests (a kind of book club) and to set up gift registries. In 2001, Amazon.com received the highest customer satisfaction score for any service company (online or offline) from the American customers who participated in the survey.

As in other dot-coms that sell tangible products, the development of efficient offline processes and information systems to complete the order fulfillment process became a major logistics challenge and a barrier to achieving profitability. Amazon.com's early success with delivery logistics as a dot-com book retailer has been attributed to its access to a major distribution infrastructure first built by another company. For example, when other dot-com companies failed to deliver on holiday sales at the end of 1999, Amazon was able to keep the trust of its customers by fulfilling 99 percent of its orders in time for the Christmas holiday. However, its expansion into

ONLINE SHOPPING AT AMAZON.COM

Amazon has won the loyalty of millions by building an online store that is friendly, easy to use, and inspires a sense of confidence and community among its customers. People trust Amazon, partly because it knows their tastes and does what it promises. Most purchases arrive on time and exactly as ordered. The company sends e-mails to tell when the order was processed and, later, when it was shipped. An order can be cancelled before it ships without going through the usual wrangling. If something goes wrong, Amazon usually forgives the shipping charge or upgrades the type of shipping.

The shopping experience is just terrific. The site is easy to navigate, even though it features 15 different departments. Searching is easy and excellent. The site intelligently personalizes the pages you see to highlight merchandise of a type you've bought before and to suggest similar items.

[Adapted from Mossberg, 2000b]

other products in 1999 also meant that the company had to execute a gigantic expansion of its warehouse and delivery systems, as well as its distribution facilities, to handle products for which it kept an inventory (including electronics).

The business rationale for this aggressive product expansion strategy was that the company had succeeded in becoming a brand name trusted by consumers for a safe online and reliable post-purchasing experience. To be successful at this strategy, however, it not only had to ensure that it still had a superior customer interface for sales and customer support but also had reliable back-office order fulfillment processes. By August 2003, Amazon.com clearly was the "department store" with the most online visitors: 43 percent of the online visits were to Amazon.com, with Wal-Mart and Target each having less than 10 percent (Hitwise, 2003). After considerable investments in its backend processes and systems, Amazon also reported its first profitable fiscal year at the end of 2003.

Dell.com

Companies in the computer hardware and software industries were early online direct-to-customer retailers because they were able to take advantage of the early penetration of Internet access in the homes of people who were likely to be more computer literate and therefore customers who would be likely to buy a computer based on catalog information and savvy about Internet security measures for online purchasing. Dell Corporation (formerly Dell Computer Corporation) was one of the first of the PC retailers to establish a customer-driven PC configuration capability that let customers customize their order.

Dell initially developed software to support this "mass customization" strategy as a direct catalog retailer. The customer representative used the software to electronically capture a customer request, translate the order data into a design with these components, and then electronically "summon the right resources" to fulfill the order. Dell's "make-to-order" business model also meant that Dell didn't need to spend money to purchase, assemble, and store products that no one might buy. It also enabled a just-in-time supply chain to keep down inventory costs. Since Dell is also assembling computers with commodity components, whose prices tend to quickly fall, its make-to-order model also can yield additional cost savings by purchasing components as needed.

Launched in July 1996, Dell's Web site therefore leveraged the original software application used by customer service representatives to create a "self-service" application.

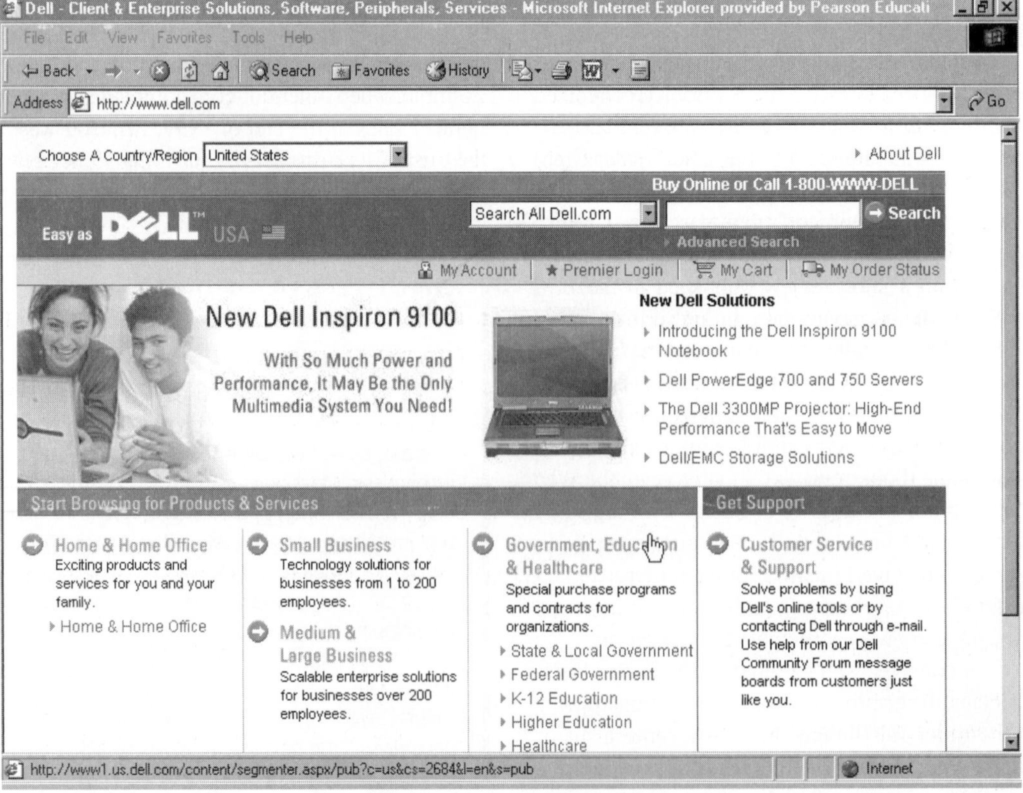

Figure 8.8 Dell.com Home Page (Used with permission of Dell Corporation.)

Businesses and individuals could bypass ordering by phone through Dell employees by ordering directly via Dell's Web site at their own convenience. Customers could also use the Web site to interactively experiment with different computer configurations using a "choiceboard" capability and could determine what the total price would be *before* finalizing their order: Without speaking to another human, a buyer chooses from menus of computer specifications, components, preloaded application software, customer support options, and delivery options, and the computer is delivered at the specified price to the requested location in a few days.

For its B2B online sales, Dell developed Premier Pages that are tailored to the needs of its business customers. For example, Dell assists procurement managers in selecting a small number of configurations to fit their infrastructure standards and employee needs, which can include the business' standard application software. These options are displayed for the business' employees on a secure Web page for this company only, and the employees can order one of the standard configurations at a prenegotiated price. By 2001, more than 50,000 business customers had Premier Pages customized for their employees (including universities that set up standard configurations for student purchases).

Dell's prior catalog model and build-to-order business model were well suited for rapid expansion to a clicks-and-mortar strategy. In contrast, build-to-channel manufacturers such as Compaq Computer and Hewlett-Packard (now merged into one company) had to evolve entirely new business processes in order to compete online with Dell's direct-to-customer online capability. By the end of 2002, Dell was No.1 in market share for desktop PCs and was also the No.1 Internet retailer (see the sidebar entitled "Dell's Way"). By leveraging its patents for process improvements, as well as its ERP and extranet systems, the company's operating costs were only 10 percent of its $35 billion revenues, compared to operational costs twice that percentage at Hewlett-Packard (Jones, 2003).

DELL'S WAY

Year	Event
1984	Michael Dell founds PC's Limited, the forerunner of Dell Computer
1988	Initial public offering of Dell stock: 3.5 million shares at $8.50 each (9 cents, adjusted for splits).
1993	Dell becomes one of the top five computer system makers worldwide. It starts selling its machines in Japan.
1996	Customers begin buying Dell computers over the Internet at *www.dell.com.*
1997	Dell opens a production and sales center in Xiamen, China. In 1999, Dell is ranked number six in China in PC shipments. By September 2002, it eclipses IBM as the top foreign PC seller. (Domestic PC maker Legend still outsells it 6 to 1.)
1999	Dell grabs the top spot in the U.S. PC market.
2000	Dell stock hits an all-time high of $58.13 a share in March.
2001	Dell overtakes Compaq in worldwide PC and U.S. server sales. It loses both leads when Compaq announces plans to merge with Hewlett-Packard.
2002	Dataquest reports that Dell has reclaimed the top spots in both worldwide PC and U.S. server sales from the merged HP-Compaq.

[Jones, 2003]

Landsend.com

Founded in 1963 as a retailer of, first, sailing equipment and then clothes and home furnishings, Lands' End traditionally marketed its products via catalog and took sales orders via telephone and mail orders. In the late 1990s it began selling its products online. Management viewed three characteristics of its traditional business as significant competitive advantages for online direct-to-customer retailing:

- a recognized brand name
- their own manufactured products (not third-party products)
- a strong, in-place distribution infrastructure from its traditional offline catalog business

Lands' End's distribution infrastructure worked well for fulfilling sales orders of items in inventory, and the company realized additional profits from the lower order-processing costs from customers using its public Web site (Piccoli et al., 2003).

In October 2001, Lands' End also began to offer custom-tailored clothing via its Web site after forming an alliance with Archetype Solutions, Inc. (ASI). ASI's founder (Robert Holloway) had previously had a 17-year career at clothing manufacturer Levi Strauss North America, which had been an early experimenter with online orders of customized clothing but relied on sales via a third-party distribution channel. Another ASI executive had been a consultant at McKinsey & Company and an engineer for a firm in the fabric industry prior to joining the startup business.

Lands' End purchased a noncontrolling interest in ASI and developed a contract that gave it a 6-month lead time in new custom-tailoring technologies. ASI's patents included the algorithms that are used to translate a customer's measurements into a pattern for cutting fabric, which is electronically sent to manufacturers of the custom clothing orders. Software to track a customer's order across non-U.S.

manufacturing sites and shippers was also put in place to monitor the handoffs between Lands' End, ASI, offshore manufacturing sites, and shippers.

Lands' End began with custom orders for chino pants (men's and women's) and added custom jeans and men's shirts by late 2002. By 2003, its Web site sales of custom chinos and jeans accounted for 40 percent of sales of those items, and repeat purchasers for custom clothing were reported to be high among those individuals making custom orders via the Web. One reason for this high customer satisfaction was that the company retained its usual return policy: even if the clothing was custom-ordered, customers could return it. They were also encouraged to "try again" by providing additional information to Lands' End to help improve the fit. In this way the company also got feedback that ASI could use to improve its software algorithms.

Successful Online Direct-to-Customer Models

These three successful direct-to-customer examples have some common, IT-related strengths. All three companies have developed B2C Web sites that use advanced technologies that support customized interactions with their customers. Amazon's Web site tailors its content to match the customer's expected preferences and Amazon customers can also personalize the Web site display for their own third-party product needs. As sellers of their own products, Dell and Lands' End take the customization a step further and provide online tools that enable a mass customization sales strategy: customers design their own products, which these companies then make to order.

In addition, all three of these companies have implemented back-office order fulfillment systems that enable them to fulfill the order quickly and reliably. As traditional catalog companies, Dell and Lands' End have continued to improve their preexisting capabilities to support their online sales. Dell has leveraged its ERP system to provide extranet links with suppliers, including providers of computer display devices that coordinate their direct shipping to the customer with Dell's shipping of the computer's custom components. Lands' End was able to create a partnership with a new firm founded by a former president of a competitor (Levi Strauss). As a new dot-com, Amazon had to develop a back-office order fulfillment capability; although it initially jump-started this new capability with an alliance, Amazon continued to invest heavily in technology and process improvements for its warehouses in order to compete with discount department stores such as Wal-Mart and Sears.

According to a 2002 survey, the most common online activities of U.S. consumers that result in a business

Figure 8.9 Landsend.com Home Page (© 2004 Lands' End, Inc. Used with permission.)

Online Activity (2002)	No. U.S. Internet Users
Buy a product	73 million (62%)
Buy or make a reservation for travel	59 million (50%)
Bank online	37 million (32%)
Participate in an online auction	22 million (20%)
Buy or sell stocks	14 million (12%)

Source: Pew Internet & American Life Project Surveys, 2002

Figure 8.10 Common Online Activities by U.S. Consumers

transaction include buying a product, making travel reservations, banking online, participating in an online auction, and buying or selling stocks (see Figure 8.10). According to a recent Ernst and Young study (Straub, 2004), individual products that sell best via the Internet are likely to be (1) specialty items or unusual, (2) information-intensive, (3) nonperishable, and (4) of small enough size and weight to have relatively low shipping costs. Among the best-selling services are those that are information-intensive, such as financial brokerages and travel reservation businesses.

For the clicks-and-mortar firm, one of the biggest challenges is how to *integrate* its online and offline channels and provide a single face to the customer and maintain efficiency. From the customer perspective, the challenge is to provide consistent services, whether the customer purchases a product online, at a retail store, or via an offline catalog service and then uses a different channel for customer service, including returning the product. To accomplish this, managers need to integrate both place (offline) and space (online) business operations; sometimes this is difficult because of incentive systems that might be in place that only reward employees for sales and customer service using a single channel (in-store, call centers, or Web-based). Similarly, the IT groups that support offline and online business operations also need to be integrated in some way in order to develop applications that support a single-face-to-the-customer goal.

INTERMEDIARY EXAMPLES

In the mid-1990s, there was a widespread belief that the Internet would primarily have a *disintermediation* effect: That is, direct-to-customer strategies could circumvent traditional intermediaries. However, the reality is that both online intermediary dot-com businesses have emerged *and* traditional intermediaries have evolved to be successful clicks-and-mortar intermediaries. In addition, as the size of the Internet has increased, a number of "hubs" have emerged that are used as gateways to other sites (Barabasi, 2002).

Weill and Vitale (2001) identify six different subtypes of intermediaries; their salient characteristics are summarized in Figure 8.11. In contrast to the direct-to-customer business model, businesses that pursue the intermediary model typically own the Customer Relationship and Customer Data, but not usually the Transaction Data. Intermediaries in general are successful when they develop a value proposition that increases their linkages to both buyers and sellers. For example, a successful auction intermediary where sales are made to the highest bidder typically requires sufficiently large numbers of buyers and sellers.

The value proposition for an intermediary also is based on the degree to which the intermediary can provide "complete" service. According to Weill and Vitale (2001), for example, the intermediary can lower costs for potential buyers by providing relevant searching capabilities, product/service specification information, and sometimes fulfillment services. An online intermediary can also create a marketplace in which the buyer determines the price, and the intermediary locates the seller—such as the intermediary model developed by Priceline.com.

Three examples of online intermediary models are described below:

- eBay, Inc. (*www.ebay.com*), a dot-com pioneer in electronic auctions that was one of the first to achieve profitability and is today not only a C2C intermediary, but also a B2C and B2B intermediary
- Yahoo! (*www.yahoo.com*), an early dot-com intermediary that has recently leveraged IT innovations and business acquisitions to become a leading portal
- Manheim (*www.manheim.com*), a traditional B2B intermediary for the sale of used cars that has leveraged the Internet to reduce purchasing and sales costs for its sellers and buyers and to provide remote, real-time bidding during physical auctions.

Intermediary Type	Intermediary Role	Revenue Source(s)
Electronic Auction	Links *high-bid buyer* & seller: sellers list items (specs), buyers bid	Listing fees, % of sale, additional services
Reverse Auctions	Links *low-bid seller* & buyer: buyers list needs (specs), sellers bid	Listing fees, % of sale, additional services
Electronic Markets (Exchanges)	Links (or matches) buyer & seller: sellers list items (specs)—sometimes fixed price, buyers purchase items	Listing fees, % of sale, additional services
Aggregators	Creates market: collects & analyzes comparative information for buyer or seller	Preference listing fees, % of sale, additional services
Electronic Malls	Creates marketspace: creates virtual site for sellers that want to leverage brand proximity	"Rents" from sellers, memberships from buyers, advertising fees, % of sale, additional services
Portals	Information hub: aggregated information, categorized and searchable	Preference listing fees, advertising fees, additional services

Figure 8.11 Key Characteristics of Six Types of Intermediaries (Based on Weill and Vitale, 2001)

eBay

eBay.com, an early dot-com auction, brings together individual buyers and sellers from all over the world who might not otherwise find each other. Launched in 1995, eBay.com captured about 80 percent of the online auction market by the year 2000, with more than $5 billion in merchandise sales from 250 million auctions and global participants. Although profitable from the beginning, its net income is still somewhat modest due to its relatively low charges for its services.

The online auction model is based on revenues captured as a percentage of the auction sale, as a listing fee, and for additional services to facilitate the transaction. Initially, the eBay business model was a consumer-to-consumer (C2C) application; that is, the typical user assumed that he or she was part of a "community" of individual buyers and sellers. However, many eBay sellers today are small businesses: liquidators, wholesalers, small retail shops, or at-home entrepreneurs (Guernsey, 2000). eBay today is therefore also a B2C and B2B intermediary, and to foster relationships with the small business in particular, the company provides extensive online advice and periodically holds workshops in various regions.

eBay has also grown its service capabilities via acquisitions. For example, it created a fixed-price trading capability for direct sales of previously owned goods when it purchased the dot-com start-up Half.com. For auction sales there is also a "Buy It Now" capability in which the buyer agrees to pay a price specified by the seller before the auction period is scheduled to be over. In 2003 it also purchased PayPal, which provided eBay with its own third-party payment capability: an account established by the user that does not depend on having a personal credit card. Since PayPal also provides payment services to other Web sites, it has become an additional revenue source for eBay. eBay also collects fees from sellers for "extras" such as additional digital photos with a listing, the highlighting of a listing, and setting a "reserved price" (such as a minimum price or a "Buy It Now" capability).

As an intermediary that hosts millions of auction sales simultaneously, in real time, eBay's IT operations are of critical importance. In addition to capacity planning for its servers, the company has also had to quickly recover from denial-of-service attacks and other security breaches in recent years. Its primary value to sellers and buyers is low search costs, so the design and execution of its site search capabilities must also be of the highest quality. It owns the relationship with its buyers and sellers and the data on the items being sold, but the transaction itself takes place between the buyer and seller.

Like other online intermediaries dealing with the public at large, eBay also faces considerable sales transaction risks, such as buyers with inadequate funds, sellers who misrepresent their goods, or sellers who do not deliver their goods. Since maintaining the trust of buyers and

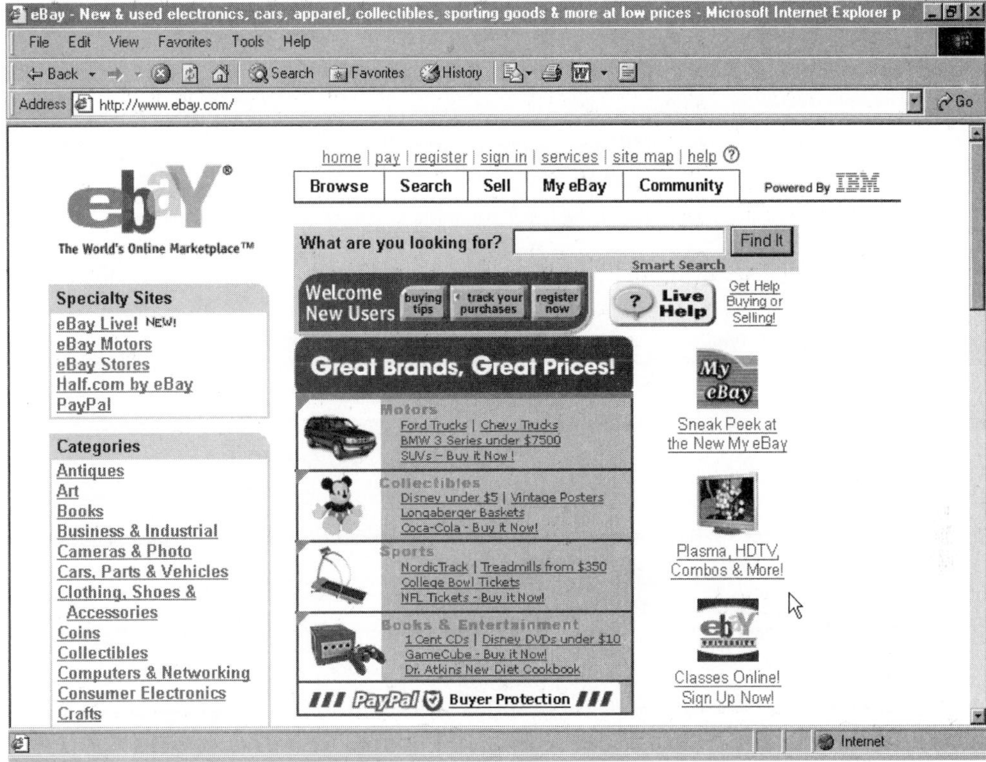

Figure 8.12 eBay.com Home Page (These materials have been reproduced with the permission of eBay, Inc. Copyright © eBay, Inc. All rights reserved.)

sellers is a key to its survival, one of eBay's early tactics for self-policing was to encourage buyers to rate their sellers, and vice versa. Nevertheless, for legal reasons, eBay also states that it is only a venue: "We are not involved in the actual transaction . . . we have no control over the quality, safety or legality of the items advertised" (Weber, 2000). The company also offers insurance coverage for items of certain types and value, plus it facilitates a process to resolve disputes between buyers and sellers.

eBay also has to continually monitor its sites for the sale of inappropriate items or even illegal items. For example, eBay has had to delete listings for items related to recent tragic events in the United States—including the 9/11 terrorist attacks on the World Trade Center and Pentagon and the explosion of the NASA space shuttle Columbia (see the sidebar entitled "eBay Items Yanked").

eBay ITEMS YANKED

eBay deleted several items billed as debris from the space shuttle *Columbia* from the online auction site Saturday, warning that anyone attempting to sell fragments from the doomed shuttle could be prosecuted. It's unclear what kind of debris was listed, but eBay spokesman Kevin Pursglove said that many of the items were pranks. The listings were immediately yanked form the site, and executives may report the sellers to federal authorities. The San Jose–based company has become a barometer of pop culture and current events. But eBay must also deal with morbid postings and attempts to capitalize on human tragedy, and it frequently pulls items.

[The Associated Press, 2003]

Yahoo!

Yahoo! was launched in April 1994 by a pair of Ph.D. candidates at Stanford University who wanted a way to keep track of Web sites for their own personal interests. It quickly became well known as a site that provided useful links, in an organized way, to help Web users link to other sites. That is, its intermediary business model is to be a Web *portal* that Web users go to first. Some of the ways that portals become hubs for large numbers of users is to offer free services. For example, Yahoo! offers free e-mail and chat rooms and allows users to customize their own home page (MyYahoo!) with specific stock quotes, the relevant horoscope, and so on. By March 2001, Yahoo! had 125 million registered users worldwide.

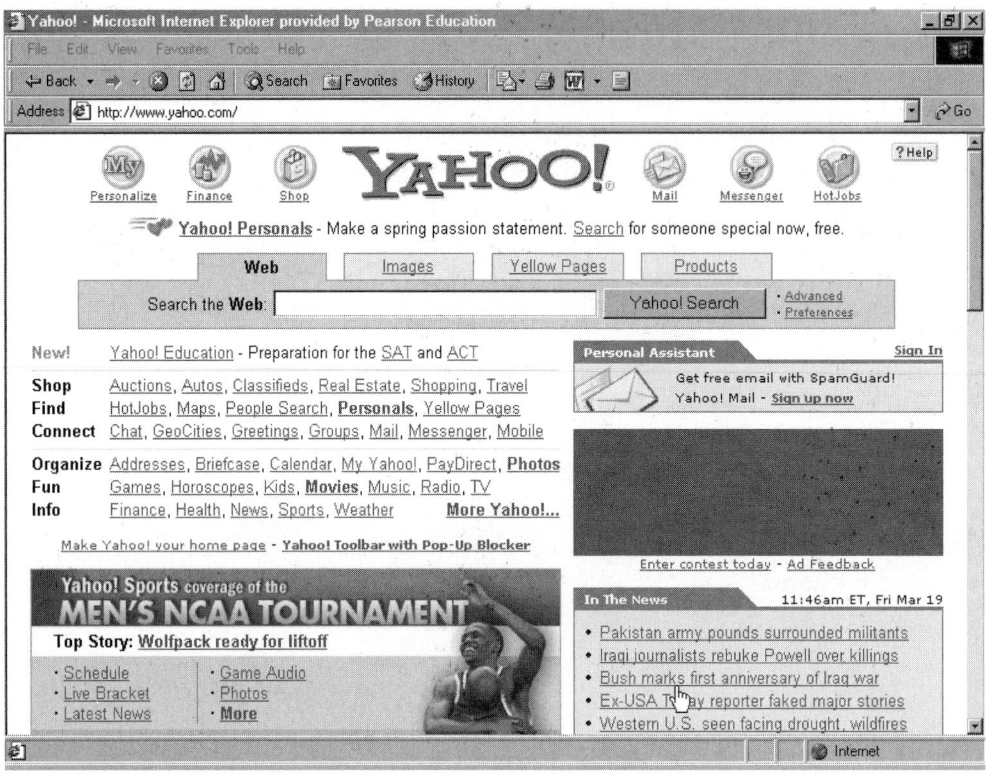

Figure 8.13 Yahoo.com Home Page (Reproduced with permission of Yahoo! Inc. Copyright © 2004 by Yahoo! Inc. YAHOO! and the YAHOO! logo are trademarks of Yahoo! Inc.)

As a portal, the site owns only the customer relationship. Its primary source of revenue has been fees for advertisements on its sites. Initially, these were direct marketing communications using "banner" ads that the user could click on to go to the advertised site. However, like other portals in the late 1990s, Yahoo! began to offer additional services to keep users on its site longer—what came to referred to as a "walled garden" approach, a term coined by the CEO of one of its competitors (Weill and Vitale, 2001). Yahoo! has also expanded its model to include revenues from sales—including online "shops (like a shopping mall) and its own auctions site. It also has attempted to be a hub for B2B marketplaces.

Under a new CEO beginning in May 2001, Yahoo! has continued to be one of the most popular Internet hubs as it has changed its business model. In late 2001 it acquired HotJobs.com, a major player in the online job-search market. In mid-2002 it launched a cobranding alliance with SBC Communications, Inc., in order to capitalize on the opportunity to become a new portal for DSL home adopters within the United States, and within the next 12 months it acquired a search technology firm (Inktomi) and an Internet advertising leader (Overture Services) in order to compete with a growing search and advertising compeititor (Google). After these acquisitions, its revenue sources included banner ads, paid searches (placing Web site links next to the results of an online search), subscriptions for services (including personal ads), and fees from its SBC broadband partnership. In late 2003 it was the third most frequented site by U.S. users at home or at work (after Microsoft and Time Warner, Inc.) and its instant messenger service was one of the top five Internet applications used (Nielsen/Net Ratings, November 2003; December 2003).

Manheim

Manheim is a used car "remarketer" that in 2003 had 32,000 employees and 116 physical auction sites worldwide, generating more than $2.4 billion in annual revenues. The company provides a marketplace where consignors that own the cars—including rental car companies, car fleet managers in corporations, leasing companies, banks, manufacturers, and licensed auto dealers—can sell their used car inventories to wholesale car retailers.

The typical auction facility has 10 to 15 physical lanes, with cars streaming down the lanes, an auctioneer who

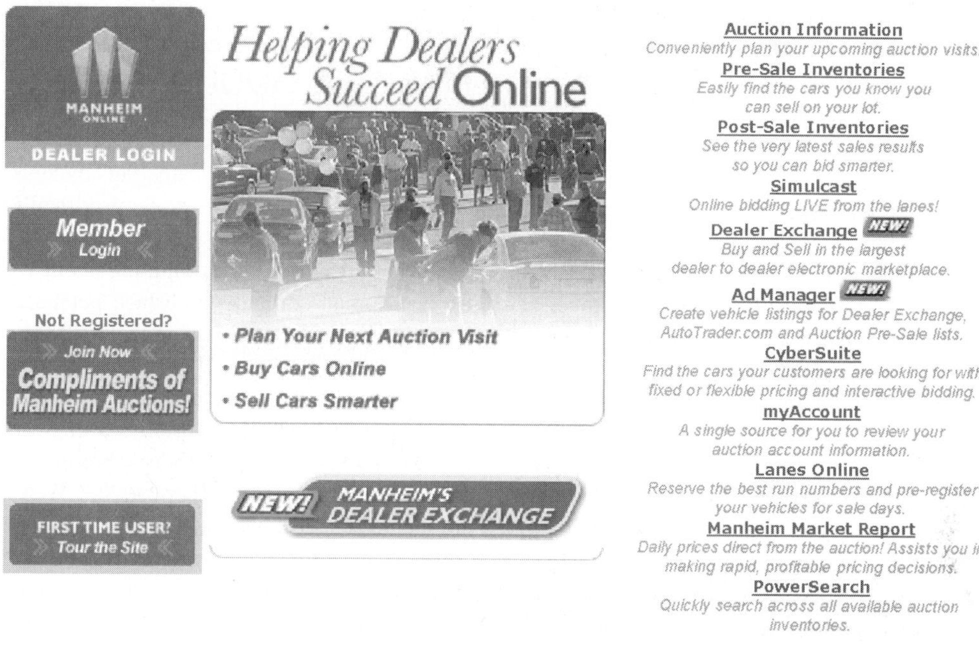

Figure 8.14 Manheim.com Home Page (Used with permission of Manheim.)

settles the bidding, a full-service reconditioning operation, precertification service, and post-sale arbitration of the vehicles. Manheim also services the transfer of car ownership to the buyer, including transport of the used car to the buyer's lot.

In early 2000, Manheim launched a new business unit (Manheim Online) to develop a B2B Web portal for a new online business as well as to provide online support for the physical auctions. For example, vehicles at a physical auction site can be inspected and registered, a sales price is set in consultation with the seller, and a full description (with digital photos) is loaded on the Web site. If a licensed used car dealer agrees to buy the car for the preset price, based on the online description, then there might be appreciable savings in depreciation and holding costs for the seller. The Web site also has a search capability that enables dealers to find used vehicles that meet their requirements. In 2002, Manheim launched Manheim Simulcast, enabling buyers to remotely view and purchase vehicles as they are being offered in the lanes at the physical auction sites.

Most U.S. states have laws that restrict car manufacturers from competing with car sales dealers, so the potential "supplier" threat of car manufacturers reaching directly to customers and bypassing car dealerships is still quite low. In the early days of the Internet, the conventional wisdom was that online car purchasing would be unlikely because consumers would want to test-drive a vehicle, However, online intermediaries that link consumers with used car consignors, either bypassing used car dealers or collecting fees from used car dealers for customer leads, have become a major threat. For example, a dot-com pioneer was Autobytel.com, which refers customers to dealers in the customer's geographical area that have cars with the characteristics that the customer is looking for and then collects fees from dealers (which by the year 2000 numbered more than 5,000 dealers). Other sites that facilitate online purchasing of used (and new) cars, which are owned by groups of dealers, have also emerged (e.g., AutoNation).

Successful Online Intermediary Models

Like the direct-to-customer examples we reviewed earlier, online intermediaries have achieved their current success by continuously innovating with IT. eBay overcame some early server reliability problems and has maintained an outstanding record for systems availability and reliability. Yahoo! grew new technology capabilities via aggressive acquisitions following the dot-com meltdown. Manheim attracted the new IT skillset that it needed by setting up a new business unit (subsidiary) and by using its central-site auction facilities to capture feedback from the used car dealers.

In addition, these three intermediaries have all continued to evolve their business models to not only increase revenues but also to provide value to their buyers and sellers. eBay has expanded into certification services in order to provide auction services for products that yield higher service fees (such as used cars). eBay has also considerably changed its original buyer/seller mix to include many small businesses selling their products online, as well as large companies, including Dell, that sell their inventory remainders. Under a new CEO, Yahoo! evolved its business model to capture new sources of revenue and to compete with a new competitor with a leading search engine technology (Google).

The sustainability of Manheim's B2B clicks-and-mortar model will depend on the continued fragmentation of its buyers and its sellers, as well as its ability to continue to provide unique value-added services to its used car dealers. Although Manheim has evolved its online Web site to facilitate purchases that bypass its own physical auction sites, other online intermediaries, including eBay, have become Manheim's competitors in the development of a capability to bring online buyers who do not need to see a car to sellers who own the car. Since in other intermediary ventures, the online buyers also include consumers, the demand for a B2B intermediary (traditional or online) for the used car industry could also significantly decline in the future.

SPECIAL ISSUE: WHAT MAKES A GOOD WEB SITE?

For e-commerce applications that use a Web site, the company's Web site *is* the company. This means that the design and operation of the Web site is of critical importance for dot-com as well as clicks-and-mortar firms.

A useful framework for thinking about Web site designs from a human-computer interface perspective is the 7Cs framework in Figure 8.15 developed by Rayport and Jaworski (2004). These 7Cs take into account both the functional and the aesthetic characteristics of a good Web site. Using Rayport and Jaworski's framework, we can analyze Web sites known for their superior customer experience and then compare them to the Web sites of other companies that are pursuing similar e-business models.

Other usability frameworks have also been widely disseminated. For example, Microsoft's Usability Guidelines (MUG), include five categories: content, ease-of-use, made-for-the-medium (including customer tailoring), promotion, and emotion (affective reactions to the site). Two acknowledged writers on human factors topics also have regularly published guidelines for Web site design on their Web sites: Walter Mossberg, a long-time columnist for the *Wall Street Journal*, and Jakob Nielsen, a human factors researcher.

Context	Site's layout and design—functionally vs. aesthetically dominant or both (integrated)
Content	Text, pictures, sound, and video that Web site contains, including offering dominant "store types"
Commerce	Site's capabilities to enable commercial transactions—functional tools and pricing
Community	Ways that the site utilizes user-to-user communication to enable feelings of membership and shared common interests
Connection	Extent to which the site is linked to other sites—links out and in
Customization	Site's ability to tailor itself to different users or to allow users to personalize the site
Communication	Ways that the site enables site-to-user, user-to-site, or two-way communications

Figure 8.15 7Cs Framework for Web Site Design (Based on Rayport and Jaworski, 2004)

M-Commerce Web Site Design Issues			
7Cs Framework		**Mobile Setting** to support consumer's limited attention	**Mobile Device Constraints** to complement the insufficient display of mobile devices
Context	*Focal Point*	Linking structure that connects pages seamlessly but efficiently	Section breakdown that organizes information in separate pages
	Interface Implementation	• Menu structured in a shallow rather than a deep hierarchy • Layered sequential process rather than field selection process	Summary and key words that give a whole picture of information separated over pages
Content	*Focal Point*	The adaptive supply of product information and promotional messages to a user's setting	Multimedia mix to utilize both visual and audio channels
	Interface Implementation	Proximate selection method that makes nearby located objects easier to choose (gas stations, bank accounts)	• Conversion of visual information to audio format • Use of non-speech sound
Community	*Focal Point*	Interactive communication by connecting the people with similar needs	To accelerate interactive information exchange despite inferior input/output devices
	Interface Implementation	Connection to shopping companions who share interests in common	SMS, and graphics describing products, transferred through a user's phone book
Customization	*Focal Point*	Tailoring enhanced by information on users' mobile setting	Filtering unnecessary information, so that a small screen contains only information that is highly useful
	Interface Implementation	Proximate selection method that emphasizes the objects of interest, by combining a user's mobile setting (location, time, and resource) with his or her personal interests	Personalized service based on known user profile (content and layout configuration without a need of log-in registration)
Communication	*Focal Point*	Broadcast messages relevant to a consumer's environment	Alternative methods for interactive communication that overcome text typing with awkward input devices
	Interface Implementation	Targeted advertising suitable at the point-of-purchase	Customer feedback in multiple-answer or multimedia formats
Connection	*Focal Point*	Pathways that present Web sites relevant to users' changing environment	To reduce the probability of feeling lost given pathways provided
	Interface Implementation	Adaptive map that shows the information about nearby stores	Icon that gives a link to the starting page with one click of the 'cancel' button
Commerce	*Focal Point*	Secure payment method demanding minimal cognitive attention	Condensed checkout process
	Interface Implementation	Insertion of authentication into mobile phones	One-click checkout process made available by storing a consumer's address, payment method, and preferred delivery options

Source: Lee and Benbasat, 2003

Figure 8.16 Designing an Interface for Mobile Devices

Given the increase in wireless networks and handheld devices that can access the Internet, today's developers must also consider what makes a good Web site display not only on desktop computer screens, but also on much smaller devices. Researchers warn that the applicability of design principles for an application intended for display on desktop computer screens should not be assumed to be the same as for an application to be displayed on a cellular phone.

More specifically, the developer needs to take into account not only the differences in hardware (e.g., screen size, keyboard, etc.), but also differences in typical usage. For example, the typical mobile user might use the device for only a short time, and in very different contexts (while traveling, shopping, walking down a street, etc.).

Lee and Benbasat (2003) have identified some of the design elements that address the consumer's limited attention as well as the deficient displays of today's typical handheld devices for each of the 7Cs shown earlier in Figure 8.15. For Commerce, for example, a secure payment method that demands minimal cognitive attention is needed, as well as a condensed checkout process suitable for a small display (see Figure 8.16).

Other key attributes of a good Web site are related to the characteristics of the operational environment—both the client side and the Web server side, as well as networks being accessed. Common technical problems that need to be anticipated include download delays and search problems, as well as security weaknesses (Straub, 2004).

For example, many users consider more than a few seconds to be an intolerable online delay for a screen to appear. User tolerance for download times will likely be a function of the users' goals, where they are working (at home versus the office), whether they are connected to a highspeed communications line or not, whether the download involves multimedia, and the user's expectations for the download time. The delay in download time can be at the server side, the client side, and/or be a function of the network infrastructure between the client and server.

SUMMARY

As this chapter is being written, we have less than one decade of experience with e-commerce applications that use the Web. The technologies have continued to evolve, although the fast rate of change in the second half of the 1990s has slowed down due to the economic slowdown in the United States in the first few years of the new millennium. The legal and regulatory environments of the United States in particular have also shaped the current e-commerce landscape, although there will be a much larger global influence in the coming decades.

Today we do have the advantage of competitive forces models at the industry level and online e-business models based on real-world examples with which to evaluate a given firm's e-business strategy and the potential opportunities and threats for a given industry. Both dot-com survivors and successful clicks-and-mortar companies pursuing direct-to-customer and intermediary e-business models provide examples of potentially viable approaches for the coming years. Less clear is the viability of B2B exchanges that are owned by an independent company or a consortium of companies. We also now have some useful frameworks for what makes a good Web site for desktop and laptop screens, although designs for m-commerce applications are still in an experimental stage.

REVIEW QUESTIONS

1. Define the terms e-commerce, dot-com, clicks-and-mortar, B2C, and B2B.
2. What major e-commerce benefit can be provided by eXtensible Markup Language (XML) but not by Hypertext Markup Language (HTML)?
3. What is meant by a first-mover advantage, and what are some of the reasons that being a first-mover might not actually be a competitive advantage?
4. Describe some U.S. laws that have influenced the nature of e-commerce via the Internet.
5. What are some of the primary benefits of e-commerce via B2C Web sites for buyers? For sellers?
6. Choose one of the five competitive forces in Porter's model and describe the opportunities and threats for a specific industry of your choosing.
7. Describe two privacy issues of consumers that are due to e-commerce applications.
8. Describe some of the distinguishing features of a direct-to-customer e-business model.
9. Describe some of the distinguishing features of an intermediary e-business model.
10. What do you see as some of the competitive strengths of Amazon.com? Dell.com? Landsend.com?
11. Describe one of the ways that eBay has extended its auction model.
12. Compare the usage of the Internet in the United States with one or more other countries.
13. Describe why expertise in Web page design is of critical importance to any online retailer.

14. What is one of the ways that the dot-com meltdowns in the early 2000s have influenced the recent growth of e-commerce?
15. What is m-commerce and why is this the next e-commerce frontier?

DISCUSSION QUESTIONS

1. Provide evidence to support the following statement: The growth of e-commerce is due to both business and technological innovations.
2. Provide an argument to either support or refute the following statement: In applications for trading partners, the customer holds the greatest power.
3. Briefly describe the potential of the Internet as a new customer service (support) channel.
4. Describe a customer experience that you have had on a retailing Web site.
5. Describe what you see as the barriers to car manufacturers developing Web applications to sell directly to consumers
6. Choose three firms within the same industry that have well-established public Web sites. Based on these sites, compare and contrast the B2C e-commerce benefits that these companies appear to be achieving.
7. Use the 7Cs framework of Rayport and Jaworski to evaluate the Web sites of two competitors.
8. Find an article that describes the current status of the automotive consortium Covisint and report on your findings.
9. Identify an article on B2B e-commerce and provide an update to the text.
10. Describe some of the ways the Internet has *or has not* impacted the way you: (1) buy groceries, (2) make travel plans, (3) read news, (4) track your favorite sports team, (5) decide which movie to see next, (6) decide what political candidate to vote for, and (7) do research for a business course.

CASE STUDY II-1

MIDSTATE UNIVERSITY BUSINESS PLACEMENT OFFICE

Midstate University is a major state university with about 35,000 students on its main campus. It is internationally known for its programs in the arts, sciences, music, engineering, education, business, and languages.

The Midstate University School of Business is a "national" school, ranking in the top 20 business schools in the country. It has outstanding undergraduate, MBA, doctoral, and executive programs. Its faculty is renowned for research, teaching, and service to the state and the business community.

The Business Placement Office (BPO) is among the handful of placement operations in the country that conduct over 15,000 interviews each year. It has an outstanding reputation among company recruiters and other business schools. Arnold Worthy, dean of the Midstate University School of Business, notes that the Business Placement Office is very important to the mission of the school:

> It is our marketing arm, and a very good one. We get good students at least partly because they know that they can get good jobs. Our school is in the top twenty in all the national rankings of business schools, but we rank highest where those who do the ranking are businessmen. That is quite a tribute to our BPO.

The director of the Business Placement Office, James P. Wine, is known among his peers as an energetic and innovative director. He is a past president of the Midwest College Placement Association, and is a frequent speaker at placement conventions nationwide. Wine has a degree in electrical engineering, an MBA in personnel management, and a Ph.D. in industrial relations. He is the author of several textbooks that are widely used in placement and career planning courses.

The primary mission of the BPO is to help Midstate University students get appropriate jobs. But, as Wine notes, "We must also serve our corporate clients, for if they don't come back year after year there won't be any jobs for our students." In 1999–2000 the BPO served about 1,700 students and over 500 employers. Over 17,000 interviews were conducted in the BPO's 34 interview rooms, an average of over 1,000 interviews each week of the interviewing season.

In order to provide outstanding service to both students and employers, the BPO makes extensive use of sophisticated computer systems. According to Wine:

> We are rapidly becoming a paperless operation throughout the BPO. Our communication to students and employers for posting jobs, scheduling interviews, and accessing our office publications is in the user-friendly, graphical environment of the World Wide Web (WWW). With the click of a button, students are able to scan job listings, schedule interviews, forward resumes, and much more from personal computers located anywhere in the world. Results of the bidding process are sent from our computers to students via e-mail.

Companies also interact with the BPO via the Web. Recruiters can set up interview dates and interview schedules via the Web, and they can watch their interview schedules fill up with students and even access those students' resumes through the Web.

The Student's View of the BPO System

The BPO is not an employment agency. It does not "get" anyone a job, but it provides many services to students to assist them in obtaining a suitable job, including teaching two required courses (Career Perspectives and Career Planning and Placement), sponsoring over 600 on-campus presentations by employers each year, making available company brochures, distributing student resumes to companies not interviewing on campus, providing the opportunity to network with Midstate University alumni, and scheduling and administering on-campus interviews with over 500 companies. From the student perspective, however, the main function of the BPO is to provide on-campus interviews with companies for which the student would like to work.

The matchmaking required to schedule 1,700 students into 17,000 interviews with 500 companies so that the students talk with their desired companies and the companies interview students with the required qualifications is a very complex, high-volume logistical problem. It is particularly difficult because all the students want to talk with the companies offering the best jobs, but these companies may have strict requirements concerning the qualifications of the students they want to interview. Some companies have far more students seeking interviews than there are interview times available, while other companies' interview schedules may not be filled.

The 1,700 students submit about 65,000 requests for the 17,000 available interview opportunities. How can the BPO be fair to all in allocating these interviews to qualified students? To deal with this problem in a fair and equitable way, the Midstate University BPO uses a bidding system, where students submit "bids" for interviews with the companies of their choice. Each student is given a fixed allotment of bids with different levels of priority. A complex process (designed to be fair to the students given their qualifications, their time availability, their graduation date, and the bid priority) is used to decide which students get the interview slots. Because the BPO receives up to 5,500 bids during a peak week, interview scheduling can only be handled with the aid of computers.

Midstate University students are introduced to the Web in their sophomore-year computer course, where they learn HTML. Because many Business School faculty communicate with their students through a class Web page, students are quite familiar with how to use the Web. All Business School students are given a computer account that provides access to network resources such as e-mail and the World Wide Web.

In order to take advantage of the BPO services a student must meet certain criteria and register at the beginning of the year. After paying a registration fee, the student can go to the BPO Web site and register to use the BPO services. Registration involves three things. First, the student must fill out a **registration information** form on the Web (see Exhibit 1). Second, the student must submit via the Web a **times not available** form indicating the times each day of the week when he or she cannot be available for interviews. Finally, the student must complete a **general resume**, save it in HTML format, and upload it via the BPO Web site. After registration has been completed the BPO sends feedback via e-mail to the student showing how the student is coded in the computer. Any errors can be corrected via the BPO Web site.

The student may submit additional specialized resumes to be used in interviewing for different types of jobs. The student is responsible for the accuracy of his or her resumes and registration information. If any information, such as GPA, changes, the student's information in the computer can be updated via the Web.

Preparation for Bidding

All the activities involved in bidding for interviews can be done through the BPO's user-friendly Web site that provides information on available interview schedules and the student's bid status, and allows the student to bid for available interview slots.

When entering the BPO Web site the student must provide his or her student identification number and password before being presented with a main menu. Clicking on "student" leads to the student menu shown in Exhibit 2 (see p. 269). In addition to allowing the student to enter bids, the Student menu provides access to much of the information needed to develop his or her bidding strategy. The *Career Street Journal* (*CSJ*) was formerly a printed weekly paper that contained helpful articles related to placement, announcements, and complete information on upcoming interview schedules. The weekly *CSJ* is now available on the Web by clicking on "Weekly *CSJ*" in another menu.

Each student is allocated only three "A" bids, three "B" bids, three "C" bids, and 30 Regular (or "R") bids each semester and is not allowed to exceed these limits. In addition to determining the qualifications that students must meet in order to be scheduled for an interview, the companies may also establish "preference lists" of students who will get priority for interview slots. Some companies will not use preference lists, others will establish half as many preferences as there are slots available, and others may include more students on their preference list than there are slots on the company's schedule. If students are interested in a company, it is important to know whether or not they are on that company's preference list, and this information may be obtained by clicking on "View Preference Lists" on the student menu.

The BPO provides many opportunities for students to meet with company recruiters, including company presentations, roundtable discussions, orientation programs connected with the career development classes, and company-sponsored receptions. In addition to the information that they may obtain, students have an opportunity to meet recruiters, give them resumes, and perhaps thereby get on company preference lists. Sign-ups for these programs are handled through the bidding system, and these opportunities appear in the *CSJ* along with interview schedules. To sign up for these events one uses a special "interest" or "I" bid instead of the A, B, C, and R bids used for interviews. There is no limit on the number of I bids a student may submit. However, attendance at these events may be limited, and the bidding system is used to determine who can attend an event if the demand exceeds capacity.

EXHIBIT 1
BPO Registration Information

Name:	George P. Burdell
Email:	burdellgp@midstate.edu
Current Address:	120 East 15th St. Midstate City
Phone:	423-345-6749
Permanent Address:	1040 Amsterdam Ave. Atlanta, GA
Phone:	205-378-5327
Pending Degree:	BS
Graduation Date:	June, 2001
Date Available:	July 1, 2001
Current Major(s):	Finance, Quant
Current GPA:	3.72
Job Targets:	
Citizenship:	U.S. CITIZEN
Home Country:	U.S.A.
Location Preference:	None - Willing to Relocate
Work Experience:	Less than 1 year
Authorized to Work Countries:	U.S.A.
Languages:	English, Spanish (3 yrs. study)
Skills:	1) Public Speaking, 2) Analysis, 3) Computer
Minimum Annual Salary:	$30,000
Desired Annual Salary:	Depends on Job Challenge & Future Prospects
Release Data?	Yes
Year of Birth:	1980
Sex:	Male
Ethnic Origin:	Caucasian

The data in the student's registration information file is used to determine whether or not a student meets the criteria established by the company for signing up for an interview or attending an event. Therefore, the student must make sure that this information is accurate and up to date. For instance, student George P. Burdell may view and update his information by clicking on "View Registration Information" on the student menu. Burdell must also provide the BPO computer with information on times when he is not available for interviewing so that he will not be scheduled at such times. Clicking on "Change My Times Not Available" on the student menu allows the student to view and/or change this availability information at any time.

In order to plan one's bidding strategy, it is helpful to know what companies are planning campus interviews and when they plan to be on campus. This information is obtained by clicking on "View Companies on Campus" on the student menu, which displays planned interviewing dates for a particular company, companies scheduled for a particular date or date range, or companies interested in various degrees and majors. Also, by clicking on "View Bid History," Burdell can review his bid history and see what bids remain available.

Submitting Bids

When Burdell is ready to enter the bidding process, he clicks on "Bidding *CSJ*" and is given the opportunity to choose whether to sort work within the *CSJ* by alphabetical order or by functional area. Choosing to work with the *CSJ* sorted by functional area, and then selecting Accounting/Finance, Burdell views interview alternatives, the first page of which is shown in Exhibit 3 (see p. 270). By clicking on a company name, Burdell can view the *CSJ* write-up for the position being offered.

EXHIBIT 2
Student Menu

Student Links

View Registration Information	Bidding CSJ
View My Personal Information Calendar	Change My Times Not Available
View Preference Lists	Edit/Upload My Resumes
View Bid History	Report Job Offers
View Internship Opportunities	Interpret Bid Result Messages
View Companies on Campus	Contact Search (Alumni Links)
View BPO Report Center	Job Fairs
Career Resources	Compare Salary Statistics
BPO Style Resume Template	Submit Trouble Log Form
Chronological Resume Template	BPO Directors
View Placement Manual	Review the Resume Preparation Guide

Burdell wishes to submit bids on three companies, so he clicks on the three left-hand boxes where the checks are shown. Proceeding to the bottom of the sorted listing, Burdell clicks on the "Continue" button and receives the screen shown in Exhibit 4 (see p. 271). Here he specifies the type of bid (A, B, C, R, or I) he wishes to use and indicates which of his resumes he wishes the company to see. Up to now, no bids have been submitted, and changes may be freely made. However, when Burdell clicks on "Submit Bids," the bids are submitted.

Each week of the recruiting season the *Bidding CSJ* is available at 9 o'clock Friday morning, and the primary bidding period for its interview opportunities extends until 4 P.M. the following Monday. All of the bids received during the primary bidding period are processed together to assign students to interview slots. First, bids of students who do not meet the qualifications set by the company are rejected and the student loses that bid. If the company has established a preference list those students are processed first in priority order (A, B, C, and R). Then the remaining students are processed in the same priority order. Finally, those students who have been selected are scheduled into time slots, taking into account the student's time availability. Students who are left over are placed on a ranked waitlist and will be given any time slots that become available before the interview date. Time slots do become available because some students may cancel and recruiters may add a schedule when the BPO sends them the resumes of all students on the waitlist. If a student who has submitted a priority bid is waitlisted, the priority bid is returned and an R bid is substituted, even if the student subsequently gets on the schedule.

Bidding Results

The computer sends bid results to students via e-mail as soon as all bid processing has been completed, usually during the early morning hours on Tuesday. The bid results list the student's name, the results of each bid placed, and how many bids remain in the student's account. For each bid the following information is listed: the bidding number, the employer's name, the type of bid that was taken, and the result of the bid (date, time and place scheduled, or waitlisted). Bid results are also placed on the Web so that they may be viewed at any time by clicking on "View My Personal Information Calendar" or "View Bid History."

After the results of primary bidding have been announced, there is a secondary bidding period that extends until 3 days

EXHIBIT 3
The First Part of the Sorted Bidding CSJ for Accounting/Finance

Accounting/Finance

Interest	Company	Position	Status	Preference
☐	ABN AMRO/LaSalle Bank	Commercial Lender Training Program	Secondary	
☐	ABN AMRO/LaSalle Bank	Finance Associate	Secondary	
☐	ACNielsen	Account Associate	Primary	
☐	ATA - Strategic Planning	Night Before Presentation	Secondary	
☑	ATA - Strategic Planning	Strategic Planner	Secondary	
☑	Acosta Sales and Marketing	Management Trainee	Primary	
☐	Allegiance Healthcare Corporation	Operational Development Program	Secondary	
☑	American Express Financial Advisors/Merrillville	Personal Financial Advisor	Primary	
☐	Arrow Electronics, Inc.	Financial Development Program	Primary	
☐	Arrow Electronics, Inc.	Financial Development Program	Primary	
☐	Bain & Company	Associate Consultant	Secondary	
☐	Bank One Corporation	National Retail Development Program	Primary	
☐	Bank of America/Charlotte	Debt Capital Raising Analyst	Primary	
☐	Bank of Louisville	Management Training Program	Primary	
☐	Bank of Louisville	Night Before Presentation	Primary	
☐	Black & Decker Corp.	Field Marketing Specialist	Primary	
☐	Black & Decker Corp.	Night Before Presentation	Primary	
☐	Bloomingdale's	Buyers Training Program	Secondary	
☐	Boise Cascade Corp.	Audit Analyst	Secondary	

before the interviews are scheduled. During this time the student may cancel a scheduled interview if necessary, although the bid that was used is lost. Also, during this time schedules that have vacancies are shown on the *Bidding CSJ* and students may bid on any such vacancies. Each day's secondary bids are processed that night and the results are sent to students by e-mail the next morning. Also, if a company cancels or changes its schedule, or a student on the waitlist is scheduled

EXHIBIT 4
Web Page for Submitting Bids

Company Name	Job Description	Bid Type	Resume Number
ATA - Strategic Planning	Strategic Planner	A	12
Acosta Sales and Marketing	Management Trainee	R	00
American Express Financial Advisors/Merrillville	Personal Financial Advisor	C	12

Submit Bids Reset

for an interview, the affected students are notified immediately via e-mail. Students who are using the BPO must check their e-mail at least once a day.

The BPO has a strict policy against "no-shows" for interviews. If a student does not show up for a scheduled interview, he or she is suspended from bidding until the student has made a satisfactory explanation to both the BPO and the company involved. Therefore, it is crucial that the student always know when his or her interviews are scheduled so that if something comes up the affected interview can be canceled at least 3 days before the interview is scheduled. By clicking on "View My Personal Information Calendar" on the student menu, the student is presented with a 2-week calendar of his or her scheduled events.

The process of obtaining suitable employment is difficult, stressful, and crucial to the graduating student. Students are competing with each other (and with students from other institutions) for the jobs that are available. Recognizing that companies have strong preferences about the qualifications of students they wish to interview, that popular companies may only be willing to interview a limited number of students, and that each interview with a popular company that is taken by one student cannot be taken by another, the BPO bidding system provides each student with a fair and convenient way to schedule interviews with the companies that come to the campus.

The Employer's View of the BPO System

Employers are very pleased with the services provided to them by the Midstate University BPO, rating it among the very best placement operations in the country. This is a great advantage to Midstate University students because the number of companies that come to the campus to interview determines the number of job opportunities the students have. Therefore the BPO goes all out to provide outstanding service to the employers, and the BPO computer system provides extensive support for most of these services.

For the employer the first step in the interview process is to schedule the dates on which to interview on campus. Whenever a company is on campus interviewing, a BPO manager attempts to set up a schedule for that company to return for interviews the next year. This tentative schedule is entered into the BPO computer system. During the summer the BPO system prepares and sends a letter to each company confirming its tentative schedule for next year. The system also produces a list of companies that have interviewed on campus in the past that are not scheduled for next year, and each of these companies is contacted by a BPO manager during the summer.

The BPO system also prepares electronic resume books that companies may order. These "books" are stored on standard computer disks and contain the resumes of all students registered with the BPO. The disk also includes software that makes it easy to select resumes (and/or mailing labels) to print based on factors such as major, degree, GPA, geographic preference, areas of interest, skills, and graduation date. The resumes may be used by companies to determine whether or not to interview on campus, or to decide who to add to their preference list. The mailing labels may be used to contact selected students prior to the bidding process. Companies that do not interview on campus may use the disk to identify students to contact directly. The student resume book is also available via the Web, and resumes for students who have been scheduled or waitlisted are available to recruiters at the click of their mouse.

Five or six weeks before a scheduled recruiting date the company must submit a Campus Recruiting Information Form (CRIF) that provides the information for the company's listing in the *Weekly CSJ* and the *Bidding CSJ*. This information may be mailed or faxed, or it may be submitted directly to the system by filling out a form that is available on the Web. All of the forms that employers submit to the BPO are available on the Web for direct submission.

A few weeks before a company is scheduled to interview, the system mails (or upon request, faxes) the company contact person a reminder notice containing the interview schedule and requesting notification of any modifications that the company wishes to make. Then, after primary bidding is completed, the system mails or faxes updated interview schedules and waitlists to the companies, which help the recruiters prepare for their visits and sometimes leads to last-minute addition to schedules for some of the waitlisted students. In addition, recruiters may look at their schedules via the Web while bidding is going on and see the names and resumes of the students who have been scheduled or waitlisted. Two days before the interviews the system prepares a packet to be given to the recruiter upon arrival that includes the final schedule and resumes for the students on the schedule.

At the end of each season the system sends each of the companies an extensive packet of information, including a report of their recruiting activities at Midstate University. This includes a review of the past year's interview dates and a listing of next year's scheduled dates. If the company is not yet scheduled for the next year, dates are suggested. The packet includes an alphabetic listing of all the students the company interviewed, accompanied by a note asking them to fill in blanks for offers and hires and return it to the BPO. The packet also includes a list of the contacts from that company along with a request to return the list after deleting the names of any persons who no longer work for the company (used to remove obsolete names from the system's database). And finally the system also produces mailing labels for the BPO yearly report sent out in August and the *Midstate University Recruiter Newsletter* sent twice yearly.

The BPO Managers' View of the BPO System

The BPO computer system forms an essential part of all of the critical activities of the BPO, and it would be impossible for the BPO to render the high level of services that it provides to Midstate University students and recruiting companies without this system.

During the recruiting year the system provides Wine and other BPO managers with a great deal of up-to-date information. For example, the system can highlight recruiting dates where there are rooms available or where extra rooms must be found to accommodate the scheduled interviews. It can compare the demand for the various majors and salary offers with past history. Moreover, the system provides a mechanism for collecting feedback from both students and recruiters so that common problems can be identified and corrective measures taken. Students who encounter problems are encouraged to report the problem via e-mail or to come to the BPO and talk to a consultant. The online system enables BPO managers to search the system to find the information necessary to investigate and resolve the problem. The BPO usually resolves reported problems within 24 to 48 hours.

The system has a reporting facility that is available to students, faculty, recruiters, BPO managers, and the general public. This reporting facility provides a wealth of information on the BPO and its activities. Its menu includes such items as salary statistics, annual reports of the BPO, registrant statistics, tentative recruiting activity, company recruiting summary, placement by company, and student interview frequency. Exhibit 5 (see p. 273) shows the initial screen of the salary statistics report generator and illustrates the various factors that can be used to tailor salary reports. A portion of the report generated by the alternatives highlighted in Exhibit 5 is shown in Exhibit 6 (see p. 274). Exhibit 7 (see p. 275) shows a portion of a student interview frequency report generated on November 3, 2000, during the recruiting season.

At the end of the recruiting season the system provides comprehensive summary information on the results of the year's placement activity for the BPO yearly report. This wealth of information on placement activity and the job market is of great interest to the dean and faculty of the Business School, and is avidly perused by students as they choose their major field of study and by recruiters as they attempt to maximize the success of their recruitment efforts. This information is also used in brochures promoting the school.

The BPO Computer System

The context diagram in Exhibit 8 (see p. 276) summarizes the inputs to and outputs from the BPO system described earlier. As shown in this diagram, the system takes a variety of inputs from client companies and students, and provides outputs for the companies, students, and BPO and Business School management. The system maintains a number of important databases, schedules student interviews, supports communication with client companies, and produces a wide variety of analysis reports for management. The computer system that provides these capabilities consists of a complex combination of networks, computer hardware, systems software, applications software, and databases.

The Computer Network

The computer hardware and network on which the system runs is depicted in Exhibit 9 (see p. 277). The Midstate University backbone network at the top of this diagram is a high-speed (100 mb/sec) fiber-optic Ethernet network that connects all of the buildings on the five Midstate University campuses. Through this network students and faculty all over the university can access university computing resources,

EXHIBIT 5

Salary Statistics Report Generator Screen

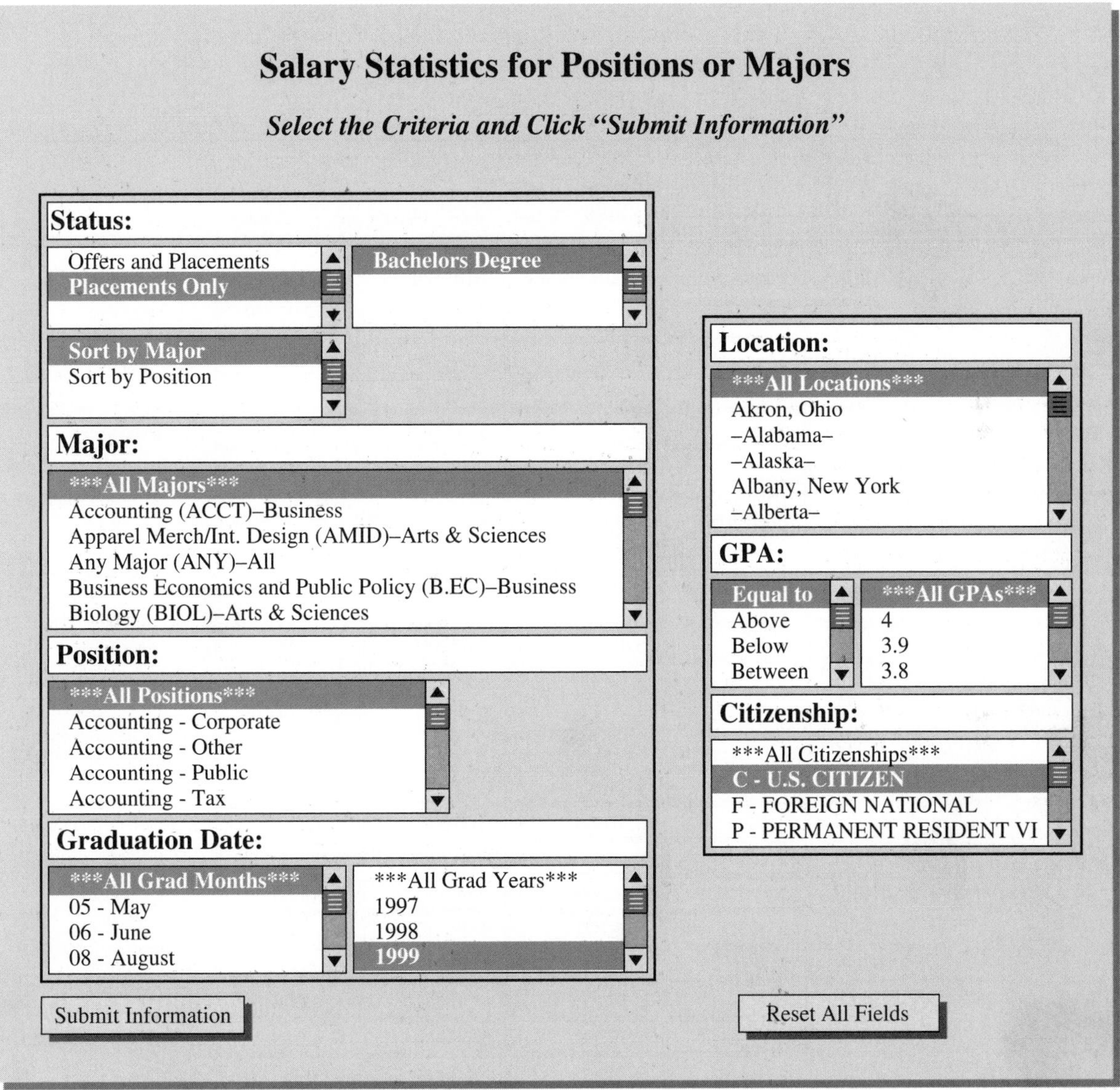

including the Internet, from PCs in computer laboratories, dormitories, libraries, and through the Internet or direct telephone lines from anywhere they may be. The university Web server (connected to the Internet), the university e-mail server, and the BPO subnet are connected to this backbone network, and are thereby connected to each other. The BPO subnet connects the BPO servers, printers, and various IBM-compatible PCs in the BPO waiting room and staff offices to each other and to the backbone network.

The BPO system all runs on the same server, an NCR Worldmark server with 2.5 gigabytes of RAM and dual Pentium III 500 megahertz Xenon processors with a 1 megabyte cache with each processor. The system's data are stored on a RAID 5 array of ten 18 gigabyte hard drives, and two more 18 gigabyte hard drives (RAID level 1) are used for the operating system, Windows 2000. There is also a smaller NCR server that mirrors the production server and is used for system development.

Although everything runs on the Worldmark server, the system uses three "logical" servers: the Web server that works in conjunction with the applications server that works with the database server. Another important function that runs on the Worldmark server is virus protection.

EXHIBIT 6
Part of a Salary Statistics Report

Salary Statistics by Major
for Placements Only

Bachelors Degree
For Graduation Dates Between 01-DEC-98 and 01-AUG-99

Major	Placements	Mean Salary	Min Salary	Max Salary
ACCT	115	$ 38557	$ 27000	$ 75000
AMID	13	$ 32846	$ 27000	$ 37000
AOTR	6	$ 36000	$ 30000	$ 43000
B.EC	6	$ 39167	$ 30000	$ 50000
BIOL	2	$ 41350	$ 36000	$ 46700
BUS	1	$ 0	$ 0	$ 0
CIS	112	$ 44019	$ 32500	$ 55200
COAS	1	$ 34500	$ 34500	$ 34500
D.T.	37	$ 42719	$ 27000	$ 52000
ECON	5	$ 40400	$ 36000	$ 50000
EDUC	1	$ 60000	$ 60000	$ 60000
ENGL	1	$ 31000	$ 31000	$ 31000
ENTP	1	$ 30000	$ 30000	$ 30000
FIN	125	$ 38387	$ 22500	$ 75000
FNRT	2	$ 31000	$ 31000	$ 31000
GNRL	1	$ 0	$ 0	$ 0
HPER	2	$ 60000	$ 60000	$ 60000
INTL	65	$ 38102	$ 28200	$ 55000
JOUR	2	$ 34000	$ 32000	$ 36000
LAMP	4	$ 41000	$ 36000	$ 50000
LEGL	6	$ 35750	$ 28000	$ 44000
MATH	2	$ 50000	$ 50000	$ 50000
MGMT	51	$ 34508	$ 20000	$ 52000
MKTG	134	$ 35137	$ 20000	$ 55000
NOTR	4	$ 33750		
	10			

The database server maintains the BPO databases, the applications server handles all the processing, including the bid processing, and the Web server presents information to and collects data from students, recruiters, and the general public. Periodically a batch of data that has been collected from the students and recruiters by the Web server is given to the applications server where the data is processed, databases are updated by the database server, and a batch of results are sent back to the Web server to update its files. The students can then access these data through the Web.

EXHIBIT 7

The Business Student Part of an Interview Frequency Report

Student Interview Frequency

Undergraduate Majors: Accounting, Business Economics and Public Policy, Entrepreneurship, Finance (also Real Estate and Insurance), Human Resource Management, Information Systems (BS), Information Systems (MBA), International Business, Legal Studies, Management, Marketing/Distribution, Not-for-Profit Management, Operations Management, Operations/Decision Tech, Other Business	**Graduation Date:** Dec-2000 to Aug-2001	Students interviewing from 09/01/2000 to 11/03/2000
Paid Status: Yes		

As of 03-Nov-2000

Number of Interviews Taken								
School **Major**	**None**	**1–5**	**6–10**	**11–15**	**16–20**	**21+**	**Ints**	**Average Interviews/Student**
Business								
Accounting	57	51	47	23	9	4	1091	8.14
Any Business	0	0	1	0	0	0	6	6.00
Business Economics and Public Policy	0	5	3	2	0	0	64	6.40
Entrepreneurship	7	12	7	0	0	0	87	4.58
Finance (also Real Estate and Insurance)	71	121	128	62	17	4	2556	7.70
Information Systems (BS)	70	142	87	18	3	0	1353	5.41
Information Systems (MBA)	0	0	1	0	0	0	6	6.00
International Business	22	62	53	21	3	1	901	6.44
Legal Studies	11	16	4	0	0	0	82	4.10
Management	34	56	25	10	0	1	482	5.24
Marketing/Distribution	68	160	105	23	3	0	1580	5.43
Not-for-Profit Management	2	0	2	0	0	0	13	6.50
Operations/Decision Tech	29	72	64	14	3	1	958	6.22
Other Business	7	20	9	5	1	0	206	5.89

In addition to Windows 2000, the system's software includes Oracle database software, HTML software for the Web pages, and ColdFusion, a special application development environment that works well as middleware between HTML and Oracle. ColdFusion includes its own HTML editor and has additions that allow one to write SQL queries to the Oracle database. Therefore, many of the applications are written in the ColdFusion language. The application software of this

EXHIBIT 8
Context Diagram for the System

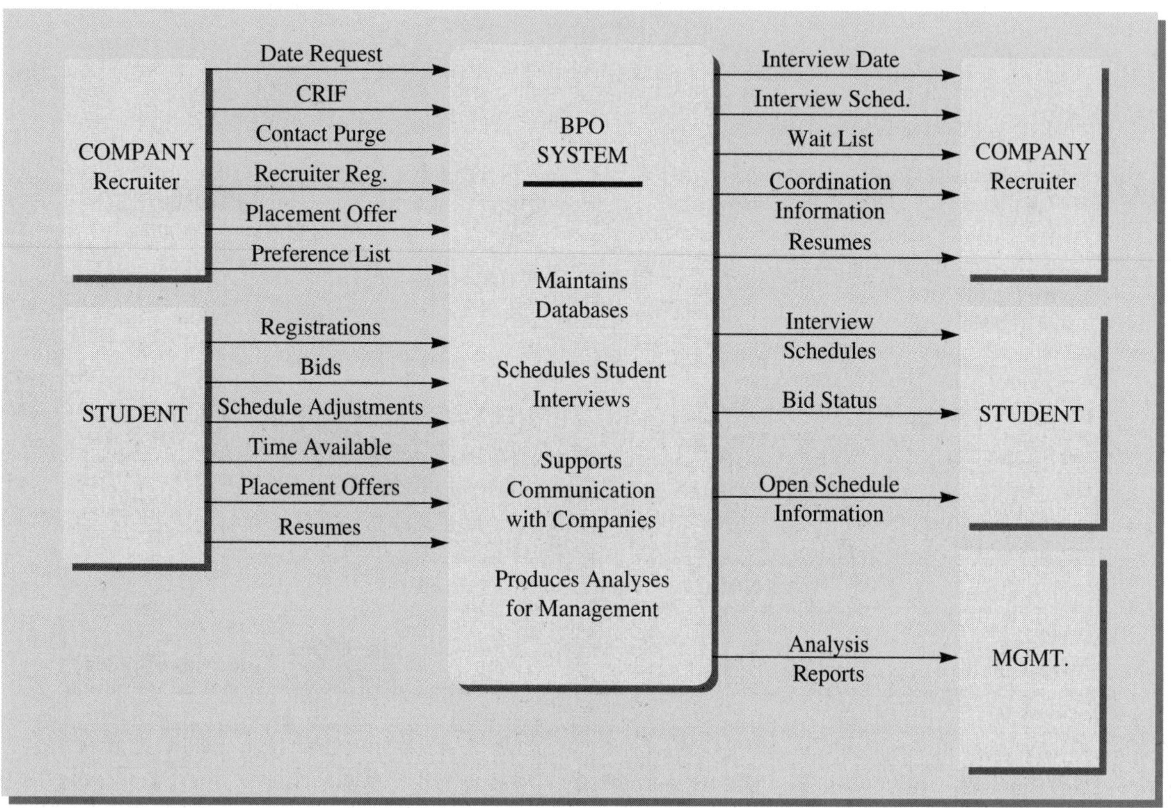

system includes some 500 programs and around 100,000 lines of code.

The Database

At the heart of this system is a comprehensive database managed by the Oracle 8 relational DBMS. There are about a dozen major tables (or relations) in this database, but there are over 150 tables in the entire BPO database. The BPO database takes up about 1.5 gigabytes of disk space. In this section we describe some of the most important of these tables, their use, and how they are maintained.

The COMPANY table, whose structure[1] is illustrated in Exhibit 10 (see p. 278), contains name and address information on each of the BPO's client companies. It is updated whenever BPO managers enlist a new client or when there is some change in the data on a current client. There is relatively little maintenance activity on this database.

The CONTACTS table, shown in Exhibit 11 (see p. 278), contains data on individual recruiters who have interviewed students through the BPO. It is updated with data from the registration forms that recruiters fill out when they arrive at the BPO to interview. Each summer the BPO sends a list of current contacts to each company and asks it to return the list after crossing off the names of those who are no longer recruiting for the company. This list is then used to purge names from the CONTACT table.

The SCHEDULE table has an entry for each planned interview schedule. Companies usually submit these data about 6 weeks prior to the interview date, and schedules are entered into the database when they are received. Changes to planned schedules occur, and when they are approved by the BPO manager in charge of the schedule, they are entered into the table. These data are an important input into the bid processing subsystem described in the next section.

[1]Each data element of a **row** in the table is listed in Exhibit 10. The COMPANY table consists of as many rows as there are companies in the database. Unfortunately, the data element names in the database examples are not always easy to relate to common terminology. Nevertheless, they give a fair idea of the contents of the database.

EXHIBIT 9
The BPO System's Technology Platform

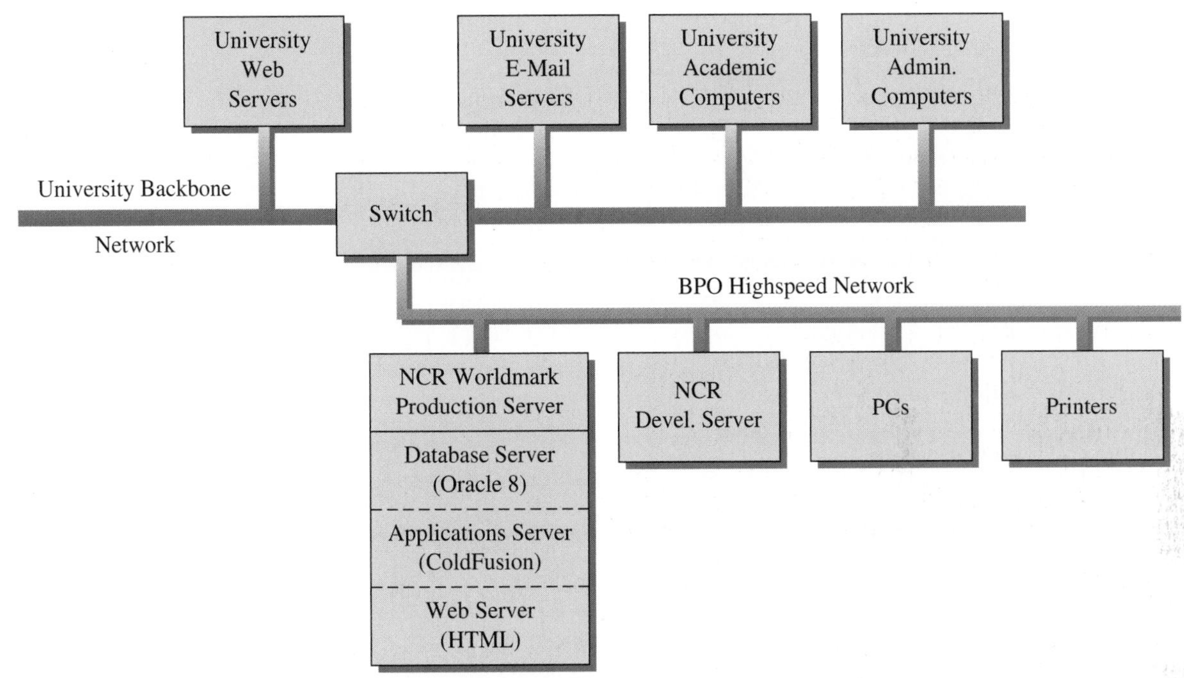

The BID_TITLES table, shown in Exhibit 12 (see p. 279), contains data describing each position offered by each company through its interview schedules and the qualifications required for a student to interview for that job. These data are provided via the Campus Recruiting Information Form (CRIF) that is submitted by the companies 5 or 6 weeks before the interview date. The CRIFs are entered into the database on a daily basis, and any changes to the data (such as positions available or required qualifications) are made as they occur. These data are used to establish the company's notice in the *CSJ* on the Web and are used by the bid processing subsystem described in the next section.

The REGISTRANTS table, shown in Exhibit 13 (see p. 279), contains data on the students who are registered with the BPO. Some of these data are collected when the student registers with the BPO, and changes during the year can be made by the student via the Web, but some data are added as codes by BPO personnel. These data are required by the bid processing subsystem. Some of this data is highly confidential and is never released by the BPO except in summary reports.

The BIDS table, shown in Exhibit 14 (see p. 280), contains the data for each bid submitted by students via the bidding system on the Web. These data provide the most important input into the bid processing subsystem.

The INTERVIEW SCHEDULE table contains the data for a line on an interview schedule. The entries to this database are produced by the bid processing system described in the next section. However, the student may make changes (such as canceling an interview or signing up for an open interview slot) via the Web after the schedule has been posted on the Web until 2 days before the interview occurs.

The WAITLIST table contains the data for unsuccessful bids for interview slots. These data are also created by the bid processing system and the results are provided to both the student and the company involved. However, if someone cancels an interview and a waitlisted person is given that slot, both the INTERVIEW SCHEDULE and the WAITLIST tables must be updated.

Changes to these tables take place quite frequently, so each table is updated on a daily basis. BPO managers are very concerned with maintaining the accuracy of each of these tables.

Primary Bid Processing Subsystem

Most interview schedules fill during primary bidding, which makes the primary bid processing system crucial to both the students and the BPO. Primary bid processing takes place on Monday evenings during the recruiting season and results are provided to the students via e-mail and the Web by early Tuesday morning. As the following description shows, a complex process is required to process the primary bids.

EXHIBIT 10
COMPANIES Table

COMPANIES
UPDATE_USER
INSERT_USER
COMPANY_NAME
ADDRESS1
ADDRESS2
CITY
STATE
ZIP
FAX
PHONE
URL
SICCODE
CLEARANCE
DIRECTOR_ID
UPDATED
INSERT_DATE
UPDATE_DATE
PIN
COM_ID
CD_CD_ID

EXHIBIT 11
CONTACTS Table

CONTACTS
UPDATE_USER
INSERT_USER
FIRST_NAME
MID_INIT
NICKNAME
LAST_NAME
ADDRESS1
ADDRESS2
CITY
STATE
ZIP
TITLE
PHONE
PH_EXT
FAX
FAX_EXT
UPDATED
SALUTATION
EMAIL
INSERT_DATE
COM_COM_ID
CON_ID
COM_COM_ID_CONTACT_THIS_PERSON

A system flow chart depicting the bid processing system is shown in Exhibit 15 (pp. 280–281). A system flow chart is composed of processes sandwiched between the inputs to and the outputs from those processes. Output data may be the input to another process. Each process is usually performed by a computer under control of a program. The lines indicate flows of data, and are read from the top down and from left to right. Arrowheads at the end of a line indicate that the flow is up or off the diagram.

All of the processes in this subsystem are performed on the BPO applications server, and the databases shown reside on the database server, although the data may have been collected via the Web and the outputs may be transferred to the Web server for access by the student. These servers are, of course, "logical servers," all of which are running on the NCR Worldmark server.

As shown at the top of the first page of the flow chart, the input to the bid validation process includes the batch of bids on specific jobs with specific companies from the students, the data from the CRIFs (in the BID_TITLES table) on the requirements to bid on each job imposed by the companies, the student data[2] used to determine the student's eligibility to bid on the job, and the preference lists. In order to validate the bids the program first checks to see if the student has been suspended for missing an interview and if he or she has the requested bid available. Then the program compares the student status from the student file with the company restrictions to determine if the student is qualified to bid on that job. If the student is on the preference list for that job he or she is certified as qualified without checking the student's status. The program also adds two data elements to the valid bids: a preference code (1 if the student is preferenced and 2 if not) and an eight digit number from a random number generator that is used to break ties between students who would otherwise have equal priority. The output from this process includes valid bids, bid errors, and an error summary report summarizing the frequency of various types of errors. The bid errors file is input to a distribution process (on page 2 of the flow chart) that e-mails the notice of the error to the student and sends the bid errors file to the Web server.

The next processing step is to sort the valid bids database on the concatenation of bidding code (which is company number and job code), preference code, priority, and the tie-breaking random number. By concatenation we mean that the

[2]The student data include the REGISTRANTS table and subsidiary tables for data elements like "Major" and "Languages" that may have several values.

EXHIBIT 12
BID_TITLES Table

BID_TITLES
UPDATE_USER
INSERT_DATE
INSERT_USER
BID_NUMBER
NOTE
SHOW_FAX
SHOW_PH
SALARY_MIN
SALARY_MAX
TITLE
LIST_GIVEN
UPDATED_DATE
BID_PROCESS_DATE
CANCEL
CONFIRMED
BOOKING_DATE
COURSE_STATUS
GRAD_DATE
FALL_PRIORITY
LIST_TYPE
MIN_GPA
GPA_SCR
WORK_EXP
EXP_SCR
OPEN_PREF_TYPE
PUBLICATION_DATE
BDT_ID
LT_LT_ID
CON_CON_ID
UTL4_UTL4_ID
TIT_DESC_TIT_DESC_ID
BID_TITLES_DESC_ID
BID_TITLES_CIT_ID
BID_TITLES_JT_ID

data elements are combined to form one long data element, starting from the left with company number, then job code, then preference code, etc. This sorting process gets all of the bids for a company-job combination together, and also arranges these bids in sequence by the complex priority scheme the BPO uses to assign bids to interview slots. Thus, if there are 12 slots available for a given company-job combination, then the first 12 bids would be given these slots.

Then (on page 2 of the flow chart) the schedule database, sorted bids, student database, and time available database are input into the interview scheduling process. As described

EXHIBIT 13
REGISTRANTS Table

REGISTRANTS
C_STATE
LAST_NAME
FIRST_NAME
MID_INIT
H_ADDRESS
H_COUNTRY
H_CITY
H_STATE
H_ZIP
H_PHONE
C_ADDRESS
C_CITY
C_ZIP
C_PHONE
DISCIPLINE_STATUS
EMAIL
GRAD_DATE
SEX
BIRTH_YR
YRS_EXP
NO_PRES_MSG
GPA
CC
DATE_AVAIL
OFP_CHECK
PAID_CODE
SAL_MIN
SAL_DESIRE
UPDATED
SALUTATION
REG_RELEASE
BIDS_USED_A
BIDS_USED_B
BIDS_USED_C
BIDS_USED_R
PIN
SOCIAL_SECURITY_NO
REG_ID
REGISTRANTS_CY_ID
REGISTRANTS_EO_ID
REGISTRANTS_DEG_ID
REGISTRANTS_CIT_ID
REGISTRANTS_CT_ID
REGISTRANTS_RT_ID
REG_LOC_ID
REGISTRANTS_CNTRY_ID

EXHIBIT 14
BIDS Table

BIDS
RESUME_ID
BID_SEQUENCE
BID_TYPE
BID_TIME_DATE
DISPOSITION
WAIT_LIST_RANK
INITIAL_BID_LETTER
FINAL_BID_LETTER
BID_NUMBER
BID_ID
STURES_STURES_ID
BDT_BDT_ID
REG_REG_ID

previously, the bids are sequenced so that determining which students get the interview slots is trivial, and the rest of the bids form the waitlist. But the time availability data must be used to determine which student interviews at each time slot. A complex algorithm is used to assign the selected students to time slots in such a way that all the students are scheduled to interview when they do not have other conflicts. The outputs from this process is an interview schedule database, a waitlist database, and an updated student database (whose bids-available data has been updated to reflect the bids that have been used).

Next the interview schedules and waitlists are printed and sent to the Web server, and some of them are automatically faxed to the companies who have requested this service. Finally, the interview schedule, waitlist, and bid errors databases are sorted together by student number, combining all bid actions for a student, and a single e-mail is sent to the student that reports the results of all of his or her bids.

Conclusion

The Midstate University BPO has developed its computerized bidding system over a period of several years. Prior to the use of the Web, accurately capturing the necessary data from the students was a difficult problem. The switch to the Web has been a tremendous success, from both the students' and the BPO's perspective. The Web offers convenience for the students and company clients, and also makes updating changes easy. Plus, the BPO has been able to continuously improve this system, even on a week-by-week basis.

EXHIBIT 15
System Flowchart of the Bid Processing Subsystem (page 1)

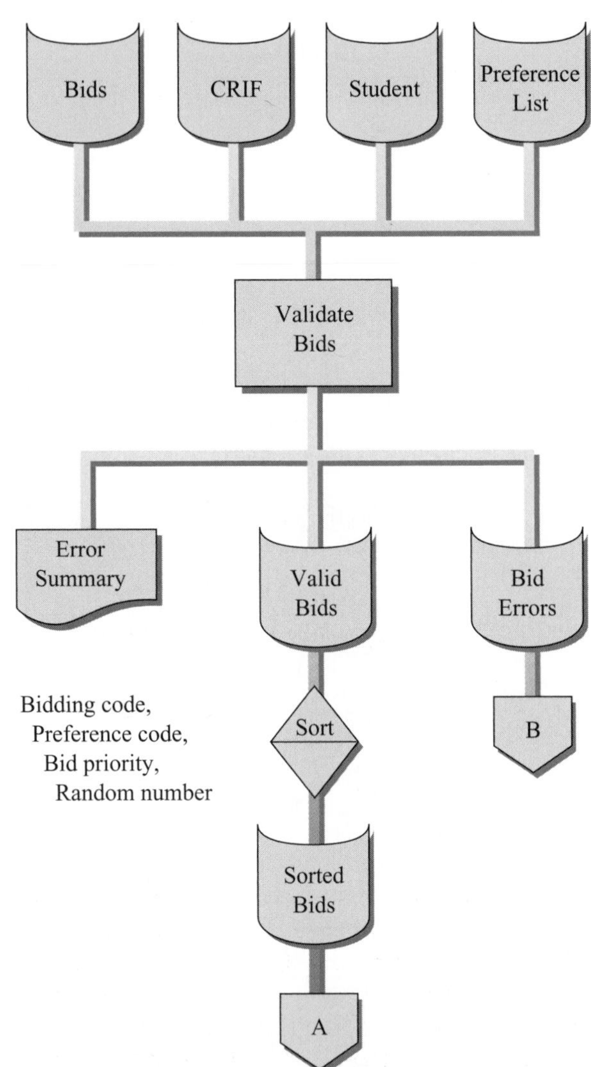

The system has worked so well that Wine has only one concern:

> My only worry now is security. It might be attractive to some students to get into the system and make changes so that they could get interviews to which they are not entitled. And, of course, there will always be hackers who get their kicks by causing trouble. We have built in lots of firewalls to protect this system, but who is to say that it cannot be penetrated?

This concern for security has dictated how the system has been designed to operate. Although the system may appear to be an online system, it is not. There is no online connection through the Web to the system's database. Rather, the Web

EXHIBIT 15
System Flowchart (page 2)

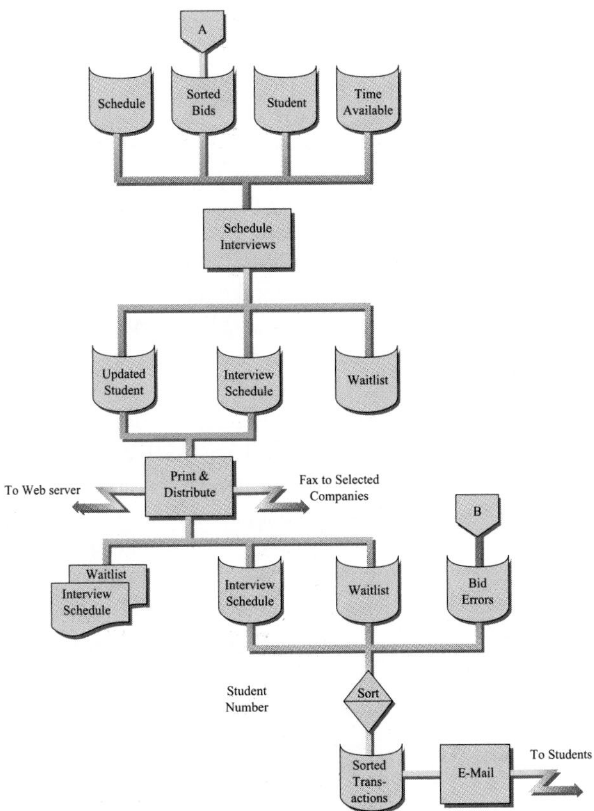

system collects the students' input and accumulates a batch of transactions that is used at night to update the system's database tables. Then the processing takes place and the results are made available to the students and companies via the Web. Thus the databases and processes on the BPO server are not available to persons who might try to penetrate and modify the data or processes of the system.

The students, however, have a major responsibility for the security of their own data. If a student leaves the system without exiting it properly by returning to the BPO or School of Business home page anyone who comes to that PC can continue to work with the student's data. Not only can this person see the student's data, but the intruder can cancel interviews, enter bids, and take other actions that may not be to the student's liking. In the manual that describes the system and explains how to use it, the BPO repeatedly cautions the students to be sure to exit the system properly.

Other large university placement operations are using the computer to assist in their operations, but the Midstate University BPO has been a pioneer in this area. Although he will continue to improve the system, Wine is very pleased with the current Web-based version:

> Since we got the system on the Web we have been able to provide outstanding service to all our clients, both students and recruiters. The Web has made a tremendous improvement in our operation!

CASE STUDY II-2

THE CHALLENGES OF LOCAL SYSTEM DESIGN FOR MULTINATIONALS: THE MAXFLI SALES FORCE AUTOMATION SYSTEM AT BAT

Will all direct-distribution markets eventually use MaxFli or a system like it? Yes. I believe yes, they will. And why? Because there is an absolute need to connect selling in and selling out together.

—*Peter Brickley, Chief Information Officer, BAT Globe House*

I have a very high view of MaxFli. [It] creates a selling process. It allows us to have a real competitive advantage in the field. It's really that ... MaxFli allows you to direct your promotion, all your marketing strategies to the right outlet at the right time. That is why it gives us competitive advantage.

—*Oscar Gonzalez, formerly at BAT Colombia, transferred to Globe House in 2001*

Until today, there are some concerns [with MaxFli]. Why is that? The problem is the cost of MaxFli, and it is not paying off. That is the big concern. Why not use a more simple system to help us to sell? Selling is our business. So we [should think about] stopping the use of MaxFli.

—*Juan Morales, a marketing executive in BAT Central America*

MaxFli was a business change initiative: a sales force automation (SFA) system created to structure and automate the sales process within multiple locations around the globe. However, after three implementations, the success of MaxFli was in question.

Background: British American Tobacco

Founded in 1902, British American Tobacco (BAT) has grown through organic growth and acquisitions to be one of the top three global players in the tobacco industry. By 2002 it ranked number 271 in the *Fortune* Global 500 list of companies. Prior to 1996, BAT Industries PLC had four tobacco businesses among a number of unrelated business interests. In 1996, this business strategy was revised to merge the four independent tobacco businesses into one. Nontobacco businesses (financial services, retailing, and others) were divested, and BAT became a stand-alone business focused only on tobacco. The company then merged in 1999 with the global cigarette company Rothmans International. In the fall of 2001 BAT's local and international brands were sold through five regional divisions: America Pacific, Asia Pacific, Europe, Latin America, and AMESCA (Africa, the Middle East, South and Central Asia). A sixth division, STC (Smoking Tobacco and Cigars), is global and operates in more than 120 countries.

The profit centers are 120 "end markets," each typically a country. End-market directors (general managers) report to regional directors, who are members of BAT's top executive board—the Tobacco Management Board (TMB). The company's strategy leverages global economies of scale while offering autonomy to end markets.

In general, end markets either distribute the product to retail outlets via their own trucks and sales force (direct distribution) or use other distribution-for-fee service companies. The direct distribution model is data- and resource-intensive and is used by many end markets worldwide. MaxFli was designed to facilitate the trade-marketing and distribution activities within direct distribution markets.

Birth of MaxFli in Latin America

The Origins of MaxFli

Several business and technical issues converged for the creation of MaxFli. The rapid maturation of trade marketing and distribution (TM&D) within BAT markets had outpaced the ability of existing technology. As sales, marketing, and cash-collection methods evolved, new systems were needed to support them. Additionally, BAT began to consider the implications of Y2K issues for their IT systems. By the mid-1990s many Latin American markets recognized the need to replace their existing

 This case was prepared by Bradley C. Wheeler and Michael L. Williams at Indiana University's Kelley School of Business. The names and titles of some informants have been camouflaged as requested. The authors would like to thank the IU CIBER office for funding the research and the many BAT employees around the world who participated in the research.

SFA system as a result of Y2K concerns and the rapid acceleration of trade-marketing and distribution practices. Because these were all direct-distribution markets with similar business processes, a codevelopment strategy emerged.

As end markets discussed strategies for a Y2K-compliant TM&D system, a new opportunity arose. BAT global headquarters (Globe House) reasoned that global economies of scale could produce a better system, at a lower per-user cost. In particular, executives at Globe House and several end markets saw the opportunity to develop a flexible, re-usable IT system to support trade marketing and distribution within direct distribution markets.

Choosing the Right Approach for Developing MaxFli

Based on experience with a recent Globe House–led IT initiative to develop a TM&D system for traditional distribution markets, there was a widely held belief that the primary design of the system should occur in the end markets, not in Globe House. Because TM&D includes many of the value-added processes that support the retailer, it was thought difficult for Globe House to understand or appreciate the nuances and complexities of regional differences. Hans Neidermann, global director of trade marketing for BAT, observed, "There are so many differences in terms of local processes relating to invoices, trading terms, taxation, etc., that we did not want to get involved in this in the first place."

In light of the complexities involved in local trade-marketing processes, Globe House decided on a distributed approach for the design and development of MaxFli. Globe House would coordinate much of the development effort in London with the help of Andersen Consulting (now Accenture), but the design would occur in the end markets of Latin America.

In February 1998, representatives from 15 markets including Colombia, Honduras, Venezuela, Brazil, Mexico, UK, USA, Belgium, and France began a 2-month feasibility study to develop the business case for MaxFli. Two specific goals for the feasibility study were to determine the "best practices" of direct distribution markets to be embedded in the software, and to determine if the direct distribution solution could fit within the existing technological platform at BAT. The business case from this feasibility study was presented to the TMB, which granted final approval to begin development in May 1998. The MaxFli steering committee planned for three separate implementation rollouts before the end of 2000: Chile, Colombia, and Central America. (See Exhibit 1.)

Chiletabacos, BAT's operating company in Chile, was selected to take the lead in designing and implementing MaxFli, for several reasons. Chiletabacos was one of the leaders among the BAT markets in Latin America. They were already a well-established company with a strong market presence in Chile. With 98.5 percent market share, Chiletabacos had demonstrated a consistent ability to develop successful business strategies and generate revenue. Additionally, Chiletabacos General Manager Roberto Friere was highly respected throughout the BAT community.

Designing and Building MaxFli

MaxFli was viewed as an important element in the continued maturation of the TM&D function in BAT direct distribution markets. Designing a system to incorporate the best practices from 15 end markets was a complex task. Much attention was given to the design objectives and issues to ensure the usefulness of the system.

Design Objectives

Hans Neidermann captured the essence of the design objectives for MaxFli by saying, "we needed a better integration of the selling process and the trade-marketing process." The goal for the system focused on four key strategic elements:

- Focusing on the in-store experience of the consumer
- Partnering with the retailer as the primary interface with the consumer
- Maximizing marketing costs by understanding in-store promotional successes
- Forecasting retail sales to maximize supply chain efficiency

To accomplish these goals, MaxFli had to provide accurate business information that would allow BAT to cross-reference retail sales and consumer information, which was the only way for BAT to continue succeeding in markets where advertising was increasingly restrictive. Finally, MaxFli needed to be integrated with accounting and inventory management to avoid the duplication of effort and accounting difficulties experienced with previous systems.

Design Issues

Because the system was to be used in markets of different sizes and market conditions, the design of MaxFli required agreement on several early decisions. According to Roberto Palacios, the MaxFli project manager in Chile, the IT strategic priorities that guided the development of MaxFli were:

- A common, reusable, and scalable technology platform
- Shared data between sales, accounting and marketing
- Appropriate use of packaged software

BAT faced a variety of options to attain these priorities. Should BAT use an existing product or develop their own?

EXHIBIT 1

A History of Handheld Sales Force Automation Systems in Latin America

Date	Event
1983	Chile's first handheld is developed
1986	Major upgrade to handheld in Chile
1983	BAT Colombia is started
1995	Six independent end markets of Central America form a single cluster market, BAT Central America
March – May 1998	2-month feasibility study of MaxFli case
May 1998	BAT Tobacco Management Board approves MaxFli concept
May 1998	BAT has commitment from Siebel Systems to build a handheld solution
May 1999	Siebel backs out of building handheld solution
Summer 1999	BAT replaces Andersen Consulting with Ernst & Young
Sept. 1999	Ciberion is started as a joint venture with E&Y and BAT
Nov. 1999	MaxFli 1.0 goes live in Chile
May 2000	MaxFli 1.0 goes live in Colombia
Nov. 2000	MaxFli 1.1 goes live in Central America

Should they develop a product independently or in partnership with a supplier? What platform provided maximum scalability, reusability, and stability? What were the implications of MaxFli for the Enterprise Resource Planning (ERP) applications being installed throughout BAT? What handheld device allowed for international support and maintenance? What implications did the variance in technical expertise throughout Latin America present?

After carefully reviewing the options, BAT negotiated with Siebel Systems to build a handheld solution for direct distribution markets within BAT. However, one month before development was to begin, Siebel withdrew to focus on other corporate priorities of its own.

Design Choices

In May 1998, BAT began developing MaxFli with the help of Andersen Consulting. The primary design work and project leadership were in Santiago de Chile and consisted of a team of BAT staff from Brazil, Chile, Colombia, Honduras, Mexico, and Venezuela. The development effort took place in London, performed by Andersen Consulting and managed by BAT personnel. The system was to be finished and first implemented in Chile in May 1999.

MaxFli was designed to deliver a globally transferable, leading-edge direct distribution system for BAT. In its final form MaxFli consisted of several interdependent systems to track sales, inventory, credit accounts, competitor information, merchandising, and outlet classification. (See Exhibit 2.)

The front end of MaxFli was a Visual Basic® application running on a handheld Hewlett-Packard Jornada 680™ using Windows® CE 2.1. This handheld was used by the sales representatives each day to place orders, issue credit, print invoices, track inventory, and monitor merchandising and competitor activity. At the end of each day, the sales reps synchronized their handhelds with the back-office system. Synchronization could occur through the office network, a dial-up connection from a land-based telephone, or from a mobile phone. The back-office system was a Siebel Systems customer relationship management system (CRM) and an Oracle 8i data warehouse running

EXHIBIT 2
Main Technological Concepts in MaxFli

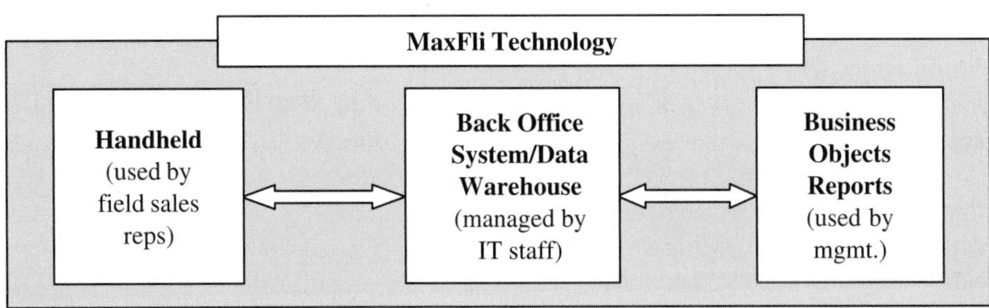

on HP servers. The reporting engine was BusinessObjects 2.0 integrated into a Lotus Notes workspace. MaxFli reported sales and competitor information, outlet classification, and promotional material effectiveness. It was designed to be used by management at all levels from junior sales manager to senior executive.

Implementing MaxFli in Chile

Chile is a long, narrow country of 15 million people surrounded by the Andes Mountains to the east and the Pacific Ocean to the west and south. It covers about 50 percent of the western edge of South America and has been receptive to BAT products over the years. Chiletabacos held command over a large percentage of the cigarette market in Chile.

The IT function at Chiletabacos was a mature function with a strong presence in the business. Despite a history of difficult IT implementations, General Manager Roberto Friere expressed great confidence in the team of IT professionals in his organization. One senior executive argued that "[implementing MaxFli] was an important move for us, because our track record with large IT system implementations was poor."

MaxFli was the largest IT project in the history of Chiletabacos. Chiletabacos shouldered $8.9 million of the development costs, which cumulatively totaled nearly $15 million. Before taking on the project Friere asserted two conditions to Globe House: it had to be first and foremost a Chilean solution (as opposed to a global solution that required Chilean adoption); and he had to have final control over project development.

Palacios was selected as the project manager on the basis of his track record of managing large projects throughout his 20 years in finance at Chiletabacos. It did not take long for Palacios to develop a clear vision about the implementation of MaxFli. From the beginning he saw MaxFli as a business change project, not just an IT project:

> The IT tool is just one of the key components of the business change program. The tool by its own will not change anything. So people, processes, and IT systems need to be aligned. MaxFli is a business change program that requires huge organizational effort with four major work-streams: management, communication, process/people, and technology.

Management

Friere and Palacios shared a belief that decisively addressing project challenges as they arose would be critical for success in the MaxFli implementation. Palacios demonstrated this by creating a well-defined plan for pre-implementation, implementation readiness, and post-implementation acceptance. Still, at one point in the development process, Friere believed that he needed to exercise his project control explicitly. When a series of events led him to question who was in charge of the project, he froze the development effort for two weeks until he was convinced that his two primary objectives, creating a Chilean solution and maintaining control, would be met. This helped the development team remain focused on the task at hand and ensured that they did the "right things, the right way, using the right tools."

Palacios also emphasized managing expectations:

> An implementation of this size represents a serious challenge; thus the organization needs to be aware that there will be problems. Delays and problems ... should be communicated and explained to the whole organization. The business and technical learning curve is unavoidable. So level of service expectations need to be managed.

Palacios demonstrated a pattern of underselling the benefits of MaxFli while over-delivering on their realization in order to manage expectations.

Communication

Palacios crafted his communications about MaxFli very carefully. MaxFli was under very close scrutiny from management because of its cost. Consequently, Palacios spent much of his energies "managing upward—making sure management understood what we were doing and why we were doing it." Palacios created "powermaps" to help monitor communication. These graphic representations displayed each important person on the MaxFli team, how they were all related, and what communications were essential. These maps helped Palacios keep management informed about the current struggles and successes of the project. This style worked well, according to GM Friere: "Everyone was well informed throughout the [different] stages of the process. It was not a 'black box' where we put in the money and hoped we got the right system."

This was important because MaxFli was intended to be a solution for many direct distribution markets in Latin America. By "managing upwards" Palacios secured the approval and protection of the most powerful force in the MaxFli implementation, the strategic steering committee.

There were several challenges to effective communication during the MaxFli development effort. First was the geographical distance between the design team based in London and the development team based in Santiago. Frequent teleconferences, video conferences, and pan-Atlantic trips helped to moderate the effect of time and distance on communication between designers and developers. A second constraint could not be moderated by travel or telephone. Most of the design team were native Spanish speakers while the development team in the UK were primarily English speakers. This issue was moderated somewhat by the fluent bilingual language skills of Friere, Palacios, and others on the team.

Processes and People

Palacios insisted that MaxFli was not primarily a technology innovation, but a business-process change project supported by technology. Therefore, successful implementation depended on much more than having a strong IT function to support it. He argued, "[T]o capture its full potential [MaxFli] requires an in-depth revision of current TM&D processes, organizational change and a strong commitment."

This view is illustrated by Exhibit 3, which Palacios used in describing MaxFli. It displays the role of the MaxFli system and the role of the implementing end market in determining system success with MaxFli. The unshaded areas represent end-market responsibilities for success while the shaded areas represent MaxFli's contribution toward system success. Accordingly, almost 75 percent of the final outcome depends on the efforts of the local end market, apart from MaxFli. MaxFli was not expected to single-handedly increase market share, streamline processes, and manage trade marketing in the end markets. It was a technological tool that enabled these desiderata but did not command them.

Palacios planned the implementation as a 13-month, 3-phase plan, consisting of awareness, presystem business preparation, and in-market implementation. Over 50 percent of the total effort was expended in end-market business process improvements and preparations before the system went live. The first 2 months were spent in developing awareness, studying the business case, and choosing a management team. The next 5 months were spent reviewing and optimizing current organizational processes to be ready to implement the system. Finally, the system implementation itself required 6 months and led to well-aligned processes, people, and systems.

Palacios gave considerable attention to training and support. Training in the new business processes as well as the MaxFli tool itself were offered in parallel with the process improvements for all employees who would use MaxFli. Palacios

EXHIBIT 3

Clarifying MaxFli and End-Market Responsibilities for Implementation Success

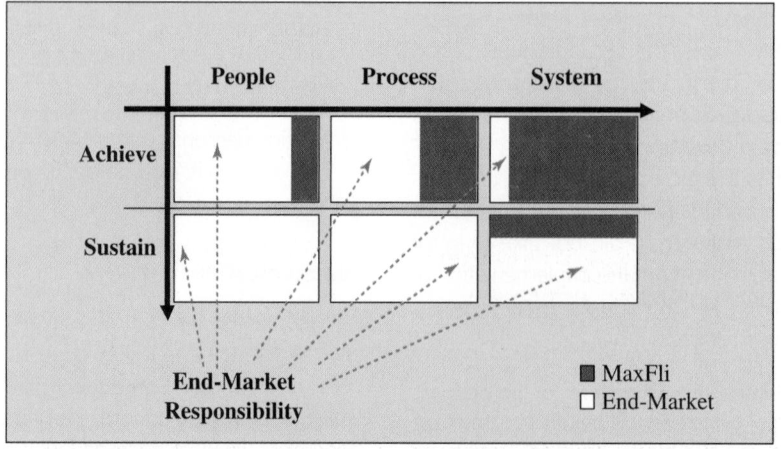

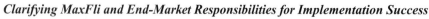

believed that ongoing support was just as critical as initial training. He argued that,

> [a]lthough thorough system testing and adequate training are essential before implementation, with any highly complex system, support plays a key role. The set-up of a local support team should be anticipated and ideally it should be in place before final implementation.

The support team had to be prepared to answer both technical questions (e.g., "How do I print an invoice?") and business questions (e.g., "Can I make a credit decision for this customer, or do I have to check with someone else?").

By focusing on training and support, Palacios wanted to preempt some of the personnel issues that often plague large IT implementations. As stated by GM Friere: "[T]here are personnel issues involved in any project this size. Treat [your people] well, but expect a lot."

Technology

Previous systems at Chiletabacos were designed to control and support basic sales rep activities, but did not provide valuable sales and marketing information. One of the primary objectives of MaxFli was to increase the information available to management, so that they could quickly identify market trends and competitor activity and make effective trade-marketing and distribution decisions. Before, MaxFli marketing managers had to rely mostly on instinct to select which marketing promotions to run in each outlet. MaxFli allowed managers to cross-index sales with promotional activities in individual outlets to better understand the effectiveness of marketing promotions in each category of outlet. This required a combination of technologies. (See Exhibit 4.)

When MaxFli was first proposed in 1997 there were no integrated, off-the-shelf systems that tied a handheld SFA system to a CRM system. The challenge faced by the MaxFli steering committee and project managers was to integrate off-the-shelf and custom components while maintaining low costs, maximum flexibility, and reliability.

Go Live in Chile

MaxFli went live in Chile in November 1999 on schedule and 2 percent over budget. Despite being over budget, the MaxFli implementation in Chile was viewed as a success: it provided valuable information to management about market trends and enabled efficient trade-marketing decisions. Chiletabacos GM Friere elaborated:

> The best thing about MaxFli is that I, or any of my managers, can sit at my desk and see exactly what happened yesterday throughout the country, region, city, or even a single outlet. That is incredibly powerful for making decisions about brands, promotions, and marketing.

By the spring of 2001 the success of MaxFli in Chile was secure: Managers at every level in the organization were using it. However, its biggest test would be its introduction to other end markets in Latin America and around the world.

MaxFli in Colombia

The next site for MaxFli was BAT Colombia. BAT Colombia planned to implement MaxFli in May 2000, 6 months after Chiletabacos completed implementation. BAT Colombia was a relatively young firm, founded by Chiletabacos in 1993. Beginning as a marketing

EXHIBIT 4
Combining Custom and Off-the-Shelf Packages

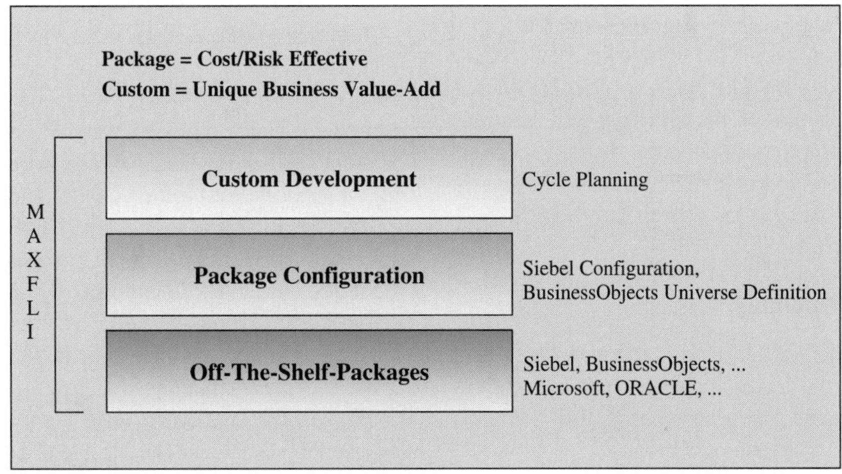

operation, it had expanded to be a complete direct distribution market. Many of its business processes were imported from Chiletabacos, along with several members of the executive team. Consequently, according to Jorge Soto, the general manager of BAT Colombia, they run a very "Chilean business." The relationship between BAT Colombia and Chiletabacos continued to be both close and supportive.

Market Forces in Colombia

Although the business processes and leadership style in Colombia were similar to Chiletabacos, the competitive environment was quite dissimilar. There were four tobacco firms competing for the market in Colombia with each having approximately 25 percent of the market. Two of BAT Colombia's competitors were Colombian companies focused on value brands, while Phillip Morris, Inc., and BAT battled over premium brands.

Chiletabacos was primarily concerned with MaxFli as a competitive information tool; BAT Colombia was more concerned with consumer information, cutting costs, and creating efficiencies with MaxFli. The new system enabled BAT Colombia to more quickly identify and understand the consumer's tastes and preferences. This information helped them produce and target premium brands to those willing and able to buy them.

Project Team in Colombia

BAT Colombia had aggressively adopted new technologies to increase efficiencies for several years, but MaxFli was their largest IT project to date. The MaxFli project team in Colombia was led by one of their senior TM&D Managers, Patricio Imbert. The IT personnel assigned to the MaxFli project included some of the best and brightest IT talent in BAT Colombia, including System Administrator Juan Carlos Hidalgo, who had already spent 1 year in Chile working on MaxFli.

In July 1999, at the beginning of the MaxFli project in Colombia, Chiletabacos hosted a "MaxFli University," and several members of the project team spent one week in Chile becoming familiar with MaxFli. Upon returning home, the IT project staff began to dive into the MaxFli program. They carefully examined each component and module to discover its purpose, inputs, and outputs. This was essential because there was little existing documentation to describe the detailed specifications of MaxFli. In addition to the "MaxFli University," Chile sent two IT personnel on monthly 2-day visits to Colombia throughout the implementation process.

Implementation in Colombia

BAT Colombia implemented MaxFli on time and 11 percent under budget. Overall, the MaxFli implementation in Colombia was considered a success. Like Chiletabacos, BAT Colombia undertook an extensive training program.

BAT Colombia GM Jorge Soto attributes the success primarily to the quality of personnel in BAT Colombia and the training: "Here in Colombia, we have a lot of young, motivated people. We have been through many changes in the past few years and they are ready to handle more changes."

Mauricio Leon, the infrastructure manager for MaxFli in Colombia, agreed: "This is a very good experience we have here ... because of the training."

Even though MaxFli was widely considered a success in Colombia, there were two major obstacles. First was the perception that MaxFli was inadequate as a trade-marketing system. This problem was exacerbated by BAT Colombia's decision to implement a multiphase rollout of the system. In May 2000 the full system went live, but only the basic sales force automation functionalities of MaxFli were used. The more advanced modules that allowed for gathering competitor activity, structuring the sales visit, and maintaining merchandising material were not activated until January 2001. BAT Colombia CIO Jaime Navas argued that this approach was beneficial because it reduced the initial complexity and smoothed the transition to MaxFli from legacy systems. While this strategy met their immediate need for a new sales system, it did not immediately tap into the true value of MaxFli as a competitive information tool.

Although the system was implemented on time and under budget, the limited initial usefulness of MaxFli may have affected some users' views of its value. One manager from trade-marketing suggested: "We need a new system for trade marketing. MaxFli does distribution very well but with it we cannot manage individual promotions or other trade marketing activities."

These concerns led to the development of a locally designed trade-marketing system named AMiT. This system was developed for use by sales managers to coach, monitor, and support individual sales reps. This system runs on palm-sized HP Jornadas and aggregates MaxFli data and automates a sales review process for the sales manager. Sales managers use this system to improve cycle planning and sales activities as well as to mentor sales reps. As of Fall 2001, AMiT was only being used in Colombia.

The second major obstacle for MaxFli in Colombia was the reliability and performance of the handheld device (Jornada 690). Based on Chiletabacos's experience, CIO Jaime Navas expected reliability problems with it. Consequently, he chose a different strategy for acquiring the devices. Instead of purchasing the devices from a local vendor and negotiating a service agreement for support, he leveraged the strength of BAT Colombia's relationship with HP to negotiate a leasing arrangement directly with HP Colombia.

While BAT Colombia experienced the same high failure rate with the Jornadas as Chiletabacos, they had lower support costs. CIO Navas claimed that this arrangement saved BAT Colombia $150,000 over 3 years compared to working with a local vendor. Eventually HP decided to provide newer Jornadas to BAT Colombia free of charge in order to reduce their support costs. Despite this beneficial leasing arrangement, the handhelds were a major obstacle for MaxFli in Colombia. Mauricio Leon described the problem:

> I think that the most important challenge was the handheld. Because the server we [could] manage. There were many new things in the server. Oracle was new for the company. All the processes that MaxFli runs were new ... we understood what the process does, and there was no problem with that. There was some problem but they fix it. So for us, Oracle was new but it was not a problem. We had experience in databases so the operating system of the MaxFli was not a problem, we knew it. We had to change the communication links; we had to double [our bandwidth]. ... That was not a problem. We put in remote access services (RAS) in order to support some salespeople who work in very far away small cities. So they just dial in. That was not a problem. But the handheld has been a continuous challenge. And we spent a lot of money in the handhelds. At the beginning, we had many problems with the handhelds. A lot of problems. So I think that is the challenge, to find a powerful device and stable device is the main challenge.

MaxFli in Central America

The next test for MaxFli was BAT Central America (BATCA). BATCA is as different from Chiletabacos as BAT Colombia is similar. BATCA is unique in organizational structure, market conditions, IT capabilities, and business processes.

BATCA operates as a "cluster market," meaning that the six countries of Central America (Costa Rica, Honduras, Nicaragua, Guatemala, El Salvador, and Panama) form a single operating unit. The markets operated independently prior to 1995. In 1995 BATCA management was centralized in San Jose, Costa Rica, and production was centralized in Honduras. Each country maintained independent marketing and sales operations. By combining resources into a cluster, BATCA was able to centralize production and create efficiencies of scale in their operations. The larger size of the cluster allowed BATCA to implement larger, more expensive IT systems like MaxFli, although none of the independent countries of Central America would have been able to.

Market Forces in Central America

Coordinating six sets of business processes in one organization created many complications for BATCA. The six countries of Central America share a common language and religion but little else. Each country differs in terms of competitive environment, taxes, regulation, currency, market share, and business strategy. (See Exhibit 5.)

An important market feature in BATCA was that the sale of nontobacco products (e.g., matches) was an important source of revenue. However, in order to limit the complexity of the new system, the global steering committee decided not to support nontobacco products in MaxFli. Since MaxFli would be the

EXHIBIT 5

Breakdown of BAT Central America by Country

Volume (rank)	Country	Market Share	World Bank Income Classification *
1	Nicaragua	95 %	Low income, severely indebted
2	Honduras	90 %	Low-middle income, moderately indebted
3	Panama	75 %	Upper-middle income, moderately indebted
4	Costa Rica	50 %	Upper-middle income, less indebted
5	Guatemala	30 %	Low-middle income, less indebted
6	El Salvador	75 %	Low-middle income, less indebted

*Based on the World Bank's Country Classification Table (n.d.) accessed from Web site 9/18/01: *www.worldbank.org/data/databytopic/CLASS.XLS.*

only system in use by BATCA sales reps, the implementation of MaxFli implied an immediate decrease in revenue from lost match sales.

IT Infrastructure and History in Central America

Prior to 1995 each country in BATCA had developed independent information systems to monitor and track sales. Two markets, Guatemala and Costa Rica, had specific concerns about migrating to MaxFli because both of these countries had developed custom IT applications that mapped well to the contours of their existing business processes. The "best practices" embedded in MaxFli required the sacrifice of those customized applications. The business case for MaxFli in Central America identified eight important risk factors associated with the MaxFli project. (See Exhibit 6.)

Items 4 and 7 represented highly probable risks that would have a high impact. From the beginning, the implementation team was concerned about MaxFli's ability to achieve and sustain improvements in the way of doing business. These concerns would continue to be present throughout the implementation process.

Item 3 addressed possible "technical constraints" based on two specific concerns. First, BATCA's IT infrastructure relied on complicated relationships with telecommunications providers in six countries. It was a challenge to create an intercountry backbone capable of running MaxFli, because each country had an independent domestic telecommunications provider (See Exhibit 7.)

Based on previous experiences with its primary telecommunications vendor, BATCA estimated that a significant portion of the ongoing costs for MaxFli would be devoted to improving the commuincations infrastructure.

EXHIBIT 6

Risk Management Table for MaxFli Implementation in Central America

#	Summary Description of Risk	Keyword	Probability	Impact
1.	Implementation delays due to staffing problems	Resources	M	H
2.	Implementation delays due to readiness not achieved by end markets	Readiness	M	H
3.	Implementation delays due to technical constraints	Technical	H	M
4.	Organization does not achieve expected level of improvement in the way of doing business	Achieve	H	H
5.	Dedicated central team's performance not optimal	Team	L	M
6.	System/network configuration does not fully support vision of doing business	System	L	M
7.	The organization does not sustain achieved level of performance in the way of doing business	Sustained	H	H
8.	External factors delay system implementation	External	L	L

EXHIBIT 7

The Intercountry Communications Backbone for MaxFli in Central America

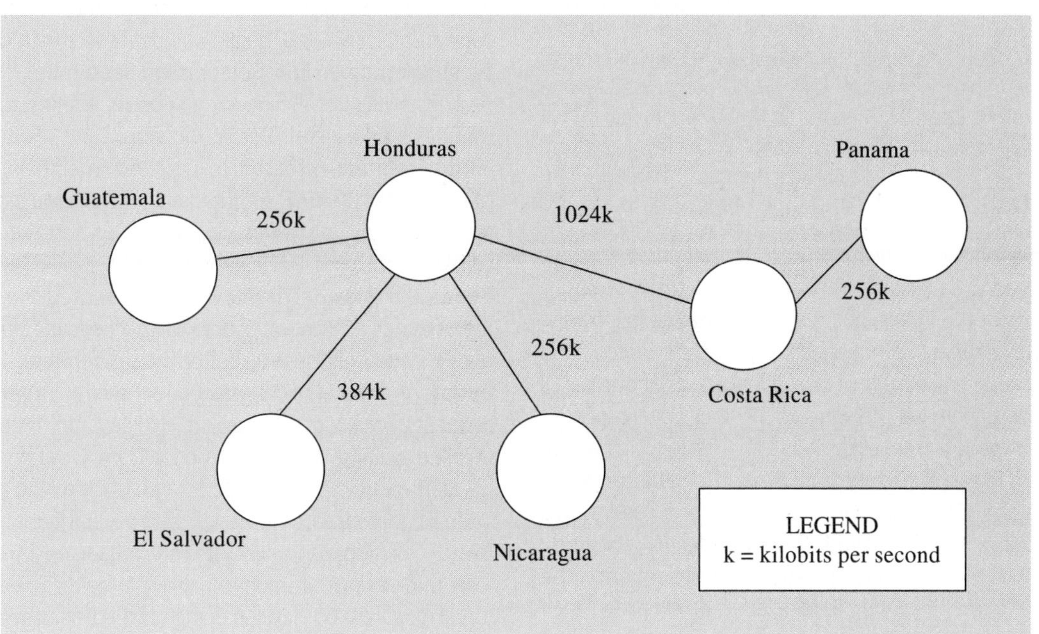

The communication infrastructure was an ongoing frustration during the initial phase of implementation. Juan Carlos Gracia, the project IT leader, noted:

> One of the challenges from an IT perspective that we faced was in terms of dealing with six different telephone companies when setting our wide-area network for centralizing the operations of MaxFli. That is something that you really have to take into consideration. Even though we are a cluster, we speak the same language, we have many things in common, even the same religion. But legally, there are many differences between countries. ... So [each] has to be treated differently. Telecoms are privatized in most countries [but are] publicly managed in Costa Rica and Honduras. [And] that's where we have most of our operations concentrated.

A second technical constraint was the challenge of finding a vendor able to support the Jornada handheld across the six cluster countries. The MaxFli project team faced a choice: find a vendor who could provide a service-level agreement to provide and maintain the handhelds locally in all six countries, or find a vendor in one country who could coordinate shipping the handhelds throughout Central America and perform all the maintenance from one country. They chose the first option and signed a service-level agreement with a vendor to provide all of the Jornada handhelds plus an additional 10 percent standing inventory to use as backups to all six countries and provide a 14-day repair/replace service locally in each country.

The Project Team in Central America

Similar to the Colombian team, the MaxFli implementation team in Central America was led by an experienced trade marketing manager. Walter Kruger had worked his way up through the BAT trade-marketing function in Central America. Unlike BAT Colombia, BATCA did not share many business practices with Chiletabacos, nor did it have strong relational ties with them.

One of the difficulties for the BATCA project team was a lack of training in MaxFli. Gracia remembers that the "flying doctors," a term he used to refer to the MaxFli support team, dogmatically insisted that no one on the implementation team needed MaxFli training. Instead, they suggested that reviewing the MaxFli documentation and system outputs were enough to prepare the implementation team. The "MaxFli University"–style training used by BAT Colombia, where several key project personnel spent time in Chile studying MaxFli, was not offered to BATCA. This was especially problematic to Gracia, who had built his IT career outside of BAT and joined BATCA at the beginning of the MaxFli project to provide expert assistance during this large system implementation. With no history within BAT, he felt at a disadvantage in learning the details of the MaxFli system. Gracia laments:

> Marco [a colleague IT manager] told me, "oh, you must go to Chile for two months where you'll be trained in MaxFli. How it

has been done, how the implementation works, what are the interfaces and fields, how do you do the change management, etc." Chile, however, decided to curtail the training to the markets embarked in this initiative. They said, "it is now your responsibility to get training" ... [I]t was a nightmare. We had to rely on one particular resource that had been an integral part of the implementation in Chile, Luis Boesch. He became very important. Definitely, he was an ombudsman. Initially we were so reliant on him that he could not leave even to provide consulting to Colombia, which was the other market implementing MaxFli.

Through a long and difficult process of examining screens, reports, and documentation, the MaxFli project team began to form ideas about the inputs, outputs, and processes involved in MaxFli. However, apart from interactions with Luis Boesch and participation in several electronic discussion groups about MaxFli implementation, there was no way to verify their conclusions.

The BATCA project team struggled to find qualified IT personnel to support MaxFli in each country. While stronger economies like Panama and Costa Rica had adequate IT personnel, it was more difficult finding qualified IT personnel in struggling economies like Nicaragua and El Salvador. Consequently, the MaxFli project team hired and coordinated all development staff in Costa Rica. To confirm the capabilities of applicants, Gracia had applicants complete a small programming scenario along with their written application for employment. Those applicants who successfully completed the programming module were further considered for hiring. This process allowed Gracia to identify qualified personnel whom he believed added value to the development process. Ultimately Gracia was very satisfied with the quality of his team.

A final challenge faced by the project team in BATCA was turnover on the BATCA executive steering committee. Six months into the MaxFli project, the GM of BATCA transferred to Europe, and a new GM, Raymond Acorda, was selected from Souza Cruz, BAT's Brazil operation. Then shortly after the project rollout, a new marketing executive, Juan Morales, joined the steering committee. While both Acorda and Morales supported MaxFli, the mid-project leadership change created additional difficulties for the implementation team.

Implementation in Central America

The MaxFli implementation in Central America struggled. It was completed on time but over budget. Much of the budget overage was caused by the necessary transition from MaxFli 1.0 to MaxFli 1.1. This transition was required because MaxFli 1.0 was designed to handle a single currency and a single management structure. It could not support the complexity of multiple countries and multiple currencies required by BATCA's cluster structure. The software development challenges associated with a major system upgrade were made more difficult by another transition occurring with BAT globally.

In May 1999 Globe House decided to phase out all projects with Andersen Consulting. To continue the development and support of MaxFli, BAT began a joint venture with Cap Gemini/Ernst & Young, called Ciberion. In September 1999 formal responsibilities for the ongoing support, training, and development of MaxFli were given to Ciberion.

Ciberion was created to develop, market, and sell the MaxFli system to BAT end markets and external companies in the consumer goods industry. The transition was difficult for Chiletabacos and BAT Colombia, but especially difficult in Central America. To Gracia, Ciberion seemed too focused on future sales to pay attention to the present needs of BAT MaxFli users. Although Ciberion had committed to a 2-week turnaround for MaxFli problems, even "urgent" support requests took an average of 60 days to resolve. Gracia recalled waiting for weeks to hear from Ciberion even when his staff had already developed a solution to the problem.

Project IT Leader Gracia felt that several requirements that BATCA considered important were neglected by Ciberion. At least three are worth mentioning. First, the disagreement about the importance of MaxFli training for the implementation team caused continual frustration. Despite continual requests for training from Kruger and Gracia, Ciberion insisted that it was not required. This had long-standing implications for the success of the MaxFli implementation in Central America. As clearly stated by Rodrigo Palacios of Chile, "MaxFli is a business change program supported by an IT program." Without proper training, the BATCA implementation team was at a severe disadvantage in implementing the system.

Second, by the time BATCA implemented MaxFli it was clear that there were problems with the Jornada handhelds used by MaxFli. Both Chiletabacos and BAT Colombia had experienced problems with the limited durability and unreliability of the Jornadas. The BATCA project team felt that these difficulties would only be worse in Central America. Central America has a tropical climate with regular, often daily, periods of heavy rain. The project team felt that the climate might be too stressful for the handheld. Additionally, many of the sales routes in Central America are in remote, rugged, and isolated locations. Gracia was convinced early on that the handhelds were not adequate:

> We assessed the handheld ruggedness and therefore knew that it was not robust enough and was going to bring lots of trouble to our sales force. However, since there was a mandate that the system had to be implemented during Year 2000 and the decision from Ciberion was "Look, we are not going to test the code on any other machine besides this handheld unless you want to defer the implementation until later," we

had no choice. If that was the decision, we had to go with it. I explicitly communicated that decision to the project stakeholders. This was, in the long term, going to create a problem. But, there was this mandate that we had to implement regardless of the robustness of the hardware. And guess what, we have an average of 10 handhelds each week that need to be replaced!

Upgrading to newer, more rugged handheld devices was more complicated than it might have appeared to Gracia. Microsoft released Windows CE 3.0 during the final stages of MaxFli development. Because the new version was a major upgrade from Windows CE 2.1, it made fundamental changes in how MaxFli could interact with the hardware. The new CE 3.0-enabled handheld devices would not run MaxFli in its current version. Ciberion directed their efforts toward making the shift from CE 2.1 to CE 3.0. The Jornada 690 in use by Chiletabacos, BAT Colombia, and BATCA could not run CE 3.0 and was thus obsolete. Neil Coupland, a senior vice president for marketing and sales in Ciberion, argued that, "because of the fact that hardware reliability was an issue, we had to support new hardware, [and] the old hardware was now obsolete. You couldn't buy it. Therefore, the code was obsolete too. The focus was put on actually producing a working version on the new hardware."

Complicating the difficulties with the Jornadas, the service-level agreement with the supplier who provided and supported the Jornadas in all six countries was unsatisfactory. The average repair/replace order required 6 weeks instead of the contractually agreed 2 weeks. The delay required an additional 20 percent reserve supply of handhelds. Eventually, Gracia switched to a vendor in Costa Rica, who agreed to support all six countries centrally and manage the shipping to the sales reps in each country.

A third technical issue important to BATCA but largely unaddressed by Ciberion was the "suggested order" functionality. The suggested order routine is intended to provide the salesperson with a suggested order of brands and quantities at each outlet. This functionality was one of the major selling points of MaxFli in the minds of the trade marketing department. By giving the salesperson an accurate, up-to-date order history for each outlet, BAT hoped to increase sales and market share. However, due to technical problems with the Siebel and Oracle systems, this functionality was not implemented in initial MaxFli versions. This frustrated the project teams in Chile and Colombia as well as in BATCA. Kruger repeatedly pressed Ciberion about the importance of the suggested order routine. As of June 2001, the suggested order functionality was still not implemented in MaxFli 1.1.

BATCA installed multiple servers to manage MaxFli across six countries. Because of the communication infrastructure issues discussed previously, the management team chose to put the servers in Honduras and the IT support team in Costa Rica. The rollout occurred in three phases. Because Nicaragua was the strongest market in Central America, they were selected to go first. Costa Rica, Panama, and Honduras went live in the second phase of implementation, and finally El Salvador and Guatemala in the third phase. Like BAT Colombia, the BATCA MaxFli project team also chose a phased implementation strategy for the rollout. Instead of implementing the full MaxFli functionality, the project team chose to focus first on the basics of ordering, invoicing, and receiving payments. The value-added features of MaxFli, like brand coverage, competitive information gathering, and cycle planning, would be integrated one at a time every other month.

As in Colombia, this implementation decision created perceptual problems for MaxFli. The system had been billed as a panacea for Central America. Unfortunately, the enthusiastic expectations for MaxFli surpassed its initial capabilities. Because the initial system only handled the basics, it was essentially a replacement for the relatively low-tech handheld system previously in use. Without the value-added features of MaxFli, Central American users felt they had the worst of both worlds. They had given up the highly customized sales force automation system they were used to, without gaining the information benefits promoted for MaxFli. The morale and enthusiasm for MaxFli waned quickly. This sentiment was expressed by Morales, who said:

> I think we oversold this as a tool. ... Our business is very, very simple. And now we're utilizing this big, big, very complicated tool. It is silly because we treat big complicated outlets like Shell, Exxon, and others the same as the little mom and pop shops. It is easy to sell this kind of system to Shell and Exxon. But when it comes to the mom and pop shops, this is not important. What they're looking for is that our salesperson will be there every week, be there on time, provide the right product, and so on. They don't care about all of this information gathering.

While initial user satisfaction was lower than in Chile and Colombia, there was reason to be hopeful. One of the technical challenges faced by the MaxFli team had become one of the technological strengths of BATCA. The MaxFli project team successfully negotiated with several telecom providers to implement the necessary communications backbone for MaxFli. As a result, BATCA now has one of the best communications infrastructures in Central America. Gracia argued:

> What I can tell you right now is that we have the best communications infrastructure in Central America in terms of a company. We have received people from telecoms who say, "Look, the network capacity you have, no one else in Central America has."

> That sounds great, though we need to make a more effective use with additional services into it. But that is one of the challenges of implementing in different countries for one market.

As of the summer of 2001, the Central America implementation of MaxFli had been the most difficult implementation to date. However, it may also have been the most important. Neil Coupland of Ciberion summarized:

> [Central America] was critical frankly. Central America proved an awful lot of things. That MaxFli could work for example. Not just in another market outside of Chile. But that it could [work]. Really [work]. In six markets simultaneously. Frankly, I don't know that anyone had thought through how difficult that would be. But it worked, and is working still.

On the other hand, Morales summarized his concerns this way:

> Our business is very, very simple. ... In my opinion, until today we have a very, very simple business and a very complicated tool. I don't think it ought to be. We need to balance our tool with our business.

For the Globe House, the questions to be answered were: Is the MaxFli approach the best way to build custom-developed IT systems that can be shared by multiple end markets? Is this the systems development approach to replicate for future multinational systems that embody a business change initiative? Or are the needs of end markets unique enough to demand a more locally-tailored solution?

CASE STUDY II-3

CRM Using Data Warehousing at First American Corporation

Introduction

In 1990, First American Corporation (FAC) lost $60 million and was operating under letters of agreement with regulators. Today, FAC is a profitable, innovative leader in the financial services industry. This change in fortune is the result of an ambitious strategic vision, and a major investment in data warehousing that made the vision possible.

FAC's strategic vision is called Tailored Client Solutions (TCS), a customer relationship–oriented strategy that positions FAC clients at the center of all aspects of the company's operations. Though many organizations espouse customer relationship management, FAC has redesigned every aspect of its operations to meet its clients' needs as well as its own profitability goals. Underlying these efforts is the recognition that, to succeed with this strategy, it must know its customers exceptionally well, and leverage that knowledge in product design, in distribution channel decisions, and in every interaction with its clients.

The execution of this strategy would be impossible without a data warehouse called VISION that maintains client behaviors (e.g., products used, transactions), client buying preferences (e.g., attitudes, expressed needs), and client value positions (profitability). Using information from VISION, FAC has

- identified the top 20 percent of its customers who provide virtually all of the consumer profits, and the 40 to 50 percent who are not profitable
- developed strategies to retain the top high-value customers
- developed strategies to move unprofitable customers to lower-cost distribution channels, different products, or pricing structures that boost profitability, while still focusing on customer needs and preferences
- developed strategies to expand relationships with all customers
- redesigned products and distribution channels to increase profitability and better meet customers' needs and preferences
- redesigned information flows, work processes, and jobs in FAC's branches in order to meet customers' needs and increase their use of profitable products

To implement TCS, FAC had to change the way its employees think about banking and about their jobs, shifting from "banking by intuition" to "banking by information and analysis." All of these actions combined have moved FAC from losses of $60 million in 1990 to profits of over $211 million in 1998.

This case describes FAC's transformation and emphasizes the information technology that was essential to its success. The first two sections discuss First American Corporation and the Tailored Client Solutions strategy. Then it presents the VISION data warehouse and the way in which it was implemented. The final sections describe the uses and applications of VISION, and the resulting benefits.

About First American Corporation

Founded in 1883, FAC is a comprehensive financial services holding company headquartered in Nashville, Tennessee. Its holdings include

- First American National Bank
- First American Federal Savings Bank
- Deposit Guaranty (acquired in 1998 and now operating as First American National Bank)
- First American Enterprises, Inc.

 The authors would also like to thank Carroll Kimball, Jay Phillips, Theresa Leahy, and Connie White from First American Corporation. An earlier version of this case report was the 1999 first-place winner of the Best Paper Award from the Society for Information Management (SIM).

EXHIBIT 2
VISION Data Supports TCS Initiatives

"About life. About you."

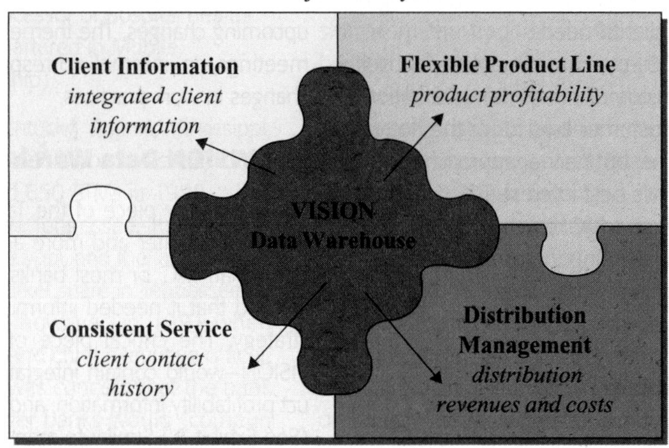

system within 3 months, and the project team began to understand which data would need to be stored in the data warehouse. In the next two phases, additional products and transaction data were added to VISION, and the profit formulas were enhanced. The data warehouse team also developed extraction and transformation processes, while developing the data models for physically storing the data in VISION.

Implementing a complete data warehouse was the major target of the final phases. FAC relied on external vendors such as NCR to provide hardware, software, and methodological support through much of the initial data warehouse development. According to Emery Hill, executive vice president of operations and technology, "we just jumped into the pool because they [NCR] said that they would jump in with us and

EXHIBIT 3
VISION Goals by Project Phase

PHASE	Phase 1	Phase 2	Phase 3	Phase 4	Phase 5
DATE	1–2Q 1996	2–3Q 1996	3Q 1996–1Q 1997	2Q 1997–1Q 1998	2–4Q 1998
Business Goals	Identify the top revenue producers	Identify the least profitable customers	Include actual transaction and product data in profitability formulas	Understand all aspects of client and product profitability	Incorporate profitability understandings in business processes
Technical Goals	Enhance the existing customer information system with retail revenue	Enhance the existing customer information system with direct contribution view for consumers	Enhance existing customer information system with net income after capital charges (NIACC) for consumers	Deploy the warehouse–proof of concept (consumer business) Commercial profitability integration	Complete production testing of the warehouse

EXHIBIT 4
The VISION Data Warehouse Architecture

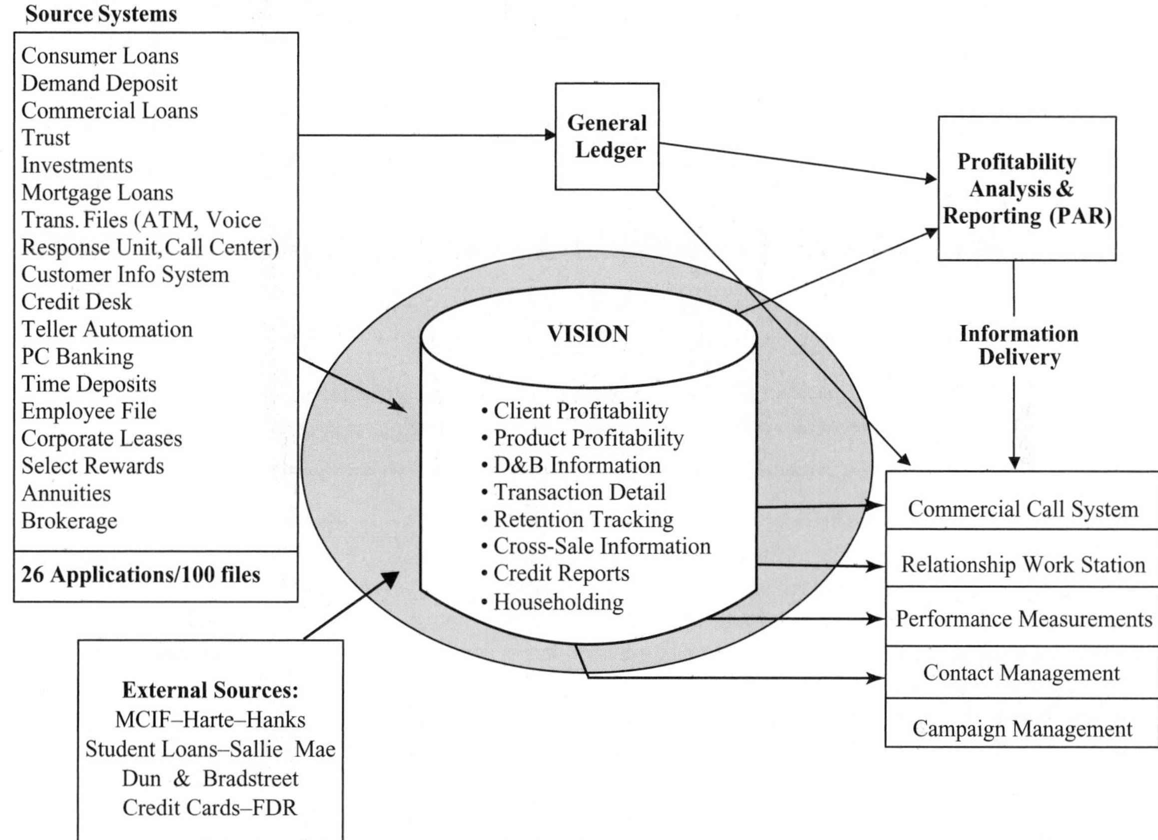

keep us afloat." Yet the company was also careful to appoint an FAC employee to manage the process. By 1997 the data warehouse proof of concept was delivered, and the data warehouse team spent 1998 validating the data, rolling out the warehouse, and helping develop applications for finance and marketing.

Warehouse Architecture

FAC's production data warehouse was an NCR platform (NCR 5150M) configured with five SMP nodes running the Teradata Relational Database System.[1] This configuration would provide FAC with 1.5 terabytes of storage. At the end of 1998 it supported 200 gigabytes (GB) of raw data, which was growing at a rate of 10 GB per month. The database held 2 million accounts and information about 1.2 million households, and FAC planned to store up to 37 rolling months of history for analysis. Exhibit 4 shows the warehouse architecture.

Data Sources

The warehouse uses more than 100 source files extracted from 26 legacy applications. From the mainframe environment, VSAM and IMS files are FTP'd to a file server, where Informatica's Powermart software applies business rules written to transform the data from the legacy systems (e.g., making account numbers consistent across banks) into data elements consistent with the relational database structure of the data warehouse. The resulting files are loaded into a warehouse staging area where business users manually validate a subset of the data (e.g., financial data is validated within five percent of the general ledger). After the users approve the data conversions, the data moves into Teradata base tables that are organized by account and by activity. Concurrently, files from external data sources, such as student loans from

[1]SMP (symmetric multiprocessing) is the processing of programs by multiple processors that share a common operating system and memory. A relational database is a collection of data organized as a set of tables from which data can be accessed or extended with little effort.

EXHIBIT 5
VISION Data

Data	Description	Source
Client Behaviors	Products Delivery channels Transactions	• IBM mainframe • Sallie Mae
Client Buying Patterns	Segments Attitudes Expressed needs	• IBM mainframe • Dun & Bradstreet geographic and demographic data • Harte-Hanks household data
Client Value Propositions	Profitability	• IBM mainframe • Profitability algorithms

Data can be analyzed at any level of aggregation, from bankwide or line of business down to individual account or client relationship.

Sallie Mae, geographic and financial data from Dun & Bradstreet, and psychographic and demographic appends to data from Harte-Hanks, are also incorporated into the warehouse. Exhibit 5 describes the various kinds of data that exist in VISION after the warehouse is populated. The entire process for populating the data warehouse currently takes approximately 10 business days, although the team plans to reduce that time by half in 1999.

Customercentric Data

All of the data are organized around the client to provide a comprehensive understanding of the client's demographic characteristics, the banking products used, transaction activities, interactions with the bank, measures of the client's relationship to the bank, and psychographic insights about client preferences and propensities. (See Exhibit 6.) The data can be analyzed in multiple ways, including "slicing and dicing" by time, products, geographical regions, and market segments as dimensions; planning marketing campaigns for specific products and markets; and detecting which clients are at risk of leaving the bank.

Data Access

About 50 marketing and finance analysts have direct access to the warehouse data. For the marketing area, the data warehouse team uses Cognos Corporation's tools to create multidimensional cubes of data that are stored on a local file server. Users can access these data cubes on the server or download the information to their desktops. They then use the Cognos tool suite, including PowerPlay, Impromptu, and Scenario, to manipulate and analyze the data.

The finance analysts access warehouse data using the same Cognos Corporation tools, as well as via a data mart extracted from the data warehouse that uses an Oracle relational database management system.[2] The data mart supports the custom-developed profitability analysis and reporting tool called PAR (Profitability Analysis Reporting), which supports ad hoc SQL queries against the mart and also provides users with predefined reports.[3]

Data Warehouse Team

Eighteen full-time IT employees comprise the team that supports all of the company's data warehousing initiatives. As shown in Exhibit 7, warehouse services manages the extraction, transformation, and load processes for the Teradata warehouse. The warehouse development team—the "gatekeepers" of the warehouse—is responsible for developing new and enhanced applications for data feeds. The business access tool support group

[2]Since FAC took an enterprise-level data management approach from the outset, and began with a large number of legacy systems that were not integrated, the VISION project focused on the enterprise data model from the outset. At FAC, the data warehouse was created first and then used to populate its data mart. A different approach often found in practice is for data marts created for departments or divisions to be used to populate an enterprisewide data warehouse.

[3]SQL is a standard query language used in querying, updating, and managing relational databases and is the de facto standard for database products.

EXHIBIT 6
The Customercentric Data Model

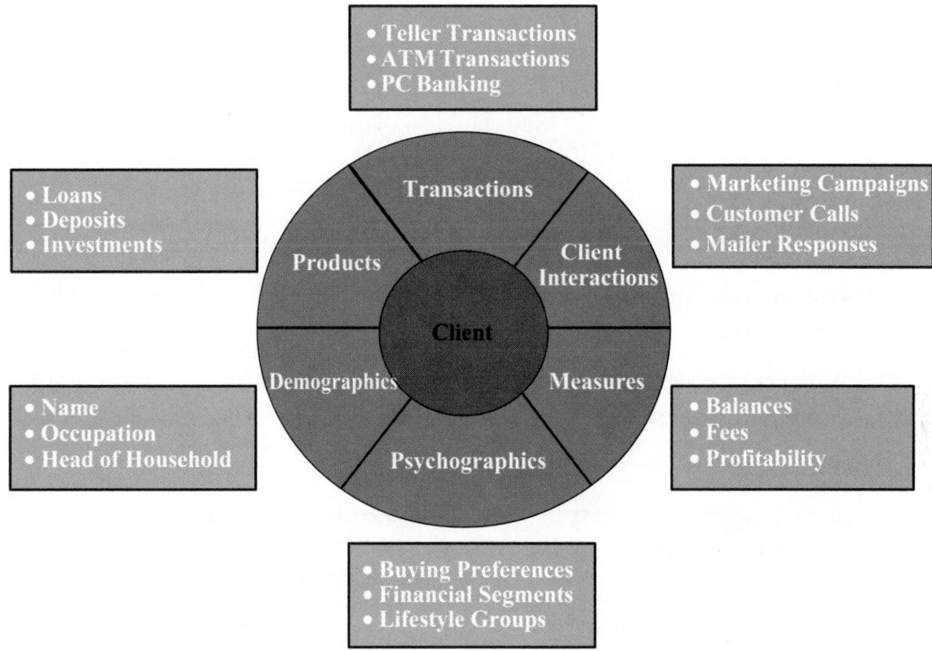

implements and supports the data access tools, such as Cognos. The analytics group performs analytical studies and *ad hoc* analyses of warehouse data. The data mart team extracts, transforms, and loads data into the VISION data mart (PAR system).

Early in the project (1996–1997), most of the data warehouse positions were filled by internal IT employees who were newly trained, because there were few experienced data warehousing professionals available on the market. Data warehousing expertise was provided by consultants and especially the vendor NCR. After the arrival of Lance Mattingly, who was hired as a new applications development manager in 1998, most new data warehousing positions were filled using a "contract-to-hire" approach: data warehousing professionals were brought into FAC first as contractors, and the bank offered them permanent positions after they had an opportunity to "take a test drive" with them.

VISION Users and Applications

The Users

The VISION data warehouse has both direct and indirect users. The direct users are the 20 marketing analysts and 30 finance analysts who directly access the warehouse data and provide the analyses that are used for decision making by FAC's management. There are also hundreds of indirect users who use reports generated from the VISION warehouse data. Exhibit 8 profiles some of these indirect users and the types of information that they receive.

Software Applications

Many applications that support the attraction, enhancement, and retention of customers rely on the VISION data warehouse. A description of the major applications, organized by the TCS strategy, follows.

Client Information

Customer Preferences and Profiles

Customer preferences are important to many banking decisions, and FAC has created preference information in VISION using a technique called "conjoint analysis." The company selected a sample of over 3,000 customers and asked each one what he or she would do under different circumstances. For example, would you use an ATM to make a deposit if the transaction were free and the same transaction performed by a teller cost fifty cents? a dollar? Based on the answers, a number of different types of customer were identified, and by

EXHIBIT 7
IT Data Warehouse Organization Chart

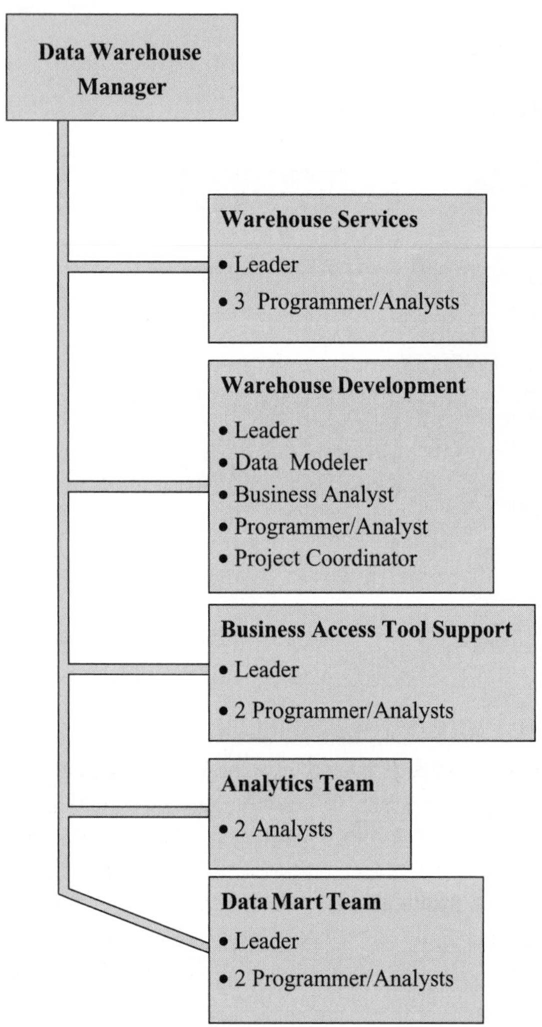

matching transaction and demographic patterns for each type of customer with those of the remaining customers, FAC was able to generate preference information for its entire customer population.

FAC also generates and uses market segmentation information. Data are purchased from Claritas, which are then appended to FAC household records by Harte-Hanks. Using financial segmentation software from Claritas, demographic and financial transaction data are used to place clients in one of 10 financial categories (e.g., wealth market, wealth preservers). A similar process is used to place customers in one of 62 lifestyle groups (e.g., young influentials, pools & patios). The category placements are based on the assumption that "you are like your neighbors."

Preference and profile information is used in many ways, such as targeting marketing efforts and designing the best mix of distribution channels for the bank.

Customer Retention

VISION calculates the profitability of every customer so that appropriate actions can be taken. High-value customers are identified and targeted for retention programs, primarily because this group is responsible for nearly all of the bank's consumer profits. The mid-value customers receive targeted messages about bank products that should be attractive to them (and will move them into more profitable relationships). Low-value customers are migrated to more profitable products and lower-cost distribution channels (e.g., PC banking rather than using tellers). However, FAC's goal is to retain all of its clients, regardless of their current profitability.

The "Top 20 List" is one example of a retention program based on VISION data. Using the results from customer profitability analysis, each branch receives a weekly list of its top 20 clients. Service representatives then discuss ways to retain these customers and to expand their use of the bank. A required approach is to telephone the top customers to thank them for their business and then to discuss their financial goals and how the bank can help the client realize them.

Retaining clients and expanding their use of the bank's products are important components of how FAC employees are evaluated and compensated. For example, the bank may have a campaign to increase the number of savings accounts and each branch makes a commitment for their contribution to the campaign. Information from VISION is used to profile customers who are most likely to open a savings account, and employee compensation is tied to how well the commitments are met. On Mondays, branch managers commit to performance objectives for the week, and on Fridays their performance is evaluated.

Select Rewards

Like airlines' frequent flyer programs, Select Rewards is designed to increase customer loyalty and to increase customers' use of the company's products. VISION data is used to analyze the profitability of the bank's products, determine the points that are awarded, and establish the point levels for different awards. With Select Rewards, a customer earns points for longevity with the bank and the breadth (number of products) and depth (average account balances) of the banking relationship. Each month a customer receives a statement that reports the points earned and a redemption certificate. (See Exhibit 9.) The points can be redeemed in a variety of ways—discounted banking services, items from a

EXHIBIT 8
Indirect Users and the Information Provided by VISION

Indirect User	Information Provided by VISION
Senior Management	Profitability by line of business
Corporate Banking Managers	Profitability by industry segment
Small Business Banking Managers	Sales performance by area
Retail Sales Managers and Sales Force	Retention of high-value households
Product Managers	Profitability of products within product groups
Distribution Managers	Channel migration opportunities
Marketing Managers	Segment profitability
Asset and Liability Managers	Product profiles
Credit Managers	Analysis of deciles and risk-taking

local retail store, gift certificates for meals at a restaurant, or free airline tickets.

Flexible Product Line

Product Profitability

It is critical for FAC to know the profitability of its various products. This is a complex calculation that requires cost-accounting equations and data from more than 20 relational database "joins"[4] using VISION data warehouse tables. Provided with product profitability information, financial analysts look at products in a variety of ways. To illustrate, an analyst might begin by examining the profitability of deposits, loans, and fee-based services (e.g., managing trust accounts). Drilling down into loans, the analyst sees that commercial loans are the least profitable when returns are adjusted for risk and capital charges, a finding contrary to conventional banking wisdom, wherein commercial loans are thought to be very profitable. The analyst sees that floor plan loans are the most profitable of the commercial loans. The analyst then rank orders all of the commercial loans to see which ones are the most and least profitable. For the least profitable loans, the analyst examines all of the loans, by the relationship managers who are responsible for them. The analyst learns that a particular relationship manager is consistently making loans at rates that do not cover their full costs. This information is marked for management's attention.

Seniors Account

Product profitability information is also used to redesign products. Like many banks, FAC offers a free checking account to customers who are age 55 and older. Working with VISION, financial analysts discovered that the bank was making money from a few senior accounts, but was experiencing a loss with many others. Further analysis revealed that the average size of the checking account balance was the key difference between profitable and unprofitable accounts.

Based on profitability information and input from clients, a redesigned product was introduced that created value for both FAC and its customers. Next, FAC implemented a marketing plan to retain profitable senior account customers while improving the profitability of the non-profitable accounts. The 20 percent of the customers whose account balances were normally high enough to make them profitable received a letter and a personal call saying that the new minimum balance requirement was unlikely to affect them. The other customers received a letter notifying them of the new minimum balance change and encouraging them either to increase their average balance or to switch to another type of account. The results of this change were impressive: there was a significant increase in average account balances, net income after capital charges, and service fees. Less than 2 percent of the clients closed their accounts and many of them ultimately returned as profitable customers.

[4]A "join" is a relational database command that results in data from multiple tables (relations) being combined based on the value of a data element (such as an account type code) common to the tables.

EXHIBIT 9

Select Rewards Statement and Points Redemption Certificate

First American

Select Rewards Update

First American National Bank
NA-7143
550 Metroplex Drive
Nashville, TN 37211

April 29, 1999 Page 1 of 12

0

Primary account number: 123456 001
Earnings period: 3/31/99 through 4/29/99

John Doe HOLD
123 Main Street
Anywhere, USA

608

Questions? Call 1(888)5REWARD(573-9273)

Save Your Points for these Rewards

Magnavox CD Boom Box

Cannon Sure Shot Camera

Sony Cordless Speakerphone

Courtyard Weekend Certificate

See catalog for more great rewards!

Summary of Points

Beginning balance	107,199
+ Points earned	2,520
+ Points adjusted	0
- Points redeemed	0
- Points expired	0
= Ending balance	109,719

Win Points in May

- Bring all of your accounts to First American, and watch your points add up!

MAY

Details of points

Points Redemption Certificate

Total points as of 4/29/99: **109,719**

You can redeem your points two ways. Complete this coupon and mail to Select Rewards; NA-7228; 550 Metroplex Drive; Nashville TN 37211, or call 1(888)5REWARD(573-9273). Your reward will be shipped to your address shown above, unless otherwise specified.

SELECT Rewards

Item Number	Item description:	Size,color,etc.	Points

YOUR SIGNATURE:

Next Most Likely Purchase

FAC is applying data mining techniques to the VISION warehouse data in order to better understand and predict customer behaviors. Applications that are either in place or under development include accurate identification of buying trends, precise definition of market segments, optimization of promotional programs, customer retention and acquisition, customer cross selling and upgrading, and fraud detection. To illustrate, one data mining application calculates the likelihood that a customer will adopt a specific product. Exhibit 10 shows the steps that are used to transition VISION data into this useful preference information for marketing campaigns.

Consistent Service

Contact Management System

The contact management system helps FAC service representatives develop a one-to-one relationship with customers by giving them a clear picture of the customer's entire banking relationship. Drawing from VISION and other data sources, it provides personal information about the customer, how profitable the customer is to the bank, how long the customer has been with the bank, buying preferences (e.g., serious saver, price shopper), the products used, transaction history, and the customer's financial goals. All of this information is accessible to the service representative's desktop computer in order to support better-informed, more personal interactions with the customer. Because it is a bankwide system, it also creates more consistent, seamless service. A customer can go into any FAC branch and the service representative has access to the same information about the client.

The service representatives and the contact management system work together to

- build a more personal relationship between customers and FAC
- provide opportunities to learn more about customers' needs and goals
- market additional products to customers

EXHIBIT 10

Analytical Steps to Determine the Next Most Likely Purchase

Step	Activity
1	Analysts determine that the target is to determine the likelihood that a household would use Product A.
2	Examples of households with and without Product A are extracted from VISION. 5,000 of each are selected.
3	Data are pulled on the 10,000 households and a file is created using an SQL query tool.
4	The file is transformed into a format readable by the data mining application and loaded into the product.
5	The data is analyzed using several statistical techniques. Each data variable is examined for importance, relevance, coverage, etc.
6	A first pass is made to select variables for the initial modeling effort. Between 40 and 60 variables are usually selected.
7	The data is divided into training, test, and validation sets.
8	A neural net makes its first attempt at predicting the target variable (use of Product A). Several hundred iterations may be made before a reasonable model is created.
9	The initial model is reviewed and tested. Adjustments are made. A new model is created. The process continues until no other improvements are seen.
10	The neural net is released in the form of a scoring algorithm, which is usually a multivariate nonlinear regression calculation.
11	Using a reporting tool, every household meeting the correct profile is downloaded from VISION.
12	The data file is formatted and then run through the data mining application. Each household is scored for its propensity to use Product A.
13	A household score file is created.
14	The household scores are appended to VISION where they are used to create target marketing lists.

When service representatives meet with clients, they follow a structured interview process that includes "meet and greet" questions that may take into account a recent conversation with a bank employee (e.g., How are you? Did your daughter enjoy her trip to Europe?), questions about financial needs (e.g., Are you still planning to buy a cottage at the lake and might you want to finance it with a home equity loan?), and questions about investment goals (e.g., Have you thought about opening an IRA to help with retirement plans?). The answers to these questions are entered into the contact management system by the service representative either during the conversation or later on. When the client is interested, the service representative prepares a detailed financial plan that ties the client's goals to appropriate bank products. The contact information is also used in identifying which customers to include in direct marketing campaigns.

Redesigning Bank Operations

FAC has redesigned its network of branch banks, how processes are performed in each branch, and the jobs that people perform in each branch, with the goal of increasing the time spent with clients in order to better understand their needs and to enhance the opportunities for marketing products. For example, the jobs of the customer service representatives (i.e., tellers) were expanded to handle routine tasks such as changes of address in order to allow personal bankers to have more time for sales-related activities.

The personal banker job itself was divided and is handled by four different types of people. The personal banker still exists to handle walk-in traffic and sell additional products as time permits. Then there are the consumer relationship managers who perform an expanded personal banker role. Because of their abilities, they are entrusted with the most valuable relationships identified by VISION and they have more time for marketing efforts. Small-business-relationship managers do the same thing for the most valuable "mom and pop" businesses. The final role is handled by investment specialists who sell an expanded set of investment products. With these changes, it is estimated that 60 percent of the time of the business relationship managers and investment specialists is spent better understanding customers' needs and marketing new and additional products.

Distribution Management

Channel Distribution Costs

In order to make good decisions about investments in the bank's multiple distribution channels, it is important to know the costs associated with each channel, and VISION data makes this possible. The cost calculations require information about how frequently the channels are used, the nature of the transactions, and the costs of operating the channels.

An interesting example of how this information can be used comes from ATM channel data. As a general rule, ATM transactions cost less than a teller. However, a recent FAC study found that the cost of accepting a *deposit* through a teller was 77 cents as opposed to $1.79 with an ATM. This surprising result was because there are fixed costs associated with processing ATM deposits (the deposits must be collected from an ATM, posted at the branch, mailed to a central location, and inspected at the central location), and these costs were being distributed across a relatively small number of ATM deposit transactions. In fact, only 4 percent of FAC's ATM transactions were for deposits, which was below the industry average. FAC's response was a program to educate customers on using ATMs for deposits and to extend the hours whereby clients would receive "same day" credit for making their deposits through an ATM. For a specified period of time, customers who were Select Rewards members also received bonus points for making ATM deposits.

Distribution Management System

The Distribution Management System (DMS) is a highly analytical application that helps FAC plan distribution channels for various market segments in a way that is profitable to the bank, yet still meets the needs and preferences of customers. Using inputs from VISION, such as household profitability, how customers currently use the bank's products, customer preferences, segments and channel costs, and external data that match potential new customers to the customer segments, DMS calculates the best way to distribute products to customers.

For example, in a particular market area, FAC was operating a main bank (a hub), three branch banks (spokes), and various ATMs. Using DMS, it was decided that closing one branch and increasing the number of ATMs would increase the bank's profits while better meeting the area clients' needs.

TCS and Data Warehousing Impacts

FAC's TCS strategy, supported by the data warehouse, has changed the mind-sets of employees, which in turn has created tangible benefits at the application and organizational levels. Further, FAC's senior management believes that the company is realizing strategic benefits thanks to the organizational transformation and the way in which the bank is now perceived within the industry.

A Change in Mind-set

The organizational transformation at First American Corporation included major shifts in the mind-sets of its staff, primarily because of the information available through the data warehouse. Jay Phillips, SVP for decision support, says, "We reengineered all of finance, changed all of the systems, and made a huge shift in marketing. You see a real change in how the lines of business do business; you see the branches really going through a redesign process." Finance has moved from being "bean counters" to aggressively working to find better ways of creating revenue. "Good customers" are now determined by the profitability of their overall relationship with FAC. Marketing has moved from a "lollipops and balloons" mentality to predicting customer actions through careful analysis, and using this information to promote profitability.

Across the bank, units that previously took a passive approach to business innovation now see themselves as responsible for creatively improving the bottom line. For example, accounts payable took an existing, internally used purchasing-card application and turned it into a product that could be sold to smaller corporate customers. (A purchasing card is basically a credit card for projects or groups to conveniently purchase items and automatically record the expenses against

EXHIBIT 11
TCS Application Benefits Realized

Application	FAC Users	Benefits
Client Information		
Customer Attrition and Retention	Segment managers Financial analysts Marketing analysts	Revenues from high value clients grew by more than 15%.
Customer Complaints	Service representatives	Improvement in NSF fee collection efforts increased fee income by more than $1.3 million in 1997 and 1998.
Select Rewards	Marketing analysts Segment managers	More than 43,000 customers are Select Rewards members, accounting for over $1.4 billion in loans, deposits, and investments.
Flexible Product Line		
Seniors Account	Marketing analysts	Improved risk-adjusted returns on equity (RAROC) from less than 25% to over 50% while maintaining deposit balances.
Repackaging of budget checking, student checking, 55 and better, and small business checking	Financial analysts	Enhanced revenues in excess of $1.8 million in 1997 and $3.2 million in 1998.
Repricing of certificates of deposit, express mortgages, NOW accounts, FAIR accounts, and savings accounts	Financial analysts	$1.7 million additional revenue in 1997 and 1998.
Next Most Likely Purchase	Service representatives	Improved sales effectiveness.
Consistent Service		
Contact Management	Sales representatives	Assisted in improving retention of high-value clients by 1%; worth $4 million in revenue.
Redesigning Bank Operations	Sales representatives Service representatives	Assisted in improving retention of high-value clients by 1%.
Distribution Management		
Distribution Management System	Financial analysts Distribution managers	In 1998, 22 higher-cost "hub" locations were replaced by 30 lower-cost "spoke" sites. Over 20% return on investment.

EXHIBIT 12

FAC's Financial Performance 1996–1998

Financial Indicators	1996	1997	1998
Return on assets	1.33%	1.40%	1.55%
Return on earnings	15.20%	15.91%	18.07%
Earnings per share	$1.98	$2.18	$2.62
Productivity ratio	58.98%	57.93%	53.44%
Average assets (in billions)	$16.6	$17.9	$19.3
Average core deposits (in billions)	$11.6	$12.4	$12.6
Stock price (as of)	$29.56 (1/17/97)	$45.875 (1/15/98)	$41.3125 (1/21/99)

their budgets). This was quite a shift in mind-set for accounts payable, which had never before been involved with revenue creation. Brian Cooper adds: "It is gratifying to see that VISION has transformed the organization. People think differently now because of it, and new employees don't even know the [old] ways we used to think."

However, this level of change has not been easy or comfortable for everyone. Throughout the organization, those who could adapt to frequent changes and could take the initiative to enhance performance prospered, while those who could not, left. Some areas experienced 100 percent turnover in one year, and many others experienced 25–30 percent turnover over 3 years. Those who stayed, however, are part of exciting changes.

Achieving the Benefits

In order to assess the success and impact of TCS, senior management initiated some project tracking metrics. Exhibit 11 describes selected applications, the users of the applications, and the resulting benefits. For example, the seniors account has seen an improvement in the risk-adjusted return on equity from less than 25 percent to more than 50 percent while maintaining deposit balances.

FAC's Tailored Client Solutions strategy, powered by the VISION data warehouse, had also fundamentally changed how the bank is managed, and had generated quantifiable financial returns. It has allowed FAC to emerge as a profitable, innovative leader in the financial services industry, as the highlighted data in Exhibit 12 show.

The TCS strategy also has favorably affected how other banks perceive FAC. The CEO of Deposit Guaranty (which FAC acquired in 1998) considered FAC to be an attractive buyer because he wanted to be part of "a financial institution of the future and not a bank of the past." He had learned of FAC's data warehousing initiatives and had not encountered banks of similar size, or even larger size, with the same capabilities.

FAC was clearly at the forefront of a new wave of enterprise systems—customer relationship management systems using a data warehouse solution—and after many years of effort was beginning to leverage its IT investments. The CEO's goal for FAC to join the "Sweet 16" was also within reach as the company's financial performance significantly improved.

CASE STUDY II-4

BATESVILLE CASKET'S WORLD WIDE WEB SITE

Batesville Casket Company is a subsidiary of Hillenbrand Industries, Inc., headquartered in the small southern Indiana town of Batesville. Batesville Casket is the world's largest producer of metal and hardwood burial caskets, having the leading position in the U.S. market. With six manufacturing plants in the U.S., one in Canada, and one in Mexico, Batesville Casket serves some 22,000 funeral homes in North America through 70 strategically located distribution warehouses.

In order to bring a spirit of entrepreneurship into Batesville Casket, in early 1996 the company reorganized from a traditional organization to a Strategic Business Unit (SBU) form. Strategic Business Units oriented around product lines include a burial urn SBU, a premium products SBU, a standard metal casket SBU, a wooden casket SBU, and an "essentials" SBU whose products are caskets made of composite materials. There are also Centers of Excellence in support functions such as finance, personnel, and sales/marketing. As a part of this reorganization, the previously centralized Batesville Casket information technology department has been decentralized to better serve the needs of the SBUs and Centers of Excellence.

Batesville Casket's Market

Batesville Casket sells its products to funeral homes. The family of the deceased person chooses the casket from the selection provided by the funeral home. Typically the funeral home will have a casket selection room with a limited number of caskets that can be seen, and there may be one or more catalogues from which other models can be chosen. Because the funeral home has a rather limited stock of caskets on hand, it is critical that the casket manufacturer be able to deliver any desired casket to the funeral home within 24 to 48 hours. In order to provide the necessary level of service, Batesville Casket has some 70 service centers (warehouses), its own fleet of trucks, and a sophisticated computer system for processing orders and managing its inventory and deliveries.

Some funeral homes deal exclusively with Batesville Casket, some stock other brands of caskets as well, and some do not provide Batesville Casket's products.

During the past few years there has been a strong trend towards consolidation in the funeral home industry, with large organizations competing aggressively to buy family-owned funeral homes. According to the December 9, 1996, issue of *Time*,[1] consolidators then owned only about 10 percent of America's 23,000 funeral homes, but these homes tended to be prime properties in key markets and accounted for about 20 percent of the country's funerals and thus about 20 percent of the U. S. market for burial caskets. In late 1996 the industry leader, Service Corporation International of Houston, owned 2,832 homes and 331 cemeteries in North America, and the Lowen Group, based near Vancouver, Canada, owned 814 homes and 265 cemeteries in North America. Both organizations were expanding as rapidly as possible in order to ready themselves for the time when baby boomers begin to die in increasing numbers.

Motivation for a Web Site

Responding to the rapid changes in its market, Batesville Casket allocated more of its information technology resources to the sales and marketing areas. Accordingly, James J. Kuisel, former director of the centralized information technology area, is now head of the sales/marketing information technology group and reports to the vice president of sales. Kuisel explains:

> Top management thought that we could grow the business by using information technology, so they decided to concentrate IT in marketing and sales to use it for generating revenue. One of our first steps was to use the Internet to build brand preference so that we can have families asking for our product.

[1]Larson, Erik, "Fight to the Death," *Time*, December 9, 1996, pp. 62–67.

> We believe that we can offer a valuable service to families of those who are terminally ill by providing them information on the decisions that have to be made when death occurs. There are a number of things where they will be sorry for a long time if they make the wrong decision, and they can do a lot of planning in advance of the death. We hope to provide a service to the community and at the same time build brand awareness for our products.
>
> There is also a lot of negative public relations information that is out about our industry, and as the number one casket company we tend to be "picked on." We think that the Internet can give us an opportunity to present our side and counter that negative publicity.

Kuisel was concerned about the possible reactions of funeral directors to the idea of setting up a home page on the Web. Some funeral homes have used the Internet to promote cut-rate funeral services, and some critics have used the Internet to attack the funeral industry. The possibility that funeral directors would associate Batesville Casket with these negative activities on the Internet troubled Kuisel, so the first thing he did was to check out the idea with Batesville Casket's customers.

> We have an advisory council composed of representatives from 30 funeral homes nominated by our regional managers. We called each one and asked them what they thought of the idea of Batesville Casket going on the Internet, and all of the response was favorable. Incidentally, we were surprised to learn that more than half these representatives indicated that they were using the Internet!
>
> We then sent out an announcement to each of our 16,000 funeral home customers. We told them that we were attempting to promote a better understanding of the funeral process, and that we had three goals for our Web site: (1) To promote the value of the funeral and the important role of the funeral home director, (2) to educate consumers on the funeral process and the product choices available, and (3) to make available resources that provide support in the human processes of grief. A section of questions that might be asked (with answers) was included.

Web Site Development

Development of the Batesville Casket Web site was begun in late February 1996, and a phase one version was up and running by early May (*www.batesville.com*). The initial home page design is shown in Exhibit 1. By clicking on the buttons on the left, this home page leads to the following sections: *Decisions to Make when a Death Occurs*; *Grief Resource Center* (see Exhibit 2, p. 312); *Funeral Products & Services* (see Exhibit 3, p. 313); *Company Profile*; *What's New*; and *Visitor Feedback*.

Each section's introductory page leads to a great deal of additional information related to its topic.[2] For example, clicking on "Casket Showroom" on the *Funeral Products & Services* page leads to Exhibit 4 (see p. 314). (Note: Additional casket models are shown farther down on this Web page.) Clicking on the "*Classic Gold*" picture in Exhibit 4 leads to the larger picture shown in Exhibit 5 (see p. 315).

Because the Batesville Casket people had no experience in developing a Web site, Kuisel employed a Cincinnati advertising agency to do the graphics work and develop the pages. Batesville people developed an outline of the various sections to be included. For each proposed section they then collected pertinent printed material that Batesville had produced over the years. The advertising agency used the plan and this material as the basis for development of the Web site, but developing the Web pages from these materials was not a trivial matter. According to Kuisel:

> We were fortunate that we had accumulated a lot of excellent material on the grieving process over the years. We have solicited the foremost authorities in this area and have purchased exclusive rights to publishing some of their materials. However, because these materials had been written at different times and for different audiences, they had to be reworked to make a cohesive presentation. The principles associated with grieving haven't changed, but the words in which they were expressed may have changed or gone out of style. Although using the existing materials was almost as much work as starting from scratch, we felt that using time-tested materials was preferable because we knew that they would not offend anyone.
>
> Similarly, much of the content of the other sections could be compiled from existing materials, but it was much more difficult than we had expected to make sure that everything was consistent. We frequently uncovered things that did not match up. For example, we would find that on one Web page we said that Batesville Casket distributed its products from 56 warehouses, and on another Web page we said that we had 70 warehouses. This was because we had used materials from different times in our history.
>
> We tried to be very careful in the development of the Web materials. For example, we had talked about entombment going back to the time of Christ, and one of our advisory panels suggested that we instead talk about it going back to Roman times so that we did not alienate other religious groups.

Kuisel questions their decision to develop the Web pages from previously published materials:

> The documents had been written to be read sequentially, whereas on the Web everything is linked. If we had started from scratch on the Web we would probably have come up with a

[2]The reader may want to explore the current version of the Batesville Casket Web site, which has been extensively modified.

EXHIBIT 1
Batesville Casket Home Page

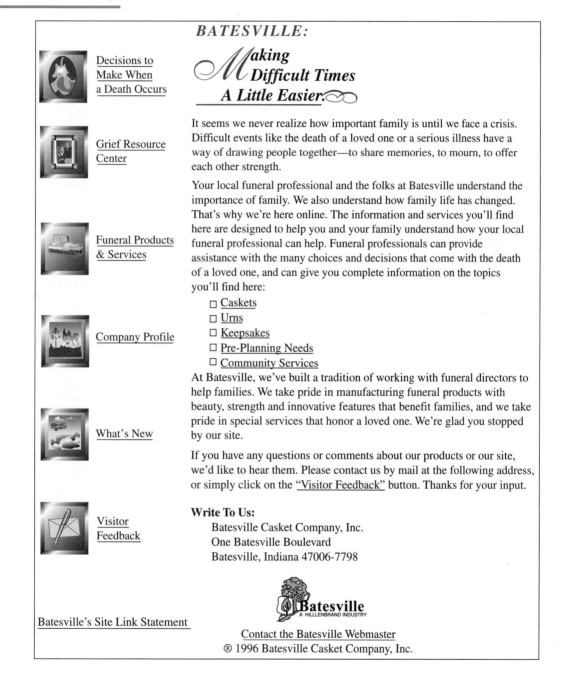

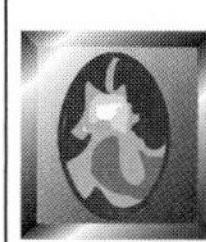
Decisions to Make When a Death Occurs

Grief Resource Center

Funeral Products & Services

Company Profile

What's New

Visitor Feedback

It seems we never realize how important family is until we face a crisis. Difficult events like the death of a loved one or a serious illness have a way of drawing people together—to share memories, to mourn, to offer each other strength.

Your local funeral professional and the folks at Batesville understand the importance of family. We also understand how family life has changed. That's why we're here online. The information and services you'll find here are designed to help you and your family understand how your local funeral professional can help. Funeral professionals can provide assistance with the many choices and decisions that come with the death of a loved one, and can give you complete information on the topics you'll find here:

- Caskets
- Urns
- Keepsakes
- Pre-Planning Needs
- Community Services

At Batesville, we've built a tradition of working with funeral directors to help families. We take pride in manufacturing funeral products with beauty, strength and innovative features that benefit families, and we take pride in special services that honor a loved one. We're glad you stopped by our site.

If you have any questions or comments about our products or our site, we'd like to hear them. Please contact us by mail at the following address, or simply click on the "Visitor Feedback" button. Thanks for your input.

Write To Us:
Batesville Casket Company, Inc.
One Batesville Boulevard
Batesville, Indiana 47006-7798

Batesville's Site Link Statement

Contact the Batesville Webmaster
® 1996 Batesville Casket Company, Inc.

more effective design of how to present the material. All in all, we felt that development of most of the pages might have been easier and more effective if we had started with a clean slate.

Batesville chose the advertising agency to do the development because it had gotten a number of awards for previous Web page designs. Unfortunately, the advertising agency had farmed out most of its previous Web design work, and its in-house Web capability was minimal. Kuisel reports:

> They did not understand the technology very well. The first design for our home page was a work of art–it had a beautiful

EXHIBIT 2
Grief Resource Center Page

Grief Resource Center

The long illness of a parent or friend. The tragic death of a young person due to an accident. The aftermath of violence. The helplessness we feel when facing our own death. No matter what the situation, grief is something that each of us must face in our lifetime.

Fortunately, many expert resources exist to help families deal with grief. Several resources are presented here, and more are available through your local funeral professional.

Whether you are helping yourself or someone else through a trying time, we hope this information gives you both practical direction and emotional comfort.

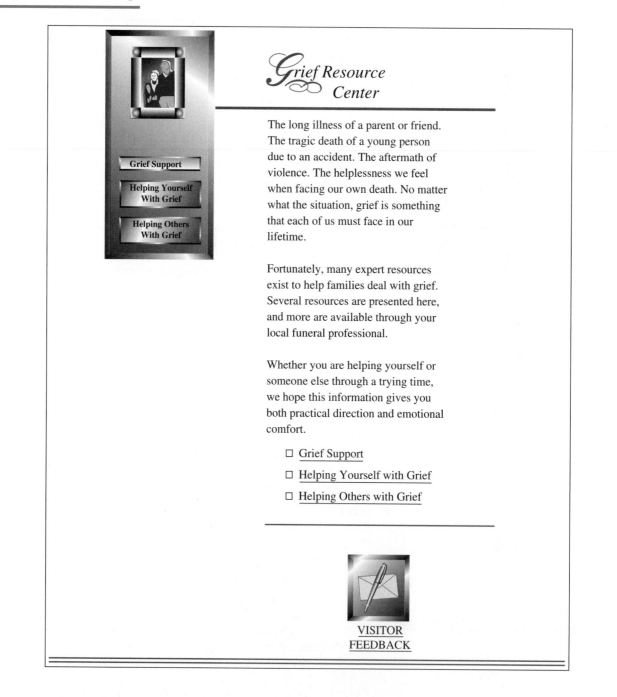

- Grief Support
- Helping Yourself with Grief
- Helping Others with Grief

VISITOR FEEDBACK

white satin background with a profusion of beautifully arranged flowers. But it took about 2 minutes to transmit the page to the PC of someone who wanted to visit our site, so it was unusable because people would not wait that long for the home page to appear. If a visitor wanted a picture of a particular casket he might wait 2 minutes for it to be transmitted, but on the home page you have to get them hooked much, much quicker.

We spent a lot of time and effort with the advertising agency editing the materials, setting up linkages, and changing the site around. It was more work to undo things that they did wrong than it would have been to do them in the first place, so

EXHIBIT 3
Funeral Products & Services Page

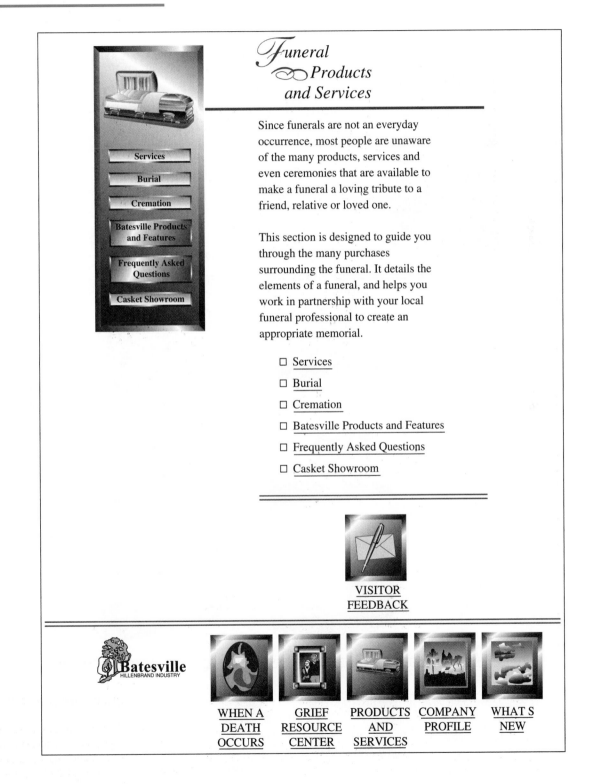

Funeral Products and Services

Since funerals are not an everyday occurrence, most people are unaware of the many products, services and even ceremonies that are available to make a funeral a loving tribute to a friend, relative or loved one.

This section is designed to guide you through the many purchases surrounding the funeral. It details the elements of a funeral, and helps you work in partnership with your local funeral professional to create an appropriate memorial.

- ☐ Services
- ☐ Burial
- ☐ Cremation
- ☐ Batesville Products and Features
- ☐ Frequently Asked Questions
- ☐ Casket Showroom

VISITOR FEEDBACK

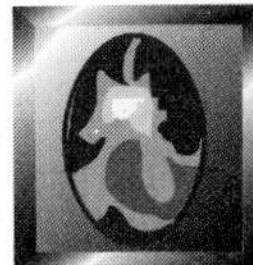

WHEN A DEATH OCCURS

GRIEF RESOURCE CENTER

PRODUCTS AND SERVICES

COMPANY PROFILE

WHAT S NEW

EXHIBIT 4
Casket Showroom Page

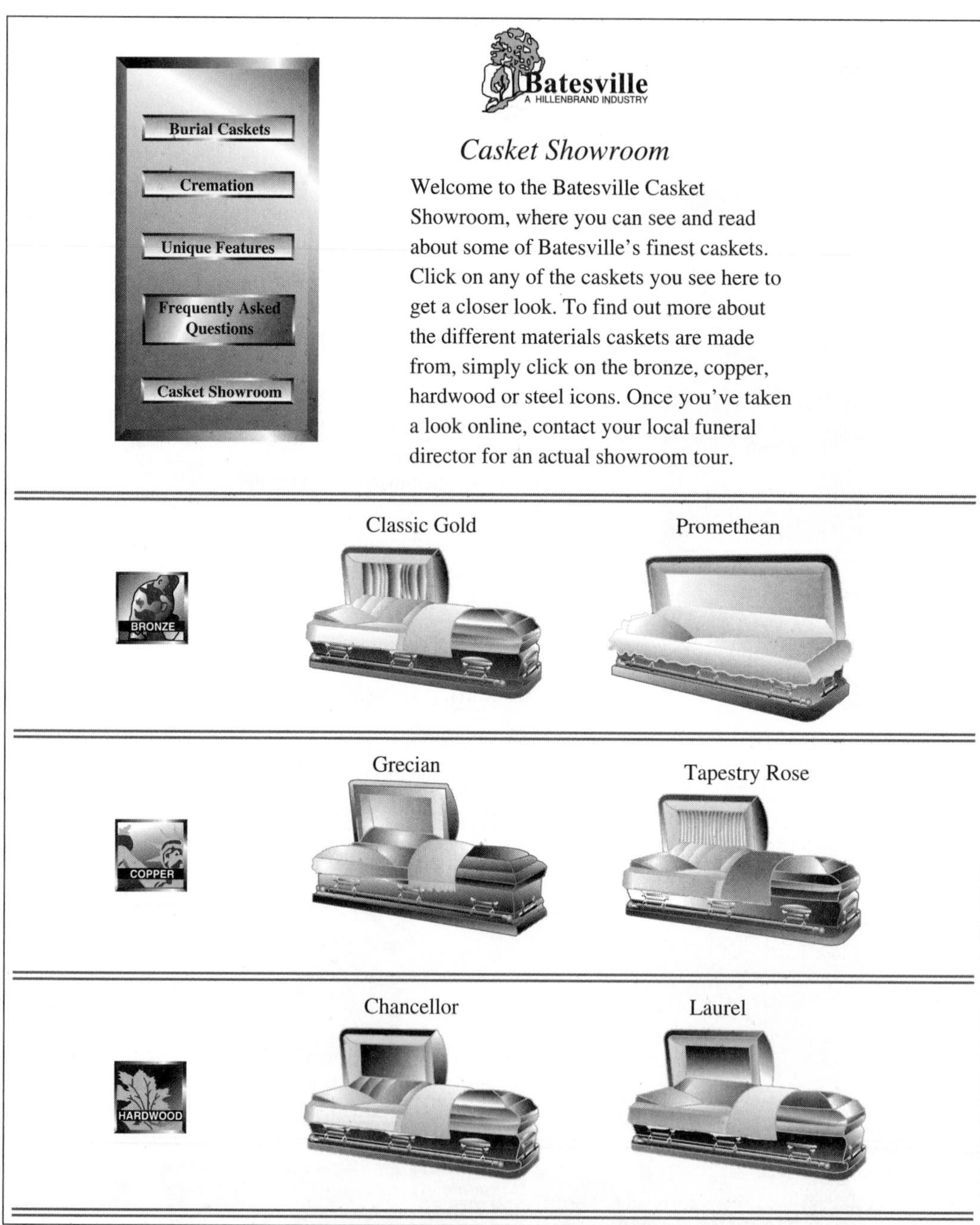

we feel that we would have been better off if we had done the development work ourselves.

The cost of developing the Batesville Casket Web site was in the neighborhood of $50,000, split about equally between the advertising agency and Batesville's internal costs.

Because of time pressures, possible security problems, and the capital costs involved, Batesville Casket decided to use an Indianapolis company, I-Quest, to provide the hardware and Web software for the Batesville Web site. This decision also significantly reduced the strain on Batesville Casket's relatively

EXHIBIT 5
Classic Gold Page

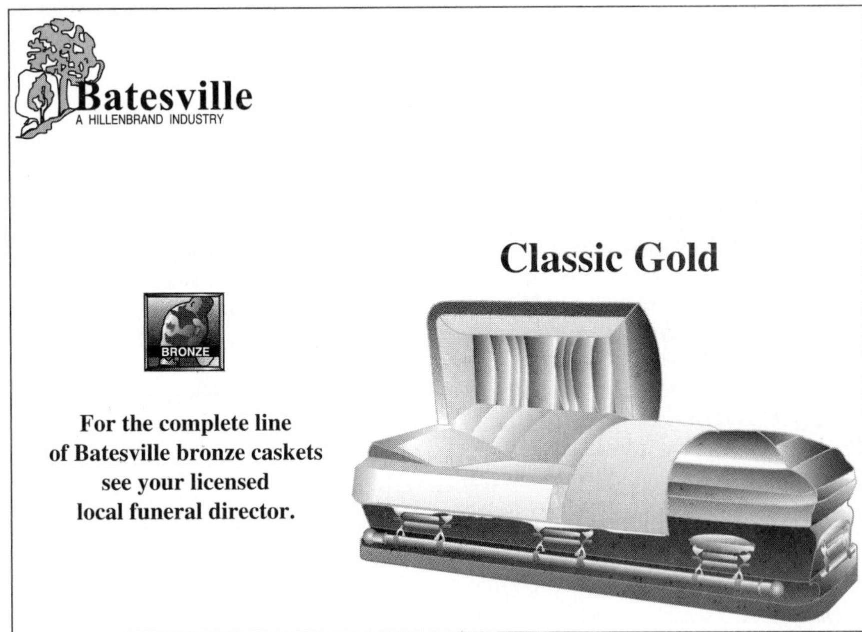

small information technology staff. Kuisel has been happy with this decision:

> We knew that I-Quest has a number of very successful sites, and ours has run very smoothly. I-Quest provides us with a lot of statistics on the number of people who visit the site and the number of pages that they access, and we think their prices are reasonable. There is a basic monthly fee, based upon the size of the site, that covers everything unless the number of hits exceeds a generous limit. If you exceed the hits limit you pay extra for each additional hit, but we never come close to the limit. We pay I-Quest less than $300 a month.

Early Results

In the first few weeks of operation, a number of other Web sites set up links to the new Batesville Casket home page. Batesville Casket encourages this, but with some reservations because of the possibility that a site hostile to the industry might link to this site. Therefore, the following notice appears when one clicks on the "link statement" at the bottom of the Batesville home page: "Batesville Casket Company encourages others to link to our Web site. Batesville reserves the right to discontinue the association if, in Batesville's opinion, any message or information communicated from the linked Web site is not consistent with the goals of Batesville Casket Company." It is not clear, however, what Batesville Casket could do to "discontinue the association."

After a few months of operation, the Batesville Web site was getting around 2,000 visitors a month, with hits from all over the world. Although this was not a large number, those visiting the site seemed to be staying a long time, accessing an average of around 45 pages a visit. Those who have provided feedback are split about 50–50 between the general public and funeral industry people.

Although the feedback received has been very favorable, evaluating the success of this endeavor is a problem. According to Kuisel:

> We know our goals, but we do not know how to easily measure our goals. Our most important goal is to establish a brand preference. Also, we would like to educate consumers so that they will not be swayed by negative TV programs on the industry. We also want to increase customer satisfaction, and we think that educated customers will make a choice that they will be more satisfied with. It is easy to measure hits and to analyze the "Visitor Feedback" messages, but these things do not measure these goals.
>
> As far as measuring our financial success, we will probably only be able to survey our customers and ask: "Has there been any change in the number of people who have come in asking for a Batesville casket since the Web site has been operating?" That would be the bottom line, but such a survey would be quite unreliable in measuring modest changes in demand.

Further Considerations

Kuisel is working to expand the number of people visiting the Batesville Web site:

> We are now working on getting our site to show up near the top of the list presented by the various search engines such as Yahoo and Netcrawler. We want to be in the top ten listings presented by each of the top five search engines, so when people query on funeral or casket or burial they will see us first.
>
> Each of the search engines uses a different algorithm to select what they show and to determine the sequence in which to present them. There are people who understand the algorithms that are used, and we are employing a consulting firm that has a good reputation in this area to help us. Although each search engine is different, our consultant knows some tricks of the trade that we think will be helpful. For example, we are considering installing a "phantom" home page that no one will ever see, but that has the attributes that the search engines use to select the sites they present at the top of their lists.
>
> We are also considering having some of the top search engines present an advertising banner for us whenever someone enters a search for a funeral-related topic.

Batesville is considering a number of interesting opportunities. For instance, Batesville produces custom caskets that are tailored to the interests of the deceased. The family of an avid sailor, for example, might want something incorporating sailing symbols into the burial. Because of the lead times involved, this could only be done in cases when someone is terminally ill. Normally a family would not contact a funeral home until after death has occurred, but if Batesville's Web site could make family members aware of the alternatives ahead of time, they might choose something special.

Batesville is also thinking about how to use the Internet to present product information to funeral homes. Kuisel explains: We depend upon our sales representatives to present product information to the potential buyer, and the Internet can provide the most up-to-date information to our funeral home customers. We have a number of large customers that our sales representatives see very frequently, and we have lots of small customers that they do not see very often. We think that it is very good to be able to supplement our sales force by getting the latest product information to our small customers and presenting it in the way the company would like to have it presented.

Kuisel sees several strategic issues to consider in Batesville's use of the Internet in the future. One issue is whether or not to list funeral homes. Kuisel explains:

> In the same city there may be a funeral home that is a 100% Batesville customer and another that is only a 30% customer. If we were to list recommended homes on our Web site, how would we deal with this disparity? If we list both homes, the 100% customer may be upset, and if we list only the 100% customer, the other customer may get upset.

Kuisel discusses other issues that Batesville is exploring:

> We were thinking about establishing an Internet mall. You would come into our page and get linkages to services and products that we do not offer, such as a vault, and you would be referred to a vault site. That raises an issue, because you might never come back to our site.
>
> Another possibility is called (in Internet terminology) planting and seeding. For example, getting insurance companies to link to our site from their sites so that when someone is thinking of insurance they might go a step further and think of funeral preplanning. And there are publications that we might like to have link to us. We also need to think of the positives and negatives of linking up with certain groups, such as various churches or cemetery organizations.

There are many opportunities and issues that Batesville Casket is considering in the use of the Web to help communicate the value of the funeral process. Therefore, the Batesville Casket Web site is likely to evolve over time.

CASE STUDY II-5

E-BUSINESS TRANSFORMATION AT THE CROSSROADS: SEARS' DILEMMA

It was December 2002, and Garry Kelly, the newly appointed CIO of Sears, Roebuck and Company, looked out of his office window and contemplated the issues he needed to discuss in the management committee meeting the following day. Garry had arrived at Sears only a few weeks earlier when the company was at a critical juncture. Sears' net income in 2001 had fallen to $735 million on a revenue level of $41.1 billion. These figures reflected only half of the profits it had recorded two years earlier, on a similar level of sales. Sears also faced intense competition from rival retailers across the nation, new dot-com e-tailers as well as from the specialty stores that had been eroding the Sears profit base for the last couple of years. Investors, stakeholders, and employees were anxiously looking for signs of turnaround at the giant in the U.S. retailing industry.

Garry was brought in after the former CIO, Jerry Miller, suddenly left the company, just days after Sears announced its acquisition of Lands' End, a premier Internet and catalog clothier company. The company appointed an interim CIO and Garry came as a replacement from the shoe retailer Payless ShoeSource.

Garry, as well as the senior managerment at Sears, clearly understood the impact of the Internet on the retailing industry and had no second thoughts about their quest to exploit the Web for boosting the company's profitability. Although Sears had made significant investments in its online e-business initiatives, it was facing significant challenges to realizing returns on these investments. A couple of issues were at the forefront of Garry's attention. These issues and challenges needed to be resolved to pave the way for future decisions and strategies pertaining to e-business.

From *Journal of Information Technology,* 19:2 (June 2004). Reprinted by permission of the Association of Information Technology Trust. The case was prepared by Professor C. Ranganathan (University of Illinois at Chicago), Analini Shetty, and Gayathri Muthukumaran as a basis for class discussion, rather than to illustrate either effective or ineffective handling of an administrative situation. It has been slightly edited for textbook publication.

While the customer base for online shopping was increasing steadily, Sears was facing severe competition. Sears sells a broad range of products, from appliances to apparel, and had followed a largely incremental approach for moving its product range online. It was not clear if Sears needed to focus exclusively on a select line of products or sell its entire set of products online. An added dilemma was whether to have multiple sites with different selling and return policies for different product categories or to have a unified, integrated site with uniform product policies across all kinds of goods.

Another issue was Sears' foray in the business-to-business e-commerce arena. In 2000, Sears joined hands with Oracle Corporation and Carrefour, a large retailer in Europe and Latin America, to form GlobalNetXchange, an online marketplace that would enable suppliers and retailers to communicate, collaborate, and manage their supply chains. Sears and Carrefour expected to cut down their combined purchasing costs, which totaled $80 billion annually, and effectively manage a fleet of over 50,000 suppliers. Despite the investments in the B2B exchange, Sears faced mixed results. Only 6 months earlier, Sears had acquired one of the largest and most successful catalog and Internet direct-only specialty clothiers, Lands' End, which had great brand appeal, sophisticated technological infrastructure, and a sound operations backbone. Moreover, Lands' End had also made impressive strides in using the Internet to attract and improve its sales.

Lands' End recorded a net profit of $66.9 million on sales of $1.6 billion at the end of 2001, and a margin of 4.3 percent, nearly double Sears' profitability percentage. Given the successful operations of Lands' End, Sears has been moving with great caution in order not to disrupt the Web sales and catalog operations of Lands' End. Both companies have significant differences in their product lines, customer base, and brand appeal. However, the merger has paved the way for immense opportunities to multichannel across stores, Web sites, and catalog operations. Sears could offer its customers the opportunity to buy everything from automobile parts to shirts through any of its channels. Considerable synergies could be exploited in back-end business operations, marketing, promotion, and distribution. Could Sears take advantage of Lands' End's strengths to improve its own e-business efforts?

The U.S. Retail Industry

Retailing is the second-largest industry in the United States in number of establishments and number of employees. In 2003, the U.S. retail industry employed more than 23 million individuals and generated more than $3 trillion in sales. Based on the type of products they sell, retailers are classified into two sectors: durable and nondurable. Durable goods include building and garden supplies, automobiles, computers, home furnishings, and furniture. Nondurables include general merchandise, food, drugs, apparel, and accessories. Since 1988, the retail industry had grown between 4 and 5 percent annually, with sales of durable goods growing a bit faster than nondurables. A major portion of the nondurable sales came from stores in the general merchandise category that included department and discount stores.

Many retailers, including department and discount stores, had pursued rapid expansion strategies in the 1970s and 1980s, fueled by the rise in consumer spending. The retail square footage increased from 8 square feet to 19 square feet per capita between the years 1976 and 1995. This rapid expansion of retail stores and selling space resulted in an environment with many mature market segments. As a result, mergers, restructuring, and consolidation activities intensified in the industry. (Exhibit 1 presents an overview of the U.S. retailing industry and Exhibit 2 presents the top retailers.)

The commercialization of the Internet in the mid-1990s led to the emergence of a number of online retailing firms. Several virtual retailers like Amazon.com posed a serious challenge to traditional brick-and-mortar retailers. In response to the competition from new e-tailers, several brick-and-mortar companies launched their own online channels in the late 1990s. By the turn of the millennium, the U.S. retail industry environment reflected a mature industry with considerable overcapacity. Exhibit 3 presents trends in the U.S. retailing industry, along with online retailing. Exhibit 4 shows the online market shares for pure play online retailers and the traditional firms. Exhibit 5 presents the online sales trends based on different product categories.

Sears, Roebuck and Co.

The seeds of Sears were sown in 1886 when Richard Sears began the R. W. Sears Watch Company in Minnesota. A year later, he moved to Chicago and teamed up with Alvah C. Roebuck, and Sears, Roebuck and Company was born. In 1888, the company started its catalog business, which was the first of its kind in the country. The catalog operations were a huge success, as Sears, Roebuck offered a wide variety of products that were not easily available to consumers. The Sears, Roebuck catalog for each season was welcomed with great anticipation and business soared. In 1925, the company expanded into retail store operations and opened its first retail store, and within four years grew to 324 stores across the country. Sears, Roebuck's retail stores carried a variety of merchandise such as apparel, jewelry, cosmetics, electronics goods, tools, household appliances, cookware, and bedding. In the following decades, Sears, Roebuck (later just Sears) grew rapidly, becoming an icon in the U.S. retailing industry.

By the early 1980s, discount stores such as Wal-Mart and Kmart had become dominant forces in the retail industry, eroding Sears' market share. In an effort to boost its competitive position and performance, Sears tried a number of different

EXHIBIT 1

Annual Sales Trends in U.S. Retail Industry (in millions)

	1992	1995	1996	1997	1998	1999	2000	2001
Discount department stores	$93,871	$118,661	$121,936	$128,049	$131,004	$135,713	$138,360	$139,895
Chain department stores	87,384	92,258	95,065	97,013	97,543	100,350	100,387	94,780
Speciality stores:								
Furniture, home furnishings, electronics, and appliance stores	97,757	130,447	137,930	144,303	154,555	167,151	178,834	179,241
Clothing and accessories stores	120,346	131,605	136,860	140,565	149,442	159,888	167,541	169,127
Total	$401,350	$474,966	$493,787	$511,927	$534,542	$565,101	$587,122	$585,044

Source: U.S. Census Bureau.

EXHIBIT 2

Top Retailers in U.S. Market

Rank	Company	Volume (in thousands)		Earnings (in thousands)		Units	
		2001	2000	2001	2000	2001	2000
1	Wal-Mart	$219,812,000	$193,295,000	$6,671,000	$6,295,000	4,414	4,190
2	Home Depot	53,553,000	45,738,000	3,044,000	2,581,000	1,348	1,134
3	Kroger	50,098,000	49,000,400	1,042,500	876,900	3,534	3,660
4	Sears	41,078,000	40,937,000	735,000	1,343,000	2,960	2,960
5	Target	39,362,000	36,362,000	1,368,000	1,264,000	1,381	1,307
6	Albertson's	37,931,000	36,762,000	501,000	765,000	2,400	2,533
7	Kmart	37,028,000	35,925,000	–244,000	403,000	2,150	2,172
8	Costco	34,797,037	32,164,296	602,089	631,437	369	335
9	Safeway	34,301,000	31,976,900	1,284,400	1,091,900	1,773	1,688
10	J.C. Penney	32,004,000	31,846,000	98,000	–705,000	3,770	3,725

Source: *Stores Magazine*, National Retail Federation.

retailing initiatives such as "store of the future," "everyday low pricing," and "stores within a store," and also diversified into financial services and real estate. But such initiatives bore little fruit. Profit margins continued to decline, taking the company almost to the brink of bankruptcy.

In 1992, Sears hired a new leader for its retail operations, Arthur C. Martinez, who was named the company's CEO three years later. Martinez faced the arduous task of turning the company around.

> Well, the company was in big trouble, really floundering. We were losing over $100 million in the catalog, retail was making zero money, and the credit business was making a couple of hundred million dollars. When you put the whole package together there was no money and very little cash flow coming out of the retail business.[1]

Martinez took several cost-cutting measures to improve profitability. He changed the product mix and placed special emphasis on middle-class female customers. The reorientation was reflected in the new slogan, "Come see the softer side of Sears." Martinez also pushed the credit card business that offered customers more flexibility in paying for their purchases at Sears.

After a spate of restructuring exercises, Sears had operations in three broad areas: retailing, service, and credit. CEO Martinez said: "After the restructuring in '92, the business did take off in 1993. The sales trend was fantastic all the way through '97."[2] However, this revival was short-lived. Sales stagnated again and several key executives left Sears. Competitors such as Home Depot, Lowe's, and Circuit City garnered considerable portions of Sears' market share. Other discount stores such as Old Navy, Target, and Wal-Mart chipped away at Sears' apparel business.

EXHIBIT 3

U.S. Retail Industry Sales—Total Retail and Online Sales (in millions)

Period		Retail Sales (in millions)	
		Total	E-Commerce
1999	4th Quarter	$784,278	$5,481
2000	1st Quarter	711,600	5,814
	2nd Quarter	771,691	6,346
	3rd Quarter	765,536	7,266
	4th Quarter	810,311	9,459
2001	1st Quarter	724,224	8,256
	2nd Quarter	805,245	8,246
	3rd Quarter	782,088	8,236
	4th Quarter	856,285	11,178
2002	1st Quarter	743,810	9,880
	2nd Quarter	825,243	10,265
	3rd Quarter	827,461	11,061
	4th Quarter	869,588	14,334

Source: U.S. Census Bureau.

[1] T. Savage, "T. Terry Savage Talks Money with Arthur Martinez," *Chicago Sun-Times*, April 29, 2001 (available online at *www.suntimes.com/savage/talk/arthur_martinez.html*).

[2] Ibid.

EXHIBIT 4

Trends in Online Sales: Traditional (Store + Catalog) Retailers vs. Online E-Tailers

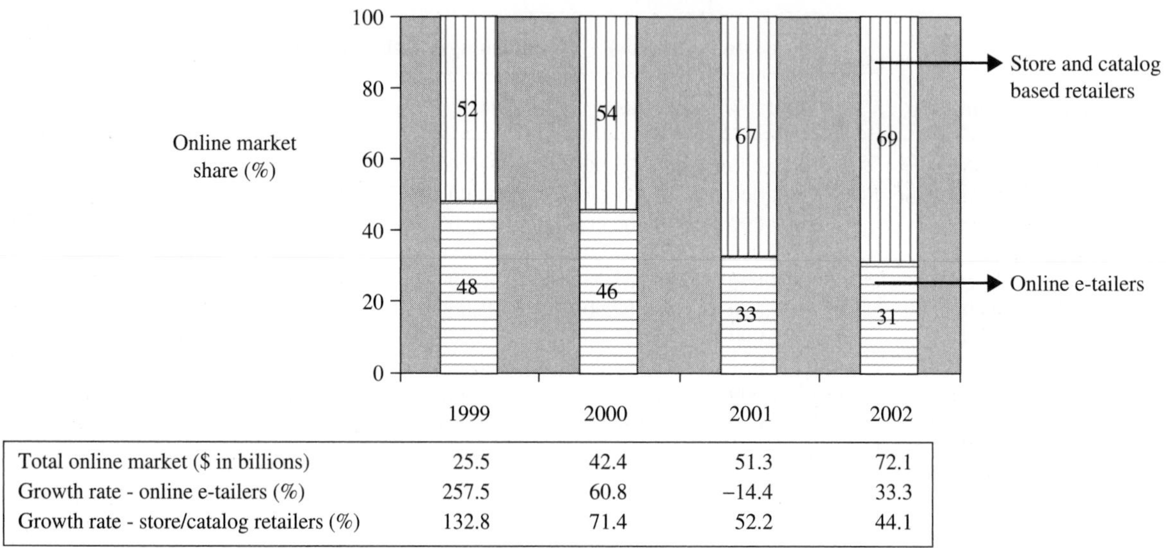

	1999	2000	2001	2002
Total online market ($ in billions)	25.5	42.4	51.3	72.1
Growth rate - online e-tailers (%)	257.5	60.8	−14.4	33.3
Growth rate - store/catalog retailers (%)	132.8	71.4	52.2	44.1

Source: *The State of Retailing Online 5.0* (Boston Consulting Group, Forrester Research, and comScore Networks. Used with permission.)

An industry analyst described this situation as, "It's been a middle market squeeze for Sears—from the department stores on one side and value-oriented business on the other."[3]

By the late 1990s, the e-commerce wave had started sweeping through corporate America. Many retailers were looking at exploiting the Web to promote, market, and sell their products. Sears was initially skeptical about the Internet. CEO Martinez remarked, "I was a serious skeptic for a long time ... I saw this as a domain of fanatics."[4] However, subsequently, Sears started taking a serious look at the Internet to improve its profitability and performance. Exhibit 6 traces the key e-business initiatives at Sears.

Crawling in Cyberspace: E-Business Initiatives at Sears (1996–1999)

Sears had all the important pieces to be an early e-commerce leader, but the process of restructuring in the mid-1990s hurt its chances. Sears, in a partnership with IBM, owned 50 percent of Prodigy, one of the first commercialized online services. This could have given a lot of momentum to its online initiatives. However, as a part of corporate restructuring, the company sold its stake in Prodigy in 1996. Sears also had good distribution, fulfillment, and direct-marketing catalog operations, fundamental building blocks of a successful e-tail business. Yet, Sears closed its catalog operations in 1993. With such handicaps, Sears had to plan its e-business moves cautiously.

Sears made its online debut in 1996 as an information-only Web site. Sears did not add any transaction or selling capabilities to its Web site, as it preferred to wait and watch to see if electronic shopping would be a lucrative channel. In 1997, it decided to sell over 3,500 of its Craftsman tools online. Sears chose Craftsman tools because it wanted to experiment in online selling with a product line that not only had a strong business potential, but also a recognized brand name. "Craftsman is a brand where quality and features are well known, so there is a high chance of customer satisfaction and even higher chance of overall success,"[5] remarked a senior Sears marketing executive. While the rival department stores were dealing with the complexities of selling apparel online, Sears started its online selling with hard goods like Craftsman tools.

In an effort to experiment in online selling of softer products, Sears decided to sell gift items from its Christmas wish-book catalog. The online experiment from Craftsman and the wish-book products generated about $10 million in sales. Despite the

[3]E. Brown, "Big Business Meets the E-World," *Fortune* (140:9), November 1999, pp. 88–98.

[4]Ibid.

[5]D. Claymon, "IT Takes Tools," *Redherring*, February 1998.

EXHIBIT 5
Trends in Online Sales by Product Category

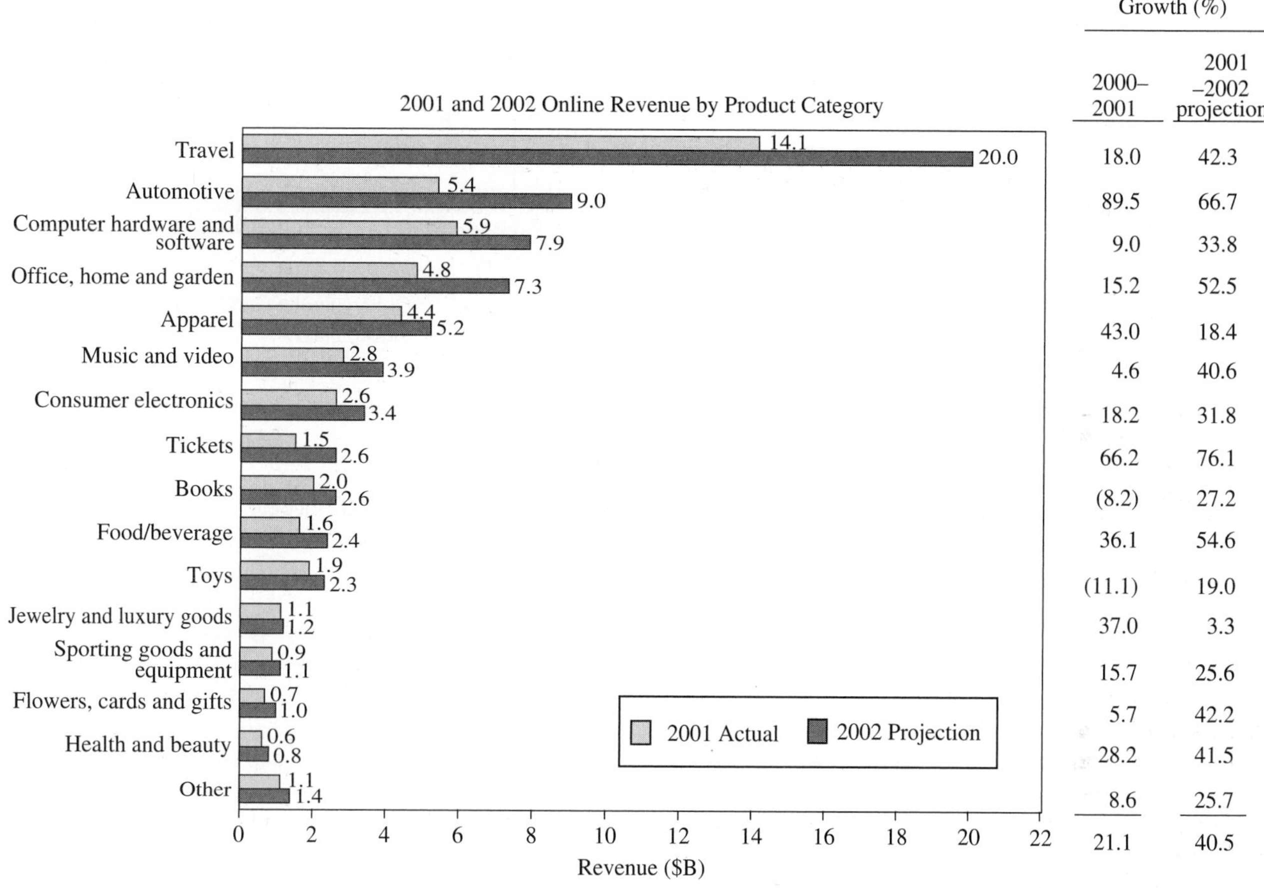

	Growth (%) 2000–2001	Growth (%) 2001–2002 projection
Travel	18.0	42.3
Automotive	89.5	66.7
Computer hardware and software	9.0	33.8
Office, home and garden	15.2	52.5
Apparel	43.0	18.4
Music and video	4.6	40.6
Consumer electronics	18.2	31.8
Tickets	66.2	76.1
Books	(8.2)	27.2
Food/beverage	36.1	54.6
Toys	(11.1)	19.0
Jewelry and luxury goods	37.0	3.3
Sporting goods and equipment	15.7	25.6
Flowers, cards and gifts	5.7	42.2
Health and beauty	28.2	41.5
Other	8.6	25.7
	21.1	40.5

Source: *The State of Retailing Online 5.0* (Boston Consulting Group, Forrester Research, and comScore Networks. Used with permission.)

encouraging results from this initial experiment, serious skepticism arose among some Sears executives as to the viability and profitability of e-business. Skeptics pointed out that Sears had earlier tried both catalog and home shopping, and the results had not met expectations. Having come full circle, Sears might face the same experience with the Internet as well. Concerns were also raised about the problems in filling orders for bulky items such as washers and dryers. Some executives also argued the risks of cannibalization. They saw the Internet as a threat that would draw customers away from their retail stores.

Among those executives who favored e-business, it was not clear if the company should adopt a faster rollout of all its products online or if it should take an incremental, category-by-category approach to e-business. The company conducted focus group sessions to understand the potential impact of its online initiatives. "We discovered through focus groups that the Internet was a great mechanism for delivering solutions. Even if customers aren't comfortable buying online, the site is important for their product search,"[6] said a general manager.

While the debates and arguments continued for several months, a clear mandate emerged from top management in favor of an incremental approach to moving online. "If we worry about cannibalization, we'll miss the opportunity,"[7] declared CEO Martinez. The CEO was convinced Sears should move online. The modest success of the initial e-business efforts resulted in stronger top management commitment. The

[6]C. Zimmerman, "Partnerships Are Important to Sears Web Strategy," *InternetWeek*, February 1998 (available online at *www.redherring.com/mag/issue51/tools.html*).

[7]N. Brumbach, "Sears Sees Web Sites as Add-On Volume for All Inventory," *Home Furnishing News*, March 1, 1999, p. 38.

EXHIBIT 6
Key E-Business Initiatives at Sears

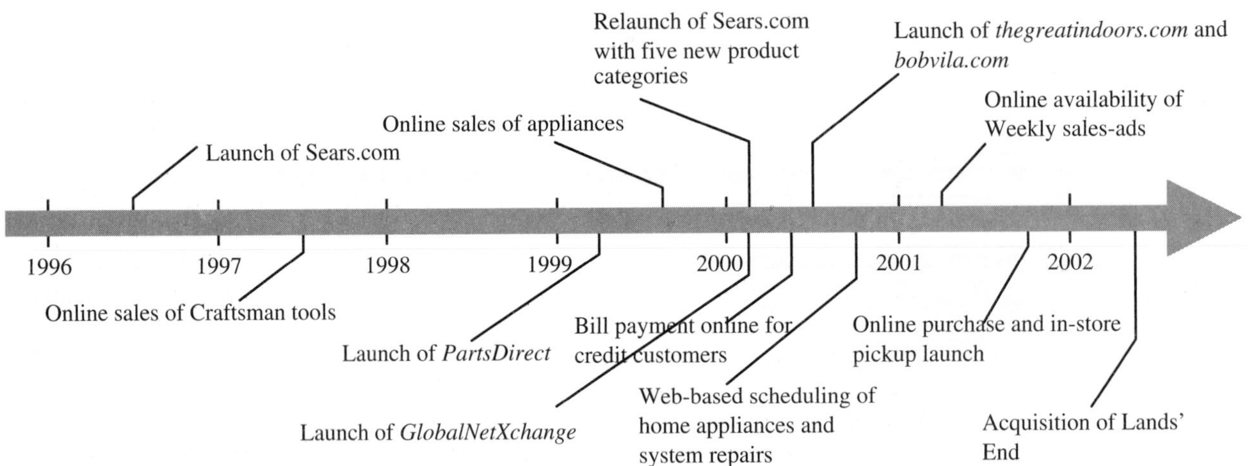

CEO decided to go ahead with converting Sears into an effective clicks-and-mortar organization:

> The notion that all old economy companies were going to be marginalized and put out of business was a [laugh] to me. The people who were advancing that view were talking out of their own self-interest, not a strategic viewpoint. We saw the Internet coming and asked ourselves how we could use it as an additional channel of distribution and an additional channel for customer relations.... It wasn't another new business model, just another tool in the toolkit of how to run your business .[8]
>
> —*CEO Martinez*

A new head was appointed for online ventures, and an internal Web team with about 35 employees was formed to focus exclusively on e-business efforts.

In early 1999, Sears launched *PartsDirect* site as a part of Sears.com to feature more than 4.2 million parts and accessories from over 400 manufacturers of appliances, power tools, and other home equipment. Apart from selling these parts, the site also offered extensive assembly and repair manuals that would aid do-it-yourself customers.

Within a month of launching *PartsDirect*, Sears added its major appliances—refrigerators, freezers, stoves, dishwashers, washers, and microwaves—to its Web site. "Major appliances are Sears' strength. We have 38 percent of the market. If you put the No. 2 through [No.] 15 retailers together, that's our market share,"[9] said an executive. Appliances were not only an area of traditional stronghold, but Sears also had the necessary infrastructure to take care of logistics, distribution, deliveries, installation, and repairs to make online selling possible. The appliance launch marked the online availability of over 2,000 brand-name appliances that included popular names such as Kenmore (Sears' brand), GE, Maytag, and Whirlpool.

Sears' approach was to treat the Web site as an additional channel, rather than as a separate business unit. The Web site served as a complementary channel for marketing and selling appliances, with Sears' 850 department stores and 680 dealer stores providing the backbone distribution infrastructure. To strongly integrate its Web operations with that of store retailing, Sears extended all the services such as repairs, warranty, pricing, etc., to online customers as well.

The company's experience from selling appliances online allayed the cannibalization fears in the minds of many in-store salespeople. Sales representatives came to realize that their jobs were getting easier as the Web site educated customers about the varied products, schemes, and services. The appliance information and the side-by-side product comparison feature in the site greatly helped customers in their product research. The in-store sales crew began to appreciate the online channel as customers started bringing in printouts of online research to the stores to complete their purchases. Through an internal study, Sears found that about 13 percent of customers who purchased goods from their stores used the Sears Web site for some research prior to their purchases.

The next logical step for Sears was to market its online channel. Sears started banner ads on Microsoft's MSN network in mid-1999. It also pushed its marketing efforts by promoting Sears.com through television and print commercials.

---

[8]Savage, op cit.

[9]R. Williams, "The Software Side of Sears," *Interactive Week*, September 2001 (available online at *www.eweek.com/article2/0,4149,1243780,00.asp*).

The company spent close to $100 million in marketing its Web site. In preparation for the holiday season, Sears also enhanced its Web site by adding holiday products and items, and by introducing new features such as product comparison aids. Sears also introduced its Sears card and gift card services online. "It's a truly clicks-and-mortar type of holiday season for Sears. Not only have online tool and appliance sales surpassed our expectations this season, but we have sold thousands of Sears gift cards online as well,"[10] said a general manager.

By 1999, Sears had invested between $75 and $100 million in its e-business initiatives. In December 1999, Nielsen/Netratings ranked Sears.com fourth on its list of fast-growing online properties. It also estimated that Sears.com had about 250 percent growth in terms of unique audience, or first-time visits to its site, during the 1999 holiday shopping season. Site-performance tracker Media Metrix also reported Sears.com to be a leader in the online retail segment in terms of unique visitors, with about 1.9 million customers logging on at least one time in a month. Further, more than 90 percent of the online orders were completed perfectly, in terms of delivery times and correct fulfillment of the product and quantities.

By the end of 1999, Sears had 100 full-time employees working exclusively for its online division. Further, 50 employees from several departments were involved in different e-business projects. The company also started involving several departments and employees in its e-business initiatives. It also empowered its divisional managers to develop ideas for expanding the online presence of the company.

The Cyber Marathon: E-Business Initiatives (2000–2002)

By the turn of the new millennium, a new crop of startups such as Homewarehouse.com, Hardware.com, and Ourhouse.com had emerged on the dot-com terrain. Moreover, some of Sears' suppliers also launched their own Web sites, trying to sell directly to customers. Discount stores such as Kmart and Wal-Mart had stepped up their online efforts. Kmart had launched an independent e-commerce spin-off, bluelight.com, and Wal-Mart had started making impressive gains through its Wal-Mart.com site. Other competitors like J.C. Penney and Home Depot had also beefed up their Web sites to increase their online presence.

In an effort to counter the frenzied online competition, Sears decided to pursue a partnership approach to enhancing its e-business efforts. To gain immediate access to capabilities not readily available within the company, Sears decided to form a number of strategic alliances and joint-venture relationships with other firms. "Our strategy has been to look for the absolute best partners to build e-business,"[11] remarked the general manager for Sears online.

Sears entered into a partnership with IBM to launch *thegreatindoors.com*, a site dedicated to home decorating ideas and products. To combat Home Depot, Sears and home improvement guru Bob Vila created an online joint venture, *bobvila.com*, as a site for home improvement solutions. According to CEO Martinez, this joint venture, "latest in the series of alliances," was a part of a "new and powerful online strategy" Sears planned to use to build its digital capabilities.[12] Sears also formed an alliance with Sun Microsystems to promote the Internet-connected home. Through this project, homes could function more safely and efficiently using Sun's networked products. Sears was responsible for installation, service, and financing of the products.

To further improve its marketing efforts, Sears entered into a partnership with America Online (AOL). The deal was to make AOL a preferred ISP for Sears, with AOL providing links to direct its customers to Sears.com. The deal also included offering Internet access through AOL's browser that would make it easier for customers to get in touch with Sears' customer service representatives. Further, AOL subscriptions could be paid online through Sears credit cards. "These deals help both sides gain deep penetration into each other's markets. It helps both Sears and AOL reach new customers that they didn't get or know about before,"[13] said an industry analyst.

As the e-business initiatives grew, Sears started building its information technology capabilities through strategic technology partnerships. Sears collaborated with Viant Corporation in planning and implementing product additions to its online offerings. Sears also teamed up with Xpedior, an e-business solutions provider, to build and integrate multiple product lines and legacy systems into the Sears.com Web site. To evaluate and monitor the online customer behavior and buying patterns, Sears worked with E.piphany to deploy a system for gathering marketing, operational, and technical metrics concerning online customers and Web site visitors.

In its efforts to become the most desired online destination for home solutions, Sears added lawn and garden power equipment to its online offerings in April 2000. The company president said,

> As a part of our online strategy to provide solutions for the home, during the past 12 months we have introduced the largest appliance store and the largest parts site for the consumers, as well as

---

[10] Sears press release, December 17, 1999.

[11] Zimmerman, op cit.

[12] Sears press release, March 3, 2000.

[13] *The Gazette* (Montreal), "AOL, Sears Forge Web Alliance: Partnership Will Focus on Expanding Each Company's Business via Internet," March 15, 2000.

expanded to 120 brands on Sears.com's tool territory. Our online efforts are designed to build relationships with our existing customers and attract new customers to Sears.[14]

In August 2000, the company relaunched its Web site with additional product offerings and a number of new features. Home electronics, computers, and office equipment, small appliances and cookware, and baby products were added to the existing set of offerings. A senior executive said,

> Our customers can go to a single online store to shop, or to comparison shop and buy in-store. This will be essentially convenient for our customers during gift-buying seasons, when furnishing a new home, getting ready for a new baby—or for all those students going back to school next month who still need an iron, coffee maker, laptop, refrigerator, or an MP3 player.[15]

Sears continued to add a number of new features to its Web site. In October 2000, it implemented a new online scheduling capability, through which customers could arrange for service and repairs to appliances and heating and cooling systems in their homes. The company also implemented an online bill payment service. Partnering with Mercado Software, Sears added an advanced search solution to its Web site to enable its customers to quickly and easily find the products or services for which they are looking. Sears formed an alliance with PCsupport.com to provide online technical support on its Web site to Sears' customers who had purchased computers. This service enables customers to diagnose the problem in a 24/7 time frame, get live technical support through e-mail or chat, and access online self-help resources.

Sears took a number of measures to increase the integration between its online and offline operations. Apart from being an additional sales channel, Sears saw the Web site as a way to drive its customers to make in-store purchases. Sears offered in-store pickup for products that were sold online. This arrangement was intended to pull shoppers into the stores so that they could make additional purchases. "Sears.com influences about 10 percent of in-store purchases of major appliances, and that's about $500 million a year. One of every 20 purchases of home office or home and garden products is influenced by the site,"[16] said a senior executive. To efficiently manage in-store pickups, Sears purchased 15,000 handheld devices for its employees to scan store merchandise and reserve products when an order came in over the Web. This ensured that the items were in stock when the customer walked into the store to pick up an order placed through the Web site.

As a part of its brick-and-click integration, Sears also introduced in-store kiosks. This enabled customers to do product research without the help of sales personnel at the retail stores. Sears also included an automotive category on its Web site, allowing customers to conduct online research on tires, batteries, and other automotive maintenance parts for their vehicles. Customers could research the parts, brands, and prices online and make the purchase from the nearest Sears store. Because the products must be installed on the vehicle, they were not available for online purchases. The main intent of the automotive category was to enable online research and in-store purchase, installation, and service.

Furthering the efforts to integrate its online and offline operations, Sears also carefully aligned the incentives of its store-based personnel with online efforts. Sears decided that the stores would receive a commission according to the zip code of the Web orders. This commission was to be divided among the employees of the particular product section. This step helped eliminate any remaining cannibalization fears among in-store personnel, who feared that customers would come into the stores to gather information and then purchase the product on the Web. "Sears.com and our stores strongly complement each other. Our aim is to maximize overall sales, whether through Web or stores," said an executive. In addition to incentives for sales personnel, the vendors are also credited for Web sales based on the category of the merchandise purchased online.

Business-to-Business Initiatives

As mentioned earlier, Sears teamed with Oracle Corporation and Carrefour, a large retailer in European and Latin American countries, to launch a business-to-business marketplace to bring their combined 50,000 suppliers under one trading platform. That e-marketplace, named GlobalNetXchange (GNX), was aimed at bringing down procurement costs and product prices in addition to streamlining purchase processes. The exchange also offered a full range of trading mechanisms, including bidding and auctions.

When it announced the initiative, Sears expected other major retailers to join the exchange so as to increase economies of operation. Soon afterward, U.S. retailer Kroger, European retailers Metro AG and J Sainsbury Plc, and Australian retailer Coles Myer Ltd. joined the exchange. However, with a volume twice that of Sears' and Carrefour's combined, Wal-Mart chose to leverage its own streamlined internal procurement process by creating its own B2B exchange. GNX also faced competition from other retailer exchanges. For instance, the Worldwide Retail Exchange (WWRE) was started with backing from some popular retailers including Target, Albertsons, Best Buy, Kmart, Walgreen's, and J.C. Penney. In fact, more than 200 retailer exchanges with different product categories emerged in 2000 and 2001. In addition, as forecast by industry analysts, several suppliers initiated

[14]Sears press release, April 12, 2000.

[15]Sears press release, July 25, 2000.

[16]Williams, op cit.

their own private exchanges in order to retain control over their distribution channels and to avoid fees charged for goods sold via the buyers' exchange.

Acquisition of Lands' End

The acquisition of Lands' End in May 2002, which at the time was the largest U.S.-based specialty apparel company, was a major step toward attracting offline and online Sears customers to its softer goods segment. An internal study showed that 70 percent of the customers who shopped at Sears for appliances shopped elsewhere for apparel. In the words of Alan Lacy, who became CEO of Sears in 2000 when Martinez retired:

> We were drawn to Lands' End's brand strength across all apparel categories, including men's, women's and children's. It is an excellent fit for Sears and our customers and will aid us in becoming the preferred shopping destination for families. We can help accelerate the growth of the Lands' End direct business through Sears' extensive customer relationships.[17]

Sears would carry and sell Lands' End merchandise in its stores, and Lands' End would assume responsibility for Sears' customer-direct business, including Sears.com. Lands' End's CEO was named the head of Sears' customer-direct business. As an initial experiment, Sears began to stock and sell Lands' End's apparel in 180 of its 800-plus stores. This acquisition would also enable Sears to re-enter the catalog business, which it had exited in 1993.

In addition to its Web and catalog operations, Lands' End operated 16 outlet stores in Wisconsin, Illinois, Minnesota, and New York, plus three outlet stores in the U.K. and one in Japan. Lands' End had launched its Web site in 1995, featuring about 100 products as well as stories, essays, and travelogues. Over time, its product range, selection, and customer base grew. The company also introduced several innovative features for shoppers on its Web site, including My Virtual Model, a tool that allowed shoppers to create three-dimensional models for their bodies to ensure a better fit for clothing they ordered. The company also offered My Personal Shopper service, which allows customers to set up a profile of their wardrobe style preferences so they receive recommendations from Lands' End. A brief comparison of the Web-site features of Sears and Lands' End is provided in Exhibit 7. Exhibits 8 and 9 present the Web sites of both Sears and Lands' End (see pp. 326–330).

The two companies also had some major differences. First, they had a different customer base. While Lands' End had built a solid brand name over the years and typically attracted affluent and brand-conscious customers, Sears catered to a broader customer base. The acquisition therefore ran the risk of diluting the Lands' End brand image if its goods were sold together with other brands at Sears. As one industry analyst remarked, "If they don't dilute the brand and they keep the quality, I think that Sears is going into a good direction."[18] Sears and Lands' End also had some differences in the way they handled product returns and in their approaches to marketing.

Both companies also had adopted different approaches to information technology sourcing as well. Sears had historically relied largely on inhouse IT development and operations, although it had partnered with other companies for some of its Web initiatives. However, Lands' End had relied much more heavily on external expertise to develop their IT infrastructure and applications. For their Web operations, they had licensed

EXHIBIT 7

Sears vs. Lands' End Web Sites: A Comparison of Online Processes and Features (2002)

Processes/Features	Sears	Lands' End
Return	In-store or by mail	By mail only
Pickup	By mail/in-store (for selected items and based on availability)	By mail only
Price matching	Within 30 days	NA
Geographical scope	U.S. only (separate site for Canada)	Global (international sites available in multiple languages for Europe, U.S., and Asia)
Product presentation	Dominantly through text and graphic images.	Text, graphic images, and advanced visual presentations through virtual models, etc.
Customer service channels	Phone, e-mail, FAQ	Live Chat, Personal Shopper, Virtual model, Shop with a friend, Call back, Phone, e-mail, FAQ
User registration	Required	Required

[17]T. Robinson, "Sears Shells Out $1.9B for Lands' End," *E-Commerce Times*, May 14, 2002.

[18]T. R. Weiss, "Sears Buying Lands' End," *Computerworld*, May 13, 2002 (available online at *www.computerworld.com/managementtopics/ebusiness/story/0,10801,71132,00.html*).

and adapted some unique technology capabilities. The company held an equity position with a technology vendor for its custom clothing design and ordering capability, which by the time of its acquisition had been implemented for selected product lines.

Garry Kelly reflected on how IT could help make Sears a successful bricks-and-clicks organization, a multichannel retailer with a Web site that would be a compelling place for customers to research, order, and shop. The $41 billion company had to return to health, while simultaneously digesting a $1.6-billion direct-sales operation. He knew that in order to fulfill this goal, he had to reorient his technology organization, reexamine and improve on the e-business initiatives for Sears, and integrate systems as necessary. The technological growth of the company had been somewhat haphazard and needed to be set in order. As CEO Alan Lacy explained,

> We've had a very fragmented approach, and we're basically trying to standardize much more so than we have in the past. ... We've got too many point-of-sale systems, too many inventory systems, too many this, that and the other thing, because we basically allowed for many, many years each business to do its own thing, which we're not going to do anymore.[19]

Given the existing financial scenario at Sears, it wasn't clear which would be the best IT direction to take for the future.

Garry rose from his desk, considering the three strategic questions on the future course of e-business that faced his company. First, what was the best way to utilize the Web site and Internet to attract and sell a varied range of products? Second, how should Sears extend and enhance its business-to-business e-commerce initiatives to stay ahead of the pack and beat the competition? And finally, could Sears utilize Lands' End's technological and operations capabilities to turn around its e-business?

[19]C. Silwa, "CEO Says Company Will Standardize Technology," *Computerworld*, January 20, 2003 (available online at *www.computerworld.com/industrytopics/retail/story/0,10801,77715,00.html*).

EXHIBIT 8

Sears' Site Map—1997 and 2003; Sears' Home Page—2003

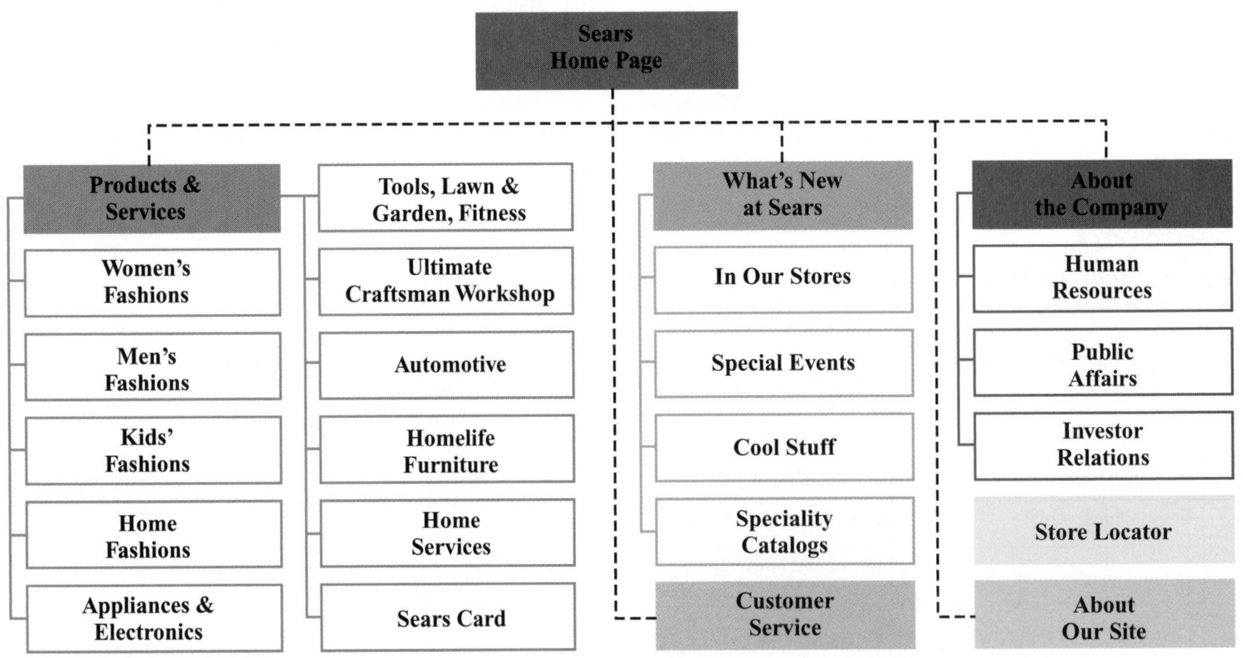

EXHIBIT 8 (Continued)

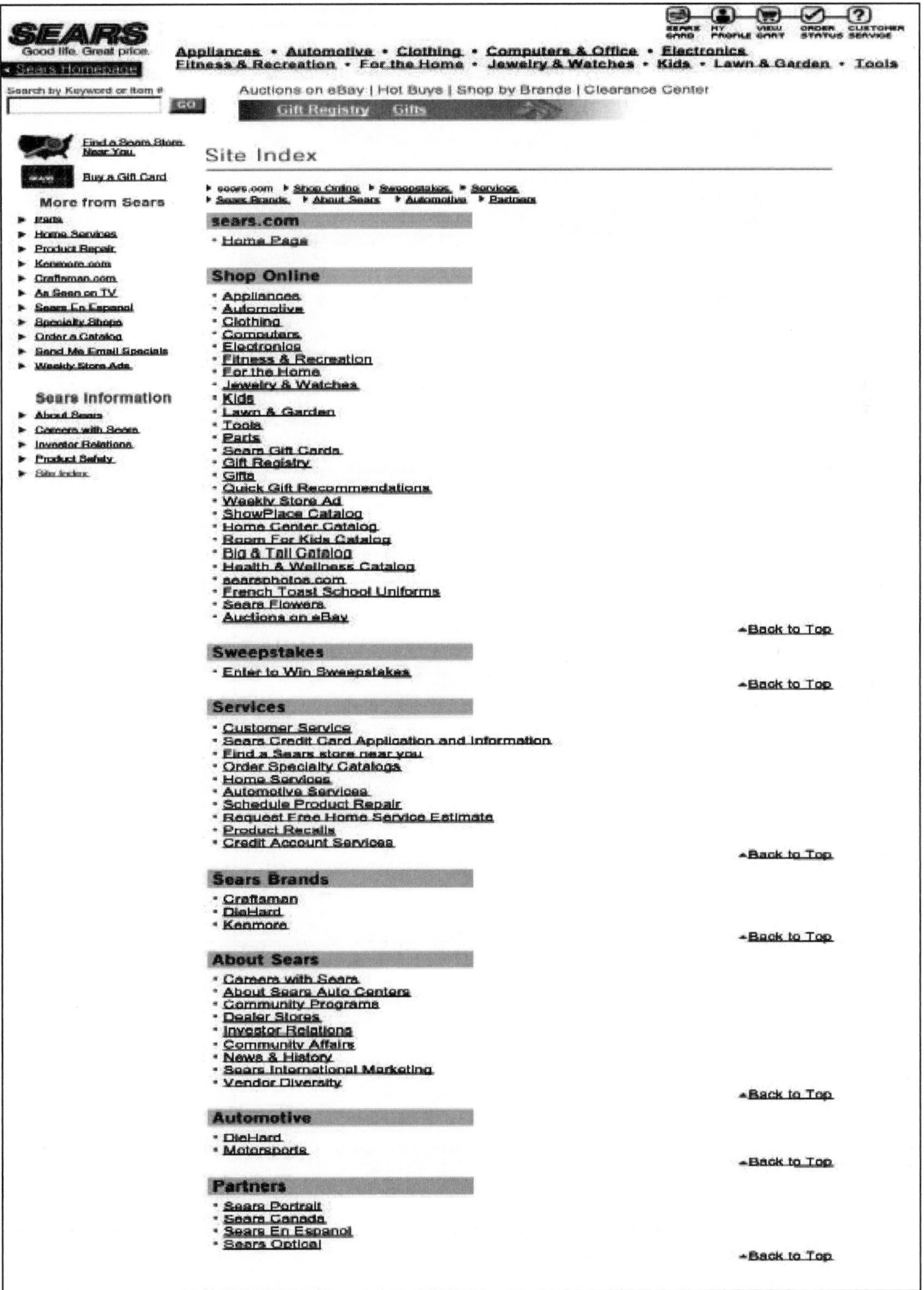
SEARS
Good life. Great price.
Sears Homepage
Appliances • Automotive • Clothing • Computers & Office • Electronics
Fitness & Recreation • For the Home • Jewelry & Watches • Kids • Lawn & Garden • Tools
Auctions on eBay | Hot Buys | Shop by Brands | Clearance Center
Gift Registry Gifts
Find a Sears Store Near You
Buy a Gift Card
More from Sears
Home Services
Product Repair
Kenmore.com
Craftsman.com
As Seen on TV
Sears En Espanol
Specialty Shops
Order a Catalog
Send Me Email Specials
Weekly Store Ads
Sears Information
About Sears
Careers with Sears
Investor Relations
Product Safety
Site Index
Site Index
sears.com
Home Page
Shop Online
Appliances
Automotive
Clothing
Computers
Electronics
Fitness & Recreation
For the Home
Jewelry & Watches
Kids
Lawn & Garden
Tools
Parts
Sears Gift Cards
Gift Registry
Gifts
Quick Gift Recommendations
Weekly Store Ad
ShowPlace Catalog
Home Center Catalog
Room For Kids Catalog
Big & Tall Catalog
Health & Wellness Catalog
searsphotos.com
French Toast School Uniforms
Sears Flowers
Auctions on eBay
Back to Top
Sweepstakes
Enter to Win Sweepstakes
Services
Customer Service
Sears Credit Card Application and Information
Find a Sears store near you
Order Specialty Catalogs
Home Services
Automotive Services
Schedule Product Repair
Request Free Home Service Estimate
Product Recalls
Credit Account Services
Sears Brands
Craftsman
DieHard
Kenmore
About Sears
Careers with Sears
About Sears Auto Centers
Community Programs
Dealer Stores
Investor Relations
Community Affairs
News & History
Sears International Marketing
Vendor Diversity
Automotive
DieHard
Motorsports
Partners
Sears Portrait
Sears Canada
Sears En Espanol
Sears Optical

EXHIBIT 8 (Continued)

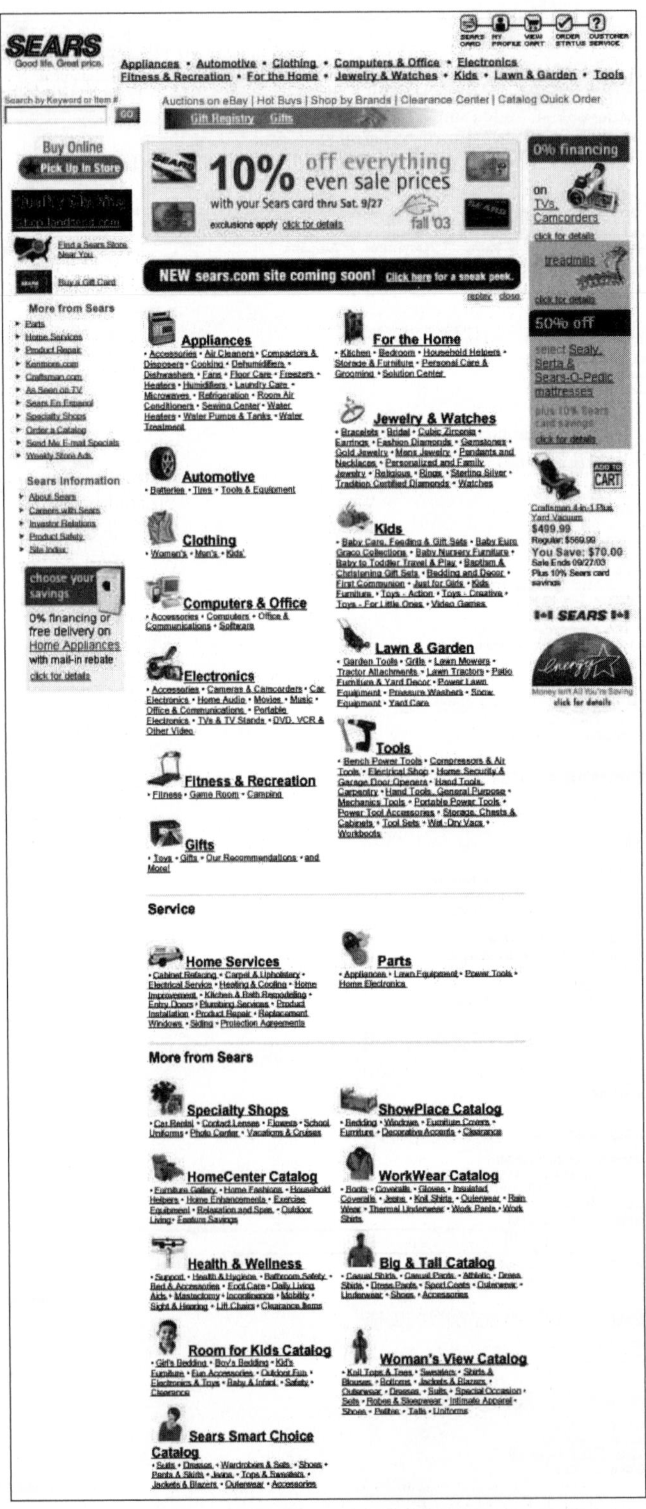

EXHIBIT 9

Lands' End Site Map—1997; Lands' End Home Page—2003

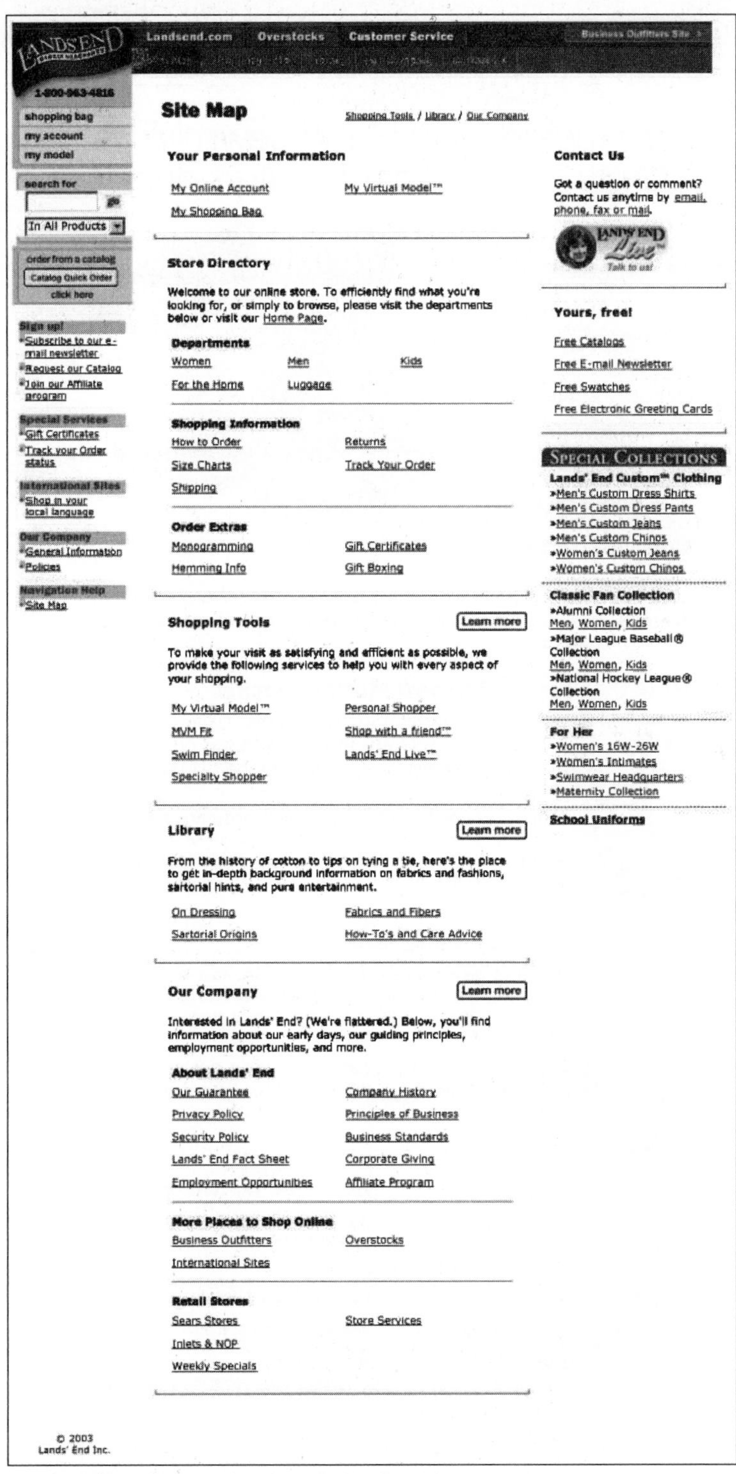

EXHIBIT 9 (Continued)

Landsend.com
Overstocks
Customer Service
1-800-963-4816
shopping bag
my account
my model
search for
In All Products
order from a catalog
Catalog Quick Order
click here
Sign up!
Subscribe to our e-mail newsletter
Request our Catalog
Join our Affiliate program
Special Services
Gift Certificates
Track your Order status
International Sites
Shop in your local language
Our Company
General Information
Policies
Navigation Help
Site Map
Introducing New Hand-sewn Mocs. Quality craftsmanship, value-priced.
If you know Land's End only for great outerwear and well-made outfits, you should walk a mile in our shoes. Start with our new Hand-sewn Mocs for Women and Men. Meticulously hand-sewn uppers, foot-hugging neoprene collars, ultra-comfy dual-density soles and genuine, weather-resistant suede make these Mocs a real treat for feet. The price? A refreshingly honest $29.50.
You'll find all of our shoes, sandals, sneakers and boots at Men's, Women's, or Kids'. Good reasons to make landsend.com your family shoe store.
Meet the remarkable new Marinac Jacket
"Soft Shell" technology is the most important advance in outerwear in years and our new Marinac™ Jacket for Men and Women is leading the way.
Our Jacket of the Year looks like ordinary fleece but it's so much more. It stretches, breathes, stops wind and water — and defies comparison – all for about a fourth of the price you'd pay elsewhere.
Sweater days are here again!
The hot days have had a good run. But summer's days are numbered. It's time to reach for the sporty Drifter™ Half-zip Mock – our Men's Sweater of the Year.
Can't get enough sweaters? Browse our entire assortment of Men's and Women's Sweaters.
Contact Us
We're here to help – by phone or e-mail.
Business Outfitters
Business solutions: quality logos, corporate gifts and more.
¿Habla Español?
Para realizar un pedido en español, por favor comuníquese al 1-800-675-7681 y un representante se complacerá en atenderle en español.
Lands' End at Sears
Sears® stores are now offering a colorful array of bestselling Lands' End products. See our Sears Store Directory for a location near you.
Special Collections
Lands' End Custom™ Clothing
Men's Custom Dress Shirts
Men's Custom Jeans
Men's Custom Chinos
Women's Custom Jeans
Women's Custom Chinos
Now in Corduroy
Men's Custom Dress Pants
Logo Apparel
Alumni Collection
Major League Baseball® Collection
National Hockey League® Collection
For Her
Maternity Collection
Women's Intimates
Women's 16W-26W
Swim HQ
Lands' End School
Top-of-its-class Dress Code Clothing and Uniforms
Stories. Fun.
Things to wear.
Join the happy multitudes who receive the Lands' End e-mail newsletter. Enter your email address to subscribe:
©2003 Lands' End Inc.

CASE STUDY II-6

THE CLIPTOMANIA™ WEB STORE

Cliptomania, LLC, a Limited Liability Corporation, sells clip-on earrings on the Internet at *www.cliptomania.com.* Cliptomania is owned and operated by the Santo family—father Jim, mother Candy, and daughter Christy. Its business is conducted from the lower level of the Santo home in Indiana, but it sells clip-on earrings throughout the United States, Canada, the U.K., Ireland, Japan, Australia, and New Zealand.

Most people who wear earrings have pierced ears, so stores offer a limited assortment of nonpierced earrings. Those who want clip-ons have a very difficult time finding appealing choices. Cliptomania sells nothing but non-pierced earrings, and it offers its customers a choice of hundreds of different styles of clip-ons. Although the percentage of people who want clip-ons is small, the total number of potential customers available to Cliptomania on the Internet is huge. The Santos have found an underserved market niche. According to Candy:

> A lot of our buyers are first-time buyers on the Internet, and some of them are older women. Recently a lady wrote to us: "I'm 83, and last week I finally broke down and got my ears pierced. This week I found you. Where were you last week?!"
>
> But you would be surprised how many teens and young twenties buy because for one reason or another they have had trouble with pierced ears. There are young mothers whose babies ripped the earrings out of their ears and their ears cannot be pierced again. And there are people like me who have problems with scar-forming keloids—and don't want any unnecessary scars. There are people for whom piercing their ears is against their religious beliefs. Some women are so thrilled to find us—they will tell me that they have this problem or that problem and ask which of the earrings will work best for them. Because there are several different types of clip mechanisms, I can often help them out.
>
> Our customers are pretty evenly distributed by age from preteens to the elderly. We had not anticipated it, but we estimate that we get some 5 percent of our sales from the cross-dresser and transgender population.

The Santos want Cliptomania to become the Kleenex[1] of clip-on earrings, that is, the first name someone thinks of when looking for nonpierced earrings. They concentrate on providing a quality product at a competitive price with outstanding customer service. They have worked diligently to provide quality, honesty, and friendliness through the Cliptomania Web site. For example, Cliptomania has a very liberal return or exchange policy that allows customers to return or exchange any item within 30 days for any reason without question. Less than 1 percent of their customers return any items.

First established as a Yahoo! store in November of 1999, Cliptomania has had spectacular growth in sales during a very difficult period for retailing. (See Exhibit 1 on p. 332.) Although it sells only clip-on earrings, by June 2003, Cliptomania was the fifth largest jewelry store on Yahoo! in terms of gross sales.

When they send their order to a Yahoo! store, customers are encouraged to rate their satisfaction (or lack thereof) with the store. If they choose to rate the store, in 2 weeks (by which time they should have received their purchases), they are sent an e-mail pointing to an on-line rating form to complete. The ratings are on the following scale:

Excellent Better than I expected. Tell everyone that Cliptomania is a great store.

Good Everything went just fine.

OK There were a few problems, but I would probably still order from Cliptomania again.

Bad There were real problems. I would be reluctant to order from Cliptomania again.

Awful I had such a bad experience that I want to warn everyone about Cliptomania.

[1] Kleenex is the brand name often used as a generic term for paper tissues.

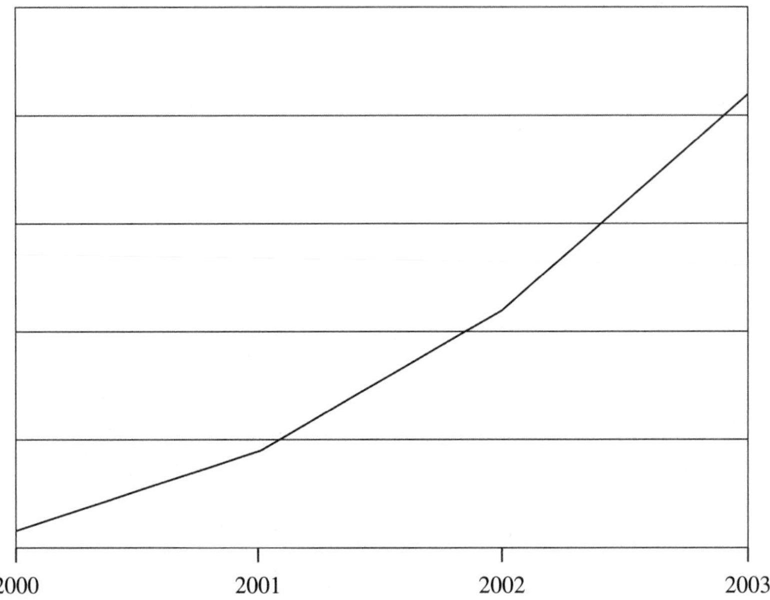

Although the default rating (already checked) is Good, an amazing 81 percent of Cliptomania's ratings have been Excellent! Ninety-eight percent of Cliptomania's ratings have been either Excellent or Good, so Cliptomania quickly earned a five-star Yahoo! rating for service.

In addition to a numerical rating, the rating form provides space for customers to submit specific comments that are available to the store through a database. Cliptomania receives a great deal of effusive praise, such as the following example:

> I am very pleased and satisfied with the service I received from Cliptomania. The customer service representative was polite, helpful, and patient with me being a new customer ordering with a credit card. The service was superb! I am also very pleased with the earrings. They are light, comfortable, and no pinching of my ears. And the cost you cannot beat. I am so thrilled with this. I plan on ordering more earrings from them, and have told several of my friends about this Web site. It is hard to find good quality clips, and I found just what I was looking for, and more. Working with the customer service representative was just like talking to a friend. I appreciated that.

They get positive feedback from other sources as well. Candy relates:

> Several times a week, without fail, we will get an e-mail or a phone call from someone saying: "You have no idea how hard it is to find clip-on earrings. I am so glad I found you!"

How Cliptomania Began

In the mid-1990s Jim and Candy Santo were living in New Jersey near New York City. Candy was the development director for a large nonprofit organization that provided a broad continuum of care for the homeless, and before that she had been executive director of a crisis line. Jim had a long-time career in insurance sales. But conditions in the insurance industry were changing radically and Jim was increasingly frustrated. According to Jim:

> Around 1995 or so, the insurance industry was deregulated so that all the financial service firms were in each other's business. Stockbrokers, bankers, and insurance agents were all selling each other's products, and the profit margins fell drastically. I went from really enjoying what I was doing to really hating it. I was ripe for a change.
>
> In 1998 I went out to buy earrings for an anniversary present for Candy, and I could not find a good selection of nice clip-on earrings anywhere. I looked everywhere I could think of in the New York metropolitan area. I could find plenty of earrings for pierced ears, but it was clear that all the stores had decided that they could not sell enough clip-ons to justify carrying an adequate stock in their stores.
>
> I knew that there must be millions of people in the world who wanted clip-ons and could not find what they wanted, so this appeared to be a great opportunity to sell them on the Internet. Because I was not enjoying the insurance business and knew little about the Internet or jewelry, I started staying up

at night and working weekends doing research on jewelry and how to sell via the Internet.

After 13 months of research, I concluded that the Internet was the ideal medium for this type of business. Earrings had a high markup, you could get started with little capital, and the Internet was the way to access the widely distributed market for clip-on earrings.

At this point the Santos needed a name for the new business, and Candy came up with the name *Cliptomania*. They decided that if the URL *www.cliptomania.com* was available and the name Cliptomania had not been registered as a corporate name, they would go forward with the endeavor. They employed a patent and trademark attorney who checked and found that the corporate name appeared to be available. And they were able to purchase the URL *www.cliptomania.com* from Network Solutions, so they decided to go ahead.

On Thanksgiving Day 1999, traditionally the beginning of the holiday sales season in the United States, the Santos went live with the Cliptomania store on the Web, operating out of one small room of their home in New Jersey. Their total capital investment was $10,000, which came from their savings. Although Jim had hopes that Cliptomania would grow, both of the Santos expected it to be a sideline activity that they would take care of in their spare time while continuing their regular jobs.

Setting Up the Web Store

Neither Jim nor Candy had any expertise in the creation of a Web site, so Jim devoted a lot of time and effort to determining how they would go about setting up the Cliptomania Web site. Jim found that one way would be to contract with an Internet service provider (ISP) for the computer resources required, purchase several software packages to perform the various functions that would be needed to run the store, and design the site and write the HTML code to set up the pages. The problem was that they did not have the personal experience or any IT development background to design the site and write the code or to integrate the various software packages. To hire someone to do all of that would be expensive and they might have little control over the process or the result.

The other alternative was to pay a vendor for hosting a store on a "Web mall." For a price, the vendor provides the computer resources and integrated software as well as "templates" for setting up the Web pages that provide the basic Web-store structure but allow you to customize pages to suit your business. The Santos chose this option and contracted with Yahoo! to establish their Cliptomania Yahoo! store.

Yahoo! provides templates for setting up home pages and the pages that display images of and describe the items offered, as well as for navigation across the site. Yahoo! makes it easy to add and delete items offered for sale and to make changes in the images and descriptions of these items. It uses a shopping-cart approach and holds selected items there until the customer wishes to place an order. Then it provides an online order form with the selected items detailed, and accepts a credit-card number and other billing information from the customer. Yahoo! then sends the completed order to Cliptomania, and presents the customer with a page confirming that the order has been placed with Cliptomania. By checking a box, the customer can request that the order also be confirmed by e-mail.

Another company, Paymentech, is integrated with Yahoo! to validate the credit card by making sure that the customer address on the order is the same as the billing address of the credit card. After Cliptomania accepts the order, Paymentech collects the money from the credit-card company and deposits it in Cliptomania's bank account once a week.

Jim was very concerned with transaction security via the Internet. When he was doing his research he had read that 40% of the transactions on the Internet were fraudulent. He also read that Yahoo! had the best security among the vendors providing support for Internet stores. In addition to encryption to restrict access by outsiders to credit-card numbers and other financial data, the Yahoo!/Paymentech combination detects and eliminates fraudulent purchases, and that was crucial to Jim. The outstanding security and the ease of setting up and operating the store were the main reasons the Santos decided to go with Yahoo! as their vendor.

The Yahoo! store also has a "back office" that collects and makes available data about Cliptomania's Web-site transactions. The Santos get a historical report for each month showing the number of customers who visited the store, the number of page views, the average number of page views per customer, the number of orders, the income, the number of items sold, the average number of items per order, and the dollar value of the average order. This report also includes daily and yearly totals. They can also print out graphs such as Exhibit 2 (see p. 334) that show the volatility and seasonality of their orders. On many orders they can find what search engine sent the customer to Cliptomania and what search terms were used, and this information can be summarized by search engine. All of this information was of great value to the Santos in managing the store and evaluating the effect of their marketing efforts.

When Cliptomania was started in 1999, there was only a $100 monthly charge for the Yahoo! store. However, over the years Yahoo! has changed its pricing structure, and as of 2003 it charges $49.95 per month for hosting, 10 cents per item carried per month, a 0.5 percent fee on all sales, and a 3.5 percent revenue share on sales that originate through a Yahoo!

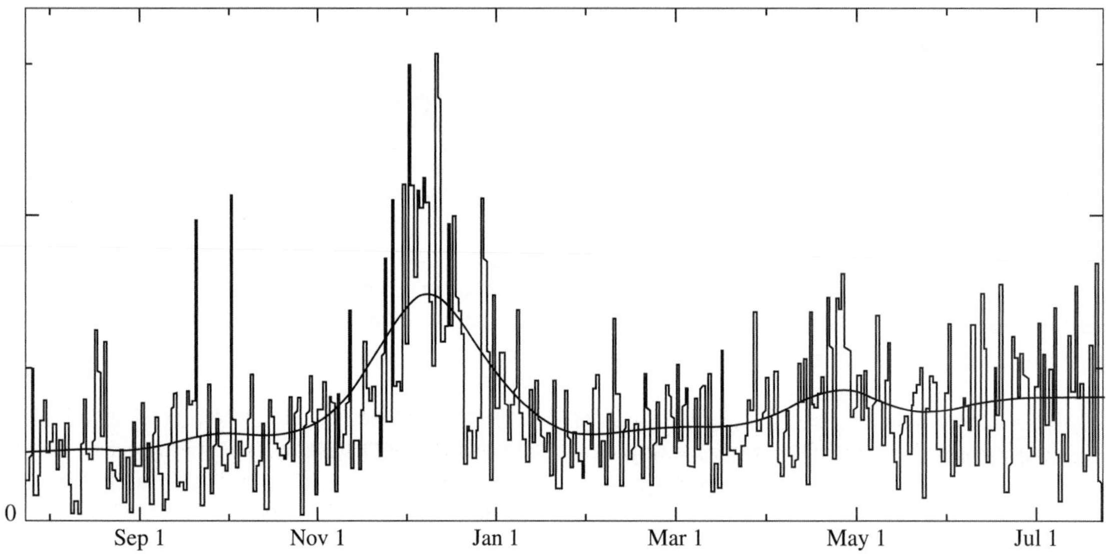

Store search.[2] Paymentech charges 20 cents for each credit card transaction it processes, in addition to the percentage of the amount of the sale charged by the credit-card company (typically 2.5 to 3.5 percent).

Designing the Cliptomania Web Site

Jim and Candy did most of the setup work on the original Web pages themselves, with some help from a freelance consultant they employed to help them with problems that were beyond their technical capability. Since then Candy has learned the basics of the HTML language. The consultant is still available to the Santos via telephone and the Internet for tougher questions, although they have had to turn to him less and less often.

Before starting the store, the Santos examined a number of Web stores, and they had a pretty good idea of what they liked and what they did not like in these Web sites. Candy explains what they wanted to do:

> I designed the logo in the banner at the top of our page. I wanted the "t" to be dangling down from the "p" like an earring hanging down. We chose the burgundy and gold colors for our page because we wanted to give the impression of a quality jewelry store and not look like the typical Web store with bright colors crying for your attention. We put our names "Jim, Candy, and Christy" on the front page and we use personal pronouns throughout the site because people need to know that we are real people. Some people call before they will place an order on the Internet because they feel the need to talk to a real person and have a sense that we are legitimate. A lot of our buyers have been first-time buyers on the Web. We are asking them to make a leap in faith, and we want them to feel comfortable about making that leap.
>
> From the start, we put the various categories of products that customers can click on down the left side of the page. The names of these categories are very important because they must guide the customers to the products that they like. I have set things up so that no more than six items appear on one page. I do this because I think that most people don't like to scroll down a page—they will only look at the top items. Also, our pages load fast, which is important when people are using Web TV and coming in through regular phone lines. Customers often mention how nice it is that our pages load so fast.

Getting Items to Sell

Initially one of their biggest problems was finding sources from which they could get earrings to offer in the Cliptomania store. They searched yellow pages on the Internet for jewelry wholesalers and manufacturers and called lots of them. Half of them did not exist any more and the rest were not very helpful. They finally found a man in Virginia who bought overruns and

[2]The current fee structure can be accessed by going to yahoo.com on the Web.

closeouts, so in the beginning most of their stock was not the most attractive. Jim remembers:

> We were very naive in the beginning. We got any stock we could get because we were almost desperate. We didn't know anything about jewelry, about what styles were popular, or about fashion. And we are in the fashion industry, so there was a big learning curve there. But somehow we survived.
>
> I knew there was a jewelry district in Manhattan, so I took a day off from my insurance business and went to the city to the fine jewelry area, the diamond district. I tromped around for 5 or 6 hours before I concluded that I was in the wrong area. Finally someone had mercy on me and told me where to find the fashion jewelry area. That was a major breakthrough.
>
> We finally found the wholesalers that would provide the kind of product we were looking for. These wholesalers had the product, but they were relatively expensive because they were several layers down from the manufacturers, and each layer tacked on its expenses and profit. After searching everywhere for manufacturers, we finally found this woman manufacturer/wholesaler out on Long Island who got all excited about what we were doing. We started getting stock from her and developed a relationship with her. She told us that we should go to the manufacturers' International Fashion Jewelry, Accessories, and Gifts (IFJAG) national show in Rhode Island, which is very difficult to get admitted to. She got us an invitation that allowed us to get into that invaluable show that we now go to each February and September.
>
> Before we went to the show, manufacturers' reps wouldn't talk to us because at that point we weren't buying in large enough quantities to interest them. But when we went to the show and got to talk directly to the manufacturers, some of them connected with our passion to offer quality products for women who don't want to pierce their ears. Some of the manufacturers would say: "I think you've got a good idea, and you remind me of my wife and I when we were your age. We're going to gamble on you. I'm going to take orders from you that I would kill any rep of mine if he came in with them." They started providing stock to us that we couldn't have gotten otherwise.
>
> That was the beginning of some mutually beneficial relationships. Since then we have grown to the point that we are ordering in such volumes that we are higher up on their customer lists. Some manufacturers will now make special manufacturing runs for us. At the 2003 February show, one of the manufacturers said it was time we had our own exclusive earrings, and that manufacturer designed some for us and we put them in the store the other day.

Early Growth

The year 2000 showed steady growth in Cliptomania's sales. The Santos had only three orders in January, but by the end of the year they were up to more than one order a day. In 2001 Cliptomania's sales continued to grow rapidly, more than quadruple the sales for the year 2000. Candy recalls:

> Jim and I both had full-time jobs and Christy was a student. We took no pay out of the business for the first two years—we just plowed everything back in. We started with pure "sweat equity."
>
> It started very, very slowly. When we got to one order a week we were celebrating. But it just grew and grew. Around October of 2001 I left my full-time development director job because I was really burning the candles at both ends at that point. I took a part-time job where I could just go to work and leave it behind when I came home.

The Move to Indiana

In December 2001, the Santos sold more than they had in the entire year 2000. They were running out of space for operating out of their small house in New Jersey. Candy was originally from Indianapolis, Indiana, and she began to think about getting away from the high costs of New Jersey to the Midwest where the cost of space was much lower. She explains:

> I could see after the holiday season of 2001 that we would not be able to handle the next holiday season out of the space in which we were working. If you needed packing material you either went up into the attic or out into the garage. We didn't have separate offices—we were all trying to work out of one room. After we searched for a suitable space in our area and found that everything available was far too expensive, it dawned on me that the people on the Internet don't care whether you are doing it out of high-cost New Jersey or lower-cost Indiana.

Jim provides another perspective on the move:

> Another reason we moved to Indiana was to change our lifestyle. Candy and I recognized that if I continued to work 80 hours a week I was going to kill myself. Our expensive lifestyle wasn't giving us any quality of life.
>
> Also, I think that the events of 9/11 had something to do with it. We lost several friends and some neighbors in the World Trade Center disaster. Moreover, after 9/11 thousands of people who felt vulnerable living in Manhattan wanted to move out of the city. They bid up real estate by 50 percent in our neighborhood across the river in New Jersey, so we could sell our house easily and at a very good price.
>
> In March 2002, we took a trip out to Indiana, and after that trip we decided to move. We sold our house in New Jersey and bought our present one in Indiana. We got twice the house for half the money; the equity in our New Jersey house paid for our new home, and we now have no mortgage. That is a big plus in enabling us to devote the time necessary to bring Cliptomania to the point where it can fully support the three of us and enable us to hire adequate help to make sales 24/7 without having to cover every day on our own.

When they moved to Indiana, Candy quit her part-time job. She has been full time with Cliptomania since then. Also, Jim cut back his insurance agent job to half time and has hired his own help to continue to build his insurance clientele in Indiana.

Cliptomania's Operations

Cliptomania now operates out of the lower level of the Santos home in Bloomington, Indiana. There is a large workroom that contains the inventory in wide, shallow drawers in cabinets and small plastic containers in cubbies along one wall. There also is room for assembling and packing orders, two desks with computers, and workspace for receiving orders. In addition there are two offices, one for Jim and one for Candy, and a storeroom for packing materials and reserve stock.

There are four PCs connected by a network, along with a fax machine and a printer. They have two high-speed lines coming into a router on the network, one from a telephone company and the other from a cable company, so that they can continue operations if one vendor's lines go down for some reason. Once a month Candy backs up key records onto a zip drive and puts it into their safe deposit box at the bank.

In addition to the security features provided by Yahoo!, they have firewalls to deter break-ins to their own computers. They have many different layers of security to make it more difficult to break into their store either physically or electronically, including central security alarm systems for their house.

When an order comes in on the computer Candy or Christy checks Paymentech's assessment of whether the billing address the customer has given matches the address for that card in a central database available to Paymentech. If these addresses are not the same, it is a red flag that the order may be fraudulent. She also looks over all orders for other indications that they may be suspicious. If it appears that there might be problems, she can call Paymentech to obtain the telephone number of the issuing bank and call it to determine whether or not the card is legitimate. If she cannot verify that the card is legitimate, she can cancel the order, which does occur, but rarely.[3] If everything seems all right, she checks the inventory to make sure the items are available and, if so, prints out the picking ticket and the mailing label for shipment.

The order is then assembled. Each pair of earrings is wrapped in plastic padding; the more expensive ones are placed in an attractive box. Once the earrings are protected, they are placed in a small corrugated cardboard shipping box. For some kinds of clip-ons a set of printed instructions for putting on the earrings is inserted. Then the box is sealed and the mailing label is affixed. Once a day the completed orders are taken to the local U.S. Post Office[4] and mailed. Most orders go out within 24 hours of when they are received. The shipping options and charges for shipping and handling are detailed on *www.cliptomania.com.*

After the orders are put into the mail, Christy, Cliptomania's customer relations manager, sends each customer an e-mail thanking her for the order, telling her it has been shipped, spelling out the return policy, and, when appropriate, encouraging her to read the instructions in the box describing how to put on the earrings. Candy explains:

> We found early on that customers were having trouble with some of the ear-clips because they didn't know how they worked—they were twisting them and breaking them. So I made a graphic and wrote directions showing how to put them on properly and we include these instructions in the box with the earrings.

Some customers are not comfortable ordering over the Web, so Cliptomania also accepts orders by mail or fax. Fortunately such orders are relatively rare (less than 2 percent) because it is more work to process them: The information has to be manually entered into the computer and the credit card processing must be done manually. Mail orders sometimes include items that were in stock when the buyer decided to make the purchase, but are sold out by the time the order is received by Cliptomania. When the mail order includes a personal check, nothing is mailed until the check has cleared Cliptomania's bank.

Cliptomania reluctantly accepts orders over the phone. They discourage phone-in orders because this requires someone to sit at the computer and enter the order while talking over the phone, which is quite time-consuming for their small staff. Despite the following plea on the "how to order" page, they still receive and handle several phone-in orders a week:

> Please do not use our phone number to place an order. We are a small family-run store and that would overwhelm us. We would be happy, however, to answer any questions you may have at that number.

One of Cliptomania's PCs is a laptop. The office printer has two trays, one with plain paper and the other with mailing labels. Things are set up so that if the Santos go on a trip they can call into the network via the laptop, process orders from the Web as though they were in the Cliptomania office, and print out the orders and mailing labels. A part-time worker can come in and pack and mail the orders so Cliptomania's operations can continue uninterrupted.

[3]Their credit-card verification process has been very effective. There have been only two instances in their four-year history where they were charged back on a credit-card transaction.

[4]The boxes are too small to make it feasible to use a package service such as UPS.

Foreign Sales

By August 2003, about 10 percent of Cliptomania's sales were to customers outside of the United States. Selling overseas has some challenging aspects. There is the language problem—their overseas sales are restricted to customers who can read and write English. The cost to a foreign customer is considerably higher than the cost to someone in the United States because of higher shipping costs and import duties that may be charged. A major problem is verifying the validity of credit cards. On the other hand, currency exchange is not a problem as the credit cards take care of that—Cliptomania bills in dollars and the customer's credit card is charged in his local currency at a reasonably good exchange rate.

Although Canadian import duties on jewelry make Cliptomania's earrings cost as much as 60 percent more to Canadians than they cost Americans, the majority of their foreign sales are to Canadians. Overseas customers may pay even more than Canadians because shipping costs are higher.

In July 2003, Cliptomania expanded into Japan. They had been told that Japan could be a big market for clip-ons. The major problem Jim encountered when he researched how they could serve Japanese customers was figuring out how to validate Japanese credit cards. After a lot of searching for information, Jim found that, although there are many different credit cards in Japan, there is one dominant card, and Paymentech will verify the authenticity of sales with that card. Therefore Cliptomania only accepts sales in Japan that pay with that credit card. The first 2 months' sales in Japan were very slow, but they also started out slow in the United States.

A few weeks ago a man from Mexico e-mailed Cliptomania and was adamant about needing three pairs of thin hoop earrings. Although they do not usually sell in Mexico, Candy worked with him and reports:

> Mail theft is rampant in Mexico and has been for at least 10 years. As the U.S. Postal Service does not serve his area, the customer said he would pay for UPS or FedEx shipping. The shipping costs exceeded the costs of the earrings as neither company would ship by ground due to theft problems. The customer was afraid a money order would not reach us, so he sent his credit card number by three different e-mails and the expiration date by a fourth. And then the whole order had to be manually done. The time it took to research this and all the e-mails sent back and forth added up to a loss to us if we add the value of my time. He was thrilled with his earrings, and I am convinced we have made the right choice not to sell in Mexico!

Despite the many problems, Jim is continuing to investigate the possibility of expanding into parts of the world that Cliptomania does not yet serve.

Candy's Role

Candy is Cliptomania's CEO. In addition to sharing responsibility for receiving and processing orders with Christy, she maintains the Web site, chooses the styles of earrings to stock, orders the stock, sets the prices, and manages the inventory.

Customers access the items for sale by clicking on one or more of the categories arranged vertically along the left side of the main page. Therefore Candy's choice of and wording of these categories is carefully selected. Candy also produces the images of the items that are shown and writes the descriptions that appear alongside the pictures. According to Jim:

> Candy describes each earring very honestly so that the customer knows exactly what she is getting. But she has the gift of wording it in such a way that the person reading about it thinks that she will look like a million bucks when she wears our $10 earrings.
>
> The quality of the pictures is critical. The customer cannot pick up an earring and look at it like you would in a brick-and-mortar store, so if she does not feel she is seeing the real thing and is not attracted to the earring, she is not going to buy it. Candy also does all of our imaging and her pictures look great! We don't tell people how she does it because that is a valuable corporate secret. You might think we have $100,000 worth of equipment here, but we don't.

Earrings are fashion items, so the market is continually changing. Candy changes Cliptomania's Web pages almost every day as new items are added, old ones are removed, items are featured during special times of the year, items are put on sale, the categories are reorganized, and so on.

About half of their sales are for fairly standard items that sell year in and year out. But the other half are fashion items that are very dynamic. Candy and Christy try to keep abreast of fashion trends to choose what to stock. There is a long lead-time in ordering and receiving fashion items—in fact, many decisions must be made at the national manufacturers' show in February. Therefore, they depend heavily on the manufacturers whose judgment they trust to help them decide what will be hot for the next year.

With Cliptomania's rapid growth and the dynamism and long lead times of the fashion business, keeping adequate stocks of the good sellers while not getting stuck with items that don't sell is a continuing challenge for Candy. She describes the problem:

> We do about 60 percent of our business in the last third of the year—September through December. September is the latest that I can order fashion items and expect to get delivery before Christmas, so I have to make decisions as quickly as I can figure out what items are going to be hot for Christmas. In mid-December the manufacturers worldwide close down, and don't open back up until mid-January. They have the IFJAG show in

> February, so they won't really start making the stock to fill the IFJAG orders until March and I will be lucky to get the new stock in May. When I order in September, I figure it is going to have to hold me until May, but I don't want to overbuy on something that will have passed its peak by the time February rolls around so I will be sitting on it forever.

Many of the newer fashion items are designed and manufactured in the U.S. Many of the standard items that do not change are made overseas where costs are much lower. Even the standard items can be difficult to maintain in inventory because the lead times on them are long and delivery schedules can be uncertain. In April 2003, Candy reported:

> I have recently run out of some of our staples that are best sellers. Refill orders from China have slowed down significantly due to shipping problems. I had to take some staple items off the site and it has taken me two months to be able to put them back on.

Candy gets lots of helpful information from the back end of the Yahoo! store that helps her with stocking decisions. She can see how many people visited, how many put items in the basket but have not bought yet, what they put in the baskets, and which search engine they came from and what search terms they used. She can get online graphs showing sales trends by item as well as for total sales. She can request summaries for various time periods and sort by gross receipts or number of items sold.

Candy also uses an Excel spreadsheet she developed that has a line for each item Cliptomania sells. It shows the Cliptomania product code, the name of the item, the cost per unit, the total number she has received, the dollars she has invested in the item, how many they have sold, the number damaged or lost in the mail, gross receipts for the item, total net margin, the vendor of the item, the vendor's product code, the current inventory, and the value of the current inventory. But even with all this information, there is still a lot of judgment involved in deciding what to stock and how much to order.

Jim's Role

Jim spends half his time as Cliptomania's vice president for marketing and half his time with his insurance business. He describes the current Web environment:

> We have plenty of major competitors who sell all kinds of earrings, jewelry, watches, necklaces, rings, etc., but none that deals exclusively in clip-ons like we do. But the Web is so dynamic that we have to keep running hard just to keep up.
>
> I look at other successful Web stores and try to learn from them. I try to take the good parts and avoid the bad. And I devote a lot of time and energy to identifying and keeping up with new developments and trends relating to the Internet.

When Cliptomania got started in late 1999, search engines on the Internet were still listing sites by "relevance" based on the site's fit with the search terms. In very quick order, Cliptomania was listed number one on all the search engines when someone searched for clip-on earrings. But soon the environment changed radically. Jim explains:

> When the dot-coms went "dot bomb" a couple of years ago, the whole environment got even more dynamic—it went ballistic. Since I was devoting lots of time to keeping up with what was going on, I quickly caught on to the fact that the industry somehow had to generate revenue and profits instead of just expanding its customer base. This is when Yahoo! went from a modest fixed monthly charge to adding fees based on volume.
>
> About this time the GoTo search engine started charging for listing position. There was not a fixed price for the top positions. You stated how much you would pay per click for each of your search terms, and if you bid high enough you could be number one or number two on a GoTo search. But if you did not pay, you might be down on the second or third page where 95 percent of the people would not find you. I jumped on this and immediately agreed to pay GoTo (which has since changed its name to Overture). We had an instant increase in our business! Within a week it was very obvious that our sales were up significantly, and they stayed up.
>
> At the start we paid one cent whenever GoTo sent a person to our site. Since then we have been paying for our position on quite a number of sites, and the cost has increased to where we are paying an average of 20 cents a click on one site and 15 cents a click on another. When you realize that only about 1.2 percent of those visiting our site make a purchase you can see that this eats up most of our profit on such sales. We are willing to pay such a high price because we view this as an acquisition cost—hopefully a good proportion of these buyers will be repeat customers who will come directly to Cliptomania without going through a search engine (which is one reason why we encourage people who visit our store to bookmark us).

The Cliptomania site includes over a hundred search terms, but most customers access them through a small number of terms such as "clip earrings" or "clip-on earrings." A Web business bids for position by search term so Jim only pays for the terms that are used by most customers. It does not make sense to pay for a search term where a person will click on your site and find that she has no interest in buying your product.

Like many Web businesses, Cliptomania also owns quite a number of URLs with names that are similar to "Cliptomania" or have to do with clip-on earrings. For example, if someone in desperation keys in the URL www.cliponearrings.com, their browser will pull up the Cliptomania Web site.

Another marketing approach involves the use of e-mail. Cliptomania has a file containing the e-mail addresses of all its customers. It also has a box on its home page where a visitor can provide an e-mail address. About eight times a year Candy sends everyone in this file a promotional e-mail. Candy cites examples:

> For the Twelve Days of Christmas (December 26 through January 12) everything in the store is a fixed percent off. I give our customers a jump on that by sending out an e-mail that lets them get the discount a few days before other visitors so that they can get the most desired stock before it sells out.
>
> These e-mails can be very effective. I sent out an e-mail around April 25 that said "Here comes Mother's Day, graduation, wedding season, and proms. If you or someone you know doesn't have pierced ears we have what you need for these occasions." That produced a tremendous spike in our sales over a 2-week period.

Jim is always seeking ways to increase sales. A year ago he joined an affiliate program through which other Web stores can add a button to their site that sends potential customers to Cliptomania. Then Cliptomania pays the affiliate store a 10 percent commission on any sales to customers who are sent from that store. This is operated through a third party, Commission Junction, which collects the commission money from Cliptomania and sends it to the affiliate store. Commission Junction also gets a 3 percent commission, so the total cost to Cliptomania is 13 percent. Jim explains:

> This was a big investment for us. Not only did we have to pay thousands of dollars to join the program, but we also took a week off to go to a training program in California. We took a risk and invested five or six thousand dollars to join this program.
>
> It started slowly. In the beginning we were getting one or two sales a week, but we are now averaging two to three sales per day from this source. It is expensive, but it gets us customers who may come back to us directly, in which case we do not have to pay a commission again.
>
> We do not participate in other stores' affiliate programs and send visitors off our site to other stores. We don't like the idea of cluttering up our store with links that send people away and they may not come back. Furthermore, we have worked hard to provide superior service and achieve an outstanding excellence rating. We have control over how you are treated when you deal with us, but if we refer you out to another site we lose that control. If someone gets bad service from a store we sent them to, they might associate that experience with us, and our good reputation is too important to risk.

The Internet is such a dynamic environment that Jim realizes that not all his initiatives will work out well. He admits:

> During 2002 I probably spent $5,000 on experiments that did not work out. I get several calls every day from people who want me to pay them up front, claiming that they will send me lots of customers. I now tell them that I only pay for performance—send me the customers and I will pay for them, but I won't pay anything up front.

However, despite the risks, Jim has to continue to search for and experiment with new marketing approaches so that Cliptomania does not fall behind.

Although the Santos have had to overcome many difficulties and problems, Cliptomania seems to be an outstanding success. During a period where most Internet retailers have had a hard time, Cliptomania has grown rapidly, and this growth shows no signs of slowing. Although Jim plans to continue in the insurance business, if this growth continues Cliptomania will be a very rewarding business for the Santo family.

CASE STUDY II-7

MEZZIA, INC.: DECIDING WHICH INFORMATION TECHNOLOGY COMPANY TO JOIN

It was Thursday, November 15, 2001, and Willis "Willie" Stahe was running late. As president of Midwest University's Computing and Information Systems student club, he had helped organize a student-alumni networking event and was relieved to find the room packed for lunch and the afternoon seminar. He threw his backpack into a corner and headed for the podium. After a short introduction and thank you to everyone for coming, he stopped at the buffet table and filled a plate.

As he reached for a crescent roll, he crossed arms with a tall, older man, dressed surprisingly casually. Willie thought his long-sleeved shirt looked like it was flannel. "Sorry. I guess I'm still rushing," Willie said.

"Quite all right. After you," flannel shirt said quietly.

"I feel like I've just been hit by a truck," Willie continued. "I just attended a presentation by this speaker in our Management of Information Systems class. He co-founded a local startup software firm."

"Sounds interesting," flannel shirt said. Willie raced on, "See, I graduate this semester and I have an offer from Hewlett-Packard to start as a software developer in January. I told them I would get back to them at the end of this week. I just told them that because I was playing it cool. But now, I'd really like to interview with this startup company. They're here today and Friday only."

"Seems to me like you should go through the interview first. That may help make the decision for you," flannel shirt said.

"The startup sounds so cool. But Hewlett-Packard—how could I turn that offer down?" Willie thought out loud.

"A lot of software startups crash and burn. But since the end of the Y2K binge, some of the large IT companies have had their problems as well. Before you turn HP down, perhaps you should really study this other company," flannel shirt said.

"The speaker did give us some handouts. Plus, I guess I could do some additional library and Internet research myself," Willie said. "Thanks for talking me through this. When did you graduate from Midwest?"

"Alum? Is that why there are so many people here? Is this an alumni event?" flannel shirt asked.

"Yes. Why? You're not an alum?" Willie asked.

"No. I'm here interviewing. We haven't done a lot of campus interviewing, so I don't know the layout here. One of the interviewers said there was a break room down the hall," flannel shirt said.

"Oh. That's down the hall the other way," Willie said.

"Whoops," flannel shirt said. "I was surprised at the crowd, but I thought Midwest was going all out to retain recruiters!" Willie and flannel shirt laughed. Then flannel shirt said, "It's time I get back. Good luck with your decision."

"Thanks," Willie said and shook flannel shirt's hand. As Willie started to ask his name, the caterer interrupted to ask what Willie wanted to do with the extra food. "Just leave it out. Someone will eat it," Willie said. "No. Wait. Put it in the Placement Office break room. For the recruiters."

As Willie picked up his backpack, he thought about what flannel shirt had said. He would sign up to interview with the startup Friday. But before that, he would need to do a lot of research. He had planned to stop by the gym after the seminar, but decided he had better stop by the library instead.

The Job Opportunity at Mezzia, Inc.

In his class, Willie had been impressed by guest speaker Scott McCorkle, co-founder and executive vice president of Mezzia, not so much by his colorful charts and demonstration of the company's software as by what he said. He had not expected the co-founder of a Midwest e-business to be so insightful about the role of the Internet in business-to-business (B2B) commerce and the need to see oneself as in the Internet software business versus being a "dot-com." He had always assumed that anybody who was somebody in the Internet business world was on the West Coast.

 This case was developed by Professor Daniel W. DeHayes at Indiana University with the help of Brian Ramsey Chabowski. The case was written to provide a basis for class discussion rather than to illustrate effective or ineffective business practices. Some figures, names, and dates have been disguised.

He found himself excited by the prospects of this company, about how he could have a huge role so early in his career. It seemed like they really understood the past and future of e-commerce and their role in it with respect to their target market. He was excited about Hewlett-Packard, too, but not about what he would be doing so much as that he would be working for Hewlett-Packard. He had already made sure all his friends knew he had been given an offer. And his mom had made sure everyone in the family, the church, her bridge group, the whole neighborhood knew it, too. Even Aunt Nellie in Saskatchewan, Canada, wrote to congratulate him on the offer. The HP opportunity was even better than when he interned in the IT group of a large public accounting firm last summer.

However, Willie also knew that the offer from HP had its uncertainties. The company had made public earlier in the year its intention to purchase rival Compaq for $25 billion. Now issues were developing that made Willie uncertain of this employment option. As he had read in the business press, several major HP shareholders had expressed their objection to the Compaq purchase. But even more worrisome was the public opposition of members of the Hewlett family to the merger. With Wall Street analysts stating the HP-Compaq union had a 50-50 chance of failing, Willie began to wonder how long he would be employed by the company—particularly if he was brought in soon after the deal.[1] He knew that he would be low on the seniority list. If the merged company ran into problems, he would be among the first to go. And, as had happened to some of his friends, the offer might be revoked after he had accepted.

In his class notes, he read that Mezzia was founded in December 1999 by Mike Robbins, Scott McCorkle, and Rich Cunningham, software veterans who had worked together for a company that was eventually acquired by IBM. All three had at one time worked for large corporations. They named the company from the Italian phrase "per mezzo di" or "by means of" to signify the company's role as a vehicle for allowing its customers to collaborate more closely with other participants in a marketing channel.

From the Mezzia Web site, Willie found some additional information about the founders and members of Mezzia's advisory board. (See Exhibit 1.) Willie knew Mezzia had not been in business long, but to its credit it had survived the bursting of the Internet bubble. Although the risk associated with working for a company that was not well established was great, so was the reward if the company grew as expected. Regardless of current corporate controversy, even Hewlett-Packard started with just two founders and a garage. He reviewed Mezzia's short history from a handout by McCorkle. (See Exhibit 2.)

The Business-to-Business E-Commerce Market

Willie then reviewed what he knew about Mezzia's market and Mezzia's competitors from McCorkle's presentation and some materials McCorkle distributed.

McCorkle said in class that the business-to-consumer (B2C) e-commerce market had grown dramatically in the late 1990s. He asserted that the next wave of Internet impact would be in the B2B market, with technology allowing businesses to seamlessly conduct online transactions with other businesses. In early 2001, analysts had predicted that B2B would dwarf B2C as e-commerce grew. Forrester Research estimated that the volume of B2B electronic commerce would grow from its 1998 level of $43 billion to $1.3 trillion by 2003, or 9 percent of all goods and services purchased in the business community.

According to McCorkle, Net Market Makers, a company that monitors online trends, estimated that more than 300 B2B trading communities were online in early 2000. They predicted more than 1,000 such trading communities in the near future. Many software companies supported the B2B industry. Some were focused on cross-industry trading communities that helped customers procure office supplies or materials in the broader maintenance, repair, and operating (MRO) supplies category. A number of companies created communities focused on indirect materials or services procured within specific vertical industries. Others focused on the direct materials used in production within vertical industries (e.g., pharmaceuticals, chemicals, steel, electronic components). Other software producers, like Mezzia, focused on helping buyers understand demand better within their company before creating an online trading community.

The Health Care Industry

When creating their business plan, Mezzia's founders decided to focus first on applying the company's software development skills to a single industry and a specific market segment within that industry that met the following niche requirements:

- Of significant size with a high volume and velocity of commerce dollars and transactions
- Readily identifiable block of buying organizations and influencers
- Need for an e-commerce company to affiliate more closely with buyers, not suppliers
- Not dominated by a short list of suppliers

[1]Singer, Michael, "HP/Compaq merger—Now a 50-50 chance," *Internet News*, November 7, 2001, *boston.internet.com/news/article.php/919071*.

EXHIBIT 1
Mezzia Management and Advisory Board

Management

Michael J. Robbins, co-founder, president, and CEO. With more than 20 years' experience in technology and software, Robbins serves as director of the Midwest Information Technology Association, which is focused on the development of technology companies in the Midwest. He has held executive-level responsibility for all aspects of a technology company, including sales, marketing, product development, and operations. He was previously VP and COO for an IBM company focused on enterprise software for customer relationship management, where he routinely overachieved all financial and operational targets. Robbins has also been senior VP for a software vendor in the consolidated service desk market (including help desk, asset management, change management, and decision support). Once this company was acquired, he became senior VP for worldwide operations, establishing global direct and indirect sales organization. Robbins directly managed the creation of the North American, European, and Asia-Pacific operations. Robbins began his career at Xerox and Honeywell in sales and sales management. He holds a B.S. degree from the University of Detroit.

Scott S. McCorkle, co-founder and executive vice president, product group. McCorkle was previously VP and CTO for IBM's Corepoint, where he had responsibility for all product and business strategy aspects. He managed a 550-person global product effort across five geographic sites and four product families. McCorkle earlier managed a shift in product direction toward integrated technologies and applications. Prior to Corepoint, McCorkle was general manager and VP for a software vendor in the consolidated service desk market (help desk, asset management, change management, decision support) where he was responsible for product development. He led the effort to launch a new business unit into the fast-growing customer relationship management (CRM) enterprise software market. McCorkle started his technology career at BorgWarner Automotive Research Center, developing advanced vision-guided robotics. He then spent several years at Eli Lilly, a leading pharmaceutical firm, developing enterprise-level applications and very large databases for Lilly Research Laboratories. McCorkle holds an M.B.A. degree from Indiana University and a B.S. degree in computer science from Ball State University.

Richard A. Cunningham, co-founder and executive vice president, marketing. Cunningham has spent 19 years in marketing management and entrepreneurial business development, working for companies ranging from start-ups to Hewlett-Packard. Previously, he was VP of worldwide marketing for Corepoint, where he was responsible for a $26 million marketing budget and 45 people across five global regions. He successfully planned and executed a comprehensive marketing launch of the company in a remarkable 12 weeks, attaining significant awareness levels within the Global 1000. Cunningham spent the first 9 years of his career at Hewlett-Packard, where he marketed UNIX-based manufacturing automation systems and software to major accounts, and consulted with the company's value-added reseller channel partners. One of these clients, a leading industrial engineering simulation and production scheduling software firm, recruited him to manage their newly formed alliance with IBM. There, he headed marketing and developed the company's first channel marketing program. For the past 15 years, Cunningham has participated as investor and director in local entrepreneurial ventures. He holds a B.S. degree in electrical engineering technology from Purdue University.

Health Industry Advisory Board[1]

Network vice president of materials management, Midwest Mega Hospital. During his 27 years in the health care industry, he has been involved in all aspects of corporate materials management. He has been responsible for a staff of

[1]The two individuals described as members of the Health Industry Advisory Board are not named and their company affiliations are disguised in order to maintain confidentiality.

EXHIBIT 1 (Continued)

80 in corporate purchasing and accounts payable across MMH's network, and has also been responsible for individual hospital receiving, shipping, sterile processing, central supply, and surgical supply distribution. His major process responsibilities include supply and equipment contracting, stockless inventory, and supply and equipment value analysis. He has a B.S. degree in business and finance from Indiana University.

Former founder and president of Hospital Supply and retired division vice president of Health Care Distributors. She has a total of 35 years in sales and executive-level management in health care products distribution. She founded Hospital Supply in 1974 and sold the company in 1993. It was later acquired by Health Care Distributors, the leading medical distributor in the United States, where she served as division VP until retiring in 1996. She also served on the Hospital Marketing Committee for the Health Industry Distributor Association. She holds a B.S. degree in economics from Syracuse University.

An additional five members will be added to this advisory council.

Source: Company Records.

- Need for decentralized buying, yet centralized accountability and control
- Unique procurement processing and documentation requirements
- Not especially sensitive to privacy issues or excessive regulatory burdens pertaining to its procured goods and services
- Not overcrowded with first or early movers

After an analysis of many industries, Mezzia's founders chose health care as their initial targeted industry. Within health care, the health service providers (or health services) market segment (e.g., hospitals) was selected as their market niche. Mezzia found the market to be of substantial size with a high potential in B2B commerce dollars and transactions. Importantly, the health service providers market was not dominated by a small number of suppliers.

Health care spending of all kinds amounted to 13 percent of the U.S. gross domestic product, weighing in at more than $1 trillion in 2000. The health services segment within health care represented a large market and was characterized by a high volume of B2B commerce among large buying constituencies and large supplying constituencies. Mezzia's research found that it was common for health service providers in each category listed in Exhibit 3 to spend between 20 and 40 percent of their annual revenue on goods and services. The prominent category specific to Mezzia's target market was the medical and hospital equipment and supplies area. This category included products ranging from consumable supplies to instrumentation and equipment.

The health services supply chain had traditionally been highly fragmented and inefficient. More than 10,000 manufacturers of medical equipment and supplies in the United States marketed their products to well over 100,000 buyer organizations, including hospitals, clinics, physicians, and long-term care facilities. The suppliers sold either directly or through a channel composed of distribution companies.

The distribution channel consisted of traditional "brick-and-mortar" distributors that acted as principals or agents for a large number of suppliers. Many, such as Cardinal Health and Owens & Minor, also offered value-added distribution services (e.g., inventory management) that served to differentiate them from less sophisticated competitors. In 1999, a newer type of competition entered the field—the online distributor (e.g., SciQuest.com and MedicalBuyer.com). Buyers could conduct purchasing transactions through these sites, saving time and money. Some traditional brick-and-mortar operations started to partner with dot-com companies to gain momentum in this new form of distribution service. The new dot-com distribution companies able to survive the Internet shakeout were most often affiliated with suppliers rather than buyers. Some were even subsidiaries of the larger suppliers.

EXHIBIT 2
Mezzia Timeline

Event	Date
Rich Cunningham, Scott McCorkle, and Mike Robbins leave their employer (all three worked for same employer).	July 1999
The three founders continue meeting socially, discussing business ideas. Decide they want to continue working together doing something in e-commerce.	Summer 1999
Meetings with business consultant, attorney, accountant. Begin drafting business plan.	October–November 1999
Meetings with stakeholders in target industries—health care, education … Narrowed down to health care.	October 1999
Meetings with hospital executives (about 50 to 60 to date) on how best to support their needs.	November 1999 to today
Mezzia incorporated.	December 1999
First business plan complete. Primary focus of the plan is to develop reverse auctions.	February 2000
Round 1 of private placement financing, exceeding goal of $3.5 million.	April–June 2000
In meetings with hospital executives, three founders discover a greater need for better internal demand planning prior to creating e-commerce capability.	May 2000
Test version of Demand Planner.	July 2000
Pilot Demand Planner in hospital.	July–October 2000
Round 2 of financing.	August–November 2000
Code complete for Demand Planner.	October 2000
Release of Demand Planner.	November 2000
New version releases of Demand Planner.	February, May, and September 2001
Two paying customers obtained	October 2001
Trading Community Product	May 2002 (est.)

Source: Company records.

Buyers' advocates had emerged in the early 1990s as cooperative buying organizations for their membership of hospitals, nursing homes, clinics, and physician groups. Group purchasing organizations (GPOs), of which there were more than 600 in 1998, negotiated multiyear contracts with suppliers and distributors on behalf of their membership. By the late 1990s, about 85 percent of purchases were covered under contracts of this type, according to the Health Industry Group Purchasing Association.

Mezzia's interviews with hospital executives in early 2000 indicated that there was room for significant cost reduction throughout the supply chain. As buyers considered the broad

EXHIBIT 3
Health Service Provider Segments

SIC	Segment	Annual Sales	Sales/ Establishment
8011–8049	Offices & clinics of health practitioners	$196B	$0.4M
8051–8059	Nursing & personal care facilities	$58B	$2.3M
8062	General medical & surgical hospitals	$360B	$37.0M
8063–8069	Psychiatric & specialty hospitals	$24B	$3.8M
8071–8072	Medical & dental laboratories	$19B	$0.8M
8082	Home health care services	$16B	$1.3M
8092–8099	Kidney dialysis & specialty outpatient clinics and health & allied services	$24B	$0.8M

Source: Dunn & Bradstreet's I-Market, Inc., 1998

implications of B2B e-commerce over the Internet, they were looking for a partner clearly affiliated with their interests rather than the interests of the suppliers. Mezzia therefore planned to create close partnerships with buyers and GPOs.

The health care industry traditionally has been slow to adopt new information technology and has spent a smaller percentage of its overall operations budget on information technology as compared with other industries. However, as Mezzia found through its interviews, buyers were uncertain how to forecast their demand and therefore effectively use B2B commerce tools.

Mezzia's Strategy

After helping members of the health services niche understand their demand better, Mezzia's strategy was to eventually draw members from the health services supplier community into an electronic market. In their interviews with buyers, Mezzia's founders discovered that buying was not the immediate problem. In order to achieve real savings, buyers must first be able to forecast demand from a number of diverse departments and labs. If this information could be aggregated somehow, then a long-term view of demand could be created. Then, the buyer could use e-commerce tools to achieve real savings.

Mezzia would create advanced software for the health service providers segment of the health care industry. The first software product (released in November 2000) helped providers plan their demand. Several upgrades to this product were released in 2001. In addition, Mezzia planned to create a Web site to connect buyers with many suppliers, creating a trading community clearly affiliated with buyers. The site would increasingly put in place supply chain management capabilities that allowed buying organizations to manage their procurement process. Over time, these capabilities would be fully integrated with the commerce capabilities of the site to provide end-to-end management of the B2B procurement cycle for members of the health services industry.

Mezzia targeted GPOs, individual buying organizations (specifically hospitals), and large multisite long-term care organizations. Mezzia worked with executives (CEOs, CFOs, and VPs of materials management) at health service provider organizations to sell their products and services. Mezzia's leaders had concluded that the tools for conducting business developed by Mezzia must be sold at the highest level in the organization. CFOs would be key customers because they could validate the real cost savings. On a day-to-day basis, executives and managers in the materials management group would be a key constituency. Suppliers would also be viewed as customers and recruited to join the community based on the needs of the buyers.

Competitors

Mezzia's executives considered their primary competition to be the current method of purchasing. Current methods entailed some degree of automation combined with a large amount of manual paper processing. Buying organizations tended to process orders from departments individually because they could not easily forecast what demand for the same product might be coming from other departments. This single order would be issued to a supplier directly or via distributor sales personnel, telesales, catalog sales, purchasing cooperatives, or, to a small extent, supplier Web sites. As the buying population became more comfortable with purchasing goods and services online, the adoption of B2B e-commerce was expected to accelerate, leading to more direct competition.

Mezzia's leaders knew that the size and newness of the health service providers B2B market opportunity had drawn and would continue to draw a large number of competitors. Online competition consisted of individual product manufacturers, wholesale distributors, industry-specific group-purchasing cooperatives, health care portals, supply chain management companies, and other trading communities. Some of the key publicly traded companies involved in B2B e-commerce in early 2000 are listed in Exhibit 4, followed by a summary of some of their strengths and weaknesses.

Willie's First Interview with Mezzia

Willie signed up to interview on campus with Mezzia Friday. He was pleased that Scott McCorkle was there to do the interviewing. Willie was excited by McCorkle's description of Mezzia's software developer job, which would position Willie closer to the road and hold him accountable for making major contributions to an application and customers.

After asking Willie about his grades (a 3.42 on a 4.0 scale), his internship experience, and the extra Computer Science courses he had taken, McCorkle asked him to come to the Mezzia offices for a second interview on Tuesday morning. Willie called Hewlett-Packard to ask if he could postpone his decision to the end of next week. His sponsor replied that they needed to know no later than Wednesday so they could extend the offer to another candidate before Thanksgiving should Willie decide not to accept. Willie would have little time to make the most important decision of his career. But he had no choice.

Over the weekend, Willie decided to look into some of the current competitors Mezzia faced. Using the information Willie had received already from the company, he looked to see how Mezzia's competitors were doing. While most were still generating sales, as seen in Exhibit 5, there were many concerns about those of Mezzia's competitors that planned to create or were creating trading communities. Willie found such B2B exchanges were having questionable results.

A specific example Willie found concerned Chemdex.[2] Though the exchange survived as Ventro, analysts were predicting the company would have little or no revenue for 2001. How could this be? According to the press Willie read, the B2B exchange models were flawed. Across industries, only about 10 percent of these Internet businesses had any traffic. Though they most often had suppliers, many large companies were not committing to purchase through the exchanges.[3]

This lack of demand created a situation common in many small technology-oriented businesses. Many of the startups were drastically altering their primary strategy. Instead of operating as an exchange, many companies had started to sell their services in software development. Desperate for cash flow, some startups would take any project just to generate cash, regardless of how well it aligned with the original company strategy.

This rapid change in strategy reminded Willie of some material covered in an entrepreneurship class he took with Professor Morphen at Midwest University. The professor pointed out that short-term cash difficulties faced by small businesses sometimes caused managers to make dramatic changes in direction with little or no notice to employees. Morphen underlined the dangerous implications of this behavior for the ability of the small company to move forward consistently toward its vision. However, Morphen also wanted to make sure the students understood the need for small businesses to change and innovate quickly when circumstances required it.

The Second Interview with Mezzia

It took Willie longer than normal to get dressed for Tuesday's interview. He was not sure whether he wanted to wear a full suit or slacks, a button-down, and tie. A full suit seemed to be the safest bet. He would make a horrible impression if he did not wear one and was expected to. But, the button-down and tie seemed to say "confident."

He opted for gray dress pants, a black long-sleeved turtleneck, and a black jacket—kind of a Steve Jobs look. He felt comfortable and well prepared.

When he entered Mezzia's office, he was surprised. Unlike the huge marbled reception area at Hewlett-Packard, there was only a desk, unstaffed, in Mezzia's entry. Two chairs and a small table with business magazines were off to the side. He was not sure whether he should just start roaming the halls or if he should sit down and hope someone showed up. He sat down.

"Has someone helped you?" Willie looked up and was surprised to see flannel shirt, the interviewer he had run into at the alumni event! "Hi. I'm Mike Robbins," Mike said as he extended his hand. "I guess we didn't introduce ourselves properly last time we met."

"Willie Stahe," Willie said as he shook hands.

"Have you solved your dilemma over whether or not to go with Hewlett-Packard?" Mike asked.

"Not yet. I'm here for a second interview," Willie said.

"Oh. So we're the cool startup you want to work for," Mike said.

"I think so," Willie answered. "It's such a huge change from where I thought I'd be and what I thought I'd be doing."

"It's a big decision, a big challenge," Mike said as he sat in the chair next to Willie. "We're less than 2 years old and have

[2]American Medical Association, "More dot-coms bite the dust," January 15, 2001, *www.ama-assn.org/sci-pubs/amnews/pick_01/tebf0115.htm*

[3]*The Economist*, "Time to rebuild," May 17, 2001.

EXHIBIT 4
Summary of Competitors

Company	Founded	1999 Revenue
Ariba (ARBA)	Sep-96	$23.5M
Chemdex (CMDX)	Sep-97	$8.5M
Commerce One (CMRC)	Jan-94	$16.9M
FreeMarkets (FMKT)	Mar-95	$7.8M
Neoforma (NEOF)	1996	$0.2M
PurchasePro (PPRO)	Oct-96	$2.6M
SciQuest (SQST)	Nov-96	$2.6M
VerticalNet (VERT)	Oct-95	$10.1M

Ariba

Advantages
- Well funded
- First mover
- Extensive partnerships (e.g., Hewlett-Packard, Andersen Consulting, major ERP players, FedEx, and large office products distributors)

Disadvantages
- Broad vision, difficult to specialize
- Buy-side application is expensive to purchase and implement
- Primarily focused on maintenance, repair, and operating (MRO) supplies cross-industry
- Acquisition integration requires significant resources

Chemdex

Advantages
- Well funded, early mover
- Partnership with laboratory products distributor with 350,000 products
- Exclusive 5-year joint marketing agreement with Biotechnology Industry Organization, largest trade organization to represent biotechnology
- Acquisitions and alliances provide significant inroads to medical community

Disadvantages
- Product distributor (customer is supplier)
- Terms and scope of partnership may deter other suppliers

Commerce One

Advantages
- Well funded, early mover
- Established distribution in U.K., Japan, Singapore
- Not competing against vertical portals
- Good system integrator channel with consulting alliances

Disadvantages
- Buy-side application expensive
- Playing catch-up to Aribaís technology
- No long-term contracts
- 1Q1999: only four customers account for 79% of revenues

FreeMarkets

Advantages
- Doing online auctions since 1995

Disadvantages
- 58% of 1999 revenues (9 months) came from two customers: GM and a canceled contract to work with Commerce One

Medibuy

Advantages
- Well funded and visible partnerships

Disadvantages
- Limited commerce capabilities

Medicalbuyer.com

Advantages
- Gaining visibility via online and offline advertising

Disadvantages
- None

EXHIBIT 4 (Continued)

Medpool	
Advantages • Business model allows for group purchasing	*Disadvantages* • Does not have content or community components
Neoforma.com	
Advantages • Gaining visibility via online and offline advertising • Strategic alliances are market leaders in their niches • Model allows for "room" planning and then purchasing supplies • Broad health care content is aggregated well	*Disadvantages* • Limited customer base on buy side
PurchasePro.com	
Advantages • Well funded • Established marketplace development agreements with prominent and emerging companies serving hospitality, health care, and construction • Revenue-sharing agreement with Ariba allowing customers to connect with Ariba network suppliers • Exclusive relationship with Dow and Monsanto, but are both investors and customers	*Disadvantages* • Members are companies that sell products/services to large hotels and resorts • Beyond hospitality industry, marketplace partners hold the industry-specific expertise
SciQuest.com	
Advantages • Well funded • Extensive list of suppliers and partnerships with other complementary health care-related marketplaces • Integrated with Ariba's OMS procurement application	*Disadvantages* • Revenues as of 11/99 consist primarity of banner ads • Only 35% of revenues ($432K) are sales of scientific products • Reliant on a few customers
VerticalNet	
Advantages • Extensive funding supported acquisition of 10 companies within 1 year • Strong advertising/sponsorship revenues • Alliance with PurchasePro to provide Internet-based procurement automation • Business model leverages Internet technology investment over many different vertical markets	*Disadvantages* • Large number of acquisitions difficult to assimilate • High long-term debt, not generating enough cash flow • May be difficult to focus/dominate one specific industry/market

Source: Mezzia Business Plan.

money in the bank to last only until January of next year, assuming the worst case. I'm out raising more equity capital now and we expect our product to continue to sell, but still … it's a challenge. Tell me, what kinds of challenges have you faced?"

"Getting to college was a big one. My Dad's business was close to filing for bankruptcy my senior year in high school. Not only did I not get to go to prom and stuff like that, but I wasn't sure I would be able to get to college," Willie said.

"That's a big hit for an 18-year-old. How'd you handle it?" Mike asked.

"I wasn't eligible for most of the government programs because need is based on the previous April's tax return, which for us wasn't great, but it was enough to make us ineligible. So I looked at holding off a year and working and saving or trying to get a bank loan and working while going to school. With my Dad's situation, it was unlikely I'd get the bank loan," Willie said.

EXHIBIT 5
Relevant Competitor Data for 2000

Company	*2000 Revenue*
Ariba (ARBA)	$279.0M
Ariba (ARBA)*	$408.8M
Commerce One (CMRC)	$401.8M
FreeMarkets (FMKT)	$170.0M
Neoforma (NEOF)	$10.4M
SciQuest (SQST)	$51.7M
VerticalNet (VERT)	$112.5M

* Ariba data for 2001, since fiscal year ends September 30.
Source: Company reports.

"So you held back a year?" Mike asked.

"No. Actually, I went to the bank anyway. My Dad and I worked on why we thought his business still had potential and then we laid all the cards out on the table and convinced the bank I'd be a good credit risk," Willie said.

"Seems like that was a creative and effective solution," Mike noted.

"In addition, we met with a financial aid counselor and ended up getting a low interest loan for most of the money," Willie paused, deep in thought. "I think what's more important is that my confidence in my Dad and his business, and working with him to look at the positives when everything seemed doomed, really helped him reenergize and get the business back on track. Of course, that helped me as well," Willie said.

"Kind of like not running from the smoke," Mike said.

"Huh?" said Willie.

"It's a saying we have here. Don't run from the smoke. If you see something's wrong, run to it, not away from it," Mike said.

"I guess it was a lot like that," Willie said.

"I see you've met Mike," McCorkle said as he walked toward them. "You'll be meeting with him later on."

"I don't think that'll be necessary, Scott," Mike said. "He's answered my questions. Willie," he extended his hand, "it was a pleasure talking with you. I hope we have the opportunity to work together sometime."

Willie wished he had been paying more attention to what he had been saying. "Wow. I didn't even know I was being interviewed," he said.

"That's what everyone says after talking with Mike," McCorkle said. "He pretty much can tell within the first 5 minutes whether someone will fit with Mezzia. Looks like you left a favorable impression. About your next interview—normally the founders don't all interview a candidate. But since you've gotten an offer from Hewlett-Packard, I thought you might like to talk with Rich."

"He's the one that started out at Hewlett-Packard, isn't he?" Willie said.

"Right. I thought he might be able to answer a lot of your questions," McCorkle said. "Hey, Rich, this is the student I was telling you about, Willie Stahe."

"Good to meet you," Rich said as he extended his hand. "Have a seat."

As he sat down, Willie was struck by how neat Rich's office was and how neatly he was dressed. Rich had a soft voice and disarming smile, and Willie immediately felt comfortable.

"Scott tells me you're interested in working with us, but that you've also gotten an offer from Hewlett-Packard," Rich said.

"I'm really torn. It's like a dream come true to be offered the chance to work for Hewlett-Packard. Move out to the West Coast. I haven't even told my family that I'm interviewing with you. I don't think they would understand," Willie said.

"What don't you think they would understand?" Rich asked.

"That I'd be turning down big bucks for incredibly smaller bucks that may or may not turn into big bucks," Willie said.

"Considering you wouldn't be living on the West Coast, I think you'll find our salary is pretty competitive. And predicting future big bucks is largely dependent on each of us who work here and how much you believe in our vision and business model," Rich said. "Disregarding salary, which job would you take?"

"Hmm—that is a tough question. I think that I would take this job," Willie said.

"Why?" Rich asked.

"Because what I'd be doing would matter, would have a significant impact. I could be part of something new that will be the leader in industry, first health care and then others after that. I'd be on the ground floor of the next Microsoft, or the next Hewlett-Packard," Willie said. "You worked at Hewlett-Packard. Why did you leave?"

"In a large corporation, if you want experience with other perspectives, you pretty much have to displace someone else. And the higher up you go, the more difficult it is to get different experiences," Rich said. He added, "With a startup like Mezzia, everyone will share in the company's good fortune and can take on additional responsibility as we grow. There's always an opportunity to expand your set of experiences."

"How come you chose to start Mezzia after you left IBM rather than take a position with another established company?" Willie asked.

"All the other opportunities I looked at were startups. I'm interested in making an impact, in creating something. To me, that's where the challenge, and the excitement, lies," Rich said. "Plus, our business is still evolving. It's exciting working in a dynamic environment. Although Hewlett-Packard changes, it's incremental change. They know their products and their markets well. Have you looked at working for other startups?"

"No. This is the only one. I fully intended to work for Hewlett-Packard. It's a goal I've had for about 2 years and I was pretty focused on attaining it," Willie said.

"Then I guess you have a big decision to make," Rich said.

"I do," Willie said sadly. "Thanks for meeting with me."

"Good luck," Rich said as he shook hands with Willie.

"What did you think?" McCorkle asked Rich.

"The main question for Willie isn't whether he wants to work with us. I think it's whether he wants to say no to Hewlett-Packard," Rich said.

Willie met with a few other software developers and the chief architect. He really liked the Web design tools and the design of Mezzia's first product. But it was all over in 2 hours. During the exit interview, McCorkle offered him a software developer job to start in January at an annual salary that was $6,000 less than the one from Hewlett-Packard, but with comparable benefits. He then showed him the space on the floor where his new cubicle would be constructed.

Decision Time

As Willie left the building, he was torn. He secretly had hoped he would not like someone—anyone—at Mezzia. But he found that not only did he like everyone he met, he felt stimulated by their enthusiasm and energy.

He could work for Hewlett-Packard for a few years and then leave to work for a startup, or maybe start his own company. But, if that was what he really wanted to do in a few years, then why not do it now while there was an opportunity? But how could he say no to Hewlett-Packard? That was a prestigious opportunity that would open many doors. Just working for them would establish his credibility.

But there was definitely reason to be concerned about this employment option. The fight between the shareholders led by the Hewlett family and Hewlett-Packard's board of directors had grown heated. Carly Fiorina, CEO of Hewlett-Packard, was fully confident in the long-term success of the merger, but she had begun to publicly question the integrity of many journalists reporting the story and financial analysts concerned only about short-term profits.[4]

If Willie chose Hewlett-Packard for employment, he was unsure of how long he would stay. He had heard from friends at Midwest University who used to work for companies that underwent mergers that many times a significant number of people were laid off as a result. Would this happen to him at Hewlett-Packard after it merged with Compaq?

However, he still questioned whether he should accept the offer at Mezzia. As he had found in his search for information on the health care industry over the weekend, many of the smaller companies were showing signs of rapid change because of a more demanding competitive environment. How would Mezzia's management team keep the direction of the company focused, but still give employees the sense of ownership they wanted? If the company began to have more serious financial troubles, would Willie be quickly asked to leave?

Again, he headed for the library instead of the gym. He needed to review his notes from the 2-day interview at HP and the visit to Mezzia. He also needed to make a list of pros and cons for working for Hewlett-Packard versus working for Mezzia. Then he would talk to some friends. Once he had the options clearer, he knew they would help him make the final decision. He had to give Hewlett-Packard his answer the next day.

---

[4]Pelline, Jeff, "Fiorina spreads cash, blame," CNET, November 15, 2001, *news.com.com/2100-1001_3-275925.html*.

PART III
ACQUIRING INFORMATION SYSTEMS

OBTAINING AND SUCCESSFULLY IMPLEMENTING A NEW INFORMATION SYSTEM IS FAR from trivial. Whether a system is custom-built for a business organization, or purchased from a software vendor, both business and information systems (IS) managers need to be accountable for achieving the business benefits and managing the potential business risks from investments in information technology (IT) applications. Thus, it is very important for business and IS managers to know how to successfully acquire and implement a new information system, as well as how to provide effective end-user computing support over the life of the system.

In Chapter 9 we focus on basic IS concepts on which modern systems are designed, built, and implemented. In Chapters 10 and 11 we describe alternative methodologies that organizations use to acquire and implement computer systems. In Chapter 12 we describe accepted practices for effectively managing IT projects. In Chapter 13 we discuss application development by end users, including the organization's role in supporting end-user computing activities. For those of you who are preparing to be IS professionals and have taken courses on systems analysis and design techniques, many portions of these chapters will be a review of system methodologies and project management techniques.

More specifically, Chapter 9 presents some fundamental systems principles on which applications are built. We describe how systems thinking underlies business process engineering and is useful for recognizing the technical *and* organizational aspects of introducing new technologies to an organization. An overall life-cycle process for systems development is introduced, as well as a variety of structured techniques, both procedural-oriented and object-oriented. The chapter concludes with a general discussion of information systems controls to ensure security and operational reliability.

Chapter 10 focuses on methodologies for developing custom software applications with IS professionals. Three approaches are described in some detail: the traditional systems development life cycle (SDLC), an evolutionary prototyping approach, and a rapid application development (RAD) approach—a hybrid methodology for delivering system modules in short timeboxes. In addition to describing methodology steps, we discuss project team roles, some project characteristics associated with successful system delivery, and advantages and disadvantages of the approach. The chapter concludes with some guidelines for managing software projects with an off-site, outsourcing staff.

Chapter 11 details a methodology for purchasing large software packages. For more than a decade, even large organizations with their own staffs of IS professionals have been purchasing packaged systems whenever it is feasible and cost-beneficial to do so. We begin the chapter by discussing the importance of the make-or-buy decision and then describe in detail the process steps for identifying, selecting, and implementing packaged software. We then discuss project team roles, some project characteristics associated with successful system implementation, and advantages and disadvantages of a purchasing approach. The chapter ends with a discussion of two special packaged system situations: the benefits and critical success factors associated with enterprise system packages and the advantages and downsides associated with implementing a packaged solution hosted by an application service provider (ASP).

Chapter 12 discusses generally accepted practices for managing IT projects. After introducing the concept of application portfolio management, the project initiation, planning, execution and control, and closing phases of an IT project are described. Techniques are then presented for addressing two IT project management challenges that also require strong IS-business relationships: managing the business risks of an IT project and managing business change. The chapter concludes with a discussion of two special issues: managing complex IT software projects and managing postmerger IT integration projects.

Chapter 13 focuses on facilitating end-user computing, including application development by employees who are not IS professionals. User application development has been common in many organizations since the 1990s, when PCs with spreadsheet programs began to be commonly found on the desktops of knowledge workers. In fact, user-developed applications are frequently used not only by the developer, but also by entire workgroups or departments. The chapter discusses the advantages and disadvantages of user-developed applications and some specific characteristics to evaluate when decided whether a user-developed application solution is the best alternative or not. Strategies and tactics for managing end-user computing in general are then described. The chapter concludes with a discussion of different categories of telecommuting, as well as both the benefits and management obstacles associated with telecommuting programs.

Ten original teaching cases accompany Part III. The Consumer and Industrial Products, Inc., case study describes the roles of managers and IS professionals when using the SDLC approach for the development of a complex system. The Zeus, Inc., case study describes the development of a large interorganizational system designed to serve a network of independent distributors—and the politics involved.

The Jefferson County School System case study provides an example of the pitfalls involved in purchasing and installing a packaged system for the first time. The Baxter manufacturing case is concerned with a make-or-buy decision for a critical software application, and the Benton Manufacturing case study describes the different viewpoints of various managers as the organization considers whether or not to acquire an enterprise resource planning (ERP) system.

Two cases are concerned with major changes to an organization's business processes. The Naval Surface Warfare Center case explores business process reengineering as a method for improving the competitiveness of the organization, as well as the role of the IS organization in supporting a BPR initiative. In the NIBCO's

"Big Bang" case, a 15-month project to implement an ERP package at a midsized manufacturing firm is described in detail. The project entails major changes to the way the organization purchases materials, manages its factories, uses its warehouses, conducts transactions with its customers, and manages its accounting functions, as well as its use of consultants as implementation partners. The BAT Taiwan case describes the challenges faced when implementing a standard ERP package in a small country office that is becoming a new profit center, with internal IS resources from area and regional support units rather than external consultants.

The Modern Materials case study describes a dilemma faced by many organizations: what to do with a runaway (troubled) IT project. And finally, the short Grandma Studor's Bakery case study describes the dilemma faced by business managers when the only user familiar with a user-developed spreadsheet application used for making critical materials purchasing decisions plans to leave the organization.

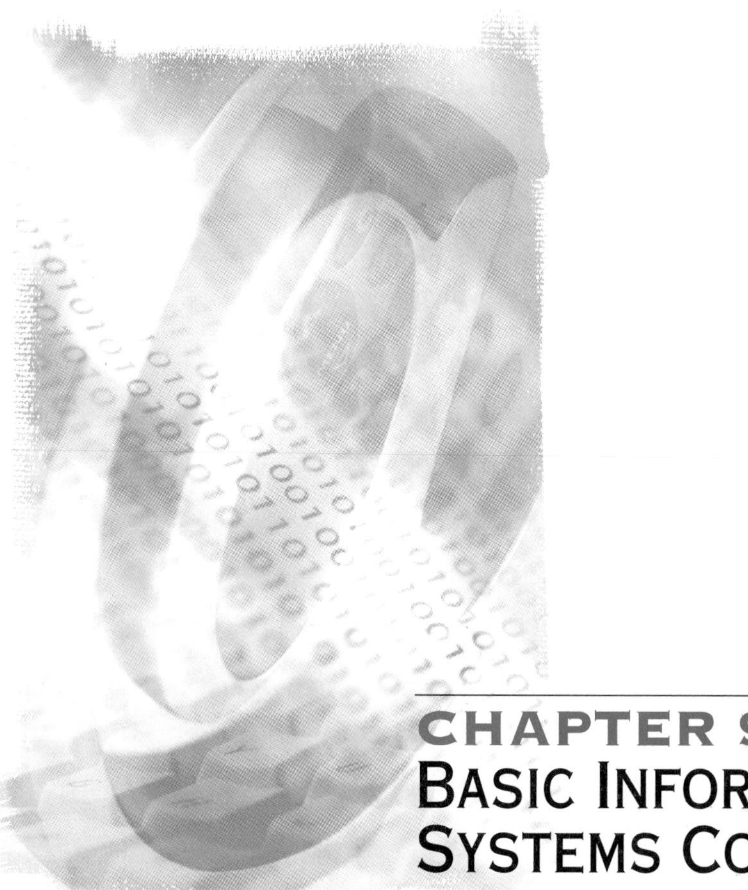

CHAPTER 9
BASIC INFORMATION SYSTEMS CONCEPTS

"It's the SYSTEM's fault!"
"The SYSTEM is down."
"My SYSTEM can't be beat!"
"Don't buck the SYSTEM."

PHRASES SUCH AS THESE REMIND US THAT THE TERM "SYSTEM" CAN BE used to refer to an information system with hardware, software, and telecommunications components (discussed in Part I) or that the term "system" can be used to refer to something much broader than an information system. For example, a systems perspective helps us to understand the complex relationships between different business units and different types of events within an organization so that when we change one aspect of a business we can anticipate the impact on the entire business. The ability to manage organizations as systems with interrelated processes is crucial for success in today's fast-changing business environments.

Today's business managers are being asked to play major roles in systems project teams with internal information systems (IS) specialists and/or outside vendors and consultants, and one of their key roles will be to help provide a high-level systems perspective on the business. Business and information technology (IT) managers must work together to determine the best scope for a systems project to meet the business's needs, as well as the business's requirements for financial returns on its IT investments. With IS personnel, business managers will also help develop and review graphical diagrams of the ways in which the organization currently works, as well as new ways. This chapter will therefore familiarize you with some of the specific methods and techniques that software developers use to describe both current (As-Is) and future (To-Be) systems in the abstract.

Today there is also a heightened sensitivity to system security and reliability. At the end of this chapter we describe a variety of controls that are associated with best practices for system development and implementation in particular. In Chapter 12 we will more fully discuss how a project manager needs to manage the business risks associated with a systems project.

THE SYSTEMS VIEW

Peter Senge and other management gurus have argued that more holistic systems thinking is needed to enable organizations to more quickly adapt to today's complex, fast-changing environments. According to Senge (1990), systems thinking is

- a discipline for seeing wholes
- a framework for seeing interrelationships rather than things
- an antidote to the sense of helplessness one feels when confronted with complexity

This section provides some templates for analyzing, describing, and redesigning systems. The systems concepts we discuss are general ones, although we will use many information systems examples.

What Is a System?

A **system** is a set of interrelated components that must work together to achieve some common purpose. An example of what happens when system components do not work together appears in Figure 9.1. This house has all the components (rooms, doors, windows, plumbing, electrical wiring) necessary for a functioning home, but the components just do not fit together. For example, the outside steps do not lead to a door. The lesson here is that even when a given component is well-designed, simple, and efficient to operate, the system will malfunction if the components do not work together.

Further, a change in one component could affect other components. For example, if the marketing group (one component part of a business) sells more of some product than expected, the production group (another component) would have to special-order materials or pay overtime to produce more than the planned amount. If the interrelationships between these functions (components) are not well managed, an unanticipated result might be a rise in the costs of goods sold, leading to the company actually losing money from increased sales.

An **information system** (**IS**) can be defined in a very broad way as the collection of IT, procedures, and people responsible for the capture, movement, management, and

Figure 9.1 An Example of Poor Design

distribution of data and information. As with other systems, it is crucial that the components of an IS work well together. That is, the components must be consistent, minimally redundant, complete, and well connected with one another.

Seven Key System Elements

Systems share the seven general system elements briefly defined as follows:

1. **Boundary** The delineation of which elements (such as components and storage) are within the system being analyzed and which are outside; it is assumed that elements within the boundary are more easily changed and controlled than those outside.
2. **Environment** Everything outside the system; the environment provides assumptions, constraints, and inputs to the system.
3. **Inputs** The resources (data, materials, supplies, energy) from the environment that are consumed and manipulated within the system.
4. **Outputs** The resources or products (information, reports, documents, screen displays, materials) provided to the environment by the activities within the system.
5. **Components** The activities or processes within the system that transform inputs into intermediate forms or that generate system outputs; components may also be considered systems themselves, in which case they are called subsystems, or modules.
6. **Interfaces** The place where two components or the system and its environment meet or interact; systems often need special subcomponents at interfaces to filter, translate, store, and correct whatever flows through the interface.
7. **Storage** Holding areas used for the temporary and permanent storage of information, energy, materials, and so on; storage provides a buffer between system components to allow them to work at different rates or at different times and to allow different components to share the same data resources. Storage is especially important in IS because data are not consumed with usage; the organization of storage is crucial to handle the potentially large volume of data maintained there.

Figure 9.2 graphically illustrates how these seven elements interrelate in a system.

These elements can also be used to describe specific computer applications. For example, in Figure 9.3 a payroll application and a sales-tracking application are described in terms of five system elements, excluding boundary and environment.

Another important system characteristic is the difference between **formal** versus **informal systems** within organizational contexts. The formal system is the way an organization was designed to work. When there are flaws in the formal system, or when the formal system has not been adapted to changes in business situations, an informal system develops.

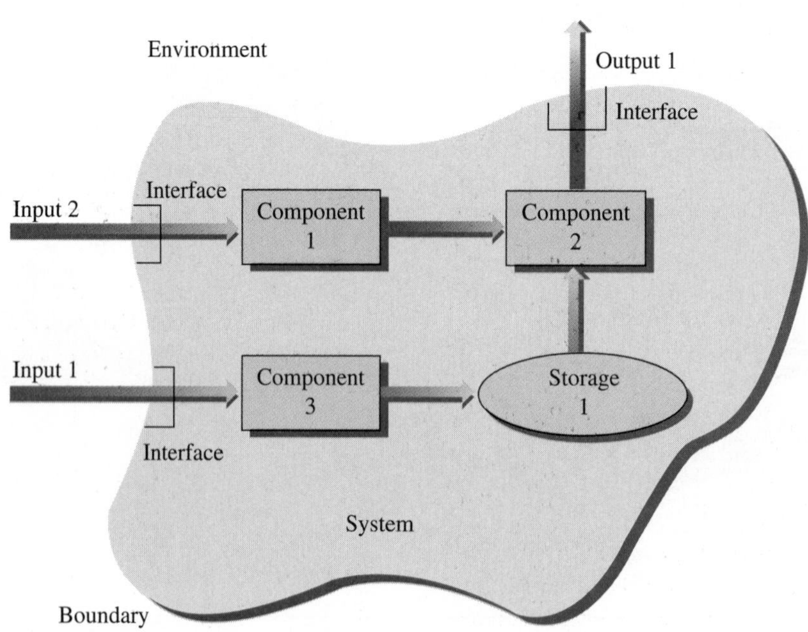

Figure 9.2 General Structure of a System

System:	Payroll	Sales Tracking
Inputs	Time cards Vouchers	Customer orders Customer returns of goods
Outputs	Paychecks W-2 forms	Monthly sales by product Monthly sales by territory
Components	Calculate total pay Subtract deductions	Accumulate sales by product and compare to forecast
Interfaces	Match time cards to employees Sort paychecks by department	Translate customer zip code into territory code
Storage	Employee benefits Pay rates	Product list Sales history Sales forecasts

Figure 9.3 System Component Examples

Recognizing that an organization's formal system is not necessarily equivalent to the real system is crucial when analyzing a business situation or process. For example, if workers continue to reference a bill-of-materials list that contains handwritten changes rather than a computer-printed list for a new shop order, an informal system has replaced the formal information system. In this case, the real system is actually the informal system or some combination of the formal and informal systems.

Three system characteristics that are especially important for analyzing and designing information systems are: determining the system boundary, breaking down a system into modules (decomposition), and designing interfaces between old and new systems.

System Boundary The system **boundary** delineates what is inside and what is outside a system. A boundary segregates the environment from the system or delineates subsystems from each other. A boundary in the systems world is often arbitrary. That is, we can often choose to include or exclude any component in the system. The choice of where to draw the boundary depends on factors such as these:

1. **What can be controlled** Elements outside the control of the project team are part of the environment, and the environment often places a constraint on the system scope. For example, if a preexisting billing system is treated as part of the environment of a new product management system, the product management system could be limited to devising products that can be priced and billed in ways already supported.
2. **What scope is manageable within a given time period** Complex systems often take so long to design and develop that the envisioned systems solution could no longer be the best choice by the time the project is complete.
3. **The impact of a boundary change** As the business changes or new information about the organization is uncovered, a different system boundary can appear to be beneficial. This decision requires careful analysis of the impact of such a change.

Component Decomposition A system is a set of interrelated components. A component of a system that is itself viewed as a system (or a set of interrelated components) is called a **subsystem (module)**. The components of a subsystem can be further broken down into more subsystems. The process of breaking down a system into successive levels of subsystems, each of which shows more detail, is called hierarchical (or functional) decomposition. An example is provided in Figure 9.4.

Five important goals of **hierarchical decomposition** of a system are the following:

1. **To cope with the complexity of a system** Decomposition of a complex system allows us to break the system down into understandable pieces.
2. **To analyze or change only part of the system** Decomposition results in specific components at just the right level of detail for the job.
3. **To design and build each subsystem at different times** Decomposition allows us to respond to new business needs as resources permit.
4. **To direct the attention of a target audience** Decomposition allows us to focus on a subset of components of importance to a subset of the total user population.
5. **To allow system components to operate more independently** Decomposition allows problem components to be isolated and components to be changed, moved, or replaced with minimal impact on other components.

Interfaces An **interface** is the point of contact between a system and its environment or between two subsystems. In an information system, the functions of an interface are generally as follows:

Filtering Disposing of useless data (or noise)
Coding/decoding Translating data from one format into another (for example, switching between two-part

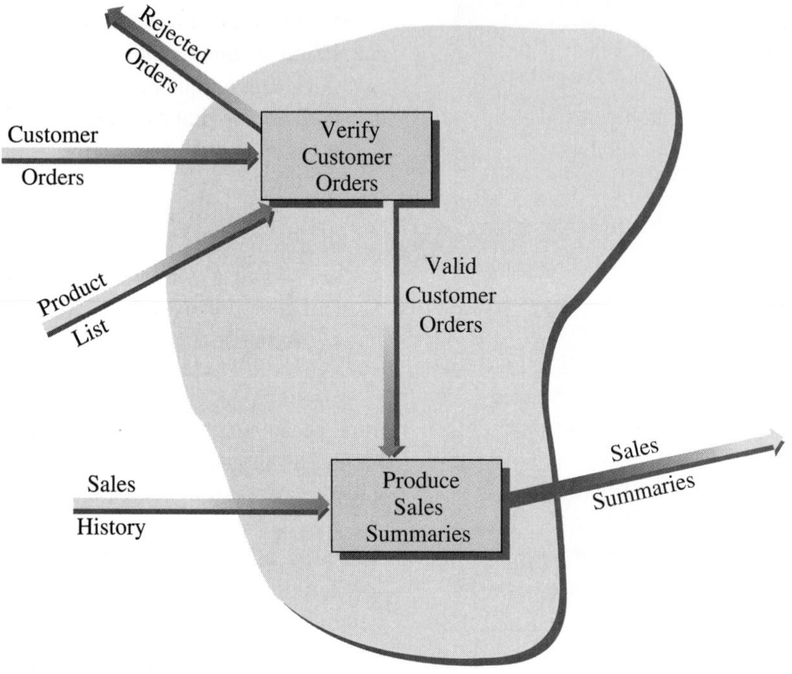

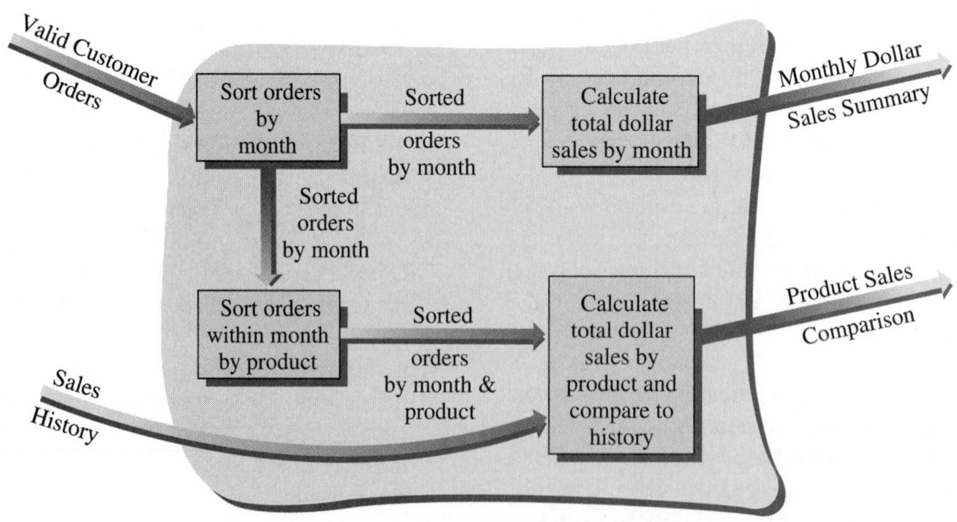

Figure 9.4 Sales Summary Reporting System and Subsystem

numbering schemes, one used by marketing and another used by engineering)

Error detection and correction Checking for compliance to standards and for consistency; by isolating this task in interfaces, other components can concentrate on their more essential responsibilities

Buffer Allowing two subsystems to work together without being tightly synchronized, as by having the interface collect data until the next component is ready to accept the data

Security Rejecting unauthorized requests for data and providing other protection mechanisms

Summarizing Condensing a large volume of input into aggregate statistics or even mathematical parameters to reduce the amount of work needed by subsequent subsystems

Interfaces also can be built between preexisting independent systems. For example, a company might contract with an outside organization (possibly a bank) to process payroll checks or with a market research firm to capture competitor sales data. In each case an interface is built that allows the external system to communicate with the company's internal systems. Different formats for data, different identifications for customers or employees, and various other differences in definitions and coding need to be translated to support this type of interface. Sometimes these interfaces are called bridges because they connect two "island" systems.

Bridge programs are relatively common. Bridges are expedient ways to accomplish the goal of expanding the capabilities of any one system. Rather than take the time to redesign two systems into one (e.g., to reduce redundant steps, to share common data, and to discontinue duplicate processing and calculations), the two systems are simply interfaced.

Another important objective of an interface is **system decoupling**. Two highly coupled system components require frequent and rapid communication, thus creating a dependence and bottleneck in the system. If one of the components fails, the other cannot function; if one is modified, the other might also have to be modified. Appropriately designed interfaces result in the decoupling of system components. The principal methods of system decoupling are these:

Slack and flexible resources Providing alternative paths to follow when one component breaks down or slows down, such as having an interface reroute data transmissions to public carriers if the company's private data communications network becomes busy

Buffers Storing data in a temporary location as a buffer or waiting line that can be depleted as the data are handled by the next component, as in collecting customer orders over the complete day and allowing an order-filling batch program to allocate scarce inventory to highest-need jobs

Sharing resources Creating shared data stores with only one program (part of the interface component) maintaining the data, thus avoiding the need to synchronize multiple step updating or to operate with inconsistent multiple copies of data

Standards Enforcing standards that reduce the need for two components to communicate, as in adopting a business policy that requires all interunit transfer of information about customers to be done using the company standard customer identification code

Decoupling allows one subsystem to remain relatively stable while other subsystems change. By clustering components into subsystems and by applying various decoupling techniques, the amount of design and maintenance effort can be significantly reduced. Because business is constantly changing, decoupling can significantly reduce an organization's systems maintenance burdens.

Organizations as Systems

Several useful frameworks exist to conceptualize how information systems fit into organizational systems. The framework in Figure 9.5, based on the Leavitt diamond, graphically depicts four fundamental components in an organization that must work in concert for the whole organization to be effective: people, information technology, business processes, and organization structure.

Figure 9.5 also suggests that if a change in IT is made in an organization—such as the introduction of a new software application—this change is likely to affect the other three components. For example, *people* will have to be retrained, methods of work (*business processes*) will have to be redesigned, and old reporting relationships (*organization structure*) will have to be modified. The important principle here is that:

> *Each time we change characteristics of one or more of these four components, we must consider compensating changes in the others.*

This raises an interesting question: With which of the four components do we start? There is no universal answer to this question, and organizational politics can play a key role in this decision. For example, organization theorists have argued that changes in technology can lead to organizational changes (technological imperative); that organizational factors can drive changes in technology (organizational imperative); and that changes are difficult to predict because

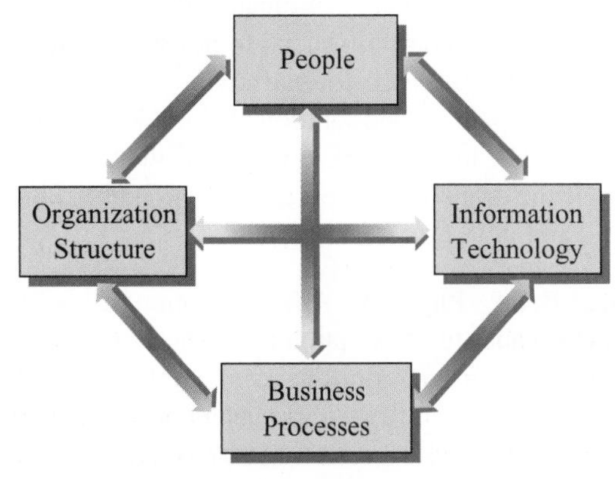

Figure 9.5 Fundamental Components of an Organization

of variations in purpose, processes, and organizational settings (Markus and Robey, 1988). In the 1990s many large U.S. companies chose to make large-scale changes in the way they conducted business by replacing custom information systems with a large software package (such as an enterprise resource planning [ERP] system) in which a vendor embedded the "best practices" for a business function or even an industry.

Systems Analysis and Design

A major process used in developing a new information system is called **systems analysis and design (SA&D)**. SA&D processes are based on a systems approach to problem solving. Here we describe several fundamental principles associated with good SA&D techniques that stem from the key system characteristics described previously.

The first two principles are these:

- *Choose an appropriate scope* Selecting the boundary for the information system greatly influences the complexity and potential success of an IS project.
- *Logical before physical* You must know *what* an information system is to do before you can specify *how* a system is to operate.

System Scope Often the fatal flaw in conceiving and designing a system centers on choosing an inappropriate system scope. Apparently the designer of the house in Figure 9.1 outlined each component separately, keeping the boundaries narrow and manageable, and did not see all the necessary interrelationships among the components. Turning to a business situation, when a salesperson sells a cheaper version of a product to underbid a competitor, that salesperson has focused only on this one sale. However, the costs of handling customer complaints about inadequacy of the product, repeated trips to install upgrades, and other possible problems make this scope inadequate.

The system boundary indicates the system scope. Defining the boundary is crucial to designing any system or solving any problem. Too narrow a scope could cause you to miss a really good solution to a problem. Too wide a scope could be too complex to handle. Choosing an appropriate scope is difficult but crucial in problem-solving in general and in IS projects in particular.

Logical Before Physical Any description of a system is abstract because the description is not the system itself, but different system descriptions can emphasize different aspects of the system. Two important general kinds of system descriptions are logical and physical descriptions. Logical descriptions concentrate on *what* the system does, and physical descriptions concentrate on *how* the system operates. Another way to say this is "function before form."

Returning to our example of a house as a system, as an architect knows, function precedes form with the design of a new house. Before the house is designed, we must determine how many people will live in it, how each room will be used, the lifestyle of the family, and so on. These requirements comprise a functional, or logical, specification for the house. It would be premature to choose the type of materials, color of plumbing fixtures, and other physical characteristics before we determine the purpose of these aspects.

We are often anxious to hurry into designing the physical form before we determine the needed functionality. The penalty for violating the function before form principle is increased costs—the cost and efforts to fix a functional specification error grow exponentially as you progress to the physical. We must get the logical or functional specifications right to understand how to choose among alternate physical implementations.

As an example of the difference between a logical and a physical information system, consider a class registration system. A **logical system** description would show such steps as submitting a request for classes, checking class requests against degree requirements and prerequisites, and generating class registration lists. A **physical system** description would show whether the submission of a request for classes is via a computer terminal or a touch-tone telephone, whether the prerequisite checking is done manually or by electronic comparison of transcript with course descriptions, and so on.

Problem-Solving Steps The three following principles, or problem-solving steps, have also been associated with good SA&D processes. In fact, they are recommended as good principles for problem-solvers in general.

- A problem (or system) is actually a set of problems; thus, an appropriate strategy is to keep breaking a problem down into smaller and smaller problems, which are more manageable than the whole problem.
- A single solution to a problem is not usually obvious to all interested parties, so alternative solutions representing different perspectives should be generated and compared before a final solution is selected.
- The problem and your understanding of it could change while you are analyzing it, so you should take a staged approach that incorporates reassessments; this allows an incremental commitment to a particular solution, with a "go" or "no-go" decision after each stage.

Later in this chapter we will introduce a generic life cycle process for developing new systems, as well as some specific techniques used by SA&D professionals. First, however, let us develop a shared understanding of the "what" that is driving many IS development and implementation projects today: systems to support cross-functional business processes.

BUSINESS PROCESSES

In the 1990s many organizations began to transform their businesses in an effort to sense and respond more quickly to global threats and demands for cost-cutting. Many of these transformation efforts were directed at moving away from a functional "silo" approach to a more process-oriented approach. Organizing work and work structures around business processes—rather than business functions or business products—requires a new mindset in which basic assumptions are challenged and change is embraced.

> A **business process** is a set of work activities and resources.

Identifying Business Processes

According to Peter Keen (1997), the identification of a firm's core processes is a key analytical task. For example, a typical manufacturing firm may have six core processes: sensing the market, developing product, sourcing of materials, manufacturing product, selling product, and fulfilling customer order. A firm's core processes should not be viewed just as its workflows. Rather, these business processes should be viewed as the firm's assets and liabilities. By evaluating the worth of a given process to a firm's competitiveness, managers should be able to identify a small number of processes that need their attention the most.

Figure 9.6 shows one way in which managers can evaluate the importance of a given business process. Folklore processes are those processes that are carried out only because they have been in the past; they are often difficult to identify because they are so embedded in an organization's tasks. When they are identified, they should be abandoned because they create no economic value. Keen also warns that the importance (salience) of a given process is not necessarily the same in different companies in the same industry or even in the same company under different circumstances.

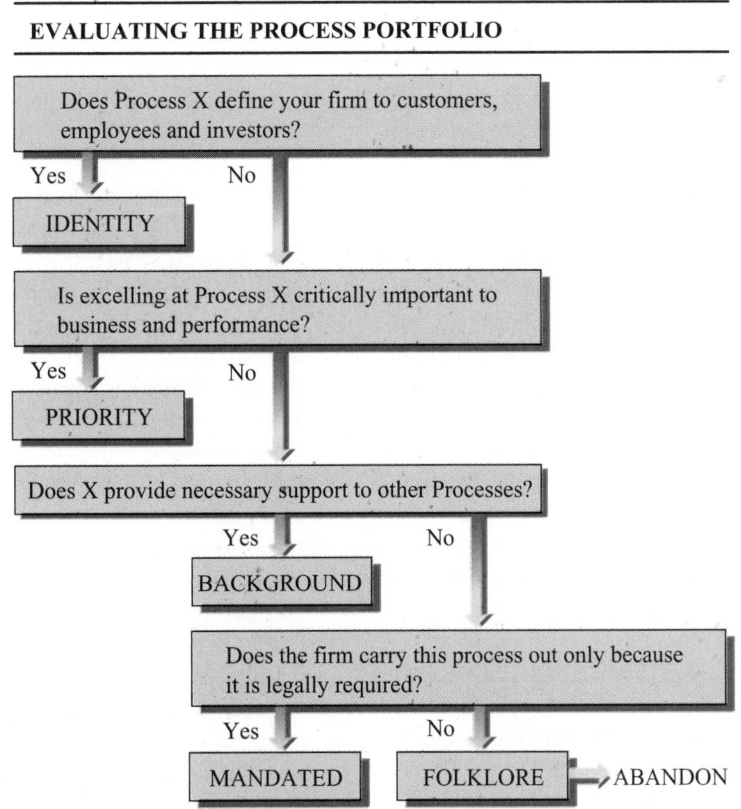

Figure 9.6 Evaluating Business Processes (Keen, 1997)

Business Process Redesign

In a seminal article published in the *Harvard Business Review*, reengineering expert Michael Hammer urged companies to start with a "clean slate" and use IT to radically change the way they did business: "Don't automate; obliterate!" By the early 1990s, consulting firms had developed expertise in what came to be referred to as **business process reengineering (BPR)**: radical business redesign initiatives that attempt to achieve dramatic improvements in business processes by questioning the assumptions, or business rules, that underlie the organization's structures and procedures, some of which could have been in place for decades.

Simple questions like "why," "what if," "who says so," and "what do our customers think," can lead to breakthrough insights that result in totally new business processes. The goal is to achieve an order of magnitude improvement, rather than incremental gains.

Two BPR success stories described by Hammer (1990) have now become classic examples.

Accounts Payable at Ford Motor Company During an initial redesign of its accounts payable process, Ford concluded that it could reduce head count by 20 percent in this department. The initial solution was to develop a new accounts payable system to help clerks resolve document mismatches. This solution was based on the assumption that problems with coordinating purchase orders, shipment documents, and invoices are inevitable. The proposed new system would help prevent the document mismatches.

Ford's managers were reasonably proud of their plans until the designers discovered that Mazda Motor Corp. accomplished the same function with just five people. The difference was that Ford based its initial system solution on the old business assumptions. In particular, Ford had not questioned its assumption that it could not pay a vendor without an invoice. When Ford questioned its assumptions, a truly reengineered solution was identified, as follows: capture the receipt of goods at the loading dock using computer scanners and use the negotiated price to pay the vendor based on a validated receipt of goods—instead of an invoice. When Ford took a "clean slate" approach, the company achieved a 75 percent improvement gain—not the original projected 20 percent.

Mutual Benefit Life Insurance Mutual Benefit Life's old insurance application processing was a 30-step process that involved 19 people in 5 departments. Rather than automating the old workflows across multiple people in multiple departments, the process was radically redesigned. Under the reengineered process, an individual case manager is empowered to handle the entire loan application process. This was accomplished by supporting the case manager with an advanced PC-based workstation, expert system software, and access to a range of automated systems. Time to issue a policy dropped from 3 weeks to about 3 hours.

In both of these examples IT played a key role as an enabler of radical business process redesign. Hammer and Champy (1993) encourage managers to go through exercises that help them think about how IT can be used to break old assumptions and rules. Three examples of rule-breaking IT are provided in Figure 9.7.

Hammer (1990) advocated the use of key principles for redesigning business processes. A consolidated list of six principles is presented below.

1. **Organize business processes around outcomes, not tasks** This principle implies that one person should perform all the steps in a given process, as in the case of Mutual Benefit Life, where one manager handles the whole application approval process. IT is used to bring together all the information and decision-making resources needed by this one person. Often this principle also means organizing processes around customer needs, not the product.
2. **Assign those who use the output to perform the process** The intent of this principle is to make those most interested in a result accountable for the production of that result. For example, Hammer reports the case of an electronics equipment manufacturer that reengineered its field service function to have customers perform simple repairs themselves. This principle reduces nonproductive overhead jobs, including liaison positions. Principles 1 and 2 yield a compression of linear steps into one step, greatly reducing delays, miscommunication, and wasted coordination efforts. Information technologies, like expert systems and databases, allow every manager to perform functions traditionally done by specialty managers.
3. **Integrate information processing into the work that produces the information** This principle states that information should be processed at its source. For example, at Ford this means that the receiving department, which produces information on goods received, should also enter this data, rather than sending it to accounts payable for processing. This puts data capture closest to the place where data entry errors can be detected and corrected, thus minimizing extra reconciliation steps. This principle also implies that data should be captured once at the primary source, thus avoiding transmittal and transcription errors. All who need these data work from a common and consistent source. For example, the true power of electronic data interchange (EDI) comes when all information processing related

Old Ways to Work	Information Technology	New Ways to Work
Field personnel (such as sales and customer support staff) need to physically be located in an office to transmit and receive customer and product data	Portable computers with communications software and secure networks that allow remote access to company data	Field personnel access data and respond to messages wherever they are working
Client data is collected in different databases to support different points of contact with the client	Centralized databases that capture transactions from different parts of the business and are accessible via a network	Client data can be accessed simultaneously by employees working in different business units
Only experts can do a complex task *(see Mutual Benefit Life Insurance example)*	Expert systems that have knowledge rules used by company experts when they do this task	Generalists can do a complex task previously only done by an expert

Figure 9.7 How IT Enables New Ways to Work

to an EDI transaction works from a common, integrated database.

4. **Create a virtual enterprise by treating geographically distributed resources as though they were centralized** This principle implies that the distinction between centralization and decentralization is artificial with IT. Technologies such as teleconferencing, group support systems, e-mail, and others can create an information processing environment in which time and space are compressed. Hammer reports on the experience of Hewlett-Packard, which treats the purchasing departments of 50 manufacturing units as if they were one giant department by using a shared database on vendor and purchase orders. The result is 50 percent to 150 percent improvement in key performance variables for the purchasing function.
5. **Link parallel activities instead of integrating their results** This principle says that related activities should be constantly coordinated rather than waiting until a final step to ensure consistency. For example, Hammer suggests that different kinds of credit functions in a financial institution could share common databases, use communication networks, and employ teleconferencing to coordinate their operations. This would ensure, for example, that a customer is not extended a full line of credit from each unit.
6. **Have the people who do the work make all the decisions, and let controls built into the system monitor the process** The result of this principle is the drastic reduction of layers of management, the empowerment of employees, and the shortcutting of bureaucracy. This principle emphasizes the importance of building controls into a system from the start, rather than as an afterthought (see the section entitled "Information Systems Controls to Minimize Business Risks" at the end of this chapter).

However, not all BPR projects of the early 1990s were successes. In fact, Keen (1997) points out that Mutual Benefit Life, whose radical reengineering example was described above, was taken over by regulators due to insolvency about the time Hammer lauded it as a success story. By the mid-1990s many firms began to acknowledge that a combination approach of both radical change and incremental change (such as continuous improvements as part of quality management initiatives) was more successful (El Sawy, 2001).

By the mid-1990s client/server versions of enterprise system packages had also become widely available, making it possible for large companies to implement systems that would support complex processes across multiple functions for the first time: Earlier attempts to become more process-oriented had been aborted because systems to support their reengineered processes were too difficult to custom develop. For example, as described in Chapter 6, enterprise resource planning (ERP) packages offered by vendors such as SAP and PeopleSoft provide integrated software modules that use the same centralized database for manufacturing, purchasing, and accounting transactions. Similarly, packages to support customer relationship management (CRM) by vendors such as Siebel Systems provide modules that can integrate customer data from multiple communication "channels," which are typically managed by different business units (marketing, sales, and customer support).

PROCESSES AND TECHNIQUES TO DELIVER INFORMATION SYSTEMS

We turn now to processes and techniques for developing information systems. Our intent here is to introduce the key concepts that underlie the toolkits of system professionals. We also emphasize topics of use to both IS specialists and business managers who are asked to participate in, or lead, systems projects.

The Information Systems Life Cycle

Figure 9.8 presents the three phases of a generic **systems development life cycle** model: Definition, Construction, and Implementation.

In the *Definition* phase, end users and systems analysts conduct a multistep analysis of the current business operations and the information system or systems in the area of concern. Current operations and systems are described via both process-oriented and data-oriented notations. Process-oriented analysis concentrates on the flow, use, and transformation of data. Data-oriented analysis focuses on the kinds of data needed in a system and the business relationships between these data. Problems with current operations and opportunities for achieving business value through new IT capabilities are identified. A business case is made for the feasibility of new systems, and one solution is chosen. This solution is detailed in a requirements statement agreed to by all parties. If a software vendor has already developed a "packaged" system that meets these requirements, this phase also includes steps to identify and select the best packaged solution. The Definition phase of the life cycle is very much a cooperative effort between business and systems professionals. Doing this phase right can have significant impact on the competitive use of IT.

The *Construction* phase entails the designing, building, and testing of a system that satisfies the requirements developed in the Definition phase. The system first is logically described, and then its physical design is specified. Programs and computer files are designed, and computer technology is chosen. Inputs such as business forms and computer screens are designed, as well as outputs such as reports. After the physical design is accepted as feasible (technically, economically, and operationally), the computer software is programmed and tested. Users play a major role in acceptance testing to verify that the system requirements have been met.

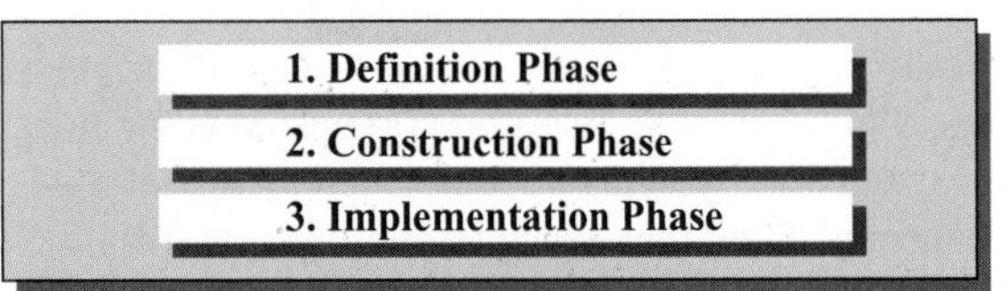

Figure 9.8 Generic Systems Life Cycle

In the *Implementation* phase, business managers and IS professionals work together to install the new system, which often involves converting data and procedures from an old system. The installation of a new system can occur in a variety of ways, such as in parallel with operation of the old system or in a total and clean cutover. The implementation phase also includes the operation and continued maintenance of the system. Maintenance is typically the longest stage of the systems life cycle and incurs the greatest costs. It includes system changes resulting from flaws in the original design, from changing business needs or regulations, and from incorporating new technologies.

In the following chapters we will discuss in more detail some specific methodologies for developing and implementing custom software solutions (Chapter 10) and for purchasing and implementing packaged software solutions (Chapter 11). All these methodologies are based on the generic three-phase life cycle for systems development described above. Although many IS organizations customize these approaches—including expansion or contraction of the specific number of phases or steps, or using different names—there is agreement among IS specialists on the generic activities that are required for developing a quality system that meets the organization's needs.

Structured Techniques for Life Cycle Development

Just as architects use blueprints as abstract representations of a house, IS professionals have developed techniques for representing system requirements and designs. In this section we describe some of these techniques.

Today, IS development projects range in size from a single-user application for a desktop machine to one that will be used by thousands of people in a large organization. The scope of today's large development projects has brought system builders up against both cognitive and practical limitations: The scale and complexity of these projects exceed the capacity of one developer or even a single team of manageable size. Effective large system development requires more systematic approaches that allow partitioning of the problem so that many developers can work on the project simultaneously. Increasing the scale also increases the number of parties involved. Systems projects today can require coordination across multiple project managers and even involve IS professionals in a customer or supplier organization (such as some e-commerce applications discussed in Chapter 8). System builders must be able to communicate with other IS professionals about what system modules do and how they do what they do. IS project managers must be able to coordinate and monitor progress and understand the commitments they are asking business managers and IS project team members to make.

A body of tools has emerged to document system needs and requirements, functional features and dependencies, and design decisions. Called **structured techniques**, these techniques exist for all phases of the systems development process, and many variations have emerged. Additionally, the techniques could be embodied within a larger approach called a **system development methodology**. A methodology is a framework consisting of guidelines, tools, and techniques for managing the application of knowledge and skills to address all or part of a business issue. A systems development methodology, then, consists of processes, tools, and techniques for developing systems. In addition to the types of structured tools discussed in the sections that follow, these methodologies prescribe who should participate and their roles, the development stages and decision points, and specific formats for system documentation.

This section will provide a conceptual introduction to the most common structured techniques in a general life cycle development framework. Two major approaches to systems building have emerged: procedural-oriented and object-oriented. Procedural-oriented systems have historically been the most common, as they appropriately represent a large class of business activities. They include data-oriented as well as sequential, process-oriented activities such as tabulating time cards and printing paychecks, inventory handling, and accounts payable. Object-oriented (O-O) techniques are a newer approach to systems development. Considered by some to be revolutionary and by others to be evolutionary, O-O techniques are better suited to the development of graphical user interfaces (GUIs) and multimedia applications, but they require an entirely new way of thinking for veteran IS professionals.

Procedural-Oriented Techniques

In the past the vast majority of IS development projects have involved automating an existing paper-oriented business process or updating and expanding an existing automated or partially automated business process. This reality is reflected in the fundamental procedural approach to systems development: describe what you have, define what you want, and describe how you will make it so.

As shown in Figure 9.9, this approach involves documenting the existing system (the As-Is model), creating a model of the desired future system (the Logical To-Be model), and then interpreting the logical future model as a physical system design (the Physical To-Be model). The motivation for following such a process derives in part from human nature. Most people find it easier to imagine the future by conceiving of how it is different from today. A systematic effort to document the existing system can also yield important insights about its deficiencies and worker ideas about improvements.

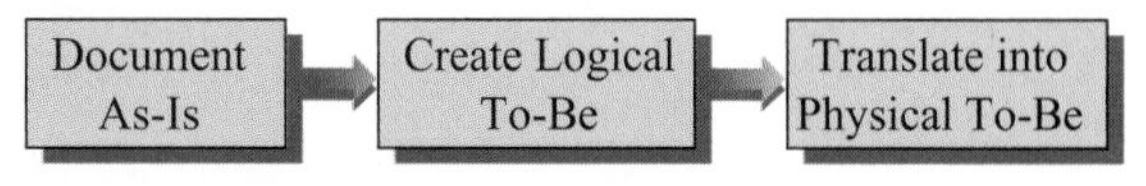

Figure 9.9 Three-Step Modeling Approach

This sequential approach is also effective when a new business process is being implemented at the same time that a new system is being implemented; it helps ensure that the new process will work in concert with the new IS, not against it. As described previously, business process redesign became increasingly common during the 1990s.

Describing the three models in Figure 9.10 requires a significant amount of effort prior to building the software. Business managers are often surprised at the demands placed on them to support this definition phase. The objective of this process is to have a thorough description of what the construction phase for the system will entail, so that the project risks can be assessed and planned for with some level of confidence or the decision can be made to abandon the project. In fact, actual software coding during the construction phase typically represents less than one-quarter of the entire systems development effort (Page-Jones, 1988).

The As-Is model provides a baseline for the system: Why build a new one if it will not do more than the old one, do it faster, or avoid existing problems? The As-Is model typically includes both logical and physical models.

Although developing the As-Is model can be user-intensive, the majority of the effort is typically involved with developing the second model: abstracting the As-Is model into the Logical To-Be. Logical To-Be modeling involves a critical appraisal of existing work processes in order to

- identify major subprocesses, entities, and their interactions
- separate processing from the flow of data
- capture relationships between data elements
- determine those entities and processes within the project scope, and those that are not

Creation of the Physical To-Be model is a task dominated by IS specialists, as it requires technology expertise to map

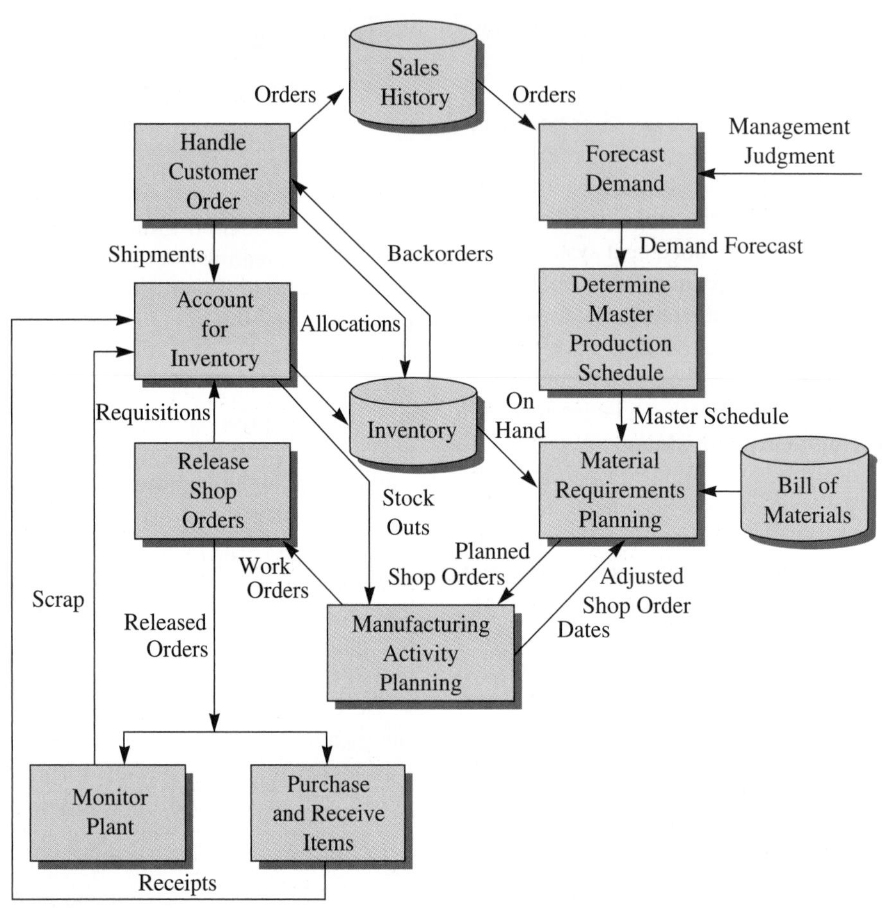

Figure 9.10 Physical Model of a System

the logical requirements to available technology. Although information systems are implemented with specific hardware and software, participants in systems development efforts are cautioned to resist the urge to make decisions related to design and implementation until as late as possible in the project. Premature fixation on a particular technology has often led to unsatisfactory outcomes because it can cause important aspects of the system to go undiscovered or put undue emphasis on *how* to do something before there is certainty about *what* needs to be done. In reality, although no IS project is truly a "clean slate," delaying judgment until the Physical To-Be stage is the recommended strategy.

After a new system has been implemented and is operational, a diagram like that in Figure 9.10 would be used to show a physical model of the key system components and their relationships. It uses the following symbols:

Boxes	for	Major modules
Cylinders	for	Databases
Arrows	for	Flow of data

Note, however, that this diagram makes no references to details such as what type of computer hosts the software or what language it is written in. Instead, the Physical To-Be model is a high-level model. It communicates how the new system will work and helps identify any dependencies that might lead to downstream impacts, such as data integrity problems or inadequate process definitions.

Distinct tools are used at each stage of procedural-oriented development. The output from one stage serves as the input for the next. As firms gain experience with systems development, they often develop a preference for certain tools or adopt variations in the notation. The following section introduces some of the most common tools, concepts, and terminology using widely recognized notation. The tools will be presented with the model (As-Is, Logical To-Be, Physical To-Be) with which they are most closely associated, using a common business example throughout: accounts payable. An accounts payable example is useful because accounts payable activities interact with other business activities (such as purchasing and receiving), are familiar to most managers and business students, and are common across industries.

Tools for the As-Is Model

Whether a system is entirely manual or highly automated, the functions and flows of the existing business activity must be captured. Knowledge of a business process is rarely entirely in the possession of a single person, and there could be disagreements on the actual or preferred processes. Procedures, policies, manuals, forms, reports, and other documentation are used along with individual and group interviews to identify existing processes, external participants such as vendors and other functional departments, other databases or applications, and the inputs and outputs of the activities concerned.

A **context diagram** positions the system as a whole with regard to the other entities and activities with which it interacts. This provides a common frame of reference for project participants and helps define the project scope. Figure 9.11 illustrates a context diagram for an accounts payable system. We can see from this diagram that the accounts payable function both receives input from vendors and sends output to them. Other accounting functions receive summary information about payables activities, whereas purchasing provides the input needed to process payables. Vendors, accounting, and purchasing are all considered to be outside the project scope for this development effort.

Another common tool for documenting the As-Is system is a work process flow diagram, as shown in Figure 9.12. This flow chart identifies the existing information sources (purchase order file, receipts file), information sources that are updated (changes to payables), the order in which steps occur (approvals before checks are printed), and some of the dependencies (need to know whether vendor is new or not). The way in which exceptions are handled should also be captured (e.g., what happens to invoices not approved). No two workflow diagrams are identical, because they capture the unique patterns and procedures—formal and informal—of a company.

The work process flow diagram and other As-Is tools serve to point out where the existing system does and does not perform as desired. Common problems include repeated handling of the same document, excessive wait times, processes with no outputs, bottlenecks, and extra review steps. This shows how systems development efforts are closely associated with business process redesign efforts.

Tools for the Logical To-Be Model

In this step systems developers build a high-level model of a nonexistent system: the system that the users and managers would like to replace the one they have now. The Logical To-Be model is an abstraction that identifies the processes and data required for the desired system *without* reference to who does an activity, where it is accomplished, or the type of computer or software used. The model describes the "what," rather than the "how." Stated differently, it separates the information that moves through the business process from the mechanisms that move it (e.g., forms, reports, routing slips). This is important because IT enables information to be in more than one place at the same time; paper does not possess this attribute. By leaving physical barriers behind, the analyst can better determine how to exploit IT. This abstraction step can be difficult for first-time business participants because it appears to ignore issues crucial to their daily work (e.g., specific forms, reports, routing slips). Understanding that the Logical To-Be model encompasses information flows, rather than physical flows (paper, money, products), is the key.

The Logical To-Be model is most closely associated with the **data flow diagram** or **DFD** (see Hoffer et al., 1999, for a thorough discussion of DFDs). The DFD notation itself is technology independent; the symbols have no association with the type of equipment or the humans that might perform the process activities or store

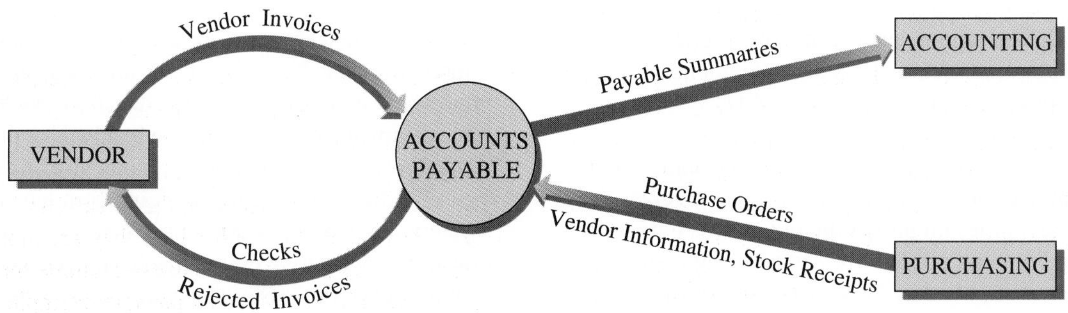

Figure 9.11 Context Diagram for Accounts Payable System

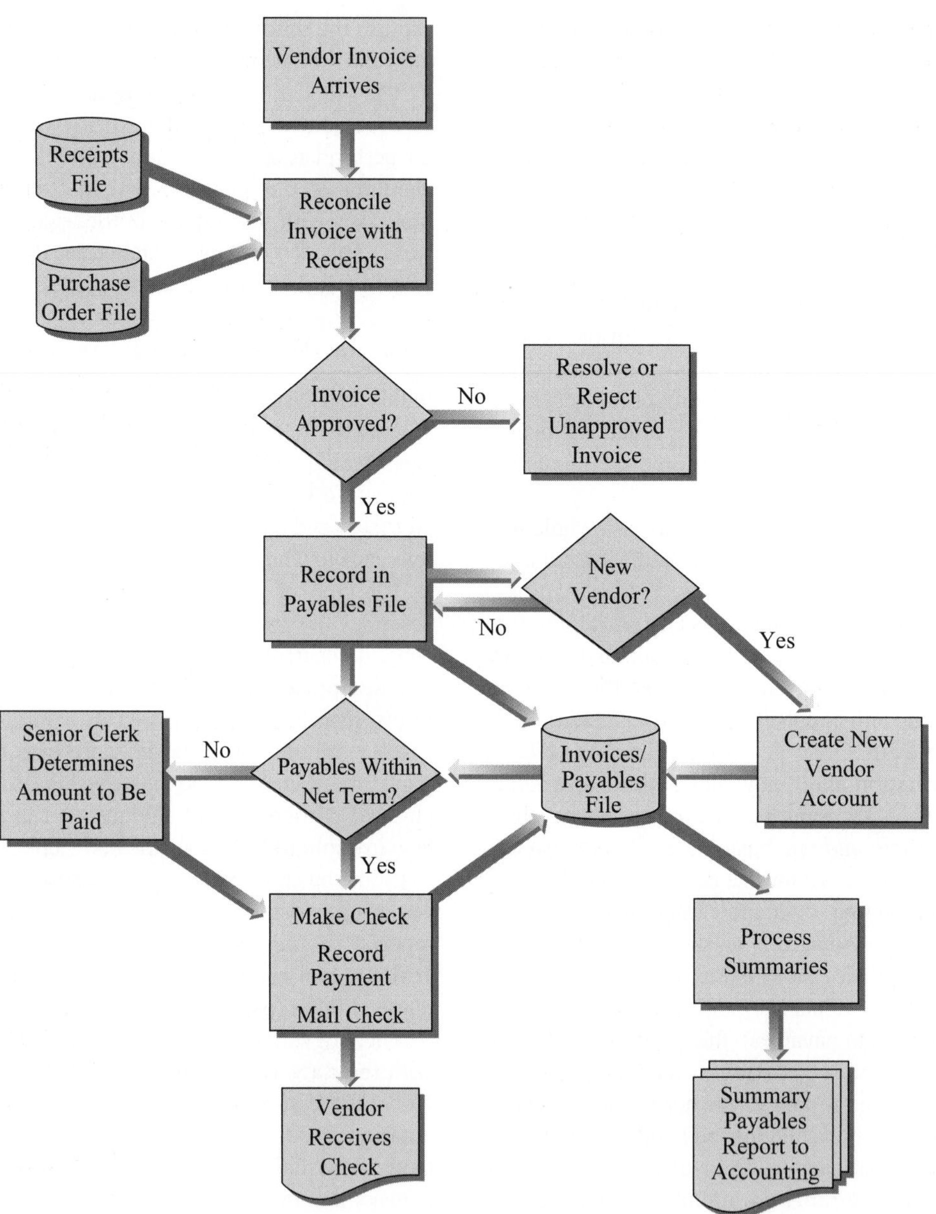

Figure 9.12 Work Process Flow Diagram for Accounts Payable

the data. DFD creation typically involves groups of people and is accomplished through multiple iterations.

Four types of symbols are used in DFDs:

External Entity A square indicates some element in the environment of the system that sends or receives data. External entities might not directly access data in the system but must get data from processing components of the system. No data flows between external entities are shown. External entities have noun labels.

Data Flow Arrows indicate data in motion—that is, data moving between external entities and system processes, between system processes, or between processes and data stores. Timing and volume of data are not shown. Data flows have noun labels. Because data flow labels often sound similar, and there could be hundreds of distinct data flows in a project, numbers might also be assigned.

Process Circles represent processing components of the system. Each process has to have both input and output (whereas an external entity may have either input, output, or both). Processes have verb-phrase labels as well as a numerical identifier.

Data Store Open rectangles depict data at rest—that is, data temporarily or permanently held for repeated reference by one or more processes. Use of a data store implies there is a delay in the flow of data between two or more processes or a need for long-term storage. Each data store contained within the system must have both input and output (i.e., be populated and be used) within the system. Data stores that are outside the system may provide only input or only output. Data stores have noun labels and a unique identifier.

The process of creating data flow diagrams is as follows:

- Identify the entities that supply or use system information.
- Distinguish processes from the data that they use or produce.
- Explicate business rules that affect the transformation of data to information.
- Identify logical relationships.
- Pinpoint duplicate storage and movements of data.

In Figure 9.13(A) a "top-level" DFD for the Accounts Payable system is shown. Consistent with the context diagram of Figure 9.11, the dashed line delineates the system boundary. The system includes four processes (circles). Data stores internal to this system (D2, D3, and D4) serve as buffers between the process components (e.g., to compensate for different processing rates of the components or to permit batch processing of transactions), as well as semi-permanent storage for auditing purposes.

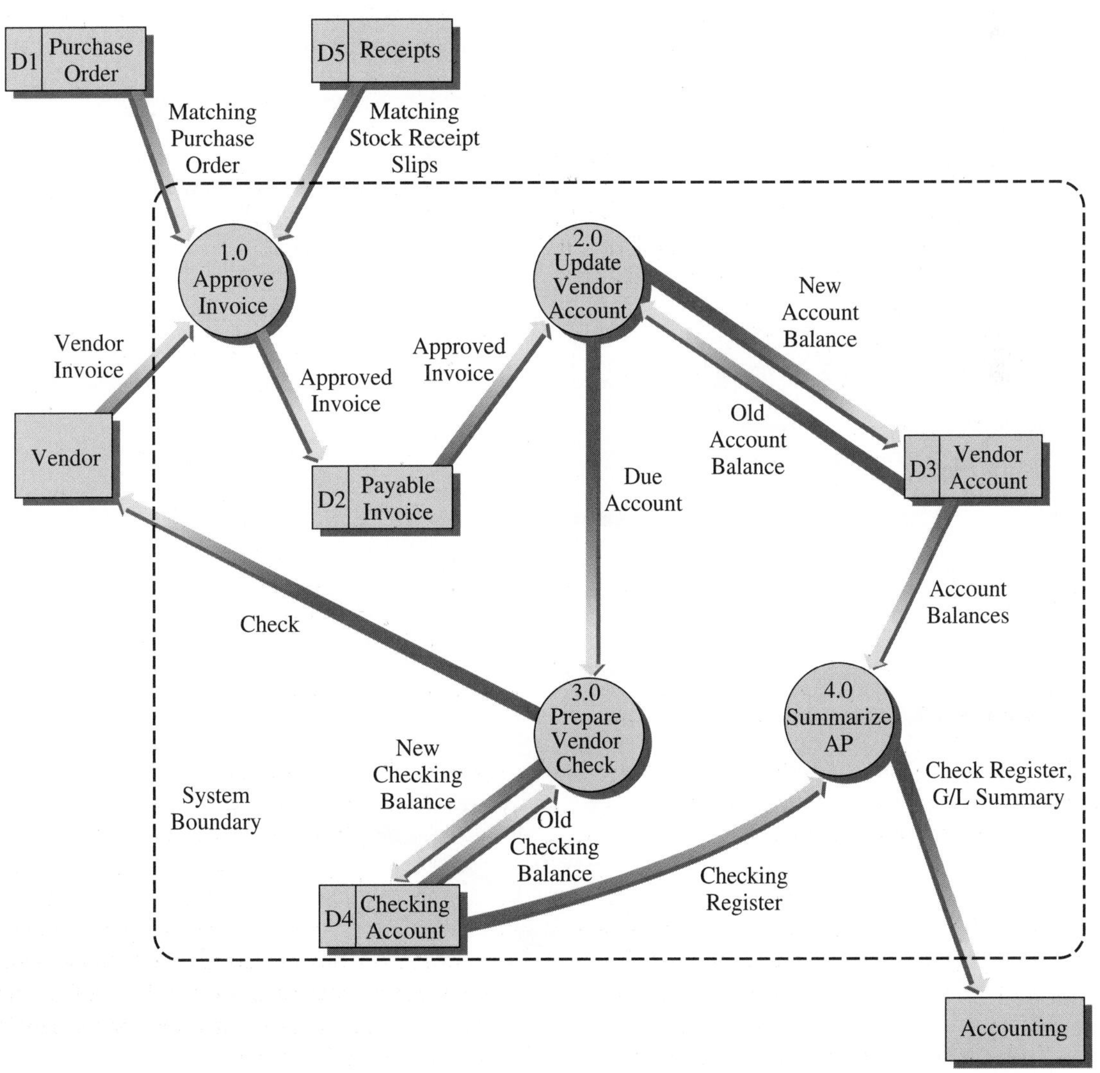

Figure 9.13(A) Top-Level Data Flow Diagram for Accounts Payable System

Because this is a top-level DFD, or macro view, processing details are not depicted. For example, this top-level diagram does not show what happens to exceptions—such as what the process does to deal with invoices that do not match purchase orders or shipment receipt records.

A key to the effectiveness of DFD modeling is the enforcement of strict hierarchical relationships. Each process (circle) on the top-level DFD has a lower-level DFD that documents the subprocesses, data stores, and data flows needed to accomplish the process task. This "explosion" continues for each subprocess until no further subprocesses are needed to describe the function. A process at the lowest level in the model must be definable by a few descriptive sentences. Figure 9.13(B) is the next-lower-level explosion DFD for Process 1.0 (Approve Invoice) in Figure 9.13(A). The process decomposition relationship is shown by the process numbering scheme (1.1, 1.2, etc.).

The lower-level DFDs can result in the identification of additional data stores and data flows as well as subprocesses, but the exploded DFDs must balance with their higher-level counterparts. All data flows identified in a lower-level DFD must be accounted for in the description, source, and destination of data flows at the higher level. During the Logical To-Be defining process, external entities and data flows sometimes will need to be added to higher-level DFDs to assure completeness. It is not uncommon for business systems to have four or five levels of DFDs before exhausting all subprocesses.

When complete, DFDs tell a story about the business process that does not depend upon specific forms or technology. The rigor imposed by the explosion, aggregation, balancing, and documentation of DFDs results in more than simple circle-and-arrow diagrams. For example, from reviewing the accounts payable DFDs, we see:

1. Purchase orders and shipment receipt records are produced by systems outside the accounts payable system (because they are shown as inputs from the environment—that is, outside the system boundary).
2. The payable invoice data store temporarily stores and groups invoices after invoice approval and before subsequent vendor account updating and check writing (data flows into and out of D2).

These statements describe two aspects of the accounts payable organizational data flows as we want them to be

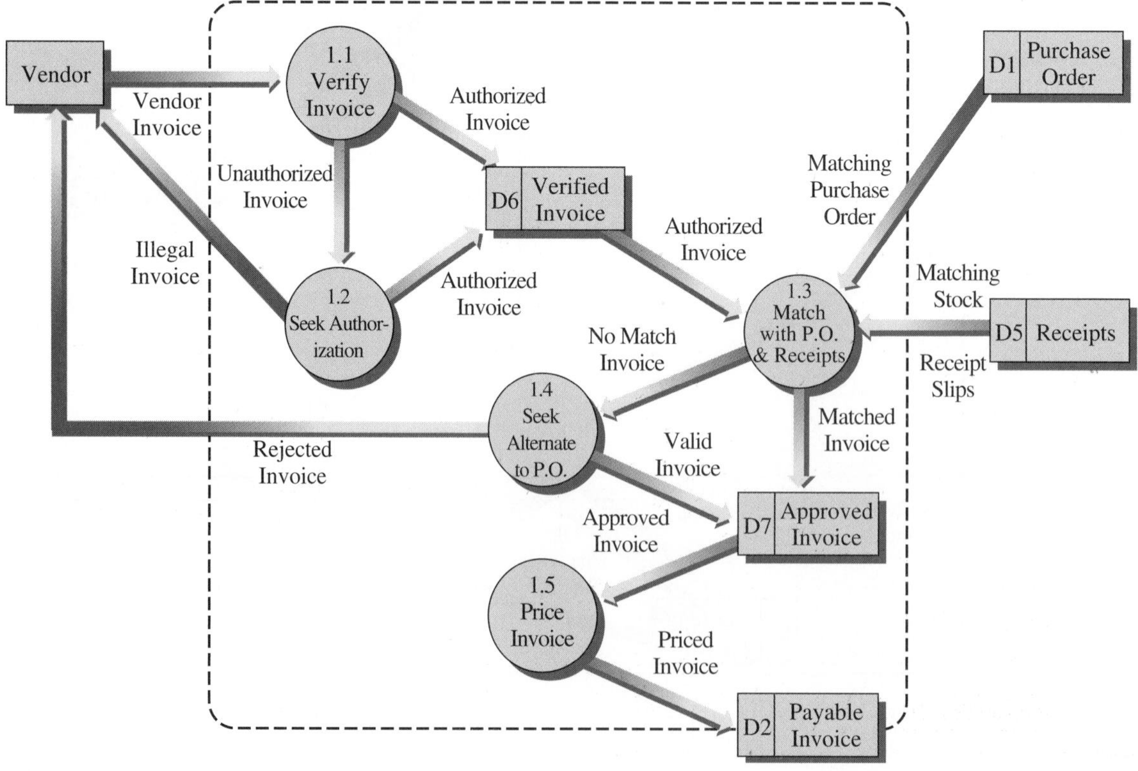

Figure 9.13(B) Second-Level Data Flow Diagram for Accounts Payable System

without implying computerization or any other form of new system implementation.

In addition to diagrams such as in Figure 9.13 (A) and (B), each external entity, process, data flow, and data store is documented as to its content. The documentation also shows how the components are related; for example, the description for the Vendor entity would include both inbound and outbound data flows. Similarly, the data store documentation includes the individual data elements that are input into the store and matches them to output descriptions.

The accuracy and completeness of a DFD model is crucial for the process of converting the Logical To-Be model into the Physical To-Be design. However, prior to commencing this physical design step, additional logical modeling is required to define the system's data elements and relationships.

A **data model** is created by logically defining the necessary and sufficient relationships among system data. The specialized terminology for the four levels of data modeling is provided here.

Data elements are the lowest unit of data. These represent individual types of data such as "purchase order number," "vendor name," or "quantity received."

Entity instances are groupings of related data elements that correspond to a single entity in the world. For example, an entity instance would be all the different data elements needed to represent an invoice.

Entities (or data entities) are groups of entity instances. As such, all the instances have the same structure because they all have the same data elements. This entity then represents a collection of like items, such as all invoices or the transactions that make up a checking account.

Data stores (or databases) are groups of entities that have a relationship. This highest level captures the relationship between entities, such as how invoices can be associated with a purchase order.

The most common approach to defining data elements in a DFD is to create a **data dictionary/directory (DD/D),** a concept introduced in Chapter 5. The goal of the data dictionary entry is to describe the data element as completely as possible; these entries should err on the side of too much information, rather than too little. This is also the place to capture whether elements are calculated, how many decimal places are required, and how an element may be referred to in external systems that reference it. Figure 9.14 shows a typical data dictionary entry for the data element Purchase Order (PO) Number.

Accounts Payable Project Data Dictionary Entry for PO Number

Label	**PO Number**
Alternate Names	Purchase Order Number. PO Number. PO#
Definition	Unique identifier for an individual purchase order: alpha character designates the division. The five digit number is assigned in sequential order at the time of creation.
Example	C07321
Field Name	PO_Num
Input Format	A##### (single alpha followed by five integers, no spaces or symbols allowed)
Output Format	Same as input format
Edit Rules	No values below 1000 allowed in numeric portion: currently using A-E as division code indicators.
Additional Notes	At conversion to the former system in 1991, numbers below 1000 were discontinued. Each division writes about 700–1,000 purchase orders per year. PO Numbers cannot be re-used.
Storage Type	Alphanumeric, no decimals
Default Value	None
Required	Each purchase order must have one PO Number.

Prepared by: JDAustin	Date: 8/27/97	Version No.: 1

Figure 9.14 Data Dictionary Sample Entry

Figure 9.15 Entity-Relationship Diagram for Invoice and PO

In addition to the detail at the data element level, the relationships between entities must be determined. A tool for capturing this information was introduced in Chapter 5: the **entity-relationship diagram**, also known as the E-R diagram or ERD. Figure 9.15 shows that the data entity "Vendor Invoice" is related to the data entity "Purchase Order" by the relation type "includes." Furthermore, the numerals next to the data entities show that a many-to-one relationship has been defined. This means that one invoice can refer to only one purchase order number but that a purchase order number can have many invoices associated with it.

The E-R diagram in Figure 9.15 thus reflects an existing business rule:

Vendor invoices cannot include items from more than one purchase order.

The motivation for such a business rule could lie in difficulties related to manual paper processing. However, IT can be used to break this rule by eliminating the problems of manually reconciling invoices to multiple purchase orders. If this decision rule is changed, the E-R diagram would be changed to reflect a new many-to-many relationship desired in the Logical To-Be system.

In summary, creating a Logical To-Be model requires the abstraction of existing business processes from the As-Is model into representations that separate data flows from processes and entities, accurately identify business rules, and capture the relationships among data. Though a demanding effort, the creation of a complete To-Be model for complex systems is our best assurance that the new system will improve upon the existing one.

The next step is to develop a physical model based on the Logical To-Be model—including all the decisions necessary to determine how the logical requirements can be met. In preparation for the following Physical To-Be model discussion, Figure 9.16 identifies relational database terminology (as used in a physical model) that corresponds to the various logical E-R model terms. For each pair of terms, a corresponding example from the accounts payable system is also provided.

Tools for Documenting the Physical To-Be System

The end deliverables from the Logical To-Be modeling process are called the **system requirements**. Any proposed system design must address the need for each requirement, provide a substitute, or justify its exclusion. Of course, the objective is to meet as many of the requirements as possible without jeopardizing project scheduling and budget constraints.

Making the Logical To-Be model "physical" requires additional analysis and a host of decisions. Tools for physical design include those that represent how processes and data stores will be partitioned, how program control will be handled, and how the database will be organized.

One of these tools is called a **program structure chart**. Figure 9.17 shows the program structure chart for a subsystem called "Handle Customer Order." Boxes represent subprocess modules, and arrows represent the flow of control during program execution. The diagram is read from top to bottom starting from the left and moving to the right. Flags (arrows with circles) come in two forms: data couples (open circle) and control flags (filled circle). Both flags direct the program modules to take action. Data couples cause action to be taken based on the data passed to the module, whereas control flags cause program execution based on the result of another module's processing. The module at the top controls all these processes and is

Logical Data Modeling Terms	Physical Data Terms	Example
Data Store	Database	Accounts Payable Database
Entity	File or Table	Purchase Order (D1)
Entity Instance	Record or Row	All information on purchase order number C07321
Data Element	Field	PO Number

Figure 9.16 Key Terms for Logical Data Modeling

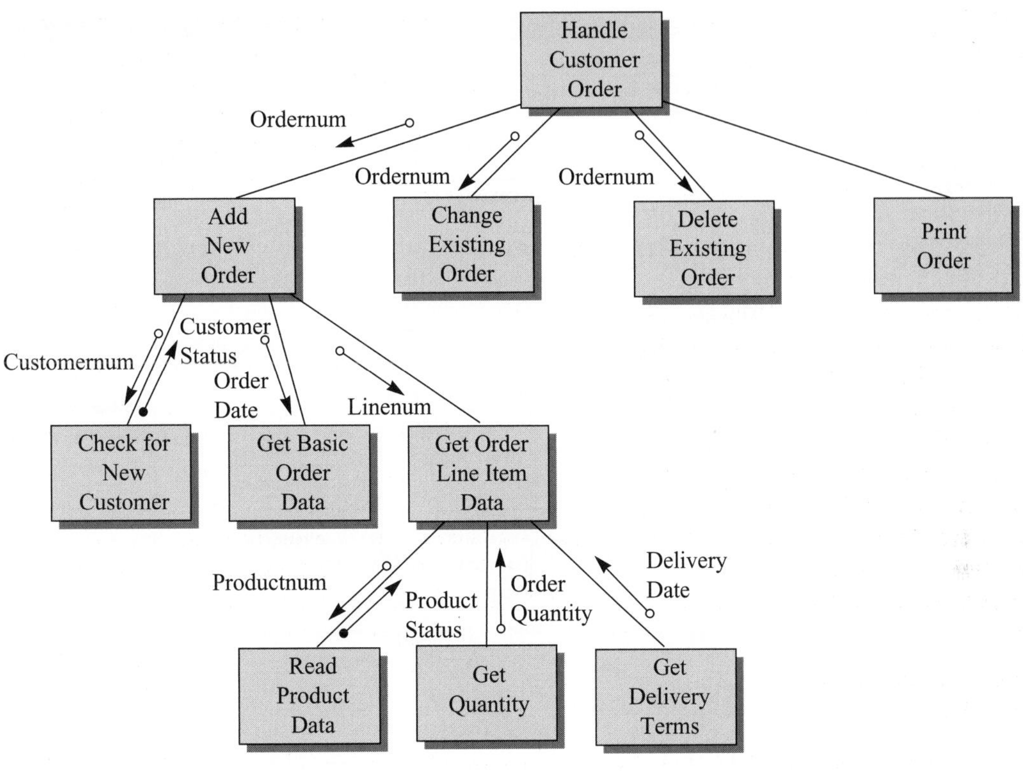

Figure 9.17 Program Structure Chart

the only means by which other program modules can interact with any of the subprocesses.

Program structure charts have rules for determining when they are complete by evaluating design factors such as cohesion and coupling (Page-Jones, 1988). Cohesion requires that each component within the system has a well-defined function and that all components cooperate to achieve an overall system goal. Coupling refers to the degree to which components are dependent on one another. Similar to DFDs, a complex system will have many program structure charts organized in a hierarchy of greater to lesser detail.

Data design issues must also be resolved for a specific database and application architecture. The number, content, and relationship of data tables and their elements must be defined. For example, a closer look at the accounts payable system reveals that purchase orders, receipts, and invoices may contain several similar data elements. An Item Master table is created into which data about all invoice items must be entered. Figure 9.18 shows the Item Master table and its relationship to other tables in the accounts payable database. The creation of this table greatly facilitates the reconciliation of receipts and purchase orders to invoices.

Our final example for the Physical To-Be model is layouts for system interfaces with end users. The most common interfaces are online screen layouts and report layouts. In the Logical To-Be modeling, the need for an interface was identified, as well as its frequency of use and information content. In the Physical To-Be modeling, the specific interface design is addressed.

Figures 9.19 and 9.20 show draft layouts for an input screen and a report for the accounts payable system. Layouts such as these are often developed in close consultation between systems designers and the end users who will be directly working with a computer display. Today's system building tools allow for easy prototyping of such interfaces by end users before the system itself is actually built. Systems today are also frequently built with some flexibility, so that the user can directly control design options for reports and data entry forms in order to adapt to changing needs of the business or the user of the report.

You have now considered some of the tools used to capture system needs, document business rules, and uncover hidden dependencies and relationships as part of the process of developing a new computer system using procedural-oriented techniques.

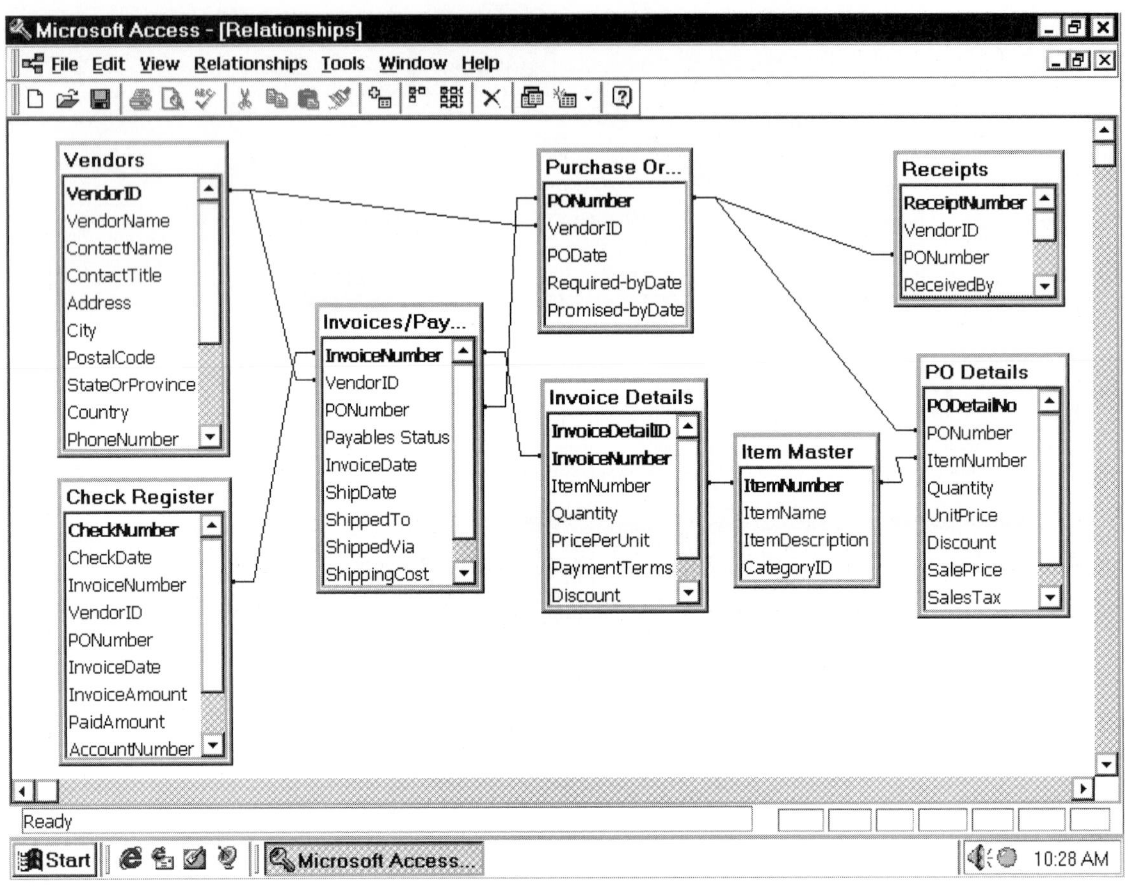

Figure 9.18 Relationships for Data Elements in Accounts Payable Tables (Access Implementation) (Screen shot reprinted with permission from Microsoft Corporation)

Object-Oriented Techniques

An object orientation (O-O) to systems development became common in the 1990s as the demand grew for client/server applications, graphical interfaces, and multimedia data. Objects can be used with any type of data, including voice, pictures, music, and video. An object approach is also well suited for applications in which processes and data are "intimately related" or real-time systems (Vessey and Glass, 1994). As described in Chapter 3, common O-O programming languages include C++, Java, and Visual Basic.

One of the primary advantages of an O-O approach is the ability to reuse objects programmed by others (see Figure 9.21). According to industry observers, successful O-O approaches can produce big payoffs by enabling businesses to quickly mock up prototype applications with user-friendly GUI interfaces. Application maintenance is also simplified.

Software objects are also a key concept behind the sharing of software for an emerging type of network-centric computing: Web services. A Web service enables computer-to-computer sharing of software modules via the Internet on an as-needed basis: A computer program (which could be another Web service) "calls" a Web service to perform a task and send back the result. This type of "dynamic binding" occurs at the time of execution and therefore greatly increases application flexibility as well as reduces the costs of software development: The computer program's owner who uses the service could pay the owner of the Web service on a subscription basis or per use. Existing examples of Web services include currency conversions (e.g., U.S. dollars to euros), credit risk analysis, and location of a product within a distribution channel. (For a discussion of the software standards, communication protocols, and development environments that enable Web services, such as .NET by Microsoft Corp., see Chapter 3.)

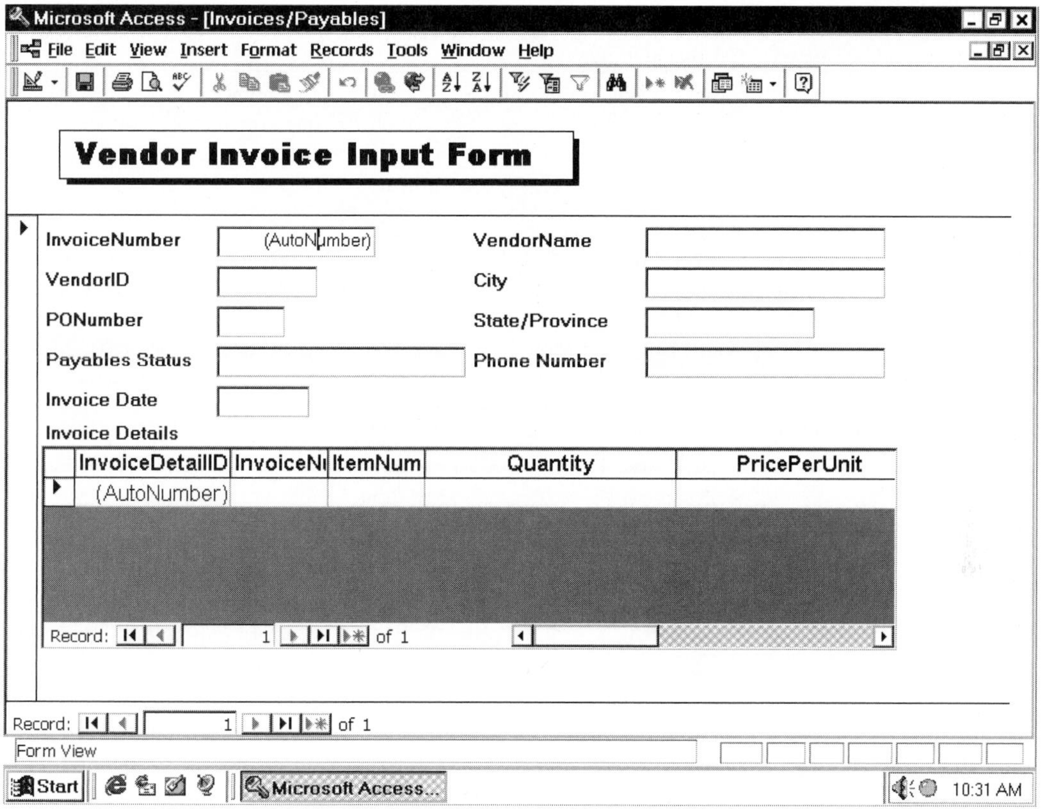

Microsoft Access - [Invoices/Payables]

File Edit View Insert Format Records Tools Window Help

Vendor Invoice Input Form

InvoiceNumber (AutoNumber) VendorName
VendorID City
PONumber State/Province
Payables Status Phone Number
Invoice Date

Invoice Details

InvoiceDetailID	InvoiceNı	ItemNum	Quantity	PricePerUnit
(AutoNumber)				

Record: 1 of 1

Record: 1 of 1

Form View

Start Microsoft Access... 10:31 AM

Figure 9.19 Input Form Layout for Vendor Invoice (Screen shot reprinted with permission from Microsoft Corporation)

Check Register

Account Number 2936

	CheckNumber	CheckDate	InvoiceNumber	VendorID	PONumber	InvoiceDate	InvoiceAmount	PaidAmount
	482441	8/3/98	C1523	178	A00702	7/20/98	1,925.50	1,925.50
	482442	8/3/98	1398752	52	C00321	7/24/98	408.92	408.92
	482443	8/3/98	E17982	104	E00052	7/23/98	1,500.00	1,200.00
	482444	8/3/98	175632	89	C00323	7/24/98	10,328.72	10,328.72
TOTAL							14,163.14	13,863.14
	482445	8/4/98	R1689	13	B00824	7/27/98	505.17	505.17
	482446	8/4/98	M568930	97	B00825	7/28/98	12,327.18	11,094.46
	482447	8/4/98	897532	152	A00704	7/28/98	765.15	765.15
	482448	8/4/98	C1527	178	D00376	7/30/98	1,534.83	1,534.83
TOTAL							15,132.33	13,899.61
MONTHLY TOTAL							29,295.47	27,762.75

Figure 9.20 Check Register Report Layout with Sample Data

	Procedural Approach	Object-Oriented Approach
Defining the Task	A team of business managers prepares a detailed design document specifying, as precisely as possible, how the program should do the task.	The O-O programmer searches alibrary of objects (prewritten chunks of software) looking for those that could be used for the business task.
The Process	Programmers divide up the design and write thousands of lines of code from scratch. If all goes well, the pieces work together as planned and the system fulfills the design requirements.	Within days, a few objects have been put together to create a bare-bones prototype. The business user gets to "test-drive" the prototype and provide feedback; by repeatedly refining and retesting the prototype, the business gets a system that fulfills the task.
Elapsed Time	Months.	Weeks.

Figure 9.21 The Promise of Object-Oriented Approaches (Based on Verity and Schwartz, 1991)

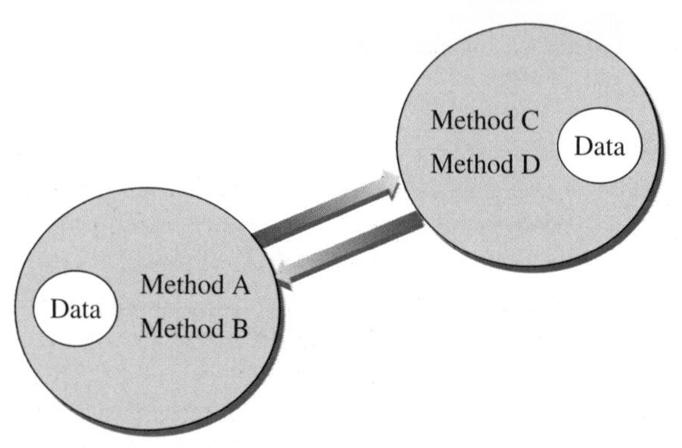

Figure 9.22 Message Passing

Core Concepts

An **object** is a person, place, or thing. However, a key difference between an entity in data modeling and an object is that data attributes as well as the methods (sometimes called operations or behaviors) that can be executed with that data are part of the object structure. The attributes of an object and its methods are *hidden* inside the object. This means that one object does not need to know the details about the attributes and methods of another object. Instead, objects communicate with each other through *messages* that specify what should be done, not how it should be done (see Figure 9.22).

Storing data and related operations together within an object is a key principle of O-O approaches, referred to as **encapsulation**. Encapsulation also means that systems developed using O-O techniques can have loosely coupled modules, which means they can be reused in other O-O applications much more easily. This is why O-O approaches should theoretically result in faster project completion times: New systems can be created from preexisting objects. In fact, vendors can sell libraries of objects for reuse in different organizations.

A second major O-O principle is **inheritance**. That is, classes of objects can inherit characteristics from other object classes. Every object is associated with a *class* of objects that share some of the same attributes and operations. Object classes are also typically arranged in a hierarchy, so that subclasses inherit attributes and operations from a superclass. For example, if a bird is a superclass, the bird object's attributes and operations could be inherited by a specific type of bird, such as a cardinal.

Unified Modeling Language (UML) for O-O Modeling

Techniques and notations for O-O analysis and design modeling have now been standardized under a Unified Modeling Language (UML).

Logical modeling begins with a use-case diagram that captures all the actors and all the actions that they initiate. (The actors are similar to external entities in a data flow diagram.) For example, the actors for a software application to support the renting of videos would include customers who are registered members, noncustomers (browsers) who could choose to become members, a billing clerk, a shipping clerk, and an inventory system. As shown in Figure 9.23, nine different functions initiated by these actors are modeled as Use Cases.

Each Use Case is also described in a text format using a standard template. Common elements in a template are Use Case Name, Actor, Goal, Description, Precondition, and Postcondition, as well as Basic, Alternate, and Exceptional

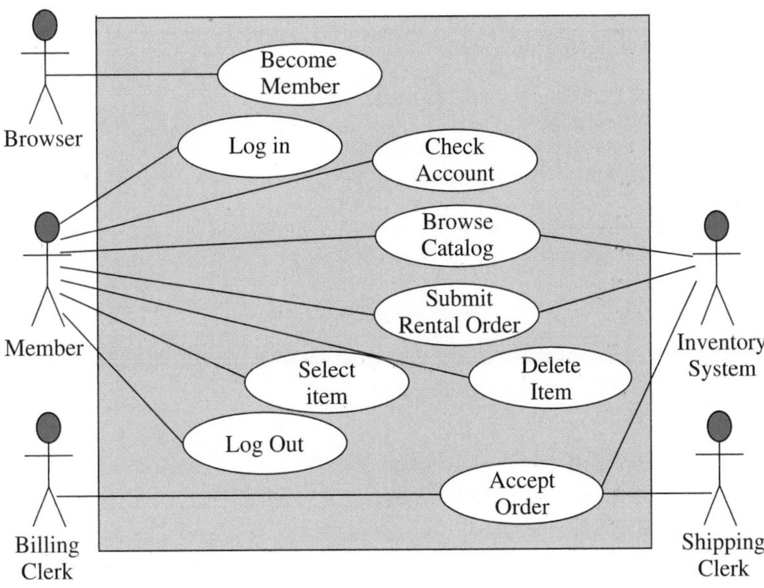

Figure 9.23 Use Case Diagram (Reprinted from Chand, 2003)

Flow events, which describe the actor's actions and the system's response. The events to be documented for one of the use cases (Become Member) in Figure 9.23 are shown in Figure 9.24.

UML also has many other types of diagrams. Three examples for a student registration system are shown in Figure 9.25:

- An extended relationship use-case diagram to logically model event flows beyond initial requirements
- A sequence diagram to capture the messages that pass between object classes
- A class diagram with each object's attributes and methods as well as a model of the relationships between object classes

INFORMATION SYSTEMS CONTROLS TO MINIMIZE BUSINESS RISKS

Suppose you and your partner with whom you have a joint savings account separately go to the bank one day to withdraw the same $500 in savings. Or suppose an inventory clerk enters a wrong part number to record the issue of an item from the storeroom, which results in an out-of-stock status, which automatically generates a purchase order to a supplier, who then begins production, and so on. These situations illustrate just some of the ways in which potential human errors when interacting with information systems can create business risks. However, they are only a small part of the potential risks associated with the use of IT.

Other common system security risks include: (1) risks from criminal acts, (2) risks due to staffing changes and project management deficiencies, and (3) risks from natural disasters. All these risks have the potential for not only dissatisfied customers, but also considerable business expenses for error correction. There is also the risk of potential losses due to lawsuits and negative publicity, which even the world's largest software vendors don't want to receive (see the sidebar entitled "Regaining Customer Trust at Microsoft").

Because of the importance of this subject, elsewhere in this textbook we will also provide discussions of potential IT-related business risks and how to manage them. For example, in Chapter 12 we provide some guidelines for managing the risks of IT projects.

Here we discuss some of the management controls to address risks that are specifically associated with the three phases of the software life cycle. Although the security and reliability issues will differ somewhat due to the nature of the software application, this list of control mechanisms provide a starting point for understanding the role of the IS professional (including project managers, analysts, and programmers) in helping to ensure that business risks have been accounted for. However, the identification of potential control risks is to a large extent a business manager's responsibility.

Use Case Name:	Become Member	
Actors:	Browser	
Goal:	Enroll the browser as a new member	
Description:	The Browser will be asked to complete a membership form. After the Browser submits the application form, the system will validate it and then add the Browser to the membership file and generate a password that is e-mailed to the Browser.	
Pre-condition:	The systems is up and the Browser is logged in as a guest	
Post-condition:	The Member password e-mailed to the Browser/ Member is logged	
Basic Flow		
	Actor action:	System response
	1. This use case begins when the Browser clicks the membership button	
		2. Display the membership form
	3. Browser completes and submits the application	
		4. Check for errors
		5. Check the membership database for prior membership
		6. Create a password
		7. Add new or updated member record to the membership database
		8. Send an e-mail to the actor with the password
		The use case ends
Alternate Flow	Prior membership handling	5.1. Update membership record
		5.2. Inform the browser
		Continue from step 6 of Basic Flow
Exception Flow	Errors in membership application	
		4.1. Identify errors
		4.2. Return errors to Browser
	4.3. Browser corrects errors	
		Continue from step 4 of Basic Flow

Figure 9.24 Become Member Use Case (Reprinted from Chand, 2003)

First we describe different types of control mechanisms that need to be considered. Then we describe specific examples of control mechanisms for error detection, prevention, and correction that need to be addressed during the three life cycle phases (Definition, Construction, and Implementation). Although these "proven" mechanisms are recommended responses, both business and IS managers also need to recognize that when new information technologies are introduced they likely will also introduce new control risks.

Types of Control Mechanisms

Control mechanisms include management policies, operating procedures, and the auditing function. Some aspects of control can be built into an information system itself,

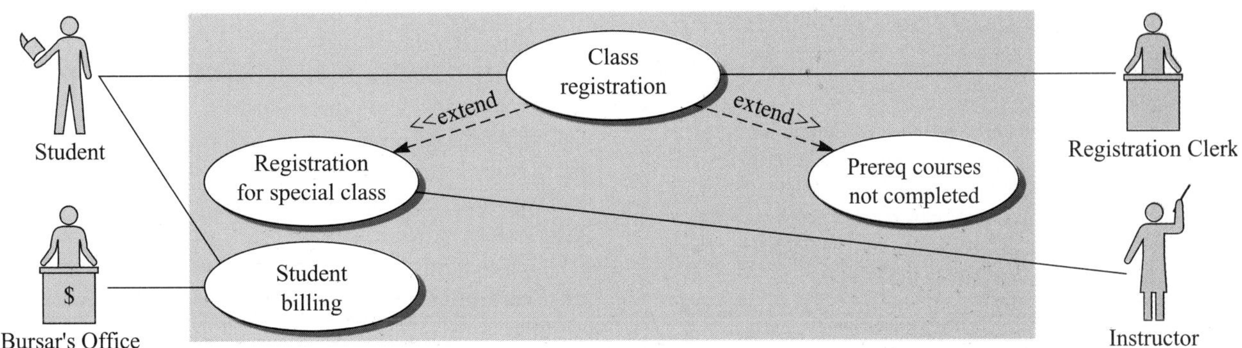

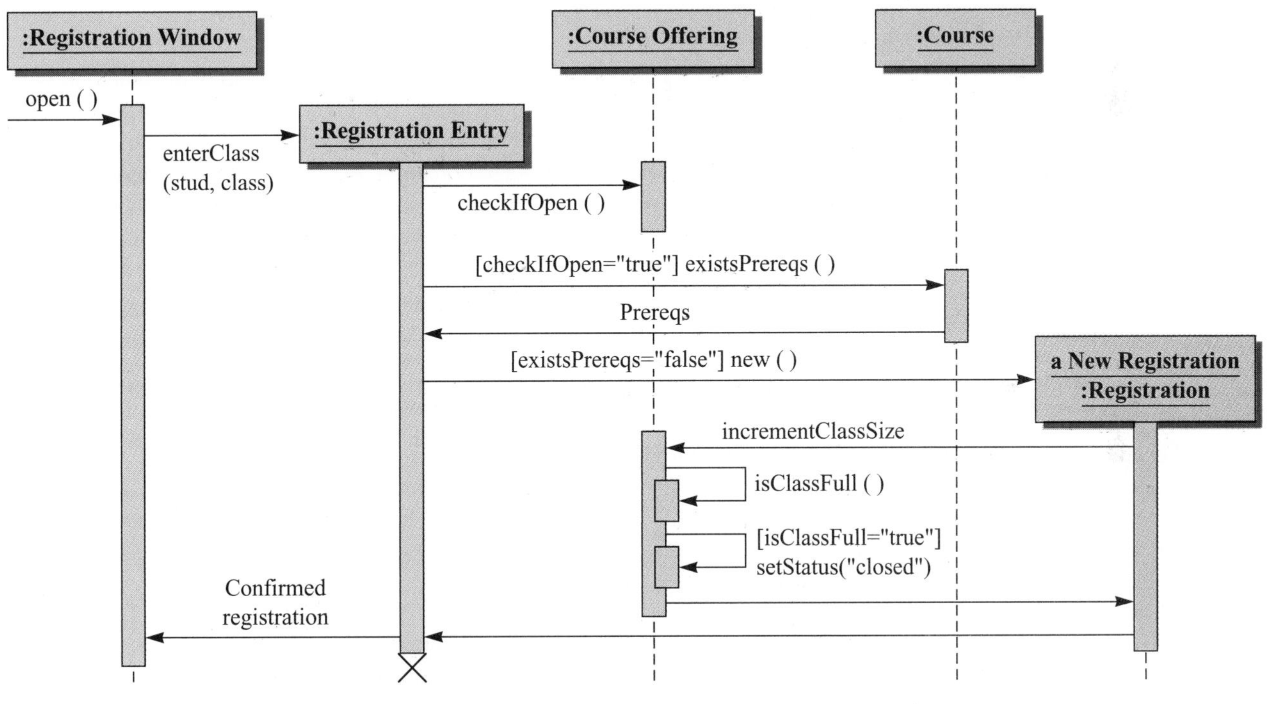

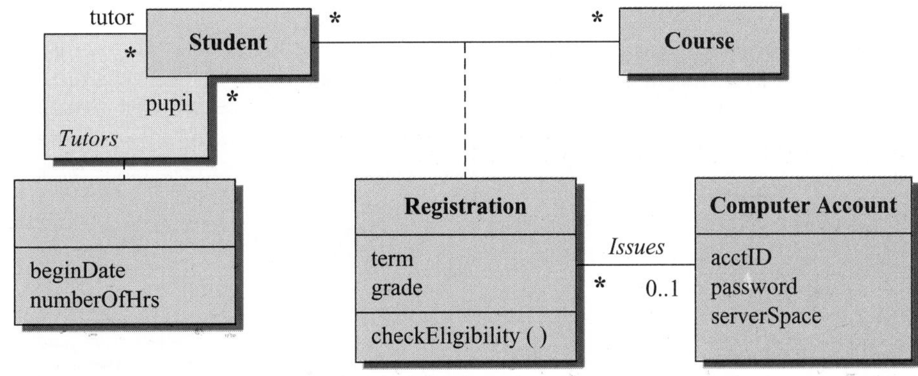

Figure 9.25 UML Diagrams for Student Registration System

REGAINING CUSTOMER TRUST AT MICROSOFT

Computer users worldwide raced to protect themselves from a malicious electronic "worm" designed to allow hackers to gain access to infected PCs. Whatever the origin of the worm, one thing is clear: The outbreak increases pressure on Microsoft to make its Windows software more reliable and secure. In 2002, Bill Gates launched an initiative, called "Trustworthy Computing," to change the way the company designs and builds software. Among other actions, Microsoft added 10 weeks of training for 8,500 of its software engineers. The company also reportedly spent more than $200 million in 2002 to improve the security of its Windows program for corporate servers.

But experts give Microsoft mixed grades for its follow-through, saying the company hasn't changed its methods enough to avoid the kinds of flaws that make attacks by viruses and worms possible in the first place. Ultimately, that could hurt Microsoft where it matters most–in the corporate wallet.

[Adapted from Guth and Bank, 2003]

whereas others are the result of day-to-day business practices and management decisions. Information system controls, for example, are needed to maintain data integrity, allow only authorized access, ensure proper system operation, and protect against malfunctions, power outages, and disasters. Throughout the systems development process, the needs for specific controls are identified and control mechanisms are developed to address these needs. Some mechanisms are implemented during the system design, coding, or implementation. Others become part of the routine operation of the system, such as backups and authorization security, and still others involve the use of manual business practices and management policies, such as formal system audits. Figure 9.26 shows some of the control approaches usually employed in the indicated phases of the systems life cycle.

Security controls related to the technology infrastructure—such as backup power supplies, network access control, and firewall protection—are typically the purview of the IS organization. In addition, IS developers will include some standard controls in all applications. However, specifying checks and balances to ensure accurate data entry and handling is a business manager's responsibility. Managers must carefully identify what are valid data, what errors might be made while handling data, what nontechnical security risks are present, and what potential business losses could result from inaccurate or lost data.

Some new technologies, such as advanced software tools for system testing, have improved an organization's control processes, whereas other new technologies (such as Web applications) have introduced new control risks. The increase in distributed computing applications over the past two decades in general has significantly increased a company's reliance on network transmission of data and software—which requires additional technical and managerial controls (Hart and Rosenberg, 1995). Below we discuss only some of the most common control mechanisms that apply to a wide range of application development situations.

Controls in the Definition and Construction Phases

In the initial two phases of the systems life cycle, the accurate and reliable performance of the system can be assured by the use of standards, embedded controls, and thorough testing.

Methodology Standards The reliable performance of a system depends upon how well it was designed and constructed. No amount of automated checks can override errors in the software itself.

Life Cycle Phase	Control Mechanism
Definition and Construction	• Methodology Standards • Validation Rules and Calculations • System Testing
Implementation	• Security • Backup and Recovery • Auditing Roles

Figure 9.26 Pre- and Post-Installation Controls

One way to avoid errors is to develop standard, repeatable, and possibly reusable methods and techniques for system developers. The use of standard programming languages and equipment means that systems developers will be more familiar with the tools and will be less likely to make mistakes. A common method is to create a library of frequently used functions (such as calculation of net present value or a sales forecasting model) that different information systems can utilize. Such functions can then be developed and tested with great care and reused as needed, saving development time and reducing the likelihood of design and programming flaws. Most organizations also have standards for designing user interfaces, such as screen and report layout rules and guidelines.

The importance of standards also extends to the documentation of the system during construction and the following period of maintenance and upgrades. If future programmers do not have access to systems documentation that is complete and accurate, they could be unaware of prior changes. Documentation for the system's users also needs to be complete and accurate so that system inputs are not incorrectly captured and system outputs are not incorrectly used.

Validation Rules and Calculations Each time a data element is updated, the new value can be checked against a legitimate set or range of values permitted for that data. This check can be performed in each application program where these data can be changed (e.g., in a payables adjustment program that modifies previously entered vendor invoices) and in the database where they are stored. Edit rules are also used to ensure that data are not missing, that data are of a valid size and type, and that data match with other stored values.

Providing a screen display with associated data can be a very useful edit check. For example, when a vendor number is entered, the program can display the associated name and address. The person inputting or modifying data can then visually verify the vendor information. Edit rules can also ensure that only numbers are entered for numeric data, that only feasible codes are entered, or that some calculation based on a modified data value is valid. These edit checks are integrity rules that control the data's validity.

Various calculations can be performed to validate processing. Batch totals that calculate the sum of certain data in a batch of transactions can be computed both manually before processing and by the computer during processing; discrepancies suggest the occurrence of data entry errors such as transposition of digits. Though they are not foolproof, such approaches, along with automated edits, go a long way toward assuring valid input.

A **check digit** can be appended to critical identifying numbers such as general ledger account numbers or vendor numbers; the value of this check digit is based on the other digits in the number. This digit can be used to quickly verify that at least a valid, if not correct, code has been entered, and it can catch most common errors.

Business managers and their staffs are responsible for defining the legitimate values for data and where control calculations would be important as a part of the information captured in the data dictionary. Furthermore, business managers must set policy to specify if checks can be overridden and who can authorize overrides. Validation rules should permit business growth and expansion, yet reduce the likelihood of erroneous data.

System Testing Certainly the most common and effective of all IS controls is complete system testing. Each program must be tested individually and in combination with the other programs in the application. Managers develop test data that have known results. Programs are run with typical and atypical data, correct and erroneous data, and the actual results are compared to what should be produced. Testing occurs not only when systems are initially developed, but also when systems are modified. (See Chapter 10 for a description of additional roles played by users when testing a system.)

Controls in the Implementation Phase

Not all the elements necessary to assure proper systems operation can be built into an application. Avoiding and detecting inappropriate access or use, providing data backups and system recovery capabilities, and formally auditing the system are all ongoing control mechanisms. As mentioned earlier, many application-level controls work in concert with managerial controls. User-managers are responsible for being familiar with any firm-wide control mechanisms and identifying when additional ones are needed for a specific application.

Security The unauthorized use of data can result in a material loss, such as the embezzlement of funds, or in losses that are harder to measure, such as the disclosure of sensitive data. In any case, the security of data and computers is necessary so that employees, customers, shareholders, and others can be confident that their interactions with the organization are confidential and the business's assets are safe.

Security measures are concerned with both logical and physical access. Logical access controls are concerned with whether users can run an application, whether they can read a file or change it, and whether they can change the access that others have. Managers work with systems personnel to identify and maintain appropriate authorization levels based on work roles and business needs. Two mechanisms for controlling logical access are authentication and authorization (Hart and Rosenberg, 1995):

Authentication involves establishing that the person requesting access is who he or she appears to be. This is typically accomplished by the use of a unique user identifier and a private password.

Authorization involves determining whether or not authenticated users have access to the requested resources. This is typically accomplished by a computer check for permission rights to access a given resource.

Encryption techniques are used to encode data that is transmitted across organizational boundaries. Data may be stored in an encrypted form and then decrypted by the application. Unless a user knows the decryption algorithm, an encrypted file will be unreadable.

The physical security of specific computers and data processing centers must also be established. Badge readers; voice, fingerprint, and retina recognition; or combination locks are common. Formal company statements about computer ethics raise awareness of the sensitivity of data privacy and the need to protect organizational data. When combined with knowledge of the use of transaction or activity logs that record the user ID, network location, time-stamp, and function or data accessed, many security violations could be discouraged.

Because no security system is foolproof, detection methods to identify security breaches are necessary. Administrative practices to help deter computer security abuses have been compiled by Hoffer and Straub (1989). Detection methods include:

- Hiding special instructions in sensitive programs that log identifying data about users
- Analysis of the amount of computer time used by individuals
- Analysis of system activity logs for unusual patterns of use

With the rise of end-user computing and use of the Internet, additional risks due to inappropriate behaviors while using these tools have emerged, as well as issues stemming from work-related use of home PCs. Some specific end-user computing risks and controls are discussed in Chapter 13. Today, organizations are developing similar controls to manage intranets and access to external Web sites from intranets.

Backup and Recovery The ultimate protection against many system failures is to have a backup copy. Periodically a file can be copied and saved in a separate location such as a bank vault. Then, when a file becomes contaminated or destroyed, the most recent version can be restored. Of course, any changes since the last copy was made will not appear. Thus, organizations often also keep transaction logs (a chronological history of changes to each file) so these changes can be automatically applied to a backup copy to bring the file up to current status.

A common flaw in backup plans is storing the file backup in the same location as the master file. If stored in the same location, a backup is no more likely to survive a fire, flood, or earthquake than its source file. A secure, off-site location for the backup must be provided, along with a foolproof tracking system.

Some organizations (such as airlines, banks, and telephone networks) can operate only if their online computer systems are working. One approach is to provide redundant systems and operations that "mirror" the production system and data located at a distant facility. This improves the chances of an effective recovery from a widespread power or network outage or a natural disaster. If data recovery processing via another location is immediately available, these locations are known as "hot sites."

Managers and IS professionals together need to determine how frequently backup copies are needed, the business cost of recovering files from backup copies, and how much should be spent on specialized backup resources. As with any security procedure, the ongoing backup and recovery costs need to be in line with the potential organizational benefits and risks.

Auditing Roles Critical business processes are subject to periodic formal audits to assure that the processes operate within parameters. As more and more organizations have become dependent on information systems in order to operate their business, the importance of IS auditing has increased. IS auditing is still frequently referred to as **EDP auditing**—a name chosen when the term electronic data processing was used to refer to computer operations. EDP auditors use a variety of methods to ensure the correct processing of data, including compliance tests, statistical sampling, and embedded auditing methods.

Compliance tests check that systems builders use high-quality systems development procedures that lead to properly functioning systems. Statistical sampling of a portion of databases can identify abnormalities that indicate systematic problems or security breaches. Embedded auditing methods include reporting triggers programmed into a system that are activated by certain processing events. The flagged records are then analyzed to determine if errors or security breaches are occurring in the system.

The most commonly used EDP auditing technique in the past has been an **audit trail**. Audit trails trace transactions from the time of input through all the processes and reports in which the transaction data are used. Audit trail records typically include program names, user name or user ID, input location and date/time stamps, as well as the transaction itself. An audit trail can help identify where errors are introduced or where security breaches might have occurred.

Managers need to participate in the identification of elements that should be captured in the audit trail to detect errors and assure compliance with all relevant laws and regulations. Furthermore, the frequency and extent of formal information system auditing is a management decision that should take into account the system's breadth and role, its relationship to other business processes, and the potential risks to the firm.

SUMMARY

Systems thinking is a hallmark of good management in general. Systems thinking is also core to many basic concepts on which modern information systems are defined, constructed, and implemented. Three systems characteristics especially important for IS work are: determining the system boundary, component decomposition, and designing system interfaces.

This chapter also introduced a generic life cycle model for software systems as well as some of the processes and techniques for systems analysis and design used by IS professionals for developing software. Procedurally oriented techniques for structured system development include notation systems for modeling processes and data separately. Object-oriented (O-O) techniques, including a new modeling language (UML), have become more prevalent as newer software applications have required graphical user interfaces, multimedia data, and support for "real-time" transactions. O-O approaches will also be important in the development of Web services. Common IS control mechanisms to minimize business risks due to internal and external threats are described; many of these controls need to be identified with the help of business managers and then addressed during the development and maintenance of an information system.

REVIEW QUESTIONS

1. Define the term *system*. Give an example of a business system and use a context diagram to show its boundary, environment, inputs, and outputs.
2. Define the term *subsystem*. Give an example of a business subsystem and identify some subsystems with which it relates.
3. Define the term *business process reengineering* and describe its importance for IS work.
4. Describe how logical and physical representations of a To-Be system will differ.
5. Describe the relationships between a context diagram, as in Figure 9.11, and the top-level and second-level diagrams of a data flow diagram, as in Figure 9.13(A) and (B).
6. What is a data dictionary and why is it important?
7. Why are software objects more "reusable" than other types of computer code?
8. Compare a context diagram (using DFD modeling) and a use case diagram (using UML); what is the same and what is different?
9. Briefly describe some common information system controls that need to be implemented by business managers, not IS professionals.
10. What is an audit trail and why is it a useful mechanism for controlling business risks due to an information system?

DISCUSSION QUESTIONS

1. Explain and give an example that supports the following statement: Each time we change characteristics of one or more of the components of the organization (organization structure, people, business processes, information technology), we must consider compensating changes in the other components.
2. Explain the function of hierarchical decomposition in systems analysis and design and discuss the reasons for viewing and analyzing systems in this way.
3. Why do informal systems arise? Why should systems analysts be aware of them?
4. Some observers have characterized business process reengineering (BPR) as evolutionary, others as revolutionary. Develop an argument to support one of these sides.
5. Explain why many companies were unable to implement new cross-functional processes that were

identified by BPR project teams in the early 1990s, before ERP packages became widely available.

6. Describe why analysts begin with the As-Is system, rather than starting with the design of a To-Be system.
7. Develop a context diagram and a top-level DFD to model the data flows involved in registering for classes at your college or university. Then model the student registration system in a use case diagram and write a textual description for one of the use cases.
8. Web services have been called a second wave of net-centric computing that will have broad implications for software development approaches in the future. Develop an argument to support or refute this viewpoint.
9. Explain why some organizations have adopted more rigid control mechanisms in recent years and whether or not you think they are justified, given the added costs to implement them.

CHAPTER 10
METHODOLOGIES FOR CUSTOM SOFTWARE DEVELOPMENT

UNTIL THE LATE 1980S, SOFTWARE APPLICATIONS THAT WERE CUSTOM-developed systems for a specific firm were very common. If an organization had its own information systems (IS) professionals, the organization's own IS staff most likely developed these custom applications in-house. If an organization did not have the resources (or IS expertise) to develop custom applications, an outside vendor would be employed either to provide IS contract personnel on a temporary basis or to completely develop the custom software for the organization. As we will discuss in Chapter 11, today's firms are likely to purchase software packages whenever they can. However, custom software development skills are still in high demand in manufacturing and service firms, as well as in software vendor and consulting firms.

In this chapter we first describe two common approaches to developing customized applications: a traditional systems development life cycle (SDLC) approach and an evolutionary prototyping approach. Although our methodology descriptions assume that the IT project is being managed in-house, most of what we describe holds true for application development approaches used today within software houses. A key difference, of course, is that when custom applications are being built for a specific organization—rather than for many organizations—business managers and end users who will use the application on a day-to-day basis will play key roles in the development process.

Next we describe two newer development approaches: rapid application development (RAD) and an "agile" development approach, including some characteristics of an "extreme programming" approach. The chapter closes with a brief description of some of the special issues related to developing custom software using external contract (outsourced) staff.

SYSTEMS DEVELOPMENT LIFE CYCLE METHODOLOGY

In Chapter 9 we introduced three generic phases of a systems **life cycle process**: Definition, Construction, and Implementation. We turn now to a detailed discussion of these three phases in the development of a new software application using a highly structured approach. This traditional life cycle process for developing customized applications is referred to as the **systems development life cycle (SDLC)**.

The SDLC approach also provides a baseline for understanding what is involved in developing an application system, whether by IS professionals employed by a manufacturing or service firm, by IS professionals employed by a software development firm or consultancy, or by some combination of internal and external IS specialists. The processes for purchasing a software package (described in Chapter 11) or developing an application as an end user (described in Chapter 13) will also be better understood after becoming familiar with the traditional SDLC approach.

The SDLC Steps

The generic SDLC methodology includes three phases and eight steps. This template is shown in Figure 10.1. The specific steps in this figure can vary across organizations. For example, an organization could have developed its own version of an SDLC methodology that includes a total of five steps or even ten steps. Nevertheless, an organization's internally developed SDLC methodology should also essentially correspond to the steps for each of the three phases in Figure 10.1.

The overall thrusts of the three phases of the SDLC are quite straightforward. The Definition phase is critical: It defines precisely what the system must do in sufficient detail for IS specialists to build the right system. In the Construction phase, the IS specialists produce a working system according to the specifications set forth in the earlier phase. These include many of the structured techniques—data flow diagrams, E-R models, structure charts—and IS control concerns discussed in Chapter 9.

A key characteristic of the SDLC approach is extensive formal reviews by project team members and business management at the end of each major step. Without formal approvals, the project team cannot begin the next step of the methodology. The completion of each phase therefore represents a milestone in the development of the system.

In the Implementation phase, the new system is installed, becomes operational within the organization, and is maintained (modified) as needed so that it continues to reflect the changing needs of the organization. These last two steps—Operations and Maintenance—are included in the life cycle as a way to formally recognize that large custom applications are major capital investments for an organization that will have ongoing operational and maintenance costs.

In large organizations in the 1980s it was not uncommon to find many custom software applications that were more than a decade old. These systems had often been modified multiple times—the Maintenance step—in response to the organization's changing requirements. As we will learn later in this chapter, it often took a major external crisis, such as potential system failures due to the program's handling of the year 2000, for the organization to invest in a replacement system after having made significant dollar investments in these systems over many years.

In Figure 10.2 a typical breakdown of IS costs is presented for these three phases for a medium-sized project with a total development cost of $1 million. This breakdown does not include costs that a business unit might bear for training or replacing a business manager who is working on the project team. As can be seen from this hypothetical example, the Requirements Definition step is the costliest. As will be emphasized in the following sections, this is a hallmark of the SDLC approach: Extensive, upfront time is spent determining the business requirements for the new custom software application in order to avoid expensive

Definition Phase
- Feasibility Analysis
- Requirements Definition

Construction Phase
- System Design
- System Building
- System Testing

Implementation Phase
- Installation
- Operations
- Maintenance

Figure 10.1 The Systems Development Life Cycle

Development Activities	Percentage of Total Cost	Dollar Cost
Definition Phase		
Feasibility analysis	5	$ 50,000
Requirements definition	25	250,000
Construction Phase		
System design	15	150,000
Coding and initial testing	15	150,000
System testing	13	130,000
Documentation and procedures	12	120,000
Implementation Phase		
Installation planning, data cleanup, and conversion	15	150,000
Total	100%	$1,000,000

Figure 10.2 Cost Breakdown for $1 Million SDLC Project

changes later in the process due to inadequate definition of the requirements.

Most SDLC methodologies result in a lot of documentation. In the early steps, before any computer code is even written, the specific deliverables from each step are written materials. An SDLC step is not complete until a formal review of this documentation takes place.

The traditional SDLC approach has often been referred to as the "waterfall" model (Boehm, 1981): The outputs from one step are inputs to the next step. However, in practice, an organization could have to take more of a "spiral" approach, returning to earlier steps to change a requirement or a design as needed. Later in this chapter (see the section entitled "Newer Approaches") we will discuss an approach that builds on both the waterfall and spiral concepts: rapid application development (RAD).

Initiating New Systems Projects

Organizations use a number of approaches to decide which new applications to invest in. In many organizations the process begins with the submission of a formal proposal by a business department. Some large organizations require that these proposals first be reviewed and prioritized by a committee at the department or division level. When substantial investments and resources are involved, the department might be required to wait for an annual approval and prioritization process to occur. Very large, high-budget projects could also require approval by the corporation's top management executive committee and board of directors. Some organizations require that a business sponsor, rather than an IS manager, present his or her proposals to these approval bodies. Smaller, low-budget projects might be approved on a much more frequent basis with fewer hurdles.

At a minimum, a proposal that describes the need for the software application with a preliminary statement of potential benefits and scope will be prepared by business management or an IS manager assigned to a particular business unit (an account manager). The extent to which IS professionals need to be involved in this preliminary phase varies greatly across organizations.

Once the proposal has been approved and IS resources are formally assigned to the project, the formal SDLC process begins. For some projects, the initial approval might only be an endorsement to proceed with a feasibility analysis, after which additional approvals will be required. The documents for the feasibility analysis then become the basis for a decision on whether or not to invest in the custom application.

Descriptions of each of the eight steps outlined in Figure 10.1 follow.

Definition Phase

Feasibility Analysis For this first step of the SDLC process, a project manager and one or more systems analysts are typically assigned to work with business managers to prepare a thorough analysis of the feasibility of the proposed system. Three different types of feasibility will be assessed: *economic, operational*, and *technical*.

The IS analysts work closely with the sponsoring manager who proposed the system and/or other business managers to define in some detail what the new system will do, what outputs it will produce, what inputs it will accept, how the input data might be obtained, and what databases might be required. An important activity is to define the scope or boundaries of the system—precisely who would it serve, what it would do, as well as what it would not do—and what data processing would and would not be included. The IS analyst is primarily responsible for assessing the system's technical feasibility, based on a knowledge of current and emerging technological solutions, the IT expertise of in-house personnel, and the anticipated infrastructure needed to both develop and support the proposed system. The business manager is primarily responsible for assessing the system's operational feasibility. In some organizations, business analysts who are knowledgeable about IT, but are not IT professionals, play a lead role in this process.

Both business managers and IS analysts work together to prepare a cost/benefit analysis of the proposed system to determine the economic feasibility. Typical benefits include costs to be avoided, such as cost savings from personnel, space, and inventory reductions; new revenues to be created; and other ways the system could contribute business value overall. However, for many applications today, some or all of the major benefits might be intangible benefits; they are hard to measure in dollars. Examples of intangible benefits include better customer service, more accurate or more comprehensive information for decision making, quicker processing, or better employee morale. (For a further discussion of system justification, see the section later in this chapter entitled "Managing an SDLC Project.")

The IS analyst takes primary responsibility for establishing the development costs for the project. This requires the development of a project plan that includes an estimated schedule in workweeks or months for each step in the development process and an overall budget estimate through the installation of the project. Estimating these project costs and schedules is especially difficult when new technologies and large system modules are involved. (Note that these costs usually do not include user department costs, which might be substantial during both the Definition and Implementation phases.)

The deliverable of the Feasibility Analysis step is a document of typically 10 to 20 pages that includes a short executive overview and summary of recommendations, a description of what the system would do and how it would operate, an analysis of the costs and benefits of the proposed system, and a plan for the development of the system. Sometimes referred to as a systems proposal document, this document is typically first discussed and agreed to by both the executive sponsor and the IS project manager and then reviewed by a management committee that has authority for system approvals and prioritization.

Before additional steps are undertaken, both IS and business managers need to carefully consider whether to commit the resources required to develop the proposed system. The project costs up to this point have typically been modest in relation to the total project costs, so the project can be abandoned at this stage without the organization having spent much money or expended much effort. As described earlier, the approval of a large system request might not actually occur until after the completion of a formal feasibility analysis. For large projects, the executive sponsor of the application is typically responsible for the presentation of a business case for the system before the approving body.

Requirements Definition If the document produced from the feasibility analysis receives the necessary organizational approvals, the Requirements Definition step is begun. Both the development of the "right system" and developing the "system right" are highly dependent on how well the organization conducts this step in the SDLC process. This requires heavy participation from user management. If this step is not done well, the wrong system might be designed or even built, leading to both disruptive and costly changes later in the process.

Although in the past new systems often automated what had been done manually, most of today's systems are developed to do new things, to do old things in entirely new ways, or both. Although the executive sponsor plays a key role in envisioning how IT can be used to enable change in what the sponsor's people do and how they do it, the sponsor is often not the manager who helps to define the new system's requirements. Rather, the sponsoring manager must make sure that those who will use the system and those managers responsible for the use of the new system are involved in defining its detailed requirements.

Also referred to as systems analysis or logical design, the requirements definition focuses on processes, data flows, and data interrelationships rather than a specific physical implementation. The systems analyst(s) is responsible for making sure these requirements are elicited in sufficient detail to pass on to those who will build the system. It might appear easy to define what a system is to do at the level of detail with which system users often describe systems. However, it is quite difficult to define what the new system is to do in the detail necessary to write the computer code for it. Many business applications are incredibly complex, supporting different functions for many people or processes that cross multiple business units or geographic locations. Although each detail might be known by someone, no one person knows what a new system should do in the detail necessary to describe it. This step can therefore be very time-consuming and requires analysts who are skilled in asking the right questions of the right people and in conceptual system design techniques. In addition, there might be significant disagreements among the business managers about the nature of the application requirements. It is then the responsibility of the IS project manager and analysts to help the relevant user community reach a consensus. Sometimes outside consultants are used to facilitate this process.

Furthermore, some new applications are intended to provide decision support for tasks that are ill-structured. In these situations, managers often find it difficult to define precisely what information they need and how they will use the application to support their decision making. Information needs might also be highly variable and dynamic over time. As noted in Chapter 9, many of today's large systems development projects might also arise in conjunction with reengineering an organization's business processes. Redesign of the organization, its work processes and the development of a new computer system could go on in parallel. The ideal is to first redesign the process, but even then work processes are seldom defined at the level of detail required for a new business application.

Because defining the requirements for a system is such a difficult and a crucial task, analysts rely on a number of techniques and approaches. Examples of these were described in detail in Chapter 9. Later in this chapter we also describe an evolutionary prototyping approach that can be used to help define systems requirements—for the user interface in particular.

The deliverable for the Requirements Definition step is a comprehensive *system requirements document* that contains detailed descriptions of the system inputs and outputs and the processes used to convert the input data into these outputs. It typically includes several hundred pages with formal diagrams and output layouts, such as shown in Chapter 9. This document also includes a revised cost/benefit analysis of the defined system and a revised plan for the remainder of the development project.

The system requirements document is the major deliverable of the Definition phase of the SDLC. Although IS analysts are typically responsible for drafting and revising the requirements specifications document, business managers are responsible for making sure that the written requirements are correct and complete. Thus, all relevant participants need to carefully read and critique this document for inaccuracies and omissions. Case studies have shown that when key user representatives do not give enough attention to this step, systems deficiencies are likely to be the result.

The deliverable from this step is typically subject to approval by business managers for whom the system is being built as well as by appropriate IS managers. Once formal approvals have been received, the system requirements are considered to be fixed. Any changes typically must go through a formal approval process, requiring similar sign-offs and new systems project estimates. All key participants therefore usually spend considerable time reviewing these documents for accuracy and completeness.

Construction Phase

System Design In this step, IS specialists design the physical system, based on the conceptual requirements document from the Definition phase. In system design, one decides what hardware and systems software to use to operate the system, designs the structure and content of the system's database(s), and defines the processing modules (programs) that will comprise the system and their interrelationships. A good design is critical because the technical quality of the system cannot be added later; it must be designed into the system from the beginning.

As shown in Figure 10.3, a quality system includes adequate controls to ensure that its data are accurate and that it provides accurate outputs. It provides an audit trail that allows one to trace transactions from their source and confirm that they were correctly handled. A quality system is highly reliable; when something goes wrong, the capability to recover and resume operation without lost data or excessive effort is planned for. It is also robust—insensitive to minor variations in its inputs and environment. It provides for interfaces with related systems so that common data can be passed back and forth. It is highly efficient, providing fast response, efficient input and output, efficient storage of data, and efficient use of computer resources. A quality system is also flexible and well documented for both users and IS specialists. It includes options for inputs and outputs compatible with its hardware and software environment and can be easily changed or maintained. Finally, it is user-friendly: It is easy to learn and easy to use, and it never makes the user feel stupid or abandoned.

Accurate	Reliable
Auditable	Robust
Changeable	Secure
Efficient	User friendly
Flexible	Well documented

Figure 10.3 Characteristics of High Quality Systems

To ensure that the new system design is accurate and complete, IS specialists often "walk through" the design first with their colleagues and then with knowledgeable business managers and end users, using graphical models such as those described in Chapter 9. This type of technique can help the users understand what new work procedures might need to be developed in order to implement the new system.

The major deliverable of the System Design step is a detailed design document that will be given to programmers. Models created by various development tools, such as diagrams of the system's physical structure, are also an important part of the deliverable. The documentation of the system will also include detailed descriptions of all databases and detailed specifications for each program in the system. Also included is a plan for the remaining steps in the Construction phase. Again, both users and IS managers typically approve this document before the system is actually built.

System Building Two activities are involved in building the system—producing the computer programs and developing the databases and files to be used by the system. IS specialists perform these activities. The major involvements of users are to answer questions of omission and to help interpret requirements and design documents. The procurement of any new hardware and support software (including the database management system selection) is also part of this step, which entails consultation with IS planners and operations personnel.

System Testing Testing is a major effort that might require as much time as writing the code for the system. This step involves testing by IS specialists, followed by user testing. First, each module of code must be tested. Then the modules are assembled into subsystems and tested. Finally, the subsystems are combined and the entire system is integration tested. Problems might be detected at any level of testing, but correction of the problems becomes more difficult as more components are integrated, so experienced project managers build plenty of time into the project schedule to allow for problems during integration testing.

The IS specialists are responsible for producing a high-quality system that also performs efficiently.

The system's users are also responsible for a critical type of testing—*user acceptance testing*. Its objective is to make sure that the system performs reliably and does what it is supposed to do in a user environment. This means that users must devise test data and procedures that completely test the system and that they must then carry out this extensive testing process. Plans for this part of the application testing should begin after the Definition phase. Case studies have shown that end-user participation in the testing phase can contribute to end-user commitment to the new system, as well as provide the basis for initial end-user training.

Both user and IS management must sign off on the system, accepting it for production use, before it can be installed. **Documentation** of the system is also a major mechanism of communication among the various members of the project team during the development process: Information systems are simply too complex to understand when they are described verbally.

Once the users sign off on this part of the testing, any further changes typically need to be budgeted outside of the formal development project—that is, they become maintenance requests.

Implementation Phase

The initial success of the Implementation phase is highly dependent on business manager roles. Systems projects frequently involve major changes to the jobs of the people who will use the system, and these changes must be anticipated and planned for well before the actual Implementation phase begins. Ideas for user training as well as other "best practices" for change management will be discussed in a subsequent project management chapter (Chapter 12).

Installation Both IS specialists and users play critical roles in the Installation step, which includes building the files and databases and converting relevant data from one or more old systems to the new system. Depending on the extent to which the data already exist within the organization, some of the data conversion burden might also fall on users. In particular, data in older systems could be inaccurate and incomplete, requiring considerable user effort to "clean it up." The clean-up process, including the entering of revised data, can be a major effort for user departments. Sometimes the clean-up effort can be accomplished in advance. In other situations, however, the data clean-up is done as part of the new system implementation. This means users that have a lot of data verifications to do and conversion edits to resolve, sometimes without the benefit of additional staff, as they also learn the new system.

Another crucial installation activity is training the system's end users, as well as training other users affected by the new system. If this involves motivating people to make major changes to their behavior patterns, planning for this motivation process needs to start well before the Implementation phase. User participation in the earlier phases can also help the users prepare for this crucial step. Similarly, user training needs to be planned and carefully scheduled so that people are prepared to use the system when it is installed but not trained so far in advance that they forget what they learned. If user resistance to proposed changes is anticipated, this potential situation needs to be addressed during training or earlier.

Installing the hardware and software is the IS organization's responsibility. This can be a challenge when the new system involves technology that is new to the IS organization, especially if the technology is on the "bleeding edge." The major problems in system installation, however, usually lie in adapting the organization to the new system—changing how people do their work.

Converting to the new system might be a difficult process for the users because the new system must be integrated into the organization's activities. The users must not only learn how to use the new system but also change the way they do their work. Even if the software is technically perfect, the system will likely be a failure if people do not want it to work or do not know how to use it. The **conversion** process therefore might require attitudinal changes. It is often a mistake to assume that people will change their behavior in the desired or expected way.

Several strategies for transitioning users from an old system to a new one are commonly used (see Figure 10.4). This is a critical choice for the effective implementation of the system, and this choice needs to be made well in advance of the Implementation phase by a decision-making process that includes both IS and business managers. Good management understanding of the options and trade-offs for the implementation strategies discussed below can reap both short-term and long-term implementation benefits.

In the *parallel* strategy, the organization continues to operate the old system in parallel with the new system until the new one is working sufficiently well to discontinue the old. This is a conservative conversion strategy because it allows the organization to continue using the old system if there are problems with the new one. However, it can also be a difficult strategy to manage because workers typically must operate both the old system and the new while also comparing the results of the two systems to make sure that the new system is working properly. When discrepancies

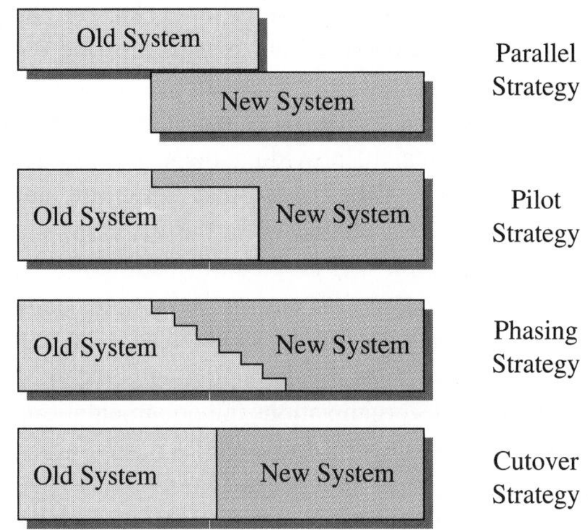

Figure 10.4 Implementation Strategies

are found, the source of the problem must be identified and corrections initiated. Parallel conversion can therefore be very stressful. A parallel strategy also might not even be feasible due to changes in hardware and software associated with the new system.

The *pilot* strategy is an attractive option when it is possible to introduce the new system in only one part of the organization. The objective is to solve as many implementation problems as possible before implementing the system in the rest of the organization. For example, in a company with many branch offices, it might be feasible to convert to the new system in only one branch office and gain experience solving data conversion and procedural problems before installing the system companywide. If major problems are encountered, companywide implementation can be delayed until they are solved. Pilot approaches are especially useful when there are potentially high technological or organizational risks associated with the systems project.

For a large, complex system, a *phased* conversion strategy might be the best approach. For example, with a large order processing and inventory control system, the firm might first convert order entry and simply enter customer orders and print them out on the company forms. Then it might convert the warehouse inventory control system to the computer. Finally, it might link the order entry system to the inventory system, produce shipping documents, and update the inventory records automatically. The downside to this approach is that it results in a lengthy implementation period. Extra development work to interface new and old system components is also typically required. On the other hand, a phasing strategy enables the firm to begin to achieve some benefits from the new system more rapidly than under other strategies.

In the *cutover* (or cold turkey) strategy, the organization totally abandons the old system when it implements the new one. In some industries this can be done over holiday weekends in order to allow for a third day for returning to the old system in the event of a major failure. The cutover strategy has greater inherent risks, but it is attractive when it is very difficult to operate both the old and new systems simultaneously. Some also argue that the total "pain is the same" for a system implementation, whether implemented as a cutover or not, and that this strategy moves the organization to the new operating environment faster.

Combinations of these four strategies are also possible. For example, when implementing system modules via a phased conversion strategy, one still has the option of a parallel or cutover approach for converting each phase of the system. Similarly, a pilot strategy could include a parallel strategy at the pilot site.

Operations The second step of the Implementation phase is to operate the new application in "production mode." In the Operations step, the IS responsibility for the application is turned over to computer operations and technical support personnel. The project team is typically disbanded, although one or more members may be assigned to a support team.

New applications are typically not moved into production status unless adequate documentation has been provided to the computer operations staff. Implementing a large, complex system without documentation is highly risky. Documentation comes in at least two flavors: system documentation for IS specialists who operate and maintain the computer system and user documentation for those who use the system.

Successful operation of an application system requires people and computers to work together. If the hardware or software fails or people falter, system operation might be unsatisfactory. In a large, complex system, thousands of things can go wrong, and most companies operate many such systems simultaneously. It takes excellent management of computer operations to make sure that everything works well consistently and to contain and repair the damage when things do go wrong.

In Part IV we consider what it takes to successfully schedule and run large applications on a large computer system in a reliable and secure production environment.

Maintenance The process of making changes to a system after it has been put into production mode (i.e., after the Operations stage of its life cycle) is referred to as

Maintenance. The most obvious reason for maintenance is to correct errors in the software that were not discovered and corrected prior to its initial implementation. Usually a number of bugs in a system do elude the testing process, and for a large, complex system it might take many months, or even years, to discover them.

Maintenance could also be required to adapt the system to changes in the environment—the organization, other systems, new hardware and systems software, and government regulations. Another major cause for maintenance is the desire to enhance the system. After some experience with a new system, managers typically have a number of ideas on how to improve it, ranging from minor changes to entirely new modules. The small changes are usually treated as maintenance, but large-scale additions might need approval as a new development request.

Because both business and technology environments change rapidly, periodic changes to large systems are typical. In the past the total costs over a typical system's life cycle have been estimated to be about 80 percent on maintenance and only 20 percent on the original development of the application. As a result, many IS organizations have to allocate a significant number of their IS specialists to maintaining systems, rather than developing new ones. In the early 1990s maintenance resources were consuming as much as 75 percent of the total systems development resources in many large organizations (see Figure 10.5). The IS organization is responsible for making the required changes in the system throughout its life, as well as for eliminating any bugs that are identified prior to launching the new system in a production mode.

To make a change in a system, the maintenance programmer must first determine what program(s) must be changed and then what specific parts of each program need to be changed. The programmer must also understand the logic of the part of the code that is being changed. In other words, one must understand the system in some detail in order to change it.

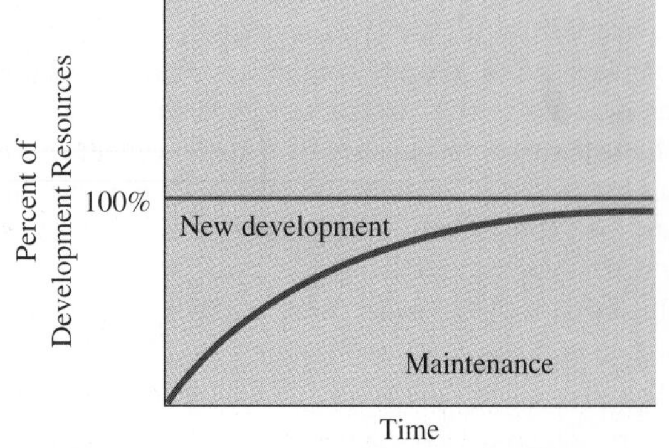

Figure 10.5 Percent of Development Resources Devoted to Maintenance

Because systems can be very complex, system documentation is critical in providing the necessary level of understanding. This brings up another difficulty—the documentation must be changed when the system is changed or the documentation will provide misleading information about the system rather than assistance in understanding it. Most programmers are primarily interested in programming and are not rewarded for updating the documentation, so in many IS organizations the documentation of old systems becomes outdated and includes inaccuracies.

Furthermore, when changes are made in complex systems, a **ripple effect** might be encountered such that the change has an unanticipated impact on some other part of the system. For example, a change in a program can affect another program that uses the output from the first program. A change to a line of code can affect the results of another line of code in an entirely different part of that program. Another change must be made to correct those problems and that change might cause unanticipated problems elsewhere.

Another major problem with maintenance is that most IS professionals prefer to work on new systems using new technologies rather than maintain old systems. Maintenance is therefore often perceived as low-status work, although it is critical to the business. Maintenance is often the first assignment of a newly hired programmer, and most organizations do not have mechanisms to ensure that really good maintenance people are rewarded well.

From the business manager's perspective, the major maintenance challenges are getting it done when it is needed and dealing with new system problems introduced as part of the maintenance process. A high proportion of operational problems are caused by errors introduced when making maintenance changes. Changes to production systems need to be carefully managed. Maintenance changes are typically made to a copy of the production system and then fully tested before they are implemented. An effective **release management** process for changing from an older to a newer version of the system is critical to avoid introducing large numbers of new problems when maintaining operational systems.

If adequate numbers of IS specialists are not available for systems maintenance projects, the manager often must suffer long delays before needed changes are made. Figure 10.6 graphically displays the widening gap that can occur between the organization's needs and the system's performance over time. Also, as a system gets older and is repeatedly patched, the probability of performance problems becomes even greater and reengineering or replacement solutions might be required.

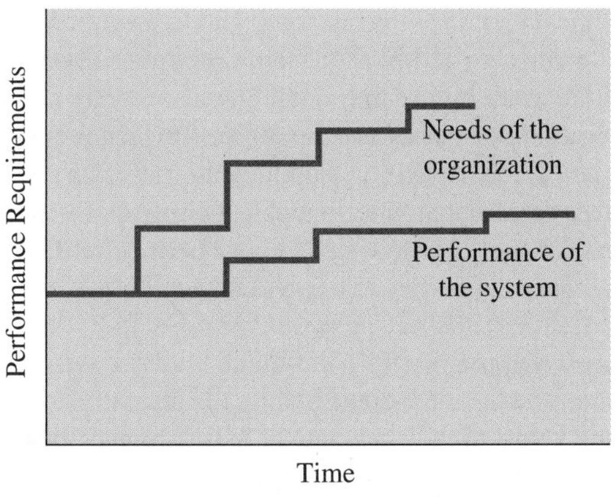

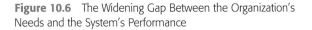

Figure 10.6 The Widening Gap Between the Organization's Needs and the System's Performance

The SDLC Project Team

Most application systems are developed by a temporary project team. When the system project is completed, the team is disbanded. Most project teams include representatives from both the IS organization and relevant business departments. If several organizational units or several levels of people within a unit will use the system, the project team might include representatives from only some of these different units, including higher-level managers and experienced end users who will work with the new application on a day-to-day basis. The selection of the project team is therefore critical to the success of a given systems project.

The project team also can vary in membership during the system's life cycle: A few members might be assigned full-time to the project for its entirety, while others might join the project team only temporarily as their specific knowledge or skills are required. In addition to an IS manager in a project leadership role, other IS personnel will be assigned as needed for the specific application, including systems analysts, application programmers, data administration specialists, telecommunications specialists, and others. It is also not unusual for IS specialists from outside the organization to also be used on systems projects. The IS specialists hired from a contract firm might bring specific IS knowledge to the project or might be needed due to the lack of internal resources available to assign to the project. These personnel could be so well integrated into the project that they are almost indistinguishable from the firm's internal IS personnel.

Historically, the **project manager** for a custom application was always an IS manager. Today, however, a business manager with information technology (IT) management knowledge might be asked to be the project manager, or a project might have two project managers: a business manager responsible for all user activities, especially for the implementation phase, and an IS manager responsible for the activities of all IS personnel. Some guidelines on whether the manager of a specific project should come from the IS organization, a business unit, or both, are provided in the sidebar "Who Should Lead the IT Project?" The practitioner press suggests that assigning both IT and business managers to lead IT projects is a way to tighten the overall alignment between the IT organization and the business. According to a recent report, Cisco Systems, Inc., is giving IT and business leaders joint responsibility for every IT project (Hoffman, 2003).

Whether or not this role is shared, the project manager(s) is held responsible for the success of the project—for delivering a quality system, on time, and within budget. Managing a systems project typically involves coordinating the efforts of many persons from different organizational units, some of whom work for the project only on a part-time or temporary basis. The project manager must plan the project, determine the SDLC tasks that must be carried out and the skills required for each task, and estimate how long each will take. The skills of the IS resources assigned to the project can be just as important as the number of resources assigned.

The system documentation produced at each step of the SDLC methodology provides a major tool for communication across team members and for assessing the quality of the development effort throughout the life of the system. Most organizations require that systems for which an SDLC process is appropriate include business management beyond those on the project team to provide formal sign-offs at each milestone of the project.

WHO SHOULD LEAD THE IT PROJECT?

If the project involves new and advanced technology,
Then it should be managed by someone from the IS department.
If the project's impact would force critical changes in the business,
Then it should be managed by someone from the business unit.
If the project is extremely large and complex,
Then it should be managed by a specialist in project management.
If a project shares all of the above characteristics,
Then senior management should consider multiple project leaders.

[Radding, 1992, based on Applegate]

The **systems analyst** role is also a critical one. These IS professionals are trained to work with business managers and end users to determine the feasibility of the new system and to develop detailed system requirements for the custom application. During the Construction phase, they work with other IS specialists in designing the system and help to monitor the adherence to the system requirements. A good systems analyst has problem-solving skills, a knowledge of IT capabilities, and a strong understanding of the business activities involved in the application. The role of the systems analyst needs to be played well in order for *multiple* user perspectives to be taken into account. Sometimes the systems analyst also provides the important function of providing checks and balances for IS specialists eager to work with new, but unproven, technologies by ensuring that the business risks associated with new technologies are accounted for in project decisions.

Other key roles, including key business roles (sponsors, champions), are discussed in the chapter on IT project management (see Chapter 12).

Managing an SDLC Project

All systems projects are typically measured by three primary success criteria: (1) on-time delivery of an IS that (2) is of high quality and meets business requirements and (3) is within project budget. Additional project management techniques for achieving these goals will be considered in Chapter 12 (IT Project Management).

Particularly critical for the success of custom development projects using an SDLC methodology are three characteristics: manageable project size, accurate requirements definition, and executive sponsorship.

Manageable Project Size Experience has convincingly shown that very large custom IT projects are very difficult to deliver within budget. On the other hand, projects that take fewer technical people a year or less to complete are more likely to meet the success criteria for the project. This suggests that large systems should be broken down into relatively independent modules and built as a sequence of small, manageable projects, rather than as a single monster project.

Accurate Requirements Definition The SDLC waterfall process is based on the premise that requirements for a new system can be defined in detail at the beginning of the process. The downside is that if the requirements are not well defined, there could be large cost overruns and the system could be unsatisfactory. Early studies have shown that about half of the total number of requirements errors (or omissions) is typically detected in the Requirements Definition step. Further, as shown in Figure 10.7, an error detected in the Implementation phase costs about 150 times as much to fix as an error detected in the Definition phase. Every effort must therefore be put into obtaining as accurate a requirements definition document as possible. This requires systems analysts skilled in eliciting requirements as well as in process and data representation techniques. It also requires *access to business users* knowledgeable about both current business operations and the envisioned system.

Executive Sponsorship Although all large systems projects require business sponsorship, the intensity and length of time involved with the typical SDLC project means that executive-level sponsorship is critical to success. Key business managers need to understand the potential benefits of the proposed system and be dedicated to contributing resources to the systems project team, as well as the sustained usage of the new custom application. Because some business managers and end users will also be assigned to the project team, business sponsors need to be willing to dedicate these resources to the project team, sometimes on a full-time basis for the life of the project.

Although not every project team has end users as formal team members, end users frequently participate by providing information about current work processes or procedures and evaluating screen designs from an end-user perspective. This, too, takes time away from normal business activities. User involvement in a systems project has in fact been associated with user acceptance and usage of the new system (Hartwick and Barki, 1994). However, business managers must be willing to dedicate these business resources throughout the project as needed, not just at the time of implementation.

Beath and Orlikowski (1994) have pointed out that systems development methodologies can differ in their assumptions about IS and user roles over the life of the project. For example, two methodologies that have been practiced more commonly outside of the United States (the ETHICS method and the Soft Systems Methodology) are specifically designed to facilitate more user involvement.

System implementation also requires managing organizational changes. Unless there is strong business sponsorship, there will not be a strong initiative to make changes to the business as part of the systems project effort. (See Chapter 12 for some guidelines for managing business change.)

SDLC Advantages and Disadvantages

The SDLC process is a highly structured approach to the development of large, complex applications for one or more business units. A summary of the advantages and disadvantages of the SDLC approach is provided in Figure 10.8 and is discussed in the following paragraphs.

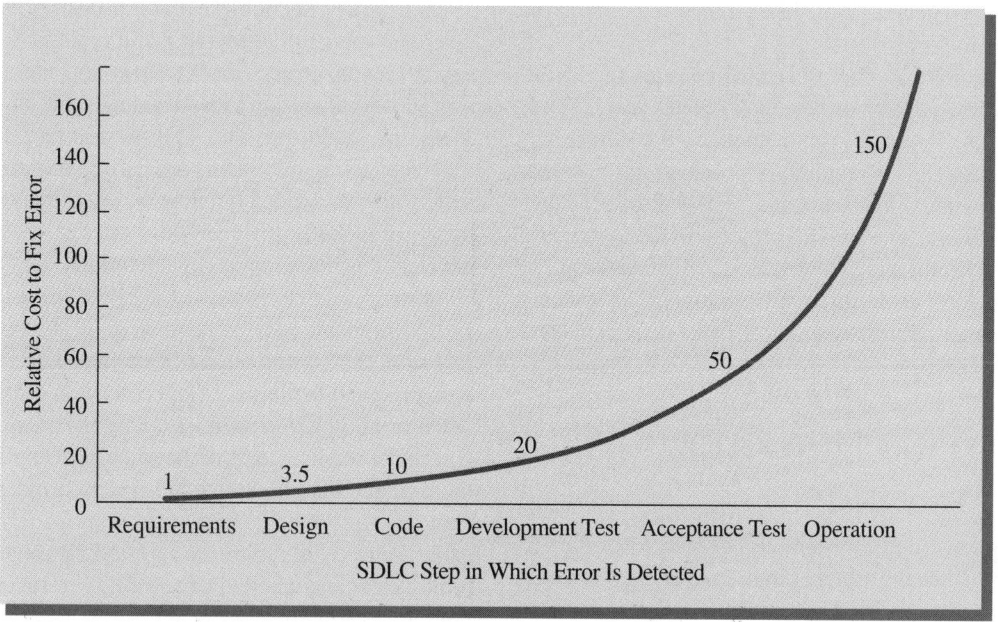

Figure 10.7 Costs of Error Correction by SDLC Step (Adapted from Boehm, 1976)

In the hands of competent IS specialists and knowledgeable business managers, the SDLC process sets up formal steps with clear IS and user roles, formal checkpoints, and techniques for analysis, design, testing, and implementation. These tools and the rigorous discipline associated with an SDLC methodology help the systems project manager produce a well-engineered system on time and within budget.

The major disadvantages are inherent in the methodology. First, the project's success depends on the accurate and complete specification of detailed requirements at the beginning of the development process (Definition phase). There are several serious problems with this dependency. For example, many customized applications today are unique solutions. Because the project begins with an incomplete understanding of what this unique information system will do, it might be necessary to try several approaches before discovering the optimal one. New technologies might also be involved, and until the capabilities of these technologies are better understood, it might be hard to develop a firm set of requirements. Another problem with upfront detailed requirements specification is that today's business environment is changing so rapidly that there can be significant differences in business needs between the time the requirements are specified and the time the system is installed.

Note that the SDLC process also requires a full cost/benefit analysis based on the initial Definition phase. The justification process can be difficult to accomplish using traditional approaches such as return on investment (ROI)

Advantages

- Highly structured, systematic process
- Thorough requirements definition
- Clear milestones with business management sign-offs

Disadvantages

- Does not account well for evolving requirements during project
- Time-consuming (and costly) process
- Top-down commitment required

Figure 10.8 Advantages and Disadvantages of Traditional SDLC Approach

calculations when new technologies are involved or requirements are incomplete.

Second, the SDLC process is time-consuming. In the 1980s the typical systems project took several years. Third, because the SDLC process is both lengthy and costly, strong executive sponsorship is required. Without strong business sponsorship, business managers and users will be reluctant to dedicate their time to a systems project instead of working on other activities for which they are typically measured.

Below we look at an alternative approach to systems development that addresses some of these disadvantages.

PROTOTYPING METHODOLOGY

The SDLC methodology is based on the premise that business requirements for the system will be static over the life of the project. Thus, the system requirements must be completely and finally specified before the Construction phase is begun. Once the requirements have been agreed upon, changing them leads to significant project costs and potential schedule delays.

In the second half of the 1980s, the growing availability of fourth generation nonprocedural languages and relational database management systems began to offer an alternative approach. These tools make it possible to initially build a system (or part of a system) more quickly and then revise it after users have tried it out and provided their feedback to the developers. Thus, rather than first initially defining the system and then building it, the initial system can be revised based upon the user's experience and understanding gained from the earlier versions.

This approach is very powerful because, although most people find it very difficult to specify in great detail exactly what they need from a new system, it is quite easy for them to point out what they do not like about computer screens that they can try out and use.

This general approach is most commonly known as **prototyping**. It is a type of **evolutionary development** process. The prototyping concept can also be applied to a process in which a real system is developed for the user to try out as well as for situations in which only a "toy" (non-operational) prototype is developed. For example, prototype input and output screens are often developed for users to work with as part of the requirements definition or detailed design steps. Other examples of prototyping include a "first-of-a-series" prototype in which a completely operational prototype is used as a pilot and a "selected features" prototype in which only some essential features are included in the prototype and more features are added in later modules (Kendall and Kendall, 1999).

In the next section we first discuss prototyping as a *complete alternative* to the traditional SDLC methodology: its steps, project management considerations, and its overall advantages and disadvantages in comparison to an SDLC methodology. This approach is particularly attractive when the requirements are hard to define, when a critical system is needed quickly, or when the system will be used infrequently (or even only once)—so that operating efficiency is not a major consideration. Note that these are all system characteristics that apply to some types of managerial support systems.

Prototyping as an alternative to an SDLC methodology is impractical for large, complex system efforts. However, when prototyping is used *within* an SDLC process to help determine requirements of a new custom application, it can increase the likelihood that the system project is a success. Prototyping provides a practical way for organizations to experiment with systems where the requirements are not totally clear and where the probability of success is unclear but the rewards for success appear to be very high.

The Prototyping Steps

Figure 10.9 presents the steps for an evolutionary methodology for developing a new, working system. The process begins with the identification of the *basic* requirements of the initial version of the system (step 1). The analyst/builder(s) and user(s) meet and agree on the inputs, the data processing, and the system outputs. These are not complete detailed requirements; rather, this is a starting point for the system. If several builders and users are involved, a joint application design (JAD) session may be used to determine requirements (see the description of JAD in the section entitled "Newer Approaches" later in this chapter).

In step 2 the system builders produce an initial prototype system according to the basic requirements agreed on in step 1. The system builders select the software tools, locate the necessary data and make these data accessible to the system, and construct the system using higher-level languages. This step should take from a few days to a few weeks, depending on the system's size and complexity.

When the initial prototype is completed, it is given to the user with instructions similar to the following: "Here is the initial prototype. I know that it is not what you really need, but it's a beginning point. Try it and write down everything about it that you do not like or that needs to be added to the system. When you get a good list, we will make the changes you suggest."

Step 3 is the user's responsibility. He or she works with the system, notes the things that need to be improved, and then meets with the analyst/builder to discuss the changes. In step 4 the builder modifies the system to incorporate the

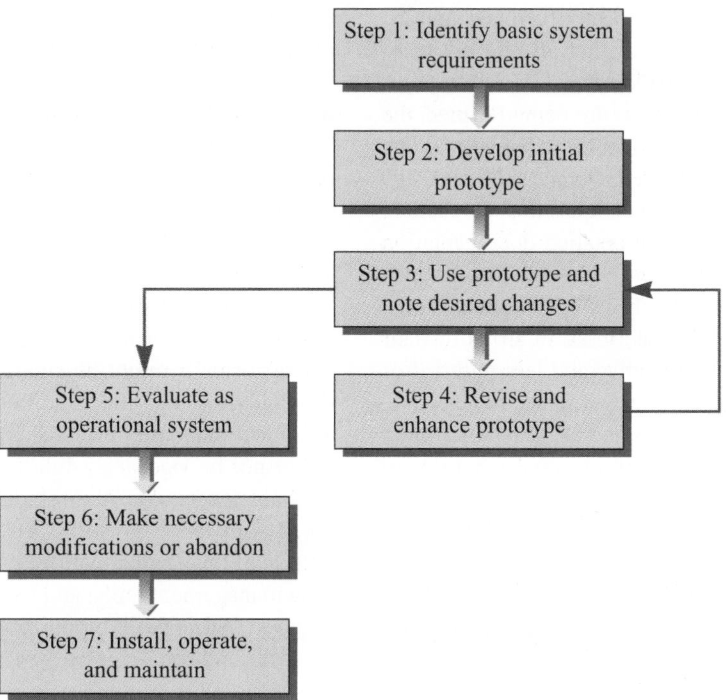

Figure 10.9 The Prototyping Life Cycle

desired changes. In order to keep everyone actively involved, speed is important. Sometimes the builder can sit down with the user and make the changes immediately; for larger systems, the changes might take several weeks. Steps 3 and 4 are repeated until the user is satisfied with the current version of the system. These are *iterative steps* within the prototyping process. When the user is satisfied that the prototype has been sufficiently developed, step 5 begins.

Step 5 involves evaluating the final prototype as an operational system. It should be noted, however, that not all prototypes become operational systems. Instead, it might be decided that the prototype system should simply be thrown away. Or, it could be decided that no additional costs should be devoted to the application because a system could not be developed that solved the original problem. That is, the prototyping process helped the organization decide that the system benefits do not outweigh the additional development or operational costs, or both, or that the expense of developing an operationally efficient system is too high. At this point it could also be decided that the system will be implemented but that the system needs to be built using different tools in order to achieve performance efficiencies.

If the prototype is to become an operational system, in step 6 the builder completes the Construction phase by making any changes necessary to improve operational efficiency and to interface the new application with the operational systems that provide it with data. This is also the step in which all necessary controls, backup and recovery procedures, and the necessary documentation need to be completed. If the prototype is only slightly modified, this step differs from the end of the Construction phase of an SDLC methodology in that most (or all) of the system has already been tested. Step 7 is similar to the Implementation phase of the SDLC: The new system is installed and moved into operational status. This is likely to be a much easier Implementation phase than under the traditional SDLC process because at least some of the intended users are already familiar with the system. Step 7 also includes maintenance. Because of the advanced tools that likely were used to build it, changes might be easier to make.

The Prototyping Project Team

Managing an evolutionary development process is clearly a joint IS and user management responsibility. Whether the project manager role is played by IS alone, business personnel alone, or both IS and business personnel, both groups need to jointly determine when to continue to request revisions to a prototype and when to end the iterative tryout-and-revise steps. The business manager needs to determine whether a satisfactory solution has been developed, and the IS manager needs to determine whether all relevant technology capabilities have been explored.

Because only basic requirements are being defined, the systems analyst and prototype builder (which might be one and the same) need to have some different skill sets than required for the SDLC process. Techniques to elicit abstract requirements and an emphasis on detailed documentation under the SDLC process are replaced by a heavy reliance on skills to build systems quickly using advanced tools. The initial prototypes are assessed more in terms of their look-and-feel from a user perspective and less in terms of technical quality from a systems performance perspective. Interactions between IS specialists and users center around creative development solutions and personal reactions to user-system interfaces and outputs.

A prototyping methodology also requires a dedicated business user role. Because there is continual user involvement with the various versions of the system, the designated business user needs to be able to be freed from other responsibilities to work with the application and to suggest changes over the life of the project. Sometimes more than one person plays this critical end-user role, which will require a structure and process for reaching agreement when suggested changes from different users are in conflict.

Managing a Prototyping Project

Managing new development projects with a methodology based on an iterative or evolutionary process requires a different mindset than managing projects using an SDLC methodology based on a highly structured development approach. IS project managers and system builders need to approach the project differently: The objective is to respond quickly to user requests with a "good enough" prototype multiple times rather than to produce a tightly engineered actual system at the outset of the project. This might require some cultural changes within the IS organization. IS professionals who have built their careers on skills and attitudes required by an SDLC approach might need to acquire new skills for prototyping approaches.

IS managers also find managing prototyping projects more problematic because it is difficult to plan how long it will take, how many iterations will be required, or exactly when the system builders will be working on the system. Project managers need to have sufficient IS resources available for system building in order to quickly respond to user requests for system changes within an agreed-upon timetable. Users who will be trying out each prototype version must be committed to the process and must be willing and able to devote the time and effort required to test each prototype version in a timely fashion. IS managers might rightfully feel that they have less control over the project's scope. One of the potential hazards of prototyping is that the iterative steps will go on and on and that the project costs will keep accumulating. Good working relationships between IS personnel and users responsible for the project are required to move to the prototype evaluation step (step 5) at the optimal time. Joint IS-user accountability would appear to be a key to success for these types of projects.

Depending on the software tools used to build the prototype, the operational efficiency of a prototype that is evaluated in step 5 might be significantly inferior to systems developed using the traditional SDLC methodology. Technical standards established by the organization also might not be rigorously followed, and the documentation might be inadequate. A substantial investment in computer-aided software engineering (CASE) tools (see the final section of this chapter entitled "Newer Approaches"), database management tools, and IS specialist training might be required before an IS organization can successfully implement the end prototype as the final system.

Prototyping Advantages and Disadvantages

The advantages of the evolutionary development methodology address the disadvantages inherent in the SDLC methodology. First, only *basic* system requirements are needed at the front end of the project. This means that systems can be built using an evolutionary approach that would be impossible to develop via an SDLC methodology. Furthermore, prototyping can be used to build systems that radically change how work is done, such as when work processes are being redesigned or a totally new type of managerial support tool has been envisioned but never seen. It is virtually impossible to define requirements for these kinds of systems at the beginning of a systems development process. Prototyping also allows firms to explore the use of newer technologies, because the expectations under an evolutionary methodology are that the builders will get it right over multiple iterations, rather than the first time.

Second, an initial working system is available for user testing much more quickly. In some cases business managers might actually use a working prototype to respond in some way to a current problem or at least to quickly learn that a given systems approach will not be the best solution. Although the complete process might take several months, users might have a working prototype in a few weeks or months that allows them to respond to a problem that exists now and is growing in importance; often a business manager cannot wait many months, let alone years, for a particular system to be built.

Third, because of the more interactive nature of the process, with hands-on use of working system models, strong top-down commitment based on a well-substantiated justification process might be less necessary at the outset of the project. Instead, the costs and benefits of the system can be derived after experience with an initial prototype.

Fourth, initial user acceptance of an application developed with an evolutionary process is likely to be higher than with an SDLC process. This is partly because the evolutionary process results in more active involvement and more joint control of the process on the part of the user.

The disadvantages of an evolutionary methodology are related to the evolutionary build process. The end prototype typically lacks some of the security and control features found in a system developed with an SDLC process. It also might not undergo the same type of rigorous testing. Documentation of the final version can be less complete because of the iterative nature of the process.

In the past the operational inefficiencies of fourth generation tools also contributed to the inadequacies of end prototypes. However, with recent advancements in hardware and software tools for developers and end users, these issues have become much less important than implementing a system that meets user needs. As described earlier, these potential deficiencies are assessed in step 5 and corrected in step 6 of the evolutionary methodology in Figure 10.9.

Another potential disadvantage is related to managing user expectations. Frequently, a prototype system appears to be so good that users are reluctant to wait for a well-functioning, well-documented operational system.

Prototyping Within an SDLC Process

As fourth generation tools have become commonplace, the incorporation of a few steps of an evolutionary process into an SDLC methodology has also become common. In the following paragraphs we describe two ways that prototyping is commonly incorporated into an SDLC process.

First, prototyping is used in the Definition phase to help users define the system requirements, particularly for the user interface (computer screens and navigation). As shown in Figure 10.10, the SDLC process still begins with a feasibility analysis. However, for the requirements definition step, IS specialists use screen-painting tools to produce initial versions of screens and reports that users can experiment with. This might be an example of a nonoperational prototype, in which the screen designs are not connected to a live database. After the requirements have been determined with the help of the prototype, the remainder of the steps in the SDLC process remain the same. However, the system builders can also make use of the screens during the design and build steps, and they may actually use computer code generated by the prototyping tools in the final system.

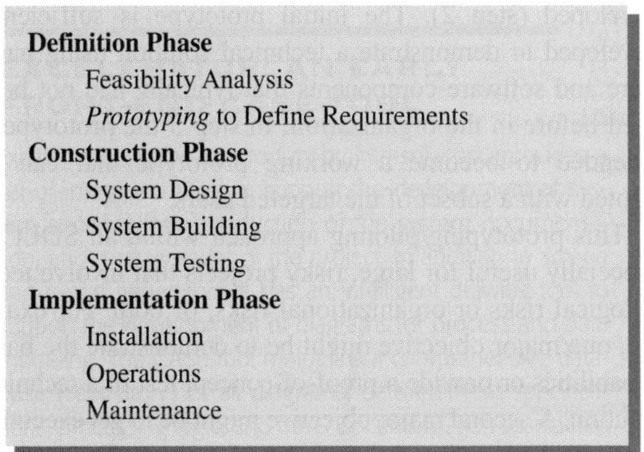

Definition Phase
Feasibility Analysis
Prototyping to Define Requirements
Construction Phase
System Design
System Building
System Testing
Implementation Phase
Installation
Operations
Maintenance

Figure 10.10 SDLC with Prototyping to Define Requirements

The second way prototyping is used is more complex, and includes a pilot implementation of a working prototype. This type of prototype is typically a first-of-a-series type of pilot system. Unlike the pilot rollout strategy discussed for the Implementation stage of the SDLC process, in which a complete system is first implemented in only a portion of the organization, here the intent is to use a scaled-down prototype in only a minimal number of locations within the organization in order to assess its feasibility in an operational setting. As shown in Figure 10.11, the Definition phase of the SDLC process is replaced by three steps in a Prototyping/Piloting phase. After basic requirements are determined (step 1), a working prototype is

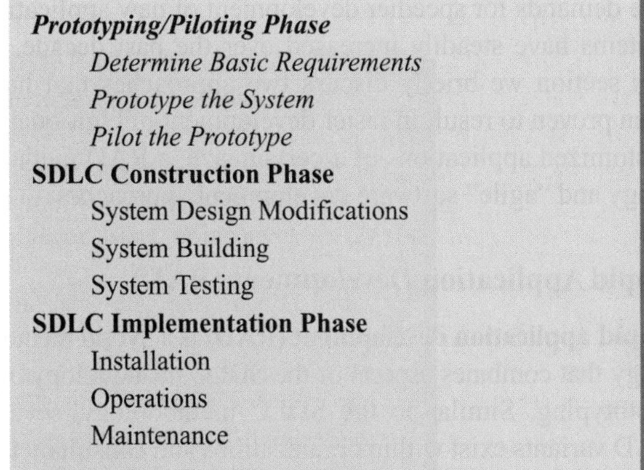

Prototyping/Piloting Phase
Determine Basic Requirements
Prototype the System
Pilot the Prototype
SDLC Construction Phase
System Design Modifications
System Building
System Testing
SDLC Implementation Phase
Installation
Operations
Maintenance

Figure 10.11 Prototyping/Piloting Phase Replaces SDLC Definition Phase

Advantages
- Dramatic savings in development time
- Focuses on essential system requirements
- Ability to rapidly change system design at user request

Disadvantages
- Quality may be sacrificed for speed
- Time-consuming commitments for key user personnel
- Possible shortcuts on internal standards and module reusability

Figure 10.14 RAD Advantages and Disadvantages

standards might be sacrificed, such as consistent user interfaces across screens and data element naming standards.

Figure 10.14 summarizes some of the advantages and disadvantages of RAD. Like prototyping, a RAD methodology is highly dependent on involvement by key users. If these key users are not freed up to work on the RAD project, the custom application might still be produced quickly, but is less likely to be an optimal software solution for the business.

In recent years a more "agile" software development discipline has emerged as an alternative methodology for smaller projects (e.g., project teams not larger than 20). The objective is to deliver software with very low defect rates, based on a set of four key values:

- Simplicity
- Communication
- Feedback
- Courage

A "whole team" approach is taken in which business representatives (customers) and technical team members (programmers) work side-by-side in an open workspace on a daily basis.

In one agile approach, called **Extreme Programming (XP)**, the programmers write production code in pairs. By using simple designs and frequent testing, the team produces small, fully integrated releases that pass all the customers' acceptance tests in a very short time period (e.g., every 2 weeks). The programming pairs then might disband to form new pairs and thus quickly share their specialized knowledge and completed code. Another hallmark of the XP approach is the obsession with feedback and testing. As team-tested programs are released to a collective repository, any pair of programmers can improve any of the collective code at any time, following the common coding standards adopted by all teams.

MANAGING SOFTWARE PROJECTS USING OUTSOURCED STAFF

Although hiring on-site contractors to help with custom software projects has been a widespread practice for decades, today there is a renewed focus on keeping down the costs of software development by outsourcing portions of the project to off-site workers, especially offshore workers in a different labor market. Other advantages of using external resources for custom development work are to make use of technical expertise not available in-house and to be able to complete the project more quickly.

Off-site outsourcing can involve contracting with companies within the same country or region ("onshore") or not ("offshore"). According to Poria (2003), the offshore alternative is likely a very favorable option when the following conditions exist:

- The system requirements can be well-defined and will remain relatively stable over the project.
- Time is of the essence and 7x24 hour availability of resources to work on the project is advantageous.
- The cost of the project (or program) is an important consideration.

Guidelines for effectively managing the day-to-day interactions with an offsite outsourcer have also been developed. For example, some of the key guidelines published by a Sourcing Interests Group (and summarized in McNurlin and Sprague, 2003) are as follows:

Manage expectations, not staff The outsourcer's staff is not under the direct control of the client company, so a facilitative mode of working is best in which the focus is on the outcomes.

Take explicit actions to integrate the offsite workers Managing projects across workgroups requires more formality, such as explicit, agreed-upon outcomes and measures. In-house staff might even benefit from moving to the outsourcer's firm in order to work side-by-side with them and learn how they work together internally.

Communicate frequently Managers responsible for the relationship with the outsourcers need to keep the lines of communication open.

Abandoning informal ways may result in increased rigor Because of their business model, a service provider might have more disciplined processes than the client organization, which can lead to higher quality solutions.

SUMMARY

The choice among the traditional systems development life cycle (SDLC), prototyping, RAD, and the newer "agile" methodologies for developing a customized application is essentially an IS management decision. Within firms that have their own capable IS staffs, the methodology choice might be based on factors such as the degree to which system requirements can be easily determined, and the application's functionality, size, and complexity. Custom application development using the multistep SDLC methodology, with well-defined signoffs, is now the traditional way to develop new computer systems and to maintain them; it is still the preferred approach when the system is large, complex, and serves multiple organizational units. A prototyping methodology is a more effective approach for small, simple projects. A prototyping approach is also used within an SDLC methodology to help users and IS professionals begin with a set of basic requirements and then develop a fuller set of functional requirements. A combination prototyping/piloting approach within an SDLC methodology is especially useful when the systems project is characterized by significant technological risks or organizational risks, or both, that can be tested out early in the project using a prototype.

Whether the traditional SDLC, prototyping, or some combination of the two is used, it is the responsibility of both business managers and IS specialists to ensure that the system that is installed meets the needs of the business at the time of installation. IS specialists typically hold primary responsibility for most system analysis and all system building steps. However, the systems project may be managed by an IS manager, a business manager, or both.

Rapid application development (RAD) methodologies have become more important as businesses seek to deliver high-quality applications within shorter time frames. A RAD methodology combines the iterative development benefits of prototyping with the quality controls of the SDLC; this approach also typically relies on JAD sessions and software automation (CASE) tools to generate code. In recent years there has also been a movement to develop more "agile" development methods based on the principles of simplicity and feedback, with relatively small project teams. One of the characteristics of an agile method called Extreme Programming is an obsession with testing code early and often, in order to have zero defects.

The chapter ends with a discussion of some guidelines for managing the interactions between project team members when there are off-site (including offshore) contract workers on a project.

REVIEW QUESTIONS

1. Briefly describe the typical steps in the typical systems development life cycle (SDLC) as presented in this chapter.
2. Describe the key activities performed by IS professionals in each step of the SDLC.
3. Select three characteristics of a high-quality application system, as shown in Figure 10.3, and provide a rationale for why each is important.
4. Describe the importance of documentation under an SDLC methodology.
5. Describe a distinct advantage of each of the four strategies for implementing a new system, as shown in Figure 10.4.
6. Why is an accurate and complete requirements definition especially critical when using the SDLC "waterfall" approach?
7. Briefly describe the steps of a pure prototyping methodology as an alternative to an SDLC approach.
8. Which disadvantages of an SDLC methodology are addressed by a prototyping approach?
9. Describe two ways that a prototyping approach can be used within the Definition phase of a traditional SDLC methodology.
10. Why are JAD techniques a key characteristic of RAD methodologies?
11. Describe how a RAD methodology builds on the strengths of both an SDLC methodology and prototyping.
12. Why does the use of contractors increase the complexity of an IT project?

DISCUSSION QUESTIONS

1. Discuss why you think the SDLC methodology for developing application systems was widely adopted in U.S.-based organizations by the early 1990s.
2. IS department managers often believe that they are responsible for making sure the requirements of the system are properly defined, but in this chapter the business manager's responsibility for defining requirements is emphasized. How can you reconcile these two points of view?
3. There have been many failures in the development of application systems using the traditional SDLC. Discuss some characteristics of the methodology that could contribute to the high failure rate under certain situations.
4. Compare the role of the systems analyst in the development of an application system using the SDLC and using a prototyping approach.
5. Some IS specialists contend that end prototypes are usually poor technical solutions. Comment on why this perception might (or might not) be valid.
6. Discuss why an application might be built using prototyping as part of the SDLC methodology, rather than by a pure prototyping methodology alone.
7. Discuss the role of the project manager in the in-house development of a customized application and in what situations both IS and business managers might serve as coleaders of a project.
8. It has been said that "a system without good documentation is worthless." Provide support for this statement. Then comment on how today's advanced tools might alleviate the documentation burden.
9. Discuss how some modern tools (such as CASE), techniques (such as JAD), and new methodologies (such as extreme programming) help IS organizations overcome the disadvantages of the traditional SDLC methodology.
10. Do a Web search on the topic of offshore outsourcing of IT project work and discuss some of your findings.

CHAPTER 11
METHODOLOGIES FOR PURCHASED SOFTWARE PACKAGES

IN MOST LARGE COMPANIES TODAY, SOFTWARE IS BOTH CUSTOM DEVELOPED by in-house information systems (IS) staff and procured from an outside source. In fact, the trend for more than a decade has been for midsized and larger organizations to purchase application packages rather than custom develop their own solutions with in-house IS personnel, whenever it is feasible and cost-beneficial to do so. Capital expenditures for implementing purchased software packages are therefore a large part of the total IS budget. Of course, many small businesses have no, or very few, IS professionals, so they essentially procure all their software from outside sources.

Firms in the software industry have grown across the globe over the past decades, so that today companies can choose from thousands of products that can be purchased as "off-the-shelf" packaged software. The software industry firms that survive attract new and seasoned IS professionals to be their employees so that they can quickly develop information technology (IT) solutions to respond to new marketplace needs. Firms that purchase a software package also typically need to purchase services from the software vendor to help install and maintain the software for their business. Besides working with the software vendor, the purchasing firm's own system and business analysts work on project teams with business managers to purchase and install new systems. Some team members also typically are part of an ongoing support team for the business users after a new purchased system has been installed.

Packaged software applications are often built today with standard Windows or Web browser interfaces for the end user. These types of interfaces are also available for large client/server systems (such as the enterprise resource planning [ERP] and customer relationship management [CRM] packages introduced in Chapter 5). Some of these enterprise-level systems have industry-specific versions of their packages to facilitate their implementation. Other software vendors develop packages for a specific industry only, such as sales and inventory management systems for retailers, commercial loan systems for banks, claim-processing systems for insurance companies or healthcare providers. Wherever there is a sizable market for a standard package, a software company is likely to be developing applications to sell to that market.

For firms that have their own IS department resources, a make-or-buy analysis is undertaken in order to decide whether to procure a product or service from an outside source or to produce the software or perform the service using internal IS resources. Below, therefore, we begin by better understanding the overall business and IT benefits that an organization needs to consider when it has a choice between purchasing a software application and developing a customized application. Next we will describe in detail the process steps for selecting, preparing for, and implementing a software application package, as well as some of the project team roles and keys to success.

THE MAKE-OR-BUY DECISION

The choice between building a custom application and purchasing a software package—a **make-or-buy decision**—should be made jointly by the business managers who need the software and the IS professionals who have the knowledge to assess the technical benefits and risks. For organizations with their own skilled IS personnel, the two most obvious advantages of purchasing software are (1) cost savings and (2) faster speed of implementation. A purchased package usually costs less than a custom solution because the software vendor will be selling the package to many organizations. That is, the companies that purchase the software will be sharing the development and upgrade costs of the package. A software package also typically can be implemented sooner than a custom application because it already exists; in today's fast-changing business environments, this can be a very important advantage.

However, there also are some downsides. One major downside of buying an application solution is that a purchased package seldom exactly fits a company's needs. For the organization that is buying a package to replace an older, custom-developed system, this type of change can have several important ramifications for the business. Most commonly, it means that business users might be asked to "give up" features of the older custom software that the package does not support. This downside alone means that organizations should have a very good process in place that will help them make the best trade-off decisions for the organization. As described below, this requires a methodology that will take into account knowledge of the package's capabilities as well as informed business and technical judgments about how well the package will meet the organization's needs.

At the end of this chapter we also briefly discuss a procurement option that includes contracting with a vendor to "host" (run) one or more applications for a business firm under a leasing contract (see the section of this chapter entitled "New Purchasing Option: Application Service Providers").

PURCHASING METHODOLOGY

Let's turn now to the detailed steps of a life-cycle process for selecting, modifying, and implementing these large software application packages. After describing the individual steps in detail, we then briefly discuss the project team roles, how to effectively manage a purchased system project, and the major advantages and disadvantages of purchasing a packaged system.

Although at first glance it appears relatively easy to purchase packaged software, many instances of systems implementation problems have arisen because an organization simply did not understand what was involved in acquiring and installing the software package that was purchased. Our description of the purchasing steps assumes that an initial approval has been received for a new system that is of sufficient size to merit a full purchasing process. As we will discuss, the package selection should be a joint decision between business managers who can assess the organizational benefits and risks and IS professionals who can help assess the benefits and risks from a technical as well as ongoing support perspective.

Note that our focus here is on what has been referred to as a "dedicated" package that offers a solution to a particular business problem, rather than a personal productivity suite (such as Microsoft Office). Our discussion also assumes that an organization has its own IS specialists. Organizations that have no IS specialists will need to rely on the vendor or outside consultants, or both, to provide the necessary IS expertise.

The Purchasing Steps

The template for the purchasing process steps is shown in Figure 11.1. The steps for purchasing application packages fit into the three life-cycle phases introduced in Chapter 9: Definition, Construction, and Implementation. In the systems development life cycle (SDLC) methodology described in Chapter 10, detailed systems specifications (what the system is to do) are documented in the Definition phase; the system is built in the Construction phase; and the system is installed, operated, and maintained in the Implementation phase.

Because customized application development using an SDLC process historically came first, the process for purchasing packages is referred to here as a *modified SDLC approach.* In the Definition phase, an organization not only defines its system needs but also then uses these requirements to identify potential vendors and solutions and then collect enough information to be able to evaluate them. In comparison to the SDLC process for custom software, the

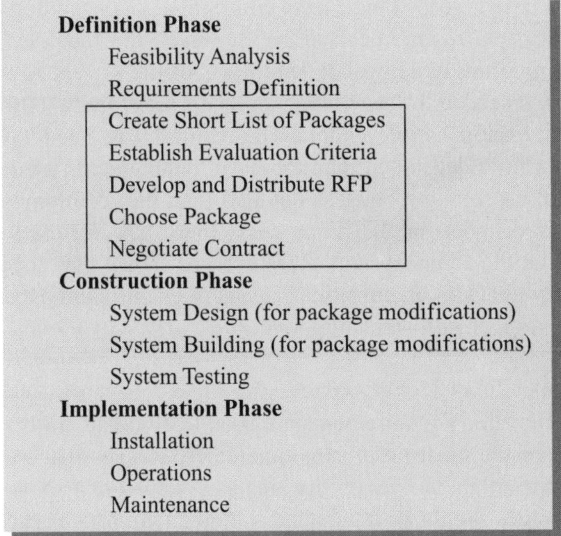

Definition Phase
Feasibility Analysis
Requirements Definition
Create Short List of Packages
Establish Evaluation Criteria
Develop and Distribute RFP
Choose Package
Negotiate Contract
Construction Phase
System Design (for package modifications)
System Building (for package modifications)
System Testing
Implementation Phase
Installation
Operations
Maintenance

Figure 11.1 The Purchasing Process

Definition phase is expanded to include five additional steps, beginning with creating a short list of potential packages.

Since an off-the-shelf packaged solution has already been designed, built, and tested by a vendor, the Construction phase is radically reduced. An exception here is when the package has not yet been fully released and the purchasing organization contracts with the vendor to serve as an **Alpha** or **Beta** site for the software vendor. Being involved as an Alpha site often means that the company can play a significant role in determining the final functionality and user interface design for the new package; in turn, this is a major commitment to providing both business and IS resources to work with the vendor. Being involved as a Beta site typically means significant involvement in a user acceptance test role for the software vendor (such as described in Chapter 10): A vendor does Beta testing with organizations that are not Alpha sites in order to closely monitor the system for potential errors in a different setting.

The Implementation phase includes the same steps as in the SDLC. For a purchased system, however, the software vendor might be highly involved in the Installation. Further, the maintenance of the package is usually a task performed by the vendor. The negotiation of this part of the purchase contract is therefore a critical step.

Initiating the Purchasing Process Similar to the decision for customized application investments, organizations use a number of approaches to decide whether to invest in a purchased system. Some organizations do not require a detailed formal request to begin an investigation of a possible system purchase because there is an assumption that fewer IS resources are needed. At a minimum, the business manager prepares a document that briefly describes the proposed application needs and outlines the potential benefits that the application will provide to the organization.

A high-level cost estimate for a proposed purchase will need to be developed with both business manager and IS analyst input. Estimating the system costs involves much more than identifying the purchase costs of candidate packages. For example, Figure 11.2 provides a hypothetical

Stages	Cost of Building System	Cost of Buying System
Definition Phase		
Feasibility Analysis	$ 50,000	$ 50,000
Requirements Definition	250,000	200,000
Construction Phase		
System Design	150,000	—
Coding and Testing	150,000	—
System Testing	130,000	100,000
Documentation and Procedures	120,000	25,000
Implementation Phase		
Installation Planning, Data Cleanup, and Conversion	150,000	175,000
Software Purchase Price	—	100,000
Total	$1,000,000	$ 650,000

Figure 11.2 Comparison of Costs and Building versus Purchasing a System

comparison of the costs for a $1 million custom-developed system using in-house resources (a midsized system) with the costs for selecting and purchasing an off-the-shelf package with the same overall functionality. The total cost for the purchased solution ($650,000) is about two-thirds of the total cost of building the system in-house. Note, however, that the software purchase price ($100,000 for purchasing the licenses to the software package) is less than one-sixth of the total costs—a characteristic that is often not fully realized by business managers who don't have extensive experience with purchasing packaged software. Further, in the Construction phase costs for this example, there is an assumption that no major modifications to the package are required and that linkages with other systems are not a part of this project.

As when building the system using the SDLC, a systems project team should be established and given the responsibility for acquiring the software. The team should include representatives from the business units that will implement the system, IS analysts, and other IS specialists who will operate and support the packaged system and other systems that will interface with the package. Some of the specific team roles will be described later in this chapter.

Definition Phase The Definition phase begins with the same two steps as in the SDLC process. However, five additional steps are specific to the purchasing process.

Feasibility Analysis Similar to the SDLC, the objective of this step is to determine whether the proposed system is economically, technically, and operationally feasible. When purchasing a system, the feasibility of purchasing rather than building a system solution is also being considered. This step would therefore include a preliminary investigation of the availability of packaged systems that might be suitable candidates, including a high-level investigation of the software features and capabilities provided by the vendors. In this step a more detailed cost-benefit analysis is undertaken for project budgeting and monitoring purposes.

Requirements Definition The requirements definition is a critical step in the SDLC approach. The SDLC deliverable is a detailed specification of what the system must do in terms of the inputs it must accept, the data it must store, the processes it must perform, the outputs it must produce, and the performance requirements that must be satisfied. It must be accurate, complete, and detailed because it is used to design and program the system and because it determines the quality of the resulting system.

When purchasing the system, this step is equally critical. In order to select the best software package, one must first have at least a high-level conceptual understanding of the system requirements. Here, however, the focus is on defining the functional requirements of the system to the degree needed for developing a request for proposal (RFP) from a short list of vendors. The requirements need to be more fully developed than the basic requirements used to build a prototype but less detailed than the requirements elicited under an SDLC process when they are used to design the actual system. Research has shown that uncertainty about an organization's needs is a significant barrier to packaged software adoption.

Create Short List of Suitable Packages In this step the organization's requirements are used to eliminate all but a few of the most promising candidate packages that were identified in the feasibility analysis step. For example, packages should be eliminated if they do not have particular required features or will not work with existing hardware, operating system and database management software, or networks. Further research on the vendor's capabilities can be undertaken to eliminate vendors due to problems experienced with other users of the package, a vendor's inadequate track record or firm size, or other concerns about long-term viability. Independent consultants with expertise on specific types of applications or specializing in a given industry can also be key resources here and might be able to help the project team eliminate inappropriate candidates.

Establish Criteria for Selection In this step both business and IS team members need to work together to determine relevant criteria about the candidate packages and vendors in order to choose the best one. Some criteria can be categorized as mandatory requirements, whereas others could be categorized as desirable features.

Some areas in which detailed criteria should be developed are shown in Figure 11.3. For example, the vendor's

The Package
- Functional capabilities of the packaged system
- Technical requirements the software must satisfy
- Amount and quality of documentation provided

The Vendor
- Business characteristics of the vendor firm
- Vendor support of the package—initial and ongoing

Figure 11.3 Key Criteria for Software Package Selection

business characteristics could include items such as how long the vendor has been in the software business, the number of employees, financial reports over the past 5 years, its principal products, its yearly software sales revenue, and the location of its sales and support offices. The packaged system's functional capabilities should include the degree to which the package allows for multiple options and the ease with which it can be tailored to fit company needs using parameters or other approaches that do not require system coding.

The technical requirements to be evaluated include the hardware and system software (system platform) required to run the system and the database requirements for the package. This information allows one to evaluate how well the package will conform to current organizational standards for hardware, software, and networks. The types, amount, and quality of the documentation provided should also be evaluated, as well as the quality and amount of vendor support available, including training, consulting, and system maintenance.

In addition to detailing the evaluation criteria, consideration should be given to the measures that will be used in the evaluation process. It is not uncommon to evaluate packages using a scale with numbers (such as 1 through 10) or qualitative labels (such as outstanding, good, average, fair, or poor). If a scale with numbers is used, each criterion can be assigned an importance weight, and a weighted score can be computed for each evaluation category for each package. Although quantitative scores might not be the sole means for selection, they help to quantify differences among the candidate packages.

Develop and Distribute the RFP A **request for proposal (RFP)** is a formal document sent to potential vendors inviting them to submit a proposal describing their software package and how it would meet the company's needs. In organizations with prior experience purchasing software, a template for the RFP could already have been developed. A sample table of contents is shown in Figure 11.4. However, the specific requirements sought in Section III in this example will greatly depend on the type of package and the specific business needs.

The project team uses the criteria for selection to develop the RFP. The RFP gives the vendors information about the system's objectives and requirements, the environment in which the system will be used, the general criteria that will be used to evaluate the proposals, and the conditions for submitting proposals. Specific questions might need to be developed to capture the system's performance characteristics, whether source code is provided,

	Page
I. Introduction	
A. Structure and Scope of the RFP	3
B. Objective of RFP	3
C. Company Background and Philosophy	3
D. Hardware/Software Environment	4
E. Current Business Environment	5
II. Guidelines for Vendor Response	
A. Guidelines	6
B. Vendor Response	8
C. General Evaluation Process	10
III. Requirements	
A. Vendor Information	12
B. Vendor Support/Training	13
C. Documentation	15
D. Package Hardware and System Software Environment	17
E. Application and Database Architecture	21
F. Tuning and Measurement	26
G. Functional Requirements	28
IV. Costs	
A. Summary	33
B. Non-Recurring	35
C. Recurring	37
D. Price Guarantee	39
E. Maintenance Agreement	40
F. New Releases	41
V. Signature Page	42

Figure 11.4 Sample RFP Table of Contents

and whether the purchasing organization is allowed to modify the package without voiding the vendor warranty. In addition to pricing information for the package itself, any additional costs for training and consulting need to be ascertained. The RFP can also be used to capture historical information about the package, such as the date of the first release, the date of its last revision, and a list of companies in which the package has been implemented—including contact information to obtain references from these companies.

This step ends when the RFP is sent to the short list of qualified vendors.

Evaluate Vendor Responses to RFP and Choose Package
In this step the vendor responses to the RFP are evaluated and additional actions are taken to evaluate the candidate packages and their vendors. The overall objective of the evaluation process is to determine the extent of any discrepancies between the company's needs as specified by the requirements and the weighting system and the capabilities of the proposed application packages. Aggregate evaluations (scores) need to be calculated for each set of criteria and for the overall package. The team then uses these figures to discuss the major strengths and weaknesses of the candidate packages. This can be a large data collection and analysis task and might involve independent evaluations by all project team members. Both IS and business team members might need to confer not only with other project team members, but also with other members of their departments.

In addition to evaluating the vendors' responses from the formal RFP process, two other types of data collection are commonly pursued, at least for the leading candidate packages. First, demonstrations of the leading packages can usually be arranged. Sometimes it is feasible for the vendor to set up a demo on-site at your organization; at other times, another location is required—either at a vendor location or at another company that has installed the package. Detailed requirements for software demos should be provided to the vendors to ensure equitable conditions for demonstrating system performance, because response times and other characteristics of system performance can vary greatly depending on the hardware and system software being used to run the package. An example of demo specifications for a financial modeling package, and a form for evaluating the demo specified, are provided in Figures 11.5A and 11.5B.

Second, references from users of the software package in other companies are usually obtained. Each vendor might be asked to provide a reference list as part of the RFP. One especially effective technique is to require the vendor to provide the names of users as well as IS specialists for each customer organization on their reference list. Task force members can then divide up the names with, for example, IS specialists contacting their counterparts in companies that have already implemented the package. Site visits to one or more of these companies might also be possible. Evaluations of the vendor's consulting and training services can also be obtained from these sources.

Presentation Directions

The format must follow the outline provided.

The mainframe to which the PC is connected for this presentation must be an IBM running under MVS. If your MVS is not exactly like ours (as outlined in the RFP) you must provide a written explanation of how the differences (i.e., response time, color, etc.) affect the demonstration.

The presentation is limited to 2 hours, including 30 minutes for questions at the end. You will be given 30 minutes to set up.

With the data and formulas provided, create a relational database so that the following Profit and Loss (P&L) statements can be modeled and reported.

Fiscal 2000 Plan:

Item P&L: by month with total year at the right.
Control Unit P&L: by item with total at the right.
Business Unit P&L: by Control Unit with total at the right.

Fiscal 2001 Projection:

Business Unit P&L: by Control Unit with total at the right.

Combined Fiscal 2000 & Fiscal 2001:

Control Unit Change Analysis: by item for total Fiscal 2000 vs. proj. Fiscal 2001.
Business Unit Change Analysis: by Control Unit for total Fiscal 2000 vs. proj. Fiscal 2001.

Provide a listing of the populated database relations and/or tables.

Provide an example listing of the programs/models and report format files for each type of P&L and Change Analysis above.

Figure 11.5A Example of Requirements for Vendor Demonstration

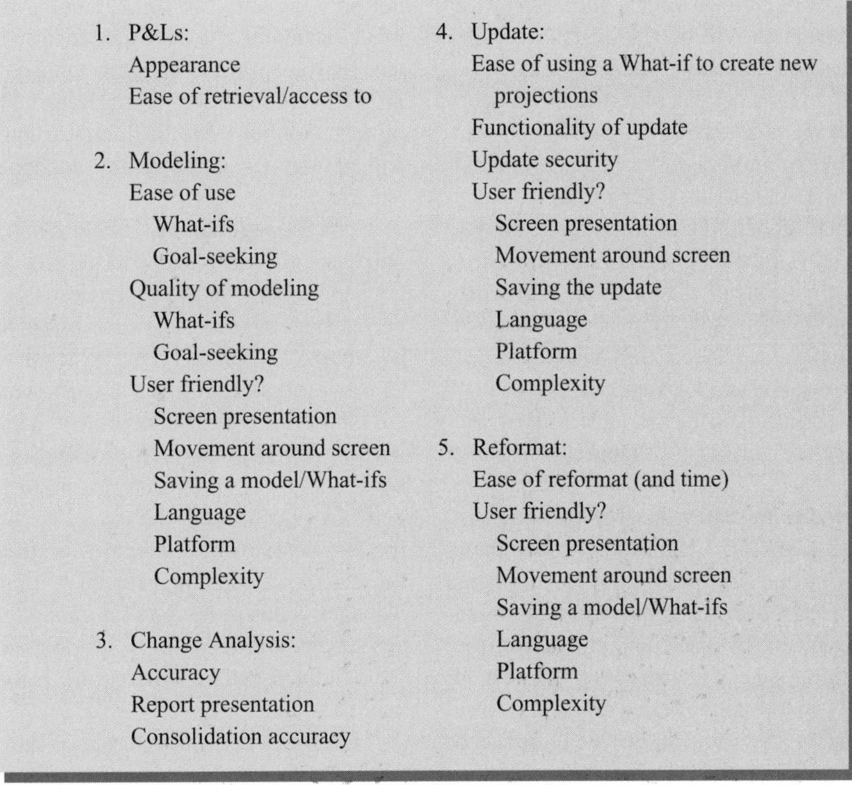

1. P&Ls:
   - Appearance
   - Ease of retrieval/access to

2. Modeling:
   - Ease of use
     - What-ifs
     - Goal-seeking
   - Quality of modeling
     - What-ifs
     - Goal-seeking
   - User friendly?
     - Screen presentation
     - Movement around screen
     - Saving a model/What-ifs
     - Language
     - Platform
     - Complexity

3. Change Analysis:
   - Accuracy
   - Report presentation
   - Consolidation accuracy

4. Update:
   - Ease of using a What-if to create new projections
   - Functionality of update
   - Update security
   - User friendly?
     - Screen presentation
     - Movement around screen
     - Saving the update
     - Language
     - Platform
     - Complexity

5. Reformat:
   - Ease of reformat (and time)
   - User friendly?
     - Screen presentation
     - Movement around screen
     - Saving a model/What-ifs
     - Language
     - Platform
     - Complexity

Figure 11.5B Example of Evaluation Worksheet for Vendor Demonstration

Based on all the above information sources, the project team needs to assess how well the company's needs match with the capabilities of the available packages (see Figure 11.6). This is a critical step that requires both business and technical expertise. The results of this process step will also have broad ramifications for the project's success.

Once the discrepancies between the package's capabilities and the company's needs are identified, the team needs to choose the best way to deal with these discrepancies for the top candidate packages. Assuming that the company decides that it still wants to invest in one of these packages, there are three major alternatives to choose from. As shown at the bottom of Figure 11.6, the company can change its own procedures to fit the package, investigate the feasibility and costs of modifying the package, or implement the package "as is" and work around the differences.

An important factor when choosing among these alternatives is fully understanding the additional development effort and costs that would be required to modify the package in order to tailor it to the company's needs and integrate it into the company's environment. These alternatives therefore need to be made in collaboration with internal IS specialists and the vendors of the top candidate packages in order to be sure that the extent of the discrepancies have been fully identified and that the feasibility and advisability of modifying a given package have been fully considered.

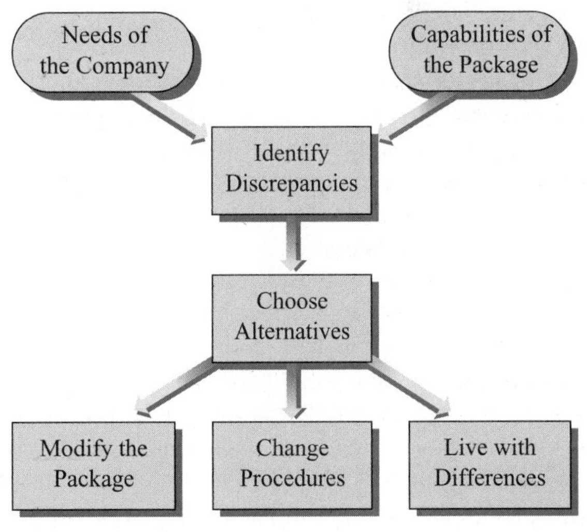

Figure 11.6 Matching Company Needs with Capabilities of the Package

If system modifications are a viable alternative, the plans for which organization will be responsible for programming the changes and the total costs of these changes will need to be taken into consideration. Further, the impacts of modifying the package need to be evaluated for not just the initial system project, but also for subsequent maintenance and package upgrade projects. For example, many companies that purchase today's large complex enterprise system packages, such as an ERP system, are advised to avoid reprogramming portions of the package in order to avoid the costs of continually modifying new releases of the package in the future (see the section below entitled "Special Case: Enterprise System Packages").

Instead, many purchasing companies have decided to take the middle alternative in Figure 11.6: Change Procedures. That is, they decide that it is better for the company to change its own procedures to match the way the software package operates than to modify the package. A company might in fact even find that the procedural assumptions incorporated into the package are better ways of doing things than those specified by the company during the Requirements Definition step of the process. This could occur if the software vendor has worked with one or more leading organizations in the same industry in order to develop the software package. For example, the vendors of today's large ERP packages might have worked with industry consortia to develop modules around industry-specific processes, and then the vendors can market their packages as having "best practices" for the industry embedded in their software package.

The decision to purchase a system is therefore not only a commitment to purchase the best of the available systems, but also a commitment to whatever organizational compromises need to be made in order to implement the system. Packaged software is a vendor's solution to a problem that is perceived to exist in a significant number of firms. Thus, it is likely that discrepancies between the organization's needs and the package's capabilities will exist. Before finalizing the purchase decision, the project team should ensure that the relevant business managers support the decision to buy the selected package and agree that they will do whatever is necessary to implement it successfully. Similarly, the project team should ensure that the IS specialists agree that the system can operate in the current environment and that they can satisfactorily support it in-house as required.

Negotiate Contract The deliverables from this stage are a legal contract with the vendor of the selected software package and a detailed plan for the remainder of the life-cycle steps. The contract with the software vendor specifies not only the software price, number of licenses, and payment schedule, but also functional specifications, acceptance-testing procedures, a timetable of the delivery process, protection of trade secrets, repair and maintenance responsibilities, liabilities due to failures, required documentation, and options to terminate the agreement (Gurbaxani and Whang, 1991).

Contract negotiations should be an integral part of the purchase process. When working with vendors to determine how to reduce the discrepancies between the company's needs and the packages' capabilities, one is actually prenegotiating a contract with the selected vendor.

Many organizations have software purchasing specialists who work with system project managers in the contract writing and negotiation steps. Because the contract will be the only recourse if the system or the vendor does not perform as specified, the use of an attorney also reduces the likelihood of future legal wrangling or a loss of rightful claims. Once the project is underway, the project manager needs to be familiar enough with the contractual agreement in order to know whether an unanticipated need for vendor services will require a formal change to the vendor contract.

The contract type also has implications for the risk level of the purchasing company. For example, under a fixed-price contract, the buyer knows in advance the total price that will be incurred for a specified product and vendor services. Under a cost-reimbursement type of contract, in which the buyer agrees to pay the vendor's direct and indirect costs, the purchasing company assumes a much greater risk.

Construction Phase In the SDLC process, the Construction phase includes three steps: system design, system building, and system testing. With purchasing, the extent to which the first two steps are needed depends on whether or not the purchased package is modified, as well as the complexity of the package itself.

Significant savings in time and money might be realized if no major modifications are made to the package's code. Looking back at the cost comparisons in Figure 11.2, the Construction phase costs are the major source of the total cost savings from purchasing a package vs. building a custom application: Even when adding in the software purchase price itself (shown under Implementation Phase), the costs for the Construction phase of a purchase package are less than half as great as the Construction costs for the customized solution. However, as stated earlier, the example in Figure 11.2 assumes that no major modifications to the package are required and that linkages with other systems are not a part of this project. The $350,000 difference in total costs between the cost of building and the cost of purchasing this particular system could therefore quickly vanish if the assumption of no system modifications does not hold true.

If no modifications to the system are to be made, the firm can move to the system testing step after the purchase contract is signed. Many off-the-shelf packages for single functions, such as accounting applications, are often not modified because the business practices they support are quite standardized and the vendor did not develop the package with modifications in mind (Rockart and Hofman, 1992). Packaged systems have typically been Beta-tested in companies in the targeted industry before they are sold on the open market. Despite the fact that the package might have been thoroughly tested and already used in other organizations, user acceptance testing still needs to be conducted to ensure that the system works properly with the company's data and on preexisting or newly installed hardware. This could require significant time and effort because the purchasing organization is not familiar with the system's detailed design. The vendor provides user documentation for those who will use the system and technical systems documentation for those who install the system and operate it. However, new procedures for the system's business users might need to be developed to fit the purchasing organization.

If the package is modified, there might be several options to consider for how to accomplish the changes: a contract with the vendor, a contract with a third party, or modifying the software with in-house resources. Many vendors routinely contract to make the desired modifications. If a vendor will furnish only the machine-language code for the application—not the source code in which the program was written—the only alternative might be to contract with the vendor to make the modifications.

If the vendor or another outside supplier makes the modifications, the purchaser also needs to test them. User acceptance testing is especially important and typically requires significant time and effort by the business users. Revised user and system documentation also needs to be reviewed. If the purchaser modifies the package, the system design and building activities in the SDLC methodology will likely be followed, similar to the way these steps would be for traditional custom development. Because IS staff must devote substantial effort to understanding the details of the software package's design and structure in order to modify it, it is not uncommon for the initial estimates of the time and costs for these steps to be insufficient.

The scope of the project might also include modifications to existing company systems in order to interface them with the new package. Creating these interface programs can be difficult and costly, and integration testing is typically time-consuming. According to Keen (1991), the total costs of system modifications can be hard to predict and the total life-cycle costs for a purchased system can be up to seven times greater than the original estimate.

Implementation Phase The Implementation phase of the SDLC involves installation, operations, and maintenance. As seen in Figure 11.1, these are all major activities in the purchasing life cycle.

Installation The installation stage in the SDLC involves installation planning, training, data cleanup, and conversion. The installation of a packaged system also includes all these activities. A key factor in a successful installation of a packaged system is the quality of vendor support during this step (Lucas et al., 1988). The package's size and complexity can also greatly affect the installation plan. For example, large ERP system packages can entail multiple years of work by in-house IS specialists as well as outside consultants to prepare for the initial installation of these integrated systems. This is because not only do these systems include many optional choices with which to configure the system to fit the organization, but also because ERP systems typically require significant changes in day-to-day business processes. As a result, the costs for installation planning, data cleanup and conversion efforts to install such packages exceed those for a custom application effort (see Figure 11.2). In large organizations, especially those with different types of business units in different geographic locations, it is also often necessary to implement the package in phases, which can also increase project costs.

Special attention also needs to be given to the training needs for a purchased system as part of the implementation activities. Depending on the extent to which the new system will require significant changes in how employees currently do their jobs, the project might require a large investment in preparing the users for the new system, including in-house or vendor-led training programs. Business managers and representative users must be actively involved in these activities and committed to devoting the time necessary to anticipate and resolve problems that arise.

To help organizations that will be making significant changes in the way people do their jobs, many consulting firms have developed an expertise in what is referred to as "change management." Some of the change management activities are specifically designed to help overcome resistance by business users to the new system being implemented. For projects implementing complex enterprise systems, for example, the systems budget for change management activities can be greater than the budgeted cost for the initial software purchase. (See the section entitled "Managing Business Change" in Chapter 12, "IT Project Management.")

Operations Ongoing operations tasks for a new application are similar whether the company purchases the system or builds it using the SDLC. However, a key to success in the initial days of operation for a new packaged system is good lines of communication with the vendor in order to quickly resolve any problems. Long-term success depends on the degree to which the organization has successfully integrated the system into the company's ongoing operations.

Maintenance As described above, it is common for a vendor to do package maintenance, and this needs to be specified in the software purchase contract. A well-designed contract can lead to considerable cost avoidance to a firm over the life of the system. The potential downside, however, is that the purchasing company becomes totally dependent upon the vendor for future system changes. Because the vendor must balance the desires and needs of all the organizations that use the system, a purchasing company might not get all the changes it wants and it might even have to accept some changes it does not want. The worst case scenarios here are as follows: (1) the purchased system has a significantly shorter useful life than originally intended, so the system costs may exceed the expected benefits for the company that purchased the software, or (2) the vendor goes out of business before the company achieves its expected return on the packaged software investment.

If the original package was modified, the installation of a vendor's new version of the package might not be the optimal solution for the purchasing organization. With the vendor's help, the company needs to compare the functionality of the new version of the package with its current modified version and then decide on the best way to deal with these discrepancies. The choices are similar to those shown in Figure 11.6, except the "do nothing" choice means that the organization might be left operating a version of the package that the vendor might or might not continue to support. If the organization modified the original package in-house or built extensive interfaces to the package's earlier version, the implementation of a new version of the package can also result in considerable maintenance costs for the organization.

In the case of large ERP system packages, the purchasing organization needs to anticipate that new releases of the software might be relatively frequent, and the vendor might continue to support prior package releases only for a certain time period. When implementing a system upgrade that includes significant new functionality, the company will need to decide whether to first implement the new version of the system and then initiate projects to make better use of the business capabilities supported by the new release or whether to implement the new business capabilities as part of the system upgrade project.

Project Team for Purchasing Packages

Successfully implementing a packaged application typically requires a major commitment on the part of business managers and users because of the extensive changes in business processes and procedures that are needed to effectively implement the purchased software. As a result, it is not uncommon for business managers to be asked to take a **project manager** role for a packaged application system project. However, because IS expertise is still required in order to manage the technical aspects of implementing a package, IS managers also need to play project leadership roles. As mentioned previously, small organizations that have no IS specialists will need to rely on the software vendor or outside consultants, or both, to provide the necessary IS expertise.

The software vendor initially provides information on the package capabilities in response to an RFP. Vendors of leading packages might then be asked to provide a demonstration and to consult with the purchaser about potential system modifications or new interfaces to older systems. The vendor company might also be contracted to perform modifications to the package prior to implementation in order to reduce mismatches between the packaged system's capabilities and the organization's needs after a careful assessment of the benefits and risks of doing so. The vendor could also play a major role in the system installation, as well as provide ongoing maintenance support for the purchasing organization. In the case of large enterprise system packages, it is also common for companies to contract with a consulting firm (that might have been certified by the software vendor) as a **third-party implementation partner** on the project.

Because of the initial and ongoing dependence on the software vendor, purchasing specialists (contract specialists) within the purchasing company can also be critical to the success of a packaged system implementation, whether or not they are formal members of the project team. For example, if an RFP is sent to vendors, a purchasing specialist will help prepare or at least review the RFP document before it is distributed to vendors. Firms with prior software purchasing experience might have developed boilerplate sections to be adapted to the type of purchase. Purchasing specialists are also skilled in negotiating contracts that provide for contingency actions that can reduce financial and other business risks for the purchasing company. For example, many of today's contracts include specific agreements about levels of service during an installation period (see the section entitled "Service Level Agreements" in Chapter 15).

As described earlier under the negotiate-contract step, attorneys (which may also be purchasing specialists) should oversee the writing and approval of the external contract with software vendors. All associated licensing agreements should also be reviewed in order to minimize the associated costs and risks for the business.

Managing a Purchased System Project

Purchased system projects are successful when the organization has selected a product, and a vendor, that is able to satisfy the firm's current and future system needs. This requires an effective project team with members who have the business and technical skills and knowledge needed, including the skills and knowledge needed for the project team roles described above. Unlike the traditional SDLC process in which a long Construction phase buffers the Definition phase from the Implementation phase, the purchase of a software package might entail large capital expenditures by the company within just a few months. The right business managers, end users, and IS specialists need to be a part of the project team to ensure that the best package is purchased from the best vendor and that both technical and business risks have been adequately considered.

A typical problem with managing the life cycle of a purchased system project is ensuring that adequate attention is given to the steps in the initial Definition phase. A common mistake is that business managers learn about a particular packaged solution from another company or a salesperson at an industry conference and they begin negotiating with the vendor without adequate attention to the functional requirements definition step. Project teams that do not do a good job identifying their requirements will not be able to do a good job assessing the discrepancies between the company's needs and the capabilities of candidate packages. This increases the short-term and long-term investment risks, because a contract with an external vendor is not as easily changed as a project agreement between users and internal IS developers. It is therefore critical that the Definition phase be performed well.

For the project team members from the business side who also have implementation responsibilities, it is also imperative that they be *representative* business managers and users. Steps should be taken to ensure that they are committed to the project goals at the outset, including the time schedule and budget.

The success of the Implementation phase also depends on how well the Definition phase was performed, because this is where the team members assessed the organizational changes needed to successfully implement the purchased system. As discussed earlier, users of the packaged system might be asked to make significant changes in how they do their jobs in order to conform to a package's features. This requires a well-planned installation step under the leadership of committed business managers who are very knowledgeable about the needed changes.

In addition, purchased system projects introduce several new types of risks. First, the success of the project is highly dependent on the performance of a third party. The quality of the implemented system will depend not only on the vendor's software engineering capabilities, but also on how well the implementing organization understands the package's capabilities and on the vendor's training and installation capabilities. As discussed earlier, a key aspect of the vendor selection process is the accurate assessment of the vendor's capabilities, not just an evaluation of the current software package.

The project's initial success, as well as the long-term effectiveness of the system being installed, is also highly dependent on the contract negotiation process. In most situations system implementation does not simply involve "turning the key." Vendor expertise might be required to install the package, build interfaces to existing systems, and perhaps modify the package itself to better match the purchasing organization's needs. Service expectations between the purchaser and vendor need to be a part of the contract developed at the end of the Definition phase. The contract will be the only recourse for the purchaser if the system modifications, vendor training, or the implementation of the package do not go well.

Purchasing Small Systems The discussion in this chapter has focused on the purchasing process for large, complex systems. If a smaller, simpler system is being considered, the time and effort put into the process can, of course, be scaled back. However, a small system can still be a major investment for a small business. Unfortunately, many small businesses have limited experience with and knowledge of evaluating and installing such systems. The services of a hardware vendor, a local software supplier, as well as external consultants might therefore be needed.

Purchasing Advantages and Disadvantages

Figure 11.7 summarizes the advantages and disadvantages of purchasing packaged systems, as well as some potential long-term advantages and disadvantages for buying packaged software solutions.

Advantages The primary project advantage is that, compared to customized application development, less time is needed to implement the system. Nevertheless, for mid-sized systems, the entire process will still require several months, and for large-scale enterprise software implementations (with packages such as ERP systems) the process can take several years.

A second major advantage is that packaged software implementations can be very attractive from an economic standpoint. For example, a small business can obtain a complete accounting system for less than $25,000, which is very low compared to the cost of developing a comparable customized application. Assuming that the vendor has more than 10,000 installations of this small package ($250 million in revenues), the vendor will have an incentive to spend millions of dollars on improving the package in order to issue new releases. Everyone comes out a winner because each purchaser has cost avoidance from purchasing a package, and the vendor makes a large enough profit to stay in business and provide upgrades and other support services on an ongoing basis. As shown in Figure 11.2, the initial purchase price of a software package might be a relatively small fraction of the total cost of acquiring and installing a software package.

A third temporary advantage is that in-house IS resources could be freed up to develop mission-critical applications that could provide the firm a competitive advantage if software packages can be implemented for relatively common processes that provide no specific strategic advantage.

Two potential long-term advantages are application quality and the infusion of external expertise. The quality of a software package might be substantially better than that of a custom system, because a vendor can afford to spend much more time and effort developing the system than an individual company. The documentation can be much better than the typical in-house documentation, and new releases of the package might incorporate improvements recommended by companies that are using the system. Furthermore, each release is usually thoroughly tested, including a Beta test in a client organization.

Finally, a packaged solution is a quick way to infuse new expertise—both IT expertise and business expertise—into the organization. Given the fast pace of technological change, most organizations today find it difficult to train and retain IS personnel with expertise in new, emerging technologies. Software vendors often have the funds and motivation to develop systems using newer technologies. Packaged solutions for a particular industry, or large ERP systems, also frequently have best-in-class processes and procedures embedded in the software. By purchasing the software, companies can also adopt better business processes.

Purchasing Advantages
- Reduced time to implement
- Lower overall acquisition costs
- High application quality (debugged)
- Reduced need for internal IS resources
- Infusion of external expertise (IS, business)

Purchasing Disadvantages
- Risks due to lack of package knowledge
- Risks due to extent of organizational changes required
- Initial and ongoing dependence on vendor

Figure 11.7 Advantages and Disadvantages of Purchasing Packaged Software

Disadvantages Two major project risks are also associated with implementing purchased packages. One risk is the lack of package knowledge. The package implementation can require significant training for IS as well as business personnel, which increases the implementation costs. Because of an organization's relative unfamiliarity with the software package, the organization might also not be as quick to leverage the capabilities of the package as it would be to leverage the capabilities of a system that members of the organization had designed and custom developed. Some organizations also make the mistake of initially modifying the package, or adding other functionality, only to learn later that the package could have provided the same functionality if it had been implemented differently.

Another related project risk is that since implementing a packaged system often requires significant business process changes, there are greater project risks. Knowledgeable business managers and skilled IS specialists need to be significantly involved in the Definition phase to understand what organizational changes need to be made. Furthermore, there often is more user resistance due to the extent of changes required in order to implement the packaged solution.

The long-term disadvantage is that the organization becomes dependent on an external IT provider not only for the initial installation and perhaps some package modifications, but also for the ongoing maintenance of the package. Although in many cases this can result in a strategic alliance of value to both the vendor and purchaser, the purchaser might not fully anticipate the coordination costs associated with managing the vendor relationship. In addition, of course, there is the risk that the vendor will go out of business or be unresponsive to the needs of the purchasing firm.

SPECIAL CASE: ENTERPRISE SYSTEM PACKAGES

By the end of the 1990s, the majority of U.S.-based Fortune 500 companies and more than one-fourth of European-based midsized organizations had invested in a first wave of enterprise system packages: enterprise resource planning (ERP) systems. Most companies purchased these systems in order to achieve business benefits, but ERP investments are also IT platform investments (see the discussion of major vendors and ERP benefits in Chapter 5).

One of the primary business benefits associated with ERP systems is to enable access to integrated data, sometimes real-time data, for better management decision making. Since most ERP systems are built to support cross-functional business processes, interfaces across separate functional systems do not need to be maintained. Further, ERP modules that can be "configured" to be used by different types of firms in different industries enable those firms that have already conducted projects to reengineer their business processes to now implement them; building custom systems to support new cross-functional processes would require a much larger system investment over a much longer time.

For the IS departments within the large firms that were among the first to purchase an ERP package, this could also be the first time that their IS personnel would be asked to configure a package in the best way possible, rather than to custom develop an application based on the requirements of their business users. IS personnel also needed to be sent to training classes, typically conducted by the software vendor, so that they could learn the packaged software as well as learn new vendor-specific languages for writing interfaces and queries. New "business analyst" skill sets could also be required to effectively manage the process steps for a packaged software project, rather than a customized life cycle methodology.

Another key characteristic of the early ERP projects was the heavy reliance on third-party consultants who were not employees of the software vendor, such as consultants in the Big 4 or smaller consulting firms. These "implementation partners" were usually invaluable for helping an organization quickly learn how the software package operates, as well as how the complex business process options embedded in each module would work. Because of the large scope and complexity of some of these ERP package implementations, one of the key management challenges, then, could have been to what extent to rely on the external consultants to lead an ERP project and how to make sure the purchasing company captured the needed knowledge to continue to operate and "fine tune" the configurations after the consultants left. Nevertheless, even with the help of third-party consultants, many initial ERP implementation projects were not successful.

According to Brown and Vessey (2003), five factors need to be managed well for an ERP project to be successful. These factors are described in some detail below.

- *Top management is engaged in the project, not just involved.* Because enterprise systems demand fundamental changes in the way a company performs its business processes, its business executives need to be visibly active in the funding and oversight of the project. Lower-level managers will not have the clout needed to ensure that not only will the ERP modules be configured to align with the best business process solutions for the company, but also that all relevant business managers buy in to the organizational changes that will be necessary to take advantage of the software package's capabilities.
- *Project leaders are veterans, and team members are decision makers.* Because ERP system implementations are extremely complex, the leaders of the project need to be highly skilled and have a proven track record with leading a project that has had a major impact on a business. The team members who are representing different business units and different business functions (e.g., finance, marketing, manufacturing) need to also be empowered to make decisions on behalf of the unit or function they represent. If the team members do not have decision-making rights, the project leaders will likely not be able to meet the agreed-upon project deadlines.
- *Third parties fill gaps in expertise and transfer their knowledge.* As described above, ERP systems are typically implemented with the help of third-party implementation partners (consultants), as well as the software vendor. The skillsets of the consultants needed will depend on the skillsets and experiences of the purchasing company's own business and IT

managers. If there are no internal project leaders with the necessary project management skills, consultants should also be used to help manage the project. However, before the consultants leave, the internal staff needs to acquire the knowledge needed to continue to operate the new system. Many organizations develop agreements with consultants that explicitly refer to the transfer of knowledge to internal staff as a part of the consultant contract.

- *Change management goes hand-in-hand with project planning.* Many of the early adopters of ERP systems underestimated the need for project resources to help prepare the business for implementing the new system. ERP systems typically require training not only in how to use the new system, but also in how to perform business processes in new ways to take advantage of the package's capabilities. Because of the tight integration of the ERP modules, workers also typically need to learn much more about what happens before and after their own interactions with the system. Companies with the fewest problems at the time of implementation began to plan for these types of changes as part of the overall project planning activities.
- *A satisficing mindset prevails.* Because of the integrated nature of the modules of an ERP package, companies typically implement the package in as "vanilla" a form as possible. This typically means that business personnel will be asked to "give up" some functionality that they had in a system that the ERP is replacing. In other words, the company needs to be in a "satisficing" mindset, as opposed to expecting an "optimal" solution. For companies with many business units across the globe, business managers will also typically be asked to accept some less-than-optimal ways of doing things in order to have a standard configuration across the enterprise. A typical rule-of-thumb here is to try and keep a standard solution for about 80 percent of the package configuration, recognizing that some local customization will even be required due to specific country or regional regulations.

Brown and Vessey also point out that later adopters of a new kind of enterprise system always have the advantage of learning from the mistakes of early adopters. For example, companies that purchased an ERP package in the second half of the 1990s could talk with other companies in their industry who had already implemented an ERP and then they could benchmark their own implementation plans in order to avoid making costly mistakes. These authors also suggest that much of what is learned from ERP projects will help the early adopters of the next wave of enterprise systems (e.g., customer relationship management and supply chain management systems).

Other researchers (e.g., Ross, 1998) have emphasized the importance of recognizing that large, complex enterprise system initiatives really don't end with the initial "Go Live" date. Rather, managers should anticipate that there will be a period of time following the initial implementation in which the system and new processes become more stabilized (a "shakedown" period). After the new ways of doing business have become more routinized and the technical operations of the new system are running smoothly, the company can begin to make smaller changes (continuous improvement) to help it achieve the promised business benefits from implementing this new type of software package. For example, many companies report having achieved cost efficiencies in materials procurement within the first calendar year after an ERP implementation, but other value-chain improvements might not be realized for several more years.

NEW PURCHASING OPTION: APPLICATION SERVICE PROVIDERS (ASPS)

A new trend related to implementing packaged solutions began to emerge in the IT industry during the first decade of the new millennium: **application service providers** (ASPs). Under this kind of purchasing option, the purchaser elects to use a "hosted" application rather than to purchase the software application and host it on its own equipment. The ASP is therefore an ongoing service provider, and the ASP option is a different kind of "make vs. buy" decision. Instead of having a software licensing agreement with a firm that developed the software, a company pays a third party (ASP) for delivering the software functionality over the Internet to company employees and sometimes the company's business partners.

The two major *advantages* associated with purchasing a package, which were discussed at the beginning of this chapter, are also advantages for choosing an ASP: (1) cost savings and (2) faster speed of implementation. A subscription-based service with an ASP typically involves monthly fees rather than large up-front IT investments in both the software package and additional infrastructure investments to host the package. For companies with widely dispersed employees requiring remote access, an ASP solution can also reduce network access and other service delivery costs. Because the package is also typically already up and running on the ASP's host computer, the implementation project should also be less time-consuming.

However, there are also some potential downsides, including dependence on an external vendor not just for the software package, but also for ongoing operations. Good processes for making the best purchasing decision and contracting for the needed service levels are even more critical when an organization enters into an ASP agreement. A purchasing process that carefully assesses the capability of an ASP to provide reliable performance and the likelihood of the ASP surviving in the marketplace are especially important for ASP contracts, because this market is still in its infancy. Some of these risks appear to be diminished when the ASP host is also a large software vendor—such as SAP or PeopleSoft for ERP modules or Siebel Systems for CRM modules.

Metrics for vendor performance and penalties for noncompliance should be a key part of the contract. As described in the sidebar "A Dream vs. a Nightmare," if you do not do a good job with the ASP selection process up front, you risk paying the price later.

A DREAM VS. A NIGHTMARE

It was an IT manager's worst nightmare. The OshKosh B'Gosh Inc. online store was open, but the orders went nowhere: The communications link between the clothing retailer and the company that hosted its Web application had gone down. Resolving the nightmare was further complicated because the ASP with which OshKosh had contracted had subcontracted with another firm to host their application. And OshKosh's telecommunications carrier needed to get into the hosting site to repair the equipment. According to CIO Jon Dell-Antonia at OshKosh, "It was like the Three Stooges and the Keystone Cops combined. If I went through the whole litany, you'd be rolling on the floor laughing. But we were not laughing at the time."

One common mistake companies make when choosing an ASP vendor is that they involve their application specialists in the meetings with the prospective ASPs, but not their computer operations specialists. According to an analyst with the Gartner Group, customers should concentrate not just on the A in ASP—the application that will be provided—but also the S—the service. You need to carefully document your needs first, before you start talking to an ASP.

[Adapted from Anthes, 2000]

SUMMARY

Purchasing packaged software is an alternative to custom software development that has been increasingly pursued by organizations of all sizes since the early 1990s. The fact that packaged solutions can be implemented more quickly than a custom-developed solution with the same, or similar, functionality is a major advantage in today's fast-changing business environment. A major disadvantage can be increased dependence on a vendor that could go out of business.

The process for purchasing an application is based on the same life-cycle phases as a custom approach: Definition, Construction, and Implementation. Even if an application is to be purchased, an organization first must define its basic system needs before attempting to select the best off-the-shelf application solution. The Definition phase also includes the development of an RFP to be sent to software vendors and an evaluation of the vendor responses. If successful, the Definition phase ends with a vendor contract, which should be negotiated with the help of contract specialists.

The time spent on Construction phase activities varies greatly depending on whether or not the source code of the package is modified, which may be done by the vendor, another outside supplier, or the purchasing company. In the case of large packaged systems for which there are expected to be frequent future releases (such as ERP modules), modifications are typically kept to a bare minimum. In contrast, the Implementation phase for a software package can be more challenging than for a custom application because of the purchasing company's lack of familiarity with the details of how the package operates as well as the need for large-scale changes in the way the company will operate once the new package has been implemented. The software vendor might be heavily involved in the installation step and is also typically relied on for ongoing maintenance. Large enterprise system vendors (such as SAP) typically release new versions on a frequent basis and support older versions of the package only for a set period of time.

Expertise in the implementation of packaged systems has become an important IT capability. In some firms new manager positions have been created in order to manage relationships with IT vendors. A new procurement option is to pay an application service provider to host a software application for remote access by company employees via the Internet.

REVIEW QUESTIONS

1. What are the major trade-offs in a make-or-buy decision?
2. Summarize the five additional steps for purchasing a system that are not part of the Definition phase of a traditional SDLC process.
3. What is an RFP, and what critical tasks does it facilitate in the purchasing process?
4. Why is making a lot of modifications to a packaged system sometimes a risky approach, and what are the alternatives?
5. Briefly summarize how the phases of the traditional SDLC are similar to or different from the phases of the modified life-cycle approach in support of the cost comparisons in Figure 11.2.
6. Describe the role of the vendor for each of the three phases of the purchasing life cycle.
7. Describe why the methodology for purchasing a small system could differ from purchasing a large system.
8. Describe what a purchasing company might want to learn from a vendor demonstration of a packaged system.
9. What do you think are the most important advantages and disadvantages of purchasing a package?
10. What are some of the major differences between a process to implement an ERP package and the process to implement a less complex package?
11. What is an ASP and why is this an attractive purchasing alternative?

DISCUSSION QUESTIONS

1. Critique the following statements: It would cost us $800,000 to build this system, but we can purchase an equivalent package for $125,000. Therefore, we can save the organization $675,000 by purchasing the software package.
2. Discuss the options an organization needs to choose from when the best packaged-system solution is not a perfect fit with the needs of the organization.
3. You run a small business. You have no IS specialists on your staff and plan to purchase all your software. What might be your three most important concerns?
4. You are a manager in a company that has a lot of in-house IS expertise. What might be your key decision rules for when to purchase a system versus when to develop it in-house?
5. Discuss why an assessment of the financial stability of the vendor can be a critical consideration when evaluating responses to an RFP.
6. Choose one of the five factors associated with successful ERP implementations (presented in the section entitled "Special Case: Enterprise System Packages") and comment on how different this really is (or is not) from other packaged system implementations.
7. Many midsized firms are investing in ERP system packages, such as SAP and PeopleSoft. Comment on what you think might be particularly important parts of the decision-making process when the purchasing organization has only a small IS department.
8. Revise Figure 11.3 to make it a list of criteria for assessing an application service provider (ASP).

CHAPTER 12
IT Project Management

THE OVERALL GOALS OF SYSTEMS PROJECTS ARE TO IMPLEMENT A QUALITY system that meets the needs of the targeted business and its users on schedule and within budget. Achieving these project goals requires not only a good systems methodology but also effective project management. The systems development methodologies (systems development life cycle [SDLC], prototyping, rapid application development [RAD], purchasing life cycle) discussed in the previous chapters are disciplined methods for acquiring an information technology (IT) solution. **Project management** for systems projects requires knowledge of these methodologies as well as other generally accepted practices for managing systems projects.

The project management practices described in this chapter include those applicable to managing projects in general, as well as practices that are specific to systems projects. Some of these techniques have their roots in military projects; since World War II, private sector firms have honed these techniques in industries highly dependent on project work, such as the construction, automotive, and aerospace industries.

The Project Management Institute (PMI), an international society of project workers, has certified thousands of project management professionals in generally accepted techniques since initiating its certification program in 1984 (Frame, 1994). The management competencies certified by the PMI include four areas traditionally associated with project management: (1) project scope, (2) time, (3) cost, and (4) human resources. However, to accommodate changing project demands in today's more chaotic world, four additional competencies are now certified by the PMI: (5) managing project communications, (6) contracts, (7) quality management, and (8) risk management. Managers of systems projects therefore need to be skilled in application systems methodologies and techniques, as well as skilled in the eight competencies summarized in Figure 12.1.

Although projects vary by size, scope, time duration, and uniqueness, most projects share the three following life cycle characteristics (PMI, 1996):

1. Risk and uncertainty are highest at the start of the project.
2. The ability of the project stakeholders to influence the outcome is highest at the start of the project.
3. Cost and staffing levels are lower at the start of the project and higher toward the end.

Project management experts also distinguish between project management and **program management**. Program management refers to a long-term undertaking that is typically made up of multiple projects. For example, in some organizations, a "program office" might be established to ensure that individual

Project scope	Project communications
Project time	Contracts
Project cost	Quality management
Human resources	Risk management

Figure 12.1 Eight Project Management Competencies

A **project** is a temporary endeavor undertaken to create a unique product or service. It typically is a one-time initiative that can be divided into multiple tasks, which require coordination and control, with a definite beginning and ending.

A **program** is a group of projects managed in a coordinated way to obtain benefits not available from managing them individually (PMI, 1996).

projects are coordinated with other projects currently underway in the same organization and that monetary and human resources are being leveraged for the benefit of the program as a whole. A program office headed by an information systems (IS) program manager might be a permanent unit, charged with overseeing multiple software development and maintenance projects in different stages of completion, each of which has its own objectives, schedule, and budget. In organizations with no permanent program office, one might be temporarily set up for a very large enterprisewide implementation project, such as an enterprise resource planning (ERP) project.

In the next sections we first discuss the growing issue of how to manage an organization's portfolio of IT projects. Then we describe some of the major approaches to managing the key stages of an IT project once it has been prioritized and initially funded: project initiation, project planning, project execution and control, and project closing. In the project execution and control section we focus on two IT project management capability areas that are especially important for successfully managing complex IT projects: managing risks and managing business change. The chapter ends with some guidelines for two special IT project contexts: (1) managing large, complex software implementation projects and (2) managing IT integration projects after two businesses have merged.

IT PORTFOLIO MANAGEMENT

As organizations have become highly dependent on IT and their investments in IT have become a very high percentage of their total capital investments, there has been an increasing emphasis on **IT portfolio management**. Typically, a steering team of senior business leaders and the senior IT executive are held accountable for managing the organization's current portfolio of IT projects and pending requests. An organization's IT portfolio usually includes investments in both "sustaining" and "strategic" IT projects (Denis et al., 2004). For example, IT infrastructure investments are typically needed to "sustain" the organization's expected availability and reliability measures. Strategic investments typically include new application software packages for one or more business functions as well as new custom applications for a single department.

An organization's **IT portfolio** includes the set of IT project initiatives currently in progress, as well as requests for IT projects that have not yet been funded.

A major part of the IT portfolio management responsibilities are to continually assess whether the organization is investing in the right set of IT projects given its current competitive environment. New IT project requests are usually submitted using an agreed-upon template that includes the expected business benefits and estimates for the level of investment needed to do the project. An example of an IT project request using an organizational template is provided in Figure 12.2.

Some executive decision makers also want to be able to review an initial return on investment (ROI) analysis, or other formal financial assessment of the capital expenditure, at the time of the initial request. For large projects, however, it is more common to require instead only a rough order of magnitude (ROM) cost estimate. At a minimum, the request should include information about three types of business risks (McNurlin and Sprague, 2004):

- the risk of not doing the project
- the risks that it is the wrong project for what is trying to be achieved
- the risk that the project will fail (for technical or organizational reasons)

To help the steering team of executives prioritize a new request for an IT project against other new requests or existing IT project, an evaluative categorization scheme for all sustaining and strategic projects is typically applied. One such scheme, based on Denis et al. (2004), would be as follows:

- *Absolute Must* A mandate due to security, legal, regulatory, or end-of-life-cycle IT issues
- *Highly Desired/Business-Critical* Includes short-term projects with good financial returns and portions of very large projects already in progress

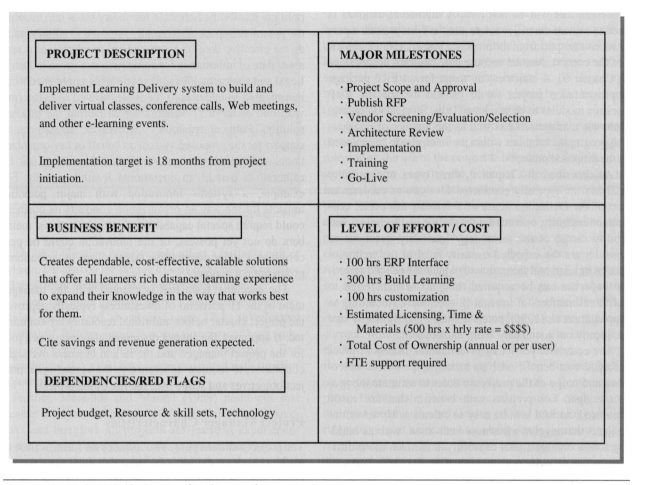

PROJECT DESCRIPTION	MAJOR MILESTONES
Implement Learning Delivery system to build and deliver virtual classes, conference calls, Web meetings, and other e-learning events. Implementation target is 18 months from project initiation.	· Project Scope and Approval · Publish RFP · Vendor Screening/Evaluation/Selection · Architecture Review · Implementation · Training · Go-Live
BUSINESS BENEFIT	**LEVEL OF EFFORT / COST**
Creates dependable, cost-effective, scalable solutions that offer all learners rich distance learning experience to expand their knowledge in the way that works best for them. Cite savings and revenue generation expected. **DEPENDENCIES/RED FLAGS** Project budget, Resource & skill sets, Technology	· 100 hrs ERP Interface · 300 hrs Build Learning · 100 hrs customization · Estimated Licensing, Time & Materials (500 hrs x hrly rate = $$$$) · Total Cost of Ownership (annual or per user) · FTE support required

Figure 12.2 Project Prioritization Template (Vavra and Lane, 2004)

- *Wanted* Valuable, but with longer time periods for returns on investment (more than a 12-month period)
- *Nice to Have* Projects with good returns, but with lower potential business value

In most organizations projects in the top two categories would most likely be funded for the budget year in which they were submitted. The "Wanted" projects would be carefully assessed and might involve the most contentious categorization decisions. The "Nice to Have" projects can be useful for helping to distinguish the projects that belong in the other categories. Many practitioners also emphasize that a team-based approach to the IT prioritization process results not only in a current prioritized list of projects but also in a better understanding among the organization's business and IT executives about the rationales for why a given IT request was funded, or not funded, and the IT budget implications for both sustaining and strategic IT investments.

Today many organizations reassess their IT project prioritization lists on a quarterly basis. Besides assessing new requests, the executive team is charged with monitoring the status of all current IT projects in order to ensure that the company's IT investments are staying aligned with the company's business goals. At AT&T, for example, a team of business and IT managers now evaluates each ongoing project on a regular basis using a Continue-Hold-Stop rating scheme (Hoffman, 2003).

PROJECT INITIATION

The first phase of a project life cycle is the project initiation phase. A key deliverable for this phase is a project charter that states in some detail the project's specific objectives, its intended scope, and any underlying assumptions and estimated results based on the feasibility analysis step of the IT project.

The scoping of a project involves setting boundaries for the project's size and the range of business functions or

In contrast to the sponsor role, the champion role is not always a formally designated one, although the champion's contribution to the project's success is widely recognized among both management and users.

PROJECT PLANNING

Three major project planning components are the project schedule, budget, and staff (project team). These components are obviously interrelated, and poor planning for one component can severely affect another. Good estimation techniques are especially important for systems projects that involve immature or emerging technologies. In general, conservative (rather than optimistic) estimations are recommended, as well as control mechanisms that focus on the areas of greatest project uncertainty and organizational vulnerability. Although we emphasize below some proven techniques for good project planning and control, it should also be kept in mind that experienced project managers will tailor their approaches to match the special circumstances of a given project or organizational situation (see the sidebar entitled "256 Project Characteristics to Be Managed").

Scheduling

Developing a project schedule typically involves a **work breakdown analysis**: identifying the phases and sequence of tasks that need to be accomplished to meet the project goals—as well as the goals for other organizational and external party obligations—and then estimating the time of completion for each task. For systems projects, the project phases as well as the detailed activities for each step and their sequence can typically be derived from the systems methodology being used for the project.

256 PROJECT CHARACTERISTICS TO BE MANAGED

Projects can have an overwhelming number of different characteristics. They can be high-risk or low-risk, long-term or short-term, state-of-the-art or routine, complex or simple, single-function or cross-functional, large or small, technology-driven or market-driven, contracted out or performed in-house, and so on. These eight characteristics alone can lead to 256 different combinations that might entail a different approach to project planning, execution, or control.

[Adapted from Roman, 1986]

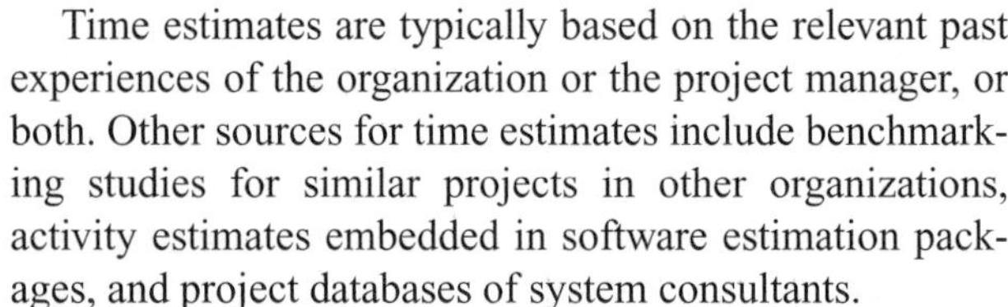

Time estimates are typically based on the relevant past experiences of the organization or the project manager, or both. Other sources for time estimates include benchmarking studies for similar projects in other organizations, activity estimates embedded in software estimation packages, and project databases of system consultants.

The detailed work activity list, the task interdependencies, and the time estimates for each task are then used to develop a master schedule for the project that identifies the **project milestone** dates and deliverables. The level of detail provided in a master schedule depends upon project characteristics such as size, functional complexity, and task interdependencies, as well as organizational practices.

Some project milestone dates will also be highly influenced by time demands particular to the organization. In particular, system implementation activities are frequently scheduled to coincide with calendar periods when transactions affected by the new system solution are much lower in number or can even be temporarily left unprocessed during the conversion process. For example, it is very common for major system tests and new system cutovers in U.S.-based organizations to be scheduled for 3-day holiday weekends. In other situations a project implementation date near the end of a fiscal period will be targeted in order to minimize historical data conversions.

The project scheduling process is somewhat different when an organization has adopted a timeboxing philosophy. The term **timeboxing** refers to an organizational practice in which a system module is to be delivered to the user within a set time limit, such as 6 months. This technique is a characteristic of the rapid application development (RAD) methodology (discussed in Chapter 10). Because the intent of timeboxing is to deliver new IT solutions as rapidly as possible, a work plan might be designed in which a given module is initially implemented during the timebox without full functionality, and then the functionality is increased in subsequent releases.

A common pitfall in developing a master schedule is a failure to understand the interdependencies among project tasks and subtasks. Including a customer verification step as part of the master scheduling process can help identify misunderstandings at an early stage of the project planning cycle.

Effective scheduling is critical to the project's success and is a key input to the project budgeting component. However, the master schedule is also meant to be a living

Work breakdown is a basic management technique that systematically subdivides blocks of work down to the level of detail at which the project will be controlled.

document. A good planning process therefore also provides for change-control procedures to request schedule changes. Aside from a process to request the necessary management approvals, changes to the master schedule should be documented with the date of the change, the nature and reason for the change, and the estimated effects of the change on other project components (budget, resource allocations) and related project tasks.

Budgeting

The project budget documents the anticipated costs for the total project. These costs are typically aggregated into meaningful categories at the level at which the project costs will be controlled.

There are two traditional approaches to estimating project costs: bottom-up and top-down. The project work plan from the scheduling process is typically used for a bottom-up process: Cost elements are estimated for the lowest level of work plan tasks and then aggregated to provide a total cost estimate for the project. According to Frame (1994), a top-down approach "eschews" the cost details and provides instead estimates for major budget categories based on historical experience. A top-down approach (also called parametric cost estimating) could be used in the project initiation stage because not enough is known about the project to do a work breakdown analysis. However, once a master schedule has been developed, a bottom-up process is recommended, especially if the project is large and complex. These two approaches can also be used as checks for each other.

No matter which approach is used, the budgeting process needs to build in cost estimates to cover project uncertainties associated with changing human resources, immovable project deadlines (that could require overtime labor), as well as changes in technology and contract costs outside the organization's control.

Like the master schedule, the project budget is a living document of anticipated total costs. A good planning process therefore also provides change-control procedures to request approvals for deviations from an estimated budget. Changes to the budget should be documented with the date of change, the nature and amount of the requested budget deviation, the reason for the change, and the estimated effects of the change on other project components (scope, schedule, resource allocations).

According to Frame (1994), inexperienced estimators typically fall into three estimation traps: They (1) are too optimistic about what is needed to do the job, (2) tend to leave components out, and (3) do not use a consistent methodology, so they have difficulty recreating their rationales. Training in estimating processes (such as that provided by the American Association of Cost Engineers) and organizational checklists of items to include in estimates can help the amateur estimator quickly improve.

Even for the experienced project manager, cost estimations can be complicated by many types of unknowns, including the lack of precedents, unpredictable technical problems, and shifting business requirements. Projects that use standard components and an evolutionary methodology are generally the easiest to estimate. Both budget padding and lowballing are apparently widely used, but both these techniques can also cause dysfunctional consequences (see the sidebar entitled "Highballing vs. Lowballing Project Costs").

Staffing

Project staffing involves identifying the IT specialist skill mix needed for the project, selecting personnel who collectively have the skills needed and assigning them to the project, preparing them for the specific project work as team members, and providing incentives to achieve the project goals.

In project work the human resource is a critical production factor. As part of the project planning, the project manager should be able to estimate the skill type, proficiency level, quantity, and time frame for human resources to execute each project phase and critical task. Some human resources need to be dedicated to the project full-time, whereas others will be shared with other project teams. Still others might not be formal team members but will be relied on for their expertise at critical points.

HIGHBALLING VS. LOWBALLING PROJECT COSTS

Budget padding is a common approach. Often there is no useful precedent to serve as a guide for a budget projection; past authorizations can be misleading or only partially applicable. Further, sometimes project budgets receive across-the-board cuts, favoring those who have submitted a padded budget in the first place. Budget padding is therefore sometimes the best defensive measure to ensure that adequate resources will be provided to get a job done.

Lowballing project costs can be conscious or unconscious. Sometimes lower estimates are provided in order to gain initial project approval. Other times the technical glitches that can arise are underestimated. Sometimes ignorance of an environmental event invalidates what was thought to be a well-informed estimate.

[Adapted from Frame, 1994, and Roman, 1986]

Wherever possible, individual employees with the best qualifications for the project work should be selected. However, in an organizational setting this is not always possible, due to the size and talent of the specialist pool internal to the organization. Because of the diverse set of specialist skills that might be needed across projects, it is not uncommon for at least a portion of the team members to undergo specialized training in anticipation of a project. Some IS organizations use a skill set "centers" approach in which IS specialists belong to a **center of excellence** managed by a coach who is responsible for developing talent and selecting personnel for project assignments based not only on project needs but also on individual development needs (see the sidebar entitled "Centers of Excellence at Bell Atlantic").

For systems projects it is also not uncommon to hire outside contractors for project work for quality or quantity reasons. This is especially desirable if a distinct specialty is required for a single project but it does not make economic sense to develop these resources in-house. It also might be impractical to use internal resources if a project requires more resources for just a short period of time. The downside in this case is that the company can become highly dependent on a talent base that is temporary. By the late 1990s, many companies began to focus on decreasing dependence on outside contractors by developing their own IT specialist talent. One way to do this is to build in a requirement for "knowledge transfer" from consultants with special expertise to internal employees as part of the consultant contract.

Another key aspect of systems project team staffing is the selection of business personnel who are not IS specialists as formal team members or as "extended" team members who help with defining the systems requirements, testing, and training over the life of the project. Careful selection of business employees can obviously be a critical step in the staffing process. IS specialists depend on users for their functional expertise (sometimes referred to as subject matter expertise, or SME). Often, formal documented procedures are not the way that work tasks really get done, and the systems team must elicit these differences as part of the Definition phase. Further, in many systems implementations, major changes in the ways of doing business are part of the project's objectives. For example, business process changes are typical when implementing a new software package that has not been modified for the implementing organization. Business personnel with enough authority to work with both business leaders and business workers who will use the new software need to be selected with the help of the executive sponsor.

Even after a well-managed selection process, there is sometimes a need for special team-building exercises to build team spirit and to help team members who have not worked together before get to know each other quickly. However, as pointed out by Frame (1994), a sports team analogy for project teams is inappropriate (see the sidebar entitled "IT Project Teams Are Not Like Sports Teams").

The degree to which team-building is needed will depend on the characteristics of the project, the prior experiences of the team members, and the degree to which the systems methodology to be used is new to the team members. Team-building and fostering ongoing motivation are easiest when team members are in the same physical location (co-located), there is a stable roster of team members, and the project manager is able to manipulate the appropriate motivating factors.

Because project incentives can influence individual performance and productivity, projects that require especially intense efforts, personal sacrifices (such as postponed vacations), and possibly geographic relocation might also have project-based incentives to help ensure that the project goals are achieved. The dot-com IT start-up culture within the United States epitomized this highly intensive lifestyle for which stock options were the primary reward. Similar behaviors are sometimes needed for IT projects with highly aggressive schedules in order to meet a schedule deadline. Unlike a dot-com start-up, however, the duration of the project is usually known and the rewards can be more certain! When designing incentives, it should be kept in mind that an individual's response to the same incentive can vary over time due to changing personal needs. For example, key project team members on ERP package implementation projects could be asked to make multiyear commitments to the project in return for special project completion bonuses or even stock options.

CENTERS OF EXCELLENCE AT BELL ATLANTIC

Beginning in the summer of 1994, Bell Atlantic began to implement 12 skill centers, also called Centers of Excellence. Each skill center was a semipermanent team of technical specialists or people trained in a specific IT skill, such as client/server, database management, or quality assurance. Each skill center was a "virtual homeroom" managed by a coach who was responsible for assigning IT personnel to specific application projects in order to achieve the project goals as well as the employee's career goals. The objective was to build an IT talent base of skilled IT professionals. Processes were developed to anticipate the skill sets needed for new development projects and to move people from older (e.g., COBOL) skill sets to newer ones.

[Adapted from Clark et al., 1997]

IT PROJECT TEAMS ARE NOT LIKE SPORTS TEAMS

The reason that project teams do not look like sports teams is that they entail the employment of borrowed resources. . . . Imagine sports events being carried out like projects: Each week the composition of the team would change, players would get their weekly playing assignments through a lottery system, team size could fluctuate, the rules of the game would be dynamic, and coaches would have no power over their players. When applied to a sports example, the standard practices employed in project management appear laughable.

[Frame, 1994]

For systems projects not as large and intensive as a major ERP implementation, the best approach is often to simply monitor factors related to how the project is being conducted that have been found to be potential demotivators. For example, the 10 items in Figure 12.5 were among 25 factors found to be counterproductive in a project environment of skilled professionals. As will be discussed below, effective communication among those associated with a project can be key to avoiding some of these demotivators.

Planning Documents

Two documents are typically created from the project planning phase: a **statement of work (SOW)** for the customer and a project plan to be used by the project manager to guide, monitor, and control the execution of the project plan.

The SOW document is a high-level document that describes what the project will deliver and when. It is in effect a contract between the project manager and the executive sponsor. It therefore can be used as a high-level guide for business managers to plan for their own unit implementation as well as to monitor the project's progress toward the project goals of on-time completion within budget.

All program managers or committees that oversee the project typically review the project plan. For example, an IS program manager and other project managers initially review the project plan, and then a project steering committee of business managers and IS leaders might be asked to endorse it.

Two types of project management charts are also typically developed during the planning phase and used during project execution: (1) PERT (or CPM) charts and (2) Gantt charts. As will be seen below, these are two complementary techniques for project scheduling and resource planning.

A PERT chart (a Program Evaluation and Review Technique developed for a missile/submarine project in 1958) graphically models the sequence of project tasks and their interrelationships using a flowchart diagram. (Note: Some organizations use an alternative method called CPM [Critical Path Method] developed by DuPont about the same time.) As shown in Figure 12.6, each major task is represented as a symbol (such as a circle or rectangle) and lines (arrows) are used to show predecessor and successor tasks. A PERT chart depicts what is referred to as a critical path—a sequence of activities that will take the longest to complete. Any delays in completing the activities on the critical path will result in slippage on the project schedule. A PERT chart therefore helps managers estimate the effects of task slippage and shows the tasks not on the critical path for which there will be some slack resources. Researchers have found that projects in which PERT (or CPM) techniques are used are less likely to have cost and schedule overruns (Meredith and Mantel, 1989).

1. Poor planning, direction, and control
2. Improper organization
3. Excessive staffing
4. Inadequate attention of management to productivity and the elimination of counterproductive elements
5. Internal communication problems
6. Insensitivity to people
7. Improper use of employees
8. An inadequate personal performance evaluation system
9. Ineffective interface with customers
10. Too many internal political machinations

Figure 12.5 Counterproductive Characteristics of Project Team Environments (Based on productivity study by Hughes Aircraft Company in Roman, 1986)

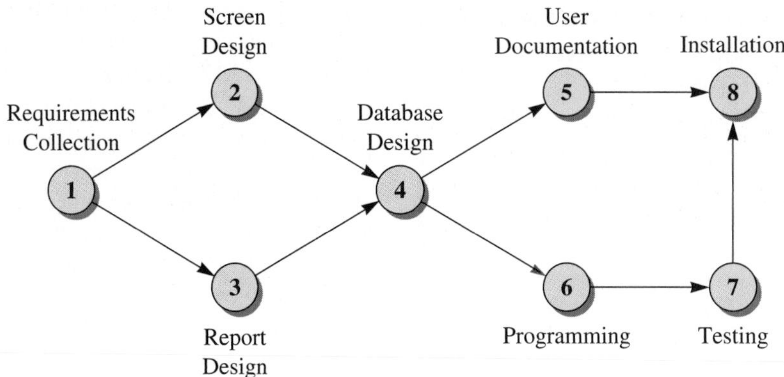

Figure 12.6 PERT Chart Example (Reprinted from Valacich, George, and Hoffer, *Essentials of Systems Analysis & Design*, Prentice Hall, 2001)

A Gannt chart graphically depicts the estimated times (and later, the actual times) for each project task against a horizontal time scale. Tasks are presented in a logical order along with a bar graph depicting the estimated time duration for each task on an appropriate linear calendar (minutes, hours, days, or weeks) for the number of months and years planned for the life cycle of the project (see Figure 12.7). The precedence relationships in the PERT/ CPM chart are reflected in the start and end dates of the activities, and overlapping tasks can be easily seen. Although time periods for tasks can also be shown on PERT or CPM charts, Gannt charts are particularly useful for displaying a project schedule and for tracking the progress of a set of tasks against the project plan (as discussed below).

An important project management skill is to determine at what level of detail to plan the project tasks. Too much detail can be stifling and result in too much time being spent on tracking rather than on more critical project tasks. Too little detail can result in inadequate project management controls and both missed deadlines and cost overruns.

PROJECT EXECUTION AND CONTROL

The *project plan* documents described in the preceding section are best recognized as living documents that need to be refined and reassessed throughout the life of the project. In large, complex projects, the planning activities still continue after a project team has been selected and some initial tasks have been undertaken, and the revised plan goes through the same endorsement procedures described above a few months into the project.

Software project management tools such as Microsoft Project are commonly used to help the project manager and other team leaders initiate and monitor the project tasks. In some cases an organization develops its own project management tools, or a consulting firm might provide such a system. Our focus here is not on the software tools used, but on three general project management practices: communication, coordination, and measuring progress.

Communication about the project to all affected stakeholders and potential users is key to successful implementation for systems projects in particular. For large projects with major business impacts, a project "kickoff" event is frequently scheduled at which the project's sponsor or champion explicitly communicates the project outcomes and perhaps also presents some general ground rules for project team members to make decisions on behalf of their constituents.

After this event, it is the project manager's responsibility to have an external communications plan appropriate for the project. This includes communicating on a regular basis (typically weekly or monthly) the project status to any oversight groups, all key stakeholders, and the user community that will be affected by the project. Using the planning charts mentioned earlier, variances from the forecasted project budget and project milestones can be reported in a way that highlights deviations from the project plan and their causes (see Figure 12.8).

Some organizations have also adopted a red-yellow-green light approach to signal what is "on track," potential problem areas, and project problems (see the sidebar entitled "Red, Yellow, and Green Lights"). This helps top managers focus on corrective actions for exceptional circumstances, such as changes in execution to avoid a bottleneck or major revisions to a project plan to better manage project risks. When outside

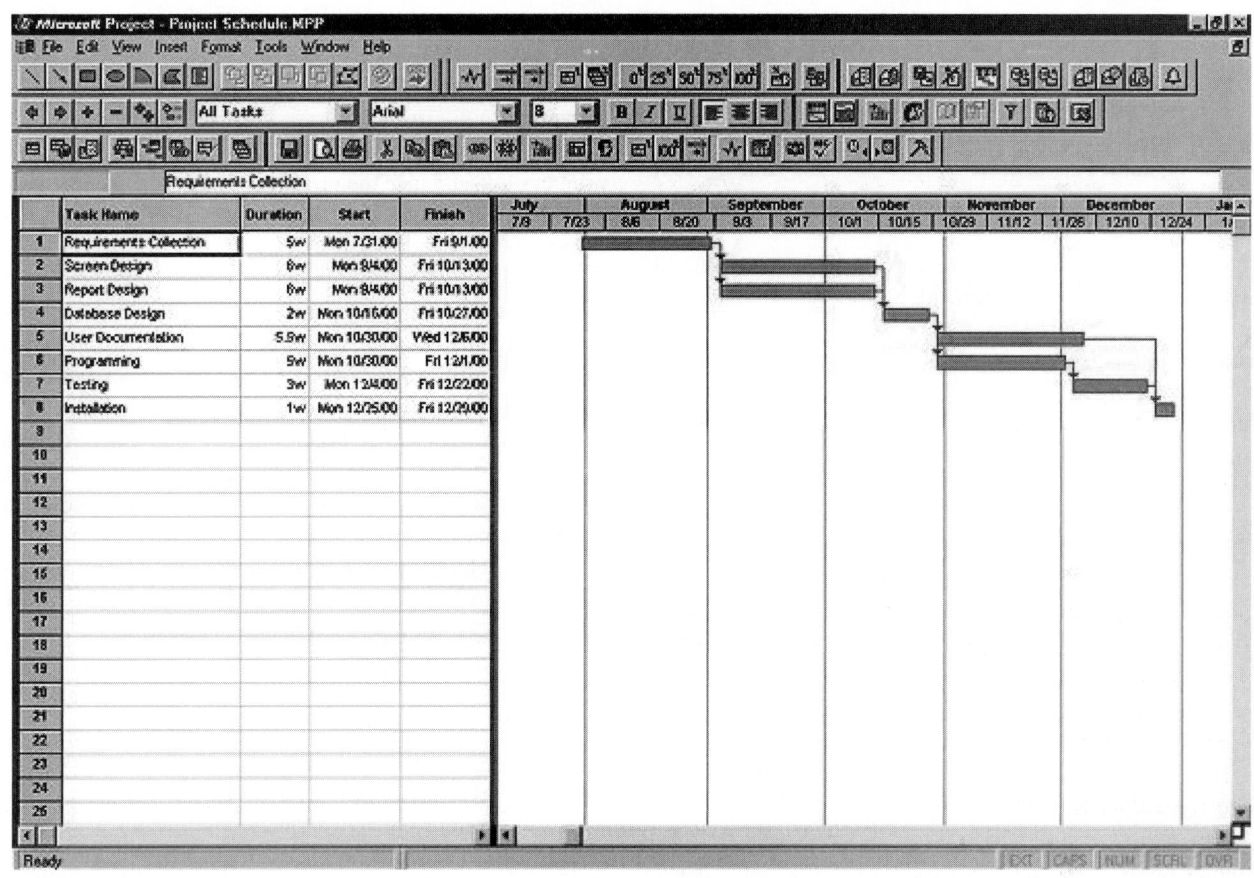

Figure 12.7 Gannt Chart Example (Reprinted from Valacich, George, and Hoffer, *Essentials of Systems Analysis & Design*, 1st Edition. Copyright © 2001. Reprinted by permission of Pearson Education, Inc., Upper Saddle River, NJ)

- **Schedule Status**
  1. Scheduled and actual or forecasted completion dates
  2. Explanations of deviation(s)

- **Budget Status**
  1. Total project funding
  2. Expenditures to date of report
  3. Current estimated cost to complete
  4. Anticipated profit or loss
  5. Explanation of deviation, if any, from planned expenditure projection

Figure 12.8 Status Reporting (Roman, 1986)

consultants are used, the tracking of consultant costs and utilization is also a key project manager responsibility.

Good communications among the project team members are also critical for task coordination and integration. The mechanisms here include both formal mechanisms (such as weekly meetings of team leaders) and informal mechanisms (such as e-mail communications and in-the-hall progress reporting).

Managing Project Risks

One of the goals of project management is to reduce the risk of failing to achieve the project objectives. All projects carry some risks. Risks can be due to a variety of causes, including human error, project scope changes, unanticipated technology changes, or internal politics. For example, Bashein, Markus, and Finley (1997) have identified 10 risk that have been associated with IT management projects. In Figure 12.9, we have categorized these IT-related risks into the four risk categories.

Risk management involves identifying the project risks, assessing their consequences, planning responses to minimize the risks, and monitoring how well the risks are mitigated and managed. Risk identification should be undertaken at the project's outset, based on experience with similar projects. A common approach is to develop a list of risk factors and then to weight them according to their potential impact, as shown in Figure 12.10. Another approach is to graph the potential impact of a given risk in relation to the extent to which it can be controlled by managers within the firm, as shown in Figure 12.11.

The highest level of project risk typically occurs at the project's outset. Once the project is underway and the team members learn more about a customer's needs, a new technology, or a vendor's software package, the project risks will typically decrease. However, in the earliest stages of the project fewer resources have been invested and it is easier to terminate the project. After more resources have been invested, the organization's stake in the project increases and thus its risk exposure also increases: More will be lost if things go wrong (see Figure 12.12). The extent of risk exposure for a given project can also vary widely across projects as well as across organizations. The culture of an organization can lead some managers to take a more defensive approach overall, while managers in a different organization might purposely pursue high-risk projects because of the potential for higher competitive rewards.

The risk assessment for a given project can result in decisions about project staffing or technical platform alternatives that lower the total risks, either in a planning stage or as a problem situation is encountered. Examples of common strategies for resource decisions are shown in Figure 12.13. For example, an exchange strategy could result in subcontracting with vendors, and a reduction strategy could result in allocating the "best and brightest" to a project team to minimize the potential for failure. Sometimes the project budget includes monetary resources allocated to a contingency fund that can be used at the discretion of project team members to resolve anticipated thorny problems that cannot be specifically defined at the outset of the project.

One of the major pitfalls in monitoring the risks of projects already underway is to ignore negative feedback. Keil and Robey (1999) warn that project managers need to be careful not to "turn a deaf ear" to bad news or to downplay symptoms of what could be major problems. Recognizing this type of problem was found to be an important first step in turning around a widely publicized IT project crisis faced by the city of Denver in the 1990s—the 16-month-late, $2-billion-over-budget project to automate airport-wide baggage handling (see the sidebar entitled "Baggage Handling Problems at the Denver International Airport"). Another lesson learned from an analysis of the Denver project crisis is that an outside consultant could be needed to evaluate a troubled project and to help devise alternative courses of action.

According to Hamilton (2000), good risk management depends on accurate and timely information on project characteristics that managers view as likely indicators of risk. Deviations from expectations need to be clearly highlighted, and this information needs to reach the right

Organizational Risks
- Competitive risk
- Reputation risk
- Technical risk

Personnel Risks
- Personnel and expertise risk
- Nonuse and unintentional misuse risk
- Internal abuse risk

Systems Project Risks
- Control design risk
- Project delay risk

External Security Risks
- External fraud, theft, or crime risk
- Extraordinary event risk

Figure 12.9 Ten IT-Related Risks and Potential Consequences (Bashein, Markus, and Finley, 1997)

RED, YELLOW, AND GREEN LIGHTS*

Some organizations use a traffic light approach to signal the status of a project on a regular basis.

- Green indicates a project is on track.
- Yellow flags potential problems.
- Red means a project is behind; the executive sponsor and project manager need to figure out a way to get the project back on track.

* Referred to in some organizations as RAG, with Amber instead of Yellow.

Technology Risk Assessment			
Risk Factor			**Weight**
1. Which of the hardware is new to the company?[a]			5
None		0	
CPU	High	3	
Peripheral and/or additional storage	High	3	
Terminals	High	3	
Mini or micro	High	3	
2. Is the system software (nonoperating system) new to IT project team?			5
No		0	
Programming language	High	3	
Database	High	3	
Data communications	High	3	
Other (Please specify)	High	3	
3. How knowledgeable is user in area of IT?			5
First exposure	High	3	
Previous exposure but limited knowledge	Medium	2	
High degree of capability	Low	1	
4. How knowledgeable is user representative in proposed application area?			5
Limited	High	3	
Understands concept but has no experience	Medium	2	
Has been involved in prior implementation efforts	Low	1	
5. How knowledgeable is IT team in proposed application area?			5
Limited	High	3	
Understands concept but has no experience	Medium	2	
Has been involved in prior implementation efforts	Low	1	

[a]This question is scored by multiplying the sum of the numbers attached to the positive responses by the weight.

Figure 12.10 Project Implementation Risk Factors and Weights (Reprinted from Applegate et al., 4th edition, 1996)

people at the right time in order for further investigation and corrective actions to be taken.

Managing Business Change

When new systems are implemented, they typically involve major changes in business processes, which in turn require changes in the way employees do their work and information flows into and out of their work activities. **Change management**, or the ability to successfully introduce change to individuals and organizational units, is therefore key to successfully implementing a new system.

When a new information system will affect organizational power structures, strategies and tactics to deal with these political aspects of the project need to be explicitly developed. According to Markus (1983), the sources for resistance to the implementation of a new information system can often be anticipated by comparing the distribution of power implied by the new system and the distribution of power existing in the organization prior to the new system. Faced with potential shifts in organizational responsibilities, key stakeholders could consciously, or unconsciously, employ counterimplementation tactics that result in preventing or delaying the completion of a new system or in modifying its initial requirements. Examples of explicit or implicit tactics include

- withholding the people resources needed for a task (including designating a representative who is not qualified to make the decisions needed)
- raising new objections about the project requirements, resulting in schedule delays
- expanding the size and complexity of the project (rescoping)

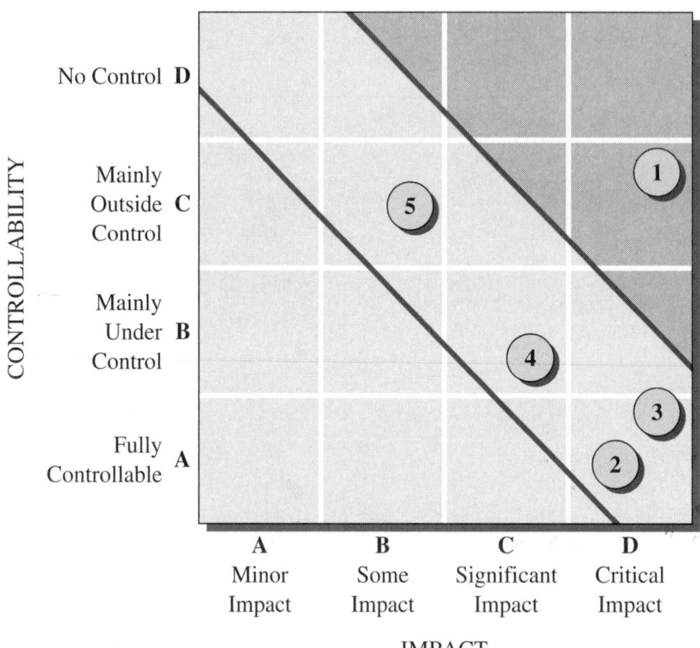

Figure 12.11 Risk Controllability and Impact Grid (Adapted from Hamilton, 2000)

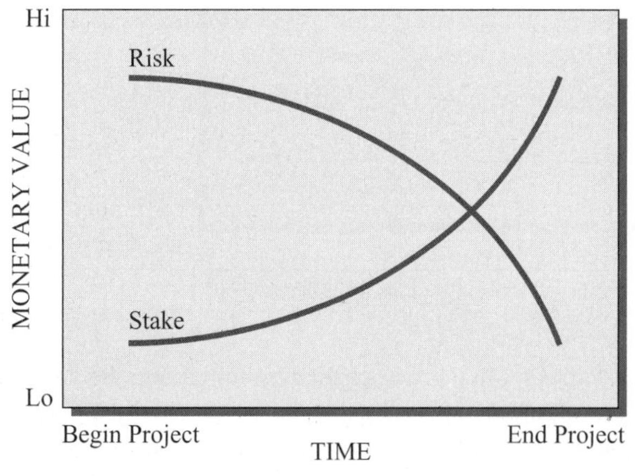

Figure 12.12 Risk Exposure: Risk Versus Stake (Adapted from Frame, 1994)

Recognizing from the beginning of a project the potential political implications and then devising solutions to avoid them is usually more effective than overtly trying to overcome resistance tactics. Devising system solutions that will be viewed as desirable by all stakeholders is of course an ideal outcome. One key way to achieve this type of win-win situation is to involve potential objectors in the implementation process so that they are involved in negotiating the requirements as well as the implementation schedule for a new system.

As business managers have come to recognize the importance of change-management practices in general, researchers have proposed multistage models for managing changes in organizations. Most of these change models have their roots in the simple three-stage **Lewin/Schein change model** shown in Figure 12.14.

In the first stage, Unfreezing, those individuals affected by the new system must realize the need for change. To help motivate change, a work environment in which it is "safe to change" needs to be created. That is, those individuals who need to change have to be convinced that giving up the old ways of doing things will not personally disadvantage them.

The Moving stage requires knowledge transfer and training. Until the knowledge and skills required for the new roles are acquired, change cannot take place. New ways to work need to be assimilated, and adequate time needs to be allocated for the people to learn these new skills and behaviors.

In the last stage, Refreezing, the new behavior becomes the accepted way of doing things. New incentive systems could be needed to reinforce the new behaviors, and the change might not be routinized until new informal norms have also been adopted within relevant workgroups across an enterprise.

Based on a study of successful and failed efforts to transform an organization, Kotter (1995) has proposed the

Exchange Strategy: An unknown risk or known critical risk is exchanged for a more acceptable level of risk. For example, the risk can be shifted to a third party by subcontracting with another organization under a fixed-cost contract for a specific project deliverable.

Reduction Strategy: By allocating to the project the best human resources available, a specific project risk can be reduced.

Avoidance Strategy: An alternative technical approach to a problem may be chosen in order to avoid risk exposure.

Figure 12.13 Common Strategies for Managing Risks (Based on Roman, 1986)

BAGGAGE HANDLING PROBLEMS AT THE DENVER INTERNATIONAL AIRPORT

Twice the size of Manhattan, the Denver International Airport (DIA) at 53 square miles was designed to be the USA's largest airport. By 1992, there was a growing realization that baggage handling would be critically important in an airport of this size and that this issue could not be off-loaded to the airlines that would be operating out of DIA. Consequently, commitment began to grow for the inclusion of an airport-wide, information technology (IT) based baggage handling system that could dramatically improve the efficiency of luggage delivery. BAE Automated Systems, Inc., a world leader in the design and implementation of material handling systems, was commissioned by the City of Denver to develop the system. An information system composed of 55 networked computers, 5,000 electric eyes, 400 radio frequency receivers, and 56 barcode scanners was to orchestrate the safe and timely arrival of every suitcase and ski bag at DIA. Problems with the baggage system, however, kept the new airport from opening as originally scheduled in October 1993. Soon the national and international media began to pick up the story, and the DIA came under investigation by various federal agencies. By the time the airport opened in late February 1995, it was 16 months behind schedule and close to $2 billion over budget. Additionally, DIA might never have opened at all if Mayor Webb had not found a way for the City of Denver to abandon its previous commitment to build an airport-wide automated baggage handling system. When DIA did eventually open, it did so with two concourses served by a manual baggage system and one concourse served by a scaled-down, semiautomated system.

[Montealegre and Keil, 2000]

following eight-step model for leaders of major organizational change efforts.

1. Establish a Sense of Urgency
2. Form a Powerful Guiding Coalition
3. Create a Vision
4. Communicate the Vision
5. Empower Others to Act on the Vision
6. Plan for and Create Short-Term Wins
7. Consolidate Improvements and Produce Still More Change
8. Institutionalize New Approaches

The first four steps bring an organization to the Moving stage (described above) by establishing a sense of urgency for the change and both creating and communicating a vision to help direct the change effort. The eighth step is similar to the Refreezing stage. According to Kotter, for a change to be institutionalized, it must be rooted in the organization's norms and values.

Today's common wisdom is that modern organizations and their people need to be able to accept change easily. This suggests that the institutionalization step, or Refreezing stage, might be pursued somewhat differently than when it was originally conceived. That is, a more

- Unfreezing
  - Establish a felt need
  - Create a safe atmosphere
- Moving
  - Provide necessary information
  - Assimilate knowledge and develop skills
- Refreezing

Figure 12.14 Three Stages of Lewin/Schein Change Model

typical organizational goal today is to have a workforce that has been reskilled but is also "change-ready," rather than becoming refrozen (Clark et al., 1997). Change-ready personnel also view change as a desirable, ongoing state for competing in today's business world.

Kotter and other change-management researchers have recently emphasized that major organizational change efforts cannot be entirely planned in advance. Instead, change efforts should be expected to be somewhat "messy" and "full of surprises" (Kotter, 1995). A successful change-management effort therefore requires both planned (pre-planned) activities as well as "improvisational" responses to unforeseen circumstances (Orlikowski and Hofman, 1997). Similar to risk management, then, a major systems project trap is to ignore negative feedback. Paying careful attention to those in the organization who are closest to the people who will be affected by the systems project will help avoid implementation failure.

Three major categories of change-management activities have been associated with successful IT projects: communicating, training, and providing incentives. Communication activities are part of good project management, and communicating the need for change (the vision) is one of the first activities that needs to be addressed. The second category, training, is part of the installation step in a systems life cycle implementation phase. According to the practitioner press, however, the amount of user training required for an initial implementation success is typically underestimated. The third category, incentive system changes (such as performance rewards), helps motivate the attitudes and behaviors needed for the Lewin/Schein moving stage and helps institutionalize the behaviors for a Refreezing stage. Special project incentives may be used for high-risk projects and be under the control of the project manager(s). However, long-term incentive schemes to influence behavioral changes are clearly beyond the scope of a single project.

Finally, it should be noted that project budgets often do not include change-management activities. Moreover, the lack of recognition of the need for change-management activities has been reported to be the greatest barrier to implementation success in IT projects that involve major business processing reengineering efforts (Grover, Jeong, and Teng, 2000).

PROJECT CLOSING

A project close-out process provides a formal opportunity to codify what has been learned as part of a post-project review step. The process begins when the IT project deliverables have been completed and a formal user acceptance has been obtained or after a failed project has been terminated. According to management guru Margaret Wheatley (Wheatley and Kellner-Rogers, 1996), in today's much more complex business environments, one of the best survival strategies is to share expertise. Yet if there is no formal post-project review step, project team leaders typically do not take the time to document what actions helped the project succeed, as well as any lessons learned that could improve the likelihood of success on a future project (Russell, 2000).

Some common questions for team members to respond to are as follows (based on Schwalbe, 2004):

- What went right on this project?
- What went wrong on this project?
- What would you do differently on the next project, based on your experience with this project?

The team member responses can be aggregated and summarized in a lessons-learned section of the report.

Project managers should also be required to document whether or not the project met its budget, schedule, scope, and other project success criteria, as well as to share their own set of "lessons learned" from managing the project. Once collected, these lessons then need to be made accessible to other project team leaders, perhaps as part of a knowledge management initiative within the IT organization.

Continuous improvements in managing IT projects based on past learnings are a hallmark of a high-quality software development capability. For example, the **Capability Maturity Model (CMM)** of the Software Engineering Institute (SEI) at Carnegie Mellon University categorized a firm's software development capability on one of five levels. Organizations in the first (Initial) level of the CMM have software development processes that are primarily ad hoc. Organizations that have established project management processes to track IT projects on cost, schedule, and scope are at a second (Repeatable) level. Standard processes across all IS staff and process steps are characteristics of the third (Defined) level, and well-defined process measurements are characteristics of the fourth (Managed) level.

Organizations that reach the fifth (Optimizing) level of the CMM are still somewhat rare. Attaining this level requires continuous project management improvements based on the software development process measurements for the organization's prior IT projects.

SPECIAL ISSUE: MANAGING COMPLEX IT PROJECTS

Experienced IT project managers or IT program managers are increasingly likely to be asked to lead large, complex systems projects across an enterprise, such as ERP package implementations. Consulting firms are also frequently contracted to help with these complex projects because of their experiences in implementing the same package in other organizations.

According to Accenture consultant Hugh Ryan (2000), complexity must be accepted as a key characteristic of systems development and implementation projects in today's world. To deliver quality solutions in this type of environment, managers must realize that complexity is inescapable and that they must manage the associated risks. A multiyear field review of how large, complex projects were implemented led to the identification of three factors that are critical to success:

1. The business vision was an integral part of the project.
2. A testing approach was used at the program level (not just at the individual application level).
3. The projects used a phased-release approach (rather than a single-release rollout strategy).

Another source of project complexity comes from the use of outside contractors on a project. As shown in Figure 12.15, project complexity increases when contract workers are offsite rather than onsite during the project and when project team members are located in a different country, commonly referred to as "offshore."

The management of offsite and offshore workers and projects is becoming an important IT project management

Type of Resource	Project Characteristics
Onsite Contract Worker	Delivery team in the U.S. Hourly charges Managed by the client company
Onsite Project Teams	Delivery team in the U.S. Hourly charges; may also be milestone fees Managed by the client company
Onsite-Offshore Projects	Project management and internal customer services in the U.S. Delivery team offshore Fees normally project-based Requires client investment in development infrastructure Requires client efforts in building trust
Pure Offshore Projects	Project management by offshore vendor Fees normally project-based Requires client investment in development infrastructure Requires client and vendor efforts in building trust Requires increased efforts to transfer intellectual capital

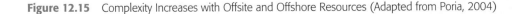

Figure 12.15 Complexity Increases with Offsite and Offshore Resources (Adapted from Poria, 2004)

capability as more programming work in particular is being outsourced to countries with significantly lower labor costs.

SPECIAL ISSUE: POST-MERGER IT INTEGRATION PROJECTS

The past two decades have witnessed an increasing number of mergers and acquisitions in which businesses seek to achieve business growth by combining with another organization. Although senior IT leaders are not always a part of the team that selects and prices the firm to be acquired, they are depended on to quickly and effectively merge IT operations to enable the newly merged organization to meet its strategic objectives for the merger. For example, if the merging firms' call center operations for customers are to be highly integrated, then so too must the IT platforms and applications to support these operations. Well-honed IT project management skills, and a program management structure, have been associated with effective IT integration in a merger situation.

Another key to success is retaining the IT talent needed for the postmerger IT integration efforts. According to a recent study by McKinsey and Company (Kay and Shelton, 2000), 76 percent of the top executives surveyed across the globe believed that retaining key talent was a "critical" success factor for postmerger integration in general. This is because many mergers have cost-reduction goals that require personnel cuts, and key employees typically receive job inquiries from other employers within 5 days after a merger announcement.

Attractive retention contracts therefore need to be quickly offered to those personnel whose IT skills and business knowledge are critical to the postmerger success. If the intent is to keep an IT professional only until a specific IT integration project is completed, the retention package should be "generous" enough so that the employee stays loyal to the firm during the period of time needed for the integration project. To help ensure that the employee's special knowledge is transferred to IT staff who will be remaining with the company, a knowledge transfer stipulation could be made part of a project completion bonus.

SUMMARY

IT project management requires competencies in general project management techniques, as well as systems methodologies. Today's IT projects can be led by an IS manager, a business manager, or both. The business manager roles of sponsor and champion are also critical to the project's success. The planning phase includes project scheduling, budgeting, and staffing. PERT charts, Gannt charts, and project management software are typically used to help execute and control project team activities.

Managing IT project risks involves assessing potential consequences, developing responses for risk minimization, and ongoing monitoring. Successfully managing business change as part of the IT project requires preplanned change management activities, as well as timely responses to unforeseen situations. Capturing lessons learned as part of a project closing phase has been associated with higher software quality and success with future projects.

The successful management of complex software projects often requires outside consulting help as well as exceptional skills in system testing and release management. The successful management of post-merger IT integration projects also requires paying special attention to human resource issues, including how to retain the necessary IT talent.

REVIEW QUESTIONS

1. Describe the difference between project management and program management.
2. What role could the Project Management Institute play in helping an organization better manage its IT projects?
3. Who is involved in managing an IT portfolio, and why is this a growing concern?
4. What information is typically included in an initial IT project request? In a project charter?
5. What skills have been identified as important for good project managers?
6. Describe the business manager roles of project sponsor and project champion.
7. What is a work breakdown analysis and why is it important?
8. Why is timeboxing a common approach for projects using new approaches such as RAD?
9. Contrast the strengths of bottom-up and top-down approaches to project budgeting.
10. What are some of the key management issues today for IT project staffing?
11. Describe the key uses of PERT, CPM, and Gannt charts.
12. Describe one technique used to manage IT project risks.

13. Describe one technique used to manage business change (change management).
14. Compare and contrast the Lewin/Schein model with the Kotter framework. What is the same and what is different?
15. Describe one key to success for managing large complex system projects.
16. Why are IT project staffing issues of special importance for postmerger IT integration projects?

DISCUSSION QUESTIONS

1. If a person has been certified by the PMI but has never been on an IT project team, would you even consider hiring that person to manage an IT project? Justify your answer.
2. Several approaches for time and budget estimations are characterized as "dysfunctional" in this chapter. Provide an argument to support or refute one of these statements.
3. Select an IT project that you are familiar with and comment on whether there was a formal project sponsor and champion, how well these project roles were carried out, and how this positively or negatively affected the project.
4. Use the Web to identify at least two project management software products for projects in general. Briefly contrast their features and costs.
5. Select an IT project with which you are familiar and evaluate how well the budget and schedule were estimated and controlled.
6. Reread the sidebar description of the red-yellow-green reporting mechanism ("Red, Yellow, and Green Lights") and comment on what you see as the pros and cons of this approach.
7. Find out more about Denver's automatic baggage handling system (described in the sidebar "Baggage Handling Problems at the Denver International Airport") and how this IT project crisis was characterized in news accounts.
8. A large number of U.S.-based mergers over the past two decades have failed to achieve the forecasted business benefits of the merger. One hypothesis for this high failure rate is that the organizations did not execute well their integration of the two businesses, including their IT systems. Develop a rationale for why this hypothesis could (or could not) be true.

CHAPTER 13 FACILITATING USER COMPUTING

THIS CHAPTER FOCUSES ON MANAGEMENT ISSUES ASSOCIATED WITH WHAT has been referred to as end-user computing. Under the broad definition we will use here, end-user computing includes the use of all the managerial support applications discussed in Chapter 7, as well as the development of applications using personal productivity tools (such as Microsoft Office), reporting tools for enterprise systems, Web-authoring tools, and so forth.

This chapter's overall objectives are to prepare you to be an effective manager of employees who are using computer applications, as well as to be knowledgeable about the benefits and risks associated with application development by workers who are not information systems (IS) specialists. An underlying theme of our discussion is that in order for end-user computing resources to be effectively leveraged, IS and business managers must both take responsibility for their management. In other words, end-user computing policies and procedures need to become institutionalized as an enterprise-wide management concern, not just as an IT management issue. Nevertheless, IS managers need to take a leadership role in providing a secure and reliable computing and communications infrastructure.

The first part of this chapter discusses end-user computing that involves *systems development* activities by users who are not IS specialists. As early as the 1970s, workers in accounting, finance, marketing, and other business departments used mainframe tools designed for end users to analyze data and to generate reports. Today's end users typically develop applications on microcomputer platforms using spreadsheet, database management, statistical analysis, and other business intelligence tools with graphical interfaces.

The second part of this chapter talks about how to effectively leverage end-user computing resources overall. Today's business managers generally recognize the productivity gains associated with end-user computing but are concerned with managing the growing costs of supporting computer users. For example, the initial purchase of a personal computer is generally only 20 percent of the total cost of supporting an employee using a networked computer over its typical 3-year life cycle. That is, the **total cost of ownership (TCO)** for desktop and portable computers includes the costs of providing application software, network access, communications services, and ongoing training and support services. This chapter therefore provides some guidelines for supporting and controlling these information technology (IT) resources, as well as the benefits and challenges associated with supporting telecommuting environments.

THE EMERGENCE OF USER APPLICATION DEVELOPMENT

When microcomputers first became available in the late 1970s, many IS specialists viewed them as inappropriate for business application development. After all, the first microcomputers were distributed by mail order to hobbyists as electronic toys with limited processing and storage capabilities compared to the mainframe and minicomputers installed in most businesses. However, when IBM Corp. introduced its first desktop microcomputer (called the "personal computer") in late 1981, microcomputers on the desktops of users began to be accepted as useful business tools. At that time IBM was the premier source of computer systems and services for the Fortune 500, and the fact that IBM thought microcomputers could play a significant business role became a wake-up call for IS managers.

Nevertheless, the growth of end-user computing was primarily an end-user "pull" phenomenon. Well into the mid-1980s, business managers in many organizations were purchasing PCs on office equipment budgets without the knowledge or support of IS professionals. That is, many IS managers were aware of PC purchases but took a hands-off approach: They viewed IBM's early desktop PCs—with less than 640K of RAM and only floppy disk storage devices—as similar to business calculators. Yet, even without proactive IS management support of desktop PCs, there was a widespread diffusion of microcomputers into businesses during this first decade of microcomputer technology for two primary reasons (see Figure 13.1).

First, during the 1980s the price/performance ratios of microcomputers continued to decline. Other PC vendors entered the marketplace, which led to frequent releases of hardware with more functionality at lower prices. Affordable nonprocedural languages (4 GLs like FOCUS, query languages like structured query language [SQL]) were also available for developing microcomputer applications, and end users could become somewhat proficient in them after only a 2-day workshop. By the early 1990s these user-friendly tools had easy-to-use interfaces that did not even require the user to know SQL or other command structures. Further, literally every business school had invested in microcomputer labs and undergraduate courses that included education in spreadsheet and other personal productivity tools. This tremendous rise in computer literacy among U.S. college graduates, not to mention children and teenagers, continues to fuel the growth of computer usage in general (see the sidebar entitled "Computer Use by Young People Hits 90 Percent Mark").

Second, business users began to submit more requests for custom-developed applications that could be worked on by the IS staffs in their organizations, creating a large *backlog* of systems requests that had been prioritized. When and if IS resources became available, the projects with the highest priority would become active projects. However, business managers knew that not all projects on the formal backlog list would be completed within the calendar year and that next year's budgeting process would bring even more new systems project requests. This typically meant that a company also had an "invisible backlog" of systems projects that

- **Availability of low-cost microcomputers**
  High-level languages for end users
  Computer literacy among college graduates and professionals
- **Increased user frustrations about new systems development project backlogs**

Figure 13.1 Primary Drivers for End-User Computing

COMPUTER USE BY YOUNG PEOPLE HITS 90 PERCENT MARK

A new government-sponsored analysis of computer and Internet use found that computer usage among young people is higher than among the adult population. About 90 percent of people between the ages of 5 and 17 use computers, and more children and teens use computers at school than at home. There is no notable difference between girls and boys. About 59 percent of young computer users also use the Internet. 60 percent of 10-year-olds and 80 percent of 16-year-olds are Internet users, and 99 percent of public schools provide Internet access.

Like adults, young people go online for a variety of reasons. Three in four use the Internet for school assignments. More than half use computers for writing e-mail, sending instant messages to friends, or playing games. However, young people are more likely to access the Internet at home than at school. Since schools now have one computer with Internet access for every five students, some suggest that the heavy home usage is because many teachers aren't yet comfortable enough with the online tool to incorporate it into their classes.

[Adapted from Associated Press, 2003]

A company's **systems backlog** includes the systems development requests by business users that members of the IS organization are not currently working on.

business management wanted but had not even formally requested due to low expectations for completion.

As business demands for more computer applications grew in the 1980s, the visible and invisible backlogs also grew, and dedicating non-IS personnel to user application development became a more attractive option (Kaiser, 1993). That is, small applications and reports could be developed quickly, as needed, without IS specialists, using tools designed for non-IS specialists.

Computer-literate business managers therefore began to invest in computing capabilities to support their own data access, reporting, and decision support needs. In many organizations the experts in the use of the new productivity tools (such as spreadsheets on a microcomputer) are in a business department, not in an IS department.

USER-DEVELOPED VERSUS IS-DEVELOPED APPLICATIONS

In Chapter 11 we described the make-or-buy decision between developing custom applications using internal IS specialists and purchasing a software package. Here we discuss the trade-offs for a different type of alternative: user-developed versus IS-developed custom applications. We begin with a discussion of the potential advantages and disadvantages of systems development by users who are not IS professionals. Then we describe three factors that need to be taken into account when making a decision about whether a specific system should be developed by end users or not: application characteristics, tool characteristics, and developer characteristics.

The overall challenge in managing user application development is to find the best combination of trade-offs that will maximize the potential benefits without creating unacceptable levels of risk.

Potential Advantages and Disadvantages

Understanding the potential advantages and disadvantages of user-developed applications is critical for making good choices about whether a new application should be user-developed or IS-developed. The lists of advantages and disadvantages in Figure 13.2 are discussed below.

Looking first at the *advantages*, **user application development** presents the opportunity for users to have total control over the initial development of the application, as well as its ongoing maintenance. Independence from IS department resources can sometimes be advantageous (Rivard and Huff, 1988). This is because users do not have to wait for IS resources to be available to work on their project; rather, the business manager can determine when the development effort is initiated. Further, users do not have to explain their information requirements to someone who might not understand the business problem; users often find it easier to communicate their computer support needs among themselves than to an IS specialist who might have only minimal knowledge about the specific area of business in which the application will be used. Also, users gain total control over the systems budget. This increased flexibility can be very attractive to the business manager: There is no cost chargeback from an internal IS organization or contractual obligations with an outside vendor if the manager's own employees develop the application. Finally, managers in organizations where an organizational committee with representatives from multiple business units determines the

POTENTIAL ADVANTAGES
Increased user control over systems development project
Increased user acceptance of systems solution
Frees up IS resources (and may reduce development backlog)
Increased IT management knowledge of users

POTENTIAL DISADVANTAGES
Loss of quality controls
Increased operational risks due to developer turnover
Potential labor/time inefficiencies
Loss of integration opportunities/capabilities

Figure 13.2 Potential Advantages and Disadvantages of User-Developed Applications

priorities for systems requests can avoid the risk of having a systems request turned down or delayed because it was not given a high enough priority. In other words, business manager control over the development of a new system can result in a timelier response to a local business unit need.

Another advantage associated with user-developed systems is the possibility of greater user acceptance of the application solution. End users tend to be more involved throughout the development process because they might be physically near the user developer. User-developed systems are also typically smaller systems that are likely to be developed using a prototyping process, which involves significant end-user involvement. Because the business unit totally "owns" the application, user application development also eliminates the possibility of "we-they" finger-pointing.

Two potential advantages for the organization as a whole are also shown in Figure 13.2. First, when IS expertise is a scarce organizational resource, it is best for the organization to use its IS resources to work on high-priority projects that require high levels of IS skills. The prolific IS guru James Martin recognized this advantage at the time of the introduction of the IBM microcomputer. In his book *Application Development Without Programmers* (1982), he shocked many IS professionals by advocating a large number of powerful software products for end users—including fourth generation languages and report writers. McLean (1979) also was an early predictor of the rise of application development by non-IS professionals. Within U.S.-based labor markets, the costs of end-user computing via a mainframe computer platform were already low enough to provide a compelling business case for user-developed applications.

> *The continuing drop in cost of computers has now passed the point at which computers have become cheaper than people.*
>
> —JAMES MARTIN, 1982

The last potential advantage of user application development listed in Figure 13.2 is also a motivator for a textbook, such as this one, that focuses on what business managers need to know about IT management. Every organization should be striving to increase the IT management knowledge of its business employees, and user application development is an experience that can contribute to this goal. As described in Chapter 1, this is an important business capability because of the role of IT as an enabler of a company's business strategy. In fact, research has shown a correlation between the IT management knowledge of key business managers and the progressive use of IT within that firm (Boynton, Zmud, and Jacobs, 1994).

However, organizations also need to manage the potential risks associated with applications that are not developed by IS specialists. These business risks are reflected in the four potential *disadvantages* shown in Figure 13.2.

First, a major concern for business as well as IS managers is the potential loss of quality controls. By virtue of their training, IS professionals are knowledgeable about how to design quality controls into a new information system: input controls, output controls, and processing controls. As in any profession, products developed by those with less training and experience will, on the average, be of lower quality. Undetected bugs in processing logic, the lack of audit trails, inadequate backup and security procedures, and undocumented systems are much more common in user-developed systems than in those developed by a trained IS professional (Schultheis and Sumner, 1991). A mid-1990s study by a leading consulting firm found that about one-third of spreadsheets contained errors (Panko, 1996). These shortcomings support the worst fears of the IS community and obviously are a major concern for all business managers (see the sidebar entitled "Errors in Spreadsheets").

In addition to quality concerns about the application design, user-developed systems also involve increased operational risks. In other words, user-developed applications that are used on an ongoing basis can pose operational risks similar to a "production system" operated by the IS department. However, the responsibilities for operations and continued maintenance of a user-developed application typically belong to the business unit that owns it and might by managed by a single employee who developed it. A common operational risk, therefore, is that the user developer could move to a different unit, or even a different organization, with little advance notice. For database applications in particular, the loss of the original user developer often results in abandoned user-developed systems due to the lack of resident operational and systems maintenance expertise within the business unit (Klepper and Sumner, 1990). The risk exposure is even greater when the application is being used as a decision support tool for decisions with high impact or as a regular transaction processing and reporting system at the workgroup or department level.

Another potential risk is the organizational inefficiencies that result when systems are being developed by persons with little or no IS training. Depending on the type and size of the application, there is an organizational cost associated with having an untrained, or partially trained, user spend considerable amounts of time on what could be much more efficiently achieved by an IS professional. There is also a learning curve associated with end-user development.

When systems are developed outside of a centralized IS organization, there is also a greater likelihood of considerable

ERRORS IN SPREADSHEETS

End users produce countless spreadsheet models each year, often to guide mission-critical decisions. In recent years several cases of spreadsheet errors have been reported. Given the reluctance of organizations to publicize embarrassments, these few cases might be only the tip of the iceberg. Some consultants have claimed that something like a third of all operational spreadsheet models contain errors. One Price Waterhouse consultant reported auditing four large spreadsheet models for a client and finding 128 errors.

Several academic researchers have done experiments to identify the different types of errors contained in spreadsheets. Even in relatively simple spreadsheets that do not require specialized business area knowledge, laboratory subjects made errors in 38 percent of their models. In a debugging phase, only 16 percent of the subjects who had made spreadsheet errors were able to identify and fix all their errors. Every research study known to us that looked for errors in user-developed systems has found them, and found them in abundance.

Spreadsheet errors can be of two types: quantitative and qualitative. Most researchers have looked at *quantitative errors*, which include the following:

- *Mechanical errors* Typing errors, pointing errors, and other simple slips. Mechanical errors can be frequent, but they have a high chance of being caught by the person making the error.
- *Logic errors* Incorrect formulas due to choosing the wrong algorithm or creating the wrong formulas to implement the algorithm. Pure logic errors result from a lapse in logic, whereas domain logic errors occur because the developer lacks the required business area knowledge. Some logic errors are also easier to identify than others: easy-to-proof errors have been called Eureka errors, and difficult-to-proof errors have been called Cassandra errors.
- *Omission errors* Things left out of the model that should be there. They often result from a misinterpretation of the situation. Human factors research has shown that omission errors have low detection rates.

Qualitative errors are flaws that do not produce immediate quantitative errors. Some qualitative errors lead to quantitative errors during later "what-if" analyses or when updates are made to a spreadsheet model. Other qualitative errors might cause users to misinterpret the model's results or make maintenance difficult, leading to increased development costs and the potential for new errors.

To err is human. We do not make mistakes all the time, but we consistently make a certain number, even when we are being careful. To reduce error rates requires aggressive techniques—similar to the discipline followed by developers of more complex applications.

[Adapted from Panko, 1996, and Panko and Halverson, 1996]

time spent "reinventing" an application with similar functionality. Duplicated efforts within the same department, let alone across business units within an organization, are common if each individual unit works independently of any IS personnel. A similar problem is faced by organizations with IS specialists decentralized to multiple business units if no mechanisms are in place to identify duplicated efforts.

Another potentially serious problem for a business unit and the organization as a whole is the possible proliferation of unit-specific customized applications that inhibit information access and sharing with others in the organization, both now and in the future. When business units throughout an organization independently develop applications using software and data definitions of their own choosing, the result is dozens, or even hundreds, of isolated islands of automation: The risks are not only unsharable data, but also conflicting information reports supposedly based on the same transaction data. (Incompatibilities across departmental systems are also a problem faced by organizations when business units have the authority to independently purchase different packaged systems for the same functions, such as payroll or the purchasing of supplies.)

The organizational risks associated with user application development therefore increase considerably when user-developed solutions are allowed to proliferate without adequate coordination. The management challenge is to find the right balance between business and IS controls without severely limiting the potential benefits.

Assessing the Application Risks

Let us turn now to the issue of whether a specific application should be developed by users or by IS professionals. As summarized in Figure 13.3, three types of factors should be considered: characteristics of the application to be developed, the tools available for user development, and the human resources needed for both a quality application and reliable operations and maintenance over the life of the completed application.

Application Characteristics Several characteristics of the application need to be taken into account. First, the organizational risks associated with user application development differ depending on the intended scope (or organizational

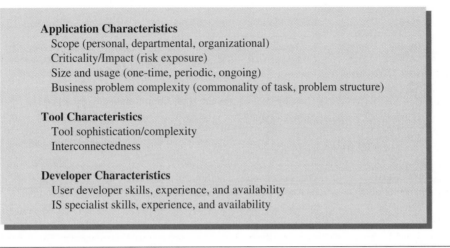

Application Characteristics
Scope (personal, departmental, organizational)
Criticality/Impact (risk exposure)
Size and usage (one-time, periodic, ongoing)
Business problem complexity (commonality of task, problem structure)

Tool Characteristics
Tool sophistication/complexity
Interconnectedness

Developer Characteristics
User developer skills, experience, and availability
IS specialist skills, experience, and availability

Figure 13.3 Application, Tool, and Developer Characteristics

usage) of the completed application. Some firms make decisions based on just two categories of risk: applications developed for personal use only and those intended to be used by more than one person. Pyburn (1986-87), however, has defined three categories of application scope that typically have significantly different risk levels:

- Personal applications developed and used (operated) by the primary user for personal decision making, often replacing work formerly done manually
- Departmental applications developed by a single user but operated and used (and perhaps enhanced) by multiple users in a department; departmental applications often evolve from applications originally developed for personal use
- Organizational applications used by multiple users across a number of departments

Personal applications typically have the least risk, whereas organizational applications have the greatest risk.

In addition to scope, the potential impact of managerial decisions based on the application, as well as the actual size of the application and its intended frequency of usage, also need to be considered. Small, one-time applications are typically good candidates for user-developed applications, but the application also needs to be assessed in terms of risk exposure for the organization as a whole.

Finally, the complexity of the business problem supported by the application needs to be assessed in two different dimensions: the task's commonality and the task's problem structure. If the application is addressing an ill-structured analytical problem, a combination of business and IS specialist expertise could be required to develop the best software application to address it. Supporting business tasks that are already well understood (common), such as a system to track the status of multiple departmental projects or to track communications with various suppliers, are usually better candidates for user-developed solutions.

Tool Characteristics Two important tool characteristics to consider are the complexity of the software tools to be used to develop the system and the degree to which the application is to be interconnected with other applications or databases. User tools vary greatly in complexity and technology sophistication. For example, spreadsheet functions are relatively simple to design and spreadsheet applications are relatively simple to implement, whereas data mining tools based on neural network technology can be much more complex.

As shown in Figure 13.4, applications also can vary greatly, depending on how much they rely on other applications for data inputs. At one extreme, "isolated" applications do not use data from any other computer-generated source and do not provide inputs to other applications. Stand-alone applications might depend on data generated by other applications, but the data is manually input. Application integration can also be accomplished in two ways: (1) manually via a specific user command (such as via file import or export commands) or (2) automatically. As organizations have implemented local area networks (LANs) and client/server computing environments, these two types of integration have become increasingly common.

Stage	Extent of Interconnectedness
Isolation	The application does not use data from another application or create data to be used for another application
Stand-alone	The application utilizes computer-generated data, which is manually entered into the application from hardcopy reports or other printouts
Manual Integration	Data is electronically transferred from another application, but this is done manually (e.g., data import command)
Automated Integration	The application is electronically connected with one or more corporate databases or applications; data is routinely transferred to this application using automated scripts designed into the applications
Distributed Integration	The application regularly utilizes data distributed via network and maintained by organizational systems under the control of IS specialists

Figure 13.4 Extent of Interconnectedness (Adapted from Huff, Munro, and Martin, 1988)

If a more integrated application is to be developed, with sophisticated tools that access data distributed via an organizational network, then an IS-developed solution could be the only suitable long-term solution. However, it is not uncommon for a stand-alone user-developed application to first be developed by users and then later to be used as a prototype for a more integrated application by IS specialists.

Developer Characteristics The application developer characteristics to be considered include the relevant skills and experience of the potential developers, as well as their availability to work on the project. A second consideration here is the *availability* of these developer resources in relation to the time constraints faced by the users.

As discussed previously, reduced dependence on IS professionals can be a considerable advantage if user developers have, or can be trained to have, the skills required for a given application. Many non-IS professionals have considerable IT-related expertise and might also even have some training in IS development methodologies. The difficulty is that the business managers in the unit responsible for the application might not have the knowledge to adequately assess the development skills needed before the project to develop the application is underway. Consultation with IS experts inside or outside the organization is therefore required to adequately assess these characteristics.

USER DEVELOPMENT METHODOLOGY

When IS specialists develop systems, IS professionals select the methodology used to develop the application. One of the responsibilities of the IS project leader is to monitor adherence to the organizational standards for the selected methodology, as well as to monitor the project's status according to the agreed-upon process steps and user-approved milestones.

For user-developed systems, the user developer (or the accountable business manager) typically chooses the development methods to be used. Panko (1988) suggests that the most appropriate methodology for a user-developed application depends on three of the application characteristics in Figure 13.5: scope, size, and business problem complexity. Many user-developed applications do not require a strict adherence to all the steps described in earlier chapters for a systems development life cycle (SDLC). For example, small and simple applications intended to be used by the person developing the application (personal scope) could be developed with a simplified ("collapsed") life-cycle approach. However, when the application for personal use is somewhat larger and more complex, a more disciplined approach needs to be taken to ensure a quality application. The Definition phase would involve thinking through what you want the system to do (inputs, processing, outputs) and

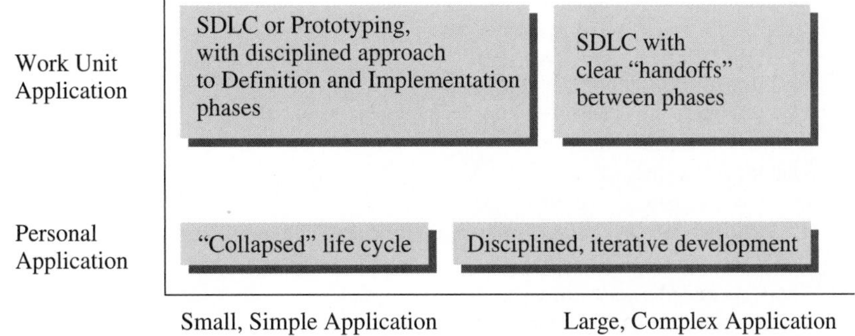

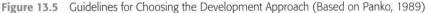

Figure 13.5 Guidelines for Choosing the Development Approach (Based on Panko, 1989)

then constructing and testing it. The developer, who is also the intended user, could try it out, modify it, and then repeat these steps as needed. However, a disciplined approach should continue to be adhered to in order to ensure that the programming logic and all modifications to the application are adequately tested.

If the application is for other users (a workgroup or department), then one or more of the intended users should be involved in the application's development, even if a formal project team is not designated for work on the application. If a large, complex application is being developed for multiple users, it should be developed using an SDLC methodology (as described in Chapter 10) with formalized user and developer roles. The Definition phase should include a reassessment of whether the project should be user-developed or IS-developed, using factors such as those summarized earlier (see Figure 13.3 in the section of this chapter entitled "Assessing the Application Risks"). This recommendation assumes, however, that the user developers are knowledgeable about the SDLC methodology and have the systems and project management skills to ensure the development of a high-quality application.

Prototyping and other iterative methods are especially well suited for user-developed applications because the end users are typically physically near the developer, the design can be tried out, and today's end-user development tools with graphical interfaces support prototyping well. As described in Chapter 10, a basic set of requirements should first be defined in order to develop the prototype; selected users then try out the prototype and suggest changes; the prototype is then modified until there is agreement that the application meets the business users' needs.

A key learning point for most first-time user developers is not to move to the Construction phase, or the building of the prototype, too soon. It is common for user developers to underestimate what it takes to define a system's requirements, especially if other users will also be using the application. In contrast, the IS professional always develops applications for other users and is typically trained in various systems analysis techniques as well as interviewing techniques to elicit requirements. The larger and more complex the system, the more critical the need for developers to devote more time to the up-front requirements analysis and Definition phase in general. In the Construction phase the design steps should take into account security features, such as input and output controls (including application backup and recovery controls).

IS professionals have also learned that a simple system that works reliably is much more useful than an elaborate failure. For user-developed applications, it is therefore often a good idea to start with a limited version of the system and then to expand it after some experience with this initial version. Indeed, user-developed systems can also become catalysts for larger systems to enable a new business strategy, which in the end will require custom development work by IS professionals.

User Development Guidelines

Figure 13.6 lists a number of important questions that can be used as a guide for user developers during the Definition and Construction phases. The first four questions need to be answered in the Definition phase when defining the system's requirements. Determining the data sources and the needed controls up front will help ensure a high-quality application. For example, can the needed data be obtained from another system, or will the data have to be collected and keyed into this system? If the data must be keyed into the system, how can the application be designed to help control for accuracy and completeness? If the data are to be extracted from other systems, separate modules might need to be constructed in order to perform this function. Today's office productivity suites, for example, allow for

DEFINITION PHASE
What outputs should the system produce?
What processes are necessary to produce the needed outputs?
What should the system be able to do?
What input data are needed?
  How can data best be obtained?
  How can data accuracy, completeness, and timeliness be assured?
CONSTRUCTION PHASE
What data must be stored in the system?
  How should data be organized?
  How can data be maintained?
How can this system be decomposed into modules?
  How do these modules relate to each other?
  In what sequence should the modules be executed?
How can the system be recovered if anything happens?
Is an audit trail necessary?
What level of documentation is necessary?
What system tests need to be run?

Figure 13.6 Questions to Guide User Developers

automatic linking of database tables (created with a database management system such as Microsoft Access) to spreadsheets that use these data for decision analysis. The data flow diagrams and other analysis tools introduced in Chapter 9 can prove helpful in these Definition tasks.

Figure 13.6 also provides questions for the Construction phase. Designing the data to be stored in the system is a critical activity. One must decide what different files or tables are required and what data elements will be stored in each record. Designing a database structure is one of the most difficult, and least understood, tasks for novice user developers. The discussion on relational database design issues in Chapter 5 should prove useful for these tasks. Data entry "forms" can be developed using a database package such as Access to facilitate record additions, changes, and deletions. A frequent design error is to use a spreadsheet program for an application that really needs database management functions such as those provided by a database management tool. These are all Construction issues in which access to IS consultants or a user developer highly experienced in database application design can help a user group avoid a costly reworking of a poorly designed system.

It is also important to consider data recovery needs; if the application is stored on a server and a multiuser version of the system is being used, some backup and recovery procedures should already be in place. However, the user developer needs to assess whether these are sufficient.

Designing an audit trail enables the tracing of activities through the system to validate transaction processing and adherence to organizational and accounting rules. This is closely related to the recovery process, and the provisions made for recovery can provide a basic audit trail.

The documentation that is necessary for a user-developed application depends upon the application's characteristics. Personal systems often have little or no formal documentation. However, if this is a system that a successor to the current user developer will also be expected to use, formal documentation should be provided and kept up to date; it should also include documentation that is not embedded in the application itself, in the event of a system crash. The documentation for a multiuser system, or a stand-alone application used by different people in different workgroups, typically requires detailed user documentation, such as that produced by IS specialists. If user-developed systems are regularly audited, it is obviously a good idea to consult with these auditors while defining and constructing the system to ensure that the organization's auditing concerns are adequately addressed.

Significant time and a rigorous test process are needed to ensure that an application works the way it is intended to. The lack of adequate testing for decision support applications can lead to serious consequences for a business. Errors in spreadsheet applications, for example, are known to have caused losses ranging from hundreds of thousands to millions of dollars (Galletta et al., 1996), and the user

USER DEVELOPER EXPERIENCES

CONTACT MANAGEMENT SYSTEM

This program was designed to better manage the contacts each member of the C workgroup has with external contacts, in order to help improve the efficiency and productivity of all members. The Contact Management System stores information about employees in the C workgroup, contacts at various sites, and the sites themselves. Contacts with other sites are captured and categorized according to their contact method. Information about a contact includes the parties involved, the time and date, the subjects discussed, and a synopsis of the communication. Reports include all contacts by individuals within a given time period, contacts on a specific topic, and contacts regarding a specific project. Visual Basic and Access were the primary tools used for this application.

The methodology used was a modified software development life-cycle approach using prototyping. I discussed the requirements of the program with several competent peers who had a desire to be a player in the development of the system. We met and discussed potential uses for the system and discussed requirements for expansion of the system to meet future goals. We utilized Visual Basic's rapid development environment to "test drive" possible screen layouts. This worked quite well, as the others were able to actually see rather than just listen to ideas and concepts for the user interface. As with most projects, this one did not progress as rapidly as predicted; the current version lacks some of the overly ambitious original goals. These will be implemented in the near future in a later release. There is a high level of anticipation for a fully functional product among the users who are currently using the program to enter the data to create the database. Their use of the product at this time is helping to finalize the interface for the final release.

Lessons Learned During the development of this project, a number of important lessons were learned. Most important was the need to stay in touch with the end users of the product throughout the development cycle. Not only does this assure that their needs are being met and the program will be useful to their productivity, but it also entices excitement, which is vital to the acceptance of the final product. Even with rapid development tools, the several months required to develop a quality product can be enough of a lapse in the anticipation of the end users such that acceptance of the product is less than enthusiastic. Another valuable lesson learned was that when the program gets close to being completed is always when the intricate, hard-to-find bugs seem to be seen.

TRACKING DATABASE

This application is a Lotus Notes project tracking database for my workgroup. It is used to track activities between my workgroup in the parent company related to current and prospective customers. In my workgroup, projects are segmented by customer. The process starts with a customer inquiry, followed by actual work done, and concluding with problem resolution. With the current version of this application, my group can track different kinds of activities with a customer: action items, call reports, incoming correspondence, internal correspondence, outgoing correspondence, meeting reports, and miscellaneous activity. The database was tailored from a template provided with Lotus Notes to meet the needs of my workgroup.

I employed the prototyping methodology. Before beginning the project, my manager and I discussed the tracking system I envisioned; I convinced him that this application would help us manage our work more effectively. In the requirements definition phase, a colleague and I developed a list of the requirements for our tracking database. During this phase, we reviewed the Lotus Notes tracking database template to verify the compatibility of our requirements with those of the template. Many of the requirements we desired, like checkboxes for project type and technology type, and activities such as internal e-mail, were not a part of the Notes template. However, many of the structural needs of our system were included in the template.

I spent most of the first couple of days working with the Lotus Notes tool to become proficient as a user before diving into the developer world. I wanted to be sure I fully understood how Lotus Notes worked, how users interfaced with it, and what its capabilities were. The Notes tool is very intuitive and, after only a couple of days, I began work on the tailored project tracking database. My goal was to have a usable prototype as quickly as possible so I could take it to three key users: my manager and two colleagues. I chose one colleague who was very computer literate and one that seems to merely know where the "ON" switch is on his workstation. I had a usable prototype in 3 days.

As expected, the majority of my effort was after the working prototype was rolled out to key users. While using the new tracking system, the key users were able to identify several items they now wanted in the system and also found a few bugs. The bugs were corrected quickly but the changes/additions to the system required several iterations. Within a few weeks, we had a fully operational system.

As with any application where the developer resides within the department, new iterations, though minor, continue. Tweaking the tracking system in this manner has allowed us to reach a point where the application is so useful that our entire department depends heavily on it for up-to-the-minute information on projects.

Lessons Learned One key lesson I learned in developing this system overshadows all others. I learned that managing user expectation is paramount to user satisfaction early in a project. My "key users" believed that since I had a prototype with the user screens developed very rapidly, that the workable system with "everything they wanted" would follow equally as fast. Another lesson I learned is the value of the prototyping methodology: It enabled our group to develop a powerful system with little time and little money invested.

[Evening MBA students, Indiana University]

developer's postdevelopment debugging practices might be a major cause (Panko, 1996; Panko and Halverson, 1996). For example, studies have found that many spreadsheet developers apparently do not attempt to reduce their spreadsheet errors systematically; it also is not a common practice to have others check their programs. Since research on the work practices of IS professionals has found that spotting errors by inspection is difficult for the original programmer, user developers should regularly involve others in debugging their applications rather than relying wholly on self-testing.

Although automatic audit features and separate audit programs (especially for spreadsheet programs) are more prevalent today than in the 1990s, research shows that organizations need to devote much more attention to spreadsheet error detection. Studies have shown that as many as one-third of spreadsheet models are likely to contain errors. The sidebar entitled "Errors in Spreadsheets" describes the types of errors that are typical in spreadsheets and some reasons why they are so common.

Complex, modular systems of course require more planning and coordination for testing and installation than simple applications for use by the person who developed the application. Even users formally educated in IS development methodologies typically face a significant learning curve as a user developer. This learning involves both tool learning and process learning. In the sidebar entitled "User Developer Experiences," knowledge workers who are not IS professionals describe the methods they used to develop their first multiuser applications and the lessons that they learned. In both instances, the user developers were also developing applications in which they were using an end-user development tool that was new to them.

User Development Roles

Depending on the development approach used, the scope of the application (personal, departmental, organizational), and its intended usage, a formal project team for the application might or might not be created. However, essentially all the roles described in Chapter 10 for custom-developed applications need to be played by the users alone or with the help of consultants. For example, consultant skills could be needed for understanding relational database and object-oriented concepts or for understanding how best to utilize a sophisticated end-user tool. IS employees within the same organization are typically the first choice for the consultant role, although sometimes the tool to be used, the skillsets needed, or the lack of availability of these IS resources results in contractual arrangements with external consultants.

For most user-developed applications, a business manager (or the business manager accountable for the application) plays the **project manager** role; for many business employees, project management is already a well-honed skill. However, developers also need to be familiar with the basic steps of a life cycle methodology, the advantages and pitfalls of alternative approaches such as an iterative or prototyping methodology, and documentation standards and best practices for auditing controls and system recovery.

Depending on the organizational context, there could also be an internal auditor or other type of oversight role to ensure that user-developed applications do not expose the organization to unacceptable levels of risk. In some organizations, the IS organization, an oversight committee of senior business managers, an internal auditing department, or all three might be formally accountable for ensuring that user-developed applications do not expose the organization to unacceptable levels of risk. Williford (2000) has identified four review methods, which range from a formal audit to a "best-guess" informal review that involves periodically questioning IS department staff about potentially problematic applications. Many organizations began taking a formal inventory of user-developed applications for the first time as part of their Year 2000 compliance initiatives and have continued this approach in lieu of a more formal (and expensive) audit.

We began this chapter by stating that in order for user computing to be effective at the individual, departmental, and organizational levels, IS and business unit managers must have a shared set of responsibilities that is appropriate for their organizational context. In the next section we present a framework to describe what types of support and control actions are commonly used, depending on the organization's overall strategy for facilitating computing by non-IS professionals.

STRATEGIES AND TACTICS FOR MANAGING USER COMPUTING

Effective management of end-user computing requires not only good procedures for making decisions about when to develop an application without the formal help of IS specialists, but also structures and personnel to support and control end-user computing activities on a ongoing basis. Figure 13.7 presents a framework that can be used to assess an organization's effectiveness in leveraging end-user computing technologies and personnel.

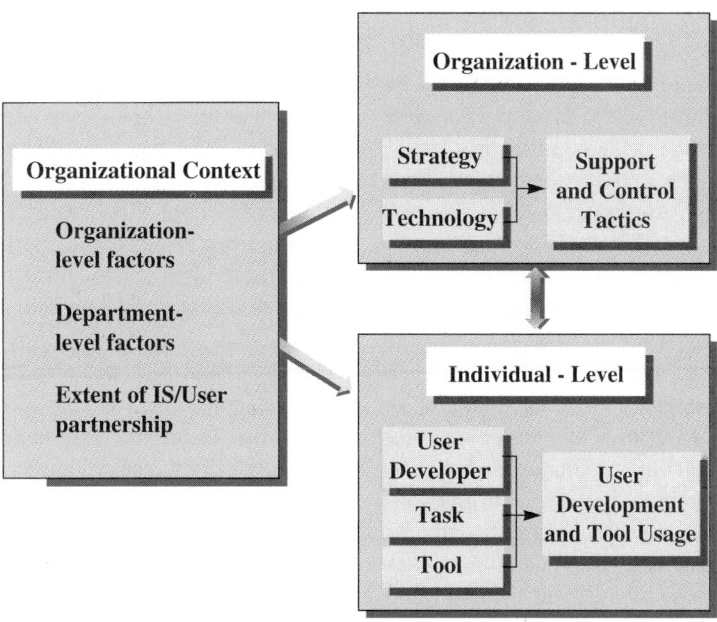

Figure 13.7 Framework for Leveraging End-User Computing (Based on Brancheau and Brown, 1993)

The box at the far left in Figure 13.7, labeled Organizational Context, explicitly acknowledges that factors such as the organization's business strategy, the way the IS professional resources are organized, the special characteristics of a given user department, and the extent of IS/user "partnering" within the organization will influence the strategies and tactics used for end-user computing as well as factors at the individual level. For example, if systems development groups have been decentralized to business unit control, there is a greater likelihood that "local" IS professionals will have a high degree of business-specific knowledge and might be more heavily relied on for playing a *consultant* role in user application development projects. Similarly, if a highly computer-literate business manager heads a given user department, there is a greater likelihood that a large amount of user application development activity will be occurring in that department. Whether or not that user department should seek a high degree of independence from the IS organization depends on the business manager's IT management knowledge and the history (status) of the IS/business partnering on other development projects.

The two-headed arrow between the Organization-Level and Individual-Level boxes on the right in Figure 13.7 reflects the linkages between an organization's strategy and tactics for end-user computing and factors at the individual end-user level. This arrow again suggests that there is no single best way to manage end-user computing; rather, an organization's approach needs to take into account unique aspects of its own organization and its own individual users.

The Individual-Level box lists four factors that were part of our discussion on user application development approaches: characteristics of the user developer, the business problem (task) being worked on, the end-user tool, and the user development process and tool usage. As pointed out in the previous section, highly skilled user developers and highly sophisticated end-user technologies exist in organizations today, but not every user department will have the same level of skills. Therefore, a one-size-fits-all approach to the development of applications by users is likely to be ill-fated.

The Organization-Level box in Figure 13.7 has three factors that are the responsibility of an organization's management—*both* IS and business managers:

- *Strategy* The strategic objectives and overall approach to end-user computing
- *Technology* The range and accessibility of end-user tools
- *Tactics for Support and Control* Support services, control policies and procedures

The technologies for end-user computing are discussed in Part I of this textbook. For the remainder of this chapter we therefore focus on the two other factors: Strategies and Tactics.

Strategies for End-User Computing

Some IS organizations did not have an explicit strategy for managing end-user computing when desktop PCs were first being brought into the organization in the early 1980s. At that time both mainframe and microcomputer tools were being used for user application development, but end-user training and support for the mainframe tools was much more likely to be in place than end-user training for microcomputer tools. The mainframe tools, of course, were installed by the IS department. However, many IS managers took a laissez-faire approach to end-user computing with desktop computers: IS managers might or might not have signed-off on business unit requests to purchase hardware and software, but end users were typically left on their own to install the equipment, learn the software, and manually organize and enter their own data into a stand-alone application. The early microcomputers were even viewed by some managers as inexpensive tools similar to calculators, in which business units were "free" to invest. LANs to connect microcomputers were not common until a decade later (the early 1990s), and few policies and procedures might have been put in place.

As shown in Figure 13.8, a laissez-faire approach was a common starting place for all organizations in the 1980s because microcomputer technologies were a new, emerging phenomenon. Although this approach still can be found, it much less common: Most organizations today have developed an explicit strategy and support staff for managing end-user computing.

Three other management approaches commonly used today can be identified based on the degree to which the organization has sought to *expand* (increase) end-user computing activities and the degree to which it seeks to *control* these activities. As shown in Figure 13.8, firms that invest heavily in end-user computing resources, but with minimal concerns about formal controls, can be said to have an *Acceleration* strategy. Their objective is to enable users to acquire and learn to use end-user technologies in order to develop their own computing solutions to business problems, with few constraints. In contrast, firms with a *Containment* strategy have opted to invest in end-user computing more slowly and carefully. Very specific controls are put in place and users are typically restricted to standard tool purchases and stricter guidelines for application development, backup, and security.

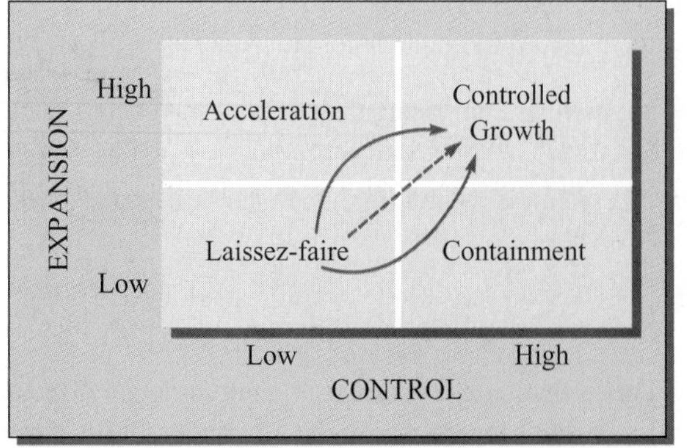

Figure 13.8 End-User Computing Strategies (Based on Munro et al., 1987–1988; Brancheau and Amoroso, 1990)

The *Controlled Growth* strategy (high expansion, but also high control) is perceived to be the most advanced or mature approach. Initially, it was expected that firms would move first to an acceleration or containment strategy and then gradually increase controls or support levels to reach a controlled growth stage. However, many organizations actually have taken a middle ground or a balanced approach, as depicted by the dotted line in Figure 13.8. This balanced strategy involves starting with small investments in end-user computing resources as well as few controls and then increasing both investments in resources and controls as the number of end users and end-user applications increases.

Finally, organizations in a mature (Controlled Growth) stage of end-user computing may still choose an Acceleration or Containment approach for introducing a new end-user technology within their organizations. For example, many organizations initially took an Acceleration approach to end-user development of Web content for organizational intranets in the late 1990s but then evolved to more restrictive approaches. Other organizations, however, chose a Containment strategy that involved committee governance and early rules for Web page content and look-and-feel (see the sidebar entitled "Different Strategies for Managing Intranets"). Today's organizations are faced with the choice among these same strategies (Laissez-Faire, Acceleration, Containment) for managing personal digital assistants (PDAs) and cellular communications devices for business computing. However, as more business employees demand linkages with personal productivity software tools and remote access to e-mail communications, organizations are likely to evolve to more "balanced" approaches.

Centralized Support (Information Center) Approaches. Some firms have established a centralized support unit for managing end-user computing activities, usually within an IS organization. The term **information center (IC)** was commonly used to describe this approach in the 1980s, because the term had previously been used to refer to supporting end-users via an separate mainframe computer on which was loaded a full copy, or extract, of one or more production databases as well as software tools for end users to develop queries, generate reports, and build decision

DIFFERENT STRATEGIES FOR MANAGING INTRANETS

As Web authoring tools designed for non-IS specialists (such as Microsoft FrontPage) became readily available in the late 1990s, managers had to develop a strategy for managing their intranets while they learned more about the best ways to do so for their organizations. (Note: intranets are internal company networks that use Internet technologies and protocols.) For example, Boeing initially took a "let-the-flowers-bloom" approach (Acceleration strategy) and deliberately sought to keep intranet restrictions to a minimum to facilitate exploration with Web tools in different units across the organization. A standard Web authoring tool was distributed without cost to user departments, and it led to a very quick growth of Web pages developed by users on the intranet. According to Graeber Jordan, who was a senior manager responsible for e-commerce at Boeing at that time, the proliferation of internal Web pages resulted in a new norm of electronic communication inside the organization, rather than communication via hard copies of newsletters, updated documents, or status reports (Jordan, 1997).

Other organizations chose a Containment strategy, in which the IS organization or a central committee first established the rules for Web page content and set specific parameters for look-and-feel formats and then continued to serve as an oversight committee. Individual employees in each department were formally designated as responsible for their department's Web pages. A separate technical committee was used to make recommendations about new technologies and to track performance for the oversight group.

Organizations like Boeing that began with an Acceleration strategy eventually implemented more rules and standards, and organizations that began with a Containment strategy also moved to a Controlled Growth strategy over time. Some of the challenges faced were how to develop a common set of terms to improve internal document searching and how to monitor and manage the deletion of outdated content.

models. By the late 1980s, the IC term was commonly used for any centralized support unit, often reporting to an IS organization, with a mandate to support end-user computing. IC managers also typically were charged with implementing appropriate control policies and procedures to help manage the business risks of user-developed applications.

A critical success factor for the effectiveness of a centralized support unit is its staffing. As with other personnel responsible for customer services, effective support staff for end-user computing need to have not only product knowledge (in this case technical knowledge), but also the ability to relate well to users. The ability to provide quick turnaround time in response to user requests for help is a key performance measure for this staff. It is also common for "power users" from a business unit to be hired into a central support unit to provide consulting and troubleshooting support for other users. In the early 1990s, a typical staffing ratio was one support member for each 100 PCs, but today ratios as low as 35 staff members supporting 10,000 users have been reported (McNurlin and Sprague, 1998).

IS/Business Partnering Approaches. Other organizations have adopted a less centralized approach to supporting users. For example, an approach based on strong user/IS partnerships and joint accountability between IS and business management, originally referred to as a *managed free economy* approach, has five components:

- An explicit strategy that reflects a support and control philosophy
- A user/IS working partnership
- An end-user support unit that is well integrated with other IS units
- An emphasis on end-user education (IS development methods, quality controls)
- A targeting of critical (high-impact) end-user applications

Focusing on applications with high payoffs was also advocated more than a decade ago by end-user computing consultants (Karten, 1990). Figure 13.9 summarizes Karten's comparison of a reactive support role (that predominated at that time) versus a more proactive support role in which investments are made in end-user applications that have the potential for significantly affecting the business. In this Stage Two role, both IS and business managers work together to focus on how to better leverage technology investments, as well as the increasing numbers of users with high levels of IT literacy ("power users") who also have an interest in developing sophisticated end-user tools for decision support.

Whether or not an organization adopts a centralized or a more distributed strategy for facilitating end-user computing, all organizations need to formulate an appropriate strategy and to implement a set of support services and control policies to help realize this strategy. Below, we present some common support and control tactics.

Common Support Tactics

A list of typical support services to facilitate user computing is provided in Figure 13.10. Services such as troubleshooting (help desk), consulting, training, assistance

STAGE ONE	STAGE TWO
Reactive services	Proactive services
Individual solutions, quick-and-dirty	Departmental solutions, in-depth
Product training	Business problem-solving
All needs supported	High-payoff needs supported
Computer literacy training	Information literacy education
One-way relationships	Alliance; IS/user partnerships

Figure 13.9 Reactive Stage One vs. Proactive Stage Two Support Roles

- *Troubleshooting* A hotline or help desk 24/7 or as needed
- *Consulting* One-on-one consulting on application development, query tools, and so on
- *Training* Technology (tool) training in classroom setting as well as self-paced e-learning modules
- *IS education* System development methodologies, security procedures, and so on
- *Product research and evaluation* Identifying and evaluating new end-user tools and recommending products for trial by users
- *Tool selection and purchasing* Hardware, software, network solutions
- *Tool installation, maintenance, and upgrading* Hardware, software, networks
- *Information sharing* Formalizing communications between support personnel and end users, as well as across end user groups; typical sharing mechanisms include newsletters, Web pages on an intranet, and periodical meetings for users to evaluate new tools and share development and technology "tips"

Figure 13.10 Common Support Services

with tool selection, maintenance, and upgrading are all services that are commonly offered today. This list also distinguishes between tool training and IS education: Training refers to learning to use a specific tool. IS education is not tied to a specific tool and addresses "best practices"—such as methodologies for developing computer applications. Sharing solutions to common problems is frequently accomplished today via Web pages on an intranet and often includes postings of answers to frequently asked questions (FAQs).

Supporting end users today also involves preparing end users for new software releases. This typically involves not only retraining users, but also refitting end-user workstations with more memory or disk storage space to support the new software. During the late 1990s many organizations adopted a 3-year replacement strategy for personal computer hardware. The rationale was twofold: (1) to take advantage of new software functionality and (2) to avoid expensive maintenance and repair costs for older PCs. However, some organizations have also found that for users who need only word processing and an Internet browser, for example, 5-year-old PCs might be sufficient (Delaney, 2003).

To save costs and keep focused on core services, many organizations contract the provisioning of user support services out to IT vendors. For example, the outsourcing of user training has become more popular as firms have begun to standardize their suites of office productivity tools. However, it should be noted that by turning over classroom training to an outside firm, an end-user support organization can lose a valuable opportunity for education on company-specific IS issues as well as an opportunity to establish a support-service relationship with end users. In other words, cost efficiencies alone should not be the only criterion for choosing whether to provide a support service in-house or via a third-party supplier. Other firms have attempted to reduce classroom training costs by providing self-paced training alternatives. Progressive firms are providing e-training via a Web-based interface to a "learning portal" that is either run by the organization or hosted by an outside vendor (see the sidebar entitled "Reinventing Training at Cisco Systems").

Another frequently outsourced service is **help desk** (hotline) support. In the past, organizations used help desk positions as an initial training ground for entry-level IS positions; in a very short time, the new employee gained a first-hand appreciation of the difficulties faced by the organization's end users. However, just as many companies today are outsourcing some of their customer service support to persons in countries with different time zones or lower labor costs, or both, many IT help desks are being outsourced to gain cost efficiencies. Like other business units with help desks, IS help desk personnel frequently are guided by expert system applications to help them diagnose a problem in order to respond to telephone inquiries from end users. Today's network administrators also have an array of tools to help them troubleshoot hardware problems at remote sites.

In addition, the software industry has made great strides in improving online self-help for the end user. For example, tools have more sophisticated help functions that include searching by key words as well as context-specific help functions. The vendors of office suites have developed various types of online "assistants"—including wizards that help users create graphs in spreadsheet programs, create tables for common entities in database management programs, and format text, spreadsheets, data entry forms, and reports. In recent versions vendors have provided cartoon characters that pop up to offer help to the user. Software tips change based on recent keystrokes by the user of the particular application and animated examples help to train end users in a specific task.

However, the costliest changes in demand for facilitating end-user computing are control actions related to security issues: preventing computer abuse due to viruses, worms, and other hacker software and preventing unsolicited bulk e-mail messages (referred to as **spam**). We briefly address both of these in the next section.

REINVENTING TRAINING AT CISCO SYSTEMS

Tom Kelly, VP of worldwide training at Cisco Systems, joined the company with a clear mandate: to make Cisco a model of Web-based excellence in the one part of its business in which it was a laggard—Cisco's training division. According to Kelly: "There are very few high-tech companies that truly respect how much learning has to happen to allow them and their people to stay current." The learning model that Kelly is building at Cisco distinguishes between "structured learning" and "emergency learning," and tries to customize each form to the needs of the individual. Each person will be able to create a customized Web page, tentatively called My Future. The My Future page will serve as a learning portal where people can chart a long-term, structured learning plan; get all relevant short-term updates; and automatically receive critical information based on their job title, area of operation, field of interest, and learning preferences—time-critical content for emergency-learning situations. Ultimately, Kelly says, e-learning will be most effective when it no longer feels like learning—when it's simply a natural part of how people work.

[Adapted from Muoio, 2000]

Common Control Tactics

Management actions directed at controlling end-user computing typically have taken the form of policies or procedures. A list of common policies and procedures for end-user computing, which include approvals for purchasing hardware and software and keeping inventories of these tools, is provided in Figure 13.11. Many organizations place the primary responsibility for developing these policies and procedures in the hands of a centralized support unit, usually within an IS department. In some organizations an IS steering committee is responsible for establishing policies, including hardware and software standards, and the IS manager of the central support unit has the primary responsibility for monitoring compliance with these standards. The degree to which organizational policies are guidelines versus mandates, and the manner in which they are enforced, varies widely across organizations and across different departments within the same organization (Speier and Brown, 1997). However, the willingness of business unit managers and individual users to comply with computing standards has increased in recent years as the advantages for access to common computing and communications networks have increased.

Keeping users up to date on the latest policies and procedures has been a challenging management issue;

Required (or recommended) product standards (hardware and software)
Requirements (recommendations) for workstation ergonomics
Approval process for product purchases
Requirements for product inventorying
Upgrade procedures

Application quality review process
Guidelines to identify high-impact applications and sensitive data
Policies for corporate data access
Guidelines for program and data backup procedures
Requirements for audit trails
Documentation standards

Policies to control unauthorized access and file-sharing
Policies to control unauthorized software copying
Virus protection procedures
Spam filtering procedures

Figure 13.11 Common Policies and Procedures

organizations have typically done a better job communicating them to new workers via orientation programs than to older ones. Today, end-user computing policies and forms for technology and password approvals are typically accessible to all employees via the company's intranet. Changes in policies and procedural deadlines can also be broadcast to all end users via e-mail.

Organizational compliance with copyrights and licensing agreements is usually a formal responsibility of the senior IS manager. Software copyright compliance has been a weak area of end-user computing control in the past, but many organizations invested in mechanisms to monitor software licenses and to inventory software on all networked machines as part of their Year 2000 compliance initiatives, and this management area is much stronger today. Although enforcing control policies for software copyrights is easier to accomplish in networked environments in general, software vendors are reportedly still losing significant revenues due to software copyright violations. To put pressure on companies to proactively monitor for copyright and software licensing violations, the large software vendors have created alliances such as the Business Software Alliance (BSA) through which they file civil suits for copyright infringement (see the sidebar entitled "Software Companies Search for Pirates").

As mentioned above, however, the greatest control challenges today are preventing, and recovering from, external threats. Although laws against hackers have existed, and been enforced, in the United States for more than a decade, IS managers are facing increasingly frequent and more costly digital attacks from viruses and worms. Although security procedures can be implemented centrally and users can be given procedures to follow to avoid these security risks, the company's network is only as secure as its weakest link. For 2003 alone, estimates of economic damage worldwide due to viruses, worms, and other hacker attacks was estimated to be more than $120 billion, which would be more than twice as large as the estimated damage for the preceding year (Langley, 2003).

Another control issue concerns the use of peer-to-peer or **file-sharing applications,** which can slow down internal networks (due to using up bandwidth) as well as create major security problems (by giving an external computer access to an internal network, creating the potential for spreading viruses). File-sharing applications therefore intensify the problems of Internet abuse, because users expose their files for search and download by other users. Further, just as the original Napster Web site facilitated access to illegal copies of songs, most file-sharing software also is facilitating the sharing of copyrighted music and videos. Lawsuits by copyright owners against individual users are also increasing the pressure on organizations to detect or block peer-to-peer access (see sidebar "New Control Challenge: File-Sharing Applications").

The current lack of U.S. laws imposing penalties for sending commercial e-mail messages also makes it difficult for organizations, and their employees, to set up controls to

SOFTWARE COMPANIES SEARCH FOR PIRATES

One of the most lucrative squealing operations in America is run out of the K Street lobbying district in Washington, D.C. The Business Software Alliance (BSA) does all the things that most D.C. lobby groups do, but it also has "power of attorney" to enforce the copyright claims of its members against companies using pirated software. The members of the BSA include large software companies like Microsoft. If the BSA finds out that your company is using more software than you have paid for, they can demand not only that you buy the programs, but also that you pay a penalty—a negotiated settlement fee that will serve as a reminder of the error of your ways. The alternative is to face a civil suit for copyright infringement, something few companies would want to risk.

The BSA has engaged in hundreds of enforcement actions over the years, bringing in a total of $70 million, including $12 million in 2002. The companies caught tend to be otherwise upstanding members of their local Chambers of Commerce, who for some reason or another are not paying for all the programs they are using; for some reason, they just do not view software inventories as important. For example, one Illinois engineer had a run-in with the BSA over unlicensed copies of the AutoCad engineering program: the penalty was $115,000. In addition to penalties, companies sometimes also endure the added indignity of having their managers being quoted in a BSA press release as lamenting how sorry they are and saying how much they respect intellectual property.

The BSA has a Report Piracy button on its Web site and a toll-free number. The money that is collected goes into the BSA's antipiracy program and is in fact, according to the software vendors, a "drop in the bucket" compared with the billions lost because of software piracy.

[Based on Gomes, 2003]

NEW CONTROL CHALLENGE: FILE-SHARING APPLICATIONS

File-sharing applications are challenges to corporate policies because they intensify the problems of old-fashioned Internet abuse. Although each uses a different architecture, these applications allow users to trade files with each other. (The old Napster music-sharing software, for instance, turned an individual's computer into a miniserver.) Users can search for and download files located on the hard drives of other users on the network. At the same time, users expose their files for search and download by other users. Almost all material that passes through file-sharing applications is copyrighted. Most of the applications help users search for MP3 music files, but some are sophisticated enough to handle the transfer of bigger files such as movies. The battle over copyright laws and file-sharing applications led to the shutdown of the original Napster site.

Corporations have long sought to regulate workers' Web access to avoid wasted time and controversial uses. Now they are increasingly taking aim at employees' use of peer-to-peer software such as Kazaa and Morpheus because they are under growing pressure from the copyright owners. In March 2003 music record companies sent about 300 U.S. corporations a letter warning that their networks had been used to swap songs. If a CIO or other company official knows of illegal use of file-sharing applications, he or she should take action.

[Adapted from Mathews, 2003; Pender, 2000]

block unwanted e-mail. According to recent estimates (Spam Calculator, 2003), the typical time lost by an employee for each spam e-mail received is only about 3 seconds; nevertheless, if an organization has a 220-day work year and 1,000 employees using e-mail, and 40 percent of their e-mail messages are spam, the annual cost in lost productivity to the organization (as well as monthly IT maintenance costs) approaches $200,000. Filtering technologies exist for identifying and destroying viruses and for bypassing e-mail messages identified as spam, but they are deterrents against moving targets: Hackers and spammers can also buy the same software and devise ways to work around them.

Support and control tactics need to continually be modified in response to new technologies, new ways of working, and new external threats. Because of the increase in security threats for organizations, in Chapter 16 we provide a more detailed discussion, including their potential impacts. We conclude this chapter by addressing the special case of facilitating user computing when the users are working remotely as telecommuters.

SPECIAL CASE: SUPPORTING TELECOMMUTERS

Providing support for workers outside of the physical walls of a business has become an important IT management and business management capability. Recent estimates are that about 20 million "white collar" workers in the United States, 10 million in Europe, and more than 2 million in Japan are part-time or full-time telecommuters, spending at least part of their workday or workweek at customer work sites, on the road, in home offices, or in satellite office facilities. Given the accelerated diffusion of mobile communication and

> **Telecommuters** spend at least a part of their regular business hours using IT to perform their jobs outside of a company's physical facilities, using a mobile office, an office in their personal home, or at a temporary office at a shared work center away from the company's main office.

computing devices and wireless networks, the number of telecommuters is likely to double before 2010.

However, not all "white collar" work (knowledge work) is suited to a telecommuting arrangement and not all telecommuters have the same needs for remote work support. One way to think about these job differences is to categorize them into three types which differ in terms of how "tethered" an employee's job is to the building that provides permanent office space for an organization's employees.

- *Office-bound* Office-bound employees are "tethered" to an office in a building, where they typically use IT that might or might not be portable.
- *Travel-driven* Travel-driven employees take their office with them to whatever location they are working in, which can change during the workday or workweek. For example, many sales force personnel have travel-driven jobs; they were likely to be among the first employees within their organizations to become telecommuters.
- *Independent* Independent workers do not have a permanent office work space owned or leased by an employer. Instead, the worker uses IT in a home office or a mobile office, or both.

However, by the end of the 1990s many organizations in the United States were implementing telecommuting options for individual employees who weren't necessarily independent or travel-driven workers, but who required more flexibility in their work arrangements. For example, an employee might normally go to an office building to work but occasionally would work at home. Some companies' programs were designed to facilitate working at home for different types of projects that might require uninterrupted work time. Other telecommuters might simply be "day extenders"—employees working full days at a permanent office but then working at home during evenings and perhaps weekends.

For those knowledge workers in positions that are not highly office-bound, the benefits from implementing telecommuting programs can be compelling. According to self-reports by telecommuters, a very high percentage of workers say that they are more productive, due to a variety of factors (including the ability to focus better and to save in commuting time). Some companies have also realized dramatic savings from real estate costs. One of the cases in this textbook describes how a division within a large company in the IT industry (IBM) was able to avoid major real estate costs by setting up sales employees with equipment and telecommunications line access, initially for home offices and subsequently for mobile offices. Over a period of 5 years more than 12,500 employees at IBM gave up dedicated office space in company buildings and the company achieved multimillion dollar savings on an annual basis (Agpar, 1998). Lucent Technologies and AT&T have reported similar dramatic savings for enterprise-wide telecommuting programs.

Further, in some geographic regions within the United States with major environmental problems (for example, Los Angeles), companies of a certain size must comply with state or local regulations designed to improve the physical environment; for example, designated companies of a certain size might be required to have only a certain percentage of employees physically commuting to a work building within a given workweek. Governments have also set up tax incentives for companies to document how their telecommuting programs help to reduce highway congestion (and therefore air pollution).

Individual telecommuters have also reported personal benefits that they believe also contribute positively to their overall performance, such as the following.

- *Increased workday flexibility* Remote workers gain flexibility in their work schedules that can reduce work stress and could allow them to avoid rush-hour traffic.
- *Improved work/life balance* Employees who work at home typically are able to spend more time with family members by working very early in the morning or very late in the evening.
- *Easier accommodation of communications across time zones* Employees who need to communicate with others in different time zones sometimes find it easier to integrate meeting times that extend their workdays if they can communicate from their homes.

Given these organizational and individual benefits, why have the number of telecommuters not increased more rapidly? One answer is that telecommuting programs typically involve an initial investment in technology, as well as ongoing IT support solutions. For example, today's telecommuters typically require portable equipment (which is still more expensive than the equivalent desktop equipment) and

DATA COMMUNICATIONS FOR TELEWORKERS

Teleworkers need to have access to all the same data communication services that are available to employees with a permanent office, although not always at the same speeds. Virtual private networks (VPN) and other remote access technologies provide seamless, location-independent access to corporate data resources. The importance of sufficient bandwidth cannot be overemphasized: It does not make sense to lower the productivity of a highly-paid professional with low bandwidth or an unreliable connection if a faster and more reliable option is available at a marginal increase in cost. Broadband connections using xDSL, cable modems, or satellite connections are the norm if connections are regularly made from the same location. For mobile workers, wireless connections are increasingly available at airports, hotels, and restaurants/coffee shops, as is connectivity in densely populated areas. Further, e-mail, instant messaging, and access to core corporate systems are increasingly available on mobile phones and PDAs: In many cases these capabilities are all a mobile worker needs in addition to voice communication.

[Based on Topi, 2003]

remote access, with sufficient bandwidth, to corporate data networks and services (see the sidebar entitled "Data Communications for Teleworkers.") Although the costs of mobile devices and networks continue to decline and not all telecommuters might need high speed connections, there are also still ongoing security and support issues that the IT organization needs to address. Telecommuters might also require immediate help desk support outside of normal work hours, due to more flexible work schedules and time zone differences. However, in large organizations, 24/7 user support at some level has become the norm.

Other reasons for the relatively slow diffusion of telecommuting arrangements over the past decade are not technology obstacles, but managerial and behavioral obstacles. For example, it has been learned that organizations need to redesign some of their work processes in order to effectively accommodate telecommuters. In particular, performance appraisal systems need to be revised to focus on performance outcomes so that the telecommuter is not penalized for different (and less visible) approaches to achieving work objectives. Some companies only allow "proven stars," not newcomers, to telecommute, and some managers believe that telecommuting weakens loyalty to the company (Dunham, 2000).

Another obstacle to telecommuting programs has been that many employees feel a sense of isolation. Remote workers don't have the opportunity for informal social interactions that working in an office building fosters. Some organizations have therefore instituted regular meetings that include telecommuters in order to increase social interactions with supervisors and among coworkers and make electronic communications more meaningful. Some telecommuters have also voiced concerns about not having the same opportunities for career advancement due to the belief that being "out-of-sight" would mean that they are less well known and therefore less likely to be considered for a given career opportunity. Many organizations have developed training programs for not only telecommuters, but also supervisors of telecommuters, in order to help avoid some of these nontechnical obstacles. Some guidelines for managers of remote workers, based on a very readable book by Jaclyn Kostner, are summarized in Figure 13.12.

Six Leadership Secrets For Managing Remote Workers

1. Aim to build trust through every interaction.
2. Create symbols and structures that unify the dispersed work group.
3. Establish ongoing opportunities for the team to learn more about each other, both professionally and personally.
4. Develop a daily alignment tool to focus the effort of the team.
5. Be scrupulously fair in treating all team members.
6. Be crystal clear about project objectives.

[Based on Kostner,1996]

Figure 13.12 Six Leadership Secrets for Managing Remote Workers

Telecommuting programs also need to take into account security and legal issues. For example, it might be necessary to develop or modify written policies about the employee's responsibility for maintaining the confidentiality of company data accessed remotely and the use of company equipment for personal reasons. Employers of telecommuters also have the right to inspect home offices that contain company equipment, and this right should also be a part of a written agreement with the employee.

SUMMARY

The development of applications by business employees who are not IS specialists has become commonplace. The pervasiveness of user-developed applications is partly due to the clear advantages associated with these applications. However, business managers should carefully consider the potential disadvantages associated with user-developed applications when characteristics of the application to be developed, the technologies to be used, and the skills and experience of the available user developers suggest that the business risks will outweigh the benefits. User developers should also use a development methodology that is appropriate for the specific application. Consultation with IS professionals and auditing personnel should be encouraged throughout the development project, as appropriate.

Effective management of end-user computing in general requires strategies and tactics that take into account unique organizational context characteristics and the range and maturity of user development activities within the specific organization. IS and business managers need to approach end-user computing management as a user/IS working partnership and focus on supporting user applications with high payoffs. Today's network technologies make it easier to provide some support services and to enforce some control policies and procedures. In particular, the increasing use of networks has made it easier to place the tasks of hardware and software inventorying and upgrading, as well as the enforcement of some security controls and procedures, in the hands of network administrators rather than individual users. The IT industry has also become more responsive to some support needs by embedding context-specific support and control mechanisms in the end-user technologies.

In order to foster organizational learning, effective strategies for managing new and emerging end-user technologies typically differ from those used for mature end-user computing environments. Supporting telecommuters requires not only new technology solutions, but also addressing unique managerial challenges. Although new technologies help facilitate teamwork by a mobile workforce across multiple time zones, both employees and managers need special training programs to increase the likelihood of successful performance.

REVIEW QUESTIONS

1. What is meant by user application development? How does this differ from end-user computing in general?
2. What are some of the reasons why business users would want to develop computer applications rather than rely on IS professionals?
3. What are some of the major business risks associated with user application development?
4. Describe one characteristic each of the potential application, tool, and developer that should be assessed when evaluating whether or not a given application should be user-developed, including what you see as the potential business risk.
5. Choose three Definition questions that the user developer should address and explain why they could be important.
6. What are some of the key causes of spreadsheet errors in user-developed applications?
7. Compare the Acceleration and Containment strategies for managing end-user computing and provide a rationale for why a firm might choose one or the other.
8. Contrast the managed free economy approach with the centralized support approach for managing end-user computing.
9. What initial approach did Boeing take to managing its intranet, and what do you see as the risks associated with it?
10. What support services do you think are most important today, and why?
11. Describe how a company policy could minimize some of the business risks associated with end-user computing.
12. Why are organizations concerned about spam in their employees' personal mailboxes?
13. Why are today's organizations more vigilant about enforcing copyright laws?
14. What are some of the technology challenges associated with supporting telecommuters?
15. What changes might a supervisor need to make to accommodate employees who are telecommuters?

DISCUSSION QUESTIONS

1. From the perspective of the organization as a whole, discuss what you see as some of the primary trade-offs between the benefits and risks of user application development.
2. Describe a situation in which one of the advantages of user-developed applications might be more important to a business manager than an IS manager. Then describe a situation in which one of the disadvantages might be more important to a business manager than an IS manager.
3. Using the factors shown in Figure 13.3, describe a scenario in which you think a business manager should endorse having a new application developed by users rather than IS professionals. Then describe a scenario in which you think a business manager should *not* endorse having a new application developed by users.
4. Comment on how typical you think some of the user developers' remarks in the "User Developer Experiences" sidebar on page 449 might be, and why.
5. Describe the extent to which you think each of the support services listed in Figure 13.10 is being offered in an organization familiar to you.
6. Develop a few guidelines for spreadsheet developers to help prevent spreadsheet errors.
7. Describe an organizational context in which you think a centralized support unit, such as an information center, would be an appropriate delivery mechanism for support services.
8. The number of telecommuters in the United States did not grow as fast over the past decade as some had predicted. Comment on the reasons that are suggested in the text; then give an additional reason for why these types of arrangements have not been embraced by as many organizations as expected.
9. Choose any three of the "secrets" for managing remote workers presented in Figure 13.12 and provide a rationale for why they might be important.

CASE STUDY III-1

MANAGING A SYSTEMS DEVELOPMENT PROJECT AT CONSUMER AND INDUSTRIAL PRODUCTS, INC.

Late Friday afternoon, T. N. (Ted) Anderson, director of disbursements for Consumer and Industrial Products, Inc. (CIPI), sat staring out the wide window of his 12th-floor corner office, but his mind was elsewhere. Anderson was thinking about the tragic accident that had nearly killed Linda Watkins, project director for the Payables Audit Systems (PAS) development project. Thursday night, when she was on her way home from a movie, a drunken driver had hit her car head on. She would survive, but it would be months before she would be back to work.

The PAS system was a critical component of a group of interrelated systems intended to support fundamental changes in how billing and accounts payable at CIPI were handled. Without Watkins, it was in deep trouble. Deeply committed to the success of these new approaches, Anderson did not know exactly what he could do, but he knew he had to take drastic action. He picked up his phone and told his secretary, "Please get me an appointment with IS Director Charles Bunke for the first thing Monday morning." Anderson would have the weekend to decide what to do.

The Origin of the PAS Project

Consumer and Industrial Products, Inc., is a Fortune 100 manufacturer of a large variety of well-known products for both individuals and industry. Headquartered in the United States, CIPI is an international company with facilities in Europe, Asia, and North and South America.

The PAS project was one of several interrelated projects that resulted from a fundamental reevaluation of CIPI's accounts payable process as part of CIPI's companywide emphasis on total quality management (TQM). Anderson recalls:

> In late 1991 we began to look at what we were doing, how we were doing it, the costs involved, and the value we were adding to the company. We realized that, even with our computer systems, we were very labor-intensive, and that there ought to be things we could do to increase our productivity and our value added. So we decided to completely rethink what we were currently doing and how we were doing it.
>
> Since we were a part of the procurement process, we needed to understand that total process and where accounts payable fit into it. We found that procurement was a three-part process—purchasing the goods, receiving them, and finally paying for them. And we concluded that our role was pretty extensive for someone who was just supposed to be paying the bills. We were spending a lot of effort trying to match purchase orders with receiving reports and invoices to make sure that everyone else had done their job properly. We typically had about 15,000 suspended items that we were holding up payment on because of some question that arose in our examination of these three pieces of information. Many of these items spent 30 to 60 days in suspension before we got them corrected, and the vast majority of the problems were not the vendor's fault but rather the result of mistakes within CIPI. For some of our small vendors for whom we were a dominant customer, this could result in severe cash flow problems, and even bankruptcy. With today's emphasis upon strategic partnerships with our vendors, this was intolerable.
>
> We finally recognized that the fundamental responsibility for procurement rests with purchasing, and once they have ordered the goods, the next thing that is needed is some proof that the goods were received, and we are outside that process also. We concluded that our role was to pay the resulting bills, and that we should not be holding the other departments' hands to make sure that their processes did not break down. And we certainly should not be placing unfair burdens upon our vendors.
>
> So we decided to make some fundamental changes in what we did and how we did it. We told the people in our organization what we wanted to do and why we wanted to do it and gave them the charge to make the necessary changes. After about 9 months we discovered that we were getting nowhere—it

 This case was prepared by Professor Martin as the basis for class discussion rather than to illustrate either effective or ineffective handling of an administrative situation. Its development was supported by the Institute for Research on the Management of Information Systems (IRMIS) of the Indiana University Kelley School of Business.

was just not moving. Obviously we could not just top-down it and get the results we wanted. With the help of a consultant we went back to the drawing board and studied how to drive this thing from the ground up rather than from the top down. We discovered that our people were very provincial—they saw everything in terms of accounts payable and had little perspective on the overall procurement process. We had to change this mind-set, so we spent almost a year putting our people through training courses designed to expand their perspective.

Our mind-set in accounts payable changed so that we began to get a lot of ideas and a lot of change coming from the floor. There began to be a lot of challenging of what was going on and many suggestions for how we could reach our strategic vision. In cooperation with the other departments involved, the accounts payable people decided to make some fundamental changes in their role and operations. Instead of thoroughly investigating each discrepancy, no matter how insignificant, before paying the bill, we decided to go ahead and pay all invoices that are within a reasonable tolerance. We will adopt a quality-control approach and keep a history of all transactions for each vendor so that we can evaluate the vendor's performance over time and eliminate vendors that cause significant problems. Not only will this result in a significant reduction in work that is not adding much value, but it will also provide much better service to our vendors.

We also decided to install a PC-based document imaging system and move toward a paperless environment. We are developing a Document Control System (DCS) through which most documents that come into our mail room will be identified, indexed, and entered through document readers into the imaging system. Then the documents themselves will be filed and their images will be placed into the appropriate processing queues for the work that they require. The Document Control System will allow someone to add notes to the document, route it from one computer system to another, and keep track of what has been done to the document. This will radically change the way we do business in the department. Things that used to take 18 steps, going from one clerk to another, will take only 1 or 2 steps because all the required information will be available through the computer. Not only will this improve our service, but it will drastically reduce our processing costs. It will also require that all of our processing systems be integrated with the Document Control System.

In addition to developing the new Document Control System, this new accounts payable approach required CIPI to replace or extensively modify five major systems: the Freight Audit System (FAST); the Computerized Invoice Matching System (CIMS), which audited invoices; the Corporate Approval System (CAS), which checked that vouchers were approved by authorized persons; the vendor database mentioned above; and the system that dealt with transactions that were not on computer-generated purchase orders. The PAS project was originally intended to modify the CIMS system.

Systems Development at CIPI

Systems development at CIPI is both centralized and decentralized. There is a large corporate IS group that has responsibility for corporate databases and systems. Also, there are about 30 divisional systems groups. A division may develop systems on its own, but if a corporate database is affected, then corporate IS must be involved in the development. Corporate IS also sells services to the divisions. For example, corporate IS will contract to manage a project and/or to provide all or some of the technical staff for a project, and the time of these people will be billed to the division at standard hourly rates.

Similarly, computer operations are both centralized and decentralized. There is a corporate data center operated by corporate IS, but there are also computers and LANs that are operated by the divisions and even by departments. Corporate IS sets standards for this hardware and the LANs, and will contract to provide technical support for the LANs.

Because the accounts payable systems affected corporate financial databases, Anderson had to involve corporate IS in the development of most of these systems. The Document Control System (DCS), however, did not directly affect corporate databases, so Anderson decided to use his own systems group to develop this imaging system.

Corporate IS had just begun using a structured development methodology called Stradis. This methodology divides the development into eight phases: initial study, detailed study, draft requirements study, outline physical design, total requirements statement, system design, coding and testing, and installation. This methodology provides detailed documentation of what should be done in each phase. At the end of each phase detailed planning of the next phase is done, and cost and time estimates for the remainder of the project are revised. Each phase produces a document that must be approved by both user and IS management before proceeding with the next phase. Stradis also includes a post-implementation review performed several months after the system has been installed.

Roles in the PAS Project

The Stradis methodology defined a number of roles to be filled in a development project: Anderson was the executive sponsor, Peter Shaw was the project manager, and Linda Watkins was the project director. (Exhibit 1 shows the Disbursements Department organization chart and Exhibit 2 shows how Corporate IS Systems Development is organized.)

Executive Sponsor

Ted Anderson, director of disbursements, is responsible for all CIPI disbursements, including both payroll and accounts payable. Starting with CIPI in 1966 in the general accounting

EXHIBIT 1
Partial Organization Chart of Disbursements Department

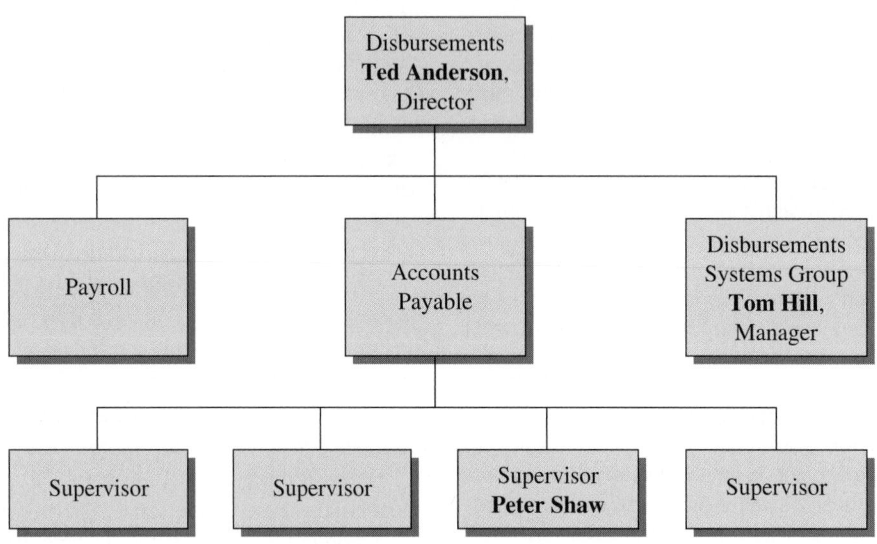

area, Anderson had a long history of working as the user-manager on systems development projects, including projects in payroll, human resources, and accounting. He spent a year doing acquisitions work for CIPI and in 1978 served a stint in Europe as area treasurer. He made steady progress up the CIPI management ladder.

In the Stradis methodology the executive sponsor has budgetary responsibility and must approve all of the expenditures of the project. He or she must sign off at the end of each phase and authorize the team to proceed with the next phase.

According to Watkins, Anderson was a very active executive sponsor:

> Ted was determined that this project would produce a quality system and get done on time and that his people would commit themselves to the project. He not only talked about these priorities, but he also led by example by attending working sessions where lower-level people were being interviewed and participating in data modeling sessions. By visibly spending a lot of his personal time on the project, he showed his people that it was important for them to spend their time.

"The area manager has to take an active role in the development of systems," Anderson asserts:

> particularly when you are trying to reengineer the processes. If you do not have leadership from the manager to set the vision of where you are going, your people tend to automate what they have been doing rather than concentrating on what really adds value and eliminating everything else, so I took a fairly active role in this project. I wanted to make sure that we were staying on track with our vision and on schedule with the project.

User Project Manager

Peter Shaw was the user project manager. He had worked for CIPI for 18 years, starting as a part-time employee working nights while going to college. Over his career he had worked in payroll, accounting, and human resources, spending part of the time in systems work and part in supervisory positions. For the past 3 years, he had been a supervisor in accounts payable.

The user project manager is responsible for making sure that the system meets the user department's business needs and that the system is completed on time. He or she manages the user department effort on the project, making sure that the proper people are identified and made available as needed. He or she is also responsible for representing the user view whenever issues arise and for making sure that any political problems are recognized and dealt with.

The user project manager and the project director work closely together to manage the project and are jointly responsible for its success. Shaw also served in the role of business analyst on this project.

Project Director

Linda Watkins, senior analyst in the corporate IS department, was the project director. Watkins, who had recently joined CIPI, had an MBA in MIS and 7 years of experience as an analyst and project manager with a Fortune 500 company and a financial software consultant. She had experience using Stradis to manage projects, which was one of the reasons she had been hired by CIPI. Because they were being charged for her time,

EXHIBIT 2
Partial Organization Chart of Corporate IS

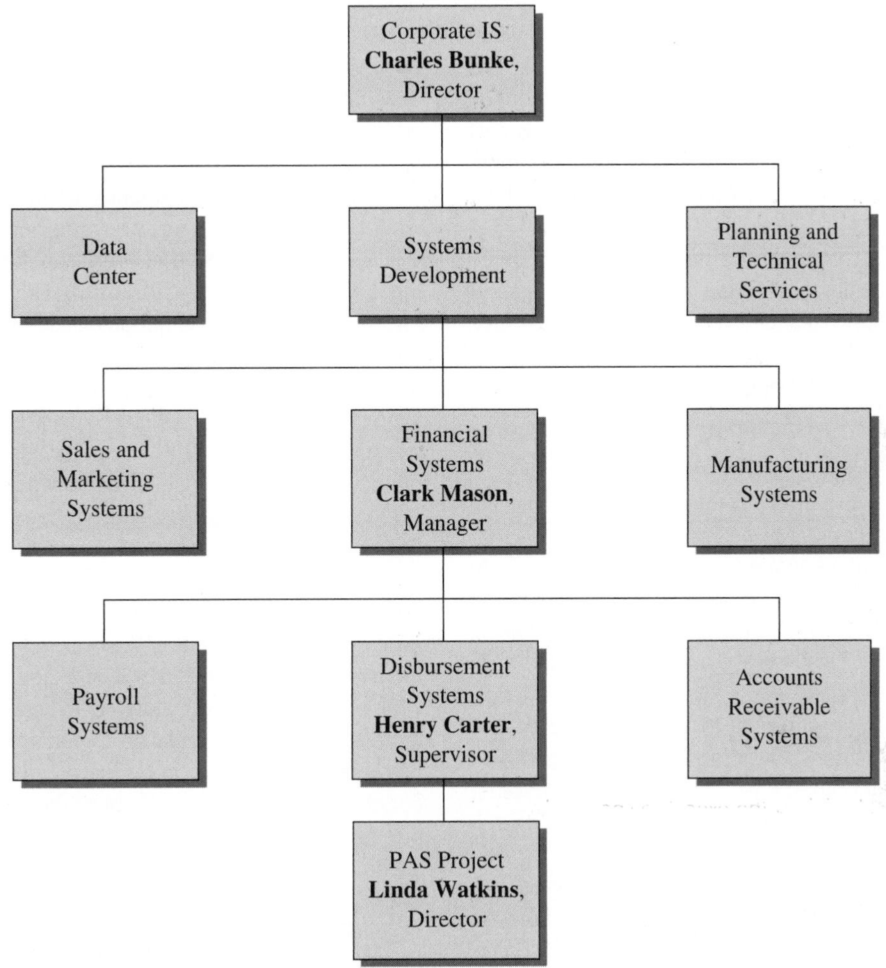

Watkins viewed the disbursement department managers as clients for whom she was working as a consultant.

The project director was responsible for managing the IS people on the project. "My job resembled that of the general contractor on a construction project who has to deal with all the subcontractors and manage the budget and schedule," Watkins explains.[1] She developed the project plans, determined what each phase would cost, managed the budget, involved the necessary technical people at the right time, and worked through Shaw to make sure that the proper client people were available when needed to be interviewed or make decisions.

"I felt like I was ultimately responsible for the success of the project," Watkins reports, "because if things fell apart I would be the one that would take the blame, both from IS management and client management. Therefore my major concern was to look ahead and foresee problems and make sure that they were solved before they impacted the success of the project."

"That is what I look for in a project manager," Ted Anderson asserts. "Most of the day-to-day work just happens if you have good people, but the crucial thing is to anticipate potential problems so that you are preventing them rather than just reacting."

Watkins also tried to make her clients aware of what was possible with computer technology so that they would not simply automate what they had been doing. "I tried to help them think about why they were doing things instead of just how they were doing them," Watkins says. "Because I was not an

[1] The interviews for this case were conducted while Watkins was recovering from her accident, a few months after the events described.

expert in accounts payable, I could ask the dumb question that might lead to a new perspective."

Another important part of Watkins' job was communication. "I tried to make sure that the client managers knew what was going on at all times and that they knew all the options when there were decisions to be made. I trusted them to make the right decisions if they had the information they needed." Anderson found that to be a refreshing change from his past experience. "Previously IS has not told its customers any more than it had to. But Linda was very open and we felt that we could trust her."

That trust was very important to Watkins, for her ultimate responsibility was to ensure that everyone worked together effectively on the project. She devoted a lot of effort to selecting technical people who had good communications skills and could interact positively with her clients.

IS Management

Henry Carter, IS supervisor of disbursements systems, was Watkins' supervisor. He was responsible for integrating all projects in the disbursements area and for allocating IS people to these projects. His role included advising and coaching the project directors, reviewing their project plans, and making sure that they got the technical assistance they needed from the IS organization.

Carter had been responsible for maintenance of the Disbursement Department's systems for many years. When the new development projects were initiated, Carter became responsible for them also, but he had little experience with systems development and was of little help to Watkins.

Carter reported to Clark Mason, IS manager of financial systems, who was aware of some of Carter's limitations but who valued him for his knowledge of the existing systems. To compensate for Carter's weaknesses, Mason had tried to get the best available project managers, and he told them to come directly to him when they had strategic questions or problems with client relationships.

Steering Group

The steering group was chaired by Anderson and included three accounts payable supervisors whose areas were affected by the project, Shaw, and the manager of the disbursements systems group, Tom Hill. Watkins and Carter were ex officio members of this group. The role of the steering group was to approve budgets, determine the business direction of the project, and make any necessary decisions.

The steering group met on alternate Wednesdays at 3:30 P.M. The agenda and a project status report, such as the one prepared for the steering group meeting on October 6, 1993 (see Exhibit 3), were distributed at least 24 hours before each meeting. Under the "Recap Hours/Dollars" section, the "Original" column refers to the original plan, and the "Forecast" column gives the current estimated hours and cost. The "Variance" column is the original plan minus the current estimate, whereas the "Actual-to-Date" column shows the hours and cost incurred up to October 5. A major function of the steering group was to deal with problems and issues. Problems require immediate attention, and issues are potential problems that will move up to the problem category if they are not dealt with.

At the start of each steering group meeting, Anderson would ask whether or not everyone had made themselves available when they were needed, and if not he would talk to them afterward. According to Watkins, "Ted was very vocal with his opinions, but he was not autocratic. When there were differences of opinion within the steering group, he would subtly hint at the direction he wanted to go, but it was still up to the interested parties to work out their own resolution of the problem. On the other hand, if he thought the project was getting off the track, he would put his foot down hard!"

Shaw was knowledgeable about the political climate, and he and Watkins would meet to plan the steering group meetings. They would discuss the issues that might come up and decide who would present them and how. If there were significant decisions to be made, Watkins and Shaw would discuss them with Anderson ahead of time to see where he stood and work out an alternative that he could support. Watkins did not try to force a recommendation on the committee; rather, she presented the problems in business terms along with a number of possible alternatives. Because the agenda was well organized and all the information was in the hands of participants ahead of time, the steering group meetings were quite effective, usually ending before the scheduled hour was up.

Several of the steering group members were the sponsors of other projects, and after the PAS steering group meetings were finished they would stay around and discuss these projects and their departmental problems with Watkins. She was pleased that she was viewed as a Disbursements Department colleague and not as an outsider.

Project Planning

The Stradis methodology requires that the project director estimate two costs at the end of each phase of the project: the cost of completing the rest of the project and the cost of the next phase. At the beginning, estimating the cost of the project was mostly a matter of judgment and experience. Watkins looked at it from several perspectives. First, she considered projects in her past experience that were of similar size and complexity and used their costs to estimate what the PAS system would cost. Then she broke the PAS project down into its phases, did her best to estimate each phase, and totaled up

EXHIBIT 3

PAS Project Status Report as of October 1, 1993

Recap Hours/Dollars	Original	Forecast	Variance	Actual-to-Date
Initial Study:				
Hours	577	448	129	434
Dollars	$20,000	17,000	3,000	16,667
Detailed Study:				
Hours	1,350	1,337	13	1,165
Dollars	$45,000	47,927	–2,927	42,050
Total:				
Hours	1,927	1,785	142	1,599
Dollars	$65,000	64,927	73	58,717

Milestone Dates	Original	Revised	Completed
Complete Context DFD—Current	8/3		8/4
Complete Level 0 DFD—Current	8/6		8/13
Complete Level 1 DFD—Current	8/22	9/12	9/14
Complete Level 0 DFD—Proposed	9/17	9/21	9/21
Map System Enhancements to DFD	9/17	9/21	9/24
Complete Data Model (key-based)	10/2	10/11	
Complete Detailed Study Report	10/8	10/15	

Accomplishments This Week:

Project Team:
- Completed the documentation library for the current system.

Lucy Robbins:
- Completed the PAS system's Business & System Objectives.
- Documented the PAS system's constraints.
- Started compiling the Detailed Study Report (DSR).
- Completed the documentation library for the current system.

Arnold Johnson:
- Completed the documentation library for the current system.

Linda Watkins:
- Reviewed the estimates and work plan for the three enhancements.
- Drafted the authorization for the enhancements.
- Initiated the Draft Requirements Statement (DRS) work plan.

Peter Shaw:
- Identified the new system's Business & System Objectives.

Carol Hemminger and Paul Brown:
- Completed the documentation of the workshop findings.
- Refined the ERM diagram.

Plans for Next Week:
- Finish and distribute the draft DSR.
- Finish the data modeling workshop documentation.
- Complete the DRS work plan.
- Distribute the finalized Initial Study Report (ISR).

Problems That May Affect the Project Status:

1. The DSR will not be finalized until the documentation from the data modeling workshops is completed.
2. Two walkthroughs are still outstanding, the key-based data model workshop and current system task force. Both will be completed when client schedules allow.

Issues:

1. Due to delays in scheduling interviews with AP, Robbins' time has not been utilized as well as possible. If this continues it may cause delays.

these costs. When she compared these two estimates, they came out to be pretty close. Finally, she went over the project and her reasoning with several experienced project managers whose judgment she respected. This initial estimate was not too meaningful, however, because the scope of the project changed radically during the early stages.

Estimating the cost of the next phase requires that the project director plan that phase in detail, and then that plan is used to set the budget and to control the project. According to Watkins:

> The Stradis methodology provides an outline of all the steps that you go through to produce the deliverables of a stage. I would go through each step and break it down into activities and then break down each activity into tasks that I could assign to people. I would estimate the time that would be required for each task, consider the riskiness of that task, and multiply my estimate by a suitable factor to take the uncertainty into account. I would also ask the people who were assigned the task what kind of effort they felt it would require and would consult with experienced people in the IS area. Finally, by multiplying my final time estimate by the hourly rate for the person assigned to the task I would get a cost estimate for each task and add them all up to get a total cost for the phase. Again I would go over this with experienced project managers, and with Peter and Ted, before making final adjustments.
>
> Then I could start scheduling the tasks. I always included the tasks assigned to user department people, although I did not need them for controlling my budget and many other project managers did not bother with them. I wanted Peter and Ted and their people to see where they fit into the project and how their activities impacted the project schedule.

To help with the scheduling, Watkins used a tool called Project Manager's Workbench that included a PERT module and a Gantt Chart module. With the possibility of time constraints and different staffing levels, she often had to develop several different schedules, for discussion with Shaw and Anderson and for presentation to the steering group.

Staffing the Project

In addition to Watkins, Arnold Johnson was assigned to the project at the beginning. Johnson had worked for Carter as a maintenance programmer for many years. Carter valued him highly as a maintenance programmer and therefore only assigned about 20 percent of Johnson's time to the PAS project. According to Watkins:

> Arnold did not see any urgency in anything he did, and being primarily assigned to maintenance, he never had any commitment to our deadlines, and he would not even warn me when he was going to miss a deadline. When you are on a project plan that has tasks that have to be done by specific times, every person must be fully committed to the project, so the project plan was always in flux if we depended on him to get anything done.

Johnson had a detailed knowledge of the existing CIMS system, and Watkins had planned for him to document the logical flow of the 14,000 lines of spaghetti code in the main program of the CIMS system. Watkins reported:

> He knew where things were done in the existing program, but he never knew why they were being done. He would never write anything down, so the only way to get information from him was verbally. We eventually decided that the only way to use him on the project was as a consultant and that we would have an analyst interview him to document the existing system.

A few weeks after the start of the project, Watkins obtained Lucy Robbins from a contractor firm to be her lead analyst. Robbins had managed a maintenance area at a medium-sized company and had also led a good-sized development project. She could program, but her main strength was in supervising programmers and communicating with the technical specialists in IS. Watkins was able to delegate much of the day-to-day supervision to Robbins so that she could concentrate on the strategic aspects of the project.

The Stradis methodology required the use of a CASE tool, and Robbins became the CASE tool "gatekeeper" who made sure that the critical project information stored therein was not corrupted. She said,

> We used the CASE tool to keep our logical data dictionary, data flow diagrams, and entity/relationship data models. The CASE tool keeps your data repository, and then uses that repository to populate your data flows, data stores, and entity/relationship models. It also assists in balancing the diagrams to make sure that everything that goes into a diagram is necessary, and everything that is necessary goes in.

Because IS had far more projects under way than it had good people to staff them, Watkins was never able to convince Henry Carter or Clark Mason to assign a qualified CIPI person to the project full time, so she had to staff the project with temporary employees from outside contractors:

> After I determined what resources I could get from CIPI, I would look at the tasks the project team had to perform and then try to find the best persons I could that fit our needs. I took as much care hiring a contractor as I would in hiring a permanent CIPI person. I tried to get people who were overqualified and keep them challenged by delegating as much responsibility to them as they could take. My people had to have excellent technical skills, but I was also concerned that their personalities fit in well with the team and with our clients.

Watkins hired two contractor analysts who had skills that the team lacked. One was a very good analyst who had experience with CIPI's standard programming language and database management system and had been a liaison with the database people on several projects. The second contractor analyst had a lot of experience in testing.

The project got excellent part-time help from database specialists in the CIPI IS department. Watkins recalls:

> We used IS database people to facilitate data modeling workshops and to do the modeling. We also used a data analyst to find a logical attribute in the current databases or set it up in the data dictionary if it was new. There were also database administrators who worked with the data modelers to translate the logical data model into physical databases that were optimized to make sure we could get the response time we needed.

Watkins also used consultants from the IS developmental methodologies group:

> Because my supervisor was not experienced in development, I used people from the methodologies group to look at my project plans and see if they were reasonable. We also used people from this group as facilitators for meetings and to moderate walkthroughs, where not being a member of the team can be a real advantage. Also, when we needed to have a major technical review, the methodologies group would advise me on who should be in attendance.

Carrying Out the Project

The project began in mid-June 1993 as the CIMS Replacement Project. The Computerized Invoice Matching System (CIMS) was an old, patched-up system that matched invoices to computer-issued purchase orders and receiving reports, paid those invoices where everything agreed, and suspended payment on invoices where there was disagreement.

The Initial Study

Because of strategic changes in how the department intended to operate in the future, a number of significant changes to the system were necessary. The project team concluded that it was impractical to modify the CIMS system to include several of these important enhancements. Therefore, Shaw and Watkins recommended that a new system be developed instead of attempting to enhance the existing CIMS system. They also suggested that the scope of this system be increased to include manual purchase orders and some transactions that did not involve purchase orders, which effectively collapsed two of the planned development projects into one. At its meeting on August 8, 1993, the steering group accepted this recommendation and authorized the team to base the Initial Study Report on the development of a new system that they named the Payables Audit System (PAS).

The Initial Study Report was a high-level presentation of the business objectives of the new system and how this system would further those business objectives. A seventeen-page document released on September 21, 1993, it discussed two major problems with the old system and described five major improvements that the new system would provide. The estimated yearly savings were $85,000 in personnel costs and $50,000 in system maintenance, for a total of $135,000. On October 9, 1993, the Initial Study Report was approved by Anderson, and the team was authorized to proceed with the Detailed Study.

The Detailed Study Report

The Detailed Study Report begins with an investigation of the current system, and with production of level 1 and level 2 data flow diagrams and an entity/relationship diagram of the existing system. Then, given the business objectives of the new system, the project team considers how the current system can be improved and prepares data flow diagrams and entity/relationship diagrams for the proposed system. Much work on the Detailed Study Report had been done before it was formally authorized, and this report was issued on October 26, 1993. This report was a 30-page document, with another 55 pages of attachments.

The major activities in this stage were initial data modeling workshops whose results were stored in the CASE tool logical data dictionary. Most of the attachments to the Detailed Study Report were printouts of data from this logical data dictionary providing information on the data flow diagrams and the entity/relationship models that were included in the report.

The body of this report was mainly an elaboration of the Initial Study Report. It included the following business objectives of the new system:

- Reduce the cost of voucher processing over the next 3 years to less than the current cost.
- Reduce the staff required for processing vouchers by 50 percent over the next 5 years.
- Significantly reduce the time required to pay vouchers.
- Provide systematic information for the purpose of measuring quality of vendor and accounts payable performance.
- Support systematic integration with transportation/logistics, purchasing, and accounts payable to better facilitate changes due to shifts in business procedures.

Among the constraints on the PAS system cited in the Detailed Study Report were that it must be operational no later than September 30, 1994; that it would be limited to the IBM mainframe hardware platform; and that it must interface with six systems (Purchase Order Control, Supplier Master, Front-End Document Control, Electronic Data Interchange, Corporate

Approval, and Payment). Four of these systems were under development at that time, and it was recognized that alternative data sources might need to be temporarily incorporated into PAS.

The estimated savings from the new system remained at $135,000 per year, and the cost of developing the system was estimated to be between $250,000 and $350,000. It was estimated that the next phase of the project would require 1,250 hours over 2.5 months and cost $40,000. The Detailed Study Report was approved on October 31, 1993, and the team was authorized to proceed with the Draft Requirements Study.

The Draft Requirements Study

As the Draft Requirements Study began, Watkins was concerned about three risks that might affect the PAS project.

> First, so many interrelated systems were changing at the same time that our requirements were a moving target. In particular, the imaging Document Control System that was our major interface had not been physically implemented and the technology was completely new to CIPI. Second, the schedule called for three other new systems to be installed at the same time as PAS, and conversion and testing would take so much user time that there simply are not enough hours in the day for the accounts payable people to get that done.
>
> Finally, I was the only full-time person from the CIPI IS department. Although the contractors were excellent people, they would go away after the project was over and there would be little carryover within CIPI.

Watkins discussed her concerns with Carter and Mason and with Anderson and the steering group. They all told her that, at least for the present, the project must proceed as scheduled.

The Draft Requirements Study produces detailed information on the inputs, outputs, processes, and data of the new system. In addition to producing level 3 data flow diagrams, the project team describes each process and produces data definitions for the data flows and data stores in these data flow diagrams, and describes the data content (though not the format) of all input and output screens and reports of the new system. The project team was involved in much interviewing and conducted a number of detailed data-modeling workshops to produce this detail.

The major problem encountered was the inability to schedule activities with Disbursements Department people when they were needed. For example, in early December, Anderson came to Watkins and told her that his people would be fully occupied with year-end closing activities for the last 2 weeks of December and the first 2 weeks of January and that they would not be available for work on the PAS project. He was very unhappy with this situation and apologized for delaying the project. Watkins told him that she understood that the business came first and that she would reschedule activities and do what she could to reduce the impact on the schedule. This potential problem had been brought up at the steering group meeting in early November, but the group had decided to go ahead with the planned schedule.

The PAS Draft Requirements Statement (DRS) was completed on March 21, 1994, 4 weeks behind schedule, but only $5,000 over budget. The DRS filled two thick loose-leaf binders with detailed documentation of the processes and the data content of the inputs, outputs, data flows, and data stores in the new system. Preparation of the Outline Physical Design was projected to require 600 hours over 6 weeks at a cost of $25,000. The DRS was approved on April 3, 1994, and the Outline Physical Design phase was begun.

The Outline Physical Design

In the Outline Physical Design phase the IS technical people become involved for the first time. They look at the logical system and consider alternatives as to how it can be implemented with hardware and new manual procedures. The approach in this phase is to map the processes in the logical data flow diagrams and the data models to manual processes and hardware and to make sure that this proposed hardware can be supplied and supported by the organization. Programming languages and utilities are also considered, so at the end of this phase the project team knows what kind of programming specifications and technical capabilities will be required.

The PAS system was originally planned to run on the IBM mainframe, but given the use of a LAN for the Document Control System, the technical people decided to move as much of the PAS system to the LAN as possible. This was a radical change that increased the estimated development cost substantially.

Watkins' new estimate of the total cost of the PAS system was $560,000. This was a substantial increase from the previous estimate of $250,000 to $350,000, and it caused some concern in CIPI management. Peter Shaw asserted:

> The company treasurer doesn't care a bit about the PAS project. All he cares about is how many dollars are going to be spent and in which year. When the cost went up so that we were substantially over budget for this year, that got his attention. If the increase were for next year it would not be a major problem because he would have time to plan for it—to get it into his budget. But this year his budget is set, so Linda and I have to figure out how we can stay within our budget and still get a usable system this year as version 1 and upgrade it to what we really need next year.

On June 27, just as the Outline Physical Design report was being completed, Watkins' car accident occurred, taking her away from work for several months.

Anderson's Concerns

Watkins' accident focused Anderson's attention on some long-standing concerns. He was worried because among the directors of the five projects he was sponsoring, Watkins was the best. All of his other projects were behind schedule and in trouble, and now he did not know what would happen to the PAS project.

Anderson was fully committed to his strategic direction for the disbursements area, and he felt that his reputation would be at risk if the systems necessary to support his planned changes could not be completed successfully. He was convinced that he had to take decisive action to get things back on track. He needed a plan of attack to present to IS Director Charles Bunke at tomorrow's meeting.

EXHIBIT 1
ZOCS Architecture Overview

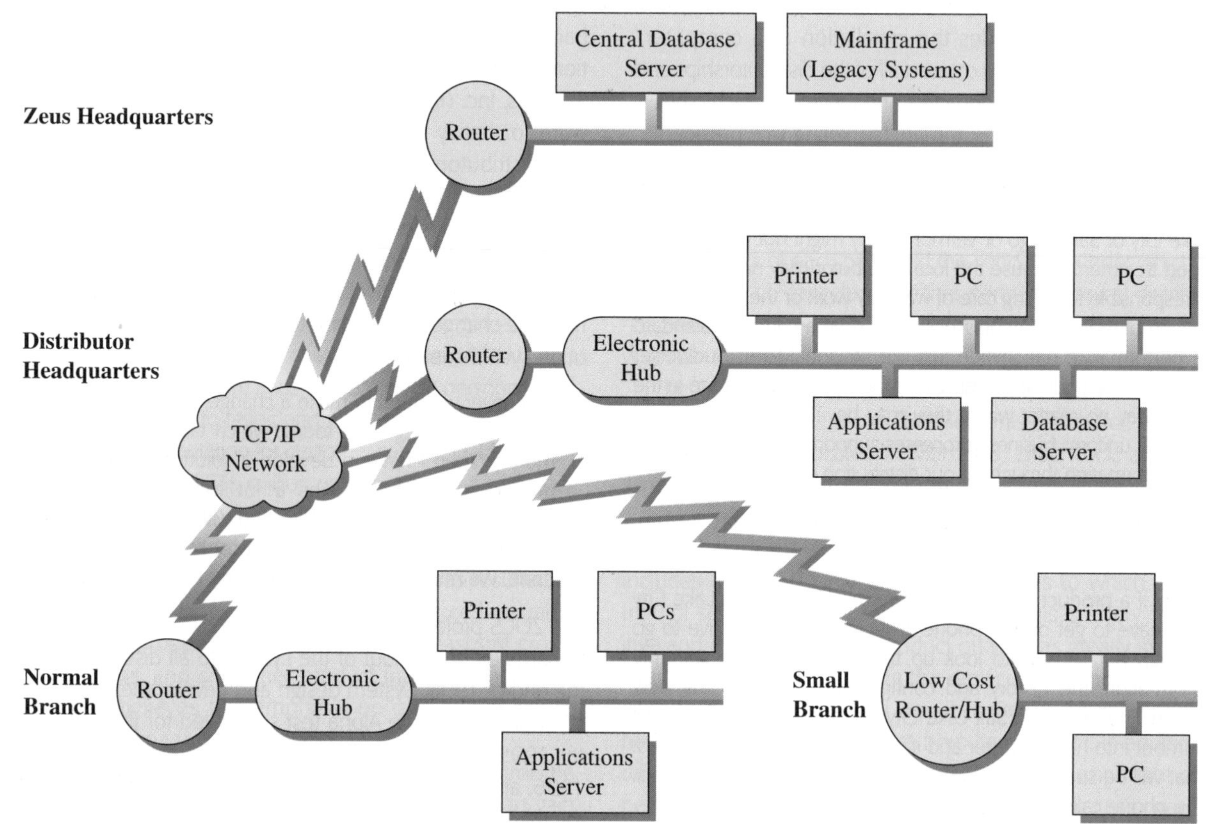

Consider first the distributor headquarters, where there is a LAN connected to the WAN through a router. The LAN connects an applications server, a database server, and various PCs and printers to each other and through the WAN to branches and Zeus headquarters, and thence to the other distributors and Zeus' subsidiaries. The applications server stores the applications software and makes it available to the PCs on the LAN, but does no processing itself. The database server maintains the databases for the distributorship and provides data to the PCs upon request. The PCs, located throughout the distributorship, run the applications software to support the business processes of the distributor.

The normal branch has a LAN similar to the one at the distributorship, except that it has no database server so its data are provided by the database server at the distributor headquarters. Again, the branch's PCs run the applications software that is furnished upon demand by the branch's applications server. A small branch with only a few people is treated like a PC on the distributor's LAN and obtains both its software and data from the distributor headquarters via the WAN.

Zeus headquarters also has a LAN that connects a national database server (which Zeus calls its central database server) to the mainframe at the Zeus Data Center that supports Zeus' legacy systems. The central database server (CDS) will provide common cross-distributor information such as the parts master database, national parts inventory database, standard repair times, and product service history summary database.

The Business Processes

A major objective of the ZOCS project was to produce and institute good, uniform business processes throughout the system so that a customer gets the same treatment no matter where he may be in the country. The ZOCS project plan has identified some 28 common processes that support all 24 distributorships' operations. The order fulfillment process, for example, includes activities from when the order is placed until the bill is paid. The preparation of a proposal to sell equipment to a particular customer is another common process. When a breakdown occurs anywhere in the United States, there is a process that determines Zeus' liability under the warranty and reimburses the distributorship that performs the required work. Many of these distributorship processes interact with corresponding processes at Zeus headquarters, so the ZOCS project must include these processes at both levels.

The Applications Software

Computer applications have been identified that support these 28 business processes. These applications are categorized in the following four areas: financial, marketing, service, and parts.

The distributorship financial applications include accounts payable, general ledger, and accounts receivable.

The main application in the marketing area is customer management, which includes maintaining contact lists, call reports, a history of proposals, and other information that assists the sales force in dealing with the customer.

The service applications include work orders, warranty, and shop management. The work orders application keeps track of progress on the work order, parts used, labor hours used, and so forth. The warranty application maintains information that enables the distributor to determine what work is required under the warranty and to assure that it is done and that the appropriate money transfers are made. The shop management application manages all the active work orders in the shop, provides standard times and costs to the work order application, and gathers data on actual times and costs that can be used to measure performance of the shop and to improve the standards when necessary. There is also a preventive maintenance application that helps manage preventive maintenance contracts. Another application is project management, where the distributor will take responsibility for a complex project that integrates Zeus equipment with other equipment for special applications.

Parts applications include order entry, inventory control, and physical inventory. Zeus also must track used or damaged components that can be reconditioned. The customer must be given credit for the component he or she provides, the component must be sent to the vendor who will recondition it, and the vendor must be billed for that component.

Reaction to the ZOCS Project

The ZOCS project received a varied reaction among the distributors, which are all independently owned businesses.

Hiram Patterson, owner of the Salt Lake City distributorship, opposed the ZOCS project:

> That project will cost me roughly a million dollars, which will eat up most of my profits for several years. Surely there is some way to allow us to share information without all that expense. Furthermore, I am not happy with Zeus trying to tell me in detail how to operate my business. This is a family business, and we've been operating this distributorship and providing excellent service to our customers for over 50 years. I seriously doubt that the people at Zeus headquarters know as much about running our business as we do!

Jack Claiborne, owner of the Memphis distributorship that uses the MSI system, saw the need for the ZOCS system and was a strong supporter of its development. He said:

> Of course I am not thrilled at having to invest over a million dollars in a new system, especially since I have a pretty good system already that I have paid a pretty penny for. However, our business will live or die on the basis of customer satisfaction, and the ZOCS system figures to give us a substantial improvement in the ability to serve our customers the way we would want to be served. It's just something that we have to do to prosper in this business.

A number of alternative approaches to developing the system were considered. The distributors who already were using the MSI system thought that the first step should be to standardize on that system throughout all the dealerships and then upgrade that system where needed. Other approaches considered were (1) having the Zeus IS group develop the new system, (2) outsourcing the development of the system to EDS or Andersen Consulting or some other organization, and (3) employing a systems integrator to put the systems together, primarily from purchased components.

After a good deal of discussion the following approach was adopted: The Zeus IS group would manage the project, but hire MSI to upgrade the existing system that was in use at 12 of the distributorships. One reason for not adopting the existing MSI system was that it was based on a minicomputer with dumb character-based terminals, and a LAN-based system with a graphic user interface (GUI) was thought to be a better approach. Although the applications would be upgraded and the systems would be integrated into the new network environment, the present MSI users would not see many exciting improvements in the basic systems.

Implementation of the ZOCS System

While MSI was developing the software, Zeus put on a big push to get the computer/communications infrastructure in place by offering to pay part of the hardware cost for distributorships that would install the equipment early. Quite a few distributorships installed this equipment before the first Beta test of the software was completed. When it was learned that some of the hardware was inadequate for the system and had to be replaced, Zeus ate the cost. The problem of deciding on the technology can be frustrating. Jacob Hickson, Zeus project manager for the ZOCS project, reflected on the problems that rapid technological change poses for a project like ZOCS that takes several years from inception to completion:

> One of the most frustrating aspects of this project is the turmoil that faces everyone in the choice of technology. Pick any component—the applications servers, the database servers, the network, the workstations—and within a 12-month period the price/performance capability changes dramatically. You are faced with rolling something out quickly, but at the same time keeping up, which is an almost impossible task! You have to draw a line somewhere, and that is the part that no one is very good at doing.

The Alpha Test

The Alpha test was started in the second quarter of 1996, 6 months late. They did not have a suitable environment for testing at that time, so they set the system up as best they could on a server and workstation at Zeus headquarters and brought in a number of distributors and walked them through the processes and applications, trying to validate functionality and capability. This testing turned out to have been inadequate, to say the least.

The First Beta Test

They started the first Beta test at the distributorship at Green Bay in July 1996, only 3 months behind schedule. It was a disaster, and the system was pulled out after only 10 weeks of attempting to operate it. According to Hickson:

> We made about every mistake that you could make. The software was full of bugs. A hardware/software component of the initial architecture was inadequate—we literally couldn't keep the server up and running for more than a 24-hour period. The users were not ready—they didn't manage the training and we didn't follow up on it the way we should have. The implementation process wasn't capable, and we didn't have the right leadership. Nothing was really up to snuff.

One of the underlying causes of this disaster was that they tried to maintain an original schedule that was totally unrealistic. They had several teams involved in different aspects of the project—information systems, the MSI development team, a business process team, a training team, and distributor people—and each team was under intense pressure to meet its deadline. The result was that there was no overall teamwork, little communication, and no understanding of where they stood on the overall process. They did not have a cohesive team that could look at the overall process, evaluate where they were at the time, and decide what they needed to do before attempting to install the system. Consequently, they launched blindly into something for which they were woefully unprepared.

The disaster at Green Bay was a tremendous blow to the Zeus team's morale, and resulted in a lot of voluntary turnover. Many of the most capable members of the team, whose skills were in great demand, transferred to other projects within Zeus or were hired away by outside firms. Also, the morale of the distributors plummeted. According to Byars:

> This was almost the end of the project. With the distributors being independently owned, there was a lot of skepticism and a lot of people saying: "You're requiring me to spend a lot of money that I'm not going to get anything for." And when you go through a disaster like that it is easy for them to resist the project. The only thing that saved the project was the unwavering support of the project sponsor, Zeus marketing VP Jonathan Buthman, who just insisted that everyone fall in line and continue the project to a successful conclusion, no matter what the problems. He made it clear that if you dropped out of the project you would not continue to be a Zeus distributor.

The Second Beta Test

The team learned a lot from the experience of the first Beta test. They spent several months working to eliminate the problems with the software and training that had surfaced in Green Bay, and then started the second Beta test at Oklahoma City in April 1997. It went much better. According to Hickson:

> The major difference in our approach was that in Green Bay we tried to implement everything at once, but at Oklahoma City we had three major phases, and some minor ones in between. We started with the finance applications on April 1, 1997, started the service applications on July 1, and started the parts applications on August 1. By the end of September the whole thing was operational, and we fixed the problems and the distributorship signed off on it on May 1, 1998.

One of the problems that they struggled with in implementing the ZOCS system was the cultural differences between the distributors and the Zeus project team. Hickson explains:

> The distributor organizations are used to operating on a crisis basis. A customer comes in with a broken-down piece of equipment and you deal with the problem and get him on his way, and then you deal with the next customer's problem. They are used to that kind of interaction. Then we come in and say: "Here is the schedule, and here is what you need to do to get the job done. Now do these things and we'll come back and see you next week." That doesn't work because that is not the way they operate. We came in and changed the rules on them, and didn't even tell them what the new rules are. So we have had to learn how to identify and develop leaders and train them to manage the implementation of all of this change that is inherent in converting to the ZOCS system.

The Memphis Pilot

The Memphis pilot began in March 1998, when the distributor started selecting process leaders. They already had the hardware up and running because they had been scheduled for conversion much earlier. On June 15 they brought up accounts payable and general ledger. Simultaneously they began training their trainers who would train the operations and service people before starting to bring up the operations components on August 15. They completed the conversion to the new system by the end of September. Incidentally, the ZOCS project was originally scheduled to have all distributors up and running by that time, so the project was seriously behind schedule, with only 2 of the 24 distributors up and running by then.

On April 15, 1999, Byars evaluated the Memphis experience as follows:

> We had a lot of problems, but have gotten to the point where our heads are above water. We haven't solved everything, but problems are not coming at us so fast and furious now. This has been a typical family squabble—there has been a lot of finger-pointing and frustration.
>
> We were the first group that the Zeus implementation team has taken through the new training process. A lot of their folks were learning at the time, and a lot of the documentation was weak. They have learned a lot from our experience and they have upgraded their training again. We are going to send some of our people to the first upgraded training session next week.
>
> Although there are a couple of things that they really have to do some work on, most of the software flaws are just a lot of irritants. The major problems are in things that Oklahoma City did not have as part of their business, or they didn't have on a big scale. For example, Oklahoma City did not have a preventive maintenance program, but we do have that business, and we had a rude awakening because that module had serious design flaws. We are still trying to work through these problems.
>
> Converting data from our old system to the new one was my most frustrating problem. The new database is really good in that it contains a lot of new data fields that will help us with marketing, keeping track of customers and equipment, etc. When we did the conversion those fields were entered as blanks. Then the first time someone used that record the system stopped him on a dime and said, "fill it in." That really frustrated the operations people who were trying to use the system to do their work for the first time. As a result of this, I had to spend a couple of months personally recreating a lot of entries. Where I usually get our books closed the third week in January, I got it done the first of April.
>
> We are concerned that we still need to make a lot of corrections, but Zeus is back on a rapid deployment plan. They argue that it is better to get a system out there that everyone is using, even if it is imperfect, and we can see the logic in that. But we still think it would be better to take a couple of extra months to get things fixed so that it will be a little easier when they go to other places. We should have devoted more time and effort to reducing the pain, but they didn't see it that way.

At this time there were four distributorships up and running, although not yet running smoothly. Zeus was pressing forward with plans to have seven more distributorships up and running by the end of 1999.

Status as of May 1, 2000

As of May 1, 2000, 17 distributorships were running or in the process of installing the new system. According to Hickson:

> We have made progress in the installation process, but they are still rough. On the basis of what we learned from the first four installations, we have developed a good plan—we know what has to happen when, and we are able to provide the right tools to support the key events that have to happen and the key work that a distributor has to do.
>
> Between the Oklahoma City and Memphis installations we took about 4 months to get the bugs out of the system that had been revealed by the Oklahoma City experience. But Memphis still had a lot of problems because of the components that had not been implemented in Oklahoma City, so we had to start back at square one with them. The reality is that some of these changes are just being put into place right now.
>
> We have had a real struggle in determining how much effort to devote to getting the system to have the kind of capability that we all want it to have. We see the need to get everyone up quickly and say "O.K., you can invoice customers and you can track inventory, so let's go." And they say, "Yeah, but how do I manage this particular activity?" Well, they did it manually before, or they didn't do it. There are lots of different dynamics that come into play there.
>
> Despite all we have learned, as we go from distributor to distributor we still have uniquenesses in terms of where they are coming from. We know where they are going to—that is crystal clear to us. What we don't know, and what we really don't put a lot of energy into, is where are they starting from. We give them the tools, and we give them a gentle nudge and tell them how to get there, but we can't attempt perfection. Our goal is 24 up and running on the system, not one running perfectly, and that has been a source of conflict.

Each of the Zeus distributorships in North America, all 24 of them, are now network capable. They have deployed 145 file servers and 145 network connections, all to the same specifications. Lotus Notes email has also been deployed to all those locations and is being used throughout the distribution system. The central database server (CDS) is up and operational, but they have had serious problems with its data because of problems with other Zeus information systems that supply the data. According to Hickson:

> One of the key pieces of information that distributors need is data about parts. Whenever a new part is released or a price changes, that information must be available to the distributors, and in the new system parts information is available to everyone through the central database server (CDS). Zeus management decided to centralize our warehousing, and in the process of doing that they installed new purchased software to manage our inventories. That has been a horrible mess, a complete disaster, and the result was that we had to turn off the CDS parts system for several months until they

could get the data cleaned up. The distributors on our new system were dependent on that information, and all of a sudden it is not there. Now what do I do?

We had a similar problem with the Zeus system that manages information on standard repair times (SRTs), the information the distributors use to do repairs. During the time when they were having those problems Zeus released four new machines, so these should have been lots of parts and SRT information going out to the distributors, but we had to shut off the system until they could get the SRT data cleaned up. The people in the field are trying to repair equipment and submit warranty claims on Zeus, and they don't have the SRT data they need for these activities. What a mess! These problems were not the ZOCS team's fault, but they damaged the credibility of the new system. And they point out how vulnerable a tightly integrated system can be.

The problems with the CDS data were extremely frustrating for the distributorships. Byars explains:

We have worked like galley slaves to get this system installed and working, and many of the most important functions are dependent upon the data available through the CDS But much of this data has not been usable for 9 months! Now, we can understand having problems with a system—we've had our share of them. But 9 months go by and the system still doesn't work! They forced us onto the system and we can't use it! What are they doing up there?

We still don't have uniform processes, which was a major objective of the new system. But putting in a system doesn't change processes, especially when the system doesn't work. The CDS not working has provided lots of excuses for not changing our processes.

Despite all the problems, there were indications that the new systems were having a very beneficial impact on those distributorships that had installed them. According to Hickson:

We have done an analysis of the sales and profit history of the first four distributorships that were implemented. We found that although there was a sharp drop during installations, sales increased by 22 percent during the first year after installation was completed, while sales only increased by 12 percent for all distributors during that period. The effect was even more pronounced for profit before income taxes—a 60 percent increase for the first four installations versus a 15 percent increase for all distributors. These are very impressive figures on year-to-year changes.

Nathan Byars was not impressed by this analysis:

We do not agree that our good performance was due to the new system. We were so tied up trying to get the new system working during the first year after installation that our good performance was in spite of the new system, not because of it. We still expect that the new system will improve our performance, but we haven't gotten to that point yet. I suspect that the first four installations performed better than average because the Zeus team chose the best-run distributorships to implement first.

In 2000 the ZOCS team was starting one new installation each month, with the process taking from 4 to 6 months depending upon the distributorship. The team anticipated that all distributors would be up and running by the end of the second quarter of 2001, almost 3 years behind the original schedule. According to Hickson:

We are implementing one distributor a month now, with a 4-month cycle from start to finish, so we have 4 to 6 of them going all the time, all in different phases. We have three two-person implementation teams that manage the contact with the distributor during the installation. Each team has one to two active projects at a time, depending on scheduling and how many delays they encounter. The teams have a predefined number of visits that they make that are scheduled around events such as kickoffs, training sessions, starting a phase, etc. The implementation teams are on site about 3 weeks during the four months, broken up into 2- to 4-day trips. There are additional training people that are used—the implementation team doesn't do much training.

Our biggest problem is the organizational adjustment that is required by the distributorships—getting their heads around the fact that this takes a different mind-set than they are used to. The notion of making changes is what is different for a lot of them. They have to understand and accept that people are going to have to go through some training and make some adjustments, and at the end do something different. This whole mind-set change has been the biggest challenge so far.

The Future

With the end of this long project in sight at last, the question for the Zeus ZOCS team is "Where do we go from here?" Hickson explains:

Zeus has distributorships in some 27 countries outside North America, and we originally thought that we would move this new system into our international distributorships after we got the system implemented in North America. However, we tried it in Taipei and had a disaster. One would think that the distributorship function would be about the same no matter where it is located, but the issues are broader than that. It is clear that, in addition to cultural differences, there are differences in financial systems, inventory management capability, repair shop operations, and a host of other areas. We definitely have learned that an overseas distributorship is not just another distributorship—it's a different animal.

We also intended to go back and do some serious reengineering of our processes. The question is "What does that mean?" We have a wealth of opportunities in many areas to tighten up the flows and improve the business. But which of them are we going to do? Where is the most value, both for Zeus and for the distributors? Although we have some ideas, we don't have a plan—we haven't had time to think about that yet. And with the distributors exhausted and in a certain degree

> of turmoil, there is a great deal of uncertainty about the future. What do we prepare for? Are we going to do something major, or are we just going to keep the system running for the time being?

The long, difficult ZOCS project has had a decidedly negative impact on the relationships between Zeus and its distributors. Nathan Byars expresses his view of the future of the system:

> We are very frustrated because there are a lot of big gaps in the system that is being installed that we have known about for years, but nothing has been done about them because all the available resources have been used getting the system running in all the distributorships. There are a lot of changes that we need, and the distributors are getting organized to see that they get done.
>
> We have set up a Z/D steering committee, half of whose members represent the distributorships and half represent Zeus. It is co-chaired by a distributor and a Zeus manager. This steering committee will study the things that need to be done and define projects and do a cost/benefit analysis of them. Then they will prioritize them and present them to the distributorship council made up of all the distributorship owners and several top Zeus managers.
>
> For the recommended projects the Distributorship Council will determine: (1) Are we going to do it? (2) How much will it cost? and (3) Who is going to pay for it? The intention, of course, is that everyone will pay their fair share. I hope that we can work through it and make good progress.

Both Byars and Hickson agree that, up to this point, the focus of the project has been on the needs of Zeus and the distributors, and the customers' needs have not had a high priority. They are hopeful that these needs will be emphasized in the future, but the distributorship council will have to determine who is going to pay for those things that primarily benefit the customer.

CASE STUDY III-3

PURCHASING A STUDENT MANAGEMENT SYSTEM AT JEFFERSON COUNTY SCHOOL SYSTEM

The Jefferson County School System (JCSS) educates about 10,000 students in fourteen elementary schools, two middle schools, and two high schools. It serves a diverse community consisting of a county seat of 80,000 with a substantial industrial base and a major state university, and the surrounding rural area.

Central High School and Roosevelt High School, located on the eastern edge of town, are spirited athletic rivals whose attendance districts split the county into approximately equal areas, with each district including about 1,450 city and rural patrons. The two middle schools each have about 750 pupils in the seventh and eighth grades and also serve diversified areas. The elementary schools are located throughout the county and range in size from rural schools with about 250 students up to almost 700 students for the largest city school.

History of Administrative Computing in JCSS

Administrative computing at JCSS began in the early 1970s when computing resources at the university were leased to do scheduling and grade reporting and to keep student enrollment data. In 1976 the school corporation purchased a DEC PDP 11/34 computer, and the student management applications were converted from the university computer. Over the next few years, financial applications were added and more student management applications were developed. In 1984 a PDP 11/44 was acquired and located in the JCSS Administration Building next to Central High. The PDP 11/34 was moved to Roosevelt High, where it was used for student management applications at Roosevelt and a nearby middle school. The payroll processing was farmed out to the data processing subsidiary of a local bank.

All of these applications, both financial and student management, were custom developed by the longtime director of data processing, David Meyer, and the two programmers on his staff. The users of these systems were satisfied with them, and when they wanted changes and improvements, Meyer and his programmers would make them. All of the systems were written in BASIC, and there was no end-user capability—if anyone needed a special report, a program to produce it was written in BASIC by one of the programmers. In 1986 the two PDP computers were replaced by two PRIME 2755 computers, and the BASIC programs were converted to run on the new machines.

In late 1993, however, the JCSS director of finance, Harvey Greene, became concerned with problems he saw developing in the data processing area. First, it was apparent that the JCSS computers were becoming overloaded, and these old machines were becoming more and more difficult to maintain. Additional capacity was going to be needed soon, but the PRIME line of computers were no longer in production, so any replacement would involve incompatible hardware and software. Mr. Greene was very concerned because he felt that converting the old custom systems to a new hardware/software environment would be time-consuming and a waste of money.

Therefore, early in 1994 the JCSS administration set up a small task force of administrators to evaluate the JCSS data processing systems and to recommend directions for the future. This task force recommended that:

- The PRIME hardware should be replaced.
- Because JCSS could not afford the time or money to convert its current systems, the JCSS systems should be replaced with purchased software packages.
- The new systems should utilize an integrated database and report-generation software so that people could share data from various applications.
- JCSS should contract with a vendor who would accept total responsibility for both the hardware and software.
- Because JCSS would no longer be doing custom development, the programming staff of the data processing department could be reduced.

EXHIBIT 1

Jefferson County School System Request for Proposal

Table of Contents

Soon after the recommendations were accepted by the JCSS administration, Meyer resigned as data processing director. In July 1994 he was replaced by Carol Andrews, who had 13 years of experience as an applications programmer, systems programmer, and systems analyst with a nearby federal government installation.

Purchasing the New System

After spending several months getting acclimated to the JCSS and her new job, Andrews set about the task of selecting a vendor to provide the hardware and software to replace the current administrative computing applications at JCSS. In late November 1994 a computer selection committee was appointed to evaluate available systems and recommend a vendor to the JCSS School Board. This 14-member committee included representatives of most of the major users of the system—assistant principals who did scheduling and were responsible for student records; deans who were responsible for attendance and student discipline; counselors; teachers; the personnel director; and the chief accountant. It also included representatives of the different levels of schools in the system and from each of the larger school locations.

By late March 1995 Andrews and the committee had prepared a 71-page request for proposal (RFP) that was sent to 23 possible vendors, asking that proposals be submitted by May 4, 1995. The RFP stated that "The proposals will be evaluated on functional requirements, support services, and a 5-year life cycle cost." The table of contents of the RFP is included as Exhibit 1. Appendices A through E listed in the contents were in

EXHIBIT 2

Application Specifications, Appendix D

Student Administration System
Attendance Accounting

Included Yes	Included No	
_____	_____	1. Provide for interactive CRT entry and correction of daily attendance information.
_____	_____	2. Provide for interactive entry and correction of YTD attendance information.
_____	_____	3. Provide for interactive entry of period by period, and half or whole day attendance.
_____	_____	4. Capable of input of attendance by CRT entry or optional scanning device(s).
_____	_____	5. Provide CRT access to student attendance records by date or course, showing period by period attendance and reason for absence for any date.
_____	_____	6. Provide "user defined" definition of ADA and ADM calculation requirements.
_____	_____	7. Provide for entry of absence reason codes by exception.
_____	_____	8. Provide for multiple attendance periods with "user defined" number of days in each.
_____	_____	9. Provide for entry of entire year school calendar.
_____	_____	10. Provide for student registers.
_____	_____	11. Provide for entry and withdrawal. Provide for student withdrawal, which retains all student information and tracks the withdrawn student's attendance as "not enrolled;" in the event the student returns to the district and reenrolls all attendance calculations will automatically be current and up to date.

Included Yes	Included No	
_____	_____	12. Daily absence worksheet phone list.
_____	_____	13. Daily absence report.
_____	_____	14. Absence report by reason.
_____	_____	15. Student Attendance Register Report. List by class and section.
_____	_____	16. Student Absence by Reason listing.
_____	_____	17. School Absence by Reason listing.
_____	_____	18. Provide attendance reports with ADA and ADM calculations from any beginning date through any ending date.
_____	_____	19. Provide attendance reports by:
_____	_____	Student
_____	_____	Absence and Absence reason(s)
_____	_____	Sex
_____	_____	Grade level
_____	_____	Course and section
_____	_____	Multiple combinations of the preceding requirements
_____	_____	20. Provide ADA and ADM calculation reports, with any "from" and "through" dates for the following:
_____	_____	Any and all schools
_____	_____	The entire district
_____	_____	Each attendance register
_____	_____	21. Provide M–F absence reports by any "from" and "through" dates, also by student, grade, sex, course and section, and/or absence reason code.
_____	_____	22. Provide daily entry and withdrawal reports.

the form of fill-in-the-blank questionnaires that defined the information that JCSS desired from the vendors.

The RFP was sent to vendors that would contract to accept responsibility for all the hardware, software, and support and training services required to install and maintain the new system. The RFP specified the number and location of the terminals and printers that were to be connected to the system in Part III-D and Appendix C. The desired requirements for the applications software were described in Appendix D in the form of characteristics that could be

EXHIBIT 2 (*Continued*)

Student Administration System
Student Scheduling

Included Yes	Included No	
_____	_____	1. Provide for interactive CRT entry and correction of student course requests and master schedule data.
_____	_____	2. Automatically process student course requests against the master schedule to produce class schedules for each student.
_____	_____	3. Provide for Arena Scheduling.
_____	_____	4. Provide for interactive CRT drop/add of students from classes after initial schedules are established, at any time.
_____	_____	5. Scheduling data must interface with student records.
_____	_____	6. Provide for course restrictions by grade level and/or sex.
_____	_____	7. Allow for addition of new courses and sections at any time.
_____	_____	8. Provide current enrollment summary of each course and section via CRT and report.
_____	_____	9. Provide for mass adds, deletes or changes based on grade, sex, etc.
_____	_____	10. On-line editing of valid course number requests during CRT entry is required.
_____	_____	11. Provide for scheduling retries without erasing previous scheduling runs.
_____	_____	12. Provide for override of maximum enrollment.

Included Yes	Included No	
_____	_____	13. Provide for each student a year-long schedule, with up to 20 different courses (excluding lunch and study hall).
_____	_____	14. Provide for "prioritizing" scheduling runs by grade level and/or student number.
_____	_____	15. Provide master schedule by teacher listing.
_____	_____	16. Preregistration "by student" course request report.
_____	_____	17. Preregistration "by course" request listing.
_____	_____	18. Provide course request tally report.
_____	_____	19. Provide potential conflict matrix.
_____	_____	20. Provide student conflict report.
_____	_____	21. Provide student schedules.
_____	_____	22. Provide course and section status summary.
_____	_____	23. Provide course rosters by teacher.
_____	_____	24. Provide room utilization report with conflict alert.
_____	_____	25. Provide teacher utilization report with conflict alert.
_____	_____	26. Provide schedule exception listing showing student and open periods (by either closed or conflict status), also show all filled periods.
_____	_____	27. Provide scheduling by quarter, semester, year-long, or trimester options.

checked off as included or not. The applications specifications for the attendance accounting and student scheduling systems from Appendix D are included as Exhibit 2.

The requirements for terminals and printers in the various buildings were determined by Andrews in consultation with someone on the selection committee who was familiar with each school. Although members of the selection committee made suggestions, Andrews determined most of the requirements for the application systems by examining what the existing systems did and talking with people throughout the JCSS.

Seven proposals were submitted in response to the RFP. Andrews was able to winnow them down easily to three serious contenders that were evaluated in detail. Each of the three finalists was invited to demonstrate its system to the selection committee. The vendors were not told in detail what to show, but they were asked to demonstrate the operation of several of the major systems. The three vendors brought in their own small computers for the demonstration, and all of the demonstrations were quite satisfactory to the committee.

The committee originally intended to visit a school that used each vendor's system, but because of time and money constraints they were only able to visit two sites—one Data Systems, Inc. installation and one Scholastic Systems Corporation installation. Andrews and Dr. Paul Faris, assistant principal at Roosevelt High, spent one day at each of these locations observing their systems in action and talking with users. In addition, members of the committee made telephone calls to their counterparts at other schools that used each vendor's systems without unearthing any major problems or concerns. Everyone seemed quite positive about all three vendors and their products.

The committee had a difficult time deciding between the three finalists. Each of the vendors proposed software packages in all the areas that JCSS had asked for, but none of these systems did exactly what they wanted in exactly the way the current systems did things. The committee finally chose Data Systems, Inc. (DSI) because the members felt they could work well with the DSI people and they felt that the DSI proposal was best on balance, as indicated in Exhibit 3, which they presented to the JCSS School Board. This table rates seven factors on a scale from 1 to 5, with a total rating for each of the finalist vendors at the bottom. The "cost of ownership" includes the purchase price of the hardware and software, installation, training, and 5 years of hardware and software maintenance and support. The "bid exceptions" rating refers to how well the proposed software fits the JCSS specifications and thus a high rating indicates that little modification of the software would be needed.

The JCSS School Board awarded the contract to DSI in June 1995, which included the following systems: financial, payroll/personnel, fixed assets, warehouse inventory, registration, scheduling, grades/transcripts, attendance, book bills, office assistant, electronic mail, and special education. These systems utilize a standard relational database management system that includes a query language called INFORM that generates ad hoc reports.

DSI agreed to make specific changes in the software packages where the committee had indicated that the packages did not meet the JCSS specifications. The contract also provided that DSI would devote up to 100 hours of programming time to making other modifications (not yet specified) in its software. Any additional changes requested by JCSS would be billed at $100 per programmer hour. JCSS also purchased DSI's standard software maintenance contract.

The operating system for the IBM RS/6000 is AIX, IBM's version of UNIX. The Administration Center and each of the 18 schools are connected via an existing TCP/IP wide area network, so each school has access to the system. The system is

EXHIBIT 3
Evaluation of Bids

Selection Criteria	Data Systems	Scholastic Systems	Orian Computer Systems
1. Vendor Profile	5	5	3
2. Vendor Services	5	4	3
3. Hardware	IBM RS/6000	DEC ALPHA	HP 9000
(Rating)	4	5	3
4. Application Software	5	4	3
5. 5 yr. Cost of Ownership	$698,600	$874,730	$495,060
(Rating)	4	3	5
6. Software support	5	4	3
7. Bid Exceptions	5	4	3
TOTAL RATING	33	29	23

character-based, using existing PCs emulating DEC VT 220 terminals for input and output.

Implementation of the Systems

The hardware arrived and the RS/6000 was installed in the Administration Center in October 1995. After the hardware was checked out, Andrews and her staff began to install the software and phase in some of the systems. They encountered their fair share of problems, and as of February 1997 they had not been able to transfer all of the old systems from the PRIMEs to the RS/6000.

Although they had some problems with the financial systems, they successfully installed most of them. However, they had major problems in installing and using the student management systems.

Andrews planned to follow the cycle of the academic year when implementing the student systems. First, they would transfer all the student demographic information from the present system to the new system's database. Then they would complete the students' fall class schedules by the end of the spring semester, as they had been doing with the old system, so that the students' schedules would be on the new system and ready to go in the fall. During the summer they would pick up the attendance accounting on the new system so it would be ready for the fall. Then they would implement grade reporting so it would be ready for use at the end of the first 6-week grading period in the fall. Finally, they would convert the student transcript information from the old system so that fall semester grades could be transferred to the transcripts at the end of the semester.

They successfully transferred the student demographic information from the old system to the new in February 1996. Then they started to work on student scheduling. Things did not go well. The training provided by DSI for the scheduling officers was a disaster. Then, after entering the student class requests and the available faculty data, they started the first scheduling run. After it had run all day without completing the schedules, they decided that there was something definitely wrong. Andrews never completely resolved this problem with DSI's experts. DSI claimed that it was caused by the way the scheduling officer set up the scheduling system—the various parameters that the system uses. Andrews was still convinced that there is some sort of bug in the scheduling program.

DSI did make some minor modifications to the program, and they sent some people out to consult with Andrews and her staff on how to set up the schedule, but they were unable to get the schedules done by the end of the spring semester as planned. This caused severe problems because the assistant principals in charge of scheduling were not on the payroll during the summer. Fortunately, Paul Faris, the scheduling officer at Roosevelt, was working summer school, and with his assistance they were just able to get all the schedules done 2 weeks before school started.

Preparation for the fall was also hindered by the fact that neither the school secretaries, who entered much of the data for the attendance module, nor the counselors, who had to work with the scheduling of new students in the system and changes to schedules of continuing students, were on the payroll during the summer. The administration would not spend the money to pay these people to come in during the summer for training on the system, so all training was delayed until the week before school started, when everyone reported back to work. The training was rushed, and again DSI did a poor job with it.

When school started in the fall, the system was a total disaster. The people who were working with the system did not understand it or know what they were doing with it. When the counselors tried to schedule a new student into his classes, the system might take 20 minutes to produce his new schedule. Needless to say, there were long lines of students waiting in the halls, and the students, their parents, the counselors, teachers, and administrators were upset and terribly frustrated.

Also, the attendance officers did not know what they were doing and could not make the system work for the first few weeks of the semester. Things were so bad that at the end of the first grading period Andrews decided that, although the grade reporting system was working correctly, it was not feasible to have the teachers enter their grades directly into the system as had been planned. Instead, she hired several outside clerical people to enter the grades from forms the teachers filled out. After some well-executed training, the teachers successfully entered their grades at the end of the semester.

By the end of the fall semester most of those working with the student systems had learned enough to make them work adequately, and a few of them were beginning to recognize that the new systems had some significant advantages over the old ones. They did get the second semester underway without major problems, and in early February 1997, they were getting ready to bring up the transcript system and start the scheduling process for the fall.

Perspectives of the Participants

Given everything that had transpired in acquiring and implementing the new system to this stage, it is not surprising that there were many different opinions on the problems that were encountered, whether or not the new system was satisfactory, and what the future would hold. The following presents the perspectives of a number of those who had been involved with the new system.

Dr. Harold Whitney, Assistant Principal, Central High School

Dr. Whitney believes that the previous system was an excellent system that really did the job for them.

> It was fast, efficient, and effective. And when we needed something, rather than having to call DSI in Virginia to get it done, our own people would do it for us in a matter of 2 or 3 days. However, the study committee (which probably didn't have enough good school people on it) decided on the new system, and we were told that we would start with the new scheduling software package early in 1996.

The first acquaintance that Whitney had with the new system was in early February when DSI sent someone in to train four or five of the scheduling people on how to use the new system to construct a master schedule. Whitney recalls:

> Over a 3-day period we took 50 students and tried to construct a master schedule. And at the end of the 3 days, we still hadn't been able to do it. It was apparent that the lady they sent out to train us, while she may have known the software, had no idea of what we wanted in a master schedule, and had never experienced the master schedule-building process in a large high school.
>
> The master schedule is the class schedule of all of the courses that we offer—when and where they will be taught, and by whom. In the past, I would take the course requests from our students and summarize them to determine the demand for each course, and then I would develop a master schedule that assigned our available teachers to the courses that they could best teach while meeting the student demand as well as possible. I had to take into account the fact that, among all the teachers who are certified to teach mathematics, some are more effective teaching algebra and geometry than they are in calculus, and similarly for other subject areas. Also, we have 15 or so teachers who are part-time in our school and therefore can only teach here during the morning (or the afternoon). Furthermore, we need to lock our 2-semester courses so that a student will have the same teacher for both semesters.
>
> With the new system we were supposed to input our teachers and their certifications and the student requests for courses, and the DSI software would generate the ideal master schedule to satisfy that demand. But we had to place quite a number of restrictions on what and when the teachers could teach and into what sections a student could be scheduled. When we tried to run the software, it just ran and ran, but it never produced a satisfactory schedule.

DSI sent one of its top executives out to talk with Whitney about these problems. The executive told Whitney that "the reason that you're unhappy is that you're placing too many restrictions on the schedule." Whitney replied, "All well and good. But are you telling me that your software package should dictate our curriculum? That it should dictate who teaches calculus, who teaches general math, who teaches advanced and who teaches beginning grammar? That's hardly sound educationally!"

Whitney ended up doing the schedule by hand, as he had done before, and the students were scheduled by the end of the spring semester. Some of the other schools continued to try to use the full system, and they had a hard time getting the schedules out by the start of school.

Whitney had a very bad impression of the system until the end of 1996, when he began to believe things were improving somewhat. The DSI people were beginning to listen to him, and he was more receptive: "I've always been able to see that somewhere down the road the new system will have capabilities that improve on our old system."

Dr. Paul Faris, Assistant Principal, Roosevelt High School

Dr. Faris, an active member of the computer study committee that chose the new system, is responsible for class scheduling at Roosevelt High. Unlike Harold Whitney at Central High, he used the system as it was intended to be used both to develop the master schedule and to schedule the students into their classes. He had a struggle with the system at first and had not completed the master schedule by the end of spring. However, he was on the payroll during the summer and was able to complete the master schedule a few weeks before the beginning of school in fall 1996.

In doing so he learned a great deal about how the scheduling system worked.

> The way your master schedule is set up and the search patterns you establish determine how the system performs. The individual principals have control over many aspects of the process, and there is a lot of leeway—whether you set up for one semester or two, whether you strictly enforce class sizes, whether or not you have alternatives to search for with specific courses, and so on. We set it up for double semester, which is the hard one, but I had generous limits on my class size and we had limited search for alternatives, which kicked the difficult ones out of the system to handle on a manual basis. And I limited certain courses to seniors, or sophomores, et cetera, and that restricted the search pattern somewhat.

Paul knew that the beginning of the fall semester would be crunch time, when lots of work would have to be done with the new system in a limited amount of time. So he prepared his people for the transition ahead of time. Paul's secretary was skilled on the old system. Early in the spring Paul told her: "We are going to change over our entire system in 4 months. And week by week I want you to tell me what files have to be changed over, and you and I are going to do it." Again, it was a matter of making sure things were done in a nonpressure situation where they could learn what they had to know.

Paul and his counselors still had many problems during the first few weeks of school in the fall, but nothing that they could not cope with. Things are going well in Paul's area now. They recently started the second semester, which was a crunch time again. The counselors got along fine with schedule changes, and they completed the new schedules faster than they had with the old system.

Paul believes that the new system is a substantial improvement over the old one.

> I can follow through and find the kids' attendance, current program, grades, past history and transcripts, and probably have everything I need in 2 or 3 minutes. Before the new system I could barely walk to the filing cabinet and find his folder in that time. And then I'd still have to go to the counseling office and get the current schedule, and then to the attendance office and get the attendance record.
>
> I'm really pleased with the new file structures. And Carol's programmer is starting to add back some of the custom things that we had in the old system. I'm looking forward to being trained on the report generator so that I can produce my own special reports without getting a programmer involved.

Dr. Ruth Gosser, Assistant Principal, Central High School

Dr. Gosser is the attendance and disciplinary officer at Central High and was a member of the computer selection committee. Ruth recalls:

> We looked at about four different companies. Several had very good packages, although I will admit that by the time you sit through four or five different presentations, they all tend to run into one another.
>
> My participation in specifying the requirements and evaluating the proposed systems was minimal. It was a big committee, and I was busy with other things, so I didn't even read the materials very carefully. I disliked spending the time that I did, and I was really turned off by the details, especially the technical details. I remember thinking: Ugh! I'm sick of this. Just go ahead and buy something!

She and her people had only 2 days of training on the system before the start of school, and Gosser thought the training provided was pretty useless. "They weren't very well-organized, and they spent too much time on the technical aspects of the system. I just wanted to know how to use the system, but they tried to give me a lot more and it really confused me and made me angry."

When school started in the fall, it was a disaster. Ruth remembers it vividly:

> It was awful! Awful! I didn't get home till after 6:30 for weeks. Just getting the information in and out was a nightmare. We had a terrible time trying to change the unexcused to excused, and doing all the little things that go with that. It was so bad that we seriously considered abandoning the system and trying to do it by hand. It was horrible!
>
> But we've just gone through second-semester class changes, and I haven't heard anyone weeping and wailing about what a crummy system this is. We're beginning to recognize that we've got the new system, and we're going to have it for a long time. They're not going to junk a system that we have paid all that money for, so we'd better work to make the very best out of it that we can. And I can see that there are some really good things about the new system that the old system didn't have, and never could have.
>
> Looking back, I don't think that the computer selection committee did a very good job. If I had known then what I know now I'd have put a lot more effort into it than I did. Since most of us didn't put in the effort to get down to the details of exactly what we needed, Carol pretty much had to do it herself. Unfortunately, we only gave her enough information to get her off our backs. Like "I need something that will chart attendance for me." That wasn't much help. Every system we considered would chart attendance, so we had no basis for deciding which system would have been best for us.

Dr. Helen Davis, Assistant Principal, Roosevelt High

Dr. Davis is the attendance and disciplinary officer at Roosevelt High School. She was not a member of the computer selection committee, and she does not think it did a very good job.

> The committee looked at a lot of different kinds of things, but they didn't communicate. Even though we all were supposed to have representatives on the committee, we didn't know what they were doing, nor did we have the opportunity to discuss any of the systems that they were looking at and whether those systems would help us or satisfy our needs.
>
> When the new system was put in last fall a lot of us had no training, no information, and didn't know what was going on. My secretary had a day and a half training in August, but I had no training at all. Some training was offered to me in August, but I had already made arrangements to be out of town, and no flexibility was provided as to when the training would be available. Furthermore, there are no user-friendly manuals for the system—the manual they gave me is written in computerese. So I've had to learn the system by bitter experience, and I still don't know what it offers me. I could go through a hundred menus and not find what I want because I don't know what they are for.
>
> Last fall when school opened my blood pressure probably went to about 300 every day! We couldn't do attendance—it wouldn't work. We couldn't print an absence list for the teachers. We couldn't put out an unexcused list. We couldn't get an excessive absence report, so it was mid-semester before I could start sending letters to parents whose kids weren't attending regularly. That really impedes the work of trying to keep kids in school.

The thing that frustrated Helen the most was that she resented being controlled by the software system.

> The system is dictating what we can do with kids and their records. It needs to be the opposite way. We ought to be driving that machine to service what we need to do as easily as possible. But the machine is driving us, and I'm really displeased with that.
>
> We're stuck with DSI and their software because we've got so much money invested in it. In time Carol will be able to make this system as compatible with our needs as it can be, but it will never be as suitable as it should be. And it will take a long, long time before we get all the things that we need.

Catherine Smith, Counselor at Central High School

Catherine Smith has been a counselor at Central High School for 20 years, but she had no experience with the computer before the training session that was held the Thursday and Friday before school started. According to Catherine:

> The first day of school was just unbelievable! It took 2 hours to schedule one new student. Everyone was running up and down the halls asking each other questions. No one knew what was going on.
>
> The first 2 days I had absolutely no control over that computer! It would bleep, and you didn't know why. But by Wednesday morning I began to get control. I knew that if I pushed this button, this would happen. And I knew how to make it do some of the things I wanted it to do.
>
> Now that I've worked with it for a semester, I'm happy with it. The system contains a tremendous amount of information that I need to help the students. The thing I like most about the system is that when I want to put a kid in a class and it's full, I can find out instantly how many kids are in each section, and I can usually find a place for the kid. I can even override it if the section is closed. Despite the fact that we almost died during that first week, now that I have control over it I think it's tremendous!

Murphey Ford, English Teacher at Roosevelt High School

Murphey has taught English at Roosevelt for 12 years, and he has had no experience with a computer beyond entering his grades into the old system.

> This new computer has been a disaster from the word go. Last fall they didn't produce a class schedule until 2 weeks before classes were to start, so I had no time to prepare to teach a class I hadn't taught for 5 years! And I wasn't even asked if I would be willing to teach it—the computer just assigned me to it.
>
> Then they relaxed the limits on class size. We ended up having some classes with 30 students and others with 40. That's not fair to either the students or the teachers. And it was a zoo around here at the beginning of the fall. It was 3 weeks before they got all the new students into their classes and things settled down a little.
>
> In this community we have very high expectations for the education system, but we never have enough money to provide the special programs we want, or get adequate supplies, or pay decent salaries. It really burns me up that we spent almost a million dollars on this new computer that doesn't work anything like as well as the old one.

Carol Andrews, Director of Data Processing

The 15 months since the new hardware arrived have been very difficult and stressful for Carol:

> I often wonder what it was that caused things to have gotten so difficult and to have raised so much negative reaction to the new system. One explanation is that we have a history of custom-developed systems, so anything that users wanted got done exactly the way they wanted it. Now we have a set of generic software that is meant to serve many school systems and it doesn't do exactly what they want in exactly the way they want it.
>
> It was hard to get effective participation from the members of the computer selection committee. Coming from the government our RFP wasn't very big to me, but when I passed it around to the committee they couldn't believe it. I couldn't even get the people to really read the RFP, let alone the responses. Actually, it should have been even more detailed. It was the lack of detail that really caused us most of our problems, because it has been the details that have determined whether or not the systems were suitable to our people.
>
> We should have paid a lot more attention to training. DSI hasn't had much experience with training, and they just didn't do a good job with it. They left me, a new user, with too much responsibility for setting up the training and making sure that everything in the system was ready for it. And they didn't provide me with the training that I needed.
>
> Money is a big constraint to the JCSS. I needed a lot more programming help in-house, and someone from DSI—a week here and a week there—to fill in for our lack of knowledge in being able to support our users.
>
> Looking back at it, 15 months seems like an extremely long time to implement a new system. But it might have been better to take even more time to do it. Maybe we should have piloted the system at one school for a year and worked the bugs out of it before installing it systemwide.
>
> Where do we go from here? How do we handle the negative reaction that has been generated from all the stumbles and falls? How do we get things turned around to take advantage of some of the things that are really positive for the school system now that we have access to all this information? I'm beginning to see little pockets here and there where people are starting to use the capabilities of the new system and are developing positive attitudes. I hope that we're getting over the hump!
>
> If we had it to do over again, would we make the decision to go with DSI? That's a question I ask myself every day! Could we have done better? Would we have had fewer problems? I don't know.

CASE STUDY III-4

A MAKE-OR-BUY DECISION AT BAXTER MANUFACTURING COMPANY

It is late Friday afternoon, and Kyle Baxter, president of Baxter Manufacturing Company, Inc., and his sister, Sue Barkley, vice president for customer relations, are discussing whether or not to purchase the Effective Management Systems manufacturing software package proposed by manufacturing Vice President Lucas Moore.

"I'm really fearful of buying such a large, complex software package given our past experience," Baxter exclaims. "What do you think?"

"I really don't know," Barkley replies. "We do need manufacturing software, and there are some obvious advantages to purchasing this software. We have had bad experiences in past attempts to buy such software, but we have learned from some of our mistakes, so we might be successful this time. But I have been impressed by the success that MIS has had in building new systems for us, so I am in a quandry right now."

"We're going to have to decide before long," Baxter notes, "but we need to talk with some of our people first."

Baxter Manufacturing Company Background

Baxter Manufacturing Company (BMC), located in a small Midwestern town, is a leading manufacturer of deep-drawn stampings, particularly for electric motor housings. (Exhibit 1 shows a few of BMC's products.) The company was founded in 1978 by its chairman, Walter R. Baxter, as a supplier of tools and dies, but it soon expanded into the stamping business. BMC is a closely held corporation, with the family of the founder holding most of the stock.

BMC's engineers have implemented some of the most complex stamping concepts in the industry, as the company has established its niche as a quality supplier of deep-drawn stampings to the automotive (85 percent of sales) and appliance (15 percent of sales) industries. BMC's major customers include Ford, General Motors, Honda of America, General Electric, Whirlpool, Amana, and Maytag. BMC puts great emphasis on quality and has achieved Q-1 status from Ford, a QSP Award from GM and quality awards from Honda, and is recognized as a world-class supplier within its niche.

Producing a deep-drawn part is a complex process requiring repeated stampings, each with a different male/female die pair. This process is performed on a heavy press, using a very complex die that consists of perhaps 10 individual dies assembled together in a line. A coil of steel of the proper width and thickness is fed into one end of the press. After each stamping cycle a precision transport mechanism moves the material forward exactly the right distance so that a part that has completed one stage is positioned correctly at the next stage to be struck by the next die on the next cycle of the press. Thus each cycle of the press performs a different forming operation on each of 10 parts, and a finished part comes off the machine at the end of each cycle. (Exhibit 2 shows the different stages of a motor housing stamping.)

EXHIBIT 1
Some of BMC's Stamped Parts

EXHIBIT 2

The Stages of a Motor Housing Stamping

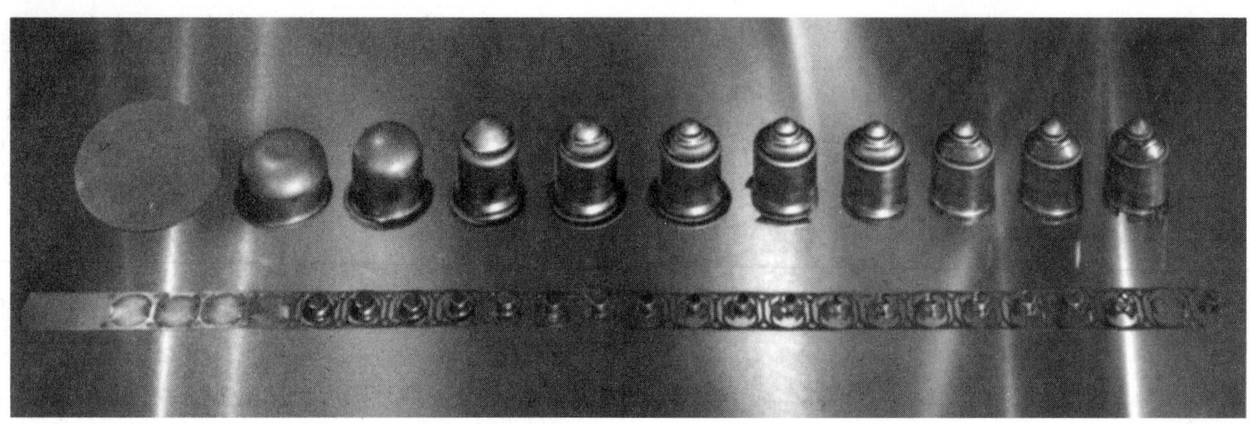

BMC's strength lies in its ability to produce efficiently large volumes of high-quality complex stampings. It may take 6 to 8 hours to install the dies and set up the huge stamping presses for a production run, so BMC cannot efficiently produce short runs and therefore does not serve the replacement market well.

BMC uses state-of-the-art equipment to develop and manufacture the necessary tooling for the needs of its customers. With the use of wire electrical discharge machines (EDM), computer numerical control (CNC) vertical machining centers, and CNC horizontal lathes, it is able to produce quality tooling efficiently. For the life of a part, BMC's computerized equipment can reproduce identical die components for replacement of worn or damaged dies.

BMC's 140,000-square-foot manufacturing facility is one of the best in the country, with 39 presses that range from 50-ton to 600-ton capacity. Every press is equipped with accessory items such as feeds, reels, and electronic detection systems. In addition to the presses, BMC has recently added the capacity to weld, drill, tap, and assemble stampings into more complex parts to suit the needs and desires of its customers.

BMC employs about 420 people and is nonunion. Management believes that these employees are BMC's greatest asset. According to Chairman Walter Baxter:

> We have a great group of people! We are fortunate to be located in a farming area where the people have a strong work ethic and a "do whatever it takes" attitude. We started out as a family company and we have a lot of families—husbands and wives, their children, aunts and uncles—working here. My son, Kyle, is now President, and my daughter Sue is Vice President for Customer Relations. We cherish our family atmosphere.

Over its 19-year history, BMC has grown at about 20 percent a year. The last 5 years of sales have been as follows:

1992	$32,000,000	1995	$61,976,000
1993	$37,292,000	1996	$74,130,000
1994	$49,900,000		

This rapid growth has caused problems at times. For example, in 1990 its sales were so close to BMC's production capacity that, even when running its production 24 hours a day 7 days a week, it became almost impossible to meet promised delivery schedules. According to Sue Barkley:

> In 1991 we had to turn down business from existing customers who wanted to give us new parts to make. For almost a year we did not accept any new business. That was the most difficult thing we ever did because we were fearful that customers who had to go to our competitors might never come back. We told our customers that we hated to refuse their business, but we had to because if we took more business we couldn't handle it—we would be late and couldn't provide the level of service that we are committed to providing. Most of our customers understood. They were not happy about it, but they respected us for being up front about it. We did lose some good orders because we weren't accepting business when they came out, but I don't think that there are any customers who haven't come back to us with more business.

By 1992 BMC had made the large investment necessary to significantly increase capacity and was back on its historical growth track.

In the late 1980s BMC's automotive customers started to go to a just-in-time (JIT) philosophy in which they carried minimal inventories of raw materials and parts. Rather than sending an order for a month's parts at a time as they had in the past, the customers began telling BMC one day what to ship on the next. BMC was provided with a blanket order for planning, but the customers reserved the right to change the amounts at the last minute.

Including the time to procure the raw materials, run them through the presses to make the parts, clean and pack them, and ship them out, BMC's production process requires at least 2 weeks if things go well. Thus the automotive companies are forcing their suppliers to maintain their inventories for them, which places great pressure on BMC to reduce its cycle times. Because of its 2-week production cycle and long setup times, BMC is often forced to maintain a finished goods inventory that is substantially above its target of a 3-day supply.

About 5 years ago its automotive customers began to pressure BMC to convert to electronic data interchange (EDI), where all paper document flows between customer and supplier are replaced by electronic flows directly between the customer's computer and BMC's computer. Thus BMC receives all purchase orders and shipping schedules electronically and sends out electronic shipping notices and bills. EDI has the potential to be quicker and more efficient for both parties, but BMC's factory computer systems were incomplete and fragmented, so for several years BMC accepted the data electronically, printed it out, and then rekeyed the data into those relevant systems that existed. The IS department is now building interfaces to enter the EDI data directly into some of BMC's systems. One reason for this delay was that their automobile customers use one EDI standard while their appliance customers use another, and each customer has its own variation on the standard it uses. BMC has had to build a separate subsystem to handle each of its customers.

Information Systems at BMC

BMC's managers have been very receptive to the introduction of new technology. They were early adopters of CAD/CAM, and are at the forefront of stamping technology. However, they have had little experience with the use of computers in business applications and have limited understanding of what the technology can do for them.

BMC got its first PCs in 1987 and a few managers started experimenting with Lotus spreadsheets. One of the first applications they set up was a spreadsheet for generating customer quotes by calculating what price to charge for a part based on estimates of raw material cost, tooling costs, the costs of stamping, and the expected quantity to be produced. Another early use of the PC was a scheduling spreadsheet developed by the company president, Kyle Baxter, when serving as vice president for manufacturing. This spreadsheet, which is still used today, contains data for each part, including the machine used, the number produced per hour, and the setup time. The quantity required and the delivery date are entered and the spreadsheet determines when each part should be started into production and generates a schedule of what should be run when on each machine group. If the schedule is not feasible (e.g., some parts must be started last week), the scheduler can make manual adjustments in due date, quantity required, overtime, and other factors to produce a feasible schedule.

Realizing that they needed someone to lead and educate them in the use of computers, in 1989 BMC management set up an MIS department and hired an MIS manager, Nancy Shaw. BMC installed a Data General MV minicomputer, and the first application was interoffice e-mail. This was a great way to start because it demonstrated how helpful the computer could be in sharing information. According to Sue Barkley:

> E-mail was very well received because we were growing so rapidly and the need to communicate within the plant was so important. It wasn't until we got on e-mail that we realized how much time we had been spending running around the plant trying to find somebody and leaving little notes on their desk. We really became dependent on our e-mail system.

During the next 2 years Shaw led the purchase and successful installation of a package of financial applications, including payroll, accounts payable and receivable, and general ledger. Also, in 1989 BMC was beginning to encounter problems in production because of its growing capacity problems and its customers' switch to JIT. When customers changed their requirements the production schedule had to be changed, which forced changes in the schedules of other parts, and production people seemed to be spending all their time rescheduling things. Because demand was so near to capacity it was difficult to get all the orders done on time and there was a lot of expediting going on, which again led to the need to reschedule. Although there was no computer support for manufacturing other than the spreadsheet used for scheduling, BMC's management decided that if scheduling could be speeded up the problems would be alleviated. Consequently, the decision was made to purchase a software package for scheduling.

Sue Barkley, who was involved in the process, remembers:

> Our MIS manager, Nancy Shaw, did some research and selected four packages from which we tried to choose the best one. That was my first exposure to software, and it was a terrible experience. Each vendor claimed that his software would do anything you wanted to do, and there were so many questions we should have asked but didn't.
>
> Vendors all offered integrated packages that included production scheduling, but you also got sales, inventory, purchasing, shipping, etc. We made our selection and paid about $120,000 for the system, including both hardware and software, which was a large expenditure for us at the time.
>
> Then we started to load the data and implement the scheduling package. The training the vendor provided was poor, the manual was full of errors, and support from the vendor was minimal. We worked and worked, and finally became so frustrated by our inability to get the system to do what we wanted it to that

> we just gave up. On top of everything else the vendor went bankrupt. It was a total disaster—$120,000 down the tube!

As mentioned previously, by 1991 the problems in meeting shipping schedules had gotten so bad that BMC began to have to turn down new business. Management again decided that they had to do something about machine scheduling, so again they decided to purchase a scheduling package. Sue Barkley remembers:

> This time things went better. Nancy Shaw and I got more people involved in the decision on what package to buy. This vendor provided some in-depth training to our MIS people, and vendor people came down here for 2 weeks to help us load the data and get the production scheduling module working. Again, we found that the manual was full of errors and that the vendor people did not fully understand the logic that the system was using. But we got the system up and working and taught the production scheduling people how to use it.
>
> The problem was that whenever we had to expedite something—give it top priority because it had to be shipped quickly—the schedule had to be regenerated, and that took 2 hours. Then we had to take the schedule for each machine and examine it to see what the impact on its schedule was and change what it was going to do. Because we were always expediting something, we were constantly churning.
>
> After about a month the production scheduler came to me and said, "I'm not getting anything done. It takes me 2 hours to regenerate a schedule. I look at it and I then have to change five or six machines because of what the system did. Then it takes me 2 more hours to generate a new schedule and I have to change another five machines, and I have to go through the cycle again. It's just a continuous process of change, change, change!"
>
> We tried for another month to make the system work for us, but we were in such bad shape with our capacity that we just couldn't take the time to try to cope with the system anymore. So we abandoned it and went back to our Lotus spreadsheet. The $150,000 that we had spent for that system was down the drain!

The Present MIS Department

In 1994 Shaw left and BMC hired Don Collins to replace her as MIS manager. Collins had 20 years of experience as a lead systems analyst with a large manufacturer and broad experience with manufacturing systems. In 1996, Collins has a programming staff of four. The 1996 capital budget for hardware, software, and other information technology items was about $200,000. The MIS expense budget for payroll, supplies, and education was about $350,000.

The MIS department is using a development tool called Cyber Query Cyber Screen (CQCS) from Cyber Science, but Collins is giving some thought to what BMC's development environment of the future should be. The Data General MV computer is becoming obsolete and is reaching capacity, so BMC will have to obtain additional capacity soon.

In order to plan a production schedule you need to know what you have in inventory, so the MIS group has created systems to track raw-material, in-process, and finished-goods inventories. MIS has also developed a minicomputer system that accepts EDI orders from customers and allows the customer service group to create a shipping schedule on the computer. Collins believes that within 2 more years the MIS group can build and install a set of manufacturing systems that will satisfy BMC's basic needs and provide quite satisfactory EDI service to customers.

This success in building new systems opened BMC managers' eyes to the possibilities for using the computer, and they have generated so many requests for new systems that an MIS steering committee has been established to approve projects and set systems development priorities. The members of the MIS steering committee are President Kyle Baxter, Controller Lou Wilcox, Sue Barkley, and Don Collins.

The New Proposal

In late 1996 Lucas Moore, vice president of manufacturing, suggested that BMC purchase and install an integrated package of manufacturing software sold by Effective Management Systems, Inc. (EMS). Moore had worked as an engineer with the company for 7 years and then took a leave for 2 years to get an MBA. The vice president of manufacturing retired soon after Moore returned, and Moore was promoted to that management position.

Moore supports the proposal that BMC install the EMS Time Critical Manufacturing package consisting of eight modules: shop floor control, EDI integration, inventory management, factory data collection, standard routings, labor collection, engineered product configurator, and general ledger. The purchase price of this software package is $220,000, including documentation, training by EMS, and consulting help during installation of the software. The cost of a software maintenance contract is $55,000 a year, and EMS will make limited changes requested by BMC at a cost of $60 per hour.

The EMS software will run on several minicomputers, including BMC's Data General MV. However, additional computer capacity will be needed whether BMC purchases the EMS package or builds its own manufacturing systems.

Moore's Views

Moore is relatively new to the manufacturing area, having taken over that area about a year ago, and was not involved in the past attempts to purchase scheduling software. Moore explained to Baxter that BMC should purchase the EMS package for the following reasons:

We are still fudging our EDI and still scheduling with a Lotus spreadsheet. The entire industry has passed us by in our use of the computer in manufacturing and we are in danger of losing our reputation as a world-class parts manufacturer. Both my MBA studies and our experience with the new inventory systems that Don has installed have convinced me that computer systems can significantly enhance our efficiency and improve our service to our customers, but we can't wait another 2 years to complete home-grown manufacturing systems that will still need to be upgraded before they are really first class.

I have had extensive discussions with EMS manufacturing specialists, read their literature, and seen the proposed systems demonstrated, and am convinced that the proposed system will do everything that we will ever want to do. EMS has assured me that there will be no problem integrating these manufacturing modules with our existing financial systems, and that we can be up and running with the entire system in 6 months.

"Given that our MIS group is doing a good job developing new systems," Baxter asked, "why should we purchase the EMS package rather than build manufacturing systems in-house?" Moore's reply was:

The time and cost differences between purchasing and building are too significant to ignore: 6 months to install this advanced system versus 2 years to build our own basic system, and a firm $220,000 to purchase this system versus over $400,000 to build our own. These costs do not include new hardware, but we will need to increase our capacity whether we purchase or build our new systems.

Furthermore, we will get a high-quality state-of-the-art system instead of a simple "first try" system. EMS has sold this system to hundreds of manufacturers, and thus has been able to spend much more time and money developing it than we could possibly afford. EMS has a large staff of more creative and sophisticated programmers than we can get, and EMS has gone through several cycles of improvement of this system based upon the experience of hundreds of users of the earlier versions of the system.

It is true that the EMS system will not always do things the way we currently do them. But is the way we do them better than the way that is based on the experience of hundreds of manufacturers? We are always making changes in how we do things, so it will not be difficult for us to make some changes to conform to this new software, and I expect that these changes will improve our operations.

"We have not been successful in two tries to use purchased software packages in the manufacturing area," Baxter noted. "What makes you think that we would be successful this time?" Moore replied:

There are a number of important differences this time. First, in the past there was little ownership of the new system by the factory people, but this time I am the champion of the new system and my people will make it work. Second, in the past the conversion strategy was flawed—BMC tried to install scheduling without having inventory data under control, but this time we will go at it a module at a time in the sequence that EMS has been very successful with in many previous installations. Third, during the previous attempts we were pushing capacity and no scheduling system was going to work when we were having to expedite everything, but today capacity is not a major problem and things are reasonably calm in our factory so we can devote our energy to making the new system successful.

Collins' Views

Baxter also talked with Collins, who argued that BMC should continue its process of building the manufacturing systems that it needed. He estimated that the needed systems could be completed in about 2 years at a cost of around $420,000—$220,000 for outside help (including training his people in new development tools) and $200,000 in internal costs.

When Baxter asked Collins why BMC should not purchase the EMS software, Collins replied:

First, the EMS software is far more complicated than we need. For most general manufacturers each part may require six operations on six different types of machines, and each part has a routing that is different than other parts. Then several parts may be assembled into a subassembly, so you have two- or three-level bills of material. We typically take a coil of steel, stamp out the part, clean it, box it, and ship it out, so both our routings and our bills of material are very simple, as is our production process. The EMS system is designed for much more complex manufacturing.

Second, we have had little or no experience with computerized production systems. Does it make sense for us to try to jump to a very complex and sophisticated system like the EMS proposal? Lucas has a very superficial understanding of this software package, and he doesn't know any of the details of how it will work. Therefore, he has no idea of the difficulties that his people will run into in adapting to this complex package. It will require them to do many tasks that they have never done, or even considered doing. And they don't need this complexity. Wouldn't it be better to build our own systems that correspond to where we are on the learning curve and plan to upgrade them as we progress in our understanding of our systems needs?

Third, it is likely that the system does not fit the way we are running the business. Do we change the system or do we change how we run our business? We probably can't change a purchased system, so we would have to change the way we run the business. Do we really want to do this?

Fourth, we are constantly changing our manufacturing facilities and processes, and they may be unique to our business. If you purchase a package you are at the mercy of the vendor to make changes in it. He may or may not make the changes that you want, and in fact he may make some changes that you do not want. If you do not expect the system to change and it is a common system, you probably should purchase it. For example, one general ledger system is just like any other, and they haven't changed in 20 years, so you should purchase this application. But we are continually changing things out in the shop, and if we build our own systems we can change them when we need to.

Finally, we have demonstrated that we can build and successfully install our own systems, but our record with purchasing and installing manufacturing systems is dismal. The EMS proposal may fulfill our needs, but then again it may not. We failed twice in the past because the system we purchased did not fit our needs. Why take that chance again?

"You seem very concerned that the EMS system might not suit our needs or that our needs might change," Baxter replied. "Could we modify this system if it does not suit our needs?" Collins said:

Because we will not have a source-code version of the software, it will not be feasible for our programmers to modify the functionality of this system. However, we can write interface software to change the form of the system's input and output.

When Baxter noted the cost and time differences between purchasing and building the system as estimated by Moore, Collins replied:

The figures Lucas quotes are very misleading. The purchase price is but a part of the total cost of buying, installing, and maintaining the software. To be sure you are choosing software that truly meets your needs, you must put a substantial effort into defining your needs and evaluating each candidate package against those needs. One of the major weaknesses of the present proposal is that this process of defining needs and evaluating possible packages has been completely ignored. In my opinion we must go through this process before buying any packaged software, and this will affect both the proposed cost and how long it will take to install the system.

Another cost of purchasing a system is the cost of modifying your existing systems so that they can feed data to or receive data from the purchased package. If the systems that must be interfaced with the purchased systems are also purchased systems that you cannot modify, you may have to create additional systems to translate from one packaged system to the other packaged system. In addition there will be costs of training the users, data conversion, and the changeover to the new system. A good rule of thumb for the total cost of installing a purchased package would be twice the purchase price of the software, which in this case would be $440,000. I doubt that we could do it for any less, and that compares with about $420,000 to build our own systems, which includes all the costs involved, such as training, conversion, and defining the needs of our manufacturing people.

It will take at least a year to properly evaluate and install a purchased system. This is less than the 2 years we will need to complete our own system, but we will be installing and using components of the new system as we complete them, so the time advantage is not that great.

When asked what it would take to do a more complete evaluation of the proposal to purchase the EMS system, Collins replied:

We would need to spend about 6 months studying our manufacturing area to determine what we are doing now and what the new systems should do. Then we would take some time to explore the many packages that are available, and winnow them down to the three or four most suitable. Then we would invite the chosen vendors to submit proposals so we could study and evaluate each of these proposals in detail and pick the best one. Meantime, we would prepare a proposal for building the new system that would describe the proposed system in detail and include a plan for its development including schedules of both time and dollars. Finally, we would compare the best proposal with the plan for building the system ourselves and decide which to do. That would take at least a year and cost between $50,000 and $90,000.

Decision Time

After his discussions with Moore and Collins, Baxter sat down with his sister, Sue Barkley, to discuss what to do about Moore's proposal. "Sue," Baxter began, "you were able to get the second manufacturing software system we bought up and running, but conditions in the shop were so chaotic that we abandoned trying to use it. Why don't we go back and try it again?" Sue replied:

We recently considered trying again to use this system, but the special computer we bought to run it died and the software vendor has gone out of business, so we were out of luck.

"Lucas claims that BMC is losing its reputation as a world-class parts manufacturer because its systems are inadequate, and therefore BMC must purchase a system without delay," Baxter said. "Do you believe that it is critical that we get these new systems immediately?" Sue thought a while before replying:

I don't think that our customers care about our systems as long as we provide high-quality products at a good price and deliver them when they are needed, which we are doing. From their perspective, we are already interacting with them via EDI, so that is a problem for us rather than for them. It would be great to have the proposed systems as soon as possible, but we have been getting along without them for a long time.

"Well, Sue," Baxter said, "I still don't know what we should do. What do you think?"

CASE STUDY III-5

ERP Purchase Decision at Benton Manufacturing Company, Inc.

Benton Manufacturing Company, Inc., is a U.S. manufacturer of a varied line of consumer durables. Although its stock is publicly traded, a single family holds a controlling interest in the company. In 1998 Benton had net sales of almost $1 billion and an operating profit of about $180 million.

Benton's 5,200 employees operate seven factories and 57 distribution centers located throughout North America. In the past few years Benton has acquired several companies, and two of Benton's factories have been added as the result of acquisitions that broadened Benton's product line. Benton's products are sold through thousands of independent dealers who may sell both Benton's and competitors' products.

Benton is the leader in its industry with its products claiming some 40 percent of the market. However, industry demand is growing very slowly while the structure of the industry is undergoing rapid change as formerly independent dealerships are being acquired by large chains. This consolidation is changing the power relationships between Benton and its dealers and causing Benton's traditional profit margins to erode.[1] Benton has responded to this pressure by pursuing a Continuous-Improvement strategy that so far has increased productivity more than 25 percent, reduced in-process inventory 30 percent, freed up thousands of square feet of factory space, and reduced new product development cycle times.

Benton has a history of continuous growth in sales and profits. In order to continue this growth in today's increasingly competitive environment, Benton management has focused on growth through the following strategies: (1) customer-driven new product development, (2) the acquisition of new businesses that complement existing ones, (3) international expansion, and (4) emphasis on the Continuous-Improvement approach.

[1]This is a disguised case. Because of confidentiality issues further details about Benton's products or its industry cannot be disclosed.

Enterprise Resource Planning Systems

As one response to growing competitive pressure, Benton management is considering acquiring an Enterprise Resource Planning (ERP) system. An ERP system is a comprehensive set of software modules that integrate a company's financial, human resources, operations and logistics, and sales and marketing information systems, storing the data for all these systems in a central database so that data are entered only once and the results of each transaction flow through the system without human intervention. An ERP system can replace many separate poorly integrated computer applications systems that a company has purchased or developed over the years. During the 1990s the use of purchased ERP packages exploded among Fortune 500 companies, making the leading vendor, Germany's SAP, the fastest-growing software company in the world.

Thomas H. Davenport[2] explains why ERP systems—sometimes called Enterprise Systems (ES)—are so popular:

> An ES streamlines a company's data flows and provides management with direct access to a wealth of real-time operating information. For many companies, these benefits have translated into dramatic gains in productivity and speed.
>
> Autodesk, a leading maker of computer-aided design software, used to take an average of 2 weeks to deliver an order to a customer. Now, having installed an ES, it ships 98 percent of its orders within 24 hours. IBM's Storage Systems division reduced the time required to reprice all of its products from 5 days to 5 minutes, the time to ship a replacement part from 22 days to 3 days, and the time to complete a credit check from 20 minutes to 3 seconds. Fujitsu Microelectronics reduced the cycle time for filling orders from 18 days to a day and a half and cut the time required to close its financial books from 8 days to 4 days.

[2]Thomas H. Davenport, "Putting the enterprise into the enterprise system," *Harvard Business Review*, July–August, 1998, pp. 123–4.

Along with the successes, however, there have been a number of resounding failures in attempts to utilize ERP systems. Davenport[3] reports on problems with enterprise systems:

> The growing number of horror stories about failed or out-of-control projects should certainly give managers pause. FoxMeyer Drug argues that its system helped drive it into bankruptcy. Mobile Europe spent hundreds of millions of dollars on its system only to abandon it when its merger partner objected. Dell Computer found that its system would not fit its new, decentralized management model. Applied Materials gave up on its system when it found itself overwhelmed by the organizational changes involved. Dow Chemical spent 7 years and close to half a billion dollars implementing a mainframe-based enterprise system; now it has decided to start over again on a client/server version.
>
> Some of the blame for such debacles lies with the enormous technical challenges of rolling out enterprise systems–these systems are profoundly complex pieces of software, and installing them requires large investments of money, time, and expertise. But the technical challenges, however great, are not the main reason enterprise systems fail. The biggest problems are business problems. Companies fail to reconcile the technological imperatives of the enterprise system with the business needs of the enterprise itself.
>
> An enterprise system, by its very nature, imposes its own logic on a company's strategy, organization, and culture. It pushes a company toward full integration even when a certain degree of business-unit segregation may be in its best interests. And it pushes a company toward generic processes even when customized processes may be a source of competitive advantage. If a company rushes to install an enterprise system without first having a clear understanding of the business implications, the dream of integration can quickly turn into a nightmare.

The ERP Study

Aware of the growing use of ERP systems and concerned that Benton might be missing an important development, Benton President and CEO Walter S. McHenry has formed a two-person team, composed of Adam T. Meyer and Jerry L. Cook, to investigate whether or not Benton should purchase such a system. Meyer is a senior systems analyst who has been a star with the Benton IS department for 15 years and has led many successful projects. Starting in engineering 12 years ago, Cook has worked in several areas throughout the company, including production, finance, and market research. Although not an IT professional, Cook is quite comfortable with computer technology and has led the introduction of CAD and LANs into engineering. McHenry told Cook and Meyer:

> ERP seems to be the direction that our industry is going, and we probably need one too. However, I don't know the specifics of what an ERP system involves or what it might bring to the company, so I want you to do a quick study and determine whether ERP is for us, and if so how we should approach it.

The study team found that there are four major ERP software vendors they might consider: SAP, J.D. Edwards, Oracle, and PeopleSoft. Each of these vendors is financially stable, supports global companies, has a full line of highly integrated modules, and is a leader in R & D. There are a number of "Tier 2" vendors, but Cook and Meyer believe that none of them is suitable for a long-term partnership.

After a great deal of study, attending a number of conferences, and talking with several people from companies that are using ERP systems, the study team is convinced that Benton should replace its legacy "back office" systems with an ERP system. Meyer explains:

> We believe that information technology is crucial to survival in today's competitive environment. Our present systems are growing old and hard to maintain, and will have to be replaced in the next few years. ERP systems have much more functionality and much better integration than our internal IT staff can possibly provide, so we have to use them just to keep up with our competitors who are starting to install them.
>
> Furthermore, Benton management has established strategic business plans that cannot be realized without an ERP system. These plans include the following emphases that cannot be fully supported by our present information systems:
>
> - International expansion
> - Mergers and acquisitions
> - Use of IT as a strategic weapon
> - Integration with suppliers and customers
> - Reduction of operational costs
> - Product line expansion
> - Process standardization across different units of the company

Adopting an ERP system will be a monumental undertaking for Benton. According to Cook:

> An ERP system is not just a huge infusion of software and technology. We have learned that this is not just an IT project. Rather, it will require wholehearted commitment from all departments. They have to be willing to change their work processes to conform to those dictated by the ERP–the software is almost an afterthought. Benton has never faced change of this magnitude!

Reactions to the ERP Proposal

Cook and Meyer know that there is strong support for an ERP system from IT management, and they are confident that, although President McHenry does not seem to want to get personally involved, he is supportive of an ERP system. To make sure that McHenry understands the issues involved in adopting an ERP, Cook and Meyer have urged him to visit with a friend of his who is the CEO of a company that installed an ERP 2 years ago and is reported to be very pleased with the results.

---

[3] *Ibid.*, pp. 122–3.

There is also a great deal of support for an ERP system from operating-level management. But the reaction of VP-level management (see the partial organization chart in Exhibit 1) is mixed. According to Cook:

> Contrary to what Benton management believed in past years, we're going to have to change. Although the structure of our industry is changing, our dealers are changing, and the economy is changing, the need for us to change is not universally recognized in the company management. We have some managers whose view is more defensive and who are less willing to embrace change.

Benton's present human resources information systems are old and inadequate. Susan R. Hamilton, human resources vice president, is an enthusiastic supporter of an ERP system. Hamilton says:

> I have talked with human resources managers who have ERP systems from several different vendors, and they are all enthusiastic about their systems. I know that an ERP system will enable us to increase productivity, serve the needs of our employees much better, and significantly improve the management of our human resources at Benton. Although I realize that converting to such a system will be a long and difficult process, I can't wait to get started.

Tracy C. Scott, vice president for distribution, has 7 years' experience with Benton and is one of the few top managers that have management experience outside the company. Scott advocates an ERP system:

> Our present computer systems work well at the distribution centers, but they only provide local information—I can't get a quick picture of the entire distribution system. Better information would enable us to significantly reduce our finished goods inventory and at the same time provide better service to our customers. The integration of sales, production, and inventory information that an ERP system provides would enable me to do a much better job of managing my department.

Pat L. Miller, vice president for manufacturing, joined Benton as an engineer 20 years ago and worked in many positions in the manufacturing area prior to becoming a vice president four years ago. Miller is concerned about the possible impact of an ERP system on the manufacturing area:

> For the past several years we have been concentrating on lean manufacturing through the Continuous-Improvement approach, and have increased productivity over 25 percent and reduced inventory by 30 percent in our factories. The Continuous-Improvement approach avoids going for the "home run." Rather, it concentrates on producing many relatively small improvements, each of which can be quickly and easily implemented. It seems to me that an ERP project costing over $30 million is the antithesis of our Continuous-Improvement approach that has been so successful. First, it is one huge step, not a progression of small improvements. Also, in the ERP approach you must use the process dictated by the designer of the ERP system, and that is inflexible. How can you do Continuous Improvement?
>
> I have another concern. We have a unique culture here at Benton that, in my opinion, is responsible for the success we

EXHIBIT 1
Partial Benton Organization Chart

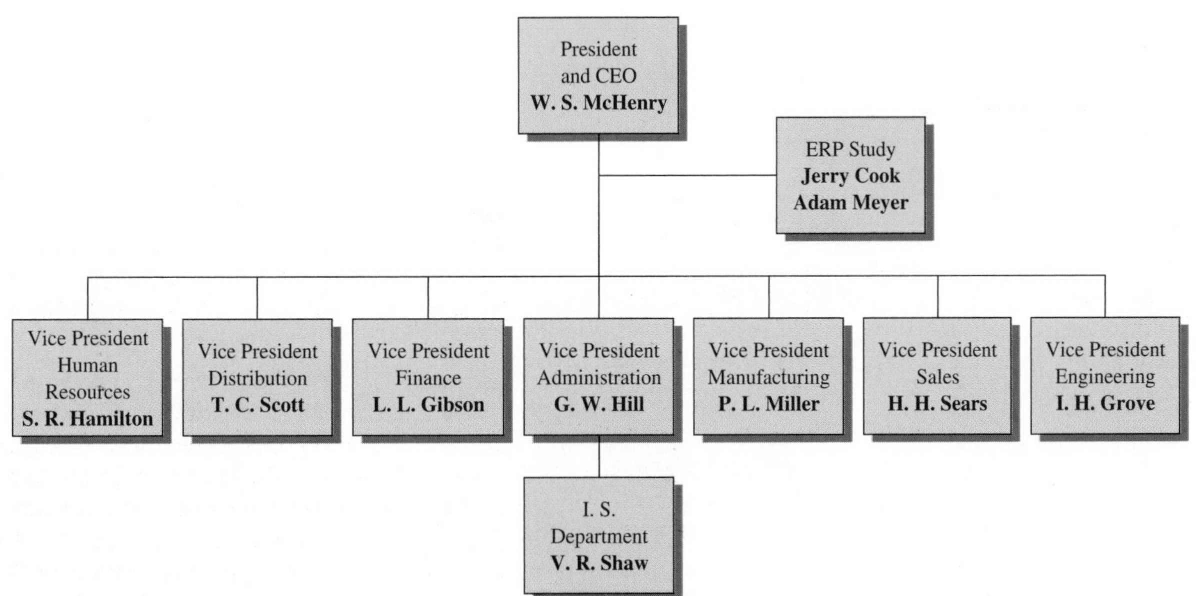

have enjoyed. I have read that installing an ERP system may well force you to change your culture to be more compatible with the ERP system. That sends shivers down my back!

Lee L. Gibson has been vice president for finance for 10 years. Until about 3 years ago the information systems department reported to Gibson. Gibson, who is responsible for financial analysis of Benton's investments, asserts:

> The IS department has developed excellent financial systems for me that are quite adequate for our needs, so I see no major need for an ERP system as far as the finance department is concerned.
>
> Also, I am very concerned about the high cost of an ERP implementation and about whether the bottom-line return from such a system would justify this huge expense. We have always subjected our IT investments to a rigorous cost/benefit analysis, and I don't see any reason why we should treat an ERP system any differently. In my view, the larger the investment the more important it is that it be carefully justified, and an ERP system would cost many times as much as the largest IT system we have ever developed.

Cost/Benefit Analysis

Meyer shudders at the thought of trying to use cost/benefit analysis to justify an ERP system:

> The costs of an ERP system are readily apparent up front, but many of the benefits are results of more complete and timely information that enable you to better manage the enterprise. These intangible benefits do occur, but they are not easy to identify and quantify beforehand.
>
> At conferences we talked with a number of people that are delighted with the results of their ERP systems, and we always asked how they cost justified the system. We got a lot of strange looks and blank stares. The identifiable cost reductions will seldom justify the cost of an ERP system, but people are installing them because they realize that they have to in order to compete in the future. And many companies are beginning to get bottomline results that they ascribe to their ERP investments.

Gibson's concern prompted Cook and Meyer to develop the analysis presented in Exhibits 2 and 3. This analysis is based on a study they obtained that reported the experience of over 60 firms that have successfully installed ERP systems and used them for at least 3 years. Using the figures from this study, the team estimates that it will cost Benton some $34 million to install an ERP system and $750,000 a year for a maintenance contract. The benefits are estimated to be about $11.593 million a year after installation is complete. Over a 7-year period this produces an Internal Rate of Return of 20 percent and a Net Present Value (at a 20 percent discount rate) of just over $156,000, which just barely meets Benton's criteria for such investments.

Cook explains how the yearly benefits were developed, as shown in Exhibit 2:

> In each area of benefits (inventory, centralized operations, etc.), the table shows the industry low and high as a percent of the Base Amount column, which contains the current cost to Benton of the category in each line, except for the last line where it contains Benton's total revenue. The three Estimated Benefits columns are calculated as follows: The Low $ column is the Base Cost times the Low percent; the High $ is the Base Cost times the High percent; and, the Medium $ is the average of the High $ and Low $ columns.

EXHIBIT 2

Industry-Based Annual Benefits of Benton's ERP

	Industry Low	Industry High	Base Amount	Estimated Benefits Low $	Medium $	High $	Benton Projected
Inventory	10%	40%	$7,800	$780	$1,950	$3,150	$780
Centralized Operations	15%	50%	$3,000	$450	$975	$1,500	$450
Procurement	10%	20%	$1,750	$175	$263	$350	$263
Logistics	5%	10%	$68,000	$3,400	$5,100	$6,800	$5,100
Incremental Revenue	1%	5%	$1,000,000	$5,000	$15,000	$25,000	$5,000
						Total Projected Yearly Benefits	$11,593

Note: Dollar figures are in thousands.

For each row we considered Benton's situation and chose a Low $ or Medium $ figure depending on our judgement, trying to be conservative. In the Inventory row we chose the Low $ column because we had already reduced inventory by 30 percent. In the Centralized Operations row we chose the Low $ figure because we think we are already pretty lean. And in the Incremental Revenue row we chose the Low $ figure because we are already growing revenues by 6 to 7 percent, and doubt that we will be able to do much better than that given the industry conditions. Incidentally, in that line we took only 50 percent of the increased revenue as the benefit because labor and materials cost is half the revenue. We think that the $11,593,000 estimate of total yearly benefits is conservative.

Meyer explains Exhibit 3:

We based our estimate of total cost of converting to an ERP on the concept of "cost per seat." The industry "cost per seat" ranges from $15,000 to $35,000, which includes hardware, networks, software, consulting, conversion, customization, and the cost of our people who work on the project. Because we expect to have to do a good amount of reengineering and will need a lot of help from outside consultants, we took $25,000 per seat and multiplied by the number of PCs we expect to have on the system (1360) to get the $34 million cost estimate. We also included $750,000 a year for a maintenance contract. We used judgement to spread both the costs and the benefits over the 7 years.

Recommendation

Although they understand that there are legitimate concerns about the cost of an ERP and that there will be many difficulties to be overcome to install an ERP, Cook and Meyer are convinced that Benton should acquire an ERP system as quickly as possible. They are aware that this proposal has generated controversy, but the team believes that most of Benton's top management is supportive of installing an ERP system. To force a decision on this matter the team has proposed to President McHenry that Benton begin the process of acquiring an ERP by employing a nationally known consulting firm to help select an ERP system vendor and assist in the process of implementation of the system. Because the recommended consulting firm has worked with each of the four major ERP vendors, it should be prepared to help select and install the ERP system that best suits Benton's needs.

EXHIBIT 3
Cost/Benefit Analysis for Benton ERP

	Year 2001	Year 2002	Year 2003	Year 2004	Year 2005	Year 2006	Year 2007
Costs	20,000,000	10,000,000	4,000,000	750,000	750,000	750,000	750,000
Benefits		6,000,000	9,800,000	11,593,000	11,593,000	11,593,000	11,593,000
Net Benefits	–20,000,000	–4,000,000	5,800,000	10,843,000	10,843,000	10,843,000	10,843,000

IRR = 20%
NPV @ 20% = $156,046.83

CASE STUDY III-6

NAVAL SURFACE WARFARE CENTER, CRANE DIVISION: IMPLEMENTING BUSINESS PROCESS REENGINEERING RECOMMENDATIONS

With less than 5 hours of sleep and after a long, hectic day, Bob Matthews was tired. He had not been getting much sleep the last 2 weeks. He wondered, while waiting outside his boss's office, how the business and process reengineering (BPR) project that he was managing would make it through this current rough spot.

He also wondered whether he would be able to see any of his son's baseball game tonight. It was already the last week of May 1999, and there was only one home game left. This was Joey's senior year at Loogootee High School, and Bob hated to miss the last game of the season. It was past 5 P.M. now and he was hoping to make the first pitch at 6 P.M.

However, he and his boss, Deputy Executive Director Bill Kaiser, were continuing a discussion they had started earlier before Kaiser had been called away to a meeting with the commander of the base. All eight of Matthews' BPR teams were running into resistance in planning for implementation. In particular, the implementation plan recommended by the financial management BPR team looked like it was stalled indefinitely.

The team was headed by Cheryl Miller and had the most support of any of the teams throughout its As-Is phase (see Chapter 9 for a discussion of As-Is and To-Be models). They, along with the other seven BPR teams, had even won the union's support for how employee transitions would be handled. But now that the financial management BPR team was ready to implement its recommendations, the leaders of Crane's directorates (the equivalent of business units in the private sector), who served on the BPR steering committee, were withholding their approval.

The financial management BPR team's process change recommendations would potentially save Crane nearly 50 percent compared to the current way of conducting certain processes. The team had recommended the development of some new information systems to automate some currently manual processes, as well as some minor organizational changes. In talking with the information systems project leader, Matthews had learned of his concern over both gaining cooperation in the systems design phase and achieving actual use of the new systems, given all the resistance.

The team also knew that there were bigger gains to be had. The average cost of financial management in the private sector was 1 to 1.5 percent of sales. Because Crane spent almost 3 percent of revenue on its financial management processes, the financial management BPR team felt there were even more significant savings to be found. To reap these more significant savings, the team had recommended establishing some common business rules across the directorates. Yet the leaders of the directorates had rejected these ideas as well.

"Hope you weren't waiting long," Bill Kaiser said, as he put his briefcase under his desk and flung his suitcoat over his chair.

"No. I was running late myself," Matthews replied. "Cheryl had stopped by my office to ask about what to do next."

"What did you tell her?" Kaiser asked.

"I told her to continue preparing for implementation," Matthews said.

"Good," Kaiser responded. "The directors may be resisting, but we have to move forward. We have a very high profile with the Navy on this project and everyone's watching, so stopping is not an option."

"No. But without the directors' support, it will be impossible for the BPR effort in financial management to succeed," Matthews said.

"We'll need to map out a strategy to make sure that doesn't happen," Kaiser said. "I went ahead and ordered dinner. It should be here in a half hour."

Matthews looked at his watch. He hoped he would catch at least the last inning or two.

Background

In May 1999, Crane was a major acquisition and support division of the Naval Surface Warfare Center, and employed about 3,200 people in 152 populated buildings over almost 100 square miles in southwestern Indiana. Beginning as a munitions production

 This case study was written as a basis for class discussion of the elements of business process reengineering and the issues involved in implementation.

and storage facility, Crane had evolved into primarily an engineering and technical support facility that included ordnance testing and evaluation, design, development, and procurement.

Crane handled diverse and highly technical product lines, including:

- **Electronic warfare** Crane's units provided comprehensive engineering, logistics, and maintenance/repair support for countermeasures systems for the Navy, Marine Corps, and Air Force.
- **Chemical/biological detection** The people at Crane built equipment and provided training and program management, technical support, alteration, installation support, and in-service engineering agent support.
- **Microwave** Crane's departments provided application engineering and product support to help sustain the microwave industry.
- **Microelectronics** The Crane facility had some of the most comprehensive failure analysis and material analysis facilities in the world.
- **Small arms** Crane personnel provided design, development, acquisition, testing, and evaluation of small arms, weapons, night vision devices, laser range finders, laser markers, and individual combat equipment in support of special operations forces.
- **Commercial technologies** Crane executives worked with business and industry leaders to apply commercial products to weapons systems.

Crane's expense budget for FY 1999 was $750 million, including payments to subcontractors. The employee payroll was about $300 million of the total.

Most of Crane's 3,200 employees worked in one of three functions: (1) munitions production and surveillance, (2) procurement of weapons, or (3) adapting commercial products for use in a military environment. There were about 450 employees involved in the munitions function. The procurement function (e.g., development of specifications, testing, evaluation, and qualification of vendors) was done for field weapons systems and employed about 800 people. The third major function, working with private business and industry to adapt commercial products for military use, employed about 700 Crane people. The remaining 1,150 employees were support (about 300) or administrative personnel (about 850).

Command Structure (Organization)

In May 1999, Crane's leadership reported to the Naval Surface Warfare Center (NSWC) which in turn reported to the Naval Sea Systems Command (NAVSEA) and then to the Chief of Naval Operations (CNO). The Chief of Naval Operations served on the Joint Chiefs of Staff for the United States Department of Defense.

NAVSEA was the largest of the Navy's five systems commands. NAVSEA engineered, built, and supported America's fleet of ships and combat systems. The NAVSEA commander, Vice Admiral George P. Nanos, reported to the CNO. As part of the NSWC, Crane's leadership reported to the NSWC commander, Rear Admiral Kathleen K. Paige, and Ira Blatstein, NSWC executive director.

At the Crane facility, there were three mission critical (line) directorates and five support directorates. (See Exhibit 1.) Each directorate was divided into departments and then branches.

The leadership of the BPR project was assigned to four people. A summary of their backgrounds follows:

Captain William E. Shotts, USN Captain Shotts was appointed commander of Crane in June 1997. (Senior Navy personnel typically rotated through this position every 3 years.) He graduated from the Naval Academy and was commissioned in 1969. Shotts served on submarines for about 10 years and then held various line management positions leading to staff leadership positions prior to coming to Crane.

Stephen P. Gootee Gootee was selected as executive director in December 1995. He previously served his entire career at the Naval Air Warfare Center, Indianapolis, working his way up the chain of command (as program manager and then branch, division, department, and directorate head). Gootee received B.A. and B.S. degrees in aerospace engineering from the University of Notre Dame. He was scheduled to retire in June 1999.

William A. Kaiser He was appointed by Gootee to the deputy executive director position at Crane in 1996. Kaiser had been employed at Crane his entire career, performing in a variety of different line and staff positions. Most recently, Kaiser served as head of the microwave systems directorate.

Robert J. Matthews Matthews was appointed as manager of the business and process reengineering project in March 1998. He had more than 25 years experience as a project manager at Crane. Previously, he led the base realignment and closure and competitive analysis activities.

The Road to Business Process Reengineering

When Steve Gootee first arrived at Crane in 1995, he and the top management at Crane attended a management seminar at Indiana University in Bloomington. Bill Kaiser, deputy executive director, said, "We realized during the program that we didn't

EXHIBIT 1
Organization Chart
Naval Surface Warfare Center, Crane Division

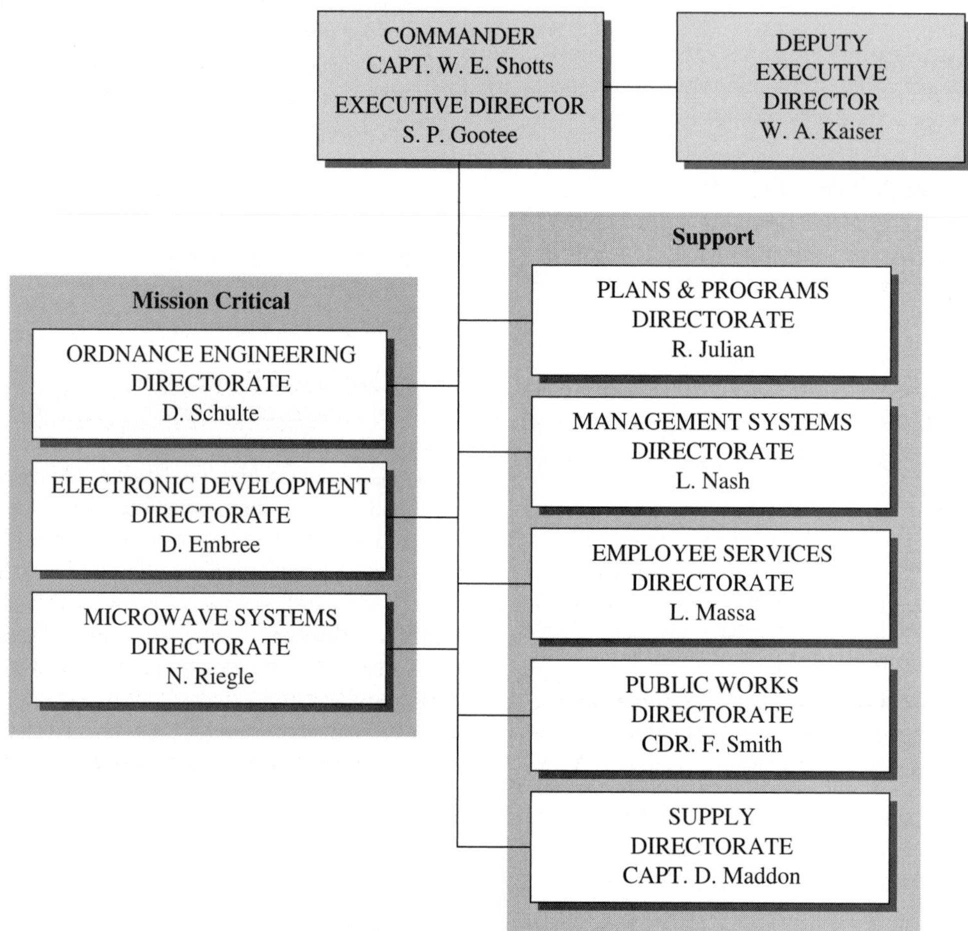

fully understand how our organization actually operated. We found that Crane lacked an overall identity. It was more like an industrial park, a conglomeration of businesses all located at the same place, but with little relationship to each other."

He added, "We realized we needed to do something to become more cohesive, to eliminate redundant operations, and to establish a strong identity. There were signs that Crane might be selected if there was another round of base closings. Our future survival depended on how efficiently we operated and how well we communicated our value to senior leadership in the Navy."

That seminar generated interest among Crane's senior management in identifying ways that the organization could become more efficient. The Navy used a process of competing for who would perform certain jobs like information systems and catering. This process was called A-76. It involved putting certain functions out for bid and allowing the private sector as well as the government to bid for operating that function. In the summer of 1997, Gootee talked with a senior staff member in the Secretary of the Navy's office. The executive informed Gootee that if Crane developed an alternative method to A-76, he would help secure support for it. The staff member cautioned, however, that any alternative would need to at least meet the 30 percent cost savings currently achieved by employing the A-76 process.

In the fall of 1997, Gootee circulated an article about process reengineering among those he thought would best be able to assess the idea for application at Crane: Bill Kaiser, the deputy executive director, and Bob Matthews, former project manager for both A-76 implementation and base realignment and closure projects. After several meetings, all three felt reengineering both the processes at Crane and the general way Crane "did business" was Crane's best hope for improving operations without cutting into the core strength of the base. They called the effort business and process reengineering (BPR). On December 20, 1997, Gootee hosted a teleconference to brief NAVSEA and NSWC staff members about BPR.

Gootee next briefed Captain Shotts on the idea and gained his approval of the BPR concept. Shotts then contacted Rear Admiral Paige, NSWC commander. After her conversation with Shotts, Paige presented the idea to the NAVSEA commander at the time, Vice Admiral Sterner, in an e-mail. His initial response was positive, "If they have a better mousetrap, I am ready to test it!" But he added a further constraint—that the implementation timeline would need to beat the time allotted for implementation of A-76.

By March 19, 1998, after Gootee and Shotts presented the idea to top leaders at NAVSEA, the commander of NAVSEA officially designated Crane as NAVSEA's pilot for BPR.

Simultaneously with gaining pilot site approval for BPR, Gootee initiated discussions with William L. Mason, the president of Local 1415 of the American Federation of Government Employees. Mason discussed the idea with his shop stewards and traveled to Washington, D.C., to present the idea at the national headquarters. Gootee and Mason signed a memorandum of agreement in October 1998.

In February of 1998, Gootee and Kaiser set a 2-year budget of $7.5 million for the BPR project. In March 1998, Kaiser recommended to Gootee that Bob Matthews be selected as the manager for the BPR project. Shortly after joining the group, Matthews selected core team members who committed to a full-time position on the team for at least 1 year. The core team reported to Bill Kaiser.

The Financial Management Team

With about 30 years of experience at Crane, Cheryl Miller had been the leader of a financial management team created earlier to look for ways to streamline the processes used to manage the financial function at Crane. Miller recalled:

> Everyone knew something was wrong with the financial management process. But no one had any data to back it up. We had just formed our team and come up with rudimentary definitions for the processes in two directorates when we joined the BPR effort in April 1998 and expanded our scope to include all of Crane. I have been through all kinds of efficiency improvement processes, but BPR is the best. It has structure and methodology and provides data for the guesses we've always had about what was broken. Implementation is tough, though.

Miller was appointed chair of the new financial management BPR team. Like all BPR teams, the financial management BPR team reported to Bob Matthews. In turn, Matthews reported to Bill Kaiser. For the BPR project, Kaiser reported to an executive steering board, made up of the eight Crane directors and the executive team. The executive team was composed of Shotts (commanding officer), Gootee (executive director), and Mason (union president). (See Exhibit 2 for the BPR organization chart.) BPR teams reported their findings to the executive steering board. The board provided oversight and guidance, reviewed and critiqued progress, acted as advocate for the BPR pilot project, and acted on recommendations.

The responsibility of the financial management BPR team was to identify and model the current financial processes, prioritize opportunities for improvement, gather and analyze data, and develop recommendations. To keep the team size manageable, Miller did not select a representative from each of the directorates.

> I wanted a group that was diverse, but not necessarily all-inclusive. I chose people who had hands-on responsibility—people who worked with the systems every day. Throughout the development of the As-Is baseline model, when we needed additional information about a specific process, we brought in detailed process experts, employees who were familiar with how that specific process actually worked. They described it and walked us through it.

The team was also supported by personnel from an outside consulting firm. Although Miller worked full-time as BPR team leader, team members committed to working about a third of the time on BPR issues. "A lot of team members were already overloaded with their current jobs so getting their supervisors to release them took a lot of effort," Miller said. "It usually took us about 2 weeks and a lot of negotiations by Matthews or Kaiser to get a person released to be on the team."

Building the As-Is Description

The development of the As-Is profile was achieved through the following five high-level steps:

1. **Define the financial processes.** The financial management BPR team modeled the financial management processes using Integrated Definition Language (IDEF), the Department of Defense's standard process modeling tool. The IDEF process model is a graphic display of business processes allowing different subprocesses to be modeled independently of each other and then integrated into the overall model. (See Exhibit 3 for an overview of the IDEF process.)

   IDEF models for the current processes in financial management were constructed by the financial management BPR team through a series of facilitated sessions with groups of employees involved in each process. "This is when we brought in the detailed process experts," Miller said. "By getting different user perspectives, we developed one common, detailed description of the business process."

EXHIBIT 2

Business and Process Reengineering Project Organization Chart Naval Surface Warfare Center, Crane Division

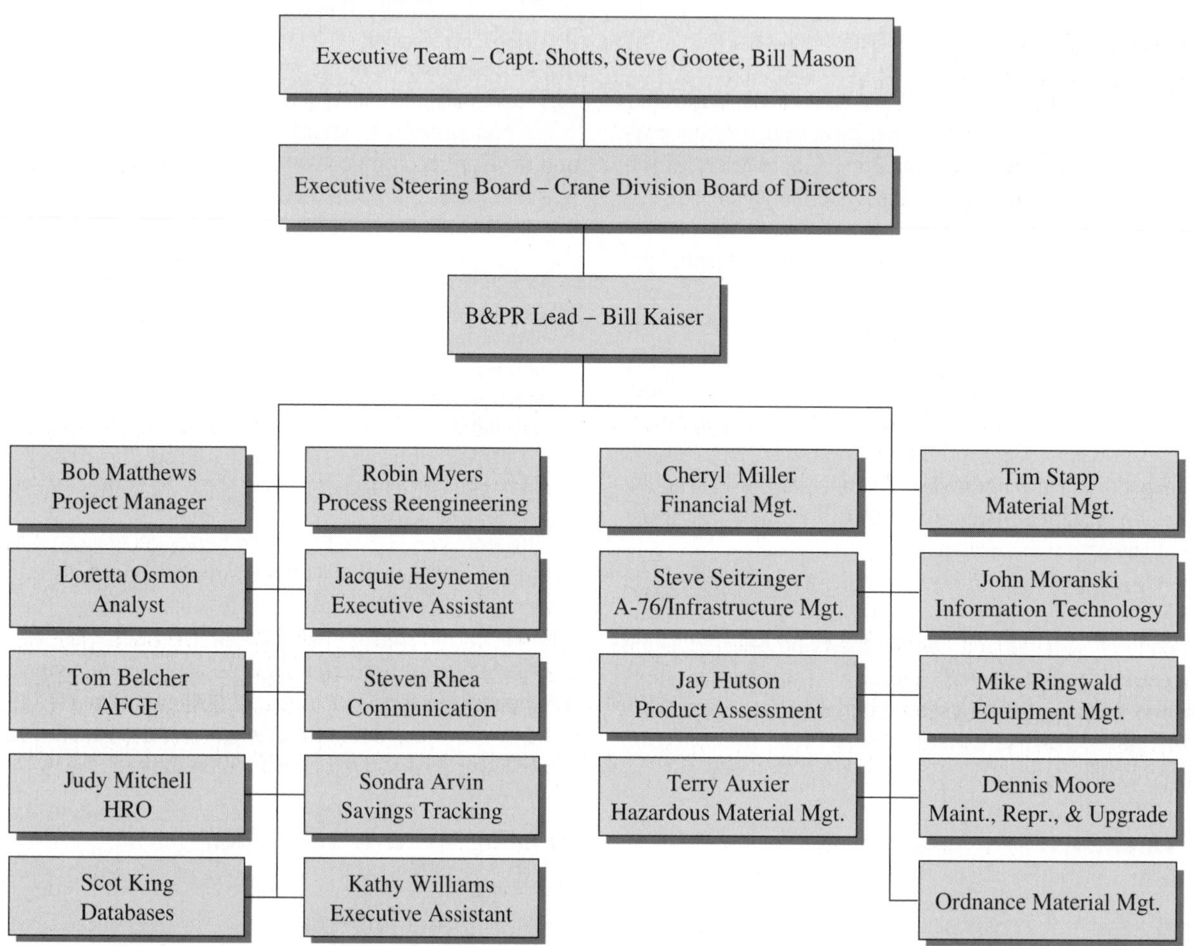

The As-Is modeling process for the financial management BPR team resulted in identifying six high-level work areas that constituted the financial management processes at Crane: workload planning, budgeting, funds administration, fiscal management, financial reporting, and financial analysis. Each high-level process contained three to four subprocesses. The list of all subprocesses is shown in Exhibit 4. The team next developed an overall model that linked together all the high-level work areas, showing how all financial management was carried out at Crane. In addition to the overall model, more detailed diagrams were developed for each subactivity.

Once the model for a process was complete, the team developed an organization-to-process matrix to map the processes into the organizational unit(s) responsible for executing each activity or subactivity. A process-to-information systems matrix was also developed to map the processes to the various information technology systems currently used in financial management at Crane.

2. **Select target processes** based on customer concerns, recognized opportunities for cost savings, and risk factors.

   The financial management BPR team used input from customer assessments and their own analysis to locate the best opportunities for gains in efficiency in order to identify which activities would be best for early reengineering. Based on the team's analysis of all the processes, four sub-subprocesses—validating/signing document, processing funding document, gathering data to monitor costs, and creating/generating reports to monitor costs—were identified as target areas for reengineering in the total financial management process.

EXHIBIT 3
Description of the IDEF Process
Naval Surface Warfare Center, Crane Division

Introduction to Process Modeling with IDEF0

The paradigm for IDEF Modeling is centered around the concept of Activity, which is an active component of a process—i.e., work. An IDEF process is represented by a collection of interrelated activities using graphic and natural language. Relationships between activities, the model, and the external environment are represented by arrows.

In an IDEF0 Model, Activities process Inputs into Outputs using Mechanisms according to the processing rules described in the Controls. This is often described with the acronym ICOM (Input, Control, Output, Mechanism).

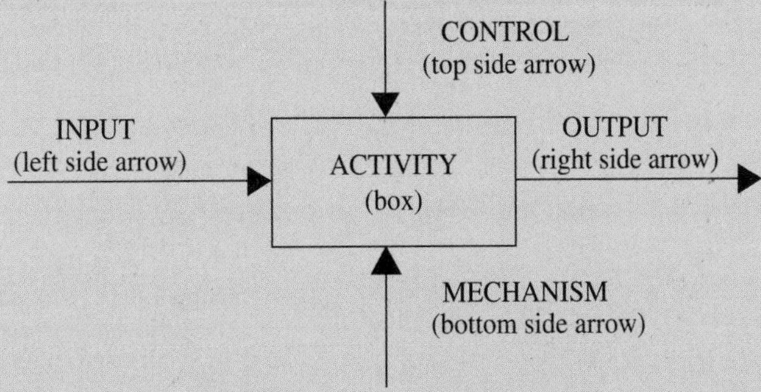

Purpose: This section explains the business reasons for why the model is constructed to help you stay focused.
Viewpoint: This section explains from whose perspective this model has been drawn.

	INPUT (I)	CONTROL (C)	ACTIVITY	MECHANISM (M)	OUTPUT (O)
Language	Describes the Input using a noun or noun phrase	Descibes the Control using a noun or noun phrase	Describes the Activity using an active verb or verb phrase	Describes the Mechanism using a noun or noun phrase	Describes the Output using a noun or noun phrase
Description	An Input is consumed as a result of the Activity process	Controls tell how the Activity should be performed	Transforms Inputs into Outputs through the Activity process	Resources used to accomplish the Activity (people, equipment, computer systems, or facilities)	Result of the Activity
Notes	Every Activity has at least one Input with some minor exceptions	Show Controls ONLY if they add value to the model you are building and support its purpose		Every Activity should show at least one Mechanism	Every Activity has at least one Output

Sample Process Model (Top Level)

Purpose: Document structure of sales order processing department to identify areas of inefficiency.
Viewpoint: Department manager

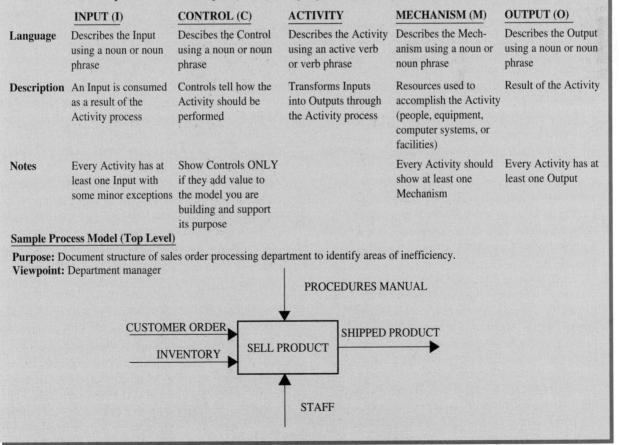

PROCEDURES MANUAL

CUSTOMER ORDER

INVENTORY

SELL PRODUCT

SHIPPED PRODUCT

STAFF

EXHIBIT 3 (*Continued*)

Activity Decomposition

IDEF0 is an hierarchical modeling method using a top-down approach to represent a process. It begins with a summary of the whole process, and progresses to the details. The top-level diagram page (A0) defines the interface of the model with external processes or real world events. The process of refining the top-level description of an Activity is called Decomposition (or drilling down). The first level decomposed pages are numbered A1, A2 A3, etc., and their progeny are A11, A12, A13, etc. (for A1); A21, A22, A23, etc. (for A2); etc., as diagrammed below. From there, the pattern continues indefinitely, adding a digit for each level. As a general rule, a decomposed activity should have 3 to 6 child activities. Node trees aid the understanding of the structure of large IDEF models. Node trees are essentially an indented outline of all the activities in the model as diagrammed below.

Decomposition Page Hierarchy: Decomposition creates a hierarchy of pages. The box numbers are used to provide context for traversing the model.

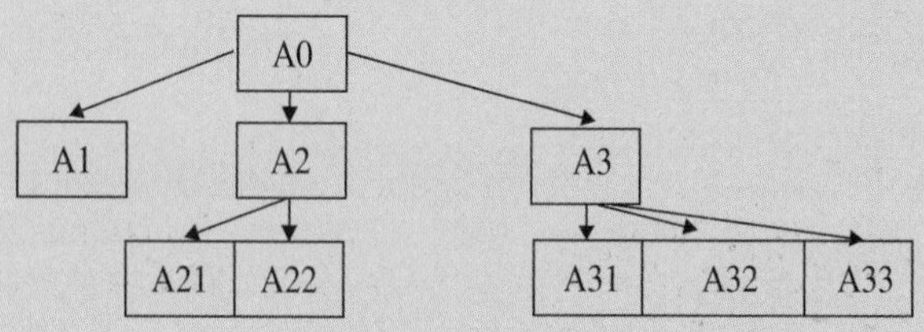

Node Tree: Node trees aid the understanding of the structure of large IDEF models by verbalizing the page hierarchy.

(A0) Sell Product
(A2) Process Order
(A21) Validate Customer Credit
(A22) Process Rejected Order
(A3) Ship Product
(A31) Fill Out Shipping Forms
(A32) Assemble Shipment
(A33) Carrier Takes Shipment

Note: The boundary for the decomposition is defined at its preceding level. ICOMs that are carried down between one activity and its decomposition page are called Ports. The port number (C1, O1, M1, I2, etc.) indicates the position of that ICOM on the parent activity ONLY.

3. **Validate the process model** in all directorates and construct a comprehensive profile of the finance function at Crane.

   Before collecting data in the directorates, members of the financial management BPR team validated the targeted process model with finance staff in each directorate by asking them to review the targeted process models and note any deviations. In addition, the financial management BPR team conducted focus groups to solicit ideas of which areas to drill down further for data.

4. **Collect data on cost, demographics, systems, and opinions** by conducting a detailed survey of all directorates.

   "What I think we did really well," Miller said, "was to go face-to-face with administrative staff in each of the directorates. We showed them our As-Is model and asked them if they had any input. Then we asked them for the names of employees in their directorates who were involved in the financial management process because we found in our initial research that there was no set job title."

   In order to calculate cost in the comptroller's office, representatives of the office allocated the cost, work-years, and people among the financial management processes. For the line directorates, the financial management BPR team collected data through a much more comprehensive survey at each line directorate.

   The survey was completed by 86 percent of the Crane employees identified as involved in some financial management process. "We conducted the survey in small groups. First we made a presentation about what we were doing. Then we gave them the survey on how they spent their time. There were four of us from the financial management BPR team present to work the room and answer questions," Miller said.

   Miller explained that the survey asked each respondent to allocate his/her hours spent in each of the six high-level processes. The survey then asked respondents for additional information in the areas of funds administration and fiscal management. These areas were selected because they contained the subprocesses deemed most fruitful for reengineering. "Overall, we had excellent participation. We had all the data collected by the end of June of 1998," Miller said. The percentage of the total population who completed the work allocation survey is shown in Exhibit 5.

   Because the percentage of coverage differed somewhat among the directorates and there was a large sample size, a proportional extrapolation of the data was performed to bring all directorates up to 100 percent, to

EXHIBIT 4

Subprocesses and Sub-subprocesses in Financial Management Naval Surface Warfare Center, Crane Division

Subprocesses	Sub-subprocesses
[A1] Workload Planning	[A11] Negotiate Workload with Sponsor [A12] Issue Data Call [A13] Update WIS [A14] Perform WIS Reporting
[A2] Budget	[A21] Develop Budget Strategy [A22] Develop All Budgets [A23] Develop Operating Plan
[A3] Funds Administration	[A31] Process Funding Document [A32] Monitor Funding [A33] Bill Customer [A34] Close Funding Authorization
[A4] Fiscal Management	[A41] Manage Costs [A42] Manage Cash [A43] Perform Fixed Asset Accounting [A44] Maintain Ledger/Subsidiaries
[A5] Financial Reporting	[A51] Publish Corporate Measures [A52] Publish Financial Statements [A53] Publish Business Systems Reports [A54] Publish External Reports
[A6] Financial Analysis	[A61] Analyze Budget to Actual [A62] Analyze WIS to Actual [A63] Analyze Operating Plan to Actual [A64] Perform Ad Hoc Financial Analysis

provide a common baseline for a more accurate comparison of data between directorates and a more accurate profile of the total cost to perform the financial management function at Crane.

Additional parts of the survey were used to collect contractor costs and noncorporate financial systems information (e.g., personal computers and file servers maintained by the directorate to perform financial management functions).

The hours collected via the survey were converted into cost by using annual labor rates. Personnel information was obtained from human resources information systems containing employee salaries or hourly rates. All salaries were converted into hourly rates and the hourly rate was multiplied by Crane's average fully-burdened labor rate for FY 1997 and FY 1998 to calculate total cost.

Based on the data collected, the total cost of financial management ($22 million) was calculated to be about 3 percent of revenue compared with the private sector range of 1 percent to 1.5 percent for financial management. Due to government regulations and requirements, achieving a cost comparable to the private sector was not considered possible by the team. However, the financial management BPR team found several areas for dramatic improvement. The division of the total cost of financial management across the six high-level processes identified by the team is shown in Exhibit 6.

Matthews said:

> A little less than one-third of Crane's workforce was identified as devoting at least part of their time to financial management. Out of the 800 employees identified, about 600 spent less than 20 percent of their time performing financial management functions. Combined with the variety of titles we found, the financial management BPR team thought there may be employees performing financial management who did not have an overall understanding of financial management. We thought that might indicate a higher cost of financial management due to these lost economies of scale.

The two major areas targeted for reengineering, funds administration and fiscal management, made up more than two-thirds of the total cost of financial management. In addition, these two areas accounted for 70 percent of the total personnel hours expended and a little less than half the number of employees identified as performing some financial management function.

Based upon the validation, the financial management processes performed were similar among the directorates. However, there were some differences in the organizational structure of financial management among the directorates—some organized financial management at the directorate/department level whereas others organized it at the branch level.

5. **Reassess target selections for redesign.** Once all the data were collected and analyzed, the team reassessed its initial target selections to identify Crane-wide reengineering opportunities. As a result of these discussions, five subprocesses in financial management were targeted for redesign: (1) monitor funding, (2) process funding documents (both in funds administration), (3) perform fixed asset accounting, (4) manage costs, and (5) manage cash (all three in fiscal management). Comments by the team about these processes are shown in Exhibit 7.

EXHIBIT 5

Response Rate of the Work Allocation Survey
Naval Surface Warfare Center, Crane Division

Directorate	Number of Employees Identified	Number of Employees Surveyed	Coverage Percent
Command	25	20	80%
Management Systems	37	33	89%
Employee Services	55	46	84%
Public Works	95	82	86%
Purchasing & Supply	75	59	79%
Ordnance Engineering	136	116	85%
Electronic Development	99	87	88%
Electronic Maintenance	126	118	94%
Microwave Systems	163	133	82%
Total	811	694	86%

EXHIBIT 6

Financial Management Processes Total Cost
Naval Surface Warfare Center, Crane Division

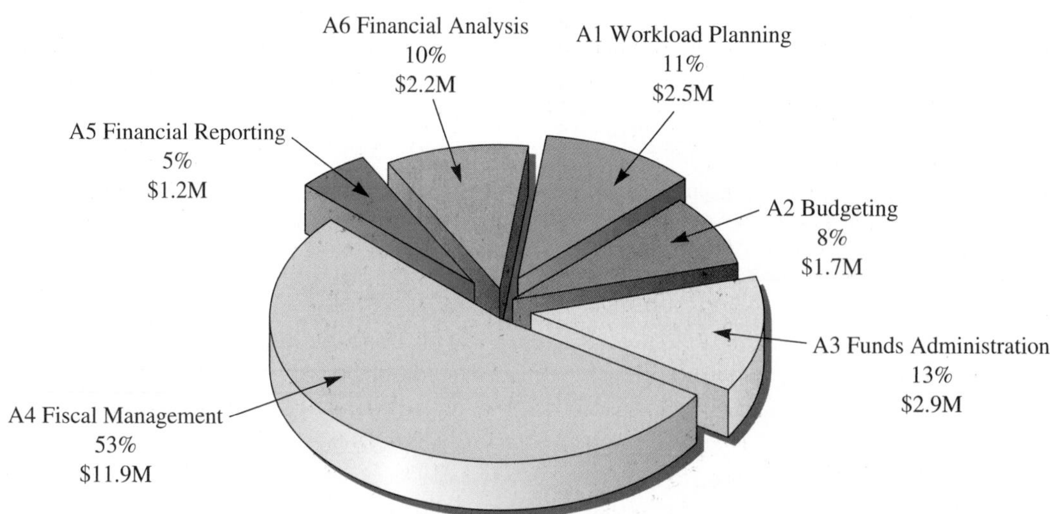

6. **Present the results.** The team presented its findings to the executive steering board in late August 1998. Exhibit 8 shows the conclusions from the financial management BPR team's As-Is report.

The board appeared to be extremely pleased with all the work the team had done. One director commented, "I knew we needed to fix some things, but the data the team collected clearly show where we need to focus our attention."

EXHIBIT 7

Financial Management Sub-subprocesses Targeted for Redesign
Naval Surface Warfare Center, Crane Division

Funds Administration

Monitor Funding. The BPR team focused on a subset of monitor funding—time and labor. This sub-subprocesses consists of processing labor and materials/equipment/service expenditures. Processing labor consists of timekeepers' duties, management certification of time, and comptroller's payroll technicians' duties. The financial management BPR team found that a majority of cost/time lies in the timekeepers' duties and that the majority of time is spent resolving errors (e.g., employees failing to clock in/out, malfunction of the time clock, and unanticipated overtime).

Process Funding Documents. Validate/sign funding documents is performed by the comptroller and process funding documents is also performed by the directorates. Funding documents are either received in the comptroller's office or the directorates (typically at the project level). Both processes are manual and circular with duplicate steps (e.g., copy and file) performed at the comptroller, directorate, department, and project levels.

Fiscal Management

Perform Fixed Asset Accounting. There are 112 people performing fixed asset accounting, which is defined as directorate and comptroller equipment custodian duties. Fixed asset accounting also includes comptroller's monitoring and maintenance of items in a property management system. Inventories take a significant amount of time to perform and often result in missing or lost items. The last physical inventory began in FY 1996, was not completed until FY 1997, and resulted in many assets reported missing or lost which have since been identified.

Manage Costs. The process of monitoring costs and funding is functionally distinct, but procedurally connected. Monitoring funding includes tracking and controlling funding from the time it is accepted through completion of the assignment. Monitoring costs is performed at the charge number level. More than 60 percent of the cost spent monitoring costs relates to gathering data and creating/generating reports. Based on information collected through the survey, reports are prepared in part due to employee dissatisfaction with the format of corporate system data and the need to integrate data from multiple sources.

Manage Cash. The team looked at a subset of manage cash—vendor pay/receipt control. This function includes the vendor pay function and consists of matching invoices with receipts and contracts, entering invoice information into a computer system, and mailing copies of all invoices to a facility in Charleston SC that manually inputs the invoice information and pays the bill. Although the vendor pay function is relatively small, it appears it is duplicated in other areas.

The executive team then approved extra funding to immediately begin designing a new vision for financial management at Crane and to construct the To-Be model for the five targeted financial management processes.

Creating the To-Be Models

"Our redesign team started right after we received approval of our report on the As-Is model in August 1998," Miller said. "We thought we could complete the To-Be models in a month or two, but we didn't complete any on schedule."

The financial management BPR team was first increased in size from 9 members to 25 members as there were now five processes to design. For each of the five processes, the team

- reviewed the As-Is model developed earlier
- conducted research on the root causes that might have created such a process
- identified best practices for the same type of process conducted either inside Crane or at another government or commercial agency

EXHIBIT 8

Conclusions of the Financial Management As-Is Report Naval Surface Warfare Center, Crane Division

Crane has a lack of integrated systems. Finance staff spend a significant amount of time gathering data from numerous systems to create reports for managers and sponsors. The data indicate that this report generation is done to present data in an integrated format versus to perform financial and performance analysis. Crane previously recognized this problem and at the time of data collection was in the process of implementing a data warehouse. As part of the redesign effort, the financial management BPR team will assess the data warehouse design and implementation and identify optimal staffing and organizational structure to complement a data warehouse.

The finance function is decentralized and fragmented. Finance consists of 333 work-years (full-time equivalent) spread over 854 employees. Seventy-five percent of finance costs are expended in the directorates. The financial management BPR team will determine the appropriate mix of centralization/decentralization in the redesign phase.

The finance function is not clearly understood. Finance should serve as a partner to operations, providing meaningful and timely financial information to management. Large numbers of employees at Crane are involved in tabulating and reformatting data. There is little value added since data are not used for analysis or for input to decision making. In the redesign phase, the financial management BPR team will design and deliver performance measurement information to support corporate strategic goals.

Employees performing the finance function do not have the appropriate financial background. Finance activities are performed by staff who are not dedicated to finance and who may not fully understand the role their activities play in Crane's overall financial management. For example, in Crane property management (and other organizations), financial activities are performed by technical staff who, although they understand the technical capabilities of the equipment they are tracking, may not understand the key role that tracking plays in financial control and reporting.

Finance is costly. Depending upon the industry, the finance function in the private sector accounts for 1 to 1.5 percent of total dollars managed. At 3 percent of total dollars managed, there is room for meaningful and substantial reductions in the cost of finance at Crane.

- developed the "ideal" way the process should be handled at Crane (the To-Be model)
- identified actions that could achieve the ideal process
- conducted a business case analysis or cost/benefit analysis for making the suggested change(s)
- selected the best course of action for stakeholder and management review

The new design for the perform fixed asset accounting process was completed in December 1998 and presented to the executive steering board in January 1999. This process tracked all significant fixed assets at Crane throughout their useful life and included updating of the fixed asset database. The team recommended that a centralized team (called the property team) be created to take over this function from smaller groups working in all the directorates. The team also recommended several changes to the information system supporting the fixed asset database. The financial management BPR team estimated that Crane could save at least $550,000 annually by implementing their recommendations. The investment in information systems development was estimated to be about $25,000.

The To-Be model for process funding documents was completed and reported to the executive steering board in January 1999. The team identified several changes that could be made to automate the processing of funding documents, including electronic processing of paper documents, electronic funds transfer processing, and Web-based funds transfer. The estimated savings exceeded $400,000 per year and would require a one-time investment of $68,000 in systems development and scanning equipment.

The redesign for monitoring funding (called the time and labor effort) was completed and presented to the board in March 1999. This team conducted an extensive best practices analysis, visiting 14 outside agencies/companies as well as several organizations inside Crane. They concluded that none of these organizations did as good a job as Crane in keeping track of personnel time associated with individual jobs.

However, they did find a concept inside Crane that was worthy of organization-wide implementation. Their proposal called for consolidating the job of tracking time and labor effort for each major organization at Crane into the duties of a single person called a scheduler. The estimated savings exceeded $550,000 annually.

The fourth redesign team focused on the receipt control/vendor payment part of the manage cash process. In March 1999, they recommended a series of changes in how this process was handled at Crane and estimated a savings of over $1,000,000 per year. An initial investment of about $70,000 for information systems development would be required.

The redesign for manage costs was put on hold until some common business rules for all Crane operations could be established. Miller said:

> One of the difficulties we ran into was that the finance function is carried out so inconsistently across, and even within, directorates. While we were able to complete most of the redesigns, we found that we really needed some overall rules that would outline how our finance business should be conducted at Crane in order to finish the last process design.
>
> As I told Bob (Matthews), thinking out of the box has also been difficult. We found that some members of the financial management BPR team were too involved in the current process of financial management in their jobs. It was difficult for them to view things objectively. We added more objective members, but the task was still very difficult for many of the members of the team.
>
> We also encountered resistance from people in the directorates. Part of the process of building the To-Be model involves validating our As-Is model, and we encountered a lot of resistance. People questioned how we derived the information. I had one department manager tell me we didn't survey all the people in her department involved in financial management. I then sent her the original list of names she gave me. She was satisfied, but the thing is that it took a great deal of time to answer her concerns. And she's not the only one. I found myself pulling actual surveys and going through them with some people to justify how we collected our data.

By May 1999, only the process funding documents and perform fixed asset accounting redesigns had received approval to start implementation planning. In addition to manage costs, the time and labor effort and vendor pay/receipt control redesigns were stalled until common business rules could be established.

Dealing with the Root Problems

After reading the As-Is report from the financial management BPR team, Bob Matthews and Bill Kaiser concluded that creating the To-Be models was needed, but new processes by themselves could not solve some of the underlying issues in financial management at Crane. Kaiser said:

> The processes observed by our team were rooted in some assumptions and practices that had developed over time at Crane. We could change the individual process but we would never achieve the full benefits of process reengineering until we changed the way we conduct our financial management business here. We had to reengineer our business, too.

Kaiser decided to ask Arthur Andersen, the outside consulting firm working on the project, for some help in surveying how the finance function was conducted at other organizations, to report back by December 1998.

The consultant's report was shared with the financial management BPR team and the resulting conclusions presented to the executive steering board in December 1998. The basic conclusion was that the years of performing financial functions both in the directorates and the central comptroller's office had created a substantial amount of redundant and excess work. As partial proof, they cited some statistics. In FY 1999 Crane had 88 projects underway. These projects in turn had created 4,701 customer order numbers and 16,692 charge numbers. Each of these items required staff processing time and put an excessive load on the organization's information systems. "At the time, there were no rules or constraints, so a project leader could do whatever he/she felt needed to be done," Matthews said.

The consultants recommended that Crane adopt a standard set of rules for conducting the financial function. For example, a single business rule establishing when and how to create customer order numbers and charge numbers would reduce the numbers and redundancy. As a result of that meeting, Kaiser and two senior executives in the corporate financial area decided that they would develop a recommended set of business rules in the finance function for consideration by the executive steering board. They presented their recommendations to senior financial managers in February 1999. About that same time, Cheryl Miller and the financial management BPR team presented their recommendations for process change to the business unit managers. All rejected the recommendations for a variety of reasons.

After several more reviews and revisions, the report on business rules for financial management was presented to the executive steering board at an off-site meeting in May 1999. Exhibit 9 contains part of the report that shows a suggested set of business rules and a set of suggested roles/responsibilities for each of the levels of management involved in the financial management process at Crane. The directors at the meeting listened carefully to the report. Afterwards, one director suggested, "These changes are too radical—do we have to change this much?" Another added, "I haven't gotten a single complaint from my customers." Kaiser asked, "But do your customers know how much it's costing them for these reports?"

EXHIBIT 9

Suggested Business Rules and Roles/Responsibilities for Financial Management Naval Surface Warfare Center, Crane Division

Business Rules Applied to Financial Management

- The departments at Crane are the primary business units, and financial management (analysis, reports, fund administration, and fiscal management) is focused at that level.
- The controller is the owner of the financial management process, but funds administration reports directly to the department managers.
- Some projects are designed with a specific focus (customer, product, group of customers, etc.) in mind, but all projects have a beginning and end.
- An estimating mechanism (for labor rates) will be established at the corporate level as a tool for the business units.
- While charge numbers are primarily accounting transaction vehicles, there is one charge number per task, instead of a separate charge number for each expense element and organizational unit.
- There is to be one customer order number (CON) per line of accounting. There will be no CON cost overruns.
- The Workload Information System will be developed at the department unit level.

Directorate Directors—Expectations/Responsibilities

- Mentoring of department managers
- Facilitating corporate business development in conjunction with each department
- Advocating and leading corporate (strategic/operational) initiatives
- Overseeing workload initiatives
- Mentoring/developing people to be future leaders
- Improving performance of individuals and the directorate
- Guiding the departments and developing policy
- Providing general oversight of the activities in the directorate

Department Managers—Expectations/Responsibilities

- Ensuring adequate project planning and execution
- Being financially accountable for budgeting, funds administration, and execution
- Planning and executing the workload
- Planning and managing the resources of the department

Funds Administrators—Expectations/Responsibilities

- Overseeing the core financial staff
- Controlling and issuing charge numbers
- Ensuring funds are not over-obligated and are expended as authorized per the CON
- Complying with the financial management business rules
- Ensuring work is planned in accordance with the appropriation requirements
- Providing support to project managers and branch managers

EXHIBIT 9 (*Continued*)

Project Managers—Expectations/Responsibilities

- Interfacing with customer with regards to tasking and meeting customer needs
- Ensuring that cost, schedule, and quality of project meet customer expectations
- Sustaining current business/customers
- Developing new business and customers
- Accepting, validating, and planning the appropriate use of funding (along with department managers)
- Using Microsoft Project (or an agreed-upon off-the-shelf software package) for project planning

Branch Managers—Expectations/Responsibilities

- Acting as the technical process owners, which requires overseeing the quality of the process output and the certification of people, facilities, and equipment, as well as an understanding of process costs, quality, and timeliness
- Delivering an output to the customer
- Managing and leading people
- Developing and maintaining technical capabilities
- Overseeing the financial support provided by the departments
- Ensuring work is accomplished within the planned appropriation

Customer Area Leaders—Expectations/Responsibilities

- Acting as the person visible to and advocate for the customer
- Analyzing existing customers' budgets, technologies, trends, and opportunities
- Focusing on total customer requirements
- Keeping command apprised of political and programmatic issues

Another director answered, "No. And they don't seem to mind or else we would have heard about it."

Another director said the changes would seriously interfere with his directorate's management of projects. Others agreed, stating that they had developed their own way of managing the financial part of projects–which was working very well. A director noted, "We created these reports because we needed them." Another director fired a parting shot: "Rather than make us implement all these new rules, just give us some time to reduce personnel since that is what this is all about anyway."

Dealing With Reductions in Personnel

Bob Matthews and Bill Kaiser realized in August 1998 that a likely result of implementing the To-Be models would be the elimination of some jobs at Crane. Yet one of the original objectives of business and process reengineering at Crane had been to make "reductions in force" (RIF) a last resort. So something had to be done to achieve the objective while being able to deliver the savings promised by BPR.

In fall 1998, the Center Resolution Committee (CRC), a group of management and union representatives, provided a framework and recommendations for movement of employees as the result of BPR. The CRC had been formed earlier to address employee grievances before they were escalated off the base. The committee had been very successful, reducing the number of escalated grievances from about 30 per year to almost nothing. But the CRC's recommendations for BPR impacts were rules- and seniority-based with little flexibility for directors to create staffing plans. When the CRC presented their recommendations to the directors in November 1998, the directors rejected the plan.

Matthews, with the help of a consultant, offered to come up with a compromise and presented his plan in early spring 1999. Administrative officers liked the new plan, but not the directors. Absent a solid agreement on employee movement, the BPR teams were stalled in implementing the recommendations in their To-Be models. In April 1999, the executive team (Shotts, Gootee, and Mason) took on the task and came to an agreement. They explained the agreement to the executive steering board during a May 1999 off-site meeting.

The agreement laid out a process for handling personnel whose positions would be eliminated due to BPR. First, each directorate would create a staffing plan when an implementation plan of some process was approved. That plan would show all remaining old positions and any new positions that were to be created. Next, individuals would be slotted into the old positions based on seniority. Any individual could apply for the new positions. All "surplus" personnel would be temporarily transferred to another job in the directorate and registered in Crane's Personnel Transfer Office (PTO) in an inventory of personnel who were to be given priority on job vacancies if they were minimally qualified for the job. In addition, voluntary separation incentives were offered to individuals to encourage retirements. Finally, the PTO manager was instructed to report monthly on the number of people registered. If too many people registered (no number was named in the agreement), discussions about a reduction in force would occur.

Moving Forward

As they sat in Kaiser's office in late May 1999, Matthews reflected, "I find my role has changed and is becoming more important in implementation. And a lot more difficult. We know fixed asset accounting and process funding can move forward. But we need business rules for time and labor effort, manage costs, and vendor pay/receipt control."

Kaiser agreed. "Securing buy-in from the directors is a real brick wall. We charged the chief financial people and the administration with talking to their business managers and directors to decide on business rules and that didn't work. Maybe we could get the executive team to finish the business rules we came up with and make their implementation a mandate—like they did with the Personnel Transfer Office."

Matthews said, "That's a possibility. We know we can't hire a consultant—an outsider can't implement changes to an internal process. The business process owner has to be the one to implement the change if it's to be effective."

Kaiser added, "Another option might be to get the employees to push for the change in business rules and processes. We seem to have the union's support for BPR."

Matthews said, "Our problem is that there are no negative consequences if the directors resist implementation. No one will lose their job for not complying. And we don't know of any upcoming rounds of base closings that would pose a threat. The directors can stall until the BPR project is effectively dead."

Matthews added, "Maybe we took on too much. We could go forward with fixed asset accounting and process funding only. Once they're successful, maybe we'd gain more support for the others."

"That will yield only a small fraction of the savings. Remember that we have to achieve a 30 percent cost savings. I don't think we have any choice other than to continue with full implementation. The project has too high a profile," Kaiser answered.

"Maybe we should back off a little. Not create mandated business rules, but create a team that would come up with less specific rules, more like guidelines, sharing of best practices," Matthews suggested.

"That's a possibility. Of course, we lose control of implementation and possibly forfeit optimal savings," Kaiser said. "It's already 7:00 P.M. We've come up with a couple of options. Let's sleep on them and meet first thing tomorrow morning."

As he drove to the ball field, Matthews thought about his options. Top management at Crane supported BPR. Navy leadership was expecting substantial results. How could middle management hold the project hostage? And if the middle managers got some control over following best practices, would they sabotage the project or would that secure their buy-in? Wasn't the size and scope of BPR bigger than the directors? Could they be successful in getting a mandate from the executive team and proceed without the directors' support? Should they even try to win the directors' support? As he pulled into a parking space, he saw his son out in right field catch a fly ball and throw to first base for a second out. If only he could think how to make a similar play and get the financial management BPR team back on track.

CASE STUDY III-7

NIBCO's "Big Bang": An SAP Implementation

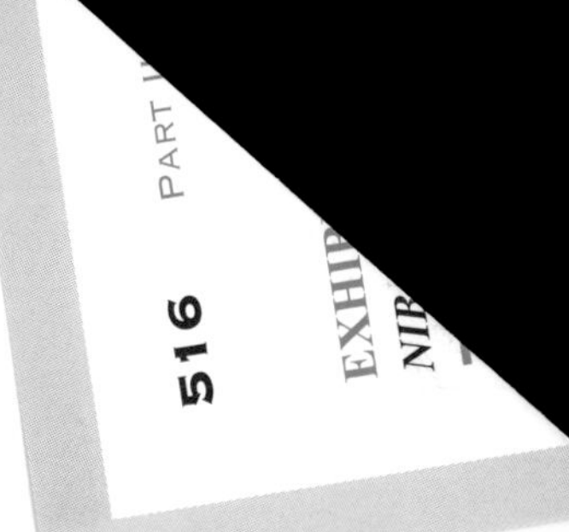

December 30, 1997, was the "Go-Live" date at NIBCO, Inc., a privately held midsized manufacturer of valves and pipe fittings headquartered in Elkhart, Indiana. In 1996 NIBCO had more than 3,000 employees (called "associates") and annual revenues of $461 million. Although many of the consultants NIBCO had interviewed would not endorse a "big bang" approach, the plan was to convert to SAP R/3 at all ten plants and the four new North American distribution centers at the same time. The price tag for the 15-month project was estimated to be $17 million. One-quarter of the company's senior managers were dedicated to the project, including a leadership triad that included a former VP of operations (Beutler), the information services director (Wilson), and a former quality management director (Davis).

> One of the major drivers of the whole thing was that Rex Martin said "I want it done now." That really was the defining moment—because it forced us to stare down these implementation partners and tell them ". . . we're going to do this big bang and we're going to do it fast."
>
> *Scott Beutler, Project Co-Lead, Business Process*

> We took ownership: It was our project, not theirs. We used the consultants for what we needed them for and that was technology skills, knowledge transfer, and extra hands.
>
> *Gary Wilson, Project Co-Lead, Technology*

> It was brutal. It was hard on families, but nobody quit, nobody left . . . Professionally I would say it was unequivocally the highlight of my career.
>
> *Jim Davis, Project Co-Lead, Change Management*

Company Background

NIBCO's journey to the Go-Live date began about 3 years earlier, when a significant strategic planning effort took place. At the same time a cross-functional team was charged with reengineering the company's supply chain processes to better meet its customers' needs (see "NIBCO's Big Bang Timeline" in Exhibit 1). One of the key conclusions from these endeavors was that the organization could not prosper with its current information systems. The firm's most recent major investments in information technology had been made over 5 years earlier. Those systems had evolved into a patchwork of legacy systems and reporting tools that could not talk to each other.

After initial talks with several consulting firms, top management brought in the Boston Consulting Group (BCG) in August 1995 to help the company develop a strategic information systems plan to meet its new business objectives.

> BCG brought in a team and what they instantly did was to start going through each of the functional areas of the company to determine the need for changes. . . . And so they went into each little nook and cranny of the company and sorted out whether we really needed to change every system we had.
>
> *Jim Davis, Project Co-Lead, Change Management*

The consensus among NIBCO's management team was that the company was "information poor" and needed to be "cut loose" from its existing systems. There were also major concerns about being able to grow the company and become more global without an integrated information capability. BCG's recommendation on December 1st was that NIBCO replace its legacy systems with common, integrated systems that could be implemented in small chunks over a 3- to 5-year time frame.

> They told us, "You really need to look at integration as a major factor in your thought processes—the ability to have common systems with common communication for the manufacturing area, the distribution area, across the enterprise."
>
> *Scott Beutler, Project Co-Lead, Business Process*

This case study published in the *Communications of AIS* 5 (January 2001). The case was prepared for class discussion, rather than to illustrate either effective or ineffective handling of an administrative situation. The authors are indebted to Gary Wilson and the other NIBCO managers who shared their insights with the authors.

BIT 1
CO's Big Bang Timeline

Time Frame	Milestone
Early 1995	Cross-functional teams charged with developing NIBCO's strategic plan and reengineering supply chain processes determined that company could not prosper with its current information systems.
May, 1995	Gary Wilson hired as new head of IS department.
August–December, 1995	Boston Consulting Group conducted strategic IT planning study. Recommended that NIBCO replace its legacy systems with integrated enterprise system on client/server platform over 3 to 5 years..
January 1, 1996	Corporation restructured into cross-functional matrix organization. Scott Beutler, former VP of operations, residential division, given responsibility for business system strategic planning, including selection of an ERP package.
July, 1996	Committee recommended purchase of SAP R/3 and "big bang" implementation. Approved by Executive Leadership Team (ELT) and Board of Directors.
August, 1996	Contracts signed with SAP for R/3 modules and IBM as implementation partner. Wilson, Beutler, and Davis form triad leadership team.
September, 1996	Completion of project-team selection and September 30th project kickoff. Begin preparation phase.
December, 1996	Final project scope and resource estimates presented to ELT and Board with Go-Live date of Monday, November 29, 1997 (30-day grace period allowed). Final scope included North America only and consolidation of warehouses to a number yet to be determined. Final project budget was $17 million.
March, 1997	Decision to consolidate warehouses from 17 to 4 by September, 1997. Incentive pay bonus in place a few months after project initiated.
April, 1997	Installation of PCs for customer service associates completed. Weekly newsletter via e-mail initiated.
May, 1997	Business review lead for materials management leaves company; role filled by business review lead for production planning.
Summer, 1997	Maintenance of legacy systems discontinued except for emergency repairs.
September, 1997	User training begins at NIBCO World Headquarters and at remote sites. Sandbox practice system becomes available.
November, 1997	Go-Live date moved from Monday following Thanksgiving to December 30 due to delays in completion of warehouse consolidation and master data load testing.
December 30, 1997	Go Live without consultants.

The company began to reorganize into a cross-functional, matrix structure in January 1996. It also initiated a new cross-functional strategic planning process. Scott Beutler was relieved of his line management responsibilities to focus on the development of a new IT strategy. Beutler had joined NIBCO in early 1990 as general manager of the retail business unit. When this business unit was restructured, he became the VP of operations, residential division. Beutler was charged with learning whether a new type of integrated systems package called enterprise resource planning systems (ERP) would be the best IT investment to move the company forward.

Information Systems at NIBCO

Gary Wilson was hired as the new head of the IS department in May 1995 and became a member of the BCG study team soon after. Wilson had more than 20 years of IS experience, including managing an IS group in a multidivisional company and leading four major project implementations. He reported to Dennis Parker, the chief financial officer.

Wilson inherited an IS department of about 30 NIBCO IS specialists, including those who ran mainframe applications on HP3000 and IBM/MVS platforms. About one-half were COBOL programmers. The IS payroll also included a number of contractors who had been at NIBCO for up to 5 years.

Four major legacy systems supported the order entry, manufacturing, distribution, and accounting functions (see Exhibit 2). The business units had purchased their own packages for some applications and plants were running their own versions of the same manufacturing software package with separate databases.

> We had a neat manufacturing package that ran on a Hewlett Packard, an accounting system that ran on an IBM, and a distribution package that was repackaged to run on the IBM. Nothing talked to each other. Distribution couldn't see what manufacturing was doing and manufacturing couldn't see what distribution and sales were doing.
>
> *Jan Bleile, Power User*

At the time of the BCG study, there was widespread dissatisfaction with the functionality of the legacy environment and data were suspect, at best, because of multiple points of access and multiple databases. The systems development staff spent most of their time building custom interfaces between the systems and trying to resolve the "disconnects."

> The systems blew up on a regular basis because we made lots of ad hoc changes. As a result, the IS people weren't a particularly happy lot . . . no one really had a great deal of respect for them.
>
> *Dennis Parker, Chief Financial Officer*

The ERP Selection Team

Beutler set up a cross-functional team to select an ERP package early in 1996. CFO Parker was the executive sponsor and it included eight other, primarily director-level, managers. Wilson played an internal technology consultant role for Beutler while still managing the IS group, which was heavily immersed in a new data warehousing project.

EXHIBIT 2
Legacy Systems at NIBCO

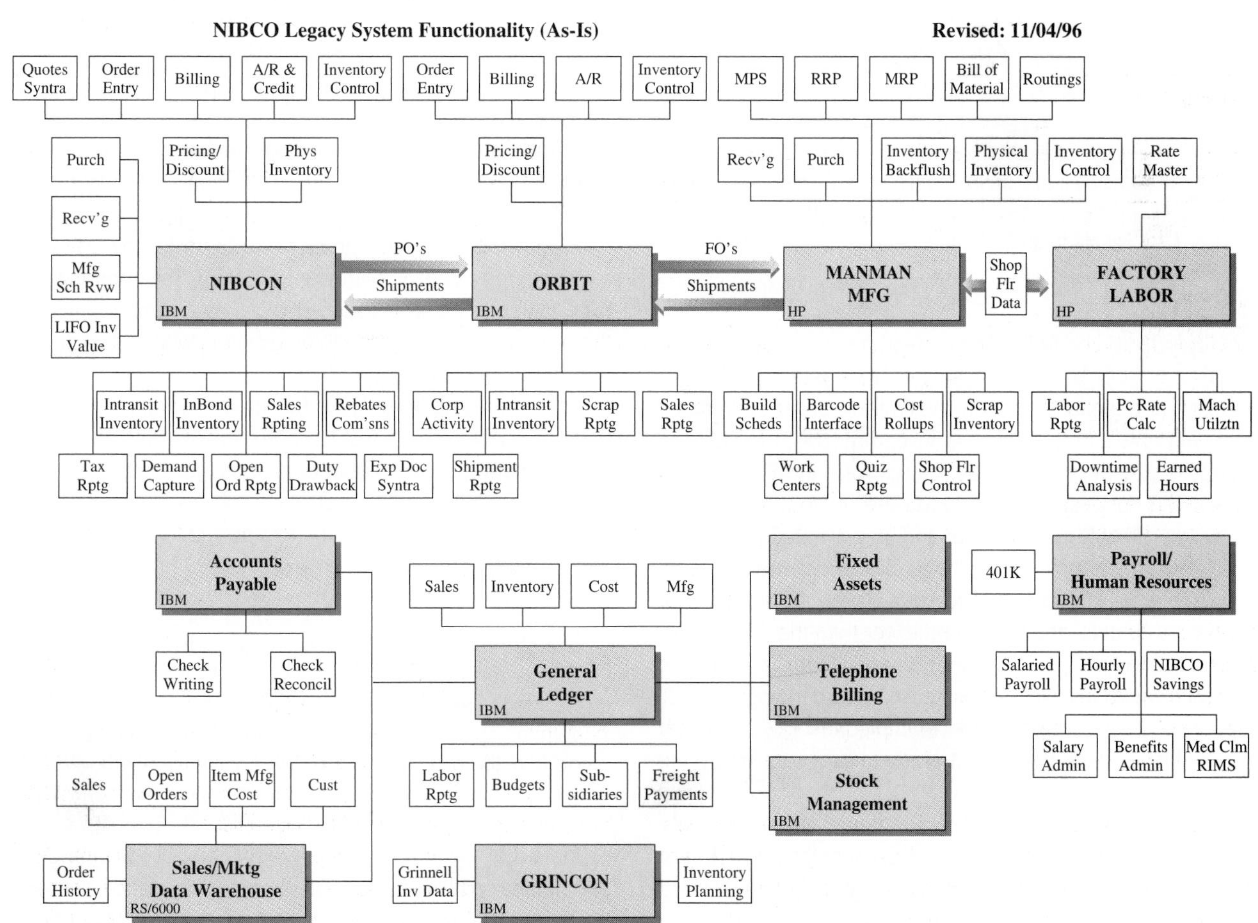

Seven ERP packages were evaluated in depth. Representatives from the various functional areas participated in walk-throughs of specific modules, and the selection team also visited several different vendors' customers. The strengths and weaknesses of each package were mapped into an evaluation matrix. One of the key decisions was whether to wrap a series of best-in-class finance and supply chain solutions around a common database, or whether to select a single ERP system that integrated all the modules.

The selection team also did some benchmarking on implementation approaches and success rates. Some of the team members sensed that the BCG recommendation for a 3- to 5-year phased ERP implementation was not the best approach for NIBCO. The fear was that the company would just get to the point where it would say "enough is enough" without executing the whole plan. Team members had also observed that some of the companies that had used a phased, "go-slow" approach were not among the most successful. At the same time business initiatives were demanding a quicker implementation.

Jim Davis, who had led a reengineering team for the strategic planning process, was asked to facilitate the selection team's formulation of a recommendation to the executive leadership team (ELT).

> Because of my facilitation experience, I was asked to facilitate that meeting so that there would be an objective person who had no particular interest or bias to help lead the discussion .... It actually was a bit of a breakthrough because in the context of that meeting we changed our approach from the point solution over 3 to 5 years to an ERP big bang.
>
> *Jim Davis, Project Co-Lead, Change Management*

In July 1996, the ERP selection team recommended to the ELT that NIBCO purchase a single ERP system: SAP R/3. Among the benefits would be multimillion dollar operational improvements and reductions in inventory costs; the ROI was based on a 6 percent forecast growth rate in NIBCO's revenues. The cost estimates included the move from a mainframe to a client/server platform and an estimated number of R/3 licenses. Although consulting costs under the big bang approach were still expected to be high—about one-third of the project budget—they would be lower than the 1,000 days estimated for the 3- to 5-year phased approach. Either approach would involve a big increase in IS spending. The ELT supported the recommendation to implement R/3 as quickly as possible—pull the people out of the business to work on it, focus, and get it done.

The R/3 purchase and big bang implementation plan were then presented to NIBCO's Board of Directors. The Board viewed the big bang approach as a high-risk, high-reward scenario. In order to quickly put in place the systems to execute the new supply chain and customer-facing strategies, which had come out of the strategic planning process, the company would have to commit a significant portion of its resources. This meant dedicating its best people to the project to ensure that the implementation risks were well managed.

A contract was signed with SAP for the FI/CO, MM, PP, SD, and HR modules and for about 620 user licenses soon afterward. The HR (human resources) module would be implemented later. Rex Martin, chairman, president, and CEO of NIBCO, assumed the senior oversight role.

The TIGER Triad

Once the team's big bang recommendation was endorsed, Beutler began to focus on the R/3 implementation project. The initial idea was to have Wilson co-lead the R/3 project with Beutler. In an earlier position, Wilson had worked on equal footing with a business manager as co-leads of a project involving a major platform change, and it had been a huge success. He therefore quickly endorsed the idea of co-leading the project with Beutler. Between the two of them there was both deep NIBCO business knowledge and large-scale IT project management knowledge. Although Beutler was already dedicated full-time to the ERP project, Wilson would continue to manage the IS department as well as co-lead the project for the next 18 months.

Shortly after the Board decision in late July, Rex Martin asked Jim Davis to join Beutler and Wilson as a third co-lead out of concern for the high strategic risk of the project. Martin had been the executive sponsor of a team led by Davis that reengineered strategic planning at NIBCO. The morning after Davis agreed, Martin introduced Davis as the third co-lead of the project, and then let the three directors work out what roles they were going to play.

As the three co-leads looked at what needed to be accomplished, it became clear that Davis' experience with total quality management initiatives could bring focus to the change management aspects of the project. Davis split his time between his quality management job and the R/3 project for about a month, and then began to work full-time on the ERP implementation.

> One of the things we did was a lot of benchmarking . . . and one of the things we kept hearing over and over was that the change management was a killer. Having been in the IT business for a long time, I realized it was a very, very key element. With the opportunity to give it equal footing, it sounded like we could really focus on the change management piece.
>
> *Gary Wilson, Project Co-Lead, Technology*

> I was pretty sensitive to change management because of my TQM role and so in the conversation I could say, "Look guys, if

we don't get people to play the new instrument here, it could be a great cornet—but it's never gonna blow a note."

Jim Davis, Project Co-Lead, Change Management

The R/3 project team came to be called the TIGER team: Total Information Generating Exceptional Results. The project was depicted as a growling tiger with a "break away" motto, symbolizing the need to dramatically break away from the old processes and infrastructure (see Exhibit 3). A triangle symbolized the triad leadership with responsibilities for technology (Wilson), business coordination (Beutler), and change management (Davis).

The three co-leads spent significant amounts of time together on a daily basis, including Saturday mornings. Each brought completely different perspectives to the project. They talked through all the issues together and most major decisions, even more technical decisions, were made as a triad.

Rex Martin was the executive sponsor for the team, and also came to be viewed as the project champion. It was Martin's responsibility to ensure that the VPs supported the project and were willing to empower the project leaders to make decisions. The project co-leads informed him of the key issues and Martin eliminated any roadblocks. Together they decided what decisions to refer to the ELT level and provided the ELT with regular project updates. In turn, the ELT was expected to respond quickly. Of the three key project variables—time, scope, and resources—the time schedule was not negotiable: The project was to be completed by year-end 1997.

EXHIBIT 3
TIGER Leadership

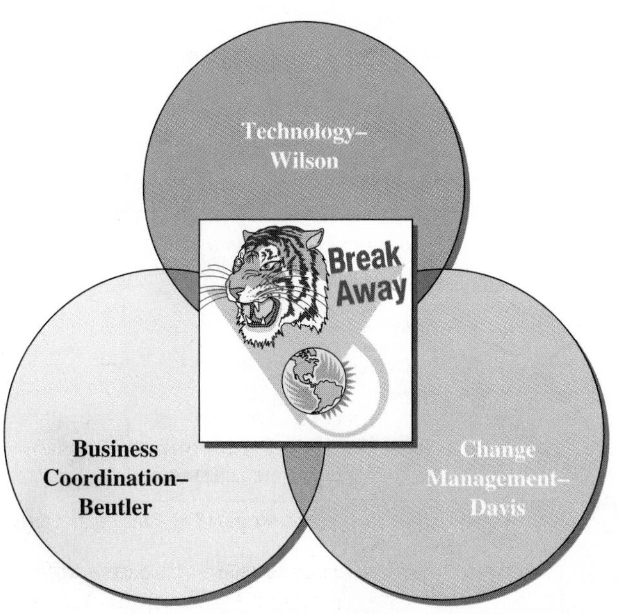

Selecting an Implementation Partner

The same NIBCO team that selected the ERP software vendor was responsible for selecting an implementation partner. It was critical that this third-party consulting firm support NIBCO's decision to take a big bang approach, which was viewed as high risk.

I remember serious counsel where people came back and said: "What you've described cannot be done. And here are all the failures that describe why it can't be done." We just kept looking at them and said: "Then we'll get somebody else to tell us how it can be done."

Scott Beutler, Project Co-Lead, Business Process

After considering several consulting firms, IBM and Cap Gemini were chosen as finalists due to different strengths: NIBCO was already an IBM shop from a hardware standpoint, but Cap Gemini had a superior change management program. The team elected to employ IBM. By contracting for a large number of services (implementation consulting, change management consulting, technical consulting, and infrastructure), NIBCO's management hoped it would have enough leverage to get a quick response when problems arose.

Not all of the potential IBM project leaders that the team interviewed believed in the viability of the big bang approach.

When we hired IBM, we hired them with the agreement that they were going to help us to do a big bang in the time frame we wanted. As far as I know, IBM had not done a successful big bang up to that point. In fact, [Michael] Hammer[1] got on the bandwagon about halfway through our project and preached that big bangs are death.

Jim Davis, Project Co-Lead, Change Management

NIBCO's triad leadership design was also not viewed as optimal for decision making, and the consultants recommended that a single project leader be designated. The three co-leads considered their suggestion, but turned it down: The triad ran the project, but designated Beutler as the primary spokesperson.

Another risk was that IBM's change management approach in mid-1996 was an off-the-shelf, generic approach that was not ERP-specific. However, it had been used successfully for business process reengineering projects, and it included communications activities and job redesign initiatives. The intent was to tailor it to the TIGER project.

When the change management consultants came to NIBCO, none of them had ever heard of ERP or SAP, so it was difficult to directly apply their principles to NIBCO's situation. They

[1]Michael Hammer has been a reengineering guru since the early 1990s. (See M. Hammer and J. Champy, *Reengineering the Corporation: A Manifesto for Business Revolution*. New York: HarperCollins, 1993.)

stayed with us for 4 or 5 months into the project so that we could get enough learning from them, couple that with our own internal understanding, and then tailor these ideas to the specific ERP change issues.

Jim Davis, Project Co-Lead, Change Management

The IBM contract was signed in late August 1996. Six functional consultants would work with the project team throughout the project. Consultants with ABAP development and training development expertise would be added as needed. Knowledge transfer from the consultants to NIBCO's associates was part of the contract: NIBCO's employees were to be up to speed in R/3 by the Go-Live date.

Selecting the Rest of the TIGER Team

The TIGER project team had a core team that included three business process teams, a technical team, and a change management team. Each business process team had seven or eight people with primary responsibility for a subset of the R/3 modules (see Exhibit 4): (1) sales/distribution, (2) financial control, or (3) materials management/production planning. NIBCO associates on the three business process teams played the following roles:

- *Business review* roles were filled by business leaders who could make the high-level business process redesign decisions based on their own knowledge and experience, without having to ask for permission.
- *Power user* roles were filled by business people who knew how transactions were processed on a daily basis using the existing legacy systems and were able to capture operational details from people in the organization who understood the problem areas.
- *Business systems analyst* roles were filled by persons with strong technical credentials who were also able to understand the business.

Wilson led the technical team of IS specialists, which was responsible for designing and building the new client/server infrastructure as well as providing ABAP programming support, PC training, and help desk support. The new infrastructure would link more than 60 servers and 1,200 desktop PCs (with standardized e-mail and personal productivity tools) to a WAN. Almost every existing PC was to be either upgraded or replaced, and the WAN would be upgraded to a frame relay network that would link headquarters with all North American plants and distribution centers. New technical capabilities would also be required for the product bar-code scanning and labeling functions that were to be implemented as part of the warehouse management changes.

Jim Davis led the three-person change management team. A public relations manager, Don Hoffman, served as the project

EXHIBIT 4
Project Team Composition

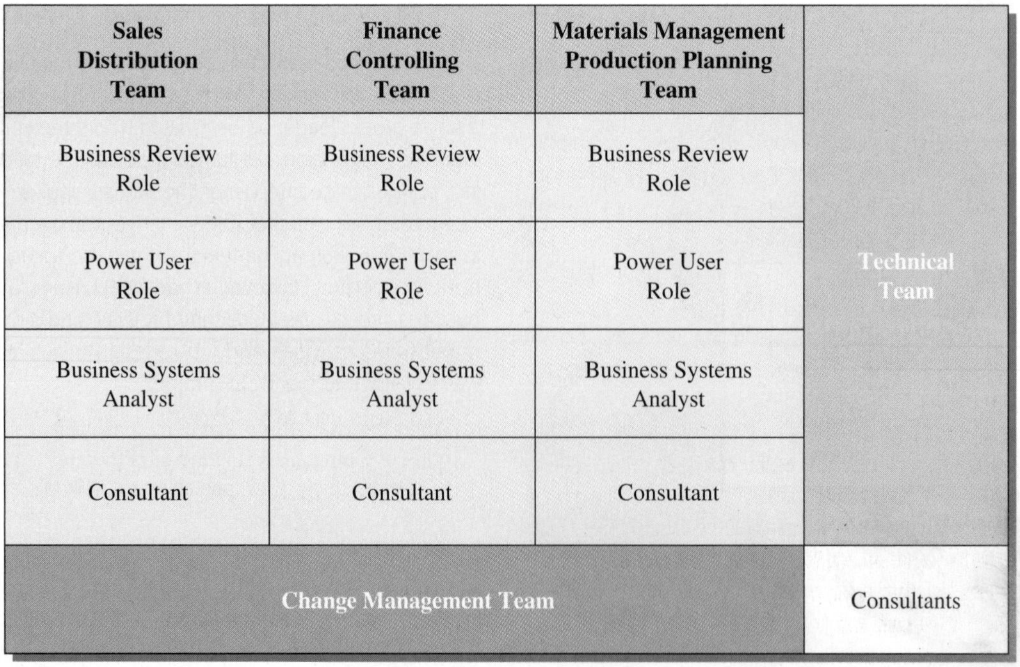

<table>
<tr><th>Sales Distribution Team</th><th>Finance Controlling Team</th><th>Materials Management Production Planning Team</th><td rowspan="6">Technical Team</td></tr>
<tr><td>Business Review Role</td><td>Business Review Role</td><td>Business Review Role</td></tr>
<tr><td>Power User Role</td><td>Power User Role</td><td>Power User Role</td></tr>
<tr><td>Business Systems Analyst</td><td>Business Systems Analyst</td><td>Business Systems Analyst</td></tr>
<tr><td>Consultant</td><td>Consultant</td><td>Consultant</td></tr>
<tr><td colspan="3">Change Management Team</td><td>Consultants</td></tr>
</table>

team's communications/PR person. Steve Hall, an environmental engineer, was responsible for ensuring that all team members and users received the training they needed. Davis had witnessed some training that Hall had done and selected him to lead the training effort for the project.

The R/3 package was to be implemented in a "vanilla" form with essentially no customization. The intent was not to try to reconfigure R/3 to look like the old legacy systems. Rather, the company would adapt to the R/3 "best-practice" processes.

> We felt like SAP had enough functionality within it that we could make, by and large, the choices that we needed to configure the system to accomplish those high-level goals . . . . We would identify what core processes we would need, we would look at the choices within SAP, we would pick the one that most closely mirrored our need, and we would adjust to the difference.
>
> We had to have some senior-level business people who could make the call on those business decisions: how would we configure and why, and what would we let go of and why . . . . We did not have a situation where we had to go ask permission; we had a situation of continuous communication and contact [with top management].
>
> *Jim Davis, Project Co-Lead, Change Management*

To find the best business people for the TIGER team, the three co-leads brainstormed with executives and managers to identify a list of 50 or 60 NIBCO associates who had the skills and competencies needed; the project would require almost half of them. A human resources representative interviewed the candidates with Jim Davis and helped to develop personality profiles, including personal ability to lead and adapt to change, and emotional fit. At some point, the core team would need to put in long hours, 7 days a week.

Four director-level leaders were chosen for business review roles, including the two leaders for sales and distribution. This meant that seven of NIBCO's twenty-eight directors (counting the three project co-leads) would be committed full-time to the project. Because the other directors were needed to keep the business running during the project, the remaining business review roles were filled with managers who had deep enough business knowledge to identify issues as well as strong enough organizational credibility to settle conflicts as they arose.

Two business systems analysts were on each business process team. As liaisons with the technical team, the analysts were to make sure that the technical implementation matched the business requirements. Because few of the IS personnel inherited by Wilson had the appropriate IT-business skill mix for this type of analyst role, Wilson started early in his tenure to use job vacancies to hire people who could fill these anticipated analyst roles. One of these new hires was Rod Masney, who had worked under Wilson a year earlier in another company.

> One of the exciting things about coming to this company was being a part of an ERP implementation. It was very exciting from a personal and career standpoint. I had been a part of a number of implementations for manufacturing businesses and those types of things, but never anything quite this large.
>
> *Rod Masney, Business Systems Analyst*

Early in the project it was decided that the project team members would be dedicated full-time to the project, but there would be no backfilling of their old jobs. Team members were expected to remain on the team throughout the project plus 4 additional months following the Go-Live date. They would then be redeployed back to business units.

IBM consultants were also assigned to each of the five project teams. The IBM project team members brought their technical knowledge to the project not only so that the business could make smart decisions among the R/3 options, but also for knowledge transfer to the NIBCO core team. Many of these consultants also brought experiences from R/3 implementations at other companies that could be used to help NIBCO avoid similar pitfalls. Consultants from the software vendor (SAP) were also occasionally brought in throughout the project—including BASIS and security consultants.

> We said all along, from day one, that we expected to become competent with the tools. We didn't take the approach of "do it to us" like it's done in many places. We took the approach of "show us how" to be an oil painter, and we'll be the artist. We wanted them to show us how the tools work and what the possibilities were. Then we'd decide how we were going to operate. We started with that from day one.
>
> *Scott Beutler, Project Co-Lead, Business Process*

> Their job was to bring to the table a deep knowledge of SAP and how it functions and enough business savvy to be able to understand the business case to help us best configure it in SAP. But we were responsible for all the decisions. We considered them critical members of the team, not somebody separate and apart. But our goal all along was that as soon as we went live, the consultants would go away and we'd manage the business on our own. We didn't want to have to live with them forever.
>
> *Jim Davis, Project Co-Lead, Change Management*

> We used the consultants for what we needed them for—and that was knowledge transfer, extra hands, and technical skills.
>
> *Gary Wilson, Project Co-Lead, Technology*

In addition to these formal team roles, extended team members would be called on to help with documenting the gaps between old and new business processes and helping with master data loads and testing. Because the business employees designated to these roles would continue to work in their business areas during the project, several of them would also be the primary user trainers in preparation for Go Live. After the cutover, many would also serve in local-expert roles.

> We probably consumed anywhere between 150 to 200 resources throughout the project in one way or another—either scrubbing master data, or training, or who knows what else. If we needed hands to key, we went and got them. That's how many people really got involved—and there were a lot.
>
> *Rod Masney, Business Systems Analyst*

The project kickoff was September 30th. It took the company 14 months of planning to get to the kickoff, and the team had 15 months to deliver the ERP system. During the first week, formal team-building exercises were conducted offsite. During the second week, IBM facilitators led the entire team through discussions about the kinds of changes the project would necessitate. For example, team members were asked to think through what it would mean to change to standardized processes from 10 different ways of doing things in 10 different plants with 10 different databases. The intent was to sensitize the entire team to potential sources of resistance and the need for early communication efforts.

Introductory-level training and training on R/3 modules were held on site; team members were sent to various SAP training sites in North America for more in-depth, 2- to 5-day courses. Altogether, the team received almost 800 days of training.

Working in the TIGER Den

Rex Martin was committed to housing the entire project team in a single physical location. The original plan was to move the team to a building across town, but Martin wanted the group to be located closer to NIBCO's senior managers.

A major remodeling project was in progress at the headquarters building, and the team was allocated 5,000 square feet on the first floor. Beutler and Davis read books on team management and came up with a plan to configure the space, which came to be called the TIGER den. The company's furniture manufacturer designed a movable desk (Nomad), which would enable flexible workspace configurations.

> In the end, we were less mobile than we thought we might be, but it created an environment of total teamwork and lack of individual space that forced us to work together and get done what we needed to get done.
>
> *Jim Davis, Project Co-Lead, Change Management*

The TIGER den had no closed doors and no private offices. A large open space called the "war room" had whiteboards on every wall. It was used for meetings of the whole project team, open meetings with other NIBCO associates, system prototyping, and for core-team training during the project. Beutler and his administrative assistant, the change management team, and the IBM project manager used an area with a 6-foot partition, that had a U-shaped conference table and workstations. Wilson kept his office within the IS area in another section of the same building, but spent about 40 percent of his time in the den.

Each business process team had its own small "concentration" room for team meetings. They configured their Nomads in different ways, and each team's space took on its own personality. There was also another open space where extended team members could work and that could be reconfigured as needed.

At one end of the TIGER den was a room with soft couches and chairs designed to facilitate informal meetings. It was also used for formal meetings as well as celebrations around significant project milestones or team members' birthdays.

Because up to 70 people could be working in the den at the same time, phones would have been very distracting. The administrative area had a few phones for outbound calls only, and all team members were given private voice mailboxes and pagers; their pager alerted them when a message went into their voice mailbox. A bank of phones was installed in a small hallway leading out of the den, and emergency numbers were given to family members.

The directors on the project team were used to having private offices, so working without privacy in an open arena alongside the rest of the team took some adjustment. They were told: "Here's a chance to 'live' change management."

Final Project Plan

During the initial months of the project, the co-leads worked with the IBM project leaders to hone in on the scope, cost, and magnitude of the project in order to develop a final project plan with a realistic budget. In early December 1996, the final project scope and resource estimates were presented to the ELT and the Board, based on a Go-Live date 12 months later.

The final project budget was estimated to be $17 million, which was 30 percent higher than the midsummer estimate. One of the major reasons for the significant increase was the inclusion of change management costs (including training) that had been missing from the summer budget. About one-third of the final budget was for technology infrastructure costs, including the R/3 software. Another third was for team costs and the education of NIBCO associates. The final third was for third-party consulting.

The December plan also addressed two major changes in project scope. One was a recommendation to include North America only. For example, sales offices outside of the United States (such as operations in Poland) would not be included in the big bang implementation.

A second scope change was driven by technology issues. At the end of 1996, NIBCO had 17 distribution centers, but its long-term strategy was to consolidate to at least half that number. An R/3 project involving 17 distribution centers would have high technology installation and operations costs as well as high project complexity due to the sheer number of locations. A distribution center consolidation prior to the ERP Go-Live date would therefore reduce both technology costs and implementation complexity.

Although the detailed planning for the distribution center (DC) consolidation was not complete when the final project plan was presented to the Board, by March 1997 the company had committed to consolidate from seventeen small DCs to four large ones: one existing facility would be enlarged, and new managers and associates would be hired to run the three new DC facilities. The goal was to complete the consolidation by September 1997 to allow time to prepare for the cutover to the ERP system.

> SAP provides opportunities for consolidation, so it's not uncommon for companies to decide on a certain amount of consolidation for something. . . . The original timing had the warehouse consolidation getting done ahead of SAP by a couple of months.
>
> *Gary Wilson, Project Co-Lead, Technology*

There were several major business risks associated with the project that also would have to be managed. First, the integration really had to work, because otherwise any one part of the organization could claim that they were no better off, or even less well off, than before the project. This meant the team would have to make decisions focused on the integration goals, which would result in killing some "sacred cows" along the way.

Second, the company could be significantly harmed during the project because most other company initiatives would basically be put on hold. The exception was the distribution center consolidation, and this would involve large-scale personnel changes and increased demands for training. At the same time, it would be important to maintain as much customer satisfaction as possible.

Management also knew that if the project ran late, it could really hurt the company. So the project had to be completed on time with a quality result.

> You can't pull 27 full-time people out of a business that runs fairly lean, and then not backfill and expect business to go merrily on its way. We actually watched one competitor of ours go live with SAP during the course of our implementation, and the first 2 weeks they were live they could not take a customer order. And so we were seeing some real-life horror stories in front of us. So, the risk management from our perspective was: We're gonna deep six this company if we do this poorly or if we don't do it on time.
>
> *Jim Davis, Project Co-Lead, Change Management*

Because there was no backfilling of the jobs held by the project team members, NIBCO associates not on the project team had to take on extra work to sustain normal operations. This meant that the whole organization needed to be committed to the ERP project. An up-front goal of participation by one-third of NIBCO's salaried associates was established to be sure they understood where the project was going, to promote buy-in, and to get the work done.

> There was a team of people who were living and breathing it everyday, but it truly was a whole company effort. I had two individuals that left my organization and were full-time members of the team. We did their work; we absorbed it. That was universal throughout the company.
>
> *Diane Krill, Director, Customer and Marketing Services*

A few months after the project began, a special incentive pay bonus was established for every salaried NIBCO associate. The bonus was tied to a half-dozen criteria (see Exhibit 5). The Go-Live schedule had to be met, or no incentive pay would be distributed: A 30-day grace period, only, would be allowed from the original date set, which was the Monday after Thanksgiving (November 29th). The incentive pay pool would be reduced by 50 cents for every dollar over budget. Four overall project "success" criteria were also established, along with specific measures. The results of these measures would be available for review by the ELT within 2 months after implementation, and the Board would make the final decision as to whether or not these results collectively met the success criteria.

> In the end, being that solid or fierce in holding firm on the timeline was probably one of the main things that made us successful. . . . There was never an option. Slippage was not an option. We had to make the milestones as we went.
>
> *Scott Beutler, Project Co-Lead, Business Process*

Stock options were also granted to all core team members in April 1997 as a retention incentive.

Achieving the Milestones

The project was conducted in four large phases: preparation, analysis, design, and implementation (see Exhibit 6).

Because few tools were available for purchase, the IS team built a number of tools to help with process scripting as well as project management. For example, Project Office was a NIBCO-developed tool for project management and project tracking that used an Access database (MS Office 95). Project Office became the repository for all project planning documents, As-Is and To-Be process scripts, tables to support the documentation for the project, testing plans and results, site visit and training schedules, issue logging, and much more. The

EXHIBIT 5

Criteria for Incentive Pay

Criterion	Measures	Impact on Incentive Pay
On Time	SAP must be live on or before 12/31/97	Required for any incentive pay
Successful	1) Client/server environment measures: - available 90% of agreed-upon time - 95% of real-time response times less than 2 seconds	Executive leadership team will review the results of these four measures and make a recommendation to the board of directors as to whether or not project was a success
	2) Business processes supported by SAP: - 1 day after Go Live, no transaction data entered into legacy systems - 45 days after implementation, less than 15 open data integrity problem reports	
	3) Core management and administrative processes supported by SAP: - close books through SAP within 15 days at first month end	
	4) Training of NIBCO associates in use of SAP and processes: - a minimum of 95% attendance at training classes across the organization	
Within Budget	Control spending to at or below project plan approved by Board 1/28/97	Every $1 over budget reduces the incentive pool by 50 cents

sales order processing script, for example, consisted of more than 100 pages of detailed documentation, and was used as the basis for classroom training documentation. This tool allowed team members to access the latest project documents and to gauge where they were in relation to the project's key milestones.

Due to the time demands of the project, all team members were provided with laptops so that they could work 24 hours a day, 7 days a week, from anywhere they wanted. Because there was no support for mobile (remote access) computing prior to the TIGER project, providing anytime/anywhere support was also symbolic of NIBCO's new commitment to helping its employees leverage their time better using information technology.

> There wasn't much of an e-mail culture before this . . . but before this project was over, we basically had pulled the whole company into this way of life.
>
> *Gary Wilson, Project Co-Lead, Technology*

Business Responsibilities

Finance and Controlling Team The business review lead for the controlling function was Steve Swartzenberg, who had spent more than 5 years in different plant positions, starting as an industrial engineer and working his way up through plant administration; he had recently been promoted to product manager. During the project Swartzenberg worked not only with his current boss, the VP of marketing, but also with the CFO—because the tactical managers of the new controlling module would be controllers within the accounting/finance group.

> My business review role responsibility was to make sure that the functional organizations who would be taking ownership for the controlling module, once we turned it on, were pulling for it. I kept them up to speed on how we were doing on the issues, on the things they needed to help with along the way, so that they knew that their role was to hit each of these critical milestones. None of us wanted to *not* make it, so we

EXHIBIT 6
Implementation Phases

Phase	Major Activities
Preparation	Final project plan—scope and cost. As-Is business analysis. Technical infrastructure specifications. Project management and tracking tools developed.
Analysis	Document As-Is processes as To-Be processes. Analyze gap between To-Be processes and R/3 processes. Identify process improvements and changes to fit R/3. Documentation of inputs, outputs, triggers, business activities, (process) roles, change categories, training requirements.
Design	Configure R/3. Develop training materials. Develop and document specifications (master data, external systems interfaces, reports). Develop prototypes: 1. Operational: module-oriented; prototyping and testing of business processes; reviewed by business review team. 2. Management: module-oriented; demonstrated functionality needed to run business. 3. Business: integrated; all key deliverables configured.
Implementation	Some overlap with design phase. New tactical teams formed with directors heading up risky areas: 1. Master data teams: data cleanup. 2. Customization team: determine customization needed across plants. 3. Implementation infrastructure team: address outstanding hardware issues; plan transition to new system. 4. Help desk team: develop post-live support processes.

knew how it had to knit together—we knew our job was to hit the milestone.

Steve Swartzenberg, Business Review Lead

There were two IBM consultants on the controlling team. One helped with the controlling (CO) module functions of product costing, cost center accounting, and internal orders; team members relied on this consultant to answer detailed questions about what the package could and could not do. The second consultant supported the team on the profitability analysis (PA) and profit center accounting (PCA) sub-modules. When the second consultant left the project, Swartzenberg helped select a replacement who not only understood R/3 details, but also had a strong financial background.

Not coming from accounting, I kind of used him as my accounting consultant—as a kind of sanity check. . . . The controlling module in SAP really is the spot where it all comes together. What you find out is no part of the organization is disconnected from another. It's all connected; the processes are all integrated. If one part falls out, it doesn't link up.

Steve Swartzenberg, Business Review Lead

A major business process change would be to centralize all accounts payable entries that had been decentralized to the plants in the past. Swartzenberg spent extra time developing documentation that included flow charts and other tools to help with the transition. For example, a check-and-balance process was designed for looking at transactions in specific areas where problems would first be visible. The accounting group did these checks every day for the first month after Go Live so that problems could be fixed as they happened, and to avoid snags at the time of the first financial close.

An extended team member from marketing helped develop profitability reporting (P&Ls) for each of the product lines—copper fittings, cast fittings, plumbing, heating valves, etc.—information that was not available under the old systems.

Materials Management/Production Planning Team

The business review lead for the manufacturing production planning (PP) module was John Hall, a NIBCO veteran of 20 years. Hall had been a member of the BCG study team and was involved in the decision to take the big bang approach.

Six months prior to the TIGER project kickoff, Hall had become director of plastics manufacturing.

> The business review teams had 100 percent support from Rex Martin and the ELT. They allowed us to only go to them for major issues. We had the freedom to make decisions.
>
> *John Hall, Business Review Lead*

One of the two power users on the PP team was Jan Bleile, a 25-year NIBCO veteran in production control who had worked on the manufacturing legacy system (Man-Man) and its predecessors. He also had a good rapport with all the old-timers in the plants.

> I was a supply chain master scheduler at that time and the position I was recruited for on the TIGER project was as a power user for the MM/PP team. One of the reasons that I was chosen was that I had been in on all the manufacturing systems implementations that have happened here at NIBCO since we've been computerized. . . . So it really was a natural for me to accept this, when offered, because of the three other implementations that I was on. This one was different in that it was 100 percent dedicated.
>
> *Jan Bleile, Power User*

From the outset, there were concerns about all the changes that would need to take place to implement both new processes and new systems at the plants. Hall worked with other manufacturing directors, the VP of manufacturing, and Scott Beutler to set up 3- to 4-day meetings with TIGER team members at every plant during December 1996. At these meetings the core project team emphasized that R/3 was the system that would be used at all plants, and that all data would reside in it. In turn, the team learned how things were done in each of the plants, including what each plant thought it did that was unique.

Although it was not initially clear whether common processes could be implemented across all NIBCO plants, the project team was able to reframe each plant's tasks into high-level generic processes. The idea was to keep things relatively simple at first. Then, as people became comfortable in using the system, the number of complex features and functionality could be increased. The project team then gained consensus for this common way of doing things, plant by plant—whether the manufacturing process was for plastics, copper, foundry materials, etc.

> We kept pounding the message home that you don't have to believe us, but just give it a try, and do it with an open mind. Every time someone would call and say, "We can't do this, we're different, we need this, we need that" we would say "you're not going to get it, so you've got to give this a try." . . . Just having the CEO as the major champion helps overcome any and all obstacles you can think of.
>
> *Jan Bleile, Power User*

Extended team members for the PP module were formally designated early on. Although they resided at the plants, they also spent time in the TIGER den at headquarters learning about the master data plans and the impacts of real-time online processing. Through these in-person interactions, the project team members learned what process changes would need to be emphasized the most when the plant workers were trained. During the final months of the project, many of these extended team members dedicated 100 percent of their time to conducting training classes at different facilities. Every NIBCO associate who would need an R/3 license was signed up for a certain number of classroom training hours.

The business review lead for the materials management module left the company in May 1997. Although this event was viewed as positive overall (due to internal team conflicts), it also left a major gap. Because this happened so late in the project, John Hall took on this role as well, with help from Beutler.

Sales/Distribution Team Several major process changes were also to be implemented for these functions. First, national accounts (which accounted for a large percentage of sales) would have dedicated NIBCO associates. Second, a much more controlled processing environment would be set up for making changes to customer master data. In the past, changes to customer data, including pricing data, could be made by all customer services (CS) personnel. Under SAP, a new, centralized marketing services group would be formed and customer master data changes would be limited to this group. This more centralized, focused approach would yield revenue gains from better response to national accounts. It would also yield dollar savings because fewer price deductions would have to be given to customers due to internal processing errors.

One of the major challenges facing the project team was the structuring of the customer master data. For example, terms of sale at NIBCO had not been defined in terms of the sales channel of the customer in the past, but in R/3, pricing distinctions are made between wholesalers and retailers. This meant that all NIBCO customers had to be classified by their sales channel. Training was also a major hurdle because about half of the CS staff had used green screen terminals in the past and had to be trained in using a PC with a mouse and graphical user interface (Windows). PCs for the CS group were installed about 8 months before the Go-Live date, and each member of this group had over 45 hours of mandatory R/3 training.

NIBCO's warehouse operations had not been highly disciplined in the past, so large-scale process changes would also be implemented for the distribution function. The risk of the warehouse management implementation was increased by the distribution center consolidation that was going on during the same time period.

> We used to run distribution centers with notebooks. John, who put stock away, put it over in bin 12 in the corner, and would write it down. He knew where the overstock was and you could get away with that in a 50,000-square-foot facility. But when running 250,000-square-foot facilities, you can't do that; you've got to have a system run your facility for you.
>
> *Larry Conn, Extended Team Member*

Technical Responsibilities

During the preparation phase, while the business process teams worked on As-Is analysis, about six IS specialists under Wilson developed a 250-page technical document that became the blueprint for building the new technology infrastructure—the PCs, servers, and networks for every NIBCO location. Over the next 9 months, the technical team worked through the installations for all the plants and distribution centers, and a trainer would travel right behind the technical team and do PC and Windows training as needed.

The TIGER project and the new client/server architecture also required new work processes for the IS organization. New processes for network management, backup and recovery procedures, system change controls, and business-client relationship management needed to be developed. Many of these changes were made under the TIGER project umbrella, and the IBM consultants helped with the IT process design and IT worker reskilling.

> The project leaders worked very hard to manage our consultants. We expanded when we needed to and we contracted very quickly. When a consultant no longer held value for us, we cut him loose. At one time, we counted 50 consultants here.
>
> *Rod Masney, Business Systems Analyst*

During the preparation phase, a new director-level position for systems development was filled with an outside hire, Greg Tipton, who began to take over the day-to-day program management responsibilities from Wilson. Tipton became the primary liaison between the TIGER team and the IS development resources during the design phase as ABAP programming needs increased. All maintenance support for legacy systems was essentially shut down by the summer of 1997 as the entire IS group focused on the R/3 implementation.

In the last months of the project, the IS area was running multiple R/3 environments: the development system, a production system, two training systems, and a test system. IS specialists were also dedicated to cleaning up and converting master data, loading master data, and stress testing the system with real data. Data from 85 different legacy system files and lots of Access databases had to be converted. Although discussions on how to accomplish these critical activities began as early as March 1997, the master data loading processes proved to be more complex than expected, and four complete heavy-duty-testing trials were run.

Change Management Responsibilities

> We were convinced we could configure a system. We were convinced we could build a technical infrastructure that would support it. We were NOT convinced that we could change people's attitudes and behaviors in a way that we could successfully use what we came up with.
>
> *Jim Davis, Project Co-Lead, Change Management*

Because IBM's change management approach was not ERP-specific, the NIBCO team had to learn how to apply it to an R/3 big bang implementation. Some of the IBM change management people had been trained in methods developed by Daryl Conner, CEO of Organizational Development Resources, Inc. Conner's book[2] heightened the leadership team's understanding of the importance of dealing with change management issues at the level of the individual. The overall change management thrust became how to ensure that the R/3 implementation would not drive NIBCO users beyond their abilities to adapt to change.

Although only Davis and two other team members were working full-time on change management issues, all team members were expected to be change leaders. During the selection process they were told that the rest of the organization would be looking to them to understand where the TIGER project was heading and why it made sense to be going in that direction. The team members also had to understand the change implications of their decisions: They were asked to identify what the major impacts would be for people performing a particular function—how they would work together differently, or need different information. The change management team used this knowledge to develop communication and training plans that would help NIBCO associates make those changes.

Identifying the Key Changes Information to help the change management team was captured as part of the business process documentation. For example, as a business process team was preparing To-Be business process documentation, the team members were asked to identify the changes a given process introduced and to categorize them (see Exhibit 7). No process documentation (and later no training script) would be approved until the change management elements were complete.

For example, an associate in accounts payable who worked with NIBCO's legacy systems in the past really had no need to

[2]Daryl R. Conner, *Managing at the Speed of Change*. New York: Villard Books, 1992.

EXHIBIT 7
Change Management Categories

New work (New) The purpose of this category is to highlight where a new job is required. Please reference which role (responsible, accountable, consulted or informed) you are referring to and any details about the job you think would be useful in defining or designing the new job. (Example: Master data is going to be managed and controlled in a centralized location. This would require the creation of a new job which is focused solely on this set of activities.)

Automation of old work (Automate) This should be used when an activity which was previously performed manually will now be automated either in whole or in part. Please note whether this activity should still remain in the same functional area or whether the automation would support its movement to another functional area. (Example: The system will automatically perform the three-way match of a PO, receiver and invoice which we currently reconcile manually.)

Elimination of related activities (Eliminate) This should be used when activities previously performed associated with this activity are no longer required because of a changed process. Please note which function previously performed this eliminated work. (Example: People spend significant time creating special reporting to summarize data in a meaningful way for analysis. The system will provide that data online in a way which allows the analysis to occur without the offline work.)

Work moved from one group to another (Transfer) This should be used when work moves from one function/department to another or when work is moved up or down from one level of management to another. The goal for this element is to track how you expect work to shift as a result of the new activity or process. (Example: Accounts receivable activities occur as a part of the customer service function because of the need for communication with CSRs. The system will now provide information in a way that allows the A/R activities to be performed in the treasury area.)

Risk of process not being done well (Risk) It is important that all new processes be performed efficiently and effectively. This change element should be used when the activity is particularly critical to activities performed downstream and you want to highlight that to the organization. (Example: The new demand pull methodology has a particular "triggering event" which drives all of the downstream events. It is imperative that this activity is performed effectively, or in a particular time frame, or with a particular frequency.)

Increased level of difficulty (Difficulty) This should be used when a new activity or process is substantially more complex or involved than previously. This will give us a heads-up for training and organizational readiness to prepare for a more difficult application. (Example: The current process calls for data to be input without any quality review or analysis. The new process requires a specific analysis to be performed or data to be reviewed and approved prior to entry into the system.)

New business partnerships (Relationships) This should be used to identify where the new activity or process requires people to work together or collaborate in new ways. This could include where information must be shared between groups that don't ordinarily work together. (Example: I currently work with the logistics function to get input for an activity I perform. In the new process, that information will come from manufacturing.)

Miscellaneous (Other) This should be used when you want to highlight an issue or concern that is not covered by one of the other change categories.

talk to the procurement department. In R/3, however, the procurement process has a significant bearing on the transaction documentation that finds its way to accounts payable. So the communication and information sharing between those two groups becomes very important. The change category here would be *relationships*.

Team members were also asked to help determine the training needs for these specific change examples. In all, 450 different business activities in 15 locations had to be addressed.

Internal Communication Plan A critical part of the change management efforts was to provide information and to keep open the communication lines between the project team and the other NIBCO associates. This involved several types of activities—some at headquarters and some onsite at the plants and distribution centers across North America.

> We basically followed the rule. . . somebody has to hear something five different times from three different sources for it to hold. So we looked for every different way that we could get ahold of somebody to get their input and to share information with them, too.
>
> *Jim Davis, Project Co-Lead, Change Management*

A communication analysis of three or four hundred people at NIBCO yielded a type of "spider web" map of internal communication linkages from which the "best connected" associates could be determined. The supervisors of associates with a score above a certain level were then asked for their permission to have these associates invited to participate in a TIGER focus group. About fifteen people at corporate, and three to six people at each plant and distribution center, were then personally invited to join the focus group. Their job was to be a "hub" within the business, to provide bidirectional feedback to the team and to those with whom they were connected in the workplace.

> We didn't say: "You have to be a cheerleader for the project." As a matter of fact we said: "We prefer that you fight back because it is only at the point of resistance that we can identify how to react" . . . . Their job was to get in our face and say: "You know what? You've got a deep problem—people are just not buying into this." Or: "Here's where you're gonna fall off the edge."
>
> *Jim Davis, Project Co-Lead, Change Management*

Another key communications activity was holding monthly "TIGER talks" in the auditorium at corporate headquarters. Jim Davis and selected TIGER team members made presentations and answered questions, and Don Hoffman facilitated the meetings. Each TIGER talk had a different main message, such as project phases, process-focused organizations, training and education plans, technology infrastructure, plans for prototype sessions, organization/role/job design, implementation phase issues, "homestretch" issues, SAP start-up plans, and post-live status.

These face-to-face sessions were open to all NIBCO associates; each session was run four times, so that people could pick a time slot to fit their schedules. Attendance was voluntary, but there was an expectation that members of the focus group would be among the attendees. A summary and internal news release highlighting the main message were published to the entire organization within 48 hours. On a monthly basis, information would be sent out to focus group members and other key players who were not at the meeting, and videotapes of the sessions were also made available.

Team members also conducted two or three rounds of onsite visits to each NIBCO plant and distribution center. That meant that all associates had an opportunity for a physical face-to-face meeting with team members once every 3 to 4 months. Again, questions and answers from these meetings were summarized and distributed within 48 hours to the entire organization.

At each meeting, the team attempted to measure the level of individual commitment to change. A change adoption curve was posted on a flip chart and the meeting leaders pointed out that their goal was to get every NIBCO associate to the buy-in point on the curve. Each participant was given a red sticker and asked to place the sticker on the curve to record "where they were" at the end of each meeting, out of sight of the TIGER team members. Over the course of the project, these scattergrams became a way to measure progress toward an effective implementation. The team could also identify which plants or distribution centers were lagging behind, and then focus on the ability of those associates to assimilate the anticipated changes.

About halfway through the project, a weekly newsletter for those associates who would be using R/3 began to be distributed via e-mail. After training had begun, the newsletter included questions asked in the training classes and the answers provided by the classroom trainers.

User Training Over 1,200 hours of training were delivered at three NIBCO training sites over the 4-month period before Go Live. Depending on their job, users received between 8 and 68 hours of training that focused on the new processes, not just individual tasks. In addition, a user ID was issued during the training classes that entitled associates to access a training "sandbox" where they could try things out and practice transactions or scenarios. User attendance at the training sessions was tracked as part of the organizational incentive scheme, but sandbox practice was not.

Delaying the "Go Live"

The original plan was to go live the Monday after Thanksgiving. This date proved not to be feasible for two primary reasons.

First, the distribution center consolidation was significantly delayed. This resulted in a somewhat chaotic state, as most of the DC managers were still focused on the consolidation, rather than on preparations for the R/3 system. The new staff hardly had a chance to get to know NIBCO's business partners, let alone be prepared for a new system by the Go-Live date.

> These new people who were in all the new facilities never had time to get involved in the SAP project. They never went through appropriate training because they were focused on the consolidation. You cannot do two astronomical projects at the same time. Distribution was not prepared for the SAP start-up and we paid for it.
>
> *Larry Conn, Extended Team Member*

Second, a complete master data load was taking about 17 to 18 days round the clock. The first loading of the master data for manufacturing was sufficiently bad that the consultants had warned them that they were in trouble. The manufacturing data alone was loaded six times. A "stress test" at the beginning of November also reinforced the need for another "full load" test, and time was running out.

> We were probably right out there at the maximum extreme as far as time to get something like this done. There were other small companies out there that had done it in like six or seven months where they just slammed it in. We didn't buy into that.

> We had a ton of master data to move around, which was a big deal for us. It was a major, major effort that slowed us down
>
> *Scott Beutler, Project Co-Lead, Business Process*

The Go-Live date was moved back to the latest possible date—the end of the 30-day grace period. The change management team used the project delay to emphasize scenario training that focused more on business process changes. Although the attendance at training had been very high, there was no formal user-certification process and user readiness continued to be a concern.

The Big Bang: December 30, 1997

On the Go-Live date, there were no consultants on site. Instead of paying the consultants to come in for 2 days in the middle of a holiday week, they were cut loose for the last week in December. Management knew that even if they struggled for those 2 days, they would be bringing the system back down and would have time to work on it over the New Year's holiday weekend to make any fixes. Core team members were on site at plants out in the field, and a help desk was manned by project team members. Besides saving some consultant costs, it was a symbolic move: The company was ready to operate R/3 on its own.

The co-leads had warned the business that "it was going to be ugly" in the beginning. Everything they had read and heard suggested that there would be an initial drop in productivity. The key was not to deny it, but to plan for it and manage through it. On Day 1 they were prepared to be able to operate at only the 50 percent level.

The project team members were kept on the team for only 2 months after the Go-Live date, rather than 4 months. The business units were clamoring for people to come back, and just did not want to wait any longer.

> Ideally, we should have had them for another 60 days because we went through a lot of growing pains, and we could have done much better if we had the team together longer. But . . . it was unraveling on us and we just had to let people go.
>
> *Jim Davis, Project Co-Lead, Change Management*

By the time they went live, most team members knew where they would be redeployed. Some went back to their old jobs, but several received promotions or new opportunities and many went into newly created jobs. Some of the extended team members found that their business groups continued to rely on them for their in-depth R/3 knowledge. A few of the power users went into SAP support positions within the IS organization.

CASE STUDY III-8

BAT TAIWAN: IMPLEMENTING SAP FOR A STRATEGIC TRANSITION

> We needed a new system to support the new business model. A/P and A/R had never been done in Taiwan before, and the timeline was very short. We told them SAP is not new to Asia, and if it works in operating companies similar to ours (like Singapore) there is no reason why it should not work for us. Furthermore, the integrated information derived from the SAP system is going to help make our jobs more efficient and meaningful. There was a huge buy-in.
>
> *Mr. Ma, BAT Taiwan Country Manager*

> Very few of our people had any experience in actually using an ERP system; they didn't have an integrated system view of things. So we depended a lot on the proven template. As a team we said there should be minimal, minimal changes to the template. We don't want to change the system and get away from those embedded best practices.
>
> *Mr. Lee, Project Co-Lead, BAT Taiwan*

The Asia Pacific Regional IT Manager, Mr. Ponce, was reflecting on the recent SAP implementation in Taiwan. The project marked an important business transition for the Taiwan market, and it also represented a big victory for insourcing an SAP implementation at BAT. What were the important lessons from the implementation approach and management of this project? How could they be amplified as best practices to other parts of the Asia Pacific region and BAT as a whole?

Company Background

British American Tobacco (BAT) is a 99-year-old company in the tobacco industry that has grown to be one of the top three global players through organic growth and acquisitions. Formerly B.A.T. Industries, it spun off its financial services business in 1998 and merged with the global cigarette company Rothmans International in 1999. BAT's local and international brands are sold in six world regions: Africa, America Pacific, Asia Pacific, Europe, Latin America, and Mesca (Middle East and Central Asia). A seventh division, STC (Smoking Tobacco and Cigars), is a global division operating in more than 100 countries. Corporate headquarters for BAT is based at Globe House in London.

The profit centers are end markets, typically at the country level. Small- to medium-sized end-markets typically report into an area cluster, a self-sufficient management unit led by an area director. An end market is headed by a country manager who reports to an area director, and each area director reports to a regional director.

For example, the Asia Pacific region has five management units: Asia Pacific North (APN), Asia Pacific South (APS), Malaysia, Australasia, and Indonesia. BAT Taiwan is part of the APN management unit, which also includes Hong Kong, The People's Republic of China, and Macau. The country manager for Taiwan has a report line to the managing director for APN, who is also the country manager for China. The APN offices are based in Hong Kong.

BAT Taiwan

BAT Taiwan is a branch office of BAT Services, Ltd., UK (BATUKE), with responsibilities for trade and brand marketing. After the tobacco market in Taiwan was liberalized in 1987, imported cigarettes were allowed to be sold via local agents. Initially, BAT brands were sold in Taiwan by Brown & Williamson and BATUKE through different distributors. Beginning in 1992, all Brown & Williamson's brands were sold through the BATUKE network worldwide. As a result of this global initiative, the importation and distribution of all BAT brands in Taiwan was consolidated, with China Merchants, Ltd., being appointed as the sole importer/distributor for Taiwan. In 1999, the BAT-Rothmans merger resulted in another realignment. Rothmans used a local agent, Taiwan International Tobacco Company, as its sole distributor. In April 2000, both distributors were merged

---

 This case was prepared for class discussion rather than to illustrate either effective or ineffective handling of an administrative situation. Personal names have been camouflaged at the request of British American Tobacco management. The authors are grateful to all of the BAT managers who were interviewed by the authors for this study.

EXHIBIT 1
Tax Law Change in Taiwan

Old Tax Law	New Tax Law
Monopoly tax at NT$830 per 1,000 sticks of cigarettes (mille)	1) Import duty levied 27% of CIF (import) price
	2) Excise tax @ NT$590 per 1,000 sticks
	3) Health tax @ NT$250 per 1,000 sticks
	4) Value added tax (VAT) @ 5% of consumer price

and now operate under a new corporate entity known as Concord Tobacco Company.

The Rothmans merger also resulted in a more progressive portfolio of brands being available to the BAT Taiwan market. Prior to the merger, BAT's major brand was SE555, but its 2.5-percent market share was declining due to its older consumer profile. After the merger, the BAT market share was slightly boosted from 4.9 percent to 5.3 percent, and the spend focus was shifted to Dunhill, an ex-Rothmans brand, which was more appealing to younger adults.[1] The Taiwan management team also rationalized its brands' stock keeping units (SKUs) to improve its marketing focus and use of resources.

Taiwan has more than 70,000 retail outlets, of which about 4,000 outlets are under five large convenience store chains: 7-11 (about 2,600 outlets), Family Mart (about 1,000), Circle K, Hi Life, and Niko Mart. These five large chain stores are still growing at a rapid pace, at the expense of the independent "mom and pop" stores and "beetle hawkers," and currently account for 43 percent of BAT's volume.

Taiwan's business environment has also been undergoing some major changes due to major bilateral negotiations in preparation for entry into the World Trade Organization (WTO). To provide a more level playing field for international tobacco companies, the Taiwan Tobacco and Wine Monopoly will have to be dissolved. Two new laws relating to the new administration and taxation of tobacco products were passed in April 2000, but have yet to be enforced, pending Taiwan's accession–which has been delayed by the deferment of China's entry. The legislated change in Tobacco Tax legislation from a specific tax per mille to a mixed tax regime will have significant impacts on pricing, market size and profitability. (See Exhibit 1.)

In the face of these changing market dynamics, and the BAT-Rothmans merger, BAT Taiwan commissioned Bain Consulting to do a full market potential study, to assess the size of the market opportunities and to identify the investment opportunities. This study identified Taiwan as one of the key profitable growth markets in the Asia Pacific region. It also highlighted various strategic options to pursue in order to realise BAT potential in this market: Besides a higher level of investment behind its "drive brand" (Dunhill), a change in business model would be necessary to grow the business and to reap supply-chain savings.

Under the new business model, Taiwan would be directly importing its own products and selling directly to key accounts (e.g., big 5 convenience chains) and its distributor, who would also focus on direct store delivery, as opposed to selling only to the wholesale trade as it had in the past. The plan was to begin direct importing by January 1, 2001. The direct-sales operation would be piloted first in Taipei and then rolled out to the rest of Taiwan sometime before mid-year 2001.

The IT Function at BAT

The information technology (IT) function within BAT mirrors the overall company structure. The global CIO is located at Globe House and has direct reports with responsibilities for IT infrastructure, IT service delivery, e-business and business system initiatives, and IT people and processes. Under the global CIO, there has been an increased emphasis on global strategies to help reduce the costs of implementing integrated IT

[1]The launch of Dunhill 1mg in July 2000 contributed to the growth of the Dunhill brand family by 170 percent in 2000.

solutions and ongoing IT service delivery. For example, the newly appointed head of business integration at Globe House has global responsibilities for IT standardization and consolidation initiatives.

BAT currently delivers IT services via three data centers geographically located in Europe (Hamburg, Germany), North America (Macon, Georgia), and Asia Pacific (Kuala Lumpur, Malaysia), and are governed by regional management. All three data centers now operate under a shared services model: by consolidating IT operational support functions at the regional level, economies can be achieved, and these cost savings contribute to the profitability of the BAT end markets that purchase their IT services via a chargeback arrangement.

Europe was the first region to extend the shared services concept beyond data center operations to include application services: In 1997 an Enterprise Center of Excellence (ECoE) began to offer hard-to-find SAP expertise to northern European countries for their R/3 implementation projects. Today the ECoE is also providing SAP services for Latin America.

In the Asia Pacific region, a data center (APDC) was established in Technology Park, Malaysia, in early 1999. Since that time, the APDC has evolved into a shared services organization (APSS) that combines two business streams: a data center and a competency center (center of excellence) for SAP. Personnel with SAP and other IT skill sets are readily available in Malaysia at a cost quite low compared to the other markets, due in part to early SAP installations in the oil and gas industries and recent government incentives for economic growth in high-technology industries.

While the data centers/shared services units are providing support for shared business system solutions, IT organizations that exist at each management unit are responsible for managing the use of IT for their respective end markets. These responsibilities include identifying business requirements, identifying IT solutions, building business cases for IT projects, and managing support services (including local, shared and outsourced services). For example, APN has an IT organization based in Hong Kong with responsibilities covering all the end markets in APN, including China, Hong Kong, and Taiwan. The smaller end markets typically operate with very few IT resources of their own but share resources from the management unit center. For example, BAT Taiwan only has one IT technical support resource onsite for desktop and LAN support, who has a dotted-line report to the IT organization for APN.

New Computer Systems for Taiwan: The ERP Choice

The new business model for BAT Taiwan created a need for a new computer system for functions and processes not previously performed. The Taiwan end market needed to have its own accounts payable and accounts receivable systems because these functions had previously been handled by BAT U.K. It also needed a system to support direct selling and inventory management for multiple sales channels, not just for a single distributor.

Two ERP platform standards had been prescribed for all BAT solutions by 1998: SAP R/3 and Sage Tetra CS/3. The Sage system was selected for less complex, smaller operations that did not need the functionality of SAP and that required a low-cost ERP solution. SAP R/3 was initially viewed as the standard solution for larger, more complex BAT markets only, because it had proven to be a very expensive system to implement and maintain. However, because the Sage system did not scale well, it was no longer viewed as the best solution for BAT organizations in rapidly growing markets. In mid-1999, for example, the former head of IT for APN (now the Asia Pacific Regional IT manager) had put an ERP implementation for the Hong Kong end market on hold because of the weaknesses of both standard options: CS/3 was not viewed as a sufficiently robust system for the Hong Kong market, but the costs of an SAP solution at that time appeared astronomical.

Although Globe House sets strategy and dictates the standard IT platforms, each end market chooses which ERP platform standard to implement, as well as when to implement it. During 1999 and the first 6 months of 2000, however, several BAT regions had gained much more expertise in implementing both ERP platforms. Some of these implementations were brought forward to achieve Y2K compliance. Other projects were undertaken as part of data integration initiatives for the Rothmans merger: Rothmans brands were transferred to BAT (according to local government restrictions) and BAT's processes and standard systems were adopted for all operations.[2]

Within the Asia Pacific region, SAP R/3 projects had been carried out in Australia, Malaysia, and Singapore. Malaysia and Singapore were originally implemented based on the Symphony template; following the merger with Rothmans, however, the Malaysian implementation was changed significantly and it is now regarded as using a different template. Australia is currently using a BAT SAP system for manufacturing, and a Rothmans SAP system for sales. Hence, the Asia Pacific region is currently using three different SAP R/3 templates to satisfy area needs. Many of these projects had been done with Andersen Consulting (now Accenture) as the implementation partner, some using SAP's rapid implementation methodology (Accelerated SAP or ASAP). Because of the success of these projects and growing pressures for common data standards, it was expected that SAP would become the

[2]Some of Rothmans' business units had implemented SAP, and other business units were using BPCS on an AS/400 platform.

solution for all end markets over time, if it could be implemented at a reasonable cost.

> When reviewing the APSS model for implementing SAP, we found that the difference in total cost of ownership between CS3 and SAP became insignificant if we use the common configuration approach. Rather than taking an interim solution for cost reason, it's more effective for us to commit a marginally higher investment and advance directly to the endgame solution—which is SAP.
>
> *Head of IT, APN*

In July 2000, a 2-day study of the SAP project for Taiwan was conducted by the APSS Applications Manager for SAP with a team that had representatives from APN, BAT Australia, BAT Singapore, and APSS. The outcome was a high-level system specification document for implementing SAP R/3. The recommendation was that R/3 modules for sales and distribution (SD), materials management (MM - purchasing and inventory management), financials (FI including fixed assets), and controlling (CO including profitability analysis) be implemented in two phases. Phase 1 would support direct importing and distribution to one customer (a former distributor) and would be operational by January 1, 2001. Phase 2 would support direct sales and distribution to key accounts and be operational within 6 months later.

Selecting an IT Partner

Although APN IT could provide project management expertise as well as PC desktop and LAN support, it had no SAP R/3 expertise. An implementation partner with functional and technical SAP experience was therefore needed. Further, Taiwan needed a contract for IT services with a BAT global data center to host the SAP application as well as a contract for ongoing application maintenance: IT resources would need to be contracted for periodic system requests such as new reports, as well as for the periodic software upgrades provided by SAP.

Following the high-level study, both the European and the Asia Pacific shared services organizations were invited to submit proposals for Taiwan's R/3 implementation as well as ongoing operations and support. Taiwan would then select the best proposal based on the R/3 template and other considerations.

The European shared services groups already provided computer support for BAT Taiwan as a user of SAP financials for the BAT U.K. operations. Because Taiwan had experienced the European data center's high-quality operational support first-hand, continuing to work with this data center was a clear option. In addition, the SAP Center of Excellence in Europe was a viable partner for the R/3 implementation project.

The SAP application services group that was part of APSS was a newer group, but had played a part in the other SAP implementations in the AP region. APSS had also been running SAP applications for Australia, Malaysia, and Singapore for more than 16 months at the time of the Taiwan proposal, so APSS also had a proven track record as a regional data center for SAP.

Although Andersen Consulting (now Accenture) had been the implementation partner on a number of BAT R/3 implementations for the AP region, such as those in Australia and Singapore, R/3 project costs using an external implementation partner had been quite expensive. For a new, still small, Taiwan end market, project costs were a very important consideration, so the decision was made to not request a bid from an external consulting firm. In addition, a regional BAT partner would be more knowledgeable about BAT business processes and existing BAT templates for SAP implementations

Proposals were received from the shared services organizations in Europe (EDC and EcoE) and the Asia Pacific (APSS). The decision was made to go with APSS for the R/3 implementation, as well as for SAP hosting and ongoing support, for a number of reasons.

First, the proposals from both Europe (EcoE) and APSS were quite similar with respect to implementing R/3. Although the European shared services group had more extensive SAP implementation experience, APSS had recently used a template (code-named "Symphony") for an SAP implementation with a similar business model in BAT Singapore. Thus, there was high confidence in the SAP functional and technical expertise in the AP region.

Second, for the ongoing operations and maintenance roles, APSS had two major advantages over the EDC: lower personnel costs in the AP region compared to Europe and the same time zone. By mid-2000, the annual operational costs at APSS for hosting an SAP R/3 user were U.S.$3,500, and were expected to drop further in 2001. BAT Taiwan would not have to purchase the SAP software licenses, which would be held by APSS.

> BAT Taiwan saves a lot of time and effort by letting APSS purchase and own the licenses and we only pay a monthly fee. We don't have to track the licenses as assets, manage maintenance contracts and payments, process procurement and track global pricing policies and terms. We also do not have to worry about selling excess licenses when the number of users comes down.
>
> *Head of IT, APN*

> It does not matter where the support group sits. What is crucial is the skill competencies, at the right price, in a politically stable region. Since we're using standard BAT operations, the quality aspect is assured. So cost and support capability become the most critical.
>
> *Mr. Ma, BAT Taiwan Country Manager*

Because Taiwan was in the same time zone as the APSS organization, its people would be able to communicate more easily about their support needs with the shared services group in APSS than with the shared services group located 7 hours away in Europe.

There were also some "natural synergies" with APSS that would help with communications: Taiwan, unlike the rest of the Mandarin-speaking world, uses only the Chinese language for business transactions.[3] The APSS staff in Kuala Lumpur, like other Malaysian businesses, includes many people of Chinese heritage, including some who speak Mandarin.

> The significant time difference between Taiwan and Europe was problematic, as was the lack of knowledge of the Chinese language. Taiwanese are not all fluent in English, and the local system requirements would include preparing invoices and printing reports in Chinese.
>
> *Major Project Management Manager, APN IT*

Taiwan's R/3 Project

The APSS project plan for Taiwan outlined a fixed-cost implementation budget of U.S.$100,000 for Phase 1 and an estimated budget of U.S.$50,000 for Phase 2. Phase 1 would involve 250 APSS man-days and consulting fees of U.S.$77,700. The other costs would include technology upgrades and direct expenses for travel and living expenses for the APSS consultants. The Phase 2 costs would include an estimated U.S.$30,000 for software development costs for unique local requirements.

The Taiwan office named this project Confucius because the project kickoff took place during the week of Confucius' birthday and it was hoped that the intellectual capability pooled from a number of areas within BAT would be as good as that of the renowned Chinese philosopher, if not better.

The project cost was based on several assumptions. (See Exhibit 2.) One key assumption of the plan related to the use of the Symphony template developed by APSS and used in Singapore (BATS). By using this template, Taiwan could leverage BAT's best practices for the new business processes, as well as take advantage of a template that was recently reported to be 95 percent compliant with the corporate data standards set by Globe House.[4]

The Symphony template initially included configuration for the financial and controlling modules, with other modules added later.

The four primary business processes would be order-to-cash (accounts receivable), requisition-to-payment (accounts payable), inventory management, and plan-and-manage-enterprise, which includes profitability analysis. However, because many of the business processes would be new to the Taiwan office and few staff members had prior in-depth experience with integrated systems in general, few changes to the template itself were anticipated. Customization would only be done for legal or statutory reporting purposes. Further, BAT Taiwan was very mindful of the dangers of customizing standard systems.

> One of the things I learned from my previous company and in BAT was that when we modified the system to suit our local operational needs, normally in the name of enhancement, we changed the system to a point beyond recognition. That's where the problems start. Later, we found that it was difficult to fit in vendors' enhancements, modules, and whatever. To me, it's the resistance to take on processes that have been established and tested as a more efficient way of doing things; we tend to hold onto old habits. It's a mind-set challenge.
>
> *Mr. Ma, BAT Taiwan Country Manager*

For Phase 1, a three-stage implementation approach, developed by APSS with reference to the ASAP methodology, was to be used. (See Exhibit 3.) The business users would participate in the detailed requirements study, in cleaning up data to be converted, verifying the data conversion, and participating in system testing and system rollout. The system would be configured by APSS personnel to reflect Taiwan's business environment, with such details as the number of warehouses and the accounts to be debited or credited in specific circumstances. The development environment would consist of a three-instance development landscape with DEV (development), QAS (quality assurance), and PRD (production) servers, all housed in Kuala Lumpur. R/3 version 3.1H would be implemented for Phase 1.

The plan for Phase 2 included potential solutions to two system requirements unique to doing business in the Taiwan end market. First, an invoicing system required by the Taiwan government (Government Universal Invoice, referred to as GUI) would need to be purchased and integrated with the SAP system. Because this capability would be required for doing business in Taiwan, it was anticipated that the module would be developed by SAP Taiwan. Second, a Chinese language module would be required because Taiwan conducts business communications almost exclusively in its official language. All reports, including those produced by the GUI, and certain parts of the system needed to be in the official Chinese language. APSS planned to request help from SAP Malaysia in producing such a module.

For Phase 1, APSS would provide an application team leader and three other full-time application consultants onsite (which could include contract employees hired by APSS from their local

[3] Taiwan uses the traditional Chinese language, rather than simplified Chinese, as its official language. Chinese is the written form of the language; Mandarin is the spoken form of the language.

[4] A recent review of BAT templates across the regions sponsored by Globe House concluded that the Symphony template had the highest compliance with the corporate data template among all the current templates.

EXHIBIT 2
APSS Assumptions for Cost Estimating Phases 1 and 2

- BATS template is extended to include BAT Taiwan in this implementation, and business requirements not supported by BATS template are considered out of scope, with the exception of Fixed Assets, which is not part of the template but will be set up for BAT Taiwan.
- BATS template remains at v3.1H and will be upgraded to v4.6x in Q2 2001. There will be no SAP upgrade during the course of this project. The cost of v4.6x upgrade shall be shared with BATS and BAT Mkt. The cost of upgrade to BAT Taiwan is estimated to be at U.S.$57,000 but the amount will be reviewed again before the upgrade commences.
- BAT Taiwan project is to commence not earlier than mid-September 2000 and a lead time of 4–6 weeks is required to mobilize the resources once the project is awarded to APSS.
- Estimate is based on the high-level understanding gathered during the 2-day SAP study in July 2000. The system specification, documented after the study, forms the basis of this proposal.
- The estimate takes into consideration efforts for 18 customized reports (please refer to Appendix B) in Phase 1.
- A total of 24 business processes will be covered in this project. Refer to Appendix A for details.
- Documents printed in Chinese are not a requirement in Phase 1.
- BAT Taiwan will use the data center services from APSS and will use the existing hardware in APSS. Please refer to Appendix C for the service-level agreement.
- Existing WAN bandwidth is sufficient but will need to reconfirm during the project.
- BAT Taiwan will assume project management, communication plan and execution, development of user procedures, and local infrastructure management.
- Project site and resources are based in Taiwan and there is no necessity to travel outside of Taiwan head office.
- Full-time resources are identified and assigned to the project as per project plan to ensure on-time delivery and quality output of project deliverables.
- The business resources assigned to the project are subject-matter experts in their respective functional areas, and are either decision makers or are in a position to influence the process owners.
- BAT Taiwan resources assigned to the project will be equipped with the knowledge to be the first-level support after Go Live.
- A single set of chart of accounts is used by BATS, BAT Mkt and BAT Taiwan. BATS finance manager has been appointed as custodian for COA. Any request for COA maintenance shall be forwarded by the respective end markets to the custodian for action.

market). These four APSS team members would work at the BAT Taiwan offices, beginning with the project kickoff at the end of September 2000 until 2 weeks after the implementation date. A part-time APSS programmer would also be assigned to the project, but would primarily work out of the APSS offices in Kuala Lumpur.

Initial Schedule

The original schedule was to implement the R/3 modules in two phases. Phase 1, to be initiated September 25 and completed by January 2, involved the modules to support direct importation: parts of the SD, MM (purchasing and inventory

EXHIBIT 3
Eight-Week, Three-Stage Project Approach

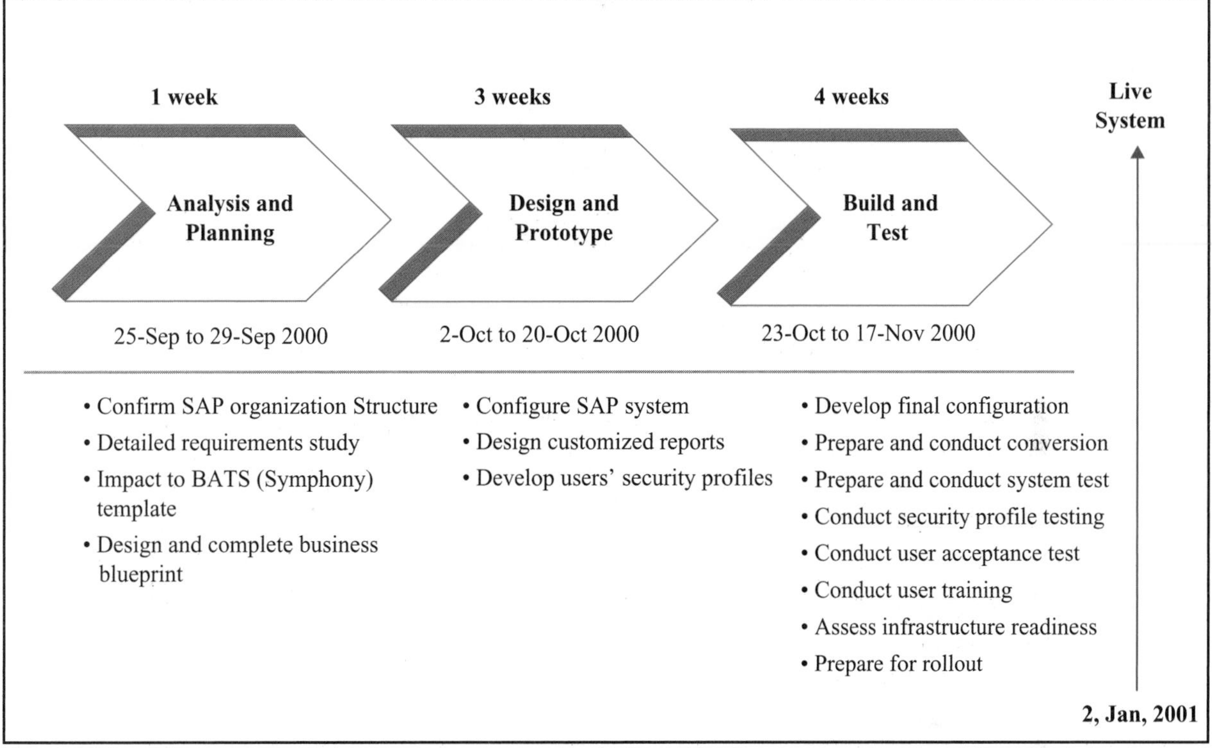

management), and FI/CO modules. Phase 2, to be completed by June 2001, would involve implementing the additional modules needed for direct sales and distribution to key accounts, as well as the specific invoicing system required by the Taiwan government and software to support the reports in Chinese for the area offices. The Phase 1 system would therefore support importing to just one customer: Taiwan's current distributor. The distributor's system would continue to be used for the GUI reporting until Phase 2 provided these customized capabilities.

Initially, the plan was to complete the Phase 1 development and testing within 8 weeks (by the end of November) to provide a buffer for training the business users in not only the new system, but also in the process changes associated with the new business model. The business users would begin with 18 customized reports.

Although the APSS staff would be full-time, the team members from Taiwan needed to continue to perform some of their current functions during the project. Further, the team members would also need to help train temporary or new personnel that would be brought in near the end of the project.

The Project Team

The leaders for the project team brought together three sources of expertise from the three organizations involved: IT project management from APN; BAT template, SAP package, and technical knowledge from APSS; and local business needs from BAT Taiwan. The country manager for Taiwan, Mr. Ma, served as the business sponsor for the project. The project leaders from APN, Taiwan, and APSS were empowered to make project decisions and formally reported to Mr. Ma and the head of IT for APN, via a project steering committee. (See Exhibit 4.)

The Major Project Manager in the IT APN organization, who had previously been a consultant for one of The Big Five consulting firms but did not have any SAP training, was the IT co-lead responsible for overall management of the project. He developed the schedule and task breakdown, the timing of each task, and the resources needed. His work plan became the final project plan, and he was responsible for monitoring the achievement of the milestones and verifying the quality and scope of the resulting system.

Initially, the lead business role for the project was played by the manager of finance for BAT Taiwan. However, at the time of

EXHIBIT 4
Project Team Composition at Time of Kickoff

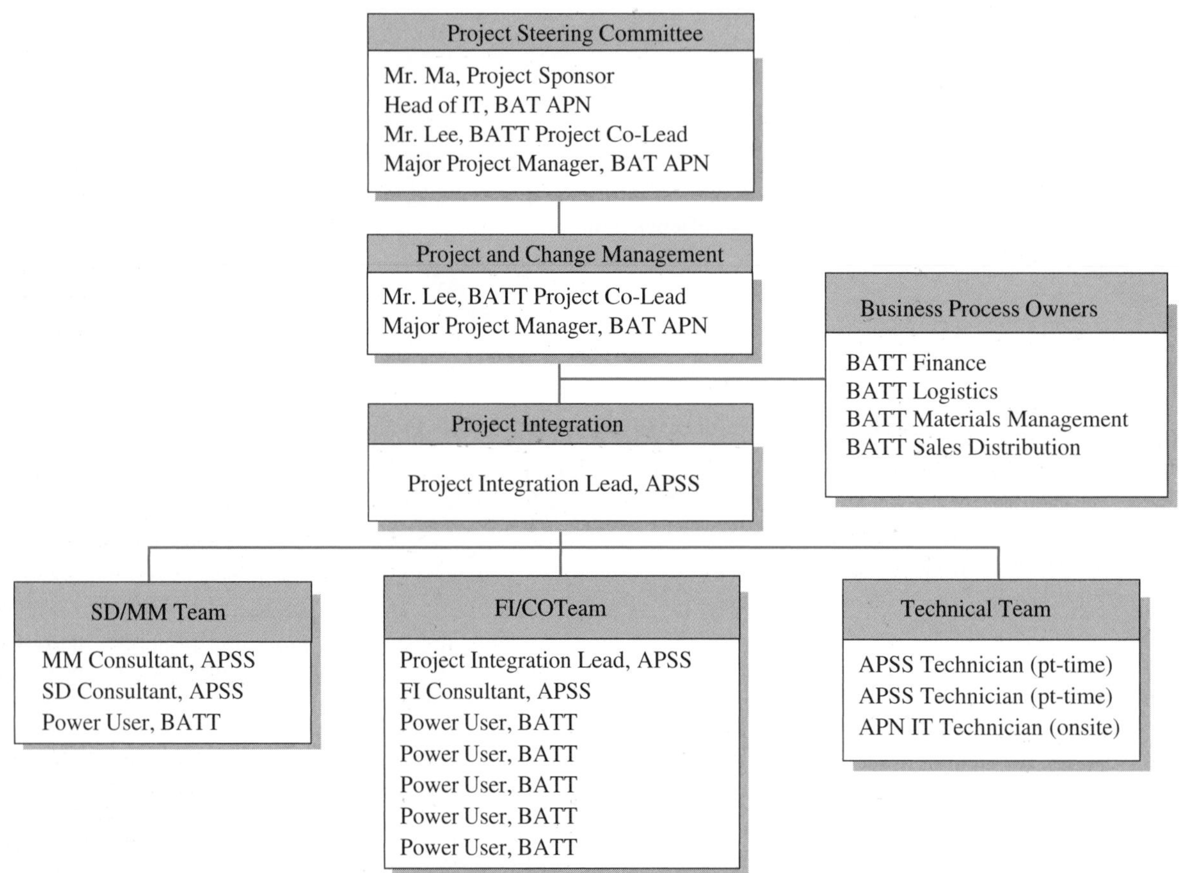

the project kickoff, she announced her resignation from BAT. The lead business manager role for the project was then assumed by Mr. Lee, who was at the time the trade marketing manager for BAT Taiwan and was the logistics process owner on the project. Lee had been Country Manager in Thailand and had experience with the core processes (such as accounts receivable and inventory management) during earlier employment at Johnson & Johnson in the U.S.

For the remainder of the project, Lee took responsibility for the business process owner role for finance as well as logistics. As project co-lead, he was also responsible for co-leading the change management efforts for the project. Two other Taiwan managers also played business process owner roles.

An APSS manager, who was a certified accountant with an MBA, was selected to play the Project Integration Lead role and to lead the APSS development team for the Taiwan project.

> This APSS manager was selected to lead the project integration because he had strong knowledge of financials, the business, and the [SAP] FI module. Plus he had managed other ERP project implementations. He also was able to speak Mandarin, to foster communications.
>
> *SAP Applications Manager, APSS*

The APSS Project Integration lead was responsible for process integration as well as the day-to-day progress of the project and the work by the APSS team members. He and one other APSS consultant were assigned to the FI/CO modules; one APSS consultant each was assigned to the SD and MM modules. There were two part-time technical team members at APSS (see Exhibit 4).

The initial plan was for the four full-time members of the APSS development team to go to Taiwan for 3 weeks at a time and then return to Kuala Lumpur (KL) for the following weekend for personal reasons. However, government regulations permitted nonresidents to work in Taiwan for only 2 weeks at a time. Therefore the return weekend visits to KL became biweekly. Further, because they could obtain a visa for only 2 months, they remained in Kuala Lumpur for 1 week every 2 months to renew their visas. The week-long visa stays in KL were staggered so that two APSS team members always remained onsite in Taiwan. Pressing issues were discussed with absent team members by phone as needed, and the Project Integration Lead provided a weekly progress report by phone to the APSS Applications manager, who was serving as the APSS lead on an R/3 project in Thailand during several weeks of the Taiwan project.

> Everything was coordinated with timelines. You could do the project at a distance, but being co-located made it a lot easier: when you hit an issue, you could say, "Let's have a meeting to discuss this."
>
> *SAP Application Consultant, APSS*

The manager of finance for BAT Taiwan was initially responsible for choosing the "power users" for the project team based on information provided by APSS about the user expertise that would be needed. Five Taiwan employees were selected to work on the FI/CO modules (see Exhibit 4). Only one user was assigned to work on the SD and MM modules because no one in the Taiwan office had previously been performing these functions; the person had gained experience with sales and logistics functions when employed at Rothmans.

None of the Taiwan users had prior experience on SAP projects, but some users had entered data into the SAP R/3 financials system (of BATUKE) and one user had some experience with Oracle systems. All team members were considered fast learners who would be able to pick up the new system quickly.

> The good thing about Taiwan is that most of the managers here are pretty new in the organization. They are young, well-educated (many have MBAs), and have a high level of computer literacy. They are open-minded and are more prepared to take on changes. They knew that whatever we were doing in the past, things were going to be different, and they knew that what we had was cumbersome, that we could not go forward with a bunch of non-integrated systems. They welcomed the [SAP] system; this was going to help them do their job. Their commitment level was extremely high. So the credit is due to the people themselves.
>
> *Mr. Ma, BAT Taiwan Country Manager*

All of the Taiwan team members continued to also do their regular jobs during the project. One manager, who had just rejoined the Taiwan office in a supervisory role, was able to devote 70 percent of his efforts to the project. The BAT Taiwan Project Co-Lead was able to juggle the workloads of the part-time project team members that reported to him. The trade marketing position was left open, but the country manager helped with that role.

> The Taiwan operations were small at that time. This made it more difficult for the project team, because they had to deal with day-to-day activities as well as the project. But they also had full senior management support.
>
> *Major Project Manager, APN IT*

There were three technical team members (see Exhibit 4). The APN IT resource already based in Taiwan was responsible for the telecommunications infrastructure to support system access by five business partners in Taiwan. The R/3 Basis expert from APSS worked offsite until a week before the Go-Live date, when he spent 2 weeks in Taiwan. The third person on the technical team was responsible for creating ABAP reports. Later in the project, she was replaced by a programmer from SAP Malaysia. Just prior to Go Live, this programmer spent 3 weeks in Taiwan to ensure that all the reports were functioning correctly.

Kickoff Meeting

A 1-day project kickoff meeting was held in Taiwan at the end of September and was run by the manager of finance for BAT Taiwan. Most of the project team members and all of the business process owners were present, as were the brand and trade marketing managers. The project co-leads from APSS and APN talked to the whole office staff—both expert and casual users—about the need to be supportive of the project team members over the coming months.

> They made a presentation to the whole office—whether they would be actual users or a final user at the end of the day. They said, "These people are taking on a lot in a short period of time...and you should not make too many unreasonable demands during this time period." They were told that the project was a critical part of the full potential initiative, so let's pull together on this one.
>
> *Mr. Lee, Project Co-Lead, BAT Taiwan*

The APSS team members worked in a conference room just down the hall from the other managers. All the team members got along well together, both in the work environment and socially—including some weekend get-togethers.

Exhibit 5 documents the High-Level Work Plan with the 8-week project milestones. During the Business Blueprint Phase (high-level requirements), the APSS team members met with the key users to explain the processes in the template and to learn about local needs. The fact that the APSS personnel knew BAT's business really helped, because Taiwan had not had to deal with accounts payable, accounts receivable, or inventory in the past.

> They added a lot of value. When we needed to decide how we wanted to configure something, they would say, "The BAT way is this."
>
> *Mr. Lee, Project Co-Lead, BAT Taiwan*

EXHIBIT 5
Work Plan and Milestones for Phase 1

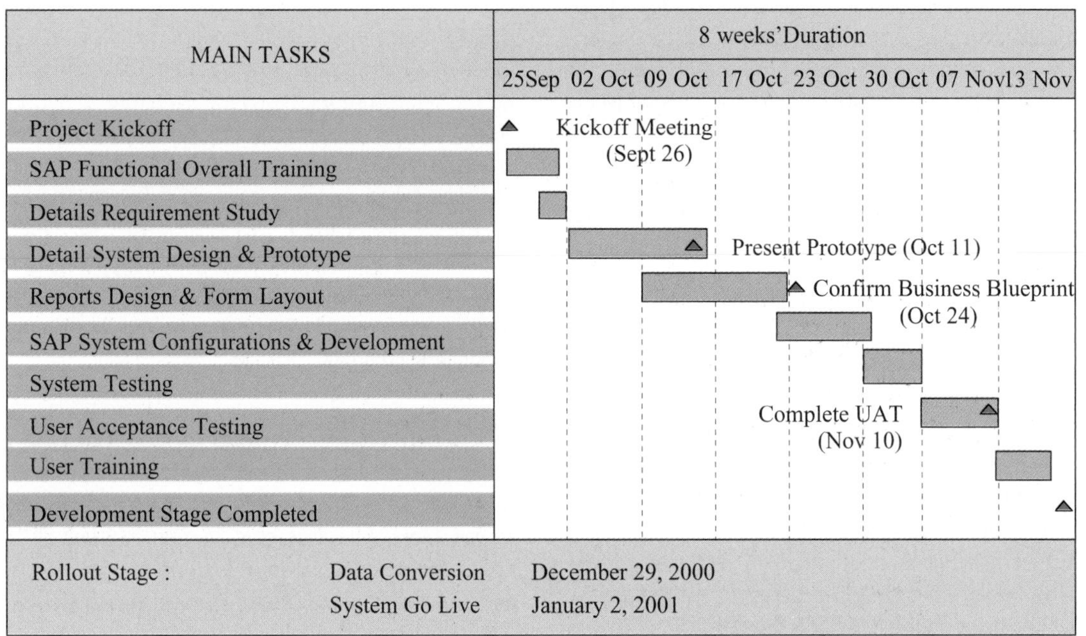

They knew the alternatives and the impact on the user and the actual process. For example, online approval of a purchase order sounds good, but they asked, "Who will approve it when the person is out of the office?" because someone must go into the system to do it. [Singapore implemented online approval, but it was not effective—so in the end it was not used.] APSS could advise us on these issues.

Major Project Manager, APN IT

The APSS people knew BAT's processes. They asked us to review the blueprint. I had worked with Oracle systems and knew how to link modules—Materials Management and Finance.

FI/CO Team Member, BAT Taiwan

The initial configuration was really good. We worked really hard. The APSS team understands our operations and our industry. Also, they spoke my primary language [Mandarin].

MM/SD Team Member, BAT Taiwan

Because BAT Taiwan had no experience with direct distribution, help was sought from some workers at the distributor. Some configuration was also done to take into account the expected future changes in government regulations regarding the payment of taxes that would affect product pricing, as well as the key accounts that would be introduced in a future phase. These changes could be activated when needed. A prototype was ready by the third week.

Scope Change: Moving Forward Phase 2

In October, the project leaders recognized that some of the Phase 2 changes would already be done in the initial configuration, so it might be possible to move Phase 2 forward. They believed that Phase 1 could be completed easily within the 8-week period and that the team had the resources to also complete Phase 2 by January, 2001. They consulted with the APSS Applications Manager, the Head of IT at APN, and the other project team members, and it was agreed to move Phase 2 forward. A revised proposal was prepared by APSS, and the phase was renamed 1A to signal that the Phase 1 resources would continue on the project team, rather than have a totally different implementation.

Changing the schedule for the two-phase implementation greatly increased the risks of the project from both an IT and a business perspective. Phase 1A included the two requirements that were specific to the Taiwan implementation: the government-designed invoicing system (GUI) and the Chinese language module. These additional requirements increased the technical complexity of the initial implementation, as well as the need for training on additional business processes. APN management therefore initiated a formal review before the end of October to reassess the risks and to determine whether the project was under-resourced.

The APN review team consisted of the IT head at APN and two finance managers from Hong Kong. The team leads walked through the project and discussions were held in Taiwan with the business sponsor. As a result of this review, BAT Taiwan made plans to hire additional temporary staff prior to the user acceptance testing phase to help relieve the business team members who would be involved. In addition, Hong Kong-based APN staff (mostly from finance, but also logistics and IT) would receive training prior to implementation in case they were needed for emergency backup support. Further, APSS staff would stay longer than originally anticipated following the rollout.

> There were a lot of concerns. It was a short timeframe and for the first time it was managed by APSS—not jointly managed with Andersen Consulting. A lot of 'teething problems' had been experienced in other project rollouts, so APSS consultants were requested to stay longer to provide onsite support.
>
> *APSS Project Integration Lead*

The functionality required for the GUI system[5] was originally expected to be part of the version 4.6 upgrade of SAP R/3 proposed for the Phase 2 project. At the end of November it was learned that SAP could not deliver a version of the GUI for the 3.1H system prior to January 1. Another vendor's GUI system would therefore need to be purchased and interfaced to the R/3 system (as a bolt-on). With advice from BAT's auditors (PricewaterhouseCoopers), a system from a local supplier that had been implemented by a number of other companies in Taiwan was identified and a contract was signed in mid-December.

The Chinese language module was needed to print reports. SAP Malaysia offered to help, but would not have the resources to do it before mid-March. Some other companies that were developing the software as a bolt-on were asked to make presentations, and a system was purchased from E-Com. The APSS Basis team member was scheduled to come to Taiwan a week before Go Live to ensure that the system would print correctly.

User Acceptance Testing and Change Management

Because of the change in Taiwan's business model, the change management activities associated with the SAP implementation involved defining new staff roles and communicating with all personnel, as well as providing training for those involved in the new system. The Project Co-lead at BAT Taiwan, Mr. Lee, was largely responsible for change management as the business lead on the project team, although all the training was done by APSS.

Temporary personnel were brought in before user acceptance testing (UAT) to perform functions usually done by project team members. Three temporary accountants were trained for 2 weeks on the general ledger, issuing checks, and paying employees. Similarly, two extra people were brought on to help in the MM/SD areas. One of these people had previously worked for the distributor and knew the existing system very well; she later became a permanent BAT employee. The other person, who used to work for a consumer products company, had considerable experience in order processing.

The UAT phase involved all of the users on the project team. Most of the other finance personnel had received exposure to the new processes during earlier phases of the project. Other Taiwan personnel were trained in early November as part of the UAT phase of the project. Few changes were required as a result of the testing. However, the integrated nature of the system did cause some problems.

> There were some hiccups here and there. During the user test phase, there were some apprehensions, partly due to the lack of understanding of the system, and the process adjustments that need to be made. With motivation and support from each other within the team, they managed to pull it through with great success.
>
> *Mr. Ma, BAT Taiwan Country Manager*

Following the UAT, an additional 20 people—mostly in marketing functions—received overview training from the APSS consultants. A key challenge here was how to convey the integrated nature of the system when most people were used to focusing on a single function.

Quality Reviews

Globe House provided funding for two quality reviews. The first one was to be a quality review after the user acceptance test, prior to implementation. The second one would be part of a post-implementation review process a few months after implementation.

The country manager decided that having a third-party independent of BAT to do the review would be a good idea, and SAP Taiwan was selected. The first review took place in early December and took the form of the quality check for the Final Preparation Phase in the ASAP methodology. The results were positive and the project team prepared for the final steps: Data Conversion on December 29 and Go Live on January 2, 2001.

> We were unconcerned about whether someone from SAP or an internal auditor did the review. The issue was: Is the system quality up to the mark? Is there anything substandard that could cause a system failure?
>
> *Mr. Ma, BAT Taiwan Country Manager*

> Globe House has sponsored some of the quality reviews. It depends on whether the project management would like to have

[5]The GUI is an official invoice that must be prepared using invoice numbers issued by the government. When a business uses up its assigned range of numbers, it must reapply for a further set of numbers, and so on. Six to eight such reports must be submitted to the government for tax purposes every 4 to 8 weeks.

it done or not. In Brazil, the reviews are being done by an external consulting partner, but it's a much bigger project: Once a week a person comes in and reviews the implementation progress.

SAP Program Manager, Business Integration, Globe House

Go Live

Phases 1 and 1A went live according to the revised project plan on January 2, 2001, with one major exception: The functionality for processing the key accounts and for printing the reports with the Chinese language module were included in this release, but the GUI interface was not integrated with SAP until mid-January. Instead, the team's contingency plan was used for the first 2 weeks in January: the sales orders were entered into BAT Taiwan's R/3 system and then submitted to the system used by the country's long-time distributor to produce the required government reports. This process made the January close very difficult, although it was still completed within a week.

There was also a delay in the installation of a new telecommunications line leased from the government-owned telecommunications company in Taiwan. This meant that a more expensive international dial-up line had to be used to connect to Kuala Lumpur via Hong Kong until early in February, when the leased line could be phased in.

Initially, there were also some order processing problems. The Go Live date was close to the Chinese New Year (January 24), which meant heavy numbers of orders had to be processed at the same time as the new business processes were being implemented. Some orders were delivered late and sometimes an order contained the wrong pricing, but within 6 weeks, these problems were worked out. The second close in February went smoothly.

The original Phase 1 plan was for all APSS consultants to remain onsite in Taiwan for 2 weeks after Go Live. Because of the new Phase 1A schedule, the business sponsor asked for 4 weeks of support. A compromise solution was to provide two APSS team members onsite for 6 weeks following Go Live. In addition to the Project Integration lead, the MM consultant from APSS remained onsite for the first 2 weeks and helped coach the users through the new processes, and then the second financial consultant and SD consultant from APSS were onsite for the succeeding 2 weeks.

As of January 2001, APSS is running three separate SAP systems for (1) Singapore, Taiwan, and Thailand, (2) Malaysia, and (3) Australia. BAT Taiwan's R/3 system is run on the same client system as those of Singapore and Thailand.[6] Because all three systems use the same template, each country shares the same organizational hierarchy, chart of accounts, and data definitions. For example, finance is subdivided into the three areas of operating, marketing, and corporate finance, while marketing is subdivided into trade and brand marketing. Each country is defined by a company code, which represents a legal entity for reporting purposes. Although the basic processes within the client are the same, some configuration is specific to the company code. For example, a country can have its own configuration to reflect how it wants to manage costs, how it structures its departments, and with codes for its own area offices and key accounts. Further, controlling area and operating concern are defined at the company code level. There is no consolidation of financials or profitability analysis at the regional level. Exhibit 6 shows the cost center hierarchy for BAT Taiwan.

Ongoing Operational Support by APSS

In the first 3 months of service, the production server running the Taiwan system had been down only once for a period of approximately 2 hours. However, in the weeks immediately following Go Live, procedural errors led to a few processing errors. For example, incorrect data was recorded on some occasions when the users specified an incorrect company code (equivalent to a country code).

A multi-tier support plan is in place. Tier 1 support is provided locally and APSS provides support services via their help line based on six priority levels. (See Exhibit 7.) Contacts with an APSS consultant on the original Taiwan project team are sometimes feasible, but not guaranteed. However, learnings from the Taiwan project and the modifications to the Symphony template for the local system requirements have been captured in a Lotus Notes database accessible to other members of the APSS support team.

User ID and authorization changes are authorized by designated business managers, and these requests are submitted to APSS via an Excel spreadsheet format. As noted earlier, APSS owns the SAP licenses and leases them to the end market as needed.

Requests for system changes (new functionality, new configuration, or new reports) for Taiwan are reviewed and authorized by the Project Co-Lead at BAT Taiwan, who is now head of finance for the Taiwan office. Some problems have surfaced over time and certain changes have been requested as users have learned more about how the system works. For instance, a differential pricing policy was not initially specified, but has been added to the configuration.

Post-Implementation in Taiwan

A project celebration was held as part of a Chinese New Year celebration for the BAT Taiwan office. It involved dinner for the heads of the Taiwan departments and all of the business users on the team. At the dinner, each Taiwan project member who

[6] The Thailand R/3 implementation was also completed in Fall 2000.

EXHIBIT 6
Cost Center Hierarchy for Taiwan's R/3 System

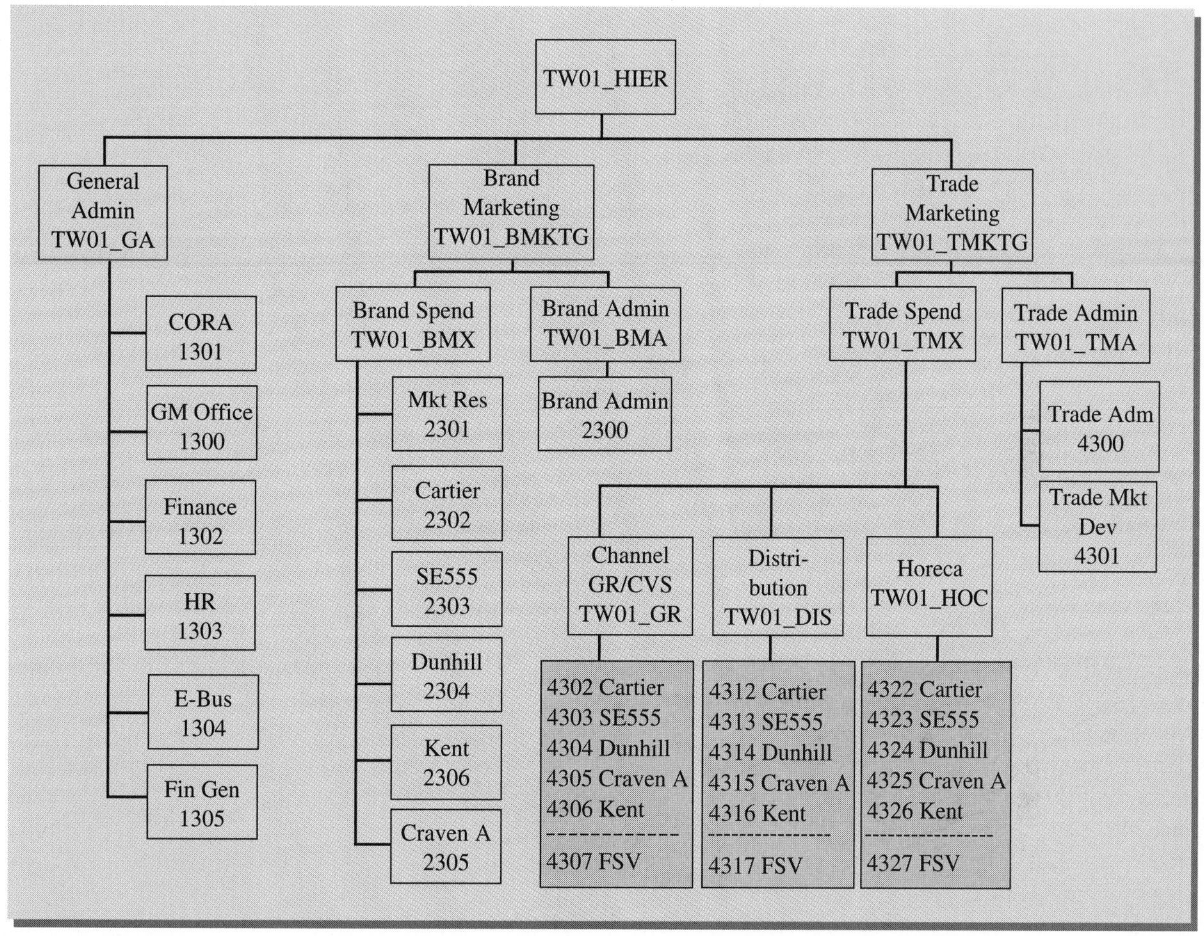

was not a department head received a surprise bonus of a month's salary in recognition of their effort and extra-long hours.

> People say that it usually takes a year to do an SAP implementation, or maybe only 6 months when you have the experience. Here it was 4 months for the implementation; it was so fast you're maybe a little afraid that things may still go wrong. But now we're starting to feel proud.
>
> *FI/CO Team Member, BAT Taiwan*

Over the past few years, BAT Taiwan has grown from 20 to 100 personnel as it first absorbed Rothmans and then evolved into a full trading company. All data entry is now done in the Taipei office, and invoices are printed at the five area offices. Within the Taipei office a few work imbalances still continued to exist because of the lack of widespread SAP expertise and the loss of some expert business users. For example, the MM/SD lead still regularly worked a few hours of overtime each evening even after the new GUI system was in place.

A system upgrade to R/3 version 4.6C is planned for July 2001, and some improvements to the process configurations could be made at the same time.

> SAP is a very powerful application for a small market. Initially you go through a stage where you learn the basics but you don't yet know all the functionality. When you become proficient with the system, you begin to look at other needs. APSS needs to be ready to show the business how to use the system better—what the more complex processes are that they couldn't absorb before.
>
> *Mr. Ponce, Asia Pacific Regional IT Manager*

A formal post-implementation review, sponsored by Globe House, was to be conducted toward the end of March 2001. Other BAT managers are expected to be interested in learning how the implementation was accomplished so quickly, at such a low cost, and whether the business users were happy with the quality of the system. Within APN, Hong Kong would probably be the next end market to implement SAP.

EXHIBIT 7
Help Desk Support by APSS

Priority	Definition	Users Affected	Examples	Minimum Service Level *
P1	The entire business is stopped, a business process has failed and/or an entire site is affected.	All	System is unavailable, billing and delivery cannot be processed, month-end processing cannot be completed.	95% resolved in 1 hour = Application & APSS (HD, Sec, Ops) – Resolution External Engineer (third party, i.e., Equant/IBM) – Active assistance
P2	Issue impacts a module, prevents a large number of users from doing their work, and/or a workaround is not available.	Group	Sales and Distribution module fails, orders cannot be taken, volume is too large for a manual workaround.	90% resolved in 2 business hours
P3	Issue impacts a module and prevents a large number of users from doing their work and a workaround is available.	Group	Financial journals cannot be posted but it does not affect third parties, volume is small for a manual workaround	90% resolved in 3 business hours
P4	User is prevented from doing work due to critical task failure, no workaround exists.	Single	User cannot print documentation, user profile is not complete.	90% resolved in 4 business hours
P5	A user is prevented from completing a function, but a workaround can be provided, and/or problem is minor.	Single	Automatic check printing fails but critical payments can still be processed with manual checks.	90% resolved in 2 business days
P6	Query or request.	N/A	How to extract data for reporting	90% resolved in 3 business days

* Minimum service level: a resolution (including workarounds) is handed to the user to confirm acceptance before it is implemented in the production environment.

CASE STUDY III-9

A Troubled Project at Modern Materials, Inc.

Modern Materials, Inc. (MMI) manufactures products that are used as raw materials by large manufacturers and the construction industry. With yearly sales exceeding $3 billion, over 10,000 employees, and four large manufacturing facilities in the United States, MMI is one of the giants in the manufacturing materials industry. Two of the facilities produce basic products and the other two process these materials further to produce products with special properties and shapes.

MMI was established under another name in 1927 and grew over time through a series of small mergers and acquisitions until 1991, when it took over a major competitor and the resulting company took the name MMI. Two of its manufacturing facilities came with this merger, which broadened MMI's product line.

The last several years have been difficult ones for the manufacturing materials industry, with overcapacity, foreign competition, and a depressed manufacturing economy putting intense pressure on profits. MMI has fared better than most of its competitors, but as can be noted in Exhibit 1, MMI has lost money in 2 of the past 5 years. Furthermore, at this time it looks like the year 2003 will be worse than 2002. MMI went through a wrenching downsizing in 1999 that has left the remaining workers stretched thin and working at a hectic pace.

Information Services at MMI

Up until 1994 MMI had a conventional internal IS structure, with a small corporate IS group and decentralized organizations serving the two major divisions created with the merger in 1991. Each premerger company became a division in MMI, and each division inherited the IS organization of the company from which it was formed. Each division had its legacy people and legacy systems modified to provide the necessary enterprise data to corporate IS.

In 1994 MMI outsourced its IS organization to STC, a major player in the IT outsourcing business. As a part of the contract, STC offered employment to all of MMI's IS people, and most of them accepted jobs with STC. Thus MMI's IS staff was pretty much the same as before, but under new management. And the hardware and software were also taken over by STC. MMI retained a small group of analysts concerned with problem definition and process analysis.

Initiation of the Supply-Chain Management System (SCMS) Project

In 1995 Harvey Woodson was hired from a smaller competitor to become executive vice president for quality at MMI. Woodson brought with him a passionate vision of how to improve MMI's competitive position and profitability through exemplary customer service—being able to take orders, produce the product, and get it to the customer with the desired quality and package type when it was needed. Everyone in the industry had similar products and similar quality, and Woodson believed that outstanding customer service could make MMI stand apart from its competition.

Providing outstanding customer service depends upon excellent supply-chain management, which involves entering an order, creating a manufacturing order to guide it through the required manufacturing processes, scheduling it into production, producing it, warehousing it, shipping and routing it so that it arrives at the proper time, invoicing and billing it, and handling any testing issues or claims that might arise. This chain of events starts with the initial order and carries all the way through the customer receiving and using the product in his manufacturing process.

Woodson understood that excellent supply-chain management depends upon efficient processes supported by appropriate information processing systems. MMI's production processes were highly automated, with exceptional computer controls, but the business processes and the supporting information systems were clearly inadequate to provide outstanding customer service. As previously noted, the information systems were mainly legacy systems from the premerger companies

EXHIBIT 1
Selected MMI Financial Data (in Millions)

Statement of Operations	1998	1999	2000	2001	2002
Net sales	$ 3,544	$ 3,142	$ 3,230	$ 3,349	$ 3,277
Cost of goods sold	3,032	2,825	2,837	2,938	3,071
Depreciation	149	147	142	154	168
Gross margin	363	170	251	257	38
Selling, general & admin.	155	160	169	163	166
Financing costs	16	15	14	32	60
Downsizing costs	30				
Net income	162	(5)	68	62	(188)

that had been jury-rigged to provide the necessary enterprise information, and each location had its own way of doing things and its own systems.

In 1996 Woodson proposed that MMI undertake a massive effort to make a quantum leap in its supply-chain management performance by reengineering its business processes corporatewide and providing adequate information systems support for the new supply-chain management (SCM) process. A task force, composed of four senior executives and chaired by Woodson, was established to develop a proposal to present to the MMI board.

MMI's senior management enthusiastically bought into the vision of gaining competitive advantage through outstanding customer service. There was unanimous agreement that making this vision a reality depended upon radical improvements in the SCM process by reengineering MMI's business processes and supporting these new processes with adequate information technology. The question was how to do this, how long it would take, and what it would cost.

The company from which Woodson had come had completed reengineering and systems development for its SCM process, and Woodson had been involved in that effort. The development of that system had been outsourced to United Consultants Associates (UCA). That system was developed for only a single-plant operation, and Woodson envisioned a much more comprehensive system, but UCA could be employed to begin with that system and expand and enhance it to suit the needs of MMI. The task force estimated that the existing UCA-developed system contained about 50 to 60 percent of the functionality that MMI would require.

Hiring UCA to develop a new SCMS for MMI was the major alternative developed by the task force. The task force also considered the alternatives of enhancing MMI's existing systems to support the reengineered processes or acquiring enterprise software, but both alternatives were rejected as impractical.

The proposal cited the following business objectives of a new SCMS:

- Reduce inventories
- Increase market share
- Enhance profits
- Reduce operating costs
- Increase customer satisfaction

The new system would be based upon reengineered processes and replace the following existing MMI systems:

- Sales-order entry
- Sales forecasting
- Order status
- Pricing
- Scheduling and planning
- Manufacturing data collection
- Inventory control
- Quality tracking
- Traffic
- Shipping
- Invoicing
- Billing
- EDI

UCA, the contractor who would provide the code for the system developed for MMI's competitor, would lead the requirements definition effort and develop the system design and program specifications for the new SCMS. UCA would also assist MMI people in reengineering the business processes. Coding, testing, and installation of the system would be done by MMI's IS outsourcer, STC. The initial system provided by UCA did not include a production scheduling module, so an existing scheduling and planning module would be purchased from another qualified vendor and integrated into the system by STC.

The SCMS project was planned to take 3 years at a cost of $60 million. This proposal was approved by the board of MMI in late 1997 and work on the project began in early 1998, with completion scheduled for early 2001.

Building the System

The project was driven by Woodson, who headed a small steering committee of MMI managers. He was the project's champion, providing the enthusiasm and push within MMI. Woodson had been through this process before, and he knew that radical reengineering was necessary to achieve the dramatic improvements in customer service that MMI was seeking. He also understood that radical reengineering was terribly hard to accomplish because it would require enthusiastic participation by workers who would have to make radical changes in how they did their jobs, and that degree of change is hard for most people. Furthermore, one of the first things business process reengineering involves is looking for work that does not contribute to what is being accomplished. Eliminating that work may eliminate people, perhaps some of the same people being asked to participate in the reengineering process. So Woodson devoted a lot of time and energy to cheerleading–generating enthusiasm and support for the project throughout the company. He spent a lot of time out at the plants explaining how important the project was to the future success of the company, encouraging people to give their best efforts, and using his clout as an executive vice president to coerce people when necessary.

Early in 1998, just as the project was getting started, the industry was hit by a serious downturn, and MMI was forced to reduce its workforce by more than 8 percent. Morale plummeted, and as the remaining workers had to assume the duties of those who were downsized, it was difficult for them to find the time to get involved in reengineering and defining requirements of the system. In order to not fall too far behind the schedule, UCA people began to design the system and develop program specifications on the basis of what they thought the processes and requirements should be. This resulted in huge problems later, when the code had been written and the systems were to be tested and installed, requiring much expensive and time-consuming rework, so the project fell further and further behind schedule.

In 1999 management realized that MMI had a serious problem with Y2K compatibility and decided that it was necessary to devote most of the STC resources at MMI to dealing with that problem, so the time spent on the SCMS project was substantially reduced during that year.

In 2000 Woodson, the driving force behind the project, suddenly left for greener pastures, and the project lost its original champion. The task force that had been driving the project was reorganized, with senior managers replaced with middle-level managers, and Woodson replaced as its leader and de facto project manager by George Leach, director of planning in the construction division.

Leach had no experience in an IS organization, but was very knowledgeable about how to run the business, and had a great reputation as a sophisticated user of information technology, having developed several impressive personal systems to assist management in running the division. These systems used PC software such as Microsoft Excel and Access to manipulate and analyze data extracted from MMI's existing IS systems, but had no documentation and were outside the regular production environment of the IS department.

Leach was an enthusiastic and forceful leader of the SCMS development effort and had a good understanding of the SCM process. When the requirements definition process for a system component fell behind schedule, Leach would step into the breach and assist in defining the requirements and specifying appropriate processes.

The first component of the system, order entry, was completed and ready for final testing in early 2001, about the time the entire project was originally scheduled for completion. Final testing did not go smoothly. The various locations insisted that the new uniform processes the system was based upon were not feasible and much rework was required to make the system acceptable. It was early 2002 before the order entry system was fully installed and in use.

New Chief Information Officer Hired

By early 2002 it was obvious that the SCMS project was seriously behind schedule and over budget, and MMI's senior management became more and more concerned with perceived problems with the project. In March 2002, Charles Hastings was brought in as chief information officer (CIO) and given the mission of straightening out the problem. Hastings was a long-time MMI manager who had been director of IS at one of the plants before becoming plant manager.

Matthew West, MMI financial vice president, had served in that position for many years. Before MMI established the CIO position, IS had reported to West, so West had some familiarity with IS projects. Shortly after Hastings became CIO, West expressed concern about the project:

> We need to admit that the supply-chain management project is a failure, minimize our losses by killing it, and move on. I realize that it is hard to abandon a project that we have invested so much time and effort in, but times are so tough for MMI that we cannot continue to pour money down a rat hole.

It took only 2 months for Hastings to agree that the project was in serious trouble. Although MMI senior management continued to believe in the vision of improved competitiveness through better customer service and the need for a new SCMS to support reengineered processes, the project had lost much of its drive when Woodson left MMI. Due to other serious business concerns, there had been no consistent personal involvement on the part of any senior manager. Consequently, there had been no top management clout to enforce the project's intent to make radical changes in how MMI did business. Furthermore, although people from MMI and at least three different outside contractors were working on the project, there was no overall project management responsibility. Hastings found a lot of finger-pointing with, for example, people from UCA saying "I'm waiting for MMI people to complete this," and MMI people saying "I'm waiting for STC." They were all correct because there was little overall coordination of what they were doing.

Hastings expressed concern about the project to George Leach, and Leach maintained that, although the project was well behind schedule and over budget, the underlying problems had been overcome and the project was now under control:

> We have had some serious problems to overcome—the downsizing that slowed down our requirements definition effort, the Y2K problem that diverted resources from the project, and Woodson's leadership was lost. We have also had some coordination problems between the four organizations that have been working on the project. We are now well past the planned completion date of the project and $4 million over the initial budget of $60 million, which is not surprising given the problems we have had.
>
> On the other hand, we have successfully installed the order-entry system and many of the rest of the components are almost completed. We are dealing with the coordination problems, have recently redone the project plan, and I am confident that we can complete the system in 18 months at a total cost of $84 million. Given the importance of a supply-chain management process to MMI's future, there is no question in my mind that we should complete the project as planned.

Wishing to get a more comprehensive picture of the health of the project, Hastings prevailed upon STC to bring in an experienced consultant, Carol Young, to study the situation and make recommendations about how to deal with any remaining problems.

Young's Findings

Carol Young was an experienced project manager who was brought in from a different STC location to conduct the study at MMI. Young had just completed an STC assignment as the project manager of a large system development project that was completed on time and on budget.

The first thing Young did was to run a quick "health check" of the project using a questionnaire that STC has used in many places. On a scale of 1 to 10, it evaluates how the project is doing in seven critical areas such as risk management, financial management, and schedule management. A score of 1 or 2 is in intensive care, 3 or 4 is critical condition, etc. When she analyzed the results, the average score was 3.1, so the project was in deep, deep trouble (see Exhibit 2).

Then Young examined the newest version of the schedule that Leach asserted would get the project completed in 18 months at a cost of an additional $20 million. She reported:

> I took two additional people and interviewed every functional person and every end user person that had anything to do with the next phase of the schedule, which was planned to take three months. All of those people said that the project was in the toilet. The major problems were that the requirements had not been correctly identified, so they were going to have to do a lot of rework to get the requirements right, and the users were terrified because there was almost no testing in the schedule—only a little time for user acceptance testing. There was no unit testing and no integration testing. The users knew that installing the system would be a disaster.
>
> I also carefully reviewed the project plan and found that it does not take into account staffing needs. Often more work is scheduled over a time period than there are people available to do the necessary work. Thus the schedule is not feasible. Furthermore, the new systems do not have the documentation and controls necessary in a production environment. It is a mess.
>
> When we included the time to define the requirements, make the necessary changes, upgrade the controls and documentation, and adequately test and install the system, the time to complete that phase went from 3 months to 6 months. All of the succeeding phases had the same problems, so the time to complete the project went from 18 months to at least 3 years, assuming that it is done right. If MMI doesn't define the requirements and do the needed testing, the project will be a complete disaster. But Leach is still planning to complete and convert to the use of each new system in about half the time it will actually take. Because MMI is burning money on this project at over $1.2 million a month, the cost goes from $20 million to $40 million.
>
> In summary, the current schedule that envisions the completion of the project in 18 months at a total cost of $84 million is totally unrealistic. The minimum time and cost that will be required for Leach to complete the system is 3 more years at a total cost of $104 million.

EXHIBIT 2

Project Health Check by Carol Young

PM Functional Area	Intensive Care		Critical		Fair		Good		Excellent	
	1	2	3	4	5	6	7	8	9	10
Communication Management		X								
Risk Management				X						
Scope Management			X							
Schedule Management (3)						X				
Quality Management	X									
Financial/Contractual Management				X						
Resource Management		X								

Note: The average score is 3.1, which means the project is in critical condition.

When Hastings asked why the project was in such deep trouble, Young replied:

> In the first place, there has been no overall project management in the professional IS sense. No one has been given overall project management responsibility and authority. What little project management the project has had has been by Leach as head of the project steering committee. There has been little coordination between the various contractors who are working on the project so one contractor has often wasted time waiting on another to complete something. During this waiting time the workers continue to work and draw their pay even though they are not accomplishing anything, wasting MMI's money as well as time.
>
> Although Leach is an enthusiastic, hard-working, dedicated manager who knows MMI and its supply-chain management problems, unfortunately he has no concept of how to develop an IS system of this complexity. His experience is in user development, where he has done an outstanding job. But in user development, where data are extracted from an existing system and manipulated with PC tools, one can get away with just building a system without too much concern for the requirements because you can easily modify it until you get it right. One does not need thorough documentation because the user is also the developer and understands the details of the system. You don't have to worry about security, risk management controls, configuration management controls, data capture issues, etc. And you do not have to coordinate the activities of various groups that are all working on the project. So Leach has tried his best to lead this project without understanding any of these crucial aspects of project management.
>
> Furthermore, the MMI legacy systems had little usable documentation, so the development team did not know the details of what these systems did or how they did it. When the downsizing came about and the users did not have time to participate in the reengineering and defining the requirements, UCA and Leach assumed that they understood the requirements and began defining the system and writing program specs without really understanding the requirements or obtaining buy-in from the users. They did not realize they had serious problems until they tried to install the systems and the users rebelled.

Hastings asked Young what she would suggest that MMI do, and this was her reply:

> I have devoted a good deal of time to determining what needs to be done, how it could best be accomplished, and how it should be managed. The bad news is that the best plan I could come up with would take 2 years for completion of the system. The good news is that the total cost would be only $84 million.
>
> My suggestion would be for MMI to designate me as the overall project manager and make sure that the entire project, including all the contractors and MMI personnel, would be directly responsible to me. Leach would continue to head the steering committee and provide vision and knowledge of MMI's supply-chain management process, but I would have direct responsibility for managing the project. The $84 million cost includes STC's fee for managing the project.
>
> I have reworked Leach's schedule to eliminate the inefficiencies, do things in the proper sequence, provide the time needed to perform the necessary activities with the people available, involve the users in requirements definition and system testing, and so on. It will take 2 years to complete the work.
>
> The project bottleneck was the rate at which the users and functional people could define the requirements. Everyone on the project had been spending a lot of useless time waiting for the users and for each other or writing code on the basis of

incomplete requirements. They were busy working, but they were not doing anything productive. When I lengthened the schedule to what was feasible and assigned the work properly, I was able to drastically reduce the staffing on the project, so we would only be spending $800,000 a month rather than $1.2 million.

Leach had been using a "big bang" approach where they worked simultaneously on all five of the remaining phases. I plan to use a "rolling wave" approach where we will concentrate on defining the requirements of the first phase. When that is completed, we will move on to programming on that phase. The people who were defining requirements for the first phase can then move on to the same task for the second phase, and so on. This way we will work at the pace at which they can define requirements and everyone working on the project will be doing useful work all the time.

Leach's Reaction

In response to Young's critique of the project and its management, George Leach made the following points:

> Carol went out and talked to a number of malcontents who do not know what is currently going on in the development process and do not understand the quality that we are now building into the system. Carol hasn't worked on this project, knows little about conditions in MMI, and just represents the viewpoint that nobody who is not an IS professional can manage a systems development project. Carol heard what Carol wanted to hear. I suspect that Carol is influenced by the desire to develop more business for STC and criticizing me is the way for STC to take over the project.
>
> I would argue that given the obstacles we have faced, the project has been remarkably successful. Remember that we lost a year to downsizing and a year to Y2K. The downsizing has made it much more difficult to reengineer the processes and to define requirements because the users are so busy trying to keep production going. Also, we lost Woodson's leadership at a crucial time.
>
> Secondly, it looks like we are farther behind than we really are. Although we have only installed the order entry system, quite a number of additional systems are almost complete and ready to go into final testing. So we are set to make a lot of progress in the next few months.
>
> Finally, experience has taught us a lot about managing development. I have thoroughly reworked our development approach, project plan, and schedule to make it more effective. I am now conducting weekly meetings with the managers of all the contractors to discuss and deal with our coordination problems. I am confident that we can complete the system in 18 months for only an additional $20 million.

Young was quick to respond to Leach's accusation that she was criticizing his leadership in order to get more business for STC:

> If my proposal to manage the project is accepted it will result in less, not more, revenue for STC than if I had recommended that the project continue under its present management. Our people are working steadily on the project now and would continue to do so for at least 3 years. Under my proposal, the number of our people working on the project would be reduced and our people would only be on the project for 2 years, so our total revenue would be substantially less. If I were trying to maximize STC's revenue I would have let things go on as they are.

West's Concerns

Vice President of Finance West believed that MMI was in such dire financial condition that the SCMS project should be shut down immediately. He asserted:

> We are losing substantial amounts of money, and if this continues for too long we will be in big trouble. We hope things turn around before long and are taking every possible measure to make sure that it does.
>
> Our stock has tanked. Our stockholders' equity, cash, and working capital have declined significantly over the last 5 years, and they will continue to decline this year. [See Exhibit 3.] We are borrowing money to cover deficits in our cash flow. We project that this year will be very tough, but we expect the economy to turn around and our position to begin to improve during 2003. [See Exhibit 4.] Although we are not in immediate danger of bankruptcy, we will be in desperate straits if our projections turn out to have been too optimistic. Borrowing more money to cover cash-flow deficits will be exceedingly difficult.
>
> It is not responsible management to spend $20 million on any project in our present situation even if that amount would not bankrupt us. There are too many better ways to use those resources. For example, that would be $20 million we would not have to borrow and $20 million less in losses. Also, we may have to downsize again in the near future, and $20 million would save the jobs of some people we desperately need.
>
> Furthermore, I doubt that this project can be completed as proposed under either Leach's or Young's proposals. Since the downsizing we do not have the user manpower to define the requirements well enough, and we also have serious political problems that are holding us back. Young will find that the lack of project management is not the only serious problem that we face in completing this project.
>
> But more importantly, even if it were to be completed it would not achieve the purpose that motivated the project in the first place, namely providing competitive advantage by a quantum jump in customer service. We might get marginally improved data processing systems, but we have not done the reengineering to obtain the radical changes in how we do business that would set us apart from our competitors. This project was never justified on the basis of quantitative returns, only on strategic grounds, and it has been doomed ever since our downsizing and the departure of Woodson. We should have killed it years ago.
>
> However, in the final analysis it doesn't matter whether or not the project is a complete failure. Even if it would be a moderate success, in these difficult times we cannot afford the huge drain on our resources that it involves. Perhaps we could

EXHIBIT 3

Selected MMI End-of-Year Financial Data (Dollars in Millions)

	1998	1999	2000	2001	2002
Cash & cash equivalents	$307	$241	$193	$215	$160
Working capital	410	305	300	350	107
Stockholders' equity	845	691	740	752	620
Stock price/share	27.25	14.00	17.75	11.50	6.25

mothball it so that if conditions improve it could be resumed, but we need to get rid of it for now.

Leach contested West's assertion that the new system would not provide the competitive advantage originally envisioned:

We have only installed one subsystem, and you cannot expect overall performance to be improved much until the entire system is installed and working. The results of this effort will be apparent when the full system is completed and installed.

Our legacy systems that run production at the plants are stand-alone systems that are not integrated with other production systems or with the support systems—administrative, financial, personnel, etc. The new system will integrate everything from the time the customer calls in an order through ordering the raw materials, scheduling and following through the production process, entering it into inventory, shipping it, billing it, and handling any problems with the use of the product.

As a result, the customer will be able to get exactly what he wants in the shortest possible time. When the customer calls with an order, it can be entered, scheduled, and the delivery date determined while the customer is on the phone. Changes to an order can be made quickly and easily. The lead time to deliver an order will be reduced from today's 120 days to 45 days, which is just a little more than a third of what it is today! That will be a huge improvement in customer service. No one else in our industry will be able to match this.

Also, this reduction in the time to deliver an order will result in tremendous savings for MMI because in-process inventory will be reduced so dramatically. And time is money for us as well as for our customers. We will be saving huge amounts of money.

Furthermore, with this integrated system, management information will be available in real time rather than months after the fact. We will be able to determine the profitability of each product and focus our marketing efforts on the most profitable products, and we will be able to plan our production and load it on our facilities so as to minimize the cost of production. Not only will we be able to radically improve customer service, but we will also be able to improve the profitability of what we produce.

I admit that the project has had its problems, but I am sure that we can complete it in 18 months for an additional $20 million. Although our financial condition is not good, this is a strategic project that will greatly improve our competitiveness. It represents a crucial top management vision, and I can't believe that we would abandon it because of temporary difficulties. MMI's future depends upon it!

EXHIBIT 4

Selected MMI Projections, End of Year (in millions)

	Projections			
	2003	2004	2005	2006
Sales	$3,217	$3,250	$3,372	$3,516
Net Income	(287)	(50)	70	180
Stockholders' equity	342	286	350	522

Mary J. Ellis, the construction division's representative on the project steering committee, believed that the project should be continued and that Leach should continue to lead it. She asserted:

Admittedly our financial condition is not the best, but $20 million is not going to make or break us. We must not let short-range problems cause us to lose the vision that can make such an important contribution to MMI's long-term success.

George has the vision, the enthusiasm, and the experience needed to complete the project. George has provided outstanding leadership, fighting through difficulty after difficulty. Without George's drive and enthusiasm the project would have failed long ago. It would be disastrous to change leadership now when the project is so close to completion.

CASE STUDY III-10

SUPPORTING END USERS AT GRANDMA STUDOR'S BAKERY, INC.

Grandma Studor's Bakery, Inc. (GSB), is a major national supplier of bread, sweet rolls, cakes, and other bakery products. In addition to its bakery products, Grandma Studor's makes and sells well-known brands of baking mixes, flour, prepared dough, and frozen pizza. GSB's industrial foods division sells a wide range of biscuit, doughnut, and other dough mixes, several types of specialty flours to bread and cereal makers, and various commodities and feed ingredients. In 1998 GSB made after-tax profits of $92 million on sales of about $1.5 billion.

Materials Management

The GSB materials management area purchased about $200 million of ingredients and commodities during 1998. One of GSB's most important commodities and ingredients is flour. GSB treats flour as a commodity that is used as an important raw material but also sells flour to others and deals in flour and wheat futures to reduce risk related to price fluctuations. In 1998 one of the senior buyers, David Prince, managed about $90 million in transactions relating to flour and wheat.

GSB uses many different kinds of flour in its various products. GSB manufactures flour as well as buying it on the open market, and since GSB produces several different kinds of flour, GSB must buy several different varieties of wheat. Prince attempts to minimize the final cost of a hundredweight of flour, which is a rather complicated task because there are so many variables involved, and they are changing all the time. The costs of flour, flour futures, milling flour, transporting flour, wheat, wheat futures, and transporting wheat are factors that may affect the cost of a hundredweight of flour.

The Flour Commodity Report System

To manage the acquisition of the flour that GSB needs each year, while controlling risk and minimizing cost, Prince needs a good deal of information in order to analyze the alternatives. Since things are always changing, timing is very important when buying and selling flour, wheat, and futures contracts for both. For this information Prince depends upon the flour commodity report system operated by his assistant, Donna Hornibrook, on her PC.

The flour commodity report system is a Lotus 1-2-3 application consisting of seven large spreadsheets, several of which contain mostly macros. This system requires manual input of data from at least three of GSB's mainframe systems that forecast future requirements for different kinds of flour and provide current cost factors for manufacturing flour, price data from several markets, reports of actions in buying and selling, and other information. It produces histories of daily flour costs by product group and location for the past month, summaries of the days of coverage of each type of flour that GSB uses, comparisons of anticipated costs of each flour based upon their inventories and futures contracts for flour and wheat, and futures contracts outstanding, among other reports. Also, someone who understands the system can use it to explore the impact of changes in the various cost factors on the future costs of the different kinds of flour.

In January 1999, Hornibrook told Prince that her husband was being transferred to the West Coast and that she would be leaving in about a month. That precipitated a crisis for Prince and the materials management area, for she was the only person in the organization who had any idea of how to run the flour commodity report system. This system was highly manual in that Hornibrook entered data from various sources and invoked many macros to process the data and produce the reports used to manage the flour and wheat positions. Neither the Lotus 1-2-3 spreadsheets nor the procedures Hornibrook used were documented. Even Hornibrook did not completely understand how the system works, and she did not think she could teach it to someone else.

History of the System

The system was begun in 1992 by Anthony Pizzo, who was in Prince's position as senior buyer for flour and wheat. Pizzo had used Lotus 1-2-3 and thought that a spreadsheet would be helpful in keeping track of his flour and wheat requirements and commitments, so he developed the first spreadsheet. Over the next year he expanded the spreadsheet and found it useful enough that when his assistant left, he decided that he would replace him with someone who knew the computer and was skillful with spreadsheet software.

He hired Elmer Smith, an enthusiastic spreadsheet jockey who began to work with Pizzo to expand the system. A year later Pizzo was promoted to a better position within GSB and was replaced by Prince, who continued to work to expand the system. Prince was not a knowledgeable PC user, and he was quite content to have Smith operate the system and enhance it from time to time as they saw opportunities to improve it. By the time that Smith left for a better job in early 1997, the system included five spreadsheets, three of which were primarily composed of macros.

Hornibrook replaced Smith, and although she was competent in entering data into a spreadsheet, she had little prior proficiency in macros. However, before Smith left, he taught Hornibrook how to use the system, and she was able to take over its operation. During the drought in the summer of 1998, Prince began to worry about possible wheat shortages if the drought continued, so Hornibrook added two more spreadsheets to the system to provide more information to help Prince track things more closely.

Hornibrook had trouble in making some of the system changes that Prince requested. She also occasionally got results from the system that did not make sense. Hornibrook felt that the system was extremely precarious and was secretly relieved to be leaving.

The IS Department Response

When Prince learned that Hornibrook was leaving, he was frantic because he would have to manage GSB's flour purchasing while flying blind. He immediately called Roy Morgan, director of the IS materials management systems group, and asked him for help. Despite the fact that the IS Department has had nothing to do with this system (and did not even know of its existence), Morgan agreed to provide all possible assistance in resolving this crisis situation.

Microsoft Excel was the standard spreadsheet package at GSB, so Morgan did not have anyone available with the depth of expertise in Lotus 1-2-3 required to analyze the system and correct its problems. The IS group was planning to develop a corporatewide material requirements planning (MRP) system starting in 2001 that would include a component that would serve the needs of flour and other commodity buyers, but that would be far too late to solve Prince's problem.

Therefore, Morgan suggested that the Gamma Consulting Group, which provided training and consulting to GSB and did have some Lotus 1-2-3 expertise, be employed to analyze the system, redesign it, and rebuild it using Excel and/or other PC software.

The Consultant's Preliminary Report

Tully Shaw, the Gamma consultant assigned to the project, spent several days working with Hornibrook and Prince and prepared the following preliminary report on the problem:

> During January I met with David Prince and Donna Hornibrook to review the existing PC-based system and to discuss revising it into a new easier-to-use system for tracking flour and wheat usage and flour and wheat costs, and to assist in the buying and selling of futures at three exchanges. The existing system does not track all flours being used in all GSB products.
>
> The existing system is made up of several Lotus 1-2-3 spreadsheets. Other than the disk files containing these spreadsheets, there is no documentation for this system. The spreadsheets making up this system were authored by several different persons and are driven by macros written in a format that makes them difficult to edit.
>
> Because the existing system is in such bad shape, I do not believe the existing system should be upgraded and reused. Rather, a new system should be built. Also, the system is not really suitable for a spreadsheet, so I would suggest that it be rebuilt using Microsoft Access and Visual Basic for Applications (VBA).
>
> Although the ranges currently being printed from the LOTUS spreadsheets can be helpful as a basis for designing the new system, a major task in developing this system will be to create a specification from the existing spreadsheets with the assistance of GSB staff.
>
> Preliminary cost and time estimates are:
>
> | | | | |
> |---|---|---|---|
> | System Design | 30 days | $75/hour | $18,000 |
> | Programming | 25 days | $60/hour | 12,000 |
> | Procedure Manual | 5 days | $60/hour | 2,400 |
> | TOTAL (estimate) | | | $32,400 |
>
> These estimates for design allow for approximately 3 days for each major section of the system. This is a minimal amount of time for specification for a system of this complexity, and it could easily require more time. I estimate that the project will require at least 3.5 calendar months to complete.
>
> This is not a fixed-cost bid for this project. In view of the uncertainties involved, we would only contract for this project on an hourly basis with the costs per hour specified above.

It appeared that Prince would be flying blind for at least 3 months.

PART IV
THE INFORMATION MANAGEMENT SYSTEM

EVERY BUSINESS MANAGER SHARES RESPONSIBILITY WITH INFORMATION SYSTEMS (IS) professionals for managing the organization's information resources. Similar to managing other resources (such as people, capital, and facilities), managing information assets requires planning, directing, and controlling. Being successful in managing these assets also requires knowledge of some of the ethical, social, and legal issues that broader access to information, which results from recent developments in information technology (IT), have helped create. The chapters in this section lay out the issues and a model system for managing information resources—one in which the business manager plays a critical role.

The first step in establishing an effective management system for IT, as in managing any resource, is for business and IS leaders to agree on a shared vision, set of values, and expected behaviors regarding the role of information and IT in the business. This shared vision needs to link the direction of the IS organization with the direction of the business. All technology investments need to be viewed as critical corporate resources. Difficult choices must also be made about how to structure the IS organization, what role IT plays in the organization, and where to place IS managers and professionals within the business. IS and business managers must also develop clear policies to guide the behavior of employees in their access and use of internal and external information.

This part of the book opens with Chapter 14, "Setting a Direction for Information Resources," which lays the critical groundwork for establishing the role of the IS organization. A process for setting a direction for an organization's information resources is described. An IS planning approach is presented that includes an assessment of current IS performance, creating a vision of the role of information in the business, designing an IT architecture, and developing strategic and operational plans for IT investments. The chapter first reviews the areas to be included in an assessment of the IS system. Next the concept of a comprehensive information vision and architecture, covering both technology and human assets, is presented. The chapter demonstrates the need for a vision and the benefits of having an IT architecture. The chapter also covers strategic planning tools (such as critical success factors) and reviews methods for identifying strategic applications of IT, including the role of a business manager in IS planning.

Chapter 15, "Managing the Information Systems Function," discusses the issues and provides recommendations for managing the IT technology and human assets, as well as the relationships with other managers both inside and outside the firm. Chapter 15 first focuses on the physical infrastructure and applications portfolio elements of the IT technology asset. (The data resource issues are covered in Chapter 5.) A central theme of this chapter is that both IS and business managers need to be responsible for managing information resources effectively. For example, both business managers and IS professionals need to take the responsibility of keeping the physical IT infrastructure current, including central and distributed computer hardware, internal networks, and links to the Internet. One of the major assets of an IT system, the applications portfolio, is also addressed in this chapter. The chapter suggests guidelines for how business managers can be active participants in designing and managing the infrastructure and the portfolio.

Chapter 15 also looks at the human and organizational aspects of leading an IS organization. Successfully managing an organization's IS resources involves making critical decisions about alternative organizational structures, reporting channels for IS units, and the potential roles of the chief information officer (CIO). Other critical issues, such as outsourcing IS work, developing staff, financing the costs of operating and developing new IS resources, and deploying IS resources globally, are discussed. The chapter also addresses the growing influence of the Internet on the effective management of IS resources.

Chapter 16, "Social, Ethical, and Legal Issues," addresses subjects of growing importance to both IS and business managers, due to the increased availability of information and the ease with which that information can be accessed, sometimes without the permission of the owner of the information. A framework for understanding the ethical issues involving the access and use of data and information is presented, as well as codes of ethics developed by various IS organizations. The changing legal environment within the United States is discussed, as well as topics such as computer crime, attacks by hackers on organizational resources, identity theft, and privacy issues. Related social issues, such as freedom of speech, spam, and intellectual property rights (including downloading of music) are also considered.

Part IV closes with 11 original teaching cases. The Clarion School for Boys case study addresses how to conduct an assessment of the use and management of IT in an organization and a process by which to build a plan for the future. The Teletron, Inc. case study describes a business proposal to convert a company from a services firm to a software firm, which involves making a major IT investment. The Advantage 2000 case study details the approach used by Owens Corning to become a process-oriented business as part of an enterprise-wide implementation of an enterprise resource planning (ERP) package.

The two Compaq-Digital teaching cases offer an inside look at the IT management challenges that are faced when two IT manufacturing giants are merging. Part A emphasizes the achievement of short-term objectives between the merger announcement and day one of the new merged business (Compaq), while Part B addresses the longer-term issues of integrating two IS organizations, including decisions about ERP implementations underway in both Digital and Compaq at the time of the merger. The case study about a fast track IT integration for the Sallie Mae merger is also an IT integration story involving multiple IS organizations with systems that have similar capabilities; this case study is also a success story of an internally led IT project using a project management office capability. The Schaeffer, Inc., case study addresses an issue being looked at by essentially all IS leaders today: the outsourcing of one or more of the IS functions.

The next two cases have an international focus. The Baxter Manufacturing Company case study involves a small company based in the Midwestern United States that made the decision to build a new manufacturing plant in Mexico and now must decide how to support the IS needs of the new plant. The BAT APSS case study describes a shared services approach to providing IS operations, applications development, and other support services to country-level offices within the Asia Pacific region of a large multinational firm (BAT).

Two short case studies, "Mary Morrison's Ethical Dilemma" and "A Security Breach on the Indiana University Computer Network," are companion cases to the final chapter of this textbook, which addresses IT security issues as part of its discussion of ethical, legal, and social issues related to IS management.

CHAPTER 14
SETTING A DIRECTION FOR INFORMATION RESOURCES

IN PREVIOUS CHAPTERS THE TECHNICAL AND OPERATIONAL GROUNDWORK crucial to an understanding of the management of the information resources in an organization was established. You should now be familiar with many of the issues of computing hardware and software, telecommunications and networking, the variety of information technology (IT) applications, and the development and maintenance of application software systems. The successful management of an organization's information resources in today's competitive business environment must combine this knowledge with a thorough understanding of business strategy to guide the development of information resources for the firm.

This chapter deals with one of the critical components for effectively managing IT in an organization—setting a direction for its information resources. The development of an overall management system for the information resources in an organization is not complete without a clear understanding by information systems (IS) professionals and business managers about how the information resources of the organization will be developed.

This chapter asserts that an information resource planning system must include: (1) an assessment of current information resources, (2) the establishment of an information vision and the IT architecture, and (3) the formulation of strategic and operational IS plans needed to move an organization's information resources from their current status toward the desired vision and architecture. It would not be appropriate here to outline detailed instructions for a specific planning system because planning needs and styles differ greatly from organization to organization and many approaches seem to work. However, the basic issues and concepts for an effective information resources planning effort are addressed in this chapter.

Likewise, the exact organization structure for IS varies widely among firms. Many large organizations have multiple IS departments, but they are treated as a single organization here. Although some parts of the detailed planning process are typically internal to the IS organization, it is helpful for the business manager to understand and to be involved in the overall process. Therefore, this chapter structures the entire IS planning process in rather broad terms. The focus is on those areas where the business manager should be involved. Examples from a variety of organizations are used to explain the concepts.

This chapter points out some of the reasons companies should set an IS direction, defines some terms, explains the planning process and each of the steps in it, and focuses on the issues that should be addressed. The chapter ends with some guidelines for developing an information resources plan and outlines the benefits to business managers and IS professionals of having a clear direction for the development of the entire organization's information resources.

WHY SET A DIRECTION FOR INFORMATION RESOURCES?

Organizations need a plan for the development of their information resources for several reasons. In some firms the management of all the diverse applications of IT is not, and never will be, organized under a single person. Yet most firms want to share information among diverse parts of the firm (and sometimes outside the firm) and use that information for strategic or operational advantage. Discussion and agreement on a common structure (or architecture, as defined later in this chapter) for the varied applications of IT in an organization can provide a shared understanding among IS professionals and business managers of how the company can best use its information resources.

Developing a plan for a company's information resources helps communicate the future to others and provides a consistent rationale for making individual decisions. Sometimes an information resources plan is created because business managers have expressed concern about whether there is some grand scheme within which to make individual decisions. The plan for information resources development provides this grand scheme. The decentralization of IS decisions and information resources makes the establishment of a well-understood overall information resources direction critical to making consistent, timely decisions by both business managers and IS professionals.

> **BUSINESS AND IT ALIGNMENT**
>
> Alignment of IT strategy with the organization's business strategy is a fundamental principle. IS managers must be knowledgeable about how new technologies can be integrated into the business (in addition to the integration among the different technologies and architectures) and must be privy to senior management's tactical and strategic plans. Both IS and business executives must be present when corporate strategies are discussed. IS executives must be able to delineate the strengths and weaknesses of the technologies in question.
>
> [Adapted from Luftman and Brier, 1996]

Planning discussions often help business managers and IS professionals in making basic decisions about how the "business" of IS will be conducted—defining the organization's basic style and values. Such discussions might be part of comprehensive programs that attempt to define or refine the culture of the overall company. In 2002, for example, a growing medical device manufacturing company believed it was necessary to instill a greater awareness about the concept of quality in the entire business to compete more effectively in the global marketplace. The effort led that company's IS director to consider more precisely the quality-related values to be embraced by the IS organization. For the first time, the IS organization began to consider the role of quality in the shared beliefs of people within the IS organization. Discussion focused on various IS quality issues such as excessive rework in the design of major systems.

Traumatic incidents sometimes create the need for an information resources direction-setting process. In September 2003, telecommunications network redundancy was a significant architecture discussion topic among some IS directors within the financial services industry. A tornado had destroyed much of a telecommunications company's critical switching center, and the extensive damage reduced data and voice circuit availability for several days. As a result, banks and other organizations that depended on the constant availability of the public telephone network for certain operations, such as automatic teller machines (ATMs), were forced to reexamine contingency plans associated with the unavailability of telecommunications service. Some organizations realized that IS management had not thought seriously about what to do when faced with such a loss. The result in many firms was an extended set of discussions on network architecture and network plans.

THE OUTPUTS OF THE DIRECTION-SETTING PROCESS

IS managers have developed project plans and budgets for many years. However, the task of formally developing and communicating an overall information resources plan, with an explicit information vision and architecture, is relatively new to many organizations. Some organizations have several years experience in developing such outputs formally. For others, building an information vision, for example, might be a very new activity. As a result, the deliverables at each step in the process take on somewhat different meanings from organization to organization. It therefore makes sense to define each output or deliverable in the planning process.

Information Resources Assessment

As outlined in earlier chapters, any organization has a set of information resources—both technological and human—through which business managers conduct the organization's business.

> An **information resources assessment** includes inventorying and critically evaluating these resources in terms of how well they are meeting the organization's business needs.

An information resources assessment includes reviewing the quality and quantity of the organization's technological resources—the hardware, software, networks, and data components of an information resources system. The human asset portion of an information resources assessment includes a review of the quantity and training/experience level of both users and IS professionals, as well as the management systems and values that drive IS decisions in the organization.

Information Vision and Architecture

At a recent meeting of IS directors, the following ideas emerged about the meaning of the information vision and architecture concept. Some executives described the term as a "shared understanding of how computing and telecommunications technology will be used and managed in the business." Others reported that they generate a "comprehensive statement about our future information resources that is part philosophy and part blueprint." The group held that a vision and architecture statement must be "specific enough to guide planning and decision making but flexible enough to avoid restatement each time a new information system is developed." Finally, several in the group asserted that a "vision and architecture statement should provide the long-term goal for the IS planning effort"—the vision and architecture statement represents the overall design target.

Several ideas common to these descriptions suggest a definition. First, the information vision and architecture statement is an ideal view of the future and not the plan on how to get there (the information resources plan is discussed later). Second, the vision and architecture statement must be flexible enough to provide policy guidelines for individual decisions but more than just fluff. Third, deliberation about both vision and architecture must focus on the long term, but exact dates are usually not specified. Finally, there is some difference between a vision and an architecture, although some firms combine the two concepts into a single statement.

With these ideas in mind, the terms can be defined as follows:

> An **information vision** is a written expression of the desired future about how information will be used and managed in the organization.
>
> The **information technology architecture** depicts the way an organization's information resources will be deployed to deliver that vision.

Much like the design of a future complex aircraft or a skyscraper, an information vision and an IT architecture together translate a mental image for the desired future state of information use and management into a comprehensive set of written guidelines, policies, pictures, or mandates within which an organization should operate and make decisions. Either the vision or the architecture might take the form of a set of doctrinal requirements (like the Ten Commandments). Other organizations create architectural diagrams or blueprints much like a building architect uses a diagram to represent a mental image of the future. As is true for a business vision, the information vision and architecture might also be a written statement. For example, one organization found it sufficient to define its information vision by stating, "We must provide quality data and computing products and services that meet our clients' needs in a timely and cost-effective manner." Regardless of the form, statements about vision and architecture should provide the business, managerial, and technical platform for planning and executing IS operations in the firm.

Information Resources Plans

The information resources planning process should generate two major plan outputs—the strategic IS plan and the operational IS plan.

> The **strategic IS plan** contains a set of longer-term objectives that represent measurable movement toward the information vision and technology architecture and a set of associated major initiatives that must be undertaken to achieve these objectives.

At the strategic level, these initiatives are not typically defined precisely enough to be IS projects. Instead, the IS strategic plan lists the major changes that must be made in the deployment of an organization's information resources over some time period, usually multiple years.

The **operational IS plan** is a precise set of shorter-term goals and associated projects that will be executed by the IS department and by business managers in support of the strategic IS plan.

The operational IS plan incorporates the precise results that will be accomplished, and often the budgets for each project are identified in the plan. In essence, the operational plan crystallizes the strategic plan into a series of defined projects that must be accomplished in the short term.

The process of generating each of these outputs and how they are linked together is discussed in more detail in the next section.

THE PROCESS OF SETTING DIRECTION

IS and Business Planning

Previous chapters have argued that IS decisions must be tightly aligned with the direction of the business. Such a maxim exists whether for the design of a particular application system or for the overall direction of the organization's information resources. Figure 14.1 depicts the relationship between setting the direction for the business as a whole and setting the overall direction for information use and management in that business. This process may be applied for the entire company, a division, or an individual business manager's department. On the left side of the chart are the general steps required to set direction for the business. On the right are the required planning steps for the organization's information resources. Note the many arrows depicting how the output of a step affects both the next step on the same side (left or right) of the figure as well as steps on the other side of the figure. This chart provides the outline for the rest of the chapter.

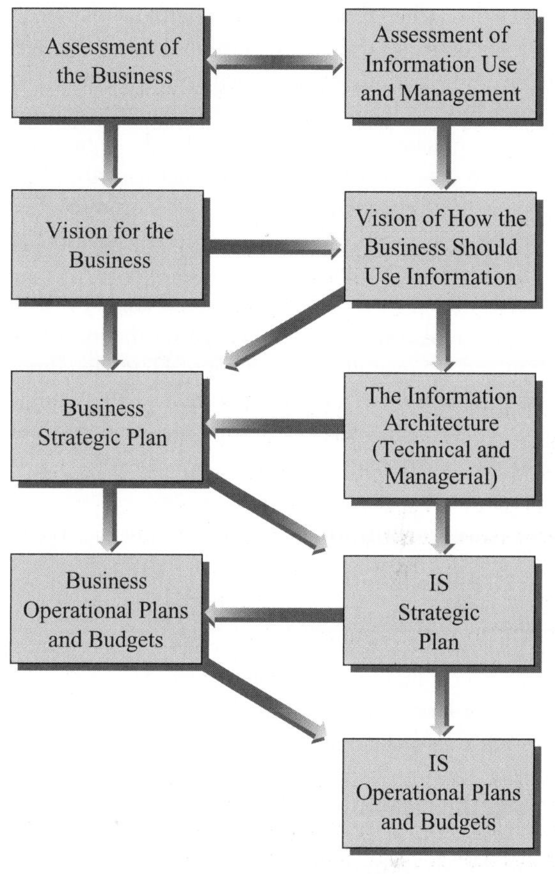

Figure 14.1 The Information Resources Planning Process

Assessment

Any organizational planning process starts with an assessment step, both for the business and for its information resources. Current performance is compared to a previous plan, to competitors, or to a set of past objectives. Operating data are collected. Surveys are often conducted to measure customer attitudes on performance. Competing organizations are "benchmarked" to determine both what is possible and what is being achieved at other organizations. Both a business assessment and an information resources assessment should be conducted. More on the information assessment step is presented later in this chapter.

Vision

The second basic step in any planning process should be to envision an ideal state at some distant point in the future. This step defines what the organization wants to become or to create. It does *not* define how to achieve this vision. For the information resources area, a technology architecture is added to the information vision for the organization.

Strategic Planning

Strategic planning is the third step and should be conducted for both the business and its information resources. **Strategic planning** is the process of constructing a viable fit between the organization's objectives and resources and its changing market and technological opportunities. The aim of any strategic planning effort is to shape the company's resources and products so that they combine to produce the needed results. Strategic *business* planning sets the basic course for the use of all resources, usually over an extended time period. It is designed to be general in nature and typically does not specify precise budgets, schedules, or operating details. Instead, it translates the organization's vision into a set of major initiatives that describes how to accomplish the organization's vision of its future. Review of the strategic plan is exercised by regularly examining the status of the major initiatives contained in it.

In parallel with the business plan, a strategic IS plan should be built considering the vision for the use of information and the overall management of IT in the company, as well as the role of the IS department. The strategic IS plan lays out the results desired for a specified time period and the necessary major initiatives.

Operational Planning

Operational planning lays out the major actions the organization needs to carry out in the shorter term to activate its strategic initiatives. It typically includes a portfolio of projects that will be implemented during some time frame in order of priority or urgency. Specific, measurable goals are established, and general estimates of costs and benefits are prepared. Quite often, capital expenditures are identified and justified. Responsibility for achievement of the objectives, actions, and projects is also specified in this plan. Review of the operational plan is more precise, often on a time-and-cost basis at the project level. Specific details, responsibilities, and dates of projects that move to the implementation stage are identified in the budget, including staffing requirements, facility scheduling, specific demand and usage forecasts, and detailed expense estimates. Once set in motion, the operational plan is naturally less flexible than the strategic plan. The operational plan relies heavily on the operating budget for control purposes. Quite often, companies develop both long-term (3 to 5 years) as well as short-term (1 year) operational business plans.

The operational IS plan, although usually coinciding in length with the business operational plan, is likely even more project-specific than its business plan counterpart. This difference is a natural result of the operational plan's purpose—to translate the general information resources direction, as defined in the strategic IS plan, into specific systems development projects or other efforts for the IS department (such as a capacity upgrade) that also meet specific initiatives for the business. In addition to defining methods by which the IS department plans to complete projects for other units in the organization, the operational IS plan lists internal projects designed to enable the IS department to better meet the needs of its internal customers.

The operational IS plan also identifies specific accomplishments to be achieved on multiyear application systems development projects. Suggestions are made for improvements in IS department operating procedures and for increasing infrastructure capacity. Specific goals, actions, due dates, and budgets are proposed for software purchases. The time of professional IS staff is allocated to major systems development projects.

Traditional Planning in the IS Organization

In many IS organizations the process of overall information resources planning has not been structured in the same way as the business planning process. Traditionally, the emphasis of IS planning was on major application systems internal development project planning rather than on overall organizational planning. Because of this emphasis on internal development projects, many IS organizations adopted a bottom-up, immediate needs-based approach to information resources planning, referred to as **needs-based IS planning**. When a specific, urgent business need called for a new information system, some form of formal project planning process was invoked to address the situation.

Over time, this **project-oriented IS planning** process was found to be largely reactive and often did not ensure that the proposed system meshed well with the organization's overall business plan. In some cases not enough consideration was given to the impact that one proposed system might have on another proposed or existing system. This orientation toward IS planning, although practical from the perspective of the IS department and perhaps the individual business manager, often resulted in lost strategic business opportunities, incompatible systems and databases, unacceptable implementation time frames, and a host of other problems. The needs-based IS planning approach often failed to adequately consider the organization's total information requirements across operating units, possible economies of scale, and avoidance of duplication of efforts. As demand for information to be shared across functional organizational lines increased and the distinction between classes of IT blurred, the shortcomings of the needs-based approach to IS planning led many companies to seek better ways to set a direction for their information resources. Thus, the concept of developing a strategic IS plan, driven by the business strategic plan and seeking to conform to an agreed-upon information vision and technology architecture for the organization, began to be used more extensively.

Although both the business planning and information resources planning processes are important for overall organizational effectiveness, the rest of this chapter deals in detail only with the right-hand side steps of Figure 14.1.

ASSESSING CURRENT INFORMATION RESOURCES

The information resources planning process should begin with an assessment of the use of information and IT in the entire organization and an assessment of the IS organization itself. The information resources assessment step is usually conducted by a committee of business managers and IS professionals, perhaps with the aid of outside experts. Outside facilitators can bring needed objectivity and experience to the process, but their value must be weighed against the added cost. Alternatively, the assessment might be conducted totally by an outside organization and presented to top business and IS department management or the IS oversight committee. As with all such outside studies, however, there is the distinct possibility that this approach might develop a "not invented here" response by the IS organization and some business managers. If carefully orchestrated, however, an outside information resources assessment can be very successful.

Measuring IS Use and Attitudes

The information resources assessment, however it is conducted, should measure current levels of information resources use within the organization and compare it to a set of standards. These standards can be derived from past performance in the organization, technical benchmarks, industry norms, and "best of class" estimates obtained from other companies. In addition to use measures, the attitudes of users and staff of the IS organization are important. Opinions about the performance of the IS organization in relating its activities to the needs and direction of the business must be measured. Likewise, a technical assessment of the IT infrastructure should be conducted. Figure 14.2 (see p. 564) contains a portion of an information resources assessment conducted in late 2001 for a Michigan-based food products company. The company president initiated the assessment after the IS director was terminated, and a team of business managers and IS personnel facilitated by an outside consultant undertook it. As should be clear from the example, the assessment will likely lead to substantial changes in overall information resources direction at this organization.

Reviewing the IS Organizational Mission

Another important part of the assessment step is a review of the IS department's mission. The **IS mission** statement should set forth the fundamental rationale (or reason to exist) for the activities of the IS department. The activities of the IS department must be assessed in light of this mission.

ASSESSING THE ORGANIZATION

In conducting an information systems department assessment, ask these questions:

- Do key executives understand the impact of IT on the company's competitive position?
- Do they understand what is possible with current and forthcoming technologies?
- Do they know how the capabilities and economies of IT will change the way the business is operated and managed?
- Does the company have the right balance between innovation and managing scarce technology resources?

[Adapted from Hildebrand, 2000]

The IS organization's mission can vary substantially from one organization to another. Some IS departments are assigned the task of improving efficiency in the firm, typically by automating processes in order to reduce costs. Often, IS departments are also engaged in improving the information environment for knowledge workers in the organization, giving them the data and software tools needed to do their job better. Finally, many IS organizations have been assigned the role of helping the organization achieve strategic or competitive advantage in the marketplace, offering information-enhanced services or through some application that attracts and holds customers.

It is not uncommon in the assessment process to find an imbalance of performance in these three areas. Traditional needs-based planning approaches often do not address the requirements of all three of the above mission areas. Instead, efficiency usually receives the majority of the planners' attention. Unfortunately, satisfying immediate needs of just one of the areas might contribute little to the other elements of the IS department mission.

Involving business managers in the assessment exercise is one way to ensure that the IS mission statement defines the most appropriate role of the IS department. This involvement also allows business managers throughout the organization to understand better why the IS department needs a mission statement and a strategic plan. Figure 14.3 (see p. 565) contains a mission statement for the IS organization of a West Coast machinery manufacturer developed by staff in the IS organization in 2003 and based on what they thought business managers wanted from the organization. The identified roles include an emphasis on secure data storage for the official records of the organization, maintaining processing capacity, managing the data network, providing access to external information resources, and offering systems development capability. Although all

- **A *single* information system does not exist in our organization.**
  A variety of disconnected information systems exists throughout our organization. Some systems are contained in isolated PCs, some on isolated mainframes/minis. Such disintegration causes needless effort on the part of staff.
- **Substantial potential exists for "cleaning up" the automation of existing work processes.**
  Significant manual processing of information currently occurs in such areas as the compilation of statistics, reporting, billing information given to finance, typing, and administrative functions. There are several work steps that our software does not treat, and there are steps where the software has a different set of requirements than is practiced at our company. Consequently, staff must override the software or supplement it manually.

  Our organization maintains several paper-based "shadow" systems created to fill in where information systems do not connect. These paper systems are costing our organization a significant loss in time.
- **Significant gaps exist in automation of the "value-added" process in our company.**
  Many of the steps involved in the value-added process are conducted either manually or, if the computer is used, operate from old data. Automating and integrating these steps will offer a significant strategic advantage for our company.
- **There is a perception that the IS organization is not a company-wide support organization.**
  The staff feels that IS seems to focus almost exclusively on the order processing function. IS has not been seen as a source of leadership for solving problems that are in other functions and PC-based. Staff associated with the distribution function seem to receive better service on their information requests and have software upgrades made more easily.
- **Except for the last year and a half, IS appears to have been a "stepchild" of senior management.**
  The staff questions whether senior management is really committed to making IS an integral part of our company. Senior management is still seen by some staff as too distant from information resource management. Active participation by senior management will be required if leadership is expected from IS.
- **There is a significant perception among the user population that IS is not particularly responsive to their needs.**
  Turnover of personnel in the PC support positions has been high, resulting in staff not understanding its role.

  There seems to be a general lack of trust between the user community and the IS organization. Requests for new software are denied with little explanation. Many people feel standards are enforced in situations that should not be subject to arbitrary standards.
- **IS personnel seem dedicated to IS and the company.**
  A strong team spirit exists in IS to operate in the current adverse situation (i.e., without a director).
- **The level of user training and support is substantially below needs and expectations.**
  Training on software is inconsistent. There is a strong feeling among staff that "tunnel training" exists (only taught enough to perform specific job). Opportunities to use software to extract data and be creative do not exist.
- **While the workload in IS is heavy at times, current staffing levels should be sufficient to meet current expectations.**
  Current IS staff are performing their regular duties consistently without a director, but nonroutine functions, many of which were previously performed by the director, are not being done. Personnel seem willing, but have not been trained in these functions, many of which require a high level of system knowledge.

  There are a number of users within our organization who would like to see IS take on a much more active role. Such a role will increase human resource requirements, both in numbers and skill levels.
- **The Internet is not used extensively.**
  Very few personnel have access from their desktops. Opportunities for use of the Internet by management seem to have been disregarded by the IS department

Figure 14.2 Example Information Resources Assessment

Information Services is responsible for a wide variety of computing systems and services for the people of our corporation.

In this role, the department:

- Provides a secure location for housing and accessing the official electronic data records of the company.
- Maintains central/shared computer processing capacity and support for file maintenance and information reporting.
- Manages a corporate data network that delivers services to departmental servers and individual workstations linked to its data center.
- Provides integrated IS development for departments in order to advance organizational strategies (systems development services are available for corporate, local area network, workstations, and supply chain applications).

Figure 14.3 IS-Prepared Mission Statement Example

these are important technical functions, this "inside-out" view of the IS organization's mission might not match a statement developed from a user-based perspective.

Figure 14.4 provides a mission statement for the same IS organization developed by some of the business managers in the organization (in this case, the nine senior managers of the corporation). The second paragraph in particular makes it clear that these business managers see the IS organization as not being in the computing business at all, but as the provider of "management tools" to increase organizational effectiveness and the developer of the information infrastructure and services needed to improve decision making in the business. Operating an IS department with this latter mission statement would clearly require a major reconsideration of the basic activities of the IS organization compared to those represented in the first statement. Indeed, some assessments reveal that an outdated mission statement is the root cause of internal customer concern about the IS department.

Assessing Performance versus Goals

The traditional goal of many IS applications was to reduce cost by increasing the operating efficiencies of structured, repetitive tasks, such as the automation of the payroll function. The scope of IS applications has expanded dramatically in recent years to include systems to assist in the decision-making process for unstructured problem situations and in providing ways by which competitive advantage is achieved for the organization. This broader scope in the uses of IT has

In order to meet the challenges outlined within the company Vision Statement and support the strategic objectives and values of our company, the mission of Information Services is to provide reliable information, data, and computing services to all clients, both within and, where appropriate, outside of the company.

To accomplish this role, it will be necessary to exercise leadership in identifying new management tools based on evolving information technology that enables management to increase their effectiveness in operating and managing the business. The department's ultimate objective is the development of an integrated information infrastructure and associated services required to facilitate the decision-making process.

Figure 14.4 Internal Client-Prepared Mission Statement Example

Table 14.1 Objectives for the IS Department

Achievement Area	2003 Objectives	2003 Performance	2004 Objectives
Percent of internal client satisfaction with applications development services	80%	71%	85%
Percent of knowledge workers with a networked workstation	75%	78%	85%
Percent of scheduled hours data network is available to internal clients	99%	99%	99%
IS department personnel turnover	12%	14%	8%
Percent of departmental computing equipment purchases that comply with the supported equipment list	85%	88%	85%
Percent of total organization computing resource capacity connected to data network	80%	85%	85%
Cost per transaction on common systems	$0.025	$0.0285	$0.02
Percent of targeted systems converted to client/server architecture	95%	87%	99%
Percent of internal client workstations with access to the Internet	85%	92%	95%

required IS and business managers to assess the IS organization based on objectives in addition to reducing cost.

Table 14.1 shows the objectives of an IS organization at a regional bank in the Midwest. Nine objectives for 2003 were identified in an earlier planning process, and data were collected during late September 2003 to estimate actual performance for the year. The assessment report noted that on some measures, such as the number of customers and network availability, actual performance during the year exceeded expectations. On other measures, notably customer satisfaction with certain services and conversion to a client/server architecture for certain systems, actual results were far short of the goal. These conclusions and a new set of objectives for the year 2004 were used as input to later steps in the information resources planning process shown in Figure 14.1.

CREATING AN INFORMATION VISION

After assessing the current use and management of an organization's information resources, the shared business and IS leadership expectations of how information will be used in the business should be specified. Developing these expectations requires both an understanding of the future direction of the business and an understanding of the role information can play in winning the competitive race.

Vision creation starts with speculation on how the business's competitive environment will change and how the company should take advantage of it. Once this business vision is specified (and written), the implications for how information should be used in the firm in the future should be outlined. The information vision for the organization may then be written.

An example might be useful to explain the process. A $35 million printing company in Atlanta was taken over by new management in early 2003 as the result of an acquisition. During three off-site, full-day discussion sessions that were held to create a new vision and direction, the group developed the following set of basic specifications for the company:

- We will compete in five major market segments, each supplied by distinct business units.
- We will have revenues of at least $100 million by 2008 and be known for our quality and leading-edge technology.
- We will be a leading "national player" in the printing industry.
- We will exploit new business lines or market niches via acquisition or joint ventures or by spinning off existing operations.

- Our centralized administrative units (personnel, accounting, purchasing, etc.) will operate in support of all business units.
- We will achieve strategic advantage in each market via our "information-based" decisions.
- Our profit margins will exceed 10 percent of revenue.

These fundamental propositions about the company in the future led to the following basic business strategy decisions:

- We must improve gross margins and lower overhead costs while achieving moderate sales growth.
- We must increase the productivity of every person in the company.
- We must shorten the job fulfillment cycle time (from customer order to delivery).
- We must strive toward "zero defects" in all we do (quality objectives and monitoring systems will exist).
- We must be able to receive jobs electronically from all our customers.
- We must improve company-wide internal management systems (e.g., budgeting, personnel evaluation).

Senior management and senior professionals in the IS department then reviewed these business priorities along with the business vision. After several sessions, they jointly arrived at a shared vision for information use and management in the company. They chose to represent this vision via the following set of bullet points.

- Our corporate network will be able to service a large number of remote nodes at high speed.
- User demand on our information system each year will experience:
  1. Medium growth in transaction volume on existing common systems.
  2. High growth in ad hoc requests for information on all shared and personal systems.
  3. High growth in transaction volume from new applications on shared and personal systems.
- New data fields will be defined and managed each year.
- The entire job acquisition and fulfillment cycle will be supported by an integrated, comprehensive, and accurate database.
- Our corporate network will be able to send and receive large files from external customers at high speed.
- All internal customers will regularly use the Internet for research and communication.
- Business managers will know how to use information to make decisions and how to use the capabilities of our information resources effectively.
- Each business unit and functional department will manage its information resources within an overall IT architecture.
- All existing business support processes (e.g., purchase order processing) will be automated via expert systems to free up time of critical human resources.
- Internal customers will have workstation tools to make all information easily accessible.

Taken together, these statements represent a specification of how senior management wants information to be used and managed in the future. These statements are not a plan—how the IS department working with business managers will create this environment must still be determined. Instead, these statements represent a vision of what is desired. The architectural decisions on how to deploy the company's data, software, people, and other IS assets are also not all specified. That is the next step.

DESIGNING THE ARCHITECTURE

Now that a vision for future information use in the organization has been formulated, the IS organization, often in cooperation with business managers, must design an IT architecture. This architecture specifies how the technological and human assets and the IS organization should be deployed in the future to meet the information vision. The plan for migrating the organization's current information resources to the deployment specified in the architecture is developed later.

Components of Architecture

Several models have been developed that define the elements that make up an architecture for IT. Traditionally, the treatment takes on a very technical definition of an IT architecture. Later models have expanded the dimensions to include more managerial and fewer technical aspects of information resources.

In keeping with the classification of IS assets outlined in earlier chapters, it makes sense to structure an IT architecture into its technological and human components. Each component in turn contains several elements. Figure 14.5 contains a list of the elements of each component.

The **technological assets** component of the IT architecture contains desired specifications about future hardware

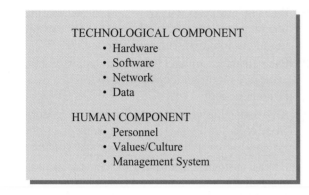

TECHNOLOGICAL COMPONENT
- Hardware
- Software
- Network
- Data

HUMAN COMPONENT
- Personnel
- Values/Culture
- Management System

Figure 14.5 Elements of an Information Technology Architecture

and operating systems, network, data and data management systems, and applications software. Some of the tradeoffs and issues in developing the specifications about these elements are dealt with in more detail in other chapters. Figure 14.6 contains an example of the technology elements of an IT architecture developed by the IS department of a rapidly growing, privately held personnel outsourcing company in Ohio in 2001. By carefully examining this part of an architecture, you should be able to picture the technical IT system being designed.

The **human assets** component of an IT architecture defines the **values architecture** and the **management system architecture** parts of an IT system. Together, these

- An effective IT architecture is dependent on a high-quality process by which data are collected and transformed into information.
- The company's process for information creation will apply regardless of the diverse source of data, the division, or location.
- The process of transforming our data into information will be carefully designed.
- Our core data will always be stored in a secure place.
- The entire information creation process will be supported by an excellent technical IT infrastructure.
- All company staff will be attached to a high-speed electronic network that provides easy access to a variety of data and computing resources both within and outside the company.
- Small, ad hoc reporting systems created to access existing core data are not covered by these specifications.
- All information systems that contain or use core data will be available on the electronic network.
- All information systems that contain or use core data will be of an "open" design.
- All systems development processes will follow the protocol developed by the Systems Development Policy Committee.
- All data management systems in the company will be relational and be selected from a list of supported data management software maintained by the Information Services organization and approved by the Data Committee.
- The Information Services organization will maintain a list of supported word processing, spreadsheet, statistical, and e-mail software.
- The Data Committee will regularly publish a list of data collection and data maintenance standards.
- A corporate data model for our core data will be developed and regularly maintained by the Data Committee, using outside consultants.
- Each manager in the company will be held responsible for the integrity of the core data maintained by his/her organization.
- Information Services will provide support for a set of hardware/operating system platforms that are approved by the Information Resources Management Committee.
- Data analysis methodologies will be regularly reviewed by the Data Committee.

Figure 14.6 Example Technology Component of an IT Architecture

- Trained external customers will be able to see appropriate information stored in our systems via secure access from the Internet.
- The entire information creation process will be supported by a responsive management system.
- The Data Committee will exercise overall responsibility for the quality and cost of using data and information in carrying out the mission of our company.
- The Information Resources Management Committee will be responsible for ensuring that the infrastructural components of individual systems comply with the architecture.
- The Systems Development Policy Committee will develop and maintain policies relating to information systems development.
- The Data Committee will oversee and update the company's data architecture.
- The Information Resources Management Committee will approve an information systems funding system.
- The head of the Information Services organization (i.e., the CIO) will lead and support the development and maintenance of an enterprise-wide information system for the organization.
- The Director of Network Services will be responsible for maintaining and improving the technical infrastructure, both within the organization and secure links to the Internet.
- The Director of Customer Development will provide for longer-term internal customer development and support.
- The Director of Data Quality will support the improvement of data integrity throughout the company.
- The Information Systems Director will be responsible for maintaining and improving existing information systems.
- Support for the development of new application systems and the maintenance/upgrade of existing systems will be housed in the Information Services organization.
- Each manager in our company will be responsible for budgeting and executing a data/systems training plan that meets our data training requirements.
- Each Vice President will ensure that each department within the organization has developed its own information systems plan.
- A plan for the migration of each information system in the company to be compatible with this architecture will be established by the Data Committee and approved by the Executive Staff.
- Each member of the staff will take at least 24 hours of IT training each year.

Figure 14.7 Example Human Component of an IT Architecture

elements specify the "business" parts of managing the IS department, how business managers will be involved, and how IS decisions will be made. These areas are dealt with in more detail in Chapter 15. Figure 14.7 shows the companion human assets component of the Ohio outsourcing firm's IT architecture developed in 2001. By carefully reviewing this part of the architecture, you should be able to understand the future culture, organizational structure, and management system for this organization's information resources.

THE STRATEGIC IS PLAN

According to Figure 14.1, the next two IS planning steps involve creating plans for the development of an organization's information resources. After the current information resources situation is assessed and a vision and an architecture are established, the first plan that should be developed for an organization's information resources is the strategic IS plan. The strategic IS plan is a statement of the major objectives and initiatives (not yet defined precisely enough to be projects) that the IS organization and business managers must accomplish over some time period to move the company information resources toward the information vision and to fit the business strategic plan. The plan should also contain a set of measurable results to be achieved during this time period in order to act as benchmarks for assessing progress toward the vision. The plan might also contain the results of an internal and external strategic analysis performed as part of the strategic IS planning process.

The Strategic IS Planning Process

The development of the IS strategic plan is accomplished in four basic steps: setting objectives or goals, conducting an external analysis, conducting an internal analysis, and establishing strategic initiatives. Although they are treated here in sequence, most planning processes involve iterations through these four steps.

Setting Objectives The setting of IS objectives is done in much the same way as strategic objectives are specified for any business or functional organization. Measures are identified for each of the key result areas for the organization. IS objectives are often established in such areas as IS department service image, IS personnel productivity, and the appropriateness of technology applications. Goals relating to increased effectiveness, access to external resources, and breadth of business manager involvement in IS applications are also possible.

A sample of strategic IS objectives for a regional bank in the Midwest was shown in Table 14.1. This organization assigned the IS department goals in several areas, including internal customer satisfaction, breadth of workstation coverage, data network performance, IS department personnel turnover, supported equipment list acceptance, pervasiveness of the data network, cost per transaction on common systems, client/server conversion progress, and Internet access. Although the choice of which results to set as goals will vary with the organization's circumstances, each objective should provide some clear benchmark toward achieving the vision and architecture for IT.

Conducting Internal and External Analyses The second step in the development of a strategic IS plan is a review of the external environment within which the organization's information resources must be developed over the planning period, say 3 to 5 years. This step should include reviews of the company's strategic business plan as well as an IT forecast. Quite often the result of this process is a series of statements called opportunities (areas in which new systems could be created or where the IS organization could take some action to the company's long-term advantage) and threats (external factors that might affect IS performance that could be corrected or for which some countermeasure could be developed).

Along with the external analysis, a review of the internal strengths and weaknesses of the IS department and how well business managers play their role in the entire IT process is also conducted. The list of strengths indicates areas where the IS department is particularly strong. Likewise, the list of weaknesses displays areas where the IS department or the role of the business manager should improve. The internal analysis parts of this step are often conducted during the assessment phase of the planning process described earlier in this chapter. These four statements together make up a **SWOT** (strengths, weaknesses, opportunities, and threats) strategic situation analysis.

A sample SWOT analysis for the Ohio outsourcing company mentioned earlier that was input into its strategic IS plan is shown in Figure 14.8. Note that the company (via a working group of business managers and IS managers) identified seven strengths related to the organization's information resources. Most relate to technical skills of IS professionals and the quality of their transaction processing systems. Six weaknesses in the use or management of information are listed, ranging from personnel issues within the IS organization to limited departmental applications beyond routine transaction processing.

These strengths and weaknesses act as either leverage points (strengths) or as limiting factors (weaknesses) for new strategic initiatives. The threats and opportunities lists contain both factual and attitudinal issues that must be dealt with in the plan. Both user and technology issues should be mentioned in the opportunities and threats sections.

Establishing Strategic Initiatives Figure 14.9 (see p. 572) contains a set of strategic initiatives resulting from a 2002 strategic information resources planning effort for a medium-sized energy company. Each statement represents an important initiative needed to enhance the role of IT at this corporation. Some of these initiatives will require substantial investment and create new operating costs for implementation. Yet none of the initiatives is spelled out well enough to be immediately translated into action. The operational planning step is required to translate these initiatives into actual projects.

Strengths

- Major transaction control systems are relatively new, functionally adequate, well-documented, maintainable, and operationally efficient.
- The IS department has demonstrated effectiveness in adding new technologies (e.g., its own access to the Internet).
- The IS department has demonstrated competence and effectiveness in applications development that facilitate group decision support.
- There is a stable, competent professional IS staff with expertise in designing and programming transaction processing systems.
- Our IS outsourcing partner seems to manage a reliable, cost-effective data center.
- There is a substantial use of our in-house electronic mail operation, frequented by most business managers in the company.
- There is substantial information technology expertise among business managers in both line and staff organizations.

Weaknesses

- A single point of IS contact for end-user operational problem diagnosis and resolution has not been established.
- There are limited data center performance measurement systems.
- There has been only limited transaction-based systems development productivity.
- There is a high degree of technology specialization (narrowness) among IS professional staff and a limited degree of business orientation.
- There is limited departmental use of information technology beyond simple decision support and participation in common transaction processing systems.
- Few business managers make effective use of the Internet.

Opportunities

- The IS department enjoys a high degree of credibility among the large and growing internal customer community.
- The role of the business manager in collaborating with the IS department has been institutionalized, facilitating ease of future system implementation.
- There is a growing base of internal customers who understand a wide range of information technologies and want to use IT for their business.
- The Internet provides data and interaction capabilities that would be of substantial strategic use to the firm.

Threats

- The IS department's effectiveness is threatened by pockets of internal customer negativism, especially among top management.
- Some business managers are developing a high degree of technical competence, which they employ in a nonintegrated fashion by developing separate workstation-based systems.
- The accelerating pace of technological change and proliferation of information technologies pose risks of control loss, obsolescence, and difficulty in maintaining IS professional staff competence.
- The extensive internal communication networks and internal customer accessibility to external databases pose security risks to our data.
- The IS department is still not an integral part of the company's business planning process.

Figure 14.8 Example SWOT Analysis

Management wants the Information Services and Systems department to develop its own long-range plan utilizing the vision, mission, values, and principles of operation outlined previously. The following is a listing of initiatives we feel should be undertaken in the ultimate formulation of this plan:

1. Manage development and operations of network architecture and security in accordance with business and internal customer requirements.
2. Help departments build individual information plans, utilizing Information Services and Systems departmental expertise and knowledge of overall company system requirements.
3. Create and maintain a short list of approved hardware and software that can be efficiently utilized within the designed network to meet end-user requirements.
4. Coordinate with other departments in the evaluation and design of telecommunication and data communication systems that meet the company's strategic and operational needs.
5. Provide and annually update a prioritized list of uses of external data that would strategically help the company.
6. Encourage active client participation in network utilization through training programs and help sessions that increase the efficiency and effectiveness of the overall company decision-making process.
7. Restructure the information services and systems departmental organization to better accomplish the mission of the department.
8. Develop a structured timetable and system of application backlog reductions.
9. Formulate a written standardization process for application development.

Figure 14.9 Sample Strategy Agenda

Tools for Identifying IT Strategic Opportunities

While building the strategic IS plan, organizations often seek help in identifying ways in which IT can provide strategic advantage. Several tools for finding new strategic insights have proven useful. None of the tools discussed here explicitly considers how an opportunity, once identified, can be translated into a comprehensive IS plan for the organization. The tools, however, have proven valuable in finding specific opportunities for IT applications and showing the role that IT might play in achieving certain business objectives. Because using these tools might result in IT applications during the operational planning process that help change the firm's strategic direction, their use is most important to effective strategic IS planning.

Critical Success Factors One well-known method for identifying strategic IT opportunities is to define information needs and processes critical to the success of a business function like sales or to the entire organization, called **critical success factors (CSFs)**. Any recent text on strategic management should contain a fuller discussion of CSFs. Generally, however, CSFs define a limited number of areas (usually four to six) that, if executed satisfactorily, will contribute most to the success of the overall performance of the firm or function. Many CSFs have either short-term or long-term impact on the use of IT. Once identified, the factors can be stated as opportunities for the application of IT. An analysis might then be conducted to determine more precisely how IT can be used to accomplish the needed task.

Analysis of Competitive Forces It is generally accepted that competitive advantage can come about by changing the balance of power between a business and the other actors in the industry. As seen from the strategic systems examples in earlier chapters, a company interested in finding a strategic initiative can

- Inhibit the entry of new competitors by raising the stakes for competing in the market or by redefining the basis for competition in at least one dimension (e.g., price, image, customer service, product features).
- Slow the application of substitute products/services by providing difficult-to-duplicate features.
- Make products/services more desirable than those of current competitors by providing unique product features or customer services or by shifting some customer product selection criterion (e.g., by being a low-cost provider).
- More strongly link with customers by making it easy for them to do business with the company and difficult to switch to a competitor.
- More strongly link with suppliers to obtain lower-cost, higher-quality materials.

An analysis of these competitive sources can identify ways in which competitive advantage can be achieved through IT. But where exactly might opportunities exist? Figure 14.10 (see p. 574) lists various questions that IS strategic planners can ask about suppliers, customers, and competitors to identify opportunities for the strategic use of IT. An individual manager can study these questions as well and use them to stimulate discussion in a brainstorming session aimed at suggesting possible applications of IT.

Value Chain Analysis Another technique frequently used to suggest strategic IS initiatives is the classic **value chain analysis** method described by Porter and Millar (1985). As depicted in Figure 14.11 (see p. 575), the value chain includes five primary and four support activities within an organization that can each add value for the customer in the process of producing, delivering, and servicing a product or service.

IT can be used in each activity to capture, manipulate, and distribute the data necessary to support that activity and its linkages to other activities. To be of strategic or competitive importance, automating an activity in this chain must, for instance, make the process run more efficiently or lead to differentiation of the product or service.

For example, an organization's goal of market differentiation by a high level of on-time delivery of products requires that operations, outbound logistics, and service activities (such as installation) be highly coordinated, and the whole process might need to be reengineered to be Web-enabled. Thus, automated IS in support of such coordination could have significant strategic value. In automotive manufacturing, for example, Internet-based systems that facilitate sharing of design specifications among design, engineering, and manufacturing (which might be widely separated geographically) can greatly reduce new vehicle development time and cost. Significant advantage also can be gained at the interfaces between the activities, where incompatibility in departmental objectives and technologies can slow the transition process or provide misinformation between major activities.

From a broader perspective, an organization's value chain is actually part of a larger system of value creation, called a supply chain, that flows from suppliers, through the firm, to other firms providing distribution, and ultimately to the end customer. Opportunities for improvement in the supply chain could thus be intercompany, such as using the Internet to automate the automobile ordering process from dealers to manufacturers. As a result, exchanging information over the Internet has been of strategic importance in several industries. It is also important to remember that activities in a value chain are not necessarily sequential because many activities can occur in parallel. In fact, significant competitive advantage can occur by using IT to allow these activities to be done in parallel, thereby developing or delivering products sooner. Thus, competitive advantage can result from improvements in either the internal value chain or the interorganizational supply chain.

A series of idea-generation and action-planning sessions is often used to generate possible strategic applications of IT for the organization. The idea-generation sessions typically include example strategic applications from other organizations (to stimulate ideas by analogy). Small groups then brainstorm on possible strategic opportunities that address the competitive assessment. Questions such as those in Figure 14.10 can be used to stimulate ideas for IT applications. A critical element of this brainstorming process is that criticism and negative comments about new ideas are prohibited.

Subsequent evaluation of these ideas involves the degree of competitive advantage expected, cost to implement, technical and resource feasibility, and risk. Based upon these criteria, ideas are then grouped into ranked categories. Top priority ideas are identified and used in the strategic IS planning process.

The constructs and opportunity identification techniques discussed here are nothing more than tools for creating a strategic IS plan. Like any tools, they can be misused or misinterpreted to the detriment of the information resources planning process and ultimately the organization. Although tools and concepts help, the key to the development of a viable strategic IS plan is clearly the ability of the IS department and business managers to work together.

Suppliers

- Can we use IT to gain leverage over our suppliers?
  — Improve our bargaining power?
  — Reduce their bargaining power?
- Can we use IT to reduce purchasing costs?
  — Reduce our order processing costs?
  — Reduce supplier's billing costs?
- Can we use IT to identify alternative supply sources?
  — Locate substitute products?
  — Identify lower-price suppliers?
- Can we use IT to improve the quality of products and services we receive from suppliers?
  — Reduce order lead time?
  — Monitor quality?
  — Leverage supplier service data for better service to our customers?
- Can we use IT to give us access to vital information about our suppliers that will help us reduce our costs?
  — Select the most appropriate products?
  — Negotiate price breaks?
  — Monitor work progress and readjust our schedules?
  — Assess quality control?
- Can we use IT to give our suppliers information important to them that will in turn yield a cost, quality, or service reliability advantage to us?
  — Conduct electronic exchange of data to reduce their costs?
  — Provide master production schedule changes?

Customers

- Can we use IT to reduce our customers' cost of doing business with us?
  — Reduce paperwork for ordering or paying?
  — Provide status information more rapidly?
  — By reducing our costs and prices?
- Can we provide some unique information to our customers that will make them buy our products/services?
  — Billing or account status data?
  — Options to switch to higher-value substitutes?
  — By being first with an easy-to-duplicate feature that will simply provide value by being first?
- Can we use IT to increase our customers' costs of switching to a new supplier?
  — By providing proprietary hardware or software?
  — By making them dependent upon us for their data?
  — By making our customer service more personalized?
- Can we use external database sources to learn more about our customers and discover possible market niches?
  — By relating buyer behavior from us to buying other products?
  — By analyzing customer interactions and questions to us to develop customized products/services or methods of responding to customer needs?

Figure 14.10 Questions to Identify Opportunities for Strategic Information Technology Applications

- Can we use IT to help our customers increase their revenues?
  - By providing proprietary market data to them?
  - By supporting their access to their markets through our channels?

Competitors

- Can we use IT to raise the entry barriers of new competitors into our markets?
  - By redefining product features around IT components?
  - By providing customer services through IT?
- Can we use IT to differentiate our products/services?
  - By highlighting existing differentiators?
  - By creating new differentiators?
- Can we use IT to make a preemptive move over our competition?
  - By offering something new because we have proprietary data?
- Can we use IT to provide substitutes?
  - By simulating other products?
  - By enhancing our existing products?
- Can we use IT to match an existing competitor's offerings?
  - Are competitor products/services based on unique IT capabilities or technologies and capabilities generally available?

Figure 14.10 *Continued*

SUPPORT ACTIVITIES	**Firm infrastructure**	Planning models				
	Human resource management	Automated personnel scheduling				
	Technology development	Computer-aided design			Electronic market research	
	Procurement	Online procurement of parts				
PRIMARY ACTIVITIES		**Inbound logistics**	**Operations**	**Outbound logistics**	**Marketing and sales**	**Service**
	Examples of IT application	Automated warehouse	Flexible manufacturing	Automated order processing	Telemarketing Laptops for sales representatives	Remote servicing of equipment Computer scheduling and routing of repair trucks

Figure 14.11 Strategic Information Systems Opportunities in the Value Chain

THE OPERATIONAL IS PLAN

After the strategic IS plan has been developed, the initiatives identified in it must be translated into a set of defined IS projects with precise expected results, due dates, priorities, and responsibilities.

The Long-Term Operational IS Plan

Operational planning differs from strategic planning in its focus, its linkage to the business, and in the specificity with which IS projects are defined and addressed (see Figure 14.1). The long-term operational IS plan is generally developed for a 3-to-5-year time period and focuses on project definition, selection, and prioritization. Resource allocation among projects and tools for providing continuity among ongoing projects are also components of the long-term plan.

The first step in preparing the long-term operational IS plan is to define long-term IS operating objectives. Key changes in the business direction should be identified and their possible impact on IS activities should be assessed. The inventory of available information resources is then reviewed to determine which needs can be met over the planning period. Alternatives to new systems are developed in light of the constraints identified by the information resources inventory process conducted earlier.

IS development or acquisition projects must next be defined and selected. The criteria for evaluating projects include availability of resources, degree of risk, and potential of the project to contribute value to the organization's objectives. Clearly, politics often play more than a minor role in the final project selection process.

Many IS planners have taken a cue from financial analysts by adopting a portfolio view of the IS long-term operational plan. They attempt to select new systems to be developed or purchased based on their association with and impact on other projects in the current systems development portfolio. Factors to consider include, but are not limited to, the level of risk of the various projects in the portfolio, the expected time until completion, their interrelation with other projects, their nature (such as being transaction processing oriented), and the amount of resources required. IS planners then seek to balance the projects in the portfolio.

Firms that ignore portfolio balance and concentrate solely on implementing lower risk transaction processing systems, for example, might lose the opportunity to develop higher risk systems offering potential competitive advantage. Conversely, a project portfolio of nothing but risky applications with unknown chances for success and uncertain economic benefits might place the firm itself in financial jeopardy. Table 14.2 shows a portion of the systems development and enhancement project portfolio developed for the Ohio-based outsourcing company referred to earlier in the chapter.

Table 14.2 IS Long-Range Operational Plan Project Portfolio

System/Project	This Year	Next Year	In Two Years	New (N) or Replacement (R)	Make (M) or Buy (B)	Risk Assessment	Project Size	Comments
Executive and retiree personal income tax assistance		X		N	B	Low	Small	Manual assistance currently provided
Fixed assets accounting		X	X	R	B	Medium	Large	Improved asset management and ability to respond to tax law changes
Corporate competitive database	X	X		N	M	High	Medium	Improved analytical capabilities, access
Common tactical sales information system		X	X	N	M/B	High	Large	An ongoing series of installations of capabilities to enhance the effectiveness of the sales organization
Order entry by field organization	X			N	M	Medium	Small	Provide more timely processing of customer orders

Table 14.3 Sample 2004 Operational IS Plan

Title	Priority	Business Requirement
CRM/Fulfillment	High	Further develop our customer relationship management (CRM)/fulfillment application; position the company as a leading provider in this area.
Server Consolidation	High	Combine the existing two servers into one. Further improve and customize our enterprise resource planning system, focusing on supply chain management, assembly, warehouse, and corporate portal.
Field Scheduling System	High	Develop a business-focused scheduling system to work with our existing cost estimating and accounting system.
Call Center Billing System	Medium	Develop and enhance the current online help desk system. Add more functional e-mail management functions.
LAN/WAN Management	Medium	Build better monitoring tools and routing protocols.
Network Infrastructure	Low	Convert telephone system to Internet Protocol.

Each IS project in the portfolio must then be subjected to a more detailed project planning process, as described in earlier chapters. The IS and other information resources enhancement projects are portrayed in the form of a budget for review by management. Once the long-term operational IS plan has been approved, it should be publicized throughout the organization. Publication of the plan will help instill a sense of commitment on the part of the organization that will hopefully have a positive impact on users. As with all business functions, the IS plan should be reviewed and updated as necessary, at least annually.

The Short-Term Operational IS Plan

The short-term operational IS plan is usually created for a 1-year time period. Its focus is on specific tasks to be completed on projects that are currently underway or ready to be started. It is linked to the firm's business priorities by the annual budget. Immediate hardware, software, and staffing needs, scheduled maintenance, and other operational factors are highlighted in detail in the short-term plan. An example of the major projects in a short-term operational plan for 2004 is contained in Table 14.3. Sometimes the long-term and short-term operational plans are combined into a single document.

GUIDELINES FOR EFFECTIVE PLANNING

Planning for the development of an organization's information resources can be a very complex, time-consuming process. Planning efforts attempt to make provisions for the rapid rate of change in IT and capture the often hazy definition of exactly what a strategic system is supposed to do. The first step in developing an organizational planning focus, as opposed to only a project focus, is to change the way in which the IS organization's professionals view their jobs. These changes include adoption of a service orientation by the IS staff in order to view users as partners. Change must also be viewed by IS professionals as a constant process to be exploited, not just an intermittent disturbance to be controlled.

Business managers can take certain actions to increase the likelihood of adoption of the proposed mindset. By taking these actions, they also increase the likelihood of the successful creation and implementation of an IS plan.

1. Early clarification of the purpose of the planning process is essential. The IS planning group must know what they are being called upon to perform prior to their work. IS professionals and business managers will not adopt the shared vision necessary for success of the direction-setting process if they do not understand the purpose of the effort, its scope, and its relevance to their individual efforts.
2. The information resources planning effort should be developed in an iterative, not serial, process. An extended planning process that generates reams of paper that are left untouched will not be as effective as a short process that generates a plan that is reviewed and modified periodically to reflect the new realities facing the organization. Many IS plans have long implementation periods. Needs and situations might change, calling for the revision of the original plan before it is implemented.

Times, of course, have changed. In their day-to-day activities, many IS professionals now act more in a consulting and planning role than in a programming one. They must help the business manager understand how his or her ideas for competitive advantage can get built into a new information system. They must be able to create a project plan for acquiring the new system.

The increased IT sophistication of business managers and the recognition that the firm's IS function should be afforded the same strategic status as such functions as marketing, finance, and manufacturing have also changed the role of the IS professional in the information resources planning process. IS professionals must be able to combine their technical skills with a sharp understanding of planning and how the organization works (and should work) to accomplish its goals.

This chapter provides only a brief summary of the duties of the parties involved in the information resources planning process. The message of the chapter, however, should be clear: Business managers and IS professionals must work together from start to finish in setting the direction for the development of an organization's information resources. Frequent review and feedback must occur.

SUMMARY

To ensure that IT is effectively utilized in today's competitive, rapidly changing world, the organization must engage in a proactive, future-based information resources planning process. To develop a meaningful IS plan, the firm must have a clear understanding of both the technology and the information resources planning process. The process must begin with a thorough assessment of the current situation. The IS mission, goal accomplishment, information use intensity, and business manager attitudes must all be reviewed.

The definition and development of an information vision and architecture is a difficult conceptual task. Yet the value of an explicit vision and architecture statement, over a period of time, usually exceeds the creation and maintenance costs. Organizations often create visions or architectures that explicitly deal with only some of the issues mentioned in this chapter. It is not always possible to deal with all critical issues in a short time. Therefore, it is important to revisit a vision/architecture statement regularly to resolve issues not dealt with earlier and to determine if the information vision still meets the needs of the business. In any case, attention to architecture decisions is critical for the business manager and IS organization leadership.

Planners must have an understanding of the environment in which they make their plans. Such understanding includes knowledge not only of the competitive marketplace in which the company operates but also of the strengths and weaknesses of its own IS department, its relative maturity, and the ways by which the IS plan will be linked to the business plan.

The information resources planning process should be documented and controlled. Documentation ranges from the broad objectives stated in the strategic IS plan to the detailed staffing requirements and expense forecasts made in the short-term operational IS plan. The overall IS plan should provide a well-documented road map from which the firm can navigate. The IS plan should mirror and be clearly linked to the business plan.

A number of tools exist for the development of an IS plan. The methodology most appropriate for the organization should be determined as the result of a conscious thought process. A number of tools can be used to identify strategic opportunities to be assimilated into the IS plan. As firms continue to realize the increased importance of information resources planning, greater emphasis will be placed on comprehensive planning methodologies.

REVIEW QUESTIONS

1. How does the information technology architecture differ from an information vision?
2. List the critical IT issues about which Figure 14.2 makes an explicit statement. Why do you think these particular areas were specified?
3. What important issues does Figure 14.2 *not* address that would normally be part of a complete information resources assessment? Why do you think these issues were not addressed?
4. How would you respond to the criticism that a particular architecture is not feasible based on today's technology?
5. What are the benefits of stating an architecture by means of a picture rather than a text statement? What are the problems?
6. Consider the objectives for the IS department shown in Table 14.1. What other functions or responsibilities normally assigned to the IS organization should have objectives?
7. Describe the basic steps in the development of the IS strategic plan.
8. Contrast the critical success factors (CSFs) and SWOT (strengths, weaknesses, opportunities, and threats) approaches to strategic IS planning.

DISCUSSION QUESTIONS

1. In addition to the reasons listed in the chapter, what other issues or events might cause an organization to recognize the need for an information resources plan?
2. What are the major implications for the business manager if a review of current practices indicates substantial inconsistency in the information vision and architecture for the company? For the IS director?
3. How might the human assets architecture described in Figure 14.7 have an impact on the company's technological assets architecture?
4. What are the user implications of the technological assets architecture shown in Figure 14.6?
5. What are some of the most important problems that would likely be encountered in working toward the architectures in Figure 14.6 and Figure 14.7?
6. Through which media can an information vision and architecture be represented? What are the advantages of each approach?
7. Making assumptions when necessary, construct an IT architecture that is consistent with the Atlanta printing company's information vision explained in the section of this chapter entitled "Creating an Information Vision."
8. Compare and contrast the mission statements contained in Figure 14.3 and Figure 14.4.
9. Given the rapid rate of change in IT capabilities, do you believe that strategic IS planning efforts are worthwhile, let alone realistic? Why or why not?
10. As information technologies continue to advance, is it reasonable to assert that in many instances the strategic IS plan will drive the business strategic plan instead of being driven by it? Why or why not? Can you think of an example where this might be the case?
11. Do you believe that strategic advantages obtained by the effective use of IT are sustainable? Why?
12. In what phases of the IS planning process is the business manager most likely to be involved? What are his or her responsibilities likely to be during each of the stages?
13. What role do you envision the business manager playing in plan justification as the benefits of proposed systems become increasingly difficult to quantify?

CHAPTER 15
MANAGING THE INFORMATION SYSTEMS FUNCTION

TO CREATE AN EFFECTIVE MANAGEMENT SYSTEM FOR INFORMATION resources, information systems (IS) leaders must create a vision, an architecture, and an overall plan for the deployment of an organization's information resources (see Chapter 14). But laying out an IS plan for reaching the information vision/architecture is only part of the task. IS leaders, with input from business managers throughout the organization, must actively manage the technology and human resources that comprise the organization's information resources. In addition, these leaders—both IS and business managers—must resolve a series of issues in order to create an effective management system for the organization's information resources. Success is attained only by actively implementing that plan via projects, policies, and an effective organization in order to build an overall management system.

Many organizations are making dramatic changes in their IS management system. Some organizations are switching from either highly centralized or highly decentralized IS organizations to a more cooperative, client/server-type structure to parallel the trend in information technology (IT) architecture. IS organizations, like other functions, suffered through the downsizing of the 1990s and early 2000s as companies worked to become more globally competitive for customers and shareholders. Also common in the early 2000s is outsourcing a portion of the IS department to an independent organization, sometimes to an offshore company. This organization may be a subsidiary of the corporation but usually is a separate service company in the business of running data centers, telecommunication networks, or systems development groups. Another major theme in IS management today is helping the organization participate in a global marketplace. As covered in this chapter, managing global systems raises unique factors and issues for an organization. Last, but certainly not least, IS organizations are responding to the fundamental influence of Internet technology as a medium for conducting business both up and down the supply and distribution channel and within the organization.

This chapter first identifies the causes of the increasing complexity in managing the IS function. Some of the issues involved in managing the human and technical resources in an IT system are then identified. Finally, the issues related to making the IS organization an effective player in the business are discussed.

THE CHALLENGES FACING IS LEADERSHIP

Almost from its inception, major external developments have required the IS function to undergo significant changes in the basic definition of its mission and the way it carries out its role. Why has the evolution of IS management—from highly centralized, low-level management units to a mixture of centralization and decentralization across all units and levels—taken place? Basically, the changes reflect trends in the technology, applications, and data; an increased understanding of IT by business managers; and changes in business environmental factors. Many of these developments have been addressed throughout this book. A few of the more critical influences are reviewed here.

These developments serve to make it difficult for IS professionals and their customers (the business managers) to determine how best to manage the IS function. Complicating this confusion is the fact that in today's (and tomorrow's) business environment, the way in which the IS function is managed and its contribution to the business are critical success factors for the entire organization. Today, IT is so pervasive that it requires the attention of every organizational unit and business manager. Ensuring payback from IT investment, being able to respond quickly to changing requirements, and leveraging technology for increased business value are now basic to conducting a successful business or other organization.

Rapid Technological Change

Small and inexpensive electronic technologies have made it possible for each knowledge worker, business manager, department, and small business to acquire sophisticated computer and communications equipment. In fact, many managers today have more data on their workstation's hard drive than in their file cabinets. With this distribution of technology comes a need for local responsibility for operations, backup and recovery, security, development, education, and planning. Even with these needs to manage the distributed technology, there is still the need to ensure that desktop and departmental systems do not become isolated.

Exploding Applications and Data

There has been very rapid growth in the number of available software systems for almost every imaginable application. Likewise, the growth of the Internet has made vast amounts of data (certainly not all of it useful) available to organizations. Gone are the days when the IS department developed the vast majority of software in-house. Also gone are the days when people could be sure that the data they are accessing have been checked for accuracy. Software development is now fragmented. Some systems are purchased; some are built in-house. Database management has become a more critical part of the IS department's responsibilities and that of the business manager as well.

Growth in Business Management Understanding of Technology

There is now a greater IT skill level among non-systems professionals, which creates higher and more diverse expectations for new and improved systems and greater confidence that business managers can develop and run systems themselves. More senior management than ever before are comfortable with data-based decisions. They want to see data—and a lot of it—before making decisions. More use and development of systems by business managers stimulates the need for additional systems (a learning phenomenon—the more one knows, the more one wants).

Frequent External Shocks

External developments have caused major changes in the IS organization. For example, the deregulation (and resulting greater competition) of the telecommunications industry forced organizations to manage aspects of data and voice communications previously entrusted to the vendor. International regulations on transborder data flows and vast differences in labor rates have caused organizations to reconsider where new systems are built and operated and where data entry is most economically conducted. The terrorist threats following the events of September 11, 2001, have caused many organizations to mount a serious effort to do a better job of protecting people, facilities, and data. The shortage of highly qualified IS professionals in the late 1990s and the economic downturn in the United States in the early 2000s encouraged organizations to expect greater productivity from existing IS staff and resulted in the distribution of more systems work to non-IS professionals.

MANAGING THE ASSETS IN AN IS ORGANIZATION

In many organizations the IS function has undergone a sequence of frequent and often nonlinear changes over the last several decades in response to rapid changes in technology and business manager expectations. As mentioned in Chapter 14, the job of IS leadership (for both professionals and business managers) starts with setting a vision for how the organization should use information, an architecture for the deployment of information resources to support that vision, and a plan to achieve the architecture. In addition, IS leadership must manage the organization's assets—its human resources, organizational data, the physical infrastructure, and the applications portfolio. The concepts and issues regarding the data asset are covered in Chapter 5. Here the focus is on the other assets critical to an effective IS function. The business manager must be an active participant in this leadership process.

The most important asset in the IS organization is clearly its people. These individuals must be kept up-to-date in the rapidly changing world of IT if they are to be effective for the organization and themselves. How IS professionals should be treated and challenged is critical for both IS leadership and business managers to understand. It is also important for IS leadership and business managers to cooperate in making basic decisions about the other two major assets of an IT system: the physical infrastructure (hardware and networks) and the applications portfolio. In both these areas difficult technological tradeoffs must be considered and key decisions must be made. Most important, these decisions can have a major impact on the business. For example, a policy to buy rather than build applications software (popular in most organizations) usually increases the speed with which a new system can be up and running. However, using a packaged software product can severely restrict the ways in which the business can operate and perhaps even limit the ability of the business to grow. It is because of these potential types of impacts that business managers need to be involved (at least enough to understand the implication for the business) in decisions about how the organization's technological resources will be managed. The key issues and tradeoffs in determining the physical infrastructure and the applications portfolio follow the human resources discussion.

Developing Human Resources

An effective IT management system will allocate significant resources to the continuing professional development of both IS personnel and business managers. A full treatment of human resource management practices for IS personnel can be found in a number of human resources textbooks. The subject is too specialized to be treated here. However, in an environment of rapid change in technology and business demand, significant effort in technology training for both IS professionals and other employees is required. The IS field is diverse and traditionally specialized. Although senior IS executives are more and more becoming general business managers, most IS professionals, whether based in the IS organization or in business units, have specific technical duties and require specialized training. With the life cycles for software products shortening, it is not uncommon for organizations to have technology training underway all the time.

Figure 15.1 lists the generic job titles and a brief description for many possible IS management positions in a typical IS organization. Depending on the IS department structure, these positions might reside in a business unit, in a divisional group, in the corporate IS unit, or in all three. All these roles are essential for the high-quality operation of the systems in the organization. This list does not include the programmers, analysts, computer operators, trainers, and consultants. Each of these professionals has substantial training requirements as well.

The business manager community and IS leaders share in the responsibility of providing IT training for all users. Figure 15.2 shows the IT training requirements for employees in a major metropolitan healthcare organization. In 2003 senior management committed the organization to a policy that all employees should have at least 24 hours of IT training each year. The required courses had to be taken in the first year of employment.

Improving the Physical Infrastructure

In addition to developing the most valuable asset (people), business managers and IS professionals must develop policies and procedures to manage an IT system's physical assets—the computer hardware and the network—on a global basis. These assets have always represented a very large investment in IT. As hardware costs have decreased and personal workstations have proliferated, many business managers have forgotten that the aggregate monetary value of network and hardware assets is now higher than ever—even in a smaller organization.

Failure of the computer network once affected only a few administrative workers. Today, however, employees at all levels in the organization all around the world interact with the computer network for essential aspects of their work. Thus, network or computer failure now has a high degree of visibility—it might disrupt plant managers, division heads, vice presidents, and even sometimes the CEO. Computer power is like electrical power—if it goes out, everything comes to a halt until service is restored. A recent week-long outage of the corporate e-mail system at an Indianapolis outsourcing company caused the firm to lose several days of files with losses in terms of time and missed opportunities estimated at several million dollars.

Furthermore, with the advent of strategic application systems, the impact of infrastructure management is no longer restricted to company employees. Poor infrastructure management might have a direct impact on the company's

Selected IS Management Positions

CIO
Most senior executive responsible for leading in the introduction of information technology across the whole organization

IS Director
Responsible for the day-to-day operations of all aspects of IS for the organization

Systems Development Manager
Coordinates all new systems development projects, allocates systems analysts and project managers to projects, schedules development work

Systems Maintenance Manager
Coordinates all systems maintenance projects, allocates the time of systems analysts and project managers to projects, schedules maintenance work

IS Planning Manager
Analyzes business and develops an architecture for hardware and software to support systems in the future; may also forecast technology trends

Data Center Manager
Supervises the day-to-day operations of the data center and possibly also data entry, the data network, and the computer file library; schedules computer jobs, manages downtime, and plans computer system capacity

Manager of Web-Based Technologies
Evaluates new ways to use the Internet, fosters experimental projects to test Web-based technologies in the organization, consults with users on appropriate application of new technologies, and approves new technologies for use in the organization

Telecommunications Manager
Plans, designs, and coordinates the operation of the corporate data and voice network

Systems Programming Manager
Provides support and maintenance of systems software (operating system, utilities, programming language compilers, etc.); interacts with vendors to install updates and request changes

Database Administrator
Plans databases and coordinates use of data management software

Project Manager
Supervises analysts and programmers working on the development or maintenance of an applications system and coordinates with customers of the system

Quality Assurance Manager
Coordinates activities that set standards and checks compliance with standards to improve the quality and accuracy of systems

Computer Security Manager
Develops procedures and policies and installs and monitors software to ensure the authorized use of computing resources

Figure 15.1 Selected IS Management Positions

IS Training Architecture

Required courses:

Hourly	Professional	Executive
Lotus Notes—Basics Windows—Basics Basic Network Navigation Microsoft Office MS Word—Basics MS Word—Advanced MS Excel—Basics MS Access—Basics	Lotus Notes—Basics Windows—Basics Windows—Advanced Basic Network Navigation Microsoft Office MS Word—Basics MS Word—Advanced MS Excel—Basics MS Excel—Advanced MS Access—Basics	Lotus Notes—Basics Windows—Basics Basic Network Navigation Microsoft Office MS Word—Basics MS Word—Advanced MS Excel—Basics MS Excel—Advanced MS Access—Basics Microsoft Project

Electives:

Windows		UNIX	Internet
MS Access—Basics MS Access—Intermediate MS Access—Advanced MS Excel—Basics MS Excel—Intermediate MS Excel—Advanced ArcView	Lotus Notes—Basics Lotus Notes—Advanced PC Anywhere MS PowerPoint—Basics MS PowerPoint—Advanced MS Project—Basics MS Project—Advanced MS Word—Advanced	UNIX—Basics UNIX—Advanced	HTML XML MS Front Page—Basics MS Front Page—Advanced

Figure 15.2 IS Training Architecture

customers or suppliers. For example, problems with a bank's network directly affect those customers who enter transactions into the bank's automatic teller machine (ATM) system. Problems with an airline's reservations system might affect travel agents worldwide. In today's world, most people depend on the successful management of one or more IT networks every day.

The same basic functions that must be performed to manage any asset successfully should be applied to the IT global physical infrastructure. It must be planned, acquired, made available, and so on. Because of the high degree of specialized skills and training required to perform these functions, however, most business managers outsource the management of the infrastructure either to the organization's IS department or to an outside vendor. For this reason, the focus here is on infrastructure management policy issues where business managers will be most affected. More information on the elements in a physical infrastructure may be found in earlier chapters.

The following are some of the issues that must be resolved in an infrastructure management system, typically through policy statements:

1. **Location** Clearly, most organizations today operate in a distributed computing environment. However, the physical location of the hardware on a network can be a critical issue from cost, control, and security standpoints. Physically distributing equipment, other than personal workstations, can create additional costs for managing the hardware and safeguarding data. Many computers and telecommunications switches benefit significantly from being housed in a secure, environmentally controlled location. Quite often, however, physical location connotes a sense of control to many business managers. A division general manager might be comforted by locating the division's servers in a room on divisional premises rather than in the IS data center in corporate headquarters a few blocks away.

Likewise, some countries might be better hosts than others for location of complex data centers.

2. **The Workstation** Policies on the future design and role of the IT workstation should be determined. Which workstations should have independent intelligence and which should be a network device slaved to some central server? Should telecommunications, such as with Voice over Internet Protocol (VoIP), and computer components of the workstation be physically integrated? Should videoconferencing capability be integrated into the manager workstation? What is the most appropriate location for each type of computing work? At the workstation? At a central server? At a remote hardware resource? On a local area network (LAN)? Or at some departmental server? What level of access should the workstation have to outside resources on the Internet? In answering all these questions, cost, convenience, and security tradeoffs must be made.
3. **Supported Operating Systems** Some vendors of technology hardware still offer a proprietary operating system, although more commonality exists now than in the past. How many and which operating systems will the organization support? Will the organization support newer operating systems such as Linux? Each different operating system creates more difficulty in sustaining a seamless network, and support costs increase rapidly as new operating systems are added. Confining the company to one operating system, however, reduces bargaining power, limits access to the best software, and makes the organization more dependent on the fortunes of a particular vendor. For example, if all workstations are required to operate only with the latest version of Microsoft Windows, the company's future in part depends on how well Microsoft sustains its leadership.
4. **Redundancy** Because organizations are so dependent today on their networks, many business managers want full redundancy of the key nodes and paths in the IT network. Yet full redundancy can be *very* expensive. How much redundancy should there be in the design of the network? Should there be full redundancy only for major nodes and high-volume pathways? The cost for full path redundancy can be very expensive because there must be at least two different paths to every node in the network from every other node. Likewise, "hot" backup sites that allow failed critical nodes to return to operation quickly are also expensive. The lack of redundancy, however, can be very expensive in terms of lost user time if the network or a critical node is not available for some period. Business managers need to express their views on the trade-offs between the cost of downtime due to network unavailability and the cost of providing continuous access.
5. **Supported Communications Protocols** As with operating systems, some hardware vendors support their own proprietary communications protocols as well as some mix of standard communications protocols. For example, most vendors support the American Standard Code for Information Interchange (ASCII) file transfer protocol, the Ethernet protocol for LANs, and the Transmission Control Protocol/Internet Protocol (TCP/IP) for use of the Internet. However, there are many other protocols to be considered. (See Chapter 4 for a discussion of protocols.) Although the selection process is complex, some set of communications protocols should be established as standards in the firm.
6. **Bandwidth** What bandwidth, or transmission capacity, should be provided between hardware nodes in the network? The decision, of course, depends on the applications to be used. Image and graphical applications require much greater transmission rates for effective use than do text-only applications. Content-rich applications are growing rapidly on the Internet. Should every workstation on the network have broadband connectivity (e.g., 1.5 megabits/second)? How much bandwidth can a company afford on a global basis? Should a company provide excess capacity to allow company employees to try new applications? Or should the network be designed to meet only current needs? Specifications about the desired technical infrastructure to meet the vision for information use are critical to help drive individual decisions. Business managers should make their views known on this issue.
7. **Response Time on the Network** In many organizations, hundreds of users are simultaneously interacting with the network, and each of them is directly affected by the system's **response time**—the delay between when the enter key is pressed and when the response from the system appears on the screen. If this delay is reasonable and consistent, the system is satisfactory. If the delay is excessively long—3 or 4 seconds when one is used to subsecond responses—it can be very frustrating and significantly hamper perceived productivity. Yet the costs needed to reduce response delays tend to increase exponentially below some level, so input from business managers is critical in making this decision.
8. **Security Versus Ease of Access** If steps are taken to make the network and its nodes more secure, quite often the result is to reduce ease of access for users of

the network. In some companies, for example, company employees cannot dial in directly to the data center from home because of security concerns. Instead, the employee calls the data center and an operator calls the user back after verification. In other organizations, systems can be much more easily accessed from the desk, from home, or from a hotel room in another part of the world. Yet horror stories about hackers breaching the security of well-known companies' Web sites make easy access a worrisome feature. Organizations should make an explicit decision to operate somewhere along the spectrum between maximum ease of access and maximum security. Business managers should provide input to the decision.

9. **Breadth of Network Access** How ubiquitous should access to the network be? Should everyone in the organization have access to all corporate data? Or should access be restricted to only those who have a "need to know"? Some organizations have gone on record as striving for access by all personnel. As soon as such a commitment is made, however, training and other support requirements increase significantly. Business managers should provide input to this policy decision.
10. **Access to External Data Services** What should be the range of data services that a business manager may receive via the network? Should access to customer and supplier databases be allowed? How active will the company be in electronic commerce and electronic data interchange with customers and suppliers? Should the network provide access to personal data services? At many firms viewing the results of athletic events (or even the events themselves) is permitted from the workstation at the desk. Others restrict even external e-mail. Some organizations provide broad access to a variety of commercial services. Some prohibit such access. Business managers must clearly state their need for such access.

Figure 15.3 shows a policy statement that addresses many of these issues for a multidivisional company in the medical device industry. The statement was the result of an assessment conducted by a major IS consulting firm in 2002 that criticized the organization for not having policies for the use of the IT physical infrastructure.

Managing the Applications Portfolio

The third IT asset discussed in this chapter is the applications software portfolio. Earlier chapters in this book have discussed alternative methods for the acquisition of individual applications. However, business managers and the IS department need to cooperate to manage the bundle of applications as a critical organizational asset.

In contrast to the physical infrastructure, too often the software portfolio is not managed as an asset. Frequently, the business manager's focus is on an individual application or a small number of applications. Applications development and maintenance costs are treated as a current expense. Software, and particularly software maintenance, is treated as an expense to be minimized rather than as an essential activity that preserves or enhances the value of a critical asset.

Most organizations have a substantial investment in their software portfolio. Some have thousands of programs and millions of lines of code that are the result of investing millions of dollars in thousands of staff-years of system development. These applications are critical assets without which the company could not operate, but many companies have never seriously thought about managing these programs as costly and critical assets. Some companies do not even know exactly what software resources they possess. They might not know the condition of their application systems, and some have no plan for replacement or renovation of critical obsolete systems.

Treating software as an asset changes how the portfolio is viewed and managed. A company should know what software it owns, where it is located, what it does, how effective it is, and what condition it is in. Companies should treat maintenance of software just as they treat plant maintenance—as an activity that is necessary to preserve the asset's value. Software managers are obligated to evaluate the effectiveness of the software inventory and to plan, organize, and control this inventory to maximize the return it provides to the company.

The development and maintenance of IS applications should be subject to a set of policy guidelines derived from the organization's IT architecture. Figure 15.4 contains a statement developed in early 2004 that outlines how applications should be developed in a distributed computing environment at a major personnel services company. The statement imposes a standard set of management controls on company-critical, computer-based applications being developed and supported by all company business units. These guidelines, developed by a committee representing the organization's central IS department, business unit IS groups, and users, define controls that must be applied to critical applications.

Other issues that applications portfolio policies should deal with include the following:

1. **Assumed User** For any applications system, some assumption is made about who will use the application. Data entry operators were assumed to be the users of

The Infrastructure of the Information Technology Network

An IT infrastructure through which video, voice, data, image, and text information may be created, accessed, manipulated, and transmitted electronically will allow our company to enhance its position in the industry. The continued enhancement of such an integrated network must be a key priority and requires the establishment of policies.

The policies are as follows:

- A standard workstation shall be used uniformly in offices, laboratories, meeting rooms, and all other facilities.
- Every shareable node on the network will operate with UNIX as one of its operating systems.
- A common set of physical distribution facilities (servers and LANs) shall be used throughout the company.
- Each physical distribution subsystem shall be designed in such a way that it can be replaced or modified without affecting the performance of the other subsystems.
- Each divisional chief executive shall designate the organization responsible for the design, operation, maintenance, and allocation of the appropriate physical distribution facilities.
- Strong consideration shall be given to the installation of adequate pathways and substantial reserve transmission capacity when new physical distribution facilities are installed or existing ones enhanced.
- The public network will be used among locations for voice, data, and video and a private data network will be developed at each site.

Figure 15.3 The Infrastructure of the Information Technology Network

many transaction processing systems. As more individuals inside and outside the company become potential users and the technology skills of people grow, some clarity about likely IS users is required. What is the training level required? Should all help facilities be resident in the system? How deep into the applications system can external users get? The design requirements for the user interface and associated security are thereby likely to change and should be made explicit. Business managers must provide input to this policy issue.

2. **Application Location** With the immense popularity of personal workstations, many applications have been developed for the workstation that would work much better on a more centralized, shareable resource. Where (at what network node) should a particular type of application be performed? For example, where in the network should word processing normally be done? For most organizations that decision seems clear. Most people find it convenient to do word processing on their personal computers. On the other hand, some organizations encourage users to save files on department servers, citing the improved ability to share and back up files. There are also many other issues about where certain applications should be performed in the network. Guidelines need to be developed with business manager input to assign applications to places in the network.
3. **Process-Driven or Data-Driven Design** It must also be determined whether future applications development is going to be data-driven or **process-driven**. Most past systems have been designed to represent a process and to collect and manipulate only the data necessary to operate the particular process. For example, under the process approach, the job classification information system would be designed

Distributed Applications Development Policy

- Information systems development in departments is best done on distributed computers when the object of the analysis (e.g., an asset type or set of transactions): (a) is local and self-contained; (b) has sufficient commitment in the department for funding systems development and operations over the life of the system; (c) is unlikely to be needed outside the department; and (d) has total life cycle development and operational cost less than on a central resource.
- Support for the development of distributed information systems is available on a coordinated basis at each division. Support participants include the local IS organization and corporate IS personnel.
- Distributed information systems development is normally expected to have been identified as a priority in an approved departmental information resources plan.
- Support software standards for information systems should be used. The list of supported software is determined at the local site in cooperation with the corporate IS organization.
- The department should be prepared to commit approximately 25 percent of the initial hardware, software, and personnel investment associated with systems development each year for the ongoing support of the system.
- Documentation standards for all application systems are published on a regular basis by the corporate IS organization. These standards may be supplemented by standards published by the local IS organization.
- The hardware on which the system is developed should be supported by the local IS organization and/or the corporate IS organization and should be attached to either the local network or to the companywide network or both.
- Units engaging in information systems development activity should review their internal policies and procedures to bring them into compliance with these policies.

Figure 15.4 Example Distributed Applications Development Policy

to mirror the job of the personnel analyst, who must review a particular job description and make a decision on rank classification. The system would require collection of the necessary information to help make that decision. The process approach is efficient for that one particular application.

Other decisions, however, such as hiring, require much of the same data. The hiring information system would collect some of the same data, add more data, and store the data in that system. Now there are two different representations of several data fields, each collected for a particular process. The alternative **data-driven** approach is to concentrate on all the data needed in an area or department and to collect these data into a database. Each application would be designed to access this common database and extract only the needed information.

4. **Evaluation Criteria for New Applications Systems** What should the requirements be for justifying new systems? Should a return-on-investment analysis be required? Should a risk assessment be performed on every application? Most organizations attempt to adopt some decision rules, such as expected return on investment, risk analysis, cost-benefit analysis, or expected payback period. These methods might prove to be beneficial when systems with benefits that are not easily quantifiable are considered for implementation. Business managers should actively participate in the process to determine how systems will be evaluated.

INFORMATION TECHNOLOGY MANAGEMENT SYSTEM ISSUES

Faced with the challenges mentioned above and assuming that the critical assets are being well managed, what major issues do IS leaders and their business manager partners need to deal with in designing a successful IT management system? What are the areas that most need attention? Ten areas for attention seem to be common across most organizations when designing a successful management system for IT. Two of these 10 areas, however, are discussed in other chapters and will not be considered here: An effective change management system was discussed in Chapter 12, and the ethical use of IT will be discussed in the next chapter. Each of the remaining eight areas is explained in the sections that follow.

The reader should realize that the IS organization introduces dramatic (and often traumatic) changes for its customers when it introduces new systems or technologies. The overall effectiveness of these changes is often related more to how well the change is managed than to the quality of the new system or technology. To be sure, many other issues are critical in certain organizations. For example, how to best effect the integration of systems across many organizations might well be critical for a multidivisional company.

1. Agreeing Upon the Role of the IS Organization

The IS organization's role is changing, and it will likely change even more. How IT is best managed depends on how the senior management of the organization sees information and IT as a part of the overall business vision. Therefore, the senior business management of an organization should ensure that there is a clear, shared understanding of the IS department's mission.

What mission or role the IS organization takes on, how it performs these duties, and how it organizes to get its job done will vary from organization to organization. Two sample IS department mission statements may be found in Chapter 14. As a general trend, however, senior business managers expect a future-oriented IS organization that can anticipate their information needs while simultaneously meeting today's information requirements. This challenge means that senior business leadership expects the IS unit to align its activities closely with the overall business activities and direction. IS must exercise leadership in providing IT solutions that will help the business in the future while also providing systems that solve today's problems. More specifically, these expectations mean

- demonstrating an understanding of the business through an awareness of business plans and strategies and close communication with business managers
- responding quickly with systems to meet changing business conditions (not waiting years for a strategically important system to be built)
- helping to reengineer business processes to be more responsive to customers, to bring product to market faster, or to improve business process quality
- ensuring that the business can participate, and maybe lead, in the growing development of e-commerce
- keeping the final customer, not just internal operations, in mind
- building systems that provide direct and identifiable benefits to the final customer, thus building stronger customer relationships
- helping business managers make better decisions with information
- using IT for sustainable competitive advantage and increased market share
- helping the business integrate IT into every appropriate part of the business

It is important to note that the traditional dominant expectation of the IS function—saving money through cost efficiencies (such as workforce reduction due to automation)—is not included in this set. Although such short-term tangible benefits are still important (yet often difficult to attribute solely to a new information system), expectations today are more comprehensive and complex than merely reducing cost.

Many CEOs and other senior executives were skeptical until the late 1990s and early 2000s that their businesses were getting enough value or return from the sizeable investment made in IT. However, that set of attitudes is definitely changing. It is now more common for business leaders to attribute gains in productivity and effectiveness to the integration of IT into the business. Indeed, many economics experts claim that the slowness of job growth in the economic recovery during 2002 and 2003 was due to the major progress made in improving productivity via IT. Because employees were much more productive, additional personnel did not need to be hired even though sales

THE DIFFICULTY OF CHANGE

Let it be noted that there is no more delicate matter to take in hand, nor more dangerous to conduct, nor more doubtful in its success, than to set up as a leader in the introduction of changes. For he who innovates will have for his enemies all those who are well off under the existing order, and only lukewarm supporters in those who might be better off under the new.

[Machiavelli, 1513]

improved. These leaders also admit that IT applications significantly change the way their organizations operate and compete. Some even claim that good systems are critical to the organization's success. It is therefore clear that effort must be expended to develop a shared understanding of what the IS organization's role should be.

In general, the role of the IS organization (both central and distributed units) is to be the steward of the organization's information and IT resources, much as the finance organization is the steward of financial resources. More specific roles include the following:

- Deploy IT resources throughout the organization in support of the organization's effort to participate in e-commerce.
- Facilitate the productive and effective use of these resources today, not just in the future.
- Lead the development of an information vision and an architecture for IT that will support the rapid deployment of new and improved systems (through both original software development and packaged products).
- Communicate this vision and architecture to the entire organization and show the implications for the business.
- Maintain managerial control and integrity over important information resources.
- Administer corporate data and the movement of data between systems.
- Make current and new IT available at the lowest possible cost.
- Help business managers become comfortable with information technologies and knowledgeable about their effective use.
- Develop a partnership with business managers to exploit technology for business value and to influence the products and services offered by the organization.

Cooperative efforts between IS leadership and senior business leaders have often proved useful in clarifying how IT is to be exploited in the firm and what the role of the IS function should be. Figure 15.5 contains an example statement of the values and beliefs about IT that was drafted by a joint IS leadership/senior business management task force. The statement was developed at a $350 million manufacturer of industrial painting systems in late 2003. More about ethical issues and value statements may be found in Chapter 16.

The need for stating these shared beliefs came from an assessment of the company's IT management system. That review revealed that the expectations of senior business management and IS leadership differed widely. Indeed, the statement in Figure 15.5 took several months of discussion to develop due to these different perceptions of the participants. Item 1 was derived from business management's belief that the IS organization spent more time generating ideas on the possible use of IT than it did delivering systems that worked. Item 2 was included because IS management felt regional managers and product managers in the company were developing systems in a haphazard, uncoordinated, and undocumented way. The interaction in developing this statement served to "clear the air" on these views. An outside facilitator later used this statement to help the organization focus on the development of the company's first e-commerce strategy and to set data sharing and other policies.

2. Selecting Effective IS Leadership

The second key factor in determining the success of the IT management system and the IS function is, not unsurprisingly, the leader. The leader's level of authority in the organization, his or her business experience and skills, and his or her leadership style are all important. Most important, however, is that the leader and his or her attributes fit the mission and expectations laid out for the IS function.

In most organizations someone can be identified as the executive to whom all centralized IT management activities report. In some enterprises this person might be the IS department manager, director, or vice president; in other organizations, this person might be a finance or administrative executive. Starting in the mid-1980s, some organizations created the role of **chief information officer (CIO)** to lead IT management. More recently, some organizations (especially those involved heavily on the Internet) have established a **chief technology officer (CTO)** to focus on how IT can be used to enhance the conduct of the business.

A true CIO is part of the organization's officer team and is one of those executives responsible for making the strategic decisions for the whole organization. It is clear that some mix of business and technical skills and duties is required for IT leadership—regardless of the title. Figure 15.6 is a fictitious advertisement for a CIO. It makes clear the challenges inherent in many senior IS leadership positions. The role defined for the CIO says much about what an organization can expect from its IS organization.

Above all, the CIO is responsible for guiding and unifying the entire organization's IT resources—Internet applications, office applications, transaction processing, telecommunications, and possibly the reengineering efforts for examining business processes. Although different divisions, lines of business, or subsidiaries might have their own information

Values Statement

1. **We stress implementation of ideas.** We have generated many new ideas and concepts that will help us develop our systems. We must refine these concepts and implement these ideas. Good ideas without implementation are insufficient.
2. **We believe in a planned, coordinated approach.** Individual decisions will be based on a well-developed and communicated information technology plan within each regional and corporate staff area. Each area will explicitly recognize information needs in the annual plan. Because many good ideas have been thought of or are being used by areas of our operations, we stress the importance of communicating these ideas to other individuals and operating units. Planning will take place at the regional level; planning and coordination will take place at the corporate staff level.
3. **Information technology will be made a valuable resource in our jobs.** We will make IT services valuable to everyone in the organization. We recognize the change that is required. We will encourage the responsible use of this important asset throughout the organization. We will help all users of information understand the effective and responsible use of the technology.
4. **We welcome the organizational impacts of information technology advances.** Improving technology will provide the potential to increase service to our clients and reduce our overall cost. These changes will create opportunities to reconsider organizational span of control, reporting lines, and communication paths. We will assess potential improvements on a regular basis and implement those changes that demonstrate enhancements to accomplish our mission.
5. **Data will be shared.** Data are not "owned" by a particular individual or department, but belong to the whole organization. Data will be made easily accessible to all authorized users. Each individual within our company should be able to access appropriate information based on her or his responsibility. Policy guidelines will be established for data to be shared.
6. **We encourage innovation in the use of information.** We are committed to the creative use of information to identify and respond to basic changes in the company's environment. We will challenge the status quo in how we use information to do our jobs. We will encourage our people to apply information technology in new ways so as to benefit our clients and owners.
7. **We expect to use information technology more frequently in our relationships with customers and suppliers.** We see the use of the Internet as an important supplement to our sales force. We hope to employ reverse auction technology to save cost on commodity purchases. We will share important data with our trading partners.

Figure 15.5 Example Values Statement

executives, central IS leadership is charged with coordinating all the resources. Often, the CIO does not have responsibilities for day-to-day IS operations.

Clearly CIOs should be able to act as business executives. They are, however, expected to bridge the gulf between the more technical IS organization and general business managers. Therefore, they need to be willing to learn some aspects of IT. Traditional IS managers spent most of their time interacting with other IS professionals and users, focusing on specific user needs. In contrast, CIOs should spend the greatest percentage of time interacting with peer general managers as part of managing the business as a whole. CIOs need to be able to see the advantages of IT and where to apply it broadly in the business. This role is most suited to those persons who can explain what IT is currently accomplishing and what can be done with IT in business terms.

Although the position is now a reality in many organizations, the role of the CIO is still emerging. In some cases, therefore, the CIO might not yet have the authority needed

Wanted

Bright, versatile, industrious individual to lead the effort in determining the information vision for the company, creating partnerships with internal clients, and ensuring that IT delivers business value. Person must be able to understand how to apply information technology to corporate strategy and transform the company so that its business processes are based on information technology. Must be able to work well under pressure and have strong analytical capabilities. Outstanding interpersonal and communication skills are required because the individual will interact with all information suppliers and customers inside and outside the company. Must add value as a member of the senior management team.

Figure 15.6 Example of a CIO Job Advertisement

to carry out the responsibilities of the position. Not all CIOs report directly to the company CEO or president. Few small and medium-sized companies have a CIO. However, some smaller firms have hired a senior IS consultant as a part-time CIO. Usually, it is organizations on the frontier of information management that have a true CIO—such information-intensive enterprises as banks, insurance companies, and airlines—although more and more manufacturing and retailing firms have created the position and are effectively implementing the concept.

Senior IS Management Issues Various studies in recent years have tracked the major concerns of senior IS executives, including the CIO. Although the exact list and ranking of issues vary from year to year, some general patterns have emerged. The following concerns summarize the kinds of expectations the business has for IS management:

- *Improving data and IT planning, especially linking IS to the business* With rapidly changing businesses and technologies (e.g., selling products and services over the Internet), such planning is not easy, but it is essential to anticipate information needs and manage resources prudently.
- *Gaining business value through IT* Systems that enable the organization to achieve sustained competitive advantage give the IS organization visibility and attention that can help to make many other changes in IT management possible.
- *Facilitating organizational learning about and through IT* This issue is consistent with the evolution of the IS organization away from an exclusively "doing" role and towards an enabling one. In particular, training on how to use information to make better decisions can now be an important function of senior IS leadership.
- *Refining the IS unit's role and position* CIOs are concerned about the IS organization's ability to be proactive and what responsibilities should be distributed to achieve the greatest payoff for the whole enterprise.
- *Guiding systems development by business managers* The development of systems by business managers or other employees directly or by IS staff in line organizations is now a major alternative way to have systems built. Determining the proper standards for programming languages, systems justification procedures, documentation, and database management is a difficult policy challenge for the CIO.
- *Managing organizational data as an asset* Much of Chapter 5 was devoted to this issue, which has been rising in the list of top concerns for the CIO.
- *Measuring IS effectiveness* Frequently the strategic and decision support systems being introduced

WHAT MAKES A GREAT CIO?

Know the business. Learn and master every aspect of it—net income, EPS (earnings per share), EBITDA (earnings before interest, taxes, depreciation, and amortization), its management, its products, its vendors, its sales channels, its customers, its competition. Hire the best people you can and delegate. The CIO belongs in the executive room working with the chairman, the CEO, and other executives in understanding and influencing the business strategy, as well as in identifying opportunities where IT can be a competitive advantage for the enterprise.

[Adapted from Karlgaard, 2003]

today are difficult to justify with hard benefit numbers. Further, it is difficult to show the contribution of information and IT planning and architecture work. Thus, IT resources might be cut in hard times unless real contributions can be demonstrated.

- *Integrating information technologies* Often, the primary role of the CIO is the unification of IS services and technologies. The history of isolated islands of automation, each with strong and protective organizational homes, usually makes integration a difficult political as well as technical problem.
- *Developing systems personnel* Finding and retaining staff knowledgeable in such strategic technologies as enterprise resource planning (ERP) systems, Web design tools, and global telecommunications networks are of special concern. Motivating systems personnel to be productive and aware of business needs is also of high concern to the CIO and other IS managers.

3. Creating an Active Partnership with Business Managers

If the CIO is truly an officer of the business, then he or she will not be the only person at that level concerned with IT issues. In many organizations issues at the officer level are issues for all senior managers regardless of title. Cross-functional management, where problems are addressed in partnership among peers, is now the culture of most businesses. Even when there is no strong consensus or collaborative culture, senior IS leadership should not address all IT concerns alone.

It is essential for the CIO (as well as other senior IS managers) to build strong working relationships with other top managers. This result cannot be achieved unless the senior IS person is a peer in authority and responsibility, the IS department's mission and vision are clearly communicated, and other business managers view IT as an area that cannot be delegated to lower-level personnel.

What must be defined is a true business-IS partnership, a cooperative relationship. Business managers must welcome such partnerships and overtly communicate this receptivity to their peers and subordinates. The CIO and other senior IS managers must be committed to working on non-IT issues. In many organizations one senior business manager, recognizing the power of such an alliance, has championed the partnership concept.

Partnership is a critical strategy for IS management. It is based on sustaining a long-term relationship between IS and business management. Partners share key common goals. Partners seek benefits not possible to each party individually. Partnership is based on mutual trust as well as shared benefits, responsibilities, and risks. Its goal is to achieve a greater contribution for IT to the benefit of the organization. Each partner understands and appreciates the critical stakeholders and business processes that influence the organization's performance. A partner respects the distinctive resources and competencies of other partners.

Although these attributes of a true partnership are the goal, partnerships sometimes start by clearly defining the authority of the partners (as a sort of "prenuptial agreement"). Figure 15.7 contains an example of a statement developed in mid-2003 that defines the authority of both business departments and the IS department. In this mid-sized manufacturer of electric motors, relations between IS and several business departments had deteriorated to the point where such a statement was needed prior to building a better relationship.

The statement in Figure 15.7 created the IS Policy Committee that is now the focal point for the developing partnership. Although working IS/business partnerships can be implemented in several ways, by far the most frequent is the steering committee for IS management. An **IS steering committee**, issue forum, or advisory board can be used to ensure frequent interaction. Much discussion of such groups has centered on how they have been misused or abused. Inadequate authority, narrow perspectives, uninformed or inappropriate membership, and a host of other problems can hamper these committees. When properly set up, however, such groups can be used effectively to

- set priorities for systems development and IS direction
- check progress against an established direction
- allocate scarce resources (especially IS staff) to achieve business objectives
- communicate concerns, issues, and possible remedies
- provide education and the development of shared mind-sets
- develop shared responsibility and ownership of actions

Such groups are not a substitute for a good CIO and good IS management. Instead, they work best when there is proactive and responsive IS management already in place. Partnership means cooperation, dealing with problems jointly, and managing the business, not empires. A good steering committee, along with professional IS leadership, can be an effective part of the management system for IT exploitation in the business.

Expectations/Responsibilities Statement

1. All user departments will be fully accountable for their use of information resources, including the skill level of people using information technology resources.
2. User departments will pay an annual fee to the IS department for workstations to include capital, software, and maintenance costs.
3. The IS department will set and enforce standards for user workstation hardware, software, and network connections.
4. User departments will pay for use of shareable information technology resources through a fair division of overhead.
5. Senior management will be kept engaged in information technology issues via regular communications by IS staff.
6. The IS department will actively initiate communication with all user departments.
7. The IS department will build its plan and budget with full knowledge of company business plans.
8. Members of the IS department will serve as internal business process improvement consultants and consultants on the use of the Internet in making the supply chain more efficient.
9. The IS department will be represented on issue-oriented or business planning teams where information definition and/or collection is crucial.
10. Policy affecting users will be determined by the IS Policy Committee, which will be chaired by a senior business executive.

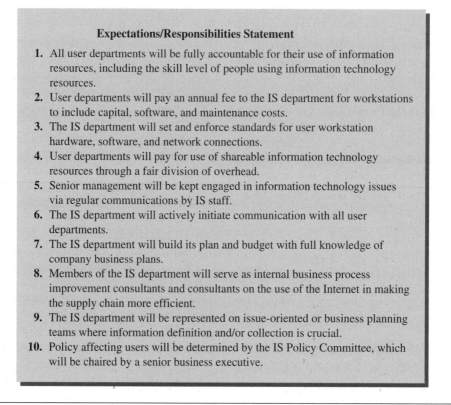

Figure 15.7 Example Expectations/Responsibilities Statement

4. Determining an Outsourcing Strategy

Many organizations have hired outside professional IS services organizations to run part of their IS operations. This approach to IT management is commonly called **outsourcing**. For many companies internal computer operations have never held a monopoly position. Public data banks, market research data processing firms, and other computing services with special software or data have been around for decades. With the cost-cutting emphasis in business since the mid-1980s, however, there has been renewed interest in outsourcing data center operations (sometimes called IS facilities management) to external service organizations. Besides the data center, an organization might outsource the management of telecommunications or traditional transaction processing systems programming. More recently, **application service providers (ASPs)** have developed that provide total systems to organizations ranging from single purpose applications like competitive intelligence to broad applications like ERPs.

Much of the outsourcing movement has been driven by the need to downsize and to respond to other significant organizational changes taking place (mergers, acquisitions, and divestitures). With these changes often come sudden shifts in demands for computing power. Sometimes the value of IS outsourcing to a company that is aggressively acquiring other firms is the speed and efficiency with which the outsourcing firm can integrate the systems of acquired firms into those of the acquirer. Alternatively, some companies report 10 to 20 percent cost savings from the economies of scale and competitive pricing provided by data center suppliers.

Outsourcing allows a company with greatly fluctuating computer processing demands to pay only for what it uses, rather than building a data center for peak load and letting it sit underutilized during other periods. For example, a using organization often pays an ASP on the basis of the number of "seats" (users) or on the number of transactions per month. Companies can invest the savings in fixed costs toward identifying and developing other high-impact IT applications. The trend toward outsourcing might also be related to the establishment of a CIO, who often is not tied emotionally to the existing data center and does not feel that the IS function has to manage the hardware to prove its value to the firm. A CIO might view data centers much as a manufacturing plant, which is a candidate for outsourcing when such an operation is not in the strategic core of the business.

Some firms have chosen to outsource IS operations because it is difficult to keep pace with technological change. Keeping up with the latest techniques requires hiring and retaining highly skilled IS staff, which might be difficult, especially in nonurban areas. Others believe that a large outsourcing supplier, with experience in many organizations, can reduce the cost of providing IS services and provide better customer service. Still other senior executives were not satisfied with the service being delivered by in-house staff and chose to outsource the job to a specialist. However, in late 2003 many firms reported that outsourcing, if not done properly, could in fact cost the company more in hard costs and various soft costs, such as delays, than if those functions were handled internally (see the sidebar entitled "Outsourcing: Look Who's Out of Sorts").

The decision to outsource must be viewed as both a remedy for service failures or cost issues and as a strategic choice. Likewise, outsourcing must be done selectively. In one of the early efforts at outsourcing, Eastman Kodak Company outsourced its data centers to IBM, its telecommunications to Digital Equipment Corporation, and its microcomputer systems management to Businessland, Inc. Kodak did not see these areas as core to its vision for IT or as a significant strength for competitive advantage. The savings from outsourcing were used in other parts of the business where Kodak felt a greater return on investment could be achieved. Other organizations, however, have outsourced critical strategic IS functions in response to short-term emergencies and subsequently have lost the competitive advantage its prior investment in IS staff had brought.

As discussed in earlier chapters, outsourcing systems development and integration is also possible and popular. Contracted systems development and programming, as well as purchasing of system and applications software, both common today, are forms of outsourcing. Because the bulk of IS costs are in personnel, and because many IS personnel work in systems development, major cost-reduction benefits might come from outsourcing if the outsourcing partner is able to bring improved productivity tools to the process.

When certain information systems have strategic value to the firm, healthy organizations should not see outsourcing, especially of sensitive development and planning activities, as a viable option. Security and privacy issues and the strategic value of some data might mean that certain applications should not be developed or operated outside the organization. For example, some systems development in support of research and product development might be considered too sensitive to outsource. Further, it might be quite difficult to bring systems development or operations back in-house if prices for outsourcing services increase or if there is a change in the need for strategic control of these system functions or for technical know-how. Hiring staff and familiarizing them with company operations, building data centers, and setting methods and procedures cannot be done quickly. Organizations with highly variable needs for computing power, however, are increasingly considering the outsourcing option.

The ideal outsourcing arrangement is a win-win partnership between the company and the outsourcer. The outsourcer should know and care about the business as much as client executives do. Sometimes an outsourcer will specialize in particular industries (for example, retail or health care) to gain a depth of knowledge. In such instances care should be taken to ensure that the outsourcer is not put in a situation where its personnel could leak competitive information. An outsourcer can also help the firm make sound technology decisions, not just solutions convenient for the outsourcer. The outsourcing contract should accommodate growth and expansion in the business. Finally, the firm should select an outsourcer who can operate over the full geographic area of the company's operations.

Several key factors in selecting an outsourcing vendor are

- vendor reputation, which includes understanding the business and technology standards
- quality of service, which means a clear comparative advantage over in-house services
- flexible pricing, which means cost effectiveness because, as processing volume increases or new services are added, costs can escalate

OUTSOURCING: LOOK WHO'S OUT OF SORTS

When the outsourcing firm blew a December 1 deadline to turn on a new Medicaid claims processing system, state officials decided to fight back. The budget had tightened, Medicaid costs were skyrocketing, and the creaky mainframes that the outsourcer was supposed to replace were partly to blame. The outsourcer was 2 months behind schedule. The state is levying a $32,000 fine.

[Adapted from Park, 2003]

5. Designing an Equitable Financing System

IT services are expensive, IT systems are complex, and IS personnel are among the best-paid employees in the company. At the same time, the value of IS services is not always clear. Systems often take years to build and are sometimes over budget. The direct business impacts (e.g., reduced personnel costs) of new systems might not be as evident as they were in the past. More and more systems are being built in order to compete better, and the impact on sales increases is not always easy to predict.

An effective IT management system must carefully measure IT costs, enable the understanding of the financial impacts of new and existing systems, and find a way to fund IS operations and new systems. Measuring the organization's investment in IT and calculating the impact of this investment on the organization's performance are still not well-understood activities. Most benefits are indirect or confounded by other organizational changes.

Managing IT Costs The typical measures used for tracking IT costs include

- total IT budget as a percentage of total organization revenues, income, premiums, deposits, or other indicators of overall financial activity of the organization
- total IT budget as a percentage of total organization budget
- IS personnel costs as a percentage of total organization professional personnel salaries and wages
- the ratio of hardware and software costs to IS personnel costs
- the costs for IT hardware and software per managerial or knowledge worker

None of these measures is perfect or complete by itself, and organizations should track several of them. Sizable changes in these measures might be more significant than the absolute values. Further, high or low values are not by themselves necessarily bad or good. All these measures require interpretation to match them with IS and business directions. Organizations that try to be pioneers and leaders should expect, for example, to have higher values on many of these measures than less aggressive firms.

Even in combination, these measures must be used cautiously because of various definitional and measurement problems:

- Some IT costs are hidden because of the highly distributed nature of information processing in most organizations. Not all costs appear as IS department budget items, and certainly not all are spent in the IS organization. Personal computer hardware, software, training, and services can be purchased as general office expenses or other expense categories.
- No relationship to benefits is directly included in these measures. Costs without benefits give a very incomplete picture.
- Benefits happen after many of the development costs occur, and the lag is not considered in these measures. Direct benefits can occur quickly, but secondary benefits of technology diffusion and new ways of doing business might not emerge for years.

Measuring Benefits There is no simple, reliable way to measure the value added benefits of IT. IT costs are easier to find; IT value is typically much more intangible (as is the value of a business education). Organizations must capture and track measures of IS performance over time to best utilize such indicators, so that values can be interpreted, changes explained, and reasonably helpful comparisons made. Some organizations now treat investment in IT like research. No matter how IT investments are valued, it is the job of the business manager, not the IS manager, to justify the investment.

Controlling IS Costs A primary mechanism for financial control of IT is the IS organization's budget. One way to divide costs creates four primary groups—personnel, equipment and software, outside services, and overhead. But not all organizations use these areas. Furthermore, statistics from studies on IS budgets vary widely across industries. Because of these reporting and measurement issues, some individual statistics can be misleading, but some general observations appear to be valid:

- The most common measure, IT expenditures as a percent of revenue, varies widely by industry and size of firm. Information-intensive industries spend the highest percentage on IT. Smaller firms suffer from a lack of economies of scale and can spend a higher percentage (all else being equal) than larger companies.
- Personnel costs are the largest piece of the IT budget, typically more than 50 percent (depending on the industry) of the total. Although increased productivity aids have helped to keep this percentage from growing much larger, the demand for new systems makes reduction of IS development staff budgets difficult to achieve unless outsourcing is employed.

Obviously, the size of the IS budget depends on the demand for new systems. As the applications portfolio increases, greater budget pressures occur due to enhancement and maintenance requirements. Without sizable productivity gains, it is easy to incur double-digit annual IS department budget increases.

Chargeback Systems Some senior business managers believe that the best way to hold IS and line organizations accountable for the impact of systems on the organization is to have the IS unit operate as a business within a business. In this instance the IS unit operates like a profit center, with a flexible budget and an agreed-upon transfer pricing scheme. This design places control of IS spending directly in the hands of those business managers who use the services. Instead of a vague annual negotiation process of capital expenditure approvals and cost allocations, the IS head or CIO and senior business managers must agree on prices for IT services that allow the IS department to make a profit or at least break even.

For business managers, the business unit or organization is affected directly by an IS **chargeback** process. If done well, a chargeback system can be a way to better understand true costs. Certainly there are many positive aspects to charging for IS services, but as with any profit-center and transfer-pricing scheme, short-term and long-term costs and benefits become difficult to balance. Business managers adapt behavior to take advantage of the pricing structure. For example, discounts for overnight processing might cause a business manager to rely less on online reporting. Thus, it is important for every business manager to understand why chargeback schemes are put in place and what characterizes a good process.

Organizations usually adopt a chargeback process for IS services for one or more of the following reasons:

- To assign costs clearly to those who consume and benefit from IT
- To control wasteful use of IT resources by encouraging users to compare the benefits with the costs and eliminate unprofitable use
- To overcome the belief that IT costs might be unnecessarily high
- To provide incentives by subsidizing the price of certain services or innovative uses of technologies
- To change the IS department's budgeting process to be more business driven, thus rewarding the IS organization for improved service and greater efficiency rather than technological change for its own sake
- To encourage line managers to be knowledgeable consumers of IS because they must directly pay for such support

A major problem in any chargeback system is that many IT costs are joint costs not easily attributed to one single organization, such as the cost to store and maintain a shared database or to place the order fulfillment process on the Internet. Further, some costs are essentially fixed, such as systems software and many components of a data center complex. Thus, calculating costs and reducing expenditures as demand varies might not be as easy as one would wish. Also, in applications in which the benefits of IT might be difficult to determine, as in education, research, and customer service, chargeback can limit creative uses of technology.

Transfer prices can be developed for a broad and comprehensive range of IS activities, including charges for

- personnel time
- computer usage or wall-clock time (or computer cycles used)
- disk file space
- number of transactions processed
- amount of computer main memory used (per unit of time)
- number of screens or Web pages accessed

Charges might be cost-based (to recover all costs) or market-based (to be comparable to market alternatives). A combination of clearly identifiable direct costs plus an allocation of other overhead costs (space, administrative staff, and so on) might be used.

Chargeback systems for IT activities can be a great source of irritation between the IS organization and business managers unless a mutually agreed-upon structure for charging can be developed. A successful chargeback system should incorporate the following characteristics:

- *Understandable* An understandable chargeback system reports use in business terms that business managers can relate to their own activities, not just to computer operations. For example, charges per customer order, invoice, or report relate more to business activity than does the number of computer input/output operations performed or machine cycles used.
- *Timely* Charges should be reported soon after the activity to which they are related so that use and cost can be closely linked and those who can control the costs can accurately monitor the total costs.
- *Controllable* The activity for which business managers are charged must be something they can control (e.g., charges for rerun computer jobs because of operator errors would not be controllable). Further, business managers must have a choice to use alternative services or to substitute one kind of usage with another (e.g., switching between two alternative database management systems or trading computer time for data storage).
- *Accountable* Managers responsible for generating IS activity must be identifiable and must be held accountable for their charges. Otherwise the charges are meaningless and useless.

- *Clearly linked to benefits* Managers must see a link between costs and benefits so they can balance the value of the IS services against what is being spent.
- *Consistent with IS and organizational goals* Charges should be designed to achieve the goals set for the business and the goals of the IS organization. Thus, charges should encourage use of important IT services, efficient use of scarce technology and services, the desired balance of internal and external sourcing of IS services, and the development of systems that comply with accepted architectural standards.

Chargeback systems must be periodically evaluated to check that the desired results are being achieved. In any case, the chargeback or funding mechanism for the IS organization is one of the keys to having an effective IT management system.

6. Deploying Global Information Systems

In the past, managing in a global environment was the sole domain of large multinational corporations whose operations spanned the globe. Today, virtually all organizations, regardless of size, must deal with the effects of competing in a global economy. Improved telecommunications infrastructures in many countries, coupled with a steadily falling cost of technology ownership, have lowered the barriers to entry for competitors worldwide. As a result, IT managers have expanded their focus to include threats and opportunities extending well beyond their own domestic borders.

Global IT managers face a number of daunting tasks. For example, systems and standards must be coordinated across geographical, legal, and temporal borders; multinational teams have members who are dispersed across countries in multiple time zones and have radically differing languages and cultures; and potentially devastating security threats can originate from a single computer located anywhere in the world. Successful navigation of the international waters of technology management can, however, result in substantial returns for an organization.

Region and Country Issues The heterogeneous nature of the multiple environments in which global IT managers operate makes managing such systems highly complex. Variations in language and culture affect leadership and communication styles. Time zone differences and physical distance make coordination a complex task. Among the unique factors influencing the global management of IT are the following:

1. **Country telecommunications infrastructures.** To fully realize the benefits of integrated global information systems, countries must be able to provide transnational companies with the necessary telecommunications infrastructure and its associated worldwide connectivity. Landlines in many developing countries, such as those in sub-Saharan Africa, are limited and are often supplanted by easy-to-setup wireless infrastructures. Unfortunately, cellular networks do not yet provide the bandwidth necessary for enterprise-wide applications and satellite connections are expensive.

   Many governments have become increasingly aware of the need for more state-of-the-art telecommunications capabilities to attract foreign direct investments. For example, Nigeria's improved telecommunications infrastructure has contributed to an increase in foreign investments in that country (Odo, 2003). Many global companies, including IBM, base their Asian headquarters in the tiny island nation of Singapore to take advantage of the fact it is one of the most wired countries in the world (Collett, 2003). Indeed, many emerging economies in Asia have created special zones for foreign subsidiaries where the telecommunications is world-class, even if the infrastructure in the rest of the country is limited. Malaysia, for example, has developed a 270-square-mile area designated as the Multimedia Super Corridor (MSC) to act as a global technological hub for the region. The MSC is supported by a high-capacity global telecommunications infrastructure with a 2.5 to 10 gigabit digital fiber-optic backbone that will link the region to the rest of the world through a 5-gigabit international gateway (MSC Web site, 2003). Global IT managers must be aware of what different countries will be able to provide before making decisions on global systems rollouts and multinational development efforts.
2. **Legal and security considerations.** In addition to being technically knowledgeable and culturally sensitive, the global IT manager must also keep constantly abreast of current legal and ethical issues in the countries of operation. Governmental regulations on technology transfers, intellectual property and copyrights, privacy laws, and transborder data flows are but a few of the areas that must be monitored. For example, the European Union's Data Protection Directive requires that companies exporting data about EU citizens across borders meet Europe's very stringent privacy standards. Failure to comply can lead to hefty fines imposed on the offending company. Such privacy requirements place a heavy burden on all non-EU companies to meet Europe's "no privacy, no trade" policy.

   In addition, global electronic commerce has led to considerable legal argument over issues of jurisdiction regarding intellectual property and Web content. For example, which country's laws should apply when objectionable Web content may be viewed in any country in the world? In November 2000 a French judge ruled that Yahoo! must ban the sale of Nazi memorabilia on its auction Web site as it was in violation of French law to do so (Essick, 2000). In 2002 an Australian judge ruled that a Melbourne-based businessperson had the right to sue Dow Jones, the financial publisher, for an allegedly defamatory article published on a U.S.-based Internet site (Legard, 2002).

Network security has also become a global concern for IT managers. With the promise of global connectivity comes the danger of network attacks from locations around the world. According to a 2003 survey by mi2g Ltd. (CIO.com Web site, 2003), Brazil leads the world as the originating point of hacker attacks on systems around the world (95,000 attacks). Brazil was followed by Turkey (14,795 attacks), with the United States a distant third (2,995 attacks). The attendees at the 2003 United Nations Conference on Global Information Security pointed out that it was critical to have greater information sharing on technology threats, illustrating the global nature of interconnecting systems today and the involvement of governments in determining information assurance policies.

3. **Language and culture.** Among the most common problems facing global IT managers dealing with a culturally diverse group of international workers is the issue of differences in language. Fluency in English is often mistaken for an understanding of western idioms. A baseball expression ("hit a home run") might make as little sense in a country whose national sport is cricket as would "bowling a googly" in the United States. Further, body language and gestures have different connotations in different countries.

   Cultural differences also play an important role in determining the effectiveness of global technology management. Global managers must understand the differences in the way individuals from various cultures interact with one another and their superiors. House, et al. (2002), identified nine dimensions of culture:

   - *Uncertainty avoidance* Extent to which members of a society avoid uncertainty (through social norms or bureaucratic processes) to improve predictability of future events
   - *Power distance* Degree to which members of a society expect and accept that power is distributed unequally within a firm
   - *Collectivism-I* Extent to which organizations and society reward collective distribution of resources and collective action
   - *Collectivism-II* Degree to which individuals see themselves as part of a group, whether it is an organization or family
   - *Gender egalitarianism* Extent to which a society or organization minimizes gender role differences and gender discrimination
   - *Assertiveness* Degree to which individuals are assertive, confrontational, and aggressive in societal relationships
   - *Future orientation* Extent to which society engages in future-oriented activities such as planning, investing in the future, and delaying gratification
   - *Performance orientation* Extent to which group members are encouraged and rewarded for performance improvement and excellence
   - *Humane orientation* Extent to which a collective encourages and rewards individuals for being fair, generous, altruistic, caring and kind to others

   Global IT managers need to adapt their management style to the cultural and social context in which they are operating. For example, when dealing with individuals from a society characterized by high power distance, the manager should be aware that those employees might be less comfortable with contradicting their superiors than are their western counterparts. This might require, for example, different communication mechanisms for project team members to avoid potential problems.

4. **Time zone differences.** Managing across time zones is often frustrating. With employees around the world separated by as much as 10 to 15 hours, finding times for synchronous meetings and discussions can be very difficult. For example, setting a 10:00 A.M. meeting in a Seattle corporate headquarters translates to 10:30 P.M. in the New Delhi office and 4:00 A.M. in Sydney, Australia.To deal with the problem fairly and avoid resentment in foreign offices, meeting times are sometimes rotated through time zones, alternating between the local workday times of the foreign and domestic offices.

   It should be noted that there are also advantages to operating across multiple time zones. By handing off work from one location to another, projects can "follow the sun." For example, when an employee leaves for the day at the U.S. office, he or she can hand off the project work to an employee in the Bangalore, India, office who is just coming in for the day. Under this model, project work continues around the world, around the clock.

Global Systems Integration and Standardization Systems integration has long been acknowledged as a critical process for most organizations. Controlling and integrating a multitude of diverse systems is exceptionally difficult in global companies. To avoid the pitfalls of nonintegration, global technology managers often rely on creating worldwide standards for systems development. For example, Unilever, the multibillion dollar consumer products company, decided to standardize its global IT servers across 80 countries to run on Linux, thus allowing the company to deploy common systems worldwide without having to worry about incompatible platforms (Weiss, 2003). In what is considered to be the company's biggest technology change ever, MasterCard International has created a globally integrated payment platform by moving its 25,000 card issuers worldwide to a standardized virtual private network (VPN)-based system (Mearian, 2002). Nestlé's commitment to an "e-revolution" has resulted in consolidation of over 140 financial systems across 70 countries to a mere handful (Wheatley, 2001).

Global Outsourcing Since the intensive Y2K reprogramming efforts of the mid and late1990s, companies have looked increasingly beyond their own national borders for partners to help design, develop, and maintain their information systems. Although India remains the leader in offshore outsourcing, many other countries vie for a share of this market. The Philippines, Vietnam, Malaysia, Brazil, Russia, Bulgaria, and South Africa are some locations that offer highly trained IS personnel at costs that seem to be a fraction of what is required in the United States. In a 2003 survey of 252 corporate IT managers in the United States, 44 percent identified cost savings as the primary reason most global companies outsource (King, 2003a). Other drivers of offshore outsourcing include the desire to gain access to skilled personnel around the world, reduce fixed IT costs, exploit follow-the-sun development to improve time to market, and compensate for gaps in the organization's internal capabilities.

Of course, there are drawbacks to global outsourcing. For example, cost savings are often overestimated or elusive, there is a perceived loss of strategic control over IT operations, there are increased security concerns, and there is a loss of jobs in the domestic market. In late 2003 several U. S. companies were criticized in the press for moving jobs overseas at a time when many Americans were unemployed.

Nevertheless, IT managers must be aware of the emerging trends in global outsourcing. A 2003 Gartner, Inc., research report suggests that by 2004, 80 percent of all CIOs will be using offshore resources for at least part of their technology operations. Some of the key trends in global outsourcing include:

- *Offshore development centers* With increasing commitments to offshore projects, some companies have established a permanent offshore presence. In this model of offshore insourcing, foreign technology workers are employees of U.S.-based companies and receive the same training, software tools, and development process guidelines as their domestic counterparts. The main difference between these workers is salary. Global Exchange Services, Inc., estimates that for every \$100 spent on its IT workers in the United States, it spends only \$30 on employees in Bangalore, India (King, 2003b). Other benefits of moving from offshore outsourcing to offshore insourcing include the ability to retain knowledge and expertise across multiple projects, greater productivity, and a sense of belonging for foreign workers who are thousands of miles away from the outsourcing company.
- *Near-shore sourcing* For certain critical projects where the costs of failure are high, IT managers often feel more comfortable sending work to low-cost countries that are geographically closer to home and in an overlapping time zone. Further, since September 11, 2001, security risks in certain countries are forcing managers to look to locations closer to home. For the United States, Canada has emerged as a popular near-shore outsourcing destination.
- *Multisourcing* It used to be commonplace for an outsourcing firm to establish a relationship with a single offshore provider for all its systems development and IT infrastructure needs. Now companies

NEW FRONTIERS: BUSINESS TRANSFORMATION OUTSOURCING

No longer merely a cheaper way to develop and test code, offshore outsourcing is now taking on more strategic areas. Business transformation outsourcing (BTO) looks to global outsourcing vendors to provide innovative technology solutions to existing business process problems.

In expanding the nature of outsourcing relationships, BTO attempts to integrate traditional IT outsourcing (ITO) and business process outsourcing (BPO) to provide a more robust outsourcing model. The ultimate goal is to achieve a technology-based transformation of business in which outsourcing vendors go beyond simply doing what they are told and become strategic partners in nurturing business innovation.

[Adapted from Bendor-Samuel, 2003 and Marguilius, 2003]

often rely on multiple service providers in a number of countries, based on price and the skills that are needed for the portfolio of IT projects. Electronic Data Systems Corporation (EDS), for example, has a "best-shore" policy in which it sends offshore work to the most appropriate offshore development centers for a given project.

Managing Global Virtual Teams Traditionally, most team-based projects have involved individual team members in the same geographical location. Today, however, the focus is often on bringing together the best possible talent for a project, regardless of their location. This change has given rise to global virtual teams in which individual members who actively collaborate on a project are dispersed across thousands of miles and multiple time zones. It is very likely that the success of global systems will hinge on the effective management of such teams. Carmel (1999) identified six "centripetal" forces that, if addressed properly, can lead to more effective virtual teams. Though Carmel's research focuses on software development teams, the issues can easily be applied to the management of any globally dispersed project team. The six forces are as follows:

- *Telecommunications infrastructure* Clearly, when team members are not co-located, reliable electronic communications are critical. Today, team members must have access to high-bandwidth network connections as well as necessary secure communication software.
- *Collaborative technology* To get the most out of globally dispersed teams, it is often useful to have a common IT platform for collaboration that allows for easy coordination of team activities and leveraging worldwide intellectual capital. Examples of such packages include Microsoft's Sharepoint Portal and IBM's Websphere Collaboration Portal.
- *Development methodologies* Given the differences in operating environments of team members, it is important to agree to a mutually acceptable project methodology or process that all participants will follow. The project manager must be sure that all project members are educated on the specific methodology.
- *Architecture and task allocation* The team manager must be able to divide the project into smaller, relatively independent pieces. By reducing the coupling between these project pieces, a number of coordination overhead costs are reduced. Carmel and Agarwal (2001) argue that reducing coordination complexity is an important tactical approach to dealing with the issues of geographical distance in such teams.
- *Team building* The need for a cohesive, focused team is important for all projects, whether co-located or dispersed. Extreme distances, both geographical and cultural, can often make the need for careful team building critical to project success. Some ways to foster such cohesion are constant communication, face-to-face milestone meetings, understanding cultural nuances and differences in communication styles, using expatriate managers (executives who leave their home country to work abroad), encouraging lateral communication between team members, and providing all team members a 360-degree view of the project via project tools.
- *Managerial techniques* A global team manager must posses certain unique traits and abilities. Carmel refers to these as the *MERIT* qualities, that is, those of (1) a *Multiculturalist*, who is able to switch easily between cultural styles of management and communication; (2) an *E-facilitator*, who can build team loyalty and cohesiveness through e-mail and other electronic communications, even when team members cannot meet; (3) a *Recognition promoter*, who understands that virtual teams must rely on the manager to keep them in the headquarters' spotlight and tout the accomplishment of the team members; (4) an *Internationalist*, who enjoys the challenges of dealing with multiple cultures and country environments; and, finally, (5) a *Traveler*, who understands that electronic communication will never completely replace the benefits of face-to-face meetings and social contact.

In summary, the job of the global IT manager is a challenging one. It requires an in-depth knowledge not only of technological and business issues, but also of world history, culture, geography, religion, politics, and international law. With ever-improving global communication networks and connectivity, global technology management is destined to become a pervasive issue in IT governance.

7. Designing an Appropriate IS Organization and Governance System

Just as the IS leader must be selected to fulfill the expectations for IT in the total organization, the IS organization itself must be designed to fit the information needs of the business. A wide variety of IS organization structures are found in small to large organizations and in all kinds of industries, and this variety has been broadened by today's distributed technologies. Although the alternatives are numerous, this section focuses on the more common IS organizational designs as well as some alternatives that establish the IS organization as a separate business.

The Classic IS Organization The earliest attempts to design organizations for the IS department followed a functional design. As can be seen in Figure 15.8, the classic IS organization had two primary functional areas: systems development and maintenance, and operations. Systems development activities included systems analysis and programming, as well as the installation of custom and purchased applications. Operations activities included computer processing and computer storage management (often run as part of a data center), network operations and maintenance, equipment maintenance, and systems programming.

At the outset these two primary IS activities were typically managed within the same unit. In midsized and small organizations, in particular, there was typically a single, centralized (or corporate) IS organization unit. However, in large organizations, each business division might have had its own IS organization—with separate systems development and operations staff—with little or no coordination across divisions. This design in large organizations resulted in what came to be called a decentralized IS organizational approach.

Decentralized IS designs are often found in organizations with highly autonomous business units that see no major benefits from sharing IS applications and resources with other business units. Stated differently, the business units want total control of their IS resources. In contrast, highly centralized IS designs are most often instituted in businesses that are most concerned about cost efficiencies, because all business units share the costs of purchasing and running computers, networks, and applications.

Newer Designs for the IS Organization In all but the smallest organizations, however, two hybrid IS governance designs are often found instead. These are a federal design and a customized design (see Figure 15.9). Organizations that choose a **federal design** are attempting to achieve the benefits of *both* the centralized and decentralized designs. These companies are seeking cost efficiencies from centralizing their operations activities under a single corporate IS unit while decentralizing their applications activities to their business divisions—in order to give each business unit autonomous control over its local application needs.

A **customized design** is a mixed design found in many large enterprises. In this design some business divisions have a centralized IS unit handle all their IT needs. Other divisions within the same parent organization have a federal or decentralized design in order to locally address their own IT needs with their own local IS staff.

It is important to note that decisions on how to distribute IS decision-making authority and oversight are separate from decisions on how to distribute computer processing power, storage equipment, and network hubs. The discussion here focuses on centralized versus decentralized decision-making authority for a set of IS activities, not on the economies of locating data processing operations close to a supplier or a specific business user.

Separate IS Business Many firms have adopted a design for the IS organization in which the IS unit is responsible for its own financial and market survival. In this approach the business units treat the IS unit much like

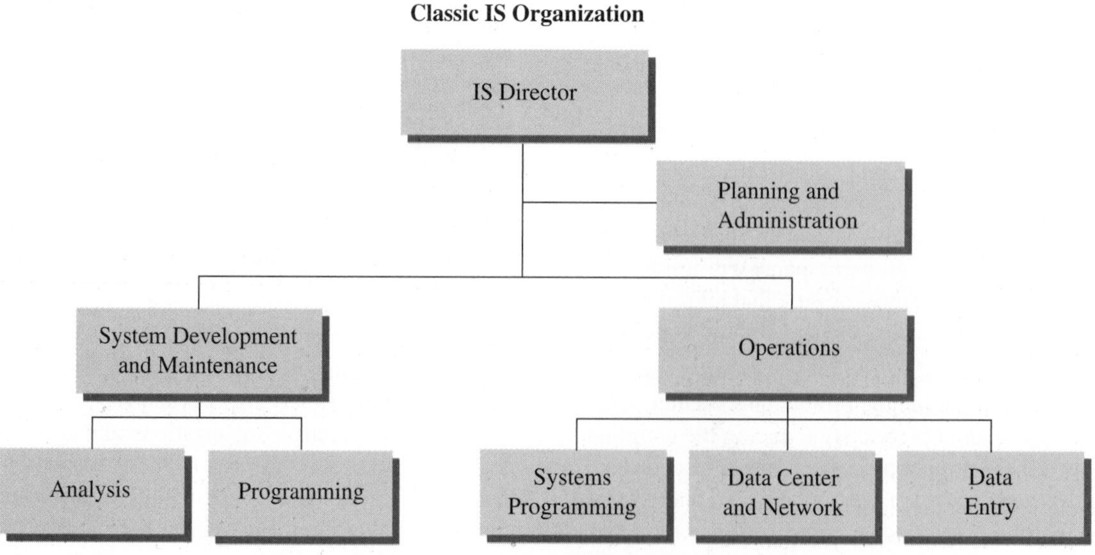

Figure 15.8 Classic IS Organization Structure

	entralized	Decentralized	Federal	Customized
Operations				
Infrastructure Planning	C	D	C	C
Computer Operations	C	D	C	C or D
Telecom/Network Operations	C	D	C	C or D
Applications				
Application Planning	C	D	D	C or D
Systems Development & Maintenance	C	D	D	C or D
End-User Support	C	D	D	C or D

C = Centralized decision making (decision rights consolidated into a single unit)
D = Decentralized decision making (decision rights dispersed to multiple units)

Figure 15.9 Common Designs for the IS Organization (Based on Brown, 2003)

a vendor, with separate cost and revenue accounting. There are two common designs for this "business within a business" approach. First, the company might create a separate IS subsidiary company. Here the IS organization operates much like an independent business with its own board of directors and governance process. Second, many other organizations have chosen to combine the IS organization and other support organizations in a "shared services" model. These groups often include human resources, legal, physical facilities maintenance, and transportation. These organizations might or might not be created as a separate legal entity. For example, Ashland Inc. operates a shared services organization in Rotterdam, the Netherlands, to support all Ashland operations in Europe.

The primary objective for both of these approaches is to gain more cost efficiencies from the same number of resources and also to increase the responsiveness of IS units to customers' needs. Sometimes these separate structures are also created as a way to determine if contracting out IS activities is more effective than performing all IS activities with internal staff.

Creating a separate IS business organization gained popularity during the late 1990s and early 2000s because the design puts the IS organization into a competitive market position. The business units in the parent company are usually free to contract with other suppliers for IS services. Sometimes the separate IS business unit is also allowed to provide IT services to outside, noncompeting organizations. Multiple shared services organizations might also be set up in large, international firms. Sometimes these units compete for service contracts with other shared services units that primarily serve other regions.

Selecting the Best Organization Design The IS organization structure needs to be aligned with the organization as a whole. The choice among the organization designs described above should depend on the following factors:

- How the rest of the business enterprise is organized, including global operations
- Other business characteristics, such as the type of customer markets, products, and geographical spread of the business units
- The conceptual and actual role of IT within the organization
- The reporting level of the most senior IS leader or officer within the organization
- The types of technologies managed by the IS organization

Since the late 1990s many firms have moved to more centralized IS organization designs in order to take advantage of commercial software developments. These developments include packaged enterprise systems with cross-functional modules for back-office transactions (ERP systems), front-office transactions (e.g., customer relationship management [CRM] systems), and business or competitive intelligence systems. However, the trend toward more hybrid IS organization designs seen at the end of the 1980s might emerge again as Web services approaches and other distributed technology approaches reemerge.

Governance Mechanisms Each of the designs discussed above has its own strengths and weaknesses in terms of achieving cost efficiencies and cross-unit synergies. Thus, one approach that many businesses use to minimize the weaknesses of a given organization design is to implement additional decision mechanisms to achieve coordination across multiple IS units, multiple business units, and business and IS units. Four common types of mechanisms are shown in Figure 15.10.

The most common type of coordinating mechanism is the implementation of a formal group that brings together stakeholders from different reporting units. For example, IS steering committees (or "advisory boards") are formal group mechanisms for linking a central IS unit and multiple business units for strategic and tactical decision making. Typically, business leaders serve on a steering committee for the senior IS leader of a centralized IS unit in order to achieve consensus on which application project requests from the business units are to be worked on first and to make IT infrastructure decisions. Another type of group governance system is a center of excellence team in which individuals from multiple reporting units are virtually (if not physically) linked for tasks such as sharing best practices and researching opportunities for new technologies.

Recent research has found that some organizations also view integrator role positions as critical for achieving cross-unit coordination. For example, in firms with a centralized IS organization design, an account manager might be assigned to "manage the account" of a specific business unit. Often the person in this integrator role will have an office physically adjacent to other business managers in the company.

Two other types of mechanisms in Figure 15.10—informal networking practices and human resource practices—are used to link IS and business managers, or IS managers who report to different business units, in a less formal way. In these cases as well, the intent of these mechanisms is to help build interpersonal networks among organizational members that will promote information and knowledge sharing to help grow and sustain the business.

8. Ensuring Regular Performance Measurement

Another key element in a modern IT management system is the regular evaluation of the IS organization by its internal customers. Some business managers complain that they are not sure they are getting their money's worth from the IS function. More important, many organizations simply do not know what the impact of IT investments has been. Often, promised cost savings were never realized, project budgets were exceeded, head count was not reduced or personnel were simply moved to other jobs, and

Four Types of IS Governance Mechanisms

Mechanism	Description
Formal Groups	Formally established councils or teams with specific linking or oversight responsibilities for IT activities (such as IS steering committees)
Formal Roles	Individual positions with formal responsibility for linking activities between a central IT unit and one or more business units (such as IS managers serving as account managers for specific business units)
Informal Networking Practices	Intentional activities or practices to link managers in two or more organizational units who may engage in or impact cross-unit problem-solving (such as physical co-location)
Human Resource Practices	Human resource management initiatives to facilitate voluntary cross-unit problem-solving (such as temporary job rotations, cross-unit input to performance reviews)

Figure 15.10 Four Types of IS Governance Mechanisms (Based on Brown, 1999)

the important benefits could not be directly attributed to the use of IT. By contrast, certain general impacts are clear. Many organizations have become very dependent on IT, and IT is often being used for competitive advantage. In these instances the IS department is critical to the organization's success.

Organizations and individual managers need agreed-upon and measurable criteria by which to judge the health and contribution of the IS organization and the systems it manages. IS organizations also need metrics to judge the quality of their work. The focus of this section, however, is on the measures of most interest to the business manager.

Measures of IS Unit Success Traditional productivity measurement approaches, such as cost-benefit analysis and return on investment, can be used to justify and evaluate individual systems. A wide variety of other criteria for evaluating the IS organization is possible, many of which are outlined in Figure 15.11. These criteria are used in

IS Evaluation Criteria

- **Meeting business objectives:** This means increasing business effectiveness and developing systems that support annual and long-term business goals and directions.
- **Responding rapidly and economically to new needs:** Reducing the length of the cycle from product idea generation to market introduction can have tremendous value in terms of cost reduction, personnel time, earlier revenue generation, and competitive advantage.
- **Expanding business or services:** Reaching new markets, adding features (often information-based) to existing products or services, or improving product service quality can be used for differentiation and revenue generation.
- **Developing an architecture and plan:** An architecture allows line managers to easily access the data now contained in data storage systems and supports the more rapid development and deployment of new systems.
- **Operating reliable and efficient technology resources:** Reliable and efficient operation of both internal systems and external services (such as order entry, reservations, and point of sale) is essential for the business to succeed.
- **Focusing on the customer:** Better customer support helps the organization to retain customers, gain new customers, and increase sales; the goal is to make it easy for the customer to do business with us and for us to know as much about the customer as he or she expects us to know.
- **Providing quality IS staff:** Indicators such as a high level of education, low turnover rate, and a large number of employees outplaced to line management jobs all suggest an IS organization of productive and useful people.
- **Reducing size of backlog:** Although a backlog of work indicates a strong demand for IS services, a large backlog can be a source of considerable frustration and unmet business opportunities; with a proper mix of end-user development, use of fourth generation languages, and purchasing package software, this backlog should be reduced to a manageable and reasonable level.
- **Satisfying users:** In the spirit of the business focusing on customer satisfaction, the IS organization can be measured by how satisfied line managers are with the technology, systems, and support services provided to them.
- **Adopting new technologies:** The IS organization can be evaluated on the basis of how soon new technologies (such as the Internet) are integrated into existing or new systems.

Figure 15.11 IS Evaluation Criteria

combination; no one or two measures adequately provide the complete picture of the IS department's contribution.

The IS evaluation criteria of Figure 15.11 require specific measures to be useful, some of which will be subjective. For example, the "meeting business objectives" criterion could be measured by an opinion survey involving such questions as:

- Does the IS plan support the corporate strategic plan?
- Would the organization be out of business without the IS unit?

Other criteria can be assessed by more quantitative and objective measures. For example, the "operating reliable and efficient technology resources" criterion could be measured by

- online response time
- network up-time as a percentage of total time during a period
- number of network crashes

As with any measurement system, an organization should measure only what is important, what needs improvement, and what is meaningful to some audience. Typically, measures of time, money, and defects are the most useful. In their classic article on the **balanced scorecard**, Kaplan and Norton (1992) called for using a set of measures that "balance" various assessment categories, including financial measures as well as the drivers of future performance:

- *Customer satisfaction* Such measures as on-time delivery of new systems, number of defects in a system
- *Internal processes* For IS, this could be the productivity of computer system developers, often measured by an industry standard of number of function points per month
- *Innovation and learning* Education level of IS staff and business managers

Service Level Agreements The IS organization can be evaluated through a **service level agreement** similar to one that would be written with an external supplier. This agreement makes expectations—from both IS and business management—explicit and defines agreed-upon criteria for a successful system and quality service.

User Satisfaction Measures If IS is viewed as a service organization, then user satisfaction is a very important measure of IS success. Such measures are an excellent way for managers to communicate their assessment of IS to senior officers and IS executives. Although not economic in nature and not related directly to business impacts such as reduced inventory, increased customer satisfaction, or improved product quality, user satisfaction measures can easily be captured and compared over time. User attitudes about systems and the IS department affect a business manager's willingness to work with IS professionals in the kinds of partnerships discussed earlier.

Typically, an annual survey would be conducted for each major system, systems that might have problems, IS support organizations, or any area of IS that is receiving criticism; that is, a user satisfaction survey can be conducted on an application system or on an IS unit. Business managers at different levels should be surveyed separately, because their different systems perspectives and roles (for example, direct user, source of funding, supervisor) can affect their evaluation.

Figure 15.12 lists some criteria that might appear on user satisfaction surveys for a specific system and other criteria that could be customized to particular IS units, such as systems development or end-user support. The survey would ask the respondent to rate the individual system or unit on, for example, a 1-to-10 scale (low-to-high performance) or ask users to respond on a strongly-disagree-to-strongly-agree scale concerning various statements involving the criteria in Figure 15.12. The survey might ask the business manager to indicate how important each criterion is, so that a weighted assessment can be derived. The survey might also include some open-ended questions that ask for problems, complaints, praise, particular system features to add or delete, and what the customer likes best or least about the system or IS unit.

SUMMARY

The nature of how organizations manage information systems and technologies is changing. Increasingly, IT is managed like other business units, with expectations for contribution to the organization and with shared responsibilities for all managers.

The IS organization's major assets (its human resources, physical infrastructure, and applications portfolio) must be treated as assets whose value needs to be increased whenever possible. In order to improve the value of assets, investment, whether in training or capital expenditures, is required.

In addition, IS leaders and their business counterparts must develop strong partnerships in their organization. Steering committees and other governance mechanisms must be designed. The importance of IT is reflected in

Criteria for User Satisfaction Surveys

User Satisfaction Criteria for Individual Systems

- Accuracy of outputs
- Quality/readability of output format
- Completeness of outputs
- Relevance of outputs
- Completeness of or accessibility to database
- Currency of database
- Response time (or other measure of work completed)
- Availability
- Mean time between failures
- Downtime or malfunction recovery time
- Charges/costs
- Quality of system documentation
- Number and severity of security breaches
- Ease of operation
- Ease of making changes
- Increased confidence in decisions and actions based on system outputs
- Extent of achieving expected benefits

User Satisfaction Criteria for IS Units

- Quality of system specification documents
- Size of request backlog or workload
- Projects completed on time and within budget
- Speed at which requested system changes are made
- Professionalism of IS staff
- Nature of relationships with IS staff
- Business knowledge of IS staff
- Quality of user training
- User feeling of involvement in systems management

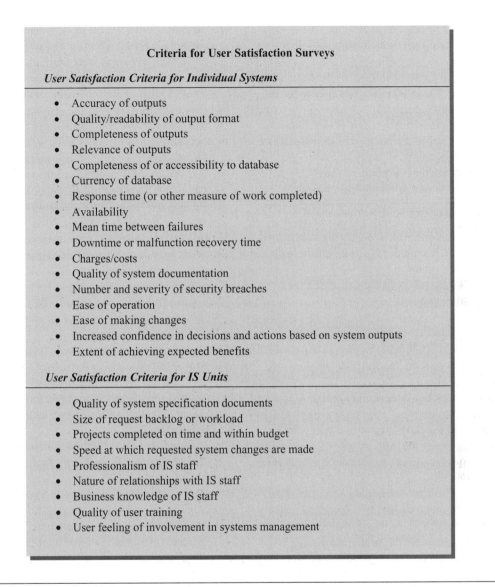

Figure 15.12 Criteria for User Satisfaction Surveys

many organizations by the establishment of a chief information officer or other senior IS executive responsible for linking the IT and business plans.

Organizations have not settled on one best way to organize the IS unit. The globalization of companies makes structuring this function even more difficult. Although history suggests that the IS function has periodically shifted between centralization and decentralization, today many organizations have very distributed IS functions.

These issues and more must be dealt with in the design of an effective management system for IT. Only when combined with direction setting (setting a vision, an architecture, and an IS plan) and excellent management of its technology assets can an IS organization perform most effectively.

REVIEW QUESTIONS

1. Why have IT management and structure changed in the past 10 years? That is, what changes in IT or the business have caused the IS unit to be restructured or to take on a new mission?
2. How have the perspectives of IS professionals changed in the past 10 to 15 years?

3. Why are strictly financial measures like return on investment and cost-benefit analysis insufficient for evaluating information systems?
4. What are the major responsibilities of the chief information officer? How are these different from the traditional IS director?
5. Outline the essential characteristics of the classic, federal, customized, and separate unit IS organization structures discussed in this chapter.
6. What is IT outsourcing? Is it good or bad?
7. What is the largest cost in the IS budget today?
8. What are the characteristics of a good IS chargeback system?
9. What are some unique issues concerning IT management that arise in multinational firms or firms doing business in many countries?
10. What should be the nature of the partnership between IT and business managers?

DISCUSSION QUESTIONS

1. If you were to write an IS department mission statement, what key words would you have used 10 years ago compared to the words you would use today?
2. Consider an organization with which you are familiar. Develop a policy for managing the applications portfolio.
3. As the manager of a major business unit (division), what would you do to implement a corporate infrastructure policy, such as the one in Figure 15.3?
4. What financial measures can be used to assess the contribution the IS organization makes to the business? What are the caveats involved with these measures?
5. What type of person in an organization should be considered for a chief information officer position? That is, what type of individual would be a prime candidate for such a job?
6. This chapter emphasizes the need for a partnership between IS and business managers for managing IT. Define your concept of a management partnership and relate this to making people accountable for business operations and functions.
7. Review the various pros and cons of distributing the systems development organization between central IS and line management organizations.
8. What type of organization would benefit most from creating an IS subsidiary? What type of organization would benefit most from outsourcing IS operations?
9. Under what circumstances would you recommend that an organization adopt a direct chargeback scheme for IS services?
10. As the manager of a statewide ATM network, how would you evaluate the quality of the IS organization serving you? If you were director of consumer marketing for a major appliance manufacturer, how would you evaluate the quality of the IS services you receive?
11. What arguments would you use to justify a career in IS management as a way to senior management in an organization?
12. How should the role of the IS department change as more of the business transactions with other firms (B2B commerce) are conducted over the Internet? How should the role of the business manager change?

CHAPTER 16
Social, Ethical, and Legal Issues

As we have seen, information technology (IT) is becoming a core resource for organizations in today's global economy and is affecting, if not determining, what organizations produce and how they are managed. Anyone with casual familiarity with today's news knows that IT is influencing the whole of society, not just the business arena. Today's generation can hardly conceive of living without the cell phone, the PC, communication satellites, FAX machines, and the Internet. IT is rapidly changing our lives, and this process of change is ongoing. The information revolution is often compared with the industrial revolution in terms of the overall impact that the industrial revolution had on civilization.

In spite of all the benefits that IT has brought, it has also given rise to a number of troubling social problems, such as loss of privacy, intellectual property issues, identity theft, spam, **computer viruses** and **worms**, sexual exploitation of children, obsoleting of workers' skills, and deterioration of working conditions. In this chapter we will explore a number of these social issues and consider their ethical and legal implications.

In the next section we discuss the legal environment as it relates to IT. Then we explore some ways to analyze social problems from an ethical perspective, after which we consider the ethical and legal dimensions of a number of social problems.

The Legal Environment

In dealing with the use of IT, individuals and organizations must work within a complex legal environment. This legal environment is incomplete and sometimes less than satisfactory, yet it is a manager's duty to know and obey the existing laws. Ignorance of the law is no excuse.

The purpose of law is to constrain behavior within a society so that its needs are satisfied and harm within it is prevented. Thus, law is related to, but not necessarily identical to, ethics. Laws are rules that must be obeyed, but it is difficult to write a rule that applies to every possible situation, especially in the case of IT, which is changing so rapidly. Also, laws must be enforceable—there must be meaningful sanctions that are invoked if the law is broken. A law that cannot be enforced or that people will not obey simply engenders a lack of respect for all law.

The information revolution has put great strain on the legal system. IT has made new forms of crime, such as identity theft, feasible. And it has changed the mechanisms for reproducing printed material, photos, art, and music to the point where what was once laborious and expensive has become a simple matter of downloading from the Web.

Technology has evolved quite rapidly and the legal system has inevitably lagged behind.

The first reaction has been to try to try to reinterpret existing laws to apply to new conditions, which they often do not quite fit. Then writing and adopting new laws takes time, and it is hard to write a law that exactly suits the problem, especially when the problems are always changing. It might take a number of iterations before a satisfactory law emerges.

Ideally, the law should reflect the best interests of society as a whole, but there is always controversy on what best serves the public interest. Laws, then, are typically compromises between the views of various interest groups. Also, the issues in regulating technology can be very complex, and members of Congress might have little expertise in dealing with these issues. Therefore, representatives may depend on the expertise and advice of lobbyists who can devote resources to developing logical positions that reflect the interests of those who are paying them.

Organizations are increasingly global, and the Internet covers most of the world. Different countries have different values and different legal systems. Whose laws apply when a possible crime has been committed? There are serious problems in determining who has jurisdiction when the person who is injured is in one jurisdiction and the perpetrator of the crime is in another. It might be virtually impossible to enforce any law in a situation where essentially anonymous people in multiple countries are involved.

ETHICS FRAMEWORKS

In this section we will be concerned with ways to analyze ethical issues that IT poses to individuals and organizations, so we will introduce some classical frameworks for considering what is moral or immoral about decisions and actions and discuss how to determine whether actions are moral or immoral.

Why are we discussing ethics in a book on management of IT? First, IT is having a growing impact on our lives, and anything that has such powerful effects on people's lives gives rise to ethical issues. Second, managers determine how IT is used, and therefore managers are responsible for the effects of the use of IT and the ethical implications of these effects.

To act ethically requires that we take *responsibility* for our actions. We need to clearly understand that the technology itself is not to blame for any harm that results from its use. Too often we hear: "We can't do that because our computer won't allow it." That might be true for the person who is making the statement, but it does not absolve the organization from responsibility—someone designed the system and programmed the computer to act in that way. And saying "the computer won't let me do that" is equivalent to saying "our organizational policy won't let me do that." Likewise, blaming the computer for a mistake is just an excuse—those who decided to use the computer and designed and implemented a system without adequate controls are responsible for any harm, not the computer! People and organizations are responsible for the results, good or bad, of the use of IT.

Most of us consider ourselves ethical persons. Most of us have an internal set of ethical standards, and if we violate these standards we lose our self-respect. There is little doubt that our self-respect is among our most valuable possessions, for if we lose our self-respect we do not like ourselves and become unhappy with ourselves.

Furthermore, in our careers as managers or professionals, there are very practical reasons to act ethically according to the society's standards. As individuals, if we are perceived as unethical we are in deep, deep trouble. If we get a reputation for being unethical, our jobs, or even our careers, might come to an inglorious end. Likewise, if an organization is perceived as unethical it might quickly be out of business. Whether it belongs to an individual or an organization, a reputation for integrity is crucial to success. Consider, for example, what happened to Enron and its managers when its books were found to be dishonest. Thus, managers must be concerned both with their individual ethics and the ethics of their organization. Managers are involved in determining the organization's ethical standards as well as in making sure that these standards are followed.

Identifying Ethical Problems

The first step in acting ethically is to recognize that a decision or action has ethical implications. In our use of IT we might do harm because we simply did not realize that our actions might be harmful—we might not consider all the implications of our actions. Therefore, we need to think about the ethical issues associated with our decisions before we take action. One purpose of this chapter is to sensitize you to the ethical issues that might arise in your use of IT so that you will not neglect the ethical implications.

How do we identify decisions where ethical problems might arise? Because our ethical makeup lies deep within us, the most common way we recognize ethical problems is by feel—when we don't feel right about a situation there might be an ethical problem. When we suspect that there might be ethical problems, a number of questions can be of help: Is this fair to everyone that will be affected? Would I want my mother to know about this? Would I care if everyone knew about this? What would be the result if everyone did this?

Identifying ethical problems associated with the use of IT might be complicated by the fact that its effects can be so pervasive. The effects of the use of IT might extend to many stakeholders—managers, workers, stockholders, customers, suppliers, communities, and the general public—and might affect them in ways that are not immediately obvious. For example, collecting information on customers for use in serving their needs might be beneficial to both the customer and the organization, but if this information is not protected against intrusion, someone might break into the system, steal personal information, and use it to harm the individual. Furthermore, if this information is sold to outside parties it might be used to harm the individual. Therefore, when trying to determine if there are ethical problems in the use of IT, a good place to start is to carefully consider all the potential stakeholders who might be affected by the system and determine how each one could be affected. If one or more of the stakeholders might be harmed, there is likely to be an ethical problem.

Analyzing Ethical Problems

There is no universally accepted way to determine whether an action is ethically justified or unethical. There are examples where almost everyone would agree that an action, such as murder, is unethical, but still there are those who believe that they are acting ethically when they kill women and children in an act of terrorism or in war. Even though there are no universally accepted rules, many concepts are helpful in analyzing ethical problems.

A number of professional organizations have recognized that IT presents many ethical issues. The Institute of Electrical and Electronic Engineers (IEEE) and the Association for Computing Machinery (ACM) have jointly developed a comprehensive code of ethics for the software engineering profession. The preamble to this Code of Ethics and Professional Practice, developed by the IEEE-CS/ACM Joint Task Force on Software Engineering Ethics and Professional Practices, contains the following paragraph:

> *Ethical tensions can best be addressed by thoughtful consideration of fundamental principles, rather than blind reliance on detailed regulations. These Principles should influence software engineers to consider broadly who is affected by their work; to examine if they and their colleagues are treating other human beings with due respect; to consider how the public, if reasonably well informed, would view their decisions; to analyze how the least empowered will be affected by their decisions: and to consider whether their acts would be judged worthy of the ideal professional working as a software engineer. In all these Judgments concern for the health, safety and welfare of the public is primary; that is, the "Public Interest" is central to this Code.*

The Association for Computing Machinery (ACM) code of ethics for its members explicitly recognizes that managers and organizations have special responsibilities that are expressed in Section 3 of this code (see Figure 16.1).

Quite a number of basic principles to guide ethical behavior have been suggested over the years. Some of these principles come from religious traditions, while others come from philosophers and others concerned with ethics. The ancient Hippocratic oath advises physicians to "do no harm." The second question of the Rotary Club's Four-Way Test is "Is it fair to all concerned?" The Ten Commandments of the Hebrew scripture forbid killing, adultery, stealing, bearing false witness and coveting. Most world religions promote the same ethic as Christianity's Golden Rule: Treat others as you would like them to treat you.

Although there are many variations of both theories, there are two basic ethical theories, one called **deontologism** and the other called **consequentialism**. Neither of these approaches is without problems, so it might be necessary to choose between them or to consider some combination of these approaches.

Deontologism Deontologism holds that an action is either ethical or unethical based only upon the action itself without regard to its consequences in the particular case. (De George, 1999, p. 52) The great moral philosopher, Emmanuel Kant, argued that it is our *duty* as humans to act according to ethical rules, and that it is our intent, not the actual result, that determines whether or not an action is ethical. Kant believed that there is a *categorical imperative* for ethical action and he gave several formulations of this imperative. Two of his formulations (paraphrased) are:

Act according to a rule that you would like to be applied universally, including to yourself. (Closely related to the Golden Rule.)

> *Act so that you treat humans always as an end and never as only a means to an end.*

In the Western world the rules by which actions are judged in the deontological approach often have their roots in the Judeo-Christian tradition. Although a large portion of the population might not be religious, these rules have become a part of our culture and provide an important foundation for our ethical reasoning. It should be noted that different cultures have different rules. For example, in some

Section 3 of the ACM Code of Ethics

3. **Organizational Leadership Imperatives.** As an ACM member and an organizational leader, I will ...

3.1 Articulate social responsibilities of members of an organizational unit and encourage full acceptance of those responsibilities.

3.2 Manage personnel and resources to design and build information systems that enhance the quality of working life.

3.3 Acknowledge and support proper and authorized uses of an organization's computing and communication resources.

3.4 Ensure that users and those who will be affected by a system have their needs clearly articulated during the assessment and design of requirements; later the system must be validated to meet requirements.

3.5 Articulate and support policies that protect the dignity of users and others affected by a computing system.

3.6 Create opportunities for members of the organization to learn the principles and limitations of computer systems.

Figure 16.1 Section 3 of the ACM Code of Ethics

Islamic cultures charging interest and drinking alcohol are unethical while polygamy is permissible. In some cultures bribery is not considered unethical, just the way you get things done.

In cultures where there is respect for the law, breaking the law is considered unethical. However, the reverse—if it is not illegal it is ethical—is usually not an accepted interpretation.

A major problem with deontologism is that the rules are absolutes that sometimes appear to produce harmful results. For example, to tell a lie is unethical, but there are circumstances where a "white lie" is best for all concerned. The weakness of deontologism is that it ignores the consequences that come from a specific action.

Consequentialism Consequentialism judges an action by evaluating all the consequences that it produces—if the consequences are predominantly good then the action is ethical, but if the consequences are predominantly bad, then the action is unethical. This is the reasoning that we might be using when we say, "the ends justify the means."

There are a number of variations of consequentialism, but we will only consider **Utilitarianism**, where *all* the parties who will be affected by the action must be identified and the consequences for each party delineated and quantified, with beneficial results measured on the positive scale and the harmful results measured on the negative scale. If the outcomes are not certain, then probabilities must be assigned to each outcome for each of the affected parties so that the expected return can be calculated. Then the action is ethically justified if the expected value of the positives and negatives is positive—that is if the good outweighs the bad.

In complex situations we should remember that there usually are a number of possible alternative actions—not just "do it" or "not do it." Especially in the case of developing and using IT, we can often devise alternatives that obtain adequate benefits while minimizing the harmful effects. And we need to be sure that we identify and include all those who will be affected by the system, not just those who will benefit from it.

There are problems in applying utilitarianism. One is quantification—how we assign numerical values and probabilities to outcomes. For example, at first glance it would seem that stealing would be ethically neutral—what one party gains is what the other party loses, so the sum is zero. But how do we factor in the emotional harm that being robbed produces? How do we factor in the possibility that condoning stealing in one case might encourage others to steal in other cases? How do we include the possibility that the person who is stolen from has so much that the theft is practically meaningless while the thief might have stolen to save his family from starvation?

Another question is how to evaluate the situation when the decision maker gets all the benefits and others bear all the harm, but the net result is positive. "This helps me more than it hurts you" does not appear to be a convincing ethical argument.

Another problem has to do with how one treats all the parties that might be affected. We might be inclined to include ourselves, those we know, members of our organization, members of our community, or members of our segment of society, while excluding "outsiders" from consideration.

Kant argued that utilitarianism is inherently flawed in that when you hurt someone to benefit others you are treating humans as means rather than as ends. Many people would argue that if an action hurts someone, then the benefits to others must vastly outweigh that hurt for the action to be ethical.

The fact that there are problems with most approaches to making ethical decisions does not mean that we are not expected to be concerned with the ethics of our actions. Rather, it means that we need to be very thoughtful and careful in our ethical reasoning. We might have to apply a combination of approaches in order to be comfortable with, and to make others comfortable with, our choices. Hopefully, these approaches will be used collectively to determine the most ethical action rather than selectively to justify an objectionable action.

In the following sections we discuss a number of topics, including computer crime, cyberattacks on computers, identity theft, the impact of IT on privacy, access to the technology and freedom of speech issues, intellectual property issues, the hazards of inaccuracy, and the impact of IT on workers. We conclude the chapter with a brief look at some long-range issues associated with IT.

Some social issues are important because managers must be aware of them and make sure that these activities are not going on in the workplace. However, they are not central to the management of IT, so for space reasons they are not included in this chapter. These omitted topics include hate e-mail, cyberstalking, sexual abuse via the Internet, and pornography. An employee might harass others via hate e-mail. Cyberstalking is the use of the Internet, e-mail, or other electronic communications devices to stalk another person. Employees can be sexual predators who are contacting minors through chat rooms using company facilities. And employees might use their office computers to access pornography while at work. These activities might subject the organization to significant penalties as well as public embarrassment, so it behooves prudent managers to make sure that they do not occur in their area of responsibility.

COMPUTER CRIME

Computer crime is big business and appears to be growing rapidly. It is very difficult to get reliable figures on the financial impact of computer crime because so much of it goes undetected and much that is detected is not reported. The National Computer Crimes Squad estimates that between 85 and 97 percent of computer intrusions are not even detected, fewer than 10 percent of those detected are reported, and only a few of those reported are solved. The Federal Bureau of Investigation (FBI) has estimated that computer crime losses in 1999 were as much as $10 billion. According to Gaudin (2003), mi2g, Ltd., a British firm supplying computer security software, asserted that the economic damage caused by all forms of digital attacks in the first 5 months of 2003 had reached between $34.7 billion and $42.4 billion worldwide.

Computer crime takes many forms, including financial crimes, businesses stealing competitors' secrets, espionage agents stealing military intelligence, attacks on computers by terrorists, grudge attacks by disgruntled employees or ex-employees, attacks by "hackers" who do it for fun, and the use of IT by criminals to run their criminal businesses and facilitate their criminal activities.

In this section we will discuss some financial crimes and attacks on computers via the Internet. Later sections will be devoted to some important issues that also might involve illegal activities, such as identity theft, privacy, and intellectual property.

Financial Crimes

Many financial crimes are old-fashioned embezzlements perpetrated by employees using company computers. For example, a person in the purchasing area might create purchase orders on fictitious suppliers, submit bills, and cash the payment checks. Life insurance company employees might create fake policies and file claims against them. Employees might transfer money to overseas banks and disappear or steal customer files or marketing plans or research and development files and sell them to competitors.

Sabotaging a crucial computer system can be a way of "getting back" at a company for real or perceived transgressions. For example, an insurance company employee was fired from his IT job, but before he was fired he planted a "**logic bomb**" that went off after he left the firm and destroyed more than 160,000 commission records used to prepare the monthly payroll (Baase, 1997). Such sabotage is a serious potential problem, so in many companies when someone is fired or quits that person's computer passwords are immediately canceled and he or she is watched while cleaning out his or her desk before being escorted off the premises. Of course, as the above example shows, when a person quits because of a grudge such measures do not provide complete protection.

Fraud is rampant on the Web. It is estimated that 5 percent of the transactions on the Web are fraudulent. Almost any scam that can be imagined can be perpetrated via the Web. The international nature of the Web has broadened the possibilities. For example, a flood of e-mails from Africa offer to share a fortune with recipients if that person will allow access to his or her bank account so that the money can be transferred there.

Some ingenious new techniques have been employed to defraud the unwary. For example, **spoofing**—setting up a Web site that mimics a legitimate site—has been employed to mislead and defraud (see the box entitled "Stock Fraud"). The spoofer might use some means, such as a message board, to direct the victim to the spurious site, or the spoofer might simply use a close variant of the site's Uniform Resource Locator (URL) to con people who make an innocent typing mistake.

STOCK FRAUD

On April 7, 1999, visitors to an online financial news message board operated by Yahoo! Inc. got a scoop on PairGain, a telecommunications company based in Tustin, California. An e-mail posted on the message board under the subject line "Buyout News" said that PairGain was being taken over by an Israeli company. The e-mail also provided a link to what appeared to be a Web site of Bloomberg News Service, containing a detailed story on the takeover. As news of the takeover spread, the company's publicly traded stock shot up more than 30 percent, and the trading volume grew to nearly seven times its norm. There was only one problem: The story was false, and the Web site on which it appeared was not Bloomberg's site, but a counterfeit site. When news of the hoax spread, the price of the stock dropped sharply, causing significant financial losses to many investors who purchased the stock at artificially inflated prices.

Within a week after this hoax appeared, the FBI arrested a Raleigh, North Carolina, man for what was believed to be the first stock manipulation scheme perpetrated by a fraudulent Internet site. The perpetrator was traced through an Internet Protocol (IP) address that he used, and he was charged with securities fraud for disseminating false information about a publicly traded stock. The Securities and Exchange Commission also brought a parallel civil enforcement action against him. In August he was sentenced to 5 years of probation, 5 months of home detention, and over $93,000 in restitution to the victims of his fraud.

[Adapted from Reno, 2000]

Cyberattacks on Computers

Cyberattacks on computers and the Web infrastructure are occurring with increasing frequency and are doing serious economic damage. Figure 16.2 shows how the number of reported incidents has exploded in recent years. Note that an incident might involve one site or even thousands of sites. Most computer penetrations exploit some security vulnerability in the software, especially the operating system.

Computer intrusions began years ago with **hackers**, usually bright young students motivated primarily by the technological challenge required to break into a computer via a communications connection. Usually they intended no harm, other than perhaps a taunting message revealing that they had been there, and some even justified their intrusions as helpful in pointing out vulnerabilities in computer security that might be exploited to do serious harm. They were also motivated by competitiveness—each hacker trying to outdo his or her compatriots. Many of them also had idealistic opinions on how things ought to be—that, for example, information and access to computers ought to be free to everyone. Many hackers insist that hackers would never harm anyone or damage anything; if they do they're something worse.

However, things soon got out of hand, with **crackers** using hacking techniques to break into computers and steal information, wipe out hard drives, or do other harm. For example, Kevin D. Mitnick broke into numerous computer networks, and (among other things) stole some 20,000 credit card numbers from NetCom, stole hundreds of programs from the home computer of a security expert at the San Diego Supercomputer Center, and wiped out some of the accounting records of an online service (Cortese, 1995). For a fascinating account of the pursuit of a West German

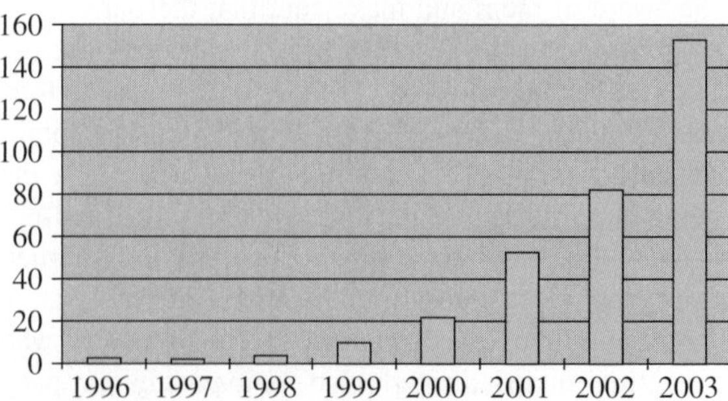

Note: These data are from CERT/CC Statistics 1988–2003, *www.cert.org/stat/cert_stats.html*, 11/1/2003. The figure for the year 2003 is projected from 9 months of data.

Figure 16.2 Number of Cyberattack Incidents Reported (in thousands)

cracker who was extracting information from defense computers in Western nations and selling it to the Soviet KGB, see Cliff Stoll's *The Cuckoo's Egg* (1989).

As indicated in the text box entitled "Digital Terrorism," it appears that political attacks are growing in frequency and intensity.

Methods of attack A number of techniques are used to impede legitimate use of computers, including viruses, worms, Trojan horses, logic bombs, **and denial of service attacks**. See Figure 16.3 for definitions of these technologies.

Although there had previously been some theoretical and experimental work on viruses, it is commonly accepted that two brothers from Pakistan created the first "wild" virus, called "Brain," in 1986. It was spread by inserting an infected floppy disk into a computer, and it mainly affected those who copied software or received data files from another computer. Today most viruses are of the worm variety that spread themselves from computer to computer via e-mail or other electronic computer-to-computer communications (see the text box entitled "Virus Epidemic").

A different approach, denial of service attacks, is quite easy for a sophisticated cracker to employ. The cracker uses a worm to infect many computers with a program that is designed to send messages to a target computer starting at a specific time or when a signal is given. Then all the infected computers start to rapidly send messages to that computer, either overwhelming the computer's input buffer

DIGITAL TERRORISM

Mi2g's November report names the United States as the nation most targeted for overt digital terrorism. As the world's only economic superpower and a bastion of human freedoms, the United States is considered the prime target for the jealous and zealous outside or inside her borders. DK Matai, Chairman and CEO of mi2g says: "The main reasons behind the escalating attacks on U.S. targets have been the rising penetration of 24/7 Internet connectivity within the American business, government, and domestic environment coupled with criminal opportunism and some antagonism towards U.S. foreign policy." With a total of 26,792 overt digital attacks so far in 2002, the attacks on the United States IT infrastructure by hacker terrorists exceeded those on the next four biggest victim countries combined.

"In 2002," Mr. Matai explains, "We have seen major hacker groups coalesce to harm and profit from Western commercial targets motivated by pro-Islamic and anticapitalist agendas as well as criminal activity such as identity theft, credit card fraud, software and data piracy."

[Abstracted from McCollum, 2002]

Techniques Used to Attack Computers

1. A **virus** is a small unit of code that invades a computer program or file. When the invaded program is executed or the file is opened the virus makes copies of itself that are released to invade other programs or files in that computer. It may also do nasty things like erase files or corrupt programs. Viruses are transmitted from one computer to another when an invaded computer program or file is transmitted to another computer.
2. A **worm** is a virus that has the ability to copy itself from machine to machine, normally over a network.
3. A **Trojan horse** is a security-breaking program that is introduced into a computer and serves as a way for an intruder to reenter the computer in the future. It may be disguised as something innocent such as a screen saver or a game.
4. A **logic bomb** is a program that is introduced into a computer and set to take action at a certain time or when a specified event occurs.
5. A **denial of service attack** is implemented by invading a large number of computers on the Internet and instructing them to simultaneously send repeated messages to a target computer, thus either overloading that computer's input buffer or jamming the communications lines into the computer so badly that legitimate users cannot obtain access.

Figure 16.3 Techniques Used to Attack Computers

VIRUS EPIDEMIC

Since early August [2003], the world's computer systems have been blitzed by hundreds of viruses—some of them real doozies. On August 11, the Blaster virus and related bugs struck, hammering dozens of corporations, including Air Canada's reservation and airport check-in systems. Ten days later, the SoBig virus took over, causing delays in freight traffic at rail giant CSX Corp. and shutting down more than 3,000 computers belonging to the city of Fort Worth. Worldwide, 15 percent of large companies and 30 percent of small companies were affected by SoBig, according to virus software tracker TruSecure Corp. Market researcher Computer Economics Inc. estimates damage will total $2 billion—one of the costliest viruses ever. All told, damage from viruses may amount to more than $13 billion this year.

[Hamm, Greene, Edwards, and Kerstetter, 2003]

and knocking it down or jamming the communications lines so that legitimate messages cannot get through (see the sidebar entitled "Denial of Service").

Protecting Security The security function in an IT organization, discussed in Chapter 15, is responsible for protecting the organization's infrastructure from intrusion.

DENIAL OF SERVICE

The scenario that no one in the computer security field likes to talk about has come to pass: The biggest e-commerce sites on the Net have been falling like dominoes. First it was Yahoo! Inc. On Feb. 6, the portal giant was shut down for 3 hours. Then retailer Buy.com Inc. was hit the next day, hours after going public. By that evening, eBay, Amazon.com, and CNN had gone dark. And in the morning, the mayhem continued with online broker E*Trade and others having traffic to their sites virtually choked off.

Experts say it's so easy, it's creepy. The software to do this damage is simple to use and readily available at underground hacker sites throughout the Internet. A tiny program can be downloaded and then planted in computers all over the world. Then, with the push of a button, those PCs are alerted to go into action, sending a simple request for access to a site, again and again and again—indeed, scores or hundreds of times a second. Gridlock. For all the sophisticated work on firewalls, intrusion-detection systems, encryption and computer security, e-businesses are at risk from a relatively simple technique that's akin to dialing a telephone number repeatedly so that everyone else trying to get through will hear a busy signal.

[Sager, Hamm, Gross, Carey, and Hoff, 2000]

However, an individual must take responsibility for protecting his or her personal computer by taking the following measures:

- Using antivirus software and keeping the virus definitions file up to date
- Making sure that all updates to the operating system are installed. These updates often fix known security vulnerabilities.
- carefully protecting passwords.
- Being very careful when opening e-mail messages. Opening attachments is especially dangerous. Even trusted sources can be harmful because some worms spread by sending infected e-mails to everyone in an infected computer's address book

Protecting a computer's security can become an ethical issue, for other people can be injured if someone breaks into your system and steals, destroys, or changes data. There might be others who use that data who could be hurt by the intrusion. Also, once a hacker has gotten into the system of a legitimate user, it can be relatively easy to invade the entire computer system, or even an entire network. Thus, effective security of the entire system or network depends upon the vigilance of each legitimate user of that system. In short, unless we take seriously our responsibility for security, we can abet penetration of, and perhaps destruction of, a network's entire contents.

Computer Crime Laws

Laws against theft, embezzlement, and fraud have existed long before the computer and the Internet were developed, and these laws can often be applied to financial crimes where IT is involved. The Computer Fraud and Abuse Act of 1986 as amended (Title 18 United States Code, Chapter 47, Sections 1029 and 1030) includes the most important laws used in U.S. Federal Courts to deal with computer crime.[1] These laws apply only to crimes that affect U.S. government computers or financial institutions or that involve interstate or foreign commerce, but this includes practically everything connected to the Internet.

Section 1029 prohibits fraud and intrusion by the use of counterfeit access devices such as personal identification numbers (PINs), credit cards, account numbers, and various types of electronic identifiers. Fines range up to $50,000 for the first offense and up to $100,000 for repeat offenses.

[1]The analysis of these laws that follows is abstracted from *Computer Crime Law Issue #1* compiled by Hooda *<webmaster@beahacker.com>* found at *www.beahacker.com/law.htm*.

Prison sentences upon conviction range up to 15 years for the first offense and up to 20 years for a repeat offense.

Section 1030 covers espionage activities and adversely affecting the use of a U.S. government computer, stealing financial information from a financial institution or a credit card issuer or a consumer reporting agency, knowingly damaging an application or a computer by hacking into it, stealing passwords, and furthering a fraud by accessing a computer. The penalties for such activities include fines and imprisonment of 1 to 5 years for the first offense and up to 10 years for a repeat offense. Espionage, of course, can result in much more severe penalties. It should be noted that traditional laws against theft and fraud and espionage can also be applied to these crimes, and they may have more significant penalties in many cases.

It should also be noted that the laws in other countries sometimes vary considerably from U.S. laws, and they may also be enforced more or less vigorously.[2] In addition, when the crimes cross national borders the difficulty of solving and prosecuting these crimes increases significantly.

IDENTITY THEFT

According to the Federal Trade Commission (FTC), **identity theft** is "someone appropriating your personal information without your knowledge to commit fraud or theft." An identity thief uses information about you, such as your name, address, social security number, credit card number, and/or other identifying information to impersonate you and obtain loans or purchase items using your credit. When the thief does not make the required payments, it is reported to **credit bureaus** and your credit rating could be ruined. Furthermore, the thief's creditors might hound you to repay the debts that have been run up in your name. Trying to clean up the mess the thief created can take a lot of time and effort and exact an emotional toll (see the sidebar entitled "Impact of Identity Theft").

Technically, identity theft may not be solely a computer crime, for the stolen information about you might be obtained by stealing your wallet, by obtaining your credit card number from a credit card receipt, by "dumpster diving" to find discarded paper records, or by disclosure by someone who has legitimate access to your personal information. However, the information can also be obtained by breaking into a computer and examining files that contain this information or even by intercepting information flowing through the Internet or dedicated communication lines. Moreover, the fraud that makes identity theft lucrative would not be possible without national credit cards and credit bureaus that depend heavily on IT.

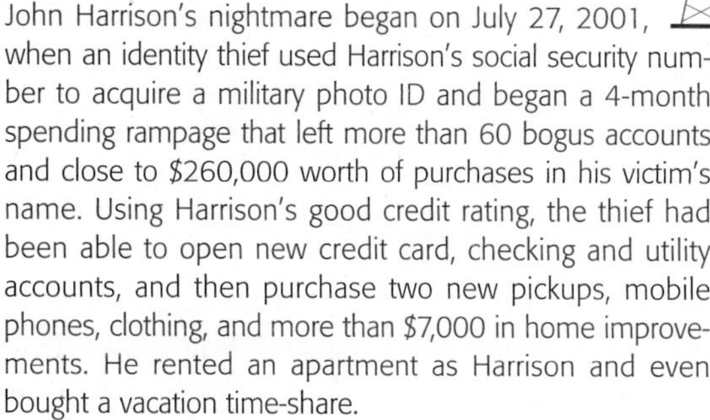

IMPACT OF IDENTITY THEFT

John Harrison's nightmare began on July 27, 2001, when an identity thief used Harrison's social security number to acquire a military photo ID and began a 4-month spending rampage that left more than 60 bogus accounts and close to $260,000 worth of purchases in his victim's name. Using Harrison's good credit rating, the thief had been able to open new credit card, checking and utility accounts, and then purchase two new pickups, mobile phones, clothing, and more than $7,000 in home improvements. He rented an apartment as Harrison and even bought a vacation time-share.

Despite a letter from a U.S. attorney stating his innocence and a copy of the identity thief's federal indictment, Harrison has struggled for over 2 years to clear his name. "I'll spend 10 minutes explaining that I'm a victim of identity theft," says Harrison of his daily battles with unremitting debt collectors. "Then they'll say, 'OK, can you start paying some of this debt?'"

Harrison's personal credit also dried up as banks revoked his spending limits. And when his 15-year-old daughter needed his help to open up her first savings account, they were turned away. "I can't put a price tag on the humiliation I felt," Harrison reported.

[Abstracted from Moritz, 2003]

Impact of Identity Theft

Identity theft crime is a serious problem, both for business and individuals. As reported by the Federal Trade Commission (2003), in 2002 there were nearly 10 million victims and a loss of almost $48 billion for business and $5 billion for consumers. As indicated, financial institutions and merchants bear most of the dollar costs of identity theft. If your credit card is misused, either the merchant or the credit card company absorbs the loss. If someone borrows money in your name, the lender is stuck with the loss. However, the dollar figures do not tell the full story of the impact of identity theft on the victim. In the first place, the victim must prove his or her innocence to every business that has been victimized, and the business might not be happy about its loss and be reluctant to admit that it erred, so it might make it difficult to erase what it assumes to be the victim's debt. Furthermore, by the time the victim finds out about the crime, the thief could have run up a lot of bad debts that end

[2]See, for example, Michael W. Kim, *How countries handle computer crime*, a paper for MIT 6.805/STSo85: Ethics and Law on the Electronic Frontier, Fall 1997 found at *http://www-swiss.ai.mit.edu/6095/student-papers/fall97-papers/kim-crime.html.*

up on the victim's credit record, thus destroying the victim's reputation and creditworthiness. Getting these records corrected can be a long, laborious process and might have to be repeated over and over as the thief continues more thievery using the victim's identity. A 2003 study found that the average identity theft victim spent over 600 hours recovering from this crime, often over a period of years (ITRC, 2003).

Police and Bank Attitudes

The banks and merchants from whom the identity thief has stolen money seldom wish to pursue and prosecute the thief, because unless the loss was quite large the costs of pursuing the matter are greater than whatever repayment, if any, they might collect. It is frustrating to the person whose identity has been stolen, but he or she is the only victim who has any direct motivation to stop the thief from further activity.

The police are sometimes reluctant to pursue identity thieves. Police agencies are underfunded, overworked, and might be untrained in how to handle identity theft investigations. Because the identity thief has not taken any money from the person whose identity has been stolen, many police officers feel that no crime has been committed, so the victim has no standing to report a crime. According to the 2003 ITRC study, 26 percent of the victims were unable to get the local police to take a report of the crime, even after multiple attempts, and only 29 percent of the victims were able to get a written report from the police. This is particularly frustrating because many businesses and banks require a copy of the police report to clear the record of the identity theft victim.

There usually is no one who looks out for the interests of the person whose identity has been stolen. The lenders, banks, credit bureaus, collection agencies, and police all are difficult to contact, unsympathetic, and unhelpful to some degree. When the identity thief persists in using the stolen identity over a long period of time, the victim could be forced to live with the fact that his or her credit and reputation is ruined and quit trying to correct the record. Then the thief can no longer get credit via the stolen identity. But if the victim repairs his or her credit rating, the thief can steal again.

Ethical Issues

There is no question that an identity thief is acting unethically. But how about the banks and merchants who simply ignore the crime rather than pursuing the thief? It is clear that the identity theft victim is often injured by that lack of action as it allows the identity thief to continue to take advantage of the victim. That inaction violates Kant's categorical imperative that one should act according to a rule that you would like to be applied universally, including to yourself.

However, the banks and merchants might justify their inaction on the grounds that the cost of taking action exceeds the amount that might be recovered from the thief, so the net result of not acting is positive—which would make the action ethical according to the utilitarian approach. Here they are not considering the impact on the victim and other possible victims of allowing the criminal to continue, so they would be misusing the utilitarian approach. If the analysis were to take into account the effect on all the parties concerned, it would almost certainly lead to the conclusion that not assisting in pursuing the criminal is unethical. Any utilitarian analysis that considers only the effect on you is seriously flawed.

Laws on Identity Theft

The Identity Theft and Assumption Deterrence Act of 1998 amended Title 18 United States Code Section 1028 to make it a federal crime when anyone "knowingly transfers or uses, without lawful authority, a means of identification of another person with the intent to commit, or to aid or abet, any unlawful activity that constitutes a violation of Federal law, or that constitutes a felony under any applicable State or local law."

Violations of the act are investigated by federal investigative agencies such as the U.S. Secret Service, the FBI, and the U.S. Postal Inspection Service and prosecuted by the Department of Justice. The act also requires the FTC to log and acknowledge such complaints, provide victims with relevant information, and refer their complaints to appropriate entities (e.g., the major national consumer reporting agencies and other law enforcement agencies).

The Fair Credit Reporting Act as amended sets the rules for how credit bureaus maintain information and what victims of identity theft must do to clear their credit records. The act is a large, complex law, and it does not adequately address the needs of identity theft victims. For example, at a time when speed is very important to the victim, the law allows 30 days for the credit bureaus to make corrections, and the credit bureau is the judge of whether any correction should be made. Always the burden of proof is on the victim. To summarize the current situation, the law on identity theft is inadequate and enforcement of the law is poor.

PRIVACY

Privacy is important to people, but it is a difficult concept to define. Violating your privacy can relate to unwanted access to your person, or to intruding into your home or office, or to observing you, or to obtaining information about you. We would like to think that we have a "right" to privacy, but legally that right is much weaker than property rights or the right to free speech.

As a legal right *privacy* was defined by Samuel D. Warren and Louis D. Brandeis in 1890 as "the right to be let alone." However, this broad right has not been enacted into law in the United States.

In our discussion we will be concerned with privacy defined as the ability to control access to information about ourselves. Control is a key word in the preceding sentence because there is information about us that we willingly share with family, or friends, or those we trust, that we would not want to share with the general public. Note that there is information about us—public information—to which we cannot control access. And there is critical information about us, such as our social security number, that by law we must provide to financial institutions so that income can be reported to the Internal Revenue Service (IRS). This is another instance of why the concept of control is so important, for we want to be able to keep our social security number away from potential identity thieves.

A person might give up his or her claim to privacy by giving permission to collect and use certain personal information. Therefore, if, after fully informing a person of how the information is to be used, you receive the person's permission to obtain and use personal information, you are not invading that person's privacy. People routinely give up personal information to someone they trust in exchange for some benefit or in order to transact business. However, privacy has been invaded when that information is used in ways that the person never intended or agreed to.

Ethics of Invasion of Privacy

In the Kantian view invasion of privacy is always unethical, for if you invade someone's privacy you are not treating that person with respect as an individual—you are violating Kant's imperative to always treat persons as an end rather than as a means. From the utilitarian view, however, whether or not invasion of privacy is ethical depends upon the result of that action, and one can argue that the total resulting good can exceed the harm that has been caused. This, of course, can be tricky as it might be very difficult to accurately value the harm caused by a loss of privacy.

Laws on Privacy

In the United States there is no comprehensive legal right to privacy, but there is a great deal of legislation that purports to offer some privacy protection. (The following is abstracted with minor changes from Baron, 2000.) The Fair Credit Reporting Act regulates the disclosure of credit application data and credit histories. The Privacy Act restricts a government agency from gathering information for one purpose and using it for another purpose or sharing it with another government agency. For example, the IRS has been prohibited from sharing income tax information with other agencies. The Family Education Rights and Privacy Act protects the privacy of students by restricting access to their student grade and disciplinary information. The Electronic Communications Privacy Act prohibits unauthorized access to e-mail. The Video Protection Privacy Act prohibits videotape service providers from disclosing information about video rentals. The Driver's Privacy Protection Act prohibits states from selling driver's license information. The Health Insurance Portability and Accountability Act protects your electronic medical records from unauthorized disclosure. The Children's Online Privacy Protection Act prohibits collecting information from children under the age of 13 unless their parents authorize it.

In total, these federal laws provide a great deal of protection in certain areas. Student information, electronic medical information, and electronic communications are reasonably well protected. However, although several federal laws relate to protection of financial data, the total result is not very impressive. The key financial data protection law is the Gramm-Leach-Bliley Act (GLBA), which purports to protect the privacy of information collected by financial institutions, but this protection is quite limited. Furthermore, there is no federal protection of the privacy of information collected by other businesses such as merchants.

Financial institutions—businesses that engage in banking, credit card issuing, insuring, stocks and bonds, financial advice, and investing—often buy and sell the information that they collect on you. The GLBA provides limited privacy protections against the sale of this private financial information, as follows:[3]

- First, financial institutions must develop precautions to ensure the security and confidentiality of customer records and information and to protect against unauthorized access to such records.
- Second, financial institutions must provide the customer with written notice of their information sharing policies when he [or she] first becomes a customer and annually thereafter
- Third, the customer has the right to opt-out of sharing his [or her] information with certain third parties, and the above privacy policy notice must explain how, and offer a reasonable way, for the customer to opt out.

[3]This information comes from the Web sites of the American Civil Liberties Union and the Federal Trade Commission.

However, the customer cannot prevent sharing this information with affiliated companies or companies that the financial institution has employed to provide certain services, or with credit reporting agencies, or as part of the sale of a business.

The requirement that the customer "opt-out" to obtain this limited privacy protection is a significant concern. Because the ability to sell this information has substantial value, the financial institution has the motivation to reduce the likelihood that the opt-out option will be exercised. So the required privacy notice might be long, written so only a lawyer can understand it, printed in small type, and included in the envelope with the customer's bill along with several advertising inserts. It takes a dedicated person to take the time and effort to read through and understand the notice, to figure out how to opt out, and to follow the required procedure. From the standpoint of the consumer, an "opt-in" policy would be much preferred, for it would force the companies to explain clearly what would be shared, with whom, and how the information would be used in order to persuade the customer to agree to the sharing.

Judging by their laws, many other countries seem to value privacy more highly than the United States does. According to Grupe, Kuechler, and Sweeney (2003), the U.S. position on privacy can be characterized as

- unprotective of data about individuals collected by businesses and government
- an unrestricted flow of data among companies
- a market-driven view of people as consumers under which data is seen as a saleable, usable commodity that belongs to the corporations
- reliant on self-regulation by companies to respect an individual's privacy
- Regulated by specific pieces of legislation (i.e., by sector) that relate to particular aspects of privacy, but not to privacy generally

The European position can be characterized as

- protective of personal rights with respect to data about individuals
- restrictive regarding the flow of personal data out of the country of origin, except to other countries honoring certain privacy principles
- having a view of the people as citizens who are in control of their personal data
- regulated by general laws, principles, procedures, and standards adopted to oversee the collection of data by governmental agencies established for this purpose

The above differences in approach have led to conflict. In 1998 the European Union issued a directive that requires that countries allow transborder personal data transfers only to countries that adhere to standards substantially equivalent to those of the European Union. That does not include the United States, which threatened to interrupt European operations of U.S. companies. After some intense negotiations, an accommodation has been worked out that allows U.S. companies to continue to transfer data back to the United States if they certify that they adhere to agreed-to "safe harbor" standards that are roughly equivalent to those that the GLBA requires for financial institutions.

The Patriot Act, passed by Congress soon after the terrorist attacks of September 11, 2001, with the purpose of protecting Americans against terrorism, significantly weakens Americans' constitutional protection against unreasonable search and seizure by allowing the FBI to force anyone—including doctors, libraries, bookstores, universities, and Internet service providers (ISPs)—to turn over records on their clients or customers by simply telling a judge that the request is related to an ongoing terrorism or foreign intelligence investigation. As of this writing, Congress is considering proposals by the attorney general to "strengthen" the Patriot Act in ways that further erode an individual's right to privacy from government.

Privacy Problems

It is clear that IT has radically affected our ability to control access to information about ourselves and thus presents serious privacy problems. Before the computer, when transactions and records were on paper, there was quite limited access even to public information about ourselves. To find information someone had to go to where it was located, find it in the file, and copy it down. Today, when the same information is in a database, it can often be obtained from anywhere in the world in a few seconds and at no cost. That ability has provided an enormous boost to productivity in our economy, but without substantial safeguards it can devastate our personal privacy.

Many of the computer crimes previously discussed result in invasion of privacy. For example, hackers and crackers who invade your computer are also invading your privacy, and identity theft is a particularly flagrant violation of privacy.

However, explosive growth of the use of IT has produced a situation where huge amounts of personal information are easily available without any need for criminal activities. For reasons of convenience and efficiency, government agencies are putting official records into online databases—birth and death records, marriages, divorces, property sales, business licenses, legal proceedings, driving records, and so on. Furthermore, personal information is valuable for marketing purposes, so it is collected whenever possible and often sold to others. Also, there are data brokers whose business is to collect and sell such information to whomever wishes to purchase it.

In the normal activities of transacting business we often must provide sensitive personal information such as name, address, and credit card number. To take out a loan from a financial institution we must provide much more personal information and allow a credit check so that the loaning institution can decide whether we are likely to repay the loan. This is quite legitimate and, as we agree to provide the information in order to transact the business, there is no invasion of privacy. However, when the business uses the information for purposes that we did not authorize or sells the information, serious privacy problems arise. People differ widely in their attitude toward this kind of invasion of their privacy. Surveys over the years have shown that about 25 percent of the public is not at all concerned with these privacy issues, 25 percent is quite sensitive to loss of privacy, and the remaining 50 percent is willing to consider trading some privacy for other benefits if given the right to make that decision.

Personal information is so valuable to marketers that they go to great lengths to obtain it. Purchasers are encouraged to fill out and return warranty cards that sometimes include a questionnaire with questions about age, income, hobbies, favorite magazines, and so forth. If you enter a sweepstakes you might have to fill out an entry form with similar questions. If you have a special shopper card that provides discounts at your supermarket you probably filled out an application that included personal information. Credit card records can provide comprehensive information about your shopping habits (see the sidebar entitled, "Credit Cards"). All this personal information is likely to end up in databases that are used to target marketing efforts.

When individuals do not know what data are being collected or by whom or how it is used, they have no control over their personal information and therefore by definition their privacy has been invaded. Furthermore, if all these marketing databases were to be combined with official information databases and financial information databases into one database the result would be a very comprehensive dossier on each person. So far this has not been done, but it would be possible.

CREDIT CARDS

In 1992, General Motors Corp. joined with MasterCard International Inc. to offer the GM Card. As a result, GM now has a database of 12 million GM cardholders, and it surveys them to learn what they're driving, when they next plan to buy a car or truck, and what kind of vehicle they would like. GM went into the credit-card business not just to build loyalty and offer cardholders rebates on cars but also because it saw the billing process as a way to harvest reams of data about consumers.

American Express Co., using massively parallel processors from Thinking Machines Inc., stores every credit card transaction. Then 70 workstations at the American Express Decision Sciences Center in Phoenix race through mountains of data on millions of AmEx cardmembers—the stores they shop in, the places they travel to, the restaurants they've eaten in, and even the economic conditions and weather in the areas where they live—in order to target special promotions to customers through its billing process.

[Adapted from Berry, Verity, Kerwin and DeGeorge, 1994]

E-Commerce Privacy Concerns

We know that unencrypted communications on the Web can be intercepted and that there are sites that mimic trusted companies for the purpose of enticing the unwary to give their personal identifying information and credit card number to potential identity thieves. But we might not be aware that legitimate, trusted businesses are collecting personal information about us and our shopping activities and selling them to others.

When you visit a Web site, that site might deposit a "cookie" on your computer in a cookie file provided by your Web browser. The cookie is a small record that identifies you to the Web site you visited and allows it to set up a file on its computer that can record information about the actions you take with that site. When you visit that site again, the cookie is retrieved and that data are used to access your file on the site. This can be very helpful to you. For example, if you have made a purchase from that store, it might have saved your name, address, and credit card number so you do not have to enter that information again (but only verify it) when you wish to make another purchase. The Web store might also maintain a record of the particular items you looked at and the purchases you made and analyze that information to determine your interests and target its advertising and promotions to those interests.

From the standpoint of your privacy the above use of cookies is relatively benign. Furthermore, it provides the basis for "target marketing" that is very beneficial to the marketer and also helps provide you with promotional material that might be of interest to you instead of just junk mail. However, you might not know about the cookie or the information that the Web site maintains about you, and if the Web site sells that information to others without your permission that is a definite violation of your privacy because you have lost control of your personal information. This information, along with similar information from other Web sites that you visit, might end up in the data base of a data broker whose business is building comprehensive dossiers on people and selling them. You might or might not care about whether a comprehensive picture of your buying habits and interests is freely available, but some people consider this to be a gross invasion of their privacy.

Cookies can also be used to develop more comprehensive information on your interests and preferences as you surf across a number of Web sites. For example, DoubleClick Inc., the leading Internet advertising service, places ads for thousands of advertisers on thousands of Web sites that employ their services. When you visit one of these client Web sites, a cookie is deposited on your computer that identifies you as described above. However, that cookie also identifies you when you visit any other of DoubleClick client's Web sites, so your record in DoubleClick's computer includes information about your viewing and purchasing behavior across all of DoubleClick's client sites. This information is extremely valuable to advertisers, for they can then display ads to you that fit your interests and you have a higher than normal probability of responding to their ads. Any improvement in the response rate is of great value to an advertiser, and you might also benefit by not being subjected to as many ads that you have no interest in.

The data collected by the use of a cookie is anonymous—the cookie only identifies your browser to DoubleClick's computers. However, in 2001 DoubleClick made a strategic investment in Abacus Direct, a direct marketing service that served direct mail and catalog marketers. Abacus had buying information on 88 million households, including name, address, telephone number, credit card numbers, income, and purchases. DoubleClick soon announced a product that provided advertising services based upon merging its Internet database with the Abacus database to serve cross-channel marketers. When this linking of databases was publicized by the news media it elicited a storm of protest and DoubleClick announced that it was withdrawing that product until suitable privacy standards had been developed. The product has since been returned to DoubleClick's product line under the following privacy guidelines:[4]

- DoubleClick will not use any personal information to target Internet ads.
- DoubleClick will allow you to opt out of its depositing a cookie on your computer.
- DoubleClick encourages its clients to also allow you to opt out of the client depositing cookies and to provide notice to its customers of the DoubleClick technologies that they use.
- DoubleClick does not develop marketing scores that indicate a user's individual health condition, detailed financial information, sexual orientation or behavior, information that appears to relate to children under 13, racial and ethnic origin, political opinions, religious or philosophical opinions, and trade union membership.

Except for the financial industry, in the United States there are no laws regulating the collection and sharing of such data. Many companies on the Web do not post a privacy policy. Many companies post privacy policies that do not fully explain what data they collect or how they use or share the data, and companies can change their privacy policies at any time without notifying those whose data they have collected.

Workplace Privacy

There is no expectation of privacy in the workplace. The U.S. courts have held that a company can monitor anything done using company computers. Employees need to be aware that e-mail is archived on company computers and preserved for a long time, so deleting an e-mail message does not remove it from company records. Furthermore, if the company is investigated by a government agency the e-mail archives might be turned over to the investigating agency. Enron employees were dismayed in March 2003 when 1.6 million personal e-mails and documents were posted on a government Web site (Berman, 2003). Embarrassing personal messages, as well as sensitive information such as social security numbers, were among the data posted.

According to an American Management Association survey released in 2000, nearly three-quarters of employers record employee Web use, voice mail, e-mail, or phone calls, review computer files, or videotape workers. Moreover, up to a quarter of companies that spy do not tell their employees (Associated Press, 1997). The only federal law that limits employer surveillance is the 1986 Electronic Communications Privacy Act, which bans employer eavesdropping on spoken personal conversations.

Companies do not want their employees to waste company time and resources on inappropriate activities such as personal online shopping, chatting with friends, gambling online, or visiting pornographic Web sites. But also, as explained in the text box entitled "Legal Liability for Employee Conduct," managers can be held accountable for certain illegal activities of employees even if they do

[4]Selected from the DoubleClick Web site *www.doubleclick.com*.

LEGAL LIABILITY FOR EMPLOYEE CONDUCT

Corporate executives are becoming increasingly aggressive about spying on their employees, and with good reason: now, in addition to job shirkers and office-supply thieves, they have to worry about being held accountable for the misconduct of their subordinates.

Even one offensive e-mail message circulated around the office by a single employee can pose a liability risk for a company. Not only that, but a wave of laws—including the federal Health Insurance Portability and Accountability Act of 1996 and the anticorruption and corporate-governance Sarbanes-Oxley Act of 2002—have imposed new record-keeping and investigative burdens on companies. Not complying with some laws can result in the personal liability of officers and directors.

[Nusbaum, 2003]

not know that these activities are taking place, so companies often monitor employees in self defense.

For practical as well as ethical reasons, it is important that the company policies for monitoring employee activities and communications be carefully considered and that they be clearly communicated to company employees.

Access

There are two sides to the access issue. The first is that IT has become such an essential ingredient of a modern economy that people who do not have access to IT are precluded from full participation in the benefits of the economy. Similarly, societies are doomed to third-world status if they do not have a computer literate population provided with access to modern IT.

The other side of the access issue is that IT allows so much access that we have lost control of information that for the good of society should not be widely available. Furthermore, the Internet provides access to your e-mail in-box to spammers who are free to fill it up with junk.

The United States is in reasonably good shape in regard to computer access and computer literacy. As reported in NCES (2001), about 90 percent of children and adolescents ages 5 through 17 use computers and about 59 percent use the Internet. Furthermore, this participation rate is growing year after year. On the other hand, there is a "digital divide"—computer and Internet use are divided along demographic and socioeconomic lines with whites having more usage than blacks, who have more usage than Hispanics. Also, those living in households with higher family incomes are more likely to use computers and the Internet than those living in lower-income households, and the lower-income children tend to have access to these technologies only at school while the higher-income children have access at both home and school. The good news is that the digital divide is getting smaller and smaller over the years as the total participation rate is growing. Rather than access to technology, our problem is likely to be functional illiteracy in both reading and mathematics.

Europe and Japan lag behind the United States in access to the computer, but are in relatively good shape. The developing countries lag far behind the developed world, but are making progress. However, in the undeveloped world the situation is virtually hopeless, for the problem is not computer literacy but any kind of literacy, and huge numbers of people have no access to any technology—80 percent of the world's population has never made a phone call, let alone used the Internet.

Freedom of Speech

The Internet is such a powerful and pervasive technology for presenting information that the question arises: Is there information that is so harmful or dangerous that for the good of society it should be prohibited from being posted on the Internet? How about detailed plans for an atomic bomb? Or instructions for making a bomb from readily available materials such as the one used in the Oklahoma City bombing? Or several different suggestions for how to poison a city's water supply? Or the names and addresses of physicians who perform abortions along with assertions that they are murderers who must be punished? Or child pornography? Or any pornography?

The increasingly pervasive use of the Internet and the World Wide Web has led to renewed controversy over the conflicts between our right to freedom of speech and the right of society to protect itself against terrorists or criminals or those who would tear down the moral basis on which our society depends. It is clear that there are limits to free speech—you cannot libel someone or threaten to harm someone without risking legal action. However, when it comes to prohibiting other types of speech, the U.S. courts have generally upheld the free speech rights granted by the First Amendment. Furthermore, the legal status might be moot because of the practical difficulties of policing the Internet, as the offender's identity might be concealed or he or she might be anywhere in the world and therefore out of the jurisdiction of U.S. law.

Spam Unsolicited commercial e-mail, commonly referred to as spam, is becoming an overwhelming burden on the Internet. Spammers acquire e-mail lists by various means—

they use special software to search the Web for e-mail addresses, they create random e-mail addresses and send them out in bulk knowing that some will get through, and they purchase e-mail lists from anyone who will sell them. Then they use special software to broadcast their spam messages to everyone on their e-mail lists.

According to Swartz and Davidson (2003), some 2 trillion junk e-mails were expected to be sent in 2003—which is more than half the total e-mail traffic—causing immense problems for both consumers and the ISPs that serve them. There is antispam software designed to identify spam and block it. ISPs spend a lot of money blocking spam and might succeed in blocking up to 80 percent of it, but the typical consumer still receives 110 unwanted e-mails a month. Some consumers are very upset or even opt out of using e-mail because of spam.

There is a continuing battle between those writing antispam software and the spammers—as soon as a way of blocking it is devised the spammers create a way of thwarting it. Furthermore, blocking or filtering software is an imperfect solution for it lets through about 20 percent of the unwanted e-mail and also might block some legitimate e-mail that the user wants. According to the Pew Internet Project (2003), this erodes confidence in the e-mail system—some 30 percent of e-mail users report a fear that filtering software might be filtering out messages that they want to receive. Furthermore, blocking spam is costly to ISPs and other businesses—estimates are as much as $2 per user per month.

Spam has become such a problem that Congress has made a number of attempts to write laws to outlaw it, but because of the free speech protection in the constitution it has been very difficult to devise a law that will not be struck down in the courts. After several false starts, the Controlling the Assault of Non-Solicited Pornography and Marketing Act (CAN-SPAM Act) was passed and signed in December 2003. According to Sorkin (2003), the CAN-SPAM Act requires unsolicited commercial e-mail messages to be labeled (though not by a standard method) and to include opt-out instructions and the sender's physical address. The law prohibits the use of deceptive subject lines and false headers in such messages and authorizes the FTC to establish a "do-not-e-mail" registry similar to a "do-not-call" list.

FTC chairman Timothy Muris has said that the CAN-SPAM Act will do little or nothing to stem the deluge of spam. The volume of spam has not been reduced, and there are indications that spammers are moving their operations overseas. The FTC has proposed much stronger legislation that recognizes that controlling spam is an international problem.

Intellectual Property Rights

There are a number of definitions of **intellectual property**, but we will use the following: Intellectual property is any product of the human mind, such as an idea, an invention, a literary creation, a work of art, a business method, an industrial process, a chemical formula, a computer program, or a presentation. One can go so far as to say that most of what we class as information is intellectual property, so IT and intellectual property are closely interrelated.

Intellectual property is quite different from physical property. If one sells or gives away something physical you no longer have it, but an idea can be shared without losing it. With the invention of the printing press the widespread sharing of intellectual property became feasible, and succeeding waves of technological development have made sharing easier. With digital representation increasingly becoming the norm, sharing intellectual property has become easy, rapid, and inexpensive.

What property can be owned differs from one society to another. For example, in a communist society individuals cannot own land and the means of production. Many Native Americans had no concept of land ownership. And in many societies today private ownership of intellectual property is uncommon. Even in the United States you cannot own an idea, but only the particular expression of that idea, and others can take that idea and use it in other ways.

Most societies have long recognized that intellectual property is so valuable to society that its creation should be rewarded, so they have copyright and patent laws that grant its creator exclusive ownership rights that allow that person to profit from the creation of the intellectual property. But societies also recognize that eventually intellectual property should be in the public domain, so the ownership rights to intellectual property are granted for only a limited time. Societies differ widely in exactly what is to be protected, how it is to be protected, and for how long. Protection for intellectual property is built into the U.S. Constitution in Section 8 on the powers of Congress, which includes these words: "To promote the Progress of Science and useful Arts, by securing for limited Times to Authors and Inventors the exclusive Right to their respective Writings and Discoveries."

The patent and copyright laws were first devised when printing was the main medium of expression that needed protection. However, IT separates the information from the media that contains it—one can no longer protect information by controlling the piece of paper on which it is written. The development of photography, motion pictures, sound recorders, copiers, computers, CDs, and the Internet have continuously changed the environment, and it has been quite a challenge to adapt these laws to each new reality. This is further complicated by the fact that each country has its own history of laws, which differ from one another. With globalization and the international reach of the Internet the result is a messy situation. We cannot begin to cover all aspects of intellectual property rights in this section of a single chapter, but in the following we will discuss two areas that are currently of great interest—software piracy and digital entertainment piracy.

Software Piracy

Software piracy is a serious problem for the software industry. According to the Business Software Alliance (2003), 39 percent of the business application software installed worldwide in 2002 was pirated, which cost the software industry some $13 billion. It should be noted that despite this loss of revenue the software industry has managed to remain profitable.

The business software piracy rate varied significantly by region, with North America the lowest at 24 percent, Western Europe at 35 percent, Mid East/Africa at 49 percent, Asia/Pacific and Latin America tied at 55 percent, and Eastern Europe leading the pack at 71 percent. In dollar terms the Asia/Pacific region leads with $5 billion, followed by Western Europe at $3.2 billion and North America at $2.3 billion in losses. China was the worst offender, with its piracy rate of 92 percent and its growing economy producing a dollar loss of $2.4 billion in 2002. Although the U.S. piracy rate of 23 was the lowest of any country, that still represents a dollar loss of nearly $2 billion.

The highest software piracy rates are in formerly communist areas where there is no tradition of intellectual property rights. Also, in developing economies there are strong incentives for the government to ignore (or even encourage) software piracy. Software is essential to becoming a modern economy, it is expensive to purchase legally, and foreign exchange resources are scarce, so low-cost domestic copies are a significant advantage to a developing country. China, for example, agrees to crack down on pirated software enough to keep the U.S. government from retaliating with trade sanctions but does as little as it can get by with to keep its promises.

The ownership rights of developers of computer software are protected by both copyrights and patents. One cannot copyright an idea, but one can copyright a specific written expression of that idea, whether it is on paper, magnetic disk, CD, or in some other electronic form. Except for certain "fair use" exceptions, the copyrighted material cannot be copied without the copyright holder's permission. Computer programs can be copyrighted, and that means that they cannot be used without the developer's permission because they must be copied into your computer memory in order to be used. For most software the copyright owner does not sell the software itself, but only the right to use it under certain specified conditions. If the user violates those conditions he is deemed to have violated the copyright.

U.S. copyright laws make it illegal to copy software and use it without the software vendor's permission, and there are severe penalties for violating these laws. Although this is difficult to enforce against individuals, software vendors have become vigilant in prosecuting large companies that have (knowingly or unknowingly) allowed software to be copied. Most well-managed companies have strict policies against copying software, and they check periodically to make sure that an individual's office PC hard drive contains only authorized software. That is why the business applications software piracy rate is so low in the United States. However, individuals can copy software for personal use without much fear of prosecution, so whether one copies software or not depends upon one's ethical position on that issue.

A copyright provides effective protection against software piracy, but it does not prevent someone else from creating another computer program that does the same thing as the copyrighted program. This is where patents come in. A patent on an invention or process gives its creator the exclusive right to the manufacture and use of a new design or method for a limited period of time. One cannot patent laws of nature, natural phenomena, mathematics, or other universal truths. We used to think of patents as protecting the inventors of machines, but in recent years some very strange things have been granted patents: plants, animals, and even genes.

Patenting computer programs has had a controversial history. At first, courts viewed computer programs as algorithms similar to mathematical algorithms that cannot be patented. However, in recent years the U. S. Patent Office has begun to issue patents on computer-implemented processes. For example, Amazon has been issued a patent on "one-click ordering" on the Web: If you are a previous customer, Amazon retrieves a cookie to locate its record containing your name, address, and credit card number, and thus can process your order without you having to reenter that information. That process seems obvious as cookies were being widely used for many similar purposes, but nevertheless the patent was issued. Amazon sued Barnes and Noble over infringement of that patent, but in March 2002 that suit was settled out of court so that patent has not yet been tested in court.

As this is being written, the European Union Parliament is considering modifications to the European Union's patent law that would not allow patents on business methods such as the Amazon "one-click ordering" patent. According to Newman (2003):

> *Under the European law, software companies would obtain exclusive rights only for programs that demonstrate novelty in their "technical contribution." This is a stricter standard than is required in the U.S.*
>
> *Companies, for example, would be allowed to patent a new software algorithm for handwriting recognition. But they wouldn't receive a patent for the general idea that handwriting could be digitally recognized. Regular computer programs, such as word processing software, are excluded.*

However, today computer programs and basic business processes are copyrighted by the thousands by such software giants as Microsoft Corp. and IBM. IBM was issued over 3,000 patents in 2002, a substantial number of which were computer program patents. This has created a great deal of controversy because it might well kill off small software developers who do not have the resources to find their way through the maze of what is allowable and what is not or to defend against infringement lawsuits. Many persons contend that if this situation continues, society will suffer because innovation will be limited and monopoly power will be encouraged.

Digital Entertainment Piracy

Digital entertainment piracy is an arena in which the technology and the laws are changing so rapidly that what we write now is likely to be obsolete by the time it is read. However, because this is likely to remain a very active issue we will attempt to summarize the situation as of the end of 2003.

Growing volumes of digital music, digital videos, and digital movies are being pirated worldwide. In developing countries most of this piracy is carried out by copying or counterfeiting CD and DVD disks and cassette tapes. The International Federation of the Phonographic Industry (IFPI) represents the international recording industry. According to IFPI (2003), in 2002 28 percent of all CDs sold worldwide were pirated and music piracy was a $4.3 billion industry. The IFPI claims that this lucrative piracy is financing both organized crime and international terrorism.

The CD piracy rate varies widely from country to country, reaching 99 percent in Paraguay, 90 percent in China, 85 percent in Indonesia, and 65 percent in Russia, while in the United States, Japan, and most of Western Europe the piracy rate is less than 10 percent. In terms of dollar value, the leading pirate markets are in China ($400 million), Russia ($240 million), Brazil ($215 million), Indonesia ($205 million), and Mexico ($175 million).

Internet File Sharing

In the United States pirate CDs are widely available at flea markets, small shops, and on the street, but the major problem for the recording industry is file sharing on the Internet. Sharing entertainment files on the Internet has become an emotional and contentious issue, with some claiming that it is leading to the demise of the entertainment industry as we know it, some saying that the industry can continue to prosper and even profit from downloading. Still others rejoice and say "good riddance" (see the text box entitled "It's All FREE!").

The Recording Industry Association of America (RIAA) has launched a crusade against sharing music on the Internet, undertaking a publicity and educational campaign, lobbying lawmakers for help, and instituting legal action against those trafficking in copyrighted files. The RIAA claims that primarily because of illegal downloading from 1999 throught 2002, unit shipments of recorded music in the United States fell by 26 percent and sales revenues were

IT'S ALL FREE!

James Phung saw *Phone Booth* before you did. What's more, he saw it for free, in the comfort of his private home-screening room. Phung isn't a movie star or a Hollywood insider; he's a junior at the University of Texas who makes $8 an hour at the campus computer lab. But many big-budget Hollywood movies have their North American premieres in his humble off-campus apartment. Like millions of other people, Phung downloads movies for free from the Internet, often before they hit theaters. *Phone Booth* will fit nicely on his 120-GB hard drive alongside *Anger Management*, *Tears of the Sun*, and about 125 other films, not to mention more than 2,000 songs. "Basically," he says, "the world is at my fingertips."

Phung is the entertainment industry's worst nightmare, but he's very real, and there are a lot more like him. Quietly, with no sirens and no breaking glass, your friends and neighbors and colleagues and children are on a 24-hour virtual smash-and-grab looting spree, aided and abetted by the anonymity of the Internet. Every month, they—or is it we?—download some 2.6 billion files illegally, and that's just music. That number doesn't include the movies, TV shows, software and video games that circulate online. First-run films turn up online well before they hit the theaters. Albums debut on the Net before they have a chance to hit the charts. Somewhere along the line, Americans—indeed, computer users everywhere—have made a collective decision that since no one can make us pay for entertainment, we're not going to.

[Grossman, 2003]

down 14 percent. The RIAA quotes surveys that show that more than three times as many 12-to-24 year-olds will download a song they like than will buy the song. According to Berman (2004), speaking for the recording industry:

> *Internet piracy means lost livelihoods and lost jobs, not just in record companies but also across the entire music community. For those who think the 10.9 percent first half sales fall in 2003 does not speak for itself, look at the other evidence. Artist rosters have been cut, thousands of jobs have been lost, from retailers to sound engineers, from truck drivers to music journalists. Surveys in five major markets—USA, Canada, Germany, Japan and the UK—show that Internet copying and file-sharing is reducing CD sales significantly more than it is promoting them.*

There are many critics of the RIAA position on the impact of sharing music files. Some contend that the downturn in music sales was mainly caused by the economic slump and the decrease in the product's quality. Some contend that price increases and the strategy of forcing the customer to pay for a complete album when he or she wants only one or two of the songs have caused much of the sales fall-off. Some people are just fed up with the major record labels, asserting that they have a long history of freezing out talented artists who are trying to be heard while cheating their chosen performers. Entertainers are split on the issue of downloading, with many artists supporting the RIAA position but many others contending that free downloading gives them exposure that they could not get otherwise.

Swapping music on the Net gained widespread popularity with the advent of Napster. Napster developed software that enabled people to make **MP3** files stored on their computers available to others through a peer-to-peer (P2P) network so that others could download music at no cost. In addition to distributing the necessary software, the Napster site maintained a directory of available songs that facilitated access to a computer containing the desired music so that the MP3 file could be obtained through the Internet. Soon most popular music, whether copyrighted or not, was available for free downloading, and millions of people worldwide were happily taking advantage of this treasure trove of free music.

Downloading free music became so popular on college campuses that many colleges started banning access to Napster on their networks because it was eating up so much bandwidth. On some campuses music downloading accounted for more than 60 percent of the school's traffic on its Internet connection.

Quickly the major record labels sued Napster in federal court on the grounds that it was violating their copyrights. Napster defended itself by arguing that it did not have any of the music on its server and did not even know what files were being sent from one user to another through the Internet. However, after a good deal of legal maneuvering the judge ordered Napster shut down by ruling that by maintaining the directory of available songs on its server Napster was clearly involved in the copyright violations.

That, of course, was not the end of sharing music on the Web. Sharman Networks developed P2P software that provided the same service as the Napster software and started the Kazaa service to distribute the file-sharing software. The Kazaa software did not use a central directory. Instead, local directories were available on the computers of users with fast connections, called supernodes. That approach worked so well that by 2003 some 143 million copies of the Kazaa software had been downloaded and the volume of free music files being downloaded on the Web continued to grow.

So the major labels sued Sharman networks, again on the grounds of copyright violations. Although Sharman is headquartered in Australia and incorporated in the Pacific island nation of Vanuatu, U.S. courts have ruled that Sharman must stand trial in California. As of this writing this case is still in litigation, and Kazaa is still in full operation.

No matter how this trial turns out, it will not end free downloading of copyrighted material because other sites and other technologies will spring up. So in 2003 the RIAA began another approach—filing lawsuits against those making large quantities of copyrighted music available through a P2P network. These individuals are identified through a complex process. The RIAA uses software that scans the public directories available to users of the P2P network. That gets the user computer's Internet address, which allows the RIAA to identify the user's ISP. The Digital Millennium Copyright Act relieves the ISP of legal responsibility for what the user transmits over the Internet, but it has a provision that allows the RIAA to easily subpoena the names and addresses of suspected users so that they can be contacted and lawsuits can be filed. This provision of the act is currently being challenged in court.

Such a lawsuit is not a trivial matter, for U.S. copyright law provides penalties of up to $150,000 for each violation. So many individuals are involved in this activity that it would be impossible to file lawsuits against even a small fraction of them, so the RIAA's strategy is to file a number of highly publicized lawsuits as a scare tactic and thereby substantially reduce the amount of music being downloaded (see the sidebar entitled "Early Downloading Lawsuits"). Most of those sued have settled out of court for

EARLY DOWNLOADING LAWSUITS

Twelve-year-old Brianna LaHara was frightened to learn that she was among the hundreds of people sued yesterday by giant music companies in federal courts. "I got really scared. My stomach is all turning," Brianna said. "I thought it was OK to download music because my mom paid a service fee for it. Out of all people, why did they pick on me?"

Those sued included a working mom, a college football player, and a 71-year-old grandpa who blamed his grandkids for the legal mess.

[Adapted from the Fox News Channel and Wired News on the Internet, September 9 and 10, 2003]

a few thousand dollars, but the message has been sent that those who share copyrighted music on the Web are not anonymous and might be subjected to expensive penalties. This might be working, as there are indications that the volume of downloading has steadily decreased during the first 3 months of this campaign. However, suing 12-year-olds and grandfathers has not endeared the music industry to its customers and the general public.

The entertainment industry is hoping that these lawsuits will motivate increasing numbers of people to sign up and use legal for-pay Internet sites such as Apple Computer's iTunes, Pressplay, Listen.com, and BuyMusic.com. Stay tuned and see how all this turns out!

Ethical Questions

It seems clear that large numbers of people are comfortable illegally downloading copyrighted entertainment on the Internet, at least as long as they don't get caught. A survey by Public Affairs (2003) of 1,000 U.S. college and university students found the following about student attitudes and behavior:

- 69 percent of the students surveyed have downloaded music from the Internet, and three-fourths of the downloaders admitted to never paying for the music they download. Thus, over half of the students surveyed had been downloading music and never paid for any of it.
- Only 26 percent of the students download movies, but 80 percent of those that do say they never pay for them.
- Only 24 percent of the students said that it is always wrong to pirate music and movies, 55 percent said it depends on the circumstances, and 21 percent said it is always all right.

People give many reasons why they think it is OK to download copyrighted music off the Internet. Consider a few examples of their rationales:

- I'm not stealing anything because people are giving it to me.
- The music industry is so corrupt that I just want to get back at them.
- I wouldn't buy this anyway, so I am not taking any revenue away from the copyright holders.
- The albums are ridiculously expensive, and I resent having to buy an entire album to get the one or two songs I really want.
- I can't find the songs of the lesser-known artists in the stores, so I have to get them off the Web.
- It is easy and risk-free, so I never even think about it one way or another.

To analyze the ethics of downloading copyrighted software, let us first consider the deontologism approach where the intent of the action determines whether is it ethical or not. Most such frameworks conclude that taking something of value from others without their consent is unethical. For example, downloading someone's music that they are trying to sell violates Kant's categorical imperative to never treat someone as a means to an end (your own pleasure).

The consequentialism approach is not so straightforward. A utilitarian analysis requires all the persons who can be affected by the action to be identified, the result of the action on each person to be determined and quantified, and then the total result to be added up to determine if the benefits outweigh the harm. In the case of someone downloading an album instead of buying it, one can argue that the money that the downloader saves equals the money the copyright holder loses, so the downloading is ethically neutral. That is not a very convincing argument, for it would justify stealing anything. Furthermore, that argument does not consider the wider implications of such action. If everyone downloaded their music without paying for it, the music industry would cease to exist, the artists would not be employed, and little recorded music would be available. Most music lovers would consider that to be a bad outcome, so the action would be unethical.

In the case of downloading music that you would not purchase, the artist has not forgone any income and the downloader has had the pleasure of hearing the music. If you extend that to the point where everyone downloaded only that music that they would not otherwise purchase, the copyright holder still has forgone no income and the industry would still be profitable, so one might conclude that that action would not be unethical. However, that is a slippery slope because it is so easy to assume that you would not have purchased the music, although you would have if you could not download it for free.

ACCURACY

As mentioned earlier, comprehensive data about individuals are contained in numerous large databases that are used to make important decisions that affect the individual. Unfortunately, much of this data is highly inaccurate or incomplete, or both. When these erroneous data items are used to make decisions about individuals, the results might have serious consequences for those unfortunate persons.

National Crime Database

For example, the FBI's National Crime Information Center maintains an integrated, real-time transaction processing and online fingerprint-matching database that includes data about suspected terrorists, fugitives, outstanding arrest warrants, missing people, gang members, and stolen vehicles, guns, or boats. This system handles millions of transactions a day while serving law enforcement officials at all levels by providing information on people who have been arrested or who have arrest warrants outstanding, stolen cars, and other items. It is used at airports to screen people who are boarding airplanes. Many police agencies have terminals in police cars so that when a police officer stops a car for a traffic violation, the officer can check whether the driver is potentially dangerous or the car is stolen before approaching the car.

Input into this database comes from thousands of agencies all over the country. The law establishing this system required the FBI to ensure that the information was "accurate, relevant, timely and complete." However, despite all reasonable efforts to keep this data accurate, inevitably information that should be in the system will not be there and obsolete or erroneous information will be included. There have been reports of innocent citizens being shot because they made some motion that the police officer, influenced by information from the computer indicating that the car's occupant was dangerous, interpreted as reaching for a concealed weapon. In other cases police officers have been injured because the computer did not indicate that the car's occupant was dangerous. Also, financial institutions and nursing homes use the FBI system to screen people for employment, and erroneous information can lead to a person being denied a job.

In March 2003 the Justice Department eliminated the requirement that the FBI ensure the accuracy of the information in the National Crime Information Center system. To justify the change, the Justice Department said that the previous restrictions on the information "would limit the ability of trained investigators and intelligence analysts to exercise their judgment in reporting on investigations and impede the development of criminal intelligence necessary for effective law enforcement." It is likely that more innocent people will be identified as criminals than in the past.

Credit Bureau Databases

The three large credit reporting services in the United States—Experian (formerly TRW), Equifax, and TransUnion LLC—maintain huge databases on 90 percent of American adults. These services purchase computer records from banks and other creditors and from public records of lawsuits, tax liens, and legal judgments. These records are compiled and then sold to credit grantors, rental property owners, employers, insurance companies, and many others interested in a consumer's credit record. If these records are not accurate, an individual might be unable to get a credit card or a loan to buy a home or an automobile or might even be denied employment. Unfortunately, a person usually does not know what is in his or her report until something bad happens, and then it is the individual's responsibility to go through a long and involved process to remove the erroneous information.

Credit report information is notoriously inaccurate. According to a study by PIRG (1998):

- Twenty-nine percent of the credit reports contained serious errors—false delinquencies or accounts that did not belong to the consumer—that could result in the denial of credit;
- Forty-one percent of the credit reports contained personal demographic identifying information that was misspelled, long-outdated, belonged to a stranger, or was otherwise incorrect;
- Twenty percent of the credit reports were missing major credit, loan, mortgage, or other consumer accounts that demonstrate the creditworthiness of the consumer;
- Twenty-six percent of the credit reports contained credit accounts that had been closed by the consumer but incorrectly remained listed as open;
- Altogether, 70 percent of the credit reports contained either serious errors or other mistakes of some kind.

Maintaining better accuracy would be costly to the credit bureaus and raise the cost of credit checks to those who depend upon them to make decisions about the creditworthiness of individuals. Credit bureaus and the businesses that provide them with information want to minimize costs and therefore do not spend any more than the law

program along with modern crisis-management facilities and tracking devices. Clarion–Milwaukee's strategy to differentiate itself from its competitors emphasized the importance of using modern information technology in combination with a caring staff attitude. Because the school typically dealt with potentially dangerous students, the ability to contact support staff and access student records quickly was considered essential to effective performance.

As operational expenses and capital requirements continued to rise, the Milwaukee school became more dependent on increased *per diem* charges and higher enrollments to balance the budget. During the 2002–2003 fiscal year (ending June 30, 2003), Clarion charged placement agencies or families $100.50 per day for each student enrolled in the regular treatment program. For students enrolled in the ISIS program, a premium care/rehabilitation facility opened in 2001 for students whose next option was a juvenile delinquency institution, the charge was $167.00 per day. Total *per diem* revenue for the 2002–2003 fiscal year was budgeted at $3,891,000, but enrollment had been running well ahead of projections. As a result, there was considerable interest in expanding the school's capacity in fiscal 2003–2004.

All capital expenditures were allocated from the Capital Assets Fund of Clarion, Inc. Each division competed with the other operations for access to this fund. Clarion–Milwaukee was proposing five major projects for fiscal year 2003–2004: the purchase of 32 more personal computers, programming upgrades of some key applications software, a hardware upgrade for the IBM AS/400 computing system, the remodeling of a living unit to expand the ISIS program, and the construction of a cottage that would accommodate 10 additional students for the regular program. Young would have responsibility for managing each of these major capital projects. All capital projects exceeding $25,000 had to be approved by the board of directors of Clarion, Inc. The board was known for reviewing each capital request carefully.

Information Systems (IS) Planning

With labor costs representing 68 percent of the school's operating budget, Young considered computerization as one way to increase staff effectiveness and productivity in accessing information and to improve communications among the staff. He did not emphasize using automation to reduce costs directly (e.g., by reducing staff). On the recommendation of Young in January 1998, the Clarion, Inc., board of directors approved the purchase of an IBM AS/400 computer and the associated applications software. Because Clarion, Inc., had many demands for its capital, Young knew that capital expenditures for computers were considered difficult to justify, especially if the purchases were not connected directly to a new revenue stream. Nevertheless, members of the board of directors exhibited interest in the new information systems project even before the approval in 1998.

As Young began to describe the capabilities of the system in detail, the board's interest rose even further. Likewise, staff from all treatment programs and support areas expressed enthusiasm for the proposed benefits. Based mostly on the treatment staff's support, the board approved the project.

The stated objective of the hardware and software investment was to save staff time by using electronic communications to accelerate routine tasks and to provide easier, faster access to computerized student data. Critical functions at the time were considered to be electronic mail, student database access, analysis of the data held in the student database, and appointment/room scheduling. Applications software was purchased for each of these functions as well as support packages for accounting and human resources. This AS/400 system supplemented the 60 personal computers that had been purchased from 1993 to 1997.

In order to synchronize implementation of the 1998 computer acquisition project with the needs of all departments, the Clarion board of directors had also approved a long-range organization plan for the Milwaukee Division. A joint effort between board members and staff from all levels had led to the adoption of the division's first 5-year plan. This comprehensive plan focused on both administrative and treatment issues and was also approved in January 1998.

Clarion–Milwaukee's Computer System

While no longer considered by some as state of the art, Clarion–Milwaukee's computer network was custom-designed for its application needs in 1998. The distributed system was networked campus-wide and included 60 linked personal computers and attached laser printers. Each personal computer was provided with the latest version of Microsoft Windows as well as the Microsoft Office applications software suite. According to the IBM sales representative, the network architecture allowed for 40–50 more personal computers to be added over time. Additional AS/400 computers could also be networked to provide peer-to-peer communications if more central computing power was needed at the school.

Clarion–Milwaukee's AS/400 computer was located in the front office building, where 14 personal computers were also located. (See Exhibit 1.) The primary system console—used for initial program loads and file backups by Jean Baker (the senior bookkeeper who worked for Young)—and Clarion–Milwaukee's PBX unit (for the telephone system) were also located in the front office. The "white house," where the offices of the assistant to the superintendent and the controller were located, housed 10 personal computers as well.

The education center contained all of Clarion–Milwaukee's classrooms and was by far the largest building on campus. Twenty-four personal computers were available in a pool in the staff lounge of the center for teachers and the education

EXHIBIT 1
Campus Computing Network
The Clarion School for Boys, Inc., Milwaukee Division

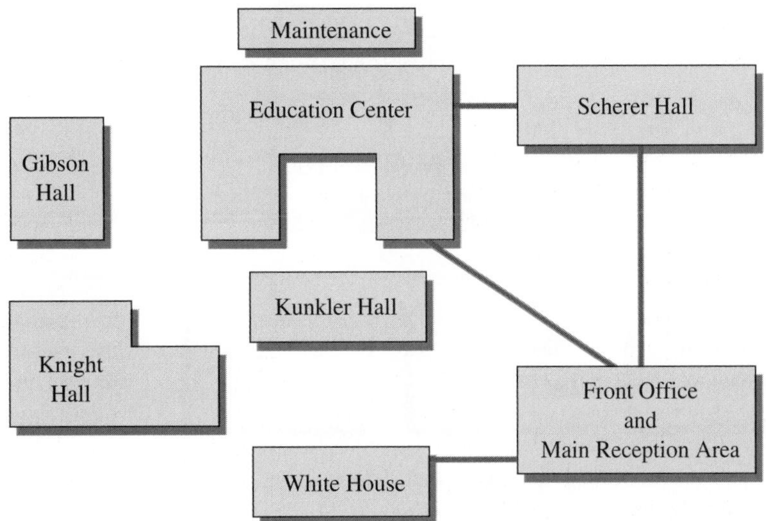

supervisor, who also shared these systems with personnel who worked under the supervisor of services and other staff who worked in the east wing of the center.

The ISIS treatment program was located in Sherer Hall. Twelve personal computers were available in a community cubicle office environment for shared use by treatment and support staff. The Knight, Gibson, and Kunkler Hall dormitories (that could each house up to 45 students) were not equipped with computers, nor were the maintenance facilities. The proposed addition would place personal computers in each of the dormitories for student use. None of the computers at Clarion–Milwaukee had Internet access for fear that residents might access inappropriate materials.

The Organization of Clarion–Milwaukee Division

Exhibit 2 shows the organizational chart for Clarion–Milwaukee. The duties of each unit are described as follows:

Social Services Department. The social services department is responsible for ensuring that those under care receive the appropriate clinical treatment. Because of the involvement of this department with the boys and their placing agencies as well as the wide variety of treatment options, access to the treatment files as well as e-mail, mail routing, and dictation is extremely important. The supervisor of social services functions as department head and is a member of the administrative council. She is also a member of the institutional treatment team.

Social services counselors handle direct counseling and casework functions, enter various progress data, and serve as members of the institutional treatment team and unit treatment teams. Most of the documents and reports that are the responsibility of the unit treatment teams require user data entry and report generation on the part of counselors.

Program Department. The program department is responsible for the group living environment, activities such as crisis intervention, recreation, and special events of the treatment program. Staff members in this department supervise part-time employees within their treatment area (child-care workers, recreation workers, and program aides). One lead program supervisor functions as the primary department head and needs access to computer treatment data and all other information resources. Seven associate program supervisors share direct supervisory responsibility for the child-care and recreation data.

Education Department. The education department is responsible for the operation of Clarion–Milwaukee's comprehensive year-round education program. Because the education department coordinates its activities with the program department, effective communication between these departments is critical. The education supervisor functions as the principal for the school. She is a member of the administrative council and the institutional treatment team. Within this department 20 teachers, assisted by teachers' aides, provide instruction to the boys in a regular classroom environment. Some teachers have telephones while others do not. Most communication is through direct contact and written memos.

Transition Department. The transition department is responsible for the treatment and care of twenty boys enrolled in Clarion–Milwaukee's "transitional living" program. In most respects,

EXHIBIT 2
Organizational Chart
The Clarion School for Boys, Inc., Milwaukee Division

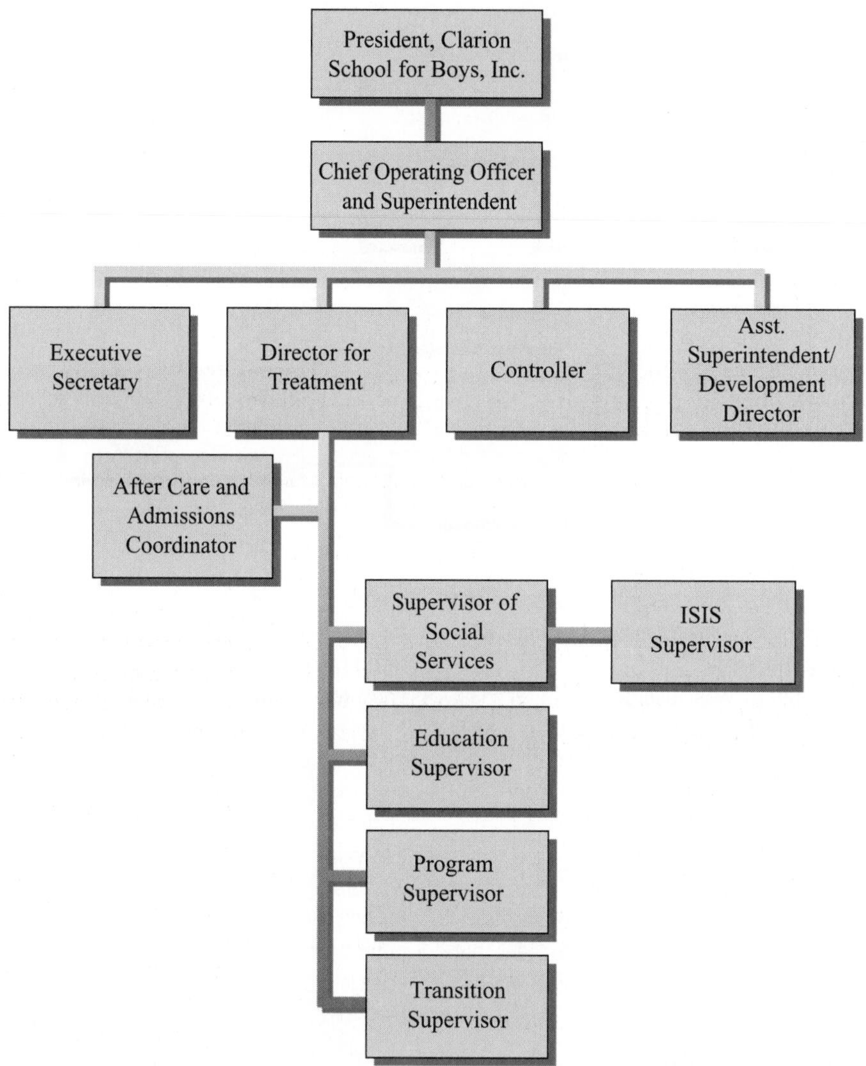

the transition program is a separate treatment entity with its own supervisory, counseling, and care staff, but most supplementary functions are still performed by main campus personnel. The transition supervisor serves as the department head and is on the institutional treatment team and the administrative council.

ISIS Department. The ISIS department was created in response to the development of the ISIS rehabilitation program. The ISIS department reports to the supervisor of social services but has its own program supervisor. ISIS social service counselors perform some of the same functions as their counterparts in the regular program. Certain treatment needs require computer access to specialized treatment data.

Development Department. The development department is responsible for all human resource issues and a variety of other tasks, including the fund-raising efforts and public relations of Clarion–Milwaukee Division. The development director also serves as assistant to the superintendent. This department has access to the AS/400-based human resources data. The director is a member of the administrative council.

Business Department. The business department performs purchasing, information systems, and financial control functions as well as all accounting and treasury functions. The controller, who also assumes overall responsibility for finance, leads the department. The head bookkeeper reports to the controller and spends about one-quarter of her time performing system operator responsibilities. Typical daily tasks include answering users' questions and performing file backups for the AS/400. The controller is also responsible for the housekeeping and maintenance departments. Neither of these departments is tied into the computer network.

Evaluating the Current System

Four years after installation, Young thought that the new computing system should be evaluated. During a staff meeting in November 2002, Young commented that he thought the decentralized campus-wide IS architecture was "leading edge" for schools like Clarion. He viewed the network as an advantage Clarion–Milwaukee had over other schools providing similar services. Young also mentioned the pride with which the board of directors still spoke when discussing the system. He then mentioned that he would like to conduct an evaluation. No one in the meeting objected.

Following his comments, Young raised the question, "What are your opinions of the system?" A sampling of the answers follows.

> We use e-mail to distribute weekly teaching plans to our aides.
>
> —*Teacher*

> We put the whole report card process on the system. Each teacher can input grades from a terminal—it saves a lot of time since the cards don't have to go to each instructor individually.
>
> —*Education Supervisor*

> I recently talked with an old classmate of mine who is using a computerized database to store addresses for frequent mailings. He addresses envelopes through the printer in a fraction of the time it used to take. I send a lot of mail to local businesses every month. Can we do that on the system?
>
> —*Executive Secretary*

> We had two programmers working for us at my last school. They would ask us about our needs in admissions and would customize software that we licensed. I enjoyed using the system since I helped design the applications. Why don't we have that kind of help?
>
> —*After Care and Admissions Coordinator*

> Since I just joined the Clarion staff about a month and a half ago, I'm not sure what is available on the system. We used computers extensively at my university. Are there training sessions offered so I can learn more about the system?
>
> —*Associate Program Supervisor for Activities and Honor Jobs*

Following the staff meeting, Young spent some time trying to determine how he could prove that the current system really was an advantage to Clarion–Milwaukee. Although it was clear that the system had potential, his inquiry showed it was not getting the level of use he had envisioned. Young realized he faced a challenge in convincing his boss of the need for any change in the current system. Superintendent McHardy had always been hesitant to incorporate any new technology into the school's operations. Young once overheard McHardy mention to a board member that he felt that "computer technology and the treatment of troubled boys just don't mesh."

A New Long-Range IS Plan

In December 2002, McHardy called Young into his office, and said,

> John, I'm hearing that you're asking questions about the computer system. Your inquiry matches my concerns about the way we are managing our information system—or should I say not managing it? From what I can tell, few people on Clarion–Milwaukee's staff fully understand how our current systems are functioning and what capabilities are available. Furthermore, we have only sketchy ideas of what our IS objectives should be over the next few years—and most of those are probably only in your head.

Young nodded in agreement, as if he truly had a vision of Clarion–Milwaukee's IS strategy. McHardy continued,

> We've also got to get a handle on the cost situation. Are you aware that we have spent more than $80,000 on hardware and software maintenance agreements alone in the last 12 months? I want you to really dig into the information systems area so you can include a long-range information systems plan for the Clarion board of directors next June along with your regular business plan and budget presentation. Can you do it?

In mid-January 2003, Young formed the Information Systems (IS) Task Force to help develop a long-range IS plan. Besides Young, the six-member task force included Christopher Larson, director for treatment; Brian Thomas, assistant to the superintendent; Ann Lyman, supervisor of social services; Lara Kirk, education supervisor; and Michael Todd, program supervisor. As indicated on the organization chart in Exhibit 2, the task force was composed primarily of department-level management.

At its first meeting, Young defined the objectives of the IS Task Force—to explore the IS needs of Clarion–Milwaukee employees and determine what enhancements (if any) should be made to the AS/400 system and software so that it would better fulfill the staff's mission-critical requirements. At the meeting, Young suggested that task force responsibilities would require only minimal time commitment by the staff. He told the group simply "to keep your ear to the ground and listen for needs that are not being met."

An IS Assessment

By their mid-February 2003 meeting, the IS Task Force members had not developed a list of new needs. Instead, they reported that they had received substantial informal input from staff indicating that the current system was not living up to expectations. In an effort to identify the root causes of these disappointments, the task force decided to conduct a staff survey with the goal of understanding the most common complaint—the lack of communications throughout the organization and the failure of the AS/400 to remedy the situation. The survey was distributed by Young's office during March 2003. Some responses were not received until a full month later. Results of the survey are shown in Exhibit 3.

An initial review of the results of the IS Task Force's survey indicated that personal contact was seen by the respondents as the most important form of communication among staff at Clarion–Milwaukee. Second was the telephone system. Third

EXHIBIT 3

Information Systems Survey Results
The Clarion School for Boys, Inc., Milwaukee Division

Mechanisms for Communication

Type	Frequency
Large formal staff gatherings	
General staff meetings	One per year, or when there was a major crisis
Convocations	Three per year
Institutional treatment team meetings	1–2 hours, once per week
In-service training sessions	One per month
Large informal staff gatherings	
Weekday lunches	Most staff were required to eat with the students
Holiday parties and banquets	Five per year
Small formal staff gatherings	
Unit treatment team meetings	One or two per week
Administrative Council meetings	One per week
Departmental meetings	One per week
Teachers' meetings	Every weekday morning
Supervisory sessions	Approximately one per month
Performance reviews	Annual, with supervisor
Scheduled one-on-one meetings	Various
Long-range planning committee meetings	Four per year
Other informal staff gatherings	
Teachers' lounge discussions	
Work space area conversations by coffee machine and mailboxes	
Service staff's break room conversations	
Unscheduled one-on-one meetings	
"Parking lot" conversations	
Written communication	
Scrap notes	Notes of all shapes and sizes, no format
Memos	A standard 4-copy form, many per day
Weekly treatment services calendar	4 to 6 pages
Special request forms	Various requests
Minutes of formal meetings and supervisory sessions	1 to 6 pages
The Clarion Record	5 to 10 page quarterly internal report of the corporation
Semester calendar	20 to 26 pages three times per year
Financial statements	6 pages issued monthly
Departmental one-year goals	2 to 6 pages annually
Annual audit	10 to 12 pages annually
Five-year plan	40 to 60 pages, updated annually

EXHIBIT 3 (*Continued*)

Summary of Detailed Data Analysis

For each of the following questions, the survey question (as it appeared on the questionnaire) precedes the summary analyses.

Question: What information sources do you rely on most to accomplish your daily job tasks?

	Direct	*Telephone*	*Written*	*Computer*	*Other*	*Total*
Responses	32	11	6	8	0	57
Percent (rounded)	56%	19%	11%	14%	0%	100%

Data from the above question displayed by job classification (percent rounded):

	Direct	*Telephone*	*Written*	*Computer*	*Total*
Treatment	65%	15%	10%	10%	100%
Management/Administration	67%	11%	11%	11%	100%
Instructional	30%	20%	10%	40%	100%
Clerical	0%	70%	0%	30%	100%
Social Services	80%	0%	20%	0%	100%

Question: Which of the following information resources would you most like to use more?

	Direct	*Telephone*	*Written*	*Computer*	*Other*	*Total*
Responses	8	5	5	19	0	37
Percent (rounded)	22%	14%	14%	51%	0%	100%

Data from the above question displayed by job classification (percent rounded):

	Direct	*Telephone*	*Written*	*Computer*	*Total*
Treatment	24%	24%	24%	28%	100%
Management/Administration	10%	0%	10%	80%	100%
Instructional	50%	0%	0%	50%	100%
Clerical	0%	25%	0%	75%	100%
Social Services	0%	0%	50%	50%	100%

Question: Which of the following computing functions have you used? (Select more than one if necessary.)

"Percent of respondents" designates percent of respondents who indicated the specific answer for this question if they indicated at least one answer for this question. "Percent of all" indicates the percent of responses as a portion of all Clarion employees.

	E-mail	*Database Entry*	*Database Query*	*Calendaring*	*Spread-sheet*	*Accounting*
Responses	36	32	23	7	3	10
Percent of respondents (rounded)	80%	71%	51%	16%	7%	22%
Percent of all (rounded)	28%	25%	18%	5%	2%	8%

EXHIBIT 3 (*Continued*)

Question: How much formal training have you had on the computer system?

"Percent of respondents" designates percent of respondents who indicated the specific answer for this question if they indicated an answer for this question. "Percent of all" indicates the percent of responses as a portion of all Clarion employees.

	None	*Demo*	*1–3 hr.*	*4–7 hr.*	*8–16 hr.*	*17–32 hr.*	*32+ hr.*
Responses	2	5	11	7	7	6	7
Percent of respondents (rounded)	4%	11%	24%	16%	16%	13%	16%
Percent of all (rounded)	2%	4%	9%	5%	5%	5%	5%

Question: Circle either I am satisfied or dissatisfied with the amount of training I have received.

"Percent of respondents" designates percent of respondents who indicated the specific answer for this question if they indicated an answer for this question. "Percent of all" indicates the percent of responses as a portion of all Clarion employees.

	Satisfied	*Dissatisfied*
Responses	18	25
Percent of respondents (rounded)	42%	58%
Percent of all (rounded)	14%	20%

Question: How much time do you spend working on a PC or the central system on the average each day?

(For this question, answers were compiled only by job classification.)

	None	*< 1 hr.*	*1–2 hr.*	*3–4 hr.*	*> 4 hr.*
Treatment	0%	50%	31%	14%	5%
Management/ Administration	0%	31%	38%	15%	15%
Instructional	0%	60%	10%	20%	10%
Clerical	0%	0%	67%	33%	0%
Social Services	0%	90%	10%	0%	0%

on the staff's list was the AS/400's electronic mail system. Most staff members were aware of the communications software products available on the AS/400, but many were not using them. Further down on the list of ways to communicate was reports. Although hundreds of different paper reports were processed regularly, the importance of these types of written communication was perceived as low.

The task force considered the possibility that the AS/400 had not proved as effective as hoped simply because it was not being used extensively by staff. By checking the system logs (an automatic record of system usage generated by the operating system), it was determined that while an employee might have been logged on the system for most of the day, he or she was actively using it less than 30 minutes each day. The task force members were not sure why the system was not being used as expected.

In addition to conducting the survey, task force members allotted time at their own departmental meetings in March 2003 and during one-on-one conversations to solicit responses from other members of the units for which they had primary responsibility. Discussion of these issues was awkward for some of the task force members because they were not well educated in the area of information systems.

Task Force Interviews

Highlights from task force personal interviews helped better define the attitudes of Clarion–Milwaukee's staff. One task force member, Lara Kirk, reported to the committee at its late-March 2003 meeting that she had conducted a group interview with instructors who had used the system for electronic mail. She recalled one teacher saying, "It was great during the first month or two when we could actually find a PC available, but after that, they got so crowded. I don't have time to wait in line." Another added, "I have found PCs available early in the morning, say between eight o'clock and nine, but whenever I try to log on, I get a message telling me the system is not available. I think it says something about backups—whatever that means."

When Kirk pursued these problems, she learned from Jean Baker that the system backup schedule took place each morning between 8:00 and 9:30. When Baker was backing up the system, she specified that no other users could log on.

Christopher Larson also relayed comments from one of his group interview sessions. "We have found that it is easier to use our old file card system to look up student records rather than walk all the way down the hall to the nearest PC to use the system. But I heard the same information is actually available online. I just don't have time to go stand in line and wait to use the system."

Michael Todd reported that although he had thought the clerical staff was using the calendaring software product on the AS/400 to help his associate program supervisors with room scheduling and personal calendar services, they were actually using the functions very infrequently. When he questioned the secretaries during the group interview, they told him that "the associate program supervisors like to keep their own calendars and they never give us enough time to schedule activities ahead of time. We usually end up rushing around trying to find an open classroom or conference room for their needs at the last minute."

Brian Thomas discovered that his assistant and the director of planned giving were using the system less than he had thought as well. "To make a long story short," he said, "no one ever told me what value I would get from the new computer system. I could use a better phone system so I could hold conference calls among potential donors rather than a better computer system. I'm sure I could raise more money if I could put donors in contact with each other one on one. I have heard that we spent a lot of money on the AS/400. Who is using it?"

Young also heard reports that staff members at Clarion–Milwaukee felt defensive when faced by what they perceived as an "interrogation" by their supervisors on the IS Task Force. It was obvious that some employees were sugar coating their answers while others simply avoided giving their opinions.

Obtaining Outside Help

One important result of the task force assessment survey and the individual interviews was the conclusion that the task force needed additional planning assistance from an objective source. At the special request of the task force, Clarion's board of directors approved funding in late April 2003 for Young to hire a consulting firm to assist with his assessment and plan.

In a hurried search for a consulting firm, the IS Task Force selected LTM Consultants, Inc., from among three companies that submitted proposals, largely because LTM had a local office in Milwaukee and had done some work for other divisions of Clarion.

LTM was a growing firm of 47 professionals and 18 support staff members based in Chicago. The firm had offices in six states, and its expertise included accounting, information technology, and general management consulting. It was Young's opinion that LTM would provide the best value to Clarion–Milwaukee for the fees charged. The final engagement letter from LTM is included as Exhibit 4. Young expected LTM to deliver an IS strategic plan for Clarion–Milwaukee by the first week of June 2003. Although Young would assume ultimate responsibility for the recommendations he would deliver to the Clarion board of directors, he considered an outside set of recommendations as well as the task force work critical to his success with the directors in June.

Young spent a full day briefing the three LTM consultants on the history of Clarion–Milwaukee's IS situation, including the results of the recent IS Task Force survey. In his position as controller, Young explained that he was responsible for making sure that major capital investments were paying off. He wanted to know if the system was filling the information needs at Clarion–Milwaukee and which long-term improvements should be made. He also pointed out organizational change issues to LTM that he thought might have affected system usage. For example, Clarion–Milwaukee had grown in 3 years from 90 to 120 students. A number of new positions had been created to take on the extra load. Full- and part-time staff had increased by almost 30 percent, and turnover and absenteeism were very low.

"I'm not sure," Young told the LTM team, "but my biggest challenge may be in selling McHardy that the system was a good investment for Clarion–Milwaukee." He went on to describe a brief discussion he had with McHardy when they bumped into each other on the way to the parking lot one evening. "When I asked Sean's opinion of the AS/400, he said that he himself hadn't found any practical use for the computer system so far besides the word-processing software on his PC (he uses it for his daily to-do lists)." Young recalled McHardy's words, "I don't use e-mail, I just make a phone call or walk over to someone's office." McHardy continued, as he headed for his car, "Sometimes I wonder if our investment was worthwhile, John. I know the Clarion board of directors is counting on you to make sure that Clarion–Milwaukee is getting full value from the system."

Regarding his own concern about use of the current system, Young remembered that his own department had a difficult time with specialized billing needs. Most of the billing was done directly through the system's accounting software, but about 10 percent was first done by hand and then manually entered into the invoicing system as adjustments at the end of a period. Young admitted to the consultants, "If I can't get invoicing to work consistently for my own staff, how can I expect others to be excited about other applications?"

Decision Time

It was 4:35 P.M. on June 9, 2003—one week before his presentation. Knowing he would have to work with his IS Task Force to finalize the report, Young poured himself a cup of coffee and flipped open the consultants' findings, which he had received earlier that day (the report's text is included as Exhibit 5). He read LTM's report with the rigor of a graduate student, hoping

EXHIBIT 4

Engagement Letter from LTM Consultants, Inc.
The Clarion School for Boys, Inc., Milwaukee Division

LTM Consultants
765 Corporate Circle
Milwaukee, WI 51744

April 18, 2003

John F. Young
Controller
Clarion School for Boys, Inc.—Milwaukee Division
Post Office Box 2217
Milwaukee, WI 51740-2217

Dear John:

LTM appreciates the opportunity to work with the Clarion School for Boys, Inc. —Milwaukee Division in identifying critical issues related to its future information systems environment and determining its future systems strategy. The primary objectives of our engagement are to:

- Evaluate the current strengths and weaknesses of Clarion–Milwaukee's information systems.
- Determine the information systems strategy required to achieve Clarion–Milwaukee's short-term and long-term business goals.

In consideration of the importance of this engagement, we have combined the unique talents of LTM consultants from three of our offices. A three-person team of consultants from LTM's Information Technology Group in Milwaukee, the Human Factors Group in Indianapolis, and the Strategy Group in Chicago will ensure that this engagement is approached from both a business and technical solution perspective.

One critical success factor of this project is to quickly gain an in-depth understanding of the needs, issues, and constraints related to Clarion–Milwaukee's information systems environment. Only then can we convert the present functional needs into a broad set of systems requirements and a subsequent strategy.

We estimate this analysis will require approximately four weeks to complete at an estimated cost for professional services of $30,000. Costs for travel and lodging expenses will be billed as incurred. An initial invoice of $20,000 will be issued fifteen days after start-up, and a reconciling invoice will be submitted upon completion of the engagement.

John, we look forward to working with you and the Clarion–Milwaukee School on this important assignment. I can assure you that we will bring the value that will make a difference to your school in the future.

Sincerely,

C. J. VanZant
Carl John VanZant
Vice President

Approved: John F. Young ______ 4/22/03
Clarion School for Boys, Inc. Date

the findings would be a panacea for Clarion–Milwaukee's information systems problems.

Young had intended to make LTM's report the basis of his own report to the board of directors. Now that he had read it, he thought it included some good ideas and suggestions, but it seemed lacking as a long-range IS plan. Young was unsure exactly what he needed to do, but he knew he would be burning a lot of midnight oil during the next few days.

EXHIBIT 5
LTM's Consulting Report
The Clarion School for Boys, Inc., Milwaukee Division

LTM Consultants
765 Corporate Circle
Milwaukee, WI 51744

June 7, 2003

John F. Young
Clarion School for Boys, Inc.—Milwaukee Division
Post Office Box 2217
Milwaukee, WI 51740-2217

Dear John:

LTM has completed our study at Clarion and we submit the enclosed written report per our agreement. As I mentioned to you during our telephone conversation, we would be happy to present our findings to Clarion, Inc.'s Board of Directors meeting in Chicago if you wish.

Please note the four main sections of the report. First, a sampling of comments from Clarion–Milwaukee's staff characterize the general attitude toward information systems (IS). Strengths and weaknesses of the current information system are highlighted. Finally, specific recommendations are presented for improving Clarion–Milwaukee's information system.

As I am sure you will agree, there are many opportunities to improve Clarion–Milwaukee's daily IS operations. We would like to meet with you soon to discuss how LTM can assist you in making our recommendations operational.

Sincerely,

C. J. VanZant

Carl John VanZant
Vice President

Enclosure

Long-Range IS Plan Final Report

Findings in this report are a result of analysis during the last week of April and the first 3 weeks of May 2003. Eighteen person-days were spent on site at the Clarion–Milwaukee school. LTM consultants began with a kickoff meeting that included six department supervisors, three directors, and the superintendent. In this meeting, the scope and purpose of LTM's engagement was defined: to identify critical issues related to

EXHIBIT 5 (*Continued*)

Clarion–Milwaukee's future information system (IS) environment with the goal of defining Clarion–Milwaukee's future IS strategy.

Included in this report is a selection of comments made by Clarion–Milwaukee staff during both formal and informal interactions with LTM consultants. The following six questions were used as a starting point for each interview. A majority of the interview time was devoted to exploring responses to initial questions using follow-up questions.

1. Are there any recommendations you would like to make regarding how the Clarion–Milwaukee school handles information—written, computer, telephone, or direct (face-to-face)?
2. What is the most useful form of information you receive?
3. In what ways do you feel this form of information is vital to your work objectives?
4. What could be done to make Clarion–Milwaukee's information system even more beneficial to your work?
5. Summarize the strengths of the current information system.
6. Are there any additional comments you would like to make regarding future enhancements to Clarion–Milwaukee's information system?

The following interviews were conducted during the first three weeks of the study:

- Six 2-hour two-on-one interviews with department supervisors (two LTM consultants and one supervisor)
- Six 1-hour interviews with the unit directors
- Twenty-three 1-hour two-on-one interviews with nonsupervisory staff

LTM consultants attended the following meetings during the last three weeks of the study:

- Two weekly administrative council meetings (comprised of the nine supervisors and the superintendent)
- One weekly institutional treatment team meeting (comprised of the superintendent, director of treatment services, deputy director of treatment services, supervisor of the program department, associate program supervisors, supervisor of social services, social service counselors, education department supervisor, and transition department supervisor)
- Two scheduled department meetings and four impromptu department meetings
- Five daily teachers' meetings
- One weekly unit treatment team meeting (comprised of one teacher, two members of the child-care workers staff, and a member of the social service staff)

LTM consultants randomly queried seventeen of Clarion–Milwaukee school employees in the halls of the school and in the parking lot by asking questions about their uses of current IS resources at the school. Staff comments were recorded during both formal and informal conversations.

The remainder of this report is divided into four main sections: Sampling of Staff's Comments, Strengths of Clarion–Milwaukee's Information System, Weaknesses of Clarion–Milwaukee's Information System, and Information System Strategy.

Sampling of Staff's Comments

I have been trying to finish this month's books for the last 2 days, but I am having the same problems as last month. The accounts receivable software program is still giving me difficulties. I think I'll just do them by hand again this month.

—*Bookkeeper*

EXHIBIT 5 (*Continued*)

I use the scheduling module all the time for my event scheduling since most of the work I do runs in biweekly cycles. The automatic messages remind me when I have something due.

—Clerical Worker

There was a lot of initial excitement about e-mail, but I haven't heard much about it since then. I know I've been too busy to learn it myself, and I missed the training sessions because of other meetings. The only thing I've heard is that a few of the teachers sent out e-mail to others, but never got a reply. Maybe the interest died down because everyone didn't get training right away.

—Education Supervisor

I'll be honest with you. Although I have been using the system for almost a year now, it is not easy to use. I think my daughter's Mac is much easier.

—Development Staff Member

I remember someone mentioning that there is an inventory management software package we might use for our kitchen supplies, but I haven't checked into it yet.

—Kitchen Manager

In my last job, we used a program on our computer to monitor the progress of our students. It was a custom package written for us by a consulting group. Although it took about 10 months to complete the software, it worked very well for our special needs.

—Transition Counselor

It would help us if we had a reliable system for keeping the student's medical records. Sometimes the note cards get misplaced, and you don't know about it until you really need one.

—Nurse

I just bypass the menu system since it slows me down … especially since I have set up generic templates for all the common reports.

—Secretary

I am responsible for producing the weekly treatment services calendar. Because I am continually making updates, my biggest complaint is that I have to walk down the hall whenever I want to get a printed copy.

—Associate Program Supervisor

Strengths of Clarion–Milwaukee's Information System

Hardware and Software

1. Dictation equipment is used extensively by treatment personnel. This use increases efficiency for both treatment staff and the secretarial staff who transcribe the dictations.
2. Personal computers are used by the controller and the director of development to generate overhead slides for presentations.
3. Software application programs are flexible enough to be useful for both beginners and advanced users.
4. Adequate software documentation manuals are available for users.
5. The AS/400 file transfer product allows data transfer between PC and mainframe units. It allows flexibility for those who use PCs a lot.
6. The AS/400 is expandable in case additional workstations or processors are needed.

EXHIBIT 5 (*Continued*)

Policy and Procedures

1. System backups are done on a daily basis and are well organized.
2. Quarterly preventive maintenance schedules coordinated through IBM representatives are effective.

Staff Perceptions

In general, interviews revealed that most of the staff, although not totally satisfied with Clarion–Milwaukee's information system, felt that the system was likely better than what existed in comparable facilities. Most frequently noted comparisons were with a local mental health facility that is experiencing severe system difficulties.

Weaknesses of Clarion–Milwaukee's Information System

Hardware and Software

1. Resultant quality of dictated memos is largely dependent on the level of experience of the secretary.
2. Some needed software is not available on the AS/400, necessitating use of personal computers for some reporting functions.
3. Self-paced tutorial software is not available for users.
4. A number of users stated that PCs were not available when they needed them late in the day. PCs are used heavily from 3:00 to 5:00 P.M.

Policy and Procedures

1. At least 90 minutes each day of the senior bookkeeper's time is spent running system backups and initial program loads (IPLs). Consequently, others cannot use the system during that time, and Ms. Baker is not available to perform her regular supervisory functions.
2. Requests for report changes are routed through department supervisors to either John Young or Jean Baker. Once each month they are reviewed and reprioritized by Baker and Young. Baker then works on requests according to priority, as time permits. Day-to-day operations require Young or Baker to answer user questions as they come up, which reduces the time they have for their primary responsibilities.
3. Only two individuals have attended college-level computer courses. A formal training schedule does not exist.

Staff Perceptions

1. Administrative council members were given very limited opportunities to provide input for the original computerization project in 1998. Thus, they perceive the current system as incapable of providing for their needs.
2. Direct personal communication has become more difficult as staff size has increased and departmental specialization has evolved.
3. Many of Clarion–Milwaukee's would-be IS users have decided not to use the system because they find it difficult to find an open PC.
4. Secretarial staff use the AS/400 application software more than any other personnel. The AS/400 is regarded by many as only a tool for performing reporting tasks.
5. Staff who use accounting applications have a sense that they are "the shoemaker's children" whose applications receive lowest priority.

EXHIBIT 5 (*Continued*)

Information System Strategy

The following recommendations are arranged in general categories, with more specific suggestions offered in the conclusion:

1. **Establish a permanent staff position for IS management.** It is difficult for a staff member to handle an information system project as a part-time assignment when he or she has a multitude of other responsibilities and projects to oversee at the same time. For this reason, a new manager-level position should be created with primary responsibility to manage Clarion–Milwaukee's information system (including computing networks, personal computers, and telephone systems). Additional responsibility should include evaluation and implementation of IS training needs. The new IS manager should report to the controller and have permanent membership on the long-range planning committee. The individual selected for the IS manager position should have extensive computer science background and information systems experience.
2. **Establish a team approach to planning.** Planning should initially be conducted by a small team with strong leadership, making sure that feedback is obtained from the various user groups in each of the departments. A feedback process should be used to motivate staff toward cooperation and support of IS projects. This feedback can be accomplished by soliciting their input and explaining system benefits so they will develop a sense of ownership. Potential "stakeholders" should also be identified as this process reduces the barriers to change.
3. **Involve and evaluate the entire system when considering all IS projects.** Telecommunications, central computer, and PC decisions should not be made in a vacuum. When IS-related decisions need to be made, Clarion–Milwaukee's entire IS must be considered. The new IS manager's responsibilities should include researching "high-impact" issues. This procedure should be regarded as an integral part of Clarion–Milwaukee's information system evolution. Overall evaluation should include input from experts within each department.

   A formal impact assessment methodology should be established to ensure a comprehensive and consistent evaluation. The methodology should include consideration of the following:

   - What are the attitudes of employees regarding the introduction and use of the new system?
   - How should Clarion–Milwaukee's business practices change as a result of the new system?
   - Should organizational restructuring occur, including changes, additions, or eliminations of staff positions?
   - How much experience does Clarion–Milwaukee have in this particular area?
   - What other current projects or strategic issues could compete with this project?

   Use of a formal impact assessment methodology will allow identification of opportunities with low, medium, and high risk that can be considered when appraising the response to future change. Furthermore, in concert with an evaluation of the entire information system, this technique facilitates development of a rolling, long-range IS plan.
4. **Install a formal approach to IS planning.** A variety of techniques can be used in matters of IS planning. "Critical success factors" and "investment strategy analysis" are common frameworks. Elements of several of these techniques should be combined in structuring planning activities. It is also vital for the Milwaukee superintendent and the Clarion, Inc., board of directors to have proposals that can be judged according to the same criteria in the process of decision making. Although the formal process will

EXHIBIT 5 (*Continued*)

undoubtedly be time-consuming, our experience with IS projects suggests that this practice will benefit the school in the long term by reducing the likelihood of inappropriate projects being implemented. A specific planning framework should include the following features:

A. **Master IS Plan.** A master IS plan involves identification of the school's strategic issues and the development of the planning infrastructure for the future. The master plan is based on an examination of Clarion–Milwaukee's formal mission statement with respect to current strategic emphases. Workshops should be held for staff with the goals of educating them as to the strategic process of IS planning and providing an understanding of broad IS management objectives. All employees at Clarion–Milwaukee should be aware of the necessity to manage all information—including text documents, voice messages, diagrams, and statistics—as valuable corporate assets. Staff should understand that computers, software, written documents, and telephones are not "theirs." Decisions and procedures regarding these assets will be based on the treatment of these elements as "Clarion–Milwaukee Division" resources addressed within the master plan. Staff should also be instructed to identify "critical success factors" vital for accomplishing Clarion–Milwaukee's objectives. This process will link specific task activities to the master IS plan.

B. **Top Management Involvement.** Primary attention should be given to techniques that facilitate top management involvement and support. The superintendent, along with the new IS manager, should play a critical role in long-range IS planning. All future IS planning decisions should also include substantial input from members of the administrative council.

C. **Systems Life Methodology.** A "systems life" methodology is recommended for use on each specific application system. It is also useful for establishing requirements definitions and project timetables. When evaluating new application systems, consideration should be given to the life-cycle stage of each component. Avoid decisions that lead to purchase of an application just prior to the release of a new option. A formal system should be developed that facilitates identification of a software product's evolutionary position with respect to Clarion–Milwaukee's current technology. Only after application systems are characterized within the spectrum of "cutting edge" to "nearing obsolescence" and compared to the Clarion–Milwaukee Division's ability to manage new technology, should tactical decisions be made.

D. **Rolling Timetable.** The master IS plan should include a rolling timetable in order to coordinate various project efforts and make effective IS investment decisions.

5. **Incorporate IS requirements in proposed long-range planning objectives.** Long-range planning (LRP) objectives must include information regarding a standard set of topics relevant to information systems. Each LRP objective should address its potential impact on Clarion–Milwaukee's information system and specifically identify any additional requirements. It is because of the highly integrated nature of IS planning and other long-range planning that the new IS manager will have to work closely with Clarion–Milwaukee's controller.
6. **Establish IS objectives within Clarion–Milwaukee Division's 5-year plan.** As Clarion–Milwaukee's IS planning requirements become more complex, it will be imperative to continually seek out new ways to make strategic decisions. For this reason, Clarion–Milwaukee should include ongoing evaluation of computer-based methodologies, which would increase planning efficiency and integrity, as part of the long-range planning process. The role of IS management must be evaluated and redefined in light of technological changes.

CASE STUDY IV-2

TELETRON, INC.: USING INFORMATION TECHNOLOGY TO TRANSFORM A COMPANY

"Come on in, guys," said Timothy C. Lybrook, founder and chief executive officer of Teletron, Inc., a Bloomington, Indiana, provider of telecommunications expense management services for corporate telecommunications users. It was April 25, 1999, and Teletron was considering the implementation of a new strategy to grow the company from about $10 million in sales to about $100 million, in part through the use of information technology.

"Thanks," replied Robert N. Jonas, director of information technology at Teletron, and Dennis M. Kirin, vice president of client services at the company, simultaneously, as they entered Tim's office.

"We want to show you the plans for the development of Virtual Analyzer and get your approval," said Bob.

"The investment will not be small, but the benefits are huge," said Dennis.

"OK," said Tim. "I am anxious to see your analysis and plan. As you know, this is one of the three legs in the transformation of our company. We gotta get it right."

Expense Management in the Telecommunications Industry

In 1999, there were approximately 6,000 telecommunications providers in the United States. However, only about 45 companies accounted for approximately 95 percent of the dollar value of the telecommunications services provided. The providers signed their customers to various plans or contracts that carried costs for specific services. The providers then invoiced the users each month.

Traditionally, telecommunications invoices from providers were sent to customers on paper—thick stacks of paper for large corporations. Often, these invoices contained internal provider codes that offered little explanation of their exact meaning. Customers were forced to determine what each charge on the invoice was for and to compare the charge to their particular plan or contract. Needless to say, this situation made the process of verifying invoices very time-consuming for the customer. As a result, many corporations merely accepted the invoice as accurate. Even checking invoices sent electronically was very difficult.

Surveys of corporate telecommunications managers often showed major dissatisfaction with the providers' billing practices, especially about errors that seemed "always in the favor of the provider." Most customers believed that these billing overcharges occurred because of poor record-keeping by the provider, complexity of the contracts, inadequate operational support systems at the provider, lack of time by the customer to verify the invoices, and internal miscommunication within either organization. These mistakes were considered by most telecommunications managers to be significant—telecommunications expenses were often rated as the fifth or sixth largest expense item in corporations, and were growing rapidly.

The size and complexity of the telecommunications expense problem increased significantly during the 1990s, and was forecast to grow significantly during the first decade of the new century. Additional services, such as broadband technology, were enabling enterprises to transfer vast amounts of digital information rapidly. In addition, cell phone use by corporate customers grew rapidly during the 1990s and was forecast to grow substantially in the new century as well. Finally, the old voice-centric telecommunications infrastructure was being replaced with new service offerings that combined voice, data, and video using the Internet Protocol (IP).

According to Gartner-Dataquest, an industry tracking firm, total telecommunications spending by the business market was estimated to grow to $175 billion in 2000 and continue to expand rapidly to over $350 billion by 2005. One reason given for this rapid growth was that many corporations recognized that their telecommunications infrastructure was critical for their company's revenue growth. Yet the cost of errors in operating this infrastructure could well be greater than the revenue benefits.

The expense management environment, characterized by numerous service offerings, frequent errors in billing, and multiple telecommunications providers, created a significant opportunity for service firms to assist enterprises in realizing cost savings and operating efficiencies. Most corporate customers did not consider telecommunications expense management to be a core competency. They typically did not possess the time, expertise, and access to the necessary information that would enable them to analyze their telecommunications bills in-house for accuracy or to investigate money-saving opportunities. According to a recent research report, procuring telecommunications services was "a pain for everyone." The researchers concluded that companies of all sizes were unhappy at every stage of the telecommunications procurement process, from ordering to installation to billing.

In the late 1990s, several experts recognized an opportunity for service firms with expertise in telecommunications billing to review complicated invoices from several providers (each with different codes) for accuracy as well as searching for and negotiating the lowest prices and the highest quality service for a corporation. Furthermore, these experts forecast a large incremental market opportunity for such firms that would go beyond traditional outsourcing to provide software tools that would empower enterprises to analyze easily and proactively their telecommunications services.

Company History

In the 1980s, Tim Lybrook was working as a consultant to the resort industry. His business took him to a variety of resort operations across the United States. As part of his work, he reviewed how his clients were spending their money. While reviewing the cost structure of his clients, Tim often noticed inaccuracies in their telephone bills. Resort operators were consistently being overcharged for their telecommunications services, often by as much as 30 percent.

After seeing this situation existing for several customers, Tim wondered if there was a business opportunity there. During 1990–1991, Lybrook investigated several other industries and found that the same problem existed. Companies were routinely overpaying their local, long distance, data, and wireless providers. These overpayments were due to the complexity of the bills, the size of the organizations, the diversity of services, and errors of the service providers. So in 1990 Lybrook incorporated Teletron to assist "companies throughout the United States to reduce their telecommunication expenditures by identifying inefficiencies and errors in their phone bills." He finished a business plan in late 1991, and Teletron started hiring employees in February 1992.

Teletron targeted customers in the United States that spent between $10,000 and $500,000 per month on telecommunications services. An inside Teletron salesperson would call the telecommunications manager, and propose that Teletron audit the company's last 12 months of telecommunications invoices. If Teletron found errors and had them corrected, Teletron would receive 50 percent of the savings. If no savings were found, the company owed Teletron nothing. A typical proposal call went something like:

> Mr. Jones, I am Mary Johnson with the Teletron Corporation. We are a telecommunications expense management firm located in Bloomington, Indiana. In our work with clients, we have discovered that over 95 percent of the telecommunications bills received from carriers or providers contain errors, often in the provider's favor. Have you ever seen that problem? . . . I thought you might have. We provide a no-risk service for our corporate clients—you send us your telecommunications bills for last month. If we find errors in the bills, we will contact the carriers and get them to send the rest of the past year bills. When we correct the errors, you pay us 50 percent of the documented savings. If we don't find anything, you owe us nothing. Therefore, our service is risk-free to you. Would you be interested in talking further?

Teletron then assigned the client to an account manager who in turn often used former telephone company personnel to conduct manual audits of the provider bills. The company maintained a library of relevant telecommunications contracts and tariffs against which the auditors would compare the bills. When errors were found, the Teletron auditor contacted the billing personnel at the telecommunication provider and worked with the provider to adjust the bill. When all the bills were audited, Teletron compiled the savings and invoiced the client for its fee. Teletron personnel also attempted to identify better plans or contracts for their clients. If future savings could be achieved by the client by implementing one of their suggestions, Teletron invoiced the client for a share of the next 12 months of savings.

After the initial engagement with the client, Teletron personnel attempted to build a longer-term relationship with the client, auditing their bills on an ongoing basis. But clients accepted this additional service very rarely. Most client engagements lasted from 6 months to a year. New clients had to be solicited on a continuing basis.

Lybrook considered the core competencies of Teletron to be its ability to interpret telecommunications bills, find errors, compare contracts and tariffs with current invoices, and effectively deal with telecommunications providers. He considered this expertise to apply equally well to the local, long distance, wireless, Internet, and data markets.

Teletron faced strong competition from a few larger firms and hundreds of "mom-and-pop" operations. However, there was no company that held more than 1 percent of the market. Most firms that audited telecommunications invoices were small operations, usually owned by a retired telephone company employee who knew contracts. Others were captives of certain service providers. Likewise, some telecommunications departments of user companies offered to audit the telecommunications invoices of other companies as a way to earn revenue.

Most competitors were privately held. Several of these privately held companies had grown to significant size. They were:

- **Cost Management Consultants:** This company assisted clients in making decisions regarding both energy and telecommunications costs. The company performed both energy and telecommunications invoice audits.
- **Optimizers:** Optimizers helped midsize businesses manage telecommunications expenses via invoice auditing, selecting and integrating telecommunications equipment, providing telecommunications management advice, and negotiating rates for telecommunications needs.
- **Teledata Control, Inc.:** TCI specialized in providing cost control solutions for voice, data, and information services. The company offered invoice auditing among a range of other services. In 1999, TCI had approximately $7 million in revenue and employed 93 people.

Teletron was very successful in its strategy from 1992–1998, amassing over 5,000 clients that ranged from small businesses to Fortune 500 companies. Exhibit 1 contains a map of where Teletron's past and current customers were located in 1999. Exhibit 2 shows a selected list of past and current clients as of December 1998.

In addition to serving many well-known clients, Teletron was generally successful from a financial standpoint, achieving a compounded revenue growth of more than 200 percent from 1992 through1998. In addition, Teletron maintained EBITDA margins on revenue in the 10 to 30 percent range during this period. See Exhibit 3 for the financial results of Teletron during 1992–1998.

Despite the financial success, in 1998 Lybrook began to question whether the company could continue to grow under its current business model. The company experienced over 90 percent yearly customer "churn," requiring a costly ongoing customer acquisition process. As carriers corrected their billing mistakes, many of Teletron's customers felt that they no longer needed Teletron's services. Other customers hired a person for finding billing errors so as to keep 100 percent of the savings rather than splitting the savings with Teletron. In addition to churn, Lybrook recognized that the auditing process was a labor-intensive operation. While the process of searching the contracts for the correct charge for a particular customer could be

EXHIBIT 1
Location of Clients in 1999
Teletron, Inc.

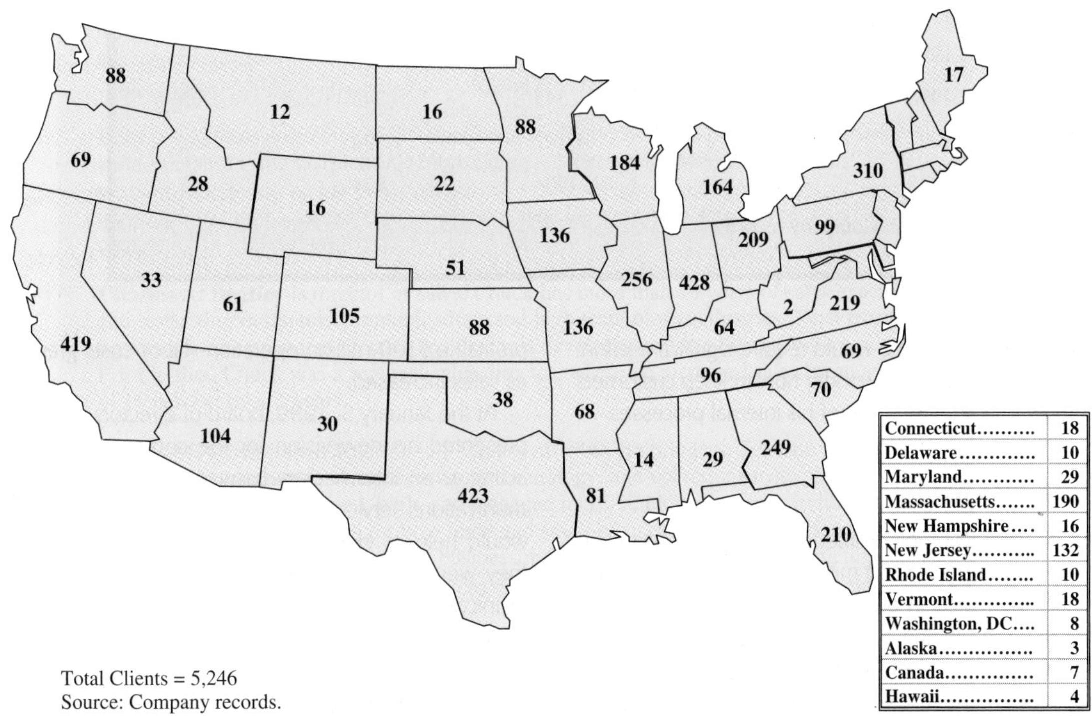

Total Clients = 5,246
Source: Company records.

management, bill management and auditing, accounts payable processing, telecommunications contract negotiations, and project management. Delivery of these services is done via a proprietary Web application, providing real-time visibility into their outsourcing services."

"Hmm . . . very interesting," said Tim. "Two out of these five companies recently received venture capital funding . . . and in large amounts. If we can develop something better, maybe we can go to the VC market as well. But that is for later . . . after we decide if we want to develop this package or not. Tell me, given all the competition out there, is what we are planning any better than the others? Or are we just being a 'me too'?"

"We figured that you might ask that question," replied Dennis. "We were able to inspect each of the competing products. From that process, we prepared a comparison table (Exhibit 5) that shows what each of these offerings can do compared to what we are planning to put in as features and capabilities of Virtual Analyzer. As you can see from the table, Virtual Analyzer will be the best offering in this market. It looks to us that Tenet is our most robust competitor, but it is targeting a different size market and the company is pretty small."

"I'm impressed so far," said Tim. "But let's discuss what you are proposing that Virtual Analyzer actually be able to do. What is the functionality you see in the product?"

"OK," said Bob. "Let's answer that question three ways:"

First, Virtual Analyzer will have six major modules corresponding to the needs we found in the market. They are Client Information Management; Move, Add, and Change Processing; Vendor Invoice Processing and Vendor Invoice Payment; Invoice Analyzer; Rate Optimizer; and Industry Information Management.

Second, Virtual Analyzer provides six primary reporting and analysis capabilities. Let me define each one:

1. Inventory management reports show the exact telecommunications services used at each site, including the exact features, the service provider, and any other tracking information desired by the client.
2. Detail tracking reports provide data on costs by site, service provider, and user-defined categories.
3. Cost allocation reports show cost by site, service, service provider, and user-defined categories. Our clients will use this report to charge back costs to groups within their organizations.
4. Usage allocation reports provide the client with a flexible way to allocate usage to projects or entities in case they want to study the actual cost of a project or organization.

EXHIBIT 5

Comparison of Virtual Analyzer to its Competition Teletron, Inc.

Company	Teletron	Quantum-Shift	Tenet International	Simplexity	Intera	Profit-Line
Service Offerings:						
Cost Management	Yes	Yes	Yes	Yes	Yes	Yes
Bill Optimization	Yes	Yes	Yes	Yes	Yes	Yes
Bill Management	Yes	No	Yes	Likely	Yes	Yes
Full Service	Yes	Some	Yes	Yes	Some	Some
Inventory/Infrastructure Management	Yes	Yes	Yes	No	Yes	Yes
Target Market	Medium to Large	Medium to Large	Small to Medium	Residential, SOHO, Medium, Carriers	Small to Medium	Small to Medium
Internet Capability	Full	Nearly Full	Nearly Full	Some	Nearly Full	Some
Name of Platform	Virtual Analyzer	InterAct	Copyrighted ASP Software	N/A	Smart Partner	Bill Manageme

Source: Company records.

5. Trend analysis reports track usage and cost trends by a variety of dimensions, allowing the user to detect abuses and areas for improved services.
6. Variance analysis reports identify any significant changes in cost or usage measures.

Through these capabilities, our clients will be able to generate many unique and customizable reports. They can create reports based on certain factors they define and produce a report that is specific to their individual needs. The software will reside on our server here in Bloomington. We will be linked electronically to the carriers or providers as well as our clients. As clients update their database, the system will automatically contact the carriers for adjustments. Likewise, when there is a new contract or an invoice for one of our customers, the carrier will send it electronically to us, and Virtual Analyzer will update the customer's database.

Third, there is a more detailed and technical description of the features and capabilities of each major routine in the software being designed. If you are interested, I have a handout on the capabilities of each of the major routines. (See Exhibit 6.)

"Maybe later," replied Tim. "Right now, I'm more interested in exactly how you are planning to bring Virtual Analyzer to market."

EXHIBIT 6
Virtual Analyzer's Features and Capabilities
Teletron, Inc.

Client Information Management—Reports and Analysis

Client Information Management	The Client Information Management System collects, processes, and presents all of a client's telecom information. This includes all of the services they use, who provides the service, locations where the services are used, what equipment is used to provide the service, how much it costs, and how it is used.
Data Acquisition	Cost and usage data are acquired from service providers in three ways: EDI, CD, and from paper bills. EDI is the preferred mechanism and will be used whenever possible. CD data will be used when EDI is not available. Paper bills will be used when they are the only available source.
Data Processing	When the data has been collected, it is processed. Processing includes aggregation and allocation of cost and usage data into user-defined categories based on user-defined time periods.
Inventory Management	An inventory of the services used, the providers of the service, the locations where the services are used, and the components (equipment) used to provide the services are maintained in the inventory. The inventory provides the basic structure by which all cost and usage information is aggregated and allocated.
Monthly Detail Tracking	All of the cost and usage information provided monthly by the service providers is captured and tracked. This includes translating each service provider's charge codes into standard (Teletron) charge codes. The data can be presented in the form of a "Teletron" invoice that breaks down the data (cost and usage) into easy to read and understandable formats.
Cost Allocation	Costs are aggregated and allocated by location, service provider, type of service, type of component, any user defined code, or any combination of these. For example, Virtual Analyzer can aggregate and allocate by service type by location. If locations are assigned a user-defined code for "Office Type," Virtual Analyzer can aggregate and allocate by service type by office type by type of component, etc.
Usage Allocation	Usage is aggregated and allocated by up to 13 categories that include the basic inventory items (location, service type, service provider, etc.) as well as categories that can be defined by the client. These include time of day, time of month, length of call, type of call, etc. Each client determines the categories into which usage data are aggregated.
Trend Analysis	Trend Analysis is performed and reported on both cost and usage data. The reports will provide the information in both words and graphical representations. Trends analyzed will include month to previous month, other time periods (such as quarter to previous quarter and year-to-date to previous year-to-date), current month to same month of previous year, etc. These reports can be run by location, service provider, service type, user-defined codes, etc.
Variance Reporting	Variance Reporting refers to reports that show changes to the client's information. This includes new accounts/components, missing accounts/components, changes in charges from one month to the next, changes to the inventory, etc.

EXHIBIT 6 (*Continued*)

User-Defined Codes	Users have the ability to assign codes to locations, services, and/or components. The user defines a category for each code, identifies the valid codes for each category, and then assigns the code(s) to the appropriate inventory item. For example, the client may have their locations assigned to "Regions." They can also assign codes that identify the type of location (sales office, distribution center, manufacturing facility, warehouse, etc.).
Chargebacks	Virtual Analyzer will create a standard ASCII delimited file that will contain user-specified data for input into the client's accounting system.

Move, Add, Change (MAC) Processing

MAC Processing	MAC Processing tracks the processing required for implementing a change. It is an external system in that it tracks the work done by the service provider and not work done by Teletron.
Online Request	Users will input their requests for changes to service through a Web-based request system. This will be linked to Virtual Analyzer's inventory so that the user can select the service provider, service, and/or component.
Service Order Creation	Service Orders will be created from the MAC Request. Templates will be developed and used for each type of Service Order. Multiple Service Orders can be generated from a single MAC Request. For example, a client may change its long distance provider from MCI to AT&T. Service Orders are created for AT&T, MCI, and every local service provider. The Service Orders created are sent electronically via e-mail or fax to the service provider.
Service Order Tracking	The progress of every Service Order issued is tracked. Each Service Order type has milestones associated with it that detail what needs to be done and when it should be done. If a milestone date passes, the person assigned to manage the Service Order is notified. As each milestone is completed, the system updates the status of the Service Order. The client can view the status of its requests at any time.
Issue Tracking	Each issue that arises during the completion of a Service Order is logged. The Teletron employee assigned to manage a Service Order, the service provider, and the client can communicate through the Issue Log.
Update Inventory	Virtual Analyzer Inventory will automatically be updated by the MAC system. New services requested will be added to the Inventory. Cancelled services will be marked and tracked until the service provider has sent the final bill.
Reporting	The MAC system will provide multiple reports that will detail information by service provider, by location, by type of MAC, by type of service, etc.

Vendor Invoice Processing (VIP) and Vendor Invoice Payment Program (VIPP)

VIP/VIPP Processing	The VIP/VIPP Processing system presents each invoice to the client. The client determines which invoice to pay, how much to pay, and when to make the payments. A payment is made for each invoice from the service providers.
Account Setup	A payment account is set up with the bank that is used to pay the bills for the client. If a service provider accepts electronic payments, the billing accounts are set up for electronic payment.
Payment Authorization	The client views each invoice and enters the amount they authorize to pay and when payment should be released. Multiple payments can be authorized for a single invoice.
Money Transfer	The money to pay the authorized amounts is transferred from an account in the client's bank to the payment account.
Payment Creation	There are two ways payments can be made: electronic and check. Electronic payments are transfers from the payment account directly into an account specified by the service provider. This is the preferred method of payment. Checks are created and mailed to those service providers that cannot accept electronic payments. One payment is created for each invoice received.

EXHIBIT 6 (*Continued*)

Payment Tracking	The date each payment (electronic or check) is processed is tracked, including the dates the payments are created, sent, and cleared in the payment account.
Reporting	The VIP/VIPP system has reports that identify the payment accounts, monthly payment log by client by account, outstanding balances, etc.

Invoice Analyzer

Invoice Analyzer	The Invoice Analyzer reviews each invoice against a set of rules that are maintained in a database, then logs every violation for evaluation by an analyst. The client determines what to do with each finding.
Specify Rules	The rules used to analyze an invoice are maintained in a database. The rules are developed by the analysts and can be applied for a specific service provider, type of service, specific billing plan, etc. For example, a rule may be to identify all short calls (i.e., calls that are less than 30 seconds). Another rule may be to identify all long calls (i.e., calls longer than 2 hours).
Review Invoices	The main logic of the system is to apply each rule to an invoice. When invoice data are found to violate a rule, this is logged in the Findings table. It is possible for a single invoice data item (such as a specific call) to violate more than one rule.
Analyze Findings	The violations identified and logged are summarized for the analyst. An analyst reviews the findings and determines whether a specific finding is legitimate or not. If legitimate, it is marked as an "opportunity" for a savings or for a credit. Analysts can review aggregate findings or each specific finding. For example, the review may have found 300 short calls and 25 long calls. All of the short calls can be classified as an opportunity at one time. Alternatively, each long call can be reviewed and only those that are questioned are marked as opportunities.
Authorize Findings	The opportunities are reviewed with the client. The client authorizes which opportunities to pursue and which ones to ignore.
Savings & Credits	Savings and Credits tables are updated with authorized opportunities. The Savings and Credits table is used to track implementation of the findings.
Generate MACs	MACs are generated for the authorized opportunities. Each MAC is for a specific service provider and can contain one or more opportunities. A Teletron analyst determines whether to combine opportunities or to submit them separately. The MAC system is used to track the progress of implementing an authorized opportunity.
Reporting	The Invoice Analyzer has reports that identify the findings, opportunities, authorized opportunities, etc.

Rate Optimizer

Rate Optimizer	The Rate Optimizer system maintains a database of Billing Plans with rates. It is used by the Invoice Analyzer to verify that proper rates were used for an invoice item. It is also used to identify rate plans that can save money. There are two primary types of Billing Plans that are kept, commercial and private. Commercial Plans are plans that are available to the general public. Private Plans are contracts negotiated between a service provider and a company. All Billing Plans must be published.
Database Maintenance	The Billing Plans database can be maintained manually. This includes adding new plans, modifying existing plans, etc. Notes about specific plans, features, rates, etc. can be made by analysts.
Database Population	Most of the data in the Billing Plans database will come from a third party. The system will use this data to populate and maintain the data. It is able to distinguish data between the third party information and the data entered manually.
Build Billing Plan Profile	Rate Optimizer analyzes the Billing Plans and develops a profile that identifies the services covered, the qualifications to obtain the lowest rates, the probability that the vendor will give discounts, etc.

EXHIBIT 6 (*Continued*)

Build Client Profile	Rate Optimizer analyzes a client's telecom requirements and builds a profile that identifies the services required, the number of sites, components, and the mix of each.
Find Potential Plans	Rate Optimizer will match a client profile against the Billing Plan profiles and identify all Billing Plans that are candidates for supplying the services needed at lower cost.
Calculate Potential Savings	For each candidate Billing Plan, the potential savings are calculated. This is done by applying the client's profile against the qualifications of the potential plans and usage and calculating the cost of the candidate plan.
Reporting	Rate Optimizer generates reports on the Billing Plans, including updates, special offers, etc. The primary report identifies potential plans for saving money with the calculated potential savings.

Industry Information Management

Industry Information Management	The Industry Information Management system aggregates client telecommunication information into a database that views the information by industry rather than by client.
Maintain Aggregation Criteria	The primary criterion for aggregation is the industry. There are additional criteria that can be specified to further refine the data such as annual revenue, number of employees, geographic region, etc.
Data Aggregation	Each client's data is aggregated into the industry database as specified by the criteria established. Once in the industry database, the identity of the client is lost.
Cost Analysis	Costs are analyzed by industry, service type, service provider, component type, time of year, etc., and any combination. It includes calculating average costs by cost category, service type, etc. For example, the average cost of a long distance call by service provider can be calculated.
Usage Analysis	Usage is analyzed by industry, service type, service provider, component type, time of day, time of month, time of year, etc., and any combination.
Service Provider Analysis	Service provider analysis includes analyzing what the actual average cost of a call is for a service provider for different volumes of calls (100 per month vs. 5,000 month vs. 10,000 per month, etc.) for calls from different geographic regions. It also includes an evaluation of performance for completing service orders, annual volume of billing errors, etc.
Trend Analysis	The system also analyzes trends in the industry, such as percent of telecom expense by service type, total expenditures, total costs by service type, etc.
Industry Reports	Virtual Analyzer will provide both standard industry reports and custom reports requested by service providers, industry analysts, and corporations who want to evaluate their performance against industry standards.

Source: Company records.

"OK," replied Dennis. "That is my area, at least for now. While we want the client to use all of the Virtual Analyzer modules as a single package, we will allow some customers to pick and choose among the various services. However, we believe that a customer must at least subscribe to the Client Information Management and Vendor Invoice Processing and Vendor Invoice Payment modules in order to realize any significant advantages from the Virtual Analyzer system.

"Next," Dennis continued. "We think that parts of the software are 'protectable' . . . we intend to file a patent application when we finish the beta test in two years."

"Great, great . . . tell me how we are planning to price the product," asked Tim. "You mentioned the customers will be able to pick and choose between the various services . . . how is that going to be figured into the pricing?" Dennis explained,

> Tim, pricing will be based on the size of the company and the number of modules they choose to use. Larger companies using only two modules would be charged about two percent of their monthly telecommunications cost while smaller companies using all the modules would be billed around six percent of their monthly telecommunications expense. So we expect our average customer revenue to be about $25,000 per month which is roughly four percent of their average monthly telecommunications bill.

"Good," replied Tim. "Tell me, how do we get to market? We have no experience in selling software. What are the channels?"

"We have three choices," replied Dennis.

We can create a sales force and go after the clients one at a time. Clearly, we will have to do some of that, but it is very expensive. Alternatively, we can use our Web site to sell the software. That method is cheap and will work for some clients, but we think that most customers won't buy our solution by seeing a demonstration package on the Internet. They will want someone to visit them. Finally, we can create a series of channel partners. These are companies who sell complementary services, like help desk companies or information technology consulting companies. Some examples might be IBM, EDS, and some of the large accounting firms. We give them a piece of the revenue in exchange for their selling the product for us. Our guess is that we will have to use all three approaches.

"OK. Well done, you guys. Give my thanks to the rest of your team," replied Tim. "You have clearly thought about the issues from our customers' standpoint. I like what I am hearing. But I can't invest money without a return, despite how good an idea we have here. Have you estimated how much this part of our transformation will cost us?"

"Now comes the bad news," offered Bob.

This is one complex piece of software. I have worked on some big projects before and this one will be among the most complex ones I have seen. We have to imbed the thought processes our auditing analysts have been using for ten plus years into computer code. So the analysis time will be significant. We looked at going outside for the systems development work, but the cost right now is out of sight. And most of the consultants don't have any capacity anyway since they are all working on Y2K problems. So we are going to have to hire our own staff.

In addition to designing and testing the software itself, there are lots of other costs that have to be considered as part of the investment. We need to buy lots of big servers. And we will need to translate all the data tables used by the providers in their contracts and invoices into a standard table that our system can use. This task by itself will be huge. We found out that AT&T alone has something like 800 different billing systems—each with a different data structure. Plus what we worked on already—the market research—costs money. And the time we are going to spend contacting customers and providers must be considered as part of the investment as well.

Our best estimate is that the project will take the rest of this year, all of next year, and be ready for alpha and beta testing by early 2001. We should not count on any revenue from Virtual Analyzer before 2002. Any revenue we get until then will come from operating our old business model.

"Yeah," added Dennis.

As this chart (Exhibit 7) shows, we expect the total investment needed to achieve this transformation will cost us over $9 million spread out over 1999 through 2001. Plus, we have to count on added costs for enhancements of between $1 million and $3 million each year from then on. That is definitely the bad news. But . . . we think that we can definitely hit your revenue targets coming from this new business model. Getting to $100 million in revenue with nearly $50 million in EBITDA is really doable. After all, look at the size of the market. We only need a tiny percent of the $5 billion market to hit our 2006 target revenue.

EXHIBIT 7

Investment and Financial Projections for 1999 to 2006 Teletron, Inc.

Year	Revenue (in $000)	EBITDA (in $000)	Investment (in $000)
1999	$11,061	$971	$3,173
2000	12,585	1,801	2,838
2001	10,271	1,124	3,382
2002	5,393	(891)	1,000
2003	16,575	5,540	1,000
2004	33,601	15,612	1,500
2005	60,343	27,947	2,000
2006	108,368	49,598	3,000

Source: Company records.

"That sucking sound you hear is my gasping for air!!" replied Tim. "I had no idea that our transformation would cost this much. So . . . you are telling me that to make this part of our transformation work, we have to spend over $9 million. That is quite a load for a $7 million company. We will have to raise that money . . . clearly Teletron won't generate that kind of cash internally."

Decision Time

"Guys," said Tim. "Again, let me thank you for your effort on this project. I need to consider whether I want to bet this company's future on this idea. And . . . I have to prepare a presentation for the board of directors that includes the return on investment from this endeavor for them to consider at its May 4 meeting in Bloomington."

As the two task force leaders left his office, Tim Lybrook began to construct his presentation to the board. (See Exhibit 8.) He started by listing some of the benefits of the idea. Tim wondered what other benefits he was missing. He then started to make a list of risks. Tim stopped for now. He knew that there were additional risks he had not yet considered. He had to go to a meeting with the builder of his new building. But he knew that he had to finish the presentation. Of course, he first had to decide whether he really wanted to go ahead with the project.

EXHIBIT 8

Preliminary List of Benefits and Risks of Making the Investment
Teletron, Inc.

Benefits

- A huge market with generally weak competitors.
- A steady revenue stream as an application service provider (ASP)—remember the value of an annuity.
- Simple support process as an ASP with all software directly under Teletron's control.
- Ease of initial installation with no on-site activity since an ASP.
- Ease of software upgrades with no requirement to change client software.
- Simpler and less expensive EDI/XML connectivity to carriers from one site.
- Simple pricing model ($ per month per user for each module subscribed to).
- An ROI of ? percent.
- High barriers to entry—requires expertise and lots of capital.

Risks

- Required reliance on the Internet, but we have no experience using this communications medium.
- Relatively untried concept.
- Market acceptance is subject to a high level of uncertainty and risk.
- Difficulty in predicting future growth rates.
- Sales cycle may be long.
- Excessive length of time until revenue starts flowing from the offering.
- Difficulty in reaching the market—have to use channel partners not under our control.

CASE STUDY IV-3

ADVANTAGE 2000 AT OWENS CORNING: BUSINESS AND IT TRANSFORMATION

By March 1997, almost 2 years after the launch of Advantage 2000, Owens Corning was well on its way toward meeting its goal of implementing common, simple, global processes. It would also be one of the first U.S.-based companies to have SAP R/3[1] globally installed. In fact, Advantage 2000 had brought the company some bottom-line gains ahead of schedule:

> A key benefit of SAP is the integration of our businesses into a common global system. This increases our purchasing leverage, and we expect to save more than $17 million over the next 3 years. SAP also gives us a powerful tool to analyze our spending. We expect to reduce material inventories by 50 percent by the year 2000.
>
> —*Chief Procurement Officer, Global Sourcing*

> The financial benefits already are appearing, and I believe they will exceed our expectations. With these systems we expect to perform our monthly closings in just 2 days by next year and in a day by the year 2000. SAP alone will give our business a full percentage point gain in productivity.
>
> —*Chief Financial Officer*

The Advantage 2000 project had also played an important role in the company's 1996 launch of System Thinking™, a growth strategy that shifts the market focus from individual products to system-driven solutions. This strategy leverages the company's brand and distribution strengths by offering whole-project solutions to consumers and industrial customers. For example, a roofing system solution not only fends off outside elements, but also lets moisture out from the inside and comes with a warranty. This solution requires not just shingles, but a full system solution of underlayment and ventilation materials as well as shingles. In the future, even Owens Corning's small building-materials customers could have one-stop shopping: With a single phone call, they could order all the construction materials they needed—not just roofing materials, but eventually exterior siding, insulation, doors, windows, and pipes as well. According to CEO Hiner:

> The System Thinking concept calls for an integrated focus, a common resolve, a new way of doing business, and a sense of team that is always at the heart of success. It is a mandate for the way we think. It spells out how we approach our markets. It is the path of growth, and no one else in our industry can lay claim to this position.
>
> —*Glen Hiner, CEO*

Advantage 2000 had also enabled the company to move toward a more process-oriented structure. Process executive roles for Finance and Sourcing were held by the CFO and chief procurement officer. In early 1997, a new process-executive position for customer fulfillment had been filled with a former business unit president. This appointment sent a clear signal that the process executives were on equal footing with the business unit presidents under a matrixed, process-oriented structure.

> The key to our new process organization is the ability of Advantage 2000 systems to deliver data. With the data it provides across our businesses, the opportunities for process improvement are tremendous. Our customer fulfillment process, which spans all of our business units and business regions, will deliver more than $30 million in cost savings over the next 2 years through gains in productivity in each part of our process.
>
> —*Process Executive, Customer Fulfillment*

Yet Hiner's management team knew that when they took the industry lead with a project as large as Advantage 2000, they would make some mistakes. There was no defined path for the

---

 This case study was prepared by Professor Carol V. Brown as the basis for class discussion, rather than to illustrate either effective or ineffective handling of an administrative situation. The author is indebted to Michael D. Radcliff, David Johns, and Robert Heinaman, who generously shared their time and insights, as well as all of the other Owens Corning managers who were interviewed by the author over a period of several years.

[1]Founded in 1972, SAP AG is based in Walldorf, Germany. R/3 is SAP's enterprise-level software solution for a client/server platform that includes modules for Accounting/Finance, Materials Management, Manufacturing/Operations, Sales and Distribution, and Human Resources processes.

organization to follow in pursuit of its vision of common, simple, global processes. But that's what industry leadership is all about: pushing forward with what you believe to be the best path and not being afraid to make a few mistakes along the way.

The Owens Corning Turnaround

Owens Corning's history began in 1935, when it was formed as a joint venture of Corning Glass and Owens-Illinois Glass to exploit a new technology: glass fiberization. By the mid-1990s, it was a world leader in building material systems and a leading producer of advanced composites and glass-fiber insulation. Its 1995 sales of $3.6 billion were primarily from five businesses that produced and marketed more than 25,000 separate products, including glass fiber and foam insulation; roofing materials; doors, windows, and outdoor vinyl siding; large industrial pipes made of reinforced glass; and glass-fibers and resins for synthetic yarns and composite products. Headquartered in down-town Toledo, Ohio, in early 1996 it had 11 business units, 17,000 employees in 30 countries, a 45-percent market share in the composites materials market, and the leading market position in glass-fiber insulation.

However, the company was heavily in debt when Glen H. Hiner took over as CEO of Owens-Corning Fiberglas in January 1992, after a 35-year career with General Electric Company. Its successful defense against a takeover bid in the mid-1980s had required major cash and stock payouts to shareholders, and it was faced with a slew of litigation related to an insulation product that contained asbestos, a product it manufactured for 14 years from 1958 to 1972. During the next 3 years, Hiner infused his management team with outside talent, including a strategic planner, a new CFO from Honeywell, a new vice president of procurement, and two other new vice presidents he had worked with at General Electric (Research & Development, and Human Resources).

Under its new management team, Owens Corning began to make its customers its first priority and renewed its focus on R&D. Noncore businesses were sold, and new plants were built in Europe, Latin America, and Asia. In mid-1996, the company's New York Stock Exchange ticker symbol was changed from OCF to OWC to reflect its name change from Owens-Corning Fiberglas to Owens Corning. By July 1996, its earnings per share had more than quadrupled and its first dividend in a decade had been declared. Its trademarked pink color and Pink Panther logo had begun to be leveraged in the new System Thinking™ campaign.

Vision 2000

By early 1994, CEO Hiner had established ambitious financial, business, and workplace goals for the year 2000, driven by three core values: customer satisfaction, individual dignity, and shareholder value (see Exhibit 1). To achieve these outcomes, the company would have to change the way it did business. The intent was to "commoditize" what did not deliver value to the customer. This would allow the company to focus on the things that did make a difference to its customers and to make its aggressive growth goals a reality.

Hiner's Vision 2000 also included a new way of working, as summarized in Exhibit 2. These eight qualities drove his design for a new world headquarters building that became a visible symbol for the abandonment of an old hierarchical culture for the new, more entrepreneurial way of working. Completed in fall 1996, the new 3-story building replaced the 28-story tower in downtown Toledo, a few blocks away from the new site on the city's riverfront. The new headquarters is of modular design and has walls of glass with views of the Maumee River. Teamwork is supported by open workspace

EXHIBIT 1
Year 2000 Goals

Sales:	$5 billion in sales
Globalization:	40% sales outside the U.S.
Earnings per share:	2 × sales growth
Workforce:	Diverse
Productivity:	6% improvement each year
Workplace:	Preferred place of employment

EXHIBIT 2
Guiding Principles

Three Core Values:

Customer Satisfaction

- Worldwide product availability, pricing, delivery commitments and accurate order status at *anytime*

***Individual Dignity** . . . for everyone*

- Global, diverse, world-class work environment with real-time information at the fingertips of *anyone* in the company who needs it *anywhere*

***Shareholder Value** . . . improve productivity*

- Improve pre-tax earnings *by more than 1%* of sales

Workplace Vision:

global	team-oriented
mobile	learning-based
paper-free	customer-focused
integrated	technology-enabled

"pods," an abundance of formal meeting rooms, and lots of informal gathering places.

> We want to leverage the breadth and depth of the organization by engaging as many people as possible in problem-solving. Our focus is on decision making closer to the customer and a culture that is more diverse and entrepreneurial.
>
> —*Process Executive, Customer Fulfillment*

As a first step toward achieving Vision 2000, three business-process reengineering (BPR) projects were initiated by Hiner in early 1994: reengineering of the logistics and customer service processes and consolidating the finance function. Deloitte & Touche Consulting Group (CG) was engaged to work with these BPR teams. It did not take long for the teams to conclude that the company's existing information systems would not be able to support the envisioned new processes. Information technology would therefore need to play a critical role in this companywide transformation.

New Role for the Information Systems Organization

Information systems at Owens Corning (OC) had been custom-developed in the past in order to support separate businesses and single functions. Computer interfaces were written to move data across separate functional systems and to consolidate business unit data for corporate information systems. In some cases, the old computer systems could not talk to each other, so inventory or production numbers had to be manually reentered. It was often impossible for a salesperson to know the availability of a product or to research an invoice problem for a major account. By 1994, the company had a complex, incompatible, and highly redundant set of more than 200 legacy systems. Due to different data definitions and years of maintenance, some of these systems now also had reliability problems.

A string of business managers had been at the helm of the information systems (IS) organization since the mid-1980s; a career manufacturing executive had most recently been the IS head. When the reduction of overall IS costs became a business priority in 1993, all IS units that had been reporting to business managers throughout North America were recentralized. The IS heads and their systems development teams were relocated to Toledo and began reporting to corporate IS. At the time of the reengineering projects, about 75 percent of the IS budget was directed at legacy systems enhancement and support. New development was done only on a limited basis.

In May 1994 Michael Radcliff was brought on board as the company's chief information officer. Radcliff and OC's chief financial officer had been executives at Honeywell at the same time. Radcliff's selection signaled top management's decision to hire a career IS executive with a significant track record who could also work well with the top management team. He arrived with a clear mandate: to help move the company into the next century by strategically aligning the IS organization to the ambitious vision for year 2000 and to significantly cut IS operational costs worldwide.

Prior to Radcliff's coming on board, top management had assumed that the newly centralized IS group would build systems to support the new processes being designed by the BPR teams. In the past the IS organization had primarily been an order-taker, rather than a key participant in exploring alternative systems solutions to meet business needs. There was no significant IS management involvement on the BPR projects.

By June 1994, Radcliff had reoriented the logistics and customer service reengineering teams to focus on global, enterprisewide BPR and common processes that could be supported with integrated systems. A global supply-chain view of the enterprise (see Exhibit 3.) was developed with the Deloitte & Touche CG consultant team as part of the enterprise process modeling over that summer.

After there was a buy-in to an enterprisewide integrated systems solution, the organization sought to identify an off-the-shelf enterprise resource planning (ERP) system that could simplify the support of common, global business processes and enable OC managers to do the following:

- *access worldwide information in real time* (for inventory, production, pricing, and distribution information)
- *customize responses to meet customer needs* (for pricing, production and delivery schedules, and purchasing forecasts)
- *make fully informed decisions*
- *communicate paper-free* (internal and external in-person communications and business transactions)

Radcliff also asked for and received an early management buy-in to an open systems client/server solution. This would mean migrating from an older mainframe architecture to a UNIX-based platform and a centralized relational database. Terminals connected to mainframes would be replaced with standard desktop technologies.

> Making fact-based decisions in real time is the new playing field. But you have to take care to avoid multiple images of an SAP or Oracle database or you may not get this benefit and you won't have a standard template to bring in an acquisition.
>
> —*Mike Radcliff, CIO*

In parallel with the selection for an ERP system, an outsourcing vendor for Owens Corning's legacy systems was also sought. Outsourcing would enable the company to move from fixed cost to variable cost funding for mainframe data center operations and legacy system maintenance until the systems were replaced. An estimated $30 million in legacy system costs would be redirected toward the funding of the ERP project.

EXHIBIT 3
Original Supply-Chain Model

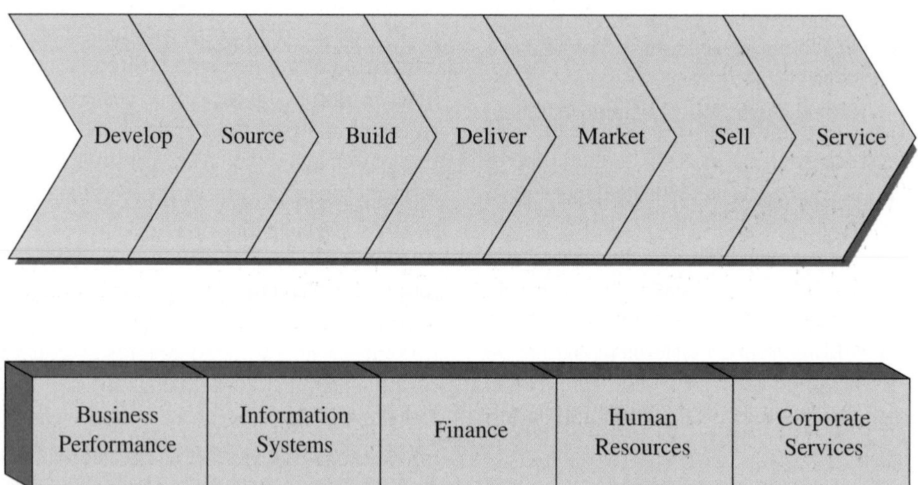

In late fall 1994, the BPR teams were brought into a lab for a hands-on investigation of SAP R/3. The feasibility of an enterprise process model and global systems solution for Owens Corning was validated. SAP's R/3 client/server enterprise system was chosen as the foundation package, and a contract was signed in December. The contract with SAP represented an enterprisewide commitment to a global initiative that would involve the redesign of most of the company's supply-chain processes and the replacement of virtually all of its major systems. It also meant a large number of business users would need to be trained on Windows and personal productivity tools, including many factory floor workers who had never used computers before.

For the first time, the IS organization would be partnering with business management on a project that would radically transform the business. The new IS role was not to be an order-taker, but to "lead the parade" by managing the project teams responsible for enterprisewide implementation of common, simple, global business process redesign and systems integration. A key challenge for the IS organization was to transform itself to be in "planetary alignment" with the business transformation.

> The company has said that we'll all use the same processes. Information systems is leading the parade here because we have told the businesses that "they will" have common processes. This is a macro systems change that takes the right mix of consultants, IS, and business folks. After this implementation, the process owners will have the tool they need to drive it to best in the business.
>
> —*VP of Global Sourcing and Logistics*

In January 1995, more than 200 legacy systems were outsourced to Hewlett-Packard for operations and support. The contract included the selling of data center assets to HP and the transfer of over 50 IS personnel who remained in the Toledo area. Outsourcing the legacy systems sent a clear signal to the whole company that the old systems were "ships to be burned" as the new systems came online. There was no turning back.

The fencing off of legacy system support via an outsourcing contract was also considered critical for another reason. It allowed IS managers to focus on acquiring the new skill sets that were needed for the ERP initiative—coined Advantage 2000.

The SAP Implementation Plan

A senior executive steering committee for the Advantage 2000 project was formed by the end of 1994. The members of the steering committee included the CFO, three business unit heads, a VP of corporate human resources, and two other functional VPs. The makeup of the committee clearly reflected the top-down leadership support that would be needed for a multiyear initiative with an estimated $100 million price tag.

By early 1995, a 100-week implementation plan had been agreed on for reengineering the company's global business processes and replacing about 200 of its legacy systems with SAP's client/server system. The 100-week schedule also helped both IS and business managers have an end in sight. However, OC's top managers also believed that no other company was trying to do an implementation of this scope so fast.

> Advantage 2000 is a bold move for Owens Corning. We're replacing 200 legacy systems across the company with a handful of systems using SAP as the backbone.
>
> —*Chief Financial Officer*

An aggressive timetable was a critical decision. The intent was to minimize the likelihood that a key senior business executive would "jump ship" or cease to support the project goals before it was completed. Top management was sure that the pain would be considerable, but the pain to achieve integration would be the same whether an aggressive schedule was followed or not. Full support and leadership at the top executive level was the only way a project of this magnitude could succeed. Some thought that the longer a project dragged on, the greater the risk that midlevel managers would design ways to protect the status quo. Weekly goals of 1 percent progress were identified and reported on each week to the project steering committee.

> We decided to learn not by studying it and then training on it, but by doing it.
>
> —*Mike Radcliff, CIO*

> The longer you take, the harder it is: managers change and the business requirements change. We have been very careful not to delay unless it was absolutely necessary. In the old Owens Corning we would have changed this schedule 50 times for all different reasons. Today we plow through.
>
> —*Global Development Leader, Sales Advantage*

The 2-year schedule for a global implementation also meant that "good enough" process reengineering would be the initial focus. Achieving an integrated process solution was the initial implementation outcome, not achieving best-in-class processes. Multiple project teams would work in parallel to identify and gain buy-in to simple, common, global process solutions across its business units. Variations would be driven by customer and product differences, not business unit differences. A perfection mentality would not work under this plan—initially there would be no bells and whistles. Instead, successive waves of process-driven change would be directed at achieving world-class outcomes by the year 2000.

> We told the division presidents we're going to piss off a lot of people, but it is more important that systems work for the whole company than to have all the bells and whistles everyone wants.
>
> —*Mike Radcliff, CIO*[2]

The development process basically had four steps. First the business team members would design the global process. Then the business and IS team members would look at SAP, identify the gaps, and work through them. A prototype was built, and then the system configuration was finalized.

Multiple SAP releases were planned over the 100-week period. The release concept entailed "shrink wrapping" several products—new processes and new systems—into a single release. This avoided the problem of business units having to contend with multiple delivery dates by multiple project teams. The number of releases was intentionally small. At a given point in time, then, the SAP global teams would be engaged in different project phases for a given release.

The release plan in effect in early 1996 is shown in Exhibit 4. Release 1 targeted a single corporate function (finance), which was one of the original reengineering projects and had computer-savvy leaders. Release 2 included a full set of manufacturing and distribution modules using version 2.2 of SAP R/3 for a major business unit outside the United States (Building Materials Europe), as well as several fabrication plants in North America. Release 3 implemented a standard client/server infrastructure in about 100 North American locations. It entailed installing wide area networks, local area networks, and about 5,000 new desktops (hardware and software) that would be able to access the centralized Oracle database in Toledo. Release 4 would begin to exploit the multinational and multilingual capabilities of a new R/3 version (3.0) that would be implemented over several waves. By 1997, the scope had grown to more than 140 locations and more than 10,000 end users.

The 4-release plan was also designed to take advantage of organizational learning from earlier releases. Release 1 would require learning the package and development tools as well as a new systems integration methodology by the project teams. It also needed to be an "early win." Release 2 would be the pilot for implementing a full global supply-chain set of modules within a single business unit and would serve as a pilot for change management and end-user training. Release 4 would have multiple waves so that mistakes made in the first business unit implementation could be corrected before the next wave. In the literature this became known as a "slow burn" type of a "big bang strategy."[3]

EXHIBIT 4

100-Week 4-Release Plan as of March 1996

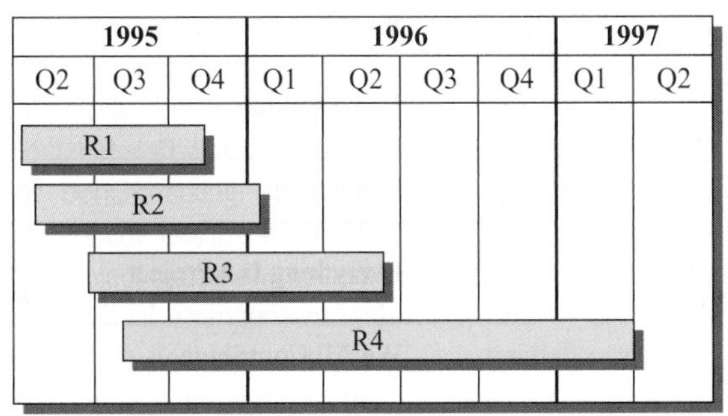

[2]Based on a quote reported in the June 19, 1995, issue of *Forbes*.

[3]For example, see Christopher Koch, "Flipping the Switch," *CIO*, June 15, 1996, pp. 43–66.

The HR staff also helped design two financial incentive plans to help retain employees critical to the project. The first incentive plan took advantage of a preexisting incentive structure at OC: a year-end bonus. OC employees already a part of this plan were eligible for a bonus of 15 to 40 percent of one year's salary; employees not on this plan were eligible for a bonus of up to 15 percent. The second incentive plan was unique to the Advantage 2000 project: a project completion bonus in the form of stock options at 20 percent of the employee's annual salary (or higher). The plans were put in place at the time of the Advantage 2000 launch.

Finding the right mix of consultants and internal employees was an ongoing challenge. Top management knew they needed external expertise for this scope and type of organizational change. However, if the external consultants were relied on to lead project teams, then project management skills and SAP knowledge might not be transferred to OC's work force as quickly. By early 1996, each D&T consultant was paired with two OC managers—one with a business focus, one with a technology focus—as part of a plan to transition out the consultants. By the fall of 1996, all full-time consultants had been transferred out of the IS organization.

> We were clear up front that we were hiring expertise for knowledge transfer. Determine what you want the consultants to do and have that as an agreement in the consultant contract. Don't hand the project over to an outside integrator.
>
> —*David Johns, Director of Global Development*

More detailed descriptions of the groups and roles represented by the three arrows in Exhibit 6 are provided in the following sections.

Global Development Teams

A Global Development Team of IS and business representatives was created for each of the global processes in the revised business process model (see Exhibit 7). The primary objective of each global team was to develop and deliver process and systems solutions on time. Five teams were given responsibility for the supply-chain processes (product development, sourcing, manufacturing, sales, and customer service). Each global development team also had subteams. For example, the Sales Advantage Team had three subteams: Field Sales Automation, Pricing, and Demand Forecasting. Two additional teams were responsible for enterprise support.

A third enterprise support team (Workplace Technology) was initially charged with selecting standard desktop tools and rolling them out to every link in the value chain. However, after release 2 it was decided that these tasks could be better achieved if these team members were integrated into the other Global Development Teams. Except for a small subset of team members who were responsible for the technology for the new headquarters building scheduled to open in fall 1996, the Workplace Technology team was disbanded and its members were reassigned.

EXHIBIT 7
Global Development Teams

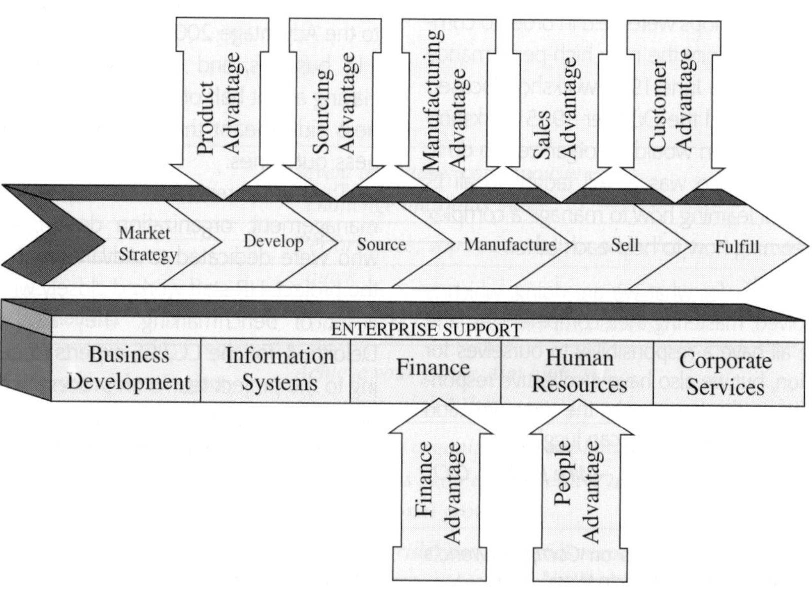

A standard report format was used to keep the Steering Committee members informed. Three "vital signs" were reported on by each project team on a weekly basis: scope, schedule, and budget. For each vital sign, there was a color code:

Red	External intervention required ("in trouble")
Yellow	Behind, but recoverable ("caution")
Green	On track (a "go")

For any vital sign not coded green, a plan "to get to green" was part of the report.

Each team had a **Global Development Leader** (GDL) who was responsible for project planning and making sure the team was "on course" in terms of both schedule and budget. Each GDL was a full-time OC employee, although some consultants were assigned to be leaders of subteams. Initially, some GDLs had responsibility for more than one project team, but as the project teams became established and the project work was launched, each project team had its own GDL.

Most of the GDLs had previously been systems development managers reporting to business unit heads a few years earlier. This meant that the typical GDL had already established extensive working relationships with key members of the business community. This IS leadership experience came to be recognized as a major work force asset for the Advantage 2000 project.

> All GDLs have experience in the business units, many in multiple businesses. That means they are credible on the business side and have a huge informal network.
>
> *—Global Development Leader, Sales Advantage*

The only external IS hire for a GDL position was David Johns who had worked with CIO Radcliff at Honeywell. Johns originally headed up both the Finance and Sourcing Advantage project teams when he arrived in fall 1994, and then he became the GDL for Finance alone. But in July 1995, it became clear that integration across the supply chain project teams needed to be focused on by someone on a weekly and daily basis, and Johns moved into the new Director of Global Development position.

> The integration of SAP is one of its biggest benefits, but also the most difficult part of it. Everything has touchpoints. Each team wants to focus on their own project, but complete integration is needed across the development teams. A director position is the best approach to fit a very aggressive timeframe. This was a big lesson learned.
>
> *—David Johns, Director of Global Development*

Multiday, intensive workshops with GDLs and other IS managers were held in order to plan a new release. When major issues arose among business executives, Johns and Radcliff helped provide "air cover" for the GDLs and their team members so that they could stay focused on the release deadlines.

Success in a GDL position required a mixture of solid technology, business, and leadership experience. They needed to be comfortable with learning new technologies, as well as leading a cross-functional team with business managers and IS professionals. GDLs also needed excellent interpersonal skills as they sometimes had to make some unpopular decisions. They also had to get comfortable with and trust the business leaders on their teams, as the success of the project relied heavily on the process knowledge and negotiation skills of these team members.

GDLs also needed to be able to help create a work environment based on the new IS organization values in which it was all right to take risks and make some mistakes. The aggressive schedule often meant that they themselves had to believe in the Advantage 2000 project goals, even though they might not yet know how they would achieve them.

Business Roles on the Global Development Teams

A co-leadership role with the GDL was played by **Business Process Leaders** (BPLs) who had primary responsibility for business process reengineering. BPLs were senior managers or other high achievers from a function or business unit who were typically assigned to an Advantage 2000 project team full-time.[5] They were the primary business interface for their team during the life of the project. Having a high-level business manager assigned full-time to an IS project was new at OC, so the BPL role was a highly visible sign that Advantage 2000 was a strategic business initiative.

For example, the Manufacturing Advantage team had four BPLs who were responsible for business process innovation across four major business units (Insulation-North America, Composites, Roofing & Asphalt, Building Materials), two smaller business units (Windows, Foam), and the VP of engineering. One BPL was assigned to each of the three global manufacturing processes (product definition, manufacturing planning and execution, plant maintenance), and the fourth BPL was a "floater."

All business team members were physically located ("co-located") with the IS team members at the Toledo headquarters. For example, all four of the manufacturing BPLs had relocated to Toledo in order to take this Advantage 2000 assignment. Team members saw each other daily, and OC's top management team shared the same building.

The BPLs were responsible for taking global business process redesign to the point of buy-in from the process owners in each affected business unit and corporate function. The business process owners were typically at the VP level within a function or business unit; in a few cases the BPL on a project team was also

[5]Some compromise arrangements were made for those from Europe: not all were full-time.

of data and infrastructure work; and actual deployment and coordination of post-installation support. Deploying a product release required coordination across multiple project teams, HR personnel responsible for training, and local business unit managers. For releases 1 and 2, the primary responsibility for deployment was in the hands of the GDLs and their team members assigned to this capability. For the desktop implementation in release 3, the capability Leader took the lead role because the focus was on infrastructure rather than system development. This meant that the global development team leaders could stay tightly focused on getting the release 4 products ready for on-time delivery.

Another capability closely tied to the GDLs was the **Intranet/Communications Capability**. Initially part of the Planning and Project Management Capability, it became a separate capability after it became clear that communications and information sharing would be key success factors for the Advantage 2000 project. Each global development team had at least one member assigned to the Communications Capability, which was responsible for communications across global project teams and the rest of the IS community as well as for communications between the IS organization and the rest of the company. Each capability member was responsible for providing monthly reports and sharing best practices for their project team. After the implementation of a standard desktop technology (Windows 95 platform) in release 3, the emphasis shifted from hardcopy reports to intranet communications. Progress reports from the project teams and new procedures could be posted on a single Web server, and documents could be quickly and easily shared across geographic distances.

Another capability that did not initially exist was the **Sourcing & Alliances Capability**, responsible for managing vendor relationships for the IS organization. At the start of the project, there was only one major outsourcing partner (Hewlett-Packard for legacy systems operation and support), and the management of the outsourcing relationship was dispersed across the IS consultants (described previously). This plan made sense because in the past systems had been custom developed for the business units. However, under this dispersed structure, the execution of the outsourcing contract with HP turned out to be a very bumpy ride. The legacy system costs continued to be a larger organizational expense than expected.

The Sourcing & Alliances capability set up a superstructure for coordinating contacts across the IS consultants who previously had acted on behalf of their business managers, not on behalf of the enterprise as a whole. Giving the responsibility for managing this strategic alliance to a high-level capability manager meant that the rest of the IS leadership team could stay focused on the systems integration goals. The capability Leader position was given a dual reporting arrangement—reporting not only to the CIO, but also to the VP of sourcing—in order to establish high-level accountability to the senior business managers. As business units encountered problems with service levels provided by the outsourcing vendor (e.g., help desk services) the IS consultants worked with the capability leader to identify the scope of the problem and to provide input to enterprise-level solutions.

An external hire who had previously worked with Radcliff at Honeywell was brought in to lead the Sourcing & Alliances Capability, and the scope of his responsibilities expanded as new vendor contracts were established. For example, HP was also contracted for wide area network support and help desk support for the new systems, and Vanstar was engaged to provide LAN and desktop support.

The transformation of the IS organization to a high-performance environment required a whole new structure for the IS organization as well as a whole new set of human resource practices and processes. Radcliff originally planned to rely heavily on OC's HR department, and a corporate HR staff member was assigned to the IS organization. However, after a few months it became apparent that the IS people were receiving inadequate attention. With the blessing of the new senior vice president of HR, a **Resource Development Capability** was established within the IS organization in August 1995, and Bob Heinaman was designated the capability leader. The establishment of this capability was a clear signal to the IS work force that the new IS organization was committed to developing a high-performance work force.

Several reasons surfaced to explain why the original plan for an HR partnership did not work. Some felt that the assigned HR employee was not in a senior enough position to expeditiously implement all of the changes needed to move an entire unit from job-based work to project-based assignments and from manager-initiated to employee-initiated career development. Others pointed out that the global development leaders and some of the other capability leaders had aggressive project milestones, and their attention was supposed to be focused on project demands, not the people side. Their incentives were directed at short-term results, not long-term development of internal human resources.

Several major HR initiatives were championed by Heinaman (see Exhibit 9). For example, a new six-level broadband compensation scheme that was competency-based was initiated in the first quarter of 1996. Each project team role was assigned a competency level and an IS capability assignment. Within each level there were three sublevels to ensure that IS employees would help each other: *learning, can do*, and *can teach*. Another early initiative was the implementation of an employee-led appraisal process with 360-degree feedback: Employees solicit evaluations from up to 10 people of their

EXHIBIT 9

Processes and Subprocesses for IS Human Resources

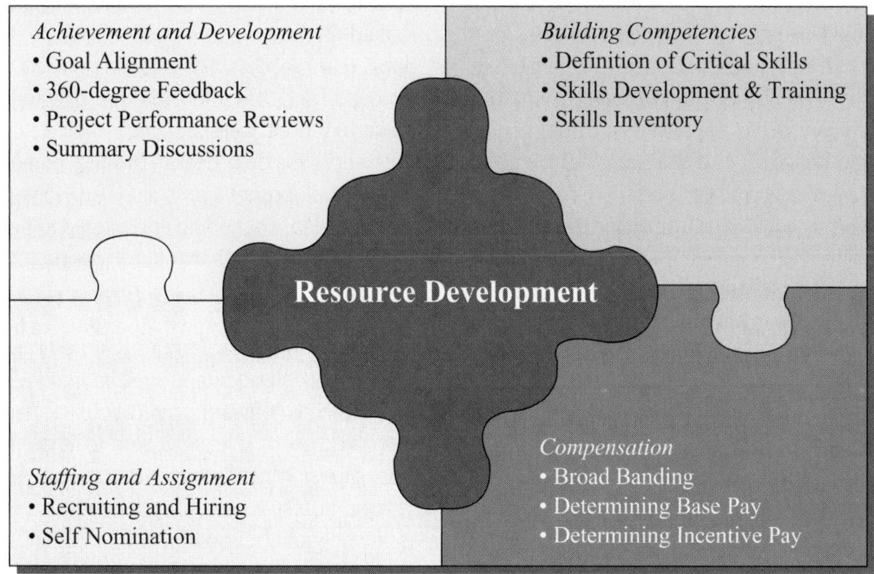

choice who are in positions below, above, and beside their own, or some other relevant sampling.

> We tried to stay aligned with the resource development of OC as a whole and act as a pilot. We didn't want to look as if we were on attack. We focused on what was IS-specific and identified individual skill sets and stretch goals for their development.
>
> —*Bob Heinaman, Resource Capability Leader*

By early December 1996, after new processes and structures had been successfully implemented for the IS organization, it was decided to "turn back the keys" to HR for these initiatives. The separate IS capability was terminated, and Heinaman moved on to the People Advantage GDL assignment responsible for HR systems.

Learning from the Early SAP Releases

Release 1: Finance Consolidation

Release 1 involved implementing SAP as part of the consolidating of financial operations, including the centralization of accounts payable, expense and travel accounts, and payroll systems. The reengineering project for Finance was one of the early ones, and the process reengineering began an entire year before Radcliff's arrival. By late 1994, these functions had pretty much been consolidated, one North American factory at a time, and operations were being run out of headquarters and out of an accounting center set up in West Virginia. The SAP R/3 system replacement was scheduled for release 1 because it would provide an SAP project experience for a corporate function that had already been heavily reengineered.

Release 1 was scheduled for October 1995 and was completed on time. This was an early, visible win for the project and bolstered confidence that the 100-week plan was on target.

> You need to do everything you can to make the first cycle happen as quickly as possible. We focused on speed. The consultants brought to the plate an understanding of SAP. Having the project teams live together and work together also helped.
>
> —*Global Development Leader, Sourcing Advantage*

That does not mean there were not some implementation problems. For example, a software glitch that delayed the printing of payroll checks was highlighted in an article published in *Forbes*.[6]

Release 2: Supply Chain Processes Pilot

Release 2 was scheduled for early 1996 and involved rolling out SAP R/3 version 2.2E at eight fabrication plants in North America, five plants in the United Kingdom (Building Materials Europe), and in the corporate research and engineering function. Release 2 was viewed as critical for finding out what it took to deploy new processes and systems within a business unit release, including SAP training and change management. This would allow for

[6]Neil Weinberg. "Think globally, act incrementally," *Forbes*, June 19, 1995, pp. 88–89.

adjustments to be made to the deployment plans before release 4, when a newer SAP version would be rolled out to all business units, including sites in Latin America and the Asia Pacific.

Building Materials Europe (BME), an organization with a total of 750 employees in the United Kingdom, served as a business unit pilot.[7] Because BME had been developed, in large part, with acquisitions from 1994 to 1996, its management had inherited multiple systems that did not provide the information they needed to run the business. The BME president and his leadership team were all willing to risk the problems associated with being first, because it would mean a major step forward toward system integration and process improvements.

BME's legacy systems were outsourced to HP shortly after a new IS manager came on board at the end of 1994 as the business unit's IS head and new corporate IS manager for all of Europe. The intent was to do only "good enough reengineering" as part of the release. The six values put together by the IS leadership team in 1994 helped serve as "navigation instruments" for this IS team, which was working in a different culture with different work habits.

> The values are all the more important for me since I'm not in Toledo. We have a laminated card that gives us three- to four-word sentences about what high performance means.
>
> —*IS Consultant for BME and Service Capability Leader for Europe*

The release 2 deployment was driven by the global development teams, along with corporate HR. BME did not have the advantage of being able to learn from other business units in the United Kingdom or any other OC business units. In fact, most companies in Europe were implementing SAP module by module, rather than in the "big bang" approach being used at OC.

One of the biggest surprises from release 2 was that the resources needed for deployment preparation and for actual deployment had been significantly underestimated. The training programs were expanded to include not just basic PC navigation skills, but also process training. This would mean a lot more business involvement in the training. Deployments also began to be planned much further in advance, and the training was timed to be as close to actual deployment as possible. The training and deployment cost estimates for 1995 to 1997 were increased to $35 million, with a projected total project cost of $110 million.

Release 2 had also significantly increased the confidence of the project team members; the consultants were gone, and the release was successful. They also had learned a lot about each other: The business process leaders better understood the trials and tribulations faced by IS managers, and the IS people learned to appreciate how changes in business executives and business processes affected the work of the business process leaders. Co-locating the project team members had helped create a learning environment. While still housed in the glass tower in downtown Toledo, the global team members worked in four-person pods alongside the consultants and global team leaders. Some building walls were even physically removed, and the CIO and his director of the SAP project worked without walls between their key administrative assistants and their own desks. The first end-of-year bonus for the global development teams also had worked well in terms of the systems release schedule and proved to be "battery-recharging."

Release 3: Developing a Global Infrastructure

Like many large organizations, OC had multiple e-mail systems and network standards as well as many different PC platforms and desktop software applications across its business units. The objective of release 3 was to implement a simple, common, global infrastructure solution that would enable reliable desktop access to the Toledo headquarters worldwide as well as lower global support costs. Initially about 80 geographic locations were involved, but the scope and complexity of the project grew over the life of the 100-week project due to acquisition activity and other growth initiatives. By the time of deployment, release 3 entailed installing wide area networks, local area networks, and about 5,000 standard desktop setups for more than 10,000 end users at more than 140 locations.

The responsibility for selecting the new standards and planning the infrastructure upgrades initially resided in an independent enterprise support team—a Workplace Technology team. Microsoft was selected as the vendor standard for microcomputer operating systems (Windows 95 and NT) and personal productivity software (Microsoft Office). In order to support the global implementation of a client/server application such as SAP, the network implementation included upgrading "by orders of magnitude" to a cost-effective solution capable of handling the anticipated increase in global communications traffic (via frame relay). At the time of release 3 deployment, most of the original team members had been reassigned and a core technology team oversaw the global implementation, including the new world headquarters.

Release 3 was therefore the first Advantage 2000 implementation that involved widespread technology change across the company. It also was on the critical path for release 4 because it established both the client/server infrastructure and the basic end-user computing skills required for the effective SAP R/3 deployment at OC's largest business units. The HR members of the Advantage 2000 project partnered with an outside vendor to deliver end-user training. The IS consultants played a key role in inventorying the pre-existing desktop tools; the knowledge they gained about end-user computing in these business units was used in the selection of local deployment teams for release 4.

[7]In January 1998, BME's organizational name was changed to International Building Materials Systems.

Release 4: Global R/3 Implementation

The primary systems objective of release 4 was to get all of the business running on a common platform. SAP was to be deployed in successive waves—a mini "big bang," one business unit at a time. In the original 100-week plan, deployment would begin in the summer of 1996. The plan was initially revised to roll out the new SAP version at BME and the three major business units (Composites, Roofing & Asphalt, Insulation North America) during the first quarter of 1997.[8] Sometime later it was determined that the company would not be able to sustain the successive 30-day deployments at these major business units, and the plan was changed to allow 60 days between waves. The deployment of a field sales automation tool would follow 4 to 6 weeks after a business unit switched over to SAP.

The holiday window at the end of December 1996 was used to upgrade the release 2 sites to version 3.0d of SAP R/3. This wave involved not only a new R/3 version, but also new configurations due to process changes as well as new functionality. December 25 was the only day the project teams were not working. The first new business unit implementation (Roofing & Asphalt) was scheduled for March 1997, with the Insulation division to follow 60 days later, followed by Composites.

> We've become experts in system testing and very good at understanding what SAP integration means. The release deployment was changed because we had significantly increased the scope. We now have 140 locations, instead of about 80 as originally planned, because of acquisitions. The scope has also increased as we have turned over the rocks; we have increased the functionality and have additional bolt-ons. We also need time to pay attention to the lessons learned from what other business units did.
>
> *—David Johns, Director of Global Development*

> The delays were greeted with mixed emotions. This is an intense project, and we wanted to be done. But the people had been giving as much as they could, and they didn't want to jeopardize the success of the project. Still, it was tough to have an installation over the holidays.
>
> *—Global Development Leader, Sourcing Advantage*

Several learnings from release 2 were incorporated into the release 4 deployment. First, more accountability for deployment activities was given to the Release Management Capability and less to the GDLs. This separation of development and deployment responsibilities meant that the project team leaders could stay focused on getting the products ready to deploy, while the capability leader could begin release planning and communications way ahead of the rollout date. For example, the local business people responsible for leading the release 4 implementation were identified one year in advance.

Another learning from release 2 was to increase the training time on the new business processes. Once the first major business unit was brought on line, it would also be possible to use a "play with sand in the sandbox" training approach: Actual production data could be used to train on different business scenarios. The business process owners would also be more involved in and have greater accountability for the deployment.

The number of business employees that would receive training at corporate headquarters was also significantly increased. Instead of the 500 "champions" in the original plan, more than 900 people were identified and trained to become the onsite trainers and support personnel at the local sites. This resulted in a champion/employee ratio of 1:7 instead of 1:10 or 1:15 in some plants. The typical-sized plant would have multiple champions trained for each process.

The March 1997 Roofing & Asphalt Rollout

Domenico Cecere had been corporate controller and a member of the original steering committee for Advantage 2000 during the release 1 financial accounting rollout. As president of Roofing & Asphalt, he opted to be the first major North American business unit to "go live" with release 4. Cecere told his plant managers that SAP R/3 would free them up to visit their large customers, to come up with new product ideas, and to move the business forward. All their paperwork would be done for them at headquarters beginning with the release 4 implementation.

The Roofing & Asphalt implementation involved 32 plants. Fifteen of these were shingle plants with an average of 100 workers. The 17 asphalt plants had about 13 workers per plant. Logistics for this division involved 700 to 900 trucks a day.

Process consolidation and simplification to improve profitability were the major release 4 goals for Roofing & Asphalt. The division did not have enough business leader resources to fully populate the project teams, so it was decided to have some of the Insulation division's business leaders represent Roofing & Asphalt's interests. The teams looked at every piece of their business in order to identify inefficiencies that had evolved over the past 20 years and to rewrite their business rules. In the past, sales transactions could be informal and inefficient, with special deals made to please a customer without knowing the ramifications for the business. Beginning with release 4, the ordering process would be consolidated and operated out of Toledo.

> I told the plants "we're the best," so we'll be the first to do it. We'll show everybody else how to do it. The project forced us

[8] In a January 1998 reorganization, BME became International Building Materials Systems, the Composites division became Composites Systems Business, and the other North American divisions were reorganized under an umbrella organization: North American Building Materials Systems, encompassing Roofing Systems Business, Insulating Systems Business, Exterior Systems Business, and System Thinking Sales and Distribution.

EXHIBIT 2

IS/IM Integration Teams - 44 Initiatives

1. Information Management Vision
2. Human Resources IS Workforce
3. IS Management Team Exchange
4. SAP R/3 Centric Business
5. Applications Portfolio
6. Intranet/Internet Deployment
7. DIGITAL Product and Services Offerings
8. Infrastructure Topology
9. Start-up Deployment Team
10. Mail and Messaging Integration
11. NT Infrastructure Integration
12. WAN Optimization
13. Remote Access
14. LAN Strategy
15. Enterprise Network Architecture
16. Enterprise Management Architecture
17. Voice Network
18. Internal Equipment Sourcing
19. Disaster Recovery Strategies
20. IT Metrics
21. Technology Integration Checklist
22. Data Warehousing/Reporting
23. Services Logistics
24. Call Management
25. Enterprise Architecture for SAP
26. Peoplesoft/SAP HR
27. Year 2000 Program
28. Project Services
29. Reference Data Strategy/Management
30. Sales Productivity Tools
31. High–Availability/High–Performance Computing
32. Operational Processes
33. Information Security
34. Desktop Support Strategies
35. Collaboration and Workflow
36. Cost Recovery for IS and Infrastructure Services
37. Merged SAP Enterprise Application Architecture
38. Alliances and Agreements
39. Sales Workbench and Transfer Manager
40. Product Management and Development Workbench
41. Document Management and Records Retention
42. Electronic Document Interchange
43. Treasury Management
44. Worldwide Trade and Compliance

acquisition. In early February 1998, four of Digital's senior IM managers went to Compaq's headquarters to lay the groundwork for the eventual integration of their two organizations. Due to legal restrictions on the kinds of information that could be shared, the discussions about existing systems and practices were very high level. In essence, each side shared presentations that they regularly made to customers. The meeting primarily served to help familiarize the two parties:

> I took notes but was told I couldn't share them. So when I came back, a lot of what I shared was "tone"—like what it was like to walk onto their campus. It felt like they were moving 800 miles an hour. They weren't fully staffed a lot of the time, and they were looking for ways to get things done.
>
> *—Technology Manager, Digital*

At a follow-up meeting in late February, a dozen or so of John White's direct reports met with Dick Fishburn and a number of his direct and dotted-line reports. The groups identified 15 key areas that needed to be integrated. They paired counterparts from the two firms' IM functions in these 15 areas to start working on an integration roadmap for both the infrastructure and mission critical applications.

They then mapped out 44 integration initiatives and created teams to work on them. (See Exhibit 2 for a list of the key areas and initiatives.) Although the focus of the meeting—and the teams—was on technical integration, issues around organizational structure quickly surfaced:

> The first thing that came to everyone's mind was that there was a huge disparity in staffing. Digital was gigantic. John [White] basically said, "You have hundreds of people too many in this group." I think Compaq was just overwhelmed by the sheer size of the Digital groups.[4]
>
> *—CIO, Tandem*

John White charged the teams with evaluating Compaq's and Digital's systems and processes. They were to present recommendations in May for adopting the Compaq, Digital, or hybrid solution for each major initiative. IM Integration leaders instituted a weekly review process for ensuring that the teams were on track, and the teams worked cooperatively toward their goals. Although Compaq was the acquiring firm, Digital had more human resources to devote to the planning.

Developing an Integrated Infrastructure

Among the 44 IM integration initiatives, management was particularly concerned with those that would establish a common infrastructure. Even before the merger was formalized, the two

[4]Digital had about 3,200 people in its IT organization the day of the merger. Compaq had about 1,500 IM employees plus 500 contractors. Tandem had a few hundred.

firms needed an efficient, secure communications channel for exchanging information between them. And soon after the merger, management wanted a technical infrastructure that would allow it to operate as a single company. To this end the IM integration leaders assigned teams to nine initiatives that they referred to as Phase One—actions that were to be implemented within 60 days after the merger was formally approved. Another 16 initiatives were referred to as Phase Two—planning efforts for post-merger activity. Enterprise network integration, enterprise application architecture, and day-one deployment were examples of Phase One initiatives.

Enterprise Network Integration

Laurence Cranwell, manager of global communications for Digital, headed a team responsible for planning the enterprise network for the combined company. Cranwell's team had the challenge of ensuring that a packet could reach across any part of the existing Digital or Compaq (including Tandem) networks, even if they had different addresses and different architectures. The two companies had different network architectures, products, and protocols. Compaq's network architecture had been developed for a highly centralized operating environment, whereas Digital's Services business required more distributed operations:

> We [Digital] had 400 sites in the U.S. They had 10. That's one thing we worked through as an organization. The stovepipe organization that does technology delivery is okay when you've got very few sites, but when you have many, you need an operating model for 1,100 global sites. You can't be there all the time.
>
> —*Laurence Cranwell, Director, Communication Technology Information Services*

Digital's networking people viewed their responsibility for the global network as an opportunity to do a "green field" design for the future. Both firms' legacy networks had become congested and both were working with carriers to design ATM networks, so these efforts were combined. They would need 6 months to turn on the green field, but they needed to design the global network in advance of the actual merger. This involved making assumptions about future site locations:

> A lot of the future communications infrastructure would depend on the data-center decisions—where they are going to be—and where the transactions are going to take place. Plans also depended on what applications would be selected to go forward, and which plant sites would remain open or closed. Plant closings were very sensitive issues; management didn't want the information to get out and scare people off prematurely, but we needed to know.
>
> —*Laurence Cranwell, Director, Communication Technology Information Services*

Although the uncertainties created challenges for planning the network, the network team could outline a high-level architecture based on the board's statement that Digital would be integrated with Compaq. They needed to know less about the structure and operations of the combined firm than the application integration teams would need to know:

> It's really like train tracks. They conform to standards, but the types of trains you can run over the tracks are pretty different. That's where you get a little more disagreement. You don't get into the politics as much about the tracks. You take care of the tracks—make sure I can get from point A to point B—and others worry about which trains, the application level.
>
> —*Ed Furilla, Sales & Marketing IM Manager*

While they planned the new global architecture, Cranwell's team worked to establish temporary linkages across the three entities. Compaq had nine CLASS B Internet addresses, and about 80 CLASS C Internet addresses.[5] Digital had one large flat address space. Consequently, if Compaq, Digital, and Tandem all had buildings in Munich, consolidating their facilities could result in having three people sitting twenty feet apart with three different IP address domains supporting them. Until the firm had a new architecture with a single address space, communications between the merged entities had to be transferred through Internet mail (i.e., through firewalls) rather than a seamless network. This was both slow and costly:

> The joke was that Compaq paid $9.6B for a CLASS A Internet address. The right answer was to redesign the network to move all of Compaq into the CLASS A address that Digital had, and at the same time rearchitect.
>
> —*Rick Fricchione, Vice President, Advanced Information Technology and Planning*

Enterprise Application Architecture

Because Compaq was the acquiring firm, its application systems were the starting point for discussions about which of the two firms' redundant systems should be retained. At the time the merger was announced, both firms were in the third year of SAP R/3 implementations to replace core transaction processing systems for finance, manufacturing, order management, and logistics. Both firms had focused first on European operations because they believed financial returns would be most immediate there. But the two firms had little else in common in their ERP implementations.

---

[5]The CLASS refers to the size of the address space. A CLASS C address space might allow for as few as 256 nodes on a network, while a CLASS B address could allow for 64,000 nodes. Large firms must cobble together their networks using multiple address spaces if they do not have a sufficiently large address space.

Digital was implementing a common, global supply chain system across its business units. It was pursuing a site-by-site implementation managed out of a central program office that leveraged the expertise of about 100 key people across the organization. A key objective of the SAP implementation was to develop consistent business processes and consistent reporting across sites. Digital had allowed just 14 modifications to SAP code. Digital had implemented SAP financials worldwide, standardizing all financial processing such that the way revenue was counted in Asia was the same as in Europe. Following about three false starts, Digital implemented SAP in its European manufacturing operations, and by June 1998 Digital had installed four instances of SAP manufacturing modules, including one U.S. manufacturing site.

Compaq's implementation was managed out of the IM organization. The central team developed a template and each geographic region customized the template to fit local needs. By June 1998, the 3-year project had included about 40 small "big bang" implementations with up to 10 projects going on in parallel. In total, it had nine separate instances of SAP. Compaq had relied heavily on Price Waterhouse consultants and had focused on a fast implementation rather than consistency across sites. Compaq had made over 1,500 modifications to SAP code as it customized the software to meet the needs of individual sites, plants, and geographies:

> We put stuff in brutally fast. We were almost up 100 percent on SAP before we bought Digital. We would just go in and make people scream; if the users didn't like it, we told them "you're going to get it anyway." Digital was just the opposite: it was very much risk-avoidance. They wouldn't "go live" unless all the issues were resolved, and everybody signed up that it was going to work. When they went live, there was never an issue. Then, again, they had very little SAP up by the time we bought them.
>
> *—Director, Global Financial Processes*

Having a common software package did not make for an easy integration of the two firms' operating processes. For a variety of reasons, including the fact that Compaq was the acquiring firm and felt that it was further along in its implementations, the SAP team eventually recommended that the firm pattern future implementations after Compaq Classic. A short-term dilemma that arose following the SAP decision was whether to continue with a Digital SAP implementation scheduled for summer 1998 in Scotland. Despite the stated new direction, the uncertainty of the timing of the merger led to the decision to implement in the Scotland plant as planned.

As part of its SAP implementation, Compaq had completed a 2-year rollout of the HR module in March 1998. In contrast, Digital, along with Tandem, had purchased PeopleSoft for its HR systems. Both SAP and PeopleSoft were asked to propose new contracts for the combined firm. Although tempted to push SAP into all of Compaq, the IM and human resource organizations chose to adopt PeopleSoft. This was the first time that Compaq employees had been in a situation where an alliance affected a platform choice:

> PeopleSoft is a business partner. We were looking for an opportunity to expand our relationship with PeopleSoft so that became part of the decision criteria. It was also important that, once the acquisition took place, 70 percent of our workforce would already be on PeopleSoft.
>
> *—Ed Pennington, Director, Corporate Administrative Services*

At the time of the PeopleSoft decision, Digital was 80 percent through its HR implementation. However, the decision was made to scrap this implementation, because it was not consistent with Compaq's processes. The combined firm would start all over again with a PeopleSoft implementation for the new Compaq.

The differences in Compaq's and Digital's approaches to enterprise application implementation were echoed in the differences in the two firms' approaches to enterprise application support. Digital had assigned responsibility for supporting its PeopleSoft implementations—and most of its other global legacy systems—to a large shared services organization called the Production Support Group (PSG). At the time of the merger the group totaled about 1,000 people, and functioned like an in-house outsourcing organization. Digital credited the PSG concept with reducing IT costs and moving spending from operations support to new investment because it forced business unit managers to decide how much support they were willing to pay for.

Compaq located responsibility for global application management within each of the geographies. Some key managers were philosophically opposed to the shared services concept, believing that it introduced unnecessary bureaucracy. Thus, PSG had no counterpart at Compaq and its head was not paired with a Compaq manager for integration planning. The design for legacy systems support defaulted to the Compaq model:

> The key issue is not shared services, but running the corporation in a geo model or a business unit/functional model. Compaq had chosen geography. Once that decision is made, other things come as a result.
>
> *—Rick Fricchione, Vice President, Advanced Information Technology and Planning*

Day-One Deployment

IM managers at the two firms worked closely to ensure some level of IT integration of the two firms as of the day the merger would be approved by the stockholders. Leveraging their experience with the Tandem merger, Compaq executives specified some aggressive day-one goals:

> One of the things done enormously well for the Tandem acquisition was to get the two networks talking within two days. So our goal with Digital was to have this capability on the day the

> merger was approved. In some of the other systems areas, the need to take immediate action wasn't quite as important. We were able to think about it a little longer.
>
> —*Fred Jones, Vice President, Information Services, Compaq*

In particular, the firms took advantage of the fact that they were both using MS Exchange for e-mail. On day one a single e-mail directory was available so that employees could easily find and mail messages to their counterparts in the other organization. Firewalls and filters that had been put in place prior to the merger came down to provide open connectivity, with no security holes to the outside world. A coordinated approach to help desk support combined Compaq's help center in Houston and Digital's in New England. And a new external Web site put a combined front end to the two firms' individual sites.

First Day as New Company

The two IS organizations viewed having the new e-mail infrastructure in place on day one as a collaborative triumph. The integration teamwork had also increased sensitivities to the cultural differences across the two organizations:

> You would hear all kinds of stories like: "Why do those folks in New England think they have to plan forever? We could have it done before they have a plan." I heard comments like these in the first 2 months, but I didn't hear them thereafter. You could almost make these deficiencies something to be proud about on both sides, because if you mixed the two, you'd have planning *and* execution.
>
> —*John Buda, Director, IS Client Management*

In addition, the premerger work resulted in some important planning decisions that would guide systems integration in the coming months. However, the Digital IT people who had worked on the integration teams did not know whether they would be tapped to play a major role in the new IM organization or not. Throughout the planning, the fact that leadership was shared by paired teams of IT managers meant that the temporary organization chart effectively had a "two in a box" look that would soon be reduced to one:

> There was plenty of tension, but it wasn't as intense as I would have expected it to be. We worked well together, especially the information services group. I think it was because there was compelling work that had to be done. The day-one set of tasks had to happen on schedule.
>
> —*Fred Jones, Vice President, Information Services, Compaq*

The public documents filed for the merger made it clear that 16,000 jobs would be cut from the new Compaq by the end of 1998, and anxieties were high, especially among those people who had been with the company the longest. The fiscal year for Digital Classic would end June 30 and, due to its strong financial results, the year-end bonus looked attractive. However, to receive the bonus, employees needed to stay with the company until the end of July.

CASE STUDY IV-5

MERGING INFORMATION TECHNOLOGY AND CULTURES AT COMPAQ-DIGITAL (B): BECOMING A SINGLE FIRM

In August 1998, within 2 months of the merger of Compaq Computer Corporation and Digital Equipment Corporation, a new chief information officer, Michael Capellas, was brought on board. Capellas arrived with a track record as an international CIO and recent stints as director of supply-chain management for SAP America and a senior VP within Oracle Corporation. At that time, he was the only senior manager within the newly integrated computer company that had been brought in from the outside.

When Capellas arrived, the basic communications infrastructure, telephone systems, and e-mail were in place, but integration of the daily operations—taking orders, shipping orders, interfacing with customers—was still underway. Nonetheless, within 4 months after his arrival, Capellas had seen the new company set a world record for the number of units shipped—4.2 million:

> Despite all the problems, we are outperforming the world in volume. At the end of the day, business results are business results. We must be doing something right.
>
> —*Michael Capellas, Senior Vice President & CIO*[1]

Creating a New Information Management Organization

The new Compaq was a combination of the old Compaq's high-growth personal computer and server businesses with Digital's mid-range computer products and highly profitable services business. According to documents filed with the U.S. Securities and Exchange Commission as part of the merger approval process, the new company was expected to achieve lower operating costs as well as increased revenues from new cross-selling opportunities. Senior management felt pressure to deliver these benefits quickly, and the information management (IM) organization's new leader felt accountable:

> In our business IT is not an enabler, it basically *is* the business. If you're not getting orders, you're not shipping product . . . and the world is ending.
>
> —*Michael Capellas, Senior Vice President & CIO*

Under its former CIO John White, Compaq had a highly centralized approach to managing IM. This structure helped the IM organization get things done quickly and kept IT spending significantly below the industry average. Although each of the geographic regions had their own IM support groups, White was tightly linked with Compaq's executive committee and IM strategy and infrastructure standards decisions were all set at the corporate level.

In contrast, under CIO Dick Fishburn, Digital had had a highly decentralized model, with each business having its own CIO. This model gave the distributed manufacturing and services businesses more personal service from their own IS groups, but it was more expensive. It also meant that the business CIOs often went off and did something on their own.

The June 1998 post-merger announcement of the top management team for the new Compaq named White as CIO—but it was well known that White planned to retire sometime before year-end. In fact, the merger integration activities had thrown a kink in the search process for a new CIO and White had signed an extension to his contract. The agreement was that he would stay on until a replacement was found and the merger activities had settled down a bit. This left plans for the new IM organization in limbo over the summer months.

> Everyone was concerned about "where do I fit on the org chart." That's what they really wanted to hear. So until we could actually tell them that, we gave them a lot about how the business is coming together, what other organizations at Compaq were doing, and where we were on our plans.
>
> —*Laurence Cranwell, Director, Communication Technology Information Services*

 This case was prepared by Jeanne Ross, Principal Research Scientist at MIT's Center for Information Systems Research, and Carol V. Brown, Associate Professor at Indiana University's Kelley School of Business. The authors would like to thank Rick Fricchione of Compaq for his insights and efforts and the many Compaq employees who participated in the research.

[1]The interviews for this case study are based on on-site interviews held between December 1998 and February 1999.

The new senior IM management team was named by White just one week before he retired in August 1998. Thus, when Capellas arrived from Oracle Corporation to head up the combined IM organization, he inherited a new management team that had not yet sorted out lower level reporting structures.

White chose primarily Compaq Classic managers for his senior management team, but as Capellas filled in the organization chart (see Exhibit 1), it became clear that IM management at Compaq would no longer be so tightly controlled from Houston. Rick Fricchione, for example, was an ex-Digital manager who was tapped to be vice president, advanced information technology and planning, and Capellas had agreed that Fricchione could fill the role from Massachusetts. Similarly, Fred Jones, a Compaq Classic manager who assumed global responsibilities for technology and process, had five former Digital managers among his eight direct reports. Only two of the five had plans to relocate to Houston. Laurence Cranwell, one of Jones' direct reports based in New England, managed a team split about 50/50 between Compaq Classic and Digital Classic.

While Compaq Classic managers lamented the increased complexity that accompanied a more distributed IM management model, they acknowledged that, in a very tight IT labor market, Houston alone could not provide sufficient IT resources for a $40 billion firm. They wanted to take advantage of the fact that Compaq's two key acquisitions were in high-tech corridors. The 1997 Tandem acquisition gave Compaq a hook into Silicon Valley, and the 1998 Digital merger gave it a hook into the Boston corridor and Route 128.

Adding to the complexity was the recognition that Compaq's newly acquired services business had different IM support needs than the manufacturing business. CEO Pfeiffer had kept the leadership for the services business in Massachusetts,

EXHIBIT 1
Compaq Information Management

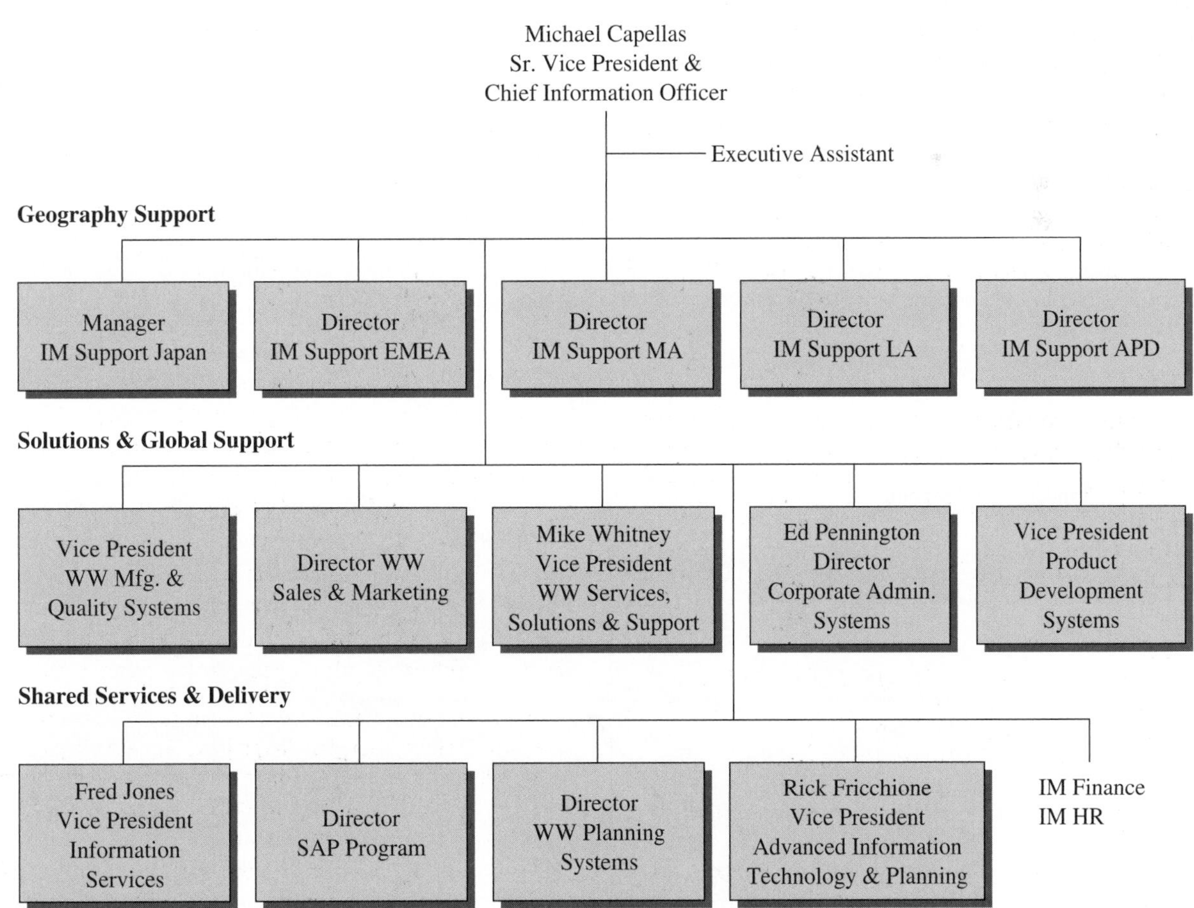

reporting to both the CEO and the geographies. Senior VP of Services John Rando had been a key player in the strategy discussions during the premerger integration process, and Rando became a member of the new Compaq's top management team as soon as the merger was finalized. The IM roadmap for services mirrored this structure. Mike Whitney, the former CIO for the Digital services group, reported to Rando, and the IM teams working on worldwide and functional systems solutions for services reported to Whitney. The IM heads working in each of the geographical services units now had a dual reporting relationship to Whitney and to their local services head:

> On Capellas' new organization chart, I'm the only person who is shown with a dotted line; everybody else is a solid line. Services makes a large percentage of the profit of the company. But it's difficult in terms of being remote from Houston and there's still concern on how well services is perceived as integrating into the rest of the company.
>
> —*Michael Whitney, CIO, Compaq Services*

While Houston IM managers were adjusting to the challenge of managing a distributed work force, those former Digital managers who had decided not to relocate to Houston had to learn when they could rely on e-mail and videoconferencing and when they needed to be in Houston. They knew that they needed to interact with other IM and business managers in order to build good working relationships, and periodically they had to be part of the action in Houston in order to influence decisions:

> Things can happen so fast, that if you're not in the middle of the floor, you're out of the decision process. The remote manager suffers a little from out of sight, out of mind, because it's been the mentality of the company.
>
> —*Michael Capellas, Senior Vice President & CIO*

Working Toward Process Integration

In order to achieve the objectives of the merger, senior management felt that process integration was critical. Immediately following the merger, a customer who wanted to buy Compaq, Tandem, and Digital products would have to submit three separate orders and later process three separate invoices. Compaq worked to provide a single customer interface within a couple months of the merger, but real process integration would take some time:

> The company had done a pretty solid job of merging the sales force, but the infrastructure was not in place to [enable all salespeople to sell all Compaq products]. The order fulfillment model still had a long way to go; it was just in its infancy. Finance was getting the books closed, but with some brute force.
>
> —*Michael Capellas, Senior Vice President & CIO*

Ultimately, management wanted an integrated supply chain across the three entities. The business vision was that a customer could call Compaq and order three DEC Alphas, two Tandem Himalayas, and 10,000 Compaq PCs on one purchase order. The order would be reflected as one entry in Compaq's systems and would arrive at the customer's location all at one time. To achieve this level of integration, management had to reconcile business model incompatibilities among the separate entities and implement integrated systems to support those enterprise-wide processes that defined the new Compaq. Management coined the term OnePaq for this integration effort. (See Exhibit 2.)

EXHIBIT 2
The OnePaq Road Map

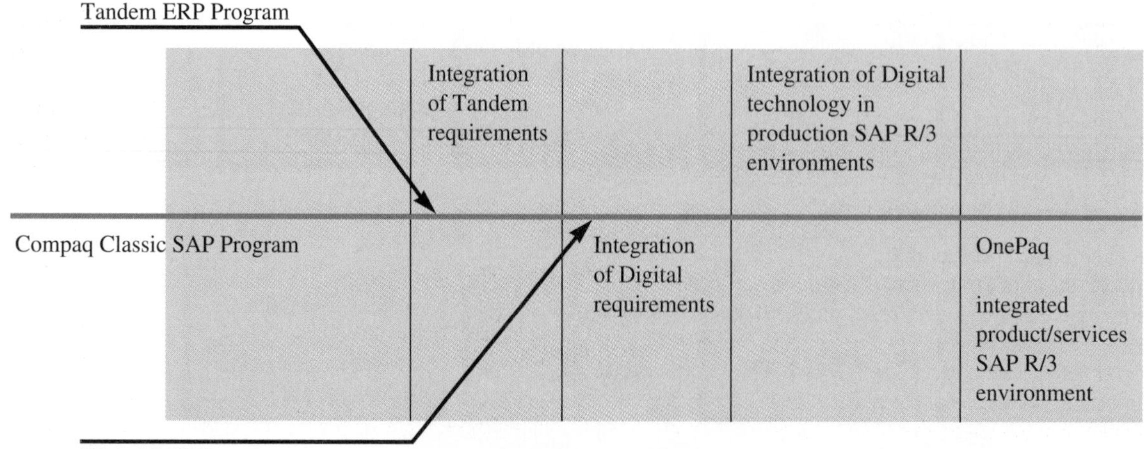

Reconciling Different Business Models

Compaq's core business processes supported large manufacturing volumes—as many as 20,000 PCs a day in a single plant, which was more than Digital manufactured in all its plants in a week. Digital's business model, on the other hand, supported direct-to-customer sales and support of smaller numbers of PCs (up to 3,000 per day) and customized mini and mainframe systems. Compaq had acquired Digital specifically because of its services business, but the opportunities it presented and the challenges of integrating services into supply-chain, customer-facing, and e-business processes were not well understood.

The services business negotiated high-end systems contracts directly with enterprise customers. Compaq Classic had not sold services. Its services unit had included a help desk, repair center, and spare-parts shipping for its products. Rather than deal with end-users, Compaq supported its channel partners, who supported Compaq's customers. In contrast, Digital had serviced its own systems and that of its competitors. In addition, Digital had sold systems integration services, while Compaq had regularly used the services of systems integrators like Andersen Consulting (now Accenture) and PricewaterhouseCoopers. These very different business models made for an uneasy transition following the merger. Some Compaq Classic managers sensed that Digital's willingness to service competitors' equipment compromised potential Compaq sales, while former Digital managers were wary of the impact of Compaq's alliances with competing service providers on service unit revenues.

Ultimately, Compaq service engagements that involved implementing systems like SAP, Siebel, or e-business applications would "pull" Compaq hardware sales. Similarly, hardware sales were expected to lead to services revenues. Because of the differences in old business models and systems, however, Whitney anticipated that it would take some time to see synergies from the merger of the Compaq, Digital, and Tandem services units. The integration would involve a global portfolio mapping of all Compaq services across the world and the implementation of the SAP baseline to support them.

An early initiative immediately following the merger was a Web-based front end for online orders via the Internet. This, of course, did not clean up the back-end systems. One vice president noted that the new front end was like "putting lipstick on a pig." But the Web-based front end was important for moving Compaq Services into the Internet space:

> The Internet world sort of changes the spin on how you want to deliver services. For the small-to-medium business environment, more than likely we'll look at a lot of Webbing and a lot of the Compaq Classic stuff, because we can't afford $100–200K service centers. But the time that it's going to take to integrate all the call-handling, all the sales and marketing, is nowhere near the speed that the business wants to go.
>
> —*Michael Whitney, CIO, Compaq Services*

The growing importance of e-business exacerbated the organizational challenges associated with the merger:

> The whole world of e-commerce came to this industry before it came to other industries. We're growing while business models are changing on top of us. Anything we build now we know is wrong. You never have your feet on the ground. What Internet technology does to the world is that you're in a continual state of aggregation and disaggregation. You're constantly putting stuff together and taking it apart.
>
> —*Michael Capellas, Senior Vice President & CIO*

Implementing Enterprise Systems

Enterprise systems implementation embodied two different challenges. One was to redefine the new firm's business processes. The other was to effectively manage ERP implementation projects in a large, complex, constantly changing organization.

Prior to the merger, Compaq had total worldwide supply-chain planning running on custom systems. Except in the U.S., this had tied into SAP for order management. IM did not immediately attempt to install these systems at Digital facilities, because supply-chain planning would be very much affected by the firm's reorganization. From June to November 1998, the firm was shutting down plants, laying off people, and consolidating operations. Thus, prior to November 1998, there was little progress in integrating the supply chain across former Tandem, Digital, and Compaq sites. Ultimately, management had to decide the extent to which the supply chain could be standardized across geographies and product lines:

> In any of these large ERP projects, if you can answer "how common is common," you'll get it right. I've never seen anybody do it gracefully or painlessly. It's a very, very difficult question—and it's much broader than IM. It's the whole world of management in the '90s. Technology is allowing you to make more things common than you used to; but on the other hand, the flexibility of that technology is also giving capabilities at the local level to people that never had it before. So it's a difficult balance of technology, management style, and just pure efficiency.
>
> —*Michael Capellas, Senior Vice President & CIO*

In addition to supply chain differences, there were significant differences in the firms' financial closing and forecasting processes. For example, both Compaq and Digital used Hyperion systems for financial consolidation. However, Digital did the currency translation at the transaction level and then fed transaction data into Hyperion in U.S. dollars prior to doing cost allocations. Compaq did all of its cost allocations and liquidations inside its new SAP system and then sent the transactions in local currencies into Hyperion where they were translated. In addition, they took different approaches to foreign currency translation. Digital translated monthly results while Compaq translated each transaction.

> How we run our closes between Compaq and Digital Classic are very dissimilar. That doesn't mean one is right or one is wrong, it's just that two companies have chosen to do it two different ways. Basically, when you look at our systems, the only thing similar is they're made by the same vendor.
>
> *—Director, Global Financial Processes*

Once the two entities moved to a common ledger system using a Compaq SAP baseline, they would have common allocation schemes, common reporting schemes, and common data. Even before formal approval of the merger, the integration team had decided to accept the Compaq SAP baseline to accomplish this financial and supply chain integration:

> We had really built a much higher-volume, high-speed environment [at Compaq]. We thought it would be much easier to add the complexity to the high volume than to add the high volume to the complexity.
>
> *—SAP Project Manager*

The services side of the business had some unique requirements that were not incorporated in the Compaq baseline. For example, services needed the project accounting module in SAP in order to determine profitability and margins by work breakdown element. The integration team had intended to adopt Compaq Classic's SAP rapid implementation approach. However, the gradual recognition of the unique needs of the services and direct sales organizations greatly increased the complexity of the implementation:

> It's a new world for Compaq. The old way we used to do it, when we were growing fast and furious, was that IM would race around and bring up SAP in big bang swoops on a Compaq Classic model, which was basically building PCs. Now, there's this giant services arm, and we have Tandem which builds giant PCs that can take a year to sell. We're getting too big for that now.
>
> *—Director, Global Financial Processes*

The OnePaq 1A project was originally intended to be simple product-order integration, but it eventually grew into a new corporate CTO (configure-to-order) initiative. Over time, the project plan evolved to include about 150 projects to be implemented in seven phases under OnePaq program managers in each geographic region. Compaq, which had traditionally defined systems projects that could be completed in 3 to 6 months, found itself constantly confronting scope creep:

> It got too big. We had master data issues. We also had to learn how services was doing things because we had never had a services group. We couldn't do it. Basically, we fell back to breaking up the project into smaller projects. In manufacturing, we're doing a phased implementation. IM gets the nasty job of saying, "how do I phase all of this into some sort of project schedule with resource constraints, cash, and all that?"
>
> *—Director, Global Financial Processes*

Meeting the Headcount Reduction Targets

At the same time that OnePaq implementations were getting underway, another challenge for the new IM organization had to be tackled: meeting the headcount reductions filed with the SEC as part of the cost savings rationalization for the merger. Achieving the quotas was a nonnegotiable issue, and funds had been put aside for termination packages. When Capellas arrived in August 1998, the "clock was already ticking" but decisions about the downsizing targets for specific IM units had been delayed until his arrival.

Most IT groups were given an 18 percent target, but a portion of the quotas would be met by attrition. Many experienced Digital managers—including the Digital CIO and eight other managers who had carried a CIO or vice president title in the Digital IS organization—had left the company before Capellas' appointment was announced. Additional "cream of the crop" employees left before the layoffs began:

> As Digital had gone through rounds of cost cutting and facility closings it was not unusual to have one or two really good people working from home in a particular area. Eventually this grew to a work-at-home program with hundreds of people (at least 100 in IS) participating. At the time of the merger, these people were viewed as a problem and the directive went out to either bring them into a Compaq office or lay them off. What many saw as progressive work practices at Digital were being eliminated. Hundreds left the company over this one alone.
>
> *—Rick Fricchione, Vice President, Advanced Information Technology and Planning*

When Capellas arrived in August, overall attrition rates were quite high. At one point "sharks" from a major IT consulting firm had camped outside of the Digital offices in recruiting vans:

> You take a very hot area like IT where the job market is on fire. You compound it with an equally red hot market like SAP. Put it together with the uncertainty of an acquisition, and you will get attrition. It was also fairly clear that the new Compaq was going to be based in Texas, and the thought of becoming cowboys was not always that appealing to those long-established Bostonians.
>
> *—Michael Capellas, Senior Vice President & CIO*

A snag in the downsizing process was caused by delays in the European labor negotiations. Late in 1998, it became clear that it would be impossible to meet the European targets for that year. The U.S. groups were told to increase their 1998 layoffs. Although this meant that the U.S. targets for 1999 would be lowered when layoffs in Europe became possible, it affected credibility and morale within IM:

> We ended up—after many of us had told everybody "that was it"—having to go back and do another [round of layoffs]. That last one in December was pretty brutal. It had big morale issues. We had said we were done.
>
> *—SAP Project Director*

The staff reductions, coupled with accelerating demands for data integration, e-commerce capabilities, and enterprise systems support, forced constant focus on attacking only the highest IM priorities.

Transforming the Firm

As the last year of the century began, Compaq's logo was appearing on Digital buildings in New England, and the rebadging of Digital Classic people was underway. IM management noted that some pieces of the IM integration were clear from the outset; others were evolving on a daily basis. In particular, IM's role was increasingly focused on enabling Compaq to transform itself from a build-to-stock to a configure-to-order model as the firm moved aggressively into e-business:

> We anticipated some of the ways that the new business would be put together, but some of the pieces were put together differently than we expected. The maturity of e-business and Web-based business all happened in the same time frame. The business priorities turned 180 degrees during the integration process. The Web project was always on the roadmap, but the urgency changed significantly during the first 9 months of integration.
>
> *—Fred Jones, Vice President, Information Services*

By early 1999, management recognized that the OnePaq initiative would not meet its initial targets, and management established new SAP target implementation dates for the next 4 quarters. These included merging general ledgers in Q2 of 1999; consolidating order management (in part) in Q3; integrating manufacturing in Q4 of 1999 and Q1 of 2000; and systems integration of the services business in Q2 of 2000. The OnePaq initiatives were critical for addressing the goals for the merger as filed with the SEC, as well as for enabling Compaq to compete in an e-business world.

Epilogue

In July 1999 Michael Capellas, Compaq's CIO, was appointed CEO. At that time, Compaq's revenues were stagnating and the firm had not yet realized the anticipated cost savings from the merger. By September 2000, Compaq's revenues had rebounded and operating costs were on the decline. Compaq reported net income of $712 million for the first two quarters of 2000 on revenues of $19.6 billion, as compared with net income of $97 million on $18.8 billion in revenues for the year-earlier period. In addition, Compaq was generating $6 million in daily sales through its Web site and about $50 million in daily sales through EDI.

Compaq's IM unit delivered GlobalNet in mid-1999, fulfilling the green-field vision established prior to the merger. In practice no one in the Compaq organization would be more than "two hops from the backbone," and the network had universal remote access. This design provided better bandwidth usage, which meant that Compaq could spend its dollars on the routing architecture rather than bandwidth. Bob Napier was brought in from GM Delphi to take the CIO role. He, in turn, placed CIOs in each of the business units, creating a federated IM structure for the new Compaq.

Capellas reorganized Compaq around global business units: consumer, commercial PCs, storage, industry standard servers, business critical servers, professional services, and customer services. Each business unit appointed a vice president for key processes such as supply chain. The services unit was originally grouped with enterprise computing, but sales languished and Compaq lost ground to IBM. Eventually Capellas moved to a direct sales force rather than channel partners, and he joined services with direct sales to better serve the needs of large corporate customers. The resulting organization was one that was prepared to be a total enterprise player.

CASE STUDY IV-6

FastTrack IT Integration for the Sallie Mae Merger

> This transaction combines our capital strength and sales capabilities with USA Group's premier service quality. ... It would be difficult to overstate the significance of this deal to our three principal constituencies: students, schools, and shareholders.[1]
>
> —*Albert L. Lord, Vice Chairman and Chief Executive Officer, Sallie Mae*

In June 2000, the two largest players in the education finance industry announced their intent to merge: Sallie Mae of Reston, Virginia, would acquire USA Group of Indianapolis, Indiana. The merger announcement in *The Wall Street Journal* highlighted the strategic role that USA Group's software applications would play in the new combined company: USA Group's loan-guarantee-processing business and its campus-loan origination and loan-processing products were expected to make the combined company more competitive.[2]

> Although Sallie Mae held a teleconference for all employees on the day of the merger announcement, new tensions about the future set in quickly. People were stunned. USA Group was our largest competitor, and there was a lot of uncertainty about how this could impact employment for all of us. There was so much anxiety on both sides. People had built their careers at these companies.
>
> —*Cindy Gunn, Vice President of Computer Operations for Sallie Mae*

Sallie Mae planned to cut its work force by 1,700 employees, or 25 percent, by the end of 2001, as it integrated its operations with USA Group. Most of these reductions (1,400) would be in its information-technology and customer-service areas; the remainder (300) would be administration and headquarters jobs.[3]

The busy season for the education-financing industry is in the summer: about 60 percent of loan processing occurs during the summer months in preparation for the fall semester, with June as the peak month. When the government's Direct Lending program had undergone a major software change about 1 year earlier, there had been a number of publicized bottlenecks and processing errors with student loans during the busy season. Sallie Mae's management team didn't want to make the same mistakes; to ensure that its own customers would not go to a competitor, customer-facing operations would need to be completed before the coming summer season, with no perceived loss of service.

> Some were afraid the merger might meet shareholder objectives but would hurt the customer. The customer concerns were that service would suffer, agility would be low, and we would create a large bureaucracy. We were combining the volume of two company's loans on one system with a new management team and brand-new architecture. And we were doing it just before peak season.
>
> —*Hamed Omar, Senior Vice President, Technology Group*

Company Histories

Sallie Mae was founded in 1972 as a government-sponsored enterprise (GSE) in Reston, Virginia, to provide a secondary market for banks and other lenders to sell their student loans. Prior to the merger, Sallie Mae had a $50 billion portfolio of student loans and was the largest funding source and servicer for student loans in the United States. The company's primary role was to purchase student loans from banks and other lenders, creating a secondary market and freeing up funds for the institutions to lend out money to other borrowers.

Albert L. Lord, Sallie Mae's CEO, had been a major catalyst in transforming the company from a GSE to a publicly held

---

 This case was prepared for class discussion by Professor Carol V. Brown in collaboration with Rebecca Scholer. The authors are indebted to Greg Clancy, Hamed Omar, Paula Lohss, and all of the other Sallie Mae managers who shared their insights and experiences with the authors via in-person interviews.

[1] *PR Newswire* (SLM Holding Corporation), June 15, 2000, "Sallie Mae and USA Group Reach Agreement to Combine."

[2] *The Wall Street Journal*, June 16, 2000, "Sallie Mae Is Set to Buy Assets of USA Group In Cash-Stock Deal."

[3] *The Wall Street Journal*, Sept. 1, 2000, "Sallie Mae Will Cut Jobs After Acquiring USA Group."

business. In the early 1990s he helped streamline the company's operations, but then left the company in 1993 when the board opposed his plans for restructuring the company. Two years later, he led a dissident slate of eight directors that was elected to the 21-member board and was able successfully to launch a plan to reposition the company from a buyer of loans to a competitive lender to students.[4]

As CEO since 1997, Lord began phasing out the company's government-sponsored status, despite some internal opposition.[5] Lord also switched its marketing focus to get closer to the customer. Rather than working solely with banks and financial institutions, the company began marketing to students through the schools. At the time of the merger announcement in June 2000, Sallie Mae was a $14 billion public firm.

USA Group was originally founded in 1960 as USA Funds, a not-for-profit company based in the Indianapolis, Indiana, area. At the time of the merger, USA Group had a $16 billion portfolio of student loans, was the largest guarantor of student loans in the U.S., and had been aggressively growing its fee-based businesses of loan origination and default collection. In 1999, the company had an excess of $150 million in revenues over expenses, and employed 3,000 people, across 20 states, the District of Columbia, and Canada.

Laying the Groundwork for the Merger

As Sallie Mae entered the new millennium, its executive team was concerned that the company could not maintain its double-digit growth in 2004 and beyond if it did not expand its servicing role. At the same time, USA Group's executive team was seeking a buyer to gain access to the capital it needed to take advantage of market opportunities to grow the company's private loans and for-profit collections businesses. USA Group became an acquisition target for Sallie Mae for three primary reasons:

1. Its complementary student loan services would result in Sallie Mae having a role in the entire life cycle of the student loan, from origination to default collection.
2. Economies of scale from combining operations would allow Sallie Mae to continue being profitable in the face of narrowing margins.
3. Sallie Mae leaders could leverage the information technology and marketing prowess of USA Group to grow revenues.

Prior to nailing down the final offer, Sallie Mae sent a team of four IT leaders to Indianapolis in May 2000 to conduct due diligence for the merger. The goals of the visit were to validate the information about the company that had been received and to report back to the CEO about any previously unforeseen issues that could materially impact the purchase offer.

> My colleagues and I were pretty impressed with what USA Group was doing from a technical standpoint. Their approach was thoughtful, strategic, and focused. We were impressed with their ability to make progress on strategic activities . . . and they had executed very effectively. . . . They were a good step ahead of us in the rollout and deployment of automated call-center technologies as well as tools to manage their hardware and software assets. We had languished behind and couldn't get focused on newer technologies. I believe this was due in part to a period of several changes in IT management in the previous years, making it difficult to focus on long-term projects. In contrast, the USA Group management team was very stable and had worked together for a long time.
>
> —*Cindy Gunn, Vice President of Computer Operations for Sallie Mae*

The New Merged Company

USA Group was acquired by Sallie Mae for $770 million on July 31, 2000. The new Sallie Mae became a single source of service for customers—from the point of loan application to successful repayment (see Exhibit 1).

The immediate financial goals for the merger were to reduce headcount by 1,700 (25 percent) and to reduce costs by 40 percent. Due to significant redundancies across the two companies, nine customer service centers would be reduced to six, and four data centers would be consolidated into one. In addition to successfully achieving its cost reduction goals for the merger, the combined company sought to attain double-digit growth in its business as a result of the merger.

Stock options were issued to all USA Group employees when the merger was finalized. Since USA Group was founded as a not-for-profit company, this was a new financial opportunity for many of its managers.

> We were really excited about getting stock options. We could exercise half of them in June 2001 and half of them in June 2002. A lot of people took advantage of the options since the stock price more than doubled.
>
> —*Paula Lohss, Manager, Application Development Support Services*

Another major change for USA Group employees was adjusting to a results-driven, for-profit culture in which risk-taking was viewed as positive as long as the risks were well managed.

> One of the biggest differences between USA Group and Sallie Mae is the increased adherence to plan and budget. We now have shareholders. Many of our employees have always

[4]*Investor's Business Daily* (Los Angeles, CA), July 11, 2001, "Sallie Mae's Albert Lord: Hard Work Helped Him Repair Lender."

[5]The privatization process is scheduled to be completed in 2006.

EXHIBIT 1
Three Basic Steps of the Student Loan Business

1) The student application originates either with a lending institution, a school financial aid office, or online through a student loan originator such as Sallie Mae.
2) After the application is submitted, a loan guarantor processes the loan; a loan approval comes with a federal government guarantee that the lender will be paid back. Guarantors are either state agencies or not-for-profit entities that provide loan insurance to lenders or holders of Federal Family Education Loan Program (FFELP) loans.
3) The loan is serviced throughout its life, which at Sallie Mae is an average of 10 years. Most students begin repayment after graduation. Default prevention and collection services work together to ensure that the highest possible percentage of loans are repaid.

worked in a not-for-profit environment and the change was somewhat of a shock.

—Larry Morgan, Senior Vice President, Application System Development

Within one calendar year from the June announcement of the merger, the IT group of the new company would integrate its most critical system applications and IT operations. To realize the publicized cost savings, a single IT headquarters location would be selected, the data centers would be consolidated, and 500 technologies within the two companies would need to be rationalized, transitioned, or retired. One of the most contentious decisions would be which of the two homegrown loan-servicing systems to eliminate.

Many mergers and acquisitions fail; more fail than succeed. So it's very important to do the right things when you're trying to bring two corporations together. You also have to do this with very good execution—do it right—or you will go out of business, or will definitely flounder.

—Hamed Omar, Senior Vice President, Technology Group

The IT Organizations

The Sallie Mae IT organization had undergone a great deal of change in the years prior to the merger. CIO turnover had been high, making it difficult for the company to maintain a coherent IT architecture. Plans for integrating the IT operations for two recent acquisitions (Nellie Mae of Braintree, Massachusetts, and Student Loan Funding Resources of Cincinnati) had not yet been completed. Several strategic applications had been totally outsourced, and the IT work force had been cut back to less than 500 just prior to the merger announcement.

In contrast, the IT organization at USA Group had a fairly stable history and had grown to 600 personnel: approximately 400 developers and 200 operations staff. CIO Greg Clancy had a 20-year tenure with the company, and his IT management team of the past 6 to 7 years was well-oiled, with a proven track record for developing complex systems and keeping operational costs low.

Within the 5 years prior to the merger, more than $100 million had been invested by USA Group in two internally developed service applications: (1) the Eagle II guarantee agency system, which tracked all federal loan origination and guarantee activities administered on behalf of guarantors, and (2) the Unity loan-servicing system.

A new call-center routing application, which routes incoming customer calls based on loan-record characteristics and the skill base of available call-center representatives, had won a Smithsonian innovation award in 1999 and led to a recognition for outstanding customer service in *CIO Magazine* Top 100 in 2000.[6]

PeopleSoft modules for financials and human resources had also been implemented under project teams led by IT groups within the business units.

The former USA Group teams had worked together for a long time. One of the major secrets of our success is that we know how to work with each other. The group in Reston didn't have the same cohesion. CIO turnover had been very high, projects took longer to complete, and there seemed to be more infighting.

—Greg Clancy, Chief Information Officer

On June 15, Clancy was privately informed that he would be CIO of the new Sallie Mae. Although the public announcement of his appointment was not made until August 1, both internal and external communications made it apparent to the Reston IT group that IT leadership at the new Sallie Mae

[6] *CIO Magazine,* Aug. 15, 2000, "IDG's CIO Magazine Honors Top 100 Companies," "CIO-100 Winners Recognized for Outstanding Customer Service."

would be primarily in the hands of the former USA Group team. For example, according to a report in *The Washington Post*, a Sallie Mae executive vice president stated in a June 16 announcement that, "Indianapolis has a . . . very high-quality work force, and in terms of the technology environment, probably a more stable one."[7]

> Those of us in [Sallie Mae] IT leadership quickly made the decision to make this work. I was 98 percent certain that I would not have a job after the merger was completed, but as a shareholder and longtime member of Sallie Mae's management team, I believed it was absolutely the best thing for Sallie Mae to do this.
>
> —*Cindy Gunn, Vice President of Computer Operations for Sallie Mae*

> Cindy Gunn really helped on the Reston side: she kept a great attitude . . . and her group was still motivated, despite the fact that many of them would lose their jobs after the merger was completed. She was the linchpin.
>
> —*Greg Clancy, Chief Information Officer*

Soon after the merger was announced, all critical systems were assigned to teams of two technology "champions"—one from Sallie Mae and one from USA Group. Together, the two champions were responsible for conducting a full disclosure and comparative analysis of the relevant systems. Knowing that Sallie Mae executives would need to have a high degree of confidence in the capabilities of the acquired USA Group team as each system alternative was examined, the USA Group IT managers encouraged their people to take advantage of every opportunity to demonstrate their abilities to develop innovative applications and to handle operations that would be triple the size of the systems they had managed in the past. They also changed their decision processes so that they could make decisions faster:

> We had to focus on making decisions quickly, so our decision-making process had to change. We went from presenting highly detailed written justifications to presenting key bullet points on PowerPoint slides. You also had only one meeting to present your case. Over time we have moved from a 5-year to a 3-year NPV [net present value]. We still use this macro-level decision-making process today.
>
> —*Sharon Vincent, Director of Network Services*

> We were told to have confidence in our ability as we exchanged and gathered information. For each application decision, we spent a lot of time and effort trying to prove that our systems were the best choice. We took charge, and we were very assertive. I think all of these interactions really helped us gain their confidence.
>
> —*Becky Robinson, Director of Systems Management*

[7]*The Washington Post*, Sept. 1, 2000, "Sallie Mae to Cut Staff 25 Percent."

> We were to be assertive, yet not burn bridges. We kept it professional. . . .And when an announcement was made, there wasn't a lot of animosity.
>
> —*Jon Jones, Director of Client Server Computing*

The IT Headquarters Decision

The decision about the physical location of the consolidated data center was not formally made until October 2000. Sallie Mae had established measurable cost-cutting goals with their merger consultants (McKinsey & Company), and each side (Reston and Indianapolis) was charged with developing a formal cost/benefit analysis for having the IT headquarters located in their city. The cost advantages became pretty clear: operating a consolidated data center out of Reston, Virginia, would be much more expensive than out of the acquired Indianapolis area facility.

- IT personnel costs in Indianapolis were estimated to be about 30 percent less than in the Reston area, which had become a mid-Atlantic Silicon Valley phenomenon.
- Running the data center out of an expanded Indianapolis facility would save an estimated annual $2 million or more in occupancy costs due to the significantly lower costs in this Midwest city.
- The new Sallie Mae data-center facility in Reston could be leased out at an attractive price.

Shortly after the relocation decision, a lease agreement with a new tenant, beginning July 1, 2001, was signed for the Reston data center.

The First Data Center Consolidation

In the months prior to the USA Group merger, Sallie Mae had been working to integrate the operations of Nellie Mae, a company Sallie Mae had purchased in 1999. Nellie Mae was a major originator of student loans based in Braintree, Massachusetts, with 150 employees. However, the integration project had been slow going. The 16 IT professionals at Nellie Mae already had severance packages in hand, but their severance pay was dependent on a successful operational move and knowledge transfer to Sallie Mae.

When Jo Lee Hayes of USA Group took on this small data center consolidation project, severance of IT professionals was only 3 months away. Working side-by-side with Nellie Mae's IT operations head and a team of six to eight people, Hayes defined the current Nellie Mae systems, established a move strategy, and worked through the systems integration and knowledge transfer issues. Successful on-time completion of this data center project was a visible early win for the Indianapolis-based IT team.

> Everybody knew where he or she stood, and there was no question about what needed to be done. We had a hard-and-fast

date, and people were motivated to combine operations successfully because severance was tied to successful knowledge transfer. . . . It was thrilling, impossible, and such a rush when we actually pulled it off.

—Jo Lee Hayes, Vice President, Business Solutions Group

Critical Application Decisions

The types of factors used to determine the fate of current applications included system functionality, scalability, performance, the number and types of interactions with other systems, whether the system was custom or purchased, and if purchased, whether the latest version of the application was currently installed.

> Now you're talking about jobs. Now you're talking about changing people's lives in a big way with whatever system is selected.
>
> *—Allan Horn, Vice President, Technology Operations*

The analyses under the two assigned champions (one for Sallie Mae, one for USA Group) led to one of three outcomes:

- A consensus recommendation was reached amicably.
- A consensus recommendation was reached, but after much conflict and strife.
- A consensus recommendation could not be reached, which meant escalating the decision to the executive level.

> Champions were technology owners who had a chance to show top management that they could make decisions and execute them. It didn't reflect well if the decision had to be turned over to senior officers.
>
> *—Jo Lee Hayes, Vice President, Business Solutions Group*

The choice between the two custom-developed loan-servicing applications was the most contentious decision and had major IT work-force effects. Larry Morgan, head of application development for USA Group at the time of the merger, had been responsible for managing the development of both loan-servicing systems. Morgan first joined Sallie Mae in the mid-1980s: he was hired away from Pennsylvania Higher Education, where he had helped to develop a loan-servicing system being used by both Sallie Mae and USA Group. Due to Sallie Mae's fast growth, a new loan-servicing system (Class) had to be developed and installed within a 2-year time frame. In 1991, USA Group lured him to Indianapolis to build a system with even more functionality (Unity), installed in 1994.

At the time of the merger, Sallie Mae's Class system was a 15-year-old application written in COBOL and CICS, maintained by more than 75 IT people in Reston. The only major change to the system had been converting it from an IMS (networked) database to IBM's DB2 (relational) database. USA Group's Unity system used a network IDMS database supported by Computer Associates.

The gap analysis that was performed for the two loan-servicing applications (see criteria in Exhibit 2) did not result in a clear choice. Although there were some concerns about the scalability of the IDMS database application, the functionality of the Unity system was more advanced. Since no consensus recommendation could be reached, the loan-servicing system decision was put into the hands of the senior officers of the company, who depended heavily on the advice of their merger consultants.

Integration risk issues began to weigh heavily on the final decision by top management. One major risk factor was the need for extensive manual review during the conversion process due to transaction complexities that had been coded into the systems to accommodate special situations. For example, updates involving retroactive changes (such as student status changes) required access to record histories, and unique decision rules (for student payment amounts) had been coded into the Unity loan processing system for lenders who had implemented incentive programs for timely student payments. Another major risk factor stemmed from the fact that these systems were servicing a population with little financial management experience (i.e., undergraduate students): System changes visible to customers therefore typically resulted in significantly higher service call volumes.

> McKinsey weighed in heavily in this decision. They generally agreed with us that the Unity system was better, but there wasn't enough difference in functionality for them to break their standard decision rule: adopt the system of the dominant company in order to reduce the merger risks.
>
> *—Greg Clancy, Chief Information Officer*

EXHIBIT 2

Gap Analysis Criteria for Loan Servicing Applications

Scalability
Cost
Performance (response time, concurrent users)
Reliability
Partnership (including customization for external partners)
Marketplace Differentiation
Quality (robustness, customer satisfaction)
Technology/Architecture
Customer Service Security
Flexibility
Compliance
Functionality Differences
Vendor Relationships
Resource Skill Set (including market availability)
Recoverability
Interdependencies

> The final point came down to risk and timing. If the conversion was to be done by April, it simply wasn't possible to convert $50 billion in loans from Class to Unity, within the time constraints required, without presenting serious problems to our operational areas.
>
> *—Larry Morgan, Senior Vice President, Application System Development*

Although the employees of both companies fought hard to keep the custom systems they had developed, and the battles were fierce, once the application decisions were made, they began working together to implement them. In the end, about 78 IT employees were retained in Reston to maintain the Class system. The plan was to add new Web functionality and to complete the implementation of an advanced call-center capability for the Class system within the second year of the new merged company.

> When you build a system, it becomes a part of you . . . both sides wanted to keep their system alive, and the battles were fierce. I was fortunate enough to have worked with both the Class and Unity teams in the construction of those systems. I was an insider to both teams. I also had established relationships with the new senior management team. . . . I had perhaps the easiest job during the integration period.
>
> *—Larry Morgan, Senior Vice President, Application System Development*

In contrast, implementation time was not the same critical concern when the back-office system for the finance function was selected. USA Group had implemented PeopleSoft modules for both finance and human resources during the second half of the 1990s. Sallie Mae was using an older and clearly less functional package for finance (Walker Interactive). Here the key trade-off was between capturing cost savings as quickly as possible by converting to the Sallie Mae package, or postponing these cost savings in order to have a more robust packaged solution that would be newly configured for the combined company.

Since this was a back-office application, rather than a customer-facing application, the Sallie Mae executive team accepted the technical team recommendation to adopt the PeopleSoft suite for both finance and human resources for the new Sallie Mae. By delaying the implementation until the fall of 2001, the company would also be one of the first large corporations to implement a Web-based version of the PeopleSoft package (version 8.0).

Retaining IT Staff

At the time when the company announced that the bulk of IT operations would move to Indianapolis, the HR department was ready with a detailed severance package program for the people in Reston who chose not to move to Indianapolis. IT jobs in the Mid-Atlantic area were plentiful at the time, and Sallie Mae's Reston data center was just across the street from Oracle's East Coast headquarters.

One third of the Reston IT staff (the most critical IT employees) were offered generous retention bonuses on top of severance pay to encourage them to stay until the merger was complete. Performance measures, including successful knowledge transfer, were built into the retention bonus contracts for the Reston staff.

> You can't pull off a project like this just through a project plan. Good people make the difference. Even if people were losing their jobs, they needed to know they had value.
>
> *—John Bennett, Project Manager for Data Center Relocation*

> The company decided to err on giving too much, and that left a good feeling in the company—that you can't be a loser in this merger. . . . When you do the right thing with employees, they pitch in and make sure that the merger is successful.
>
> *—Hamed Omar, Senior Vice President, Technology Group*

> The team had pride in what it had built and wanted to turn it over with their heads held high. The severance packages and retention bonuses were certainly better than industry standard. . . . Members of my team also knew early on when their jobs were scheduled to end. . . . All of these factors contributed to the success of the transition. . . . We leveraged what could have been negative into something positive. . . . Several took their severance money and used it to start a business and pursue a dream. Others took a year off to do something that was important to them personally.
>
> *—Cindy Gunn, Vice President of Computer Operations for Sallie Mae*

Only a small number of Indianapolis staff (e.g., critical Unity team members) were offered retention packages, because other IT jobs in the company were likely to be available to them. USA Group was viewed as a great place to work by people in central Indiana. Since there was a high differential in skill costs between Indianapolis and the DC area (e.g., $65 in Indianapolis compared to $75 or more in DC for application developers), the IT leaders could expect to retain the Indianapolis-based IT employees that they wanted to keep.

Placing the Bet on Internal Project Management

The McKinsey consultants strongly recommended that IT consultants be brought in to help with the data-center consolidation project and put forth several conditions for selecting the consulting firm. This narrowed the field to five very large players. Reston VP Cindy Gunn strongly encouraged hiring a specific IT firm because of an already established vendor relationship with Sallie Mae and the firm's recognized expertise in risk management.

The IT consultants were brought in at the end of November 2000 to work on a plan for moving the Reston data center. The consulting team hosted an IT integration kickoff meeting in Reston, during which they provided instruction on how to move equipment and applications effectively across the country. But the meeting did not go well.

> Their approach was not received well by those of us who had to carry out this move. The approach seemed generic, and they weren't showing us how their tactics could be applied in our situation.
>
> —*John Bennett, Project Manager for Data Center Relocation*

> From the beginning, we felt as if we were stretching them. They had one methodology, and if we wanted to succeed, we needed to adhere to it pretty closely. From day 1, they said it would take 12 to 18 months. We asked if we could accelerate the methodology, and they were uncomfortable with approaching it that way.
>
> —*Becky Robinson, Director of Systems Management*

Following the kickoff meeting, the IT consulting team lead advised Sallie Mae's executive team that the aggressiveness of the Indianapolis group's (FastTrack) approach was high risk. Instead of attempting to complete the data center move in 7 months, as proposed by the internal team, the consultants recommended that it be scheduled across 12 to 18 months, under their leadership.

This event proved to be a catalyst for the Indianapolis and Reston IT leaders to join together and take over the leadership for the data-center relocation project from the consultants. CIO Clancy presented to his Chief Operating Officer a counterproposal prepared by the internal IT team that would complete the data-center relocation project, including the conversion of the $15 billion loans from Unity to Class, by May 2001 (see timeline in Exhibit 3).

The CIO's plan called for managing the project internally using a project management office (PMO) structure that had been used for the $80 million USA Group Eagle II guarantee

EXHIBIT 3
IT Integration Timeline and Market Responses

Activity	Date Accomplished	Stock Price
Merger announced	June 15, 2000	$36.63 (June15)
Merger finalized; CIO announced	Aug. 1, 2000	$43.88 (Aug.1)
Data center location and Unity/Class decisions announced	October 2000	$48.69 (Oct.2)
IT consultants hired for data center relocation (DCR) project	November 2000	$57.56 (Nov.1)
Decision to lead DCR project internally	December 2000	$57.87 (Dec.1)
Move elements identified and major milestones established	January 2001	$62.81 (Jan.2)
Reston data center moves began	February 2001	$66.00 (Feb.1)
Initial enhancements to customer-facing applications completed	April 2001	$74.80 (April2)
Reston mainframe move completed	May 13, 2001	$66.20 (May 14)
Peak loan processing season begins	June 1, 2001	$69.60 (June1)
	Date Scheduled	
PeopleSoft Financials implementation	November 2001	
Full enhancements to call center routing application	April 2002	

system a few years earlier. Because of the minimal consulting role, the savings in consulting fees were projected to be $3.5 million.

> Sallie Mae's executives knew that in this day and age where everything has to be done at Internet speed, the merger had to be incredibly fast and incredibly successful. Otherwise the marketplace would really punish you. . . . The longer a merger goes, the more uncertainty there is of how well you're going to pull it off, the more your products or services have a mixed reception by your customer, and the more your leadership is uncertain. In two or three quarters, if you're not saying, "we're getting it done," you will see your stock price being affected. . . . We decided that if the consultants weren't helping us reach our goals, we didn't need them.
>
> —*Hamed Omar, Senior Vice President, Technology Group*

Sallie Mae's management decided to back the internal IT leaders. For the Indianapolis team members, an extra motivation to succeed was a rumor that a consulting partner on the loan-servicing system gap analysis had bet a Sallie Mae executive that the Indianapolis team could not pull off the FastTrack integration plan. This had made everyone mad, and created a reason for breaking the boundaries of 60-hour weeks.

The Data Center Relocation Team

The team structure for moving the IT headquarters to Indianapolis is shown in Exhibit 4. The data center relocation (DCR) team had its own steering committee of six direct reports to the CIO, chosen because of the criticality of their areas of responsibility within the two IT organizations. The primary objectives of the

EXHIBIT 4
Data Center Relocation Team Structure

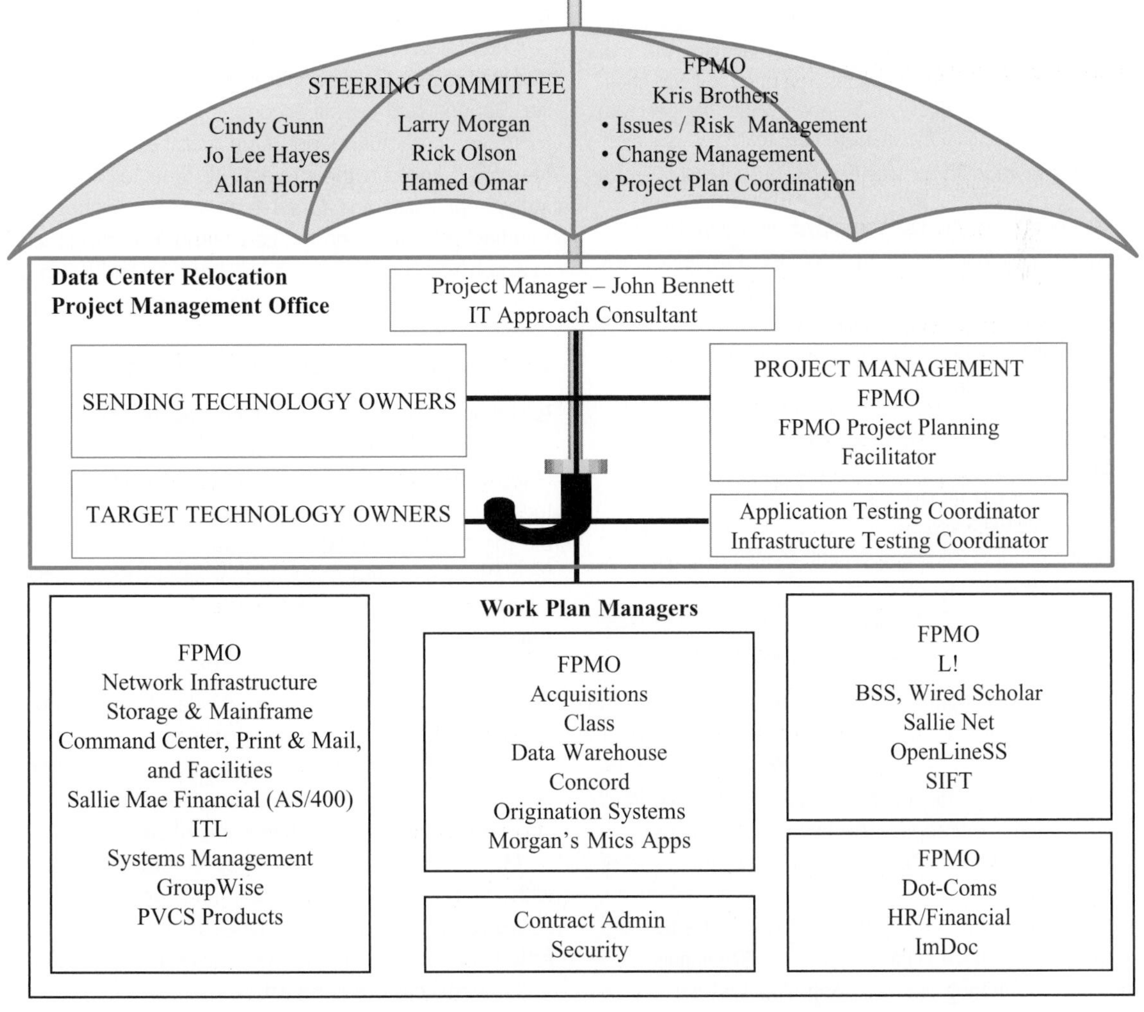

steering committee were to make top-level decisions and to keep obstacles out of the way so that the project team members could get the job done. They were responsible for setting strategic direction and mitigating the risks of the project, while still actively managing their own IT functions.

> Along the way, I questioned things quite a bit from a financial and risk standpoint. I didn't want to put the company at risk by moving the integration along too quickly. We had a number of checkpoint meetings to ensure we'd be successful at a reasonable cost.
>
> —*Greg Clancy, Chief Information Officer*

> You have to trust your people. Give them autonomy. Listen, and don't hold them back. A jockey who pulls too hard on the reins will never have a winning horse. We told them, "Guys, run like your hair's on fire." . . . We only got involved with approvals if the group couldn't agree on what needed to be done, or if the decision involved a high-risk issue. For example, the steering committee got involved when we were deciding whether to have two or three T1 lines.
>
> —*Allan Horn, Vice President, Technology Operations*

> In merger mode, you have to behave a certain way. People are watching your confidence. You're not only managing the project, but you're managing perceptions. You need to keep confidence high that the merger can be done within budget, with acceptable risks, and that the management team can pull it off.
>
> —*Hamed Omar, Senior Vice President, Technology Group*

The project office for the DCR employed some of the same team members who had managed the Eagle II system a few years earlier. The detailed processes and review mechanisms developed for Eagle II had been extensively reviewed by the McKinsey consultants before the decision was made to manage the IT integration internally.

> After our processes were reviewed at an executive level, [the consultants] spent about two weeks with us hand in hand to evaluate whether our project office was ready to manage this integration. They were very impressed with the size of Eagle II and how we handled risk management, change management, and progress stewardship.
>
> —*Cheri E. Dayton, Senior Manager, Guarantee Systems Development*

Oversight for the integration activities for the merger as a whole was provided by Rob Autor, who was Sallie Mae's VP for integration. Autor and his group of three global project managers, based in Reston, monitored the data-center move from a business perspective, keeping the key players (the board, CEO, McKinsey, institutional clients, and auditors) informed of the DCR team's progress.

Under the authority of the larger project office, the focused project-management office (FPMO) for the DCR initiative was responsible for monitoring and reporting global issues related to the data-center integration, including status of project plans, timing, codependencies, risks, and financial issues. The criteria for success for the DCR project are presented in Exhibit 5.

EXHIBIT 5

Success Criteria for Data Center Relocation

1) No unplanned interruptions
2) Meet scheduled dates
3) Meet budget
4) Continuity of staffing
5) Knowledge transfer
6) Maintain data integrity
7) Resulting service levels will be consistent, with contractual agreements met
8) Successful integration of application and infrastructure teams

The project leader for the DCR team was John Bennett, who had started as a Unity programmer at USA Group 15 years earlier. Bennett had overall accountability for planning, management, and communications. One member of the IT consulting team was kept on the project full time to help infuse best industry practices and to serve as a coach. During the kickoff meeting in Reston, Bennett had seen this particular consultant in action and liked his strong collaboration and communication skills, strong work ethic, and willingness to listen.

Defining and Implementing by Move Element

Based on guidelines from both the steering committee and the project manager, the other managers on the DCR team were responsible for specific deliverables from each phase. Sending-technology owners (primarily based in Reston) were responsible for assuring the viability and functionality of the pre-move technology area and ensuring that all necessary activities had taken place for the target (receiving) technology owner (primarily based in Indianapolis) effectively to take over the assigned technology.

Each work-plan manager had overall accountability for a specific area, and managed the tasks that needed to be done prior to the move, shutting down the application, and executing the move. This required a detailed understanding of the infrastructure and business requirements of each move element.

Move-element leaders helped create the detailed plans with their work-plan managers and were held technically accountable for relocating assigned move elements within the scheduled time frame, with no unplanned application outage and minimal customer impact.

As shown in Exhibit 6, move elements were defined in an early planning phase. Greater detail was then added to each move plan: Equipment and software were specified, dependencies defined, and testing plans prescribed. Templates were provided to improve communication across work plans, projects, and aggregate planning activities. Each move was considered complete after the relocated application had been successfully put into operation. The post-move execution ended when all unused infrastructure was disposed of, and the support of the application had become a responsibility of the regular operational support team. (See Exhibit 7 for the move-element project plan.)

One major difference between the approach adopted by Sallie Mae and the approach introduced by their IT consultants was that move elements were first identified, and managed, from a business-application perspective, rather than a technology-infrastructure perspective. As described in Exhibit 8, the software application view provided a vertical business perspective, and the technology infrastructure view provided a horizontal cross-application perspective. Move elements were therefore managed as a set of interdependent hardware and software components. Large business applications were divided into smaller logical move elements to better facilitate project planning and move flexibility.

[The IT consultants] had us looking at this move from a technology viewpoint. The way we looked at it, the superstructure was the application. We defined move elements as a set of hardware and/or software components that can and should move together because of interdependencies.

—John Bennett, Project Manager for Data Center Relocation

The systems development people became the team leads. They understood the dependencies, the integration points. . . . It was a hard decision to make, and it was difficult to let someone else be in charge of the data-center move. But it was critical that we didn't lose sight of the applications because they were our primary concern. It then became our job to focus on a higher level of coordination, resolving the dependencies. It took time to get to an organized state . . . the whole structure shook out over about two months.

—Becky Robinson, Director of Systems Management

The plans were incredibly detailed, and they were written from an application-owner point of view. The trick was to see the dependencies. The IT applications people knew those dependencies and were able to align them with what they had to do.

—Allan Horn, Vice President, Technology Operations

Move-element freeze policies (see Exhibit 9) required that no application changes be implemented for a 2-week

EXHIBIT 6
Data Center Relocation Approach

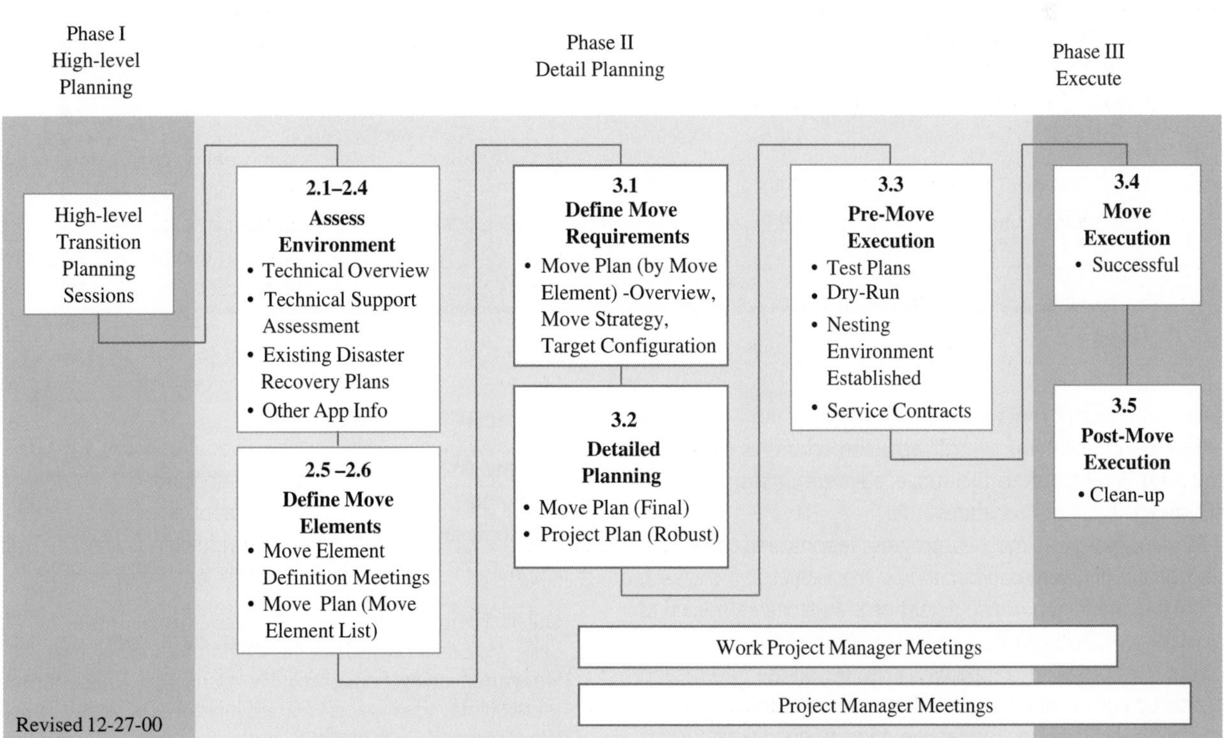

EXHIBIT 7

Move Element Project Plan

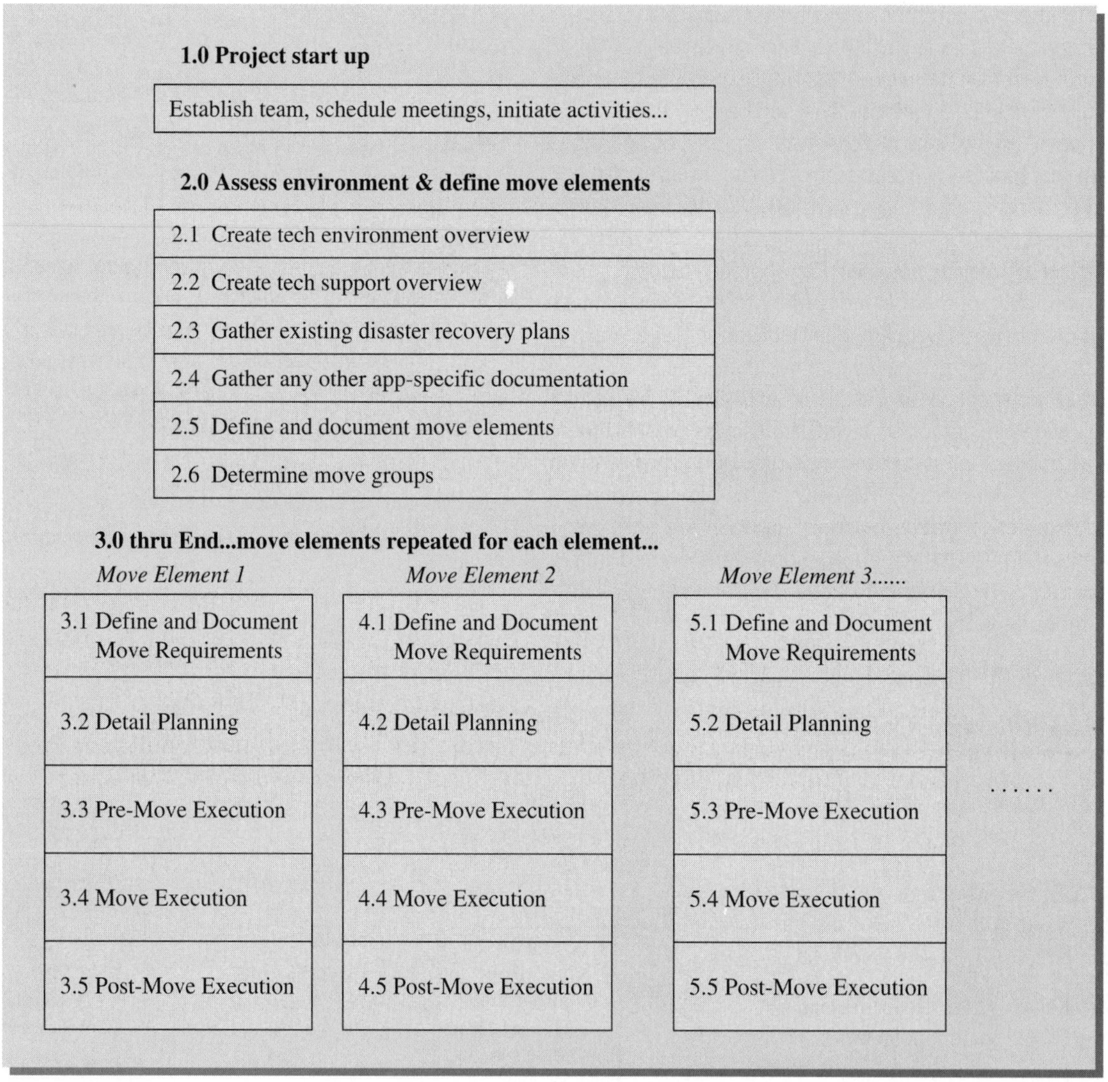

1.0 Project start up

Establish team, schedule meetings, initiate activities...

2.0 Assess environment & define move elements

2.0 Assess environment & define move elements
2.1 Create tech environment overview
2.2 Create tech support overview
2.3 Gather existing disaster recovery plans
2.4 Gather any other app-specific documentation
2.5 Define and document move elements
2.6 Determine move groups

3.0 thru End...move elements repeated for each element...

Move Element 1	*Move Element 2*	*Move Element 3......*	
3.1 Define and Document Move Requirements	4.1 Define and Document Move Requirements	5.1 Define and Document Move Requirements	
3.2 Detail Planning	4.2 Detail Planning	5.2 Detail Planning	
3.3 Pre-Move Execution	4.3 Pre-Move Execution	5.3 Pre-Move Execution	......
3.4 Move Execution	4.4 Move Execution	5.4 Move Execution	
3.5 Post-Move Execution	4.5 Post-Move Execution	5.5 Post-Move Execution	

period prior to the move-element implementation and for a 1-week period afterwards. Infrastructure changes were not allowed 4 weeks before the move element implementation and for a 1-week period afterwards.

All plans, policies, timelines, progress reports, and other relevant documents were coordinated by the FPMO staff for each area of the integration. These documents were then e-mailed to key managers and posted on Sallie Mae Central, the company's intranet. This provided companywide access to the information needed by both IT and business managers to manage the project effectively as well as to manage ongoing operations.

Equipment Move Strategies

One of the first steps in moving the data center was to make decisions on how all of the equipment from Reston would fit into the Indianapolis facility. A number of approaches were used to redesign the space to accommodate the new equipment.

> Our first impression, and theirs, was "this will never fit." The Sallie Mae data center was the length of a football field. Once we started doing floor plans, we found that Sallie Mae was underutilizing their space. We used a number of strategies here. We eliminated local monitors and keyboards on storage racks,

EXHIBIT 8
Move Element Definition Approach

1) Define move element from the applications point of view (vertical).

2) Then define from the infrastructure point of view, to catch any gaps (horizontal).

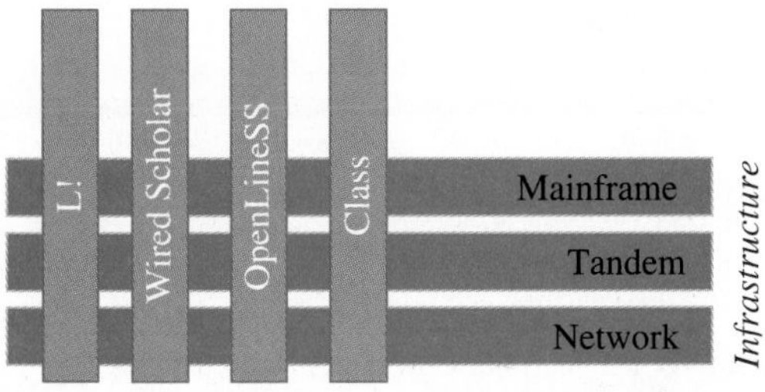

for example. This saved a lot of space. Replacing old equipment with smaller new equipment helped too.

—*Jon Jones, Director of Client Server Computing*

Excellent vendor relationships were key to rationalizing equipment, making infrastructure improvements, and carrying out the project on time and within budget.

When we were negotiating with vendors for USA Group, we weren't really a big player in the market and had less latitude. . . . As part of Sallie Mae, we were nearly able to write our own terms and conditions. In some cases, we were working with vendor reps in D.C., and they were able to make better and faster deals and were more flexible. We told them what we wanted, and they delivered.

—*Becky Robinson, Director of Systems Management*

Three different strategies were used for installing computer equipment in the Indianapolis facility that had been used in Reston. (Improvements to infrastructure components—such as backup equipment and more secure firewalls—were also built into the migration plans.)

1. The *Asset Swap* method was used for equipment in Reston ready to be retired. New equipment was purchased from the hardware vendor for the Indianapolis facility. Once the applications on the old equipment had been moved to (installed on) the new equipment in Indianapolis, the old equipment in Reston was traded in to the vendor.
2. The *Push/Pull* strategy was used for select equipment in Reston that was not ready to be retired and difficult to replace: the old equipment was taken out, moved, and reinstalled in Indianapolis.
3. The *Swing* method was used for equipment that existed in multiples. New equipment was purchased for Indianapolis for the earliest moves. After the initial applications were successfully installed on the new equipment, the relevant piece of equipment was removed from Reston and shipped to Indianapolis for the next move, and so on.

The strategy choice for each move element was based on allowable downtime for the application(s) involved, vendor prices for replacement equipment and trade-ins, and physical move costs. The overall objective was to decrease integration risks by minimizing the hardware assets that would be physically moved from Reston to Indianapolis. For example, a Reston data warehouse was stored on a Sun E10K server. Since this was a very expensive piece of equipment, an asset swap strategy would have been very costly. However, it was learned that the business could tolerate up to a week of downtime outside of the peak processing season, so a push/pull strategy was used instead. The vendor tore down the machine in Reston, trucked it to Indiana, and rebuilt it at the Indianapolis facility.

Lack of backup was the biggest risk. We determined the maximum downtime that the operation could handle without losing customers, and we established backup and system redundancies as needed.

—*John Bennett, Project Manager for Data Center Relocation*

In contrast, the company couldn't afford much downtime for the mainframe on which the Class loan-servicing system was run: the service centers needed to be able to communicate with customers. The push/pull method required too much downtime, so the asset swap method was used. For DASD storage, a new vendor was selected in order to provide newer technology that would better handle the company's increased storage needs, as well as reduce the maintenance risks associated with older technologies.

Redundancies were built in wherever possible to minimize the business impact of the "go live" dates of critical applications. For example, beginning in March 2001, three T1 lines were leased from AT&T in order to have a fast electronic backup for the major moves.

We spent a lot of money, almost a million dollars in two months, to create a pretty significant pipe between the two centers, in order to have a very fast link, so that you could essentially run the business out of either center if your migration had a problem. Fortunately, most of our migrations went well, and they did not have any problems, but that was a great big insurance.

—*Hamed Omar, Senior Vice President, Technology Group*

Prior to any move, the sending technology owners worked with the target (receiving) technology owners to transfer the knowledge needed by the Indianapolis operations staff to

EXHIBIT 9
Move Element Freeze Policies

Production Environment

The production environment move element freeze standard requires that:

- No application changes affecting the move element to be moved are implemented for a two-week period prior and one-week period after the move element implementation date.
- No infrastructure changes affecting the move element to be moved are implemented for a four-week period prior and one-week period after the move element implementation date.

In addition it is desirable that any application changes be implemented in time to have been executed successfully in production.

This generally would mean the following:

1) For changes that impact monthly processing, no changes should be made after the month-end execution proceeding the move element transition date.

2) For changes that impact weekly processing, no changes should be made after the weekly processing immediately proceeding the move element transition date.

3) For changes that impact daily processing, no changes should be made for two weeks prior to the move element transition date.

Example: If a move element is scheduled to move on 3/17, any application changes affecting month-end processing should be implemented in time to process for February month end. If the application change cannot make the February month-end implementation, it should be held and implemented after 2/24.

Quality Assurance and Development Environment

The QA and Development Environment move element freeze standard requires that:

- No application changes affecting the move element to be moved are implemented for a three-day period prior and three-day period after the move element implementation date. Any changes made during the two-week period prior to the move must be documented and given to the WPM for inclusion in the Move Control Book prior to the move occurring. This way issues caused by normal development will not be mistaken for move issues.
- No infrastructure changes affecting the move element to be moved are implemented for a four-week period prior and one-week period after the move element implementation date.

Appeal Process

In cases where the move freeze policy presents unusual hardships for the business, an appeal process is available. Any change requests falling within the standard movefreeze period require prior approval bythe Data Center Relocation Steering Committee. Information to be presented to the Steering Committee for them to consider a change within the freeze period includes:

- Explanation of the move element, the move approach, and the level of complexity
- Explanation of the requested change and primary business contact
- Increased risk associated with implementing the change during the freeze period
- Effect on the business of holding the change
- Benefits associated with completing the change during the freeze period

Questions concerning the freeze should be directed to the individual Work Plan Managers and then to their vice presidents for initial resolution. Issues that cannot be resolved through the Work Plan Manager should be documented and raised to the Data Center Relocation project manager (John Bennett). If not resolvable, the project manager will raise the issue to the Data Center Relocation steering committee and if necessary to Greg Clancy.

Move Element Freeze Communication Responsibility

Work Plan Managers are responsible for communicating to affected technology and business area management the freeze periods associated with each move element. The freeze dates will also be posted on the Data Center Relocation Web site. Any freeze period issues must be communicated to the Work Plan Manager and, if necessary, to the Data Center Relocation project manager (John Bennett).

handle the changes in applications, hardware, and large increases in transaction volume.

> Early in the process, we asked teams to start planning and scheduling tasks related to training. The approach was tell them, show them, watch them.
>
> *—Allan Horn, Vice President, Technology Operations*

The Major Data Center Moves

The DCR team began moving applications in February 2001, as they were ready (see Exhibit 10). From the director level down, the IT staffs at Reston and Indianapolis were paired by function to work on knowledge-transfer issues—including computer operators, help-desk people, database administrators, and other technical support people.

Trial runs were conducted as needed to determine the length of time that various transitions would take. Individual move element teams met every day, and a project room was dedicated for this purpose. Anyone on the DCR team was authorized to call a meeting.

> The Data Center Relocation team had an action orientation. They weren't waiting for someone to tell them what to do . . . they were off doing it. We had a number of moves from March to mid-June, and none were failures. Very little didn't work. It was truly amazing.
>
> *—Greg Clancy, Chief Information Officer*

> We clicked. We had a mission. No confusion, illusions, or secrets. . . . It was critical that we maintained people's confidence.
>
> *—Allan Horn, Vice President, Technology Operations*

Starting February 1, DCR team members were responsible for written status reports and updated project plans on a weekly basis. Plans were submitted to the FMPO staff on Mondays, and 2-hour meetings were held via videoconference every Tuesday to discuss project status. About 20 people in

EXHIBIT 10

Calendar for Data Center Moves

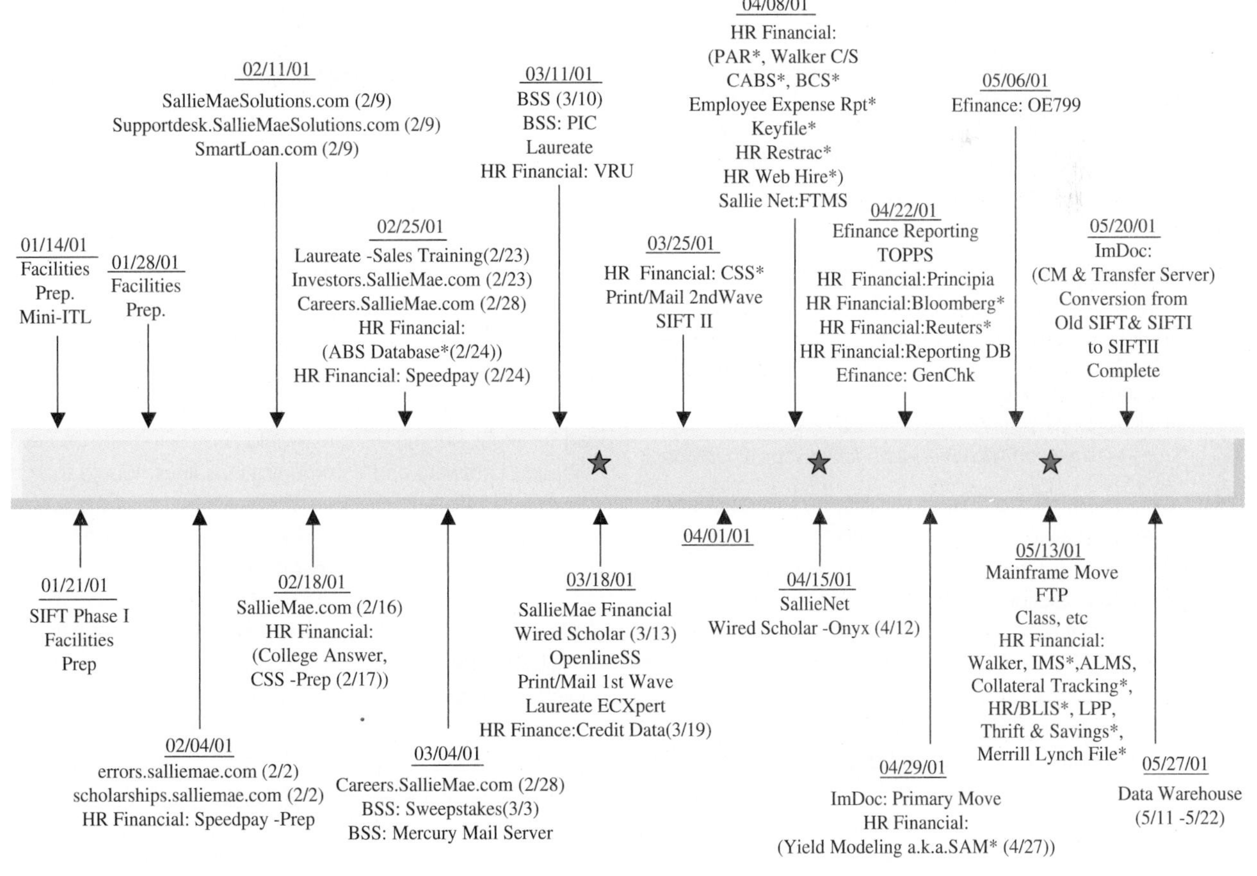

Indianapolis participated in the meetings, with about 15 people participating from Reston. Meetings were held with the steering committee two times a week.

> Videoconferencing was a key medium for us. This merger was an emotional event. In Reston, people were losing their jobs, and in Indianapolis, people were struggling to keep their jobs. Body language was everything. If you couldn't see people, you didn't know what was going on. Videoconferencing also helped us create the impression of a big group working together toward a common goal.
>
> *—John Bennett, Project Manager for Data Center Relocation*

During this time, the typical workday was 12 hours long. Since weekends afforded some downtime for executing a move element, there were many weekends when IT people couldn't go home. A command center was set up in the Indianapolis office every weekend to help monitor move activities; full command centers were set up for the three most critical weekend moves in mid-March, mid-April, and mid-May.

> On the weekends with very large numbers of move elements, complicated moves, or very integrated move elements, we created move control books that listed everything that would be moving, implementation plans, vendor information, contingency plans, risks, disaster-recovery plans, and the possible impact to the business if a move failed. We manned the PMO communications center with team members, PMO members, vendors, and specific key contacts related to the implementation.
>
> *—Cheri E. Dayton, Senior Manager, Guarantee Systems Development*

> We took every opportunity for community building. On those long weekends we set up games for them to play. About once a week, we held informal luncheons to recognize successes along the way. We had an open budget on food: it was delivered around the clock every day. You can't take too good care of your people, and you can't communicate too much.
>
> *—Allan Horn, Vice President, Technology Operations*

The movement of the Reston mainframe operations for the loan-servicing application was studied the most. Timings were made for truck hauls between Reston and Indianapolis, including loading and unloading times. The T-1 lines would allow the company to revert back to operations in Reston if a glitch in Indianapolis precluded running the loan-servicing system from its new location.

The mainframe move was scheduled to take place over a weekend in mid-May. A full command center was in place, and about a dozen representatives from hardware and software vendors were required to be on site for the weekend. In addition, all vendors were required to have plans in place to provide immediate access to other people and resources should there be a problem with their equipment or software. The team members were on location round the clock.

> The technical part of that weekend was challenging, but it wasn't the hardest part. The political and business ramifications of that move were huge. The mainframe is the lifeblood of the company. The call centers use it every minute of every day. It was the most critical part of the entire move.
>
> *—John Bennett, Project Manager for Data Center Relocation*

> You have to tell yourself that you can be the first ones to do it, that you're not an average company and can find a way to succeed. That can-do attitude is critical to success.
>
> *—Hamed Omar, Senior Vice President, Technology Group*

Before the mainframe switch was flipped, John Bennett pulled the team together for a go/no-go decision at 2 a.m. Sunday morning.

> I got a lot of flack for having a meeting at that time of morning: people wanted to know why it couldn't wait until 7 a.m. We couldn't wait that long to know if there was a problem. We had duplicated enough tapes so that we could start installing manually in Reston, and a corporate Learjet was waiting to fly the other tapes back to Reston. We never used this backup, but it was good to know it was there. We had spent a lot of time working to make sure the mainframe move went smoothly, and it went grand.
>
> *—John Bennett, Project Manager for Data Center Relocation*

> A month before the Reston data center move was even completed [the IT consultant firm that lost the contract] knew we would be successful. They told us that they planned to come up with a "FastTrack" method for mergers based on what they had learned through the engagement.
>
> *—Greg Clancy, Chief Information Officer*

The Challenges Ahead

The new IT group at Sallie Mae would soon be tested during peak lending season: not only would the transaction processing load be larger, but the systems would also be running on newly upgraded hardware and communications lines. Would they be able to avoid the bottlenecks and processing errors the government's direct lending program changeover had caused in a previous year? So far, the stock market reaction had been positive, but if there were a servicing failure, how would the market react? Would Sallie Mae be able to retain its customer base?

Still ahead were more IT application challenges—including implementing the advanced call-center routing capability for the new combined company, getting both companies on the same intranet and e-mail systems, and moving the corporate staff based in Reston onto PeopleSoft financial and human resource systems. With IT headquarters in Indianapolis and corporate headquarters in Reston, would the IT project team be able to successfully navigate the political challenges of these integrations as well?

CASE STUDY IV-7

OUTSOURCING DECISION AT SCHAEFFER CORPORATION

Schaeffer Corporation, headquartered in the small Midwestern town of Vilonia, is a diversified manufacturer. In 2002 Schaeffer Corporation's consolidated sales were around $2.5 billion and its profit after taxes was about $220 million. Schaeffer's stock is publicly held and its value has held up well over the past few years.

Founded by Frederick W. Schaeffer in 1877, Schaeffer Corporation originally manufactured small machines for use on the farm, such as churns, cream separators, corn shellers, apple peelers, and the like. Frederick had one son and four daughters. The daughters married men who joined the business: Hiram C. Colbert, George Kinzer, James Hunter, and Heinrich Reitzel. Each of these men led the development and expansion of a new product line, and today Schaeffer Corporation is composed of four product line divisions: the Colbert division, the Kinzer division, the Hunter division, and the Reitzel (pronounced "rightsell") division.

Each division is relatively autonomous, with the responsibility for design, manufacturing, and marketing of its product line. Each division has its own manufacturing plants and distribution facilities. Each of Schaeffer's many products is branded with its division's name rather than with the Schaeffer name. Although the financials of the divisions are closely monitored by Schaeffer corporate headquarters, each division is held responsible by corporate management for its bottom-line performance, and the bonuses of the managers of each division depend upon the bottom-line performance of that division.

The first three of these divisions have profitable, but very stable, product lines. However, the Reitzel division is in a more dynamic market with substantial opportunity for growth in both sales and profitability. The other divisions operate only in North America, but Reitzel has operations in 10 European countries as well as North and South America. Furthermore, most years Reitzel contributes one-third of Schaeffer's dollar sales and 40 percent of its total profits.

Historically, Schaeffer Corporation has been a rather stodgy company satisfied to be profitable while growing slowly but solidly. However, in the last 10 years the Schaeffer board of directors has become much more concerned with growth and has identified the Reitzel division as the corporate growth engine. Recently corporate executive management set ambitious goals for the Reitzel division to create 10-percent growth in Schaeffer's corporate revenues and 15-percent growth in Schaeffer's corporate profits each year. Reitzel management was encouraged to achieve these goals by expanding its product line, by expanding into new geographical areas, and by acquiring other companies.

Information Technology at Schaeffer Corporation

For years each of the operating divisions had its own information technology resources—data centers, systems development people, desktop support—the whole ball of wax. However, 4 years ago the corporate vice president of information technology decided to centralize all of this into a shared-services IT department for the entire corporation. The corporation consolidated four data centers into one, eliminated a number of servers, brought their support and system development people together, established a corporate help desk, etc.

Also, prior to this consolidation each division had its own unique applications systems, and to some extent they still do. However, recently Schaeffer completed the installation of enterprise software throughout the corporation to handle the basic areas of finance, human relations, manufacturing, and distribution. That was a difficult process, but it is now complete and things are going very well.

The corporate data center has an IBM mainframe computer, some 200 servers, and a staff of 100, including desktop support and help desk people. Computer operations are going well, with good response time and excellent availability. There have been complaints about the help desk, and the performance of the WAN (wide area network) has not been as good as users would like, but IT is working to improve performance in these areas. The system development group, consisting of about 70 people, is not a part of the data center.

Each of the Colbert, Kinzer, and Hunter divisions has a straightforward portfolio of applications that are well integrated and easily maintained. The Reitzel division, on the other hand, is much more complex. As compared with any other division, Reitzel has triple the network capacity, triple the number of servers, and more problems than the other three divisions combined. If one diagrams Reitzel's applications portfolio and draws lines showing the relationships among applications, the result looks like a plate of spaghetti. And Reitzel has a long history of making poor decisions with respect to its applications infrastructure.

The Outsourcing Study

In January 2001, shortly after the Schaeffer board announced its ambitious growth goals for the Reitzel division, Pedro A. Moreno, Reitzel's vice president of human resources, proposed that Schaeffer outsource its IT resources. Moreno argued:

> Information technology is not one of Schaeffer's core competencies, and I am confident that we can save some money by outsourcing. However, the reason that we must do it is that for us to achieve our ambitious growth goals we must have improved IT services. Expanding into additional countries and acquiring new companies will require extraordinary IT support efforts. We are doing reasonably well now, but our IT people are stretched to the limit just supporting our day-to-day activities. There is no way that we are capable of crash efforts of the magnitude that we will need. But an outsourcer has a large supply of well-trained, capable people, as well as plenty of hardware and software resources, so they can adjust to our dynamic, unforeseeable needs with little difficulty.

Schaeffer Corporation is a very conservative company and Moreno's proposal to outsource information technology was met with skepticism from many directions. However, Audrey Stewart, corporate vice president of information technology, thought that Moreno's proposal had sufficient merit that it should be carefully considered, and she established a task force, headed by Moreno, to investigate thoroughly whether or not Schaeffer Corporation should outsource its information technology.

Knowing very little about how to approach outsourcing, Moreno and the task force engaged Gartner Consulting Group to assist in exploring this issue. It quickly became apparent that this would not be a quick or easy study. Moreno recalls:

> Gartner was very helpful. They said, "Before you decide to outsource you have to know what you have in great detail, and right now we don't think you know that. You know you have a data center, you know you have a network, but you need to be very specific. You need to know each piece of machinery in every city. You need to understand your processes. You need to know what your employees are doing, both in the scope of the outsourcing and out of that scope. And most of all, you have to know every service that you are providing in each area that you are considering outsourcing. There usually are 'assumed' services done without much thought, but if they are not specified they will not be provided by the outsourcer and you will have to continue to provide them or pay extra to the outsourcer."
>
> Gartner gave us dozens and dozens of templates to be filled out and we spent months collecting data about ourselves. We did not consider outsourcing our development resources, but we studied the resources of what the outsourcers call our "towers," which were the data center, distributed computing (all the desktops), voice (telephones), data networks, and our help desk. We spent over 12 months collecting data about the local and wide area data networks, and once that was complete we started doing the same thing for the data center, our help desk, and our voice communications. We spent a total of 18 months learning about ourselves.
>
> Then we spent another 3 months preparing a 200-page Request for Proposal (RFP) to give to potential outsourcing business partners. The RFP described our infrastructure and services, indicated exactly what we wanted to outsource, and asked for bids specifying how these services would be provided and what it would cost. Incidentally, we did not want to take the risk of moving our processing to a big remote data center, so we specified that the data center must remain in Vilonia.
>
> Because of our international scope, Gartner advised us that there were only two companies that could satisfy our needs, ABC Corporation and DEF Corporation. We brought each of them in for an all-day kickoff meeting where we told them what we had learned about ourselves and what we wanted them to do for us, and gave them the 200-page RFP. It took them about 2 months to analyze the RFP and formulate a response.

Outsourcing information technology is different from buying an automobile where you have a car, negotiate its price and options, and that is it. However, when Schaeffer oursourced its information technology, it was contracting for services for a number of years in the future, and neither Schaeffer nor an outsourcer knew what would happen to the volume of transactions processed or even the locations to be served during that time. Therefore, the bids from the outsourcers could not be in the form of a total dollar cost over the 7-year length of the contract. Rather, the bids would need to include a detailed set of costs for each of the services that Schaeffer had requested, together with the penalties that would be incurred if they did not provide the specified level of service. The quoted costs were unit costs, and Moreno describes how they evaluated the two proposals:

> Everything that they will do has a price per something. If they go touch a desktop, there is a price for that. If they answer a phone, there is a price for that. If they replace a phone, there is a price for that. If we increase the number of servers or databases, we will have to pay more. And it works both ways—if things decrease we will pay less. We started with a baseline level of activity to get the projected cost to compare with our current costs, but it took us some time to go through the

process of calculating things out so that we could arrive at a projected cost for each bidder.

When the bids had been evaluated ABC Corporation was the lowest bidder. The good news was that the people on the task force felt very comfortable with the idea of having ABC as their business partner. The bad news was that the bid was projected to cost $220 million over the 7 years, which was about $20 million more than it was projected to cost Schaeffer to continue to provide its information technology in house. There was no way that Schaeffer Corporation management was going to go for that. Moreno explains:

> We were quite disappointed when the bids came in. Instead of saving some money as we had originally hoped, we were going to have to spend substantially more to outsource. Although I believed that there were still good reasons to outsource even if it cost more, I knew that our management would never agree to a deal costing that much.
>
> Gartner had told us during the data gathering part of the study that we were not likely to save any money by outsourcing because we were already pretty efficient. The work we had done ourselves in creating a consolidated shared services infrastructure had already picked all the low-hanging fruit. We had already consolidated four data centers into one. We had already eliminated about 50 headcount out of 150 and were down to 100. We had already done server consolidation and reduced our server count from 300 to 200. So the things that an outsourcer comes in and does for you we had already done. We had a very lean, efficient organization to outsource.
>
> The other reason that the bids were so high was that when we developed the specifications in the RFP we asked for a number of improvements over what we were currently doing. We asked for a Cadillac when we could only afford a Buick. The representatives of ABC understood this and agreed to work with us to get the total cost down to something that we could afford.
>
> The negotiation process was arduous and detailed. This was a big agreement, and we had 10 countries in Europe that we had to include as well. It ended up taking 8 weeks, but it was a good process. In the end we changed some of our ideas about what we needed. We took away some of the whiz-bang options that we had told ABC we absolutely had to have, which allowed them to come down in price somewhat, and they also took out some of their margin. We got the projected cost down to $200 million over the 7 years, about the same as the projected cost of doing it ourselves. Given that we have been able to make it cost neutral, I strongly believe that we should outsource because of the quality and flexibility we will obtain.

Reactions to the Outsourcing Proposal

The task force that Moreno headed recommended to Audrey Stewart that Schaeffer outsource all of its IT except system development. The task force's report included a description of the process that had been followed to obtain the bids and negotiate the proposed contract with ABC Corporation, and included the following argument in support of the recommendation:

> Schaeffer's board has set the strategic goal of growth through acquisition and through expansion overseas. However, we cannot achieve these goals without high-quality and very flexible IT resources. We have decent IT resources for serving a static situation, but we cannot handle the unforeseen and dynamic requirements that these new strategic directions will place upon our IT resources.
>
> When we have an acquisition our demand for resources is going to spike, but then it will flatten out after a few months. Not only will ABC bring access to numbers of people, but they will be capable of spiking with our demand and then flattening back out. We would have to hire people or not hire people. It is impossible for us to hire 20 experts in a field to help us for a relatively short time and then have them go away again.
>
> We are global and intend to expand into other countries. We are in 10 countries in Europe, and Europe is a bigger mess than domestically. We have only seven people working in all of Europe in the infrastructure, so we are going to have to double or triple our staff over there. So it makes sense to give the responsibility to ABC who already has resources overseas, both where we are now and where we will be going in the future.
>
> ABC has a very deep bench—hundreds of thousands of employees for them to pick from to serve our needs as opposed to our one hundred. If someone leaves it generally takes us 3 to 6 months to find a suitable replacement because it is hard to get people to move to Vilonia. ABC provides an attractive career path for its employees and can attract and keep people with outstanding talents that would never come to Vilonia to work for Schaeffer. ABC can afford to invest in extensive training and can offer a variety of challenging opportunities to its people, so we will have access to substantially higher-quality people resources.
>
> In short, Schaeffer is anticipating exciting opportunities that will be almost impossible to achieve with our existing IT support. With ABC as our business partner we will be much better positioned to exploit the dynamic opportunities for growth that we are seeking.

When the task force report was circulated there was strong reaction throughout Schaeffer Corporation, with some managers voicing enthusiastic support and others equally strongly opposed. Vivian D. Johnson, vice president for information technology of the Kinzer division, expressed the following concerns:

> Perhaps information technology is not one of Schaeffer's core competencies, but it is a critical factor in our long-term success. Do we want to turn over such critical resources to an outside organization?
>
> We will be getting married to ABC Corporation. Although it has a good reputation and we feel comfortable with its people, what happens 3 years down the road when these people have gone on to greener pastures within ABC? Today Schaeffer may be a high priority with ABC, but before long other opportunities will appear and the good people that we will start out with will

CASE STUDY IV-8

SYSTEMS SUPPORT FOR A NEW BAXTER MANUFACTURING COMPANY PLANT IN MEXICO

Baxter Manufacturing Company (BMC), located in a small midwestern town, is a leading manufacturer of metal stampings, particularly deep-drawn electric motor housings. The company was founded in 1978 by its chairman, Walter R. Baxter, as a supplier of tools and dies, but it soon expanded into the stamping business. BMC is a closely held corporation, with the Baxter family holding most of the stock.

BMC's major customers include Ford, General Motors, Honda of America, General Electric, Whirlpool, Amana, and Maytag. BMC has two markets. It makes brackets and other components sold directly to appliance and automotive assemblers to go straight into the end product. But BMC also makes motor casings and the like that go to intermediate suppliers that make components (such as motors) that then go to the appliance and automotive assemblers of the finished products. For example, BMC ships a motor housing to a motor manufacturer who makes the motor, and BMC also makes the bracket that holds the motor onto the frame and ships it directly to the manufacturer who assembles the motor and bracket into the finished product.

BMC's 170,000-square-foot manufacturing facility is one of the best in the country, with 43 presses that range from 50- to 800-ton capacity. Every press is equipped with accessory items such as feeds, reels, and electronic detection systems. In addition to the presses, BMC has recently added the capacity to weld, drill, tap, and assemble stampings into more complex parts to suit the needs and desires of its customers.

BMC employs about 420 people and is nonunion. Over its 22-year history, BMC has had steady growth. The most recent 6 years of sales were:

1994	$49,900,000	1997	$85,785,000
1995	$61,976,000	1998	$97,550,000
1996	$74,130,000	1999	$112,337,000

 This case study was prepared to be the basis for class discussion, rather than to illustrate either effective or ineffective handling of an administrative situation. It is a continuation of the case study entitled "Make-or-Buy Decision at Baxter Manufacturing Company" (see pp. 489–494); one can find further information about the history of the company and its use of the computer there.

Before joining BMC in 1994, MIS manager Don Collins had 20 years of experience as a lead systems analyst with a large manufacturer and broad experience with manufacturing systems. In 1997 the MIS department had five people, but there was some turnover and Collins was unable to hire replacements because of the high salaries commanded by people with the necessary skills. Therefore, the MIS department was down to three people, including Collins, and in a maintenance mode for the past 3 years. BMC management has recognized that improved systems are a high priority, and Collins has recently been authorized to hire two more people at competitive salaries.

BMC managers have generated so many requests for new systems that an MIS steering committee has been established to approve projects and set systems development priorities. The members of the MIS steering committee are President Kyle Baxter, Vice President for Customer Service Sue Barkley, Controller Lou Wilcox, and Don Collins. Sue Barkley is a sister of Kyle Baxter and has been a champion of information technology within BMC.

Recent Developments

In May 1999, a major appliance manufacturer customer contacted BMC President Kyle Baxter and encouraged BMC to consider building a plant in Mexico to serve the needs of the customer's Mexican operations. This customer had carefully studied its suppliers and selected a small number to invite to become favored parts suppliers in Mexico.

In January 2000, the BMC board approved the decision to build a plant in Mexico. BMC management had been thinking about building a plant in Mexico for some time, for about 20 percent of BMC's production was being shipped to factories located in Mexico. Although Mexican wage rates are much lower than those in the United States, BMC management was not primarily motivated by the prospect of low Mexican wages. Stamping is very capital intensive and semiautomated, so labor costs are not a big part of the total cost of production, and there will be additional costs that will make up for any wage savings. But the cost of shipping, the problems in getting products across the border, and the difficulty in predicting exactly when a shipment will be delivered all make customers prefer to have their parts produced locally for their Mexican factories. BMC management decided that in order to be an important factor in the growing Mexican market, BMC must have a factory in Mexico.

BMC has assured its U.S. workers and the community in which its current plant is located that no present production will be moved to Mexico—everything produced there will be new business. The U.S. plant has been expanded 18 times since the first unit was built, and there is little room for further expansion on the site. If BMC's sales are to continue to grow, new plants will have to be built, and those in the United States will probably be built closer to major customers.

BMC decided to build the new plant in Queretaro, a thriving metropolis located about a 3-hour drive northwest of Mexico City. The city of Queretaro has a population of about 500,000, and its metropolitan area has a population of about a million. It has excellent infrastructure for Mexico, with progressive city leadership and a university. This university is paperless. All course work and homework is completed on computers—no paper at all! There is a lot of technology education available, including tool and die training programs. Also, some major U.S. consulting firms have offices there. This environment is why BMC's customer and other manufacturers are locating in Queretaro.

The new factory will be located reasonably close to the customer plant that it will serve. However, Kyle Baxter intends to expand BMC's business in Mexico, so in the long run this plant will supply parts to other customers. The new plant will start out small, but BMC has plenty of land and the plant has been designed so that it can be easily expanded as the need arises. The plant's initial planned dimensions are about 200 by 200 feet, providing 40,000 square feet of space. It will start with six presses (two 125-ton, two 200-ton, and two 300-ton presses) but with none of the huge 600- to 800-ton presses that BMC has in the main plant. It will have some welders, a toolroom, and a tooling facility where dies can be maintained. There will be offices in the plant for quality control, plant engineering, and a shift supervisor, and office space along the front for the plant manager, accounting manager, human resources manager, clerical workers, and a computer room. In addition it will have a break room, a training room, and shower and locker facilities—most plants provide shower facilities in that part of Mexico. And there will be a small kitchen where the workers can cook meals.

Don Collins designed the computer room for the Mexican plant. It is located in a secure area next to a permanent wall and will have adequate power, air conditioning, emergency lighting, and everything that is needed for a computer room. The plant will be wired with category-5 copper wiring throughout. There are plans for fiber-optic cable as the plant expands, so internal communications will not be a problem. They may or may not install a central computer at the start. An Ethernet LAN will connect the PCs in the plant.

Initially this plant will employ about 35 people in a single shift operation. As of May 1, 2000, the plant manager, Jesus Salazar, and the financial and human resources manager, Maria Alvarez, had been hired. Both were from the locality and speak some English. It is expected that the other managers will speak some English, although they may not be completely fluent. But the rest of the workers will not be English-speaking. Initially two experienced BMC managers, one from the toolroom facility and the other from plant engineering, will be sent to Queretaro to help with the start-up and training. These two expatriate managers have no international experience and neither speaks Spanish. They are scheduled to return to the United States within 2 years, after which the staff in Mexico should be entirely local.

For the foreseeable future BMC will do all engineering, designing, and building of the dies in its U.S. facility and ship them to the Mexican plant. They will have to do some final tuning down there. Die maintenance will be done locally, so BMC will have to develop some skilled people there. That is one reason BMC is sending the two managers from the United States to help them get started.

The Mexican plant was designed, the land was acquired, and ground was broken for construction in January 2000. The Mexican plant was scheduled to begin to deliver parts to its major customer in December 2000.

For tax and legal reasons, BMC has established a wholly owned subsidiary corporation to own and operate the Mexican plant. BMC will treat the Mexican plant just like an outside contractor—customers will place orders with the BMC home office and pay the home office for the parts. Then the home office will pay the Mexican subsidiary for the work it performs and the service it provides. The Mexican plant will ship the parts it produces directly to the customer, and will work directly with the customer on operational issues such as quality.

IS Issues

When BMC management decided to build a plant in Mexico, Don Collins' first concern was how to deal with the systems needs of a plant in Mexico. When this question arose BMC President Kyle Baxter's first reaction was:

> We want to have good systems down there, and we ought to use this opportunity to consider the long-range systems needs of the entire company. It would be nice if we could get something in Mexico that we can use for the entire company.

In January 2000, Kyle Baxter established a small task force to develop a plan for systems support of the Mexican plant and report to the BMC executive committee. The designated task force leaders were Collins and Virginia (Ginnie) Mease, BMC's controller. The task force also included Sue Barkley, Jesus Salazar, and Maria Alvarez.

The stated mission of the task force was:

> To implement the desired business processes and to select, implement, and support the appropriate business system that will exceed the needs of BMC Mexico.

The goals of the task force included the following:

1. Business processes will be defined to facilitate optimum effectiveness.
2. Software will match the business processes.
3. Software will enable integrated processes.
4. The business system selected can also be implemented throughout BMC.
5. Language and currency needs will be met.
6. The business system investment will provide the best cost/benefit.
7. Support of the system will be available in Mexico.

For some time BMC managers had been thinking about the possibility of acquiring an enterprise resource planning (ERP) system to replace and expand the operational systems of the company, and an ERP would meet most of the previously stated goals, so the initial focus of the task force was to investigate the possibility of acquiring an ERP.

Collins was a member of an IS management group sponsored by a local university, and through this contact he was able to get access to three nearby companies who had experience with an ERP. Collins and Mease developed an interview guide covering the questions they thought were important, interviewed managers at the three companies, and summarized the results of the interviews. Two things stood out from the interviews: First, there was not enough time to implement an ERP package properly by the end of the year, and, second, BMC management could not simultaneously cope with the disruption of starting a new plant and the disruption of installing an ERP. Therefore, on May 25, 2000, the BMC executive committee decided to eliminate the goal of considering the long-term needs of BMC from the task force charter and to concentrate exclusively on developing systems support for the Mexican plant.

Alternatives Considered

After the decision to abandon consideration of an ERP, Collins and Mease defined the following three approaches to supporting the Mexican plant:

1. Connect the Mexican plant to BMC's existing systems through a high-speed communications line.
2. Contract through an application service provider (ASP) to provide systems support to the Mexican plant.
3. Employ a piecemeal solution where they would acquire a number of software packages that could run on the networked PCs in Mexico that would serve the basic needs of the Mexican plant.

Initially the Mexican plant would be a relatively small operation, and transaction volumes would be quite small. Collins and Mease felt that at the start they would only need to handle basic things—control inventory, ship, print reports, handle EDI to and from the major customer—the things necessary for the operation to run. On the other hand, they expected the Mexican operation to grow rapidly, so transaction volumes and the complexity of managing production would grow over time.

The first alternative—using the existing BMC systems in Mexico through a high-speed communications line—was quickly eliminated. In the first place, there was the language problem. BMC's existing systems were in English and would have to be translated into Spanish for use in Mexico, and that was deemed impractical. Second, because of the language problem, they could not support these systems in Mexico. The availability of local support was a crucial factor in determining how to serve the systems needs of the Mexican plant. There must be people who can help install the applications software, handle any problems that arise, and train people in using the software. And there must be support for the hardware platform that the applications run on.

An application service provider (ASP) is a company that has one or more large data centers and furnishes a portion of that processing and file storage capacity to each of its clients via communications facilities. For years it has been anticipated that, sometime in the future, information processing power would be available through a wall plug just like electrical power. An ASP is the current embodiment of that dream. Thus, the customer of an ASP does not have to invest in computer hardware and systems software or manage a data center. Rather, the customer pays a monthly fee to the ASP based on the amount of file storage, RAM, and computer processing cycles used. The customer also pays for the use of the communications facilities used.

The ASP may also provide some applications software, but the customer usually buys applications software from software vendors that work with the ASP. The ASP provides help desk support and deals with hardware problems, but applications software problems are handed off to the individual software vendors.

Collins had difficulty exploring the ASP option. He contacted his local IBM representative, but it took a long time to get in touch with a person who represented IBM's ASP business. It was early August before Collins could get definite information on what ASP services IBM could provide to the Mexican plant.

IBM would be able to serve the Mexican plant through communications facilities linking the Mexican plant to IBM's Rochester, N.Y., data center. Applications software would be obtained from a number of software vendors with whom IBM has partnership arrangements. Many of these vendors provide Spanish language versions of some of their software. IBM provides a Spanish language help desk that hands off applications software problems to the appropriate vendor's Spanish language help desk.

The cost of IBM's ASP service would be $60,000 per year. There would, of course, be additional charges for the applications software, training, data conversion, and start-up. These costs seemed excessive in comparison to the third alternative and the ASP solution seemed overly complicated for the start-up operation, so BMC abandoned consideration of the ASP option and concluded that the piecemeal solution was the only viable option for supporting the Mexican operation at the start. However, after the Mexican plant is in operation and things have settled down, BMC intends to reconsider both the ERP and the ASP options for the entire company.

Nagging Difficulties

Collins, Mease, and Barkley had encountered major communications difficulties in dealing with the BMC people in Mexico. Salazar and Alvarez had not been active participants in the task force, and there had been little effective communication with either of them. According to Collins, there were four things contributing to these communications problems:

1. *Language*. When we talk to each other we don't always understand the true meaning of what the other guy is saying. We nod our heads, but we may not be on the same page.
2. *Cultural*. They give the distinct impression of wanting to be self-sufficient, and therefore any help we give may be considered paternalistic. This may be the result of sensitivities relating to America's dominant position ever since the Mexican War.
3. *Distance*. It would be different if we could drive there in a couple of hours. But it is a major disruption for them to come up here or us to go down there.
4. *Mind-set*. Their mind-set has been on getting up and running and producing parts, not on any supporting activities. We just cannot get their attention, and you can't communicate without attention!

Collins, Mease, and Barkley have also begun to reconsider the task force's role in providing systems support to the Mexican plant. Barkley explains their dilemma:

> We feel that we are responsible for helping them get started right, but it is clear that they would like to do it on their own. We don't want their local pride to result in them falling on their faces, but if they have the capability they definitely need to have a major role in making the decisions. But we can't tell whether they have the capability.
>
> Right now they are concentrating on getting the plant operational so that they can get parts out the door. We are ready to help, but they don't seem to have the time or the urgency. We are afraid that once they get past the hurdle of getting into production, then they are going to expect to get the systems installed and running in the next week.
>
> The broader question is: How much should we dictate to them in all areas down there? Do we want to let them reinvent the wheel because of the cultural gap between us and them? Or should we insist on providing some guidance from our functional areas (human resources, quality, materials control, production planning, etc.) to assist them with getting the basics up and going? On the other hand, do we really want to pass on any of our "bad habits" to them?

Status on September 12, 2000

Construction of the Mexican plant is on schedule, and it will be ready to begin production no later than December 1. As of September 12, Collins and Mease felt that they had made little progress in providing systems support for the Mexican operation. They had decided to pursue a piecemeal approach, so they needed to find vendors who could provide and support the basic Spanish language software packages that would be needed to support the small start-up operation.

Maria Alvarez, the human resources/financial manager, had experience with a small financial software package from Contpaq and she would like very much to use that package at the Mexican plant. Contpaq has a Web site, but it is in Spanish, so Collins has not been able to find out much about the software from that source. Grant Thornton, BMC's U.S. consultant for establishing a Mexican operation, has an office in Queretaro. This firm will be the Mexican plant's auditor, and it recommends the Contpaq financial software, so it appears that local support for that package would be available. Unfortunately, Collins has been unable to find out if this package will run on the peer-to-peer PC network planned for the Mexican plant. Collins has contacted Grant Thornton's Mexican office, but has not been able to get this information from its people. Collins is also trying to determine if Grant Thornton can provide local support for the Mexican plant's PCs.

The Mexican plant now has two customers. Collins and Mease have contacted both of them to determine what kind of interaction they will require at the start. Fortunately, neither of them is using EDI in Mexico, so they will fax shipping orders and schedules to the plant. They are both using standard labels, so it should be possible to find a simple barcode package to produce the labels. They also do not have any special requirements for packing slips and bills of lading, so BMC should be able to find a simple package to produce this

EXHIBIT 2

IT Governance at Asia Pacific Shared Services

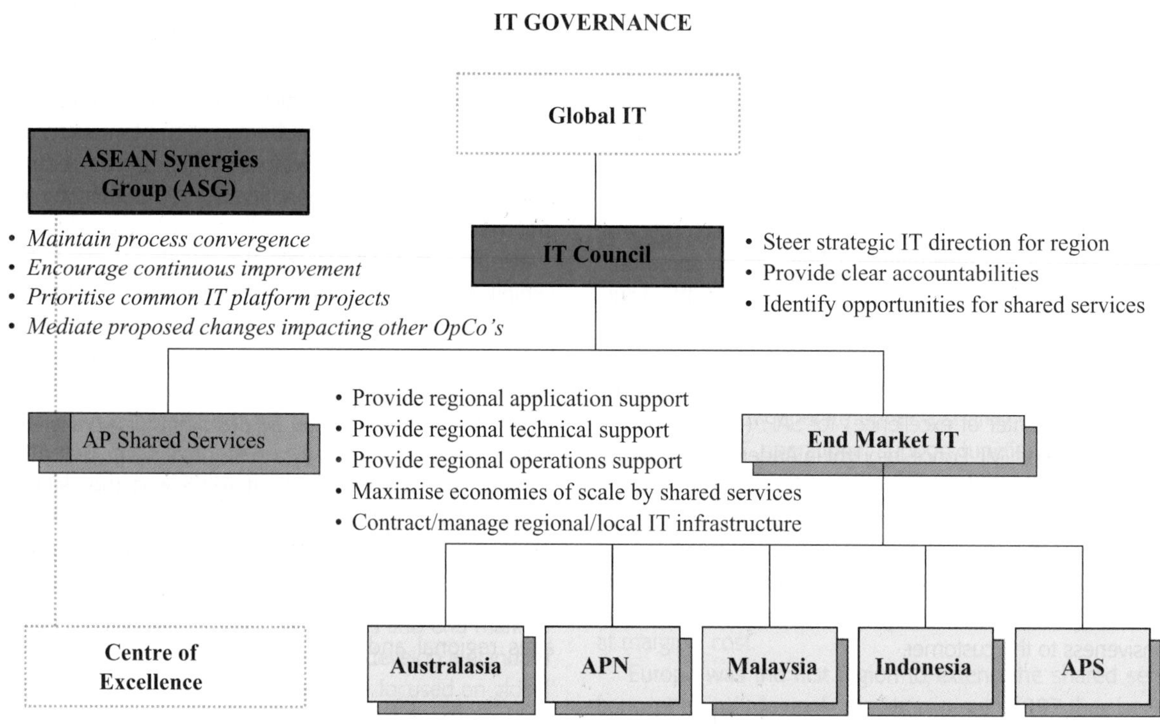

instances involves the management of outsourcing contracts. APSS also runs other shared systems for the region, such as a human resources system (Bucks), which is used by eight countries. An SAP applications manager is responsible for the SAP development and maintenance projects. A second applications manager provides other application development services for Malaysia and other countries in the region. Other centers of excellence for information technology also exist in the AP region outside of Malaysia. For example, Australia and Hong Kong provide Internet access for other end markets in the region.

In a recent 9 to 12 month APSS study, the costs for the data center, the servers, and desktop machines were examined for the whole AP region. The conclusion was that they could not achieve any additional cost efficiencies by outsourcing. In the year 2000, the annual cost via APSS for hosting an SAP R/3 user, which includes hardware, software lease, and support for hardware and applications, was U.S.$3,500. The expectation is that this figure will decrease still further by the end of 2001: three SAP instances will be running systems for ten end markets in the region and a total of 1,500 users, at an average cost of U.S.$3,000 per user. In contrast, if those end markets were to host SAP R/3 by country, their annual costs were estimated to be in excess of U.S.$9,000 per user.

Staffing Issues

External contract personnel are regularly used by APSS in order to expand and contract their resources for application development projects. APSS has formed partnerships with local service providers who can provide experienced personnel. APSS also has contracts with freelance consultants. Contract personnel are generally put first on new projects so that they understand the problems of the end markets and are then rotated into support roles. On average, APSS employs 10 to 15 contractors, with a mix of short- and long-term contracts.

For example, a new APSS contract employee with extensive SAP knowledge who was hired for the BAT Taiwan implementation was given about 3 weeks' training on the Symphony template and APSS methodology prior to going onsite to Taiwan for the kickoff of their R/3 implementation project. During those weeks, she had access to written documentation and an APSS staff member who provided support for another end market walked through the template with her.

Currently, APSS is concentrating on cross-training full-time personnel to gain more flexibility. For example, APSS personnel go to SAP training for multiple modules as well as cross-functional training so that they have exposure to how R/3 is integrated across modules. Expertise is also built via a Lotus

EXHIBIT 3
Organization Chart for Asia Pacific Shared Services

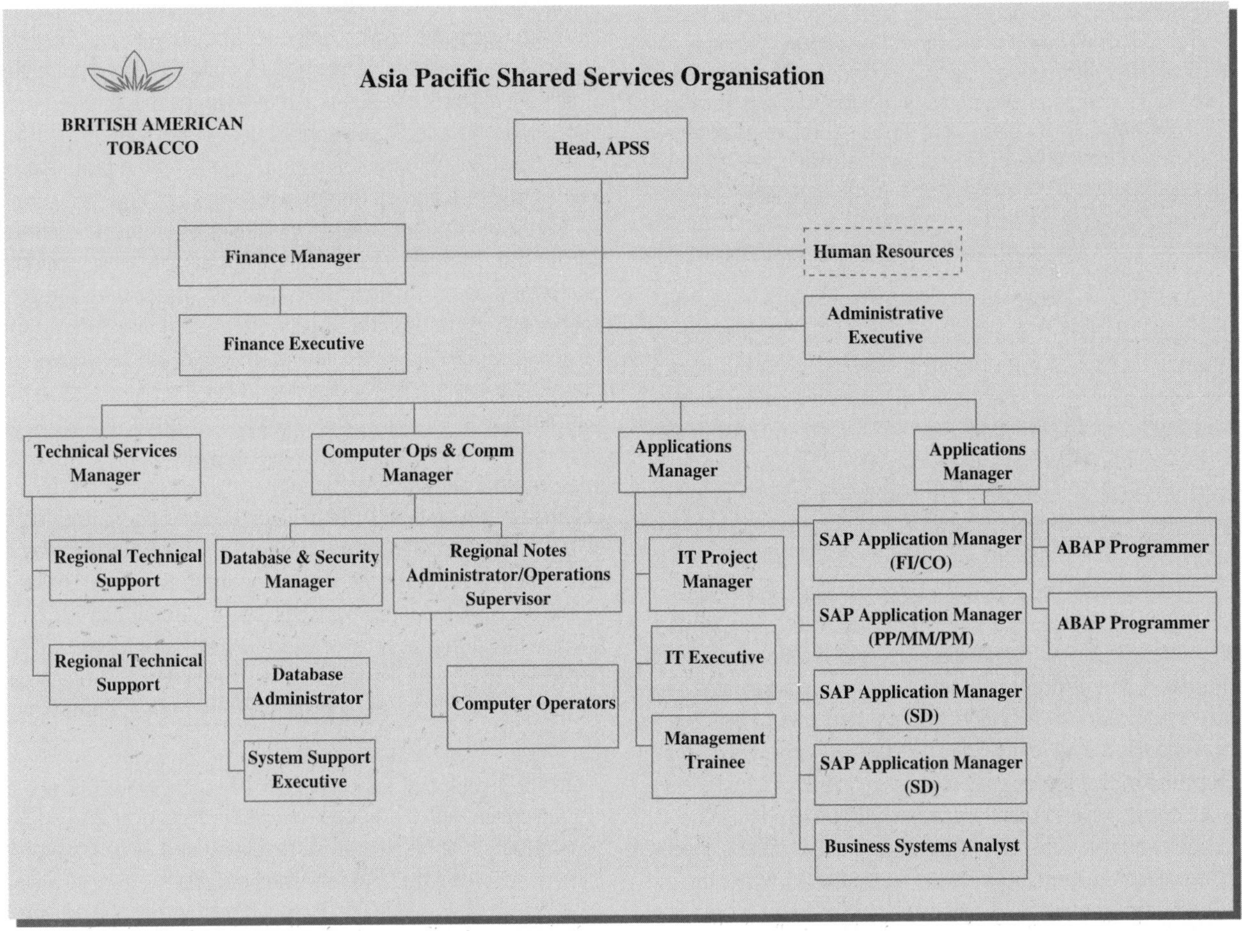

Notes database that is used for knowledge transfer. This tool is used as a repository for project documentation and for a help desk system. Knowledge transfer also occurs following each implementation: When project team members complete an implementation, they run through the design and any special requirements the country has with all members of the SAP application team.

Managing IT resources for a growing shared services operation will continue to be a challenge. APSS needs not only to recruit the best people, but also to train them and retain them.

> A key challenge is how to quickly mobilize resources and put the right people on projects.
>
> —*SAP Applications Manager, APSS*

> BAT sells itself as a company that is human-centric: it cares for its people and their development. There are numerous opportunities to grow within BAT: high-potential employees can move into many different functions worldwide throughout their career. Given that there may be limitations to grow within certain end markets, opportunities will be made available to high-potential employees and especially to those who are mobile.
>
> —*Mr. Lam, IT Director, Malaysia*

Leveraging SAP Templates and Implementation Expertise

During the past 2 years, the APSS staff has gained a lot of expertise in implementing SAP systems. An external consulting partner (Andersen Consulting) had been used for the Australia, Malaysia, and Singapore projects, and also projects that involved data integration initiatives for the Rothmans merger. Much of this experience was used to good advantage in Fall 2000 for the Taiwan and Thailand R/3 implementation projects that were completed by APSS without external consultants.

However, the opportunity for the Taiwan implementation almost eluded them.

> We were deploying resources for the merger and were not really thinking about how to bring the figure down for Taiwan because it didn't have the resources. The thinking behind it was not whether they needed ERP or not, because they needed it: we wanted them to have the scalability to grow, and grow fast. But Taiwan had an offer from ECoE [European Center of Excellence for SAP] and we realized that someone would be eating our own grass. We revised the implementation process and found that we could take time out of it.
>
> *—Mr. Ponce, Asia Pacific Regional IT Manager*

The fixed-cost contract for the two-phase Taiwan implementation was U.S.$150,000, and the less complex Thailand implementation was U.S.$50,000. The Taiwan implementation required two functions specific to Taiwan: a government-mandated invoicing system and Chinese (Mandarin) language capabilities. These projects were considered a quantum leap from the earlier Singapore implementation, which included manufacturing modules and was done with external consultants (Andersen Consulting) at a cost of U.S.$5 million.

Both the Taiwan and Thailand implementations involved converting the end markets to a new business model by January 2001. These business model changes involved not only direct importation, but also direct distribution, two activities that had been done previously by independent distributors of BAT products. Although neither of the markets was very large, the change in business model meant a big change in operations. In addition to their prior functions, both needed an ERP system for accounts receivable, accounts payable, as well as purchasing and inventory management, and they needed it in less than 6 months.

The two implementations had overlapping schedules. The first phase of the Taiwan implementation (without bolt-ons) was scheduled for 8 weeks, and the kickoff was the end of September 2000. The Thailand implementation was scheduled for 5 weeks, initiated in October, and completed before the Taiwan implementation. BAT's operations in Taiwan were much larger than those in Thailand: The office has evolved from a 20-person to a 100-person office in less than 5 years. In addition, the Taiwan implementation had two unique requirements (a government-required invoicing system and a Chinese-language module), neither of which was supplied by the R/3 version currently used by APSS. The BAT Thailand office had only two finance people prior to the R/3 implementation, and the project had one unique requirement: invoices in the Thai language.

Each project had a project manager from the area IT organization (APS for Thailand, APN for Taiwan), a full-time APSS development team, and a technical team with part-time APSS resources. For both projects, the APSS development team members worked onsite and part-time ABAP and Basis personnel worked primarily from Kuala Lampur. The SAP applications manager at APSS served as the APSS lead for the Thailand project. She also did the high-level project plan for Taiwan and had an oversight role for that project. One of her direct reports was the APSS lead on the Taiwan project. Because the Symphony template was to be implemented for both Taiwan and Thailand in the same client in a single R/3 instance along with the Singapore system, it was critical that changes made to the template for either site were carefully coordinated. APSS had formal procedures for how to go about changing the template, as well as the time frames for doing it.

The Taiwan project was treated as a one-off implementation and the project team spent a lot of time in a business blueprint stage, in which users typically determine the R/3 best practices that will be used for their company.[2] When the business processes were new to the end market, however, the APSS team members explained how the processes in the template worked, and then asked the users about local requirements. This approach was modified for the Thailand implementation: The APSS team set up the template in a conference room pilot (CRP), which allowed users to interact with a working model of the proposed system. In this way, a few special requirements were identified. Because Thailand would be using shared services out of Singapore for their finance function, the finance module for the Symphony template had to be strictly adhered to. The Thailand project was therefore more of a "straightjacket" implementation in which the APSS team drove the project.

> Thailand could not have transformed itself from Rep Office to Trading Co. with the speed required if the processes had not been determined already; it enabled Thailand to scale up its operations with very few additional resources.
>
> *—Mr. Ponce, Asia Pacific Regional IT Manager*

> The Taiwan case is a demonstration of how you can take a complex enterprise application and deploy it in a business situation in reasonable cost and time.
>
> *—Mr. Pottrick, Head of Business Integration, Globe House*

The approaches used for the Taiwan and Thailand implementations are expected to be applicable to other small locations with changing business models and few unique business requirements. However, some countries will require more complex implementations. For example, some end markets will have additional modules to implement their manufacturing operations. Other end markets that currently operate manually will require a totally new technical infrastructure as well as additional types of training.

> The oil-and-gas industry had 50 to 60 organizations sharing the same template. The same convergence can also be achieved in

[2] In a one-off implementation, the business problem has distinct characteristics that need to be assessed independently.

> the tobacco industry because the industry is not that complex. The challenge is to find the right balance between convergence and flexibility.
>
> —*Mr. Tan, Head, APSS*

IT Shared Services: The Future

APSS is a young organization building credibility based on BAT process knowledge and low-cost solutions. The next challenges will be to expand its services and to learn to market its shared services to a broader arena.

Partnerships with other BAT shared services units may also become increasingly important. Although the AP region has demonstrated that SAP R/3 implementations can be affordable to smaller end markets, IT cost efficiencies alone may not be a strong enough business driver for an end market to adopt a standard template. For example, a business model that includes a price discount for subscribing to financial shared services as well as SAP R/3 was "proven" in Thailand and is likely to be adopted by other country managers. That is, a discount per named SAP user is given to the end market based on cost savings from the sharing of help desk services: The APSS help center funnels finance calls to the financial shared center in Singapore.

> There are some restrictions when using a template, which a business is more willing to accept if it sees that it is possible to have business-focused shared services, such as for financials.
>
> —*SAP Programme Manager, Globe House*

> In Thailand there is a very conscious recognition that "I don't need to worry about all this back office work. This is all done for me. I have more time to focus on the business, just look at [the output from SAP] and analyze my profitability and what we need to do."
>
> —*Mr. Ponce, Asia Pacific Regional IT Manager*

In the future, APSS may also be in a position to offer its services outside the AP region. The European shared-services organizations already support end markets in Latin America and other regions outside of Europe, and the AP are beginning to see that SAP is affordable. The learnings from template-based R/3 implementations could also be leveraged for other package implementations—such as a standard customer relationship-management (CRM) system. Global BAT could also decide to commercialize its shared services organizations, rather than retaining these units as internal service providers.

CASE STUDY IV-10

MARY MORRISON'S ETHICAL DILEMMA

Mary Morrison, a second-semester sophomore business major at Big State University, was unpacking the new PC that her mother had given her for Christmas when she discovered that, except for the Windows operating system, no software was included with the machine. Although the new PC was an adequate computer, it was a stripped-down off-brand machine, and one way that the store kept the price low was to not include software. Mary was upset because she knew that she would need a good word processor, a spreadsheet program, and some presentation software, and she had expected that this software would be included with the computer.

According to her friends, Microsoft Office Professional was the recommended suite of software for business students. Mary quickly checked around the university and found that she could buy Microsoft Office Professional at the special price of $199, or she could get some shareware software that would have the basic capabilities that she needed for only $25. Knowing that she could not afford the $199 for Microsoft Office Professional, Mary was about to buy the shareware when a friend, Frank Taylor, offered to let her copy his Microsoft Office Professional onto the new machine. Mary was tempted, but she was also uneasy about accepting Frank's offer because she had learned from her computer literacy class that copying his software was tantamount to stealing it. She told him that she needed to think about it. Frank could not understand her hesitation. "Everybody does it," he explained.

Mary's Background

Mary's mother, Caroline Morrison, grew up on a tenant farm near Minifee, Arkansas, the second of eight children of a hard-working but poor couple. Although her parents had only an elementary school education, Caroline graduated from the local high school with outstanding grades. Seeing little future in Minifee, after her graduation Caroline left for St. Louis where she found work as a janitor in a nursing home.

Caroline soon met and married James Morrison, also from the South, who had a job driving a local delivery truck. They had four children, Mary being the oldest. Things went well for them for a few years, but James developed a drinking problem, was fired from his job as a driver, and, when Mary was nine, he abandoned his family and left town. Caroline had four children aged three, five, seven, and nine to feed, clothe, and take care of, and she was forced to go on welfare.

Caroline hated being on welfare, so when her youngest child entered school she got a job as a nurse's aid on the night shift at a nearby hospital. Working at night, she could get the children off to school in the morning and be home to greet them in the afternoon. In a few years the hospital sponsored Caroline in a part-time training program to become a Licensed Practical Nurse (LPN), which she completed in 2 years. Thus, she became an LPN at the hospital, still a low-paying job, but better than her previous job. She also worked part-time as a housekeeper, in addition to her night work at the hospital.

Mary grew up to be an excellent, highly motivated student, and graduated from high school near the top of her class, despite working at a succession of part-time jobs to augment the family finances. Knowing that her mother could not afford to send her to college, Mary applied for scholarships at several colleges and universities. She was accepted by all the schools that she applied to, and was offered a full scholarship—tuition, room, and board—at Big State. The scholarship was for 4 years, subject to maintaining good grades.

Because her mother could not help her financially, Mary worked at a part-time minimum-wage job 20 hours a week so that she would have money for books and clothes. Despite this, and despite the handicap of coming from an inner-city high school, Mary had been able to maintain her grades and keep her scholarship.

Mary's Analysis

Mary could not imagine how her mother had gotten the $1,000 to purchase the PC that she had given her for Christmas, so she knew that Caroline could not help her buy Microsoft Office Professional. Mary was barely keeping her head above water with her expenses, so she could not possibly afford $199 for this software. Therefore, her choices were to accept Frank's offer to copy his Microsoft Office or to obtain the shareware software.

Mary considered the following rationale for accepting Frank's offer:

- Although it was illegal, there was no chance that she would get caught.
- Although it would be stealing in a sense, it would be a victimless crime—it would not cost Frank anything; and, because she could never buy the software, Microsoft would not be losing any revenue.
- Even if Microsoft were losing revenue, it would go to Bill Gates, who already had more millions than Mary's whole family had tens of dollars.

Mary considered the following arguments against copying Frank's software:

- She knew that copying Frank's software was stealing the product of someone else's effort. She viewed herself as an honest person. Despite growing up poor in a tough neighborhood, she had never stolen anything. She knew that she would never consider shoplifting something worth $199 from a store, even if she knew she would not get caught. In fact, if she had found a wallet containing $200 in cash she would go to great lengths to return the wallet and its contents to its owner.
- She could get by using the shareware software.

After carefully considering her analysis, Mary picked up the phone to call Frank and tell him her decision.

CASE STUDY IV-11

A Security Breach on the Indiana University Computer Network

On Wednesday, March 12, 1997, over 2,000 Indiana University (IU) faculty received the following e-mail message: "Are you aware that Indiana University put your privacy at risk? Have they contacted you about it?"

The sender of this message was Glen Roberts of Oil City, Pennsylvania, who describes himself on his Web home page as a talk show host, privacy advocate, and Internet entrepreneur. Searching the Internet, Roberts had located an IU file containing the names of 2,760 IU faculty, along with their Social Security numbers, addresses, and phone numbers, which Roberts had downloaded and posted on his Web site. The file had been created by the University Graduate School to provide information on the research interests of the faculty members so that they could be notified of funding opportunities that might be of interest to them.

All IU information on the Web is supposed to be protected by a "safeword card." According to Norma Holland, director of university computing services: "We have what is called a 'firewall,' an Internet term that essentially prevents access to data which are not public. The safeword card allows only authorized and authenticated users to get to those data." But this sensitive file apparently was not protected. According to Jeffrey Alberts, associate dean, this was an obsolete file that escaped unnoticed when the system was being upgraded to make it more secure. The university immediately removed the file and disabled the old gateway service.

The situation was called "an eye-opener" by IU vice president for public affairs Christopher Simpson: "It was fortunate that more sensitive data was not compromised. Although we are very sensitive to the release of information like this, this is vastly different from having individual access to the university's most sensitive proprietary information. This is a good wake-up call. That is exactly how we are viewing it."

But Roberts posed a question of other potential security problems. "You must remember that even though my page may have brought this to your attention in an unpleasant manner, the real danger lies in those who may have silently obtained the information from your site with no one the wiser," he wrote in a Web page dialogue with Mark S. Bruhn, IU information security officer.

Roberts claims the Privacy Act of 1974 "forbids such agencies (as IU) from even asking for Social Security numbers in other than specifically enumerated situations. That the SSN is included in any such faculty Internet research database is outrageous," Roberts wrote on his Web conversation with Bruhn. "Even if the files are not meant to be available to the public, the wholesale collection of such information in an 'Internet database' demonstrates a clear failure to understand even the most basic precepts of personal privacy."

Roberts' Justification

Roberts was described by people at two Pennsylvania newspapers as "an interesting fellow and a computer whiz-bang." According to the *Erie Times*, which did a profile on Roberts several months prior to this incident, he came to Oil City from the Chicago area, where he published a paper that dealt with privacy issues. He has done a short-wave radio program and now does a radio program on the Internet. Also, he has been a network television consultant and appeared on local talk shows. Roberts also publishes several Web pages and works as a computer consultant.

Roberts said he came across the IU file during a check of his own domain. By typing "SSN" into the Infoseek search engine, Roberts said, he called up a list of entries that showed a name and Social Security number. By opening that file, he found the IU research database.

Roberts said he has been involved in publicizing privacy issues for about 15 years. His interest began, he said, by using the Freedom of Information Act and obtaining copies of government documents. He said he was surprised at the amount of information available of which people are not usually aware. He has been particularly interested in the seemingly widespread availability of individuals' Social Security numbers, which are pathways to other information and whose disclosure raises the potential of unauthorized use of a person's identity.

Roberts states that the issue is this: "Should the university be collecting this information and putting it in databases, with maybe not the intent to pass it out all over the world but with intent that a fair number of people may be accessing that information?"

Roberts said he published the IU list because the privacy issue does not usually become tangible to people until they experience an invasion themselves. "The bottom line is privacy is an extremely important issue but it is only important when you see it affect yourself firsthand," he said. "That's what I have done with other Web pages. People can experience it firsthand, and with that experience can be more public debate and action on the issues."

He added that he is disturbed that people are unhappy with him for posting names and Social Security numbers where they can be obtained free, but no one seems concerned that the same kind of information is being sold all over the country. "The same outrage should apply to companies for however long they've been selling this kind of information," Roberts said. "Unless it is in your face, it does not seem to matter."

Faculty Reaction

Many of the IU faculty members on the published list disagree with Roberts' tactics. They were primarily concerned, for the obvious reasons, that their Social Security numbers were made easily available, and over a hundred faculty e-mailed protests to Roberts.

"I go to Roberts and say 'I like people who are watchdogs, but do you need to post this information in a convenient location to make your point?"' said Kurt Zorn, of the IU School of Public and Environmental Affairs. "I think he might have done more damage by doing this than the university did in its oversight. There might have been more effective ways of calling attention to the problem."

Law professor Ed Greenebaum added that he believes Roberts made a judgment about the university without any information, which is unfair. "The impact is to expose us to a danger he says he is trying to prevent, and it's much more than it otherwise would have been," Greenebaum said. "My concern is not with the university's intent but why this individual feels the need, inconsistently in my view, to facilitate the distribution of our Social Security numbers."

With IU threatening to take legal action and the heavy volume of protests from IU faculty, Roberts removed the IU file from his Web page and said he has no intention of posting the names and Social Security numbers again.

The Consequences

On March 27, religious studies professor James Ackerman said he had recently been billed for phone lines, Internet access, and credit card accounts that are not his own. Although it has not been verified, he believes someone picked up his name and Social Security number from Roberts' Web page.

Within two weeks of the posting, Ackerman received a bill for a month's Internet time, had a call from AT&T saying it was ready with a conference call he did not order, got an inquiry from Ameritech asking if he made a call from Germany to Portland, Oregon, and discovered there were calling card accounts opened in his name.

William Boone, an education professor, said his wife received an inquiry from MCI's fraud department about calls originating from Germany using the Boones' calling card number. Although there has been no proof that Roberts' Web page was the source of the information used in the fraud, Boone and others believe the incidents are more than a coincidence. "What are the chances two IU professors are getting unauthorized calls from Germany? What are the chances this is not related to the World Wide Web issue?" Boone said.

Boone's wife said the issue is unsettling. "It feels like such a violation," she said. "You feel like someone knows you but you don't know them. That is very uncomfortable."

The situation has been frustrating to Ackerman, who said the credit card companies told him they could not put a block on his Social Security number. He was told he could contact three credit agencies, which many banks use to check a person's credit, and they could put a hold on his records.

Ackerman also contacted the office of IU's legal counsel, which was unable to offer much assistance. "At this point, we don't even know if his experience relates in any way to Roberts' Web page," said Michael Klein, associate university counsel. "There are some timing coincidences, but you just don't know." However, the university is exploring whether there is any legal liability Roberts might incur if faculty members are damaged, financially or otherwise.

Klein added that the university is reviewing the issue of using Social Security numbers in the course of running the school. "As an institution, we are taking a look inward to determine if there are some alternatives," he said.

GLOSSARY

Active Desktop A feature of newer versions of Microsoft Windows, which Microsoft describes as a customizable "dashboard" for the PC. With Active Desktop, the user may place both Windows icons (shortcuts to programs) and HTML elements (links to frequently visited Web sites) on the Windows home screen.

AI *See* Artificial intelligence.

Alpha testing The testing of a commercial software package inside a customer organization, similar to a user acceptance test in an SDLC approach, during which changes to the package are typically made. *See also* Beta testing.

American National Standards Institute (ANSI) The United States standard-setting body for many IT standards.

Analog network The electronic linking of devices, where messages are sent over the links by having some analogous physical quantity (e.g., voltage) continuously vary as a function of time. Historically, the telephone network has been an analog network.

ANSI *See* American National Standards Institute.

Applet An application program written in the Java object-oriented programming language; usually stored on a Web server and downloaded to a microcomputer with a mouse click and executed by a Java-compatible Web browser. A major advantage of a Java applet is that it can be run on virtually any IT platform. *See also* Web browser, IT platform.

Application independence The separation, or decoupling, of data from application systems. Application independence means that applications are built separately from the databases from which applications draw their data; application independence results in lower long-term costs for systems development.

Application service provider (ASP) An information technology vendor that hosts applications for which it holds the licenses, typically using Web-based front ends and Internet access. The vendor provides one or more complete applications to client organizations on a pay-per-use or flat-fee basis. The vendor may be the vendor of the software (e.g., SAP or PeopleSoft) or a third-party service provider. ASP aggregators host multiple applications with a common interface. *See also* Outsourcing.

Application suite *See* Office suite.

Applications software All programs written to accomplish particular tasks for computer users. Examples include programs for payroll computation, inventory record keeping, word processing, and producing a summarized report for top management.

Archie An Internet application, or tool, that allows the user to search the publicly available anonymous File Transfer Protocol (FTP) sites to find the desired computer files. *See also* File Transfer Protocol.

Arithmetic/logical unit The portion of a computer system in which arithmetic operations (such as addition and multiplication) and logical operations (such as comparing two numbers for equality) are carried out.

ARPANET The forerunner of the Internet; a network created by the U.S. Department of Defense to link leading U.S. research universities and research centers.

Artificial intelligence (AI) The study of how to make computers do things that are currently done better by people. AI research includes six separate but related areas: natural languages, robotics, perceptive systems (vision and hearing), genetic programming (also called evolutionary design), expert systems, and neural networks.

Artificial intelligence (AI) shell *See* Expert system shell.

Assembler A program (software) that translates an assembly language program—a program containing mnemonic operation codes and symbolic addresses—into an equivalent machine language program.

Assembly language Second generation computer language in which the programmer uses easily remembered mnemonic operation codes instead of machine language operation codes and symbolic addresses instead of memory cell addresses. Such a language is considerably easier to use than machine language, but it still requires the programmer to employ the same small steps that the computer has been built to understand.

Asynchronous Transfer Mode (ATM) An approach to implementing a network, especially a WAN or a backbone network, based on high-speed switching technology to accomplish fast packet switching with short, fixed-length packets. With ATM, connectivity between devices is provided through a switch rather than through a shared bus or ring, with line speeds up to 1.24 billion bits per second possible. *See also* Packet switching.

ATM *See* Asynchronous Transfer Mode.

Attribute In data modeling, the actual elements of data that are to be collected, for example, customer last name, customer first name, customer street, and customer city.

Audit trail An EDP auditing technique that allows a business transaction to be traced from the time of input through all the processes and reports in which the transaction data are used. An audit trail is used to identify where errors are introduced or security breaches may have occurred.

B2B Business-to-business e-commerce utilizing electronic applications for transactions and communications between two or more businesses. B2B e-commerce includes direct-to-customer sales with business customers.

B2C Business-to-consumer e-commerce utilizing electronic applications for transactions and communications between a business seller (or a business intermediary or distributor) and individual end-consumers.

Backbone In a telecommunications network, the underlying foundation to which the other elements attach. For example, NSFNET served as the backbone for the Internet until 1995 by providing the underlying high-volume links of the Internet to which other elements attached. *See also* Backbone network.

Backbone network A middle-distance network that interconnects local area networks in a single organization with each other and with the organization's wide area network and the Internet. The technology employed is at the high end of that used for local area networks, such as FDDI, Fast Ethernet, or ATM running over fiber-optic cabling or shielded twisted pair. *See also* Asynchronous Transfer Mode, Fast Ethernet, Fiber Distributed Data Interface.

Balanced scorecard A management technique that translates an organization's goals and strategy into a "scorecard" of measures in order to predict financial performance.

Bandwidth The difference between the highest and the lowest frequencies (cycles per second) that can be transmitted on a single medium. Bandwidth is important because it is a measure of the capacity of the transmission medium.

Bar code label A label consisting of a series of bars used to identify an item; when the bar code is scanned, the data are entered into a computer. There are a variety of bar code languages, the most widely known of which is the Universal Product Code, or UPC, used by the grocery industry. The use of bar codes is very popular for high-volume supermarket checkout, department store sales, inventory tracking, time and attendance records, and health care records.

Baseband coax A simple-to-use and inexpensive-to-install type of coaxial cable that offers a single digital transmission channel with maximum transmission speeds ranging from 10 million bits per second (bps) up to 1 billion bps. Baseband coax was widely used for LANs and for long-distance transmission within the telephone network, although much of this coax has now been replaced by fiber-optic cabling.

Batch processing A mode of transaction processing in which a group or "batch" of transactions of a particular type is accumulated and then processed as a single batch at one time. For example, all sales for a firm would be accumulated during the day and then processed as a single batch at night.

Baud Number of signals sent per second; one measure of data transmission speed. Baud is often equivalent to Hertz (another measure of transmission speed) and to bits per second.

Benchmarking A procedure used to compare the capabilities of various computers in a particular organizational setting by running a representative set of real jobs (jobs regularly run on the organization's existing computer) on each of the machines and comparing the resulting elapsed times.

Beta testing The testing of a commercial software package at one or more organizations after the package has been modified based on Alpha testing at one or more customer sites. *See also* Alpha testing.

Bit Widely used abbreviation for a *bi*nary digi*t,* i.e., a 0 or a 1. Coding schemes used in computer systems employ particular sequences of bits to represent the decimal numbers, alphabetic characters, and special characters.

Bluetooth Short-range radio technology that has been built into a microchip, enabling data to be transmitted wirelessly at a speed of 1 million bits per second. The use of Bluetooth technology eliminates the need for many cables and permits the control of Bluetooth-equipped appliances from a cellular phone—all from a remote location, if desired.

Boundary Identifies the scope of a system. A boundary segregates the system from its environment.

Bridge A hardware device employed in a telecommunications network to connect two local area networks (LANs) or LAN segments when the LANs use the same protocols, or set of rules. A bridge is smart enough to forward only messages that need to go to the other LAN.

Broadband A general designation applied to the higher-speed alternatives for accessing the Internet from a home or small office, namely digital subscriber line (DSL), cable modem, and satellite connections.

Broadband coax A type of coaxial cable—more expensive and harder to use than baseband coax—that originally used analog transmission, but increasingly employs digital transmission. A single broadband coax can be divided into multiple channels so that a single cable can support simultaneous transmission of data, voice, and television. Broadband data transmission rates are similar to those for baseband coax, and high transmission speeds are possible over much longer distances than are feasible for baseband coax. Broadband coax is still widely used for cable television and LANs that span a significant area, often called metropolitan area networks.

Browser *See* Web browser.

Bus topology A network topology in which a single length of cable (coax, fiber-optic, or twisted pair)—not connected at the ends—is shared by all network devices; also called a linear topology.

Business intelligence The focus of newer fourth generation languages; these software tools are designed to answer queries relating to the business by analyzing data (often massive quantities of data), thereby providing "intelligence" to the business that will help it become more competitive.

Business intelligence system *See* Competitive intelligence system.

Business process The chain of activities required to achieve an outcome such as order fulfillment or materials acquisition.

Business process reengineering (BPR) The redesign of business processes to achieve dramatic improvements in efficiency and responsiveness by taking advantage of information technology. Also referred to as business process redesign.

Byte A memory cell that can store only one character of data. *See also* Memory.

Cable modem A high-speed, or broadband, connection to the Internet using the coaxial cables already used by television. Cable television companies had to reengineer the cable television system to permit the two-way data flow required for Internet connections. Cable modem speeds may be degraded as the number of users goes up because users are sharing the bandwidth of the coaxial cable.

Cache memory A very high-speed storage unit used as an intermediary between elements of a computer system that have a significant mismatch in speeds (e.g., the very fast data channel and relatively slow direct access storage device). An entire block of data is moved from the slower element to cache memory, so that most requests for data from the faster element can be satisfied directly from the very high-speed cache memory.

CAD *See* Computer-aided design.

CAE *See* Computer-aided engineering.

CAM *See* Computer-aided manufacturing.

Capability Maturity Model (CMM) A five-stage model of software development and IT project management processes that are designed to increase software quality and decrease development costs due to standard, repeatable approaches across multiple projects within the same organization. The model was developed by the Software Engineering Institute at Carnegie Mellon University. A level-5 CMM certification is required for some contractors to bid on software development projects for high-risk, government-sponsored projects today, such as for custom development projects for the U.S. Department of Defense.

CAPP *See* Computer-aided process planning.

CASE *See* Computer-aided software engineering.

CD An abbreviation for compact disk, a commonly used optical storage device with a standard capacity of 700 megabytes of data or 80 minutes of audio recording. *See also* CD-ROM, CD-R, CD-RW, DVD, DVD-ROM, DVR-R, DVD-RW, Optical disk.

CD-R An abbreviation for compact disk-recordable, formerly called a WORM (write once-read many) disk, a type of optical disk that can be written on by the user once and can then be read many times. CD-R technology is appropriate for archiving documents, engineering drawings, and records of all types.

CD-ROM An abbreviation for compact disk-read only memory; the first common type of optical disk storage for personal computers. CD-ROM can only be read and cannot be erased and is particularly useful for distributing large amounts of relatively stable data to many locations.

CD-RW An abbreviation for compact disk-rewritable, a type of optical disk that can be written on and read many times, then rewritten and read many times, and so on. Rewritable optical disks are the most versatile form of optical storage, and falling prices make them an attractive alternative to the standard floppy disk.

Cellular telephone A telephone instrument that can be installed in a car or carried in a pocket or briefcase; this instrument can be used anywhere as long as it is within the 8 to 10 mile range of a cellular switching station.

Center of excellence An organizational structure in which internal experts in a technology, IT process, or both, are brought together in order to provide internal consulting and transfer their knowledge to others in the organization. For example, a multinational firm may establish an SAP center of excellence in order to more effectively leverage what personnel throughout the company have learned about how best to design and implement SAP software modules for the company's business processes.

Central processing unit (CPU) The name given to the combination of the control unit, which controls all other components of a computer, and the arithmetic/logical unit, in which computations and logical comparisons are carried out; also referred to as the processor.

Chargeback The process that is used to internally charge client units for IS services provided. These internal charges may be established to recover costs or may represent market prices.

Check digit One or more digits appended to a critical value for validation purposes; the check digit has some mathematical relationship to the other digits in the number.

Chief information officer (CIO) The executive responsible for information technology strategy, policy, and service delivery at the corporate level; a general manager responsible for IS leadership, similar to a chief financial officer who is responsible for the finance function. Sometimes CIOs have no direct operating responsibilities because the organization has decentralized these responsibilities to IT leaders reporting to division heads. In dot-com businesses, the CTO may also play a CIO role. *See also* Chief technology officer.

Chief technology officer (CTO) Senior manager responsible for identifying and recommending ways in which information technology (IT) can be applied in an organization. The title is most often used in dot-com businesses or companies with a substantial presence on the Internet. *See also* Chief information officer.

CIM *See* Computer-integrated manufacturing.

CIO *See* Chief information officer.

Clicks-and-mortar A term that emerged in the late 1990s to refer to traditional companies (bricks-and-mortar, including catalog retailers) that had implemented new business strategies based on e-commerce opportunities. Used synonymously with the term "clicks-and-bricks."

Client/server system A particular type of distributed system in which the processing power is distributed between a central server computer, such as a midrange system or a powerful workstation, and a number of client computers, usually desktop microcomputers. The split in responsibilities between the server and the client varies considerably between applications, but the client often handles data entry and the immediate output, while the server maintains the larger database against which the new data are processed. *See also* Distributed systems.

Coax *See* Coaxial cable.

Coaxial cable (coax) A common transmission medium that consists of a heavy copper wire at the center, surrounded by insulating material, then a cylindrical conductor such as a woven braided mesh, and finally an outer protective plastic covering. The two kinds of coaxial cable in widespread use are baseband coax for digital transmission and broadband coax for both analog and digital transmission.

Collaboration A term used as a synonym for groupware. *See also* groupware.

Collaborative environment *See* Collaboration.

COM *See* Computer output microfilm.

Commercial software package *See* Software package.

Compact disk *See* CD.

Competitive forces model A model of five competitive forces faced by companies within the same industry, developed by Michael E. Porter for strategic assessment and planning.

Competitive intelligence system An executive information system (EIS) that emphasizes competitive information. *See also* Executive information system.

Compiler A program (software) that translates a third generation or fourth generation language program into an equivalent machine language program, translating the entire program into machine language before any of the program is executed.

Computer-aided design (CAD) The use of computer graphics (both two-dimensional and three-dimensional) and a database to create and modify engineering designs.

Computer-aided engineering (CAE) The analysis of the functional characteristics of an engineering design by simulating the product performance under various conditions.

Computer-aided manufacturing (CAM) The use of computers to plan and control manufacturing processes. CAM incorporates computer programs to control automated equipment on the shop floor, automated guided vehicles to move material, and a communications network to link all the pieces.

Computer-aided process planning (CAPP) A computer-based system that plans the sequence of processes that produce or assemble a part. During the design process, the engineer retrieves the closest standard plan from a database and modifies that plan rather than starting from scratch.

Computer-aided software engineering (CASE) A set of integrated software tools used by IS specialists to automate some or all phases of an SDLC process. Upper-CASE tools support project management, the Definition phase, and the initial steps of the Construction phase, including the creation of a DD/D. Lower-CASE tools are back-end code generators and maintenance support tools. *See also* Integrated-CASE.

Computer-integrated manufacturing (CIM) A broad term that encompasses many uses of the computer to help manufacturers operate more effectively and efficiently. CIM systems fall into three major categories: engineering systems, which are aimed at increasing the productivity of engineers; manufacturing administration, which includes systems that develop production schedules and monitor production; and factory operations, which include those systems that actually control the operation of machines on the factory floor.

Computer output microfilm (COM) A computer output method using microfilm or microfiche (a sheet of film) as the output medium. A computer output device called a COM recorder accepts the data from memory and prepares the microfilm output at very high speeds.

Computer telecommunications network The type of network emanating from a single medium-sized, large, or very large computer or a group of closely linked computers; usually arranged in a tree topology.

Computer virus A small unit of code that invades a computer program or file. When the invaded program is executed or the file is opened, the virus makes copies of itself that invade other programs or files in that computer. It may also erase files or corrupt programs. Viruses are transmitted from one computer to another when an invaded computer program or file is transmitted to another computer.

Computer worm A computer virus that has the ability to copy itself from machine to machine over a network.

Consequentialism An ethical theory that judges an action by evaluating all of its consequences; if the consequences are predominantly good, the action is ethical, but if the consequences are predominantly bad, the action is unethical.

Contention bus A design standard for a local area network based on a bus topology and contention for the use of the bus by all devices on the network. Any device may transmit a message if the bus is idle, but if two devices start to transmit at the same time, a collision will occur and both messages will be lost. *See also* CSMA/CD protocol.

Context diagram A logical model that identifies the entities outside the boundaries of a system with which the system must interface. *See also* Data flow diagram.

Control unit The component of a computer system that controls all the remaining components. The control unit brings instructions (operations to be performed) from memory one at a time, interprets each instruction, and carries it out—all at electronic speed. *See also* Central processing unit, Stored-program concept.

Controller A hardware unit used to link input/output or file devices to the CPU and memory of large computer systems (through the data channel). The controller is a highly specialized microprocessor that manages the operation of its attached devices to free the CPU from these tasks (e.g., a DASD controller handles direct access storage devices, and a communications controller handles multiple terminals or PCs acting as terminals).

Conversion The process of changing to a new system, such as with a pilot or cutover (cold turkey) conversion strategy.

Cookie As used with the Web, a message given to a Web browser by a Web server. The browser stores the message on the user's hard drive, and then sends it back to the server each time the browser requests a page from the server. The main purpose of cookies is to identify users and possibly prepare customized Web pages for them.

Cordless telephone A portable telephone instrument that can be used up to about 1,000 feet from its wired telephone base unit; this permits the user to carry the instrument to various rooms in a house or take it outdoors.

Corporate data model A chart that describes all the data requirements of a given organization. This chart shows what data entities and relationships between the entities are important for the organization.

Corporate information policy The foundation for managing the ownership of data; a policy describing the use and handling of data and information within the corporation.

Coverage model A common data model used in geographic information systems in which different layers or themes represent similar types of geographic features in the same area (e.g., counties, highways, customers) and are stacked on top of one another.

CPU *See* Central processing unit.

Cracker A person who breaks into a computer system to steal information, wipe out hard drives, or do other harm.

Credit bureau An organization that acquires computer records from banks and other creditors and from public records of such things as lawsuits, tax liens, and legal judgments. These records are compiled and then sold to credit grantors, rental property owners, employers, insurance companies, and many others interested in a consumer's credit record.

Critical success factor (CSF) One of a limited number of organizational activities that, if done well, will contribute most to the success of the overall performance of the firm or function.

CRM *See* Customer relationship management system.

CSF *See* Critical success factor.

CSMA/CA Protocol An abbreviation for Carrier Sense Multiple Access with Collision Avoidance, the protocol used in a wireless design for a local area network. CSMA/CA is quite similar to CSMA/CD used in traditional Ethernet, but it makes greater efforts to avoid collisions. *See also* CSMA/CD Protocol.

CSMA/CD Protocol An abbreviation for Carrier Sense Multiple Access with Collision Detection, the protocol used in the contention bus design for a local area network. With this protocol, any device may transmit a message if the bus is idle. However, if two devices start to transmit at the same time, a collision will occur and the messages will become garbled. Both devices must recognize that this collision has occurred, stop transmitting, wait some random period of time, and then try again.

CTO *See* Chief technology officer.

Customer relationship management (CRM) system A computer application that attempts to provide an integrated approach to all aspects of interaction a company has with its customers, including marketing, sales, and support. A CRM system often pulls much of its data from the organization's data warehouse; most CRM packages depend upon capturing, updating, and utilizing extensive profiles of individual customers.

Customized design A mixed type of IS organization design, found in many large enterprises, where some business units have a centralized IS unit handle all their IT needs, while other divisions within the same parent organization have a federal or decentralized design in order to locally address their own IT needs with their own local IS staff.

DASD *See* Direct access storage device.

Data administration The name typically given to an organizational unit created to lead the efforts in data management; the group often reports as a staff unit to the IS director, although other structures are possible.

Data analysis and presentation application An application that manipulates data and then distributes information to authorized users. These applications concentrate on creating useful information from established data sources and, because they are separate from data capture and transfer systems, can be individually changed without the expense of changing the data capture and transfer systems.

Data architecture *See* Data model.

Data capture application An application that gathers data and populates databases. These applications allow the simplification of all other applications that then transfer or report data and information.

Data center A computer installation that stores, maintains, and provides access to vast quantities of data; includes computer hardware (servers, workstations/midrange systems, mainframes, and/or supercomputers), communications facilities, system software, and technical support and operations staff.

Data channel A specialized input/output processor (hardware) that takes over the function of device communication from the CPU. The data channel corrects for the significant speed mismatch between the slow input/output and file devices and the fast and critical CPU.

Data dictionary/directory (DD/D) Support software that provides a repository of metadata for each data element in a system—including the meaning, alternative names, storage format, integrity rules, security clearances, and physical location of data—that is used by the DBMS and system users.

Data-driven design An approach to systems development that concentrates on the ideal and natural organization of data, independent of how or where data are used. *See also* Process-driven design.

Data flow diagram (DFD) A common diagrammatic technique for logical As-Is and To-Be models. Symbols are used to represent the movement, processing, and storage of data in a system and both inputs from and outputs to the environment. Each process in a top-level DFD is decomposed to a lower level, and so on.

Data independence A highly desirable characteristic of data stored in a database in which the data are independent of the database structure or the physical organization of the data. Thus data can be selected from a disk file by referring to the content of records, and systems professionals responsible for database design can reorganize the physical organization of data without affecting the logic of programs.

Data mart A smaller, more focused version of a data warehouse created for "drop-in shopping," much like a neighborhood convenience mart. *See also* Data warehousing.

Data mining Searching or "mining" for "nuggets" of information from the vast quantities of data stored in an organization's data warehouse, employing a variety of technologies such as decision trees and neural networks. *See also* Data warehousing.

Data model A map or blueprint for organizational data. A data model shows the data entities and relationships that are important to an organization. *See also* Entity-relationship diagram.

Data standards A clear and useful way to uniquely identify every instance of data and to give unambiguous business meaning to all data. Types of standards include identifiers, naming, definition, integrity rules, and usage rights.

Data transfer application An application that moves data from one database to another. These applications permit one source of data to serve many localized systems within an organization.

Data warehouse A very large database or collection of databases, created to make data accessible to many people in an organization. *See also* Data warehousing.

Data warehousing The establishment and maintenance of a large data storage facility containing data on all or at least many aspects of the enterprise; less formally, a popular method for making data accessible to many people in an organization. To create a data warehouse, a firm pulls data from its operational transaction processing systems and puts the data in a separate "data warehouse" so that users may access and analyze the data without endangering the operational systems. *See also* Data mining.

Database A shared collection of files and associations between these files. A database reduces redundancy and inconsistency compared to file processing, but this lack of natural redundancy can cause risks from loss of data or breaches of authorized data access or manipulation.

Database administrator (DBA) The person in the data administration unit who is responsible for computerized databases. A DBA is concerned with efficiency, integrity, and security of database processing.

Database architecture A description of the way in which the data are structured and stored in a database.

Database machine *See* Database server.

Database management system (DBMS) Support software that is used to create, manage, and protect organizational data. A DBMS is the software that manages a database; it works with the operating system to store and modify data and to make data accessible in a variety of meaningful and authorized ways.

Database server A separate computer, attached to another computer, that is responsible for only processing database queries and updates. A database server is usually part of a local area network and serves the database needs of all the personal and larger computers on this network.

DBA *See* Database administrator.

DBMS *See* Database management system.

DBMS engine A computer program that handles the detailed retrieving and updating of data for a wide variety of other DBMSs, electronic spreadsheets, and other software. Use of a DBMS engine allows the other software to concentrate on providing a convenient user interface while the DBMS engine handles the common database access functions.

DDD *See* Direct Distance Dialing.

DD/D *See* Data dictionary/directory.

Decision support system (DSS) A computer-based system, almost always interactive, designed to assist managers in making decisions. A DSS incorporates both data and models and is usually intended to assist in the solution of semistructured or unstructured problems. An actual application that assists in the decision-making process is properly called a specific DSS; examples of specific DSSs include a police-beat allocation system, a capacity planning and production scheduling system, and a capital investment decision system.

Decision support system (DSS) generator Computer software that provides a set of capabilities to build a specific DSS quickly and easily. For example, Microsoft Excel, a spreadsheet package, can be used as a DSS generator to construct specific financial models that can be used in decision making.

Denial of service attack A method of crippling a computer by invading a large number of computers on the Internet and instructing them to simultaneously send repeated messages to a target computer, thus either overloading that computer's input buffer or jamming the communications lines into the computer so badly that legitimate users cannot obtain access.

Deontologism An ethical theory that holds that an action is either ethical or unethical based only upon whether the action conforms to certain ethical precepts without regard to its consequences in the particular case.

Desktop computer The most common type of personal computer, which is large enough that it cannot be moved around easily. The monitor and the keyboard, and sometimes the computer case itself, sit on a table or "desktop." If the computer case sits on the floor under the table or desk, it is called a "tower" unit.

DFD *See* data flow diagram.

Digital divide A term that emerged in the late 1990s to refer to societal inequities due to the lack of computer skills and access to the Internet by portions of the population. Also used to refer to a global digital divide.

Digital network The electronic linking of devices, where messages are sent over the links by directly transmitting the zeros and ones used by computers and other digital devices. Computer telecommunications networks and LANs are digital networks, and the telephone network is gradually being shifted from an analog to a digital network.

Digital signal processor (DSP) A type of semiconductor chip that converts analog images or sounds in real time (i.e., with essentially no delay) to a stream of digital signals. DSP chips are used at the heart of digital cellular telephones and in traditional products such as kitchen appliances and electric motors.

Digital subscriber line A high-speed, or broadband, connection to the Internet using already installed telephone lines. DSL service, which is available from telephone companies in many parts of the United States, uses a sophisticated modulation scheme to move data over the wires without interfering with voice traffic.

Digital video disk *See* DVD.

Direct access file A basic type of computer file from which it is possible for the computer to obtain a record immediately, without regard to where the record is located on the file; usually stored on magnetic disk. Computer files, also called secondary memory or secondary storage, are added to a computer system to keep vast quantities of data accessible within the computer system at more reasonable costs than main memory.

Direct access storage device (DASD) The device on which direct access files are stored. *See also* Direct access file.

Direct Distance Dialing (DDD) The normal way of using the long-distance telephone network in the United States in which the user directly dials the number with which he or she wishes to communicate and pays for the service based on the duration of the call and the geographical distance; may be used for voice and data communications between any two spots served by the telephone network.

Direct file organization *See* Direct access file.

Disposable application An application that can be discarded when it becomes obsolete without affecting the operation of any other application; this is made possible by application independence. Also referred to as a disposable system. *See also* Application independence.

Distributed data processing *See* Distributed systems.

Distributed systems Application systems in which the processing power is distributed to multiple sites, which are then tied together via telecommunications lines. Distributed systems have computers of possibly varying sizes located at various physical sites at which the organization does business, and these computers are linked by telecommunications lines in order to support some business process.

Documentation Written descriptions produced during the systems development process for those who use the system (user documentation) and for IS specialists who operate and maintain the system (system documentation).

Dot-com A term used to describe a cyber business that receives revenues entirely based on customer transactions or other usage of its Web site. Also referred to as "pure-play" dot-com businesses, as distinguished from clicks-and-mortar businesses.

DSL *See* Digital subscriber line.

DSP *See* Digital signal processor.

DSS *See* Decision support system.

DVD An abbreviation for digital video disk, an optical storage device that holds much more data than a conventional CD and therefore can be used for very large files such as video; standard capacity for a two-sided DVD is 4.7 gigabytes. Also called a digital versatile disk. *See also* CD, CD-ROM, CD-R, CD-RW, DVD-ROM, DVR-R, DVD-RW, Optical disk.

DVD-R An abbreviation for digital video disk-recordable, a type of optical disk that can be written on by the user once and can then be read many times. DVD-R technology is appropriate for archiving documents, engineering drawings, and records of all types.

DVD-ROM An abbreviation for digital video disk-read only memory, a type of optical disk that can only be read and cannot be erased. DVD-ROM is particularly useful for distributing large amounts of relatively stable data to many locations.

DVD-RW An abbreviation for digital video disk-rewritable, a type of optical disk that can be written on and read many times, then rewritten and read many times, and so on. Rewritable optical disks are the most versatile form of optical storage, and falling prices make them an attractive alternative to the standard floppy disk.

E-mail *See* Electronic mail.

EDI *See* Electronic data interchange.

EDP auditing A variety of methods used by trained auditors to ensure the correct processing of data. EDP auditing combines data processing controls with classical accounting auditing methods.

EIS *See* Executive information system.

Electronic commerce The electronic transmission of buyer/seller transactions and other related communications between individuals and businesses or between two or more businesses that are trading partners. By the late 1990s the Internet became the major platform for conducting electronic commerce or e-commerce. *See also* B2B, B2C, Dot-com.

Electronic data interchange (EDI) A set of standards and hardware and software technology that enables computers in independent organizations to exchange business documents electronically. Although typical transactions include purchase orders, order acknowledgments, invoices, price quotes, shipping notices, and insurance claims, any document can potentially be exchanged using EDI. The transaction standards are typically established by an industry consortium or a national or international standards body (such as ANSI).

Electronic mail A system whereby users send and receive messages electronically at their workstations. Electronic mail, or e-mail, can help eliminate telephone tag and usually incorporates such features as sending a message to a distribution list, resending a message to someone else with an appended note, and filing messages in electronic file folders for later recall.

Encapsulation A principle of object-oriented programming in which both data and operations (methods) to be performed using the data are stored together as an object.

Encryption An encoding system used for transmission of computer data to ensure confidentiality and security of the data.

End-user computing Hands-on use of computer resources by non-IS specialists to enter data, make inquiries, prepare reports, communicate, perform statistical analyses, analyze problems, develop Web pages, and so forth.

Enterprise modeling A top-down approach to detailing the data requirements of an organization. Enterprise modeling employs a high-level, three-tier approach, first dividing the work of the organization into its major functions (such as selling and manufacturing), and then dividing each of these functions into processes and each process into activities.

Enterprise resource planning (ERP) system A set of integrated business applications, or modules, to carry out the most common business functions, including inventory control, general ledger accounting, accounts payable, accounts receivable, material requirements planning, order management, and human resources. ERP modules are integrated, primarily through a common set of definitions and a common database, and the modules have been designed to reflect a particular way of doing business, i.e., a particular set of business processes. The leading ERP vendors are Oracle, PeopleSoft, and SAP.

Enterprise system Large applications designed to integrate a set of business functions or processes. Enterprise resource planning (ERP) system packages were the first wave of such systems, which today also include customer relationship management (CRM) systems and supply chain management (SCM) systems.

Entity In data modeling, the things about which data are collected, for example, a customer or a product.

Entity-relationship diagram (ERD) A common notation for modeling organizational data requirements. ER diagramming uses specific symbols to represent data entities, relationships, and elements.

ERD *See* Entity-relationship diagram.

ERP *See* Enterprise resource planning system.

Ethernet The name of the original Xerox version of a contention bus local area network design, which has come to be used as a synonym for a contention bus design. *See also* Local area network, Contention bus.

Evolutionary design *See* Genetic programming.

Evolutionary development Any development approach that does not depend upon defining complete requirements early in the development process, but, like prototyping, evolves the system by building successive versions until the system is acceptable. *See also* Prototyping, Rapid application development.

Executive information system (EIS) A computer application designed to be used directly by managers, without the assistance of intermediaries, to provide the executive easy online access to current information about the status of the organization and its environment. Such information includes filtered and summarized internal transactions data, as well as "soft" data, such as assessments, rumors, opinions, and ideas.

Expert systems The branch of artificial intelligence concerned with building systems that incorporate the decision-making logic of a human expert. Expert systems can diagnose and prescribe treatment for diseases, analyze proposed bank loans, and determine the optimal sequence of stops on a truck route.

Expert systems shell Computer software that provides the basic framework of an expert system and a limited but user-friendly special language to develop the expert system. With the purchase of such a shell, the organization's system builder can concentrate on the details of the business decision being modeled and the development of the knowledge base.

eXtensible Markup Language (XML) An emerging standard in markup languages that is used to facilitate data interchange among applications on the Web. An XML specification consists of tags that are intended to convey the meaning of data, not the presentation format.

Extranet An e-commerce application in which a business has electronic access to a trading partner's intranet using a Web browser. *See also* Intranet.

Extreme Programming (XP) A so-called "agile" software development approach in which programmers develop computer code in a very short time period using programming pairs, common coding approaches, and frequent testing of each other's work.

Factory automation The use of information technology to automate various aspects of factory operations. Factory automation includes numerically controlled machines, material requirements planning (MRP) systems, computer-integrated manufacturing (CIM), and computer-controlled robots.

Fast Ethernet An approach to implementing a high-speed local area network, operating at 100 million bits per second (mbps). Fast Ethernet uses the same CSMA/CD architecture as traditional Ethernet and is usually implemented using either a cable of four twisted pairs (this is called 100 Base-T) or a multimode fiber-optic cable (this is 100 Base-F). *See also* Contention bus, CSMA/CD protocol, Ethernet.

FDDI *See* Fiber Distributed Data Interface.

Feasibility analysis An analysis step in the systems development life cycle in which the economic, operational, and technical feasibility of a proposed system is assessed.

Federal design A type of IS organization design that centralizes certain functions where economies can be substantial and decentralizes other functions to be closer to the IS customer. Often operations activities are centralized under a single corporate IS unit to achieve cost efficiencies, while systems development activities are decentralized to business units to give these units autonomous control over local application needs.

Fiber Distributed Data Interface (FDDI) An American National Standards Institute (ANSI) standard for building a local area network that offers a transmission speed of 100 million bits per second and fault tolerance because of its double-ring architecture; FDDI utilizes either fiber-optic cabling or a cable containing four twisted pairs.

Fiber optics A transmission medium in which data are transmitted by sending pulses of light through a thin fiber of glass or fused silica. Although expensive to install and difficult to work with, the high transmission speeds possible with fiber-optic cabling—100 million bits per second (bps) to 100 billion bps—are leading to its use in most new long-distance telephone lines, in backbone networks to connect multiple LANs, and in LANs where very high speeds or high security needs exist.

File-sharing application A computer program that facilitates the sharing of files across computers, client-to-client, using peer-to-peer networking rather than a traditional server. See also P2P.

File Transfer Protocol (FTP) An Internet application, or tool, that allows users to send and receive files, including programs, from one computer system to another over the Internet. The user logs onto the two computer systems at the same time and then copies files from one system to the other.

Firewall An electronic device, such as a router, personal computer, or workstation, that inhibits access to an organization's internal network (intranet) from the Internet.

Flash memory A type of memory used in digital cameras and music players, as well as in keychain drives for PCs. *See also* Keychain drive.

Formal system The way an organization or business process was designed to work. *See also* Informal system.

Foundry As used in the semiconductor industry, a foundry operation involves the production of chips for other companies that have been designed by those companies.

Fourth generation language A computer language in which the user gives a precise statement of what is to be accomplished, not how to do it. No procedure is necessary; the order of statements is usually inconsequential. Examples include IFPS, SAS, FOCUS, and CA-Ramis.

Free agent A type of telecommuter who works as an independent contractor.

FTP *See* File Transfer Protocol.

Full-duplex transmission A type of data transmission in which data can travel in both directions at once over the communication line.

Functional information system An information system, usually composed of multiple interrelated subsystems, that provides the information necessary to accomplish various tasks within a specific functional area of the business, such as production, marketing, accounting, personnel, or engineering.

Gateway A hardware device employed in a telecommunications network to connect two or more local area networks (LANs) or to connect two different types of networks, such as a backbone network and the Internet, where the networks may use different protocols. The gateway, which is really a sophisticated router, forwards only those messages that need to be forwarded from one network to another. *See also* Router.

Genetic programming The branch of artificial intelligence that divides a problem into multiple segments, and then links solutions to these segments together in different ways to breed new "child" solutions; after many generations of breeding, genetic programming might produce results superior to anything devised by a human. Genetic programming has been most useful in the design of innovative products, such as a satellite support arm and an energy-efficient light bulb.

Geodatabase model A relatively new approach for representation and analysis of spatial data that draws on object-oriented database concepts; this approach results in fewer problems with data accuracy while accommodating raster, vector, address, coordinate, and other spatial data in one database.

Geographic information system (GIS) A computer-based system designed to capture, store, manipulate, display, and analyze data spatially referenced to the Earth; a GIS links data to maps so that the data's spatial characteristics can be easily understood.

Gigabit Ethernet An approach to implementing a high-speed local area network, operating at 1 billion bits per second (gbps) and higher. One-gigabit Ethernet (1 GbE) comes in several versions, including 1000 Base-T running over a cable of four twisted pairs, 1000 Base-SX running over multimode fiber-optic cabling, and 1000 Base-LX running over either multimode fiber or single-mode fiber depending on the distances involved (much longer distances are possible with single-mode fiber). 1 GbE is often used in backbone networks. *See also* Backbone network, Fast Ethernet.

GIS *See* Geographic information system.

Gopher A menu-driven Internet application, or tool, that allows the user to search for publicly available data posted on the Internet by digging (like a gopher) through a series of menus until the sought-after data are located. Gopher has largely disappeared, subsumed by the greater capabilities of the World Wide Web.

Graphical user interface (GUI) An interface between a computer and a human user based on graphical screen images such as icons. With a GUI (pronounced gooey), the user selects an application or makes other choices by using a mouse to click on an appropriate icon or label appearing on the screen. Windows 2000, Windows XP, and the OS/2 operating system employ a GUI.

Grid computing The cooperative utilization of many (even several thousand) computers in a network to solve a problem that requires a lot of parallel computer processing power.

Group support system (GSS) A variant of a decision support system (DSS) in which the system is designed to support a group rather than an individual. The purpose of a GSS is to make group sessions more productive by supporting such group activities as brainstorming, issue structuring, voting, and conflict resolution.

Group technology (GT) A computer-based system that logically groups parts according to physical characteristics, machine routings through the factory, and similar machine operations. Based on these logical groupings, GT is able to identify existing parts that engineers can use or modify rather than design new parts.

Groupware Application software designed to support groups; the functionality varies but may include electronic mail, electronic bulletin boards, computer conferencing, electronic calendaring, group scheduling, sharing documents, meeting support systems, electronic forms, and desktop videoconferencing.

GSS *See* Group support system.

GT *See* Group technology.

GUI *See* Graphical user interface.

Hacker A person who breaks into a computer for the challenge of it without intending to do any harm.

Half-duplex transmission A type of data transmission in which data can travel in both directions over the communication line, but not simultaneously.

Handheld computers The smallest type of computing device, which can easily be held in one hand while using the other hand to enter instructions or data via a keyboard or stylus; also called palmtop computer or personal digital assistant.

Hardware The physical pieces of a computer or telecommunications system, such as a central processing unit, a printer, and a terminal.

Help desk A support service for the users of IT that can be accessed via phone or e-mail. The service is either provided by IS specialists within the organization that owns, operates, or develops the resource, or is provided by IS specialists external to the organization that have been contracted to provide this service (i.e., an outsourcing vendor).

Hertz Cycles per second; one measure of data transmission speed. Hertz is usually equivalent to baud (another measure of transmission speed) and to bits per second.

Hierarchical decomposition The process of breaking down a system into successive levels of subsystems. This recursive decomposition allows a system to be described at various levels of detail, each appropriate for a different kind of analysis or for a different audience.

HTML *See* Hypertext Markup Language.

HTTP *See* Hypertext Transfer Protocol.

Hub A simple network device employed in a telecommunications network to connect one section of a local area network (LAN) to another. A hub forwards every message it receives to the other section of the LAN, whether or not the messages need to go there. Another use of a hub is to create a shared Ethernet LAN; in this case, the hub is a junction box containing up to 24 ports into which cables can be plugged. Embedded inside the hub is a linear bus connecting all the ports.

Human assets A component of the IT architecture outlining the ideal state of the personnel, values, and management systems aspects of an IT system.

Hypertext As used on the World Wide Web, the linking of objects, such as text, pictures, sound clips, and video clips, to each other so that by clicking on highlighted text or a small icon, the user is taken to the related object.

Hypertext Markup Language (HTML) A specialized language to "mark up" pages to be viewed on the World Wide Web. The "markups" consist of special codes inserted in the text to indicate headings, boldfaced text, italics, where images or photographs are to be placed, and links to other Web pages, among other things.

Hypertext Transfer Protocol (HTTP) The underlying protocol used by the World Wide Web. HTTP defines how messages are formatted and transmitted and what actions Web browsers and Web servers should take in response to various commands.

I-CASE *See* Integrated-CASE.

IC *See* Information center.

Identity theft The act of appropriating an individual's personal information without that person's knowledge to commit fraud or theft. An identity thief uses information such as name, address, social security number, credit card number, and/or other identifying information to impersonate someone else and obtain loans or purchase items using his or her credit.

IM *See* Instant messaging.

Imaging A computer input/output method by which any type of paper document—including business forms, reports, charts, graphs, and photographs—can be read by a scanner and translated into digital form so that it can be stored in the computer system; this process can also be reversed so that the digitized image stored in the computer system can be displayed on a video display unit, printed on paper, or transmitted to another computer or workstation.

In-line system A computer system in which data entry is accomplished online (i.e., a transaction is entered directly into the computer via some input device) but the processing is deferred until a suitable batch of transactions has been accumulated.

Indexed file organization A method of organizing a computer file or database in which the control keys only are arranged in sequence in a separate table, along with a pointer to the complete records associated with each key. The records themselves can then be arranged in any order.

Informal system The way the organization or business process actually works. *See also* Formal system.

Information Data (usually processed data) that are useful to a decision maker.

Information center (IC) An organizational unit whose mission is to support end-user computing by providing services such as education and training, application consulting, assistance in selecting hardware and software, facilitating access to computerized data, and so forth. An IC may also be responsible for policy setting for end-user computing, including the selection of standards for PC tools.

Information resources assessment The act of taking inventory and critically evaluating technological and human resources in terms of how well they meet the organization's business needs.

Information system (IS) A computer-based system that uses information technology, procedures (processes), and people to capture, move, store, and distribute data and information.

Information systems (IS) organization The organizational department or unit that has the primary responsibility for managing information technology (IT).

Information technology (IT) Computer hardware and software for processing and storing data, as well as communications technology for transmitting data.

Information technology architecture A written set of guidelines for a company's desired future for information technology (IT) within which people can make individual decisions that will be compatible with that desired future; should include components relating to beliefs or values, data, the technology infrastructure, applications, and the management system for IT.

Information vision A written expression of the desired future for information use and management in an organization.

Inheritance A principle of object-oriented approaches in which subclasses inherit all of the properties and methods of the class to which they belong.

Instant messaging (IM) A synchronous communication system (a variant of electronic mail) that enables the user to establish a private "chat room" with another individual to carry out text-based communication in real time over the Internet. Typically, the IM system signals the user when someone on his or her private list is online, and then the user can initiate a chat session with that individual.

Instruction An individual step or operation in a program, particularly in a machine language program. *See also* Machine language, Program.

Integrated-CASE (I-CASE) A set of full-cycle, integrated CASE tools, in which system specifications supported by the front-end tools can be converted into computer code by the back-end tools included in the system. *See also* Computer-aided software engineering.

Integrated Services Digital Network (ISDN) A set of international standards by which the public telephone network offers extensive new telecommunications capabilities—including simultaneous transmission of both voice and data over the same line—to telephone users worldwide.

Intellectual property Any product of the human mind, such as an idea, an invention, a literary creation, a work of art, a business method, an industrial process, a chemical formula, a computer program, or a presentation.

Interactive system A computer system in which the user directly interacts with the computer. In such a system, the user would enter data into the computer via some type of input device and the computer would provide a response almost immediately, as in an airline reservation system. An interactive system is an online system in which the computer provides an immediate response to the user.

Interface The point of contact where the environment meets a system or where two subsystems meet. Special functions such as filtering, coding/decoding, error detection and correction, buffering, security, and summarizing occur at an interface, which allows compatibility between the environment and system or two subsystems. *See also* Graphical user interface.

Internet A network of networks that use the TCP/IP protocol, with gateways (connections) to even more networks that do not use the TCP/IP protocol. The two primary applications on the Internet are electronic mail and the World Wide Web. *See also* B2B, B2C, Electronic commerce, Electronic mail, Transmission Control Protocol/Internet Protocol, World Wide Web.

1,000 or more parallel CPUs is considered an MPP if the different CPUs must all carry out the same instruction at the same time. *See also* Parallel processor.

Material requirements planning (MRP) A computer-based system that accepts the master production schedule for a factory as input and then develops a detailed production schedule, using parts explosion, production capacity, inventory, and lead time data; usually a component of a manufacturing resources planning (MRP II) system.

MegaFLOPS (MFLOPS) Shorthand for millions of floating point operations per second, a commonly used speed rating for computers. MegaFLOPS ratings are derived by running a particular set of programs in a particular language on the machines being investigated.

Memory The primary area for storage of data in a computer system; also referred to as main memory or primary memory. In a computer system all data flows to and from memory. Memory is divided into cells, and a fixed amount of data can be stored in each cell.

Mesh topology A network topology in which most devices are connected to two, three, or more other devices in a seemingly irregular pattern that resembles a woven net, or a mesh. Examples of a mesh topology include the public telephone network and the network of networks that makes up the Internet.

Metcalfe's Law A theory in which the value of a network to each of its members is related to the square of the number of users; more formally, the value is proportional to $(n^2 – n)/2$, where "n" is the number of nodes on the network.

MFLOPS *See* MegaFLOPS.

MICR *See* Magnetic ink character recognition.

Microcomputers The category of computers with the least cost ($200 to $3,000) and the least power (20 to 400 MFLOPS), generally used for personal computing and small business processing and as a Web client and a client in client/server applications; also called micros or personal computers (PCs).

Microwave Considered a transmission medium, although strictly speaking it is line-of-sight broadcast technology in which radio signals are sent out into the air. With transmission speeds of 50 thousand bits per second (bps) to 100 million bps, microwave transmission is widely used for long-distance telephone communication and for corporate voice and data networks.

Middleware A term that covers all of the software needed to support interactions between clients and servers in client/server systems. Middleware usually includes three categories of software: server operating systems to create a "single-system image" for all services on the network; transport stack software to allow communications employing a standard protocol to be sent across the network; and service-specific software to carry out specific services such as electronic mail.

Midrange systems The subcategory of computers that can be viewed as "small mainframes" in that their technical architecture is derived from mainframe architecture; formerly called minicomputers or superminicomputers. It is now difficult to distinguish midrange systems from workstations because of significant overlaps, resulting in the creation of the workstations/midrange systems category. *See also* Workstations/midrange systems, Workstations.

Minicomputers *See* Midrange systems.

MIPS An acronym for millions of instructions per second executed by the control unit of a computer; a commonly used maximum speed rating for computers.

Modem An abbreviation for modulator/demodulator, a device that converts data from digital form to analog form so that it can be sent over the analog telephone network and reconverts data from analog to digital form after it has been transmitted.

Module A self-contained unit of software that performs one or more functions. Ideally it has well-defined interfaces with the other modules in the program so that changes in a module affect the rest of the program only through the outputs from that module. *See also* Subsystem.

MP3 A standard coding scheme for compressing audio signals into a very small file (about one-twelfth the size of the original file) while preserving the original level of sound quality when it is played. MP3 is the most popular Internet-audio format that allows users to download music from the Internet.

MPP *See* Massively parallel processor.

MRP *See* Material requirements planning.

MRP II *See* Manufacturing resources planning.

Multimedia The use of a microcomputer system to coordinate many types of communication media—text, graphics, sound, still images, animations, and video. The purpose of a multimedia system is to enhance the quality of and interest in a presentation, whether it is a corporate briefing or a school lesson.

Multiprocessing The method of processing when two or more CPUs are installed as part of the same computer system. Each CPU works on its own job or set of jobs (often using multiprogramming), with all the CPUs under control of a single operating system.

Multiprocessor A computer configuration in which multiple processors (CPUs) are installed as part of the same computer system, with each processor or CPU operating independently of the others. *See* Multiprocessing, Parallel processor, Symmetric multiprocessor.

Multiprogramming A procedure by which the operating system switches back and forth among a number of programs, all located in memory at the same time, to keep the CPU busy while input/output operations are taking place; more specifically, this is called event-driven multiprogramming.

Multitasking The terminology used for microcomputers to describe essentially the same function as multiprogramming on larger machines. In preemptive multitasking, the operating system allocates slices of CPU time to each program (the same as time-driven multiprogramming); in cooperative multitasking, each program can control the CPU for as long as it needs it (the same as event-driven multiprogramming). *See also* Multiprogramming, Time-sharing.

Natural language A computer language (often termed a fifth generation language) in which the user writes a program in ordinary English (or something very close to it). Little or no training is required to use a natural language.

Needs-based IS planning The process of assembling the IS plan by addressing only the stated needs of users.

Negotiation support system (NSS) A special type of group support system designed to support the activities of two or more parties in a negotiation. The core components of an NSS are an individual decision support system for each party in the negotiation and an electronic communication channel between the parties.

.NET A platform for application development on the Web, using the OOP paradigm, created by Microsoft. .NET programming can be done in variety of languages, including VB.NET, C#, and J#, but can only be run on a Windows platform.

Network interface card (NIC) In general, a specialized card that must be installed in a computer to permit it to access a particular type of network, usually a local area network. For wireless LANs, the NIC is a short-range radio transceiver that can send and receive radio signals.

Network operating system (NOS) *See* Server operating system.

Network protocol An agreed-upon set of rules or conventions governing communication among elements of a network, or, more specifically, among layers or levels of a network.

Networking The electronic linking of geographically dispersed devices.

Neural networks The branch of artificial intelligence concerned with recognizing patterns from vast amounts of data by a process of adaptive learning; named after the study of how the human nervous system works, but in fact uses extensive statistical analysis to identify meaningful patterns from the data.

NIC *See* Network interface card.

Nonprocedural language *See* Fourth generation language.

Normalization The process of creating simple data structures from more complex ones; this process consists of a set of rules that yields a data structure that is very stable and useful across many different requirements.

NOS *See* Network operating system.

Notebook computers The type of personal computer that can easily be carried by the user; this type of PC is similar in size to a student's notebook and it typically weighs no more than 5 or 6 pounds. The terms "laptop" and "notebook" PC are now used almost interchangeably, although the notebook PC originally was a smaller machine than a laptop.

NSS *See* Negotiation support system.

Object A chunk of program code encompassing both data and methods. *See also* Object-oriented programming.

Object-oriented programming (OOP) A type of computer programming based on the creation and use of a set of objects and the development of relationships among the objects. The most popular OOP languages are C++ and Java. *See also* Object, Object-oriented techniques.

Object-oriented techniques A broad term that includes object-oriented analysis and design techniques as well as object-oriented programming.

Object program The machine language program that is the result of translating a second, third, or fourth generation source program.

OCR *See* Optical character recognition.

Office automation The use of information technology to automate various aspects of office operations. Office automation involves a set of office-related functions that might or might not be integrated in a single system, including electronic mail, word processing, photocopying, document preparation, voice mail, desktop publishing, personal databases, and electronic calendaring.

Office suite A collection of personal productivity software packages for use in the office (e.g., word processing, spreadsheet, presentation graphics, database management system) that are integrated to some extent and marketed as a set. Microsoft Office is the leading office suite; other suites include Corel WordPerfect Office, Lotus SmartSuite, and Sun StarOffice.

OLAP *See* Online analytical processing.

Online analytical processing (OLAP) Querying against a database, employing OLAP software that makes it easy to pose complex queries along multiple dimensions, such as time, organizational unit, and geography. The chief component of OLAP is the OLAP server, which sits between a client machine and a database server; the OLAP server understands how data are organized in the database and has special functions for analyzing the data. *See also* Data mining.

Online processing A mode of transaction processing in which each transaction is entered directly into the computer when it occurs and the associated processing is carried out immediately. For example, sales would be entered into the computer (probably via a microcomputer) as soon as they occurred, and sales records would be updated immediately.

Online system *See* Online processing.

OOP *See* Object-oriented programming.

Open systems Systems (usually operating systems) that are not tied to a particular computer system or hardware manufacturer. An example is the UNIX operating system, with versions available for a wide variety of hardware platforms.

Open Systems Interconnection (OSI) Reference Model An evolving set of network protocols developed by the International Standards Organization (ISO), which deals with connecting all systems that are open for communication with other systems (i.e., systems that conform to certain minimal standards) by defining seven layers, each of which will have one or more protocols.

Operating system Very complex software that controls the operation of the computer hardware and coordinates all the other software. The purposes of an operating system are to get as much work done as possible with the available resources and to be convenient to use.

Operational IS plan A precise set of shorter-term goals and associated projects that will be executed by the IS department and by business managers in support of the strategic IS plan.

Operational planning The process of outlining the shorter-term goals and tactics that detail how the IS organization and other organizations are implementing the strategic IS initiatives.

Optical character recognition (OCR) A computer input method that directly scans typed, printed, or hand-printed material. A computer input device called an optical character reader scans and recognizes the characters and then transmits the data to the memory or records them on magnetic tape.

Optical disk A medium upon which computer files can be stored. Data are recorded on an optical disk by using a laser to burn microscopic pits on its surface. Optical disks have a much greater capacity than magnetic disks.

OSI *See* Open Systems Interconnection Reference Model.

Outsourcing Contracting with an outside organization to perform one or more functions. IT outsourcing most often involves the operation of computers and networks.

P2P Peer-to-peer networking, in which client computers also act as servers. For example, computers running the same P2P application can gain access to files stored on other computers running the application at that time.

Packet assembly/disassembly device (PAD) A telecommunications device used to connect an organization's internal networks (at each of its locations) to the common carrier network in order to set up a packet-switched network.

Packet-switched network A network employing packet switching; examples include vBNS+, the Internet, and many WANs. *See also* Packet switching.

Packet switching A method of operating a digital telecommunications network (especially a WAN) in which information is divided into packets of some fixed length that are then sent over the network separately. Rather than tying up an entire end-to-end circuit for the duration of the session, the packets from various users can be interspersed with one another to permit more efficient use of the network.

PAD *See* Packet assembly/disassembly device.

Palmtop computers *See* Handheld computers.

Parallel processor (PP) A multiprocessor configuration (multiple CPUs installed as part of the same computer system) designed to give a separate piece of the same program to each of the processors so that work on the program can proceed in parallel on the separate pieces.

Partnership A coordinating strategy for IS management. Partnership creates strong working relationships between IS personnel and peer managers in business functions and often results in more effective information systems and IS management.

PBX network The type of network emanating from a *p*rivate *b*ranch e*x*change, or PBX, which is a digital switch operated by a built-in computer with the capability of simultaneously handling communications with internal analog telephones, digital microcomputers and terminals, mainframe computers, and the external telephone network; usually arranged in a star or a tree topology.

PC *See* Microcomputers, Laptop computers, Notebook computers.

PDA *See* Personal digital assistant.

Perceptive systems The branch of artificial intelligence that involves creating machines possessing a visual or aural perceptual ability, or both, that affects their physical behavior; in other words, creating robots that can "see" or "hear" and react to what they see or hear.

Personal computers *See* Microcomputers.

Personal digital assistant The smallest microcomputers, also called palmtop or handheld computers, which weigh under a pound and cost from $200 to $800.

Personal productivity software Software packages, usually microcomputer-based, designed to increase the productivity of a manager or other knowledge worker; examples are word processing, spreadsheets, database management systems, presentation graphics, and Web browsers.

Physical system or model A depiction of the physical form (the how) of an information system. *See also* Logical system or model.

Pocket PC The name given to handheld or palmtop PCs running Microsoft's Windows Mobile for Pocket PC operating system (formerly known as Windows CE). Pocket PCs on the market include the Hewlett-Packard iPaq line, the Dell Axim, and products from Toshiba, Audiovox, and ViewSonic.

Portal A standardized entry point to key information on the corporate network. Many organizations have created carefully designed portals to enable employees (and perhaps customers and suppliers) to gain easy access to information they need. *See also* Intranet.

PP *See* Parallel processor.

Private branch exchange (PBX) network *See* PBX network.

Procedural language *See* Third generation language.

Procedural-oriented techniques *See* Structured techniques.

Process-driven design An approach to systems development that designs systems based on the process they are intended to support. With such an approach, only the data necessary to operate the particular process are collected and manipulated.

Processor *See* Central processing unit.

Productivity language Another name for a fourth generation language. This type of language tends to make the programmer or user more productive, which explains the name.

Program A complete listing of what the computer is to do for a particular application, expressed in a form that the control unit of the computer has been built to understand or that can be translated into such a form. A program is made up of a sequence of individual steps or operations called instructions. *See also* Control unit, Instruction.

Program management Techniques for coordinating multiple projects in order to obtain benefits not achievable from managing each project individually.

Program structure chart A common diagrammatic technique for showing the flow of control for a computer program.

Project champion A business manager who has the motivation or influence, or both, to drive a systems project through to successful implementation; helps to remove obstacles and motivate users to accept changes associated with the system. *See also* Sponsor.

Project management Techniques for managing a one-time endeavor (project) that includes multiple tasks, including the management of project scope, time, cost, and human resources.

Project manager The manager accountable for delivering a project of high quality, on time and within budget; may be an IS manager, a business manager, or both.

Project milestone A significant deliverable for a project and its assigned deadline date for completion.

Project-oriented IS planning An approach to building the IS plan that assembles the IS plan from individual projects.

Proprietary systems Systems (usually operating systems) that are written expressly for a particular computer system. Examples are Windows 2000 and Windows XP, which are Microsoft's current operating systems for personal computers, and MVS and VM, which are the two alternative large machine operating systems offered by IBM.

Prototyping A systems methodology in which an initial version of a system is built very quickly using fourth generation tools and then is tried out by users, who recommend changes that are the basis for building an improved version. This iterative process is continued until the result is accepted. *See also* Rapid application development.

Pull technology Refers to the mode of operation on the Internet where the client must request data before the data are sent to the client. For example, a Web browser represents pull technology in that the browser must request a Web page before it is sent to the user's screen. *See also* Push technology.

Push technology Refers to the mode of operation on the Internet where data are sent to the client without the client requesting the data. Examples of push technology include electronic mail and the delivery of news or stock quotations to the user's screen. *See also* Pull technology.

Query language A 4 GL, nonprocedural special-purpose language for posing queries to the database, often built into the DBMS, that allows users to produce reports without writing procedural programs by specifying their content and format.

RAD *See* Rapid application development.

Radio frequency identification (RFID) An approach to item identification being considered as a possible successor to bar codes. RFID tags, which are about the size of a postage stamp, combine tiny chips with an antenna. When a tag is placed on an item, it automatically radios its location to RFID readers on store shelves, checkout counters, loading bay doors, and possibly shopping carts. With RFID tags, inventory is taken automatically and continuously. RFID tags can cut costs by requiring fewer workers for scanning items; they can also provide more current and more accurate information to the entire supply chain.

RAID *See* Redundant array of independent disks.

Rapid application development (RAD) A hybrid systems development methodology based upon a combination of SDLC, prototyping, JAD techniques, and CASE tools, in which the end-prototype becomes the actual system. *See also* Prototyping, Joint application design, CASE.

Raster-based GIS One of two basic approaches for representation and analysis of spatial data in which space is divided into small, equal-sized cells arranged in a grid; these cells (or rasters) can take on a range of values and are "aware" of their location relative to other cells. Weather forecasting employs a raster-based approach.

Reduced instruction set computing chip *See* RISC chip.

Redundant array of independent disks (RAID) A type of storage system for large computers in which a large number of inexpensive, small disk drives (such as those used in microcomputers) are linked together to substitute for the giant disk drives that were previously used.

Relational DBMS A particular type of database management system (DBMS) that views each data entity as a simple table, with the columns as data elements and the rows as different instances of the entity. The records are then related by storing common data, e.g., customer number, in each of the associated tables. Relational DBMSs are the most popular type of DBMS today.

Release management A documented process for migrating a new system, or a new version of an older system, from a development environment to a production (operations) environment within a given organization.

Repetitive stress injury (RSI) Injury occurring from repetitive motions, such as frequent mouse clicking.

Request for proposal (RFP) A document that is sent to potential vendors inviting them to submit a proposal for a system purchase. It provides the objectives and requirements of the desired system, including the technical environment in which it must operate; specifies what the vendor must provide as input to the selection process; and explains the conditions for submitting proposals and the general criteria that will be used to evaluate them.

Response time The elapsed time between when a user presses the enter key to send data over the network and when the response from the system appears on the screen.

RFID *See* Radio frequency identification.

RFP *See* Request for proposal.

Ring topology A network topology in which all network devices share a single length of cable—with the ends of the cable connected to form a ring.

Ripple effect The result that occurs when a change in one part of a program or system causes unanticipated problems in a different part of the program or system. Then changes necessary to correct that problem may cause problems somewhere else, and so on.

RISC chip Very fast processor chip based on the idea of reduced instruction set computing, or RISC; originally developed for use in high-powered workstations, but now used in other machines, especially midrange systems.

Router A hardware device employed in a telecommunications network to connect two or more local area networks (LANs), where the networks may use different protocols. The router forwards only those messages that need to be forwarded from one network to another. *See also* Gateway.

RSI *See* Repetitive stress injury.

SA&D *See* Systems analysis and design.

SAA *See* Systems Application Architecture.

Satellite communication A variation of microwave transmission in which a communications satellite is used to relay microwave signals over long distances.

Satellite connection A high-speed, or broadband, connection to the Internet using a satellite dish at the home or office to communicate with a satellite.

SCM *See* Supply chain management system.

SDLC *See* Systems development life cycle.

Sequential access file A basic type of computer file in which all of the records that make up the file are stored in sequence according to the file's control key (e.g., a payroll file will contain individual employee records stored in sequence according to the employee identification number); usually stored on magnetic tape. Computer files, also called secondary memory or secondary storage, are added to a computer system to keep vast quantities of data accessible within the computer system at more reasonable costs than main memory.

Sequential file organization *See* Sequential access file.

Server operating system Support software installed on the network server that manages network resources and controls the network's operation. The primary server operating systems are Microsoft's Windows NT, Windows 2000, and Windows 2003, Novell's NetWare, several variations of UNIX, and Linux.

Service level agreement An agreement between IS and a client that specifies a set of services to be provided, the amount of those services to be provided, the quality of these services and how it is to be measured, and the price to be charged for these services.

SFC *See* Shop floor control system.

Shared Ethernet The original Ethernet design, which employs a contention bus as its logical topology but is usually implemented as a physical star arrangement. The usual way of creating a shared Ethernet LAN is to plug the cables from all the devices on the LAN into a hub, which is a junction box containing up to 24 ports into which cables can be plugged. Embedded inside the hub is a linear bus connecting all the ports. *See also* Ethernet, Switched Ethernet.

Shop floor control (SFC) system A computer-based system that provides online, real-time control and monitoring of machines on the shop floor; for example, the SFC system might recognize that a tool on a particular milling machine is getting dull (by measuring the metal that the machine is cutting per second) and signal this fact to the human operator on duty.

Simplex transmission A type of data transmission in which data can travel only in one direction over the communication line. Simplex transmission might be used from a monitoring device at a remote site back to a central computer.

SMP *See* Symmetric multiprocessor.

SNA *See* Systems Network Architecture.

Software The set of programs (made up of instructions) that control the operations of the computer system.

Software package Computer software that is sold as a self-contained "package" so that it may be distributed widely. In addition to the computer programs, a package may include comprehensive documentation of the system, assistance in installing the system, training, a hot-line consulting service for dealing with problems, and even maintenance of the system.

SONET *See* Synchronous Optical Network.

Source program A program written in a second, third, or fourth generation language.

SOW *See* Statement of work.

Spam Unsolicited electronic mail that is broadcast to a large list of e-mail users in an attempt to reach potential customers. Spam is the Internet equivalent to the "junk mail" that is physically sent as bulk mail and delivered by a postal service to recipients who often discard it without even opening it.

Specific DSS *See* Decision support system.

Speech recognition software Software package used to convert the human voice into digitized computer input so that users can "dictate" a document or message to the computer and, eventually, control the computer by oral commands.

Sponsor The business executive who is responsible for funding a new system and ensuring that the necessary resources are available to a systems project team. Also may be called business owner. *See also* Project champion.

Spoofing A way of misleading or defrauding a Web surfer by setting up a Web site that mimics a legitimate site. The spoofer may use some means, such as a message board, to direct the victim to the spurious site, or he or she may simply use a close variant of the site's

Uniform Resource Locator (URL) to con people who make a typing mistake.

SQL A standard query and data definition language for relational DBMSs. This standard, endorsed by the American National Standards Institute (ANSI), is used in many personal computer, midrange system, and mainframe computer DBMSs.

Star topology A network topology that has some primary device at its center with cables radiating from the primary device to all the other network devices.

Statement of work A high-level document that describes the deliverables of the project and the key project milestones, which can be used as a contract between the project manager and the executive sponsor of a systems project. *See* Project milestone.

Stored-program concept The concept of preparing a precise list of exactly what the computer is to do (this list is called a program), loading or storing this program in the computer's memory, and then letting the control unit carry out the program at electronic speed. The listing or program must be in a form that the control unit of the computer has been built to understand.

Strategic IS plan A set of longer-term objectives that represent measurable movement toward the information vision and technology architecture and a set of associated major initiatives that must be undertaken to achieve these objectives.

Strategic planning The process of constructing a viable fit between the organization's objectives and resources and its changing market and technological opportunities.

Structural dependence A characteristic of a database in which, if the structure of the database changes, all programs accessing the data must be changed as well; hierarchical and network databases both have this undesirable characteristic.

Structural independence A characteristic of a database in which programs that access the data do not need to know the database's structure; in other words, if the structure of the database changes, programs accessing the data do not have to be changed; relational databases have this desirable characteristic.

Structure chart *See* Program structure chart.

Structured programming A technique of writing programs so that each program is divided into modules or blocks, where each block has only one entry point and only one exit point. In this form, the program logic is easy to follow and understand, and thus the maintenance and correction of such a program should be easier than for a nonstructured program.

Structured techniques A body of structured approaches and tools to document system needs and requirements, functional features and dependencies, and design decisions. Also referred to as procedurally oriented techniques. *See also* Structured programming.

Subsystem A component of a system that is itself viewed as a set of interrelated components. A subsystem has a well-defined purpose that must contribute to the purpose of the system as a whole. *See also* Module, Hierarchical decomposition.

Supercomputers The most expensive and most powerful category of computers, ranging in cost from $1,000,000 to $100,000,000 and power from 4,000 to 100,000,000 MFLOPS; used for numerically-intensive computing and as a very large Web server.

Superminicomputers Large minicomputers; the upper end of the minicomputer or midrange systems category. *See also* Midrange systems, Workstations/midrange systems.

Supply chain management (SCM) system A computer-based system for the distribution and transportation of raw materials and finished products throughout the supply chain and for incorporating constraints caused by the supply chain into the production scheduling process.

Support software Programs that do not directly produce output needed by users, but instead support other applications software in producing the needed output. Support software provides a computing environment in which it is relatively easy and efficient for humans to work, enables applications programs written in a variety of languages to be carried out, and ensures that computer hardware and software resources are used efficiently. Support software includes operating systems, language compilers, and sort utilities.

Switch A hardware device employed in a telecommunications network to connect more than two local area networks (LANs) or LAN segments that use the same protocols. For example, a switch might connect several low speed LANs (16 Ethernet LANs running at 10 mbps) into a single 100 mbps backbone network running Fast Ethernet.

Switched Ethernet A newer variation of Ethernet that provides better performance than shared Ethernet at a higher price. A switch is substituted for the shared Ethernet's hub, and the LAN operates as a logical star as well as a physical star. The switch is smarter than a hub—rather than passing all communications through to all devices on the LAN, which is what a hub does, the switch establishes separate point-to-point circuits to each device and then forwards communications only to the appropriate device. *See also* Ethernet, Shared Ethernet.

SWOT analysis A situation analysis conducted as part of strategic IS planning; SWOT refers to strengths, weaknesses, opportunities, and threats.

Symmetric multiprocessor (SMP) A multiprocessor computer configuration in which all the processors (CPUs) are identical, with each processor acting independently of the others. The multiple CPUs equally share functional and timing access to and control over all other system components, including memory and the various peripheral devices, with each CPU working in its own allotted portion of memory.

Synchronous Optical Network (SONET) American National Standards Institute (ANSI) approved standard for connecting fiber-optic transmission systems; this standard is employed in a range of high-capacity leased lines varying from the OC-1 level of 52 mbps to the OC-768 level of 39.812 gbps.

System A set of interrelated components that must work together to achieve some common purpose.

System decoupling Reducing the need to coordinate two system components. Decoupling is accomplished by creating slack and flexible resources, buffers, sharing resources, and standards.

System development methodology A framework of guidelines, tools, and techniques for developing computer systems. *See also* Systems development life cycle, Prototyping.

System requirements A set of logical and physical capabilities and characteristics that a new (or modified) system is required to have upon its implementation (or installation).

Systems analysis and design (SA&D) Major activities performed by IS specialists that are part of systems development and implementation methodologies. *See also* Systems development life cycle, Prototyping, Rapid application development.

Systems analyst IS specialist who works with users to develop systems requirements and help plan implementations and who works with systems designers, programmers, and other information technology (IT) specialists to construct systems based on the user requirements.

Systems Application Architecture (SAA) An evolving set of specifications, under development by IBM, defining programming, communications, and a common end-user interface that will allow applications to be created and moved among the full range of IBM computers. IBM has stated its intention of supporting both SNA and OSI protocols in its future efforts under the SAA umbrella.

Systems backlog The number of new systems development requests or maintenance requests, or both, that have not yet been assigned IS resources to work on them. An "invisible backlog" refers to systems requests not even formally submitted by business managers due to the size of the existing "visible" backlog.

Systems development life cycle (SDLC) The traditional methodology used by IS professionals to develop a new computer application that includes three general phases: Definition, Construction, and Implementation. Also referred to as a "waterfall" process because of its sequential steps. The SDLC methodology defines the activities necessary for these three phases, as well as a framework for planning and managing a development project. Operations and maintenance are included in the Implementation phase. A modified SDLC approach is used to purchase packaged systems.

Systems integrator A firm that will take overall responsibility for managing the development or integration of large, complex systems involving the use of components from a number of different vendors.

Systems Network Architecture (SNA) A set of network protocols created by IBM to allow its customers to construct their own private networks using the wide variety of IBM communication products, teleprocessing access methods, and data link protocols. SNA was first created in 1974 and is still widely used.

Systems software *See* Support software.

T-1 lines The most common leased communication lines, operating at a data transmission rate of 1.544 million bits per second. These lines, which may be leased from AT&T or another long-distance carrier, often provide the basis for a wide area network (WAN).

Tablet computer A variation of a personal computer where the user writes on an electronic tablet (usually the video screen folded flat on top of the PC) with a digital pen. Please note that a tablet PC can also be used as a standard notebook computer.

TCO *See* Total cost of ownership.

TCP/IP *See* Transmission Control Protocol/Internet Protocol.

Technological assets A component of the IT architecture that contains desired specifications about future hardware and operating systems, network, data and data management systems, and applications software.

Telecommunications Communications at a distance, including voice (telephone) and data (text/image) communications. Other similar terms used almost interchangeably with telecommunications include data communications, datacom, teleprocessing, telecom, and networking.

Telecommuter A person who works at home or at another location that is not part of a regular office environment and who uses computers and communications to connect to organizational resources to accomplish his or her work; includes mobile workers, other "road warriors," and free agents. *See also* Free agent.

Telnet An Internet application, or tool, that allows users to log onto a remote computer from whatever computer they are using at the time, as long as both computers are attached to the Internet.

Terminal A computer-related device that has input (keyboard, mouse) and output (video display) capabilities, but does essentially no processing, and thus operates as a "slave" to a "master" computer, usually a midrange system or a mainframe. For some applications, a microcomputer may emulate a terminal so that it can operate with a large computer system.

Third generation language A programming language in which the programmer expresses a step-by-step procedure devised to accomplish the desired task. Examples include FORTRAN, COBOL, BASIC, PASCAL, and C.

Third-party implementation partner Outside consultants who are contracted to manage a packaged software implementation project at a client's site as employees of an independent consulting firm, not employees of the vendor of the software package. For example, the large enterprise system vendors typically certify large consulting firms (such as the "Big 4"), IT industry consultants (such as IBM), and smaller consulting firms on different versions of their software packages, and these third-party businesses provide employees who work on project teams at the client site, while the vendors' employees only provide on-site technical support as needed.

Three-tier client/server system A variation of a client/server system in which the processing is split across three tiers, the client and two servers. In the most popular three-tier system, the user interface is housed on the client, usually a PC (tier 1), the processing is performed on a midrange system or workstation operating as the applications server (tier 2), and the data are stored on a large machine (often a mainframe or midrange system) that operates as the database server (tier 3).

Timeboxing Establishing a maximum time limit for the delivery of a project or project module; typically 6 months or less.

Time-sharing A procedure by which the operating system switches among a number of programs, all stored in memory at the same time, giving each program a small slice of CPU time before moving on to the next program; also called time-driven multiprogramming.

Token bus A design standard for a local area network based on a bus topology and the passing of a token around the bus to all devices in a specified order. In this design, a given device can transmit only when it has the token and thus collisions can never occur. The token bus design is central to the Manufacturing Automation Protocol (MAP).

Token ring A design standard for a local area network based on a ring topology and the passing of a token around the ring to all devices in a specified order. In this design, a given device can transmit only when it has the token and thus collisions can never occur.

Total cost of ownership (TCO) Total cost of ownership for a computer system or device, including initial investment and implementation as well as ongoing support costs. For example, the TCO for a desktop PC includes not only the purchase and installation of the PC hardware, but also the software and network installation costs, as well as the cost of supporting the use of the PC (user training, help desk, software upgrades, backups, etc.)

Transaction processing system A very common type of computer application in which transactions of a particular type are processed in order to provide desired output. Examples include the processing of employee work records (transactions) to produce payroll checks and accompanying reports and the processing of orders (transactions) to produce invoices and associated reports. Transaction processing systems might be batch, online, or in-line.

Transborder data flow Electronic movement of data across a country's national boundary. Such data flows may be restricted by laws that protect a country's economic, political, or personal privacy interests.

Transmission Control Protocol/Internet Protocol (TCP/IP) A popular network protocol used in many versions of the UNIX operating system, many packet-switched networks, the Internet, and intranets operating within organizations. Although not part of the OSI model, TCP/IP corresponds roughly to the network and transport layers of the seven-layer model.

Tree topology A network topology that has some primary device at the top of the tree, with cables radiating from this primary device to devices further down the tree that, in turn, may have cables radiating from them to other devices still further down the tree, and so on; also called hierarchical topology.

Trojan horse A security-breaking program that is introduced into a computer and serves as a way for an intruder to re-enter the computer in the future. It may be disguised as something innocent such as a screen saver or a game.

Twisted pair The most common transmission medium, with two insulated copper wires (about 1 millimeter thick) twisted together in a long helix. Data transmission speeds of 14,400 to 56,000 bits per second (bps) are possible with twisted pairs on the analog telephone network, with higher speeds of 128,000 bps up to 1.544 million bps attainable over the digital telephone network or up to 100 million bps on local area networks (LANs).

Two-tier client/server system The original implementation of a client/server system in which the processing is split between the client (usually a PC) and the server (workstation, midrange system, or mainframe). If most of the processing is done on the client, this is called a fat client or thin server model; if most of the processing is done on the server, this is called a thin client or fat server model.

Ubiquitous IT An environment in which computer and communications devices are almost everywhere and become an unremarkable part of almost all aspects of people's lives.

UML *See* Unified Modeling Language.

Unified Modeling Language (UML) A general-purpose notational language for specifying and visualizing complex software, especially large, object-oriented projects. Examples of such UML-based CASE tools are IBM's Rational Rose and Borland's Together.

Uniform Resource Locator (URL) An address for an Internet file; the address includes the name of the protocol to access the resource (usually http), a domain name for the computer on which the file is located, and perhaps specific locator information. For example, the Web URL for the publisher of this textbook is *http://www.prenhall.com.* Also known as Universal Resource Locator.

Upper-CASE *See* Computer-aided software engineering.

URL *See* Uniform Resource Locator.

Usenet newsgroups An Internet application, or tool, setting up discussion groups, which are essentially huge electronic bulletin boards on which group members can read and post messages.

User application development Development of business applications by employees who are not IS professionals, but rather are primarily in traditional business roles such as accountants, financial analysts, production schedulers, engineers, and brand managers. In most but not all instances, the people who develop the applications also directly use them in their work.

User-friendly A perceptual measure of how easy it is to navigate and use particular hardware or software from the perspective of a person who is not an IS specialist.

User interface That part of a system through which the user interacts with the system. As examples, it might use a mouse, a touch-screen, menus, commands, voice recognition, a telephone keypad, output screens, voice response, and printed reports. *See also* Graphical user interface.

Utilitarianism An ethical theory, a variation of consequentialism, in which *all* the parties that will be affected by an action must be identified and the consequences for each party delineated and quantified, with beneficial results measured on the positive scale and the harmful results measured on the negative scale. If the outcomes are not certain, then probabilities must be assigned to each outcome for each of the affected parties so that the expected return can be calculated. The action is ethically justified if the expected value of the positives and negatives is positive, that is, if the good outweighs the bad.

Value added network (VAN) Formerly, the name given to the practice of contracting with an outside vendor to operate a packet-switched wide area network (WAN) for an organization. Today such a packet-switched WAN is usually called a managed network.

Value chain analysis A method developed by Michael E. Porter to identify possible strategic uses of information technology. A firm's value chain contains the activities in the business that add value to a firm's products or services.

Values architecture That part of an IT architecture that specifies the basic beliefs of the managers and employees about IT in the organization.

VAN *See* Value added network.

vBNS+ A very high-speed network, operated by MCI and developed through a cooperative agreement between MCI and the National Science Foundation

(NSF), that links NSF-supported supercomputer centers across the United States and provides points-of-presence (POPs) where other users may link to vBNS+ from the Internet.

Vector-based GIS One of two basic approaches for representation and analysis of spatial data in which features in the landscape are associated with either a point (e.g., customer address, power pole), a line (road, river), or a polygon (lake, county, zip code area). The vector-based approach is in widespread use in public administration, public utilities, and business.

Vector facility A specialized multiprocessor configuration (multiple CPUs installed as part of the same computer system) used to handle calculations involving vectors. Parallel microprocessors perform the same operation simultaneously on each element of the vector. A vector facility can be attached to a mainframe or other large computer to handle numeric- or compute-intensive portions of programs.

Veronica An Internet application, or tool, that allows the user to search publicly available Gopher sites using key words until the sought-after data are located. Veronica, like Gopher, has largely disappeared, with both subsumed by the greater capabilities of the World Wide Web.

Vertically integrated information system An information system that serves more than one vertical level in an organization or an industry, such as a system designed to be used by an automobile manufacturer and the associated independent dealers.

View integration A bottom-up approach to detailing an organization's data requirements. View integration analyzes each report, screen, form, and document in the organization and combines each of these views into one consolidated and consistent picture of all organizational data.

Virtual memory A procedure by which the operating system switches portions of programs (called pages) between main memory and DASD so that portions of enough programs are stored in main memory to enable efficient multiprogramming. To the user it appears as though an unlimited amount of main memory is available, whereas in fact most of each program is stored in DASD.

Virtual organization An organization that regularly uses the services of workers who are not regular (long-term) employees or have no real office or headquarters, or both. *See also* Free agent.

Virtual private network (VPN) The equivalent of a private packet-switched network that has been created using public telecommunications lines. A VPN provides a moderate data rate (up to 2 mbps) at a very reasonable cost, but the network's reliability is low. Most commonly, a VPN is created using the Internet as the medium for transporting data, employing encryption and other security mechanisms to ensure that only authorized users can access the network and that the data cannot be intercepted. *See also* Packet-switched network, Packet switching.

Virtual reality (VR) The use of computer-based systems to create an environment that seems real to one or more senses (usually including sight) of the human user or users. Examples of practical uses of VR include tank crew training for the U.S. Army, the design of an automobile dashboard and controls, and retail store layout.

Virtual team A work team where members of the team are not co-located, and where they are not necessarily even in the same time zone. A virtual team is often supported by groupware or a group support system that facilitates a "different time, different place" meeting format.

Virus *See* Computer virus.

Visual programming A type of computer programming built around a graphical programming environment and a paint metaphor for developing user interfaces. The most popular visual programming languages are Visual Basic and Java.

Voice response unit A computer output method using the spoken voice to provide a response to the user. This output method is gaining increasing acceptance as a provider of limited, tightly programmed computer output, often in conjunction with touch-tone telephone input.

VPN *See* Virtual private network.

VR *See* Virtual reality.

W3C World Wide Web Consortium, an international consortium of companies involved with the Internet and the World Wide Web. W3C is the chief standards body for the Web with the purpose of developing open standards; among W3C's standards are Hypertext Transfer Protocol (HTTP) and Hypertext Markup Language (HTML).

WAN *See* Wide area network.

WAP *See* Wireless access point.

WATS *See* Wide Area Telephone Service.

Web Shorthand for World Wide Web. *See* World Wide Web.

Web browser Software application that runs on a microcomputer, enabling the user to access Web sites and Web pages; the most common Web browsers are Microsoft Internet Explorer and Netscape Navigator.

Wi-Fi An abbreviation for wireless fidelity, this name is commonly used to refer to a wireless LAN.

Wide area network (WAN) A type of network over which both voice and data for a single organization are communicated among the multiple locations (often far apart) where the organization operates, usually employing point-to-point transmission over facilities owned by several organizations, including the public telephone network; also called a long-haul network.

Wide Area Telephone Service (WATS) A service available from the telephone company in which an organization pays a monthly fee for unlimited long-distance telephone service using ordinary voice circuits. WATS is an easy way to set up a wide area network (WAN) and costs less per hour than standard Direct Distance Dialing (DDD).

Wireless Considered a transmission medium, although strictly speaking it is broadcast technology in which radio signals are sent out into the air. Examples are cordless telephone, cellular telephone, wireless LAN, and microwave.

Wireless access point (WAP) A radio transceiver that serves as the central device in a wireless LAN and that connects the LAN to other networks. The WAP receives the signals of all computers within its range and repeats them to ensure that all other computers within the range can hear them; it also forwards all messages for recipients not on this wireless LAN via the wired network.

Wireless LAN A local area network employing wireless communication between the various devices in the network. Compared to a wired LAN, a wireless LAN is easier to plan and install, less secure, and more susceptible to interference. Most wireless LANs operate in the range of 6 to 11 million bps, with a few newer wireless LANs operating at speeds up to 54 mbps.

Word A memory cell that can store two or more characters of data; alternatively, the amount of data handled by the CPU as a single unit. *See also* Memory.

Work breakdown analysis Identification of the project phases and detailed activities for each phase, including the task sequencing and time estimates, usually based on a particular systems methodology.

Workstations Generally, any computer-related device at which an individual may work, such as a personal computer or a terminal. Specifically, the subcategory of computers based on powerful microprocessor chips and RISC chips—really grown-up, more powerful microcomputers. Because of strong price-performance characteristics, workstations have made inroads into the domain of traditional midrange systems so that it is almost impossible to decide which machines should be considered "workstations" and which should be considered "midrange systems," resulting in the creation of the workstations/midrange systems category. *See also* Workstations/midrange systems, Midrange systems, RISC chip.

Workstations/midrange systems A broad middle-of-the-road category of computers stretching all the way from microcomputers to the much larger mainframes and supercomputers, with costs ranging from $3,000 to $1,000,000 and power ranging from 40 to 4,000 MFLOPS; used for departmental computing, specific applications such as computer-aided design and graphics, midsized business general processing, and as a Web server, file server, local area network server, and a server in client/server applications. Historically, workstations and midrange computers were considered as distinct categories of computers, but they now overlap so much in cost, power, and applications that they have been combined in a single category. *See also* Workstations, Midrange systems.

World Wide Web An Internet application, or tool, that uses a hypertext-based approach to traverse, or "surf," the Internet by clicking on a link contained in one document to move to another document, and so on; these links may also connect to video clips, recordings, photographs, and images.

Worm *See* Computer worm.

WORM disk *See* CD-R.

WWW *See* World Wide Web.

XML *See* eXtensible Markup Language.

XP *See* Extreme programming.

Year 2000 (Y2K) problem Computer calculation errors that would have occurred (without programming changes) beginning with the year 2000 due to the earlier coding of a four-digit year as a two-digit data element; sometimes called the "millennium bug." Billions of dollars were spent worldwide to achieve Y2K compliance for computer software and hardware.

REFERENCES

CHAPTER 1

Brown, Carol V., Ephraim R. McLean, and Detmar W. Straub. 2000. "Partnering roles of the IS executive," in C. V. Brown and H. Topi (eds.), *IS Management Handbook*, 7th ed. New York: Auerbach.

Brown, Carol V., and V. Sambamurthy. 1999. *Repositioning the IT Organization to Enable Business Transformation*. Cincinnati, OH: Pinnaflex.

Byrne, John A. 2000. "Management by Web." *Business Week* (August 28): 84–96.

Carr, Nicholas G. 2003. "IT doesn't matter." *Harvard Business Review* (May): 41–49.

Clemons, Eric K. 1991. "Evaluation of strategic investments in information technology." *Communications of the ACM* 34 (January): 23–36.

Clemons, Eric K., and Bruce W. Weber. 1993. "Using information technology to manage customer relationships: Lessons for marketing in diverse industries." *Proceedings of Hawaii International Conference on Systems Sciences*, January: 860–866.

[*Communications of the ACM*] 2001. "The Next 1000 Years," 44:3 (March), pp. 28–145.

Coy, Peter. 2003. "Still getting stronger." *Business Week*, September 15: 32–35.

Dell Computer Corporation. "About Dell: Direct access: Who we are." Dell Web site, *www.dell.com*, October 2000.

Gomes, Lee. "How *Internet Time*'s fifteen minutes of fame ran out." 2002. *The Wall Street Journal*, October 28, B1.

Hardwick, M., and R. Bolton. 1997. "The industrial virtual enterprise." *Communications of the ACM* 40 (September): 59–60.

Hartwick, Jon, and Henri Barki. 1994. "Explaining the role of user participation in information system use." *Management Science* 40 (April): 440–465.

Hilsenrath, Jon E. 2003. "Behind surging productivity: Immune sectors catch the bug." *The Wall Street Journal* (November 7): A1, A8.

Jones, Kathryn. 2003. "The Dell Way," *Business 2.0* (February): 63.

Kappelman, Leon. 2001. "The future is ours." *Communications of the ACM* 44:3 (March), pp. 46–47.

Lohr, Steve. 2003. "A new technology, now that new is old." *The New York Times*, May 4: Section 3, pp. 2, 13.

Mandel, Michael J. 2002. "How prosperous are we?" *Business Week*, April 29: 38–39.

McWillliams, Gary. 2003. "Innovation on Hold." *The Wall Street Journal*, May 29: B1–B2.

Piccoli, Gabriele, Bill Bass, and Blakes Ives. 2003. *MIS Quarterly Executive,* 2:2 (September): 74–84.

Pine, B. J. II, B. Victor, and A. C. Boynton. 1993. "Making mass customization work." *Harvard Business Review* 71: 108–119.

Porter, Michael E. 1980. *Competitive Strategy*. New York: Free Press.

Pottruck, David S., and Terry Pearce. 2000. *Clicks and Mortar: Passion Driven Growth in an Internet Driven World.* San Francisco: Jossey-Bass.

Rockart, John F. 1988. "The line takes the leadership." *Sloan Management Review* 29:4 (Summer): 57–64.

Ross, Jeanne W., Cynthia Mathis Beath, and Dale L. Goodhue. 1996. "Develop long-term competitiveness through IT assets." *Sloan Management Review* 38:1 (Fall): 31–42.

Samuelson, Douglas A. 2003. "The Netwar in Iraq." *OR/MS Today* (June): 19–26.

Stewart, Thomas A. 1997. *Intellectual Capital: The New Wealth of Organizations*. New York: Doubleday.

Weill, Peter, and Marianne Broadbent. *Leveraging the New Infrastructure: How Market Leaders Capitalize on Information Technology.* Boston, MA: Harvard Business School, 1998.

CHAPTER 2

2003. "Top 15 desktop PCs." *PC World* 21 (October): 144–146.

Alwang, Greg. 2002. "Better (but still not perfect) speech recognition." *PC Magazine* 21 (December 3): 46.

Alwang, Greg. 2003. "From your lips to the PC's ears." *PC Magazine* 22 (May 6): 52.

Ante, Spencer E., Otis Port, Bruce Einhorn, and Andrew Park. 2003. "The chips are falling IBM's way." *Business Week* (May 26): 91–92.

Ante, Spencer E., and David Henry. 2002. "Can IBM keep earnings hot?" *Business Week* (April 15): 58–60.

Armstrong, Larry. 2002. "A keychain never forgets." *Business Week* (August 5): 24.

Burrows, Peter. 2003. "How to milk an Apple." *Business Week* (February 3): 44.

Cray Inc. 2002. "Cray Inc. announces Cray X1 system, world's most powerful supercomputer product." Cray Inc. Web site, *www.cray.com/news/0211/X1announce.html* (November 14).

Dongarra, Jack J. 2003. "Performance of various computers using standard linear equations software." Computer Science Department, University of Tennessee, and Computer Science and Mathematics Division, Oak Ridge National Laboratory, No. CS-89-85 (August 28).

Edwards, Cliff, Moon Ihlwan, and Pete Engardio. 2003. "The Samsung way." *Business Week* (June 16): 56–61, 64.

EMC. 2003. "EMC Symmetrix DMX 1000, DMX 2000, and DMX 3000." EMC Web site, *www.emc.com/products/systems_DMX1000.jsp* (September).

Ewalt, David M. 2003. "PDAs make inroads into businesses." *Information Week* 946 (June 30): 27.

Foley, John. 2003. "Review: Tablet PCs." *InformationWeek.Com* Web site, *www.informationweek.com/story/showArticle.jhtml?articleID=12803350* (July 30).

Greene, Jay. 2000. "If at first you don't succeed . . ." *Business Week* (April 24): 120–130.

Greene, Jay, and Andrew Park. 2002. "Is the pen finally mightier than the keyboard?" *Business Week* (November 11): 60–62, 64.

Greenemeier, Larry. 2002. "Mainframes are still a mainstay." *Information Week* 911 (October 21): 74, 76, 78.

Grossman, C. P. 1985. "Cache-DASD storage design for improving system performance." *IBM Systems Journal* 24: 316–334.

IBM. 2000. "IBM introduces commercial version of world's fastest supercomputer." IBM Web site, *www-1.ibm.com/servers/eserver/pseries/news/pressreleases/2000/jul/com_super.html* (July 24).

IBM. 2002. "Merck selects IBM eServer for next-generation drug design." IBM Web site, *www-1.ibm.com/servers/eserver/pseries/news/pressreleases/2002/apr/drug_design.html* (April 5).

IBM. 2002. "IBM to build world's fastest supercomputers for U.S. Department of Energy." IBM Web site, *www-1.ibm.com/servers/eserver/pseries/news/pressreleases/2002/nov/asci-purple.html* (November 19).

IBM. 2003. "IBM introduces new high-end eServer systems powered by POWER4+ processors." IBM Web site, *www-1.ibm.com/servers/eserver/pseries/news/pressreleases/2003/may/annc_506.html* (May 6).

IBM. 2003. "IBM debuts world's most sophisticated server." IBM Web site, *www-1.ibm.com/servers/eserver/zseries/news/pressreleases/2003/z990_05-13-03.html* (May 13).

IBM. 2003. "3995 Optical Library." IBM Web site, *www.storage.ibm.com/tape/optical/3995/index.html* (September).

IBM. 2003. "Midrange servers: iSeries." IBM Web site, *www-132.ibm.com/content/home/store_IBMPublicUSA/en_US/eServer/iSeries/* (September).

Intel. 1997. "Intel delivers the next level of computing with the new Pentium II processor." Intel Web site, *www.intel.com/pressroom/archive/releases/DP050797.HTM* (May 7).

Intel. 1999. "Intel launches the Pentium III processor." Intel Web site, *www.intel.com/pressroom/archive/releases/dp022699.htm* (February 26).

Intel. 2000. "Intel introduces the Pentium 4 processor." Intel Web site, *www.intel.com/pressroom/archive/releases/dp112000.htm* (November 20).

Intel. 2002. "Intel delivers hyper-threading technology with Pentium 4 processor 3 GHz milestone." Intel Web site, *www.intel.com/pressroom/archive/releases/20021114comp.htm* (November 14).

Iomega Corporation. 2003. Iomega Web site, *www.iomega.com/na/landing.jsp* (September).

Judge, Paul C. 1999. "The inside story of how Mike Ruettgers turned EMC into a highflier." *Business Week* (March 15): 72–80.

Keenan, Faith, Spencer Ante, and Cliff Edwards. 2002. "Everybody wants to eat EMC's lunch." *Business Week* (September 2): 76–77.

Keenan, Faith. 2002. "PCs and speech: A rocky marriage." *Business Week* (September 9): 64, 66.

Park, Andrew and Irene M. Kunii. 2002. "A downturn well spent." *Business Week* (July 22): 64–65.

Port, Otis. 1996. "The silicon age? It's just dawning." *Business Week* (December 9): 148–152.

Rendleman, John. 2002. "A smaller, faster future for chips." *Information Week* 874 (February 4): 47.

Top 500. 2003. "Top 500 list for June 2003." Top 500 Web site, *www.top500.org/lists/2003/06/?page* (June 23).

Wildstrom, Stephen H. 2000. "Kiss the floppy good-bye." *Business Week* (June 12): 34.

Wildstrom, Stephen H. 2002. "The liberation of laptop design?" *Business Week* (November 25): 24.

Wildstrom, Stephen H. 2003. "Desperately seeking simplicity." *Business Week* (July 14): 24.

Wildstrom, Stephen H. 2003. "Tablet PCs: Getting better, but. . . ." *Business Week* (August 4): 22.

Zetie, Carl. 2002. "PDA wars: Round two." *InformationWeek.Com* Web site, *www.informationweek.com/story/showArticle.jhtml?articleID=6501265* (April 1).

CHAPTER 3

2003. "Best products of 2002: Desktop software." *PC Magazine* 22 (January): 92, 104.

ACCPAC International, Inc. 2003. "ACCPAC Advantage Series Corporate Edition." ACCPAC International Web site, *www.accpac.com/products/finance/accwin/sbs/* (October).

BackWeb Technologies. 2003. "Our offline infrastructure extends the reach of the Web to the disconnected mobile community." BackWeb Technologies Web site, *www.backweb.com/* (October).

Ewalt, David M. 2002. "The next Web." *Information Week* 910 (October 14): 34–36, 40, 44.

Foley, John. 2003. "Staring down Linux." *Information Week* 959 (October 13): 36–44.

Greene, Jay. 2003. "Pecked by penguins." *Business Week* (March 3): 84–86.

Greenemeier, Larry. 2003. "Adolescent angst." *Information Week* 942 (June 2): 30–32, 34, 36, 38.

Hines, Matt. 2003. "Microsoft still rules server OS market." *CNET News.com*, ZDNet Web site, *zdnet.com.com/2100-1104-5088233.html* (October 8).

IBM. 2003. "The mainframe renaissance." *The Mainstream* 3, IBM Web site, *www-3.ibm.com/software/swnews/swnews.nsf/n/lsco5pxvv7?OpenDocument&Site=swzseries* (August 12).

Information Builders, Inc. 2003. "Host-based reporting (FOCUS)" and "Enterprise business intelligence (WebFOCUS)." Information Builders, Inc. Web site, *www.informationbuilders.com/products* (October).

Jenkins, A. Milton, and Bijoy Bordoloi. 1986. "The evolution and status of fourth generation languages: A tutorial." Institute for Research on the Management of Information Systems (IRMIS) Working Paper #W611, Indiana University Graduate School of Business.

Kerstetter, Jim, Steve Hamm, Spencer E. Ante, and Jay Greene. 2003. "The Linux uprising." *Business Week* (March 3): 78–82, 84.

Kontzer, Tony. 2003. "Pervasive portal connections." *Information Week* 932 (March 24): 47.

Lindholm, Elizabeth. 1992. "The portable 4 GL?" *Datamation* 38 (April 1): 83–85.

MacVittie, Lori. 2002. "Business intelligence with smarts." *Network Computing* 13 (September 30): 42–55.

Peachtree Software Inc. 2003. "Peachtree Complete Accounting 2004." Peachtree Software Web site, *www.peachtree.com/peachtreeaccountingline/complete/* (October).

Peachtree Software Inc. 2003. "ePeachtree." Peachtree Software Web site, *www.peachtree.com/epeachtree/* (October).

Port, Otis. 2002. "The next Web." *Business Week* (March 4): 96–100, 102.

Radding, Alan. 1999. "XML: The language of integration." *Information Week* 759 (November 1): 141–148.

Radin, G. 1996. "Object technology in perspective." *IBM Systems Journal* 35, 2: 124–127.

Ricadela, Aaron. 2002. "The challenge that is Linux." *Information Week* 887 (May 6): 110, 112.

van der Linden, Peter. 1999. *Not Just Java*, 2nd ed. Mountain View, CA: Sun Microsystems Press.

Weiss, Todd R. 2003. "Is Linux on the desktop inevitable?" PCWorld.Com Web site, *www.pcworld.com/news/article/0,aid,109266,00.asp* (February 7).

Yakai, Kathy. 2003. "Neaten your number crunching." *PC Magazine* 22 (March 11): 34–36, 38.

CHAPTER 4

2003. "Making Wi-Fi work." *Business Week* (April 28): 92.

Associated Press. 2003. "Knight Ridder newspaper sites hit by denial-of-service attacks." Informationweek.com Web site, *www.informationweek.com/story/showArticle.jhtml?articleID=14700461* (September 10).

Babcock, Charles. 2003. "Fast-moving virus slams e-mail systems." *Information Week* 952 (August 25): 22.

Bluetooth. 2003. "The official Bluetooth Web site." Bluetooth Web site, *www.bluetooth.com* (October).

Bridis, Ted. 2003. "Internet attack's disruptions more serious than many thought possible." Informationweek.com Web site, *www.informationweek.com/story/showArticle.jhtml?articleID=6512203* (January 28).

Clark, Matthew. 2003. "Bluetooth is booming: Report." *ElectricNews.Net*, *www.enn.ie/news.html?code=9377022* (October 2).

Crockett, Roger O., Heather Green, Andy Reinhardt, and Jay Greene. 2002. "All Net, all the time." *Business Week* (April 29): 100–104.

Crockett, Roger O., Charles Haddad, and Steve Rosenbush. 2003. "The Bells gang up to combat cable." *Business Week* (June 30): 41.

Crockett, Roger O., Moon Ihlwan, and Catherine Yang. 2003. "How to get U.S. broadband up to speed." *Business Week* (September 8): 92, 94, 96.

Dennis, Alan. 2003. *Networking in the Internet Age.* New York: John Wiley & Sons, Inc.

Elstrom, Peter, Heather Green, Roger O. Crockett, Charles Haddad, and Catherine Yang. 2002. "What ails wireless?" *Business Week* (April 1): 60–64.

Miller, Michael W. 1992. "A story of the type that turns heads in computer circles." *Wall Street Journal* (September 15): A1, A8.

Orfali, Robert, Dan Harkey, and Jeri Edwards. 1999. *Client/Server Survival Guide*, 3rd ed. New York: John Wiley & Sons, Inc.

Orzech, Dan. 2001. "Make mine vanilla, part 1." Earthweb Web site, *itmanagement.earthweb.com/entdev/article.php/760301* (May 7).

Orzech, Dan. 2001. "Make mine vanilla, part 2." Earthweb Web site, *itmanagement.earthweb.com/entdev/article.php/760891* (May 8).

Polycom, Inc. 2003. "iPower 9000 Series: Ultimate multimedia conferencing platform," and "ViaVideo II: The industry's best personal video communications system." Polycom Web site, *www.polycom.com* (November).

Ruber, Peter. 1997. "Client/server's triple play." *Beyond Computing* 6 (March): 32–34.

SAP. 1997. "SAP announces Motorola's Semiconductor Products Sector is now live with the largest North American R/3 payroll implementation." SAP press release, SAP Web site, *www.sap.com* (June 16).

SAP. 2000. "Premier financial services company, MassMutual Financial Group, to streamline its operations using mySAP.com." SAP press release, SAP Web site, *www.sap.com* (September 25).

SAP. 2003. "Toyota Motorsport accelerates Formula One operations with SAP." SAP press release, SAP Web site, *www.sap.com* (October 8).

Schwartz, Karen D. 2003. "CRM apps get vertical." *Information Week* 950 (August 4/11): 45–48.

Singer, Peter. 1999. "Finding the right house for your data." *Beyond Computing* 8 (September): 24–28.

Singer, Peter. 2000. "Leveraging the power of your data warehouse." *Beyond Computing* 9 (May): 50–53.

Varney, Sarah E. 1996. "Will intranets lay waste to groupware?" *Datamation* 42 (December): 72–80.

Vollmann, Thomas E., William L. Berry, D. Clay Whybark, and F. Robert Jacobs. 2004. "Chapter 4, Enterprise resource planning (ERP) – integrated systems," *Manufacturing Planning and Control for Supply Chain Management.* New York: McGraw-Hill/Irwin, 108–132.

Ware, Lorraine Cosgrove. 2003. "CRM: Desperately seeking success." *CIO Magazine* 16 (August 1): 20.

Ware, Lorraine Cosgrove. 2003. "Enterprise systems show results." *CIO Magazine* 17 (November 1): 38.

Whiting, Rick. 2003. "Warehouse worries." *Information Week* 922 (January 13): 20.

Whiting, Rick. 2003. "The data-warehouse advantage." *Information Week* 949 (July 28): 63–66.

Wilde, Candee. 1999. "Citrix sees fortunes rise with thin-client model." *Information Week* 763 (November 29): 92–96.

Wreden, Nick. 1999. "ERP systems: Promise vs. performance." *Beyond Computing* 8 (September): 16–22.

CHAPTER 7

1995. "How organizations are becoming more efficient using expert systems." *I/S Analyzer Case Studies* 34 (March): 1–16.

1995. "Precision farming's 'garden' grows in Midwest." *GPS World* (April).

1996. "GIS and Sears Roebuck and Co.: Logistics and distribution moves toward 21st century." *ArcNews* (May): 1.

1997. "How businesses are cutting costs through virtual reality." *I/S Analyzer Case Studies* 36 (March): 1–16.

2000. "Comshare Decision delivers intuitive analysis solution to Petro-Canada." *DM Review*, *www.dmreview.com* (March).

2003. "Federated Department Stores, Inc. uses GIS for advanced market research." *ArcNews Online*, Environmental Systems Research Institute Web site, *www.esri.com/news/arcnews/summer03articles/federated-department.html* (Summer).

Allaway, Arthur W., Lisa D. Murphy, and David K. Berkowitz. 2004. "The geographical edge: Spatial analysis of retail loyalty program adoption," *Geographic Information Systems in Business*, edited by James Pick. Hershey, PA: Idea Group Publishing.

Baker, Sunny, and Kim Baker. 1993. *Market Mapping*. New York: McGraw-Hill.

Baum, David. 1996. "U.N. automates payroll with AI system." *Datamation* 42 (November): 129–132.

Blough, Kay. 2002. "Virtual reality to aid stroke therapy." *Information Week* 876 (February 18): 20.

Davis, Beth. 1999. "Data mining transformed." *Information Week* 751 (September 6): 86, 88.

Dennis, Alan R., and Iris Vessey. 2003. "Knowledge markets, knowledge hierarchies, and knowledge communities: Toward a theory of knowledge management strategy." Indiana University Working Paper.

Dickey, Sam. 1999. "OLAP and data mining put profits first." *Beyond Computing* 8 (October): 18–22.

Exsys Inc. 2003. "Case study: Credit analysis advisor and report system," "Case study: Detecting insider trading," "Case study: Individual development plan advisor," "Case study: Maximum yield/minimum resources farm advisors," "Case study: Pension fund advisor." Exsys Inc. Web site, *www.exsys.com* (December).

Fowler, Bob. 2000. "Dow AgroSciences Global Competitive Intelligence." Personal correspondence (September). At the time, Mr. Fowler was Global Competitive Intelligence/Data Compensation Leader, Dow AgroSciences.

Gaudin, Sharon. 2003. "Data mining and business intelligence product of the year—SAS Text Miner." Earthweb.com Web site, *itmanagement.earthweb.com/datbus/article.php/2203211* (May 8).

Geac Computer Corporation Limited. 2003. "About us," "Comshare chosen by world leader in pizza delivery to support field operations," "Krispy Kreme doughnuts manages explosive growth and creates value with Comshare," "Dean Health System creates an enterprise-wide corporate performance management system with Comshare." Geac Web site, *www.comshare.com* (December).

GroupSystems.com. 2003. "About the company," "Customer success stories: Nokia Telecommunications," "Customer success stories: Problem solving." GroupSystems.com Web site, *www.groupsystems.com* (December).

Gupta, Vijay, Emmanuel Peters, Tan Miller, and Kelvin Blyden. 2002. "Implementing a distribution-network decision support system at Pfizer/Warner-Lambert." *Interfaces* 32 (July–August): 28–45.

Gwynne, Peter. 2000. "OLAP and data mining: Making the right decisions." *Beyond Computing* 9 (September): 42–45.

Haskin, David. 2003. "Years after hype, 'expert systems' paying off for some." Earthweb.com Web site, *itmanagement.earthweb.com/netsys/article.php/1570851* (January 16).

Houdeshel, George, and Hugh J. Watson. 1987. "The management information and decision support (MIDS) system at Lockheed-Georgia." *MIS Quarterly* 11 (March): 127–140.

Hulme, George V. 2002. "Cadavers go virtual." *Information Week* 889 (May 20): 20.

Internet Pictures Corporation. 2003. "Company info," "Showcase," "Security and surveillance solutions." Internet Pictures Corporation Web site, *www.ipix.com* (December).

Konicki, Steve. 2002. "How to design cars and scare children." *Information Week* 891 (June 3): 42.

McCarthy, Vance. 1997. "Strike it rich!" *Datamation* 43 (February): 44–50.

National Center for Health Statistics (NCHS). 2004. "GIS and the public health." Centers for Disease Control and Prevention Web site, U.S. Department of Health and Human Services, *www.cdc.gov/nchs/gis.htm* (January).

NeuroDimension, Inc. 2000. "Application summaries: Portfolio management," NeuroDimension Web site, *www.nd.com* (December).

Nunamaker, J. F., Alan R. Dennis, Joseph S. Valacich, Douglas R. Vogel, and Joey F. George. 1991. "Electronic meeting systems to support group work." *Communications of the ACM* 34 (July): 40–61.

O'Dell, Carla, and C. Jackson Grayson, Jr. 1998. *If Only We Knew What We Know: The Transfer of Internal Knowledge and Best Practice.* New York: The Free Press.

Ormsby, Tim, Eileen Napoleon, Pat Breslin, and Nick Frunzi. 1998. *Getting to Know ArcView GIS 3.x.* Redlands, CA: Environmental Systems Research Institute, Inc.

Ortiz, Joseph. 2003. "Immersive images—not just pretty pictures anymore." *National Hotel Executive, www.hotelexecutive.com/premium/library25/57.asp* (July).

Orzech, Dan. 2002. "Using neural networks to beat hackers." CIO Update Web site, *www.cioupdate.com/news/article.php/1561971* (December 27).

Paul, Lauren Gibbons. 2003. "Why three heads are better than one (How to create a know-it-all company)." *CIO* 17 (December 1): 94–104.

Perkins, William C., James C. Hershauer, Abbas Foroughi, and Michael M. Delaney. 1996. "Can a negotiation support system help a purchasing manager?" *International Journal of Purchasing and Materials Management* 32 (Spring): 37–45.

Port, Otis. 2000. "Thinking machines: Special report on smart manufacturing." *Business Week* (August 7): 78–86.

Slater, Derek. 2000. "Household Financial Corporation: Loan star." *CIO* (February 1): 100–106.

Sprague, Ralph H., Jr., and Eric D. Carlson. 1982. *Building Effective Decision Support Systems*. Englewood Cliffs, NJ: Prentice-Hall, Inc.

Superscape Inc. 2003. "About Superscape," "Superscape delivers interactive 3D for safety training at Ford," "Discovery.com teams with Superscape Inc. to develop interactive 3D content," "Make it Swerve." Superscape Web site, *www.superscape.com* (December).

Vitolo, Theresa M., and Robert J. Vance. 2002. "STEP-UP: A decision support system for transforming the dislocated U.S. defense workforce." *Interfaces* 32 (July–August): 75–83.

Whiting, Rick. 2002. "Analysis gap." *Information Week* 885 (April 22): 51–57.

Whiting, Rick. 2003. "Look within." *Information Week* 922 (January 13): 32–43.

Whiting, Rick. 2003. "Intelligence or info overload?" *Information Week* 963 (November 10): 86–92.

Wohl, Amy D. 2000. "Brave new virtual worlds." *Beyond Computing* 9 (October): 14, 16.

Yu, Gang, Michael Argüello, Gao Song, Sandra M. McCowan, and Anna White. 2003. "A new era for crew recovery at Continental Airlines." *Interfaces* 33 (January–February): 5–22.

Z Solutions, Inc. 2003. "Demonstration for a public health agency." Z Solutions Web site, *www.zsolutions.com/consulting.htm* (December).

Zeiler, Michael. 1999. *Modeling our world: The ESRI guide to geodatabase design.* Redlands, CA: Environmental Systems Research Institute, Inc.

CHAPTER 8

1999. "How to talk dot-com like a webmaster." The New York Times (September 22): E-commerce, 3.

2001. "Jakob Nielsen Interview." *www.webreference.com/new/nielsen.html*, January 2.

2001. "The top 25 managers of the year." Business Week (January 8): 68.

Anders, George. 2001. "Marc Andreessen, Act II." Fast Company (February): 110–121.

Applegate, Lynda M., Clyde W. Holsapple, Ravi Kalakota, Franz J. Radermacher, and Andrew B. Whinston. 1996. "Electronic commerce: Building blocks of new business opportunity." Journal of Organization Computing and Electronic Commerce 6 (1): 1–10.

Applegate, Lynda M., F. Warren McFarlan, and James L. McKenney. 1996. *Corporate Information Systems Management*, 4th ed. Chicago: Irwin.

[The Associated Press] 2003. "eBay items yanked." (February 2).

Barabasi, Albert-Laszlo. 2002. *Linked: How Everything is Connected to Everything Else and What It Means for Business, Science, and Everyday Life.* New York: Perseus Books Group.

Brown, J. 2000. "Signing on the digital line." CIO (October 15): 273.

Clemons, Eric K. 1991. "Evaluation of strategic investments in information technology." Communications of the ACM 34 (January): 23–36.

Copeland, Lee. 2000b. "Ford, GM almost ready to shut own exchanges." Computerworld (December 11): 16.

[Cyberatlas] 2002. "B2B e-commerce headed for trillions." *http://cyberatlas.internet.com/markets/b2b/print/0,,10091_986661,00.html.* (March 6).

DeJesus, Edmund X. 2001. "EDI? XML? Or both?" Computerworld (January 8): 54–56.

[E-tailing Group] 2002. 4Q 02 Mystery Shopping Summary Conducted by the e-tailing group, inc. *www.e-tailing.com/research/mysteryshop/2002/summary.html.*

Elgin, Ben. 2003. "Yahoo! Act two." Business Week (June 3): 70–76.

Elgin, Ben. "Can Yahoo make 'em pay?" *Business Week* (September 9): 92–94.

Frei, Frances X. 2001. "E-Bay: The Customer Marketplace (A)." Boston, MA: Harvard Business School, Case No. 9-602-071 (rev. May 2, 2002).

Gates, Bill. 1995. The Road Ahead. New York: Viking Penguin.

Ghosh, Shikhar. 1998. "Making business sense of the Internet." Harvard Business Review (March–April): 126–135.

Greenspan, Robyn. 2004. "Internet not for everyone." *cyberatlas.internet.com/big_picture/demographics/article/0,1323,5901_2192251,00.html.*

Guernsey, Lisa. 1999. "Web surfers' fears prompt privacy seals." The New York Times (April 29): D9.

[Hitwise] 2003. Top online department stores ranked by visits, U.S. (August).

Hopper, Max D. 1990. "Rattling SABRE—New ways to compete on information." *Harvard Business Review* (May–June): 118–125.

Jones, Kathryn. 2003. "The Dell Way," *Business 2.0* (February): 61–66.

Kalakota, Ravi, and Andrew B. Whinston. 1996. *Electronic Commerce: A Manager's Guide*. Reading, MA: Addison Wesley Longman.

King, Julia. 2000. "B2B's surprise: The survivors," *Computerworld* (December 11): 1, 16.

Lee, Young Eun, and Izak Benbasat. 2003. "Interface design for mobile commerce," *Communications of the ACM*, 46:12 (December), 49–52.

Louie, Dickson L. and Jeffrey F. Rayport. 2001. "Amazon.com (D)." Boston, MA: Harvard Business School, Case No. 9-901-022.

Magretta, Joan. 1998. "The power of virtual integration: an interview with Dell Computer's Michael Dell, *Harvard Business Review* (March–April): 73f.

Mossberg, Walter S. 2000. "The Amazon Way is still the best model for Web shopping." *Wall Street Journal* (September 21): B1.

[Nielsen/Net Ratings] November 2003. Table 1.

[Nielsen/Net Ratings] December 2003. Table 1.

[Pew Internet & American Life Project Surveys] 2002. Growth in selected online activities by U.S. consumers: 2000–2002.

Piccoli, Gabriel, Bill Bass, and Blake Ives. 2003. "Custom-made apparel at Lands' End." *MIS Quarterly Executive* 2:2 (September).

Porter, Michael E. 1985. *Competitive Advantage: Creating and Sustaining Superior Performance*. New York: Free Press.

Porter, Michael E. 2001. "Strategy and the Internet." *Harvard Business Review* (March): 53–68.

Porter, Michael E., and Victor E. Millar. 1985. "How information gives you competitive advantage," *Harvard Business Review* 63 (July–August): 149–160.

Pottruck, David S. and Terry Pearce. 1999. *Clicks and Mortar*. San Francisco: Jossey-Bass.

Ranganathan, C. 2003. "Evaluating the options for business-to-business e-commerce." *IS Management Handbook*, 8th edition. Carol V. Brown and Heikki Topi (eds.). New York: Auerbach: 651–662.

Rayport, Jeffrey F., and Bernard J. Jaworski. 2004. *Introduction to e-Commerce*. New York: McGraw-Hill/Irwin.

Rivkin, Jan W., and Michael E. Porter. 1999. "Matching Dell." Boston, MA: Harvard Business School: Case study 9-799-158.

Schwartz, John. 2001. "New economy." *The New York Times* (January 8): C4.

Seib, Gerald F., and Jim VandeHei. 2000. "On the levy: A lobbying machine springs up to revive issue of Internet taxes." *Wall Street Journal* (June 29): A1, A10.

Senn, James A. 2000. "Expanding the reach of electronic commerce: The Internet EDI alternative." *IS Management Handbook*, 7th ed. Carol V. Brown and Heikki Topi (eds.) New York: Auerbach Publications: 635–648.

Stackpole, Beth. 2000. "Apps of steel." CIO (October 15): 164–180.

Straub, Detmar. 2004. *Foundations of Net-Enhanced Organizations*. Hoboken, NJ: Wiley.

Taylor, Alex. 2000. "Ralph's agenda." *ECompany* (July): 97–101.

Weber, Thomas E. 2000. "Recent flaps raise questions about role of middlemen on Web." *Wall Street Journal* (June 5): B1.

Weill, Peter, and Michael R. Vitale. 2001. *Place to Space: Migrating to eBusiness Models*. Boston, MA: Harvard Business School Press.

Woodham, Richard, and Peter Weill. 2001. "Manheim interactive: selling cars online." MIT, Center for Information Systems Research, WP 314.

CHAPTER 9

Chand, Donald R. 2003. "Use case modeling." Carol V. Brown and Heikki Topi (eds.), *IS Management Handbook*, 8th ed. New York: Auerbach.

Dennis, Alan, and Barbara Haley Wixom. 2000. *Systems Analysis and Design*. New York: John Wiley & Sons, Inc.

El Sawy, Omar A. 2001. *Redesigning Enterprise Processes for E-Business*. Boston: Irwin/McGraw Hill.

Fitzgerald, Jerry, and Alan Dennis. 1999. *Business Data Communications and Networking*, 6th ed. New York: John Wiley & Sons, Inc.

Guth, Robert A., and David Bank. 2003. "Online 'worm' puts new stress on Microsoft." *The Wall Street Journal* (August 15): B1, B5.

Hammer, Michael. 1990. "Reengineering work: Don't automate, obliterate." *Harvard Business Review* 68 (July–August): 104–112.

Hammer, Michael. 1996. *Beyond Reengineering*. New York: HarperCollins.

Hammer, Michael, and James Champy. 1993. *Reengineering the Corporation*. New York: HarperCollins.

Hart, Johnson M., and Barry Rosenberg. 1995. *Client/Server Computing for Technical Professionals: Concepts and Solutions*. Reading, MA: Addison-Wesley Publishing Company.

Hoffer, Jeffrey A., Joey F. George, and Joseph S. Valacich. 1999. *Modern Systems Analysis and Design*, 2nd ed. Reading, MA: Addison-Wesley Publishing Company.

Hoffer, Jeffrey A., and Detmar W. Straub, Jr. 1989. "The 9 to 5 underground: Are you policing computer crimes?" *Sloan Management Review* 30 (Summer): 35–43.

Keen, Peter G. W. 1997. *The Process Edge*. Boston: Harvard University Press.

Markus, M. Lynne, and Daniel Robey. 1988. "Information technology and organizational change: Causal structure in theory and research." *Management Science* 34 (May): 583–598.

McFadden, Fred R., Jeffrey A. Hoffer, and Mary B. Prescott. 1999. *Modern Database Management*, 5th ed. Upper Saddle River, NJ: Prentice Hall.

McNurlin, Barbara C., and Ralph H. Sprague, Jr. 2004. *Information Systems Management in Practice*, 6th ed. Upper Saddle River, NJ: Prentice Hall.

Page-Jones, Meilir. 1988. *The Practical Guide to Structured Systems Design*, 2nd ed. Englewood Cliffs, NJ: Yourdon Press.

Senge, Peter M. 1990. *The Fifth Discipline*. New York: Doubleday.

Valacich, Joseph S., Joey F. George, and Jeffrey A. Hoffer. 2001. *Essentials of Systems Analysis & Design*. Upper Saddle River, NJ: Prentice Hall.

Verity, John W., and Evan I. Schwartz. 1991. "Software made simple." *Business Week* (September 30): 92–100.

Vessey, Iris, and Robert L. Glass. 1994. "Applications-based methodologies." *Information Systems Management* (Fall): 53–57.

CHAPTER 10

Beath, Cynthia M., and Wanda J. Orlikowski. 1994. "The contradictory structure of systems development methodologies: Deconstructing the IS-user relationship in information engineering." *Information Systems Research* 5 (December): 350–377.

Boehm, Barry. 1976. "Software engineering." *IEEE Transactions on Computers* C-25 (December): 1226–1241.

Boehm, Barry. 1981. *Software Engineering Economics*. Englewood Cliffs, NJ: Prentice Hall.

Bollinger, Terry B., and Clement McGowan. 1991. "A critical look at software capability evaluations." *IEEE Software* (July 1): 25–46.

Clark, Charles E., Nancy C. Cavanaugh, Carol V. Brown, and V. Sambamurthy. 1997. "Building change-readiness capabilities in the IS organization: Insights from the Bell Atlantic experience." *MIS Quarterly* 21 (December): 425–455.

Colter, Mel A. 1984. "A comparative examination of systems analysis techniques." *MIS Quarterly* 8 (March): 51–66.

Davis, Gordon B. 1982. "Strategies for information requirements determination." *IBM Systems Journal* 21: 4–30.

DeMarco, Tom. 1982. *Controlling Software Projects*. New York: Yourdon Press, Inc.

Gane, Chris, and Trish Sarson. 1979. *Structured Systems Analysis: Tools and Techniques*. Englewood Cliffs, NJ: Prentice Hall.

Hartwick, Jon, and Henri Barki. 1994. "Measuring user participation, user involvement, and user attitude." *MIS Quarterly* 18 (March): 59–79.

Hoffman, Thomas. 2003. "Corporate execs try new ways to align IT with business units." *ComputerWorld* (October 27): 13.

Keen, Peter G. W. 1991. "Managing the economics of information capital." *Shaping the Future: Business Design Through Information Technology*. Boston: Harvard Business School Press.

Kendall, Kenneth E., and Julie E. Kendall. 1999. *Systems Analysis and Design*. 4th edition. Upper Saddle River, NJ: Prentice Hall.

Lindstrom, Lowell, and Ron Jeffries. 2003. "Extreme Programming and Agile Software Development Methodologies." *IS Management Handbook*. 8th edition. Carol V. Brown and Heikki Topi (eds.). New York: Auerbach.

McNurlin, Barbara C., and Ralph H. Sprague, Jr. 2004. *Information Systems Management in Practice*, 6th ed. Upper Saddle River, NJ: Prentice Hall.

Parker, Marilyn M., and Robert J. Benson. 1987. "Information economics: An introduction." *Datamation* 33 (December 1): 86–96.

Poria, Bharat C. 2004. "Strategic Outsourcing." *CIO Wisdom*. Upper Saddle River, NJ: Prentice Hall.

Radding, Alan. 1992. "When non-IS managers take control." *Datamation* 38 (July 1): 55–58.

Robey, Daniel. 1987. "Implementation and the organizational impacts of information systems." *Interfaces* 17 (May–June): 72–84.

Valacich, Joseph S., Joey F. George, and Jeffrey A. Hoffer. 2001. *Essentials of Systems Analysis and Design*. Upper Saddle River, NJ: Prentice Hall.

CHAPTER 11

Anthes, Gary H. 2000. "Asking the right questions up front can mean the difference between a dream relationship and a nightmarish one." *Computerworld* 34 (October 10): 21.

Applegate, Lynda M., Robert D. Austin, and F. Warren McFarlan. 2003. *Corporate Information Strategy and Management*, 6th ed. Boston: McGraw Hill.

Bailey, Jeff. 1999. "Trash haulers are taking fancy software to the dump." *The Wall Street Journal* (June 9): 1.

Brown, Carol V., and Iris Vessey. 2003. "Managing the next wave of enterprise systems: Leveraging the lessons from ERP projects." *MIS Quarterly Executive* 2:1 (March).

Everdingen, Yvonne van, Jos van Hillegersberg, and Eric Waarts. 2000. "ERP adoption by European midsize companies." *Communications of the ACM* 43 (April): 27–31.

Gurbaxani, Vijay, and Seungjin Whang. 1991. "The impact of information systems on organizations and markets." *Communications of the ACM* 34 (January): 59–73.

Hoffman, Thomas, and Sarwar Kashmeri. 2000. "Realistic ASPirations." *Computerworld* 34 (August 7): 46.

Keen, Peter G. W. 1991. "Managing the economics of information capital." *Shaping the Future: Business Design Through Information Technology*. Boston: Harvard Business School Press.

Lucas, Henry C., Jr., Eric J. Walton, and Michael J. Ginzberg. 1988. "Implementing packaged software." *MIS Quarterly* 12 (December): 525–549.

Markus, M. Lynne, and Robert I. Benjamin. 1997. "The magic bullet theory in IT-enabled transformations." *Sloan Management Review* 38 (Winter): 55–68.

Martin, E.W. 1988. "Halsted, Inc." Indiana University teaching case.

Rockart, John F., and J. Debra Hofman. 1992. "Systems delivery: Evolving new strategies." *Sloan Management Review* 33 (Summer): 21–31.

Ross, Jeanne. 1998. "The ERP revolution: Surviving versus thriving." MIT Sloan School CISR Research Paper.

Schwalbe, Kathy. 2004. *Information Technology Project Management,* 3rd ed. Canada: Thomson Learning.

CHAPTER 12

Applegate, Lynda M., F. Warren McFarlan, and James L. McKenney. 1996. *Corporate Information Systems Management*, 4th ed. Chicago: Irwin.

Bashein, Barbara J., M. Lynne Markus, and Jane B. Finley. 1997. *Safety Nets: Secrets of Effective Information Technology*

Controls. Morristown, NJ: Financial Executives Research Foundation.

Clark, Charles E., Nancy C. Cavanaugh, Carol V. Brown, and V. Sambamurthy. 1997. "Building change-readiness capabilities in the IS organization: Insights from the Bell Atlantic experience." *MIS Quarterly* 21 (December): 425–456.

Clemons, Eric K. 1991. "Evaluation of strategic investments in information technology." *Communications of the ACM* 34 (January): 22–36.

Denis, Bob, Maureen Vavra, and John Dick. 2004. "Budgeting." *CIO Wisdom*. Upper Saddle River, NJ: Prentice Hall.

Duffy, Dainty. 1999. "Making lemonade." *CIO* (December 1): 71–77.

Duncan, William R., and Duncan Nevison. 1994. "Software methodology vs. project management." *SIM Executive* 4:14 (Spring).

Frame, J. Davidson. 1994. *The New Project Management*. San Francisco: Jossey Bass.

Grover, Varun, Seung Ryul Jeong, and James T. C. Teng. 2000. "Reengineering project challenges." *IS Management Handbook*, 7th ed. Carol V. Brown and Heikki Topi (eds.) New York: Auerbach.

Hamilton, Stewart. 2000. "Information and the management of risk." *Competing with Information*. Donald A. Marchand (ed.) Chichester, England: John Wiley & Sons, Ltd., 195–207.

Highsmith, Jim. 2000. "There are projects—and there are Internet projects." *ComputerWorld* (March 27): 64.

Hoffman, Thomas. 2003. "Corporate execs try new ways to align IT with business units." *ComputerWorld* (October 27), 13.

Kay, Ira T., and Mike Shelton. 2000. "The people problem in mergers." *The McKinsey Quarterly* 4.

Keil, Mark, and Daniel Robey. 1999. "Turning around troubled software projects: An exploratory study of the deescalation of commitment to failing courses of action." *Journal of Management Information Systems* 15 (Spring): 63–87.

Kotter, John P. 1995. "Leading change: Why transformation efforts fail." *Harvard Business Review* (March–April): 59–67.

Lewin, Kurt. 1947. "Frontiers in group dynamics." *Human Relations* 1:5–41.

Lindstrom, Lowell, and Ron Jeffries. 2003. "Extreme programming and agile software development methodologies." *IS Management Handbook*, 8th ed. Carol V. Brown and Heikki Topi (eds.) New York: Auerbach.

Markus, M. Lynne. 1983. "Power, politics, and MIS implementation." *Communications of the ACM* 26 (June): 430–444.

McNurlin, Barbara C., and Ralph H. Sprague, Jr. 2004. *Information Systems Management in Practice*, 6th ed. Upper Saddle River, NJ: Prentice Hall.

Meredith, Jack R., and Samuel J. Mantel, Jr. 1989. *Project Management: A Managerial Approach*, 2nd ed. New York: John Wiley & Sons.

Montealegre, Ramiro, and Mark Keil. 2000. "De-escalating information technology projects: Lessons from the Denver International Airport." *MIS Quarterly* 24 (September): 417–447.

Orlikowski, Wanda J., and J. Debra Hofman. 1997. "An improvisational model for change management: The case of groupware technologies." *Sloan Management Review* 38 (Winter): 11–22.

PMI Standards Committee. 1996. *A Guide to the Project Management Body of Knowledge*. Newton Square, PA: Project Management Institute.

Poria, Bharat C. 2004. "Strategic Outsourcing." *CIO Wisdom*. Upper Saddle River, NJ: Prentice Hall.

Roman, Daniel D. 1986. *Managing Projects: A Systems Approach*. New York: Elsevier.

Russell, Lou. 2000. "Managing the end for new beginnings: Post-project review for year 2000." *Cutter ITJournal* 13 (July): 28–39.

Ryan, Hugh W. 2003. "Managing development in the era of complex systems." *IS Management Handbook*, 8th ed. Carol V. Brown and Heikki Topi (eds.) New York: Auerbach.

Schwalbe, Kathy. 2004. *Information Technology Project Management*, 3rd ed. Canada: Thomson Learning.

Valacich, Joseph S., Joey F. George, and Jeffrey A. Hoffer. 2001. *Essentials of Systems Analysis and Design*. Upper Saddle River, NJ: Prentice Hall.

Vavra, Maureen, and Dean Lane. 2004. "Strategic Planning." *CIO Wisdom*. Upper Saddle River, NJ: Prentice Hall.

Wheatley, Margaret, and Myron Kellner-Rogers. 1996. *A Simpler Way*. San Francisco: Berrett-Koehler.

CHAPTER 13

Agpar, Mahlon IV. 1998. "The alternative workplace: changing where and how people work." *Harvard Business Review* 76:3 (May/June): 121–136.

[Associated Press.] 2003. "Computer use by young people hits 90% mark." *The Wall Street Journal* (October 30): D4.

Boynton, Andrew C., Robert W. Zmud, and Gerald C. Jacobs. 1994. "The influence of IT management practice on IT use in large organizations." *MIS Quarterly* 17 (March): 299–318.

Brancheau, James C., and Donald L. Amoroso. 1990. "An empirical test of the expansion-control model for managing end-user computing." *Proceedings of the 11th International Conference on Information Systems*: 291–303.

Brancheau, James C., and Carol V. Brown. 1993. "The management of end-user computing: Status and directions." *Computing Surveys* 25 (December): 437–482.

Delaney, Kevin J. 2003. "Old computers don't fade away anymore." *The Wall Street Journal* (May 1): B3.

Dunham, Kemba J. 2000. "Telecommuters' lament." *The Wall Street Journal* (October 31): B1, B18.

Galletta, Dennis F., K. S. Hartzel, S. Johnson, J. Joseph, and S. Rustagi. 1996. "An experimental study of spreadsheet presentation and error detection." *Proceedings of the 29th Hawaii International Conference on System Sciences*: 336–345.

Gerrity, T. P., and John F. Rockart. 1986. "End-user computing: Are you a leader or a laggard?" *Sloan Management Review* 27 (Summer): 25–34.

Glick, James. 2003. "Tangled up in spam." *The New York Times Magazine* (February 9): 42–47.

Gomes, Lee. 2003. "Software companies flex real muscle in search for pirates." *The Wall Street Journal* (October 20): B1

Hall, M. J. J. 1996. "A risk and control oriented study of the practices of spreadsheet application developers." *Proceedings of the 29th Hawaii International Conference on System Sciences*: 364–373.

Hammond, L.W. 1982. "Management considerations for an information center." *IBM Systems Journal* 21 (2): 131–161.

Hansel, Saul. 2003. "How to unclog the information artery." *The New York Times* (May 25): BU1, 10.

Harmon, Amy. 2003. "Re: What people love to hate." *The New York Times* (May 11): WK7.

Huff, Sid L., Malcolm C. Munro, and Barbara H. Martin. 1988. "Growth stages of end-user computing." *Communications of the ACM* 31 (May): 542–550.

Jordan, Graeber. 1997. "The Boeing Web." Keynote Address at SIM Interchange, San Francisco.

Kaiser, Kate M. 1993. "End-user computing," *Encyclopedia of Computer Science and Technology.*

Karten, Naomi. 1990. "The two stages of end-user computing," *Mind Your Business: Strategies for Managing End-User Computing*. Wellesley, MA: QED Information Sciences, Inc. pp. 3–24.

Klepper, Robert, and Mary Sumner. 1990. "Continuity and change in user developed systems," *Desktop Information Technology.* K. M. Kaiser and J. J. Oppelland (eds.) Amsterdam: North-Holland, 209–222.

Kostner, Jaclyn. 1996. *Virtual Leadership—Secrets from the Round Table for the Multi-Site Manager*. Warner Books, Inc.

Langley, Alison. 2003. "Computer viruses are frustrating insurers, too." *The New York Times* (October 12).

Martin, James. 1982. *Application Development Without Programmers*. Englewood Cliffs, NJ: Prentice Hall.

Mathews, Anna Wilde. 2003. "As workers grab web freebies with 'peer-to-peer' software, employers move to prevent it." *The Wall Street Journal* (June 26): B1, B7.

McLean, Ephraim R. 1979. "End users as application developers." *MIS Quarterly* 3 (4): 37–46.

McLean, Ephraim R., L. A. Kappelman, and J. P. Thompson. 1993. "Converging end-user and corporate computing." *Communications of the ACM* 36 (December): 79–92.

McNurlin, Barbara C., and Ralph H. Sprague. 1998. *Information Systems Management in Practice*, 4th ed. Upper Saddle River, NJ: Prentice Hall.

Munro, Malcolm C., Sid L. Huff, and G. C. Moore. 1987–1988. "Expansion and control of end user computing." *Journal of Management Information Systems* 4 (Winter): 5–27.

Muoio, Anna. 2000. "Cisco's quick study." *Fast Company* (October): 286–295.

Panko, Ralph R. 1988. *End User Computing: Management, Applications, and Technology*. New York: Wiley.

Panko, Ralph R. 1996. "Minitrack on risks in end-user computing." *Proceedings of the 29th Hawaii International Conference on System Sciences.*

Panko, Ralph R., and R. P. Halverson, Jr. 1996. "Spreadsheets on trial: A survey of research on spreadsheet risks." *Proceedings of the 29th Hawaii International Conference on System Sciences*: 326–335.

Pender, Lee. 2000. "How personal is the personal computer?" *CIO* (October 15): 185–192.

Pyburn, Philip J. 1986–1987. "Managing personal computer use: The role of corporate management information systems." *Journal of Management Information Systems* 3 (3): 49–70.

Rivard, Suzanne, and Sid L. Huff. 1988. "Factors of success for end-user computing." *Communications of the ACM* 31 (5): 552–561.

Rockart, John F., and L. S. Flannery. 1983. "The management of end-user computing." *Communications of the ACM* 26 (10): 776–784.

Schultheis, Robert A., and Mary Sumner. 1991. "The relationship of application risks to application controls: A study of microcomputer-based database applications." *Computer Personnel* 13 (3): 50–59.

[Spam calculator]. 2003. *www.trendmicro.com/en/products/gateway/spam/evaluate/spam-calculator.htm* (August 13).

Speier, Cheri S., and Carol V. Brown. 1997. "Differences in end-user computing support and control across user departments." *Information & Management* 32 (February 15): 85–99.

Topi, Heikki. 2003. "Supporting telework: Obstacles and solutions." *IS Management Handbook*, 8th ed. Carol V. Brown and Heikki Topi (eds.) New York: Auerbach: 807–817.

Williford, Steven M. 2003. "Reviewing user-developed applications," *IS Management Handbook*, 8th ed. Carol V. Brown and Heikki Topi (eds.) New York: Auerbach: 781–798.

CHAPTER 14

Allen, Brandt R., and Andrew C. Boynton. 1991. "Information architecture: In search of efficient flexibility." *MIS Quarterly* 16 (December): 435–445.

Crane, Darlene B., and Margery Mayer. 2003. "A three step assessment." *Darwin Magazine* 4 (September): 4–7.

Evans, Philip, and Thomas S. Wheeler. 2000. *How the New Economics of Information Transforms Strategy*. Boston, MA: Harvard Business School.

Feeny, David F., and Leslie P. Willcocks. 1998. "Core IS capabilities for exploiting information technology." *Sloan Management Review* 26 (Spring): 9–21.

Hildebrand, Carol. 2000. "The art of the new deal." *Darwin Magazine* 1 (June/July): 9–15.

Hoenig, Christopher. 2000. "The master planner." *CIO* 13 (May 1): 76, 78.

Luftman, Jerry, and Tom Brier. 1996. "Achieving and sustaining business-IT alignment." *California Management Review* 42 (Issue 1): 109–122.

Malan, Ruth, and Dana Bredemeyer. 2003. "Architecture strategy." Bredemeyer Consulting Web site, *www.bredemeyer.com/ArchitectingProcess/ArchitectureStrategy.htm* (April).

McKeen, James D., and Heather A. Smith. 2003. *Making IT Happen: Critical Issues in IT Management*. New York: John Wiley & Sons.

Newman, David. 1996. "Data warehouse architecture." *Data Management Review* 19 (October): 34–39.

Oliver, Dan. 2002. "Build your skills: Four steps in building an enterprise data architecture." TechRepublic Web site, *www.techrepublic.com* (March 18).

Pearlson, Keri E. 2001. *Managing and Using Information Systems: A Strategic Approach*. New York: John Wiley & Sons.

Porter, Michael E., and Victor E. Millar. 1985. "How information gives you competitive advantage." *Harvard Business Review* 63 (July–August): 149–160.

Rechtin, Eberhardt, and Mark Maier. 1997. *The Art of Systems Architecting*. Boca Raton, FL: CRC Press.

Seger, Katherine, and Donna B. Stoddard. 1993. "Managing information: The IT architecture." Harvard Business School 9-193-059.

Varon, Elana. 2000. "Be nimble, be quick." *CIO* 13 (June 15): 84–94.

Wunder, John, and Will Tracz. 2003. "An information architecture strategy." *Journal of Defense Software Engineering* (October): 17–34.

CHAPTER 15

Bender, Ray. 2000. "CIO priorities 2000." *Executive Edge* 6 (June/July): 9.

Bendor-Samuel, Peter. 2003. "BTO reinvents the wheel to create strategic impact." *BPO Outsourcing Journal* 12 (October): 35–42.

Bennis, Warren. 1999. "Lessons in leadership." *CIO* 12 (June 15): Section 1, 34–36.

Birge, Eileen M. 1999. "How to measure IT performance." *Beyond Computing* 8 (January/February): 67–71.

Brown, Carol V. 1999. "Horizontal mechanisms under differing IS contexts." *MIS Quarterly* 23 (September): 421–454.

Brown, Carol V. 2003. "The IT organization of the future." *Competing in the Information Age: Align in the Sand,* 2nd ed. Jerry N. Luftman (ed.) New York: Oxford University Press: 191–207.

Brown, Carol V., and Sharon L. Magill. 1994. "Alignment of the IS functions with the enterprise: Toward a model of antecedents." *MIS Quarterly* 18 (December): 371–403.

Brown, Carol V., and V. Sambamurthy. 1999. *Repositioning the IT Organization to Facilitate Business Transformations.* Cincinnati, OH: Pinnaflex.

Carmel, Erran, and Ritu Agarwal. 2001. "Tactical approaches for alleviating distance in global software development." *IEEE Software* 18 (March/April): 22–29.

Carmel, Erran. 1999. *Global Software Teams: Collaborating Across Borders and Time Zones*. Upper Saddle River, NJ: Prentice Hall.

Carr, Nicholas G. 2003. "IT doesn't matter." *Harvard Business Review* 81 (May): 41–49.

Chang, Edward S. 1999. "Managing cyber security vulnerabilities in large networks." *Bell Labs Technical Journal* 27 (October–December): 252–256.

CIO.com. 2003. "Metrics: Most digital attacks originate from Brazil." CIO.com Web site, *www2.cio.com/metrics/2003/metric612.html* (September 26).

Cline, Jay. 2002. "Coping with Europe's data blockade." *Computerworld Online, www.computerworld.com/securitytopics/security/privacy/story/0,10801,76823,00.html* (December 17).

Clawson, James G. 2000. "The new infocracies: Implications for leadership." *Ivey Business Journal* 14 (May/June): 76–80.

Collett, Stacy. 2003. "Singapore." *Computerworld* 37 (September 15): 42.

Daily, John C. 1995. "What it takes to be CIO." *Datamation* 40 (November 1): 61–62.

Dickey, Sam. 2000. "Protect your information assets." *Beyond Computing* 9 (January/February): 31–36.

Duffy, Daintry. 2002. "Continental divide." *CIO* 15 (April 15): 92–96.

Edberg, Dana, Fritz H. Grupe, and William Kuechler. 2001. "Practical issues in global IT management." *Information Systems Management* 18 (Winter): 34–46.

Essick, Kristi. 2000. "Yahoo told to block Nazi goods from French." *The Industry Standard* 66 (November 20): 6.

Gupta, Anil K., and Vijay Govindaranjan. 2000. "The rising cost of waiting." *CIO* 13 (July 15): 54–56.

House, Robert, Mansour Javidan, Paul Hanges, and Peter Dorfman. 2002. "Understanding cultures and implicit leadership theories across the globe: An introduction to Project GLOBE." *Journal of World Business* 37 (1): 3–10.

Hubbard, Douglas. 1999. "The IT measurement inversion." *CIO* 12 (April 15): Section 2, 26–31.

Judge, Paul C. 1998. "What've you done for us lately?" *Business Week* (September 7): 68–70.

Kaplan, Robert S., and David P. Norton. 1992. "The balanced scorecard—Measures that drive performance." *Harvard Business Review* 70 (January–February): 71–79.

Karlgaard, Rich. 2003. "What makes a great CIO?" *Forbes* 163 (November 24): 43.

King, Julia. 2003a. "IT's global itinerary." *Computerworld* 37 (September 15): 26–27.

King, Julia. 2003b. "The best of both shores." *Computerworld* 37 (April 21): 37–38.

Koch, Christopher. 2000. "ASP and ye shall receive." *CIO* 13 (May 1): 94–106.

Kouakou, Koffi M. 2001. "Africa awaits." *CIO* 15 (November 1): 48–50.

Legard, David. 2002. "U.S. Web site may face defamation suit in Australia." *IDG News Service* 32 (December 10): 3.

Machiavelli, Niccolo. ca. 1513. *The Prince*. Translation by Hill Thompson (1988). Palm Springs, CA: ETC Publications.

Mackie, Andy. 2002. "Outsourcing outlook." *Computer Dealer News* 34 (October 18): 22–24.

Marguilius, David L. 2003. "Betting on BTO." *CIO* 17 (October 15): 146–152.

McKeen, James D., and Heather A. Smith. 2003. *Making IT Happen: Critical Issues in IT Management*. New York: John Wiley & Sons.

Mearian, Lucas. 2002. "MasterCard nears finish of payment system rollout." *Computerworld* 36 (December 2): 19.

MSC. 2003. "What is the MSC?" MSC Web site, *www.msc.com.my* (December).

Odo, Austine. 2003. "Improved telecom has increased investments." *Daily Trust (Abuja)*, (October 31): 4.

Park, Andrew. 2003. "Outsourcing: Look who's out of sorts." *Business Week* (December 29): 46–47.

Pearlson, Keri E. 2001. *Managing and Using Information Systems: A Strategic Approach*. New York: John Wiley & Sons.

Pearson, David. 1999. "The hidden costs of data integration." *CIO* 12 (May 1): Section 1, 38–43.

Riemenschneider, Cynthia. 2000. "What small business executives have learned about managing information technology." *Information & Management* 15 (August): 257–263.

Ross, Jeanne W., and Peter Weill. 2002. "Six IT decisions your IT people shouldn't make." *Harvard Business Review* 80 (November): 3–9.

Rutherford, Emelie. 2000. "Is this any way to build an intranet?" *CIO* 13 (April 1): 124–136.

Scheier, Robert L. 2001. "Averting disaster." *Computerworld* 54 (January 15): 46–47.

Schifrin, Matthew. 1997. "The new enablers—chief information officers." *Forbes* 158 (June 2): 138–143.

Trapasso, Ed. 1999. "The outsourcing option." *Beyond Computing* 8 (September): 15–21.

Weiss, Todd R. 2003. "Unilever dumping UNIX for Linux in global move." *Computerworld* 37 (January 27): 1, 14.

Wheatley, Malcolm. 2001. "Nestlé's worldwide squeeze." *CIO* 14 (June 1): 52–56.

Williams, Oakie. 1998. *Outsourcing—A CIO's Perspective*. New York: St. Lucie Press.

Yudkowski, Chaim. 1999. "Info system management is more than dealing with cost." *Business First—Louisville* (June 21): 15.

CHAPTER 16

Associated Press. 1997. "Survey: Bosses watching workers." *The Bloomington Herald-Times* 120 (May 5): A3.

Baase, Sara. 1997. *A Gift of Fire—Social, Legal, and Ethical Issues in Computing*. Upper Saddle River, NJ: Prentice Hall.

Baron, David P. 2000. "DoubleClick and Internet privacy." Case Number P-32, Graduate School of Business, Stanford University.

Berman, Dennis K. 2003. "Online laundry: Government posts Enron's e-mail." *The Wall Street Journal* (October 6).

Berman, Jay. 2004. "IFPI's Jay Berman sets out industry's global Internet strategy for 2004." *IFPI Quarterly Newsletter* (January 7). *www.ifpi.org/site-content/press/20031216.html.*

Berry, Jonathan, John Verity, Kathleen Kerwin, and Gail DeGeorge. 1994. "Database Marketing." *Business Week* (September 5): 56–62.

Business Software Alliance. 2003. "Trends in software piracy, 1994–2002." Eighth Annual BSA Global Software Piracy Study by the International Planning and Research Corporation.

Cortese, Amy. 1995. "Warding off the cyberspace invaders." *Business Week* (March 13): 92–93.

De George, Richard T. 1999. *Business Ethics*, 5th ed. Upper Saddle River, NJ: Prentice Hall.

[FTC] 2003. "Federal Trade Commission—Identity Theft Survey Report." Prepared by Synovate (September). *www.ftc.gov/os/2003/09/synovaterepor.pdf.*

Gaudin, Sharon. 2003. "May breaks record for digital attacks." *IT Management* (May 21). *itmanagement.earthweb.com/secu/article.php/2210321.*

Grossman, Lev. 2003. "It's all FREE!" *TIME* (May 5): 61.

Grupe, Fritz H., William Kuechler, and Scot Sweeney. 2003. "Dealing with data privacy protection: An issue for the 21st century." *IS Management Handbook.* Carol V. Brown and Heikki Topi (eds.) Boca Raton, FL: Auerbach.

Hamm, Steve, Jay Greene, Cliff Edwards, and Jim Kerstetter. 2003. "Epidemic." *Business Week* (September 8): 28.

Horowitz, Janice M. 1992. "Crippled by computers." *Time* 140 (October 12): 70–72.

IFPI. 2003. "The recording industry commercial piracy report 2003." International Federation of the Phonographic Industry, *www.ifpi.org/site-content/library/piracy2003.pdf.*

ITRC. 2003. *Identity Theft: The Aftermath—2003.* The Identity Theft Resource Center. *www.idtheftcenter.org.*

Koepp, Stephen, Charles Pelton, and Seth Shulman. 1986. "The boss that never blinks." *Time* 135 (July 28): 46–47.

McCollum, Scott. 2002. "Mi2g: Digital attacks decline worldwide while attacks on USA rise." *WorldTech Tribune, www.worldtechtribune.com/worldtechtribune/asparticles/buzz/bz12022002.asp* (December 2).

Moritz, Robert. 2003. "When someone steals your identity." *Parade Magazine* (July 6): 3–4.

NCES. 2001. "Current Population Survey." *The National Center for Education Statistics* (September).

Newman, Matthew. 2003. "EU improves software patent, but outlaws Amazon One Click." *Dow Jones* (June 17). *news.morningstar.com/news/DJ/Mo6/D17/1055868063730.html.*

Nusbaum, Marci Alboher. 2003. "New kind of snooping arrives at the office," *The New York Times* (July 11).

Pew Internet Project. 2003. "Spam: How it is hurting email and degrading life on the Internet." A report funded by the Pew Charitable Trusts.

PIRG. 1998. "Mistakes do happen." The sixth study on credit report accuracy by the Public Interest Research Group (March).

Public Affairs. 2003. "Internet piracy on campus, a survey of 1000 U.S. college and university students and 300 U.S. college and university educators." Washington, DC (September 16).

Reno, Janet. 2000. "The electronic frontier: The challenge of unlawful conduct involving the use of the Internet." Report of the President's Working Group on Unlawful Conduct on the Internet (March).

Sager, Ira, Steve Hamm, Neil Gross, John Carey, and Robert D. Hoff. 2000. "Cyber Crime" *Business Week* (Feb. 21).

Sorkin, David E. 2003. Spam Laws Web page, *www.spamlaws.com* (November 26).

Swartz, Jon, and Paul Davidson. 2003. "Spam thrives despite effort to screen it out." Cover Story, *USA Today* (May 8).

Stoll, Cliff. 1989. *The Cuckoo's Egg: Tracking a Spy Through the Maze of Computer Espionage.* New York: Pocket Books.

INDEX

Prentice Hall

MANAGEMENT INFORMATION SYSTEMS

MIS:

Alter, *Information Systems: The Foundation of E-Business 4/e*

Jessup & Valacich, *Information Systems Today*

Laudon & Laudon, *Essentials of Management Information Systems 6/e*

Laudon & Laudon, *Management Information Systems 8/e*

Luftman et al., *Managing the IT Resource*

Malaga, *Information Systems Technology*

Martin et al., *Managing IT: What Managers Need to Know 5/e*

McLeod & Schell, *Management Information Systems 9/e*

McNurlin & Sprague, *Information Systems Management In Practice 6/e*

Miller, *MIS: Decision Making with Application Software (Cases) 2/e*

Senn, *Information Technology 3/e*

Electronic Commerce:

Awad, *Electronic Commerce 2/e*

Oz, *Foundations of Electronic Commerce*

Turban, *Electronic Commerce 2004, A Managerial Perspective*

Turban, *Introduction to E–Commerce*

Database Management:

Bordoloi & Bock, *Oracle SQL*

Bordoloi & Bock, *SQL for SQL Server*

Hoffer, Prescott, McFadden, *Modern Database Management 7/e*

Kroenke, *Database Concepts 2/e*

Kroenke, *Database Processing: Fundamentals, Design, and Implementation 9/e*